The Macrodynamics of Advanced Market Economies

The Macrodynamics of Advanced Market Economies

Alfred S. Eichner

M. E. Sharpe, Inc.
Armonk, New York
London

Available in the United Kingdom and Europe from M. E. Sharpe,
Publishers, 3 Henrietta Street, London WC2E 8LU.

Library of Congress Cataloging-in-Publication Data

Eichner, Alfred S.
    The macrodynamics of advanced market economies.

    Bibliography: p.
    1. Capitalism. I. Title.
HB501.E4   1987   330.12′2   87-9693
ISBN 0-87332-439-0 (pbk.)

Printed in the United States of America

To Joan Robinson who, by first putting together into a coherent whole the alternative post-Keynesian paradigm, showed us the path out of the Valley of Darkness that is the neoclassical theory.

Contents

Preface

This text is intended to provide a comprehensive and coherent exposition of the theory that has emerged since 1956 as an alternative to the prevailing neoclassical synthesis. In this respect, it is meant to be a follow-up to the 1975 *Journal of Economic Literature* article co-authored with Jan Kregel, "An Essay on Post-Keynesian Theory," and the subsequent collection of articles, by various authors, published first in *Challenge* magazine and then brought out in 1979 as *A Guide to Post-Keynesian Theory* (Sharpe). The intellectual debt to the many post-Keynesian (and neo-Marxist, institutionalist, and behavioralist) economists responsible for most of the important new ideas to surface over the past three decades will be obvious from the references in the chapters that follow. Indeed, this textbook is as much their work as mine.

The text is, in addition, meant to be a successor to Gardner Ackley, *Macroeconomic Theory* (Macmillan, 1961), and Michael K. Evans, *Macroeconomic Activity* (Harper & Row, 1969) as the definitive treatment of macroeconomics. It was, in fact, Gardner Ackley, Daniel Suits, Robert Eisner, and Otto Eckstein who first convinced me that it is possible to place economics on a solid empirical foundation, and thus the considerable intellectual debt to these and other more orthodox macro economists needs to be acknowledged.

What follows is only a first, provisional edition. It has not been possible to revise parts of the larger work sufficiently to permit publication of all the planned chapters at this time. Missing are chapter 11, covering the rest-of-the-world; chapter 14, covering the complete model, and chapter 15, covering epistemology and methodology—as well as parts of chapters 12 and 13. The reason for rushing into print is that nearly a decade has already elapsed since the project was begun, and the chapters now available can be further improved only through whatever comments and criticisms readers may have to offer. Indeed, this provisional edition has been brought out to elicit just such a response—with the reader further warned that, despite the many revisions the text has already gone through, errors and omissions abound. If the text is to serve the purpose for which it is intended, it is necessary that those errors and omissions be pointed out. This, in turn, is possible only if the text is widely available in a provisional edition, even if not a complete one.

I would like to acknowledge the assistance of the many persons who have already commented on earlier drafts of the manuscript. I would especially like to thank Matthew Fung and Philip Arestis for their help in editing the book as a whole. In addition, I have had valuable help from John Blatt, Jan Kregel, Ray Canterbery, Peter Earl, Alessandro Roncaglia, Fernando Carvalho, Doug Woodward and Gideon Gill on chapters 1–6; from Wassily Leontief and Will Milberg on chapter 5; from David Howell on chapter 8; from Marc Lavoie on chapter 12, and from Eileen Appelbaum on chapter 13.

Alfred S. Eichner
Closter, N.J.
May, 1987

Chapter 1

Introduction

Contents

Chapter 1

Introduction

1.1 Overview

The subject matter of this textbook is the macrodynamic behavior of an economy with social institutions similar to those of the United States and the other member countries of the Organization for Economic Cooperation and Development (OECD). Macrodynamics refers to the set of principles governing the expansion of such an economic system, or economy, over time. These principles are meant to explain two types of observable phenomena:

1. The long-term increase in the total output of material goods that is discernible when any fluctuations in the relevant set of figures are averaged out. This is the "secular" growth rate, and it is derived by fitting a trend line (which itself may vary over time) to the data on economic output. (See exhibit 1.1).

2. The short-run deviations from that secular trend line. This is the "cyclical," as distinct from the "secular," behavior of an economic system. (In exhibit 1.1, the cyclical behavior is represented by the difference between the actual levels of output and the fitted trend line.)

It is usually the second of these two phenomena that arouses public concern. A sudden fall in output with an accompanying rise in unemployment is a manifestation of the economy's cyclical behavior. However, it is a premise of the theoretical approach underlying this textbook that any such cyclical behavior can be understood only in relation to the secular growth rate from which it represents a deviation. The analysis of the economy's cyclical behavior must therefore proceed hand-in-hand with an analysis of the trend. Indeed, the two are interdependent—the cyclical movements influencing the trend and the trend, in turn, defining the cyclical movements. The two together, trend and cycle, constitute the economy's macrodynamic behavior.

While it is the uneven rates of increase in the output of material goods over time that is the principal focus of the book, two closely related phenomena will also be analyzed. One is the pattern of human resource utilization, particularly the rate of growth of employment, and the other is the secular rise in the aggregate price level. All three of these phenomena—the growth of real output, G; the growth in employment, N; and the growth of the aggregate price level, P—are to be explained as different manifestations of the same macrodynamic process.

The book proceeds by first distinguishing the economic system from the other three institutional dimensions of society—the normative, the political and the

Exhibit 1.1

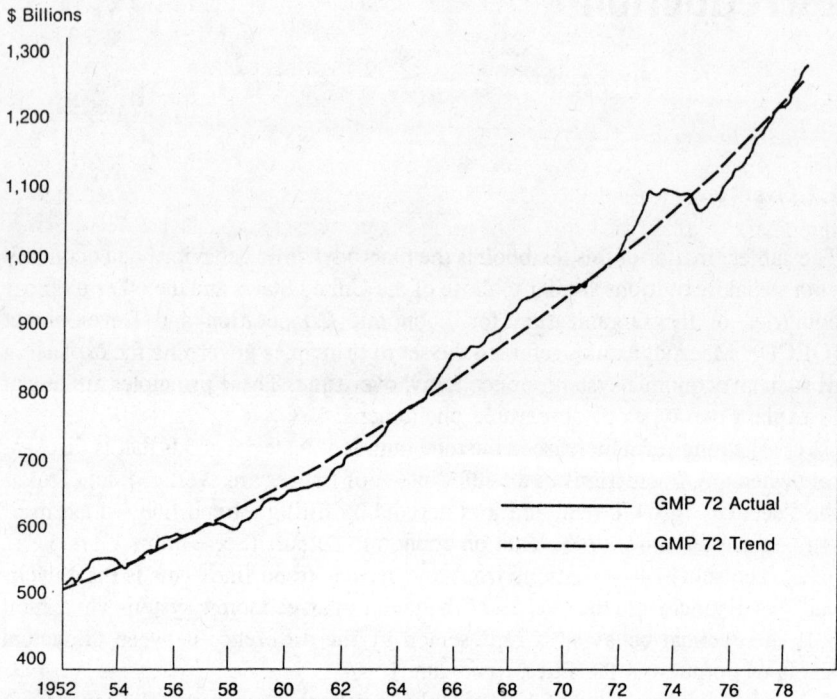

human developmental, or anthropogenic. This broader social context in which the economic system *qua* system needs to be placed is described in the second half of this introductory chapter where a systems approach to social analysis is outlined. In the book's subsequent chapters, a model is developed to explain the macrodynamic behavior of an economic system with advanced institutions like those of the United States and the other OECD countries.

The macrodynamic behavior of an advanced market economy will be "explained" by constructing a model, based on a set of posited theoretical relationships, that can be used to simulate the actual behavior of such a system over time. The term "model" will be used in this text to describe the entire set of relationships needed to explain the observed behavior of some phenomenon while the term "theory" will be used to describe the specific relationships on which the model is based—in particular, the factors identified as the determinants of the behavior being modeled. Thus, while a "model" and a "theory" are not the same thing, they are so closely related that the two terms can, and will, be used interchangeably. Indeed, it is difficult to distinguish one model from another except by referring to the differences in the underlying theory.

The model to be developed in the subsequent chapters of this text is based on post-Keynesian theory, and this distinguishes the model, along with the textbook itself, from their counterparts based on neoclassical theory. More will be said shortly about the differences between the two bodies of economic theory. First, however, it should be noted that models may differ not only in terms of the theory on which they are based but also in terms of the phenomena they claim to explain. Here, too, important differences need to be noted between the model developed in the subsequent chapters of this text and other models. These other differences are twofold: First, the model to be developed in the subsequent chapters of this text is intended to explain the actual behavior of an advanced market system like that of the United States. It is not intended to trace out the logic of rational choice nor in any other way provide a normative standard against which to compare the behavior of some actual economic system. Second, the model is meant to apply to an economic system with the types of advanced institutions found in the United States and the other OECD countries. It is not meant to abstract from, and thereby ignore the role played by, such important institutions as large corporations or megacorps, industrial trade unions, credit money and the state. The first of these other differences reflects a particular view of how economics, considered to be a form of intellectual activity, should be pursued while the second of these other differences reflects a particular view of how best to capture the complexity of an advanced market economy. It is as a consequence of these differences in purpose and method that the model developed in this textbook is based on post-Keynesian theory rather than on the alternative body of neoclassical theory. Again, more will said about these differences shortly. At this point, it is the particular type of economic system to be modeled—as distinct from the particular type of theory to be used in constructing the model of that system—which needs to be made clear.

1.1.1 The nature of an advanced market economy

The economic system to be modeled has the following characteristics: (1) its output consists of material goods that are not only "allocated" or distributed, but also first produced; (2) the firms that, collectively as industries, produce those material goods are linked together through markets; and (3) the transactions that are carried out through those markets are based on the exchange of goods for money or, looking at the same phenomenon from the opposite side, the exchange of money for goods. In other words, the economic system to be modeled is characterized by production, markets and money. These terms need to be carefully defined—along with the term "economic system" they describe.

An economic system can be defined as the set of institutions which have evolved over time so as to enable the individual members of a society to satisfy their material needs. These material needs can be satisfied only by transforming whatever resources are found in nature so that they have the qualities—and the location—essential for human use. This transformation of the natural endowment is what is meant by "production." It implies that resources, both human and natural, must first be mobilized as part of a social process so that the necessary transformations can be carried out.

In the model to be developed in the succeeding chapters of this textbook, it will be assumed that these transformations are carried out by a specialized type of social institution—the business firm or "enterprise." Each of the firms producing the same type of output can be grouped together as members of the same industry, and it is the complete set of n such industries (with n a number considerably greater than 2) which constitutes the enterprise sector, or production system, for the economy as a whole. To say that the economic system is characterized by production is to stipulate, then, that it encompasses a subsystem of production—one that includes the full set of industries needed to produce all of the items that are required to satisfy the society's material needs.

At least two different types of business firms, or enterprises, will be distinguished in the chapters which follow. One is the large corporation, or megacorp. It is characterized by a professional managerial group, separate and distinct from the stockholders, or nominal owners; by multiple plants, each of which reflects in the capital goods it embodies whatever sophisticated cost-minimizing technology was available when the plant was constructed, and by membership in one or more oligopolistic industries. Indeed, the megacorp will be viewed as the representative firm in the technically more advanced sectors of the economy, those in which just a few large firms dominate the market. The other type of firm is the neoclassical proprietorship, or small family-controlled enterprise, emphasized in the more conventional textbooks. It will be viewed as the representative firm in the nonoligopolistic sectors of the economy. Together, megacorps and neoclassical proprietorships, as members of n separate industries, constitute the enterprise sector, or production subsystem, of the economy.

Still, it is not enough that the economic system encompass a subsystem of production. It is also necessary that whatever goods are produced be distributed, or "allocated," in some manner. This is especially the case when the system of production involves specialization, with individual firms, and the persons associated with those firms, concentrating on the provision of just a single good. Those who devote the greater part of their time to producing a particular item must have some means of obtaining the other goods they need in order to satisfy the full range of their material needs. Thus a system of production, when it involves specialization, must be accompanied by some means of distributing, or "allocating," the output of the system. (The goods can be said to be "distributed" when they are made available for some final use, or consumption, and to be "allocated" when they are merely transferred from one producing unit to another prior to being made available for final use. This distinction is not always kept in mind, however, and in that case the two terms would be used interchangeably, with "allocation" the more general term.)

The problem of how to distribute, or "allocate," the system's output can be handled in a number of ways. For example, the society can rely on rules based on tradition or backed by the coercive power of the state. (How the rules are to be determined or even what are the best rules to adopt are separate questions.) However, the mechanism for allocating the output of the economic system which is relied upon for the most part, though not exclusively, in an advanced society like that of the United States is the market.

A market is a social arrangement for bringing persons together so that they can engage in trade. What is meant by trade is the exchange of one thing for another—a voluntaristic *quid pro quo*. A person about to make a trade may be under strong pressure, economic and other, to accept the terms being offered. Indeed, the situation may be such that he or she really has no choice in the matter. Still, as long as some overriding power is prepared to enforce rules against direct, physical coercion and this in turn leaves the individual with the option of holding on to whatever it is that the other party desires rather than completing the transaction, the trade retains some essential element of a voluntaristic act. The point is that, under a market system of allocation, nothing can be obtained except by giving up something else in exchange. That is, there must be a *quid pro quo*.

What has been said so far about the market mechanism applies to a barter as well as to a monetarized economy. The latter is distinguished by the fact that instead of goods or commodities being exchanged directly for one another, they are first exchanged for something which, being specified either in law or contract as the means of payment, meets the definition of money, with the money then in turn being exchanged for goods. That is, the simple barter relationship

$$\text{Goods} \longrightarrow \text{Goods}$$

is replaced by the more complex relationship

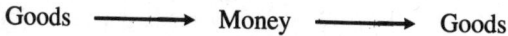

$$\text{Goods} \longrightarrow \text{Money} \longrightarrow \text{Goods}$$

The intrusion of money into the exchange relationship obviates some of the difficulties encountered when trade is based on barter arrangements. With money serving both as a common denominator of economic value, or unit of account, and as a generalized claim against all commodities, trade that involves both a large number of items and a large number of parties can be carried out more easily.

Much as the development of a monetarized economy represents an improvement over a barter system, it nonetheless introduces its own set of difficulties. First, there must be some social mechanism for supplying the money used in transactions. The failure of this mechanism to work properly is one of the things that can go wrong in a monetarized economy, and no description of such a system that aims at completeness can avoid specifying in some detail the process by which money is introduced into the system. In the model to be developed in this book, it will be assumed that money is introduced into the system through the process of credit expansion. Thus the model assumes the existence of "credit" money as distinct from "commodity" or even "fiat" money. Moreover, the existence of money creates a fundamental duality between the real, or physical, flows within the system and the monetary flows. The real flows reflect the movement of goods and other resources between different parts of the system, and the monetary flows, the countermovement of money claims in exchange for those goods and other resources. That the two flows may become unbalanced is another of the things which can go wrong in a monetarized system.

The model developed in the succeeding chapters of this book is thus intended to explain the macrodynamic behavior of a *monetarized production* system. This, it should be noted, is not the type of economic system typically analyzed by economists. Usually either the process by which production takes place and/or the role played by money is abstracted from in order to make the model mathematically more tractable. Moreover, even though markets are usually the focal point of the analysis, the markets emphasized are those linking producers to consumers rather than those linking producers to one another. With the process of production thus not explicitly modeled, the most important types of markets within a monetarized production system are likely to be ignored. These are the markets through which pass the interfirm, and hence the interindustry, flow of goods and services (involving the "allocation," as distinct from the "distribution" of those goods and services). The explicit allowance made for both production and money is, however, only one of several ways in which the model developed in the succeeding chapters of this textbook differs from the conventional approach to economics. Other differences include the following:

1. The model is based on the behavior of groups, such as business firms, households and government agencies. These groups are viewed as complex social systems in which the behavior of any individual person is role-determined. Thus, in constructing a model of the economic system's macrodynamic behavior, the textbook does not rely solely on the presumed logic of individual choice.

2. The model constructed to explain the macrodynamic behavior of the system as a whole is derived from, and is fully consistent with, the model constructed to explain the behavior of the system at the microeconomic level—that is, at the level of the individual firm and household. Thus the textbook does not accept the distinction which is usually made in economics between a macro theory based on one set of principles, both substantive and epistemological, and a micro theory based on a quite different set of principles.

3. The model used to explain the economic system's macrodynamic behavior is limited to those variables which can be observed empirically and which therefore have a counterpart in reality. Thus the textbook avoids basing its argument on factors which cannot be assigned a numerical value—or cannot even be shown to exist.

These differences are not just a means of distinguishing the model to be developed in this textbook from the models found in other textbooks. It also reflects, perhaps even more fundamentally, a different view of how one should "do economics."

1.1.2 The purpose and method of economics

Economics as an academic discipline is defined not only by its subject matter but also by the analytical techniques used to establish the validity of the propositions that constitute the theoretical core of the discipline. In both these essential aspects of how economics is to be defined, the book in hand differs radically from other texts.

The majority of economists, following Lionel Robbins, would define economics as the study of how "scarce resources are allocated among competing ends." The method they favor, in tackling this and other questions in economics, is axiomatic reasoning. This requires that they specify an initial set of conditions, or assumptions, and then show what logically follows from those premises. The standard textbooks are permeated by this view of how to do economics. Even the textbooks in macroeconomics, in examining the sources of cyclical instability, try to explain, largely by means of axiomatic reasoning, why the optimal allocation of resources which the market is thought to assure in the long run may not quite be realized in the short run.

This textbook reflects a quite different view as to what are the purpose and method of economics. The discipline's core subject matter is assumed to be the same as that of the textbook itself: the macrodynamic behavior of that particular set of institutions which enable the individual members of society to satisfy their material needs. The question of how resources are allocated will be taken up, but only as a subsidiary point to the more basic question of what determines the growth over time in available resources. Furthermore, it will be assumed that the purpose of economics—to explain the macrodynamic behavior of the economic system—is best served by constructing a model that can meet certain empirical tests, including the ability to simulate the economy's actual historical experience. It is by constructing such a model, and not simply by carrying out an exercise in axiomatic reasoning, that one does economic theory. The approach to economics reflected in the standard textbooks is rejected for two reasons: (1) it precludes economics from ever becoming a science in the sense that term is used to describe certain bodies of knowledge; and (2) it leaves the behavior of what has been termed the economic system largely unexplained.

To be considered a science, a discipline such as economics must develop a body of theory which, as a set of general statements about the phenomena it is concerned with, can be empirically validated. This means the theory must be capable of being tested against the reality it claims to explain—and then it must succeed in explaining that reality. While it is possible to make general statements about the allocation of resources which are empirically testable, these are not the types of statements which form the core of the orthodox theory in economics today. That core consists instead of statements which merely follow logically from certain assumptions, without either the conclusions or the assumptions necessarily being a description of any observable reality. The standard, or orthodox, approach to economics in fact reflects an epistemology which is alien to science, based as it is on certain fallacies which scientists over the centuries have learned to avoid. They are: (1) the solipsistic fallacy; (2) the dualistic fallacy; and (3) the Cartesian fallacy.

The solipsistic fallacy involves the belief that the external reality, indeed the very notion of an external reality, is little more than a construction of the mind with no separate existence. This belief can be traced back to the idealistic philosophy of the British bishop William Berkeley (1685–1753) and as such, it violates one of the fundamental assumptions of modern science. This is the belief that there is an external reality, independent of the mind that is perceiving that reality. To the extent that economists develop models of economic systems that do not exist, justifying this type of analysis on the grounds that such models are a logically valid construction of the mind, they engage in a form of solipsism. Perhaps more serious a matter, they implicitly deny that the purpose of economics is to explain the external reality—such as is required of any discipline that would claim to be a science.

The dualistic fallacy involves the belief that there is more than one external reality. Dualism became a prominent aspect of Western thought during the late Middle Ages when, in response to the challenge from the rediscovered Greek texts, the dominant group of scholastic philosophers adopted the Thomastic synthesis as a means of reconciling faith with reason. While the prohibition on metaphysical arguments has largely eliminated all traces of dualism from modern science, the fallacy survives in economics today in the form of the neoclassical synthesis. Like the Thomastic synthesis, it attempts to reconcile faith with reason—in this case, a belief in the self-correcting nature of a market economy with the widespread evidence of dynamic instability. Thus the neoclassical synthesis posits two separate realities—one the reality that the pre-Keynesian microeconomic theory is thought to describe and the other, the reality that the Keynesian macroeconomic theory is meant to explain. It is precisely this dualism that the textbook in hand, by presenting a single body of integrated micro and macro theory, rejects.

The Cartesian fallacy involves the belief that knowledge of the world external to the mind can be derived solely through thought experiments—without the need for any other type of experiment, empirical or otherwise, to confirm what has been deduced. This notion can be traced back to Plato, who argued in *The Republic* that mathematics, especially geometry, represents the highest form of knowledge since its truths are not subject to the confusing variability displayed by natural phenomena. However, it was René Descartes (1596–1650) who, by seeking to found an entire philosophical system based on axiomatic reasoning, was the

Exhibit 1.2
Subject and Method of Economics

	As defined in other textbooks	As defined in this text
Subject matter of economics	How scarce resources are allocated	The macrodynamic behavior of the economy
Method of analysis	Axiomatic reasoning	Construction of an empirically valid model of the economy

first modern scientist to suggest that formal, or mathematical, proofs are sufficient to establish the validity of any proposition. Indeed, he managed to combine both the dualistic and Cartesian fallacies within the same philosophical system. Under the attack of the empiricists, beginning with Galileo (1564–1642), Robert Boyle (1627–1691) and Isaac Newton (1643–1727) and continuing with John Locke (1632–1704) and David Hume (1711–1776), the axiomatic view of knowledge has been abandoned by scientists and philosophers of science, and they would now argue that formal proofs are, at most, only necessary—not sufficient. Indeed, with the demonstration by Bertrand Russell (1872–1970) and Alfred Whitehead (1861–1947) that mathematics is simply a logical language dependent on an axiomatic structure that cannot be shown to be unique, formal proofs are now recognized to be little more than tautological statements, without the prior standing that Plato claimed for them. Economists nonetheless continue to insist that formal proofs are sufficient to establish the validity of any model. In this regard, they have embraced the Cartesian fallacy.

This textbook seeks to avoid all three fallacies—and thereby place economics on a path of development which will enable it to meet the same epistemological standards as any scientific discipline. The view reflected by the textbook is that economics can—and ought to—be a science. It is merely a matter of doing economics properly. This requires, first, that the subject matter of economics be correctly identified as the macrodynamic behavior of the institutions which enable the individual members of society to satisfy their material needs; and then, second, that economics as a discipline concern itself with constructing an empirically valid model to explain the dynamic behavior of those institutions (see exhibit 1.2). The latter is the type of model which the subsequent chapters of this text will attempt to develop as a demonstration that economics can, in fact, become a science.

Thus, while the immediate objective is to explain the macrodynamic behavior of an advanced market economy like that of the United States, the ultimate purpose is to show that it is possible to do economics in a way that is scientifically valid. The reasons for doing so are twofold. One is to provide the knowledge base needed to inform public policy, and the other is to create the necessary precondition for the cumulative growth of economic knowledge. The two purposes are, of course, complementary rather than opposed to one another.

1.1.3 Economics viewed as a social science

The premise of this textbook is that economics, viewed as an intellectual activity, should be considered a social science. Two major implications follow from this view of economics. The first is that the primary purpose of economics is to provide an empirically valid explanation for the phenomena that fall within its domain. This domain is demarcated by where the economic system *qua* system fits within the hierarchy of natural systems which are the subject matter of the sciences more generally. The other major implication is that economic theory must be fully consistent with what has been empirically established by the other sciences, both natural and social. It cannot exist in a separate realm, either substantively or epistemologically.

A hierarchy of natural systems, external to the observer, can be postulated, proceeding from the level of subatomic particles to the level of the individual atom and from there to the level of the individual molecule. At that point the hierarchy of natural systems divides along two main lines, with one line of ascent represented by the inorganic molecules which form the earth, together with the other planetary bodies, and the other line represented by the organic molecules which form various biological systems, beginning with the individual cell and proceeding from there to the higher levels of organization represented by organs and organisms. This second line of ascent within the hierarchy of natural systems is the domain of the biological sciences, which are concerned with the study of human beings, among other species. It is only at the next higher level of organization, the one represented by groups of human beings, that one enters the domain of the social sciences. Economics, as one of those social sciences, is concerned specifically with how groups of human beings are organized to satisfy their material needs. Its purpose is to provide an empirically valid explanation for the phenomena which fall within that domain.

The nature of economic theory follows from what is deemed to be the purpose of economics. If that purpose is to provide an empirically valid explanation of economic phenomena, then the body of theory which constitutes the core of the discipline's knowledge must itself be empirically valid. Indeed, that body of theory should be regarded as nothing more than the most general set of empirically valid statements which can be made about economic phenomena. It is these statements which, brought together to form an integrated whole, constitute the "best" available model of the economic system. This is not to deny that the theory must, at the same time, be logically consistent, or coherent. If the theory is not logically consistent, then it can hardly describe phenomena which, as a second basic postulate of science, must be assumed to be not illogical. Rather it is to argue that coherence is only a necessary, and not a sufficient, condition for considering any body of theory, economic or other, to be scientifically valid. In addition, the theory must correspond to what can be observed empirically.

The requirement that economic theory correspond to what can be observed empirically imposes a number of constraints on those attempting to construct a model of the economic system. For one thing, it means that any variables used in the model must themselves be observable. Even if a numerical value cannot be assigned to one of the variables, it should at least be possible to determine empirically whether, at any given point in time, that factor is making its influence felt. This first requirement is the reason why the textbook begins, in the chapter immediately following this one, by examining the principal sources of empirical data—not just the better known National Income and Product Accounts (NIPA) but also the input-output tables on which the National Income and Product Accounts are based as well as the Flow of Funds Accounts (FOFA) which enable the countermovement of monetary flows to be traced out. This first requirement is also the reason why the model developed in the subsequent chapters of the textbook is restricted, in terms of explanatory factors, to the variables which can be found within the data base described in chapter 2.

A second requirement, if the theory underlying a model of the economy is to be empirically valid, is that it apply at the micro level no less than at the macro level. This means the model must be a "structural" one, based on the behavior of what are the actual decision-making units within the system. It is for this reason that the macroeconomic model developed in the succeeding chapters is constructed by first modeling the behavior of the characteristic type of organization found within each of the sectors of the economy—the business firm in the case of the enterprise sector, the family in the case of the household sector, the state and its various agencies in the case of the government sector and other countries in the case of the rest-of-the-world sector. Indeed, the second of the three main parts into which the textbook is divided is concerned with developing an appropriate microeconomic theory for modeling the behavior of the characteristic types of decision-making unit found within each of the economy's relevant sectors.

A third requirement, if the model is to be an empirically valid one, is that it must be comprehensive, in the sense of being able to encompass all the essential features of the economic system, while at the same time not losing any of its coherence. This means, on the one hand, that the theory underlying the model must be formulated so as to represent the behavior of the institutions characteristic of an advanced market economy. It also means, on the other hand, that even with this degree of institutional detail, the theory must still be capable of providing a logical explanation for the macrodynamic behavior of the system. It is because of this third requirement that the model which is to be developed in the subsequent chapters of this text is based on the systems approach described in the second half of this introductory chapter. With a systems approach, it is possible to take into account the entire set of relevant institutions, both economic and noneconomic, without becoming lost in detail or losing sight of the coherence which the system as a whole has.

To develop a model which can satisfy all of the above requirements for economics becoming an empirically valid social science, it will be necessary to reject large parts of the established theory in economics. What will remain, once this necessary surgery has been performed, is a body of theory which, to distinguish it from the neoclassical theory expounded in other textbooks, can be termed post-Keynesian.

1.1.4 Post-Keynesian and other paradigms

The post-Keynesian theory that will be expounded in the chapters to follow represents the full flowering of the seeds planted in the minds of economists by John Maynard Keynes in 1936 with the publication of *The General Theory of Employment, Interest and Money*. Based originally on the work of Keynes's closest colleagues in England, such as Joan Robinson, Nicholas Kaldor, Roy Harrod and Piero Sraffa, the theory continues to be nurtured by a minority within the economics profession the world over. Despite the inhospitable soil in which they must try to implant their ideas, the members of this small group have further refined and extended the theory to the point where it offers a comprehensive alternative to the reigning orthodoxies in economics—West and East. Although only a minority of economists as yet consciously regard themselves as post-Keynesians, they reflect the unease of the majority about the validity and usefulness of the prevailing paradigms. Indeed, one purpose of this text is to demonstrate to the majority of economists who are uncomfortable with more orthodox approaches that post-Keynesian theory represents a better way of organizing the empirical evidence which exists about economic institutions and historical events.

At a critical, early stage in the development of the new paradigm, there was an important grafting of ideas from the Polish economist Michal Kalecki. Since that time, there have been two distinct strains within post-Keynesian theory: a Keynesian strain emphasizing the role of monetary institutions, and a Kaleckian strain emphasizing the role of real factors. There have been other important graftings as well, especially with respect to the micro foundations of post-Keynesian theory. These include the work of Wassily Leontief in developing input-output analysis and of Piero Sraffa in analyzing the relationship between pricing and distribution. Also important has been the work of the Oxford Pricing Group in England and certain of the institutionalists, especially John M. Clark and Gardiner C. Means, here in the United States. Indeed, as will be clear from what follows, post-Keynesian theory provides the essential core for synthesizing a great deal of the work previously done in economics which falls outside the conventional framework, ranging from that of the behavioralists and managerial theorists on the one side to that of certain Marxists on the other side. It even provides a better explanation for much of the empirical work which has been done by mainstream economists.

As it has now finally emerged from its incubation period with certain readily distinguishable features, post-Keynesian theory can be compared to the other two major paradigms in economics. They are: (a) the neoclassical theory which predominates throughout the English-speaking world; and (b) the Marxian theory which, though barely tolerated in the West, represents the orthodox viewpoint in the Communist countries of Eastern Europe and Asia.

Because they have common roots in classical political economy—in particular, the writings of William Petty, Francois Quesnay, and David Ricardo—the contrast is less between post-Keynesian and Marxian theory. Indeed, there are many similarities between the two types of analysis, at least insofar as the "laws of motion," or dynamics, of a "capitalist" system are concerned. The most important difference, as chapter 8 will bring out, is the refusal of post-Keynesian economists to accept as valid the labor theory of value in the form originally put forward by Marx. While there are some Marxists who themselves have abandoned the labor theory of value (many of whom consider themselves to be post-Keynesians as well), other Marxists regard this step as heretical, and they can be expected to reject post-Keynesian theory for this reason. In their view, the labor theory of value is central to Marxian analysis.

There is another important difference, at least between the version of post-Keynesian theory to be presented in this text and Marxian theory. To the extent the economic system is viewed as only one of three parallel and coequal systems (and only one of four coequal institutional dimensions, taking into account the society's value orientation), the argument of this text runs counter to the materialistic interpretation of history which is part of Marxian theory. According to the latter, it is the "mode of production," representing the technological imperatives for obtaining material sustenance, that constitutes the base of any society; and it is upon this base that the "superstructure," consisting of economic as well as other types of social institutions, is erected. Underlying the analysis which follows is the belief that it is arbitrary to assign the primary causal role, as the Marxian analysis does, to the economic dimensions of society; and that, moreover, the technology which determines the "mode of production" actually derives, along with other types of validated knowledge, from the normative dimension. Just as there may be other sources of "value" besides the labor inputs used directly in the production process, so too the primary thrust in the current social dynamic may come from some other dimension besides the economic (see section 2.4). In this respect, the analysis which follows is less constricted than the original Marxian theory permits.

Still, it is between the reigning neoclassical orthodoxy in the English-speaking countries and post-Keynesian theory that the contrast is most striking. The accompanying table (see exhibit 1.3) brings out some of the more important differ

Exhibit 1.3

Contrast between Post-Keynesian and Neoclassical Theory

Aspect	Post-Keynesian Theory	Neoclassical Theory
Dynamic properties	Assumes pronounced cyclical pattern on top of a clearly discernible secular growth rate	Either no growth, or steady-state expansion with market mechanisms assumed to preclude any but a temporary deviation from that growth path
Explanation of how income is distributed	Institutional factors determine a historical division of income between residual and nonresidual shares, with changes in that distribution depending on changes in the growth rate	The distribution of income explained solely by variable inputs and the marginal productivity of those variable factor inputs
Amount of information assumed to be available	Only the past is known; the future is uncertain	Complete foresight exists as to all possible events
Conditions that must be met before the analysis is considered complete	Discretionary income must be equal to discretionary expenditures	All markets clear, with supply equal to demand in each of those markets
Microeconomic base	Imperfect markets with significant monopolistic elements	Perfect markets with all micro units operating as price-takers
Purpose of the theory	To explain the real world as observed empirically	To demonstrate the social optimality if the real world were to resemble the model

Reprinted from Alfred S. Eichner and J. A. Kregel, "An Essay on Post-Keynesian Theory: A New Paradigm in Economics," *Journal of Economic Literature*, December 1975.

ences between the two paradigms, and the chapters that follow will elaborate on these differences. For now, it need only be noted that neoclassical theory is the theory rooted in the general equilibrium analysis of Leon Walras and his intellectual descendents. Though not always recognizable in the partial equilibrium framework of Alfred Marshall in which it is often presented, this is the theory expounded in virtually all the standard microeconomic textbooks published in

English. Its primary concern is with the conditions necessary for an "optimal" allocation of economic resources, and thus its purpose is normative and exhortory rather than explanatory.

1.1.5 Limitations of the model

The model to be developed in the chapters that follow applies, in full, only to the economic system of an advanced society like that of United States and the other members of the OECD. It is therefore limited in at least two important ways that need to be carefully noted. First, it is a model of a national economy, and not of the larger global economic system. Second, it applies only partly, if at all, to (a) less developed countries, and (b) centrally planned economies (those in which production is not market coordinated).

The fact that the text covers only the case of a single national economy, and not the larger global system, is perhaps the most serious limitation of the analysis that follows. This deficiency is partly overcome in chapter 11 when, after discussing the rest-of-the-world sector of a national economy, the rudiments of a global model are outlined. Still, the perspective throughout the text is primarily that of a single national economy, and for this reason the dynamics of the larger world economy, which is more than just the sum of its individual parts, may not be fully captured. Indeed, developing an adequate world model remains an essential task of economic theory, as pointed out in chapter 11.

Even in limiting the analysis to nation states, the text focuses primarily on the case of advanced market systems, and it thereby ignores the other two types of economic systems which can be found among the nations of the world: the economies of the less developed countries and the economies in which production, rather than being market-coordinated, is centrally planned. Since there will be subsequent reference to countries which are less developed or in which production is not market coordinated, these two distinctions need to be clarified.

The term "less developed" refers to countries in which the entire set of social institutions, and not just the economic ones, have yet to evolve to the point where they are able to perform the variety of functions, with the same degree of effectiveness, as those in the United States and the other OECD countries. The less developed countries are located primarily in Africa, Asia and Latin America.

The countries in which "production is not market coordinated" are the countries that rely on a centralized planning body, rather than the market, to allocate resources among the different branches of industry. These countries may use the market to distribute among households a portion of the goods produced. But this is a relatively unimportant matter compared to the fact that the production process itself—as well as the balance of production between consumer and other types of goods—is governed by other than market mechanisms. Such countries can be described as having "centrally planned" or "command" economies, and they are found primarily on the Eurasian continent, from the Oder River in the

West to the Pacific Ocean in the East.

Both less developed countries and centrally planned economies (the two categories may, in certain cases, overlap) need to be distinguished from the type of advanced market economy which is the focus of this textbook. While some parts of the model to be developed in the subsequent chapters can be applied to each of these other two types of economies, it would be a mistake to apply the model as a whole either to a less developed country or to a centrally planned economy. Each requires its own, quite different model—the construction of which is beyond the scope of this textbook.

1.2 The Systems Context

The economic system which is to be modeled in the subsequent chapters of this text needs to be placed in its proper social context. This involves the use of a systems approach to help map out the larger social structure of which the economic system is a part. This section begins by outlining the systems approach upon which the rest of the textbook is based. Adoption of a systems approach, it will be argued, is essential for three reasons. The first is so that the question of causation can be adequately addressed, the second is so that different types of nonhomeostatic (disequilibrium) states can be analyzed, and the third is so that a general framework for integrating the subject matter of the social sciences can be developed. Each of these three reasons for basing the analysis on a systems approach will be elaborated on once the systems approach which underlies this textbook has been described in the first of the four subsections which follow.

1.2.1 The systems approach

This effort to model the economic system is based on a systems approach—as distinct from the simultaneous, and hence noncausal models on the one hand and the simple mechanistic models on the other that economists have traditionally relied upon. Based on such an approach, the economy can be conceptualized as a system which, first of all, is comprised of various subsystems (e.g., a production subsystem, a monetary-financial subsystem), and second, is itself part of a larger system (the society as a whole). Each such system, whether the society as a whole, the economic system alone or one of its subcomponents, can be analyzed in terms of (1) its structure, and (2) its dynamic behavior.

A system's structure consists of the various elements that, through their interaction, produce the system's dynamic behavior. In the case of the larger society, these elements are the economic system and its parallel institutional dimensions—a stock of inherited values, the political system and the human developmental, or anthropogenic, system. In the case of just the economic system alone, the elements are the production and monetary-financial subsystems, together with the household, government and other sectors which are supplied with goods and services by the enterprise sector.

In modeling any one of these systems, the following type of systems diagram will be found useful since it enables the essential output of the system to be distinguished both from the other elements which constitute the system's structure and from the relevant inputs.

Inputs   *Internal Process*   *Output*

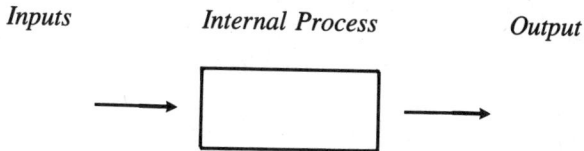

The first step in any systems analysis is to identify the output which, being unique to the system, distinguishes it from other systems. Only after this distinctive output has been identified will it be possible to identify the elements which comprise the system—and thus indicate what are the system's boundaries. For the elements which comprise the system's internal structure will be the elements which, through their interaction, produce the system's distinctive output. Since the same elements are often parts of more than one system—with the only difference being how those common elements are linked together, or organized, to produce different types of output—it is essential to have the system's distinctive output clearly in mind before beginning the analysis. For example, households, business firms, and government agencies are the elements of the political system as well as of the economic system; and it is only by first defining the economic system as the system which, by producing physical goods, or commodities, uniquely enables the individual members of society to satisfy their material needs that one can then link households, business firms and government together as the elements of an economic system separate and distinct from the political system.

What, then, differentiates one system from another is each system's distinctive output. In the case of the economic system, that distinctive output is the amount of goods (and services) produced, G, and it is therefore G which needs to be shown, in a systems diagram of the economy, under the output heading (along with the amount of employment, N, and the price level, P). Since no other social system produces goods, it is G which, as an output, distinguishes the economic system from the other major social systems. While the amount of employment, N, and the level of prices, P, are also outputs of the economic system, they are merely derivative of the process by which goods are produced and hence, for the sake of simplicity, can be subsumed under G. Thus a systems diagram for the economy would, at its simplest, take the following form:

Inputs   Internal Process   Output

$$\longrightarrow \quad \boxed{} \quad \longrightarrow \quad G$$

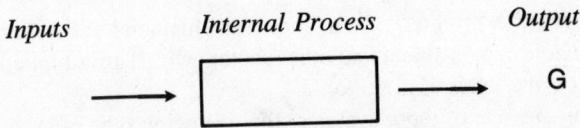

Once the output that uniquely characterizes a system has been identified, the next step is to describe the internal process by which that output is produced. In the parlance of systems theorists, this requires penetrating the "black box" that serves, even if only metaphorically, to conceal the system from the observer. Once the black box (represented in the above systems diagram as a rectangle) has somehow been penetrated and an understanding gained of how the system works, the internal process which characterizes the system can be described with varying degrees of specificity. At the very least, it is necessary to identify the factors, or elements, which are part of the system's internal structure, and then to indicate what are the relationships among these various factors which underlie the process by which the system's distinctive output is produced. This can be done through a set of prose statements alone—such as the statements that (1) G depends on F, (2) F depends on E, (3) E depends on D, etc. For greater clarity, however, especially if these relationships are subsequently to be specified more precisely, it is useful to present these statements in a mathematical form as follows:

$$
\begin{aligned}
B &= f(A)\\
C &= f(B)\\
D &= f(C)\\
E &= f(D)\\
F &= f(E)\\
G &= f(F)
\end{aligned}
\tag{1.1}
$$

which is simply another way of saying that G depends on F, F depends on E, E depends on D, etc. Alternatively, these same sets of relationships can be represented by means of a matrix, such as the one shown in exhibit 1.4, with each cell of the matrix (aside from the principal diagonal) taking either a positive value, +, or a negative value, 0. The + sign indicates that the factor identified in the column to the left has some effect on the factor shown in the top row while an 0 indicates that it has no effect.

The above set of equations, together with their relationship matrix, describe a system whose internal dynamic is based on a simple causal chain. It is only one form, the simplest one, that the relationships representing the system's internal dynamic can take—and thus it is only one form that a model of the system itself can take. The argument that is frequently made in macroeconomics—namely, that a change in the money stock will lead to a change in the interest rate, that will in turn lead to a change in investment, that will in turn lead to a change in aggregate output—is but one example of such a causal chain being postulated by economists.

There are other forms which a model can take, even a model that only identifies the underlying relationships without specifying those relationships in any greater detail. For example, the above six equations could instead take the following form:

$$B = f(C, D, E, F, G)$$
$$C = f(B, D, E, F, G)$$
$$D = f(B, C, E, F, G)$$
$$E = f(B, C, D, F, G) \qquad (1.2)$$
$$F = f(B, C, D, E, G)$$
$$G = f(B, C, D, E, F)$$

with exhibit 1.5 as the relationship matrix for this model. The model specified in these equations is a completely interdependent one in which every factor, or component of the system, depends on every other factor. (Notice that A, the seventh factor, must either be eliminated from the model or a seventh equation added, with A dependent on each of the other six factors and with A a further factor whose effect needs to be taken into account in each of the other six equations.) The neo-Walrasian general equilibrium model which forms the microeconomic foundation of the neoclassical synthesis is an example of such a completely interdependent model being postulated by economists.

Both the simple causal chain and the completely interdependent model are extreme examples of the more general systems model that will be relied upon in this textbook. Another example, one that avoids either of those two extremes, is given by the following set of equations:

$$C = f(B, E, F, G)$$
$$D = f(B, C, E, F, G)$$
$$F = f(B, C, E, G) \qquad (1.3)$$
$$G = f(B, C, E, F)$$

with exhibit 1.6 as the relationship matrix for this model. The model specified in these equations is a more general one in the sense that (a) each component, or factor, is not affected by just one other factor alone, as in a simple causal chain; and (b) each component, or factor, is not affected by, and in turn affects, every other factor, as in a completely interdependent model. Rather, each factor may be affected by two or more other factors. Moreover, each factor may be affected only by some, not all, of the other factors. Thus a systems model is not limited, on the one hand, to just simple causal chains and, on the other hand, to completely interdependent systems.

In modeling any system, it is usually not enough just to identify the set of relationships that underlie the system's dynamic behavior. One needs to specify the relationships in sufficient detail so that the system's behavior, as represented

Exhibit 1.4
Relationship Matrix
Simple Causal Chain (Mechanistic Model)

Effect of → on ↓	A	B	C	D	E	F	G
A	—	X	O	O	O	O	O
B	O	—	X	O	O	O	O
C	O	O	—	X	O	O	O
D	O	O	O	—	X	O	O
E	O	O	O	O	—	X	O
F	O	O	O	O	O	—	X
G	O	O	O	O	O	O	—

Exhibit 1.5
Relationship Matrix
Completely Interdependent (Closed) System

Effect of → on ↓	B	C	D	E	F	G
B	—	X	X	X	X	X
C	X	—	X	X	X	X
D	X	X	—	X	X	X
E	X	X	X	—	X	X
F	X	X	X	X	—	X
G	X	X	X	X	X	—

Exhibit 1.6
Relationship Matrix
General Systems Model

Effect of → on ↓	B	C	D	E	F	G
B	—	X	X	O	X	X
C	O	—	X	O	X	X
D	O	O	—	O	O	O
E	O	X	X	—	X	X
F	O	X	X	O	—	X
G	O	X	X	O	X	—

by the change occurring in one or more output variables, can actually be simulated. This means that the undefined functional relationships represented by f in the above equations need to be replaced by a more precise set of specifications which indicate: (a) how the variables within the parentheses are to be defined and measured; (b) what numerical values, if any, are to be attached to those functional relationships; and (c) under what circumstances, if any, those numerical values will vary over time. Indeed this is the type of model, with a set of mathematical equations used to represent the system's internal process, which will be developed in the chapters that follow in an effort to describe the behavior of the economic system. However, even the simpler type of model, with only the linkage between the various elements identified, makes it possible to fill in the rectangle labeled "internal process" in the corresponding systems diagram.

Thus, in completing the systems diagram for the economic system, there are three possibilities, depending on whether the equations used to represent the system's internal process are similar to those specified in equation set 1.1, equation set 1.2 or equation set 1.3. In the first case, the internal process would be that of a simple causal chain; in the second case, the internal process would be that of a completely interdepedent system, and in the third case, the internal process would be that of a more general type of systems model, with each variable or component of the system affected by more than one factor but not by every other factor.

Once all the relationships necessary for explaining how the system's output is produced have been correctly identified—and thus the system's internal process has been specified—the inputs into the system will become clear. The inputs are the variables which, like factor A in the simple causal model specified in equation set 1.1 and factors B and E in the more general systems model specified in equation set 1.3, affect at least some of the other components of the system but are not themselves affected by any of those same variables. These input variables can easily be identified from exhibits 1.4 and 1.6 by glancing up and down the columns and seeing which factors have only 0s in their column. The absence of + s means that, rather than being determined through the system's internal process, these factors are derived from without—usually as the output of some other, parallel system. As can be seen from exhibit 1.5, a completely interdependent system has no inputs. The significance of this fact will be brought out in the following subsection.

One can also glance back and forth across the rows of these same relationship matrices, seeing which factors have only 0s in their row. These factors must necessarily be an output of the system. However, any of the other factors which are part of the system's internal structure can also be an output of the system, depending on what the analysis is meant to explain. Indeed, the only factors which cannot be an output of the system are the input variables. That would render meaningless the distinction between inputs and outputs.

The various models which are to be examined in the chapters that follow, beginning with the simplest type of Keynesian macroeconomic model, will all be presented within this type of systems framework, with any exogenously determined variables treated as inputs which, through a process internal to the system, produce the output that uniquely characterizes the economic system—along with any other variable, or output, which is of interest. The various bodies of economic theory will be presented as sets of postulated relationships for filling in the rectangle labeled "internal process" in the systems diagram for the economy, with each set of postulated relationships capable of being summarized by means of the type of matrix shown in exhibits 1.4–1.6. In this way, it will be possible to identify the causal sequence by which the economic system's output is produced—not just the amount of goods and services, G, but also the amount of employment, N, and the level of prices, P. First, however, it is important to understand what, within a systems framework, is meant by causation.

1.2.2 Causation

Once the inputs into any system have been correctly identified, it is then possible to explain what causes the system to behave as it does. A system's behavior will be determined by what change, if any, is occurring in its inputs. While the other factors internal to the system also play a role—indeed, the system would not be what it is were any of those other factors absent or exerting a different type of influence—the role they play becomes a constant, or parameter, once the relationships which constitute the system's internal process have been specified. It is only the inputs that, not being affected by any of the other factors, are free to vary in such a way that the behavior of the system will be altered. Thus any change in the system's behavior, as represented by a change in one or more output variables, must be due to a change in some input. That is why it is so important to be able to identify the system's inputs correctly.

There are two separate ways in which the system's inputs will determine its behavior, depending on which of two possible forms each of the different inputs takes. If the input represents a continuous quantitative flow of some sort, it will be part of the system's internal dynamic. This is the case, for example, of factor A in the causal chain specified in equation set 1.1 (as well as factors B and E in the more general systems model specified in equation set 1.3). A change in the value of A will lead to a change in the value of the output variable, G, with A, as the determinant of B, part of the system's internal process. Indeed, it is possible to trace out the entire causal sequence by which a change in A will lead to a change in G as follows:

$$A \longrightarrow B \longrightarrow C \longrightarrow D \longrightarrow E \longrightarrow F \longrightarrow G$$

As will soon become clear, it is precisely this type of causal sequence, with the arrows pointing in one direction only, which distinguishes a completely mechanistic model, such as the simple causal chain represented by equation set 1.1, from a more general systems model.

Alternatively, the input may represent one of several possible states in which the system may find itself, with each of those states denoting a different behavioral pattern—and hence a different internal process. In the latter case, the input determines what the internal process will be but is not itself a part of that internal process. It is simply a parameter of the system, though a critical one. The difference between the two types of inputs can perhaps be better understood by taking a stereophonic system as an example. The continuous inflow of electricity when the system is "plugged in" and turned on, along with the continuous inflow of radio signals when the dial has been set for AM or FM, represent the first type of input. The on or off state, together with the settings for the other dials, represent the second type of input. For the moment, we will focus on the first type of input, one that represents a continuous flow of some sort and hence is part of the system's internal dynamic.

The series of steps by which a change in some continuous flow input leads to a change in one or more of the variables, or components, internal to the system and thence, after whatever interaction there may be among the factors internal to the system, to a change in one or more of the output variables is the causal sequence underlying the system's behavior. The principal challenge, in modeling any system, is to identify correctly that causal sequence (which necessarily depends on being able to identify correctly not just the inputs into the system but also the system's internal dynamic). Often, in what is termed the "reduced form" of the model being used to represent the system, the input variables are linked directly to the output variables, thereby omitting the intervening steps by which the change in one or more of the system's inputs leads to a change in its output. This is permissible as long as it is recognized that the inputs are not determining the change in the system's output directly, but rather only indirectly through a process which is, for the moment, being ignored. Indeed, with any complex system necessarily consisting of subsystems which themselves are combinations of subsystems, this truncation of the causal sequence may be necessary in order to avoid so much detail that one cannot see the larger picture.

Thus the six equations needed to bring out the causal sequence in the simple causal chain specified in equation set 1.1 can be eliminated from the systems diagram when a reduced form of the model will suffice, and the systems diagram can then take the following, more simplified form:

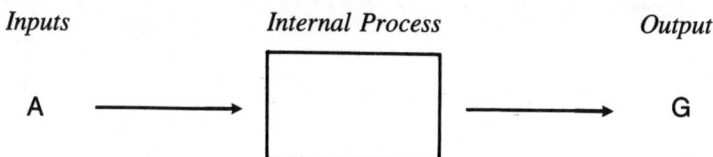

Inputs   *Internal Process*   *Output*

A ⟶ [ ] ⟶ G

Indeed, in that case, the systems diagram becomes superfluous and the original causal sequence,

$$A \rightarrow B \rightarrow C \rightarrow D \rightarrow E \rightarrow F \rightarrow G$$

which is that of a completely mechanistic system, becomes, in the reduced form of the model,

$$A \longrightarrow G$$

One must not forget, however, that this is a simplification of a more complex set of relationships—even if the causation still remains unidirectional and the model itself, mechanistic.

A completely mechanistic model, such as the simple causal chain specified in equation set 1.1, is almost always inadequate to represent any actual social system—even as a reduced form of model. This is because any complex system usually involves a feedback relationship between its output and one or more of its inputs. For example, the argument that a change in the money stock will lead to a change in the interest rate, that in turn will lead to a change in investment, that in turn will lead to a change in aggregate output ignores the fact that the size of the money stock will itself be affected by the level of aggregate output. What this means is that, if A denotes a change in the money stock and G denotes a change in the level of aggregate output, the one-way line of causation shown above needs to be replaced by a two-way line of causation as follows:

$$A \rightleftharpoons G$$

While G is still affected by A, A is now in turn affected by G. The two variables are, in fact, interdependent—as is the case, for example, in the type of accelerator-multiplier relationship which is also frequently postulated in macroeconomics and which will form an important part of the model to be developed in this text.

Any feedback effect of this sort can be depicted, in a systems diagram, as follows:

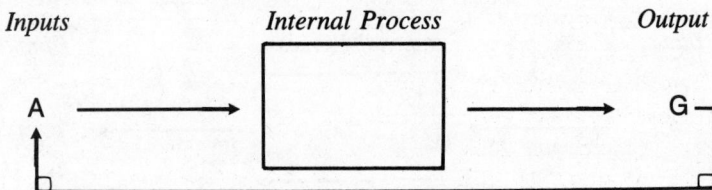

Inputs   *Internal Process*   *Output*

with the line marked by the squares at the corners indicating the feedback effect of the system's output on its inputs. The systems diagram makes it clear that what is being analyzed is not just the behavior of a single system in isolation but rather the interaction between that system and the larger environment, or system, of which it is a part. Thus, while showing A and B linked by two arrows, each pointing in the opposite direction, is sufficient to indicate their dependence on one another, this mode of presentation obscures what is actually a more complex set of relationships.

Indeed, even the above systems diagram is a somewhat overly simplified view of the actual relationships which need to be taken into account. For a system's output will feed back on, and thus affect, one or more of the system's inputs only if that output serves as an input into one or more parallel systems, with the output of those parallel systems serving, in turn, as an input back into the first system. Those parallel systems will, in fact, constitute the environment in which the system being analyzed operates—with those parallel systems, together with the system actually under examination, constituting *in toto* some larger system. This more complex set of relationships can be brought out in a systems diagram which includes each of the relevant systems and the various links between them. However, to avoid introducing too many complications all at once, it may be necessary to focus on just one system alone, with any feedback effects between the output of that system and the system's inputs (via the system's influence on the other, parallel systems which form its external environment) shown as in the above diagram.

The advantage of a more general systems framework, then, is that it allows for any interdependence which may exist, not only among the elements, or factors, which constitute the internal structure of any system but also between the output of the system and its inputs through any feedback effect. Indeed, since any interdependence among the elements constituting the internal structure of a system is usually only the interrelationship among the different subsystems which make up the larger system, the two types of interdependence are essentially the same—the only difference being the level within the extant hierarchy of systems at which the analysis is being carried out. It is because it can take into account this type of interdependence that a more general systems model is to be preferred to a simple causal chain, or completely mechanistic model. A systems framework is in fact meant to make intelligible the interrelationship, and hence interdependence, among factors that is frequently observed in economic and other types of biological systems while still making it possible to trace out what are the lines of causation. This last proviso is important because it explains why not only simple causal chains but also any model of complete interdependence is to be avoided.

A completely interdependent model, such as the one specified in equation set 1.5, represents a system which, as already noted, has no inputs. This means it is a "closed" system, and as such it runs counter to the observation that, with the possible exception of the universe as a whole, there is no such thing in practice as a closed system. Every system, beginning at the level of subatomic physics and even including the galaxies, is part of a larger system from which it must obtain inputs and to which it contributes its own distinctive output. The fact that a completely interdependent system has no inputs also means that once it has somehow come into being its behavior will, from that point on, be governed solely by its own internal dynamic, without that behavior being subject to change. The system will thus constitute a perpetual motion machine whose behavior cannot be said to be caused by anything except what enabled the system to come into being in the first place. The limitations of such a model are obvious. As the most serious criticism of all, it makes no allowance for causation in the form of the external factors which influence the behavior of the system.

At the very least, any model of an actual social system must include one or more inputs. To encompass all the possibilities, at least one of the inputs must be a state variable indicating which of several possible internal processes applies and thus how the system might change over time as the result of exogenous influences. In this way, the same systems framework can be used to analyze the historical evolution of various social systems, including the economic. Still, it is not enough merely to posit various state variables. In the case of any actual social system, it is likely that some of the inputs will take the form of various quantitative flows per unit of time. This is certainly true of the subsystems that constitute the economic system—as it is true of the economic system itself. It is primarily through a change in these continuous flow inputs that the behavior of the economic system and its subcomponents will be altered. Thus a model which does not allow for any such inputs is a model which cannot trace out the causal process by which the system's behavior is determined. It is for this reason that, if the causal sequence underlying the behavior of the economic system is to be identified, the model of a completely interdependent system, such as the one specified in equation set 1.2, needs to be replaced by a more general systems model.

One can therefore posit the following four-fold matrix of systems models, depending on whether the model allows for (a) interdependence, and/or (b) causation:

Interdependence

		Yes	No
Causation	Yes	General Systems Models	Mechanistic Models
	No	Completely Interdependent Models	Taxonomic Models

Notice that only the general systems model allows both for interdependence and causation while a taxonomic model—one which, like this delineation of possible systems models, merely provides a set of categories—encompasses neither interdependence nor causation. The deficiency of both the simple causal chain and the model of complete interdependence is that they are able to encompass only one, and not the other, of these two salient features of real-world systems, such as the economy.

1.2.3 *The dynamic adjustment process*

Many systems, including the economic, need to achieve one or more output states in order to avoid breaking down in some important way. Economists use the term "equilibrium" to describe that output state, but following the practice of systems theorists, this text will use the term "homeostatis" since equilibrium suggests the type of mechanistic model which is inappropriate to a social system.

The prevailing method of analysis in economics is to assume that the homeostatic condition is necessarily satisfied by the existence of markets and then to indicate what values for the relevant set of output variables are consistent with that homeostatic condition. Thus, in the conventional microeconomic analysis the assumed homeostatic condition is that demand and supply will be equal to one another in each of the markets and this assumption then enables the price and quantity variables to be derived once a set of production and/or utility functions has been specified. Even the neo-Ricardian critics of the conventional microeconomic theory, by substituting an equal rate of return on capital across industries for the balance between demand and supply, merely replace one homeostatic condition with another before proceeding to derive, in the same manner, the relevant set of prices.

The text in hand departs from this method in two critically important ways. First, it identifies a number of homeostatic conditions as being of far greater significance than either the balance between demand and supply emphasized by orthodox economists or the equal rate of return on capital emphasized by the neo-Ricardians. One of those more significant homeostatic conditions is an extension of the Keynesian argument that aggregate savings must be equal to aggregate investment. The other four conditions will be identified as the argument is further developed (see, for example, chapter 4, section 1.4). The emphasis throughout the text on a quite different set of homeostatic conditions radically transforms the analysis. As an even more striking departure from the usual mode of analysis in economics, however, the text in hand avoids assuming that these homeostatic conditions will necessarily be satisfied. On the contrary, it assumes that if the homeostatic conditions are by any chance satisfied at some one point in time, they will soon no longer be satisfied as exogenous factors continue to exert an influence on the behavior of the economic system. This enables the text, at certain key points in the argument, to focus on the dynamic adjustment process which is initiated whenever one of the homeostatic conditions is not satisfied.

In each case, the dynamic adjustment process will be analyzed as a series of steps which has the effect of either bringing the economy closer to the required output state or causing the system to depart still further from that homeostatic condition. When the first type of sequence occurs, the dynamic adjustment process can be described as a stabilizing one, with the economic system itself functioning, at least in this regard, as a self-correcting cybernetic mechanism. This means that the economic system's internal process is such that it leads to a gradual reduction, via the feedback relationships that characterize the system, in the discrepancy between the system's actual output state and the homeostatic condition. When the dynamic adjustment process causes the economic system to deviate even further from that homeostatic condition, the process can be described as a destabilizing one, and unless that process is counteracted by some other dynamic, the economic system will be prone to periodic breakdowns as the prelude to some fundamental reorganization of the system.

In analyzing the economic system's dynamic adjustment processes, each of the separate steps in the process will be identified. Whether each of those separate steps can be observed in practice is the empirical test that will be insisted upon to determine whether such a dynamic adjustment process actually operates within the economy. In this way, it will be possible to carry out in the chapters that follow a "disequilibrium" analysis to complement the more usual type of equilibrium analysis in which economists engage. The latter, it should be noted, is merely a logical inference from whatever homeostatic conditions can be shown to be necessary for the continued viability of the economic system and, in contrast to what is true of the disequilibrium analysis that will be developed in this text, it depends for its validity on a set of mathematical rather than empirical proofs.

The disequilibrium analysis that will be carried out is possible because of the systems framework that is adopted in this text. It is a systems framework that makes it possible to view any "disequilibrium" as simply a discrepancy between the system's current output state and some homeostatic condition—and then to analyze, as a series of steps, the process by which the system either moves closer, via the system's feedback relationships, to that homeostatic condition or, alternatively, departs still further from one of the conditions which need to be satisfied if a breakdown of the system is to be avoided.

1.2.4 The economic system in context

Finally, a systems framework makes it possible to place the economic system in its proper social context.

The economic system can be viewed as one of three operative systems which, along with a set of inherited values, or beliefs, encompass all of the observable social reality. Together, these systems and the stock of inherited values constitute the four institutional dimensions of any social system. The other two systems which operate parallel to the economic system are the political and the anthropogenic. The former, which produces societal and other group decisions in the course of resolving conflict among the individual members of society, has long been recognized by social scientists, and hence there is no need to describe the political system in greater detail, at least yet. The anthropogenic system, however, is a different matter. Although its component parts—the family, the school, and the employing organization—have also long been known to social scientists, the way in which these component parts function as a single system to produce the various skills, or competences, which the individual members of society possess has been identified only within the last few years. Thus, some further description of the anthropogenic system is in order.

The competences which the anthropogenic system produces represent the highest level of human development. They consist of the ability to use various skills, motor as well as cognitive ones, in a social setting. These competences are acquired through the process of successive affiliation with different types of developmental institutions, beginning with the family, continuing with the school system and then ending with one or more employing organizations. The competences acquired in this manner build on the individual's prior physical, emotional, intellectual, and inter-personal development; and they enable the individual to assume the many different roles as citizen, worker, parent, and even savant that are necessary to the functioning of an advanced industrial society. Indeed, without the competences produced by the anthropogenic system, the other societal systems would be without the human resource inputs they require. This is no less true of the economic system, since the anthropogenic system is the only source of the labor needed to staff the system's capital facilities and supervise the other workers. The anthropogenic system is, in turn, dependent on the economic system for the employment opportunities that enable the competences only partially acquired within the family and at school to be more fully developed. The interdependence between the economic and anthropogenic systems which has just been described is but one of the ways in which the three operative systems interact with one another. Along with the interdependence between the economic and political systems, it is particularly important, as later chapters will bring out, for understanding the macrodynamic behavior of the American economy. (Chapter 10 describes the interrelationships between the economic and political systems, as well as desciding the political system itself more fully. Chapter 13 describes the interrelationships between the economic and anthropogenic systems more fully, as well as describing the anthropogenic system itself more fully.)

Exhibit 1.7 compares the three operative systems in terms of various attributes. What is common to all three systems is the fact that they can be analyzed as systems. This implies the following:

1. Each consists of various components, which themselves are likely to be systems whose components are subsystems.

2. Each system obtains from its environment the inputs that activate the rest of

Exhibit 1.7

Summary of Key Attributes of the Three Operative Systems

System	Political	Economic	Anthropogenic
Function	To produce decisions through conflict resolution	To meet material needs	To develop individual competence through instruction and training
Quintessential activity	Coalition formation	Exchange	Affiliation
Key components	Formal and informal organs of government; executive, legislative, and judicial branches of government	Business firms, financial institutions, households, and government	Family, schools, employing organizations
Nature of feedback	Voting behavior (electoral system only)	Consumer and other final purchases (market system only)	Time, energy commitments

the system. That environment consists of either: (a) one of the other institutional dimensions, or (b) one of the natural systems which coexist on this planet with human societies.

3. Each system relies on an internal process, or dynamic, to transform the inputs that it obtains from its environment into a unique set of outputs that distinguish it from the other, parallel social systems. Some of that output will trigger a response, in the form of feedback, from the environment in which the system operates. That feedback enables the system to move closer to attaining the goals that can be attributed to it from the function that the system serves within the larger society.

What has just been said applies to the economic system no less than to the other two operative systems of any society. Its component parts are the enterprise, household, government and, in anything less than the global economy itself, the rest-of-the-world sectors, with the enterprise sector divided, among other ways, into financial and nonfinancial subsectors. The economic system obtains its inputs—for example, economic policies and skilled workers, raw materials and sunshine—from the other institutional dimensions of society as well as from the natural systems that constitute the ecological environment. The economic system's output consists of the physical goods that are produced by the enterprise sector using those inputs. (The question of whether the economic system produces any but physical goods so that its output can be described as goods *and services* must wait for the more extended discussion, in the next chapter, of how the economic system's output is to be defined.) In the case of a market system, the goods produced generate a response, in the form of sales behavior, that will guide the enterprise sector in its subsequent production activity. Indeed, the description of this feedback mechanism in Adam Smith's *The Wealth of Nations* (1776) is probably one of the first explications of cybernetic principles in the social science literature.

The fourth institutional dimension is occupied not by an operative system but rather by the stock of prevailing assumptions that guide the everyday behavior of society's members. This is the value orientation, or normative dimension, and it includes not only all beliefs about what ought to be but also—given the epistemological principle that what passes for truth is simply what has not yet been disproven—all supposed knowledge as well. The value orientation permeates every other dimension of society, for it provides the subjective underpinnings of the patterned behavior that can be observed along each of those dimensions. Again, this is no less true of the economic system. The importance of the value configurations known as mercantilism, laissez-faire and socialism in economic history, along with the cumulative growth of technical and other types of validated knowledge for organizing economic activity, attest to this point.

The value orientation, though coequal with the other three institutional dimensions of society in every other respect, cannot be regarded as a system. Rather it is only a stock which, though it may change systematically over time in a way that can be made intelligible, is nonetheless likely, when considered as a whole at any given moment, to lack one essential characteristic of a system. What the value orientation is likely to lack is the logical structure that gives a system its coherence. A particular value orientation may be logically coherent. But, since it resides in the memory of the society, collective as well as individual, it need not be. Indeed, one of the things philosophers and other intellectuals attempt to do is to make value configurations, or value systems, coherent. Still, they will not necessarily be successful in this effort— even for themselves, let alone for the society as a whole. To a considerable extent, this is because the reality they are attempting to understand will itself be changing—largely as a result of any better understanding they may gain of that reality.

Thus, the value orientation of a society need not be coherent and, in this sense, will not constitute an integral system. Indeed, the nonsystematic nature of the value orientation is an important source of the dynamism of human societies. It is the reason why, in advanced societies, the state is normally precluded from using its coercive powers to force adherence to any particular value orientation, be it a particular religion or some other set of beliefs. Like the institutions found along the other three dimensions of society, however, the value orientation can be viewed, and thereby judged, as a means of enhancing the options that the individual members of the society have. It is just that the value orientation has to be assessed in terms of its appropriateness—that is, how valid are the assumptions which its various components represent—and not how effective it is in producing a certain type of output, whether decisions, material goods or competences.

What has just been outlined is a systems framework both for integrating the study of various aspects of social life and for placing the economic system in a larger social context. It is this framework, based on the delineation of four separate institutional dimensions—the normative, the political, the economic and the anthropogenic—that will be relied on in the subsequent chapters of this text to indicate the relationship between the economic system and the other institutional dimensions of society. In particular, it will be used to identify the relevant inputs into the economic system so that the question of what causes the economic system to behave as it does, macrodynamically, can be answered.

Recommended Readings

In connection with the purpose and subject matter of economics, see Ron J. Stanfield, "Institutional Analysis," in *Why Economics is not yet a Science*, Alfred S. Eichner, ed., Armonk, N.Y.: M. E. Sharpe, 1983; Janos Kornai, *Antiequilibrium*, New York: American Elsevier, 1971; Lionel Robbins, *An Essay on the Nature and Significance of Economic Science*, London: Macmillan, 1937.

In connection with post-Keynesian theory and its relationship to neoclassical theory, see Alfred S. Eichner, *A Guide to Post-Keynesian Economics*, Armonk, N.Y.: M. E. Sharpe, 1979; Alfred S. Eichner and J. A. Kregel, "An Essay on Post-Keynesian Theory: A New Paradigm in Economics," *Journal of Economic Literature*, December 1975; Nina Shapiro, "The Revolutionary Character of Post-Keynesian Economics," *Journal of Economic Issues*, September 1977; E. Ray Canterbery, *The Making of Economics*, 3rd ed., Belmont, Calif.: Wadsworth, 1986; Paul Davidson, "Post Keynesian Economics," *Public Interest*, special issue, 1980; Geoffrey C. Harcourt, "Post-Keynesianism: Quite Wrong and/or Nothing New?" *Thames Papers on Political Economy*, Summer 1982.

The classic work on systems theory is Norbert Wiener, *Cybernetics*, Cambridge, Mass.: MIT Press, 1948 (a nonmathematic exposition of which is Norbert Wiener, *The Human Use of Human Beings*, Boston: Houghton Mifflin, 1950). See also W. Ross Ashby, *An Introduction to Cybernetics*, London: Chapman & Hall, 1961; Jiri Klir and Miroslav Valach, *Cybernetic Modeling*, London: Iliffe Books, 1967; Ervin Laszlo, *Introduction to Systems Philosophy*, New York: Gordon & Breach, 1972; L. von Bertalanffy, "General System Theory: A New Approach to Unity of Science," *Human Biology*, 1951, pp. 303–61; Russell L. Ackoff and Fred E. Emery, *On Purposeful Systems*, Chicago: Aldine, 1972; Gerald M. Weinberg, *An Introduction to General Systems Thinking*, New York: Wiley, 1975; C. West Churchman, *The Design of Inquiring Systems*, New York: Basic Books, 1971.

On the use of systems theory in the social sciences, see Walter Buckley, *Sociology and Modern Systems Theory*, Englewood Cliffs, N.J.: Prentice-Hall, 1967; Alfred Kuhn, *The Study of Society*, Homewood, Ill.: Irwin, 1963. For an attempt to apply systems theory to economics, see Oskar Lange, *An Introduction to Economic Cybernetics*, New York: Pergamon, 1970; Kenneth E. Boulding, *A Primer on Social Dynamics*, New York: Free Press, 1970.

On alternative approaches to integrating the social sciences, see Talcott Parsons and Neil J. Smelser, *Economy and Society*, New York: Free Press, 1956; Immanuel Wallerstein, *The Modern World-System*, New York: Academic Press, 1976.

Chapter 2

The Accounting Framework

Contents

Chapter 2

The Accounting Framework

In order to construct an empirically valid model of the economy, it is necessary to have an adequate data base. That is why the development of the National Income and Product Accounts (NIPA) in the 1930s and '40s was no less critical than the contemporaneous Keynesian transformation of theory in enabling economics to take the very first steps toward becoming a science. Even today these accounts are the principal source of data for measuring the real flow of resources and the counterflow of income in an advanced market economy like that of the United States. Still, they are only one element in a larger set of accounts with which an economist needs to be familiar. No less important in modeling a monetarized production system are the input-output tables which capture the interindustry movement of material goods and the Flow of Funds Accounts (FOFA) which track the system's financial flows. These three separate elements, with the input-output tables and the Flow of Funds Accounts to a large extent dictating the form which the National Income and Product Accounts will take, constitute the essential accounting framework for studying the macrodynamic behavior of the economy. All three of these essential elements will be described in the sections which follow, beginning with the crucial input-output tables. What needs to be understood are what types of data are available and what are the sources of those data.

The National Income and Product Accounts, together with the input-output tables and the Flow of Funds Accounts, are more than just a source of data, however. They are also a means of specifying the categories under which data are to be organized. The categories themselves are neither predetermined nor self-evident. Rather they reflect the choice which must be made as to how the economic process is to be conceptualized. That choice can only be made on *a priori* theoretical grounds (subject, however, to later revision as the theory itself improves). Thus, in laying out the accounting framework, there is a prior set of theoretical issues which needs to be resolved before the categories can be established. These theoretical issues include even so basic a question as how the Beconomic system's output is to be defined. It turns out that the statistic most commonly used—the Gross National Product, or GNP—is not necessarily the best measure. What will become clear in the sections which follow is that, in constructing an empirically valid model of the economy, theory must serve as the guide—even in assembling the necessary data base. That is why it is so important that the theory not be misleading.

Exhibit 2.1
Hypothetical Input-Output Table
(1978, $billion)

Inputs obtained from industry ↓ \ Outputs sold to industry →	A	B	C	D	E	Other output flows	Industry gross output
A	—	23.7	85.0	22.8	35.3	217.1	383.9
B	43.1	—	3.5	14.6	47.8	549.2	658.2
C	16.9	3.8	—	43.1	16.4	268.7	342.9
D	24.1	22.5	19.5	—	56.6	614.5	737.2
E	51.6	132.1	65.4	15.3	—	99.4	363.8
Other outlays (value added)	248.2	476.1	169.5	641.4	213.7	1,748.9	
Total outlays	383.9	658.2	342.9	737.2	363.8		4,235.0

2.1 The Input-Output Model

The production subsystem, consisting of n different industries, constitutes the very core of the economic system. It is this subsystem which produces most, if not all, of the economy's output. The flow of material goods (and services) among these n different industries is best captured by the type of input-output model first developed by Wassily Leontief. An understanding of this model is essential, not just because it will be used throughout the rest of this text to analyze the behavior of the enterprise sector but also because it now serves as the conceptual basis for the National Income and Product Accounts themselves. While the NIPA were originally constructed on a somewhat different basis, the input-output tables which are produced quinquennially by the U.S. Department of Commerce's Bureau of Economic Analysis now provide the "benchmark" estimates of aggregate economic output and its various components. It is not possible to understand how these aggregate measures are derived without first understanding how an input-output table, as the empirical implementation of an input-output model, is constructed.

2.1.1 The interindustry flows

An input-output table, such as the one shown in exhibit 2.1, shows the interindustry flow of goods (and services) in value terms, that is, without those nominal quantities being broken down into their separate components, a physical quantity, q, and a value, or price, p, per unit of physical quantity. Thus, if one glances along the first row of the input-output table shown in exhibit 2.1, one can see what disposition is made of the output produced by industry A. Of the total $383.9 billion worth of goods industry A produces within a given year (shown as the very last entry in that row, under the heading, "Industry Gross Output"), $23.7 billion flows as sales to industry B, $85.0 billion flows as sales to industry C, $22.8 billion flows as sales to industry D, etc. Similarly, by glancing along each of the other rows in the table, one can see what disposition is made of the output produced by each of the other industries. For example, as shown in the fourth row down, of the $614.5 billion worth of goods industry D produces within a given year, $24.1 billion flows as sales to industry A, $22.5 billion flows as sales to industry B, $19.5 billion flows as sales to industry C, etc.

Once the amount of each industry's output sold to other industries is known, the same input-output table can be used to see where each industry obtains its inputs of material goods (and business services). One need only glance down that particular industry's column. Thus, in the case of industry A, one can see that it purchases as inputs to be used in its own production process $43.1 billion of industry B's output, $16.9 billion of industry C's output, $24.1 billion of industry D's output, etc. Similarly, by glancing down the fourth column one can see that industry D purchases as inputs to be used in its own production process $22.8 billion of industry A's output, $14.6 billion of industry B's output, $43.1 billion of industry C's output, etc.

The rows showing the flow of each industry's output to other industries and the columns showing the source of each industry's inputs from the same other industries constitutes the input-output table's *inner matrix*. It is an n-by-n matrix, with n the number of different industries represented in the table. While only five separate industries are shown in exhibit 2.1 so as to keep the table as simple as possible, n is a much larger number in the case of the actual input-output tables which has been constructed for the U.S. and other economies, as will be brought out shortly. Still, the principles underlying the input-output table remain the same, whatever the value of n and thus whatever the size of the input-output table's inner matrix.

This inner matrix can be described in either of two ways, depending on the perspective which is adopted. On the one hand, viewing it as the combined flow of each industry's output to each of the other industries, the inner matrix can be described as the enterprise sector's *intermediate output*. This is the output of each industry which, instead of flowing outside the enterprise sector to the other sectors of the economy, remains within the enterprise sector as inputs into the other industries that, as a group, constitute the enterprise sector, or subsystem of production. This intermediate output of each industry (its sales to each of the other industries, or the sum of the first five figures shown in each row of the table in exhibit 2.1) can be subtracted from the industry's total output (the last figure in each row, denoted as "industry gross output"), with the difference being that particular industry's contribution to the net, or final, output of the enterprise sector as a whole (the next to last figure in each row, denoted as "other output flows"). Indeed, the difference can be termed the industry's *final output* (or rather, more accurately, the output available for final use or consumption).

On the other hand, the inner matrix can be viewed as the combined outlays by each industry on the output produced by each of the other industries. These are the outlays on material inputs (and business services) produced within the enterprise sector itself as distinct from the outlays on labor and the other inputs available only from without. These outlays for material inputs (the first five figures shown in each column of the table in exhibit 2.1) can be subtracted from the total revenue obtained by each industry from the sale of its output (the last figure in each column, denoted as "total outlays," which, as can be seen, is the same as the figure for the industry's "gross output"), with the difference represented by three additional chargeable items. They are: (1) whatever must be paid to workers in wages and salaries (the industry's wage bill); (2) whatever must be paid to the government to cover any excise or other indirect taxes (the industry's *ad valorem* tax bill); and (3) whatever remains left over as property income (the industry's profits). These three items constitute the industry's *value added*.

Looking at the inner matrix in this second way makes it possible to do two things. The first is to specify a production function, in value terms, for each of the *n* industries represented in the table. For it is the figures shown in each of the vertical columns which indicate how much of every other industry's output is required to enable the industry listed at the head of the column to produce a given amount of output.

The point can perhaps be better grasped from exhibit 2.2, where the nominal flows shown in exhibit 2.1 have been converted to direct requirements ratios by dividing the figures in each column of the table in exhibit 2.1 by the figure for total outlays at the bottom of each column. Thus, as can be seen from exhibit 2.2, industry A, in order to produce a dollar's worth of output, must obtain 11.2 percent of its inputs (in value terms) from industry B; another 4.4 percent of its inputs (in value terms) from industry C; another 6.3 percent of its inputs (in value terms) from industry D, etc.—with the material inputs (and business services) obtained from all the other industries representing 35.4 percent of industry A's total input requirements (in value terms). The remaining 64.6 percent of industry A's inputs (in value terms) are the labor and capital inputs the cost of which, together with any government services that are provided, must be covered by what the industry is able to add, in setting its price, to the cost of material inputs (and business services). Indeed, that difference between the price of the output

Exhibit 2.2
Direct Requirements Ratios

Inputs obtained from industry ↓ \ Outputs sold to industry →	A	B	C	D	E
A	—	0.0360	0.2479	0.0309	0.0973
B	0.1122	—	0.0105	0.0199	0.1313
C	0.0440	0.0058	—	0.0584	0.0285
D	0.0628	0.0342	0.0565	—	0.1555
E	0.1345	0.2007	0.1907	0.0208	—
(Value added) (labor and capital)	0.6465	0.7233	0.4944	0.8700	0.5874
Total	1.000	1.000	1.000	1.000	1.000

sold and the cost of the inputs purchased from other industries is the industry's value added.

The production function, in value terms, which is given for each industry in the vertical column of the input-output table under its heading is in effect the industry's cost function. All that is necessary to complete the analysis of costs is to divide the figure for value added into its wage, tax and profit components. Before taking this next step, however, it is best to replace the production functions, in value terms, represented by the columns in exhibit 2.2 with individual industry production functions—in physical terms. This can be done by breaking down the nominal values shown in exhibit 2.1 into their two components, a physical quantity, q, and a value, or price, p. Indeed, this is how individual industry production functions, in physical terms, will be derived when the analysis of production and costs is resumed in chapter 5.

The second thing which can be done once the inner matrix is viewed as the set of combined outlays on material inputs (and business services) is of more immediate relevance. This is to develop an accounting framework for deriving the various aggregate measures of economic activity, particularly the national product and the national income. It turns out that such a framework has the important advantage of providing a cross-check on any estimates that are obtained. Indeed, it is for this reason that, as will be explained in the next section, the quinquennial "benchmark" estimates of the national product and the national income for the United States—the basis for all the annual and quarterly data used in empirical research—are obtained by first constructing an input-output table for the U.S. economy.

The net, or final, output for each of the industries which make up the enterprise sector has already been identified as the gross, or total, output (the last figure in each row of the table in exhibit 2.1) less the intermediate output (all but the last two figures in each row). This net output for each industry (the next to last figure in each row) can then be summed up for all n industries to obtain the net, or final, output for the enterprise sector as a whole. (In the case of the economy represented in exhibit 2.1, the net output for the enterprise sector as a whole is $1,748.9 billion, a figure obtained by adding up all the figures shown in the next-to-last column of the table.) This net output for the enterprise sector as a whole is the portion of the national product that originates within the business, or enterprise, sector. If business firms were the only source of economic output—and we shall see, in the next major section of this chapter, the extent to which this is the case— then the net, or final, output for all n industries would, when aggregated, constitute the entire national product (in value, or nominal, terms).

Assuming, for the moment, that business firms are the only source of economic output, the national product can be calculated simply by adding up all the figures in the next-to-last column of the input-output table. This estimate can then be cross-checked, once the inner matrix of the input-output table and the final column have been filled in. For while the net, or final, output produced by any one industry (the last figure in each row less all but the last two figures in the same row) need not be equal to the value added by the same industry (the last figure in each column less all but the last two figures in the same column), the *sum* of the final output produced by each industry (the total for the figures in the next-to-last column in the table) must necessarily be equal to the *sum* of the value added by each industry (the total for the figures in the next-to-bottom row). The reason is that, since the funds used to cover each industry's outlays (plus any profits) are the funds obtained by each industry from the sale of its gross ouput, the figures in the final column are necessarily the same as the figures in the bottom row.

The point can perhaps be better grasped from exhibit 2.3, which partitions the input-output table shown in exhibit 2.1 into five segments: (1) the inner matrix, which represents both the value of the enterprise sector's intermediate output and the value of the material inputs (and business services) needed to produce the sector's total output; (2) the enterprise sector's net, or final, output (the next-to-last column in the input-output table, here redesignated as the value of the net, or final, output); (3) the enterprise sector's gross, or total, output (the last column in the table, here redesignated as the value of total output); (4) the value added by the enterprise sector (the next-to-bottom row); and (5) the enterprise sector's total outlays (the bottom row, here also redesignated as the value of total output to

Exhibit 2.3

The Component Parts of an Input-Output Table

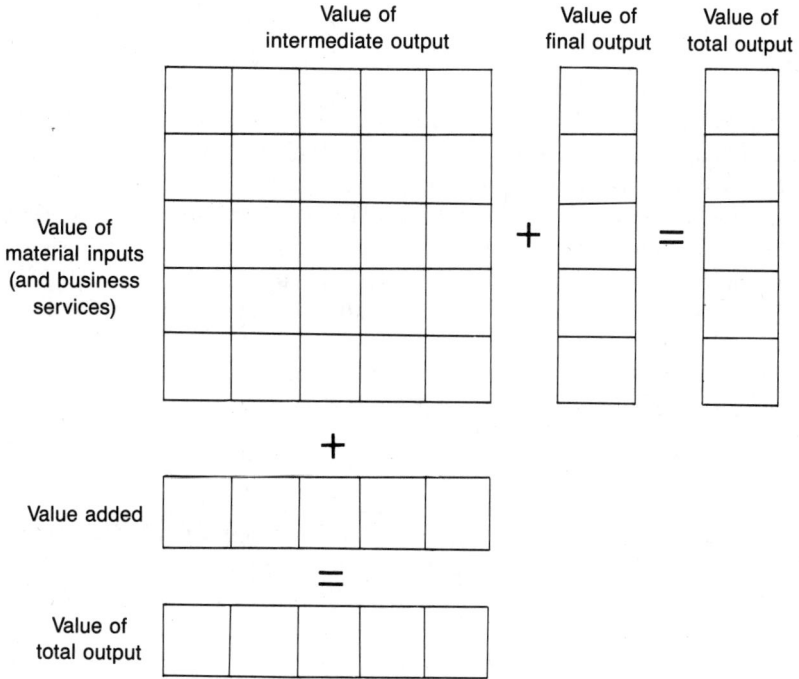

indicate that it is necessarily the same as the last column in the input-output table).

What can be seen from exhibit 2.3 is that the value of the enterprise sector's total output is equal to the value of its intermediate output plus the value of its final output—and thus that the value of the enterprise sector's final output is equal to the value of its total output less the value of its intermediate output. But what can also be seen from exhibit 2.3 is that the value of the enterprise sector's total output is equal to the value of material inputs (as well as business services) plus the value added—and thus that the value added is equal to the value of total output less the value of the material inputs (and business services) used to produce the total output. Moreover, with the value of total output and the value of the intermediate output/material inputs the same in both cases, it follows that the value of the enterprise sector's final output is necessarily equal to its value added. This result takes on particular significance when it is realized that the value of the enterprise sector's final output is in fact the national product which originates within the enterprise sector while the value added in that sector, the sum of the wages and taxes paid as well as any profits earned, is in fact the national income originating in that sector. Indeed, it is in this way that it can then be shown that the national product originating in the business sector is necessarily equal to the national income originating therein.

It should be noted, however, that this does not "prove" that the national product (or at least that portion which originates within the enterprise sector) is necessarily equal to the national income. Rather, they turn out to be equal to one another because the various categories used to construct the input-output table have been defined in such a way that the national product originating in the business sector will be equal to the national income originating therein. Specifically, this result is assured by including a residual component, profits, in the value added measure which, by the very way it is calculated, equates the revenues earned with the costs, or outlays, incurred. Still, it is useful to have the national product originating in the enterprise sector equal to the national income originating in the same sector, even if this is only true by virtue of the definitions employed, since it enables the estimates of national product and national income to be cross-checked for the years in which the interindustry flows are captured by an input-output table. What next needs to be understood is how such an input-output table is actually constructed for the U.S. economy.

2.1.2 Constructing the U.S. tables

There are three critical tasks in constructing any input-output table. The first is to delineate the set of n industries to be shown both at the top of the table and on the far left side. The second task is to fill in the cells both of the inner matrix and of the last column and row. The third and final task is to decompose the aggregates that, as the sum of the figures shown in the next-to-last column, constitute the national product originating in the enterprise sector and, as the sum of the figures in the next-to-bottom row, constitute the national income originating in the same sector. This subsection will describe how, in constructing an input-output table for the U.S. economy, the first two of these critical tasks is carried out. The next subsection will describe how the third task is carried out—an essential one if a detailed set of national income and product accounts is to be obtained.

Defining the relevant set of industries is no less a theoretical than an empirical task. The theoretical issues, however, will be put to one side, at least for now (see chapter 5, section 1.1). As a practical matter, the U.S. government has adopted a Standard Industrial Classification (SIC) which the Department of Commerce's Bureau of Economic Analysis then uses as the basis for delineating the set of n industries in the input-output table it assembles once every five years following the Census of Manufacturing and related business surveys. Based on the SIC, more than 5,000 separate industries can be delineated, each consisting of all the business establishments (separately standing plants or offices) that, as determined by the applicable census, produce the same type of good or service. However, since many of the products are only marginally distinguishable from one another, these 5,000 industries are combined into fewer than 500 somewhat broader industries when the input-output table for the American economy is actually constructed. To provide a less unwieldy table, the 496 industries are further aggregated into 79 major industry groupings. (These 79 major industry groupings are identified in chapter 5, exhibit 5.1.) Still, it is on the basis of the 500 separate industries that the quinquennial input-output table for the United States is actually constructed. This means that its inner matrix consists of 496^2, or 246,016, cells. The major part of the statistical task involved in actually constructing an input-output table for the U.S. economy consists of filling in those cells so that the totals for both the next-to-last column and the next-to-last row will balance.

The data necessary for filling in those cells is obtained from the various censuses of business activity which the U.S. government conducts every five years (in years ending in either 2 or 7). The sources are primarily the censuses of manufacturers and of mineral industries but also, to a lesser extent, the censuses of trade and services, construction, transportation, governments and agriculture. These censuses provide information on the inputs used by each of the plants and offices, or establishments, that comprise a particular industry. Based on this information, one can derive the preliminary estimates for all the cells of the inner matrix as well as the cells in the next-to-bottom (value added) row. Adding up these figures vertically gives the total outlays for each industry. Meanwhile, from the information obtained on the output of the various plants, it is possible to derive a preliminary estimate of each industry's gross output. The fact that the gross output of each industry must be the same as its total outlays provides an important check on the estimates. If this control condition is not satisfied, the estimates are then revised, relying on supplemental sources of information and the "experienced judgment" of the estimators. Since a change in the estimate for any particular cell will affect the totals for two separate industries, considerable juggling of the data is required before a consistent set of estimates for all 246,016 cells can be obtained. Indeed, it is for this reason that it usually takes an additional five years, even after all the results of the various censuses have become available, for the input-output table covering that "benchmark" year to be completed.

Once the flow, in value terms, between any two industries has been estimated in this manner for the benchmark year, and thus the main entry for that particular cell in the inner matrix has been filled in, two additional figures for each cell can then be calculated. One set of figures consists of the direct requirements ratios shown in exhibit 2.2 which, as already explained, are calculated by dividing the value of each industry's inputs, material and other, by the value of the industry's total output. These direct requirements ratios can, among other things, be used to gauge the effect on other industries of an increase in a particular industry's level of production. This is because an industry's direct requirements ratios can be interpreted as the fraction of a dollar's (or cents') worth of other industries' output that is required to produce a dollar's worth of its own output. Thus, as an illustration, if industry A is the coal industry and industry C is the steel industry, the direct requirements ratios shown in exhibit 2.2 imply that 4.4 cents' worth of output by the coal industry is required as inputs by the steel industry for every dollar's worth of steel produced (first row, third column). Should steel production increase by $10 billion, the amount of coal required by the steel industry will increase by $440 million ($10 billion multiplied by 0.0440).

But this last figure represents only the direct requirements for additional coal as a result of any increased steel production. There are also the indirect requirements. As the table in exhibit 2.2 indicates, 24.8 cents' worth of steel output is required to produce an additional dollar's worth of coal (first column, third row). Thus the $440 million additional output of coal will require $109.1 million more of steel output ($440 million multiplied by 0.2479), and the $109.1 million additional output of steel will, in turn, require $4.8 million additional output of coal ($109.1 million multiplied by 0.0440). By continuing to trace through in this manner the additional need for coal as a result of the $10 billion increase in steel production, it is possible to determine the total indirect requirements for coal. These indirect requirements, together with the direct requirements, give the total requirements for coal as a result of expanding steel production.

Using a computer to simulate the iterative process, one can derive a "total requirements" coefficient for each cell of the inner matrix. This indicates the dollar's worth of the other industry's output which is required, both directly and indirectly, to meet an additional dollar's worth of demand for the output of the industry shown at the top of the column. The total requirements coefficient is particularly useful in determining what will be the effect on other industries of a change in the demand for some industry's final output. Nearly all the studies of the impact that a shift in the composition of final demand is likely to have, such as a cutback in military expenditures or the displacement of oil by other forms of energy, rely on the estimates of these coefficients. Even more important, the entire set of these total requirements coefficients constitutes the Leontief inverse, the basis for both the output and dual price solution to the Leontief model of production (see chapter 5, section 2.3).

The total requirements coefficient is the second figure, besides the direct requirements ratio itself, which can be derived once the flows, in value terms, between any two industries have been estimated. In the wall chart which can be obtained from *Scientific American* showing the U.S. input-output table for 1972, the interindustry flow, in value terms, is the larger of the three figures shown in each cell, the direct requirements ratio is the smaller figure shown in the bottom left-hand corner of each cell and the total requirements coefficient is the smaller figure shown in the bottom right-hand corner.

It is only the inner matrix of interindustry flows in value terms and the last column and the bottow row of the input-output table—the latter two showing the value of the total output produced by each industry—that are derived from the quinquennial business censuses. The next-to-last column representing the national product originating in the enterprise sector and the next-to-bottom row (representing the national income originating in the same sector) are both then derived as residuals (by subtracting the set of figures comprising the inner matrix from the set of figures shown in the last column and from the same set of figures shown in the bottom row). Still, the input-output table cannot be considered complete until one further step has been taken. This is to decompose the next-to-last column (representing the national product orginating in the enterprise sector) and the next-to-bottom row (representing the national income originating in the same sector) into its significant component parts by drawing upon additional data sources. Indeed, this step serves as a further check on the results obtained.

2.1.3 Decomposing the enterprise sector aggregates

The next-to-last column of the input-output table is the one which has been labeled "other output flows" in exhibit 2.1 (and relabeled "value of final output" in exhibit 2.3). These "other output flows" are, in fact, the flows from the various industries which constitute the enterprise sector, or production subsystem, to the other sectors of the economy—the household, governnment and rest-of-the-world sectors. It is useful, both for the purpose of collecting data and for understanding the shifting composition of final demand, to divide that next-to-last column into a subset of flows, or sales, to each of these other sectors as shown in exhibit 2.4. In this way, the flows can be modeled based on the observed behavior of the type of social entity which distinguishes one sector from another—an individual or family in the case of the household sector, the business firm in the case of the enterprise sector and some other country in the case of the rest-of-the-world sector.

The flow of output to each of these other sectors can be further divided, as shown in exhibit 2.5 (a more detailed rendering of the next-to-last column in exhibits 2.1 and 2.4), into a flow of nondurable goods and services on the one hand and a flow of durable goods on the other. According to the definition employed in national income and product accounting, a nondurable good is one that is usable for less than three years. The further breakdown of the input-output table's next-to-last column into nondurable and durable goods is essential for understanding the economic system's macrodynamic behavior since it is the durable goods purchases by each of the sectors that are the most volatile of their expenditures. Indeed, a further breakdown of the durable goods component into structures and other durables is no less essential a distinction to make in attempting to model that macrodynamic behavior.

In the breakdown of the next-to-last column which has been outlined so far, representing the decomposition of the national product which originates in the enterprise sector into its constituent parts, the only flows which have been taken into account are those between the enterprise sector and the other sectors of the economy. This is perfectly adequate for measuring the flow of the enterprise sector's net, or final, output in the long period—that is, after averaging out any

Exhibit 2.4
Value of Final Output and its Components
(1978, $billion)

Industry	Sales to households	Sales to government	Net sales abroad	Total value of final output
A	157.0	27.3	1.1	185.4
B	397.5	68.3	3.2	469.0
C	194.5	33.3	1.6	229.4
D	444.8	76.4	3.7	524.9
E	72.0	12.3	0.6	84.9
Total	1,265.8	217.6	10.2	1,493.6

cyclical fluctuations in that flow over time. It is not adequate, however, for measuring the flow of the enterprise sector's net, or final, output in the short period—that is, in the real historical time of actual observation.

In the short period, the inner matrix represents only the interindustry flow of material inputs (or services) used directly in the production process. It does not include the material inputs which, as additions to the capital stock (consisting of new plant and equipment), are necessary for expanding capacity in the long period. Those capital inputs, to the extent they are being produced in the short period by the specialized industries that constitute the investment goods sector, need to be included, as shown in exhibit 2.6, as a separate component of the enterprise sector's net, or final, output—and hence as a separate component of the national product originating in the enterprise sector. Indeed, the convention in national income and product accounting is to include not just the purchase of new plant and equipment (what, looking at the same transaction from the opposite side, is termed "sales to other industries on capital account") but also any change in the amount of inventories held by business firms.

As the argument in this and the succeeding chapters unfolds, it will become clearer why the treatment of business investment—whether it is to be included as part of the enterprise sector's net output and hence as a component of the national product originating in the enterprise sector or whether, alternatively, it is to be included as part of the inner matrix and hence excluded from the measure of

Exhibit 2.5

Value of Final Output and its Components Further Disaggregated

(1978, $billion)

Industry	Sales to Households				Sales to Government				Net Sales Abroad				Value of Final output			
	ND	S	D	Total	ND	S	D	Total	ND	S	D	Total	ND	S	D	Total
A	65.8	53.2	38.0	157.0	5.1	13.5	8.7	27.3	7.8	−12.3	5.6	1.1	74.7	63.6	47.1	185.4
B	166.6	134.8	96.1	397.5	12.9	33.7	21.7	68.3	11.7	−15.8	7.3	3.2	189.0	160.9	119.1	469.0
C	81.5	65.9	47.1	194.5	6.3	16.5	10.5	33.3	6.4	4.2	−9.0	1.6	92.4	78.7	58.3	229.4
D	186.4	150.8	107.6	444.8	14.4	37.7	24.3	76.4	3.7	0	0	3.7	211.5	180.1	133.3	524.9
E	30.3	24.1	17.6	72.0	2.3	6.2	3.8	12.3	0.6	0	0	0.1	34.2	29.2	21.6	84.9
Total	530.6	428.8	306.4	1,265.8	40.8	107.6	69.2	217.6	30.2	−23.9	3.9	10.2	601.6	512.5	379.5	1,493.6

Exhibit 2.6
Expanded Input-Output Table
(1978, $billion)

Inputs obtained from industry ↓ / Outputs sold to industry →	A	B	C	D	E	Intermediate output	Change in inventories	Sales to other industries on capital account	Sales to households	Sales to government	Net sales abroad	Final output	Total
A	—	23.7	85.0	22.8	35.3	166.8	2.8*	28.9*	157.0*	27.3*	1.1*	217.1	383.9
B	43.1	—	3.5	14.6	47.8	109.0	7.0*	73.2*	397.5*	68.3*	3.2*	549.2	658.2
C	16.9	3.8	—	43.1	10.4	79.2	3.5*	35.8*	194.5*	33.3*	1.6*	268.7	342.9
D	24.1	22.5	19.5	—	56.6	122.7	7.8*	81.8*	444.8*	76.4*	3.7*	614.5	737.2
E	51.6	132.1	65.4	15.3	—	264.4	1.2*	13.3*	72.0*	12.3*	0.6*	99.4	363.8
Total													Total

										Total
Employees' compensation	188.9*	362.3*	129.0*	488.1*	162.5*					1,330.8
Property income	43.4*	83.3*	29.7*	122.2*	37.4*					306.0
Indirect business taxes	15.9*	30.5*	10.8*	41.1*	13.8*					112.1
Total, other outlays (value added)	248.2	476.1	169.5	641.4	213.7				1,748.9	
Total outlays	383.9	658.2	342.9	737.2	363.8					2,486.0
Total						757.1	22.3	233.0	1,265.8	217.6	10.2

*Estimated

aggregate output—depends on what is being analyzed, the economy's secular rate of expansion or its cyclical movements. It will also become clearer why the change in business inventories, if the focus is the amount of marketed output, can be excluded altogether from the flows shown in the input-output table. For now, however, we will simply follow the convention in national income and product accounting by including both the purchase of new plant and equipment and any change in business inventories as part of the enterprise sector's net, or final, output—and thus we will implicitly assume a short-period time frame with the emphasis on the level of production rather than the amount of marketed output. (The difference between the two perspectives can be seen by comparing the totals for the final output of the enterprise sector in exhibits 2.5 and 2.6.)

With business investment added to the final demand shown in the next-to-last column of the input-output table, and thus the basis for decomposing the national product which originates in the enterprise sector into its constituent parts complete, we can turn to the question of how the data necessary for filling in that additional set of categories are obtained. It would in fact be a relatively simple matter to fill in those cells if the various censuses of business activity, in addition to collecting information on the value of each industry's output (sales plus the change in inventories) and the value of inputs purchased from other industries, determined which were the other industries and which were the other sectors that purchased each industry's output. Indeed, this would provide an important cross-check on the inner matrix itself. Unfortunately, the latter type of information is not available from the various censuses. To be in a position to provide the necessary data, each plant would have to record its shipments to customers in terms of 500 different industries, with additional codes to cover any shipments to households, governments or foreign customers. Since it is not reasonable to insist on this degree of detail in response to the various business censuses, the data must come from other sources. Specifically, the data on purchases by households comes from monthly surveys which focus on the buyer rather than the seller, and they are then supplemented by the annual data collected on foreign trade and government purchases. These data must then be reconciled with the data obtained from the quinquennial business censuses.

Combining the data from these various sources, one can construct a set of accounts, such as the one shown in exhibit 2.7, giving the national product originating in the enterprise sector (the net, or final, output of the enterprise sector which is derived, in the manner already explained, from the next-to-last column of the input-output table) as well as the various items which make up that figure. Because not all the data necessary to cross-check the latter breakdown are collected, the reliability of the estimates of these various components of the national product originating in the enterprise sector, as distinct from the estimate of the aggregate figure itself, is open to question. That matter is taken up in appendix A (not available for this first, preliminary edition of the textbook). The more immediately pertinent question is whether this aggregate figure on the national product originating in the enterprise sector includes all of the output produced by the economic system—or whether, alternatively, this figure needs to be supplemented in order to derive a measure of aggregate economic output. This is the question that will be taken up in part 2 of this chapter. First, however, it is necessary to turn, at least briefly, to the decomposition of the national income which originates in the enterprise sector (the value added shown in the next-to-bottom row of the input-output table) that is also shown in exhibit 2.7.

Here the problem is somewhat different. The data on the amount of wages and indirect taxes paid by each industry, together with any profits earned, are available from the various business censuses. Moreover, these data can be cross-checked against the data obtained, for the same census years, from the tax returns which are separately filed by business firms annually as well as from other sources. Thus the reasons for questioning the reliability of the breakdown of the national income originating in the business sector are somewhat different, as appendix A brings out, having more to do with the underreporting of income for tax purposes than with the failure to obtain certain essential information from the quinquennial censuses of business. However, there is a more serious problem with the breakdown of the national income originating in the enterprise sector given in exhibit 2.7 than the reliability of the estimates for its various components. This more serious problem is whether the categories represent the relevant income flows. It is a question that will be taken up in part 3 of this chapter, after the relationship between the national product originating in the enterprise sector and aggregate economic output has been clarified.

2.2 Aggregate Economic Output

The economic system has previously been defined as the set of institutions through which the individual members of a society are able to satisfy their material needs (see chapter 1, sections 1.1 and 2.4). From this definition it would seem to follow that the aggregate output of the system would consist of all the physical goods produced in response to those needs. However, a number of problems arise when, in deriving a measure of aggregate output, one attempts to apply this definition.

One problem derives from the fact that certain entities, households in particular, are able to satisfy a portion of their material needs without having to rely on market mechanisms. Indeed, historically the market economy has emerged as a spreading network of trading relationships within what is predominantly a system of subsistence agriculture; and even today, in many countries, the nonmarket sector of the economy dwarfs the market sector. This, incidentally, is one of the reasons why a comparison of living standards between less developed and more advanced countries, based on per capita income, is likely to be misleading: Most nonmarket activity is not reflected in official national income statistics.

Though relatively small, the nonmarket sector remains important even in an

Exhibit 2.7

Consolidated Business Income and Product Account
(1978, $billion)

Income originating in business		Consolidated net sales (value added)	
Employees' compensation	1,081.3	To households	1,159.7
Wages and salaries	880.3	Durable goods	200.3
Supplements to wages and salaries	201.0	Nondurable goods	530.6
Employer contributions to social insurance	94.6	Services	428.8
Other labor income	106.4	To government	217.6
Property income	121.8	Structures	45.5
Net interest	19.5	Durable goods	23.7
Proprietor's income	102.3	Nondurable goods	40.8
Financial investment	−17.2	Services	107.6
Other	119.5	Abroad	−10.3

Corporate profits			167.7	Exports	207.2	
	Corporate tax liability	84.5		Imports	217.5	
	Net dividends	47.2		To business (on capital account)		329.1
	Corporate undistributed profits	74.3		Structures	182.6	
	Inventory valuation adjustment	−25.2		Private, nonresidential	76.5	
	Capital consumption adjustment	−13.1		Residential	106.1	
Adjustment to market price			161.1	Producers' durable goods	146.5	
	Indirect business taxes	152.8		Change in business inventories		22.3
	Business transfers	9.2				
	Less: subsidies less current surplus					
	of government sector	4.2				
	Statistical discrepancy	3.3				
Net National product originating in business			1,531.9			
Capital consumption allowance			186.5			
Charges against business product			1,718.4	**Business gross product**		1,718.4

advanced country like the United States, with the food, clothing and other items produced for each family's own use contributing significantly to the material standard of living. Even if most families do not grow their own food, they are likely to prepare most of their meals. And even if they do not weave and sew any of the clothes they wear, they are likely to do the washing and the other things necessary to maintain their wardrobe.

The distinction between market and nonmarket production poses a serious dilemma for national income and product accounting. By its very nature, nonmarket production is difficult to measure since it is not likely to be recorded in any of the business censuses. The amount of such production can only be crudely estimated, with any figures that are obtained apt to be far less reliable than the estimates of marketed output—if figures on nonmarketed output can be obtained at all. And yet, unless nonmarket production is taken into account, the extent to which the material needs of society and its individual members are being met will not be known. This dilemma gives rise to the conflicting objectives which can be discerned in the present official National Income and Product Accounts (NIPA) for the United States and most other advanced market economies. On the one hand, the objective is to provide as accurate a measure as possible of the levels of market activity so those levels can be monitored and then, through government policies, perhaps influenced. On the other hand, the objective is to provide a single "best" measure of economic welfare—that is, of the extent to which the material needs of society, individually and collectively, are being met—so that the economy's performance can be assessed. The Gross National Product, or GNP, is the measure usually relied upon to serve both these purposes.

The argument of this section is that the two objectives cannot be served by the same aggregate measure. Since the macrodynamic behavior of the economic system, which is the focal point of public policy and thus of this text, involves only the market sector—nonmarket output tends to be relatively immune to the factors producing the cyclical movements in the economy—the more important objective is to determine, as accurately as possible, the rate at which market output is being produced. Once that rate has been determined, the question of how the resulting measure of market activity needs to be further refined, and perhaps even supplemented, in order to assess the level of economic welfare can be addressed. This is the approach that will be adopted in this part of the chapter in deriving a set of alternatives to the GNP estimate typically used as the measure of aggregate economic output. The problem created by services, especially government services, will first be examined. Once this problem has been resolved and a suitable measure of market activity obtained, a subsequent set of problems—how to obtain more current estimates of this measure than those available based on the quinquennial "benchmark" estimates and how to distinguish the real from the nominal changes in those and the other data—will be taken up. Then, and only then, will the problem of how to measure a society's economic well-being, or welfare, be addressed.

2.2.1 Services

A second problem that arises in attempting to derive a measure of aggregate economic output, besides that posed by nonmarketed output, concerns the treatment of services. Up to now, the discussion has been carried out as though business firms supplied only goods. This clearly is not the case. Firms also supply services. And yet services, since they provide the purchaser with nothing material, would seem to fall outside the definition of economic output given above.

In one sense, this is true. Defined most narrowly, economic output consists only of physical goods. The rate at which the material well-being of a society is being enhanced is the rate at which the output of physical goods is being increased. Similarly, any difference in the material well-being of two societies will be due to the difference in their ability to produce physical goods (as well as, and in part due to, the difference in the stock of physical goods in the form of productive capacity they have inherited from the past). The best aggregate measure of this ability to produce physical goods is Gross Physical Output, or GPO. Exhibit 2.8 shows how this measure would be derived, based on data for 1978. GPO, it should be noted, is not one of the aggregate measures provided in the official NIPA but rather is derived from that data base. As can be seen, all the items which make up GPO are taken from the right-hand column of the Consolidated Business Income and Product Account shown in exhibit 2.7 (which, in turn, was derived from the breakdown of the enterprise sector's net, or final, output shown in exhibit 2.6).

The narrow definition of economic output reflected in the GPO figure is consistent with what, in classical economic theory, was termed the "labor-embodied" theory of value. According to this view, the only value created by an economic system is the value of the labor incorporated in the physical goods produced. However, there was also, in classical economic theory, a "labor-commanded" theory of value. According to this view, value was created not only by the labor embodied in physical goods but also by the labor commanded in any, more general way by wage payments. In effect, the question of how to treat services in measuring aggregate economic output simply reflects the old controversy among the classical economists as to whether a "labor-embodied" or a "labor-commanded" theory of value is the more appropriate one. Adding the value of all services to GPO yields what is defined in exhibit 2.8 as Gross Marketed Product, or GMP; and it is this more inclusive measure that is consistent with a "labor-commanded" theory of value. (The question of whether only labor is responsible for creating an economic surplus, and thus whether the labor theory of value itself is valid, is a question that will not be taken up until later. See chapter 8, section 4.2. At this point, the question is only how the value of any net output is to be measured, not what "creates" that value.)

The position taken here is that both GPO and GMP are useful measures of aggregate output, that each has validity, depending on the question being ad-

Exhibit 2.8
Measures of Aggregate Economic Output
(1978, $billion)

Structures		228.1
Private, nonresidential	76.5	
Residential	106.1	
Government	45.5	
+ Durable goods		366.6
Producers' durables	146.5	
Consumer durables	200.3	
Government durable goods purchases	23.7	
Net export of durable goods	−3.9	
+ Nondurable goods		541.2
Consumer nondurables	530.6	
Government purchase of nondurables	40.8	
Net export of nondurable goods	−30.2	
= Gross physical output (GPO)		1,135.9
+ Services		560.3
Consumer services	428.8	
Government purchases of services	107.6	
Net export of services	23.9	
= Gross marketed product (GMP)		1,696.2
+ Government employees compensation		218.0
= Gross national income (GNI)		1,914.2
+ Imputations		213.3
Change in business inventories	22.3	
Other imputations and rental income	191.0	
= Gross national product (GNP)		2,127.5

dressed. While GPO is the better measure of the economic system's ability to satisfy material needs, GMP is the better measure of market activity. For the income given up in exchange for services is no different in the purchasing power it represents from the income given up in exchange for physical goods. Services are simply a different way of commanding labor, the difference being the lack of anything physical that remains after the labor has been commanded.

Following this line of reasoning, one must view services as the equivalent of physical goods which are used up, or consumed, instantaneously. It is for this reason that, in measuring the level of market activity, the distinction between goods and services becomes largely meaningless. Indeed, if nondurable goods are goods that are used up within three years (as the definition used in collecting the official statistics would have it), then services are simply nondurable goods with even less durability. For most purposes, then, nondurable goods and services can be grouped together. The more important distinction is between nondurable goods and services on the one hand and durable goods on the other. Thus, in the model to be developed in the subsequent chapters of this text, GMP, not GPO, will be used as the measure of market activity.

Moreover, while GPO may be the better measure of how well the society's material needs are being met by the economic system, GMP is the better measure of how the current level of physical output, GPO, is being used to satisfy both the society's material *and* its nonmaterial needs. For services represent the use of material resources, in particular the goods required to meet the physical needs of those providing the services, so as to be able to achieve various nonmaterial objectives. What this means is that there are two components to any increase in the material standard of living. One is the greater amount of physical goods available, on average, to the members of society, with that greater availability of physical goods reflected by the rate of growth of GPO per capita. The other component is the greater amount of labor by others which can be commanded, aside from the labor embodied in the physical goods consumed, with that greater amount of labor by others which can be commanded reflected by the rate of growth of services alone. For this reason GMP can be viewed as the better measure not just of market activity but also of overall economic well-being.

Still, the two measures are not unrelated to one another. While the historical shift to a service economy that can be observed from the increasing share of GMP represented by services implies a more rapid rate of growth of GMP relative to GPO, the growth of services is nonetheless limited by the growth of GPO. This is because the growth of services depends on the size of the work force that can be maintained in the service sector, and the size of the work force that can be maintained in the service sector depends, in turn, on the availability of the physical output needed to satisfy the material needs of those who are members of that work force. While the use of any income to purchase services reduces the amount of physical output which must be made available to the workers in the service sector, this only shifts to one stage further back in the production process the amount of physical output which must be made available to workers.

Indeed, the size of the work force which can be maintained throughout the economy (and not just in the service sector) will depend on the rate at which physical output per worker is increasing, so that ultimately the material standard of living, as measured by GMP or some even more inclusive aggregate figure, depends on the relationship between two variables: (1) the growth of physical output, GPO; and (2) the growth of the work force (or population) that must be maintained. These points will become clearer following the discussion of production in chapter 5 and the discussion of the human resouce, or labor, constraints on economic expansion in chapter 13. For now it need only be noted that GMP, aside from being the best measure of market activity, also indicates the combined material and nonmaterial uses to which the current level of physical output is being put. Relying primarily on that aggregate measure, as is done in the chapters that follow, does not obscure what is happening to the level of economic welfare.

GMP, as defined in exhibit 2.8, differs significantly from the GNP measure more typically used in aggregate analysis. To bring out some of these differences, it is necessary to face up to a third problem that arises in trying to apply the definition of economic output given earlier. This is the problem of how the government sector should be treated—in particular, whether it produces any output of its own which needs to be included in the measure of aggregate economic output. Although there is some overlap between this question and the problems of nonmarketed output and of services already discussed, the question of how to treat the government sector involves yet a further complication. Up to now, it has been possible to equate the output of the economic system with the net, or final, output produced within the enterprise sector. Now we shall have to consider whether the government sector or, for that matter, the household sector as well, produces any output of its own and thus whether aggregate economic output exceeds or in some other way differs from the national product originating in the enterprise sector.

2.2.2 Value added by government

The government, as a separate sector of the economic system, can be viewed in either of two ways. The predisposition among economists, ever since Adam Smith, has been to view the government as the equivalent of another household, one that merely consumes a portion of the economic output produced by the enterprise sector. Indeed, "economic" derives from the Greek word for household, and thus "political economy," the original term for the discipline of economics, was the science of managing the royal households which had become the new nation states of the 17th and 18th centuries. Alternatively, the government can be viewed as the equivalent of another enterprise, one that merely produces a different type of output in the form of public goods which cannot be marketed at a price sufficient to cover the full cost of production. This latter view is one that has gained increasing acceptance since the end of World War II when the Keynesian revolution led to a vast expansion of the governent's role in the economy. Which is the more appropriate way of looking at the government sector depends, again, on the question being addressed.

If the concern is with the overall social welfare, then one must fall back on the conceptual framework developed in the previous chapter, in which the political system is but one of four institutional dimensions, each contributing to the well-being of society in a different way. Just as the economic system adds to the well-being of society by supplying material goods, so the political system, including the government as the formal component of that system, contributes to the same end by producing societal decisions (in the form of laws, rulings and policies). From this perspective, it follows that the political system has a different type of output, one that is measured in a different unit of account from the economic system, and it is a mistake to confuse the two. Indeed, a monetary value cannot be placed on the decisions of government—not without providing a distorted view of the political process. All that can be determined is the economic cost, in terms of the physical resources used up (including the physical resources consumed by the individuals employed by the government), in making those decisions. What this line of argument implies is that the government is simply the equivalent of another household (albeit one that overshadows all the others), consuming part of the economic system's output while producing the nonmaterial output that is unique to the political system. Indeed, any governmental services which may be provided are, from this perspective, simply another use of the economic system's output to achieve some nonmaterial objective.

The government, however, has an additional role besides that of producing, in a formal way, societal decisions. It is also the final recourse when other parts of the social structure, including the economic, go awry. Taking into account this back-up function it serves, the government can also be viewed as the equivalent of an enterprise, producing as its output certain types of "public goods." Some of these public goods are political in nature, such as the "law and order" which the government provides to supplement and reinforce the private norms which limit individual behavior in the interests of the larger society. Other public goods are anthropogenic in nature, such as the education which the public schools provide either at no cost to the individual or at a considerably subsidized rate. In the case of these types of public goods, it makes little difference whether the government is viewed as simply another household or whether, alternatively, it is viewed as an enterprise. It is still using a portion of the economic system's output of material goods to achieve some nonmaterial objective without itself adding to the output of material goods.

However, some of the public goods which the government provides are economic in nature. This is true of those governmental activities, such as constructing roads and making other transportation improvements, that fall under the category of adding to the economic infrastructure. In the case of these types of public goods, the government is acting no differently from a private firm when, in purchasing new plant and equipment, it adds to the productive capacity of the economic system. The fact that the outlays are being made by the government rather than by a private firm does not make them any less a form of social investment. Like expenditures by private firms on new plant and equipment, the government's investment in the economic infrastructure needs to be included in the measure of aggregate economic output, at least when considering the variations in aggregate economic output which occur in the short period (as distinct from the expansion of output over the longer run, see section 2.1.3).

And yet, as can be seen from exhibit 2.8, the measure of aggregate economic output to be used in the subsequent chapters of this text, the Gross Marketed Product, or GMP, excludes entirely the compensation received by government employees. It also makes no provision for a profit or any other type of residual income for the government sector. The GMP thus fails to include any value added by the government sector. This does not mean that none of what the government contributes to the economic infrastructure is counted as part of GMP. For example, in the case of a newly built highway, the GMP, as calculated in exhibit 2.20, would include, under the heading "Structures, Government," the total cost of the road if it had been constructed by a private firm under contract to the government. The highway would show up as part of the net output of the construction industry which was then purchased by the government sector. Even if the road had been built by a state highway department, the GMP would include, under the heading "Government purchases of nondurables," the cost of any materials purchased from private firms such as asphalt or concrete. Still, the GMP would not include any value added by the government itself, especially the wages paid government employees, either in overseeing the work of the private contractor or, as part of a more ambitious effort by the government, in actually constructing the road itself.

In part, this failure to take into account any value added by the government reflects the lack of a suitable set of economic accounts for the government and nonprofit sector. The task of distinguishing the provision of public goods which are economic in nature from the other activities of government has yet to be carried out, along with the task of correctly specifying the costs—both labor and capital—of supplying any and all public goods. Thus, the lack of a suitable set of economic accounts for the public sector reflects a conceptual deficiency, as will be brought out in chapter 9 when the government's role in the economy will be analyzed in some depth and indeed a more appropriate set of accounts for the public sector developed. Still, this is not the only reason that the GMP figure does not include any value added by the government. The more important reason is that the nature of the public goods supplied by the government precludes any profit while the government's wage bill—all except the portion incurred in connection with any addition to the economic infrastructure—falls outside the definition of economic output.

The value added, it will be recalled (see section 2.1.1), is equal to the compensation of employees (the wage bill) plus any property income (such as profits). The latter is the residual obtained when the cost of all purchased inputs, material as well as labor, are subtracted from the total revenue obtained from the sale of the output produced. The residual, in the case of any public goods, would have to be imputed since the distinguishing characteristic of a public good is that a price sufficient to cover its cost cannot be obtained. In the absence of a market-derived price, the usual method of calculating the residual—by subtracting the cost of any purchased inputs from the sales revenue—cannot be applied. One can only estimate what the residual would be under circumstances that do not actually hold. And while, if one could determine the capital cost of providing various types of public goods, a reasonable estimate could be obtained, it would still not be a measure of any actual income flow. As will soon be argued more generally, the inclusion of imputed values, no matter how useful this may be for other purposes, makes the aggregate figure on which they are based less reliable as a measure of market activity.

The problem with the employees' compensation component of the value added by government is of a different sort—though the reasons for excluding it amount to essentially the same argument. While the labor costs of public goods are easily enough determined from the available data—one need only look at the government's wage bill as reported in various budget documents—there are other reasons for excluding these costs from any measure of market activity. One is that these costs, unlike all the other costs so far taken into account as part of the value added, and hence the national product, are not market mediated. This means that, rather than being induced by the market demand for a certain type of output, the government's wage bill actually represents a unilateral requisition of human resource inputs from the household sector, backed by the taxing power of the state. Labor is indeed commanded—but not from the proceeds of any market sale. Still, the more fundamental reason, since the physical goods purchased by the government are no less directly commanded (though from the enterprise rather than from the household sector), is that the government's wage bill does not fall within the definition of economic output which has emerged from the discussion so far.

The output of the economic system, based on an input-output model of the system, consists of only the physical goods which are produced net of the physical goods used up in the production process itself (see section 2.1.1), together with any services which are purchased in lieu of spending the income on the net output of physical goods (section 2.2.1). Any nonpurchased physical goods would fall within this definition (even if they are then excluded from the measure of marketed output), but not any nonmarketed services (unless they have contributed directly to the output of the physical goods produced by the economic system, in which case they would be included as part of the cost of providing those physical goods and not as part of the net output produced by the economic system). The definition of economic output which emerges from a consistent application of the systems approach adopted in this text, including the input-output model outlined at the start of this chapter, thus excludes any non-marketed services, such as those provided by government employees.

While it would be erroneous to infer from this definition of economic output that government employees are not productive, the fact remains that they are productive only in a broader social sense. They contribute to the output of the political system, not the economic system. In this respect the wages and salaries they receive represent payment for services which are economically nonproductive (no matter how valuable those services may be to the functioning of the political system). It is this fact which justifies the treatment of government employees' compensation as, in effect, a transfer payment. Indeed, all of the other income which is paid directly to households by the government—both the interest on the national debt and the other nonwage transfer payments, such as Social Security and public assistance—is already treated this way in the NIPA. It is the wages and salaries received by government employees which are the exception, and were it not that transfer income has the connotation of being "unearned income," there would be no reason to treat the government's wage bill differently from the other types of income flowing from the government directly to households.

It is, of course, possible to argue that government employees' compensation represents the purchase of services from the household sector and that, like the purchase of services from the enterprise sector, it should be included as part of aggregate economic output. In that case, aggregate economic output would be measured, not by GMP but rather by what is defined in exhibit 2.8 as Gross National Income, or GNI. This means that the government's wage bill, instead of being charged against the tax revenues shown on the income side of the accounts for the enterprise sector given in exhibit 2.7 and thus being netted out, would be combined with the value added within that sector to yield a larger figure. The argument of this section, as opposed to the treatment of government employees' compensation in the NIPA, is that the larger figure exaggerates the output of the economic system. It treats as an output of the system what is, in effect, only a transfer of purchasing power from the government to the household sector, and thus only an increased claim against the available economic output without any offsetting increase in that output. Incidentally, the same argument applies to any wages paid by one household to the members of another household. Those wages, too, are best viewed as a transfer payment—though, like the compensation of government employees, as an earned rather than an unearned one.

One important exception to treating all of the compensation received by government employees as, in effect, a transfer payment should be noted. To the extent the government supplies public goods of an economic sort—that is, adds to the economic infrastructure—any wage and salary payments should be included as part of both the national product and the national income. That this has not been done, in the set of accounts presented in exhibit 2.8, reflects two considerations. One is a practical one. The government's wage bill has yet to be broken down between infrastructure and other types of programs (see chapter 10, section 2.3, for a more complete discussion of the problem). The other consideration is that by excluding all of the government's wage bill—even that incurred in connection with any addition to the economic infrastrcture—one can obtain a better measure of the level of market activity in the short period. As for the long period, the most appropriate measure of aggregate economic output, as will shortly be brought out, excludes all investment, public (such as additions to the economic infrastructure) as well as private.

2.2.3 Imputations

The compensation of government employees is only one of the items that have to be added to GMP in order to arrive at the GNP figure more commonly used in aggregate analysis. All of the other items are imputed ones, which means that they do not represent actual transactions. They are instead estimates of what the market value would be if those items were to pass through a market.

One of these imputed items is the change in business inventories. Business inventories are of three types: (1) the inventory of unprocessed, or raw, materials, consisting of inputs purchased from other business firms but not yet actually used up in the production process; (2) the inventory of goods in process, consisting of those goods whose transformation into a final product has been started but not yet completed; and (3) the inventory of unsold goods, consisting of the output which has been produced but not yet sold. All three types of inventory are essential to the maintenance of normal production. Stocks of raw materials must be kept on hand for use as needed, production takes time to complete and not all that is produced can be sold immediately. In other words, inventories reflect the fact that production is a time-delineated process.

As already pointed out (see section 2.1.3), the change in business inventories needs to be included when accounting for the total output of the various industries shown in an input-output table. The change in inventories is in fact the balancing item since it represents the difference between the total output of each industry and the output which is then sold, either to other industries as an addition to their stock of capital goods or outside the enterprise sector to one of the other sectors which make up the economic system. Still, since this output has not yet been sold, it should not be included in any measure of market activity. It is for this reason that the GMP, along with the GNI, excludes the change in business inventories, even though that item is counted, in the official NIPA, as part of the GNP. This is not to suggest that the change in business inventories is unimportant. Quite the opposite. As will be pointed out in the next chapter, it is a key indicator of any disequilibrium in the final product markets, and thus of the relative balance between investment and savings or, in the somewhat broader theoretical framework of this text, between discretionary expenditures and discretionary funds in the aggregate. It is just that the change in inventories, since it represents goods not yet sold, should not be included in any measure of market activity such as GMP.

Of the other imputations which enter into GNP, the most important is the implicit rent assumed to be paid to themselves by those who own their own homes. Actually, insofar as the official NIPA are concerned, there is a fourth type of firm besides the three that will be described in section 2.3.4. This fourth type of firm is an imaginary one, and it consists of households which, though they own their own homes, are nonetheless assumed to be in the business of renting space to themselves. A rental income is imputed to these imaginary firms, based on the revenue it is estimated they could obtain from leasing the home to others. This rental income, when aggregated for all households which own their own homes, constitutes the "Rental Income of Persons" found on the income side of the official NIPA. Against this rental income are charged all the expenses of maintaining an owner-occupied home, and the difference represents the value added by those imaginary firms. The provision of the dwelling space itself shows up, on the product side of the official NIPA, as one of the services purchased by households. (Both this item, shown on the product side, and the rental income, shown on the income side, have been omitted from exhibit 2.7 and, in this one way, exhibit 2.7 deviates from the official set of accounts for the enterprise sector.)

The rental value of owner-occupied dwellings represents about three-fourths of the imputations included in the GNP (ignoring any change in business inventories). The remaining quarter includes such diverse items as the value of the food consumed on farms, the value of the food and clothing supplied to workers by their employers, etc. All of these imputed items, including the rental value of owner-occupied housing, suffer from the same shortcomings: (1) by the very nature of these items, the estimates which are available for them are subject to considerable error; (2) in any case, the list is an incomplete one, for it includes only a portion of the economic system's nonmarketed output; and (3) the imputations are irrelevant insofar as any measure of market activity is concerned. It is for all three reasons, but especially the third, that the imputed items are excluded from GMP.

Thus it is GMP which serves as the best estimate of aggregate economic output—at least in the short period, when the capacity of the enterprise sector can be assumed to be fixed and any fluctuations in business investment affect primarily the level of aggregate demand rather than aggregate supply capability. In the long period (after any cyclical fluctuations in the level of economic activity have been averaged out so that business investment can more appropriately be viewed as simply another material input into the production process rather than part of the sector's net output, see section 2.1.3), Total Domestic Consumption, or TDC, can be substituted for GMP as the more appropriate measure of aggregate economic output. TDC is the amount of goods and services flowing from the enterprise sector, both at home and abroad, to the other sectors for final use. As can be seen from exhibit 2.9, it is the sum of private (household) consumption and public (government) consumption plus net imports (net exports with the sign reversed). Alternatively, it can be derived by subtracting the following from GMP: (1) business investment; (2) net exports; and (3) net financial investment abroad (the latter being the net cash balance of the rest-of-the-world sector, an

Exhibit 2.9
Total Domestic Consumption and its Relationship to Gross Market Product
(1978, $billion)

Private consumption		1,265.8
Residential construction	106.1	
Consumer durables	200.3	
Consumer nondurables	530.6	
Consumer services	428.8	
+ Public consumption		217.6
Government structures	45.5	
Government durable goods purchases	23.7	
Government purchase of nondurables	40.8	
Government purchase of services	107.6	
+ Net imports		10.2
Net import of durable goods	3.9	
Net import of nondurable goods	30.2	
Net import of services	− 23.9	
= Total domestic consumption (TDC)		1,493.6
+ Additions to domestic productive capacity		223.0
Private nonresidential structures	76.5	
Producer durables	146.5	
+ Net investment abroad		− 10.2
= Gross marketed product (GMP)		1,696.2

item which, as will be explained in part 3 of this chapter, derives from the FOFA). Whichever measure of aggregate economic output is the more appropriate one, however, whether it be GMP or TDC (or, for that matter, GNI or GNP), the figure can easily be derived from the official NIPA. All that is necessary is to decompose the net, or final, output of the enterprise sector in the manner shown in exhibits 2.5 and 2.7—and then to rearrange the various items in the manner shown in exhibits 2.8 and 2.9. Still, what has been described so far is only the means by which estimates of these aggregate measures can be obtained every five years based on the benchmark data obtained from the quinquennial business censuses. What still remains to be explained is how these benchmark estimates are continually updated so as to provide annual and quarterly estimates of the same aggregate measures.

2.2.4 The annual and quarterly updates

The quinquennial benchmark estimates, though they represent the most reliable set of figures on aggregate economic output and its components that it is possible to obtain at the present time for the U.S. economy, become available only with a considerable time lag. As matters now stand, about eight years are required to compile the data from the various economic censuses, construct an input-output table and derive the benchmark estimates. This means that the benchmark estimates, when they become available, describe the economy as it was nearly a decade earlier. While such a schedule more than meets the needs of those writing economic history, it suffices not at all for policymakers and others who must act in response to current economic conditions (as best those current economic conditions can be determined). For this reason, the benchmark estimates are continuously being projected forward, both on a quarterly and on an annual basis. This is done by relying on more immediately available, though less comprehensive, data. While estimates of a more current nature can thereby be obtained, the estimates are subject to a considerably greater error margin. (See appendix A for a discussion of these and other limitations of the data available for macrodynamic analysis.) Indeed, obtaining estimates of aggregate economic output, together with its components, is best viewed as an ongoing *process*, with the preliminary estimates that are published being continuously revised until, with the release of new benchmark data, a final revised figure is published.

New data sufficient to project the estimates ahead another three months become available only two weeks after the end of the calendar quarter being reported on. The new data consist primarily of reports on wage and transfer income and the results of a survey of retail trade. Together with the latest figures for certain proxy variables and the extrapolation of past trends, these data are sufficient to provide a preliminary (flash) estimate of aggregate economic output (GNP) and its major components (from which GMP can be derived). By combining these preliminary estimates with the figures for the preceding three quarters, it is possible to obtain a preliminary estimate for the preceding calendar year as early as mid-January. This preliminary estimate for the previous year is then revised four weeks later when additional quarterly data become available, and again in July of the same year and each of the next two years as additional annual data become available. When the next benchmark data have been obtained, these annual and quarterly estimates are then revised, either up or down, to match the benchmark estimates.

The manner in which the annual and quarterly updates of the National Income and Product Accounts are derived has a number of implications for those who must rely on these data in their work. One thing to keep in mind is that any of the more recent figures for the U.S. economy—in particular, the data which have been projected forward since the last benchmark estimates became available—are still only preliminary figures subject to revision. At the present time, this would be true of any annual or quarterly data covering the period since 1977. While it might seem that this problem can be avoided if one relies only on the data for the earlier period, the fact is that the institutional features of the economy may be changing so rapidly that any results based on the older data may no longer pertain. As a practical matter, then, one may have no choice but to include the more recent data in any empirical study—if only to see if the results based on the older data still hold.

A second thing to keep in mind is that the quarterly estimates, as the measure of the economy's cyclical volatility, are subject to a certain amount of error which cannot even be determined, let alone then corrected in a subsequent revision of the figures. This is because the quinquennial benchmark estimates provide no clue as to the variability of the output and income flows over the course of any one year—and the annual data are no more revealing in this regard. Although the figure for the year as a whole may be revised, either up or down, depending on what the new annual estimates indicate, the relative amount of that output attributed to any given quarter will remain unchanged (see appendix A for a further discussion of this point). While this might suggest that a model based on annual data is likely to be more reliable than a model based on quarterly data, the fact is that cyclical movements occur with greater frequency than is reflected in annual data. As a practical matter, then, it is necessary to base any model of the economy's cyclical movements on quarterly data even though the quarterly data are subject to an error factor of an unknown but certainly greater magnitude than the quarterly data. Indeed, it is for this reason that quarterly data will be relied on in the chapters which follow for most of the empirical evidence as to the cyclical behavior of the U.S. economy.

These two limitations of the data notwithstanding, annual and quarterly estimates of aggregate economic output and its components, as shown in exhibits 2.8 and 2.9, are available for the United States for most of the post-World War II period. However, the estimates given in exhibits 2.8 and 2.9, and indeed the estimates as originally derived, are in nominal terms, that is, without taking into account the change in prices over time. To obtain estimates in real terms, that is, holding prices constant, one needs an appropriate set of deflators. While a means of deriving these deflators endogenously will be outlined in chapter 5 as part of the discussion of prices, these estimates need to be checked against actual empirical data. For this purpose, a set of empirically derived price indexes is essential.

2.2.5 Deflators and price indexes

A series of deflators, measuring the change in the relevant set of prices over time, provides the means by which any estimates in current, or nominal, terms can be converted to estimates in constant, or real, terms. The relationship between these deflators and the estimates, both in current and in constant terms, is as follows:

$$R = \frac{N}{P} \qquad (2.1)$$

and

$$N = P^*R \qquad (2.2)$$

where R is the estimate in real terms, N is the estimate in nominal terms and P is the price index and/or price deflator.

The price indexes used to deflate the annual and quarterly estimates of aggregate economic output and its components derive from an entirely different source from either the NIPA or the FOFA. They are based on the collection of price data, for the most part by government agencies, and the subsequent transformation of those price data into price indexes. Three major types of price indexes are compiled by the U.S. government. They are: (1) the Bureau of Labor Statistics producer price index (formerly the wholesale price index), covering the prices of goods and services purchased by firms from other firms; (2) the BLS consumer price index, covering the price of goods and services purchased by households; and (3) the Department of Commerce's cost of construction indexes. The derivation of all three indexes is governed by the same set of principles—and is beset by the same types of problems.

Before a price index can be derived, three preliminary steps must be taken. They are: (a) specifying the items whose prices are to be included in the index; (b) determining the relative weight each of those items is to have in the index; and (c) collecting data on the prices of those items over a period of time. Once these preliminary steps have been taken, a price index can be calculated based on the following formula:

$$P = \frac{\sum\limits_{i=1}^{n} w_i p_{ij}}{\sum\limits_{i=1}^{n} w_i p_{i0}}$$

where w_j is the relative weight (with a value between 0 and 1) attached to the ith item in the index, p_{ij} is the price of the ith item in time period j and p_{i0} is the price of the ith item in the base time period, 0.

In the base time period, whether a single year or longer, the numerator will necessarily be equal to the denominator so that the index takes the value of 1.00 (customarily multiplied by 100 to avoid the use of decimal points). At other times, with the p_i varying, the index will either be less than 100, indicating that prices are below the base-year level, or greater than 100, indicating that prices have risen. A price index of 90, for example, means that prices are 10 percent below those in the base year, while an index of 125 means that prices are 25 percent higher than in the base year. Essential to being able to make this type of inference is that the weights, the w_j's, not change. While it is not necessary that the weights be taken from the base year—though this will generally be more convenient—it is essential that the weights, once decided upon, remain the same for all the years covered by the index. An index which meets this criterion is termed a "fixed-weight" price index. Since the calculation of the index is a relatively mechanical task, once the preliminary steps of specifying the items to be included, determining the weights and collecting the data have been taken, it is the preliminary steps which warrant further discussion.

Collecting price data on all the differentiable items which pass through the market in an economy like that of the United States would overtax the resources of any agency, including the government. Even in the case of a single product like steel, there are thousands of different items. Thus, in constructing a price index, it is necessary to pick only certain selected items—those which, one hopes, are in some sense representative of the whole—for inclusion in the "basket of goods" (and/or services) that is to be priced over time. The problem is that, no matter how conscientiously carried out and how defensible the selection of items may be initially, the passage of time will make the items increasingly less representative of what is being produced and/or sold. New varieties of the same item are likely to come on the market and, because of the additional features they offer, features which better serve the needs of buyers, they are likely to become more representative of the product than certain of the items covered by the index. This leads to a dilemma: If the items in the index are left unchanged, they become increasingly unrepresentative of the products being sold in the market. Yet, if the items in the index are changed with the frequency needed to reflect the current product mix, the index will no longer represent the changing price of the same "basket of goods" over time. As a practical matter, the dilemma is usually resolved by gradually substituting over time more representative items for less representative ones. But while this expedient prevents the index from becoming too unrepresentative, it also means that (1) the index is seldom fully representative of the current product mix, and (2) it does not really measure the changes over time in the price of a fixed basket of goods.

It is not just a matter of which items should be included in the index. There is also the question of what weights should be attached to those items. The weights are typically based on some measure, such as the value added or the value of shipments (total sales). The weight attached to a particular product, or even to a particular item, is then the proportion of the total value added or value of shipments which it accounts for. The problem here is similar to that encountered in the choice of individual items to be included in the index. As a result of the changing composition of demand over time, whatever weights were originally chosen as being the most appropriate will become less so over time. New products will be underrepresented or excluded altogether while older products which have declined in importance will be overrepresented. Again, the same sort of dilemma arises: If the weights used in calculating the index are revised, the index will no longer measure the changing price of a fixed basket of goods. The mix will be changing along with the price of the goods. Yet, unless the weights are revised, the index will become increasingly unrepresentative of what it purports to measure. The practical resolution of this dilemma is similar. The weights are, from time to time, revised—but only infrequently and then only after a census or some other survey has provided more current data on the measures used in determining the index's weights.

Even after the problems of specifying the items in the index and determining their relative weights have been resolved, there is still the problem of collecting the necessary price data over an extended period of time. Here the problem is of a somewhat different sort. For there is a difference between the list price publicly quoted by the seller, in the case of industrial products, and the transaction price. The latter is the price at which the good or service is actually sold. The common practice is for price indexes to be based on list prices, not transaction prices, since transactions prices are, by their very nature, not easily ascertained. It is not just that both sellers and buyers feel their interests are better served by keeping the actual transaction price a secret from rivals. It is also that, with discounts allowed for payments that are made in cash, premiums granted for expedited delivery and other trade practices which affect the actual price paid, not even the buyer and the seller can say for certain what is the actual transaction price for the good itself. Efforts have been made to develop price indexes based on transaction rather than list prices. However, it has not proven practical to do this in the case of the price indexes compiled by the Bureau of Labor Statistics and other government agencies. While this is not necessarily a failing of these indexes, it is nonetheless something to be kept in mind, along with the other problems mentioned, when considering the deflated values which are reported as part of the NIPA.

For each of the components of aggregate output listed in exhibit 2.8, the NIPA provide estimates both in current dollars—that is, in nominal terms; and in constant dollars—that is, in real terms. The latest base year is 1982, but the constant dollars shown in exhibit 2.10 are 1972 dollars. Dividing the estimates in current dollars, as shown in column 1 of exhibit 2.10, by the estimates in constant dollars as shown in column 2, produces what is known as the "implicit price deflator" for each of these components. These implicit price deflators are shown in column 3. Though based on fixed-weight price indexes, they are not themselves fixed-weight price indexes. This is because of the way in which the estimates in constant dollars, or real terms, are derived.

Each of the major components of aggregate output shown in exhibit 2.10— structures, other durable goods, nondurable goods and services—represents an aggregate of subcategories covering a large number of items. Exhibit 2.11 lists all the items included within the major categories of structures and other durable goods. For each of these separate items, as well as for each of the similar but separate items included within the major categories of nondurable goods and

Exhibit 2.10
Measures of Aggregate Output in Current and Constant Dollars
(1978, $billion)

Category	Current dollars	Constant 1972 dollars	Implicit price deflator
Structures	228.2	129.5	176.2
Other durable goods	380.4	270.0	140.9
Nondurable goods	549.6	369.4	148.8
Services	969.3	630.3	153.8
Gross marketed product	2,127.5	1,399.2	152.1

services, a price index is generated as part of the estimating procedures by which the NIPA are produced. The index is based on the formula given in equation 2.3, and it relies, for its price data, on the information assembled by other government agencies in preparing the producers, consumers and construction indexes. The current dollar estimates for each of the separate items are then divided by the most appropriate price index to provide an estimate in real terms. These constant dollar estimates are then added together to produce the constant dollar estimates for whatever larger aggregates are reported. This is true not only for the broad categories of structures and durable goods but also for all the other components of aggregate output, such as private fixed domestic investment, consumer expenditures and government purchases.

As a result of this procedure, the deflators that are reported reflect not one but two quite different movements. One is the change in the prices of the various items which constitute the broad category, and the other is the changing composition of the aggregate itself. The result is a measure not of the changing value of a given basket of goods and services, such as a fixed-weight price index would provide, but rather of the changing value of a changing basket of goods. As the output of any particular subcomponent increases relative to the others, its price carries a greater weight. In terms of the formula given in equation 2.3, w_i is replaced in the numerator by a new weight, w_k, so that the deflator, P, depends on w_k/w_k as well as on p_i/p_0. This is not to say that the constant dollar estimates for the various components of aggregate output, when added together, are not the best measure of the changing real value of aggregate output over time. Indeed, the procedure for deriving the constant dollar estimates is the correct one. The point is rather that the deflators obtained by dividing the current dollar estimates by the constant dollar estimates are not the best measure of changing price levels. Still,

Exhibit 2.11
Items Included in Structures and Other Durable Goods

Structures

Other durable goods

Nonresidential structures:
  Industrial buildings
  Commercial buildings
  Religious buildings
  Educational buildings
  Hospital and institutional buildings
  Other, nonfarm
  Railroads, telephone and telegraph
  Electric light and power
  Gas
  Petroleum pipelines
  Farm
  Mining exploration shafts and wells
Residential structures:
  New housing units, nonfarm
  Additions and alterations, nonfarm
  Nonhousekeeping, nonfarm
  New Housing units, farm
  Additions and alterations, farm
Government structures:
  Residential buildings, excluding military
  Industrial buildings, excluding military
  Educational buildings, excluding military
  Hospital buildings, excluding military
  Other buildings, excluding military
  Highways and streets
  Military facilities
  Conservation development
  Sewer systems
  Water supply facilities

Nonresidential:
Furniture and fixtures
Fabricated metal products
Engines and turbines
Tractors
Agricultural machinery (except tractors)
Construction machinery (except tractors)
Mining and oilfield machinery
Metalworking machinery
Special industry machinery, n.e.e.
General industrial, including materials
  handling equipment
Office, computing, and accounting
  machinery
Service industry machinery
Electrical transmission, distribution,
  and industrial appartus
Communication equipment
Electrical equipment, n.e.e.
Trucks, buses, and truck trailers
Autos
Aircraft
Ships and boats
Railroad equipment
Instruments
Other

as can be seen from exhibit 2.12, the difference between the behavior over time of the implicit GNP deflator and the behavior of a fixed-weight index derived from the same price data is not that great.

Thus, it is possible to obtain estimates of aggregate output and its components not just in current dollars but in constant dollars as well. The same breakdown shown in exhibit 2.10 for 1978 is also available on a quarterly basis, and it is in fact this breakdown of GMP into structures, other durable goods, nondurable goods and services flowing to the household, government and rest-of-the-world sectors (as well as structures and other durable goods remaining within the enterprise sector as additions to its capital stock) which will be used in the chapters to follow as the empirical basis for constructing a macrodynamic model of the U.S. economy. All that remains to complete the accounting framework is to bring in the monetary flows which are measured by the Flow of Funds Accounts—and thereby capture the relevant income flows. This will be done in the next and final part of this chapter. First, however, it is necessary to say something about the relationship between the aggregate figure which best measures the level of market activity, GMP, and the level of economic welfare.

2.2.6 Economic welfare

As was explained at the outset, there is a conflict between attempting to measure the level of market activity and attempting to measure the level of economic welfare—with the considerable amount of nonmarketed output only one of the several factors which make it difficult to reconcile these conflicting objectives of national income and product accounting. The conflict has been resolved so far in this chapter by focusing, in the short period, on the level of market activity—with GMP rather than GNP put forward as the more appropriate measure—and by focusing, in the long period, on Total Domestic Consumption (TDC). However, as should be clear from the discussion in section 2.2.4 of the various imputed items (besides the compensation of government employees) that account for the difference between GMP and GNP, the latter is not even a good measure of economic welfare. In discussing the level of economic well-being, it is better to ignore the GNP estimate altogether and start instead with what has been defined as TDC, supplementing this measure of the goods and services supplied by the enterprise sector for use by the other sectors with other indicators of how well the material needs of the society are being met.

Clearly, the amount of goods and services which individuals produce for themselves, outside the market economy, has an important bearing on the level of economic well-being. But rather than attempting to place a market value on this nonmarketed output, as the GNP estimate makes a pretense of doing, a different tack will be taken in the chapters which follow. This is to rely on the figure for TDC to measure the amount of goods and services supplied through the market and then, after taking into account the amount of each individual's time required to produce that level of output, to calculate how much time this leaves an indivdual to pursue nonmarket activities of all sorts. This estimate of the leisure time available to individuals—that is, the amount of time they do not have to spend in compensated employment of one sort or another (including working for themselves if they are independent businessmen, or proprietors)—is an important supplement to TDC in indicating the level of economic well-being.

The amount of leisure is actually the product of two separate sets of influences. One is the number of years which individuals are able to spend outside the work force (which is the difference between the average life expectancy and the average number of years spent in the work force). The other determinant of leisure time is the average number of hours worked each year by those in the work force (itself the product of the average number of weeks worked each year and the average number of hours worked each week). The amount of leisure available to individuals, once they become a part of the work force, is, then, the difference between the 8,766 hours in each year and the average number of hours worked each year. Thus the amount of leisure, as a key determinant of the level of economic welfare, depends on: (1) the average life expectancy; (2) the average age at which individuals enter the work force; (3) the average age when individuals retire or otherwise leave the work force; (4) the average number of weeks worked each year by individuals; and (5) the average number of hours worked each week.

To provide the basis for a meaningful assessment, however, the figures on leisure time need to be considered in conjunction with various other indicators of economic well-being. They are: (1) a measure of the amount of involuntary unemployment, and thus how much of the leisure time is imposed on the individual rather than being the individual's preference; (2) a measure of the relative inequality in the amount of income available to different households, and thus how great is the variance around the mean insofar as the distribution of TDC is concerned; (3) a measure of the "bads" (e.g., pollution and congestion) as well as the "goods" produced by the enterprise sector and thus how great is the enterprise sector's net contribution to economic welfare; (4) a measure of the product component, particularly the noneconomic product component, of government expenditures as distinct from the income transfer component, and thus how much the overall social welfare is being enhanced by the resources flowing into the public sector; and (5) a measure of how equitably the most desirable types of jobs, those which provide the greatest intrinsic satisfaction to the individual, are distributed among the population. No attempt will be made, at least in this chapter, to provide any of these additional measures. The purpose in listing them is only to indicate the extent to which it is necessary to go beyond just the figure on TDC in order to assess the level of economic well-being, or welfare. In other words, determining the value of TDC and its components in real terms is only the first step toward being able to measure the level of material well-being that the economic system is able to provide the members of a society like the United States. Still, it is the essential first step.

2.3 The Flow of Funds Accounts

So far the focus in this chapter has been on the flow of real goods and services which, when aggregated in the next-to-last column of the input-output table, constitutes the national product originating in the enterprise sector. The thrust of the preceding main section was that, with the possible exception of whatever wage bill is incurred by the government in adding to the economic infrastructure, the national product originating in the enterprise sector, and thus the next-to-last column of the input-output table, constitutes the entire national product. In this section the focus will shift to the next-to-bottom row of the same input-output table and thus to the national income originating in the enterprise sector. As already explained (see part 1 of this chapter), the national income originating in the enterprise sector must necessarily be equal to the national product originating in the same sector so that, again with the possible exception of the government's wage bill in adding to the economic infrastructure, the next-to-bottom row of the input-output table constitutes the entire national income.

Paralleling the flow of real goods and services which the national product measures is a counterflow of funds which, in the aggregate, constitute the economic system's monetary flows. The various components of the value added by the enterprise sector which are aggregated in the next-to-bottom row of the input-output table are one way of representing those monetary flows (see exhibits 2.6 and 2.7). Another, analytically more useful, way are the Flow of Funds Accounts, based on the pioneering work of Morris Copeland in measuring the money flows of the U.S. economy. The emphasis in this section will be on the relationship between these two means of representing the economy's monetary flows. In the subsections that follow, the Flow of Funds Accounts, together with the balancing condition on which they are based, will first be described. Next, an alternative set of categories will be introduced for decomposing the national income which originates in the enterprise sector so as to bring out more clearly the link between the FOFA and the income flows represented by the next-to-bottom row of the input-output table. Finally, it will be explained how a set of sectoral accounts can be derived from the FOFA to show the discrepancy, if any, between savings and investment or, more broadly, between discretionary expenditures and discretionary funds in each of the relevant sectors of the economy.

2.3.1 The structure of the FOFA

The unit of observation in the FOFA is a sector rather than an industry (with at least one of the sectors consisting of n industries as subcomponents). The sectors into which the economy is divided in the FOFA fall under two main categories, financial and nonfinancial. Thus, what in the input-output table for the U.S. economy is only one of 79 industries becomes, in the FOFA, a principal subdivision. Still, in this chapter and indeed until chapter 12 when the monetary constraints on economic expansion are analyzed, the focus will be primarily on the nonfinancial sectors delineated in the FOFA.

These nonfinancial sectors include the four principal sectors already identified—the enterprise, household, government and rest-of-the-world sectors. The FOFA, however, further divide certain of these sectors into subsectors, making seven nonfinancial sectors in all for which data are available through this set of accounts. They are the corporate, the noncorporate nonfarm, and the noncorporate farm sectors as three separate components of a more inclusive enterprise

Exhibit 2.12

Year	Implicit price deflator for GNP 1972 = 100	Fixed-weight price index for GNP 1972 = 100
1958	66.06	68.1
1959	67.52	69.1
1960	68.67	70.3
1961	69.28	71.1
1962	70.55	72.0
1963	71.59	72.8
1964	72.71	73.7
1965	74.32	75.0
1966	76.76	77.2
1967	79.02	79.5
1968	82.57	83.0
1969	86.72	87.1
1970	91.36	91.6
1971	96.02	96.1
1972	100.00	100.0
1973	105.80	106.0
1974	116.02	116.3
1975	127.15	127.7
1976	133.71	134.8
1977	141.70	143.5
1978	152.05	154.2

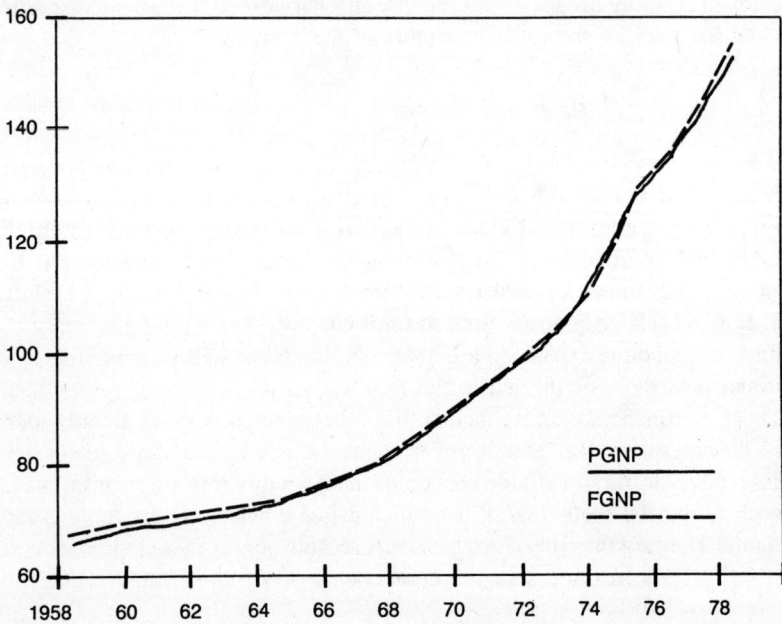

Exhibit 2.13
Sectoral Flow of Funds Account

	Uses	Sources
Gross saving	—	500
Tangible investment	200	—
Net financial investment	300	—
Total	500	500

	Net acquisition of assets	Net increase in liabilities
Stocks and bonds	200	—
Mortgages	100	—
Bank deposits	100	—
Bank loans	—	100

sector; the household sector, including not-for-profit organizations; the federal government and the state and local government sectors as two separate components of a more inclusive government sector; and the rest-of-the-world sector. Indeed, this more detailed sectoral breakdown is one reason for basing the model to be developed in the subsequent chapters of this text on both the format of the FOFA (with some minor changes) and the data available within that format. Specifically, the FOFA make it possible to distinguish the subsector of the enterprise sector which is dominated by large corporations, or megacorps, from the subsectors in which the neoclassical proprietorship is more likely to be the representative firm.

For each of the sectors into which the economic system is divided by the FOFA, a balance sheet is drawn up, showing the uses of any funds on the one side and the sources of those funds on the other (see exhibit 2.13). The sources of funds vary, depending on the sector. In the case of the enterprise sector, the sources of funds are sales revenues; in the case of the household sector (narrowly defined to exclude nonprofit organizations), they are wage and other types of income payments, and in the case of the government sector, they are net tax revenues. (These sources of funds are described in greater detail below, section 2.3.4.) The FOFA are concerned, however, not with the total inflow of funds into each of the different nonfinancial sectors but rather only with the net inflow. This is what is left after certain types of payments to the other nonfinancial sectors— for example, to the enterprise sector for any nondurable goods purchased, to the household sector for any labor inputs obtained, or to the government sector in taxes—are subtracted from the total inflow of funds. In this way, the FOFA are able to capture precisely those monetary flows which are missing from an input-output table, making the two systems of accounting complementary to one another. The net inflow of funds into each sector, as determined in the above manner, is then denoted as that sector's "gross savings."

Offsetting the net cash inflow, or gross savings, as sources of funds are the various uses to which those funds are put. The FOFA distinguish two major uses of funds. One is to purchase durable goods, and this use is termed "tangible investment." The other is to acquire financial assets of various types. Indeed, whatever net inflow of funds, or gross savings, is not spent on durable goods will necessarily show up in the FOFA as an additional financial asset which has been acquired, even if that asset is only a Federal Reserve note (currency) or a deposit at some bank or similar financial institution against which a check or some other type of draft can be written. The acquisition of such assets is termed "net financial investment."

The FOFA is thus based on the fact that any inflow of funds into a sector in excess of that sector's outlay of funds to some other nonfinancial sector—what, in the FOFA, is termed the sector's gross savings and what, in the chapters which follow, will be redefined as the sector's net cash inflow, or discretionary funds—must necessarily take the form of either "tangible (physical) investment" (the purchase of some durable good) or "financial investment" (a net addition to the stock of financial assets held by the sector). That is,

Gross Savings = Tangible Investment + Financial Investment.

Shifting terms, this can be rewritten as follows:

Gross Savings − Tangible Investment = Financial Investment

which, within a conventional Keynesian framework, means that any discrepancy between savings and investment will lead to a net change in the amount of financial assets held by the sector. For a sector such as the one represented in exhibit 2.13, this means that, with gross savings equal to $500 million and tangible investment equal to $200 million, its financial investment, or the net change in the amount of financial assets held, must be $300 million.

The FOFA provide a detailed breakdown of each sector's financial investment (that is, the change in its financial position), distinguishing the net acquisition of assets during the period covered from the net increase in liabilities. Indeed, it is in this manner that the U.S. Federal Reserve Board, the policymaking body for the Federal Reserve System, is able to construct the Flow of Funds Accounts. By supplementing the data from the balance sheets of the financial institutions it oversees, the Board is able to determine the change in assets and liabilities for each of the sectors covered in the FOFA, and thus the change in each sector's net financial position. This change in each sector's net financial position can then be compared with the balance between tangible investment (durable goods purchases) and gross savings (net cash inflow) for the same sector, based on the data available from the National Income and Product Accounts.

What is thus unique to the FOFA (as distinct from what is derived from the NIPA and then converted to a FOFA format) is the breakdown of the net financial investment for each sector into (a) the sector's net acquisition of assets, and (b) its net increase in liabilities. This breakdown is shown in the bottom half of exhibit 2.13. The figures there indicate that the sector in question acquired $200 million in stocks and bonds and $100 million in mortgages over the interval covered while still adding $100 million to its bank deposits. Offsetting this $400 million increase in assets, however, was $100 million in additional bank loans, or liabilities, incurred during the same time period, and thus the sector's financial investment was only $300 million.

The specific types of financial assets and liabilities shown in the FOFA vary by sector. Whatever form the assets and liabilities take, however, they must balance one another, not just within any one sector but also, even more significantly, for the economic system as a whole. The latter is true since a change in the financial position of any one sector, as a result of a change in either its gross savings or tangible investment, must be matched by an equivalent change in the financial position of some other sector. Indeed, this is the second balancing condition, aside from the uses of funds by each sector being equal to its sources of funds, upon which the FOFA are based.

2.3.2 The sectoral balances

The FOFA are constructed in such a way that the net financial investment for all sectors, financial as well as nonfinancial, must, in the aggregate, be equal to zero. It is this condition which provides the same statistical control for the FOFA that the equality between the national product and national income originating in the enterprise sector provides for an input-output table. As a result, any change in one sector's net financial investment must lead to a corresponding change in some other sector's net financial investment. There are two possibilities.

One is that the change in the sector's financial position will occur without any increase in the overall amount of funds in circulation. In that case, any improvement in one sector's net financial position, because its gross savings have increased relative to tangible investment, can only be at the expense of some other sector. Thus, unless there was an increase in the overall amount of funds in circulation, the $300 million improvement in the financial position of the sector depicted in exhibit 2.13 meant there had to be a $300 million deterioration in the financial position of one or more other sectors. The other possibility is that the change in the sector's financial position will be accompanied by a change in the overall amount of funds in circulation, with the amount of those funds increasing as part of the process leading to the sector's greater financial investment (the result of some other sector making a payment to that sector which has been financed by a loan from some bank). In that case, an improvement in the financial position of the one sector will be possible without some other sector necessarily experiencing a deterioration in its financial position. The increase in the overall amount of funds in circulation, and in particular the way the additional funds are put into circulation (through a bank loan), is what makes this possible. (While the sector making the payment will have increased its financial liabilities as a result of the bank loan it received, it will also have increased its financial assets in the form of the additional bank deposits credited to it in the process. Even when those funds, i.e., the bank deposits, are then shifted, in payment, to the other sector, the sector which obtained the bank loan has presumably acquired something of equivalent value in exchange. Indeed, what it has acquired is likely to be some asset, either physical or financial—this having been done so as to enable it to qualify for the bank loan in the first place.)

The second of the two possibilities is pointed out because an error frequently made in economics is to assume that an improvement in the financial position of any one sector must necessarily be at the expense of some other sector—and thus that the overall amount of funds in circulation is fixed. As will be brought out in chapter 12, with the existence of a credit-based system of money, no such limitation on the amount of funds in circulation can be assumed. Indeed, under a credit-based system of money, an increase in the amount of funds in circulation will occur as an endogenous response whenever one of the nonfinancial sectors uses loans from the banking system to finance its outlays, including any expenditures on durable goods (the sector's tangible investment). While the condition that the net financial investment for all sectors, financial as well as nonfinancial, must be equal to zero will still hold, it remains true in the second of the two cases just delineated because the overall amount of funds has increased, and not because funds have been shifted from one sector to another.

As the FOFA are actually compiled, this condition—that the net financial investment for all sectors must be equal to zero—does not strictly hold. It is not possible, as a practical matter, to record all the financial transactions which take place in an economy as complex and intricate as that of the United States and the other OECD countries; and as a result of this and other sources of errors, it is not possible to reconcile the figures on the balance between tangible investment and gross savings for each sector, which are derived from the NIPA, with the figures on the net acquisition of assets and the net increase in liabilities which the Federal Reserve Board itself compiles. To make the items balance, so that both the difference between gross savings and tangible investment and the difference between the net acquisition of assets and the net increase in liabilities will be equal in the accounts to the net financial investment for each sector, a discrepancy figure is added for each sector. The discrepancy figures aside, however, the net financial investment for all the sectors must be equal to zero; and an increase in the net financial investment for one sector must be balanced by a change in the net financial position of some other sector (or group of sectors), whether this simply reflects an intersectoral shift of funds or, alternatively, a simultaneous increase in both the assets and liabilities of two or more sectors through the process of credit expansion.

Exhibit 2.14 is a replica of the FOFA for 1973 as actually published by the Federal Reserve Board. It shows, in detail, both the different sectors, financial and nonfinancial, delineated in the FOFA and the various items included under gross savings, tangible investment and net financial investment. The Federal Reserve Board no longer publishes the FOFA in such detail in its monthly *Bulletin*. However, the data are still available, both on a quarterly and annual basis, from the Fed on computer tapes.

The advantage of the FOFA format is that it not only shows the balance between savings and investment in the aggregate (just as the alternative NIPA do) but also, by dropping the implicit assumption of the standard Keynesian models that only households save and only business firms invest, it shows the balance between savings and investment for each of the seven different non-financial sectors represented in the accounts—with the balance between savings and investment then linked to the change in each sector's financial position. Indeed, this is a second reason why the model to be developed in the subsequent chapters of this text follows the FOFA format. The format will enable us to focus on the sectoral balances between savings and investment as the key to any change in either the economy's real flows or in monetary-financial conditions. First, however, it is necessary to show how the net inflow of funds into each of these different sectors (their "gross savings ") can be derived from the national income categories which constitute the value added row of the input-output table.

2.3.3 The national income categories

The economic system's internal process involves two separate flows. One is an open-ended flow of physical goods. This is the flow represented by the diverse items which constitute the net, or final, output of the enterprise sector, as shown in the next-to-last column of the applicable input-output table (see exhibit 2.6). Together, these items constitute the national product originating within the enterprise sector. The other flow is the flow of funds among the various sectors of the economy. It is this flow, the monetary flow, which the circular flow diagrams of the economy found in most introductory textbooks are supposed to capture. These diagrams are misleading, however, in suggesting that the real, or physical, flows are also circular. The fact is that the goods and services produced by the enterprise sector simply flow at a certain rate to the other sectors of the economy where they are either used up within three years, as in the case of nondurable goods and services, or consumed more slowly—in which case they constitute an addition to the accumulated stock of durable goods. The only circular flow, then, is the monetary one which the Flow of Funds Accounts measure.

Exhibit 2.14
Summary of Flow of Funds Accounts for 1973
(Seasonally adjusted annual rates: $ in billions)

Transaction category	Private domestic nonfinancial sectors								Rest of the world	
	Households		Business		State and local governments		Total			
	U	S	U	S	U	S	U	S	U	S
1 Gross saving	229.6		112.6		.2		342.5			.1
2 Capital consumption	115.7		95.2				211.0			
3 Net saving (1–2)	113.9		17.4		.2		131.5			.1
4 Gross investment (5 + 10)	235.6		98.8		5.4		329.1		2.1	
5 Private capital expenditures	174.1		160.5				334.7			
6 Consumer durables	130.3						130.3			
7 Residential construction	37.5		19.5				57.0			
8 Plant and equipment	6.3		125.7				132.0			
9 Inventory change			15.4				15.4			
10 Net financial investment (11–12)	61.5		61.7		5.4		5.6		2.1	
11 Financial uses	130.8		43.9		7.9		182.6		17.4	
12 Financial sources		69.3		105.5		13.3		188.1		15.3
13 Gold and official foreign exchange										.2
14 Treasury currency										
15 Demand deposits and currency	13.1			.3		.3	12.5		2.5	
16 Private domestic	13.1			.3		.3	12.5			
17 U.S. Government										
18 Foreign									2.5	
19 Time and savings accounts	67.7		1.4		7.2		76.3		2.9	
20 At commercial banks	39.5		1.4		7.2		48.1		2.9	
21 At savings institutions	28.2						28.2			
22 Life insurance reserves	7.3						7.3			
23 Pension fund reserves	24.4						24.4			
24 Interbank items										
25 Corporate shares	8.2			7.4			8.2	7.4	2.8	.2
26 Credit market instruments	29.7	72.8	9.1	77.6	.4	12.3	39.3	162.7	.7	7.7
27 U.S. Government securities	20.4		1.8		.2		18.8		.3	

Exhibit 2.14

Summary of Flow of Funds Accounts for 1973

(Seasonally adjusted annual rates: $ in billions)

Financial sectors

U.S. Government		Total		Federally sponsored credit agencies		Monetary authority		Commercial banks		Private nonbank finance		All sectors		Discrepancy	National saving and investment	
U	S	U	S	U	S	U	S	U	S	U	S	U	S	U		
	8.2		10.5		.2		.1		4.4		5.7		344.7		344.7	1
			3.1						1.7		1.4		214.1		214.1	2
	8.2		7.4		.2		.1		2.7		4.3		130.6		130.7	3
7.7		13.7		.3		.1		6.0		7.4		337.3		7.4	337.6	4
		5.0						3.0		2.0		339.7		5.0	339.7	5
												130.3			130.3	6
		.2								.2		57.2			57.2	7
		4.8						3.0		1.8		136.8			136.8	8
												15.4			15.4	9
7.7		8.7		.3		.1		2.9		5.4		2.4		2.4	2.1	10
4.3		217.8		22.0		7.8		100.2		87.7		422.1		2.4	15.3	11
	12.0		209.1		21.8		7.7		97.3		82.3		424.6		17.4	12
		.2				.2						.2	.2			13
	.4	.4				.4						.4	.4			14
1.8		2.4	16.0	.1		3.4		.3	12.6	2.0		15.0	16.0	.4		15
		2.4	15.0	.1		3.9		.3	11.0	2.0		14.9	15.0	.1		16
1.8			1.5				.5		1.0			1.8	1.5	.3		17
			2.5				.1		2.6			2.5	2.5			18
.2		.1	79.1						50.9	.1	28.1	79.1	79.1			19
.2		.1	50.9						50.9	.1		50.9	50.9			20
			28.1								28.1	28.1	28.1			21
	.1		7.2								7.2	7.3	7.3			22
	2.1		22.3								22.3	24.4	24.4			23
		7.9	7.9			1.6	3.5	9.5	4.4			7.9	7.9			24
		13.4	.8					.1	1.2	13.4	.4	8.0	8.0			25
3.0		9.7	188.3	51.2	20.3	19.6	9.2	86.6	10.6	72.2	21.0	231.3	231.3			26
	9.8		10.3	19.6	1.3	19.6	9.3		1.3		.9	29.4	29.4			27

Exhibit 2.14

Summary of Flow of Funds Accounts for 1973

(Seasonally adjusted annual rates: $ in billions)

	Private domestic nonfinancial sectors								Rest of the world	
	Households		Business		State and local governments		Total			
Transaction category	U	S	U	S	U	S	U	S	U	S
28 State and local obligations	4.3		.1	1.8	.2	11.9	4.4	13 7		
29 Corporate and foreign bonds	1.1			9.2			1.1	9 2	.1	1.0
30 Home mortgages	.9	44.2		.9			.9	43.3		
31 Other mortgages	1.4	1.4		28.4			1.4	29.8		
32 Consumer credit		22.9	3.3				3.3	22.9		
33 Bank loans n.e.c.		1.8		34.0				35.8		2.8
34 Other loans	3.5	2.5	7.8	5.1		.3	11.3	7.9	.3	3.9
35 Security credit	.2	4.6					.2	4.6		.2
36 To brokers and dealers	.2						.2			
37 To others		4.6						4.6		.2
38 Taxes payable				2.3	.6		.6	2.3		
39 Trade credit		.6	24.1	20.1		1.1	24.1	21.8	1.0	1.9
40 Equity in noncorporate business	4.4			4.4			4.4	4.4		
41 Miscellaneous claims	1.5	.4	9.6	2.5			11.1	2.9	7.6	6.3
42 Sector discrepancies (1–4)	6.0		13.8		5.6		13.4		2.2	

The point of interface between the two flows—the open-ended flow of real output shown in the next-to-last column of the input-output table and the circular flow of funds measured by the FOFA—is the flow of income which the next-to-bottom row of the same input-output table is supposed to represent. Indeed, properly defined, the gross flow of funds into each sector is indistinguishable from the flow of income. To show the connection, it is necessary to rearrange the items which constitute the value added by the enterprise sector (the next-to-bottom row of the input-output table)—and thereby produce a quite different set of categories for decomposing the national income into its component parts.

As already indicated, the value added by the enterprise sector consists of three principal types of outlays, or charges against the value of each industry's total

Exhibit 2.14

Summary of Flow of Funds Accounts for 1973

(Seasonally adjusted annual rates: $ in billions)

U.S. Govt		Financial sectors										All sectors		Dis-crep-ancy	Natl. saving and invest.	
		Total		Fed. spons. credit agencies		Mone-tary auth.		Coml. banks		Pvt. nonbank finance						
U	S	U	S	U	S	U	S	U	S	U	S	U	S	U		
		9.3						5.7		3.6		13.7	13.7		28	
		11.3	2.3					.5		10.9	2.3	12.5	12.5		29	
1.2	.1	43.9	1.5	6.4				11.0		26.5	1.5	41.7	41.7		30	
.6		28.1	.3	4.0				8.8		15.4	.3	30.2	30.2		31	
		19.7						10.6		9.0		22.9	22.9		32	
		52.1	13.5					52.1	5.1		8.4	52.1	52.1		33	
3.6		13.7	17.0	8.5				.8	5.5	5.9	11.5	28.8	28.8		34	
		8.0	3.4					3.4		4.6	3.4	8.2	8.2		35	
		3.2	3.4					3.2			3.4	3.4	3.4		36	
		4.8						.2		4.6		4.8	4.8		37	
2.2					.3	.1			.1		.1	2.8	2.7	.1	38	
.3	.1	.7								.7		26.0	23.7	2.3	39	
												4.4	4.4		40	
1.0	.4	12.8	27.8	1.7	2.2	.8		7.2	17.5	.9	7.4	32.4	36.7	4.3	41	
.5		3.3						1.6		1.7		7.4	7.4		42	

output. They are: (1) whatever must be paid to workers in wages and salaries (the industry's wage bill); (2) whatever must be paid to the government to cover any excise and other indirect taxes (the industry's *ad valorem* tax bill); and (3) whatever remains left over as property income (the industry's profits, or "residual income"). According to the conventional view in economics, the wage bill represents payment to the "labor" factor of production and the profits, payment to "capital." The national income originating in the enterprise sector—and indeed the national income for the economy as a whole—is then defined as the sum of all factor payments, or the sum of the wage bill for each of the n industries plus the sum of the profits earned by each of the same n industries (see exhibit 2.7). Since this definition of national income excludes any indirect taxes which might be paid as well as various other "charges against business gross product," it is then necessary to add a third item, "adjustment to market price," to the wage bill (employees' compensation) and the profits (property income), so that the national income originating in the enterprise sector will be equal to the net national product originating in the same sector (see exhibit 2.7, which represents the actual format used in the NIPA).

This set of categories for decomposing the national income originating in the enterprise sector is unsatisfactory for two reasons. The first is that it is based on a model of production to which serious objection can be, and has been, made. This is the neoclassical model, with an "aggregate" production function which takes the form of $Q = f(K, L)$. More will be said about this point shortly (see chapter 4, section 3.5). The second and, in the present context, perhaps more important reason the categories shown in exhibit 2.7 are unsatisfactory is that they fail to bring out the relationship between the flow of funds which the FOFA measure and the flow of income which the next-to-bottom row of an input-output table, as the income originating in the enterprise sector, is supposed to represent. The relationship between the two flows is obscured because, in addition to assuming that a neoclassical production function applies, the NIPA are constructed on the assumption, common to the orthodox viewpoint in economics, that the household sector is the ultimate recipient of all income. Thus, both wages and salaries and any profits are regarded as income received by the household sector. Since this is not the case—some of the income originating within the enterprise sector is retained by that sector while some of it flows to the government in the form of various direct taxes—the categories are not entirely appropriate ones. The point can be seen perhaps more clearly by taking a closer look at the different items included in exhibit 2.7 under the categories of employees' compensation and property income—the latter especially.

The figure for net interest shown in exhibit 2.7 measures, not the total interest paid by the firms in each of the different industries but rather, only the interest paid out less any interest received from other firms. It thus measures only the net outflow of interest from the enterprise sector, including financial institutions, to the other sectors as payment for the use of any funds which have been borrowed. Indeed, since any interest paid to the government is treated as a transfer payment (see section 2.2.2) and thus as an offset to whatever subsidies have been obtained by the enterprise sector, it measures only the net outflow to the household sector. The net interest differs from the other items under property income in that it represents a relatively "fixed" obligation. The amount of interest is usually specified in advance, and generally does not vary with economic circumstances. The payments, once contractually established, must continue if bankruptcy is to be avoided. Economists refer to this type of payment as "rentier" income.

The other items under property income all involve what can be termed the residual income of different types of enterprises. This is the income which remains from the total revenues earned once all the other obligations of the enterprise, including any interest on loans, have been met. Since the total revenues can be expected to vary with economic circumstances, the residual income, too, will vary. Those who receive the residual income therefore incur a certain risk due to the uncertainty about the larger economic forces shaping the fortunes of any particular industry or firm. As will be brought out later (see chapter 7, section 3.1), there is no way to organize an economic system without this risk being borne by at least some group in society. In the case of a market economy the risk falls, at least in the first instance, on the various enterprises; and this fact is reflected in the variability—one might even say the volatility—of their residual income. The different ways in which this residual income is recorded in exhibit 2.7 reflects the different types of firms which, in the case of the United States, are found within the enterprise sector. At least three different types of firms need to be taken into account (excluding the fictive type of enterprise on which the imputed rental income of the NIPA is based). They are: (1) proprietorships; (2) corporations; and (3) government enterprises.

The proprietary form of business organization antedates all the others. In its most rudimentary form, it consists of the family unit acting as an economic enterprise, with the paterfamilias serving both as the head of the household and as the head of the firm. In more complex cases, the proprietary form of business enterprise consists of a partnership among two or more heads of households, the arrangement usually being formalized through a legally binding agreement. In either case, the distinction between firms and households is blurred, especially insofar as any savings are concerned. The savings of the household are the savings of the firm—even though it is necessary, from a legal standpoint, that the funds be held in the name of one or the other. The residual income for all proprietorships, part of which may consist of retained earnings, or savings, is recorded in the NIPA, and thus in exhibit 2.7, as proprietors' income. It encompasses not only a return on whatever funds have been invested by the firm's principals but also compensation for whatever labor inputs have been contributed by them and their families. The combined role of owner and manager which the principals play makes it impossible to distinguish the one type of income from the other in the accounts.

The corporate enterprise, though its origins can be traced back to the medieval guild and other civic and philanthropic organizations of that earlier epoch, has become the predominant type of business enterprise only within the last century. It is distinguishable from the proprietorship in that it is created by a charter obtained from the state, with a group of owners, or stockholders, who need have no involvement in the day-to-day operations of the firm once they have supplied any required initial funds. Indeed, in its most advanced form, that of the mega-corp, this type of business enterprise is managed by a separate group of executives, chosen for their professional skills in various areas of business and who may, in fact, own no stock in the company whatsoever. Legally, the executives are accountable to the stockholders and, in theory, are chosen by them. However, as will become clear from the discussion below (see chapters 6, section 2.1, and chapter 8, section 1.1), the executives are likely to be a largely self-perpetuating group enjoying considerable discretion, with the stockholders playing a mostly passive role.

The residual income for all corporations is recorded in the NIPA as corporate profits. As can be seen from exhibit 2.7, these profits are divided into three parts. The corporate tax liability is the portion that goes to the government, the dividends are the portion that goes to the stockholders, and the undistributed profits are the portion that is retained by the corporations themselves. Only the first two of these three components represent a flow of income outside the enterprise sector—and only the dividends, a flow to households. Moreover, since the flow of dividends is nearly as steady, or "fixed," as the flow of interest, the dividends can be regarded as another form of rentier income. The corporate sector's residual income, then, consists of both the undistributed profits and the corporate tax liability—with the former the residual income that goes to the corporations themselves and the latter, since the tax liability is calculated as a percentage of total profits, the share that goes to the government.

Government enterprises are firms which have been organized and financed by government to carry out marketable activities, with no separate set of owners or stockholders. They are thus to be distinguished, on the one hand, from government itself and from nonprofit organizations whose efforts do not give rise to any marketable output; and, on the other hand, from the nationalized enterprises whose stock may be held, in whole or in part, by the government but which in every other way are similar to privately owned corporations. Because government enterprises have no separate set of owners or stockholders—indeed, it is often difficult to determine even how much in the way of capital resources have been invested in these firms—their residual income is recorded in the NIPA, and thus in exhibit 2.7, as the current surplus of government enterprises. The amount of any subsidies received by the enterprise sector as a whole from the government are then subtracted from the current surplus of government enterprises to give a net figure for the amount of income emanating from the enterprise sector.

As can be seen from exhibit 2.7, this net figure is included, in the NIPA, not as part of the national income originating in the enterprise sector but rather, together with other items, including any indirect business taxes, as part of the adjustment to market price. The indirect business taxes, it should be noted, are sales and other excise taxes levied as a percentage of the transaction price (as distinct from the direct taxes levied as a percentage of the income received by labor and the other "factors" of production); business transfers consist primarily of bad debts which have been written off as uncollectable, and the statistical discrepancy will be explained shortly. The reason the net surplus of government enterprises, along with the other items included under the adjustment to market price, is not shown in exhibit 2.7 as part of the national income originating in the enterprise sector is that none of these items can be described, even nominally, as a payment to some factor of production—that is, as payment for something that is used as an input in the production process. These various "adjustment items," when added to the national income originating in the enterprise sector, constitute only the net national product originating in business. The rest of the value of the national product originating in the enterprise sector (what is denoted in exhibit 2.7 as the Charges against Gross Business Product) consists of what is termed the capital consumption allowance. This item covers both what the U.S. Treasury allows for depreciation and any actual losses in plant and equipment due to fire, theft and other misfortunes.

2.3.4 An alternative format

It is possible to rearrange the various items shown in exhibit 2.7—and thus the categories for decomposing the national income originating in the enterprise sector—so as to bring out more clearly what are the actual income flows from the enterprise sector to each of the other sectors. This is done in exhibit 2.15, where the same items shown on the left-hand side of exhibit 2.7 have been rearranged and then listed under the following categories: (1) income paid out; (2) income retained; and (3) other income. The income paid out is then further divided into (a) the income received by households and (b) the income received by government, making four categories in all. The last of the four categories, other income, includes any income which, rather than being directly available to finance the purchase of current output, merely represents a change in the net financial position of one of the sectors. For example, the other compensation of employees consists of contributions to private pension plans and hence represents an accumulation of financial assets by the household sector, with those financial assets being used to provide workers with income once they retire. (The assets are actually held in trust for the household sector by the various financial institutions which manage pension and other retirement funds.) Business transfers and the various capital consumption items, on the other hand, represent a change in the net worth of the enterprise sector and hence a change in the value placed on the enterprise sector's physical and financial assets (independently of the actual flow of income into and out of the sector).

In rearranging the data according to this format, only a little additional detail is necessary—all of it readily available from the same NIPA. For example, the amount of wages and salaries withheld for payment of personal income taxes as well as the individuals' own contributions to social insurance needs to be ascertained so that, by subtracting these two items from the total compensation of employees, one can determine the workers' actual take-home pay. Similarly, the amount of proprietors' financial investment—the amount of their income retained by proprietary forms of business—needs to be ascertained so that, along with the amount of personal income taxes paid, it can be subtracted from the total amount of proprietors' income. Thus the income paid out by the enterprise sector to households—what is actually available to cover the cost of any personal outlays—

Exhibit 2.15

Recommended Consolidated Business Income and Product Account
(1978, $billion)

Charges against business gross product

Income paid out		737.9
To households		
Wages and salaries	880.3	
Net interest	19.5	
Net dividends	47.2	
Proprietors' net income	119.5	
Gross income	102.3	
Less financial investment	−17.2	
Less personal contributions for social insurance	69.6	
Less personal tax and nontax payments	259.0	
To government		651.2
Indirect business taxes	152.8	
Corporate tax liability	84.5	
Employers' contributions to social insurance	94.6	
Personal contributions to social insurance	69.6	
Personal tax and nontax payments	259.0	
Less subsidies	9.3	

Consolidated net sales (value added)

To households		1,245.8
On capital account	286.4	
Structures	92.0	
Durable goods	194.4	
Other	959.4	
Nondurable goods	530.6	
Services	428.8	
To government and nonprofit institutions		223.5
On capital account	75.1	
Structures	45.5	
Durable goods	29.6	
Other	148.4	
Nondurable goods	40.8	
Services	107.6	
Abroad		−10.3
Exports	207.2	
Durable goods	84.7	
Other	122.5	
Imports	217.5	
To business on capital account		237.1

Other			Structures		90.6
Other compensation of employees	106.4	263.8	Residential	14.1	
Business transfers	9.2		Nonresidential	76.5	146.5
Other capital consumption	186.5		Producers' durable goods		
Inventory valuation adjustment	−25.2		Change in business inventories		22.3
Capital consumption adjustment	−13.1				
Income retained		62.2			
Corporate undistributed profits	74.3				
Proprietors' financial investment	−17.2				
Current surplus of government sector	5.1				
Statistical discrepancy		3.3			
Charges against business gross product		1,718.4	Business gross product		1,718.4

includes: (a) wages and salaries net of all deductions (workers' take-home pay); (b) net interest; (c) proprietors' income net of personal taxes and net of financial investment; and (d) net dividends. Meanwhile, the income paid out by the enterprise sector to the government includes: (a) the workers' personal contribution to social insurance; (b) employers' contribution to social insurance; (c) personal taxes and nontax liabilities; (d) corporate tax liabilities; and (e) indirect business taxes, with any (f) subsidies then subtracted from this total.

The advantage of the format used in exhibit 2.15 is that it indicates how the income originating in the enterprise sector is actually distributed among the various sectors as funds which can then be used to finance any outlays (as distinct from how the national income originates as a series of charges against sales revenues). This format, however, is not just an alternative to the format in which the NIPA data are usually presented, as in exhibit 2.7. It also represents the intervening step in transforming the three major components of the value added by the enterprise sector—employees' compensation, property income and indirect business taxes—into the discretionary funds (gross savings) and discretionary expenditures (tangible investment) shown in the sectoral Flow of Funds Accounts. How that intervening step needs to be carried out can be seen from exhibit 2.16, where the 18 items shown in exhibit 2.7 have been regrouped into the four categories delineated in exhibit 2.15. Indeed, once that intervening step has been taken, only two additional income flows need to be taken into account in order to derive the sectoral flow of funds accounts. They are (1) the compensation received by government employees (the government's wage bill), and (2) any nonwage (unearned) transfer payments made by government. The two together constitute the flow of income from the government sector to the household sector.

The government's wage bill and the amount of transfer payments, when added to the income paid out by business firms to households shown in exhibit 2.15, equals the household sector's disposable income. The household sector's disposable income, in turn, represents the total cash inflow into the household sector—just as the government's tax revenue less its wage bill and any transfer payments represents the total cash inflow into the government sector (see section 2.3.1). Thus the additional two income flows, the government's wage bill and the amount of transfer payments, need to be added to the income paid out by business firms to households while simultaneously being subtracted from the income paid out to the government in order to determine the total income, or funds, available to the household and government sectors respectively to purchase the goods and services produced by the enterprise sector (see exhibit 2.17). The net cash inflow into the enterprise sector, meanwhile, is the income retained within that sector, that is, its "cash flow." This net cash inflow is the income retained within the enterprise sector, as shown in exhibit 2.15. It consists of the following: (a) proprietors' financial investment; (b) corporate undistributed profits; (c) the surplus of government enterprises; and (d) capital consumption allowances.

Exhibit 2.16
Relationship between NIPA and FOFA Income Categories
(1978, $billion)

Employees' compensation		Business income paid to households	
1. Employee's take-home pay	551.7	1. Employees' take-home pay	551.7
2. Other labor income	106.4	6. Net interest	19.5
3. Personal contribution to S.S.	69.6	8. Proprietors' net income	119.5
4. Employer contribution to S.S.	94.6	10. Net dividends	47.2
5. Personal tax and nontax payments	259.0		737.9
	1,081.3	Net tax payments by business	
Property income		3. Personal contribution to S.S.	69.6
		4. Employer contribution to S.S.	94.6
6. Net interest	19.5	5. Personal tax and nontax payments	259.0
7. Proprietors' financial investment	−17.2	9. Corporate tax liability	84.5
8. Proprietors' net income	119.5	14. Indirect business taxes	152.8
9. Corporate tax liability	84.5	16. Less subsidies	9.3
10. Net dividends	47.2		651.2
11. Corporate undistributed profits	74.3		
12. Inventory valuation adjusted	−25.2	Other income paid out and changes in firms' net worth	
13. Capital consumption adjusted	−13.1	2. Other labor income	106.4
	289.5	12. Inventory valuation adjusted	−25.2
Adjustments to market price		13. Capital consumption adjusted	−13.1
		15. Business transfers	9.2
14. Indirect business taxes	152.8		77.3
15. Business transfers	9.2		
16. Less subsidies	9.3	Income retained by business	
17. Surplus of government enterprises	5.1	7. Proprietors' financial investment	−17.2
18. Capital consumption allowance	186.5	11. Corporate undistributed	74.3
	344.3	17. Surplus of government enterprises	5.1
		18. Capital consumption allowance	186.5
			248.7

The breakdown of the national income originating in the enterprise sector shown in exhibit 2.15—in particular, the four-fold distinction that is made between the income paid out to the household sector, the income paid out to the government, the income retained by the enterprise sector and any other income— is therefore the more appropriate one for decomposing the value added shown in the next-to-bottom row of the an input-output table. With the national income presented in this format, it is possible to show the link between the three sets of accounts—an input-output table, the National Income and Product Accounts and

Exhibit 2.17
Derivation of Household and Government Net Cash Inflow
(1978, $billion)

Household income originating in the enterprise sector		626.7
1. Take-home pay (private sector employees)	440.5	
2. Net interest	19.5	
3. Proprietors' net income	119.5	
4. Net dividends	47.2	
Plus wage and nonwage transfers		326.1
1. Government employees' take-home pay	111.2	
2. Nonwage transfers	214.9	
Equals household disposable income		1,031.4
Less household purchase of nondurable goods and services		959.4
Equals household net cash inflow (personal savings)		72.0
Government net revenues originating in the enterprise sector		660.5
1. Personal contributions to Social Security	69.6	
2. Employer contributions to Social Security	94.6	
3. Personal tax and nontax payments	259.0	
4. Corporate tax liabilities	84.5	
5. Indirect business taxes	152.8	
Less nonwage transfers		293.5
Equals government net revenues		367.0
Less compensation of government employees		218.0
Equals total government cash inflow		149.0
Less government purchase of nondurable goods and services		148.4
Equals government net cash inflow (surplus or deficit)		0.6

the Flow of Funds Accounts—which, together, constitute an integrated and comprehensive accounting framework for macrodynamic analysis. It is also possible to show the connection between the economy's income and product flows on the one hand and the monetary flows on the other. Indeed, after making certain modifications in the format and, even more important, in the nomenclature of the FOFA, this will be the next step in developing an integrated set of accounts.

2.3.5 Discretionary expenditures and discretionary funds

The key insight of John Maynard Keynes was to distinguish investment and savings from the other types of spending and income-disposition choices which individuals make—and thereby, because of the critical influence which investment and savings have on the circular flow of funds, to lay the foundation for modern macroeconomic analysis. The distinction that is now routinely made by

Exhibit 2.18
Discretionary Expenditures and Discretionary Funds
Corporate Sector
(1978, $billion)

Discretionary Expenditures		174.2	Discretionary Funds			174.1
Plant and equipment	170.0		Undistributed profits		55.8	
Residential construction	4.2		Foreign branch profits		5.2	
			Capital consumption allowance		125.1	
			Capital consumption adjustment		−12.0	
			Net borrowing			68.6
			Net increase in liabilities		146.9	
			Long-term		49.2	
			Equity	9.9		
			Mortgages	16.0		
			Bonds	23.3		
			Short-term and other		97.7	
			Net acquisition of assets		78.3	
			Liquid assets	5.3		
			Trade credit	54.9		
			Other	18.1		
			Discrepancy			−68.5

economists between investment and savings has a more profound implication for economic analysis than is commonly realized, however. For with investment and savings there must also be growth and technical progress.

It is the technology underlying modern production techniques—what Marxists refer to as an advanced economy's "mode of production" and what, beginning with chapter 5, will be denoted the A, L, and K matrices—which assures that, in a monetarized system, there will be both savings and investment as part of the accumulation process. Decisions by individual households or business firms may influence the rate at which accumulation proceeds, but they are not the reason why accumulation itself takes place. The fact is that, in order to derive the benefits of the productivity, or increased output per worker, which modern techniques afford, production must be organized so as to utilize not only the

Exhibit 2.19
Discretionary Expenditures and Discretionary Funds
Noncorporate, Nonfarm Sector
(1978, $billion)

Discretionary expenditures	34.4	Discretionary funds			30.4
Plant and equipment	24.2	Capital consumption allowance		31.9	
Residential construction	10.2	Proprietors' net investment		−1.5	
		Net borrowing			4.0
		Net increase in liabilities		8.4	
		Mortgages	2.7		
		Loans	5.6		
		Trade debt	.1		
		Net acquisition of assets		4.4	

Exhibit 2.20
Discretionary Expenditures and Discretionary Funds
Farm Sector
(1978, $billion)

Discretionary expenditures	16.0	Discretionary funds			−.8
Plant and equipment	15.2	Net saving		−.8	
Residential construction	.8	Capital consumption		15.7	
		Proprietors' net investment		−16.5	
		Net borrowing			16.8
		Net increase in liabilities		18.8	
		Bank loans NEC	2.5		
		Mortgages	10.2		
		Other loans	5.4		
		Trade debt	.7		
		Net acquisition of assets		2.0	

Exhibit 2.21
Discretionary Expenditures and Discretionary Funds
Household Sector
(1978, $billion)

Discretionary expenditures	292.3	Discretionary funds			338.3
Residential construction	92.0	Personal savings		72.0	
Consumer durables	200.3	Capital consumption allowance		181.0	
		Other		85.3	
		Net durables	57.5		
		Credit government insurance	27.1		
		Capital gains dividends	.7		
		Net borrowing			−81.9
		Net increase in liabilities		166.4	
		Mortgages	103.8		
		Consumer credit	49.6		
		Bank and other loans	7.2		
		Other	5.8		
		Net acquisition of assets		248.3	
		Demand deposit and currency	18.2		
		Time deposits	105.2		
		Credit market instruments	58.0		
		Other	66.9		
		Discrepancy			35.9

human and natural resources which are exogenous inputs into the economic system but also the sophisticated pieces of equipment (usually housed in specially designed plants) which are an output of the system. To make these sophisticated pieces of equipment (and the plants to house them) available for use within the production process, resources which would otherwise flow to households in the form of consumer goods must somehow be retained within the enterprise system in the form of producers', or investment, goods which are then used as capital inputs.

It is therefore not possible to model a technologically sophisticated economic system without making allowance for the fact that a part of the output flow of

Exhibit 2.22
Discretionary Expenditures and Discretionary Funds
Federal Government
(1978, $billion)

Discretionary expenditures	23.4	Discretionary funds		−17.7
Structures	7.9	Total receipts, NIA	432.1	
Durable goods	11.7	Less: nondiscretionary spending	442.6	
		Less: insurance contribution to households	7.2	
		Net borrowing		34.6
		Net increase in liabilities	63.5	
		Net acquisition of assets	28.9	
		Discrepancy		6.5

Exhibit 2.23
Discretionary Expenditures and Discretionary Funds
State and Local Government
(1978, $billion)

Discretionary expenditures	45.8	Discretionary funds		50.5
Structures	37.6	Total receipts, NIA	331.0	
Durable goods	7.7	Less: nondiscretionary spending	261.1	
		Less: insurance contribution to households	19.9	
		Net borrowing		−.5
		Net increase in liabilities	24.6	
		Net acquisition of assets	25.1	
		Discrepancy		−3.7

Exhibit 2.24
Discretionary Expenditures and Discretionary Funds
Nonprofit Sector
(1978, $billion)

Discretionary expenditures	5.9	Discretionary funds		5.4
Plant and equipment	5.9	Capital consumption allowance	5.4	
		Net borrowing		2.4
		Mortgages	1.0	
		Trade credit	1.4	
		Discrepancy		−1.9

Exhibit 2.25
Discretionary Expenditures and Discretionary Funds
Rest-of-the-World Sector
(1978, $billion)

Discretionary expenditures	84.7	Discretionary funds		95.0
Durable goods exports	84.7	Total imports	217.5	
		Less: nondiscretionary imports	122.5	
		Net borrowing		−12.7
		Net increase in liabilities	43.0	
		Net acquisition of assets	55.7	
		Discrepancy		2.4

goods (and services) is being retained within the enterprise sector, in the form of accumulated plant and equipment, rather than being sold to households or government. Even if the technology is stagnant, so that there is no need to scrap obsolescent pieces of equipment (along with the plants to house them), and even if there are no other sources of growth, there will still be the need to replace the existing plant and equipment as it wears out. In reality, of course, the technology is unlikely to remain stagnant, at least across the broad range of industries, and there will be other sources of growth as well. What this means is that any model that is to be used to explain the dynamics of an advanced market economy must, along with the set of economic accounts used to construct that model, make allowance for the investment which takes place within the enterprise sector.

There are three characteristics of business investment which make this type of expenditure especially important insofar as the macrodynamic behavior of the economic system is concerned. The first is the postponability of investment expenditures. A firm can decide either to add new plant and equipment immediately or else wait for a more propitious moment. It can even postpone the purchase indefinitely. Whatever the firm decides, however, it will not be prevented from continuing to operate at its present level—for it will still have its existing capacity. The postponability of business investment without impairing the firm's current ability to operate is, in turn, what marks this type of spending as being discretionary and thus a problematical factor insofar as maintaining the circular flow of funds is concerned.

A second important characteristic of business investment is its external financeability. Even if internal funds are the primary source of financing, as indeed they are, the availability of external funds, and especially the fact that those funds will, to some extent, be tapped, is critical—for the business investment which is financed externally provides the means by which the gross savings of some other sector besides the enterprise sector can be reincorporated back into the circular flow of funds. The external financeability of business investment, in turn, derives from the durable nature of the plant and equipment being purchased. On the one hand, since the plant and equipment can be expected to remain usable for some time, enabling the firm to derive additional revenue in the interval, it makes sense to spread the cost over several years through an amortized loan—if funds are not more immediately available from internal sources. On the other hand, since the purchase will yield additional revenue to the firm over time and the new plant and equipment can be offered as security in the meantime, banks and other lending institutions have a prudent basis for making the loan.

The third important characteristic of business investment is its supply-enhancing effect. The new plant and equipment purchased will add to the enterprise sector's capacity and thus will enlarge the economic system's aggregate supply capability. This last effect is the basis for whatever possibility exists of expanding economic output over time. Ironically, while the supply-enhancing effect is what economists usually emphasize in distinguishing business investment from other types of spending, it is the only one of the three characteristics of investment just enumerated which is not critical to Keynes's argument in *The General Theory* and thus not critical to explaining the cyclical movements of the economy. Indeed, as will be pointed out in chapter 4, it was by taking this supply-enhancing effect of business investment into account that Roy Harrod was able to go beyond Keynes, transforming the static analysis of *The General Theory*, with its focus on the *level* of national income, into the type of growth model which is basic to post-Keynesian theory.

Still, it is the first two characteristics of business investment—its postponability and its external financeability—that are critical to explaining the cyclical movements of the economy. Moreover, and this is the reason for making such distinctions, these two characteristics are not limited to business investment in new plant and equipment. They are just as true of other durable goods pur-chases—for example, the purchase of a new home, an automobile, or appliance by the household sector. This type of spending is no less discretionary in the sense just described, and no less problematical insofar as maintaining the circular flow of funds is concerned. Consequently, the analysis which follows will be based on the broader category of "discretionary expenditures," which includes all durable goods purchases, not just the purchase of new plant and equipment by the enterprise sector. Within the broader category of discretionary expenditures, the term "investment" will indicate that, in addition to postponability and external financability, the purchased item has a supply-enhancing effect. Private invest-ment in new plant and equipment, together with any public investment in the economic infrastructure, will thus be treated as a subcategory of discretionary expenditures, with the latter the more important concept insofar as understanding the cyclical movements of the economy is concerned and the former more important for understanding the secular rate of expansion.

Just as the category "investment" needs to be broadened somewhat if one wishes to understand the macrodynamic behavior of an advanced market econo-my like that of the United States, so the category "savings" needs to be expand-ed. It is not only that acknowledgment needs to be made of the savings by other sectors besides the household sector, with the enterprise sector in particular accounting, through its own retained earnings and depreciation allowances (that is, its "cash flow"), for most of the funds used to finance private investment. It is also that, with the household sector carrying out discretionary expenditures of its own, and not just providing savings for the use of the other sectors, savings can no longer be defined, as they are in the standard Keynesian models, as simply the difference between the income received by the household sector and any sums spent by it on consumer goods. Rather, savings need to be redefined as the difference between the income received by any one sector and the sums spent by it on nondiscretionary items (nondurable goods and services). To avoid confusing this broader concept of savings with the more prevalent, narrower definition, it is better to refer to the former as a sector's "discretionary funds." Thus,

$$F_i = Rev_i - Nond_i \qquad (2.4)$$

where F_i is a sector's discretionary funds, Rev_i is the same sector's gross income, or revenue, and $Nond_i$ is the sector's nondiscretionary expenditures (on nondurable goods and services). Similarly, it is better to refer to savings in the narrower sense as a sector's "net cash balance." This net cash balance may be either positive or negative. In the latter case, it can be referred to as the sector's cash deficit.

The essential point here is that a sector's discretionary funds, whether they be those of the household sector or those of some other sector, include not only the balance between the total income, or revenue, received and any sums spent on nondiscretionary items—the net cash balance, or "savings," in the usual sense—but also any sums spent on discretionary items. That is,

$$F_i = E_i + Bal_i \qquad (2.5)$$

where E_i is the ith sector's discretionary expenditures, and Bal_i is its net cash balance. Alternatively, since a sector's negative cash balance is its deficit,

$$E_i = F_i + Def_i \qquad (2.6)$$

where Def_i is the sector's cash deficit. Although the two formulations are equivalent to one another, the latter equation, since any deficit must be financed by borrowing from external sources, better serves to bring out the relationship between business firms, households and other spending units on the one hand and the financial structure, including banks, on the other hand.

2.3.6 The sectoral accounts

Equation 2.6 can be used to construct a set of accounts for each of the sectors delineated in the FOFA, based on the data which is available in that format from the Federal Reserve Board. The discretionary expenditures, E_i, are the tangible investment shown in the FOFA for each sector; the discretionary funds, F_i, are the gross savings; and the cash deficit, Def_i, is the net financial investment, with the net acquisition of assets subtracted from the net change in liabilities rather than the opposite and thus with the sign reversed. Exhibits 2.18 through 2.26 constitute a complete set of these sectoral accounts.

A number of important differences between this set of accounts and the FOFA themselves need to be pointed out. One is that the change in inventories, both for the corporate and noncorporate sectors, has been eliminated from the measures of discretionary expenditures. The reason for this, as already explained in the preceding main section, is that inventories are not a marketed output of the economic system. Rather they are the output which has not yet been sold—and hence they play no role in determining the current cash balance within the enterprise sector. This is not to suggest, however, that the change in business inventories is unimportant and hence need not be monitored. As will be brought out in the next chapter, quite the opposite is true. It is just that the change in inventories does not represent any actual flow of funds either into or out of the enterprise sector. Not surprisingly, the elimination of the change in inventories from the measures of discretionary expenditures reduces rather than increases the discrepancy item for the corporate and noncorporate sectors.

The measures of discretionary expenditures for the government and rest-of-the-world sectors, as given in exhibits 2.22, 2.23 and 2.25, also differ from the treatment of those sectors in the FOFA. The latter ignore any purchase of durable goods (including structures) and instead consider only the overall balance between income and outlays (the difference between total tax revenues and total spending, or the public sector's "deficit," in the case of the government sector and the difference between exports and imports, or the trade "deficit," in the case of the rest-of-the-world sector). Thus, as the FOFA are presently derived, there is no tangible investment for the government and rest-of-the-world sectors, and the gross savings in these two sectors are simply offset by the net financial investment (plus any discrepancy). In contrast, the sectoral accounts presented in exhibits 2.22, 2.23 and 2.25 record the purchase of any durable goods (including structures) as the government and rest-of-the-world sectors' discretionary expenditures. These discretionary expenditures are counterbalanced by the sectors' discretionary funds (total income less whatever has been spent on nondiscretionary items, both nondurable goods and services). The difference is the sectors' deficit, the same net financial investment reported in the FOFA (though with the sign reversed). In this way, the definitions and format are consistent across all the sectors, including the government and rest-of-the-world sectors.

It should be noted that the accounts for the noncorporate sector, both farm and nonfarm, have no discrepancy item. This is because the item "equity in non-corporate business" or, as given in the more detailed sectoral accounts, "proprietors' net investment" serves the same purpose. The equity in noncorporate business, as the difference between discretionary expenditures on the one hand and whatever funds are set aside for capital consumption plus any net borrowing on the other hand, includes both the owner-entrepreneurs' own financial investment in their enterprises and any errors or omissions. The proprietors' net investment, instead of being placed at the bottom, just ahead (as item 40) of the sector discrepancies (item 42) in the FOFA shown in exhibit 2.14, is included, along with any errors and omissions, as part of the gross savings, or discretionary income, in the accounts for the noncorporate sector presented in exhibits 2.19 and 2.20. Finally, it should be noted that the items which pertain to nonprofit organizations have been extracted from the household sector's account and transposed to form a separate account for the nonprofit subsector as part of a more inclusive government and nonprofit sector.

The sectoral accounts shown in exhibits 2.18 through 2.25 will be used as both the format and the empirical basis for the model to be developed in the subsequent chapters of this book. This is because the accounts enable the discretionary expenditures and the discretionary funds for each of the eight nonfinancial sectors into which the U.S. economy can be divided to be compared with one another as an extension and generalization of the argument more typically made in macroeconomic theory about investment and savings. The same format—since the starting point for determining the amount of discretionary funds is the total income, or revenue, obtained by each of the eight sectors—also suggests what are the relevant categories for decomposing the national income originating in the enterprise sector, and thus what should be the categories on the income side of the NIPA. The next step will be to show how this set of accounts can be used to construct an empirically valid model of the U.S. economy.

Recommended Readings

The best extended treatment of the material covered in this chapter will be found in Hector Correa, *Integrated Economic Accounting*, Lexington, Mass.: Lexington Books, 1977. See also Amit Bhaduri, *Macroeconomics, The Dynamics of Commodity Production*, Armonk, N.Y.: M. E. Sharpe, 1986.

The pathbreaking work which led to the development of input-output tables will be found in Wassily Leontief, *The Structure of the American Economy, 1919–1929*, Cambridge, Mass.: Harvard University Press, 1941. See also Leontief, *Input-Output Economics*, 2nd ed., New York: Oxford University Press, 1986; William H. Miernyk, *The Elements of Input-Output Analysis*, New York: Random House, 1965 (1st ed., Northeastern University Press, 1957); Peter M. Lichtenstein, *An Introduction to Post-Keynesian and Marxian Theories of Production and Value*, Armonk, N.Y.: M. E. Sharpe, 1983. Students should be warned that the exposition of input-output analysis found in Robert Dorfman, Paul A. Samuelson and Robert Solow, *Linear Programming and Economic Analysis*, New York: McGraw-Hill, 1958, and in William J. Baumol, *Economic Theory and Operations Research*, Englewood Cliffs, N.J.: Prentice-Hall, 1961, two of the most widely used texts in mathematical economics, fails to recognize the profound implications which this body of empirical work has for the traditional theory of production.

On the limitations of the National Income and Product Accounts, see Advisory Committee on Gross National Product Data Improvement, *Report*, Washington, D.C.: Government Printing Office, 1977; Oskar Morgenstern, *On the Accuracy of Economic Observations*, Princeton, N.J.: Princeton University Press, 1950. See also Nancy and Richard Ruggles, *The Design of Economic Accounts*, New York, N.Y.: National Bureau of Economic Research, 1970; Carol S. Corson, "The History of the United States National Income and Product Accounts: The Development of an Analytical Tool," *Review of Income and Wealth*, June 1975.

The classic work on which the Flow of Funds Accounts are based is Morris Copeland, *A Study of Moneyflows in the United States*, New York: National Bureau of Economic Research, 1952. For a survey of the literature on the FOFA, see Jacob Cohen, "Copeland's Moneyflows after Twenty-Five Years: A Survey," *Journal of Economic Literature*, March 1972, pp. 1–25. For a description of the accounts themselves, see Board of Governors of the Federal Reserve System, *Introduction to Flow of Funds*, February 1975.

Chapter 3

From Statics to Dynamics

Contents

Chapter 3

From Statics to Dynamics

The appearance of John Maynard Keynes's *The General Theory of Employment, Interest and Money* in 1936 marked an important turning point in the development of economic theory. Previously, economics had been concerned almost exclusively with the analysis of individual markets. Its purpose was to demonstrate, *a priori*, that an economic system organized on the basis of such markets was self-regulating—that is, that it required no intervention from without in order to function in a socially optimal manner. In contrast, *The General Theory* offered a model of the economic system in which markets were but one significant feature. Its purpose was to explain not only how persistent unemployment on a large scale could be the outcome of such a system but also how public policies could ameliorate, if not entirely avoid, such a consequence. The model to be found in *The General Theory*, as a further break with the tradition in economics, was based on testable propositions so that both the conclusions to be drawn from the model and the elements comprising the model could be subjected to empirical verification. This possibility was soon realized with the availability of time series data for the United States from the contemporaneously developed National Income and Product Accounts. Thus the existence of a body of macro theory—and indeed of any theory—that could meet the needs of economics as a scientific discipline goes back only as far as the appearance of *The General Theory*. The rival "quantity theory," though much older than the Keynesian model, purported to explain only the aggregate price level, leaving the analysis of real output and employment to micro theory. It is for this reason that macrodynamic theory can be truly said to begin with Keynes.

There is, to be sure, some distortion—not to mention irony—in singling out Keynes's work in this way. For one thing, as is now recognized, the priority in publishing what has come to be known as the Keynesian model belongs to the Polish economist, Michal Kalecki (though not the priority of publishing that model in English). Moreover, Keynes was opposed to the idea of attempting to test empirically the model he had developed. In a letter to the Norwegian economist Jan Tinbergen, who would later receive the first Nobel prize in economics for doing precisely what Keynes warned against, Keynes wrote, "My expectation would be that the broad problem of the credit cycle is just about the worst case to select to apply the method [of multivariate statistical analysis], owing to [the problem's] complexity, its variability, and the fact there are such important influences which cannot be reduced to statistical form." (Keynes, *Collected Writings*, XIV, pp. 294–5.) Finally, there is the fact that, in light of subsequent theoretical and empirical work by economists, it is necessary to reject certain features of the model to be found in *The General Theory*. Indeed, as will shortly be brought out, it is necessary to reject some of the most important aspects of that model—including its static framework and its microeconomic base.

Nonetheless, there is good reason to regard *The General Theory* as the starting point for macrodynamic analysis. This is not just because Keynes's preeminent position within the economics profession at the time he wrote *The General Theory* made his unorthodox viewpoint more acceptable to other economists and thereby stamped those ideas indelibly in the public mind as "Keynesian." The more important reason is that *The General Theory* introduced a series of key concepts, such as effective demand and the multiplier, as well as the distinction between investment and savings, which lie at the heart of macrodynamic analysis. By so doing, even if some of the ideas to be found in *The General Theory* have had to be significantly modified, Keynes provided economists the world over, regardless of the everyday language they speak, with the basic vocabulary for the scientific study of how actual economic systems behave over time.

The purpose of this chapter is to show, in broad outline, how the simplest version of the static model that can be found within *The General Theory*—what may be termed the basic Keynesian model—can be modified and extended so as to better capture the actual macrodynamic behavior of an advanced market economy like that of the United States. The chapter begins by presenting the basic Keynesian model (not to be confused with Keynes's own model) in the form in which that model is usually first encountered by students. The purpose is to identify the features of the basic model which apply even in the most complex of cases—and thus the features that will be retained as part of the macrodynamic model to be developed in subsequent chapters. The second part of the chapter then shows what changes need to be made in the basic Keynesian model so as to encompass the short-period disequilibrium adjustment process which is such an intrinsic aspect of any market economy. The purpose is to set the stage for the macrodynamic analysis that follows. Thus one needs to distinguish the model found in *The General Theory* from (a) the "Keynesian" model found in most textbooks, and (b) the macrodynamic model that will be developed in the subsequent chapters of this text. Though they share certain features in common, especially their macroeconomic perspective, the three are quite different. Indeed, it is one of the purposes of this chapter to bring out those differences.

3.1 The Basic Keynesian Model

The most basic of the models that owe their inspiration to Keynes is the simple expenditure model that is taught in introductory economics courses. It is easily recognized, in its geometric version, by the depiction of the consumption and investment curves intersecting a 45° line, and, in its algebraic version, by the three equations with three unknowns which uniquely characterize the model. While this model ignores or oversimplifies many of the arguments made in *The General Theory*, and thus cannot be attributed directly to Keynes himself, it does have heuristic value, especially since the features it retains of Keynes's more sophisticated model are sufficient to bring out some of the key processes at work in a market economy like that of the United States. It therefore serves as a useful starting point for developing a body of macrodynamic theory. In the subsections that follow, the basic Keynesian model will first be specified. The resulting three-equation model will then be used to make clear the distinction between endogenous and exogenous factors. Finally the way the basic Keynesian model is usually estended to cover other sectors besides just the enterprise and household sectors will be described.

3.1.1 Setting up the basic model

There are at least three assumptions underlying the basic Keynesian model which, since they need to be relaxed or dropped altogether in order to make the model more applicable to an actual market economy like that of the United States, should be identified at the outset. They are:

1. The economic system consists of only two sectors—a household sector, in which all consumption takes place and which is the source of all labor inputs; and an enterprise sector, which produces all the economic output using, in part, the labor inputs supplied by the household sector.

2. The economic system is a monetarized one—which means that money plays an intervening role in all market transactions (see chapter 1, section 1.1)—but the mechanism by which money enters into the system is left unspecified.

3. All savings are generated within the household sector—there are no business savings—and all investment is carried out by the enterprise sector.

There are, of course, other assumptions underlying the basic Keynesian model, a number of which will be challenged in the chapters that follow. Still, these are the most important of the initial assumptions, with only the first then being relaxed in the extension of the basic model that is found in most macroeconomics textbooks—including those written for advanced students. Given all three of these initial assumptions, it is possible to specify a simple macroeconomic model as follows:

$$NP = C + I \tag{3.1}$$

$$C = f(Y) \tag{3.2}$$

and
$$I = d \tag{3.3}$$

where NP is the national product, C is the output of consumption goods, I is the output of investment, or capital, goods, f is an unknown but stable functional relationship and d is an unknown but fixed quantity. These are, in fact, the three equations with three unknowns (excluding the parameters f and d) that define the basic Keynesian model. More will be said about these three equations shortly.

First, however, it is essential to recognize that they provide a determinate solution (that is, they yield values for C, I and Y once the parameters f and d are given) only because a fourth equation defines the necessary macrodynamic balance, or "equilibrium," condition. This fourth equation is as follows:

$$NP = NI \qquad (3.4)$$

where NI is the national income.

A common perception is that equation 3.4, like equation 3.1, is simply an accounting identity, and indeed it is possible to view equation 3.4 in this way—as, for example, in deriving both an input-output table and the National Income and Product Accounts (see chapter 2, part 1). In a Keynesian model, however, equation 3.4 is a condition which need not be satisfied, at least initially (at the point in time at which, borrowing the language of the Swedish school, the term "*ex ante* can be applied, meaning "before everything has worked itself out"). This quite different interpretation of equation 3.4 follows from Keynes's critical insight that the flow of income in a monetarizied system need not match the flow of output—and hence that the national income need not be equal to the national product at every historically observed moment in time. However, Keynes did believe there was a tendency for the two flows to be brought back into balance with one another since the income spent on goods and services could not fail to be equal to the value of the goods being both produced *and* sold while the income *not* spent of goods and services would reduce the sales of output and thus, eventually, the amount produced as well. Indeed, this way of looking at the dynamics of a market economy is what lies behind the Keynesian principle of effective demand—namely, that it is the level of aggregate demand, reflecting what various groups are willing to spend, that determines the level of aggregate supply (or output), and not the reverse as was previously assumed in keeping with Say's law. Thus, while equation 3.4 need not hold at any particular point in time, it does represent a condition which, were it to be satisfied, would enable the economic system to remain indefinitely at a fixed level of activity (measured by the output of the system)—assuming no further change in the factors determining that level of activity. This homeostatic condition (see chapter 1, section 2.3, for the definition of the term), with the flow of output equal to the flow of income, can be termed the macrodynamically balanced, or "equilibrium," level of economic activity. In a Keynesian model, the necessary condition for macrodynamic balance is usually expressed in terms of aggregate investment being equal to aggregate savings. However, the latter condition, as can readily be shown, is actually derived from equation 3.4.

Based on the three assumptions identified at the outset of this section, the national income, NI, can be defined as the amount of income received by the household sector in the form of wages and property income which will be used to purchase consumption goods plus the additional amount of such income which, by not being used for that purpose, constitutes the household sector's savings.

That is,

$$NI = C + S_H \tag{3.5}$$

where S_H is the amount of household savings. Substituting equations 3.1 and 3.5 for NP and NI respectively in equation 3.4 and then cancelling the C term on both sides of the resulting equation, we can see that equation 3.4 is equivalent to the following:

$$I = S_H \tag{3.6}$$

which is the form in which the necessary condition for macrodynamic balance is usually specified. What can be seen more clearly when the macrodynamic balance condition is specified in this form is that for the amount of income available to purchase the output of the economic system to be equal to the value of that output, it is necessary that any leakage from the spending stream, as represented by household savings, be offset by the amount of funds being put back into circulation through the purchase of investment goods by the enterprise sector. Otherwise, the total income flows will not be sufficient to purchase the national product at the existing set of prices. More will be said in the second part of this chapter about the role played in the model by this macrodynamic balance condition. For now it need only be pointed out that equation 3.6, along with equation 3.4 from which it is derived, denotes a condition which, were it to be satisfied, would lead to no further change in the values for C, I and, most importantly, NP (which, assuming the necessary condition for macrodynamic balance is satisfied, will be equal to NI).

Indeed, in recognition of the fact that NP and NI must be equal to one another when the model is solved, NP and NI are usually denoted by the same symbol, Y. The discussion which follows will adopt this convention. However, it should be kept in mind that, even though denoted by the same symbol, the national product and the national income are not the same. They are merely equal to one another or, if not actually equal to one another, they are approaching the point where they will be equal to one another, thereby enabling the model to be solved mathematically. Thus, while it is possible for the national product and the national income to be *numerically* equal to one another (i.e., NP = NI), this does not mean that they are qualitatively identical (i.e., NP $\equiv$ NI)—despite the convention that exists of denoting them by the same Y symbol.

While S_H might appear to be a fourth unknown, it is in fact uniquely determined, given the model's assumptions, once the other three variables, Y, C and I, are known. For the amount of household savings, S_H, is simply the difference between Y and C (with Y, in this case, representing the national income when it is equal to the national product). Thus the model reduces to three unknowns (aside from the parameters, f and d). Since the model consists of three equations (all that are necessary to determine the value of the three unknowns), the model is fully determinant.

3.1.2 The three types of equations

Aside from being sufficient to yield a determinant solution, the three equations illustrate each of the three types of relationships that can be used to construct a model. These three types of relationships are: (1) accounting identities; (2) behavioral equations; and (3) exogenously determined variables (i.e., inputs insofar as the system being modeled is concerned).

Equation 3.1 is an accounting identity. It is called an accounting identity because it merely defines the national product as the sum of consumption and investment. While accounting identities may be necessary, indeed essential, in constructing a model, they have no separate explanatory power of their own. They merely serve as logical links between other parts of the model which, since they are behavioral equations, do have explanatory power. Any accounting identities which are relied upon simply contribute to the coherence of the model as a whole. Indeed, if the model were to consist solely of accounting identities, it would amount to little more than a set of tautological statements and, though true, would have no informational content.

Equation 3.2 is the Keynesian consumption function, considered by some economists the key component of the basic Keynesian model. Indeed, the model is sometimes referred to as the consumption function model. The significance of the consumption function specified by Keynes is severalfold. First, it shifts the level of analysis, insofar as demand is concerned, from that of the individual household to that of the household sector as a whole. In this way, it lays the foundation for a macro, as distinct from a micro, model. Second, it identifies the level of household income—which, in the basic Keynesian model, is equal to Y— as the primary determinant of the sums spent on consumption. In this way, it places the emphasis on income effects rather than on the price effects emphasized in the pre-Keynesian (and contemporary neoclassical) theory. Third, by positing a function in which the amount spent on consumption depends on the level of income and thereby basing his argument on a behavioral equation which is empirically testable, Keynes pointed economic theory in a wholly different direction.

The Keynesian consumption function is a behavioral equation. It purports to explain the behavior of the household sector insofar as its purchases of consumption goods are concerned. Following Keynes, economists usually specify the function f in equation 3.2 as follows:

$$C = a + b(Y) \qquad (3.7)$$

where a is some constant term greater than zero (that is, it has a positive sign attached to it) and b is a coefficient with a value that falls between 0 and 1 (that is, it also has a positive sign attached to it but the coefficient itself is some fraction). Any model, to be empirically testable, must contain at least one such behavioral equation, like equation 3.2 or, in the more fully elaborated version specified by Keynes himself, like equation 3.7.

The coefficient *b* in equation 3.7 is what Keynes termed "the marginal propensity to consume," and as such it plays a key role in the basic Keynesian model. A great deal of effort has been made by economists to derive equation 3.7 empirically—in particular, to see if the estimates of a and b fall within the range postulated by Keynes. Indeed, most of the early work on macroeconomic model building using econometric techniques centered on this effort (see chapter 9, section 2.1, for a description of that early work). Equation 3.8 which follows is but one of the many empirically derived consumption functions which were obtained as part of this effort. (It is based on annual data for the 1929–1941 period. Since the methods used to obtain these results would no longer be considered acceptable by econometricians, the equation is reported only for its heuristic value.)

$$C = \$26.5B + 0.75Y \tag{3.8}$$

The estimated value of the constant term (what is denoted as *a* in equation 3.7) implies that the purchase of consumption goods by the household sector will be at an annual rate of $26.5 billion independently of what may be the level of national income while the estimated value of the *b* coefficient implies that, for every dollar increase in national income, consumption expenditures by the household sector will rise by 75 cents. Notice that the values for *a* and *b* fall within the limits specified above. The above results are typical of those obtained when a consumption function like that specified in equation 3.7 is empirically derived. The estimates of *b* vary from 0.50 to 0.92, depending on the period covered, the definition of "income" and other considerations. (The above equation is reported in Gardner Ackley, *Macroeconomic Theory*, New York: Macmillan, 1961, p. 226.)

Equation 3.3, the third of the three equations representing the basic Keynesian model, is an investment function. However, it is not to be confused with the investment function which Keynes himself specified in *The General Theory*, for it is not, like the Keynesian function, a behavioral equation. Instead, it merely posits an exogenously determined level of investment, *d*. Nonetheless, equation 3.3 plays a key role in the basic Keynesian model, for without at least one variable that is exogenously determined, the model would be that of a closed system. (See chapter 1, section 2.2, for the reasons why a model of a closed system must be considered inapplicable in the case of any social system.) Equation 3.3 makes investment the exogenously determined variable in the basic Keynesian model and thus I the critical factor influencing the behavior of the system. To appreciate fully the significance of this treatment of investment, it is necessary to place the basic Keynesian model within a systems framework and then derive the Keynesian multipler as the key relationship within what then constitutes the reduced form of that model.

3.1.3 *The Keynesian multiplier*

Using the systems framework described earlier (see chapter 1, section 2.1), one can view equations 3.1, 3.2 and 3.3 as describing the internal process of the economic system captured by the basic Keynesian model. The output variable is Y (along with possibly C and I), while the inputs, as a relationship matrix would make clear, consist of the flow variable d and the state variables a and b (the latter two variables representing the model's parameters).

The model, in its reduced form, can be derived by substituting equation 3.2, the consumption function, and equation 3.3, the investment function, for the C and I variables in equation 3.1 as follows:

$$Y = a + bY + d \tag{3.9}$$

Shifting terms, we obtain

$$Y - Yb = a + d \tag{3.10}$$

Factoring out the Y term, we next obtain

$$Y(1 - b) = a + d \tag{3.11}$$

Finally, dividing both sides of the equation by $(1 - b)$, we obtain

$$Y = \frac{1}{1 - b}(a + d) \tag{3.12}$$

The term $\frac{1}{1 - b}$ can be defined as the multiplier, k, such that

$$k = \frac{1}{1 - b} \tag{3.13}$$

Alternatively,

$$k = \frac{1}{s} \tag{3.14}$$

where s is the marginal propensity to save, or $1 - b$. If equation 3.8 were the actual consumption function, with b equal to 0.75 and s therefore equal to 0.25, then k would be equal to 4. Equation 3.12 can therefore be rewritten as follows:

$$Y = k(a + d) \qquad (3.15)$$

Equation 3.15 can be used to determine the macrodynamically balanced, or equilibrium, level of national income, Y_e. With a, as reported in equation 3.8, equal to \$38.1 billion and with d, for heuristic purposes, assumed to be equal to \$30 billion, then with the multiplier, k, equal to 4 (also based on equation 3.8), the macrodynamic balanced level of national income, Y_e, will be equal to \$272.4 billion (four times the combined sum of \$38.1 billion and \$30 billion). The same argument, it can be shown, applies to the *change* from one macrodynamically balanced level of income to another. That is,

$$\Delta Y_e = k(\Delta a + \Delta d) \qquad (3.16)$$

where a discrete change in any of the variables is denoted by the Greek letter Δ. Since the parameters of the Keynesian consumption function are usually assumed to be stable, and hence unchanging, Δa can be set equal to zero and equation 3.16 reduced to the following:

$$\Delta Y_e = k(\Delta d) \qquad (3.17)$$

With k still assumed to be equal to 4 and with investment assumed, again for heuristic purposes, to increase from \$30 billion to \$40, the macrodynamically balanced level of national income will rise by \$40 billion (four times the \$10 billion increase in investment, Δd), causing the level of national income to increase from \$272.4 billion to \$312.4 billion.

The fundamental point of equation 3.17—that changes in the macrodynamically balanced level of national income are to be explained by changes in the amount of business investment—can be broadened, making it more applicable to the actual contemporary situation, by letting Δd denote the somewhat broader category of "autonomous" expenditures (which includes not just the change in the amount of business investment but also any change in the government's purchases of goods and services and any change in the level of exports). These are the expenditures which have already been fully determined as to amount and thus are unaffected by the current level of national income (in contradistinction to the consumption goods purchased by the household sector). While broadening what is denoted by Δd may make the multiplier analysis more cogent, it also, as will be explained shortly (see section 3.1.5), makes the derivation of the multiplier more complicated and indeed invalidates the formula given by equation 3.13 or, alternatively, equation 3.14.

Although equation 3.17 brings out quite clearly the mathematical relationship between Δd and ΔY_e, it is important to elaborate, in prose, on that algebraic statement to see what economic sense, if any, it makes. Following Marshall (see A. C. Pigou, ed., *Memorials of Alfred Marshall*, p. 427), we can say that, if the statement cannot be translated into intelligible prose, one has reason to suspect that, insofar as any actual economic process is concerned, it may well be non-sense.

If the level of expenditures on investment or some other autonomous component of aggregate spending were to increase by $10 billion, it is clear, from the set of accounts developed in the preceding chapter, that the national income would, by that very fact, increase by $10 billion as well. This is because the value added created in producing that additional $10 billion in goods and services would have to show up as additional income for households, whether in the form of increased wage payments or some type of property income. (This is on the assumption that there is no government to siphon off a portion of the value added in the form of taxes and on the further assumption that only households account for any savings so that all the income received by enterprises passes into the hands of house-holds.) What is not so clear—and indeed did not become clear until Keynes incorporated Richard Kahn's multiplier concept into his model—is that the additional $10 billion in household income will lead to still further household consumption expenditures. Indeed, with the marginal propensity to consume, b, equal to 0.75, three-fourths of the additional household income of $10 billion will be spent, in the first instance, on consumption goods, and the national product, along with the national income, will rise by another $7.5 billion. The process, however, does not end there, for the additional $7.5 billion in spending, output and income will give rise to another round of consumption expenditures—in this case, three-fourths of $7.5 billion or roughly another $5.6 billion more—and so on *ad infinitum*. The $40 billion figure which can be quickly calculated, using equation 3.17, when $k = 4$ and $\Delta d = 10 billion simply indicates the ultimate mathematical limits to the process, and one point to keep in mind is that while equation 3.17 has no time dimension associated with it, the actual process that takes place historically does. This point will be returned to after the distinction between a timeless equilibrium model and a time-specified disequilibrium model has been brought out in the second part of this chapter.

It is the process which has just been outlined in prose which needs to be kept in mind—and not just the mathematical limit to that process—when describing the multiplier. The process, of course, also works in reverse. Thus, if autonomous expenditures were to fall rather than rise by $10 billion, then the macrodynami-cally balanced level of national income would, under the other conditions just stipulated, decline rather than increase to the limit of $40 billion.

3.1.4 Endogeneity vs. exogeneity

The process by which a change in autonomous expenditures leads to a manyfold change in the equilibrium level of national income is the fundamental causal relationship underlying the basic Keynesian model. The multiplier relationship given by equation 3.17 thus lies at the heart of the model. The process is an "endogenous" one, which means that once it has been set in motion by a change in autonomous expenditures, it depends entirely on factors which are internal to the model. These internal factors, in the case of the multiplier, are the progressively smaller increments in household income at each succeeding round of the process, with these progressively smaller increments of income, in turn, giving rise to progressively smaller increments in consumption expenditures, as determined by the marginal propensity to consume, b.

The endogenous nature of the multiplier process can be contrasted with the exogenous nature of the change in business investment or whatever other type of autonomous expenditures engenders the multiplier process. The latter is "exogenous" because it depends entirely on factors which are external to the model. Indeed, the model offers no explanation as to why there has been the change in autonomous expenditures (which, as we shall see, is an important limitation of the basic Keynesian model when autonomous expenditures include business investment, since it is not very realistic to consider business investment as being entirely exogenous). Rather the model only indicates what can be expected to ensue, insofar as the macrodynamically balanced level of national income is concerned, once a change in autonomous expenditures has occurred.

This important distinction between a change in the exogenous factor which sets the internal process in motion and the internal process itself can be seen perhaps more clearly from the following systems diagram, representing the reduced form of the basic Keynesian model.

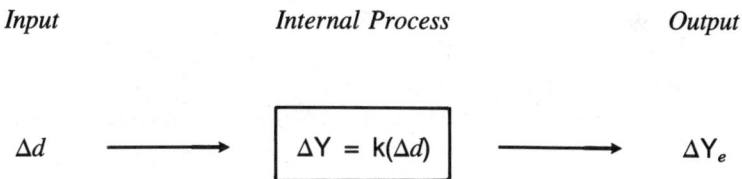

Input	*Internal Process*	*Output*

$$\Delta d \longrightarrow \boxed{\Delta Y = k(\Delta d)} \longrightarrow \Delta Y_e$$

What the above systems diagram makes clear is that it is the change in autonomous expenditures, Δd, which, as an input into the basic Keynesian model, then leads, via the internal process represented by equation 3.17, to a change in the stipulated output variable, ΔY_e. The latter can be said to be endogenously determined within the model, given the value of Δd, the flow variable which serves as the exogenous input into the model, as well as the value of b, the state variable which is also exogenously determined (and which, as the determinant of the multiplier, k, serves as a parameter of the model).

It should be noted that the endogenously determined variables may include more than just the output of the model itself. For example, in the basic Keynesian model, the level of consumption expenditures by the household sector is also endogenously determined and indeed, if that is what is of interest, C can even be considered an output of the model. More important, however, are the endogenously determined variables which, as the output of one part of the model, then serve as an input into other parts of the model—even though they are not necessarily the variables which the model is meant to explain. For example, in the model actually found in *The General Theory*, investment depends, in part, on the change in the interest rate, Δi, and any change in the interest rate depends, in turn, on the actions of the central bank in altering the supply of money, ΔM. Thus the systems diagram for this model would be as follows:

Input   *Internal Process*   *Output*

$$\Delta M \rightarrow \boxed{\Delta i = I(\Delta M)} \; -\Delta i \rightarrow \boxed{\Delta I = a(\Delta i)} \; -\Delta I \rightarrow \boxed{\Delta Y = \frac{1}{1-b}(\Delta I)} \rightarrow \Delta Y$$

In this model, the endogenously determined variables include Δi and ΔI as well as ΔY. Indeed, Δi and ΔI could just as well be regarded as the output of the model (if someone were particularly interested in explaining those variables). At the same time, ΔM replaces Δd as the variable which, as the input into the model as a whole, is exogenously determined. The systems diagram makes it easier to identify those exogenously determined variables since they are listed to the left as inputs into the model.

Obviously, there can be more than one of these exogenously determined variables. Indeed, in *The General Theory*, investment is regarded as being influenced by, not only the change in the interest rate, depending on the actions of the central bank in altering the supply of money, but also by the state of business expectations as it affects the "animal spirits" of the individuals carrying out the investment. These animal spirits reflect primarily psychological factors, and hence they are exogenous to the economic system—though they are no doubt affected by current economic conditions. Thus a more complete systems diagram of the model actually found in *The General Theory* would be as follows:

Input   *Internal Process*   *Output*

$$\Delta M \rightarrow \boxed{\Delta i = I(\Delta M)} \; -\Delta i \rightrightarrows \boxed{\Delta I = a(i) + f(Exp)} \; -\Delta I \rightarrow \boxed{\Delta Y = \frac{1}{1-b}(\Delta I)} \rightarrow \Delta Y$$

Exp ————————————

where Exp is the exogenously determined state of business expectations.

ΔM and Exp each represent a different type of exogenously determined variable. Since the money supply is something which the central bank is thought to control through its open market operations, ΔM can be regarded as an instrumental variable. This means that public officials can, as a matter of policy, determine what value the variable takes. (Actually, as will be brought out in chapter 12, the central bank can only determine the change in free bank reserves, not the change in the money stock. However, since the change in free reserves will affect interest rates in the manner attributed to the stock of money by Keynes, the change in free reserves, ΔRes_F, can replace the change in the money stock, ΔM, as the exogenously determined variable in the above systems diagram, leaving the rest of the model unchanged.) On the other hand, since the state of business expectations reflects subjective judgments being made by persons outside the government, Exp must be regarded as a noninstrumental variable. This means it cannot be manipulated by public officials (as Herbert Hoover discovered to his chagrin). It depends on factors beyond the immediate control of those officials.

The distinction between endogenously and exogenously determined variables and, in the case of the latter, between instrumental and noninstrumental variables is a critical one, as subsequent chapters will bring out. Upon it rests the question of whether the economic system is a self-regulating mechanism, as the majority of economists before Keynes simply assumed; and if not, the extent to which it is possible for a society through its political institutions to affect the macrodynamic performance of the economy. For the economic system can be considered a self-regulating mechanism only if there are no exogenously determined variables that affect the system's behavior and the system's behavior therefore depends solely on internal, or "endogenous," processes—either the price adjustment mechanisms emphasized by economists before Keynes or the other types of "automatic stabilizers" identified by economists subsequently. On the other hand, it is only by changing some exogenously determined variable critical to how the economic system functions, one that is also an instrumental variable, that the society can through its political institutions hope to affect the system's performance.

3.1.5 Extending the basic model

The basic three-equation Keynesian model which has just been explicated is useful largely because, while still a relatively simple model, it encompasses perhaps the most important of the several macrodynamic processes. This is the process represented by the Keynesian multiplier. Yet, since the model is such a simple one, it cannot bring out all the relevant macrodynamic processes. Thus, to account fully for the behavior of an advanced market economy like that of the United States, it is necessary to elaborate on the basic model in a number of ways. One of these ways has just been pointed out. The model actually found in *The General Theory* assumes that investment depends on both the interest rate and the state of business expectations rather than just being exogenously determined. Extension of the basic model along these lines will be deferred, however, until chapter 7. In this chapter we will instead focus on two other extensions of the basic model. They are (a) the incorporation of more than just two sectors into the model, and (b) the allowance for a dynamic adjustment process and, hence, for disequilibrium. Each of these extensions of the basic Keynesian model will be taken up in turn, the first in this subsection and the second, the more fundamental extension of the basic model, in the second part of this chapter.

The basic three-equation model assumes that the economic system encompasses only two sectors, an enterprise sector and a household sector. This is true even of the somewhat more elaborate model found in *The General Theory*. One of the first modifications that was made in the Keynesian model was therefore to extend it to incorporate additional sectors. The need to include a government sector was already strongly implied by Keynes himself in *The General Theory* and the need to incorporate a foreign, or rest-of-the-world, sector was no less obvious. These elaborations on the basic model turned out, for those who followed in Keynes's path, to be relatively easy ones to make.

In the case of the government, all that is required, at least as a first step, is to add the government's purchase of goods and services, denoted by Gov, to those being made by the enterprise and household sectors when one calculates the national product. Thus the accounting identity previously given (equation 3.1) becomes instead

$$Y = C + I + Gov \qquad (3.18)$$

The additional variable, Gov, means that another equation must be added so that the value of all four unknowns can then be determined. With the inclusion of a government sector, then, the basic three-equation model must be augmented to include at least a fourth equation.

The easiest way to provide that fourth equation is to regard Gov, like I, as being exogenously determined so that

$$Gov = e \qquad (3.19)$$

where e, like d above, is a constant sum greater than zero. Indeed, since the government's budget is based primarily on political rather than on economic considerations, there is greater justification for treating Gov as being exogenous than there is for treating I in the same way. What this means is that equation 3.16, representing the model in its reduced form, needs to be modified as follows:

$$\Delta Y_e = k(\Delta a + \Delta d + \Delta e) \qquad (3.20)$$

with the Δe term that has been added to equation 3.17 also shown, in the corresponding systems diagram, as an additional exogenously determined input into the model. In this case, the exogenous input is quite clearly an instrumental variable.

While this would seem to complete the modifications that need to be made in order to incorporate the government sector into the basic Keynesian model, there is actually one further matter that needs to be attended to. The offsetting flow to the government's purchase of goods and services consists of the taxes which it collects. These taxes reduce the purchasing power of the household sector, making it less than the value added by firms. Thus disposable income, the income actually available to households for making purchses, will be less than the total national income by an amount equal to the government's tax receipts. That is,

$$Y_D = Y - T \qquad (3.21)$$

where Y_D is disposable income and T is the total amount collected in taxes by the government.

With the offsetting influence of tax revenues taken into account in this way, the four-equation model for an economy with a government sector actually becomes, at the very least, a five-equation model. An additional equation is needed to explain the amount of taxes collected by the government. The value of T can, of course, be viewed as merely another exogenously determined variable, again of an instrumental nature. Indeed this is how the matter is usually handled at the introductory level. However, as will be brought out below in chapter 10, this is not a very realistic way of explaining tax revenues. The fact is that the government's tax revenues depend on the level of economic activity and hence are, to a large extent, endogenously determined. With T an endogenously determined variable, the model will no longer be a simple one. For one thing, the value of the multiplier will depend on more than just the marginal propensity to save.

In whatever way the complication is handled—and it is usually handled by making tax revenues, like the household sector's consumption expenditures, a function of income—the amount of tax revenues, T, must be included as part of the income flows represented by Y. Indeed, shifting terms in equation 3.21, we obtain the following:

$$Y = Y_D + T \qquad (3.22)$$

Setting the national income, as given in equation 3.22, equal to the national product, as defined in equation 3.18, and then subtracting the amount of consumption outlays, C, from both sides of the equation while keeping in mind that $S_H = Y_D - C$, we obtain the following as the necessary condition for macrodynamic balance:

$$I + G = S_H + T \qquad (3.23)$$

The amount of tax revenue, T, shown on the right-hand side of equation 3.23, represents an additional leakage from the spending stream, besides the income saved, or not spent, by the household sector, and the total leakage from the spending stream must be offset by the funds being put back into circulation through business investment and the government's purchases of goods and services if the economic system's total income flows are to be in balance with the output flows in value terms. This new condition for macrodynamic balance is—

aside from the amount of goods and services purchased by the government, Gov, that must now be included as part of autonomous expenditures and the change that must be made in the formula for calculating the multiplier—the most important difference which the addition of a government sector makes in the basic Keynesian model.

By making a similar set of changes, it is possible to incorporate a rest-of-the-world sector into the model as well. First, the definition of aggregate output needs to be broadened to include the value of any goods or services sold abroad. However, the value of those exports, denoted by Ex, cannot just be added to the purchase of goods and services by the enterprise, household and government sectors. The value of any goods and services imported from other countries, denoted by Im, also needs to be taken into account. It is the difference between the two, or $(Ex - Im)$, which represents the additional output of the domestic economy. Just as the value of goods and services purchased from other enterprises needs to be subtracted in calculating the value added by the enterprise sector, so the value of any goods and services obtained from other national economies needs to be subtracted in calculating the value added for the same enterprise sector, relabeled the domestic economy to distinguish it from its counterpart in other countries. Thus, with the rest-of-the-world sector incorporated into the model, the accounting identity needs to be further modified as follows:

$$Y = C + I + Gov + (Ex - Im) \qquad (3.24)$$

where Ex is the value of any goods and services exported from the domestic economy and Im is the value any goods and services imported.

The need to take into account both exports and imports adds two more unknowns to the model. In the case of exports, the simplest approach is again to regard Ex as being exogenously determined so that

$$Ex = f \qquad (3.25)$$

where f, like d and e above, is a constant sum greater than zero. This means that the complete model, in its reduced form, has to be represented by the following equation:

$$\Delta Y_e = k(\Delta a + \Delta d + \Delta e + \Delta f) \qquad (3.26)$$

with the systems diagram then being modified to include Δf as another exogenously determined input into the model (though not an instrumental variable). But as already indicated, one cannot incorporate exports into the model without also incorporating imports. While the simplest approach would be to treat Im as yet another exogenously determined variable, this would again not be a very realistic way of explaining imports. Indeed, it can be questioned whether even exports should be treated in this manner. A more satisfactory treatment of the rest-of-the-world sector must therefore wait until chapter 11—just as a more satisfactory treatment of the government sector must wait until chapter 10. Again, however, in whatever way the complication of the endogenous influence on a country's imports is handled, both the amount of exports and the amount of imports need to be taken into account in specifying the necessary condition for macrodynamic balance. In this case, with the value of imports simply subtracted from the value of exports, the necessary condition is as follows:

$$I + Gov + (Ex - Im) = S_H + T \qquad (3.27)$$

Alternatively, the macrodynamic balance condition can be specified as follows:

$$I + Gov + Ex = S_H + T + Im \qquad (3.28)$$

thereby making it clear that the value of any imported goods, like household savings and the government's tax revenues, represents a leakage from the domestic spending stream which must, *in toto*, be offset by the additional funds being put back into domestic circulation through business investment, the government's purchases of goods and services and the value of exports if the economic system is to be in macrodynamic balance.

As has just been demonstrated, the basic Keynesian model can be extended to encompass more than just two sectors. Although the condition that must be satisfied if the system is to be in macrodynamic balance becomes more elaborate—not just I and S_H but rather I, Gov and Ex on the one hand and S_H, T and Im on the other must be equal to one another—no significant change in the mode of analysis is required. The macrodynamically balanced level of national income, Y_e, is still the output variable which the model is intended to explain. And that macrodynamically balanced level of national income is still determined by (a) the level of autonomous expenditures (now broadened to include the government's purchases of goods and services, if not net exports), and (b) the size of the multiplier. The only serious problem is that, because of the additional endogenous influences which must be taken into account, especially insofar as government tax revenues and imports are concerned, the value of the multiplier cannot be so easily determined. Still, since there are endogenous factors affecting the level of business investment no less than the amount of government tax revenues and imports, this criticism applies to the simpler, three-equation model as well. Thus it is not because of any inability to encompass the government and rest-of-the-world sectors in addition to the enterprise and household sectors that the basic Keynesian model has been found to be seriously deficient by the economists who have followed in Keynes's path. Rather it is for other reasons.

One of these reasons is the static nature of the model Keynes developed—that is, its focus on why the economic system tends to settle down at a particular level of activity. As Victoria Chick has correctly noted, even the more sophisticated model found in *The General Theory* is a static model of a dynamic process. While the model has proven to be extraordinarily useful precisely because it was conceived with the dynamics of an advanced market economy in mind, still the static framework in which it was cast has placed an inherent limit on what can be explained by that model. It is therefore necessary to escape from those limitations by shifting from a static to a dynamic version of the basic Keynesian model. This will be done in small incremental steps, beginning with the dynamic properties of Keynes's own model.

3.2 The Cyclical Adjustment Process

In describing a model as being dynamic, economists usually have in mind one of three things: (1) that the model describes a growth process in which one or more variables increase at a certain fixed rate over time; (2) that the model posits some homeostatic, or "equilibrium," state which is not immediately achieved and which may be either more closely approximated or further deviated from over time; or (3) that the model encompasses one or more variables whose influence will be felt only after a certain interval of time. Thus one can distinguish three different types of dynamic models. They are (1) steady-state growth models; (2) disequilibrium models; and (3) distributed lag models. What is common to all three uses of the term dynamic is the explicit allowance made for the influence of time in delineating one possible outcome from another. A dynamic model, then, is one which is meant to explain a time delineated process—as distinct from a static model in which time plays no role.

Usually what economists have in mind when they describe a model as being dynamic is only the last of these three ways in which the term can be used. By now, it has become commonplace to include lagged explanatory variables in macroeconomic models—if only to guarantee a high R^2. In this and the succeeding chapters of the text, the emphasis will instead be on the other two meanings of the term. The primary objective will be to explain what determines the uneven rates of expansion which such economic systems exhibit, and thus it might seem that the first meaning of the term dynamic would be the more relevant one. However, it is not possible to account for those uneven rates of expansion except by being able to explain the deviations of the economy from some secular, or trend, growth rate. This means that the second way in which the term dynamic is used in economics is no less relevant. Indeed, a disequilibrium analysis, as distinct from an analysis of steady-state rates of expansion, provides a second important link, besides the multiplier, between the static model found in *The General Theory* and the type of dynamic model which is to be developed in this text. We shall therefore begin by making explicit the cyclical adjustment process on which the basic Keynesian model is predicated (this as the starting point for the type of disequilibrium analysis that will be employed throughout the rest of the text), before turning in the next chapter to the other type of dynamic model which underlies a post-Keynesian approach.

3.2.1 The change in the meaning of 'equilibrium'

Prior to Keynes, homeostasis, or equilibrium, was defined in terms of a particular market being able to clear, with the prerequisite condition being that demand and supply be equal to one another. Aggregate equilibrium was simply the homeostatic state achieved by the economic system when demand and supply in all markets, both those for final goods and those for any inputs, were in balance. Keynes's most fundamental departure from orthodoxy, the one which it has been perhaps most difficult for economists trained in the conventional theory to accept, is the underlying contention of *The General Theory* that not every market need clear, in the sense of demand being equal to supply, for the economic system to be in "equilibrium." All that is required is that investment be equal to savings—or, with the model extended to encompass more than just two sectors, that investment and the other components of autonomous expenditures be equal to household savings and the other leakages from the spending stream.

What needs to be appreciated is how liberating a step this was in the development of an empirically testable model to explain the cyclical behavior of the economic system. In the flux of daily events, there is seldom not some market clearly in disequilibrium, as evidenced by unsold inventories, unemployed workers, queues of purchasers awaiting a renewed supply, unstable prices, etc. If one must wait until all markets have cleared to confirm the correctness of the analysis, then the confirmation will never be forthcoming (and economic theory can never be put to an empirical test). Paraphrasing Keynes, we can say that the truth will be known only in the long run when we are all dead. Even if one is prepared to shift from a Walrasian general equilibrium framework to the partial equilibrium analysis of the Marshallians, the problem of confirmation remains. For then the analysis hangs on the *ceterus paribus* assumption that there is no spillover effect from other markets, and such an assumption can be tested only by shifting back to a general equilibrium framework.

Keynes was able to cut through this epistemological thicket by implicitly denying that any particular market need be in "equilibrium" as long as aggregate investment and aggregate savings—what will, more broadly, be referred to in subsequent chapters as total discretionary expenditures and total discretionary funds—are in balance. Of course, aggregate investment and aggregate savings, like demand and supply, are unlikely ever to be observed in balance with one another. Indeed, this is the point of departure for the disequilibrium analysis to be presented below. Still, it is easier to deal with one set of relationships out of balance than with a very large number, such as characterizes demand and supply conditions in all markets.

Moreover, Keynes was able to make an assumption, a not unreasonable one as it turns out, to do away with the possibility that aggregate investment and aggregate savings may, in fact, not be equal to one another—at least initially. The assumption is that if they are out of balance, then the level of savings will adjust to the level of investment, rather than the reverse, so that the change in investment or other types of autonomous expenditures can be viewed as governing the macrodynamic behavior of an advanced market economy like that of the United States or Great Britain. It turns out that the second, or corollary, part to this assumption—namely, that the change in investment and other types of autonomous expenditures is what governs the macrodynamic behavior of the economic system—is a testable proposition. It is also one of the ways to distinguish a Keynesian and thus a post-Keynesian model from a pre-Keynesian one. Unfortunately, the argument is not as well spelled out in *The General Theory* as it should be—in part because Keynes failed to pick up on the suggestion made by the Swedish school of economists that he make a distinction between the *ex ante* situation insofar as investment and savings are concerned and the *ex post* result. With the argument further refined in this way, it is then possible to explain how a disequilibrium situation, even in the more limited sense in which Keynes used the term "equilibrium," could arise in the first place, thereby necessitating an adjustment in the aggregate income and product flows.

3.2.2 The onset of disequilibrium

Let us assume that investment and savings, previously in balance with one another, are now about to diverge as a result of business enterprises deciding to increase their capital outlays. The change in capital outlays can, from the perspective of the next time period, be regarded as a change in *ex ante* investment since the change is only being planned or contemplated, and the decision has not yet been acted on. Households, it can be further assumed, expect the current level of economic activity to be maintained and are therefore planning to continue their current level of consumption. The resulting savings—the difference between the current level of household income and the current level of consumption—can be regarded as the *ex ante* savings for the next time period. Clearly, since enterprises are planning to increase their investment (beyond the current level) while households are planning to maintain the same level of consumption (and hence of savings), the *ex ante* investment for the next time period must necessarily be greater than the *ex ante* savings. This situation is depicted in exhibit 3.1, where I' (not I) is the *ex ante* level of investment for the next time period, given the capital expenditure plans of business firms, and S (equal to I) is the *ex ante* level of savings planned by households.

Exhibit 3.1

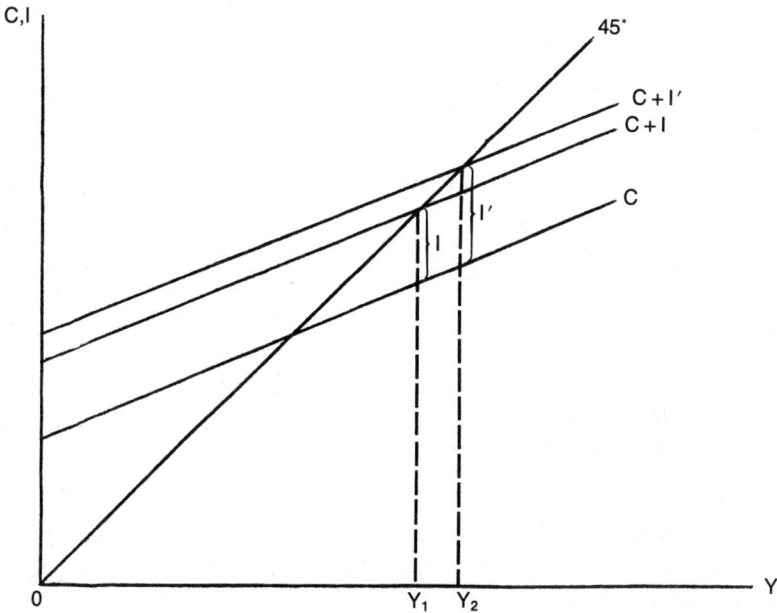

It is, of course, only in an *ex ante* sense—that is, looking ahead to the next time period before enterprises and households actually carry out their plans—that investment and savings can diverge in this way. Once business firms and households act on those plans, committing their funds accordingly, investment and savings must necessarily be equal to one another. This is because, in looking back to see how the national product and the national income have been apportioned, what has not been taken up by household consumption must be equal, on the product side, to business investment and, on the income side, to household savings. Business investment and household savings will necessarily be equal to one another because of the way household savings are defined *ex ante*—as the income not used to purchase the output of consumption goods. Thus it is only in an *ex post* accounting sense, that is, after the figures for the national product and national income have been tallied up, reflecting the spending decisions actually carried out by business firms and households (with an allowance then made for profits and any other residual forms of income), that investment and savings will necessarily be equal to one another.

Keynes, assuming that household savings would adjust to the level of business investment (the opposite of what economists had previously assumed), was content simply to point out the new level of income toward which the system would gravitate—which, in the situation depicted in exhibit 3.1, is Y_2. That is why he stressed only the necessary *ex post* condition for the economic system to be in macrodynamic balance, namely, that aggregate investment be equal to aggregate savings. However, it is just as important to indicate how the likely *ex ante* inequality between investment and savings will be eliminated so that, *ex post*, the two flows will be in balance with one another at a level of national income equal to Y_2. Otherwise, one cannot be certain that Y_2 is the level of national income toward which the economic system will tend to gravitate. Y_2 may, in fact, be only a transitory point in the movement of the economy toward some quite different level of national income—and thus Y_2 may be of no real significance. To demonstrate that Y_2 is not just a transitory point in the continuous movement of the economy, it is necessary to specify the dynamic adjustment process that is initiated whenever, as is likely to be the case *ex ante*, business investment and household savings are *not* equal to one another and then to show that this dynamic adjustment process causes the economic system to gravitate toward Y_2 rather than to some other level of national income.

3.2.3 The dynamic adjustment process

Because of the way in which the basic Keynesian model is constructed, the precipitating factor requiring subsequent adjustment by the other income flows will be a change in business investment (or, in the extended version of the same model, some other type of autonomous expenditure). The reason business investment plays this role is that it is the only one of the two components of aggregate demand which, in the basic model, is not income-constrained. The level of investment depends instead on the availability of credit. If banks and/or other financial institutions are both willing and able to provide the necessary credit and if business firms are, in turn, willing to go into debt as a consequence, then the enterprise sector can increase its expenditures on new plant and equipment independently of the current level of national income. What this line of argument implies, insofar as the role played by money and credit is concerned, will not be pursued any further until chapter 12. The more immediately relevant implication is that, for at least one sector of the economy, the constraint on expenditures which is usually assumed in circular flow models of the economy—namely, that outlays cannot exceed income—does not hold. Outlays can exceed the current level of income if the necessary credit arrangements can be worked out to cover the resulting cash deficit. Indeed, it is in this way that the enterprise sector will be able to shift the total expenditure curve depicted in exhibit 3.1 from C + I to C + I', thereby creating a disparity between the flow of investment goods on the product side and the flow of savings on the income side—a disparity equal to the distance between the two curves shown in exhibit 3.1.

In effect, the claims being put forward to purchase the national product will exceed that level of output by an amount equal to the excess of investment over savings. The manifestation of this excess of investment over savings, insofar as observable phenomena are concerned, will be a pick-up in business orders so that the level of sales, relative to the current level of production, will increase. This will lead to a fall in business inventories since firms will have to satisfy the additional demand, at least temporarily, out of their finished goods inventory. However, once firms become convinced that the increased level of sales which has led to the fall in inventories is likely to persist, they will act to restore the normal inventory-sales ratio by stepping up their levels of production. As a result, the currently employed work force will either have to put in longer hours or its size will have to be expanded. The wage bill, if not the number of persons employed, will increase, thereby adding to household income. At the same time, the purchase of material inputs from other firms will have to be expanded, with the result that the increase in sales will quickly spread to other parts of the enterprise sector—with consequences similar to the initial increase in business orders. In this way, the national product will rise and, with it, the national income—including wages and any property income.

As household income increases, so too will consumption. Savings, however, will increase more rapidly, due to the marginal propensity to save being greater than the average propensity. The flow of savings will therefore expand quickly until it matches the higher level of investment, I'. When the economy reaches that point, equal to Y_2 in exhibit 3.1, there will be no further tendency, as a result of the endogenous forces at work, for the level of national income either to continue rising or to recede. The economy will be poised at a new point of macrodynamic balance, with the amount of income being returned to the spending stream through the purchase of capital goods by the enterprise sector equal to the leakage from the spending stream due to household savings.

The same dynamic works in reverse. If the enterprise sector decides to reduce, rather than to increase, its capital outlays, then the total expenditures curve, as shown in exhibit 3.1, will shift downward from $C + I'$ to $C + I$. In that event, it will be the flow of household savings which exceeds the level of business investment, and not vice versa. In effect, the claims being put forward against the national product will be less than the current level of output, and in this case the manifestation, insofar as observable phenomena are concerned, will be a fall-off in sales and a rise in finished goods inventory. Again, once firms become convinced that the change is likely to persist, they will respond by attempting to restore the normal inventory-sales ratio—only in this case they will act to cut back on production. Overtime will be eliminated and workers perhaps even let go. Orders for material inputs will also be reduced, thereby causing the decline in sales, followed by a decline in output, to spread throughout the rest of the enterprise sector. As the national product decreases, so too will the national income, with household savings falling more rapidly than consumption. Again, the process will come to a halt only when the flow of savings has been reduced to the level of business investment. This will be the new point of macrodynamic balance, Y_1.

The dynamic adjustment process which has just been described can be represented as a four-step sequence of events, each of which can be separately observed once the shift in the level of business investment from I to I' has created a disequilibrium situation in which I = S. The four-step sequence is as follows:

1. $I \neq S$ $\longrightarrow$ Δsales and hence Δ(inventory/sales)
2. Δ(inventory/sales) $\longrightarrow$ Δproduction and hence Δoutput.
3. Δoutput $\longrightarrow$ Δ(wage bill + property income) and hence ΔY_D
4. ΔY_D $\longrightarrow$ ΔC, ΔS until S = I'

The dynamic process just outlined serves to explain why a change in investment (or some other type of autonomous expenditure) will lead, in a Keynesian model, to a change in the macrodynamically balanced level of national income, with this new level of economic activity toward which the economic system will then tend to gravitate being determined by the change in autonomous expenditures. The process just outlined also explains why it is household savings that will adjust to the level of investment rather than the reverse. (The point is further explicated in chapter 12, section 1.5.) Some economists, however, would deny that the new level of national income is a true "equilibrium" one as long as any of the markets linking the various income and product flows have failed to clear, with the demand and supply in those markets equal to one another. Indeed it can be argued that as long as any one of these markets fails to clear and thus is in disequilibrium, further changes can be expected, with Y_2 not necessarily the level of activity toward which the economic system will tend to gravitate.

In the dynamic adjustment process just outlined, it must be admitted that important markets remain uncleared. With sales affected by the disparity between investment and savings, the final goods markets are clearly in disequilibrium. Moreover, with employment varying with the level of sales, what economists term the labor market is also clearly in disequilibrium. Finally, the disparity between investment and savings betokens disequilibrium in the credit markets. Thus, to show that Y_2 will be the new level of national income toward which the economic system will gravitate when, as in exhibit 3.1, *ex ante* investment shifts from I to I', one must be able to demonstrate that any concurrent disequilibrium in the final goods, labor and credit markets will have no effect on the outcome.

3.2.4 Disequilibrium in individual markets

The dynamic adjustment process outlined above begins with a disparity between *ex ante* investment and savings which is experienced by business firms as a change in their level of sales. The theory from which Keynes struggled to free himself assumed that the response of firms to this disequilibrium condition would be quite different from that just indicated. Rather than absorbing the change in sales through a change in finished goods inventory with production then being adjusted accordingly, firms were viewed as maintaining production at the same level, with the output that was produced then sold in the market for whatever price it could command. Only if the change in industry demand were to lead to a change in the industry price, and hence to a change in the profit-maximizing level of output, would firms alter their production levels. They would, however, continue selling all they produced at whatever happened to be the new industry price, with any change in the amount produced being the result of the change in the industry price. In other words, the pre-Keynesian theory—the theory still taught in micro-economics courses—assumed that it was primarily through the influence exerted by the price variable, and not the quantity variable, that any imbalance between demand and supply in the final goods markets would be corrected.

The General Theory does not touch on this point of difference—in part because the dynamic adjustment process is left unexplicated (it would remain for Lloyd Metzler to make it explicit) and in part because Keynes was reluctant to make the attack on the prevailing Marshallian theory any broader than necessary to drive home his point about the types of policies needed to reduce unemployment. One must also recognize that Keynes himself did not realize how much of an obstacle the orthodox microeconomic theory was to a correct understanding of an advanced market economy's macrodyanmic behavior. The difference between the pre-Keynesian and Keynesian adjustment processes, insofar as disequilibrium in the final goods markets is concerned, has become clear only as a result of the subsequent work by other writers following in Keynes' footsteps.

The pre-Keynesian theory is based on what has been observed in the commodity markets which have long existed for internationally traded goods such as wheat (what Europeans term "corn"). In these markets, enterprises (usually family-operated farms) or large agricultural producers, are relegated to the role of "price-takers," which means they must accept the current market price as given since they are in no position to affect it. Their individual output is such an insignificant portion of the total world supply that, whatever action they may take, they will have little or no influence on the market price. The price is determined by impersonal market forces, which are reflected in the shape of the applicable demand and supply curves—over which the individual firm has no control. If demand should fall, the resulting shift in the industry demand curve will lead to a lower industry price; and if demand should rise, the resulting shift will lead to a higher industry price. In either case, enterprises can be expected to continue producing at some profit-maximizing level of output (as determined by the intersection of their marginal revenue and marginal cost curves), throwing the goods on the market for whatever price the goods can command (see chapter 6, section 4.1, for a more complete explanation of how prices are determined in commodity markets).

However, in the industrial sector, which constitutes the core of any advanced market economy, enterprises find themselves in an entirely different situation and behave in accordance with those different circumstances. A decline in demand is experienced as a decline in sales rather than as a weakening of the market such that the industry price will necessarily fall. Similarly, an increase in demand is experienced as an increase in sales rather than as a market-mediated rise in price. This is because the relatively small number of firms in the industries which

constitute the industrial sector must make their own markets—there are no organized markets such as those which exist for commodities—and this they do by
establishing a price list, offering to sell the items on the list to all those willing to
pay the stipulated price. In other words, the enterprises in the industrial sector are
"price-setters" rather than "price-takers," and this leads them to respond differently to changes in market conditions (see chapter 5, section 1.2, and chapter 6,
section 4.2, for a more complete explanation of how prices are determined in
industrial markets). Rather than continuing to maintain production, allowing the
change in market price to bring demand and supply into balance, they try to hold
to their price lists as long as possible, allowing the change in output to bring
demand and supply into balance. (This, of course, does not prevent them from
shading the list price in order to make a sale they might otherwise lose if they can
do so without it becoming generally known.) Thus the shift from a pre-Keynesian
to a Keynesian scenario insofar as the dynamic adjustment process in the final
goods markets is concerned is simply a belated recognition that industrial markets, and not commodity markets, are the dominant feature of an advanced
economy like that of the United States and the other OECD countries. This and
related points will be further developed in chapter 6 when the pricing behavior of
the enterprise sector will be analyzed in greater depth. For now it will suffice to
point out that the response to disequilibrium in the final goods markets posited
above as part of the overall dynamic adjustment process is fully consistent with
what is known about the nature of those markets.

Any disparity between *ex ante* investment and savings will also have an impact
on the market for human resource inputs. Once enterprises decide to alter their
output levels in response to the change in sales, they will be forced to make a
corresponding adjustment in their use of inputs. As already pointed out, while the
demand for material inputs will also be affected, it is primarily the demand for
labor, or human resource, inputs that will bear the brunt of any adjustment that
must take place. This is because the demand for material inputs is primarily a
demand for labor inputs one step removed (see chapter 5, section 4.1). Indeed, it
is for this reason that the fall-off in the demand for labor will spread rapidly
throughout the enterprise sector as a whole, extending well beyond the firms
experiencing the initial decline in sales. With the supply of labor assumed to be
unchanged, at least initially, what is usually thought of as the labor market will be
in disequilibrium, with the demand and supply of human resource inputs no
longer in balance with one another.

As this point, the pre-Keynesian theory posits a quite different scenario from
the one outlined above. Rather than the amount of employment varying, it is
assumed that wage rates will adjust. As soon as workers recognize that their
"commodity"—their time or "laboring power"—has been either overpriced or
underpriced given the current labor market conditions, they will come to accept
the necessary change in the wage rate so that the demand for and supply of labor
will once again be in balance. Only if, at the new "equilibrium" wage rate,
workers prefer more or less "leisure" will the supply of labor be affected. In this

market, too, it is the price variable, and not the quantity variable, that is assumed to play the major role in bringing demand and supply back into balance with one another so as to restore "equilibrium"; and if this dynamic adjustment process seems to take longer than one might wish, this is the fault of workers for refusing to accept the inevitable adjustment in wage rates which must occur.

In *The General Theory*, Keynes takes direct issue with this line of argument. The principal point he makes is that even if a general reduction in wages could somehow be managed—as distinct from a reduction in the wages of one group of workers relative to those of other workers—this would only make matters worse. Observing a general decline in wages, businessmen could hardly look to the future with confidence, and the resulting cutback in investment outlays would have an adverse effect on output and employment, via the multiplier, far greater than any additional workers hired because the cost of labor has declined relative to that of other inputs. In other words, the income effect from a fall in the wage rate can be expected to outweigh the substitution effect.

Keynes, in making this argument, was simply attempting to explain the observed rigidity of wage rates in the face of pronounced shifts in the demand for labor. Since workers realize they cannot improve their position by accepting lower wages, it is hardly surprising that they should vehemently resist any wage cuts. It should be noted that the point does not rest on the existence of a trade union movement able to bargain collectively on behalf of all workers. Indeed, the tendency of wages to remain "sticky" was apparent in the United States even before the growth of industrial trade unions in the 1930s. Clearly, however, the emergence of a powerful trade union movement only strengthens the argument about wages being inflexible, at least downward. (It should be noted that since wages are likely to be inflexible downward, even in the absence of a powerful trade union movement, it will not necessarily help matters to weaken or even destroy the trade unions.)

Subsequent work by other economists has helped clarify why it is that the wage rate cannot be counted to play the equilibrating role in the labor market that pre-Keynesian theory assigns it. While part of the answer has to do with the institutionally determined rigidity of wage rates, other factors are important as well. The most important of these other factors are the relatively fixed ratios, at least in the short period, at which labor and other inputs need to be combined in the production process (see chapter 5, section 3.2) and the seemingly inexhaustible supplies of human resource inputs which enterprises can count on. These and related points will be explored in greater depth in chapters 8 and 13 when the human resource inputs are analyzed, first in connection with the income of the household sector and then as a supply constraint on production. For now it will suffice to point out that the response to disequilibrium in the labor market can be expected to follow the Keynesian scenario, as outlined above, rather than the pre-Keynesian one. The stickiness of wages assumed in the former case, it turns out, is more consistent with what is known about the labor "market."

There is a third type of market involved in the dynamic adjustment process.

Pre-Keynesian writers regarded it as a market for "savings," and it was assumed that if this market were to be in disequilibrium—as a result of the amount of savings which enterprises wished to borrow for investment purposes being out of line with the amount of savings which households were willing to supply—a change in the interest rate, or price of "savings," could be expected to restore the balance. Keynes, by insisting that savings depend solely on household income, with the interest rate playing little or no role, largely cut the ground from under this argument. Changes in the interest rate can no more play an equilibrating role insofar as the demand for and supply of savings are concerned than the wage rate can in the labor "market." Nevertheless, while it may be inappropriate to talk about a market for "savings," there are still the financial markets to be taken into account. Any disparity between investment and savings, as the initiating factor in the dynamic adjustment process outlined above, will necessarily affect those markets. At the very least, with household savings varying so as to match the *ex ante* level of investment, financial institutions such as banks will be forced to adjust to a changing level of deposits.

This disequilibrium situation in the financial markets is not one that need concern us at this point. The financial markets, it can be assumed, are such that they can absorb any flow of funds into and out of them arising from a disparity between investment and savings. If the disparity is such that sales decline, along with employment and household income, banks will simply experience a loss of deposits, while if the disparity is such that sales rise, along with employment and household income, banks will gain deposits. But no further consequences will follow—as long as the central bank, in keeping with its primary responsibility for protecting the liquidity of the financial system, makes sure that the banks have adequate reserves.

This capacity of the financial markets to absorb funds is the result of the elasticity which a credit-based—as distinct from a commodity-based—form of money provides. It was largely because they were thinking in terms of commodity money, exemplified by a gold-based currency, that most economists prior to Keynes equated the flow of household savings into the banking system with the funds available to finance business investment. But under a credit form of money, the amount of funds available to finance investment depends far more on the lending policies of the banks, including the central bank, than on the willingness of households to forego consumption. In any case, it is the banks which supply the funds, not households. Keynes, because he combined the knowledge of an academic monetary theorist with that of a financial market manager, better understood this implication of credit money than any his contemporaries. Indeed, it is the existence of credit money which underlies the entire argument of *The General Theory*, including any possible disparity between *ex ante* investment and savings. These and related points will be covered in greater depth in chapter 12 when the role played by credit and financial institutions will be analyzed. For now it will suffice to point out that, because of the nature of the monetary-financial system— in particular its ability to "neutralize" the ensuing change in the cash balances of the nonfinancial sectors—any disequilibrium in the financial markets as a result of investment and savings no longer being equal to one another will have little or no feedback effect on the level of real economic activity. What has just been said will, of course, have to be modified if the central bank refuses to play its part in providing the necessary funds for business investment. That exception to the general argument will also be taken up in chapter 12. Until then, we shall simply adhere to the logic of the basic Keynesian model by assuming a fully accommodating policy on the part of the central bank.

Thus, whatever the type of market—final product, labor and other inputs, or financial—any imbalance between supply and demand within that market can be ignored in attempting to determine the level of economic activity, as measured by Y_e, toward which the system will tend to gravitate. In the basic Keynesian model, that macrodynamically balanced, or "equilibrium," level of national income depends solely on the level of business investment, with the amount of savings then adjusting to that level of investment. From this way in which equilibrium is defined in the basic Keynesian model follows one of the more important Keynesian propositions—namely, that while there is an almost unlimited number of possible "equilibrium" levels of national income, depending on the amount of investment, there is only one equilibrium level of national income at which all available productive resources, including labor, will be fully employed. Thus the "full employment" level of national income, rather than being the point toward which the economic system eventually moves, is but one of a great many possible equilibrium levels of national income—and indeed is no more likely to be realized than any of the other possible levels. Economists before Keynes (and those who still reject his basic model) could assume that there is only one equilibrium level of national income, and that is the level of national income at which all productive resources are being fully utilized, because they believed that any imbalance between demand and supply within individual markets would be eliminated through the necessary price adjustments. Keynes, believing that no price adjustments could bring demand and supply back into balance with one another in those markets, instead argued that there was no one "equilibrium" level of national income. Rather there are a great many possible equilibrium levels of national income, only one of which results in the "full employment" of all productive resources— with that one "full employment" equilibrium no more likely to be realized than any of the others.

The chapters that follow will continue to maintain that there is no one "equilibrium" level of national income—or at least no one level of activity, as measured by national income, toward which the economic system tends to gravitate. Moreover, the same reason will continue to be given as to why this is true—namely, the inability of relative price changes to restore the balance between demand and supply in individual markets. In this sense, the present text can be said to be Keynesian rather than pre-Keynesian. It will nonetheless depart radically from the basic Keynesian model in a number of ways. One way is by denying that the condition even for aggregate "equilibrium" within that model—namely, that investment be equal to savings or, more broadly, that discretionary expenditures be equal to discretionary funds—need actually hold. Indeed, in what follows the concept of equilibrium will be replaced by the notion of a necessary condition which, when it is not satisfied (as it is almost certain not to be in practice), will give rise to a dynamic adjustment process applicable to that disequilibrium situation. In this way, the equilibrium model of Keynes will be replaced by a disequilibrium analysis, as one part of the more inclusive dynamic model that needs to be constructed.

3.2.5 The cash-flow feedback effect

With the specification above of the dynamic adjustment process which ensures that any disparity between *ex ante* investment and savings will tend to be eliminated, the basis for a disequilibrium analysis has already been established. Should investment exceed savings—or, more generally, should discretionary expenditures exceed discretionary funds—then the endogenous response outlined in section 2.3 of this chapter will lead to an expansion of economic activity and an increase in output. Should the situation be reversed, with household savings along with other types of discretionary funds exceeding business investment and other discretionary expenditures, the endogenous response will lead to a contraction in economic activity and a decline in output. What is important, however, is not whether investment and savings or, more broadly, discretionary expenditures and discretionary funds will eventually be brought into balance with one another. Given the volatility of business investment and other discretionary expenditures, the eventual balance between investment and savings (representing the broader categories of discretionary expenditures and discretionary funds) is unlikely ever to be actually observed. The *ex post* equality that can be observed in the National Income and Product Accounts or, alternatively, in the Flow of Funds Accounts is simply the result of the definitions employed, particularly, the definition of profits and the other forms of residual income. Rather what is important is the thrust given to the level of economic activity by any disparity between investment and savings.

The thrust given to the level of economic activity by a disparity between investment and savings can be summarized in terms of the following dichotomy:

A	*OR*	B
If $I > S$, then ΔY will be positive.		If $S > I$, then ΔY will be negative.

These opposing results follow from the fact that if investment exceeds savings, more claims are being injected into the spending stream through the capital outlays of business firms than are being withdrawn through household savings; while if savings are greater than investment, the opposite is true. It is for this reason that, in the chapters that follow, the thrust given to the level of economic activity, whether positive or negative, by the relative balance between investment and savings—or, more broadly, between discretionary expenditures and discretionary funds—will be termed the "cash-flow feedback effect."

As a disequilibrium process, the cash-flow feedback effect is to be distinguished from the multiplier. The latter—at least as derived in the usual way, as the inverse of the marginal propensity to save (see equation 3.14)—is an equilibrium outcome since it represents the ultimate possible effect, insofar as additional household consumption is concerned, of increasing business investment or some other type of autonomous expenditures by a fixed amount. As such, the multiplier effect has no time dimension. The full effect may be experienced relatively quickly (say within two or three years) or it may take centuries. The way in which the value of the multiplier is determined mathematically—to wit, as the limit approached by an infinite series (the infinite series being the amount of income left to purchase additional consumption goods after subtracting, at each successive stage in the process, the proportion saved)—leaves the time dimension unspecified.

The multiplier effect, however, can be derived in a quite different manner so as to give it a time dimension. One can attempt to determine *empirically* the relationship between the change in autonomous expenditures in time period zero and the subsequent change in the total national income which occurs in each succeeding time period. That is, the following behavioral equation can be estimated:

$$\Delta Y_{1 \rightarrow t} = k_1(\Delta A_0) + k_2(\Delta A_0) + k_3(\Delta A_0) + \ldots + k_t(\Delta A_0) \quad (3.29)$$

where ΔY is the total increase in the national income from time period 1 through t (with t a finite number) and is calculated as follows:

$$\Delta Y_{1 \rightarrow t} = \Delta Y_1 + \Delta Y_2 + \Delta Y_3 + \ldots + \Delta Y_t \quad (3.30)$$

with ΔY_1, ΔY_2, ΔY_3, ... , ΔY_t the increase in the national income in each of those individual time periods; k_1, k_2, k_3, ..., k_t is the multiplier effect in each of the same individual time periods; and ΔA_0 is the increase in autonomous expenditures in time period 0. Once equation 3.29 has been estimated, the value of the multiplier, k, can be calculated as follows:

$$k = \sum_{j=1}^{t} k_j \quad (3.31)$$

where the j subscript represents the time periods 1 through t.

While in theory the value of k should be the same, whether it is derived by means of equations 3.14 or, alternatively, by means of equations 3.29 and 3.31, the estimates will, as a practical matter, differ significantly for the following reasons:

1. Equation 3.14 is no longer the relevant formula for deriving the multiplier mathematically when the basic Keynesian model is expanded to include both a government and rest-of-the-world sector (see section 3.1.5). The appropriate formula is, in fact, considerably more complex. It is predicated on a series of additional behavioral equations, besides the consumption function, which require a further elaboration of the basic Keynesian model that will take another seven chapters—indeed, the entire middle portion of the text—to complete.

2. Both equation 3.29 and the additional set of behavioral equations, besides the consumption function, which need to be estimated if the value of k is to be derived mathematically for an economy with a government and rest-of-the-world sector are subject to considerable error, reflecting both the data problems and the limitations of multiple regression analysis which are discussed in the two appendices to this text. This means that the estimates will vary even if the basic Keynesian model is expanded to encompass all the relevant sectors of the economy.

3. The estimate based on equation 3.14 assumes an infinite amount of time for the full impact of the multiplier process to be felt while the estimate based on equations 3.29 and 3.31 assumes only a finite amount of time. This difference is less significant than the other two reasons which have so far been given for why the estimates of k are likely to vary, depending on which formula is used. Both the theoretical argument and the empirical evidence would suggest that most of the multiplier effect will be felt within the first few rounds so that, with the value of t in equation 3.29 set to cover even less than a year, little of the model's explanatory power is lost. However, if this is true, then it means that the other two considerations should weigh all the more heavily when it comes to deciding whether to use equation 3.29 or equation 3.14 as the basis for incorporating the multiplier effect into the macrodynamic model that is to be constructed in the subsequent chapters of this text.

The advantage of equation 3.29 is that it converts the multiplier from a timeless, equilibrium outcome into a time-delineated process, one that can then be modeled empirically. Moreover, in this form, the multiplier can be better compared with the cash-flow feedback effect so as to bring out the essential difference between the two separate consequences of an *ex ante* change in business investment and/or other types of autonomous expenditures. Both the multiplier and the cash-flow feedback effect lead to a change in the level of national income, and thus the difference between them is not the variable through which their influence will be felt. Rather the difference is as follows:

a) The multiplier effect depends solely on the change in the level of investment (or, more generally, on the change in the amount of autonomous expenditures) while the cash-flow feedback effect depends on the *disparity* between investment and savings which any change in *ex ante* investment creates. Thus, k represents a functional relationship between the change in investment, ΔI, and the subsequent change in the level of national income, ΔY, while j, the cash-flow feedback effect, is the functional relationship between any *discrepancy* between investment and savings, (I − S), and the subsequent change in the level of national income, ΔY.

b) The multiplier, k, increases in value as additional time periods are taken into account (albeit in increasingly smaller increments) until it reaches the limit given by 1/s or whatever, in a more comprehensive version of the basic Keynesian model, is the appropriate formula while the cash-flow feedback effect diminishes until it equals the zero value associated with it at the Keynesian "equilibrium" level of national income. Thus, as additional time periods are encompassed within the model, k → X where X is a number greater than 1 while j→0.

The cash-flow feedback effect as just delineated, together with the multiplier as specified in equations 3.29 and 3.31, will form the core of the macrodynamic model that is to be developed in the subsequent chapters of this text. The only difference is that the multiplier will be applied to the somewhat broader category of total discretionary expenditures (in real terms) rather than just business investment—while the cash-flow feedback effect will be related to any discrepancy between total discretionary expenditures and total discretionary funds (in nominal terms) rather than just the discrepancy between business investment and household savings. Both the multiplier and the cash-flow feedback effects will thus be incorporated into the model as time-delineated adjustment processes which, at any given point in time, are likely to be incomplete. Indeed, if only the ultimate value of the cash-flow feedback effect were to be taken into account, its influence on the level of economic activity could be ignored entirely—as is done in all the more conventional Keynesian models. For with the value of j approaching zero as more time periods are taken into account, the cash-flow feedback effect disappears from the "equilibrium" solution. It is only prior to that eventual level of economic activity being reached, and thus only in actual historical time, that the influence of the cash-flow feedback effect can be observed—and measured. This is, in fact, one argument for developing a disequilibrium, as distinct from an equilibrium, model. Only a disequilibrium model can capture all the relevant dynamic adjustment processes.

Both the multiplier and the cash-flow feedback effect do not influence just the *level* of economic activity. They also have an impact on the economic system's rate of expansion. Indeed, the influence they have on the *level* of economic activity is simply a corollary to the impact they have on the rate of economic expansion. Thus, before these two cyclical adjustment processes can be adequately captured within a macrodynamic model, the focus has to shift from the concern of *The General Theory* and the numerous static models it has inspired with what determines the *level* of economic activity to the concern of the several types of growth models *The General Theory* has also inspired with what determines the economic system's *rate* of expansion over time. This will, in fact, be the subject of the next chapter.

Recommended Readings

The classic work on the basic Keynenian model is, of course, John Maynard Keynes, *The General Theory of Interest, Money and Employment*, London: Macmillan, 1936. The classic introductions to this work are Alvin Hansen, *Guide to Keynes*, New York: McGraw-Hill, 1953, and Lawrence R. Klein, *The Keynesian Revolution*, New York: Macmillan, 1947. See also Robert Lekachman, ed., *Keynes' General Theory, Reports on Three Decades*, New York: St. Martin's Press, 1964. A better guide to *The General Theory*, however, is Victoria Chick, *Macroeconomics After Keynes, A Reconsideration of The General Theory*, Cambridge, Mass.: MIT Press, 1983. See also Hyman P. Minsky, *John Maynard Keynes*, New York: Columbia University Press, 1975; Joan Robinson, *Economic Philosophy*, Chicago: Aldine, 1962, ch. 4; Luigi L. Pasinetti, *Growth and Income Distribution, Essays in Economic Theory*, London: Cambridge University Press, 1974, ch. 2.

For the earlier version of the same model developed by Kalecki, see Michal Kalecki, *Selected Essays on the Dynamics of the Capitalist Economy, 1933–1970*, London: Cambridge University Press, 1971. On Kalecki's contribution, see Malcolm Sawyer, "Towards a Post-Kaleckian Macroeconomics," *Thames Papers in Political Economy*, Autumn 1982, and *The Economics of Michal Kalecki*, Armonk, N.Y.: M. E. Sharpe, 1986.

The only useful discussion within the extant literature of the dynamic process by which any discrepancy between savings and investment is eliminated will be found in Lloyd A. Metzler, "Factors Governing the Length of Inventory Cycles," *Review of Economics and Statistics*, February 1947. This article, as well as the other writings by Metzler on the role played by business inventories in generating business cycles, has been republished in his *Collected Papers*, Cambridge, Mass.: Harvard University Press, 1973, part III. The cash-flow feedback effect, as something separate and distinct from the multiplier, has not otherwise been previously identified.

For a discussion of the proper use of the homeostatic, or "equilibrium," concept in economic analysis, see Jacques Henry, "Aggregate Supply and Demand Analysis from a Post-classical Point of View," Research Paper no. 8302, University of Ottawa, April 1983, and "On the Notions of Equilibrium and 'Inequilibrium' in Economics," paper presented at Ottawa-ISMEA Conference on Cyclical Behavior and Long-Term Structural Movements of Contemporary Economics, Ottawa University, October 3–6, 1984.

Chapter 4

Growth Models

Contents

Chapter 4

Growth Models

The basic Keynesian model has probably contributed more to the welfare of the world's population than any other advance in social science knowledge so far this century. Largely as a result of the prescription for public policy implicit in that model, governments throughout the OECD community of nations have been able to avoid the severe depressions and widespread unemployment which, prior to World War II, periodically racked the world's market economies. Even those living in the less developed countries have benefited from the general economic prosperity that has marked the post World War II era. Still, as valuable a contribution to our understanding of economic phenomena as the basic Keynesian model may be, its limitations must be recognized.

The two most important of these limitations are the following:

1. *The model is static rather than dynamic.* This means that it attempts to identify only the factors determining the *level* of economic activity at a particular moment in time, not the factors determining the continuous *change* in output over time. While the basic Keynesian model, as already demonstrated, can easily be modified to encompass discrete changes in output from one time period to the next, this is not the same as offering an explanation for the process of cumulative, compounded growth over a succession of time periods.

2. *The model focuses solely on output and employment*, to the exclusion of other variables important to public policy. Indeed, the model offers no explanation for price movements so that a change in real income cannot be distinguished from what is merely a change in nominal income. Thus the basic Keynesian model, without being supplemented in some way, has little to say about what determines the secular growth of prices, that is, the rate of inflation.

Given the historical context in which *The General Theory* was written, these limitations are hardly surprising. Unemployment was the overriding problem in Keynes's day, and the priority, quite understandably, was to find some way to ameliorate its effects. It was only in the subsequent post-World War II period, once the spectre of severe depression and widespread unemployment had been dispelled, that economists were able to turn their attention to the almost equally important problems of secular growth and inflation. At that point it became necessary to move beyond the static framework of *The General Theory*, with its singular emphasis on the problem of unemployment, to develop a new mode of analysis.

This new mode of analysis owes its inspiration largely to the work of Keynes's Oxford colleague and biographer, Roy Harrod. It was Harrod who, even as Keynes was completing *The General Theory*, sought to place its arguments in a growth framework. However, the Harrodian vision was not enough. The new mode of analysis also required the insights of the Polish economist and independent author of the basic Keynesian model, Michal Kalecki. It was Kalecki who, combining the Rosa Luxemburg and Mikhail Tugan-Baranovsky strands within Marxian theory, was able to integrate into the Keynesian model the struggle over income shares that underlies both the growth and the inflationary processes.

The person responsible for bringing the Keynesian, Harrodian, and Kaleckian visions together in a single work of original synthesis was Joan Robinson. Her 1956 book, *The Accumulation of Capital* (a title honoring Rosa Luxemburg's memory), marks the beginning of the new mode of analysis, an approach that has been termed post-Keynesian both to indicate its roots in *The General Theory* and its transcendence of that work's static framework. It is when the arguments about the multiplier and effective demand found in *The General Theory* are joined to the type of growth model developed by Harrod (as well as the distributional model derived from Kalecki) that Keynesian theory becomes post-Keynesian. Thus the next step in the transition from the static framework of the basic Keynesian model to the type of dynamic model encompassing both growth and disequilibrium that characterizes the post-Keynesian approach is to derive the model of steady-state expansion that Harrod was able to construct by recognizing the supply-augmenting, as well as the demand-enhancing, effects of business investment. Once that model of steady-state expansion, with its warranted growth rate, has been laid out, it will be possible to discuss, in the last two parts of the chapter, both the exogenous constraints on the economic system's rate of expansion and the tendency of any secular expansion path to exhibit significant cyclical movements.

4.1 Steady-State Expansion

The simplest of the models for explaining the continuous expansion of an economic system over time is a model which Roy Harrod (along with the American economist, Evsey Domar) was able to construct by taking Keynes's own model, in particular the multiplier, as his starting point. Harrod's critical insight was his recognition that business investment, once the gestation period is over, has a capacity or supply augmenting effect which is in addition to the demand enhancing effect the same investment will have operating through the multiplier. By taking into account the simultaneous impact of the two separate effects, Harrod was able to construct a model of continuous, or steady-state, expansion which is relatively easy to grasp and, at the same time, quite revealing as to the underlying determinants of economic growth. Indeed, any of the more sophisticated models of economic growth which have subsequently appeared in the literature are, if they take a mathematical form, merely an elaboration of the Harrod-Domar model. (The model, though first put forward by Harrod to explain the economy's cyclical instability, was then presented by Domar in a slightly different form and given a somewhat different interpretation so as to account instead for the secular rate of economic expansion.) Thus, any effort to incorporate growth into a model of the economy's macrodynamic behavior must begin with the same simple model. In this respect, the Harrod-Domar model is as fundamental to post-Keynesian theory as the basic Keynesian model itself.

4.1.1 The Harrod-Domar model

The Harrod-Domar model is constructed on the basis of two relationships. One is the Keynesian multiplier in the following form:

$$ Y = \frac{1}{s}(\Delta I) = \frac{\Delta I}{s} \tag{4.1} $$

which is obtained by substituting the formula for the multiplier, given above in equation 3.14, for k in the reduced form of the basic Keynesian model (equation 3.17, where the change in business investment, ΔI, is represented by Δd).

The other relationship upon which the Harrod-Domar model is based is what is known as the incremental capital-output ratio, or ICOR. It indicates how much output, valued in dollars or some other unit of account, must be diverted from current consumption and instead added to the economy's stock of capital inputs in order to have the increased capacity needed to produce in the future an extra unit of output, again valued in dollars or some other unit of account. That is,

$$ v = \frac{\Delta K}{\Delta Y_p} \tag{4.2} $$

where v is the incremental capital-output ratio, ΔK is the change in the capital stock, and ΔY_p is the change in potential output, or capacity. Since a change in the capital stock, in particular the addition of new plant and equipment, is what is meant by investment, equation 4.2 can be rewritten as follows:

$$ v = \frac{I}{\Delta Y_p} \tag{4.3} $$

where I is the amount of business investment, valued in current dollars. (The role of public investment, particularly expenditures on the economic infrastructure, will for the moment be ignored.)

The terms in equation 4.3 can be rearranged as follows:

$$\Delta Y_p = \frac{I}{v} \tag{4.4}$$

This relationship indicates the increase in aggregate output, or the national product, that will be possible once a given amount of investment has been carried out. The increase in potential output will be equal to the amount of investment divided by the incremental capital-output ratio. Thus, if $10 billion in investment is currently being carried out and the incremental capital-output ratio is 3 (i.e., if it requires $3 in investment expenditures in order to be able to increase the national product by $1), then the increase in potential output as a result of the $10 billion investment will be $3.3 billion.

Clearly, the value of the incremental capital-output ratio, v, like the value of the multiplier, k, is a critical one for economic policy. Once the value of v has been ascertained, then investment planning at the national level can proceed on a more intelligent basis. This is because v is the reciprocal, or inverse, of the social rate of return on investment. The denominator, ΔY_p, indicates how much the society as a whole will be able to benefit, in the form of increased economic output, as a result of acquiring the additional capital inputs while its numerator, I, indicates the cost to society, in the form of current output that will thus not be available for consumption, of carrying out that amount of investment. Letting ϱ denote the social rate of return on investment, equation 4.4 can be rewritten as follows:

$$\Delta Y_p = I * \varrho \tag{4.5}$$

A number of points about the incremental capital-output ratio, v, and its inverse, ϱ, the social rate of return on investment, need to be clarified before it can be incorporated into a macrodynamic model without leading the argument astray. First, only the *incremental* capital-output ratio, not the *average* capital-output ratio, can provide a meaningful basis for analysis. The latter is defined as the total capital stock, valued in money terms, needed to produce a given level of aggregate output, again valued in money terms. It is thus equal to K/Y_p. Unfortunately, the value of the capital stock, K, cannot be determined empirically. While the potential output, Y_p, can be approximated by using the figures on capacity utilization to adjust the data on actual output, there is no similar way of estimating K which does not involve either circular reasoning or the substitution of something quite different for the value of the capital stock. This is the main point of the "Cambridge criticism" of capital theory to be discussed in chapter 5, section 5.1. The source of the difficulty is the "vintage" component of the capital stock—the plant and equipment which no longer embodies the latest technology and/or was purchased at a price which no longer reflects the relative value of investment and consumption goods. For this component of the capital stock, the "historical" cost is clearly irrelevant to current allocation choices, and some other measure must be found to take its place. (The same argument, it should be noted, does not apply to the most recent addition to the capital stock, the amount of current investment, since its "historical" cost is the price enterprises are presently willing to pay in order to be able to divert resources from consumption into capital formation.) The only alternative to "historical" cost is either a "capitalized" value or a "replacement" value. Neither is satisfactory. The "capitalized" value depends on how much output the capital stock is capable of producing and therefore, relying on this approach, we cannot determine the value of K independently of Y_p. We know Y_p but not K/Y_p. The replacement value, on the other hand, depends on what it would cost to produce the same output with entirely new plant and equipment and therefore, relying on this approach, we ignore the differential productivity that distinguishes the latest additions to the capital stock from the vintage component. We know ΔK but not K. Indeed, it is best to admit that we know only ΔK, or I, along with ΔY_p, and base the analysis on that incremental rather than the average capital-output ratio.

Second, the incremental capital-output ratio and its reciprocal, the social rate of return on investment, should not be confused with the "marginal productivity of capital" which plays so critical a role in the neoclassical theory of income distribution. The latter is calculated by varying the "capital" inputs, like plant and equipment, while holding other types of inputs constant. It is thus a mathematical relationship, derived by applying the differential calculus to a "production function" with "capital" as one of the inputs, on the assumption that this input can be varied independently of the other inputs. (It should be noted that in the production functions identified in chapter 2, section 1.1, no such singular "capital" input was included. The possibility that production requires the use of multiple types of durable material, or "capital," inputs will be allowed for in the analysis that follows. See chapter 5, section 5.1. But then it is no longer clear what is being varied and what is being held constant—just one of the "capital" inputs, some of the "capital" inputs, or all of the "capital" inputs—when the differential calculus is applied in order to derive the "marginal product.")

The social rate of return on investment, on the other hand, and thus the incremental capital-output ratio, is calculated without holding any of the other inputs constant. This is because there is no intention of imputing the additional output, or "productivity," to any particular input. Rather the purpose is simply to determine the extent to which aggregate output can be increased by varying all the inputs together, in whatever combination the current technology requires. The "capital" input merely serves as the proxy for all inputs which are to be increased in fixed ratios to one another. The fact that the incremental capital-output ratio and its inverse, the social rate of return on investment, can be calculated without having to assume that the proportion of different inputs used in the production process can be freely varied is one advantage which this construct has over the "marginal productivity of capital." (See section 4.3.7 as well as chapter 5, section 4.1, and chapter 8, section 4.3, for a further discussion of this point.)

With the incremental capital-output ratio and its inverse, the social rate of return on investment, clearly defined so that they are not confused with either the average capital-output ratio or the marginal productivity of capital, it is then possible to show the dual effect that any increase in investment is likely to have and, based on that dual effect, construct a model of continuous economic expansion, without leading the argument astray. Equation 4.4 (or, alternatively, equation 4.5) represents the effect which an increase in investment will have on aggregate supply while equation 4.1 represents the effect the same increase in investment will have on aggregate demand.

The key consideration, in assessing the ability of an economic system to continue expanding over time, is whether the growth of aggregate demand and the growth of aggregate supply will be able to keep pace with one another. If the growth of demand is less than the growth of supply, then, in a market economy, business enterprises will experience declining sales and find themselves burdened with greater-than-desired capacity. They can be expected to respond by cutting back on production, employment, and investment, thereby dampening—if not ending altogether—the process of expansion. Alternatively, if the increase in demand exceeds the growth of capacity for any extended period of time, firms will find themselves running up against supply bottlenecks which, in a system of interdependent production, will lead to a slowing down of output, employment and capital accumulation. In this case, the growth of the economy will be checked not for lack of effective demand but rather for lack of sufficient productive capacity. Only if the growth of aggregate demand is matched by the growth of aggregate supply can one be certain that the economy will be able to continue expanding without serious disruption.

What is necessary to ensure this continuous, uninterrupted expansion of the economy can be seen by setting the increase in potential output, ΔY_p, as given in equation 4.4, equal to the increase in actual output, ΔY, as given in equation 4.1. With the growth of aggregate supply thus the same as the growth of aggregate demand, it follows that

$$\frac{\Delta I}{s} = \frac{I}{V} \tag{4.6}$$

Rearranging terms, equation 4.6 then takes the following form:

$$\frac{\Delta I}{I} = \frac{s}{v} \tag{4.7}$$

It is usually then assumed that, with the growth of aggregate supply equal to the growth of aggregate demand, the following relationship also holds:

$$\frac{\Delta Y}{Y} = \frac{\Delta I}{I} \tag{4.8}$$

Equation 4.8 is an important one in its own right. As a key assumption of the Harrod-Domar model, it defines one of the conditions that must be satisfied if the expansion is not to be interrupted by some cyclical movement. More will be said in elaboration of this point shortly. For the moment, it simply enables us, after denoting the aggregate growth rate, $\Delta Y/Y$, as $\dot{G}$, to equate this growth of aggregate output with the growth of aggregate investment, $\Delta I/I$. We can then substitute $\dot{G}$ for $\Delta I/I$ in equation 4.7 and obtain the following:

$$\dot{G} = \frac{s}{v} \tag{4.9}$$

Equation 4.9 is known as the Harrod-Domar formula—and it can be interpreted in either of two ways. First, it can be viewed as a model of what determines the economy's rate of expansion over long periods of time. In that interpretation, it is the parameters of the model that are primarily of interest. These parameters are: (1) the marginal propensity to save, s (which, with investment assumed to be equal to savings and to increase as savings increase, becomes the rate of accumulation, $\Delta I/\Delta Y$); and (2) the incremental capital-output ratio, v (the inverse of the social rate of return on investment). The Harrod-Domar formula, as a model of economic growth, then takes the following form:

$$\dot{G} = f(s, v) \tag{4.10}$$

As we shall see in the next major section, this is a valid way of viewing the Harrod-Domar formula—as long as it is understood that equation 4.10 represents only a hypothesis and not an axiomatic result. However, there is a second way of looking at the Harrod-Domar formula that is no less valid. This is to see it as defining a set of conditions that must be satisfied if the economic system is going to be able to expand continuously, without interruption, along a certain growth path. In that case, equation 4.9 defines not the actual growth rate but rather what Harrod termed the "warranted" growth rate. It is then the model's assumptions, rather than its parameters, which become critically important.

4.1.2 The warranted growth rate

The warranted growth rate is the rate of expansion that could be maintained

Exhibit 4.1

Twenty-Year Expansion Path of Alpha Economy
(with $Y_0 = 100$, $C_0 = 67$, $s = 0.33$, $v = 3$)

Period	Y	ΔY	$\dot{Y}$	C	ΔC	$\dot{C}$	I	ΔI	$\dot{I}$
0	100.0	—	—	67.0	—	—	33.0	—	—
1	110.0	11.0	11.0%	74.4	7.4	11.0%	36.6	3.6	11.0%
2	123.2	12.2	11.0	82.5	8.1	11.0	40.7	4.1	11.0
3	136.8	13.6	11.0	91.7	9.2	11.0	45.1	4.4	11.0
4	151.8	15.0	11.0	101.7	10.0	11.0	50.1	5.0	11.0
5	168.5	16.7	11.0	112.9	11.2	11.0	55.6	5.5	11.0
6	187.0	18.5	11.0	125.3	12.4	11.0	61.7	6.1	11.0
7	207.6	20.6	11.0	139.1	13.8	11.0	68.5	6.8	11.0
8	230.5	22.9	11.0	154.4	15.3	11.0	76.0	7.5	11.0
9	255.8	25.3	11.0	171.4	17.0	11.0	84.4	8.4	11.0
10	283.9	28.1	11.0	190.2	18.8	11.0	93.7	9.3	11.0
11	315.1	31.2	11.0	211.2	21.0	11.0	104.0	10.3	11.0
12	349.8	37.4	11.0	234.4	23.2	11.0	115.4	11.4	11.0
13	388.3	38.5	11.0	260.2	25.8	11.0	128.1	12.7	11.0
14	431.0	42.7	11.0	288.8	28.6	11.0	142.2	14.1	11.0
15	478.4	47.4	11.0	320.6	31.8	11.0	157.8	15.6	11.0
16	531.0	52.6	11.0	355.8	35.2	11.0	175.2	17.4	11.0
17	589.5	58.5	11.0	394.9	39.1	11.0	194.5	19.3	11.0
18	654.3	64.8	11.0	438.4	43.5	11.0	215.9	21.4	11.0
19	726.3	72.0	11.0	486.6	48.2	11.0	239.6	23.7	11.0
20	806.2	79.9	11.0	540.1	53.5	11.0	266.0	26.4	11.0

indefinitely—if all the assumptions underlying the Harrod-Domar model were to hold. It therefore refers to a hypothetical rather than an actual growth rate. With s equal to 0.33 and v equal to 3, the Harrod-Domar formula indicates that the warranted growth rate, $\dot{G}_w$, will be 11 percent. This is the rate at which all the relevant variables, including Y itself, will be increasing from one period to the next on into an indefinite future—or until s and v change.

Exhibit 4.1 traces out the changing value of these critical variables over 20 periods for an economic system, the Alpha economy—on the additional assumption that the initial level of national income (and national product) is equal to $100 billion, with $67 billion of that sum being used to meet the consumption needs of Alpha's citizens. The $33 billion of output which this leaves for investment will, assuming a one-year gestation period for all capital projects and an incremental capital-output ratio equal to three, lead to an $11 billion, or 11 percent, increase in the national product (and national income) by the end of the first year, with $7.4 billion of the increase being used for additional consumption (based on a marginal propensity to consume of 0.67, or 1 less the marginal propensity to save of 0.33) and the rest being used for further investment. The $111 billion national product at the beginning of the next year will then be divided into $74.4 billion of consumption and $36.6 billion of investment, with the latter leading to a $12.2 billion further increase in the national product by the end of the second year, a growth rate again of 11 percent. And so on *ad infinitum*. Although the expansion path of the Alpha economy is traced out for only 20 periods, the necessary calculations could easily be extended beyond that. For however long the growth path of Alpha is traced out, all the critical endogenous variables—Y, C and I—continue to increase by the same 11 percent each period. It is because of this constant rate at which each of these variables increases over time, with the initial ratios among the variables thereby being maintained, that the warranted growth rate given by the Harrod-Domar formula can be said to represent a balanced, steady-state growth path.

What that warranted growth rate is, and thus what is the balanced, steady-state growth path which the economy could in theory follow, depends on the parameters of the model. A change in the value of either s or v will lead to a change in the warranted growth rate and thus to a change in the balanced, steady-state growth path implied by the model. This point will be further developed in the next major section of this chapter. The more immediately relevant question is whether a market economy is likely to follow the type of balanced, steady-state growth path traced out in exhibit 4.1. The question arises because of the quite stringent assumptions upon which the Harrod-Domar model is based. Among the more important to these assumptions are the following:

1) That whatever the amount of savings generated, it will be matched by an equal amount of investment by business firms. Within the growth context of the Harrod-Domar model, this means that not just investment must be equal to savings at every point in time (this being the Keynesian condition for macrodynamic balance, or "aggregate equilibrium") but also, as a corollary, that the growth of investment, $\Delta I/I$ or $\dot{I}$, must be equal to the growth of savings, $\dot{S}$. This can be termed the aggregate demand condition since it is a necessary one for avoiding any cyclical fluctuations in output and employment due to either a positive or a negative cash-flow feedback effect (see chapter 3, section 2.5).

2) That whatever the rate of economic expansion, as given by the value of $\dot{G}$, it will be matched by an equal rate of growth of investment, $\dot{I}$. This necessary condition has already been pointed out (see equation 4.8). It can be termed the aggregate supply condition since it must hold if supply bottlenecks, and thus a slowing down of output, due to shortages of capacity, are to be avoided.

These assumptions, or necessary conditions, can be stated more succinctly by first defining a marginal propensity to invest, $\Delta I/\Delta Y$ or a, as the counterpart of the marginal propensity to save, $\Delta S/\Delta Y$ or s. The first assumption, or necessary condition, can then be stated as follows:

$$a = s \qquad (4.11)$$

In prose, this means that the marginal propensity to invest must be equal to the marginal propensity to save.

By substituting a for s in equation 4.9 and isolating a on the left-hand side, one can then state the second assumption, or necessary condition, as follows:

$$a = \dot{G}v \qquad (4.12)$$

Equation 4.12 means that the marginal propensity to invest must not only be equal to the marginal propensity to save. It must also, at the same time, be equal to the product of the aggregate growth rate and the incremental capital output ratio (or, alternatively, substituting $1/\varrho$ for v, it must be equal to the ratio of the aggregate growth rate to the social rate of return on investment).

As can be seen from exhibit 4.1, both these necessary conditions hold in the case of an economic system like the Alpha economy, that is proceeding along the steady-state growth path given by the Harrod-Domar formula (what Harrod, using a somewhat different notation, termed his "fundamental equation"). The two conditions hold, however, not because any behavioral relationship integral to the model ensures that the necessary amount of investment will be forthcoming in each and every subsequent time period. Rather the two conditions are satisfied simply because it is assumed that they are satisfied. This can be seen by examining more closely the logic of the model, as traced out in exhibit 4.1.

The $11 billion increase in the level of national income that occurs during the first period will, given the value of s, lead to $3.6 billion in additional savings. But what reason is there to believe that this $3.6 billion in additional savings will be matched by $3.6 billion in additional investment? The answer to this question is that there is nothing within the model itself to ensure so felicitous a result. The amount of additional investment needed in time period 1 to match the growth of savings is simply assumed to occur—as is true of the $4.1 billion in additional investment needed in time period 2, the $4.4 billion in additional investment needed in time period 3, etc.

It was Harrod's doubts that the requisite amounts of ever greater additional investment would be carried out in each and every subsequent time period that led him to view his model as explaining why continuous, uninterrupted growth was unlikely to be observed in the case of an advanced market economy. Harrod's point was that, given the volatility of business investment, a steady-state rate of expansion was all but precluded. This conclusion served as the basis for what Harrod termed the "knife-edge" problem.

As can be seen from exhibit 4.1, only a single constant rate of growth of investment (which must necessarily be equal to the rate of growth of savings and of aggregate output) is consistent with the continuous, uninterrupted expansion of the economy. Just the slightest decline in investment below the necessary rate of growth of that variable, Harrod pointed out, will lead to a subsequent fall in output and, with the expectations upon which even that level of investment was based being disappointed, to a further cumulative decline in investment and output. On the other hand, even the slightest rise in investment, because of the effect it is likely to have on output and business confidence, will lead to a disproportionate—and unsustainable—rise in investment and the level of economic activity. The economic system is, then, according to Harrod, poised on a "knife-edge," with the odds strongly against the economy being able to maintain its macrodynamic balance as the twin effects of business investment on the rate of expansion are felt. If the economy does not enter into a cyclical downturn immediately, based on the fact that aggregate demand is unable to keep pace with the growth of supply capacity, then it is likely to be expanding at a rate which, given the inability of aggregate supply to keep pace with the growth of demand, will lead to a downturn at some later point in time. Whether an advanced market economy is in fact so unstable is a question that will be taken up more systematically beginning in part 4 of this chapter. The point to be noted here is that, for Harrod, the warranted growth rate, as determined by equation 4.9, is not a growth path that the economic system is likely to actually follow but rather only a hypothetical growth path—the dividing line between too slow and too rapid a rate of expansion. In Harrod's view, the volatility of business investment all but precludes the economic system from actually following any such steady-state growth path.

Harrod's point about a market economy being poised on a knife-edge can perhaps be better understood by substituting, at any point along the growth path traced out in exhibit 4.1, a different level of investment other than one equal to the amount of savings that is currently being generated, and then seeing what effect this different level of investment has on the Alpha economy's expansion path. If, for example, the amount of investment during time period 2 were to be only $36.6 billion (the same as during the previous time period), instead of equaling the $40.7 billion in savings that would be generated with the national income rising to $111 billion, then the flow of savings will exceed the amount of business investment. With the Alpha economy thereby displaced from the steady-state growth path traced out in exhibit 4.1 because the level of investment and hence the level of aggregate demand is insufficient to sustain the warranted growth rate, two quite separate adjustment processes are likely to ensue. One of these is the adjustment process associated with the cash-flow feedback effect described in the preceding chapter.

With *ex ante* savings equal to $40.7 billion and therefore greater than the $36.6 billion in investment that will be carried out in time period 2, business firms are likely to experience a decline in sales, followed by a rise in their inventory/sales ratios. They can be expected to respond by cutting back on production and, in this way, causing both the national product and the national income to decline. As the national income declines, so too will savings until it no longer exceeds the $36.6 billion in investment being carried out by business firms. In this way, both the level of savings and the level of aggregate output will adjust to whatever happens to be the amount of investment occurring in that period. Conversely, if the amount of investment in time period 2 were to be $42 billion, thereby exceeding *ex ante* savings by $1.3 billion, then business firms would experience a rise in sales, followed by a decline in their inventory/sales ratios. They would almost certainly respond by increasing their levels of production and, in this way, causing both the national product and the national income to rise as well. As the national income rose, so too would savings until they matched the $42 billion in investment being carried out by business firms. In this way, again, both the level of savings and the level of aggregate output can be expected to adjust to whatever happens to be the amount of investment (see chapter 3, sections 2.3 and 2.5).

If the cash-flow feedback effect were the only adjustment process that needed to be taken into account once the amount of business investment either fell short of or exceeded the amount of *ex ante* savings, then tracing out the subsequent growth path of an economic system like Alpha's would not present so much of a problem. While the growth path would no longer be a balanced, steady-state one, it could still be readily enough determined: The economy's expansion over time would simply match the erratic path of business investment itself. Indeed, there would be no need to elaborate on the basic Keynesian model presented in the preceding chapter. The long-period rate of expansion could be explained as simply the sequence of short-period movements brought about by whatever happened to be the amount of business investment in each successive time period. There is, however, a second adjustment process which is likely to ensue whenever the amount of *ex ante* savings is not matched by business investment—one that has not yet been described. This is the adjustment process associated with what economists term the "accelerator" effect. Once this second adjustment process is taken into account, the economy's subsequent growth path becomes more difficult to trace out. Indeed, the accelerator effect as an endogenous response lends support to Harrod's view that an advanced market economy is poised on a "knife edge," with the warranted growth rate simply the hypothetical dividing line between too slow and too rapid a rate of expansion.

4.1.3 The accelerator effect

The dynamic adjustment process previously identified as the cash-flow feedback effect can be expected to ensue whenever *ex ante* savings diverge from the business sector's planned expenditures on new plant and equipment (or whenever, more generally, total discretionary funds are not matched by total discretionary expenditures). As the second step in that causal sequence, business firms can be expected to respond to any change in their inventory/sales ratio by adjusting their levels of production to match the level of sales (see chapter 3, section 2.3). This adjustment of production to the current level of sales has a further implication, however. It means that the current output relative to potential output, or capacity, will change. That is, the rate of capacity utilization within the enterprise sector will be affected, with this rate of capacity utilization, Cap, falling as output declines and rising as output increases.

The parallel effect of the change in sales on the rate of capacity utilization is usually ignored in economic analysis because it is assumed that firms have no excess, or reserve, capacity. In the conventional microeconomic models, firms consist of but a single plant—which is then used more or less intensively. Any change in the amount of productive capacity within an industry requires either the entry of new firms or the exit of older, already established firms. Within this framework, the notion of excess, or reserve, capacity has no meaning—except perhaps to describe firms which, because of their technologically obsolescent plants, are in the process of being forced out of business. As we shall see, however, it is the practice of business firms—especially the megacorps which dominate the oligopolistic sector—to maintain a certain amount of reserve capacity so as to be able to handle any fluctuations in demand (see chapter 5, section 3.2). Moreover, it is the practice of these firms to add continuously to their productive capacity by constructing new plants, or plant segments, in line with what is perceived to be the secular growth of sales. Rather than waiting until they are caught short without sufficient capacity to satisfy the current level of demand—thereby risking a loss of market share—they try to anticipate what will be the growth in the demand for their product as part of the exercise they go through before deciding on a capital spending program for the next year (see chapter 7, section 2.1).

As a result of this practice, any reduction in output following a decline in sales will, if it continues beyond a certain point, leave business firms with a certain amount of excess capacity—or more reserve capacity than they would like to have. (The evidence for this will be the decline in the actual operating rate below the average, or standard, operating rate.) Conversely, any increase in output beyond the same point, due to a rise in sales, will leave business firms with less reserve capacity than they are accustomed to maintaining. In either case, whether the rate of capacity utilization is falling or rising, firms are likely to reconsider their capital spending plans for the next period. If the actual operating rate is less than the standard operating rate, the likelihood is that firms will decide to slow down and/or reduce their investment outlays while if the actual operating rate exceeds the standard rate, the likelihood is that they will decide to speed up and/or increase their investment in new plant and equipment. What this implies is that, contrary to what is assumed in the basic Keynesian model (see chapter 3, section 1.2), investment is not independent of the level of aggregate demand as measured by Y—at least not when the analysis is extended beyond just a single time period. Rather, as was suggested in the preceding subsection, one needs to be able to determine the marginal propensity to invest, a, no less than the marginal propensity to consume, b (the complement of, or 1 less than, the marginal propensity to save, s). Economists use the term "accelerator" to denote the marginal propensity to invest, and this is how it will be referred to from this point on. However, one must not forget that what is really meant when that term is used is the marginal propensity to invest.

Economists sometimes fall into the error of viewing the accelerator, a, as a necessary technical relationship, dependent on the value of the incremental capital-output ratio, v. It is true, of course, that the value of v will determine the amount of investment that business firms will need to have carried out in some previous period so that supply capacity will have increased by a certain amount in the interval. For example, in order to have the additional capacity needed to produce the 11 percent increase in aggregate output, $123.2 billion, shown in exhibit 4.1 for time period 2, the amount of investment in time period 1 would have had to be $36.6 billion. But this does not ensure that business firms will actually carry out that much investment in time period 1—no more than it ensures that business firms will carry out the $40.7 billion in investment that is required in time period 2, the $45.1 billion that is required in time period 3, etc. so that the Alpha economy can remain on that steady-state growth path. Moreover, if there should happen to be any reserve capacity, the Alpha economy can increase input by 11 percent in any of those periods even without the requisite amount of investment in the previous period. The fact is that, while the value of the incremental capital-output ratio is fixed by the nature of the technology being employed (see below, chapter 5, sections 5.2 and 5.3, for a further elaboration of this point), the accelerator is free to take any value. It depends solely on how business firms decide to respond to the change in sales which they are experiencing. In other words, the accelerator is a behavioral relationship, one that needs to be determined empirically, without any necessary relationship, at least in the short period, to the value of v. Indeed, this is how the accelerator will be viewed when it is examined, along with other models of investment, in chapter 7.

What can be said at this point, even without knowing the precise value of a, is that the relationship between a change in sales and the subsequent response by business firms, insofar as their capital outlays are concerned, is likely to be a positive one. When, following a rise in sales, firms decide to increase their output, this will necessarily mean a higher rate of capacity utilization. Firms can then be expected to step up the rate at which they are expanding their capacity through investment in new plant and equipment. Conversely when, following a decline in sales, firms decide to reduce their output, this will necessarily mean a lower rate of capacity utilization. Firms can then be expected to slow down their rate of investment. One can therefore posit the following four-step sequence of events as the counterpart, on the supply side, of the adjustment mechanism operating on the demand side when, with investment no longer equal to savings, a disequilibrium situation arises:

1. $\Delta I \neq \Delta S \longrightarrow \Delta$sales and hence Δ(inventory/sales)
2. Δ(inventory/sales) $\longrightarrow \Delta$production and hence Δoutput

3. Δoutput ⟶ Δ(Cap)
4. Δ(Cap) ⟶ ΔI next period

The response on the supply side will thus be a two-fold one: first, a change in output (based on the change in sales and the change in the inventory/sales ratio) and then, second, a change in capital outlays, or investment, based on the change in the rate of capacity utilization, Cap. It is the second of these two responses that produces an accelerator effect, as part of the dynamic adjustment process on the supply side, which is separate and distinct from the adjustment taking place on the demand side via the cash-flow feedback effect.

As a result of this accelerator effect, investment in the next period will be greater if sales and hence the level of national income have risen in the previous period. (Investment will, of course, be lower if sales and the national income have fallen in the previous period.) The greater amount of investment in the next period will permit the necessary adjustment so that the aggregate supply condition for continuous economic expansion—namely, that I be equal to G—can eventually be satisfied. That same increase in investment, however, will not necessarily satisfy the aggregate demand condition for continuous economic expansion—namely, that I be equal to Ṡ. It will depend on how great is the increase in investment compared with the *ex ante* increase in savings. It will, in other words, depend on the value of a relative to s.

Indeed, if a is less than s—as would be the case, for example, if investment in time period 2 were to be $36.6 billion rather than the $40.7 shown in exhibit 4.1—then the reduction in the growth rate during that period (it will fall to zero in this case) will be followed in the next period, because of the accelerator effect, by a decline in investment (below $40.7 billion) which will then lead, via the multiplier and cash-flow feedback effects, to a contraction of the economy (that is, to a negative growth rate). Alternatively, in the opposite situation that can be posited, with a greater than s—as would be the case, for example, if investment were to be $42.0 billion in time period 2 rather than $40.7 billion—the rate of expansion will exceed the warranted rate of 11 percent, which is possible if there is any excess, or reserve, capacity. This greater-than-warranted growth rate, to the extent it means that firms are left with less reserve capacity than they would like to have, will cause them to step up their rate of investment in new plant and equipment in the next time period, with the combined multiplier and cash-flow feedback effect of this increased growth of investment leading to a still more rapid rate of economic expansion. Only if a is equal to s—as it would be if investment in the second time period, as shown in exhibit 4.1, were actually $41.7 billion—will the *ex ante* growth of savings be matched by the actual increase in investment so that not just the necessary aggregate demand condition but also the necessary aggregate supply condition will be satisfied, thereby permitting the Alpha economy to continue expanding, uninterruptedly, at the warranted growth rate given by the Harrod-Domar formula.

The accelerator, then, normally operates to reinforce whatever thrust has been given to the economy by the change in business investment and/or the other types of autonomous expenditures, whether that thrust is below, above or exactly in line with the warranted growth rate. Indeed, this is the basis for the type of combined multiplier-accelerator model that will subsequently be developed in this text in elaboration of the Harrod-Domar model. There is, however, one set of circumstances under which the normal accelerator response will be truncated and perhaps even nullified altogether. This is when, for lack of the necessary supply capacity, a change in aggregate demand is not followed by a change in aggregate output, or supply, as is normally the case.

With investment increasing by more than $4.1 billion in the second time period, there are thus two possibilities insofar as the Alpha economy is concerned, depending on whether or not the economy at that point has any reserve capacity. If all of the capacity, including any addition to capacity from the $36.6 billion that was invested during the preceding period, is required to produce the $123.2 billion of national income in time period 2, then any increase in investment in excess of $4.1 billion can only be at the expense of consumption. If investment increases, for example, by $5.4 billion instead of $4.1 billion, then consumption will rise in the second period by only $6.8 billion rather than $8.1 billion. Thus, because of the limit on aggregate supply that the amount of existing capacity imposes, consumption will fall short, by $1.3 billion, of the $82.5 billion shown in exhibit 4.1 for time period 2, and the rate at which consumption is increasing will be less than the 11 percent required to maintain the economy on its warranted growth path. Eventually, reflecting the need of business firms to adjust their capital spending plans to the growth in the demand for their product, investment will have to be lowered as well to match the rate at which consumption is increasing, and when this happens the combined multiplier, cash-flow feedback and acclerator effects will place the economy on a downward path of contraction.

If, however, the economic system has excess capacity, then the national income in the second time period can increase to more than $123.2 billion. The level of national income will then depend solely on the amount of business investment. With investment equal to $42 billion and consumption equal to $82.5 billion, the national income will in fact rise to a level of $124.5 billion, a growth rate equal to 12.2 percent. If this higher growth rate leads to an even more rapid rise in investment, then the aggregate growth rate will continue to accelerate—until the limit on aggregate supply that is set by the amount of productive capacity is reached, at which point the alternative scenario, based on the absence of any reserve capacity, will become the operative one. In either case, a rate of expansion greater than the warranted growth rate cannot be maintained, at least for long.

Moreover, just as a rate of expansion greater than the warranted growth rate cannot be maintained for long, so too a rate of expansion less than the warranted rate cannot long be sustained. This can be seen from the first example that was given when, in time period 2, investment falls below \$40.7 billion. In both cases, it is the combined multiplier, cash-flow feedback and accelerator effects that, once both the necessary aggregate demand and aggregate supply conditions are no longer being satisfied, cause the economy to be displaced from the steady-state growth path given by the Harrod-Domar formula.

4.1.4 The necessary conditions for continuous expansion

The steady-state rate of expansion given by the Harrod-Domar formula is an even more precarious one than has so far been indicated. The warranted growth rate, it turns out, is predicated on at least three additional assumptions, or necessary conditions. One is that the same relative composition of final demand be maintained as the economy expands. This can be termed the sectoral balance condition. In the Harrod-Domar model such a condition is easily satisfied, given the other properties of the model, since final demand is represented by only two aggregates, consumption and investment. All that is required is that these two aggregates increase at the same constant rate each period (which, as can be seen from exhibit 4.1, they do as long as the rate of growth of investment remains unchanged). In the disaggregated growth model that will be developed beginning in the next chapter, this condition is not so easily satisfied. Either all the different components of both consumption and investment must increase at the same rate or, since this is unlikely to happen in the face of changing technology and tastes, any disproportionate increase in one component must be offset by a less than proportionate increase in some other component so that the two aggregates, C and I, will continue to increase at the same constant rate. Moreover, when the model is extended to cover more than just the enterprise and household sectors, it is not only C and I which must grow at the same constant rate but also any output flowing to those other sectors, for example, to the government as public consumption.

The second further condition that must be satisfied if the rate of economic expansion is to be continuous and uninterrupted is that the price of each item being produced to satisfy final demand must be sufficient to cover the cost of production. This can be termed the necessary value condition. Since the Harrod-Domar model does not include any explicit price variables, it is difficult to discuss the necessary value condition within the context of that model. Indeed, the neglect of prices is one of the several limitations of the Harrod-Domar model which the subsequent chapters of this text will attempt to overcome. Once the relevant set of prices has been incorporated into the model of growth, as they will be in chapter 6, the necessary value condition can then be explained more fully.

The third, and last, further condition that must be satisfied if the rate of economic expansion is not to be disrupted is that whatever serves as the means of payment must increase at the same rate as the value, in money terms, of aggregate output. This can be termed the necessary monetary condition. It means that the growth of real output, $\dot{G}$, and the growth in the price level, $\dot{P}$, must be matched by the growth of whatever serves as the means of payment, $\dot{M}$, plus whatever increase has occurred in the efficiency of effecting transations, V. Although the necessary monetary condition would thus appear to be the same as the equation of exchange upon which the quantity theory of money, and hence the monetarist mode of analysis, is based, one must keep in mind that, like the other conditions for continuous, uninterrupted expansion which have now been identified, the monetary condition is not a causal relationship. Rather, it is an equality which, if not satisfied, will set in motion some type of dynamic adjustment process such as those already described in connection with the aggregate demand and aggregate supply conditions. More will be said about the necessary monetary condition when, as part of a more general discussion of the monetary and financial constraints on economic expansion, the nature of credit money is explained in chapter 12. The monetary condition is mentioned here, along with the sectoral balance and value conditions, only to give a complete listing of all five conditions that must be satisfied if the warranted growth rate given by the Harrod-Domar formula is to be maintained. These five conditions are:

1) the aggregate demand condition (that $\dot{I}$ be equal to $\dot{S}$);
2) the aggregate supply condition (that $\dot{I}$ be equal to $\dot{G}$);
3) the sectoral balance condition (that $\dot{I}$ be equal to $\dot{C}$);
4) the value condition (that prices not be less than the costs of production); and
5) the monetary condition (that $\dot{M} + \dot{V} = \dot{G} + \dot{P}$).

Once it is realized that the first two of these necessary conditions requires that the marginal propensity to investment, a, be a constant (despite the considerable evidence that business investment is in fact quite volatile) and also, at the same time, equal both to the marginal propensity to save, s, and to the product of the growth rate, $\dot{G}$, and the incremental capital-output ratio, v, one can readily see why these two conditions are unlikely to be satisfied in practice—with the third condition not then likely to be satisfied either. Indeed, there is another assumption underlying the growth path traced out in exhibit 4.1 which has not yet even been mentioned. This is that the marginal propensity to save (and hence the marginal propensity to invest) must be equal to the average propensity—which is the opposite of the assumption made by Keynes (see chapter 3, section 1.1). To show that this is a necessary condition for any steady-state rate of expansion, one need only try to trace out a growth path, such as the one shown in exhibit 4.1, without assuming that the average propensity to save is equal to the marginal propensity to save—that is, by making the initial division of the national income between consumption and investment for time period 0 different from that based on the value of s. (As for whether the marginal and average propensities to save and consume are in fact the same, see chapter 9, section 2.2).

In light of how unlikely it is that the economy will be able to follow the steady-state growth path given by the Harrod-Domar formula, it might seem best to abandon, as some economists have urged, the concept of a warranted growth rate altogether. The concept will nonetheless be retained, and indeed made the starting point for the analysis of the growth process which follows, for two reasons:

First, the theoretical construct of a warranted growth rate may help explain the secular trends which can be observed historically. Even if the economy's actual growth path deviates significantly from the balanced, steady-state growth path that is implied by a warranted growth rate, the secular trends may be no different from what would be traced out if the economy were in fact following such a growth path. Thus the warranted growth rate given by the Harrod-Domar formula may be the rate at which, based on the value of s and v, the economy will actually expand over long periods of time (after any cyclical fluctuations in output and employment have been allowed for)—in which case the Harrod-Domar model may help to explain what determines the economy's secular rate of expansion. At least this is a possibility that needs to be considered and not simply dismissed out of hand.

Second, once it becomes clear that the necessary conditions for the economy to expand at the warranted growth rate are unlikely to be realized, the focus of the analysis can shift to what happens when those conditions are not satisfied. One can then attempt to model the subsequent adjustment process, and the cyclical fluctuations in output and employment which ensue, whenever the economy is displaced from the steady-state growth path implied by a warranted growth rate.

The adjustment process will of course differ, depending on which condition necessary for continuous, uninterrupted expansion is not being satisfied. As already indicated, if it is the aggregate demand condition that is not being satisfied, then the adjustment process based on the cash-flow feedback effect is the one that will come into play, with the growth of savings subsequently adjusting to the level of investment. If it is the aggregate supply condition that is not being satisfied, then the adjustment process based on the accelerator is the one that will come into play, with the growth of investment subsequently adjusting to the growth of aggregate output—unless some absolute supply bottleneck should be encountered first, in which case the usual supply response to a change in aggregate demand may be precluded. While the adjustment process associated with each of the other three necessary conditions for continuous, uninterrupted expansion cannot be adequately explained until the Harrod-Domar model is extended to include more than just two types of output along with a price vector and a monetary-financial sector, still the adjustment process that applies in each of those other cases can, for the sake of completeness, be briefly touched on here. If it is the sectoral balance condition that is not being satisfied, then the adjustment process based on the accelerator is again the one that will come into play, with the rate of growth of investment subsequently adjusting to the growth in the demand for all the various items of final consumption. If it is the value condition that is not being satisfied, then the adjustment process based on the pricing power of individual firms is the one that will come into play, with the firms either able to increase their prices or else forced to go out of business. Finally, if it is the monetary condition that is not being satisfied, then the adjustment process associated with credit rationing, falling asset values and/or higher interest rates will be the operative one.

Thus, once the parameters of the Harrod-Domar model and its underlying assumptions have been identified, the analysis can proceed in either of two ways. One approach involves varying the parameters of the Harrod-Domar model to see what difference this makes in terms of the steady-state growth path which is then traced out, as in exhibit 4.1. This is the comparative dynamics approach that will be adopted in part 2 of this chapter. The other approach involves relaxing one or more of the model's underlying assumptions to see what sort of non-steady-state growth path will then be traced out. However, to analyze this more likely growth path, one must turn to the type of disequilibrium model that was introduced toward the end of the last chapter. The model constructed must be capable of explaining what prevents the necessary conditions for continuous, uninterrupted expansion from being satisfied and thus what endogenous process is responsible for the initial deviation from the warranted growth rate. But it must also be capable of then replicating the type of cyclical pattern which characterizes the actual growth path of advanced market economies like that of the United States.

The latter type of model, it should be noted, shifts the analysis from the post-Keynesian long period, in which timeless growth models apply, to the post-Keynesian short period with its emphasis on the actual historical experience of market economies. However, these two quite different modes of analysis, long-period and short-period, should not be seen as being opposed to one another. Rather, as the subsequent parts of this chapter will attempt to demonstrate, the two approaches are complementary, with the analysis of alternative possible steady-state growth paths necessarily preceding, and thus laying the foundation for, the analysis of the economic system's cyclical movements.

4.2 Comparative Dynamics

A post-Keynesian long-period analysis attempts to identify the factors most directly responsible for the expansion of an economic system over time—with any short-period fluctuations in economic activity abstracted from, relying on one statistical device or another. This is done so the secular movements of the economy can be distinguished from the cyclical and the two then analyzed separately before taking into account the interaction between them.

The Harrod-Domar model, and the steady-state rate of expansion which the model gives rise to, is the starting point for a post-Keynesian long-period analysis. The model, to be sure, has serious limitations. It is based on a number of assumptions that, as pointed out in the preceding part of this chapter, are unlikely to be satisfied in practice. Moreover, it fails to take into account not only the short-period fluctuations in output and employment which are so conspicuous a part of the historical experience of actual market economy but also the institutional setting in which that growth, both secular and cyclical, occurs. Perhaps most serious of all, it provides no explanation of what keeps the subsequent uneven expansion of a market economy within certain bounds once the economy has been displaced from the steady-state growth path represented by the warranted growth rate. Nonetheless, once these limitations are frankly acknowledged and kept in mind, the model, by its very simplicity, serves to highlight the most important determinants of an economic system's secular rate of expansion. They are: 1) the rate of accumulation (as determined by the propensity to save, s), and 2) the social rate of return on investment, ϱ (the inverse of the incremental capital-output ratio, v). These two factors together are what, within the context of the Harrod-Domar model, determine an economic system's warranted growth rate, $\dot{G}_w$; and a change in either of these two parameters will place the economy on an alternative steady-state growth path.

In addition, if the concern is with the material standard of living at any subsequent point in time, a third factor becomes important. This is the initial endowment of capital, as reflected in the level of output, and hence the level of national income to which it gives rise. A change in this parameter, while not affecting the warranted growth rate, will place those who draw their material sustenance from the economic system on an alternative consumption path. (Should the marginal propensity to save differ from the average propensity, as Keynes argued it would, then a fourth factor becomes important. This is the initial level of consumption, which will then determine the beginning point on the consumption path that is then traced out.)

The post-Keynesian long-period analysis is based on what is known as comparative dynamics. This involves comparing two growing economies which are alike in every respect except one—with the difference represented by some parameter of the Harrod-Domar model. Whatever is the difference in the warranted growth rate of the two economies can then be attributed to the difference in the value of that parameter. In this way, as a sort of controlled thought experiment, one can determine the effect which that one factor has on an economic system's rate of expansion over time.

What distinguishes a comparative dynamic analysis from the more typical comparative statics approach is the fact that two separate economic systems are being examined simultaneously, each assumed to be expanding over time rather than producing just a fixed amount of output. While it might seem that the same purpose could be served by focusing on just a single expanding system, with a change then made in one of the model's parameters, this procedure would in fact violate the logic underlying the warranted growth rate and the steady-state rate of expansion which it implies. For with a change in any one parameter of the

Harrod-Domar model, the economy's steady-state expansion is likely, as was demonstrated in the preceding main section, to be punctuated by a cyclical movement of unknown amplitude and duration. It was Joan Robinson who, following Harrod's lead, showed how this complication could be avoided through the technique of comparative dynamics analysis.

4.2.1 The rate of accumulation

The rate of accumulation is the rate at which the economy's productive capacity is being increased through expenditures on new plant and equipment (as well as through any expenditures by the government on the economic infrastructure). It is thus equal to the rate of "capital formation" as that term is generally understood. In the case of the Alpha economy, whose expansion is tracked over 20 periods in exhibit 4.1, the rate of accumulation, based on the value of s, is 33 percent. A crucial assumption here, one that will continue to be made unless otherwise noted, is that the 33 percent of the national product which is thereby not available for consumption is then used, within one period, to expand productive capacity through investment in new plant and equipment. This rate of accumulation, together with an incremental capital-output ratio of 3, implies, within the context of the Harrod-Domar model, a warranted growth rate, $\dot{G}_w$, equal to 11 percent. One may then ask: What is the effect of varying the rate of accumulation? The answer can be seen by comparing the expansion path of the Alpha economy, as shown in exhibit 4.1, with the expansion path of the Beta economy which is traced out in exhibit 4.2. For in Beta, while all the other parameters are the same as in Alpha, the rate of accumulation, as given by the value of s, is only 10 percent.

The first important difference to note is that, in the case of the Beta economy, all the critical variables, including C and Y, expand by only 3.3 percent each period—in contrast to the 11 percent rate at which they increase in Alpha where the rate of accumulation is 33 percent. Thus, other things being equal, *a higher rate of accumulation will be accompanied by a higher rate of economic expansion*, and vice versa. This is one of the key propositions which emerges from a comparative dynamics analysis. The consequences of the higher growth rate in Alpha can be seen from exhibit 4.3, where the number of periods required to double the initial standard of living at alternative rates of expansion is shown. In Alpha the standard of living will, within a single generation of 20 years, increase eightfold from what it was initially whereas in Beta it will, over the same interval, increase only twofold. Were this the whole story, Alpha's expansion path would clearly be the preferable one—as indeed would be that of any economy with a higher rate of accumulation.

While the rate of expansion is higher in Alpha, the level of consumption, at least initially, is lower. Indeed, it is not until three periods have passed that the level of consumption in Alpha will reach the level it was to begin with in Beta, and

Exhibit 4.2
Twenty-Year Expansion Path of Beta Economy
(with $Y_0 = 100$, $C_0 = 90$, s = 0.10, v = 3)

Period	Y	ΔY	Ẏ	C	ΔC	Ċ	I	ΔI	İ
0	100.0	—	—	90.0	—	—	10.0	—	—
1	103.3	3.3	3.3%	93.0	3.0	3.3%	10.3	0.3	3.3%
2	106.8	3.5	3.3	96.1	3.1	3.3	10.7	0.4	3.3
3	110.3	3.5	3.3	99.3	3.2	3.3	11.0	0.4	3.3
4	114.0	3.7	3.3	102.6	3.3	3.3	11.4	0.4	3.3
5	117.8	3.8	3.3	106.0	3.4	3.3	11.8	0.4	3.3
6	121.7	3.9	3.3	109.6	3.5	3.3	12.2	0.4	3.3
7	125.8	4.1	3.3	113.2	3.6	3.3	12.6	0.4	3.3
8	129.9	4.1	3.3	116.9	3.7	3.3	12.9	0.3	3.3
9	134.2	4.3	3.3	120.8	3.9	3.3	13.4	0.5	3.3
10	138.7	4.5	3.3	124.8	4.0	3.3	13.8	0.4	3.3
11	143.3	3.3	3.3	129.0	4.2	3.3	14.3	0.5	3.3
12	148.1	4.8	3.3	133.3	4.3	3.3	14.8	0.5	3.3
13	153.0	4.9	3.3	137.7	4.4	3.3	15.3	0.5	3.3
14	158.1	5.1	3.3	142.3	4.6	3.3	15.8	0.5	3.3
15	163.4	5.3	3.3	147.1	4.8	3.3	16.3	0.5	3.3
16	168.8	5.4	3.3	152.0	4.9	3.3	16.8	0.6	3.3
17	174.5	5.7	3.3	157.0	5.0	3.3	17.4	0.6	3.3
18	180.3	5.8	3.3	162.2	5.2	3.3	18.0	0.6	3.3
19	186.3	6.0	3.3	167.7	5.5	3.3	18.6	0.6	3.3
20	192.5	6.2	3.3	173.2	5.5	3.3	19.2	0.6	3.3

not until five periods have passed that consumption in Alpha and Beta will finally be on a par with one another. The initially lower level of consumption in Alpha is the necessary consequence of having to divert resources from consumption into capital formation in order to achieve a higher rate of accumulation. Thus, *a higher rate of accumulation also implies a lower level of consumption, at least temporarily.* This is another key proposition which emerges from a comparative dynamics analysis. Eventually, of course, consumption levels, and therefore the material standard of living, will be greater in Alpha, the economy with the higher rate of accumulation. This eventual outcome points out the fundamental trade-off reflected in whatever choice is made about the rate of accumulation. This is the trade-off between present and future consumption.

It would seem a relatively easy matter for a society to place itself on a more rapid growth path. All that needs to be done, based on the Harrod-Domar formula, is increase the rate of accumulation as measured by s. For example, if Beta were to decide that it preferred Alpha's growth rate to its own, it would only

Exhibit 4.3
**Number of Years Required to Double Standard
of Living at Different Growth Rates**

Growth rate	Years
2	36
3	24
4	18
5	15
6	12
7	11
8	10
9	9
10	8
11	7
12	7

have to reapportion its national income between consumption and investment so that, instead of the ratio being 90–10, it was 67–33. This line of reasoning has given rise to the simplest type of exercise in development planning. The analyst, after having first determined in some manner the optimal, or desired, rate of economic expansion, then calculates the rate of accumulation that, given the overall incremental capital-output ratio, is needed to achieve that rate of expansion. In this type of exercise, the warranted growth rate given by the Harrod-Domar formula, $\dot{G}_w$, becomes the target, or desired output, variable and the rate of accumulation, as measured by s, becomes the instrumental, or key input, variable—with v serving as a parameter. The systems diagram of the model underlying the analysis then takes the following form:

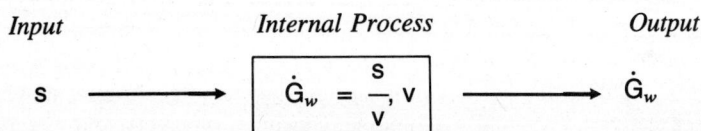

Input	*Internal Process*	*Output*
s $\longrightarrow$	$\dot{G}_w = \dfrac{s}{v}, v$	$\longrightarrow \dot{G}_w$

It turns out, however, that development planning, based on the overly simplistic Harrod-Domar formula, is not so easily carried out or executed.

First, there is the problem of determining the optimal rate of expansion. The problem arises because of the inescapable trade-off between present and future consumption. While it is true that a society, by choosing a higher rate of accumulation, will enjoy higher levels of consumption in the future, it is also true that the society will experience lower levels of consumption during some interim period.

Only if the economy's producing units, its enterprises, should happen to have excess, as distinct from just reserve, capacity (an unlikely situation in a less developed country) can the rate of accumulation be increased without having to reduce current consumption—and even then the need to cut back on current consumption so that capital formation can proceed more rapidly will only be postponed, not avoided. Thus within the framework of a long-period analyis, the possible existence of excess capacity can be ignored since it makes no difference, ultimately, in the argument. The higher rate of accumulation that a more rapid rate of expansion requires implies at least some sacrifice of current consumption.

What this means in the specific case of the Beta economy is that if a switch to Alpha's growth path is to be effected, consumption and hence the material standard of living will have to be cut back by more than a quarter, from $90 billion to $67 billion, and that it will take at least five periods before consumption will catch up to what it would otherwise have been. Is this sacrifice of current consumption levels justified? How, indeed, are the two—the immediate reduction in the standard of living and the higher standard of living that will be possible in the future—to be equated? Despite what some economists have argued, there is no objective answer to this question—or at least not one that any market mechanism is able to provide. The answer must instead come from outside the economic system as an output—that is, a decision—of the political system.

Those who are in a position to determine a society's expansion path are therefore confronted by a dilemma. Do they simply accept the current rate of expansion, whatever it may be—even zero—on the grounds that this is the society's preferred trade-off between present and future consumption? Or do they act to bring the rate of expansion more closely into line with what they believe to be the socially optimal rate? The first choice favors the *status quo*, limiting the hopes for the future, while the second choice lends itself to abuse, with the broader mass of society forced to make a sacrifice which, were they canvassed, they might well oppose and from which the elite holding political power are quite likely to succeed in exempting themselves. Still, the dilemma cannot be avoided. It even transcends the type of economic system. "Socialist," or, centrally planned, economies must face up to it the same as "capitalist," or market-oriented, ones, and developed countries, the same as less developed ones. It is just that the dilemma becomes all the more agonizing if consumption levels are already at or close to subsistence and/or the sacrifice will be borne largely by one generation while the rewards will accrue primarily to another.

But even if the optimal rate of economic expansion could somehow be ascertained through political mechanisms that enable a society to avoid both an intolerable *status quo* and the abuse of their position by the members of a political elite, there is still the problem of how to bring about the necessary change in the rate of accumulation. Two quite separate sources of difficulty immediately arise once the rate of accumulation that a particular growth path requires has been determined. First, the higher rate of accumulation implies a reduction in the level of consumption. This is the fundamental trade-off already identified. Whatever the increased value of s required, those whose standard of living will be adversely affected can be expected to offer resistance. While the technical aspects are easily enough handled—price and profit margins, along with tax rates, can usually be manipulated in such a way as to ensure the necessary decline in consumption—the political consequences are another matter. A reduction in the standard of living is likely to lead to social unrest, even more so than any failure of living standards to improve, thereby jeopardizing the continued rule of those holding power. Any decision about the value of s will therefore almost certainly have to be tempered by a consideration of the political consequences.

The second source of difficulty is that while a higher rate of accumulation implies a reduction in the level of consumption, the reverse argument does not hold. Just because the level of consumption has been reduced, it need not follow that the rate of accumulation has been increased. This derives from the fact that the rate at which income is not being spent on consumption goods, as measured by s, is not the same as the rate at which the capital stock is being augmented through investment in new plant and equipment. As pointed out in part 1 of this chapter, one of the critical assumptions underlying the Harrod-Domar model, namely, that whatever income is saved will be matched by investment outlays, does not necessarily hold. Usually, when this assumption is relaxed, it shifts the analysis from the post-Keynesian long period to the post-Keynesian short period. That is because, when savings are not matched by investment, cyclical movements of the economy can be expected. However, it is possible to relax the same assumption while still remaining in the long period.

For example, the value of s in Beta may actually be 0.33 rather 0.10. But if 23 cents out of every national income dollar collected by the government in taxes is then used to finance projects that are economically unproductive (such as weapons acquisition programs) then the result will be the same in terms of the rate of expansion, G_w, as though the value of s were only 0.10. Meanwhile, the material standard of living, as measured by the amount of resources available for current consumption, will be the same as that of an economy in which s is equal to 0.33. In other words, the citizens of Beta will bear the same immediate burden insofar as foregone consumption is concerned as those in Alpha but will not enjoy the same subsequent reward insofar as the growth of consumption, and hence the material standard of living, is concerned. Lest this example be thought of as far-fetched, it should be pointed out that the differential in growth rates between Japan and Germany on the one hand and the United States and Great Britain on the other hand during the post-World War II period is to be explained less by the share of national income accounted for by private consumption than by the share of national income accounted for by defense expenditures, a form of public consumption (see exhibit 4.6).

It is, of course, possible to redefine s so that public consumption as well as private consumption is first subtracted. Indeed, this is how s should be calculated. The point nonetheless remains a valid one: While the government can readily reduce household consumption by increasing the level of taxation, this is not the same as adding to the capital stock. Only when the resources thereby diverted from household consumption are used to expand productive capacity through the purchase and/or the installation of new plant and equipment—or used to expand the economic infrastructure through the construction of transportation, communication and other basic utility systems—can capital formation be said to have occurred.

The second part of the process, that of getting the new productive capacity in place and operating, is what is likely to defeat the government's best intentions. This is because it requires that the government act as an enterprise would, with all the organizational problems attendant upon that type of activity. In other words, it requires that the government act in ways that are quite different from the normal functioning of political institutions. At the very least, the government must be capable of operating as would the central headquarters of a large, diversified enterprise, or megacorp, determining which investment projects in different industries or sectors are to be financed from the funds obtained from tax revenues and/or public credit, and then following up to make sure that the desired results have been achieved (see chapter 7, section 3.6). It is hardly surprising, therefore, that higher taxes or whatever other means are employed to reduce private consumption seldom translate, even when that is the intention, into a higher rate of accumulation.

The argument about reduced household consumption not being the same as capital formation applies even more generally, however. Unless the enterprise sector itself is able to use the resources diverted from current consumption so as to add to productive capacity, the results will be little better, in terms of increased economic output, than from any similar effort by the government itself. This will be the case, for example, if the enterprise sector, as but one manifestation of the more general state of the social institutions which are found within a less developed country, lacks the necessary technical and organizational proficiency. It will even be the case, within a more advanced society, if the investment being carried out by enterprises is intended primarily to protect and reinforce market positions rather than to expand capacity and/or lower costs. In either of these cases, the incremental capital-output ratio will appear to be very high, thereby implying a very low social rate of return on investment. This last possibility points out the importance of the second key determinant of the long-period rate of economic expansion within a Harrod-Domar model, the social rate of return on investment.

4.2.2 The social rate of return on investment

The incremental capital-output ratio, v, is the other parameter in the Harrod-Domar model of steady-state, or long-period, expansion. The effect of varying v

Exhibit 4.4

Twenty-Year Expansion Path of Gamma Economy
(with $Y_0 = 100$, $C_0 = 90$, s = 0.10, v = 2.5)

Period	Y	ΔY	Ẏ	C	ΔC	Ċ	I	ΔI	İ
0	100.0	—	—	90.0	—	—	10.0	—	—
1	104.0	4.0	4.0%	93.6	3.6	4.0%	10.4	0.4	4.0%
2	108.2	4.2	4.0	97.4	3.8	4.0	10.8	0.4	4.0
3	112.4	4.2	4.0	101.2	3.8	4.0	11.2	0.4	4.0
4	116.9	4.5	4.0	105.2	4.0	4.0	11.6	0.4	4.0
5	121.6	4.7	4.0	109.4	4.2	4.0	12.1	0.5	4.0
6	126.5	4.9	4.0	113.8	4.4	4.0	12.6	0.5	4.0
7	131.5	5.0	4.0	118.4	4.6	4.0	13.1	0.5	4.0
8	136.8	5.3	4.0	123.1	4.7	4.0	13.6	0.5	4.0
9	142.3	5.5	4.0	128.0	4.9	4.0	14.2	0.6	4.0
10	148.0	5.7	4.0	132.2	5.2	4.0	14.8	0.6	4.0
11	153.9	5.9	4.0	138.5	5.3	4.0	15.3	0.5	4.0
12	160.1	6.2	4.0	144.0	5.5	4.0	16.0	0.7	4.0
13	166.5	6.4	4.0	149.8	5.8	4.0	16.6	0.6	4.0
14	173.1	6.6	4.0	155.8	6.0	4.0	17.3	0.7	4.0
15	180.0	6.9	4.0	162.0	6.2	4.0	18.0	0.7	4.0
16	187.2	7.2	4.0	168.5	6.5	4.0	18.7	0.7	4.0
17	194.7	7.5	4.0	175.3	6.8	4.0	19.4	0.7	4.0
18	202.5	7.8	4.0	182.3	7.0	4.0	20.2	0.8	4.0
19	210.6	8.1	4.0	189.6	7.3	4.0	21.0	0.8	4.0
20	219.1	8.5	4.0	197.2	7.6	4.0	21.9	0.9	4.0

instead of s can be seen by comparing the expansion path of Beta with that of Gamma, as shown in exhibit 4.4. Gamma differs from Beta only in that v equals 2.5 rather than 3. This means that the social rate of return on investment in Gamma, as measured by ϱ, is 40 percent rather than 33.3 percent. As a result of this one difference, the rate of expansion in Gamma is 4 percent compared with the 3.3 percent growth rate in Beta. Thus, other things being equal, *a lower incremental capital-output ratio (and thus a higher social rate of return on investment) leads to a higher rate of economic expansion.*

With this additional determinant of the long-period rate of economic expansion now explicitly allowed for, it follows that if Beta were to prefer Gamma's rate of expansion to its own, it would have two options. It could increase its rate of accumulation, as measured by s, from 10 to 12 percent, thereby needing to maintain only the present social rate of return on investment. Alternatively, it could increase the social rate of return on investment so that v fell from 3 to 2.5, with the rate of accumulation left unchanged. Insofar as achieving a particular warranted growth rate is concerned, the two options would lead to the same result. Nonetheless, the expansion path, as traced out in exhibits 4.2 and 4.4, would be different. While an increase in the rate of accumulation would require a one-time decline in the level of consumption, from $90 billion to $88 billion, an increase in the social rate of return on investment would not. Moreover, while consumption would thereafter grow at 4 percent whichever option was chosen, the initial decline in the level of consumption that is required if the rate of accumulation is to be increased would mean a lower base from which consumption would then grow (albeit at the same rate), and thus the one-time decline in the level of consumption would never be recovered. It is in this sense that the two options lead to quite different growth paths, at least insofar as the material standard of living is concerned. Clearly, were an increase in the social rate of return on investment as easily accomplished as an increase in the rate of accumulation, it would represent the more attractive policy option.

Unfortunately, an increase in the social rate of return on investment is even more difficult to achieve than an increase in the rate of accumulation. Both, it should be pointed out, are subject to asymptotic limits. Exhibit 4.5 gives the long-term growth rates for many of the OECD nations during a significant portion of the post-World War II period, together with the corresponding values of s and v. (The values shown for v are not derived independently but rather are calculated from the estimated values of $\dot{G}$ and s and therefore are only implicit estimates.) As can be seen from exhibit 4.5, no country was able to achieve a rate of accumulation, as measured by s, greater than 30 percent. Similarly, no country was able to bring its incremental capital-output ratio down to less than 3. This suggests that 33.3 percent may be the upper limit on the social rate of return on investment—just as 30 percent may be the upper limit on the rate of accumulation. Of course, within these limits, there have been significant differences among countries, both with regard to the rate of accumulation and with regard to the incremental capital-output ratio. For example, if Norway, with the second highest rate of accumulation, had had the same incremental capital-output ratio as Japan, the country with both the highest rate of accumulation and the lowest incremental capital-output ratio, its growth rate would have averaged 8.6 percent instead of the 4.2 percent actually realized. For that matter, if the United States had been able to realize the same social rate of return on investment, its growth rate, even without any increase in the rate of accumulation, would have been 5.8 percent instead of only 3.7 percent. A quick glance at exhibit 4.3 will indicate what this would have meant in terms of the improvement in the standard of living in those two countries. In truth, however, there is less scope for lowering the value of v, and thereby increasing the social rate of return on investment without having to reduce the standard of living, than these figures might suggest.

The aggregate figure for v is actually a weighted average of v for all the different sectors of the economy (see chapter 5, section 5.3). The value of v will therefore vary by sector, depending on how capital intensive, or mechanized, the

Exhibit 4.5
**Growth Rates and Savings Propensities
for a Selected Group of OECD Countries 1951–1970**

	$\dot{G}$	s	v
Japan	9.5	29.6	3.1
Germany	5.7	25.0	4.4
Italy	5.1	20.6	4.0
Netherlands	5.0	24.9	5.0
France	5.0	21.9	4.4
Canada	4.6	23.5	5.1
Belgium	4.4	18.8	4.3
Norway	4.2	26.7	6.4
United States	3.7	17.9	4.8
United Kingdom	2.7	16.9	6.3

Source: John Cornwall, *Modern Capitalism* (New York: St. Martin's Press, 1977), tables 2.1, 2.11.

method of production is. Thus one of the ways to hold down the aggregate figure is to manipulate, or bias, the composition of final demand so that less reliance has to be placed on sectors with above-average incremental capital-output ratios. For example, both transportation and housing are sectors where v is likely to be particularly high, and there is an observable tendency for less developed countries, especially at the onset of rapid industrialization, to skimp as much as possible on investment in those two sectors. Still, there are important differences, in terms of the consequences which such a strategy is likely to have, between the two sectors. Skimping on investment in transportation, especially freight, is likely to create a bottleneck situation which, unless eased or eliminated, will eventually stall the industrialization effort. Skimping on housing, however, only serves to reduce the real standard of living and therefore does not work against more rapid industrialization. On the contrary, by freeing up resources so that the enterprise sector's capital stock can be increased at the expense of the household sector, this policy actually abets the industrialization effort. Moreover, since the only consequence is that families are forced to put up with inferior housing for longer than they would prefer, the reduction in the real standard of living is not reflected in any official national income statistics. This is one of the deficiencies of those statistics, as a measure of economic welfare, that has already been alluded to (see chapter 2, section 2.6). The post-World War II experience of Japan illustrates the point. One reason for the low value of v shown in exhibit 4.5 for that country was undoubtedly the decision by its economic policy makers to discourage investment, not only in housing but also in other types of consumer-oriented services, such as retail distribution and health care.

Exhibit 4.6

**Growth Rates, Defense Outlays and Average Unemployment
Rates for a Selected Group of OECD Countries**

	G (1951–70)	Ratio, average defense outlays to aggregate output (1965–70)	Average unemployment rates (1961–73)
Japan	9.5	0.9	1.3
Germany	5.7	3.8	0.6
Italy	5.1	3.0	3.6
Netherlands	5.0	3.7	N.A.
France	5.0	4.7	2.2
Canada	4.6	2.7	5.2
Belgium	4.0	3.0	N.A.
United States	3.7	7.9	4.9
United Kingdom	2.7	5.3	3.6

Sources: John Cornwall, *op. cit.*, tables 2.1, 2.8; U.S. Arms Control Agency, *Report*, 1979.

Another reason for the low value of v for Japan was the virtually uninterrupted expansion of the Japanese economy during that period. As can be seen from exhibit 4.6, the two countries with the highest rate of growth between 1951 and 1970, Japan and Germany, were the two countries which, by largely avoiding any major cyclical downturns, were able to hold their unemployment rate well below that of the other OECD countries. On the other hand, two of the three countries with the highest average unemployment rates, the United States and the United Kingdom, experienced the lowest growth rates. This inverse relationship between the growth rate and the average unemployment rate is hardly surprising. A cyclical decline in economic activity will necessarily reduce the average rate of expansion over a given period, with the indirect effect being an increase in the average unemployment rate. Since the value of v in exhibit 4.5 has been calculated by dividing the savings rate, s, by the average growth rate, $\dot{G}$, a cyclical downturn in the level of economic activity will also lead to a higher value of v, with the implication being that the social rate of return on investment has fallen. Indeed, such an apparent decline in the social rate of return on investment is consistent with the fact that, coincidental with a cyclical downturn, the average rate of capacity utilization will fall and thus the realized return on the investment that has produced that capacity will also fall. Here one can see a possibility of being able to bring down the value of v, and thereby increase the social rate of return on investment, without having to reduce consumption, either overtly or otherwise. All that is required is to lower the average percentage of unutilized capacity (and of unutilized workers) over the cycle by minimizing the fluctuations in the level of economic activity. The chapters that follow are, in fact, intended to show how the social rate of return on investment can, in this way, be increased. For the moment, however, the focus must remain on the economy's secular, rather than its cyclical, movements.

Actually, once allowance is made for Japan's bias against investment in capital-intensive sectors and for the differentially greater cyclical movements of the U.S. and British economies, the values for v shown in exhibit 4.5 fall within a relatively narrow range—somewhere between 4, implying a social rate of return on investment equal to 25 percent, and 5, implying that ϱ equals 20 percent. To be sure, this is a significant range. The point, however, is that, just as there would appear to be an upper limit on the rate of accumulation, so too there appears to be a lower limit on the incremental capital-output ratio (and thus an upper limit on the social rate of return on investment). The reason why there might be such a lower limit becomes clearer once it is realized that, any cyclical fluctuations in output aside, the value of the incremental capital-output ratio depends on the nature of the technical progress that accompanies, and indeed underlies, economic growth.

A systematic examination of technical progress must wait until the next chapter. For now it need only be pointed out that, for v to fall below its current level, technical progress would have to go beyond just increased "mechanization." That is, it would have to involve more than just a greater amount of investment per worker. The new types of capital goods being acquired would have to be more efficient in their own right, meaning that they would have to be capable to producing more output relative to the investment required. This type of "hyper" technical progress is much more difficult to bring about, and indeed it is not clear how it can be achieved through any conscious design. It may well be that all a society can hope is to prevent v from rising. At least this is what the historical experience of the OECD countries would suggest. The best they have been able to do is to maintain a certain rate of growth of output per worker over time, this as a result of increased mechanization, while v, as nearly as can be determined, has remained unchanged. The value of v must therefore be viewed as being largely beyond the ability to the society to control, and it is for this reason that, in the above systems diagram of the Harrod-Domar model, v is treated as a parameter rather than as an instrumental variable.

4.2.3 The initial endowment of capital

Two economies may have the same rate of accumulation as measured by s, the same social rate of return on investment as measured by v, and therefore the same rates of expansion as given by the Harrod-Domar formula. Yet the material standard of living in the two economies, as measured by the level of consumption at any particular point in time, may be quite different. Compare, for example, the situation in the Delta economy, as represented in exhibit 4.7, with that of the Beta economy. As can be seen, the consumption level in Beta is only half that of Delta initially and remains so during each of the subsequent 20 periods. The reason for this difference in the material standard of living is the initial level of national income in Beta, which is only half that of Delta.

In exhibit 4.8, the levels of national income and of consumption in both Beta and Delta are plotted on a logarithmic scale and then connected to trace out the two economies' ''growth curves.'' In the case of each curve, the slope is equal to the rate of expansion—the value of G_w as determined by s and v—and the vertical intercept is equal to the initial level of national income. The latter, as can be seen, establishes the base from which any subsequent expansion proceeds. The usefulness of these growth curves is that they enable one to see at a glance which of the two possible factors—the relative rates of expansion or the relative base from which the expansion begins—accounts for any difference in the subsequent levels of national income (and of consumption) between any two economies. Comparing Beta's growth curve with Delta's, for example, one can see that the difference in subsequent income levels is due to the difference in the vertical intercepts, and thus to the difference in the initial levels of national income, since the slopes of the two curves, and hence the two economies' rates of expansion, are the same.

Why the initial level of national income in Beta should be only half that of Delta can readily be surmised. If real output in Beta is only half that of Delta, it necessarily follows (since everything else about the two economies, including the size of the labor force, is the same) that output per worker in Beta is also only half that of Delta. While differences in social organization may account for some of this gap in labor productivity between the two economies, the more important explanation is likely to be the size of the capital stock which, as a result of past investment, the two economies have available to them. Indeed, whatever differences there may be in social organization between the two societies are likely to be closely related to this difference in the size of the capital stock. One can therefore assume that Beta's capital stock at the beginning of the 20-period interval—and indeed each year thereafter—is only about half that of Delta. Even though it is not possible, as already pointed out, to measure the value of the capital stock independently of the aggregate output the capital stock is capable of producing, still one can be fairly certain that any difference in the levels of national income between two economies such as Beta and Delta will be due primarily to the difference in the accumulated stock of plant and equipment (as well as of economic infrastructure) which constitutes each economy's productive capacity. To the extent that Beta relies upon more labor-intensive, or less mechanized, methods of production—and with the same size labor force producing only half as much output, this is almost certain to be the case—its capital stock may in fact be even less than half that of Delta. Whatever may be the exact ratio, it is this difference in their respective capital endowments that is the reason for the difference in the initial levels of national income—and thus the reason for the difference in the level of national income and consumption between the two economies in each successive period. Indeed, given this difference in initial

Exhibit 4.7
Ten-Year Expansion Path of Delta
(with $Y_0 = 200$, $C_0 = 180$, $s = 0.10$, $v = 3$)

Period	Y	ΔY	$\dot{Y}$	C	ΔC	$\dot{C}$	I	ΔI	$\dot{I}$
0	200.0	—	3.3%	180.0	—	3.3%	20.0	—	3.3%
1	206.6	6.6	3.3	186.0	6.0	3.3	20.6	0.6	3.3
2	213.4	6.8	3.3	192.1	6.1	3.3	21.3	0.7	3.3
3	220.5	7.1	3.3	198.4	6.3	3.3	22.0	0.7	3.3
4	227.7	7.2	3.3	204.9	6.5	3.3	22.8	0.8	3.3
5	235.3	7.6	3.3	211.7	6.8	3.3	23.5	0.7	3.3
6	243.0	7.7	3.3	218.7	7.0	3.3	24.3	0.8	3.3
7	251.0	8.0	3.3	225.9	7.2	3.3	25.1	0.8	3.3
8	259.3	8.3	3.3	233.4	7.5	3.3	25.9	0.8	3.3
9	267.9	8.6	3.3	241.1	7.7	3.3	26.8	0.9	3.3
10	276.7	8.8	3.3	249.0	7.9	3.3	27.7	0.9	3.3
11	285.8	9.1	3.3	257.3	8.3	3.3	28.6	0.9	3.3
12	295.3	9.5	3.3	265.8	8.5	3.3	29.6	1.0	3.3
13	305.0	9.7	3.3	274.5	8.7	3.3	30.6	1.0	3.3
14	315.1	10.1	3.3	283.6	9.1	3.3	31.6	1.0	3.3
15	325.5	10.4	3.3	292.9	9.3	3.3	32.6	1.0	3.3
16	336.2	10.7	3.3	302.6	9.7	3.3	33.7	1.1	3.3
17	347.3	11.1	3.3	312.6	10.0	3.3	34.9	1.2	3.3
18	358.8	11.5	3.3	322.9	10.3	3.3	36.0	1.1	3.3
19	370.6	12.3	3.3	333.6	10.7	3.3	37.2	1.2	3.3
20	382.9	12.3	3.3	344.6	11.0	3.3	38.5	1.3	3.3

capital endowment, Beta can never hope to catch up with Delta—not as long as the rate of expansion in the two countries is the same. Thus, other things being equal, *a higher initial endowment of capital means a higher level of income (and consumption) in all subsequent periods.* (Exhibit 4.8 makes this point graphically.)

The initial endowment of capital is part of an economic system's historical legacy. Being the result of past investment decisions, it is something that, at least for the moment, cannot be changed. This does not mean, however, that a disparity in income that is the result of a lower initial endowment of capital cannot be overcome in time. For example, if Beta, by increasing its rate of accumulation from 10 to 33 percent, were to shift from its own expansion path to that of Alpha, the level of national income in Beta would be the same as in Delta ten periods later. Although the level of consumption in Beta would still be lower because of the higher rate of accumulation, even this gap would be closed within 14 periods after the shift to the more rapid growth path. Thus, *a higher rate of accumulation*

Exhibit 4.8

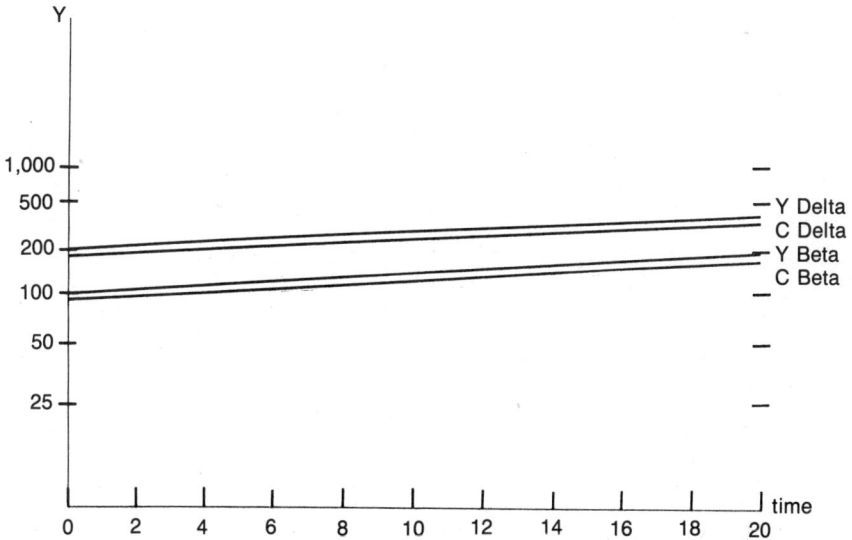

can, in time, offset a lower initial endowment of capital. This is illustrated in exhibit 4.9, where Alpha's growth curves, both for national income and consumption, have been added to those of Beta and Delta. Despite the lower vertical intercepts, Alpha's growth curves do eventually cross Delta's, and beyond these respective points, the levels of national income and consumption in Alpha (as well as in Beta if it were to shift to Alpha's growth path) exceed those in Delta.

For Beta to shift to Alpha's growth path, and thereby eventually overtake Delta, it must, as already pointed out, increase its rate of accumulation, with all the attendant sacrifice of current consumption and living standards which this implies. The sacrifice is measured by the downward shift of the vertical intercept for Beta's consumption curve from $90 billion to $67 billion. This 25 percent decline in the standard of living—indeed any decline in the material standard of living—is likely to prove socially traumatic. For Alpha, assuming that the $67 billion in initial consumption represents no departure from the historical growth path, there will be no trauma. But for Beta, since it has already achieved a higher material standard of living, the situation is quite different. While it might appear that increasing the social rate of return on investment, by lowering v, may be a better way for Beta to overtake Delta—one that would enable it to avoid the trauma of having to reduce its material standard of living—this is unlikely to be a real option for the reasons given above. An increase in the rate of accumulation and, with it, a reduction in the standard of living is, as a practical matter, the only way Beta can shift to Alpha's growth path (or some other more rapid growth path) and thereby eventually overtake Delta. It is for this reason that economic policy-makers, under pressure to eliminate any disparity in the material standard of

Exhibit 4.9

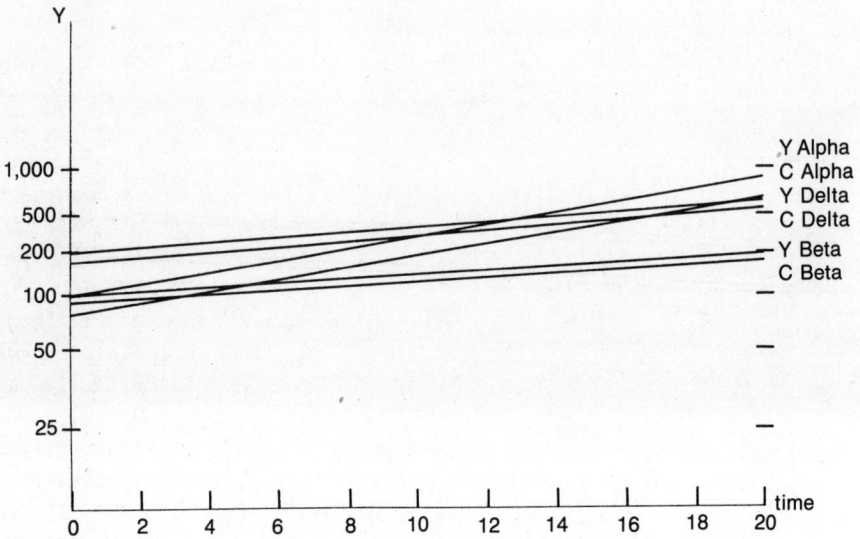

living due to a lower initial endowment of capital, face a dilemma.

4.2.4 Traumatic and nontraumatic accelerated growth

There is, it should be noted, an expansion path which, if followed, will enable Beta to overtake Delta without having to reduce its material standard of living. The expansion path, however, is a not a steady-state one. Take Eta's growth path, as shown in exhibit 4.10. In contrast to the situation in the other economies which have been tracked, Eta's critical variables do not all expand at the same constant rate, at least initially during what can be termed the "acceleration period." Instead, consumption is held constant at $90 billion and all of the increment in aggregate output is devoted to capital formation until the rate of accumulation, as measured by s, reaches the 33 percent needed to match Alpha's warranted growth rate of 11 percent. This occurs midway through time period 6. Up to that point, while the growth of consumption is zero, the growth of investment is 33 percent per period. The growth of the national income, meanwhile, increases each year until it reaches 11 percent. From then on, consumption, investment and the national income all grow at the same 11 percent as in Alpha. With Eta proceeding along this growth path, its level of national income exceeds that of Delta by the end of time period 14 and its level of consumption, by time period 18. (See Eta's growth curve, added to the others, in exhibit 4.11.) Thus Beta, by emulating Eta, would be able to overtake Delta without having to suffer the trauma of a reduction in its material standard of living. It would only have to wait longer to catch up with Delta.

Exhibit 4.10
Twenty-Year Expansion Path of Eta Economy

Period	Y	ΔY	Ẏ	C	ΔC	Ċ	I	ΔI	İ
0	100.0	—	—	90.0	—	—	10.0	—	—
1	103.3	3.3	3.3%	90.0	0	0	13.3	3.3	33.0%
2	107.7	4.4	4.3	90.0	0	0	17.7	4.4	33.0
3	113.5	5.8	5.4	90.0	0	0	23.6	5.9	33.0
4	121.4	7.9	7.0	90.0	0	0	31.4	7.8	33.0
5	131.9	10.5	8.6	90.0	0	0	41.9	10.5	33.0
6	145.9	14.0	10.6	97.3	7.3	8.1%	48.6	6.7	16.0
7	161.9	16.0	11.0	108.0	10.7	11.0	53.9	5.3	11.0
8	179.8	17.9	11.0	119.9	11.9	11.0	59.9	6.0	11.0
9	199.5	19.7	11.0	133.1	13.2	11.0	66.5	6.6	11.0
10	221.5	22.0	11.0	147.7	14.6	11.0	73.8	7.3	11.0
11	245.8	24.3	11.0	164.0	16.3	11.0	81.9	8.1	11.0
12	272.9	27.1	11.0	182.0	18.0	11.0	90.9	9.0	11.0
13	302.9	30.0	11.0	202.0	20.0	11.0	100.9	10.0	11.0
14	336.2	33.3	11.0	224.2	22.2	11.0	112.0	11.1	11.0
15	373.2	37.0	11.0	248.9	24.7	11.0	124.3	12.3	11.0
16	414.3	41.1	11.0	276.3	27.4	11.0	138.0	13.7	11.0
17	459.9	45.6	11.0	306.7	30.4	11.0	153.2	15.2	11.0
18	510.5	50.6	11.0	340.4	33.7	11.0	170.1	16.9	11.0
19	566.7	56.2	11.0	377.8	37.4	11.0	188.8	18.7	11.0
20	629.0	62.3	11.0	419.4	41.6	11.0	209.6	20.8	11.0

Eta's growth curve, as shown in exhibit 4.11, represents but one of many "nontraumatic" accelerated growth paths which an economy can follow. The critical choices are: (1) the length of time consumption is to be "frozen" at the existing level; and (2) the differential between the growth of investment and the growth of consumption once the latter is "unfrozen." Eta's expansion path, since it involves no growth of consumption at all until the desired rate of accumulation has been achieved (thereby maximizing the differential between the growth of investment and the growth of consumption throughout the acceleration period), simply falls at one extreme along a continuum. At the other end of the continuum is a growth path which involves only a slightly higher rate of growth of investment than of consumption, with consumption frozen only long enough to achieve that differential between the two growth rates. A shift from the one extreme to the other reduces the delay before the material standard of living again begins to improve. However, it also increases the time required to overcome the disparity in the initial endowment of capital. Thus, even with the more limited set of options that exist for avoiding the trauma of a reduction in the standard of living if

Exhibit 4.11

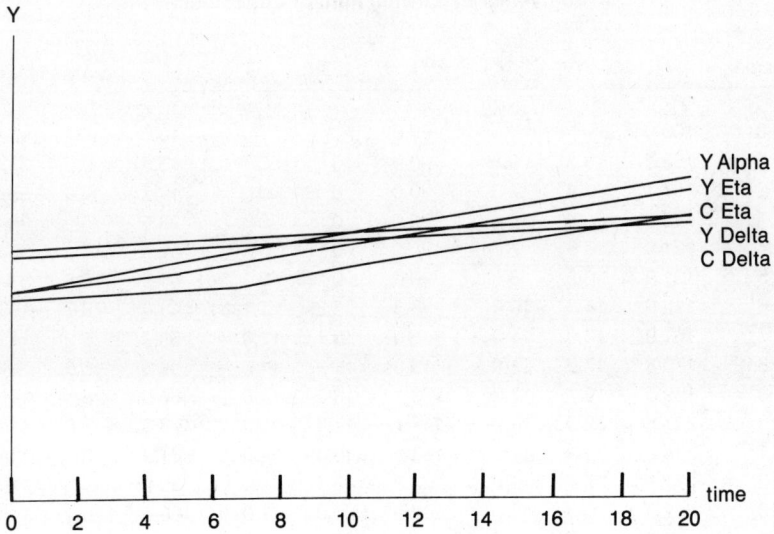

the rate of growth is to be increased, there is still a choice to be made between higher levels of consumption sooner or higher levels of consumption later, and thus a trade-off between present and future material standards of living.

Actually, for Beta, the difference between emulating Alpha and emulating Eta is not a difference between an accelerated and a nonaccelerated growth path but rather a difference between a traumatic and a nontraumatic acceleration period. To shift from its own growth path to that of either Alpha or Eta, Beta cannot avoid an acceleration period of some sort. It is just that by moving at once to Alpha's growth path, all of the acceleration—and trauma—occurs within a single period, and it is this immediate and abrupt shift to a higher rate of accumulation which requires that the standard of living be not just lowered but lowered sharply. By opting instead for Eta's growth path—or even some less extreme variant—Beta would be able to stretch out the period of acceleration and would thereby be spared both a decline in the level of consumption and the social trauma associated with any such fall in the material standard of living.

Still, in choosing Eta's expansion path over Alpha's, Beta would only avoid a reduction in the material standard of living. It would not avoid a period of accelerated growth. And this period of accelerated growth would mean, as it does in Eta's case, that the necessary equality between the growth of income, consumption and investment would not hold and thus that the aggregate demand, the aggregate supply and the sectoral balance conditions for continuous, uninterrupted expansion would not be satisfied. It seems unlikely, therefore, that any growth path traced out by Beta in imitation of Eta would be a balanced steady-state one. Rather it is likely to involve some sort of cyclical movement, or fluctuation. What the actual growth path will then be cannot be determined until the discussion has been broadened, as it will be shortly, to encompass the short period as well as the long. All that need be noted for now is that, in calculating the rate at which output in Beta would then increase—including the output of consumption goods—one would have to take into account that likely cyclical movement. Indeed, this is the problem of how to model the "traverse" from one steady-state growth rate to another. (The problem will not be taken up, in any systematic way, until the government's ability to place the economy on a different secular growth path can be analyzed. See chapter 10, part 4.)

While it might seem that Beta could avoid any cyclical fluctuation by opting instead for Alpha's growth path, this would be true only if one could assume that the necessary shift to a higher rate of accumulation, with s equal to 0.33 rather than 0.10, will occur instantaneously. Otherwise, there would be some interval, even within the one period, during which the growth of investment would be temporarily greater than the growth of aggregate output, and thus some interval during which the aggregate demand, aggregate supply and sectoral balance conditions were temporarily not being satisfied. It is wrong, however, to assume that any shift to a higher rate of accumulation, particularly one as pronounced as would be required if Beta were to emulate Alpha, could occur instantaneously. To do so is to confuse historical time, during which events unfold in sequence, with logical time.

The growth path characterized by Beta's initial conditions and a subsequent rate of accumulation equal to Alpha's does have some heuristic value in that it represents an extreme, or limiting, case within the broader category of traumatic accelerated growth periods—just as Eta's growth path represents a limiting case within the broader category of nontraumatic accelerated growth periods. The other traumatic accelerated growth periods may be more feasible in that they do not require an instantaneous shift to the higher rate of accumulation. Still, they are traumatic in that they require some immediate reduction in the material standard of living.

Important as the distinction between traumatic and nontraumatic growth paths may be, the distinction between accelerated and nonaccelerated growth paths is just as important. Only the latter involve the type of steady-state rate of expansion on which the Harrod-Domar model is based. The former, whether represented by Eta's growth path or by some other noninstantaneous shift from Beta's to Alpha's rate of accumulation, include a period of accelerated growth which is likely to be the beginning of some cyclical movement of the economy. This likely cyclical movement takes on added significance once it is realized that only by switching to an accelerated growth path can an economy like Beta overcome any disparity in the material standard of living of its citizens, compared with that of other countries, due to a lower initial endowment of capital.

4.2.5 A look at the empirical evidence

The preceding discussion of the factors determining an economy's steady-state rate of expansion, together with any change in the material standard of living over time, has identified certain key propositions. They are as follows:

1.   A higher rate of accumulation, s or $\Delta I / \Delta Y$ (as approximated by I/Y), will be accompanied by a higher rate of expansion for the economy as a whole as measured by $\dot{G}_w$.

2.   A higher rate of accumulation also implies a lower level of consumption, C, at least initially.

3.   A lower incremental capital-output ratio, v (and thus a higher social rate of return on investment, ϱ) leads to a higher growth rate.

4.   A higher initial endowment of capital, as reflected by a higher initial level of income, Y_0, means a higher level of income (and of consumption) in all subsequent periods.

5.   A higher rate of accumulation can, in time, offset a lower initial endowment of capital.

The intent in this section is to examine the extent to which these propositions are consistent with the empirical evidence. Since the propositions are derived from a comparative dynamics analysis, the relevant empirical evidence is that which pertains to the experience of different national economies over long periods of time, particularly the experience of the advanced market economies which belong to the OECD community of nations.

Historically, these countries have experienced not steady-state rates of expansion but rather, expansion marked by pronounced cyclical movements. The concept of a warranted growth rate, $\dot{G}_w$, would therefore seem inapplicable. Nonetheless, as an approximation of the warranted growth rate, one can examine the secular growth rate, $\dot{G}_s$, derived by using the appropriate statistical technique to fit a trend line to the data. The secular growth rate derived in this manner will be lower than the warranted growth rate to the extent that an economy's expansion is punctuated by cyclical downturns, and it will be higher than the warranted growth rate to the extent that the current secular rate is unsustainable. From this it follows that, the smaller the deviation from the trend line, the more closely the secular growth rate will approximate the warranted growth rate. In any case, when it comes to examining the long-period empirical evidence, there is no alternative to using $\dot{G}_s$ as a proxy for $\dot{G}_w$—at least until all cyclical fluctuations in economic activity have, through a better understanding of the macrodynamic relationships and the implementation of the appropriate policies, been eliminated. (With cyclical fluctuations eliminated, $\dot{G}_s$ will be equal to $\dot{G}_w$.) This is the approach that will be followed throughout the rest of the text whenever an empirical estimate of the warranted growth rate is needed. The treatment of investment and the other variables which are critical to a long-period analysis will be similar: A secular growth rate will be calculated by using the same statistical technique to factor out the cyclical movements.

The strong correlation between the rate of accumulation, as measured by s, and the rate of economic expansion, as measured by $\dot{G}_s$, can readily be seen from the data presented in exhibit 4.5. John Cornwall, in an important work examining the reasons for the differential growth rates among the OECD countries, has further refined the analysis based on these types of data. (See his *Modern Capitalism*, St. Martin's Press, 1977.) Drawing upon earlier studies showing that the aggregate growth rate is closely related to the growth of the manufacturing sector, Cornwall sought to explain what determines the growth of the manufacturing sector and hence of the economy as a whole. (That the manufacturing sector should play such a key role in the growth process is hardly surprising in view of its strategic position, both with respect to any capital accumulation which occurs and as the source of material inputs for the rest of the economy. See chapter 5, section 1.1)

One of the factors determining the growth of manufacturing, Cornwall found, is the ratio of investment to output in that sector. This ratio $(I/Q)_m$, can be regarded as an alternative way to measure the rate of accumulation. Indeed, since it more closely reflects the diversion of physical resources from consumption, it is in some ways a better measure of accumulation than s. According to Cornwall's statistical analysis, the elasticity of the growth of manufacturing output, with respect to the above investment ratio, falls somewhere between .229 and .365. That is, a one percent increase in the ratio of investment to output in the manufacturing sector is associated with an increase of about one-third of a percent in the growth rate for manufacturing. This finding tends to support the first of the key propositions just advanced, namely, that a higher rate of accumulation will be accompanied by a higher growth rate. It also suggests that the incremental capital-output ratio, at least in manufacturing, is approximately 3 and that therefore the social rate of return on investment in that sector is approximately 33.3 percent. Indeed, this last point, together with the higher aggregate values for v for most of the countries listed in exhibit 4.5, lends credence to the argument made earlier that countries which, unlike Japan up until the 1970s, have given greater priority to nonmanufactured output will have a lower social rate of return on investment, at least as measured by physical output. The social rate of return, as measured by nonphysical output, may, of course, be higher.

The only other factor Cornwall found to be significant in explaining the growth of manufacturing output was the disparity in per-capita income between each of the OECD countries included in his sample and the United States as the country with the world's highest per capita income during the period surveyed. The greater that disparity, Cornwall's statistical analysis indicated, the more rapid a country's rate of economic expansion. For example, in the case of Japan, the disparity apparently added 8.1 percentage points to the growth rate in the immediate post-World War II period when per-capita income in Japan was only 12 percent of that in the United States, and 4.3 percentage points in the 1960s when per-capita income in Japan had risen to 22 percent of that in the United States. In the case of Germany, the disparity apparently added 3.7 percentage points to the growth rate in the immediate post-World War II period when per-capita income was only 25 percent of that in the United States, and 2 percentage points in the 1960s when per-capita income had risen to 48 percent that of the United States. One must say "apparently" since Cornwall did not attempt to control for the effect of either lower defense outlays or less pronounced cyclical movements. With this qualification, it can nonetheless be said that Cornwall's findings tend to support the argument made earlier by Alexander Gerschenkron about the advantage of "relative backwardness" in enabling a country to grow more rapidly. (See his *Economic Backwardness in Historical Perspective*, Harvard University Press, 1962.) The disparity in per capita income can be regarded as a measure of the country's "relative backwardness," even among the group of advanced OECD nations. It can also be regarded as a measure of a country's "late start" in the rush to industrialize or, what in some ways is the same thing, the setback caused by wartime destruction of the capital stock.

Any industrial capacity which a late-starting or war-devastated country acquires can be expected to embody the most efficient production techniques currently available—especially if the country has access to capital goods from the United States or whatever other country is the source of the most advanced technology. Indeed, the ability to import the best available technology, along with the capital goods themselves, may even give the late-starting country an advantage over the country that is the source of the technology. This is because the late-starting country does not have the same problem of a vintage capital stock embodying less-than-optimal production techniques. The problem arises not just because the vintage capital reduces the overall labor-output ratio, making the country with the vintage capital a high-cost producer, but also because the vintage capital often precludes the use of the most advanced technology even at the margin. A country with a substantial industrial capacity already in place cannot, as soon as improved techniques become available, immediately scrap all of its existing facilities so they can be rebuilt at the more favorable locations and with the more appropriate plant designs needed to take advantage of the new technology. This is one of the reasons Japanese and German steelmakers were able to gain a competitive edge over their American counterparts in the 1960s, and one of the reasons that the Japanese and German steelmakers are now being overtaken by their rivals in the newly industrializing countries. In effect, the late-starting (or re-starting) country is able to offset the disadvantage of a lower initial endowment of capital with a lower incremental capital-output ratio. It is for this reason that the rate of growth will be greater than one might expect from just the rate of accumulation alone.

Another proposition, besides the first, which is readily confirmed by the empirical evidence, is the fifth. Exhibit 4.12 presents, for the most recent period, the relative per-capita income and growth rates for a selected group of OECD countries. As can be seen from the data presented, all of the other countries

Exhibit 4.12
**Relative Per Capita Income and Growth Rates
for Selected OECD Countries, 1960–1977**

	1960 per capita income (in U.S. $)	Relative per capita income (compared to U.S.)	G	Pop	G/P	1977 per capita income (in U.S. $)	Relative per capita income (compared to (U.S.)
Japan	1,594	.28	8.7	1.0	7.7	5,708	.67
France	3,643	.64	5.3	1.1	4.2	7,327	.86
Italy	1,724	.33	4.4	0.7	3.7	3,408	.40
Germany	4,724	.83	4.2	0.9	3.3	8,179	.96
U.S.	5,692	1.00	3.7	1.3	2.4	8,520	1.00
U.K.	1,935	.34	3.6	0.7	2.9	4,430	.52
Sweden	5,692	1.00	3.0	0.5	2.5	9,287	1.09

Source: World Bank, *World Development Report*, 1979, tables 1,17.

shown (except Sweden) began the period with per-capita income levels below that of the United States. Yet, because these other countries experienced higher growth rates subsequently (on a per-capita basis, that is, after taking into account the growth of population), the relative income gaps were narrowed. Indeed, by the end of the period, in 1977, Germany was poised to overtake the United States in per-capita income, with France not far behind. Meanwhile, Sweden, which was on a level even with the United States in 1960, had a per-capita income that was 9 percent greater 17 years later—though here the reason was the slower growth of population rather than a higher growth of real output. These data amply support the fifth proposition advanced above, namely, that the higher growth rate produced by a higher rate of accumulation will, in time, offset a lower initial endowment of capital. Exhibit 4.13 makes the same point graphically by showing the growth curves for some of the countries included in exhibit 4.12.

The strong evidence in support of the first and fifth propositions helps make up for the fact that the other three propositions are not so easily verified—at least not at the present time given the aggregate data which are currently available for a representative sample of OECD countries. Aside from the problems of measurement, this is due, in large part, to the difficulty of making sure that the *ceteris paribus* assumption on which the propositions rest is not so badly violated as to vitiate any empirical findings. In time, this difficulty is likely to be overcome. For now it need only be noted that there is no empirical evidence to disconfirm any of the three other propositions. The model as a whole therefore stands up quite well as an explanation for the determinants of economic expansion in the long period. At least there is no reason to reject on empirical grounds either the model or the propositions which are derived from it.

Exhibit 4.13
**Growth Curves, Actual and Projected,
for U.S., Germany, France and Japan**

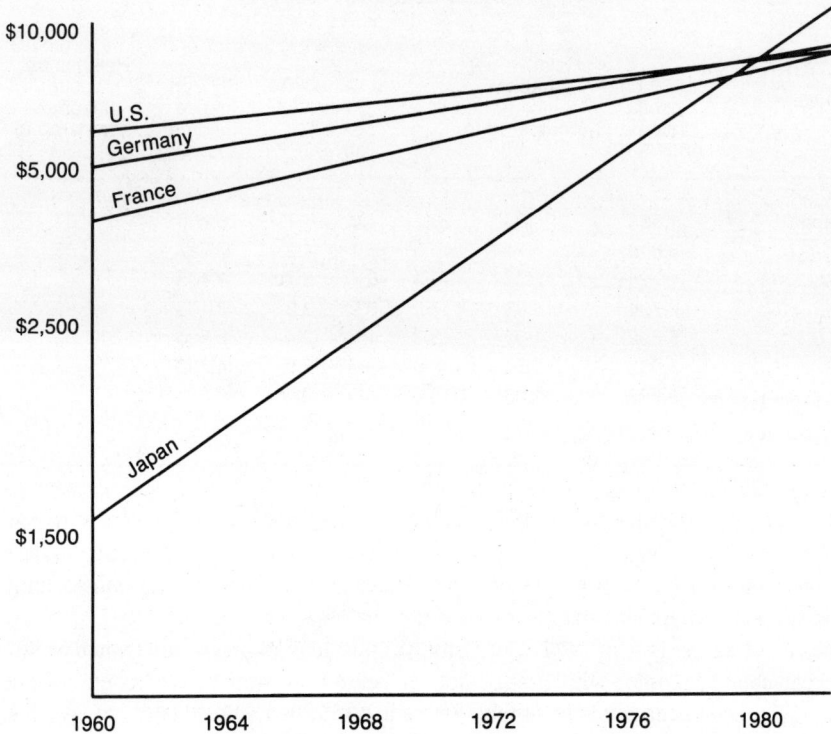

4.3 Exogenous Constraints

The steady-state rate of expansion given by the warranted growth rate, $\dot{G}_w$, reflects only the growth process that is endogenous to the economic system itself. This is the process which ensues when a part of aggregate output is withheld from consumption and used instead to expand productive capacity. Once a rate of accumulation has been determined in this manner, the expansion can be expected to feed upon itself, with the attendant investment both creating a demand for greater output and providing the capacity to satisfy that increased demand. However, the economic system is not self-sufficient, and thus it cannot expand indefinitely solely on the basis of its own endogenous processes. It requires inputs from without—specifically, labor or human resource inputs from the anthropogenic system and raw materials or natural resources from the ecological system that constitutes the natural environment. It also requires inputs from the political system as well as an inherited set of values from the normative structure, but the focus, at least for the moment, will be on the human and natural resource inputs without which the production of goods and services would immediately come to a halt. If these exogenous inputs are not available in sufficient quantity, then the rate of endogenous expansion will be constrained.

Thus, in carrying out a long-period analysis, it is necessary to examine not only the warranted rate at which the economy can expand indefinitely—assuming the endogenous accumulation process proceeds uninterruptedly—but also the rate at which the exogenously supplied inputs can be expected to become available. The latter rate is the potential growth rate, $\dot{G}_p$, as distinct from the warranted rate, $\dot{G}_w$, and it is determined by the growth in the amount of available human and natural resources. In the sections that follow, this potential growth rate will first be explained more fully and then its relationship to the warranted growth rate analyzed. The key point is that, since the warranted and potential growth rates each have different determinants, they need not be identical. The question, then, is what happens when the two growth rates diverge.

One possible result of any gap between the warranted and potential growth rates is increasing unemployment or, alternatively, secular inflation. Another possibility, however, is that the one growth rate will adjust, in whole or in part, to the other. Before being able to resolve this question fully, it will be necessary to consider the neoclassical growth model that has been developed as one extension of the basic Harrod-Domar model—an alternative to the quite different elaboration of the same basic model that will be relied on in the chapters that follow. This is because, while the neoclassical growth model implies that the warranted growth rate will simply adjust to whatever is the potential growth rate, the argument to be made in this section is that the potential growth rate is not independent of the warranted growth rate. An increase in the warranted growth may well lead to an increase in the potential growth rate, though without the increase in the warranted growth rate being fully offset. What this means is that the potential growth rate, rather than being a fixed benchmark by which to judge the performance of the economy, is better viewed as an asymptotic limit which the economic system can approach but not exceed. This, in turn, means that while a gap between the warranted and potential growth rates can explain an increase in the secular unemployment rate, it cannot account for the secular inflation that has bedeviled advanced market economies like that of the United States in the period since the end of World War II. The explanation must be sought elsewhere.

4.3.1 The potential growth rate

The potential growth rate, $\dot{G}_p$, is the rate at which the economy can expand, given the availability of essential inputs from without. Although first Malthus, later Jevons and now, most recently, the environmentalists have stressed the availability of natural resource inputs, the emphasis by economists since Keynes's time has been on the availability of human resource inputs. Indeed, it is in connection with this essential input that the most sophisticated types of analysis have been carried out. Because it makes little difference at this level of generality which type of input is seen as the limiting factor—the important thing is to recognize the existence of external contraints on the rate at which the economy can expand— the emphasis which economists are wont to place on the availability of human resource inputs will, for the moment, be maintained. Later, when the question of supply constraints is taken up more systematically, the limiting role of natural resource inputs will be given the attention it warrants (see chapter 13, part 3).

In modern growth theory, drawing on Harrod's original work, the availability of human resource inputs has been viewed as reflecting underlying demographic trends. The growth of the labor force, it was assumed, would match the increase in population. It was for this reason that the potential growth rate was originally termed the "natural" rate and equated with the growth of population. This formulation, however, is an oversimplification. The most serious objection is that it ignores the crucial role of technical progress in enabling an increasing amount of output to be produced with the same size labor force—thereby obviating the need for any increase in the labor force. But even without taking into account the labor-saving effects of technical progress, the equating of the potential growth rate with the growth of population oversimplifies the actual relationship that exists between the growth of the labor force and demographic factors. In particular, it ignores the following intervening variables.

1. *The age composition of the population.* The labor force is generally drawn from only a portion of the total population, with both the very young and the elderly excluded. Although the upper and lower age limit is sometimes thought to reflect physical capacity, it also depends on the societal judgments embedded in such institutional arrangements as the number of years of free schooling that are provided and the age at which workers become eligible for retirement benefits. In the case of the United States, one can distinguish the legally sanctioned years of work, age 16 to age 65, from the prime years of work, age 25 to age 45. The latter are usually the years of steady, full-time employment when earnings are highest, and it is only the individuals who fall within that age group, or cohort, who constitute what may be termed the "prime" labor force.

These distinctions are important because the population is unlikely to be distributed evenly among the different age cohorts. Frequently, because of wars and other dislocations, some age segments of the population are larger than others, with consequences that can extend, once patterns of family formation and procreation are taken into account, over many decades. In the case of the United States, the post-World War II "baby boom" is still complicating long-term projections of the labor force, just as the heavy casualties suffered by the Soviet Union's male population during World War II are doing the same in that country. Because certain age cohorts are larger than others, the growth of the prime-working-age group cannot be equated with that of the population as a whole.

2. *The labor force participation rate.* Even within a given age cohort, the

extent to which individuals want to enter into paid employment, rather than spend their time in other ways, will vary over time. In part, the labor force participation rate depends on broad social trends. In recent years, particularly in the United States, the most significant of these trends has been for women within the prime-working-age group to seek employment outside the home. But other trends, such as a reduction in mental and other types of debilitating illness or the tempering of discrimination against minority groups, also need to be taken into account. To the extent these trends lead to an increase in the labor force participation rate, they will cause the growth of the labor force to exceed the growth of population.

Besides the longer-run influence of broad social trends, there is the more immediate effect which the level of aggregate demand has on the labor force participation rate. The higher the unemployment rate, the larger the number of "discouraged workers." These are workers who, having become convinced they will be unable to find jobs, no longer actively seek employment and who therefore are not officially counted as part of the labor force in the statistics compiled by government agencies. While the variation in the labor force participation rate as a result of the "discouraged worker effect" is largely a cyclical phenomenon that cancels itself out over time, still, to the extent that the unemployment rate is on the average higher or lower from one cycle to the next, there may be a secular change in the labor force participation rate independent of the broad social factors determining the trend.

3. *The average hours worked each year.* Even with a labor force of fixed size, the number of hours spent on the job during any given year may change over time. Like the labor force participation rate, the average number of hours worked each year will depend on broad social trends—particularly, any trends affecting the norm as to what constitutes "full-time employment." As ideas about the length of the work week and about the frequency of such work interruptions as holidays, vacations and leaves of absence change, so too will the average number of hours worked each year. The changing view as to what constitutes full-time employment is another reason that the growth of the labor force will not necessarily be equal to the growth of population. In this case, however, any trend toward fewer hours worked each year will offset the trend toward a higher labor force partipation rate.

4. *The rate of net inmigration.* Even with no change in any of the other three factors, the growth of the labor force will exceed the growth of population by the rate at which inmigration exceeds outmigration. In the case of an advanced economy, with its higher material standard of living compared with less developed countries, this rate of net inmigration is likely to be positive. However, it need not be constant. Indeed, it is likely to change, depending on the state of the domestic economy, in much the same way the labor force participation rate itself will change. The rate of net inmigration is therefore an additional factor determining the growth of the labor force.

The secular growth in the availability of human resource inputs, $\overset{\circ}{H}$, can therefore be explained in terms of the following functional relationship:

$$\overset{\circ}{H} = \overset{\circ}{e} + f(\Delta f + \Delta h + \Delta m) \tag{4.13}$$

where $\overset{\circ}{e}$ is the secular growth of the working-age population (as defined by the previously specified lower and upper age limits), Δf is the secular change in the labor force participation rate (with any purely cyclical fluctuations in that figure thereby ignored), Δh is the secular change in the average number of hours worked each year (which rate may well be negative) and Δm is the secular change in the rate of net inmigration among the working-age population (the difference between the rate of inmigration and the rate of outmigration, a difference which can be assumed to be positive). In the discussion that follows the value of $\overset{\circ}{e}$ and Δh, along with the upper and lower limits defining the working age population, will be assumed to be fixed parameters so that equation 4.13 reduces to the following:

$$\overset{\circ}{H} = f(\Delta f + \Delta m) \tag{4.14}$$

Still, should one of those parameters change, equation 4.13 would then become the operative one, serving as the basis for determining the potential growth rate, $\dot{G}_p$. The significance of this last point can be more readily appreciated once the necessary policies for achieving better utilization of the labor force are considered (see chapter 13, part 4) since it is these parameters, especially Δh and the upper and lower limits on the working age population, that identify some of the options that exist for reducing persistent unemployment among a portion of the labor force.

It is not enough, however, just to know the value of $\overset{\circ}{H}$ if one wants to determine the most rapid rate at which the economic system can expand without its growth being slowed for lack of the necessary human resource inputs. One more factor needs to be taken into account. This is the labor-saving effect of most technical progress. To the extent the same number of workers can produce a larger amount of output, this as a result of the improved techniques which the investment in new plant and equipment makes it possible for enterprises to adopt, the potential growth rate will be even greater. Indeed, the increased productivity of labor, as measured by the growth of output per worker, is the equivalent of adding new workers to the labor force. A 1 percent increase in labor productivity will have essentially the same effect, at least insofar as potential output is concerned, as a percent increase in the size of the labor force itself. Thus the potential growth rate, $\dot{G}_p$, depends not only on the growth of available human resource inputs, $\overset{\circ}{H}$, but also on the secular growth of output per worker, $\overset{\circ}{Z}$. That is,

$$\dot{G}_p = \overset{\circ}{H} + \overset{\circ}{Z} \tag{4.15}$$

(Only the secular growth of output per worker is meaningful because the change in the rate of capacity utilization over the cycle has a separate effect on labor productivity which is unrelated to any technical progress and which, in any case, cancels out over time.)

4.3.2 Growth and the material standard of living

It is not unusual for economists to abstract from the effects of technical progress so that the potential growth rate then depends on $\overset{\circ}{H}$ alone. This is done, it is said, to "simplify" the argument. However, the absence of technical progress, as measured by $\overset{\circ}{Z}$, leads to a peculiar result insofar as any economic expansion is concerned. With the economy growing at the warranted rate given by the Harrod-Domar formula, the labor force must expand at the same rate if that "potential" growth rate is to be realized. Yet with the labor force expanding at the same rate as the economy itself, there can be no increase in output per worker, and hence no increase in real income or real consumption per worker (and, to the extent the growth of population matches the growth of the labor force, no increase in real income or real consumption per capita either). In other words, despite the rapid expansion in the economy when, for example, s is equal to 0.33 and v is equal to 3 (as in the case of the Alpha economy), the material standard of living would, in the absence of any technical progress, remain unchanged. All of the additional output will be needed just to maintain the existing standard of living as the labor force increases at the requisite rate. Only if, as a result of technical progress, output per worker were to increase will the warranted growth of 11 percent for Alpha lead to a higher material standard of living. Thus, when it was argued in the preceding section that the material standard of living in Alpha was increasing by 11 percent each period, the implicit assumption was that output per worker was also increasing by 11 percent each period.

It is therefore the growth of output per worker, $\overset{\circ}{Z}$, which will determine the rate at which the material standard of living is increasing. While growth is possible without an increase in the material standard of living—and indeed such growth may be essential for avoiding a decline in the standard of living when the labor force is increasing—an increase in the standard of living is possible only if there is technical progress in the form of increased output per worker. Thus a model which does not allow for technical progress, however much the omission may simplify the argument, cannot account for what is perhaps the most significant established fact concerning the historical experience of the advanced countries over the past 300 years. This is the steady increase in the material standard of living equal to approximately 3 percent per annum. Indeed, in the chapters that follow, a number of the most widely used models in economics will be rejected for precisely the reason that they cannot encompass continuous technical progress without the argument losing its coherence. These include virtually all neoclassical models (the one exception being the Valanvanis-Vail and Solow extentions of the J. B. Clark aggregate model to be taken up later in this chapter part) and all

Sraffian models (the one exception being the Pasinetti extension of the Leontief input-output model on which the arguments of the subsequent chapters are based).

The phenomenon of a steady improvement in the material standard of living is readily accounted for, however, while the model still remains a relatively simple one, in the opposite type of situation which can be postulated. This is with the size of the labor force assumed to remain unchanged, and thus with the potential growth rate equal to $\overset{\circ}{Z}$ alone. In this case, as can be seen by the example of the Alpha economy, there is both a continuous increase in aggregate output and a continuous improvement in the standard of living—a result that better fits the historical experience of the last 300 years. It is also a result that avoids the adverse effects on the natural environment that a concurrent growth of the labor force and population may have (see chapter 13, section 3.3, for a discussion of this point).

Still, this result is conditional on there being no increase in population and/or the size of the labor force. While there are some advanced countries which, as a consequence of past economic growth, have now nearly succeeded in halting the growth of population (see exhibit 4.12), this is not true of all the advanced countries—and not even true in the past of the countries which have now succeeded in reducing the growth of population to nearly zero. The problem is that, with the size of the labor force increasing, along with output per worker, the outcome is no longer so clearcut. On the one hand, the growth of the labor force may simply lead to increased unemployment. This is the possibility of the warranted and potential growth rates diverging that will be explored in some depth in the subsection which follows next. On the other hand, an increase in the size of the labor force, if the additional workers cannot be employed as productively as the existing labor force, may have an adverse effect on output per worker, thereby reducing the rate of economic expansion which is sustainable and/or exacerbating the conflict over the distribution of income which underlies the inflationary process. While it will not be until chapter 13 that the necessary foundation for fully understanding this second possibility will have been laid, it, too, must be kept in mind when examining the possible divergence between the warranted and potential growth rates.

What needs to be stressed here, before turning to the possibility of an increase in the size of the labor force, is that the potential growth rate does not depend on that one factor alone but rather on the growth in the amount of "effective" human resource inputs—with this growth in the amount of "effective" human resource inputs being equal to the growth of the labor force *plus* the growth of output per worker. Whatever the warranted growth rate, as given by the Harrod-Domar formula, the "effective" amount of human resource inputs will need to increase accordingly (as will the amount of natural resource inputs) if that rate of economic expansion is to be sustainable—that is, persist without leading to supply bottlenecks of one sort or another that will slow down or even halt completely the expansion process. By the same token, the rate at which the "effective" amount of human resource inputs increases over time will then define the potential growth rate—that is, the rate at which the economy can expand through its internal process of accumulation without being slowed for lack of human resource or other types of exogenous inputs.

While it might seem that including the growth of output per worker, $\overset{\circ}{Z}$, as one of the determinants of the potential growth rate is what complicates the argument, it is actually the growth of the labor force, $\overset{\bullet}{H}$, that is the source of the difficulty. With $\overset{\bullet}{H}$ equal to zero and $\overset{\circ}{G}_p$ thus equal to $\overset{\circ}{Z}$, the warranted growth will necessarily be equal to the potential growth rate as can be seen from the example of the Alpha economy. However, with $\overset{\bullet}{H}$ greater than zero, either the warranted growth rate must be less than the potential growth rate or the rise in the material standard of living will be less than the growth of output per worker. In either case, the warranted growth rate will not necessarily be equal to the potential growth rate, and it is therefore necessary to consider what will be the consequences of these two growth rates diverging.

4.3.3 Divergence between the warranted and potential rates

Joan Robinson refers to the situation in which the warranted and potential growth rates are equal to one another as a "golden age." It represents, from more than one perspective, the best of all possible growth paths. This can be seen from the example of the Alpha economy which, with its labor force remaining unchanged, has a potential growth rate equal to the 11 percent at which output per worker is increasing each period. With a 33 percent rate of accumulation and an incremental capital-output ratio of 3, Alpha's warranted growth rate will thus be the same as its potential growth rate, and it will experience a Robinsonian golden age. Not only will the rate of economic expansion be a sustainable one, with the growth of aggregate supply (both the increase in the amount of capacity and the increase in the effective size of the labor force) matching the growth of demand but, in addition, the material standard of living will improve at the same rate that the economy itself is expanding—without any increase in the unemployment rate.

Unfortunately, there is nothing to ensure that an economic system will be able to expand along this best of all possible growth paths. The reason is that the warranted growth rate and the potential growth rate each have different determinants. The former depends on the rate of accumulation and the incremental capital-output ratio (the inverse of the social rate of return on investment) while the latter depends on the growth of output per worker and the growth of the labor force. If the two sets of determinants should produce results that are identical, it could only be fortuitous. Indeed, this is true even if the growth of the labor force is zero and the potential growth rate therefore equal to the growth of output per worker. The warranted growth rate, since it depends on the rate of accumulation and the social rate of return on investment, will still not necessarily be the same as the potential growth rate. This was in fact the essential point Harrod and Robinson hoped to make when they first drew the distinction between the warranted growth rate on the one hand and the potential (or "natural") growth rate on the other.

The more likely situation, then, given the different determinants of each, is that the warranted and potential growth rates will diverge. The question then becomes, what is the dynamic adjustment process which follows from any divergence between the two growth rates. It turns out that, while the type of dynamic adjustment process will be the same whenever the two growth rates diverge, the outcome will be different, depending on whether it is the potential growth rate that exceeds the warranted growth rate, or vice versa.

Let us begin by examining the possibility that the potential growth rate, as determined by both the growth of output per worker and the growth of the labor force, will exceed the warranted growth rate. In this case, with the effective labor force expanding more rapidly than the number of employment opportunites, not everyone who wants a job will be able to obtain one. The result, at least initially, will be a secular rise in the unemployment rate that depends on how great is the difference between $\dot{G}_p$ and $\dot{G}_w$ (as well as on how large, initially, was the secular unemployment rate, $\bar{U}n$). This situation, one of increasing underutilization of the labor force, is what Robinson termed a "limping golden age."

The conventional theory in economics denies that any such underutilization of the labor force can occur except as a "temporary" phenomenon. It does so by postulating a dynamic adjustment process, or endogenous reponse, such that an increase in the secular unemployment rate, $\bar{U}n$, leads to the adoption of more labor-intensive methods of production, thereby reducing, if not eliminating altogether, the rise in the unemployment rate. While it is true that a secular rise in the unemployment rate will lead to a dynamic adjustment process such that the secular unemployment rate (at least as officially calculated) will then fall, this does not mean that the labor force will, as a result, be any less underutilized. Nor does it mean that more labor-intensive methods of production will be adopted so as to provide more jobs for those who need them. On both these points the conventional neoclassical theory can be disputed.

Rather what will happen as the secular unemployment rate increases is that the lack of employment opportunities at the entry level will lead, over time, to the withdrawal of "discouraged workers" from the labor force and thus to a secular decline in the labor force participation rate, f. At the same time, the lack of employment opportunities beyond the entry level will slow the rate of advancement, forcing a growing number of workers to remain at jobs which fail to fully utilize their abilities. The officially calculated unemployment rate will, to be sure, decline—but only because that figure does not take into account the offsetting rise in the number of discouraged or underemployed workers. Thus a decline in the unemployment rate, to the extent it is simply the result of an offsetting increase in the number of discouraged or underemployed workers, does not represent any real improvement in the extent to which the labor force is being fully utilized.

As for the argument that more labor-intensive methods of production will be adopted, thereby assuring that the labor force will be fully utilized even if the potential growth rate should exceed the warranted growth rate, this argument will be examined shortly in connection with the neoclassical model of growth which depends so critically on it. Anticipating the conclusion that will be reached (see section 4.3.5 as well as chapter 13, section 3.2), one can say that the postulated adjustment mechanism is largely a fictive one. At most, the rate of mechanization (i.e., the replacement of labor by machines and other capital inputs) will be slowed. However, this is not the same as adopting more labor intensive methods of production. In other words, a reduction in the rate at which workers are being given more equipment, or capital inputs, to use on the job is not the same as increasing the number of workers per machine. There is thus no endogenous mechanism, insofar as the economic system itself is concerned, that can be counted on to prevent the increasing underutilization of the labor force that a potential growth rate in excess of the warranted growth rate implies. The response, if increasing underutilization of the labor force is to be avoided, must be an exogenous one—through the measures taken by the government to increase the warranted growth rate and/or otherwise expand employment opportunities. Indeed, this only extends to the post-Keynesian long period the same argument made by Keynes in *The General Theory.*

The other possibility, once it is realized that the warranted and potential growth rates are almost certain to diverge from one another, is that it is the warranted growth rate that will exceed the potential growth rate rather than the the reverse. In considering this possibility, a distinction needs to be made between a warranted growth rate greater than the potential growth rate which is preceded by a period of exceptionally high levels of unemployment (and underutilized capacity)—such as occurred in the 1930s and again in the early 1980s—and one that is not. The former can be termed, following Robinson, a "galloping golden age" and the latter, a "restrained golden age." Still, with aggregate output increasing more rapidly than the availability of the necessary human resource inputs, it will be only a matter of time until the former is transformed into the latter.

A restrained golden age, with aggregate output increasing more rapidly than the availability of the necessary human resource inputs, might at first appear to provide a description of, and an explanation for, the secular inflation that has plagued the United States and the other OECD countries since the end of World War II. What this interpretation of the recent historical experience ignores, however, is the likely supply response insofar as human resource inputs are concerned once the warranted growth rate exceeds the potential growth rate. Indeed, there is a third type of supply response—in addition to the two that have already been identified: the drawing down from or adding to inventories and/or the acceleration or deceleration of capacity expansion (see section 4.1.3). This third type of supply response, unlike the other two, is a response of the anthropogenic system, as distinct from the economic system, and thus it is not endogenous to the economic system itself. It nonetheless plays a critical role in the dynamic adjustment process that follows whenever the warranted and potential growth rates diverge.

4.3.4 The induced change in the potential growth rate

With the output of the economic system increasing more rapidly than the availability of the necessary human resource inputs, the anthropogenic system can be expected to respond by increasing its own rate of output. The various anthropogenic institutions, the schools and employing organizations in particular, will act to step up the rate at which they produce individuals with the requisite types of competence. This is possible because of the considerable ''slack'' that characterizes the anthropogenic system as the complement of the ''reserve capacity'' that firms, especially megacorps, normally maintain. The slack consists both of those queued up seeking entry-level positions and those who, already employed, are waiting to be promoted to more responsible and demanding positions.

As that slack, particularly the queue of individuals seeking entry-level positions, is reduced below the normal levels, the secular unemployment rate, $\bar{U}n$, will fall, the reverse of what happens when the potential growth rate exceeds the warranted rate. To restore the normal amount of slack, employing organizations (along with the schools that provide them with candidates for entry-level positions) will step up their recruitment efforts, thereby enlarging the pool from which workers (and students) can be drawn. If the pool cannot be increased sufficiently by tapping groups within the country's borders who were previously excluded from consideration (e.g., women, ethnic minorities), then it will be enlarged by increasing the rate of net inmigration, m—either formally through ''guest-worker'' programs or informally through relaxed enforcement of the laws barring alien workers. Meanwhile, encouraged by the more rapid rate at which openings are occurring, native-born individuals, particularly in the critical decade before they turn 25, are more likely to take the steps needed to become a part of the ''permanent'' labor force. This involves undergoing whatever prior training may be required, waiting for an entry-level position to open up and then retaining the job long enough to acquire a minimum degree of competence—with a consequent rise in the labor force participation rate, f. In this way (rather than through an increase in the entry-level wage rate, the availability of human resources will be increased, with H rising and the normal amount of anthropogenic slack thereby restored, at least partly. (For a more complete discussion of the process, see chapter 13, part 2.) It should be stressed, however, that it is only a secular decline in the unemployment rate, and not the cyclical movement of that variable, which will initiate the type of response on the part of the anthropogenic system which has just been described.

One can therefore specify the following dynamic adjustment process, insofar as the anthropogenic system is concerned, whenever the warranted growth rate exceeds the potential growth rate:

1. $\dot{G}_w > \dot{G}_p \longrightarrow -\Delta\dot{U}n$
2. $-\Delta\bar{U}n \longrightarrow +f, +\Delta m$
3. $+\Delta f, +\Delta m \longrightarrow +\Delta\overset{\circ}{H}$ (as well as $+\Delta\bar{U}n$)

The result of this dynamic adjustment process, at least when the warranted growth rate exceeds the potential rate, is that the availability of human resource inputs, as measured by $\overset{\circ}{H}$, will increase. Since the potential growth rate depends on $\overset{\circ}{H}$, the potential growth rate will itself be increased. Thus it turns out that the potential growth rate is not independent of the warranted growth rate. Indeed, the potential growth rate, $\dot{G}_p$, will depend, at least in part, on the warranted growth rate, $\dot{G}_w$ (or, as an empirical approximimation, on the secular growth rate, $\dot{G}$).

The same type of response by the anthropogenic system can be expected, it should be noted, when the potential growth rate exceeds the warranted rate. It is only the outcome that will be different. With the secular rate of unemployment then rising rather than falling, employing organizations (and schools) will reduce their recruitment efforts, with further inmigration perhaps banned altogether. Meanwhile a larger proportion of the indigenous working-age population, convinced there are no jobs to be had, will join the ranks of discouraged workers who have withdrawn from the labor force. Thus the growth of human resource inputs, $\overset{\circ}{H}$, will slow, with the gap between the potential and warranted growth rates narrowing. That is,

1. $\dot{G}_w < \dot{G}_p \longrightarrow +\Delta\bar{U}n$
2. $+\Delta\bar{U}n \longrightarrow -\Delta f, -\Delta m$
3. $-\Delta f, -\Delta m \longrightarrow -\Delta\overset{\circ}{H}$ (as well as $-\Delta\bar{U}n$)

Again, it turns out that the potential growth rate is not independent of the warranted growth rate. A change in the warranted growth rate, $\dot{G}_w$, because of the effect it will have on the labor force participation rate, f, and the rate of net inmigration, m, will lead to a change in the potential growth rate, $\dot{G}_p$.

However, it is not just through the effect on the labor force participation rate and the rate of net inmigration that the potential growth rate depends on the warranted growth rate. A change in the warranted growth rate also implies a change in investment relative to savings and thus to the first of the four steps in the dynamic adjustment process previously identified as the accelerator (see section 4.1.3). Indeed, a change in the warranted growth rate, $\dot{G}_w$, will lead to a change in the average rate of capacity utilization over time, $\bar{C}ap$ (the counterpart of the reduction occurring simultaneously in the secular unemployment rate and hence in the degree of anthropogenic slack), and this change in the average rate of capacity utilization over time will, in turn, lead (to the extent it is perceived as being more than just a cyclical phenomenon) to a change in the rate of growth of investment, $\dot{I}$.

This accelerator effect which accompanies any increase in the warranted growth rate (see section 4.1.3) is important to keep in mind when discussing the potential growth rate because the increased pace at which accumulation will then be taking place is likely to lead to a more rapid growth of output per worker. With new plant and equipment being added to the capital stock at a faster pace, a larger proportion of the economy's productive capacity will embody the latest labor-saving technology, and the effect of the vintage capital stock in holding down the growth of output per worker will be correspondingly reduced. The result will be an increase in the rate of technical progress and a more rapid growth of output per worker. Conversely, a decline in the warranted growth rate and thus a slowing in the growth of investment, will mean a fall in the growth of output per worker. Again, this point will be elaborated on more fully (see chapter 5, part 4). For now it need only be noted that the growth of output per worker, $\overset{\circ}{Z}$, depends in part on the rate of growth of investment, and hence on the warranted growth rate.

What has thus been brought out are two quite separate ways in which the potential growth rate depends on the warranted growth rate. First, an increase in the warranted growth rate relative to the potential growth rate is likely to result in a more rapid growth in the size of the labor force, $\overset{\circ}{H}$, and in this way affect that determinant of the potential growth rate. Second, an increase in the warranted growth rate, since it implies a more rapid rate of growth of investment, is likely to lead to an increase in the growth of output per worker, $\overset{\circ}{Z}$, and in this way affect that other determinant of G_p. While this dependence of the potential growth rate on the warranted rate, in each of the two ways just indicated, might at first seem to preclude the possibility of a determinant outcome, the lack of independence between $\dot{G}_p$ and $\dot{G}_w$ actually poses no problem.

The response of the potential growth rate, $\dot{G}_p$, to a change in the warranted growth rate, $\dot{G}_w$, can be assumed to be slower than the change in the warranted growth rate itself so that, at any given moment in time—prior to a change in the warranted growth rate (or, as an empirical approximation, prior to a change in the secular growth rate)—the difference between $\dot{G}_p$ and $\dot{G}_w$ will be only partly eliminated. What this means is that the potential growth rate, rather than being a fixed benchmark, is an asymptotic limit which the warranted growth rate can approach but not exceed. With any increase in the warranted growth rate leading to at least a partial increase in the potential growth rate, the potential growth rate will always be greater than the warranted rate—with the gap between them either narrowing or widening depending on whether the warranted growth rate has increased or declined. However, this does not make the difference between the warranted and potential growth rates indeterminant. As long as the potential growth rate changes by less than the warranted rate, with the functional relation-ships governing each of the two growth rates both known and stable, the differ-ence at any given point in time can still be ascertained. Indeed, this is only the beginning of the effort that will be made in this text, using a systems approach, to address the problem of interdependence among key variables which, though frequently encountered in economic analysis, is usually then just glossed over because it cannot be handled within the type of simple causal model being relied upon.

Once the potential growth rate is correctly understood to be an asymptotic limit that the economic system can approach but not exceed, a number of points then follow. For one thing, it becomes clear that the secular inflation of the post-World War II period cannot be explained in terms of the warranted rate exceeding the potential growth rate. The inflation, as will be brought out in chapters 8 and 14, must be explained on entirely different grounds. Indeed, the notion of the inflation problem as merely the obverse side, or mirror image, of the unemployment problem has to be abandoned. It also becomes clear that, insofar as the full utilization of resources is concerned, the potential growth rate must be viewed as the target variable and the warranted growth rate's determinants as the instrumental variables. The former measures the extent to which resources are being fully utilized within a long-period, dynamic perspective, and the latter identifies the means by which it is possible to come closer to realizing that goal. If what appears to be the current warranted growth rate is failing to utilize human resource and other inputs at the same rate they are becoming available, then the only remedy is to increase the warranted growth rate.

Finally, once it is understood why the potential growth rate is only a hypothetical asymptotic limit, it becomes clear that while the warranted growth rate can be increased, in all of the ways brought out in the preceding section, any success in doing so is likely to increase the potential growth rate as well—though not by an equal amount. It is possible to narrow the gap between $\dot{G}_p$ and $\dot{G}_w$, but not to eliminate it altogether. This last point has an important corollary. It suggests that the expansion of an advanced market economy is not likely to be constrained for lack of the necessary human resource inputs—not as long as there are other, less developed regions from which workers can be drawn. While there may be a limit to how quickly the warranted growth rate can be increased, because of the time required to make all the necessary anthropogenic adjustments, there is no limit, at least insofar as the availability of human resource inputs is concerned, to how high the warranted growth rate can ultimately be pushed. Unless there is some limit imposed either by the rate of technical progress (a possibility that will be taken up in part 4 of the next chapter) or by the availability of natural resource inputs (a possibility to be considered in chapter 13, part 3), the rate of expansion must be constrained by some endogenous factor—such as an unwillingness to accept the sacrifice of present consumption that is implicit in the higher rate of accumulation needed to achieve a more rapid growth rate.

There is, as already pointed out, an alternative view of the matter. This alternative view is represented by what is known as the neoclassical growth model. Since this is the model which is usually favored by economists when they have concerned themselves with problems of dynamic expansion over time—and indeed since that model in effect denies many of the points which have just been made—it needs to be examined at some length.

4.3.5 The alternative growth model

The neoclassical growth model departs from the Harrod-Domar model (and from the post-Keynesian extensions of that model) by making the warranted growth rate depend not only on the rate of accumulation but also on the labor intensity of production. This is done by first postulating a production function as follows:

$$Q = f(K, L) \qquad (4.16)$$

where Q is aggregate output, K is the capital stock and L is the size of the labor force. The function, moreover, is assumed to be such that "capital" can be substituted for labor, and vice versa—though only if, as a reflection of the decreasing productivity of the two inputs at the margin, disproportionately more of one input is used in place of the other. In this way, it is possible for aggregate output to increase even if one (though not both) of the two inputs is held constant. A production function of this sort, it should be pointed out, is unacceptable on a number of grounds. First, it assumes that the capital stock, rather than just the additions to the capital stock, can be measured in a meaningful way (see section 4.1.1). Second, it assumes that capital is an input that can take a single value denoted by K. Finally, it assumes an unrealistic degree of flexibility in terms of the ratios at which labor and other inputs can be combined in the production process. (These last two criticisms will be elaborated on shortly in chapter 5, sections 1.4, 3.1 and 5.1). Still, since these objections are not the main point of difference between the neoclassical growth model and a post-Keynesian dynamic analysis, they need only be noted in passing.

As the next step in developing the model, the production function given by equation 4.16 is divided through by L so that the size of the labor force becomes a denominator of the other variables rather than a separate determinant. The production function can thus be written as follows:

$$q = f(k) \qquad (4.17)$$

where q is output per worker, Q/L, and k is capital per worker, K/L (with k not to be confused with the Keynesian multiplier). With the levels transformed into rates of growth over time, this equation becomes

$$\dot{q} = f(\dot{k}) \qquad (4.18)$$

where $\dot{q}$ is the rate of growth of output per worker with respect to time and $\dot{k}$ is the rate of growth of capital per worker. To make the formulation less objectionable from a post-Keynesian perspective, one can view $\dot{k}$ as the growth of investment per worker. (This is because the problem of how to value the capital stock does not arise when one is basing the argument only on the current flow of capital, or investment, goods.) The $\dot{q}$ term, however, should not be confused with $\overset{\circ}{Z}$. The former denotes the growth of output per worker which would occur in the absence of technical progress (as a result of the increasing investment per worker) while the latter denotes the growth of output per worker that derives from technical progress itself. Even though it may be difficult, if not impossible, to differentiate between the two empirically—a point soon to be stressed—it is nonetheless essential to the argument underlying the neoclassical growth model to be able to distinguish $\dot{q}$ from $\overset{\circ}{Z}$.

Exhibit 4.14 presents geometrically the production function given by equation 4.16. Notice that the growth of output per worker, $\dot{q}$, first rises more rapidly than the growth of capital (or rather investment) per worker, $\dot{k}$, and then less rapidly. This is a manifestation of the variable (first increasing and then diminishing) returns to capital and the other inputs which, even more than the flexibility in the use of different types of inputs, is an essential characteristic of a neoclassical model. Any point along the production function OF, it should be noted, marks a possible steady-state expansion path, and thus a possible warranted growth rate, within the framework of the neoclassical growth model.

Using the same set of axes, one can represent the potential growth rate by means of a ray OE emanating from origin with a slope equal to $\overset{\circ}{H}/s$. This is because the slope of any such ray is equal to $\dot{q}/\dot{k}$, and thus equal to the inverse of the incremental capital-output ratio, v (on the assumption that the change in actual output per worker, $\Delta(Q/L)$, is the same as the change in potential output per worker, $\Delta(Q_p/L)$, and there are no price movements so that the change in real output, ΔQ, is the same as the change in nominal output, ΔY). Since the potential growth rate in the absence of technical progress can be equated with the growth of the labor force, $\overset{\circ}{H}$, and since, moreover, for the economy to expand along that growth path the following condition must hold,

$$\overset{\circ}{H} = \frac{s}{v} \tag{4.19}$$

it is possible to rearrange terms so that the value v must take if the economy is to expand at the potential growth rate can be ascertained. That value of v is given by the following equation:

$$v = \frac{s}{\overset{\circ}{H}} \tag{4.20}$$

Exhibit 4.14

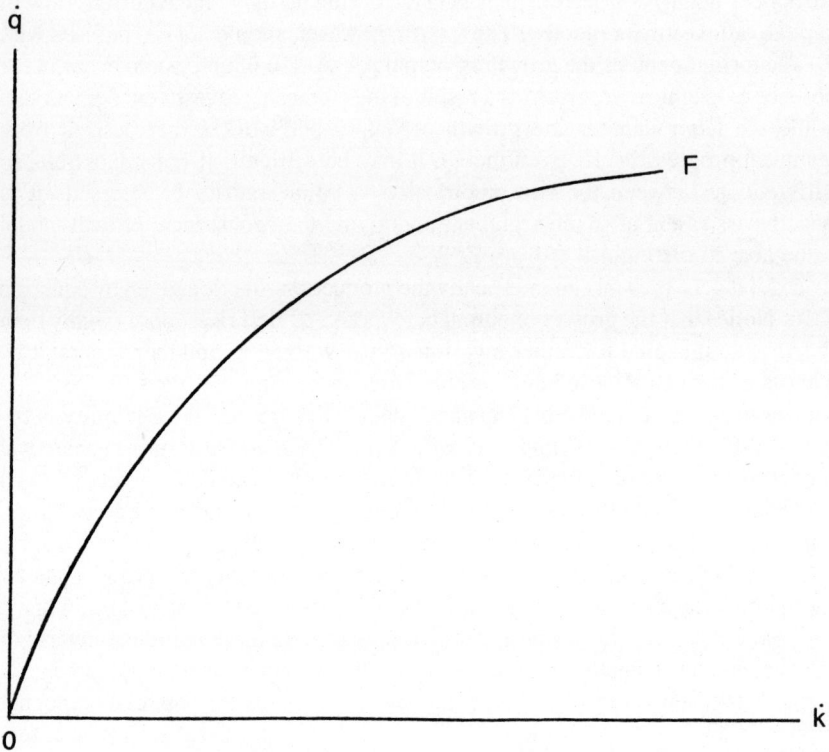

Its inverse is, of course, $\overset{\circ}{H}/s$. Thus the ray emanating from the origin in exhibit 4.15 with a slope equal to $\overset{\circ}{H}/s$ identifies the inverse of the potential growth rate at any point along the production function OF.

As can be seen from exhibit 4.15, the ray OE intersects the production function OF at one point and one point only. (This necessarily follows from the assumption of variable returns and from the fact that the production function OF passes through the origin.) To the left of this point (point A in exhibit 4.15), the warranted rate will be less than the potential growth rate. This is because a ray emanating from the origin which intersects the production function to the left of point A would have a slope greater than $\overset{\circ}{H}/s$, thereby implying that the rate of accumulation, as measured by s, was *less* than is required for the economy to expand at the potential rate. Alternatively, if the economy were located to the

Exhibit 4.15

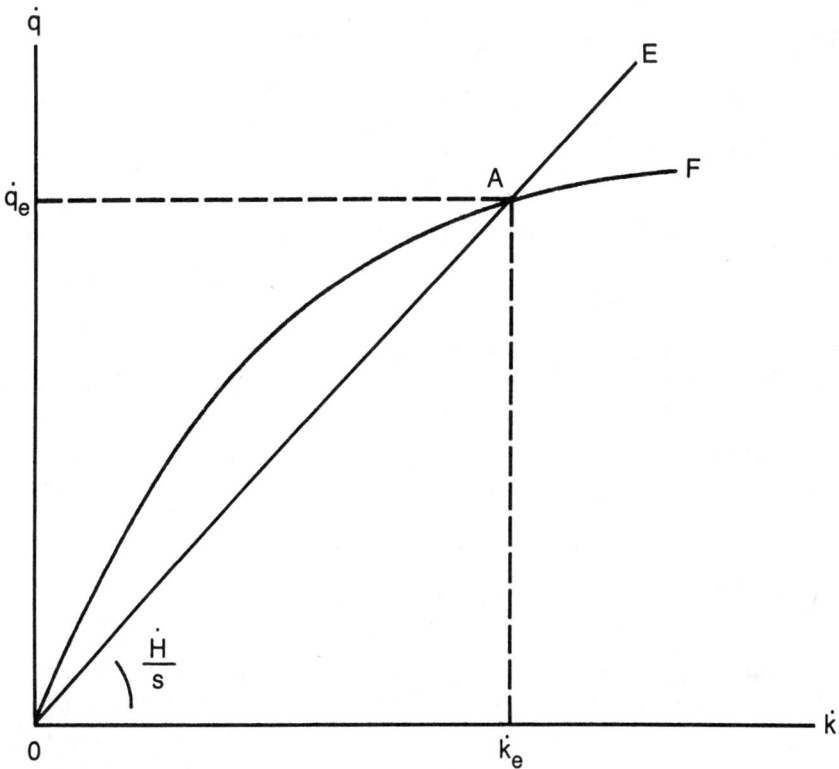

right of point A, it would be expanding at a rate greater than the potential rate, in this case because the rate of accumulation was *more* than is necessary for the economy to achieve its potential growth rate. Thus, as can be seen from the diagram shown in exhibit 4.15, there is but one set of values for $\dot{q}$ and $\dot{k}$ which will bring the warranted and potential growth rates into line with one another. This is the set given by the coordinates, $\dot{q}_e$ and $\dot{k}_e$, at the point A where the ray OE intersects the production function OF.

The import of the neoclassical growth model, however, is not just that there is but one growth path among many which will give rise to a true "golden age." That would add little to what can be learned from the simpler Harrod-Domar model. The more significant result is that, should anything happen to push the economy either to the right or to the left of the point of intersection shown in exhibit 4.15, there are self-correcting market forces that will bring the economy back to A. It is this inferred tendency of the economy to return to the optimal growth path given by the potential growth rate, $\dot{G}_p$, should it be displaced from that expansion path which gives rise to the principal implication of the neoclassical growth model insofar as public policy is concerned. This is that, since the warranted growth rate will simply adjust over time to whatever, given the growth of the labor force, happens to be the potential growth rate, there is little point in trying to place the economy on a different growth path by varying the rate of accumulation. In other words, the warranted growth rate (and thus the long-period rate of economic expansion) depends not on the rate of accumulation as was previously argued. It is instead uniquely determined by the potential growth rate, thus turning the argument of the preceding subsection on its head.

This conclusion, however, depends critically on the argument that any displacement of the economy from the steady-state growth path given by the potential rate, $\dot{G}_p$, will automatically be corrected through a change in the capital-labor ratio, k, so that the economy will, over time, return to that growth path. To determine the validity of the neoclassical growth model as an alternative to the extension of the basic Harrod-Domar model that will be relied on in the subsequent chapters of this text, it is therefore necessary to examine the dynamic adjustment process which underlies the neoclassical growth model.

4.3.6 The neoclassical dynamic adjustment process

Basic to the results obtained from the neoclassical growth model is the presumed existence of a dynamic adjustment process such that, whenever the two growth rates deviate from one another, it is the warranted growth rate that will change as a result of endogenous market forces until it is again equal to the potential growth rate. The dynamic adjustment process which brings the warranted growth rate back into line with the potential growth rate is usually not made explicit when the neoclassical model is presented. This adjustment process can nonetheless be inferred from the model's "equilibrium" solution.

If the warranted growth rate should fall short of the potential growth rate so that the economy finds itself to the left of point A in exhibit 4.15, then the growth in the supply of human resource inputs will be greater than the demand for those inputs, leading to an increase in the secular unemployment rate, $\bar{U}n$. The increase in unemployment, it is then inferred, will lead to a fall in the average wage received by labor, w, with the resulting decline in the wage bill increasing the share of national income going to the owners of capital inputs. The fall in wages will thus increase the return on capital (or, rather, the return on investment), r. The higher rate of return on investment will, in turn, induce enterprises to step up their capital spending, which can be expected to take the form of adding more capital, that is, more plant and equipment, per worker. Even if the ratios at which capital and labor inputs are combined cannot be altered in the short run (a point soon to be argued—see chapter 5, section 3.1), there will still be a strong incentive, because of the increased rate of return on investment, for enterprises to build new facilities which embody a higher capital-labor ratio; and therefore over the long period covered by the analysis there will be a tendency for the "capital-intensity" of production to increase. The existing technology, it is assumed, is sufficiently rich in the number of choices it offers that, even without technical progress, this flexibility as to the capital-intensity of production exists. With the capital-intensity of production therefore increasing, the value of $\dot{k}$ will rise; and this will cause the economy to shift along its production function OF back toward point A.

On the other hand, if the warranted growth rate should exceed the potential rate so that the economy finds itself to the right of point A, then the growth in the supply of human resource inputs will be less than the demand for those inputs, leading to a growing secular shortage of workers. As enterprises bid among themselves for the available supply of workers, wage rates will rise, it is argued, and the return on investment will fall. The lower rate of return on investment will, in turn, cause enterprises to cut back on their capital spending, with the result that investment per worker will decline. With the capital intensity of production thereby decreasing, the value of $\dot{k}$ will fall; and this will cause the economy to shift along its production function, again toward point A but in this case from the opposite direction.

The key causal links in the dynamic adjustment process just described are as follows:

1. $\dot{G}_w \neq \dot{G}_p \longrightarrow \Delta \bar{U}n$ (with $\Delta \bar{U}n$ negative $(-)$ if $\dot{G}_w > \dot{G}_p$, and $\Delta \bar{U}n$ positive $(+)$ if $\dot{G}_w < \dot{G}_p$)
2. $+ \Delta \bar{U}n \longrightarrow - \Delta w$
3. $- \Delta w \longrightarrow + \Delta r$
4. $+ \Delta r \longrightarrow + \Delta \dot{k}$
5. $+ \Delta \dot{k} \longrightarrow + \Delta \dot{G}_w$ until $\dot{G}_w = \dot{G}_p$

There are thus five steps in the causal sequence by which, according to the neoclassical growth model, any deviation of the economy from its potential growth rate will be eliminated, with the economy thereby returning to the growth path given by $\dot{G}_p$ (at point A long the production function OF shown in exhibit 4.15). While it cannot be denied that any discrepancy between the warranted growth rate (or, as an empirically observable approximation, between the secular growth rate) and the potential growth will lead to a change in the secular rate of unemployment, the logic of the argument at each successive step in the sequence just outlined can be challenged.

The second step in the sequence assumes that any disparity between the demand for and supply of human resource inputs, such as can be expected to occur should the warranted growth rate differ from the potential growth rate, will lead to a change in the economy-wide average wage rate, w. It is unclear, however, whether the wage rate thought to be affected by the change in the secular unemployment rate is the money wage rate or the real wage rate. Although the argument is usually framed in terms of the latter, it is the money wage rate which is more likely to be directly affected by a change in the secular rate of unemployment. In order for the real wage to change as well in the way that is required for the argument underlying the neoclassical growth model to hold, the impact which the change in the unemployment rate has on the money wage must be greater than the impact it has on the price of the goods being purchased with those wages. Otherwise, the real wage, rather than varying inversely, will either be unaffected by or will move in the same direction as the unemployment rate. It should be noted that this distinction between the money wage and the real wage is but one of the complications already alluded to (see chapter 1, section 1.1) that the existence of a separate set of monetary flows, independent of the real flows, introduces into the analysis.

The empirical evidence would suggest that the secular rate of unemployment has only a negligible effect—if indeed it has any effect at all—not just on the money wage but also on the real wage as well (see chapter 8, parts 1 and 2). Thus there is reason to doubt the validity of the argument at the second of the five steps in the causal sequence by which, according to the neoclassical growth model, any deviation of the warranted growth rate from the potential growth rate will be eliminated. Nonetheless, since a decline in the warranted growth rate (as distinct from an increase in the secular unemployment rate) is likely to lead eventually to a decline in the *growth* of real wages while an increase in the warranted growth rate is likely to lead to a more rapid rise in real wages—though for quite different reasons and through a quite different mechanism from that assumed by the neoclassical growth model—the argument can be accepted, at least for the moment, so we can proceed to what is an even more serious flaw in the chain of reasoning.

The third step in the causal sequence assumes that a change in the economy-wide average wage rate, w, will lead to a change in the return on capital (or, more accurately, to a change in the return on investment), r. However, even if increasing secular unemployment should lead to a fall in the wage rate, there is no reason to believe that this will necessarily increase the return on investment (just as there is no reason to believe that a rise in the wage rate, were that to follow from a decrease in the secular unemployment rate, will necessarily lower the return on investment). The confusion here is between the return on "capital" (as an input) holding other inputs (such as labor) constant and the return on any additions to the capital stock (i.e., investment) when any other inputs that are required, such as labor, are also being increased in the required proportions. It is only in the former case—an artificial one that contrasts sharply with what actually happens when new capacity is being added—that a decline in the compensation received by workers necessarily implies an increase in the return on "capital."

The truth is that a decline in the demand for labor as a result of a lower warranted growth rate, whether it leads to a fall in the wage rate or not, is more likely to be accompanied by a decline than an increase in the return on "capital." This is because the same aggregate demand factors that reduce the demand for human resource inputs will also lower the average rate of capacity utilization, and the amount of profit earned by business firms—the return on "capital"—depends first and foremost on the rate of capacity utilization (see chapter 7, section 3.1). Indeed, to the extent that, as the orthodox theory would suggest, the price of the goods being produced can also be expected to fall with any increase in the secular unemployment rate (because the average rate of capacity utilization has declined), the return on investment will be further depressed. Still, the point is not so much that the return on investment will fall as the secular rate of unemployment increases. It is rather that the opposite relationship on which the adjustment mechanism underlying the neoclassical growth model depends—that a fall in wages implies a higher return on investment and vice versa—does not necessarily follow. The flaw in the line of reasoning represented by this *non sequitor* is then compounded by an even more serious error at the next step in the causal chain.

The fourth step in the dynamic adjustment process outlined above assumes that a change in the return on investment will lead to a change in the capital intensity of production. However, even if the secular rise in the unemployment rate should somehow lead to a greater return on investment or, alternatively, that a growing shortage of workers is possible and that this will somehow lead to a lower rate of return on investment, there is still reason to question whether the capital intensity of production will be affected in the way the neoclassical growth model implies. Here the error lies in confusing the result which might follow from increasing the amount of capital inputs per worker (this result, putatively, being an increase in the net revenue of the individual firm) with what it is that induces business firms to make that type of investment in the first place.

The reason business firms are willing to increase the amount of capital inputs, or investment, per worker is that by doing so they can lower the costs of production. Indeed, it is the subsequent reduction in the wage bill and the other costs of production that constitutes the "return" on this type of investment. (For a more complete discussion of the factors governing this and other types of business investment, see chapter 7, section 2.2.) An increase in the secular rate of unemployment, to the extent it leads to a decline in labor costs (or, perhaps more realistically, to a less rapid rise in the wage bill), will therefore give business firms *less* rather than more of an incentive to increase the amount of investment per worker. That is because it is the growth of money wages, and hence of labor costs, that provides the principal incentive to adopt less labor-intensive methods of production. In other words, a change in the wage rate, w, will have the opposite effect on the capital intensity of production, k, from that assumed by the neoclassical growth model. Indeed, it is at this point that the argument by which it is concluded that the warranted growth rate will automatically adjust to the potential growth rate goes completely awry. This can be seen by substituting, for steps 3 and 4 in the causal sequence previously outlined, the more reasonable proposition that a decline in the economy-wide average wage rate, w, will lead to a decline (rather than an increase) in the capital-output ratio, k, while a rise in w will lead to an increase (rather than a fall) in the value of k.

What happens when this change is made in the dynamic adjustment process outlined above is that the results are reversed. Any displacement of the economy from the point on its production function represented by the potential growth rate (point A in exhibit 4.15) will lead to a still further movement away from, rather than a return to, that "golden age" growth path. A lower warranted growth rate, and therefore a higher secular unemployment rate, will, to the extent it leads to a fall in the industry-wide average wage rate (or at least to a less rapid growth in labor costs), result in the eventual adoption of less, rather than more, capital-intensive methods of production since business firms will then have less, rather than more, of an incentive to replace workers with machines. Investment per worker will decline rather than increase, with the warranted growth rate itself then being reduced still further. The same thing happens when the warranted growth rate exceeds the potential rate, only in reverse. To the extent shortages of human resource inputs ensue, with a consequent acceleration in the growth of wages and labor costs, business firms will have more, rather than less, of an incentive to adopt more capital intensive methods of production. Investment per worker will increase rather than decline, and the warranted growth rate will exceed the potential growth rate by an even greater margin. In this way, any deviation of the warranted growth rate from the potential rate, rather than being self-correcting, will only lead to an even greater discrepancy between the two growth rates.

This is not to say that the economic system itself is unstable. The point rather is that the neoclassical growth model, as an explanation for what happens as the economy expands over time, is seriously flawed in its logic. Once the economic system is displaced from the "equilibrium," or "golden age," growth path represented by point A in exhibit 4.15, there is no plausible mechanism to ensure that it will be able to return to that growth path. On the contrary, it is likely to find itself being pushed further and further away from that optimal growth path. The neoclassical growth model thus implies that, in the words of Joan Robinson, the economy is either in equilibrium or it is not viable.

This conclusion that the economic system would not be a viable one if the neoclassical growth model were the model that applies to an economy that is expanding over time seems to fly in the face of the considerable empirical evidence that has been accumulated about the U.S. and other advanced market economies based on that model. It is therefore necessary to take a closer look at the evidence.

4.3.7 The evidence in support of the neoclassical growth model

Perhaps no model, not even the Keynesian model itself, has inspired so large a body of empirical work as the neoclassical growth model. It may therefore come as a surprise to learn that the neoclassical growth model has yet to be empirically validated. One must distinguish between a model that, having been subjected to various empirical tests without being disconfirmed, can be said to have been empirically validated and a model that, upon merely being assumed to be correct, then permits certain inferences to be drawn from the empirical evidence. The neoclassical growth model, it turns out, falls in the latter category. Indeed, there is good reason, not just on the basis of the empirical evidence but also from the logic of the model itself once technical progress is taken into account, to doubt that the neoclassical growth model applies to an advanced market economy like that of the United States.

Although a production function of the type represented in exhibit 4.15 can be traced back to the writings of John Bates Clark before the turn of the century, it was not until the work of Charles Cobb and Paul Douglas in the 1920s that an effort was made to test this formulation against the empirical evidence. In order to reflect the properties shown in exhibit 4.15—particularly the variable returns and, as the obverse of those variable returns, the decreasing marginal productivity of the inputs themselves—Cobb and Douglas specified an aggregate production function for the U.S. economy as follows:

$$Q = K^{(1-\alpha)}L^{\alpha} \tag{4.21}$$

where α is an exponent with a value that falls between 0 and 1. Equation 4.21, it should be noted, represents what has come to be known as the Cobb-Douglas production function, the most general form that a neoclassical production function can take. With the values of K and L converted to logarithms, equation 4.21 can be rewritten as follows so that the value of α (and thus of $1-\alpha$ as well) can be estimated using standard regression techniques (which require that the equation being estimated take a linear rather than an exponential form):

$$\log \text{ of } Q = 1\text{-}\alpha \ (\log \text{ of } K) + \alpha \ (\log \text{ of } L) \tag{4.22}$$

The empirical test which Cobb and Douglas devised was to see whether the estimated values of α and $1\text{-}\alpha$ would, as predicted by the neoclassical theory of income distribution, match the distribution of the national income between wages and property income. Using annual data for the U.S. manufacturing sector over the period from 1899 to 1922, Cobb and Douglas were able to obtain an estimate for α that was remarkably similar to the 75 percent share of the national income going to labor in the form of wages. From this study, it could be argued that there was evidence, in the case of the U.S. economy, for the existence of the postulated neoclassical production function. At least the value of α predicted on the basis of the underlying theory had been confirmed. In 1952, however, better data became available, largely as a result of the work of Simon Kuznets and Raymond Goldsmith; and when S. Valanvanis-Vail reestimated the value of α using the Kuznets-Goldsmith data his results were nearly the opposite of those obtained by Cobb and Douglas. The value of α now appeared to be 0.25 rather than 0.75, and thus it was no longer equal to the share of the national income represented by wages. This negative finding was in addition to the growing evidence from input-output and other types of studies that there was perhaps not the flexibility in the use of inputs that the neoclassical model assumed.

At this point, a curious development occurred. Further efforts to test the empirical validity of a neoclassical production function ceased. Instead, a neoclassical production function, such as that represented by equation 4.18 and by the curve OF in exhibit 4.14, was simply assumed to be the correct specification. It was as though the neoclassical production function had been empirically validated when in fact the opposite was more nearly the case. This change in the status of the neoclassical production function, from an unsubstantiated proposition to an unquestioned premise, was the result of the way technical progress was subsequently incorporated into the neoclassical growth model by Robert Solow and others.

So far, in discussing the endogenous adjustment of the warranted growth rate to whatever, within the context of a neoclassical growth model, happens to be the potential growth, no allowance has been made for technical progress. The potential growth rate, $\dot{G}_p$, has been viewed as depending solely on the growth of the labor force, $\dot{H}$, with the increase in output per worker, $\overset{\circ}{Z}$, either ignored or assumed to be zero. This has been done deliberately, for once the effect of increasing output per worker on the potential growth rate is taken into account, the neoclassical growth model is no longer necessarily a determinant one. If, as a response to the higher secular unemployment that ensues when the economy finds itself to the left of point A in exhibit 4.15, business firms were to shift to more capital-intensive methods—with those more capital-intensive methods (as measured by k) leading to greater output per worker (as measured by q)—then the potential growth rate, to the extent it depends on the growth of output per worker, would also increase. In other words, the ray OE representing the potential growth rate would not then be independent of the growth of output per worker, $\dot{q}$. As the economy shifted back along the production function OF toward point A in the manner suggested by the neoclassical growth model, the change in $\dot{q}$ would lead to a shift in the ray OE and thus to a shift in A, the point of intersection with the production function OF. With no mechanism to ensure that the shift in the ray OE will be less than the movement along the production function OF so that a new point of intersection is possible, the neoclassical growth model becomes indeterminate, insofar as the long-period growth path is concerned, once the model is elaborated on, as it should be, to encompass technical progress.

The only way out of this logical impasse is to assume that technical progress occurs independently of the amount of capital, or investment, per worker. Indeed, this was precisely the approach adopted by Solow when, in 1956, he presented an analysis of technical progress within the context of a neoclassical growth model. Solow assumed that technical progress involves the shift of the production function OF itself over time so that a change in the capital-labor ratio, $\dot{k}$, can be distinguished from technical progress. This was done by rewriting equation 4.18 as follows:

$$\dot{q} = \dot{A} * \dot{k}^{\alpha} \qquad (4.23)$$

where $\dot{A}$ is the growth of output per worker, $\dot{q}$, due to technical progress and α is now the elasticity of substitution between labor and "capital." Alternatively, $\dot{A}$ can be interpreted as the rate at which the neoclassical production function, OF, shown in exhibit 4.14 shifts over time as a result of technical progress. Equation 4.23 can be rewritten as follows so that its parameters, A and α, can be empirically estimated:

$$\text{log of } q = \text{log of } A + \alpha \text{ log of } k \qquad (4.24)$$

In this way, Solow was able to divide the growth of output per worker into two parts: first, the growth of output per worker due to greater investment per worker; and second, the growth of output per worker due to technical progress—with the latter a residual derived by substracting the estimated growth of output per worker due to greater investment, or "capital," per worker from the total growth of output per worker.

Even so, Solow and the others who have followed in his steps would not have been able to estimate the value of $\dot{A}$ had they not been willing to make a further assumption. This is that the value of will necessarily be equal to the share of national income represented by wages. Only in this way could they obtain a figure for α so that, by then substracting the product of that ratio and the growth of "capital" per worker from the total change in output per worker each period, they could derive an estimate of $\dot{A}$. By adopting this expedient, however, they were no longer carrying out an empirical test of the neoclassical model. Instead they were simply assuming the model to be correct so that, based on that model, they could then draw certain conclusions from the results they obtained.

The assumption that the share of wages in national income reflects the marginal productivity of labor is not the only critical assumption underlying this body of work, however. No less critical is the assumption that technical progress is "disembodied"—that is, the assumption that the rate of technical progress is independent of the rate of investment (or accumulation). If, as will be argued shortly (see chapter 5, part 4), technical progress is capital-embodied, then the growth of output per worker due to greater investment cannot be distinguished, at least empirically, from the growth of output per worker due to technical progress. The two are one and the same. Indeed, the results obtained by Cornwall showing that the growth of output in manufacturing depends on the ratio of investment of manufacturing output (see section 4.2.5) strongly suggest that technical progress is in fact capital-embodied (see also the articles by Paul Davenport cited in the suggested readings for this chapter). This, in turn, means that the movements along the putative production function OF cannot be distinguished from a shift in that curve over time.

There are thus two reasons for believing that the results which have been obtained from "fitting" a neoclassical growth model to the data available for the United States and other advanced market economies cannot be taken as evidence in support of the model or the theory on which it is based. The first is that the results depend critically on the assumption that the share of national income accounted for by wages reflects the marginal productivity of labor—with the remaining share reflecting the marginal productivity of "capital"; and the second is that the results depend no less critically on the assumption that all technical progress is "disembodied." Both assumptions are belied by the available evidence, and this invalidates the results which have been obtained based on that model.

Both on logical and on empirical grounds, then, the neoclassical growth model, together with the dynamic adjustment process which underlies it, can be rejected as an explanation for the secular rate of expansion that be observed in the case of advanced market economies like that of the United States. While this does not necessarily invalidate other versions of the neoclassical model—particularly, the static microeconomic versions associated with Walras and Marshall that will be considered in chapters 5 and 6—it does eliminate the one version which can be said to encompass technical progress and economic growth. With the neoclassical growth model rejected as being inapplicable to an expanding economy, there is little choice but to fall back on some other variant of the basic Harrod-Domar model, one that does not rely on the same dynamic adjustment process to ensure that the warranted growth rate will always match the potential growth rate. This remaining growth model is the extension of the Harrod-Domar model along post-Keynesian lines upon which the chapters that follow are based.

4.4 Cyclical Movements

The discussion so far has been confined to steady-state growth models. The warranted growth rate, as given by the Harrod-Domar formula, was first identified, and this growth rate then distinguished from the potential growth rate. However, as already pointed out (see section 4.1.2), the steady-state growth path that the Harrod-Domar model's warranted growth represents can be maintained only as long as investment increases each period at the same constant rate as savings. Given the volatility of business investment, it seems unlikely that a market economy will actually follow the sort of growth path implied by the Harrod-Domar model. Indeed, it seems that anything but steady-state growth is possible. This conclusion is only reinforced by the realization that any deliberately induced change in the warranted growth rate, even a nontraumatic one, will preclude the possibility of steady-state growth, at least in the period immediately following, since it implies a period of accelerated (or decelerated) expansion with an accompanying change in the rate of accumulation.

It is therefore necessary to supplement the long-period analysis, based on the Harrod-Domar model and the balanced, steady-state growth path to which it gives rise, with an analysis of what happens when one or more of the conditions necessary for balanced, steady-state growth is not satisfied. In this way a dynamic model in the two most important senses of that term—as a description of the economic system's expansion over time and as a description of the non-steady-state, or "disequilibrium," nature of the growth process itself—can be constructed. The focus, in this concluding section, will be on what happens when the aggregate demand condition, namely, that the growth of savings be matched by the growth of investment, is not satisfied. The chapters that follow will explain what happens when the other necessary conditions for continuous, uninterrupted expansion—the aggregate supply, the sectoral balance, the value and the monetary conditions—are not satisfied.

The starting point for the analysis in this section is the recognition that there are only two possibilities insofar as the necessary condition for macrodynamic balance is concerned. One possibility—the least likely—is that the growth of savings will be matched by the growth of investment and there will be no cash-flow feedback effect as described earlier (see chapter 3, sections 2.3 and 2.5). The far more likely possibility is that the two growth rates will differ and that, with $\dot{I} \neq \dot{S}$, the cash-flow feedback effect will become an important factor in determining the economic system's subsequent growth path. In the subsections that follow, a set of analytical tools, based on the geometry of macrodynamic balance, will first be developed so as to make it possible to analyze what happens when, with the growth of savings no longer matched by the growth of investment, a disequilibrium situation is created and there is a subsequent adjustment process based on the cash-flow feedback effect. These analytical tools, in the form of separate investment and savings growth curves, will then be used to indicate what is meant by saying that an economic system is either endogenously stable or unstable. Finally, the groundwork will be laid for determining, in the chapters that follow, whether in fact an advanced market economy like that of the United States is endogenously stable or not.

4.4.1 The geometry of macrodynamic balance

With the growth rate of investment, $\dot{I}$, no longer assumed to be necessarily equal to the growth of savings, $\dot{S}$, once the economic system deviates from the steady-state growth path given by the warranted growth rate, $\dot{G}_w$, it is useful to examine geometrically the relationship among these several variables. This can be done by measuring the growth rates for investment and savings along the vertical axis of a two-dimensional diagram, as shown in exhibit 4.16, and the growth rate of aggregate output along the horizontal axis. It is then possible to draw separate investment and savings curves, indicating how $\dot{I}$ and $\dot{S}$ vary as the growth of aggregate output, $\dot{G}$, varies. The argument can be generalized, as it will be shortly, by replacing the variables $\dot{I}$ and $\dot{S}$ along the vertical axis with the growth of discretionary expenditures, $\dot{E}$, and the growth of discretionary funds, $\dot{F}$.

As long as the economy can be assumed to be expanding along the steady-state growth path given by the warranted growth rate, the $\dot{I}$ and $\dot{S}$ curves will coincide, as shown in exhibit 4.17, and together they will, in the absence of any feedback effect of the warranted growth rate on the social rate of return on investment, lie along a 45° line drawn from the origin. This simply means that, whatever the warranted growth rate may be, the growth of investment and the growth of savings will be equal to one another as well as equal to the warranted growth rate itself (as evidenced by the expansion paths for the Alpha and the other economies traced out in exhibits 4.1 *et al.*). If, as seems unlikely for the reasons already discussed (see section 4.2.2), the social rate of return on investment increases as the warranted growth rate itself rises, then the line representing the coincidence of the investment and savings growth curves will rise from the origin with a slope of less than 45°, as shown in exhibit 4.18—with the difference between the $\dot{I}$ and $\dot{S}$ curves (which coincide) and the 45° line indicating the feedback effect that the warranted growth rate has on the social rate of return on investment (the inverse of the incremental capital-output ratio).

Neither of these last two diagrams, since the investment and savings growth curves coincide, is of much analytical value by itself. Still, they make an important point, one that helps to locate the two growth curves in the type of disequilibrium situation shown in exhibit 4.16. For one of the growth rates measured along the horizontal axis in exhibit 4.16 can be identified as the warranted growth rate, $\dot{G}_W$ (see exhibit 4.19); and as such it serves as a benchmark for any other growth rate measured along the same axis (including the actual growth rate, $\dot{G}$). It indicates, for any other growth rate, the extent of the displacement of the economy from the steady-state growth path given by the warranted growth rate. Moreover, as can be seen from exhibit 4.19, while the investment and savings growth curves may well diverge from one another at any of those other growth rates, at the warranted growth rate they must necessarily be equal to one another and thus intersect or in some other way occupy the same point along that vertical plane. Finally, unless there is some feedback effect of the warranted growth rate on the

Exhibit 4.16

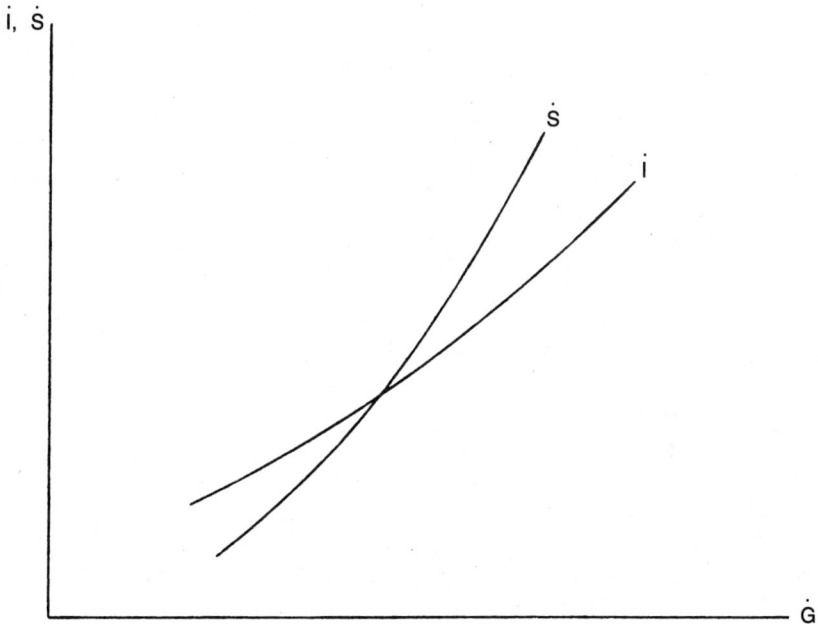

social rate of return on investment, that common point on the vertical plane for both the investment and savings growth curves will lie along a 45° line drawn from the origin.

The investment and savings growth curves shown in exhibit 4.19 are derived from more general investment and savings growth functions—just as the demand and supply curves of traditional microeconomic analysis are derived from more general demand and supply functions. The investment growth function takes the following general form:

$$\dot{i} = \dot{i}_w + f(\dot{G} - \dot{G}_w, X_1, X_2, \ldots, X_m) \qquad (4.25)$$

while the savings growth function takes the following general form:

$$\dot{S} = \dot{S}_w + f(\dot{G} - \dot{G}_w, Y_1, Y_2, \ldots, Y_n) \qquad (4.26)$$

where $\dot{i}_w$ and $\dot{S}_w$ are the rates of growth for investment and savings respectively that would prevail if the economy were expanding along a warranted growth path (which means they would then be equal to one another and, with ϱ constant, also equal to $\dot{G}_w$); $\dot{G}$ is the actual growth of output as distinct from the warranted

Exhibit 4.17

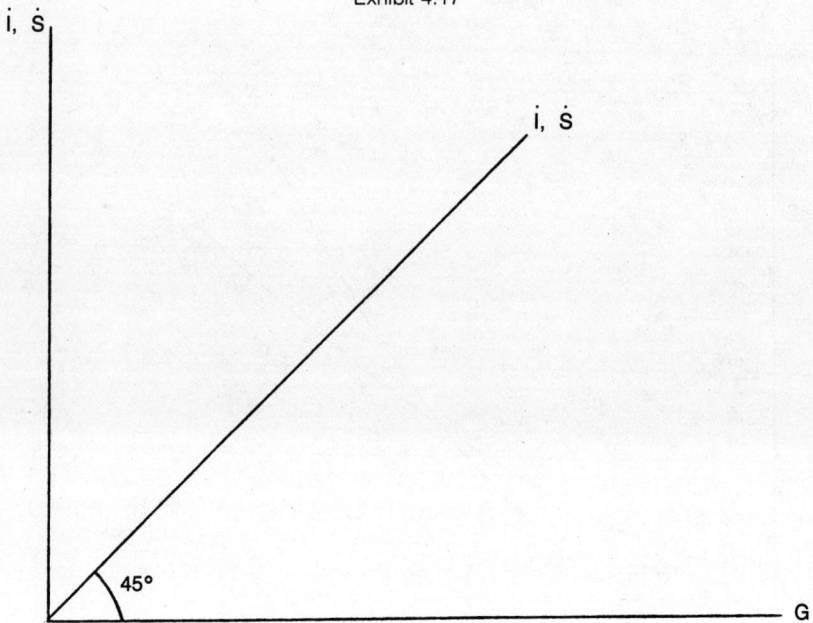

Exhibit 4.18

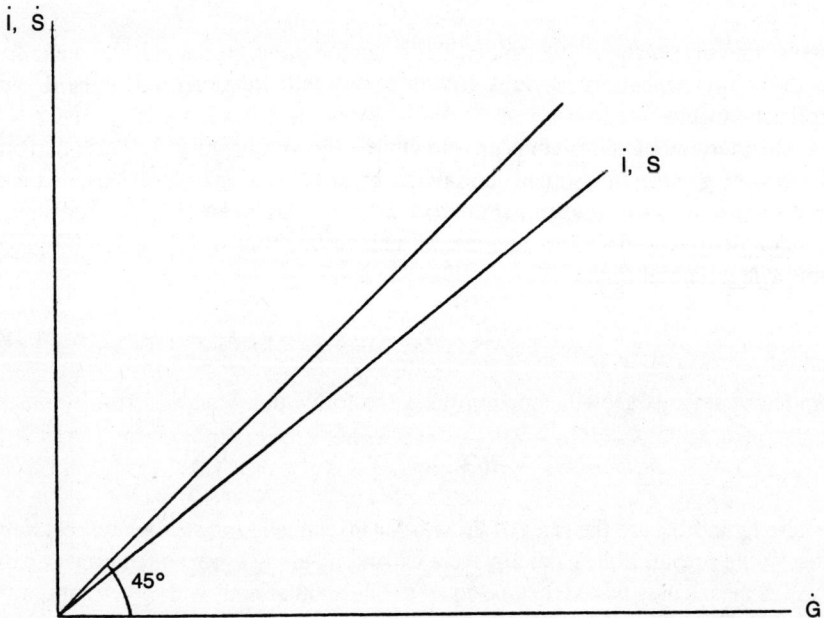

Exhibit 4.19

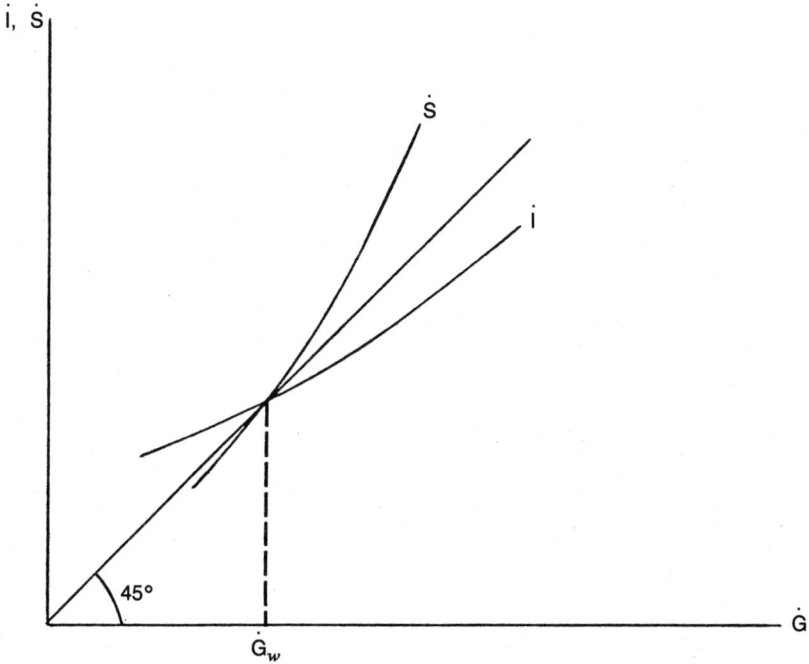

growth rate, $\dot{G}_w$; X_1, X_2, . . . , X_m are a set of other factors that influence the growth of investment, and Y_1, Y_2, . . . , Y_n are a set of other factors that influence the growth of savings. The latter two sets of factors, to be further specified in the chapters that follow, serve as the parameters of the investment and savings curves shown in exhibit 4.19; and it is only as a result of a change in one of these parameters that one or the other curve will shift. The two curves indicate how $\dot{I}$ and $\dot{S}$ each vary, relative to $\dot{I}_w$ and $\dot{S}_w$, as the actual growth rate, $\dot{G}$, deviates from the warranted growth rate, $\dot{G}_w$—other factors (i.e., the parameters of the two curves) remaining unchanged.

Actually, once there is any deviation from the warranted growth rate, that term no longer applies. The secular growth rate, $\dot{G}_s$ or $\overset{\circ}{G}$, as an empirical approximation of what is meant by the warranted growth rate, must be used instead. This means that, in constructing a model that is to be empirically applicable, equations 4.21 and 4.22 need to be rewritten as follows:

$$\dot{I} = \overset{\circ}{I} + f(\dot{G} - \overset{\circ}{G}, X_1, X_2, \ldots, X_m) \qquad (4.27)$$

and

Exhibit 4.20

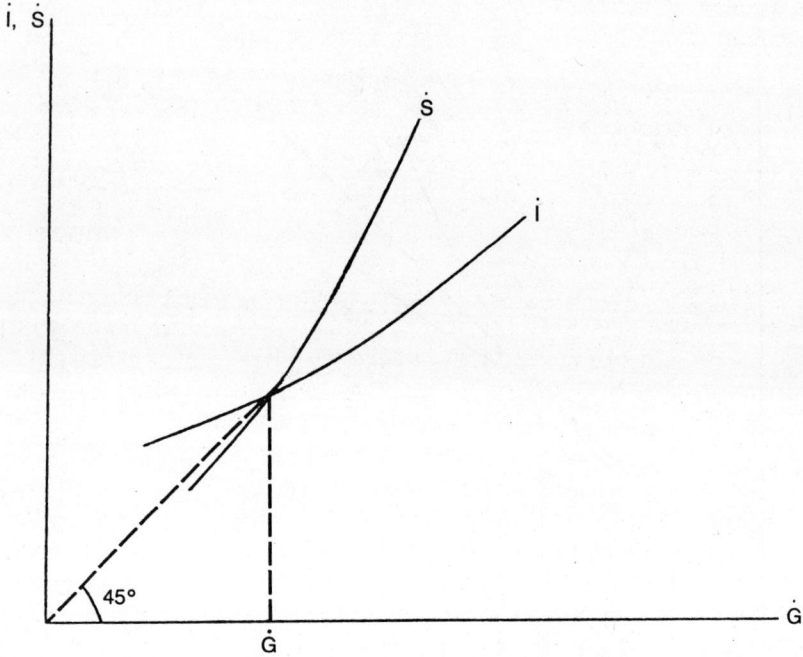

$$\dot{S} = \mathring{S} + f(\dot{G} - \mathring{G}, Y_1, Y_2, \ldots, Y_n) \qquad (4.28)$$

with the warranted growth rate shown in exhibit 4.19 replaced by the secular growth rate, $\mathring{G}$, as shown in exhibit 4.20. In other words, the growth of investment and savings during any one time period is equal to the secular growth of those two variables (the constant term in equations 4.21 and 4.22), as modified by a set of additional explanatory variables, the most important of which is the cyclical movement of aggregate output, $\dot{G} - \mathring{G}$. Once the investment and savings growth curves that are appropriate to a disequilibrium situation have been correctly drawn based on equations 4.21 and 4.22, and all the $X_1, X_2, \ldots, X_m$ and $Y_1, Y_2, \ldots, Y_n$ parameters identified, it is then possible to examine what happens when and if the economy should be displaced from the steady-state growth path given by the warranted growth rate.

4.4.2 The stability properties of an economic system

In analyzing the stability properties of an economic system, it is useful to distinguish between the endogenous and the exogenous sources of instability. The endogenous sources of instability are the processes internal to the system which, should the economy be displaced from the steady-state growth path represented by the warranted growth rate and approximated by the secular growth rate, will prevent it from returning to that growth path—and indeed may even cause it to be displaced still further. The exogenous sources of instability are the factors which, though external to the system, may nonetheless deliver a "shock" to the economy such as to cause it to deviate from the warranted, or secular, growth rate in the first place. Since the economy's vulnerability to external shocks makes the question of endogenous stability all the more crucial, it is perhaps best to begin by discussing the latter.

Whether or not an economic system is endogenously stable depends on the relative slope, and thus on the relative elasticity, of its investment and savings growth curves. Two possibilities exist. One is the situation depicted in exhibit 4.20. Notice that the savings growth curve has a greater slope than the investment growth curve both to the right and to the left of the benchmark growth rate, $\mathring{G}$ (as an empirical approximation of the warranted growth rate, $\mathring{G}_w$). This means that, if aggregate demand is cyclically high, causing the actual growth rate to exceed the secular growth rate, savings will increase more rapidly than investment. Alternatively, if aggregate demand is cyclically low, causing the actual growth rate to fall short of the secular rate, savings will fall more rapidly than investment. In either case, with savings and investment initially equal to one another, the disproportionate change in savings relative to investment means that, both to the left and to the right of $\mathring{G}$, savings and investment will no longer be equal to one another. To the right of $\mathring{G}$ savings will, because of their disproportionate increase, be greater than investment while to the left of $\mathring{G}$ savings will, because of their disproportionate decline, be less than investment.

But with savings and investment no longer equal to one another, the cash-flow feedback effect, and thus the Keynesian dynamic adjustment process described above in chapter 3, sections 2.3 and 2.5, will come into play. To the right of $\mathring{G}$, with $\dot{S} > \dot{I}$, the growth of income and output will be dampened so that the actual growth rate, $\dot{G}$, will decline until, as it approximates $\mathring{G}$ the cash-flow feedback effect becomes negligible. To the left of $\mathring{G}$, with $\dot{S} < \dot{I}$, the growth of income and output will be stimulated so that the actual growth rate, $\dot{G}$, will rise until, as it approximates $\mathring{G}$, the cash-flow feedback effect again becomes negligible. Under the conditions depicted in exhibit 4.20, then, any displacement of the economy from its secular growth rate as an empirical approximation of the warranted growth rate will trigger an endogenous response, in the form of a dynamic adjustment process, that will bring the economy back to that growth path. An economic system with investment and savings growth curves such as those depicted in exhibit 4.20 can therefore be described as being endogenously stable. This means that, should the economy for some reason deviate from its secular growth rate, it can be expected to return to that growth path as a result of its own endogenous processes.

The other possibility is the situation depicted in exhibit 4.21. In this case, it is

Exhibit 4.21

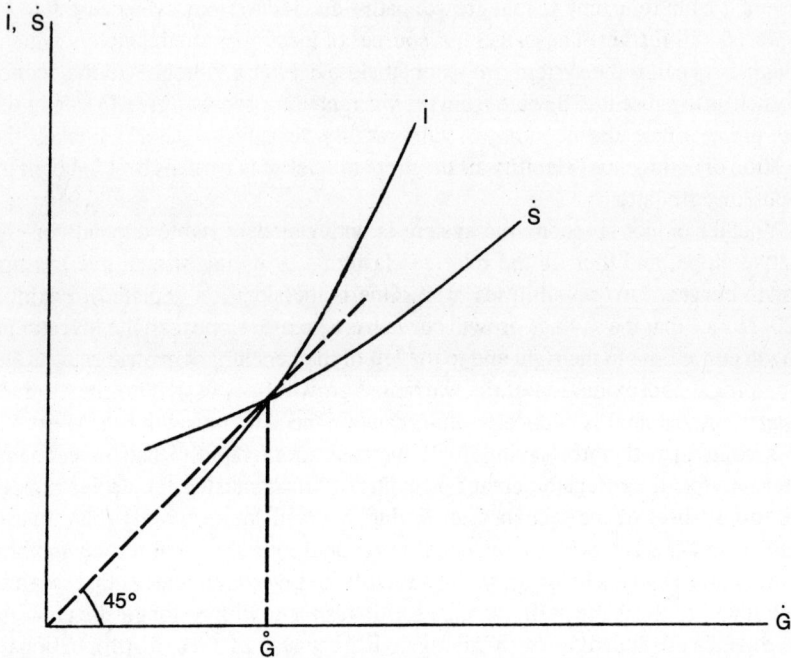

the investment growth curve that has the greater slope, both to the right and to the left of the benchmark growth rate, $\overset{\circ}{G}$. As a result, if aggregate demand is cyclically high, causing the actual growth rate, $\dot{G}$, to exceed the secular rate, investment will increase more rapidly than savings; and if, alternatively, aggregate demand is cyclically low, causing the actual growth rate, $\dot{G}$, to fall short of the secular rate, investment will decrease more rapidly than savings. In either case, there will be a disproportionate change in investment relative to savings, and this in turn will mean that the two, investment and savings, will no longer be equal to one another. To the right of $\overset{\circ}{G}$ investment will exceed savings and, to the left, investment will fall short of savings.

Again, the cash-flow feedback effect, and thus the Keynesian dynamic adjustment process, can be expected to come into play. To the right of $\overset{\circ}{G}$, with $\dot{I} > \dot{S}$, the growth of income and output will be stimulated rather than dampened, leading to a disproportionate increase in investment, a further growth of income as a result of the multiplier effect and a still further deviation from the secular growth rate; while to the left of $\overset{\circ}{G}$, with $\dot{I} < \dot{S}$, the growth of income will be dampened rather than stimulated, leading to a further disporportionate decline in investment, a further fall in income and output, and a still further deviation from the warranted growth rate. In either case the economy, instead of returning to $\overset{\circ}{G}$, will find itself displaced even further from that growth path until finally, encountering some ceiling or floor, the process is either halted or reversed. An economic system with investment and savings growth curves such as those depicted in exhibit 4.21 can therefore be described as being endogenously unstable. This means that, if displaced from the growth path represented by the secular growth rate, it will deviate still further from that growth path as a result of its own endogenous processes.

How serious a matter it is for the economic system to be endogenously unstable depends on how susceptible it is to an external shock such as will cause it to deviate from the secular growth rate in the first place. This, in turn, depends on the nature of the investment and savings growth curves' parameters. Here one needs to distinguish between the weight and the volatility of any given parameter. The weight of a parameter is the influence which that variable exerts on the growth of either investment or savings relative to the influence of the endogenous change in $\dot{G}$. It thus depends on the elasticity of $\dot{I}$ and $\dot{S}$ with respect to that parameter compared with the elasticity of $\dot{I}$ and $\dot{S}$ with respect to $\dot{G}$. The volatility of a parameter is the frequency with which a change in that variable can be expected to occur. It thus depends on the probability of a change in that variable. The greater the weight and volatility of any given parameter, whether of the investment or of the savings growth curve, the more likely it is that there will be a significant shift of the affected curve so as to displace the economy from the growth path given by the secular growth rate. Consider, for example, the situation depicted in exhibit 4.22—with the savings growth curve having shifted, as a result of a change in one of its parameters, from $\dot{S}$ to $\dot{S}'$. The decline in what would have been the growth of savings at the previous warranted growth rate, from $\dot{S}_0$ to $\dot{S}_1$, indicates the extent of the shift produced by the change in that parameter. Comparing this decline in the growth of savings with the decline in the growth of savings that would have occurred from an equal percentage decrease in the aggregate growth rate from $\mathring{G}$ to $\dot{G}_1$, and thus a movement along the savings growth curve from $\dot{S}_0$ to $\dot{S}_1'$, indicates the weight exerted by that parameter. The likelihood of such a shift in the savings growth curve occurring, meanwhile, indicates the volatility of that parameter.

In the situation depicted in exhibit 4.22, the economy will then tend to stabilize around a new growth rate, $\mathring{G}'$, with the initial decline in the growth of savings more than offset as the cash-flow feedback effect arising from the disparity between investment and savings pushes the economy up on to a more rapid growth path. But this is only because the savings growth curves, $\dot{S}$ and $\dot{S}'$, are represented as having a greater slope than the investment growth curve, $\dot{I}$. It has nothing to do with the magnitude and probability of the shift in the savings growth curve (or with the magnitude and probability of any analogous shift in the investment growth curve, as a result of some change in that curve's parameters, which would cause a similar displacement of the economy from the previous warranted, or secular, growth rate). If, in fact, the savings growth curve has a

Exhibit 4.22

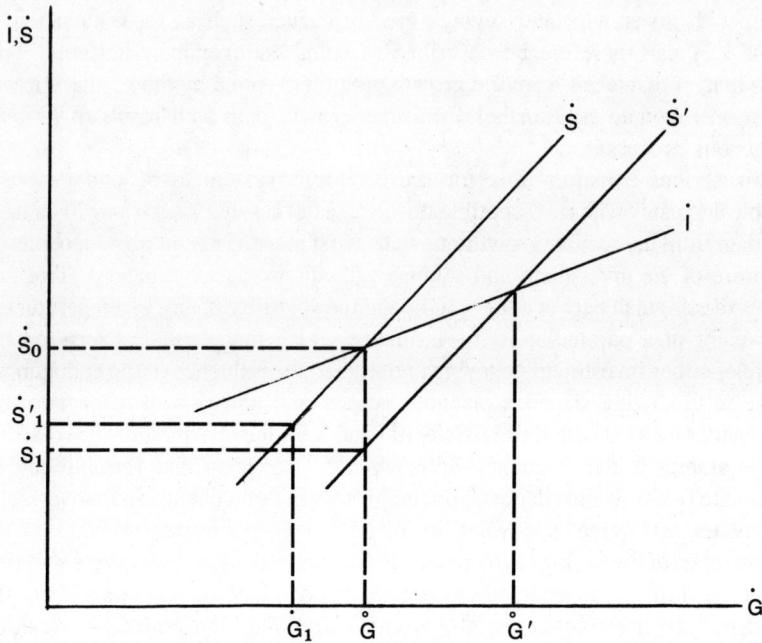

lesser slope than the investment growth curve (this is the alternative possibility depicted in exhibit 4.21), then any displacement of the economy from the warranted growth rate, as a result of a shift in either the savings or the investment growth curve, will lead, not to the stabilization of the economy around some new growth rate but rather, to a process of cumulative and unsustainable expansion or, if the shift should push the economy to the left of the warranted growth rate, to a process of cumulative decline.

The importance of being able to determine the slope of both the investment and savings growth curves, together with the weight and volatility of any parameters, should therefore be obvious. On this determination depends how stable is the U.S. or any other advanced market economy. However, the question is not one that can be answered solely on theoretical grounds—as was done, for example, by Harrod in formulating the "knife-edge" problem and by other economists in opposing his argument with the alternative neoclassical growth model. Rather the issues are empirical ones, and need to be resolved on those grounds. Indeed, this will be the task of the chapters that follow. First, however, it is necessary to elaborate on the argument up to this point in two ways. One is to shift the analysis from the macro to the sectoral level and the other is to generalize the argument about the relative responsiveness of investment and savings so that it applies to all sectors, and not just to the business sector insofar as investment is concerned and to the household sector insofar as savings are concerned.

4.4.3 The argument generalized for more than two sectors

The two functions given by equations 4.23 and 4.24 are aggregates of investment and savings growth functions for each of the sectors previously identified (see chapter 2, section 3.1). That is,

$$\dot{I} = \Sigma w_i \dot{I}_i \tag{4.29}$$

and

$$\dot{S} = \Sigma w_i \dot{S}_i \tag{4.30}$$

where $\dot{I}_i$ and $\dot{S}_i$ are the growth of investment and savings in the ith sector and w_i is the relative importance of the ith sector in determining each of the two aggregate figures. With only one sector, say the enterprise sector, viewed as carrying out all investment and with only one sector, say the household sector, viewed as being responsible for all savings as in the basic Keynesian model, the aggregate curves reduce to the curve of the one or the other sector. However, even with investment and savings defined narrowly, this is not a sufficiently realistic view of what happens in an advanced market economy like that of the United States. At the very least, the model needs to take into account any savings by business firms (which savings, in the case of the U.S. economy, represent all but about 10 percent of the funds used to finance domestic private investment). Moreover, at least part of total investment—that represented by expenditures on the economic infrastructure—is carried out by government. With investment and savings defined more broadly, as they are in the Flow of Funds Accounts, it is even less appropriate to view aggregate investment and savings as depending on the actions of any one sector.

Indeed, what is critical in determining the macrodynamic balance of a economy that is expanding over time, at least insofar as aggregate demand is concerned, is not the growth of investment and savings narrowly defined but rather the growth of what has previously been defined more broadly as discretionary expenditures and discretionary funds. It is the net cash inflow of each sector, or its "discretionary" funds, that represents the leakage from the circular flow of funds, and it is the durable goods purchases of each sector, or its "discretionary" expenditures, that represent an injection of additional funds back into the spending stream (see chapter 2, section 3.5). What this means is that wherever the argument with respect to the cash-flow feedback effect has previously been based on the relative balance between investment and savings, it needs to be modified so that it now depends on the relative balance between total discretionary expenditures (the sum of all durable goods purchases) and total discretionary funds (the net cash inflow of all sectors together). Similarly, the multiplier, k, will depend, not just on the change in investment or even on the growth of investment narrowly defined but rather on the growth of all durable goods purchases—those by the household, government and rest-of-the-world sectors as well as those by the enterprise sector. That is, it will depend on the growth of total discretionary expenditures, $\dot{E}$.

The aggregate supply condition, it should be noted, and thus the adjustment process based on the accelerator effect, is a different matter. Since only the discretionary expenditures of the enterprise sector (investment in the narrow sense) has a supply-augmenting effect in addition to its demand-enhancing effect, the aggregate supply condition remains unchanged. The growth of investment, $\dot{I}$, must still match the growth of aggregate output, $\dot{G}$, and the growth of total discretionary expenditures is irrelevant. It is only the aggregate demand condition for macrodynamic balance, and the cash-flow feedback effect that comes into play when that condition is not satisfied, that depends on the relative balance between the growth of discretionary expenditures and the growth of discretionary funds.

Thus equations 4.27 and 4.28 need to be rewritten as follows:

$$\dot{E} = \overset{\circ}{E} + f(\dot{G} - \overset{\circ}{G}, X_1, X_2, \ldots, X_m) \qquad (4.31)$$

and

$$\dot{F} = \overset{\circ}{F} + f(\dot{G} - \overset{\circ}{G}, Y_1, Y_2, \ldots, Y_n) \qquad (4.32)$$

where $\dot{E}$ is the growth of discretionary funds as measured by the durable goods purchases, or "tangible investment," shown in the Flow of Funds Accounts and $\dot{F}$ is the growth of discretionary funds as measured by the net cash inflow, or "gross savings," shown in the same FOFA and $\overset{\circ}{E}$ and $\overset{\circ}{F}$ are the secular growth of discretionary expenditures and discretionary funds respectively. This, in turn, means that equations 4.29 and 4.30 need to be rewritten as follows:

$$\dot{E} = \Sigma w_i \dot{E}_i \qquad (4.33)$$

and

$$\dot{F} = \Sigma w_i \dot{F}_i \qquad (4.34)$$

where $\dot{E}$ is the growth of discretionary expenditures in the ith sector and $\dot{F}$ is the growth of discretionary funds in the same sector. The growth of discretionary expenditures function for any one sector can then be specified as follows:

$$\mathring{\dot{E}}_i = \mathring{\dot{E}} + f(\dot{G} - \mathring{G}, X_1, X_2, \ldots, X_m) \tag{4.35}$$

while the growth of discretionary funds function for the same sector can then be specified as follows:

$$\dot{F}_i = \mathring{\dot{F}} + f(\dot{G} - \mathring{G}, Y_1, Y_2, \ldots, Y_n) \tag{4.36}$$

To determine whether or not an advanced market economy like that of the United States is endogenously stable, it is therefore necessary to estimate, using multivariate or some other statistical technique, the $\dot{E}$ and $\dot{F}$ functions for each of the different sectors of the economy so that, by aggregating the sectoral $\dot{E}$ and $\dot{F}$ curves derived from those functions (by examining the relationship between $\dot{E}$ and $\dot{F}$ on the one hand and $\dot{G}$ on the other), one see whether it is the aggregate $\dot{E}$ and $\dot{F}$ curves shown in exhibit 4.23 that apply or, alternatively, it is the aggregate $\dot{E}$ and $\dot{F}$ curves shown in exhibit 4.24 that apply. If it is the former, with the slope of the aggregate $\dot{F}$ curve being greater than that of the aggregate $\dot{E}$ curve, then the economy can be regarded as being endogenously stable; and if it is the latter, then the economy can be regarded as being endogenously unstable.

Deriving the $\dot{E}$ and $\dot{F}$ functions for each of the different sectors is, however, a much more formidable task than might at first appear to be the case. For the functions cannot be estimated without first identifying all the relevant parameters, and the parameters cannot, in turn, be identified until each of the sectors has been examined in some detail to determine what precisely are the factors influencing the growth of the sector's discretionary expenditures and the growth of its discretionary funds. Thus the analysis must shift from the macro to the sectoral level, with each of the four major sectors—the enterprise, the household, the government and the rest-of-the-world—along with any important subcomponents taken up in turn. This will be the task of the next seven chapters, which will focus on the determinants of each sector's discretionary expenditures and its discretionary funds. In the process, it will be necessary to revise much of the existing body of microeconomic theory, beginning with the theory of production and pricing.

One last point should be noted. The substitution of the secular growth rate for the warranted growth in the above diagrams is justified only if the fluctuations in the level of economic activity in the short period are in some way bounded. Otherwise, the averaging out of those cyclical fluctuations to produce an estimate of the secular trend is little more than an exercise in arithmetic, with the resulting figure unrelated to the dynamic processes outlined in this chapter. In other words, unless the economic system is stable at least to the extent that an upper and lower limit is placed on any cyclical movements by the various endogenous adjustment

Exhibit 4.23

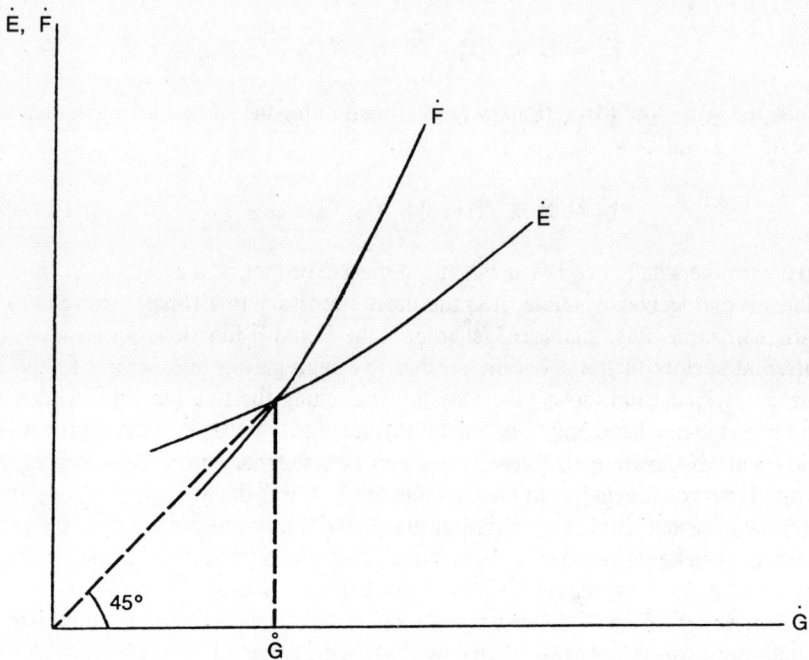

processes (for example, by the cash-flow feedback effect), the secular growth rate cannot be viewed as an empirical approximation of the warranted growth rate. The intention here is not to prejudge the issue of whether an advanced market economy is stable. That remains to be determined, on empirical grounds, in the chapters that follow. Thus, should it turn out that an advanced market economy is not endogenously stable, at least to the extent just indicated, most of what has been argued in this chapter—indeed, all but the identification of the "knife-edge" problem—can be dismissed as simply a product of the imagination rather than an explanation of the economic reality.

The minimal degree of stability necessary for the argument of this chapter to hold—namely, that any fluctuations in aggregate output be bounded—still leaves room, it should be pointed out, for pronounced cyclical movements. Indeed, it even leaves room for cyclical movements which, if economic institutions do not continue to evolve or if the government fails to adopt the appropriate policies, may become unbounded. While this last possibility cannot be excluded, still the analysis of the subsequent chapters will be predicated on the assumption that the economic system's dynamic growth path over time is characterized by pronounced cyclical movements of varying—though bounded—amplitude. It is for this reason that the concept of a warranted growth rate will be replaced by that of

Exhibit 4.24

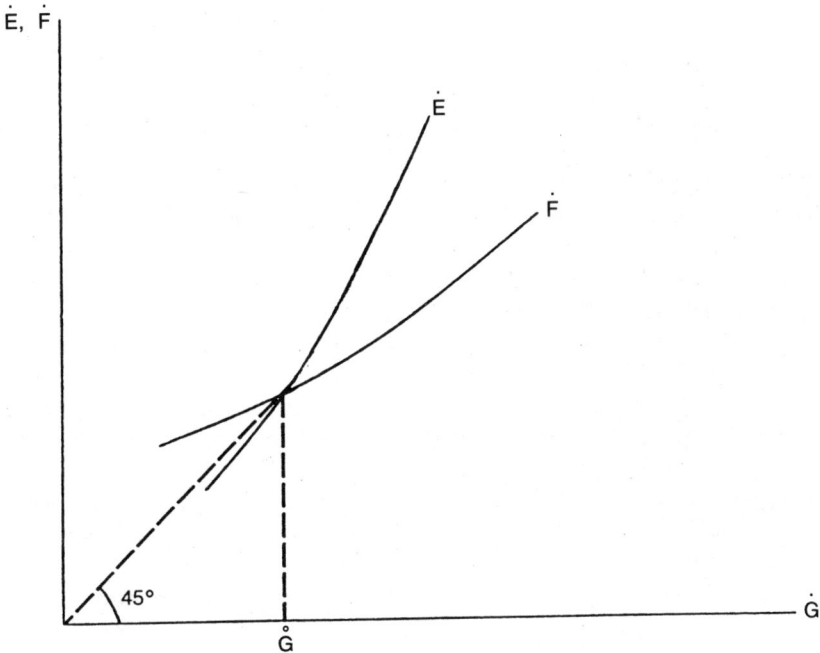

a sustainable rate of economic expansion. Unlike the warranted growth rate, the sustainable rate of economic expansion is not a steady-state growth path. It is instead a growth path that varies, within certain bounds, around a certain trend line, $\dot{G}$, with the relationships that hold, on the average over each cycle, being such that all the necessary conditions for continuous, uninterrupted expansion already identified are satisfied (see section 4.1.4). The sustainable rate of expansion is therefore like the warranted growth rate in that it is a growth path which, at least theoretically, can be maintained indefinitely. As a result, all the arguments which have been made in connection with the warranted growth rate—including the determinants of $\dot{G}_w$ and the relationship of that growth rate to the potential growth rate, $\dot{G}_p$—can be assumed to apply to the sustainable rate of economic expansion as well.

What this means is that, among the set of all possible secular growth rates, only some will be sustainable—that is, satisfy all five necessary conditions. However, until the analysis of the subsequent chapters has been completed, it is not possible to say how many such sustainable rates of economic expansion, if any, can exist. There may be one, many, or none. The answer will depend on the extent to which the arguments made in this chapter need to be modified when one takes into account, not just the pronounced cyclical movements of the macroeconomic system but also the additional relationships which hold at the micro level when the analysis is disaggregated by sector and, within the enterprise sector, by industry.

4.4.4 Summary

In analyzing the dynamics of cumulative economic expansion over time, it is necessary to differentiate the following:

1. The warranted growth rate, $\dot{G}_w$. This is the steady-state rate of expansion which the endogenous economic forces give rise to, provided certain conditions are met. The most important of these conditions, in the case of the Harrod-Domar model, is that the rate of growth of investment, $\dot{I}$, remain unchanged and that it be equal to both the rate of growth of savings, $\dot{S}$, and the rate of growth of aggregate output, $\dot{G}$. According to the Harrod-Domar model, the warranted growth rate depends on both the rate of accumulation, as determined by the marginal propensity to save, s, and on the social rate of return on investment, the inverse of the incremental capital-output ratio, v. That is, $\dot{G}_w = \frac{s}{v}$. Since the warranted growth rate is only a theoretical construct and cannot, because of the economy's cyclical movements, be observed directly, one needs to substitute for it, as an empirical approximation, the secular growth rate, $\mathring{G}$. The latter is calculated by fitting a trend line to the data.

2. The potential growth rate, $\dot{G}_p$. This is the steady-state rate of expansion which the economic system is capable of, based on the availability of exogenously supplied inputs, consisting of both human and natural resources. The potential growth rate is sometimes referred to as the "natural" growth rate in the mistaken view that it depends solely on the growth of population. Even if one ignores the need for natural resource inputs, however, and focuses only on the availability of human resource inputs, the potential growth rate depends on the growth of the labor force, $\mathring{H}$, and the growth of output per worker, $\mathring{Z}$, with the latter setting the upper limit on the rate of increase in the material standard of living. That is, $\dot{G}_p = \mathring{H} + \mathring{Z}$.

3. The actual growth rate, $\dot{G}$. This is the rate of expansion that can actually be observed in the case of any economic system by accepting as real phenomena the recorded changes in aggregate output over time. The actual growth rate can be explained in terms of two separate movements: one, the continuation of an existing trend, as measured by the secular growth rate, $\mathring{G}$, and two, a cyclical movement around the trend, as measured by the difference between the actual growth rate and the secular growth rate. That is, $\dot{G} = \mathring{G} + (\dot{G} - \mathring{G})$.

4. The sustainable rate of economic expansion. This is the secular growth rate at which all five of the necessary conditions for continous economic expansion are satisfied. Cyclical movements around some trend line, $\mathring{G}$, are allowed for but the arguments which have been made in connection with the warranted growth rate, $\dot{G}_w$, then apply to that secular rate of economic expansion.

It is because the warranted growth rate and the potential growth rate have different determinants that they may diverge from one another, creating the possibility of increasing or decreasing underutilization of the labor force in the long period. And it is because the necessary conditions for maintaining the steady-state growth path given by the warranted growth rate are not likely to be satisfied that the actual growth rate can be expected to diverge from the warranted growth rate and hence, because of that divergence, from the secular growth rate as well. Indeed, it is because the warranted growth rate may diverge from the potential growth rate, and the actual growth rate may, in turn, diverge from the warranted or secular growth rate, that both a long-period and a short-period analysis are necessary as part of the same post-Keynesian macrodynamic analysis. The examination of the warranted or secular growth rate relative to the potential growth rate constitutes the long-period analysis of post-Keynesian theory; and the examination of the actual rate of expansion relative to the warranted or secular rate constitutes the short-period analysis.

The neoclassical growth model, since it assumes the existence of an implausible adjustment mechanism whereby the warranted growth rate necessarily adjusts to whatever is the potential growth rate, is of little help in understanding the secular trends—or even the sources of long-period expansion. Indeed, it is able to encompass technical progress within its framework only by making the additional implausible assumption that technical progress is not capital-embodied. On the other hand, the static Keynesian model, which serves as the short-period complement of that long-period model in the "neoclassical synthesis," makes no distinction between the actual and the warranted growth rate (or even between the actual and the secular growth rate), and is therefore no less flawed. Indeed, that model ignores the process of cumulative economic expansion altogether. Only the post-Keynesian approach incorporates both a realistic long-period analysis with a disequilibrium short-period analysis as integral parts of the same overall conceptual framework.

Now that the long-period backdrop has been sketched, it is possible to proceed with an analysis of the short period during which economic events actually take place. (The long-period backdrop is necessary to explain the secular trends from which the short-period movements are deviations.) In seeking to understand why the actual growth rate is likely to be different from the warranted or secular rate, it is important to focus on the factors determining the growth of investment on the one hand and the growth of savings on the other. For it is the relative balance between investment and savings—or, more generally, between discretionary expenditures and discretionary funds as measured in the Flow of Funds Accounts—that will determine the cash-flow feedback effect and thus, together with the multiplier effect of discretionary or autonomous expenditures alone, the cyclical movements of the economy. However, the separate determinants of discretionary expenditures and of discretionary funds cannot be discerned from just a macroeconomic perspective. It is necessary to look at each of the different sectors separately so as to be able to identify the relevant factors that need to be included as the parameters of that sector's $\dot{E}$ and $\dot{F}$ curves. Hence the focus must now shift from the macro to the sectoral level with the analysis, in this way, disaggregated.

Recommended Readings

Harrod's own model was first presented in the *Economic Journal* in 1939 ("An Essay in Dynamic Theory," March) and then further elaborated on in his 1948 book, *Towards a Dynamic Economics*, London: Macmillan. See also J. A. Kregel, *Rate of Profit, Distribution and Growth: Two Views*, Chicago: Aldine, 1974, ch. 8, and "Economic Dynamics and the Theory of Steady Growth: An Historical Essay on Harrod's 'Knife-edge'," *History of Political Economy*, Spring 1980; Luigi L. Pasinetti, *Growth and Income Distribution*, London: Cambridge University Press, 1974, ch. 4. For Domar's own version of the same model, see his "Expansion and Employment," *American Economic Review*, March 1947, and *Essays in the Theory of Growth*, London: Oxford University Press, 1957. See also Frank Hahn and R. C. O. Matthews, "The Theory of Economic Growth: A Survey," in *Surveys of Economic Theory*, Vol. II, New York: St. Martin's Press, 1965, pp. 5–9, 26–31; John R. Hicks, *Capital and Growth*, London: Oxford University Press, 1965, chs. 10–11.

The classic exposition of the comparative dynamic approach, and indeed of the post-Keynesian long-period mode of analysis in general, will be found in Joan Robinson, *The Accumulation of Capital*, London: Macmillan, 1956. This source should be supplemented by her *Essays in the Theory of Economic Growth*, London: Macmillan, 1956, written in further explication of the argument found in *The Accumulation of Capital* when it appeared that the argument of the earlier work had passed over the heads of most of the economics profession. See also Kregel, *Rate of Profit, Distribution and Growth: Two Views*, Chicago: Aldine, 1971, ch. 11.

For the empirical evidence by Cornwall referred to in the text, see his *Modern Capitalism, Its Growth and Transformation*, Armonk, N.Y.: M. E. Sharpe, 1983 [1st ed., London: Martin Robinson, 1977]. This book is notable for its effort to test empirically the different theories of long-term economic growth. Cornwall's findings have been confirmed by others. See, for example, the work of S. Gromulka cited by Paul Stoneman, *The Economic Analysis of Technological Change*, Oxford: Oxford University Press, 1983, p. 183. As for the argument about the advantages of relative backwardness, see Alexander Gerschenkron, *Economic Backwardness in Historical Perspective*, Cambridge, Mass.: Harvard University Press, 1962.

For Harrod's original discussion of the potential growth rate under the rubric of the "natural growth rate," see his article, "An Essay in Dynamic Theory," and his later book, *Towards a Dynamic Economics*. See also Kregel, *Rate of Profit, Distribution and Growth*, ch. 8; Robinson, *The Accumulation of Capital*, pp. 404–06; Pasinetti, *Growth and Income Distribution*, ch. 4. On the possible divergence between the warranted and potential growth rates, see Robinson, *The Accumulation of Capital*, and *Essays in the Theory of Economic Growth*.

On the neoclassical growth model, see Robert M. Solow, "A Contribution to the Theory of Economic Growth," *Quarterly Journal of Economics*, 1956, and "Technical Change and the Aggregate Production Function," *Review of Economics and Statistics*, 1957; T. W. Swan, "Economic Growth and Capital Accumulation," *Economic Record*, 1956; James E. Meade, *A Neo-Classical Theory of Economic Growth*, London: Allen and Unwin, 1961. For an earlier review of the literature and an exposition of the type of geometric diagram used in this section to represent the neoclassical growth model, see Hahn and Matthews, "The Theory of Economic Growth: A Survey," pp. 9–15, 31–33, 47–55. For later surveys of the empirical literature, see M. Ishaq Nadiri, "Some Approaches to the Theory and Measurement of Total Factor Productivity: A Survey," *Journal of Economic Literature*, December 1970, pp 1137–77; Charles Kennedy and A. P. Thirwell, "Technical Progress: A Survey," *Economic Journal*, March 1972. See also C. W. Cobb and Paul H. Douglas, "A Theory of Production," *American Economic Review*, 1928, pp. 139–65; S. Valanis-Vail, "An Econometric Model of Growth, U.S.A. 1969–1953," *American Economic Review*, May 1955, pp. 208–21; Paul Davenport, "Investissement, progres technique et croissance economique," *L'Actualite Economique*, nos. 1–2, Janvier-Juin 1982; Stoneman, *The Economic Analysis of Technological Change*, pp. 181–86.

The line of argument presented in part 4 of this chapter can be traced, in its historical development, through the following works: Robinson, *Essays in the Theory of Economic Growth*, p. 48; Alfred S. Eichner and J. A. Kregel, "An Essay on Post-Keynesian Theory: A New Paradigm in Economics," *Journal of Economic Literature*, December 1975; Eichner, *The Megacorp and Oligopoly: Micro Foundations of Macrodynamics*, Armonk, N.Y.: M. E. Sharpe, 1980 [1st ed., Cambridge University Press, 1976], ch. 6; Eichner, "The Geometry of Macrodynamic Balance," *Australian Economic Papers*, June 1977; "Macrodynamic Modeling and Post-Keynesian Theory," *Thames Papers in Political Economy*, Summer 1983. See also Pasinetti, *Growth and Income Distribution*, ch. 3.

Chapter 5

The Enterprise Sector: A Disaggregated Model of Production

Contents

Chapter 5

The Enterprise Sector: A Disaggregated Model of Production

The radically different theory which has emerged since the 1930s is primarily macroeconomic in its orientation. This means that it is concerned with the behavior of the economy as a whole. Clearly, however, the behavior of the whole depends, at least in some ways, on the behavior of its component parts. And this means that, underlying the macroeconomic model, there must be a microeconomic foundation. Now that the outline of a macrodynamic theory has been broadly sketched, the task of the next seven chapters will be to provide that microeconomic foundation.

The overall objective, in these next seven chapters, will be to identity the various factors determining the growth of discretionary expenditures and the growth of discretionary funds so that separate E and F curves can be derived for each of the different sectors. However, in the case of the enterprise sector, the first of the sectors to be examined in detail, there is an even more immediate goal. This is to overcome the other shortcoming, besides its static nature, which has limited the usefulness of the basic Keynesian model. That other shortcoming is the model's inability to distinguish real from nominal changes in output, and thus to provide a satisfactory explanation for the secular inflation that has bedeviled the U.S. and other advanced market economies in the post World War II period. It is the need to account for the rise in the price level that explains why the analysis of investment and finance in chapter 7, the penultimate step in deriving the enterprise sector's E and F curves, is preceded by an analysis in chapter 6 of the individual firm's pricing behavior. Indeed, as will be made clear, the price and investment decisions are inextricably linked and therefore need to be analyzed within the same comprehensive model of individual firm behavior—one that is set in the context of an industry that is expanding over time at a certain rate relative to other industries and thus expanding at a certain rate relative to the growth of the economy as a whole.

Still, before the pricing and investment behavior of the individual firm can be analyzed, there is a prior question that needs to be taken up. This is the question of how much will be produced, not just by the enterprise sector as a whole but also by each of the industries which make up the enterprise sector. Thus, the model that has been developed up to this point now needs to be disaggregated, first by sector and then, within the enterprise sector, by industry. The basis for doing this will be the type of input-output model already examined in connection with the system of accounts by which aggregate output and its principal components are measured. The distinguishing characteristic of this type of model, at least insofar as production is concerned, is the assumption that inputs can be used only in fixed combinations with one another, without the degree of substitutability usually assumed in orthodox models.

This "fixed-coefficient" model of production can be termed the Leontief model in recognition of Wassily Leontief's preeminant role not only in formulating the model but also in giving it empirical substance. The model, however, is part of a larger family of fixed-coefficient models of production that go back in economics to the *tableau economique* of François Quesnay (1694–1774). Thus the approach to be followed in this and the succeeding chapters has more in common with the classical tradition in economics than with the neoclassical theory which has come to prevail since 1870. It owes more to Smith and Ricardo than to Walras and Marshall. Indeed, the construction of a post-Keynesian macrodynamic model, erected on the micro foundation of an input-output model, represents a return to that classical tradition. Here the key contribution, besides that of Leontief himself, is the work of Piero Sraffa in reconstructing Ricardo's arguments so as to highlight the distributional issue and of John von Neumann in showing how a fixed-coefficient model of production can be used to analyze the process of growth itself. Yet, it was not until Luigi Pasinetti's recent work of synthesis, *Structural Change and Economic Growth* (1981), that an input-output model of production suitable for analyzing the problems of growth and distribution could be said to have been fully integrated with the rest of post-Keynesian theory.

5.1 The Input-Output Model Further Refined

This chapter picks up where the discussion of the Leontief input-output model left off in chapter 2. That model needs to be elaborated on and further refined in a number of ways before it can serve as the micro foundation for a macrodynamic model—particularly one meant to explain the secular rise in prices. One thing that needs to be done is to specify the n different industries into which the enterprise sector is divided so that some of the more important distinctions—in particular, the distinction between commodity and industrial markets—can be brought out. A second way the model needs to be further refined is to break down the nominal flows shown in the input-output table's cells into their price and quantity components. Once this has been done, it will be possible to manipulate the model by means of matrix algebra, and the stage will then be set for explaining what determines the level of output in each of the n different industries which constitute the enterprise sector.

5.1.1 Plants, firms, industries and sectors

The individual plant, or establishment, is the smallest unit of business organization with which we shall need to be concerned. It consists of a certain type of physical structure, together with the necessary complement of equipment, work force and managerial personnel, for supplying a uniquely delineated good or service. The individual plant can readily be identified since it is the only facility, at that particular address, producing that particular good or service. The plant may actually include two or more plant segments, each of which has the full complement of equipment and personnel needed to operate at the lowest possible cost. However, except for being able to make a certain point about the nature of the cost curves confronting the individual firm (see section 5.3.2), it is not necessary to probe below the level of the individual plant.

The firm, consisting of one or more separate plants, is the relevant social unit for analyzing decision-making within the enterprise sector. As already pointed out (see chapter 1, section 1.1), two quite different types of firms can be identified. They are the family-controlled neoclassical proprietorship and the megacorp. The latter is controlled by an executive group, drawn from a professionally trained managerial class and chosen for reasons other than family ties or equity holdings. Indeed, the members of the executive group may own little or no stock in the company they direct. This distinction between family-controlled and professionally managed enterprises is even more basic than the distinction between proprietary and corporate forms of business since many family-controlled firms, in order to obtain the tax and other benefits, have become incorporated while a number of managerially controlled firms, in order to preclude the possibility of a takeover, have now gone "private" by purchasing their publicly traded shares. Although there are other features which distinguish the megacorp from the neoclassical proprietorship, the authority exercised by a professional class of managers is the crucial one insofar as the analysis of decisionmaking is concerned. This is because the behavior which decisionmaking represents depends on motivation, and motivation, in turn, depends on the nature of the individuals or group making the decisions.

In an earlier and simpler period, when each firm consisted of but a single plant, there was no need to define the plant and the firm separately. With its single plant, the firm necessarily belonged to only one industry—the industry consisting of all the other single-plant firms producing the same good or service. However, with multiple-plant operation being one of the distinguishing features of the megacorp and with those multiple plants producing a variety of goods and services, matters are no longer so simple. Plants can now be grouped together in either of two quite different ways: (a) into firms (all the plants under the control of the same management), and (b) into industries (all the plants producing the same good or service). While it is the first way of grouping plants that is crucial for understanding decision-making within the enterprise sector, it is the second way that is crucial for understanding the enterprise sector as a system of production.

Although an industry has already been defined as the set of all firms with plants that produce the same good or service (see chapter 1, section 1.1), it is quite another matter to be able to say which goods or services are identical to one another. The very fact that the goods are being supplied by different firms, each under a separate label, may be sufficient to make them different in the mind of the purchaser. Indeed, the use of brand names and similar means of differentiating one firm's product from that of another means that, in effect, no two firms actually supply the same good or service. It is therefore necessary to fall back on a somewhat looser definition of what constitutes an industry. An industry, it can said, consists of all the firms with plants that produce a *similar* type of good or service rather than an "identical" one.

As for what is meant by a similar type of good or service, two answers can be given. One is based on the behavior of the firms supplying the goods or services. The goods or services supplied by different firms can be said to be sufficiently similar that the firms must be considered part of the same industry if it is necessary for any one of those firms to know the price being quoted for that type of good or service by each of the other firms. On this behavioral basis, an industry can be said to consist of all the firms whose salesmen keep watch on, and therefore monitor, the same set of prices. This is the definition of an industry which is most appropriate for analyzing the pricing behavior of firms and it depends empirically, as will be brought out later (see chapter 6, sections 2.2 and 4.3), on the cross-elasticity of demand within the given set of firms. However, the definition of an industry that is most appropriate when it comes to constructing an input-output table, and hence for to analyzing the enterprise sector as a production system, is somewhat different. For that purpose, what matters is the technology on which the firms depend. The goods or services supplied by different firms can be said to be sufficiently similar that the firms must be considered part of the same industry when the goods or services are produced using the same types of inputs and is considered, in turn, by other industries or by final consumers to be the same type of input into their own production process or household operation. On this technological basis, an industry can be said to consist of all the firms (or parts thereof) which obtain their material inputs from the same group of suppliers and sell their output to the same group of buyers. The two definitions of an industry, while different, are not necessarily incompatible with one another.

Still, as a practical matter, any attempt to report data on the U.S. economy's enterprise sector, broken down into mutually exclusive industry categories, must take into account the Standard Industrial Classification (SIC) developed by the Federal government. This is because, as already pointed out (see chapter 2, section 1.2), the Federal government, in collecting industry data through the quinquennial economic censuses and other surveys, uses the SIC categories. The SIC schema is based on a four- to seven-digit code, the first two digits of which are used to delineate 84 major industry groups, beginning with 01, agricultural crop production, and ending with 99, nonclassifiable establishments. The steel industry, for example, is included in the major industry group 33, primary metal products. With the addition of a third digit, these major industry groups can be broken down into more narrowly defined industry groups. For example, industry group 331 covers blast furnaces, steel works and rolling and finishing mills, while industry 332 covers iron and steel foundries—the two groupings together encompassing the entire steel industry. The other industry groups within major group 33 cover aluminum, copper and other nonferrous metals. With the addition of a fourth digit, the industry groups can be broken down into even more narrowly defined industries. For example, industry 3312 encompasses blast furnaces, steel works and rolling mills; industry 3313, electrometallurgical products; industry 3315, steel wire drawing, steel nails and spikes; industry 3316, cold rolled steel sheet, strip and bars, and industry 3317, steel pipe and tubes. The major industry groups, then, are what are often referred to as "two-digit SIC industries;" the industry groups, what are often referred to as "three-digit SIC industries," and the industries, what are often referred to as "four-digit SIC industries." At the four-digit level, the SIC schema is able to delineate up to 10,000 separate industries, with about half that number of industry code numbers actually being used.

In the construction of the input-output table for the U.S. economy, as was pointed out earlier (see chapter 2, section 1.2), the 5,000 separate industries delineated in the SIC schema are reduced to 496 industries by combining wholes and parts of various four-digit SIC categories. This is the level of detail which the experience gained in constructing input-output tables has shown to be necessary for bringing out the economy's interindustry flows. The 496-industry breakdown is therefore the most detailed one available for analyzing the enterprise sector as a production system. Four hundred ninety-six, however, is a larger number of industries than can easily be handled within a single graphical display, or even within a single model of the enterprise sector. To make the analysis more manageable, the 496 industries can be reduced to 79 major industry groupings which, together with six dummy sectors to account for the income generated outside the enterprise sector, represent the industry breakdown for the 85-fold input-output matrix, the smaller of the two available for the U.S. economy. The 79-industry breakdown is therefore the minimal one for disaggregating the enterprise sector into individual industries.

Exhibit 5.1 lists these 79 major industry groupings. The number in parenthesis is the number of more narrowly defined industries from among the 496 which have been combined to form the industry grouping, and the percent of value added shown in the last column indicates the relative importance of the industry grouping insofar as total value added, or national income, is concerned. The steel industry, it will be noted, no longer falls between groupings but rather constitutes the whole of industry 37.

Exhibit 5.1

Industrial Structure of the Enterprise Sector

	Percent value added
I Primary Activities	4.3
A. Agriculture, forestry and fisheries	2.7
1. livestock and livestock products (3)	0.8
2. other agricultural products (13)	1.7
3. forestry and fishery products (1)	0.1
4. agricultural, forestry and fishery services (1)	0.1
B. Mining	1.6
5. iron and ferroalloy ores mining (1)	*
6. nonferrous metal ores mining (2)	0.1
7. coal mining (1)	0.3
8. crude petroleum and natural gas (1)	1.0
9. stone and clay mining and quarrying (1)	0.1
10. chemical and fertilizer mineral mining (1)	*
II Secondary Activities	39.4
C. Construction	6.4
11. new construction (32)	4.6
12. maintenance and repair construction (17)	1.8
D. Manufacturing	24.7
13. ordnance and accessories (6)	0.3
14. food and kindred products (44)	2.8
15. tobacco manufactures (4)	0.4
16. broad and narrow fabrics, yard and thread mills (4)	0.5
17. miscellaneous textile goods and floor coverings (10)	0.1
18. apparel (7)	0.9
19. miscellaneous fabricated textile products (8)	0.1
20. lumber and wood products (13)	0.7
21. wood containers (1)	*
22. household furniture (6)	0.2
23. other furniture and fixtures (7)	0.1
24. paper and allied products, except containers (12)	0.6
25. paperboard containers and boxes (1)	0.3
26. printing and publishing (15)	1.2
27. chemicals and selected chemical products (10)	0.9
28. plastics and synthetic materials (4)	0.3
29. drugs, cleaning and toilet products (5)	0.6
30. paints and allied products (1)	0.1
31. petroleum refining and related industries (3)	0.6
32. rubber and miscellaneous plastic products (6)	0.8
33. leather tanning and finishing (1)	*
34. footwear and leather products (8)	0.2
35. glass and glass products (2)	0.3
36. stone and clay products (23)	0.6
37. primary iron and steel manufcturing (9)	1.3
38. primary nonferrous metals manufcturing (14)	0.5
39. metal containers (2)	0.1
40. heating, plumbing and structural metal products (10)	0.5
41. screw machine products and stampings (4)	0.4
42. other fabricated metal products (11)	0.6
43. engines and turbines (2)	0.2
44. farm and garden machinery (2)	0.2
45. construction and mining machinery (3)	0.3
46. matrials handling machinery and equipment (4)	0.1

47. metalworking machinery and equipment (6)	0.4
48. special industry machinery and equipment (6)	0.3
49. general industrial machinery and equipment (7)	0.4
50. miscellaneous machinery, except electrical (2)	0.2
51. office, computing and accounting machines (5)	0.3
52. service industry machines (5)	0.3
53. electric industrial equipment and apparatus (8)	0.4
54. household appliances (7)	0.2
55. electric lighting and wiring equipment (3)	0.2
56. radio, TV and communications equipment (4)	0.7
57. electronic components and accessories (3)	0.4
58. miscellaneous electrical machinery and supplies (5)	0.2
59. motor vehicles and equipment (4)	1.8
60. aircraft and parts (3)	0.7
61. other transportation equipment (7)	0.4
62. scientific and controlling instruments (7)	0.3
63. optical, opthalmic and photographic equipment (3)	0.3
64. miscellaneous manufacturing (20)	0.4
E. Transportation, communication, electric, gas and sanitary services	8.3
65. transportation and warehousing (8)	3.8
66. communications, except radio and TV (1)	2.2
67. radio and TV broadcasting (1)	0.2
68. electric, gas, water and sanitary services (3)	2.1
III Tertiary Activities	44.6
F. Wholesale and retail trade	14.0
69. wholesale and retail trade (2)	14.0
G. Finance, insurance and real estate	15.6
70. finance and insurance (5)	3.7
71. real estate and rental (2)	11.9
H. Services	13.8
72. hotels, personal and repair services, except auto (3)	1.5
73. business services (3)	4.0
74. eating and drinking places (1)	1.8
75. auto repair and services (1)	1.0
76. amusements (2)	0.6
77. medical, educational and nonprofit organizations (9)	4.9
I. Government enterprises	1.2
78. federal government enterprises (4)	0.7
79. state and local government enterprises (3)	0.5
IV Other Value Added	11.7

The 79 major industry groupings listed in exhibit 5.1 are themselves grouped together by subsector—e.g., agriculture, mining, construction, etc. In some cases, it is more useful to disaggregate the enterprise sector by these ten subsectors than by individual industries. This is because the nature of the economic activity, or mode of production, varies less within these subsectors than between them. For example, the various agricultural industries have more in common with one another, in terms of how production is organized and carried out, than with any of the other types of industries; and the same is true of the various mining, construction and other types of industries.

The ten subsectors listed in exhibit 5.1 can be further grouped together in terms of primary, secondary and tertiary levels of economic activity. Industries at the primary level are concerned with the extraction of basic raw materials, both biological and mineral; industries at the secondary level, with the further processing of those raw materials; and industries at the tertiary level, with the distribution of the goods thereby produced, along with the provision of other services. Again, the mode of production varies less among industries at the same level than between industries at different levels. Indeed, at each level, the key to production is a different type of input. In the primary sector of the economy, the key to production lies in the nature of the land, or natural resource, inputs; in the secondary sector, the key lies in the nature of the capital inputs, and in the tertiary sector, the key lies in the nature of the human resource inputs. It should be noted that the importance of the capital inputs in the transportation, communications and other regulated utilities sector is the principal reason why that sector, even though its output is a service, is included among the secondary level industries rather than among the tertiary level. This sector is therefore an intermediate one between the secondary and tertiary levels, just as the mining sector, given the important role played in that sector by capital inputs as well as land resources, is an intermediate one between the primary and secondary levels of economic activity.

The primary, secondary and tertiary levels thus delineated can be said to constitute the commodity, industrial and service sectors of the economy respectively. In terms of economic output, the industrial sector is the most crucial one. All but about 10 percent of the commodity sector's output is sold to the industrial sector for further processing and, except for that 10 percent, all of the Gross Physical Output (GPO) is put into final form by either the construction industries (in the case of structures) or the manufacturing industries (in the case of all other physical goods). The industrial sector is the crucial one not only because virtually the entire GPO emanates from it in the physical form it finally takes but also because the type of market through which the output of the industrial sector is sold is also the type of market through which the output of the service sector is sold. This leads to the important distinction between the commodity markets found in the primary sector and the industrial-type markets which operate throughout the rest of the U.S. economy.

5.1.2 Commodity vs. industrial markets

Commodity markets are not just the type of market associated with the commodity, or primary, sector. They are also, even more importantly, the type of market in which the individual sellers, because they are so numerous and so small relative to the size of the market, are able to exert no perceptible influence on the price. They must instead take as a given, when deciding what quantity to produce, the current price as determined by demand and supply factors. The price itself can thus be described as being market-determined, rather than seller-determined, meaning that the price is controlled by impersonal market forces. The control over the price which the market exercises is usually reinforced by the existence of a speculative class of middlemen, trading on their own account, who buy when they perceive the price to be low relative to the "normal" or long-period price and who sell when they perceive the price to be high. Much of the existing price theory in economics, particularly the body of theory that falls under the rubric of the "competitive model," applies only to commodity markets of this sort, in which the individual producer is thought to face a perfectly elastic demand curve for its output. The distinguishing feature of this type of model is that the firm, once it has decided how much to produce, is assumed to throw that amount of output on the market for whatever price can be obtained. The market then functions so as to validate what has been termed the Walrasian excess demand hypothesis. This means that any imbalance between demand and supply will be eliminated through a change, of the appropriate kind, in the price variable (see chapter 6, section 4.1).

In sharp contrast to the commodity markets found in the primary sector are the industrial markets which predominate throughout the rest of the economy. In these markets, sellers are sufficiently few in number and/or enjoy a sufficiently well protected market position that it is not impossible for them to influence the market price directly. Indeed, the price they quote, either individually or collectively, is the price that can be expected to prevail in those types of markets. The sellers, then, are price setters rather than price takers. This means that, instead of being limited to deciding only what quantity to produce, they can also determine the price that buyers will have to pay. The price itself can be described as being seller-determined rather than market-determined, with the result that a supply curve as usually formulated in economic theory does not govern the market price. In an industrial market of this sort, the firm does not simply throw its output on the market for whatever price can be obtained. It sets a price and then sells whatever quantity it can at that price. In the absence of middlemen speculators, the firm has a reasonable chance of being able to hold to its announced price (see chapter 6, section 4.4). What this means is that, at least over the range which can be empirically observed, the supply curve or, more accurately, the supply-offer curve is perfectly elastic. It is therefore the Marshallian excess price hypothesis rather than the Walrasian excess demand hypothesis which holds. This, in turn, means that when there is an imbalance between demand and supply, the necessary adjustment will occur through the quantity variable rather than through the price variable. Indeed, it is precisely this type of adjustment process which, as already pointed out (see chapter 3, section 2.4), is implicit in the basic Keynesian model and its various extensions. The basic Keynesian model, then, is a model of an economy dominated by industrial markets, as distinct from commodity markets.

The distinction between commodity and industrial markets is one that a number of economists have pointed out. Gardiner C. Means, in contrasting the behavior of firms in what he termed "trading" markets with that of firms in "administered price" markets, was one of the first to make this distinction. More recently, John Hicks has noted the difference between "flex-price" markets and "fix-price" markets. Following Paul Davidson, one can also relate the difference to the distinction which economists make between "spot" and "forward" markets —that is, between markets where, since goods are being sold for immediate delivery, current demand and supply factors dictate the price and markets where, since goods are being sold for future delivery, long-period considerations instead govern. The "trading" or "flex-price" markets, then, are the markets in which "spot" prices dominate or at least are important while the "administered" or "fix-price" markets are the markets in which, if "spot" prices exist at all, they play a relatively insignificant role.

Unfortunately, the prevailing theory in economics focuses almost exclusively on commodity markets—to the virtual neglect of industrial markets with their "administered" or "fixed" prices. That this is a serious omission can be seen from exhibit 5.1, which indicates the relative importance of the primary sector compared with the secondary and tertiary sectors. Even within the primary sector, it should be noted, not all the markets are commodity or "spot" markets. In mining, especially, the extractive activities which are carried out are often part of larger integrated operations, with the raw materials simply flowing from one division to another at the direction of the company's central headquarters staff. At most, as in the case of the steel, aluminum, copper and petroleum industries, a small "spot" market exists for supplies not already tied up through long-term contracts or intra-firm commitments. On the other hand, it also needs to be pointed out that some of the manufacturing sector's output is handled through commodity markets. This is true of the more simply processed materials, such as vegetable oils and steel ingots. Still, the distinction between the primary sector on the one hand and the secondary and tertiary sectors on the other hand—with the latter accounting for all but about 10 percent of all value added—marks the dividing line between that part of the enterprise sector in which commodity markets prevail and that part in which industrial markets predominate. It is for this reason that the lack of an adequate theory of explain the process of price determination in industrial markets is such a serious omission—and why it will be necessary, in chapter 6, to correct that omission.

The industrial sector can be further divided into oligopolistic and nonoligopolistic subsectors. Although not as fundamental as the distinction between commodity and industrial markets, it is nonetheless an important one since the oligopolistic sector includes nearly all of the technologically more advanced and more rapidly growing industries. The oligopolistic subsector consists of the industries with a certain type of market structure and a certain type of representative firm. The market structure is one of oligopoly, with a few firms producing most of the industry's output and with entry significantly limited by the existence of various types of barriers. The representative firm, meanwhile, is a megacorp easily identified by: (1) the *de facto* control exercised by a professional group of managers (with the nominal owners, the stockholders, playing a largely passive role); (2) the multiple plants which the firm operates; and (3) the substantial market share which the firm holds in at least one oligopolistic industry. The nonoligopolistic subsector consists of all the other industries within the industrial sector. These industries, too, have a certain type of market structure and a certain type of representative firm. The market structure is one of numerous firms, none of which is very large either absolutely or relative to its rivals, and of minimal barriers to entry. The representative firm, meanwhile, is the same neoclassical proprietorship found in the primary, or commodity, sector—in agriculture especially. This type of representative firm can be differentiated from the megacorp by its three distinguishing features. They are: (1) the control exercised by the small group that, bound together by family or other close personal ties, serves as both the firm's managers and its owners; (2) the single or at most two plants the firm operates; and (3) the negligible share of the market the firm holds in the one industry to which it belongs—an industry which, though it is likely to be nonoligopolistic, need not be since some neoclassical proprietorships also round out the membership of many oligopolistic industries.

The oligopolistic sector encompasses approximately two-thirds of manufacturing and at least an equal portion of the transportation, communications and public utilities industries. To the extent that the megacorps which are the representative firm within the oligopolistic sector are integrated backward into mining and the other extractive industries, the oligopolistic sector also encompasses a part of the U.S. economy's primary level of activity. The nonoligopolistic sector, on the other hand, encompasses the larger share of agriculture, construction, wholesale and retail trade, and services. It also encompasses the minority portions of manufacturing and mining which are not oligopolistic. Exhibit 5.2 presents the breakdown of the strategically critical manufacturing sector between its oligopolistic and nonoligopolistic components.

Based on exhibits 5.1 and 5.2, it is possible to be more specific not only in identifying the n industries which constitute the inner matrix of the relevant input-output model for the U.S. economy but also in distinguishing, first, the commodity from the industrial sector and then, within the industrial sector, the oligopolistic from the nonoligopolistic subcomponents. The next step in further refining the input-output model will be to divide the nominal flows shown in each cell of an input-output table into their price and quantity components.

5.1.3 From nominal to real flows

It has already been explained how an input-output table, such as the one depicted in exhibit 2.1, can be partitioned into five segments: one, an inner matrix representing the interindustry flow of direct material inputs; another, a column representing the enterprise sector's net, or final, output; the third, a column

Exhibit 5.2

**Oligopolistic and Nonoligopolistic Components
of the Manufacturing Sector, 1966**

SIC No.	Industry	Percent of value added in manu-facturing	Percent of value added produced by four-digit industries with four-firm concentration ratios of at least 60 percent
Oligopolistic			
34	Fabricated metals	6.4	25.0
30	Rubber	2.5	32.5
20	Food	10.1	37.0
35	Machinery	10.9	42.6
27	Printing and publishing	5.4	45.4
38	Instruments	2.6	50.5
36	Electrical machinery	9.5	50.8
32	Stone, clay, glass	3.4	70.5
33	Primary metals	8.5	74.0
28	Chemicals	9.2	77.0
21	Tobacco	0.8	84.6
37	Transport equipment	11.8	86.7
29	Petroleum	1.9	86.7
Nonoligopolistic			
25	Furniture	1.6	0
31	Leather	1.0	1.4
24	Lumber and wood	1.9	2.3
23	Apparel	3.7	3.0
22	Textiles	3.2	10.6
26	Paper	3.8	13.8

Sources: William G. Shepherd, *Market Power and Economic Analysis* (New York, Random House, 1970). See also Shepherd, "Causes of Increased Competition in the U.S. Economy, 1939–1980," *Review of Economics and Statistics*, November, 1982, pp. 613–26.

representing the enterprise sector's gross, or total, output; the fourth, a row representing the value added by the enterprise sector; and the fifth and final element, a row representing the enterprise sector's total outlays. (See exhibit 2.3, along with exhibit 2.1). Since the third and fifth segments are identical once the total outlays are broadened to include any profits, or residual income, the last of these five elements is redundant and can therefore be ignored.

The numbers shown in each of the cells in exhibit 2.1 are value figures. They represent some quantity (e.g., tons of steel, barrels of oil, kilowatts of electricity) multiplied by some price. While the product of the two is known, the separate multiplicands themselves are not. This means the figures shown in each cell represent only the flow in nominal terms, without the real flow of goods and services being distinguishable from whatever change is occurring in the price of those goods. To develop a model of the enterprise sector that can be used to explain not only the level of production in each industry but also price movements, it is essential that we be able to break these value figures down into their price and quantity components.

Exhibit 5.3 indicates what must be done. First, the output of each industry in nominal terms (covering each industry's intermediate output, its net or final output, and its total output) needs to be divided through by the relevant price in order to determine the quantities represented in each cell. In this way, the value figures can be transformed, at least insofar as the top three segments of the input-output table are concerned, into a quantity figure multiplied by some price. Second, the value added row needs to be disaggregated into the wage bill for each industry and—ignoring for the moment any indirect business taxes—the profit or residual income. The wage bill for each industry can then be divided through by the wage rate to determine the total amount of labor inputs used by each industry. In this way, a similar breakdown can be obtained, at least for one of the two rows that compose the value added segment of an input-output table. However, the other row, representing the residual income obtained by each industry, cannot be broken down, in this or any other way, into its price and quantity components. The significance of this point will become clearer as the discussion proceeds.

The production system depicted in exhibit 5.3 and similar input-output models, with the value figures (all except the residual income) broken down into their price and quantity components, can be then rewritten as a set of algebraic equations in the following manner:

$$
\begin{array}{l}
\left.
\begin{array}{l}
p_1 q_{1.1} + p_1 q_{1.2} + p_1 q_{1.3} + \ldots + p_1 q_{1.n} \\
p_2 q_{2.1} + p_2 q_{2.2} + p_2 q_{2.3} + \ldots + p_2 q_{2.n} \\
p_3 q_{3.1} + p_3 q_{3.2} + p_3 q_{3.3} + \ldots + p_3 q_{3.n} \\
\cdot \qquad\quad \cdot \qquad\quad \cdot \qquad\qquad \cdot \\
\cdot \qquad\quad \cdot \qquad\quad \cdot \qquad\qquad \cdot \\
\cdot \qquad\quad \cdot \qquad\quad \cdot \qquad\qquad \cdot \\
p_n q_{n.1} + p_n q_{n.2} + p_n q_{n.3} + \ldots + p_n q_{n.n}
\end{array}
\right| +
\left|
\begin{array}{l}
p_1 q_{1.n+1} \\
p_2 q_{2.n+1} \\
p_3 q_{3.n+1} \\
\cdot \\
\cdot \\
\cdot \\
p_n q_{n.n+1}
\end{array}
\right| =
\left|
\begin{array}{l}
p_1 Q_1 \\
p_2 Q_2 \\
p_3 Q_3 \\
\cdot \\
\cdot \\
\cdot \\
p_n Q_n
\end{array}
\right|
\end{array}
\quad (5.1)
$$

$$+ \qquad + \qquad + \qquad\qquad +$$

$$
\left|
\begin{array}{l}
w L_1 + w L_2 + w L_3 + \ldots + w l_n \\
\Pi_1 + \Pi_2 + \Pi_3 + \ldots + \Pi_n
\end{array}
\right|
$$

where $p_1, p_2, p_3, \ldots, p_n$ is the price that must be paid for the output of industries *1, 2, 3, . . . , n* respectively; $q_{1.2}$ is the physical quantity of output produced by industry 1 which is needed as an input to produce industry 2's

Exhibit 5.3
Input-Output Table with Price and Quantity Components Delineated

Inputs obtained from industry ↓ / Outputs sold to industry →	A	B	C	D	E	Other output	Total output
A		118.5 @ $0.20	425.0 @ $0.20	114.0 @ $0.20	176.5 @ $0.20	1,085.5 @ $0.20	1,919.5 @ $0.20
B	431.0 @ $.10		35.0 @ $.10	146.0 @ $.10	478.0 @ $.10	5,492.0 @ $.10	6,582.0 @ $.10
C	33.8 @ $.50	7.9 @ $.50		86.2 @ $.50	20.8 @ $.50	537.4 @ $.50	685.8 @ $.50
D	16.1 @ $1.50	15.0 @ $1.50	13.0 @ $1.50		37.7 @ $1.50	409.7 @ $1.50	491.5 @ $1.50
E	51.6 @ $1.00	132.1 @ $1.00	65.4 @ $1.00	15.3 @ $1.00		99.4 @ $1.00	363.8 @ $1.00
Human resource inputs	97.6 @ $2.00	214.9 @ $2.00	77.9 @ $2.00	28.8 @ $2.00	91.6 @ $2.00		
Residual	$53.0	$46.3	$13.7	$65.4	$30.5		

output; $q_{2.1}$ is the physical quantity of output produced by industry 2 which is needed as an input to produce industry 1's output; $q_{1.n+1}$, $q_{2.n+1}$, . . . , $q_{n.n+1}$ is the other output, besides the output needed as inputs by other industries, produced by industries *1, 2, 3*, . . . , *n* respectively and can be termed the net or final output, as distinct from the intermediate output, of those industries; Q_1, Q_2, Q_3, . . . , Q_n is the total output of industries *1, 2, 3*, . . . , *n* respectively; L_1, L_2, L_3, . . . , L_n is the quantity of human resource inputs, measured in hours of labor, needed by industries *1, 2, 3*, . . . , *n* respectively; w is the wage rate, and Π_1, Π_2, Π_3, . . . , Π_n is the residual income of industries *1, 2, 3*, . . . , *n* respectively. The four sets of boxed lines which have been drawn—the square enclosing the inner matrix, the two rectangles to the right and the other rectangle below—serve to demarcate the four separate segments of the input-output system represented by this set of equations.

Equation set 5.1 is the basic mathematical representation of the Leontief model of production. As one feature of this model, each column defines the production and cost function for the industry shown in the column. The column itself indicates the physical quantity of direct material inputs that must be obtained from every other industry in order to produce the industry's output, the price that must be paid for each of those direct inputs, the quantity of human resource inputs that is needed, the wage that must be paid for those human resource inputs, and the amount of any residual income. The quantity variables alone represent the industry's short period production function (predicated on an already acquired stock of plant and equipment) while the product of the price and quantity variables represents the industry's short-period cost function (on the latter point, see chapter 2, section 1.1). The Leontief model of production, as given by equation set 5.1, thus incorporates the short-period production and cost function for each of the 79 (or, using a more detailed breakdown, the 496) industries delineated in the input-output table for the U.S. economy. Indeed, any subsequent reference to an industry's short-period production or cost function will be to the quantity variables or the value terms (quantity multiplied by the price) shown in the column of the input-output model representing that industry.

Relying on data from Peter Marcus's *World Steel Dynamics* (New York: Paine Webber Mitchell, Hutchins, Inc., 1978), it is possible to fill in, at least partially, the column for steel, industry number 37 in the U.S. input-output table. Exhibit 5.4, based on these data, shows how the cost of producing a ton of carbon steel in 1978 can be broken down into its material input, labor input and residual components. The figures shown under the price heading correspond to the p_1, p_2, p_3, . . . , p_n variables in equation set 5.1 and the figures under the quantity heading, to the $q_{1.37}$, $q_{2.37}$, $q_{3.37}$, . . . , $q_{n.37}$ variables. The figures under the cost/ton of steel produced heading, the product of the other two sets of figures, meanwhile correspond to the value figures which are normally all that is shown in an input-output table.

Unfortunately, this type of data is not available for all industries, at least not

Exhibit 5.4
Production Function for American Carbon Steel Industry

Item	Price	Quantity	Cost/per ton of steel produced	% of costs
Material inputs				
Coal	$38.32/ton	.95 tons	$ 36.40	13.0
Iron ore	35.25/ton	1.65 tons	41.66	14.9
Steel scrap	67.50/ton	.10 tons	6.75	2.4
Energy	1.90/mbtu	11 mbtu	21.00	7.5
Fluxes, alloys	NA	NA	20.00	7.2
Refractories and rolls	NA	NA	9.00	3.2
Other materials	NA	NA	41.00	14.6
Human resource inputs				
Labor	11.66/hr.	8.15 hrs.	95.03	34.0
Overhead expense				
Net interest	—	—	3.25	1.2
General taxes			5.50	2.0
Total costs			$279.59	100.0
Residual income			29.92	10.7
Price, carbon steel	$309.51/ton	1 ton	$309.51	110.7

Source: Peter Marcus, *World Steel Dynamics* (New York: Paine Webber Mitchell, Hutchins, 1978).

from any single source. It is therefore necessary to adopt either of two expedients. Price indexes exist for each of the 79 major industry groupings shown in the input-output table (see chapter 2, section 2.5, for a discussion of how these price indexes are derived), and the nominal flows shown in each cell of the input-output table can be divided by these price indexes to derive an estimate of the real (deflated) flows over time. It should be noted, however, that relying on this approach, one cannot obtain the same detailed breakdown of an industry's actual physical inputs and their price (or per unit cost) that is shown for the steel industry in exhibit 5.4. The other expedient is to derive the relevant set of prices from the Leontief model of production itself. Indeed, this will be the approach followed in the chapters which follow. The price indexes which are available for the same 79 industries can then be used to check the reliability of this endogenously generated set of prices. For the moment, however, it will be necessary simply to assume that the physical quantities implicit in the value figures shown in each cell of an input-output table can be factored out and the amount of these physical goods and services thereby distinguished from their price so that an input-output table like that shown in exhibit 2.1 can be transformed into one like that shown in exhibit 5.3, with equation set 5.1 the algebraic representation of that system of production. On this assumption, it is then possible to identify the technical coefficients, and thus the technology, that underlies the system of production.

5.1.4 Technical coefficients and matrices

Basic to the Leontief model of production, as represented by equation set 5.1, are the technical relationships between the inputs obtained from other industries and the output produced by each industry. These relationships can be made explicit by means of a set of technical coefficients, with each coefficient, $a_{i,j}$, defined as the amount of industry i's output which industry j needs to obtain in order to produce one physical unit of its own output (the total amount of industry i's output needed to produce all of industry j's output, $q_{i,j}$, relative to industry j's total output, Q_j). That is,

$$a_{i,j} = \frac{q_{i,j}}{Q_j} \tag{5.2}$$

where $q_{i,j}$ is the amount of industry i's output supplied to industry j and Q_j is the total output of industry j. For example, according to exhibit 5.4, it required 0.95 tons of coal in 1978 to produce one ton of carbon steel in the United States. Thus the technical coefficient, with coal the ith industry and steel the jth industry, was 0.95. (The per ton figure given in exhibit 5.4 corresponds to the total flow of coal to the steel industry divided by the total tons of steel produced.) Similarly, since it required 1.90 million BTUs of energy to produce the same ton of steel, the technical coefficient, with energy the ith industry, was 1.90. These technical coefficients, it should be pointed out, are assumed to derive from the technology employed by each industry, and thus will vary only as the technology itself changes. More will be said on this point shortly.

By shifting the terms in definitional equation 5.2 so that $q_{i,j}$ is isolated on the left-hand side as follows:

$$q_{i,j} = a_{i,j}Q_j \tag{5.3}$$

it is possible to replace the $q_{i,j}$ terms in equation set 5.1 with $a_{i,j}$. The set of equations representing the inner matrix of the Leontief model of production will then take the following form:

$$p_1 a_{1.1} Q_1 + p_1 a_{1.2} Q_2 + p_1 a_{1.3} Q_3 + \ldots + p_1 a_{1.n} Q_n$$
$$p_2 a_{2.1} Q_1 + p_2 a_{2.2} Q_2 + p_2 a_{2.3} Q_3 + \ldots + p_2 a_{2.n} Q_n$$
$$p_3 a_{3.1} Q_1 + p_3 a_{3.2} Q_2 + p_3 a_{3.3} Q_3 + \ldots + p_3 a_{3.n} Q_n$$

$$\vdots$$

(5.4)

$$p_n a_{n.1} Q_1 + p_n a_{n.2} Q_2 + p_n a_{n.3} Q_3 + \ldots + p_n a_{n.n} Q_n$$

This inner matrix can be specified more simply relying on the notation of matrix algebra. There is, first of all, a square matrix with n columns and n rows that encompasses all the $a_{i \, j}$ technical coefficients. (A square matrix is one in which the number of columns is equal to the number of rows.) This n-by-n **A** matrix can be specified as follows:

$$\mathbf{A} = \begin{Bmatrix} a_{1.1} & a_{1.2} & a_{1.3} & \cdots & a_{1.n} \\ a_{2.1} & a_{2.2} & a_{2.3} & \cdots & a_{2.n} \\ a_{3.1} & a_{3.2} & a_{3.3} & \cdots & a_{3.n} \\ \vdots & \vdots & \vdots & & \vdots \\ a_{n.1} & a_{n.2} & a_{n.3} & \cdots & a_{1.n} \end{Bmatrix}$$

(5.5)

Leontief refers to this **A** matrix as the technological "recipe" of the economy—though it would be perhaps more accurate to view it as the list of ingredients used in following the economy's technological recipes. This **A** matrix and the inverse derived from it, $(\mathbf{I} - \mathbf{A})^{-1}$, play the same key role in the Leontief model of production, as will soon be brought out (see section 5.2.3), as the marginal propensity to save, s, and its inverse, the multiplier, k, play in the Keynesian model of effective demand.

In addition to the **A** matrix, we need a column vector to represent the total output of each industry, Q_j, and a row vector to represent the prices, p_i, paid for the output of each industry. These are an n-by-1 **Q** vector and a 1-by-n **P** vector, specified as follows:

$$\mathbf{Q} = \begin{Bmatrix} Q_1 \\ Q_2 \\ Q_3 \\ \cdot \\ \cdot \\ \cdot \\ Q_1 \end{Bmatrix}$$

(5.6)

and

$$\mathbf{P} = \{p_1, p_2, p_3, \ldots, p_n\} \tag{5.7}$$

(A vector is a matrix with a single column or row, the column vector consisting of but a single column and the row vector of but a single row.)

In order to derive the inner matrix of a Leontief production system, as represented by equation set 5.4 above, it is therefore necessary only to multiply the **A** matrix by the **P** and **Q** vectors. However, because of the rules which apply when multiplying one matrix by another, it is first necessary to convert the **P** vector into a diagonal matrix such that

$$\mathbf{P} = \begin{Bmatrix} p_1 & 0 & 0 & \ldots & 0 \\ 0 & p_2 & 0 & \ldots & 0 \\ 0 & 0 & p_3 & \ldots & 0 \\ & \cdot & \cdot & & \cdot \\ & \cdot & \cdot & & \cdot \\ & \cdot & \cdot & & \cdot \\ 0 & 0 & 0 & \ldots & p_n \end{Bmatrix} \tag{5.8}$$

(A diagonal matrix, as can readily be seen, is one in which the values are all equal to zero except along the principal diagonal. It is used so that a matrix or another vector, when multiplied by it, will still remain a matrix or vector. A diagonal matrix is denoted by a ^ or "hat" above it.) To carry out the multiplication process, the **Q** vector, too, needs to be converted to a diagonal matrix. The inner matrix of the Leontief production system can then be specified as simply $\hat{\mathbf{P}}\mathbf{A}\hat{\mathbf{Q}}$.

The other three segments of the input-output model represented algebraically in equation set 5.1 can also be specified more simply using the notation of matrix algebra. The total output of each industry (the second of the two rectangles at the top) is the **P** vector multiplied by the **Q** vector. It becomes $\hat{\mathbf{P}}\mathbf{Q}$. The other two segments, however, require that additional matrices (or vectors) first be specified.

The net, or final, output of the enterprise sector (the other rectangle constituting the top portion of equation set 5.1) is the portion of each industry's total output which is not needed as inputs by any of the other industries. It is therefore the portion of each industry's total output which is available to meet the needs of the rest of society—the household and government sectors in particular—for goods and services. It is for this reason that the column in equation set 5.1 representing the net, or final, output of the enterprise sector has been designated the $n+1$ column. The designation serves as a reminder that the quantities shown in that column represent the net output of each industry, that is, the output in excess of what must be used by the enterprise sector itself as direct inputs into the production process. As already pointed out (see chapter 2, section 1.1), this net output of each industry, when aggregated for all n industries, constitutes the national product. Thus the $n+1$, or next-to-last, column in equation set 5.1 is the national product (in value terms). Reflecting the Keynesian view as to what determines the national product, and hence the national income, this $n+1$ column is sometimes termed the "final demand" column. Indeed, this is how it will usually be referred to henceforth.

The $n+1$ column cannot be reduced to a set of technical coefficients in the same way the inner matrix can. It instead reflects the social factors—economic, political and other—that determine what use will be made of the surplus that the enterprise sector, and thus the economic system itself, is able to generate. Rather than being technologically fixed, the quantities shown in the $n+1$ column are free to vary, within certain constraints still to be identified, as the level and/or the composition of final demand changes in response to those social forces. These variable quantities—the consumption goods and services purchased by the household and government sectors along with any investment goods purchased by the enterprise sector itself—can be represented, using matrix notation, as an n-by-1 **D** (for final demand) vector, defined as follows:

$$
\mathbf{D} = \begin{Bmatrix} q_{1.n+1} \\ q_{2.n+1} \\ q_{3.n+1} \\ \cdot \\ \cdot \\ \cdot \\ q_{n.n+1} \end{Bmatrix} \tag{5.9}
$$

with $q_{1.n+1}, q_{2.n+1}, q_{3.n+1}, \ldots, q_{n.n+1}$, the net, or final, output in real terms produced by industries $1, 2, 3, \ldots, n$. Once this **D** vector has been defined, the $n+1$ column representing the level of final demand can be specified as simply $\hat{\mathbf{P}}\mathbf{D}$.

It is sometimes useful to distinguish a change in the *level* of final demand from a change in the *composition* of final demand. This can be done by first specifying a set of final output ratios, with each ratio, y_i, defined as the share of aggregate output in value terms, $\hat{\mathbf{P}}\mathbf{D}$ or **G**, produced in industry i. That is,

$$
y_i = \frac{p_i q_{i \cdot n+1}}{\sum\limits_{i=1}^{n} p_i q_{i \cdot n+1}} = \frac{p_i q_{i \cdot n+1}}{\hat{\mathbf{P}}\mathbf{D}} = \frac{p_i q_{i \cdot n+1}}{\mathbf{G}} \tag{5.10}
$$

where **G** is the aggregate output in nominal terms, that is, the sum of all the nominal values (quantities multiplied by price) shown in the $n+1$ column. The $n+1$ column can then be represented as follows:

$$
\begin{aligned}
& Gy_1 \\
& +Gy_2 \\
& +Gy_3 \\
& \quad \cdot \\
& \quad \cdot \\
& \quad \cdot \\
& +Gy_n \\
& =G = \hat{P}D
\end{aligned}
\tag{5.11}
$$

In matrix notation, this becomes $GY = G$ where G is a scalar (a matrix with but one column and one row) and Y is an *n*-by-*1* column vector defined as follows:

$$
Y = \left\{ \begin{array}{c} y_1 \\ y_2 \\ y_3 \\ \cdot \\ \cdot \\ \cdot \\ y_n \end{array} \right\}
\tag{5.12}
$$

such that all the y_i terms sum up to one, that is, $\Sigma\, y_i = 1$. (Note that the scalar G is in light-face type and the vector Y, like all matrices, is in bold-face type). This Y vector can be used not only to denote the composition of final demand but also to weight the relative importance of the different industries insofar as any physical output is concerned. In either case, since Y can only be calculated if the set of relative prices or values is known, it presumes the simultaneous determination of the price vector, P.

The fourth, and last, separate segment of the Leontief model of production represented algebraically by equation set 5.1 consists of the value added by each of the same *n* industries. The value added by each industry is equal to the value added by each industry per unit of output, v_j, multiplied by the total output of each industry, Q_j. The value added by each industry per unit of output can then be represented, using matrix notation, as a *1*-by-*n* V vector defined as follows:

$$
V = \{v_1,\ v_2,\ v_3,\ \ldots,\ v_n\}
\tag{5.13}
$$

where v_j is the value added per unit of output by the *j*th industry. The fourth segment of the Leontief model, the valued added row, can therefore be specified as simply $\hat{V}Q$. The V vector can, in turn, be divided into two rows. However, before one of these rows can be specified using matrix notation, an additional set of technical coefficients needs to be identified.

The system of production, as represented by the Leontief model, requires that each industry obtain not only a certain amount of material inputs from other industries but also a certain amount of human resource inputs as well from the parallel anthropogenic system. These human resource inputs, like the direct material inputs, can be represented by a set of technical coefficients, with each coefficient, l_j, defined as the amount of human resource inputs required to produce a single physical unit of industry j's output (the total amount of human resource inputs required to produce all of industry j's output, L_j, relative to industry j's total output, Q_j). That is,

$$l_j = \frac{L_j}{Q_j} \qquad (5.14)$$

For example, according to exhibit 5.4, it required 8.15 manhours to produce a ton of carbon steel in 1978. The labor (technical) coefficient for the steel industry in that year was therefore 8.15. The next-to-bottom row of equation set 5.1 can then be rewritten in terms of these labor coefficients as follows:

$$wl_1Q_1 + wl_2Q_2 + wl_3Q_3 + \ldots + wl_nQ_n \qquad (5.15)$$

where the wage rate, w, is to be interpreted as the price of the required human resource inputs. The labor coefficients alone can then be represented by a 1-by-n L vector defined as follows:

$$L = \{l_1 \ \ l_2 \ \ l_3 \ldots l_n\} \qquad (5.16)$$

With the labor (technical) coefficients represented by only a row vector, as in equation 5.16, one is implicitly assuming that the human resource inputs into the production process consist of but a single type of undifferentiated labor service—for example, that all production workers in the steel industry have the same skill level or competence. This assumption can be relaxed to take into account the different types of skilled workers that each of the n industries requires—including any managers. In that case, the 1-by-n L vector would become an m-by-n L matrix, with m the number of different types of labor, or skill categories, that need to be taken into account in deriving the technological coefficients of production. The scalar w, representing the average hourly wage rate paid, would then have to be expanded to an m-by-1 column vector indicating the different hourly wage rates paid each group of workers. This further complication will, however, be avoided—at least for the moment (but see chapter 8, section 3.2)—and the labor coefficients specified simply as a row vector. These labor coefficients, no less than the direct material coefficients given by the A matrix, constitute the fixed ingredients of the economic system's technological "recipe," at least in the short period. The labor coefficients, multiplied by the wage rate, equal the unit labor costs for each industry, wl_j; and the unit labor costs, multiplied by the total output, equal the wage bill of each industry wl_jQ_j.

The wage bill for each of the different industries, as represented by $w\hat{L}Q$, is only one component of the value added by those same industries. The other component is the residual income of each industry, Π_j, shown in the very bottom row of equation set 5.1. This residual sum, it will be recalled (see chapter 2, section 1.1), represents the balance between each industry's sales revenue and its outlays for all the direct inputs needed to produce that output. In attempting to explain the derivation of this residual income, one must avoid a common error in economic analysis. Just as it is not possible to reduce the $n+1$, or final output, column to a set of technical coefficients, so too it is not possible to represent the bottom, or residual, row in the same way. However, in this case the reason is different. It is not that there are quantity variables which cannot be reduced to a set of technical relationships. It is rather that the residual income per unit of output, Π_j, cannot be broken down into separate price and quantity components as the unit labor costs, wl_j, can.

While it might seem reasonable, from the perspective of the conventional neoclassical theory, to interpret the residual income per unit of output, Π_j, as the "return on capital," and thus to specify both a quantity of "capital" used by each industry and a price, or rate of compensation, received by that "input," this is not possible as a practical matter. There is no unique physical unit, such as tons, BTUs or manhours, in which such an "input" can be denominated. As pointed out by Joan Robinson in launching the post-Keynesian attack on neoclassical theory in the 1950s, the capital inputs consist of the heterogeneous physical items which constitute each firm's plant and equipment, and there is no physical unit of measurement common to all those heterogeneous items. Later, we shall see how the capital inputs can nonetheless be incorporated into the analysis—though only as a vector from which the incremental capital-output ratio for each industry is derived, and not as any singular physical input (see part 5 of this chapter). For now, however, the capital inputs must be viewed as a given, the legacy of past accumulation which has provided each industry with its existing capacity. The only manifestation of that past investment, insofar as current production is concerned, is the set of technical coefficients represented by the A and L matrices. The capital inputs do not otherwise affect the set of equations that define the Leontief model of production, at least in the short period. Indeed, those capital inputs cannot be separately identified—let alone related to the residual income of each industry. Thus it is not possible to specify a quantity variable for the capital inputs used by each industry so that its residual income can be broken down into some quantity multiplied by some price.

What this means is that while it is necessary to add a bottom, or residual, row when the value relationships within a Leontief production system are being taken

Exhibit 5.5

$$\hat{P}A\hat{Q} \quad + \quad \hat{P}D \quad = \quad \hat{P}Q$$

$$+$$

$$[\hat{V} = w\hat{L} + \hat{\Pi}]Q$$

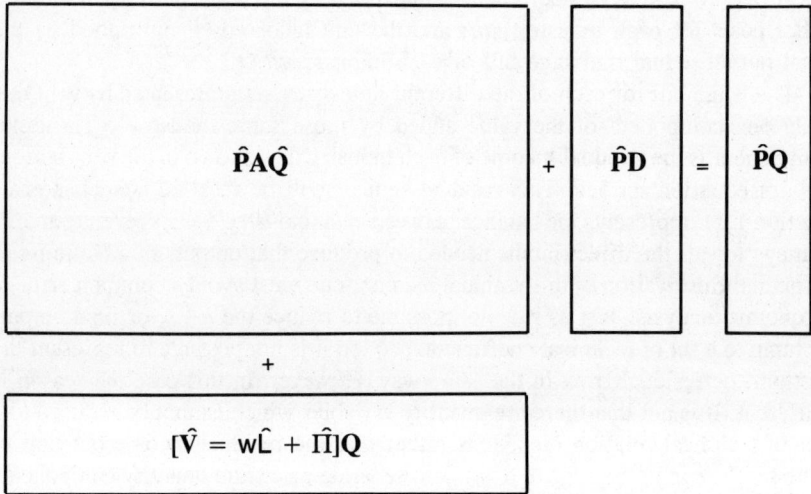

into account, that bottom row cannot be decomposed into any more basic units once the level of industry output, Q_j, has been taken into account. It must instead be represented as simply a 1-by-n $\boldsymbol{\pi}$ vector, specified as follows:

$$\boldsymbol{\pi} = \{\pi_1 \ \pi_2 \ \pi_3 \ \ldots \ \pi_n\} \tag{5.17}$$

where π_j is the amount of residual income earned by each industry per unit of output produced. This unit residual income, when added to the unit labor costs, wl_j, equals the value added by each industry per unit of output, v_j. That is,

$$V = w\mathbf{L} + \boldsymbol{\pi} \tag{5.18}$$

With the Leontief model of production, as represented by equation set 5.1, rewritten using matrix notation, it is a relatively simple matter to identify the basic elements of that model. They are the following:
1. The material technical coefficients represented by the $\mathbf{A}$ matrix.
2. The labor coefficients represented by the $\mathbf{L}$ matrix.
3. The net output of each industry represented by the $\mathbf{D}$ vector.
4. The total output of each industry represented by the $\mathbf{Q}$ vector.
5. The prices for the output of each industry represented by the $\mathbf{P}$ vector, and
6. The residual income of each industry represented by the $\boldsymbol{\pi}$ vector.
In addition, there is the level of aggregate output in value terms represented by $\mathbf{PG}$ (instead of, as in previous chapters, by Y); the relative composition of final

demand represented by the **Y** vector; and the wage rate (or set of wage rates) represented by w (or the **W** vector). The four segments of the Leontief model of production can then be specified, using this notation, as follows: 1) the inner matrix, $\hat{P}A\hat{Q}$; 2) the final demand vector, $\hat{P}D$, or, so as to be able to distinguish a change in the level from a change in the composition of final demand, GY; 3) the total output of each industry vector, $\hat{P}Q$, and 4) the value added by each industry, $\hat{V}Q$ (with the value added per unit of output by each industry, V, equal to w**L** + π. (See exhibit 5.5, a reformulation of equation set 5.1 using matrix notation.) It is in this form that the Leontief model of production will be used, in the next major section which follows, to explain what determines the level of output, industry by industry, in the short period.

5.2 Determining the Level of Industry Output

The set of equations representing the Leontief model of production can be solved, once the final demand vector is known, so that the level of output by each industry is then uniquely determined. The same set of equations can also be solved, once the value added vector has been determined, to indicate the set of prices that must be established if each industry is to cover its costs of production. In this way, it is possible to disaggregate the analysis of the preceding two chapters, explaining the level of output in each industry as well as the price that needs to be obtained, without having to alter the explanation that was given in those two chapters for what determines the level of aggregate output.

It turns out that the key parameter in explaining both the level of output in each industry and the price that needs to be obtained is the **A** matrix and the Leontief inverse, $(I - A)^{-1}$, representing the underlying technology of the system of production. This raises the question of what determines the actual values taken by the **A** matrix. Three possible answers have been suggested in the literature, only one of which is dealt with in this part of chapter 5. This is the argument of the alternative neo-Walrasian model that the **A** matrix depends on the set of relative prices given by the **P** vector. The other two possible explanations—that the values taken by the **A** matrix depend on the scale of operation and/or that they depend on the rate of technical progress—will be examined in the subsequent parts of this chapter.

5.2.1 The quantity solution

As previously demonstrated (see chapter 2, section 1.1, and this chapter, section 1.3), the total output produced by each industry, in value terms, is equal to the intermediate output (the output needed as inputs by other industries) in value terms plus the net, or final, output (the output available for final use by one of the other sectors or by the enterprise sector itself for capital accumulation) also in value terms. In matrix notation, this means that, as can be seen from exhibit 5.5,

$$\hat{P}A\hat{Q} + \hat{P}D = \hat{P}Q \qquad (5.19)$$

If it is not inappropriate to divide through by P (actually, to multiply both sides of equation 5.19 by P^{-1} since, strictly speaking, it is not possible to perform the operations of division with a matrix), the price vector can be canceled (since it appears in all three terms) and the above equation reduced to the following:

$$AQ + D = Q \qquad (5.20)$$

Whether, in fact, it is permissible to eliminate the P term in equation 5.19 in this manner is a question that will be taken up shortly. For the moment let us assume that it is permissible so that, by then solving equation 5.20 for Q, we can explain what determines the level of total output, in real terms, in each of the n industries which comprise the enterpise sector.

Equation 5.20 can be solved for Q by first shifting terms as follows:

$$Q - AQ = D \qquad (5.21)$$

and next factoring out the Q vector as shown below:

$$(I - A)Q = D \qquad (5.22)$$

where I is what is known as an indentity matrix, such that

$$I = \begin{Bmatrix} 1 & 0 & 0 \ldots 0 \\ 0 & 1 & 0 \ldots 0 \\ 0 & 0 & 1 \ldots 0 \\ . & . & . \qquad . \\ . & . & . \qquad . \\ . & . & . \qquad . \\ 1 & 0 & 0 \ldots 0 \end{Bmatrix} \qquad (5.23)$$

and plays a role in matrix algebra similar to that of the number 1 in elementary algebra. (An identity matrix, as can be seen, is a diagonal matrix with only 1's along its principal diagonal.) To isolate Q on the left-hand side, it is necessary only to divide both sides by $(I - A)$. This can be done by multiplying each side by $(I - A)^{-1}$, thereby giving rise to the following equation:

$$Q = (I - A)^{-1} D \qquad (5.24)$$

Equation 5.24 is the quantity solution to the system of equations representing the Leontief model of production. It indicates that the total output of each industry in real terms, as given by the **Q** vector, depends on 1) the final demand vector in real terms, **D**, and 2) what is known as the Leontief inverse, $(\mathbf{I} - \mathbf{A})^{-1}$. As previously explained (see chapter 2, section 1.2), the latter indicates the direct and indirect material requirements for each industry, and is represented by the set of coefficients shown in the bottom right-hand corner of each cell in the input-output table for the U.S. economy published by *Scientific American*. More will be said about the Leontief inverse shortly. The final demand vector, meanwhile, is the level of aggregate output in real terms which the basic Keynesian model, as elaborated on and extended in the last two chapters, is meant to explain. Thus once the secular growth of aggregate output, $\overset{\circ}{G}$, and the cyclical movements in aggregate output, $G - \overset{\circ}{G}$, have been explained within a single comprehensive macrodynamic model so that the level of aggregate output at any given point in time is known, it is possible to extend the analysis and, based on the Leontief inverse, explain what will be the total output in real terms produced by each of the *n* different industries that constitute the enterprise sector—any intermediate output (inputs supplied to other industries) as well as any final, or net, output. To extend the analysis in this way, it is necessary only that the composition of final demand in real terms, as given by the **D** vector, be known.

Not until the disaggregated, sectoral analysis of the next seven chapters has been completed will it be possible to explain, in a precise way, how the composition of final demand, and thus of aggregate output, is likely to change as the economy expands unevenly over time. It is therefore not yet possible to link the Leontief model of production to the type of macrodynamic model outlined at the end of the last chapter. Still, this will not prevent us from continuing to develop the Leontief model itself. All that need be noted, at least for the moment, is that the composition of aggregate output will change, due both to the cyclical movement of discretionary expenditures in the short period and to the changing pattern of final demand in the long period; and that this change in the composition of aggregate output, as given by the **D** vector, will in turn lead to a change in the output of each industry, as denoted by the **Q** vector. The Leontief model of production, as a subcomponent of a larger macrodynamic model of the economy, can then be represented by means of the following systems diagram:

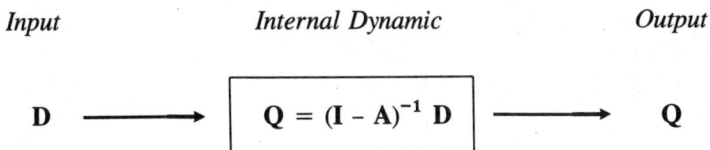

Input	*Internal Dynamic*	*Output*
D $\longrightarrow$	$\boxed{\mathbf{Q} = (\mathbf{I} - \mathbf{A})^{-1}\,\mathbf{D}}$ $\longrightarrow$	**Q**

with the final demand vector, **D**, the exogenously determined variable (at least exogenously determined insofar as the subsystem of production is concerned) that, in conjunction with the Leontief inverse, $(\mathbf{I} - \mathbf{A})^{-1}$, will then determine the total output of each industry in real terms, $\mathbf{Q}$.

The quantity solution to the Leontief model of production, as given by equation 5.24, depends critically on being able to factor out or in some other way either eliminate altogether or take as a given the price vector, $\mathbf{P}$. Otherwise, it is not possible to proceed from equation 5.19 to equation 5.20 before deriving equation 5.24 itself. Thus, before elaborating any further on the Leontief model of production, it is necessary to explain under what circumstances it is permissible to factor out the price vector, $\mathbf{P}$.

There are, in fact, three different sets of circumstances under which the price vector can be either eliminated altogether or simply taken as a given—with each situation having a quite different implication insofar as any subsequent analysis is concerned. The first set of circumstances is when, as under a system of direct, central planning such as that of the Soviet Union and some other Eastern European countries, material inputs are allocated among industries directly without relying on markets. In that situation, the appropriate model of production is the purely physical version of the Leontief model, as given by equation 5.20 (rather than equation 5.19). The price vector can be eliminated because, for all practical purposes, it does not exist. Based on this purely physical version of the Leontief model, it is then possible to carry out a series of planning exercises by varying the proportions between various types of final demand—e.g., between consumption (wage) goods and investment goods or between civilian and military goods—and seeing what difference this makes in terms of the $\mathbf{Q}$ vector. Indeed, this purely physical version of the Leontief model is the more appropriate one when, as in the Soviet Union or even in the United States and other market economies during wartime, the role of markets and prices has been superseded by the direct physical allocation of the inputs critical to the production process.

The Leontief model formulated in purely physical terms is, however, not the appropriate one for an advanced market economy like that of the United States in which, under normal circumstances, the allocation of resources among industries is governed by market prices. Equation 5.19 with the price vector included (rather than equation 5.20 with the price vector omitted) is then the correct starting point. This, in turn, means that the price vector must be dealt with explicitly.

There are only two options. One is to treat the price vector as being exogenously determined and then to proceed with the analysis solely in value terms, that is, with the $\hat{\mathbf{P}}\mathbf{AQ}$, $\hat{\mathbf{P}}\mathbf{D}$ and $\hat{\mathbf{P}}\mathbf{Q}$ matrices and vectors not broken down into their separate price and quantity components. Indeed, because of the deficiencies in the available data as already noted (see section 5.1.3), this is the way the Leontief model is usually applied in the case of the United States and other market economies for which input-output tables are available. In this version of the model, what is being explained is not the total output of the various industries in physical terms, $\mathbf{Q}$, but rather the total output in value terms, $\hat{\mathbf{P}}\mathbf{Q}$. In fact, to avoid any confusion on this point, the $\hat{\mathbf{P}}\mathbf{Q}$ vector as well as the $\hat{\mathbf{P}}\mathbf{A}\hat{\mathbf{Q}}$ matrix and the $\hat{\mathbf{P}}\mathbf{D}$ vector need to be respecified, using a single variable, one which is not factorable into separate price and quantity components, to denote the value relationships. This means that equation 5.19 needs to be rewritten as follows:

$$\hat{\mathbf{B}}\mathbf{X} + \mathbf{Z} = \mathbf{X} \qquad (5.24)$$

where $\mathbf{X}$ is the vector of total output by each industry in value terms (replacing $\hat{\mathbf{P}}\mathbf{Q}$), $\mathbf{Z}$ is the vector of final demand in value terms (replacing $\hat{\mathbf{P}}\mathbf{D}$), and $\mathbf{B}$ is an n-by-n matrix, indicating the value in dollars (or whatever else happens to be the appropriate monetary unit) of the direct material inputs required of one industry by another (replacing the $\mathbf{A}$ matrix). The elements of this new $\mathbf{B}$ matrix, it should be noted, are not strictly speaking technical coefficients but rather are direct requirements ratios, such as those shown in exhibit 2.2 (see chapter 2, section 1.2). With this equation solved for $\mathbf{X}$, equation 5.24 can then be rewritten as follows:

$$\mathbf{X} = (\mathbf{I} - \mathbf{B})^{-1}\, \mathbf{Z} \qquad (5.26)$$

The Leontief model formulated in value terms, as in equations 5.25 and 5.26, may be suitable for analyzing the differential impact on industries which a change in either the level or composition of final demand may have in a market economy like that of the United States. It may even suffice, once the nominal flows shown in each cell of the input-output table have been deflated by the appropriate price indexes, for analyzing the real flows over time. The model is nonetheless not a satisfactory one when it is the secular rise in the price level that is of particular concern because the model leaves the price vector unexplained. Prices are simply a parameter—one that is not determined within the model itself. In this respect, the Leontief model, when it is specified only in value terms, is no better than the static Keynesian model or even the more dynamic Harrod-Domar model. All three models leave the set of relative prices, as well as the price level itself, unexplained. If the analysis is to not to remain incomplete, with the relationship between production and prices left unclear, the price vector must be endogenously determined within the model itself. Indeed, the next step to be taken in developing the Leontief model of production is to show how the necessary set of prices can be determined simultaneously, once the output solution has been obtained.

5.2.2 The dual price solution

It is not just that, in a Leontief model, the total output produced by each industry is equal to the intermediate output plus the net output and that therefore, as indicated by equation 5.18, $\hat{\mathbf{P}}\mathbf{A}\hat{\mathbf{Q}} + \hat{\mathbf{P}}\mathbf{D} = \hat{\mathbf{P}}\mathbf{Q}$. It is also that, as shown in exhibit 5.5 and reflecting the value conditions that must simultaneously hold, the total outlays by each industry must be equal to the outlays on intermediate goods plus any value added. In matrix notation, this means that

$$\hat{P}A\hat{Q} + \hat{V}Q = \hat{P}Q \qquad (5.27)$$

In this case, however, what can be canceled out because it appears in all three terms is not the price vector, P, but rather the total physical output of each industry vector in real terms, Q. Indeed, dividing through by Q (i.e., multiplying both sides by Q^{-1}) reduces equation 5.27 to the following:

$$PA + V = P \qquad (5.28)$$

Again, one has to ask under what circumstances is it permissible to eliminate the Q term. This question will be taken up shortly. For the moment let us simply assume it is permissible so that, by solving equation 5.28 for P, we can derive the dual price solution to the Leontief model of production. This requires that we first shift terms as follows:

$$P - PA = V \qquad (5.29)$$

and then factor out P as shown below:

$$P(I - A) = V \qquad (5.30)$$

It is then possible to isolate P on the right-hand side by dividing both sides by $(I - A)$, thereby giving rise to the following equation:

$$P = V(I - A)^{-1} \qquad (5.31)$$

Equation 5.31 represents the dual price solution to the Leontief model of production. What it explains is not the set of relative prices that will actually be established but rather the set of relative prices which must prevail in the long period if each industry is to cover its costs of production. It therefore defines what has already been identified as the value condition for continuous, uninterrupted growth—including the value condition for zero growth, with no increase over time in aggregate output (see chapter 4, section 1.4, as well as below, chapter 6, part 1). This value condition, as indicated by equation 5.31, depends on the same Leontief inverse, $(I - A)^{-1}$, as the quantity solution. The difference is that while it is the final demand vector D that needs to be premultiplied by the Leontief inverse in order to determine the total output of each industry in real terms, as given by the Q vector, it is the value added vector, V, that needs to be postmultiplied by the Leontief inverse in order to determine the required set of prices, as given by the P vector.

The value added vector, as already pointed out (see equation 5.18), is equal to the unit labor costs, wL, plus the unit residual income, π. With the set of labor coefficients, as denoted by the L vector, viewed as a technologically determined parameter like the A matrix, this means that the value-added vector—and thus the price vector—will depend on the wage rate, w, and the unit residual income, π. The systems diagram, insofar as the necessary set of prices is concerned, therefore takes the following form:

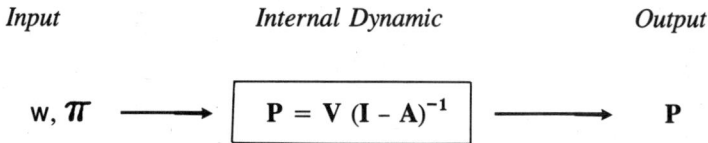

Input   *Internal Dynamic*   *Output*

$$\text{w}, \pi \longrightarrow \boxed{P = V(I-A)^{-1}} \longrightarrow P$$

with w and the exogenously determined inputs into the system of production which will then determine the necessary set of prices, **P**. What still remains to be explained is what determines both the wage rate, w (or, taking into account the different wage rates in each industry, **W**), and the unit residual income earned by each industry, π. Explaining what determines each industry's unit residual income will be the task of chapters 6 and 7, and explaining what determines the wage rate, the task of chapter 8.

Before proceeding any further, two points need to be clarified. The first is under what set of conditions it is permissible to eliminate the **Q** terms in equation 5.27 so as to be able to derive equation 5.31, and the second is how the different time frames of the quantity and dual price solutions are to be reconciled.

The three sets of circumstances under which it is permissible to cancel the **P** vector before proceeding to derive the quantity solution to the Leontief model have already been pointed out in the preceding subsection. One such set of circumstances is when the interindustry flow of material inputs depends on some nonmarket system of planning or direct control and there is, as a consequence, no real price vector. This purely physical version of the Leontief model has its counterpart, on the price side, in the model of a pure exchange economy—one that has no production subsystem.

With no output produced by any industry, there is no **Q** vector. This means the economic system must necessarily be a parasitical one, obtaining all the goods and services it needs to satisfy the material needs of its members from some external source. It is therefore quite different from the type of economic system found in the United States or indeed in any other country, excepts perhaps at the end of a devastating war. It is for this reason that the pure exchange model—one without an explicit production subsystem—has already been rejected as being inapplicable to the type of economic system that is the focus of this text (see chapter 1, section 1.1). A **Q** vector must therefore be assumed to exist—just as in a market economy a **P** vector must also be assumed to exist.

The second set of circumstances which makes it possible to cancel the **P** vector is the same as the second set which makes it possible to cancel the **Q** vector. This is when the Leontief model is specified in value terms only, with no effort made to break those nominal values down into their price and quantity components. Indeed, this is the very model specified in the preceding subsection with $\hat{B}X$ replacing $\hat{P}A\hat{Q}$ as the inner matrix, Z replacing $\hat{P}D$ as the final demand vector and X replacing $\hat{P}Q$ as the total output of each industry vector. To derive the dual solution to this model, it is necessary only to replace the value added by each industry, $\hat{V}Q$, in equation 5.27 with a single vector, U (in addition to replacing $\hat{P}A\hat{Q}$ with $\hat{B}X$ and $\hat{P}Q$ with X). Equation 5.31, as the dual solution, then takes the following form:

$$X = U(I - B)^{-1} \qquad (5.32)$$

with U a vector representing the value added by each industry.

This method of proceeding, however, suffers from the same limitation already pointed out in connection with the quantity solution to the same model. Although the total output of each industry in value terms, as represented by the X vector, can now be determined by multiplying either the final demand in value terms, Z, or the total value added by each industry, U, by the Leontief inverse, the model still fails to explain how those value terms break down into their price and quantity components. Indeed, how much is actually produced in physical terms by each industry, along with the necessary set of prices that must be obtained for that output, remains indeterminant. To develop a disaggregated model that can shed light on the inflationary process, it is therefore necessary to proceed to the third set of circumstances under which it is permissible not only to cancel the P terms in equation 5.19 and thereby derive equation 5.24 as the quantity solution to the Leontief model but also to cancel the Q terms in equation 5.27 and thereby derive equation 5.31 as the dual price solution. This is when equations 5.24 and 5.31 are solved simultaneously as part of the same comprehensive model of a production system. First, however, another point needs to be made clear.

The dual solution to the Leontief model, as already noted, represents not the set of prices that will actually prevail but rather only the set of prices that needs to be established if each industry is to cover its costs of production. In other words, the P vector, as determined by equation 5.31, specifies a value condition that must be satisfied in the long period. In contrast, the model of production, as developed so far, applies only in the short period. Production in the long period, with the capital inputs no longer remaining unchanged, is something quite different. It requires its own distinctive model, one that can incorporate the output of the capital goods sector within the inner matrix rather having it simply remain as part of the enterprise sector's net, or final, output. Thus equations 5.24 and 5.31, although derived simultaneously from the same Leontief model of production, do not hold within the same time frame. Not until the Leontief model has been extended, as it will be in the final part of this chapter, to encompass the long period as well as the short will this discrepancy in the time frame of the two equations be eliminated. In the meantime, the dual price solution simply needs to be noted and recognized for what it is—the value condition that must be satisfied if each of the different industries is to obtain sufficient revenue from the sale of its output to purchase all the inputs needed to produce the level of aggregate output, or final demand, given by the **D** vector.

Even at this preliminary stage in the development of the Leontief model, however, the key role played by the **A** matrix and its inverse, henceforth to be denoted as $\dot{\mathbf{A}}$, should be clear. Once either **A** or $\dot{\mathbf{A}}$ has been determined empirically—and they are in fact approximated by the elements of the **B** and $\dot{\mathbf{B}}$ matrices available for the U.S. economy each year that the various economic censuses are conducted—it is then possible to derive simultaneously both the quantity and dual price solutions to the Leontief model of production. One needs to know, in addition to the **A** (or **B**) matrix, along with its inverse, only the composition of final demand as given by the **D** vector on the one hand and the wage rate and residual income of each industry as given by the **W** and $\boldsymbol{\pi}$ vectors on the other hand. The **A** matrix and its inverse, $\dot{\mathbf{A}}$, is therefore the key parameter insofar as the Leontief model of production is concerned—just as the marginal propensity to save, s, and its inverse, the multiplier k, is the key parameter in a Keynesian model. While a common sense explanation for what the **A** matrix represents has already been given, this still remains to be done for the Leontief inverse.

5.2.3 The Leontief inverse

Production occurs, not instantaneously but rather, over time. Before any output can be produced, the necessary inputs must be obtained and, if those inputs are material ones, they must themselves be produced—in some prior time period after the necessary inputs have first been obtained. Any goods (or services) produced during the current time period will therefore embody some combination of material inputs produced during the immediately preceding time period. These are the direct material inputs. They, in turn, will embody some combination of material inputs produced in yet a previous time period—and so on back through an infinite regress in time. It is the material inputs needed to produce the other material inputs in the time periods prior to the immediately preceding one that constitute the indirect material requirements for any current production.

While one might think it necessary to use time subscripts to denote each of the successive "rounds" in the production process, they can be omitted in a system of continuous production that has stabilized at a certain level of output. The successive "rounds" are, in fact, occurring simultaneously as each industry both supplies inputs to other industries and in turn uses the output of other industries as inputs into its own production process. Indeed, even if the level of output should vary, the time subscripts can still be omitted—as long as the system of production will then stabilize at some new level of output. In other words, the time dimension can be ignored, and the direct and indirect material requirements treated as though they were contemporaneous, as long as one is concerned only with the inputs needed to maintain a certain level of continuous output. The significance of the Leontief inverse is that it indicates what these "contemporaneous" direct and indirect material input requirements are.

The Leontief inverse, $\mathbf{A}$, is an n-by-n matrix with each element, $\ddot{a}_{i,j}$, representing the fraction of industry i's output which industry j needs, both directly and indirectly, in order to produce a single physical unit of its own output. That is,

$$\mathbf{A} = \left\{ \begin{array}{ccccc} \ddot{a}_{1.1} & \ddot{a}_{1.2} & \ddot{a}_{1.3} & \cdots & \ddot{a}_{1.n} \\ \ddot{a}_{2.1} & \ddot{a}_{2.2} & \ddot{a}_{2.3} & \cdots & \ddot{a}_{2.n} \\ \ddot{a}_{3.1} & \ddot{a}_{3.2} & \ddot{a}_{3.3} & \cdots & \ddot{a}_{3.n} \\ & \cdot & \cdot & \cdot & \cdot \\ & \cdot & \cdot & \cdot & \cdot \\ & \cdot & \cdot & \cdot & \cdot \\ \ddot{a}_{n.1} & \ddot{a}_{n.2} & \ddot{a}_{n.3} & \cdots & \ddot{a}_{n.n} \end{array} \right\} \tag{5.33}$$

where $\ddot{a}_{i,j}$ is the total amount of material inputs supplied, directly and indirectly, by industry i to industry j, $\ddot{q}_{i,j}$, relative to the total output of industry j. That is,

$$\ddot{a}_{i,j} = \frac{\ddot{q}_{i,j}}{Q_j} \tag{5.34}$$

As already noted, the elements of this inverse matrix, $\mathbf{A}$—or rather, the elements of its empirical approximation, $\mathbf{B}$—are shown in the bottom right-hand corner of each cell in the input-output table for the U.S. economy published by *Scientific American*. Together, they constitute what is termed the set of total requirements coefficients for the enterprise sector as a whole.

To understand not only how the Leontief inverse is derived but also what it represents, it is best to begin with the $\mathbf{A}$ matrix—and in particular with the set of technical coefficients, $a_{i.1}, a_{i.2}, a_{i.3}, \ldots, a_{i.n}$, that denotes the row occupied within that matrix by the ith industry, and the set of technical coefficients, $a_{1.j}, a_{2.j}, a_{3.j}, \ldots, a_{n.j}$, that denotes the column occupied within the same matrix by the jth industry. One can then specify the *rate* at which the ith industry generates net output—or a physical surplus, $q_{i.n+1}/Q_i$—as well as the *rate* at which the jth industry generates value added—or a value surplus, v_j/Q_j—as follows:

$$\sigma_i = 1 - (a_{i.1}, a_{i.2}, a_{i.3}, \ldots, a_{i.n}) \tag{5.35}$$

and

$$s_j = 1 - (a_{1.j}, a_{2.j}, a_{3.j}, \ldots, a_{n.j}) \tag{5.36}$$

where σ_i is the net output of industry i in physical terms, $q_{i.n+1}$, as a proportion of industry i's total output in physical terms, Q_i; and s_j is the value added by industry j through wage payments and any residual income, v_j, as a proportion of the total value, or price, placed on industry j's output, p_j. It follows that

$$s_i + (a_{i.1}, a_{i.2}, a_{i.3}, \ldots, a_{i.n}) = 1 \qquad (5.37)$$

and

$$s_j + (a_{1.j}, a_{2.j}, a_{3.j}, \ldots, a_{n.j}) = 1 \qquad (5.38)$$

In other words, a certain portion of each industry's output, $(a_{i.1}, a_{i.2}, a_{i.3}, \ldots a_{i.n})$, must be used as inputs by other industries, leaving only the remaining portion, σ_i, to satisfy any final demand. On the other hand, a certain portion of the value, or price, placed on an industry's output, $(a_{1.j}, a_{2.j}, a_{3.j}, \ldots a_{n.j})$, is the value of the inputs purchased from other industryies, leaving again only the remaining portion, s_j, as the value added by the industry itself through wage payments and any residual income.

The $a_{i.j}$ terms in equations 5.37 and 5.38, it should be noted, are ratios with values that fall between 0 and 1. Indeed, it is a necesary condition that not only each of these technical coefficients be some positively valued fraction but also that, together, they sum up to less than 1 for at least some of the industries. Otherwise, none of the σ_i and s_j terms would be positive, indicating that the enterprise sector was not capable of producing any net output. Since this would mean that the economic system was not able to meet the needs of the rest of the society for material goods—that of the household sector for consumption goods in particular—the social system would not be economically, indeed even biological- ly, viable.

One can add together for all n industries the physical surplus, σ_i, generated by each industry (that is, the rows specified in equation 5.35) or, alternatively, the value surplus, s_j, generated by each industry (that is, the columns specified in equation 5.36). The result, in either case, is an n-by-n $(\mathbf{I} - \mathbf{A})$ matrix. Whether this matrix is viewed as the sum of all n rows (the physical surplus produced by each of the n industries) or, alternatively, as the sum of all n columns (the value surplus created by each of the same n industries) will depend on whether $(\mathbf{I} - \mathbf{A})$ is being premultiplied (as in equation 5.30) or postmultiplied (as in equation 5.22). If $(\mathbf{I} - \mathbf{A})$ is being premultiplied—that is, if some other vector or matrix, such as $\mathbf{P}$, is multiplied by it—then $(\mathbf{I} - \mathbf{A})$ is the set of n rows. If $(\mathbf{I} - \mathbf{A})$ is being postmultiplied—that is, if it is instead being multiplied by some other vector or matrix, such as $\mathbf{Q}$—then $(\mathbf{I} - \mathbf{A})$ is the set of n columns. Indeed, it is to indicate that the $(\mathbf{I} - \mathbf{A})$ matrix is to be viewed as the set of n rows, each of which takes the form specified in equation 5.35, that equation 5.30 is written with the $\mathbf{P}$ vector preceding it. And it is to indicate that the $(\mathbf{I} - \mathbf{A})$ matrix is to be viewed as the set of n columns, each of which takes the form specified in equation 5.36, that equation 5.22 is written with the $\mathbf{Q}$ vector following it. However, whether premultiplied or postmultiplied, the $(\mathbf{I} - \mathbf{A})$ matrix denotes the same n-by-n set of positive fractions, or ratios.

With a common sense interpretation given to the $(\mathbf{I} - \mathbf{A})$ matrix, it is now possible to do the same for its inverse, $\dot{\mathbf{A}}$ or $(\mathbf{I} - \mathbf{A})^{-1}$. This inverse, as represented by equation set 5.33, is a matrix the elements of which indicate the number of times each element of the $(\mathbf{I} - \mathbf{A})$ matrix would have to be multiplied in order to obtain the identity matrix, $\mathbf{I}$. It is therefore analogous to the Keynesian multiplier, the inverse of the marginal propensity to save, s.

The Keynesian multiplier, k, can be thought of as the number of times the marginal propensity to save, s, would have to be multiplied to equal 1—and therefore the number of times the fraction saved out of any increase in income would have to be multiplied to equal 100 percent of the increase in income. It thus marks the end, or at least the theoretical limit, to the multiplier process since, with 100 percent of the increase in income saved, no further rounds of consumption would be possible (see chapter 3, section 1.3). Similarly, the Leontief inverse, $\dot{\mathbf{A}}$, when it is being premultiplied and thus represents the set of n rows, can be thought of as the number of times the rate at which a physical surplus is being generated by each industry, as represented by the $(\mathbf{I} - \mathbf{A})$ matrix, would have to be multiplied to equal the identity matrix, $\mathbf{I}$. It therefore represents the number of times the fraction of the total physical output produced by each industry which its net output represents would have to be multiplied before 100 percent of that total output would be used up in producing both the intermediate output needed as inputs by other industries and the net, or surplus, output needed to satisfy any final demand. The same Leontief inverse, when it is being postmultiplied and thus represents the set of n columns, can be thought of as the number of times the rate at which a value surplus is being generated by each industry, as represented by the same $(\mathbf{I} - \mathbf{A})$ matrix, would have to be multiplied to equal the identity matrix, $\mathbf{I}$. It therefore represents the number of times the fraction of the total value, or price, placed on the output of each industry which the value added by that industry represents would have to be multiplied before 100 per cent of that total value would be accounted for both by the value added to the output of other industries (through the inputs supplied to those other industries) and the value added directly by the industry itself.

Indeed, this is why, in the quantity solution to the Leontief model given by equation 5.24, the Leontief inverse is postmultiplied by the $\mathbf{D}$ vector in order to determine the total output that must be produced by all n industries, $\mathbf{Q}$, and why, in the dual price solution as given by equation 5.31, the same inverse is premultiplied by the $\mathbf{V}$ vector in order to determine the price that must be obtained by each of the same n industries, $\mathbf{P}$, if they are to cover all their costs of production. Just as the Keynesian multiplier can be used to indicate the total demand generated from a given amount of investment and other types of autonomous (or discretionary) expenditures, so the Leontief inverse, $\dot{\mathbf{A}}$, can be used to indicate the total output that must be produced by each industry if a certain amount of net output is to be obtained from those same n industries (when the Leontief inverse is premultiplied) or, alternatively, it can be used to indicate the total value, or price, that must be placed on the output produced by all n industries if the set of relative prices is going to be sufficient to cover the value added in the form of wages and other income payments by each of those same n industries (when the Leontief inverse is postmultiplied).

The Leontief inverse, $\dot{\mathbf{A}}$ or $(\mathbf{I} - \mathbf{A})^{-1}$, can be derived from the $\mathbf{A}$ matrix by making use of the following formula:

$$x^{-1} = 1 + x + x^2 + x^3 + \ldots + x^\infty \qquad (5.39)$$

where x is some scalar or matrix the value or values of which fall between 0 and 1. With x some positive fraction, its value will be close to zero when raised to the 20th power so that, for all practical purposes, the above series need not be carried beyond that point. Thus the values taken by the elements of the Leontief inverse can be calculated as follows:

$$\mathbf{A} = \mathbf{I} + \mathbf{A} + \mathbf{A}^2 + \mathbf{A}^3 + \ldots + \mathbf{A}^{20} \qquad (5.40)$$

with the matrix that is thereby obtained then transposed so that its columns represent the rows and its rows, the columns of the Leontief inverse, $\dot{\mathbf{A}}$. The first two terms in the above equation, $\mathbf{I} + \mathbf{A}$, represent the direct material requirements for any current production and the other terms, $\mathbf{A}^2 + \mathbf{A}^3 + \ldots + \mathbf{A}^{20}$, represent the indirect requirements. (Inclusion of the identity matrix, $\mathbf{I}$, has the effect of adding a 1 to the technical coefficients represented along the principal diagonal of the A matrix. It thus indicates that each industry, in order to produce enough to meet its own internal needs—when firms within the industry sell part of their output to other firms within the same industry—must produce as direct inputs 100 percent of the fraction it supplies other industries plus whatever fraction is needed internally.)

With the Leontief inverse the mathematical equivalent of an identity matrix, $\mathbf{I}$, plus the $\mathbf{A}$ matrix as an infinite series raised to successively higher powers, the critical importance of the technical coefficents represented by that matrix becomes even clearer. Once those technical coefficients are known, the inverse, $\dot{\mathbf{A}}$ or $(\mathbf{I} - \mathbf{A})^{-1}$, can be derived and the Leontief model of production then solved, relying on equations 5.24 and 5.31, so as to be able to explain how much will be produced by each industry, given the level of final demand, and what value, or price, must be placed on that output if each industry is to cover its costs of production. What next needs to be explained is what determines the values taken by the elements of the **A** matrix itself, along with the elements of the **L** vector that serves to further specify the production subsystem's necessary inputs (the "ingredients" for the economic system's technological "recipe").

5.2.4 The determinants of the technical coefficients

There are three factors which have been identified in the economics literature as being likely to cause the technical coefficients of production (the **A** and **L** matrices) to change. They are: (1) a change in relative prices (or, in the absence of a price system, a change in the relative scarcity of material and human resource inputs and thus a change in what are termed relative "shadow" prices); (2) a change in the scale of production; and (3) technical progress. In the remaining part of this section, only the first of these three possible determinants of the technical coefficients will be examined. The other two possible determinants will be taken up and discussed in the subsequent, last two parts of chapter 5.

To suggest that the technical coefficients of production depend on relative prices—or, in other words, that **A**, **L** $= f(\mathbf{P})$—is to throw into question the validity of the Leontief model of production. For if the technical coefficients depend on relative prices, then the values which can be observed for $a_{i\,j}$ and l_j, as in exhibit 5.4, are merely epiphenomena. To analyze the economy as a production system, one needs to start, not with the **A** matrix, using the inverse derived from that matrix to explain both the **P** and **Q** vectors, but rather with the price vector itself. It is the latter which, by determining the technical coefficients of production, actually explains how much each industry will produce in real terms, as denoted by the **Q** vector. Indeed, this is precisely the argument of the neoclassical theory of production, based on the neo-Walrasian model of the economy developed initially by John Hicks and Paul Samuelson and later extended by Kenneth Arrow, Gerard Debreu and Frank Hahn.

In a neo-Walrasian model, what are significant are not the technical coefficients of production but rather the demand and supply functions applicable to each industry. These demand and supply functions are what govern the market for the output of each industry, determining the quantity produced and the price changed (the elements of the **P** and **Q** vectors as previously defined). With 79 separate industries, there would then have to be no less than 79 separate sets of these demand and supply curves (not counting those for labor or any other nonmaterial inputs)—with each set of these curves taking the following form:

$$Q_d = f(p_1, p_2, p_3, \ldots, p_n) \tag{5.41}$$

and

$$Q_s = g(p_1, p_2, p_3, \ldots, p_n \tag{5.42}$$

where Q_d is the quantity of each material input demanded by a particular industry; Q_s is the quantity supplied by the same industry; $p_1, p_2, p_3, \ldots, p_n$ is the price of the material inputs produced in industries $1, 2, 3, \ldots, n$; and f and g are different functional relationships, the first indicating that the quantity of any particular input demanded by an industry varies inversely with (i.e., is negatively related to) its price and the second indicating that the quantity of any particular input supplied by an industry varies directly with (i.e., is positively related to) its price.

It is usually further specified, as part of the same neo-Walrasian model, that it is possible to substitute in the production process any one of the n inputs for another (subject only to diminishing returns) so that the relationship among any two of the inputs included within the industry's cost and/or production function can be represented by a set of isoquants like the ones shown in exhibit 5.6. Each isoquant implies not only that is it possible to substitute one input for another but also that, in so doing, it is possible to maintain the same level of output. The only drawback, should one input be substituted for another, is that it will be necessary to use disproportionately more of the one input in place of the other. This condition of diminishing returns, insofar as the substitution of one input for another is concerned, is represented by the increasingly greater quantities of each input that are required toward either end of the isoquants shown in exhibit 5.6.

What first needs to be pointed out in connection with this alternative neo-Walrasian model of production is that the 79 separate sets of demand and supply functions that would be needed, at the very least, to explain the interindustry flows of the U.S. economy have yet to be derived empirically. There is thus no evidence to indicate that these 79 different demand and supply curves—not to mention the isoquants which are said to represent the relationship between each of the 79 different material inputs included within each supply curve—actually exist. They remain only a theoretical speculation, unsupported by any empirical evidence. Indeed, it is usually acknowledged that, because of the identification problem created by the fact that the demand and supply functions depend on the same set of price variables, it is not possible to observe directly the critical parameters of the neo-Walrasian model of production, these being the cross elasticities of substitution among the different inputs and hence the slopes of the postulated isoquants.

The evidence available from studies of production and costs in the short period would, in fact, argue against the existence of any isoquants, such as those shown in exhibit 5.6. These studies suggest that the technical coefficients, rather than than being flexible and therefore capable of varying in response to a change in relative prices, are immutable, or fixed—at least in the short period. The lack of empirical support for the neo-Walrasian model of production does not mean that industries are without any flexibility insofar as the direct material inputs are concerned. In the steel industry, for example, it is possible, within limits, to

Exhibit 5.6

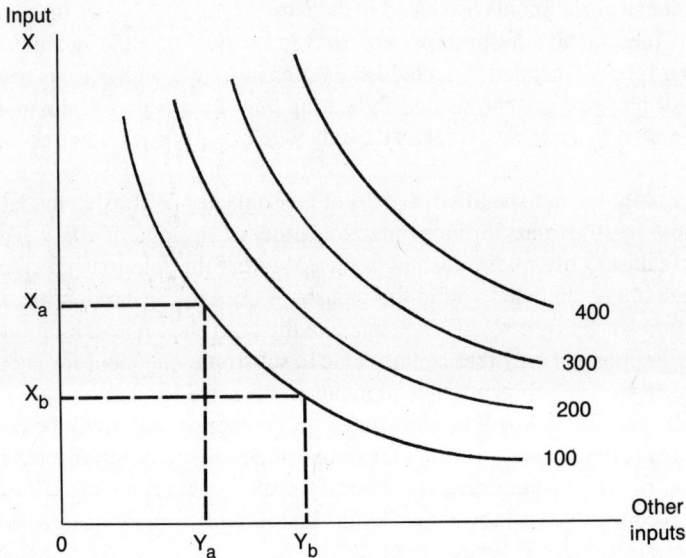

substitute steel scrap for iron ore as the basic raw material and vice versa, depending on relative prices. It is even possible to learn how to economize on the use of certain inputs whose relative price has risen, such as energy, by taking advantage of previously overlooked opportunities to eliminate what Harvey Leibenstein has termed "X-inefficiency." The empirical evidence nonetheless suggests that the degree of flexibility, insofar as the choice of material inputs is concerned, is too restricted to make the neo-Walrasian model of production the appropriate one. In the steel industry, for example, it is not possible—not without a major change in technology and the investment in new plant and equipment needed to effect that change—to substitute other inputs for the coal used in coking. Nor is it possible to substitute other inputs for whatever combination of iron ore or steel scrap is used as the basic raw material. What has been observed in the case of the steel industry insofar as the substitution of one material input for another is concerned holds true for most, if not all, of the technologically sophisticated industries which constitute the core of an advanced market economy.

And indeed no claim is made that the neo-Walrasian model of production applies in the short period—or, using the neoclassical theory's own terminology, in the short run. Instead, what is asserted is that each of the different markets governing the inter-industry flow of material inputs (one for each of the 79 different industries) can be expected to clear, at least in the long run; and that when this homeostatic condition is not satisfied, the response of the market will be a change in the price of the input so as to bring the supply and demand for that input back into balance with one another. This is the Walrasian excess-demand hypothesis already alluded to (see section 5.1.2). Two points need to be made in connection with this argument. The first is that, to the extent the necessary adjustment is assumed to occur only in the long run, it cannot be used to explain the set of technical coefficients, as represented by the A and L matrices, which govern the levels of production within each of the n industries in the short period, the time frame of the Leontief model that has been developed so far. It would, at most, explain the actual values taken by those technical coefficients only in the long run (or, using the terminology of post-Keynesian theory, only in the long period). The second point is that, even insofar as any long-run (or long-period) change in the technical coefficients is concerned, the neo-Walrasian model implies the existence of an adjustment process which, once it has been properly specified, can then be tested against the evidence. This adjustment process can be outlined as follows:

1. $Q_d \neq Q_s$ → Δp (If $Q_d > Q_s$, then $+\Delta p$; if $Q_d < Q_s$, then $-\Delta p$)
2. $+\Delta p$ → $-\Delta q_{i,j}$ until $Q_d = Q_s$ within each of the n^2 cells that
   constitute the inner matrix.

In view of the "administered" or "fixed-price" markets which generally prevail throughout the industrial sector, this adjustment mechanism can be dismissed as being largely inoperative—at least within that sector in the short period. The long period, however, is a different matter. Relative prices clearly change within that extended time frame. The question is whether they change as a result of a shift in the parameter of some demand or supply curve, with the resulting change in relative prices then leading to a change in the technical coefficients that characterize the production and/or cost function of some industry or whether, alternatively, it is a change in the technology that first produces a change in the technical coefficients and then leads, via the dual price solution, to a change in the price vector. The question will be put to one side until the Leontief model of production has been extended to cover the long period as well, and it can then be compared directly with the neo-Walrasian model (see chapter 6, section 4.1). For now, however, the neo-Walrasian model can be rejected, at least as an explanation for what determines, in the short period, the value of the technical coefficients represented by the A (and L) matrix. This in turn means that, when it comes to explaining the level of output produced in the short period by each of the n different industries, the A matrix and its inverse, $\dot{A}$, must be considered to have a prior existence not dependent on any existing set of prices. The Leontief inverse, $\dot{A}$ or $(I - A)^{-1}$, can thus be regarded as a previously determined parameter—as was done in presenting the systems diagrams for the quantity and dual price solutions to the Leontief model of production (see sections 5.2.1 and 5.2.2).

5.3 Scale of Production and Costs

One of the critical assumptions underlying the Leontief model of production has just been examined and found not to be unreasonable. This is the assumption that the values which the technical coefficients represented by the **A** and **L** matrices take are determined prior to and therefore are independent of the price vector, **P**. Indeed, based on the available evidence, this seems to be a more reasonable assumption than the argument of the alternative neo-Walrasian model that $A = f(P)$. In this third part of chapter 5, a second critical assumption underlying the Leontief model of production will be examined. This is the assumption that, within certain limits, production can be either expanded or contracted at constant returns to scale.

The assumption of constant returns to scale implies that if production in some subsequent period were to be $1 + \lambda$ of what it was when the values of the technical coefficients were ascertained (with λ a scalar denoting a certain fraction that may be either positive or negative), then the output of the different industries, as given by the **Q** vector, would change by the same $1 + \lambda$ factor. In other words, both sides of equation 5.24, representing the quantity solution to the Leontief model, can be multiplied through by $1 + \lambda$ without affecting the **A** (and **L**) matrix. This, in turn, means that the level of aggregate output, **G**, can be increased by $1 + \lambda$, with the only result being that the output of the different industries, **Q**, will increase by $1 + \lambda$. The proportions of the different types of material (and labor) inputs required to produce that greater or lesser amount of output, as represented by the **A** (and **L**) matrix, will be left unchanged.

The assumption of constant returns to scale when production is varied by some scalar, like the assumption that the **A** and **L** vectors are independent of the **P** vector, flies in the face of the conventional theory in economics. Only in this case it is the Marshallian partial equilibrium analysis—and in particular the so-called "law" (it is actually only a hypothesis) of variable returns to scale—which represents the alternative line of argument. This section begins therefore with an examination of the variable returns to scale hypothesis before proceding to construct a set of cost curves which, because they take into account the effect of the megacorp's multiple-plant operation, are more consistent with the situation typically faced in the short period by the representative firm within the industrial sector of the U.S. economy.

5.3.1 Variable returns to scale

Variable returns to scale may be said to be a plausible hypothesis whenever the method of production requires that some inputs—those which are free to vary in quantity as the level of output itself changes—must be used in combination with inputs which are fixed in quantity, at least in the short period. These fixed inputs are usually assumed to be the plant and equipment or, in some formulations, the control and direction provided by the firm's management. Clearly, only one combination of the variable and fixed inputs will be the optimal one which enables the firm to produce at the lowest possible cost. Indeed, plants are usually designed with this optimal, or cost-minimizing, level of output clearly in mind. (The optimal level of output may be a certain range rather than just a single point, but this does not alter the argument in any signficant way.) It therefore follows that, whenever the level or scale of production is varied, the costs of production will be affected. Only one level (or limited range) of output will be the optimal one, resulting in the lowest possible costs; and any other levels (those outside the limited range) will be less than optimal.

This argument leads to the type of cost curves usually postulated as part of a Marshallian, partial equilibrium analysis (when the focus is on a single firm or industry rather than on all n industries simultaneously). They are the types of cost curves shown in exhibit 5.7. The curve in the top half of the exhibit shows the behavior of total costs as output varies and the curves in the bottom half, the behavior of unit costs (i.e., total costs divided by the quantity of output per time period, Q/t). As indicated by the vertical intercept of the total cost curve, there are certain costs incurred irrespective of the level of output. These are the fixed costs associated with the prior provision of plant and equipment as well as with any managerial inputs. The term "overhead costs" is sometimes used instead of the term "fixed costs." There is nonetheless a subtle distinction between the two. The fixed costs refer to the costs of those inputs which cannot be varied in the short period while the overhead costs refer to those costs which cannot be attributed, through the system of cost accounting, to any particular unit of output. While the two categories largely overlap, still they are not the same. For example, certain of the overhead costs, e.g., the cost of R&D and other staff personnel, can be varied in the short period and thus are not necessarily "fixed." In the steel industry, according to Marcus's *World Steel Dynamics*, about 10 percent of the material costs and about 25 percent of the labor costs—or about 15 percent of the total costs—are fixed. These fixed costs are in addition to the overhead expense from depreciation and interest charges which can be assumed, as in exhibit 5.4, to come out of the industry's residual income.

In addition to the fixed and/or overhead costs, there are the firm's variable costs—the cost of the material and labor inputs the quantity of which can be varied as the level of output itself varies. The individual firm's total costs are therefore equal to its fixed costs plus its variable costs. That is,

$$TC = FC + VC \qquad (5.43)$$

where TC denotes the firm's total costs, FC its fixed costs and VC its variable costs. Notice that, in the case of the TC curve shown in the top half diagram of exhibit 5.7, the total costs first increase at a decreasing rate as output rises (the increase in costs is less than the increase in output), then increase at a constant rate

Exhibit 5.7

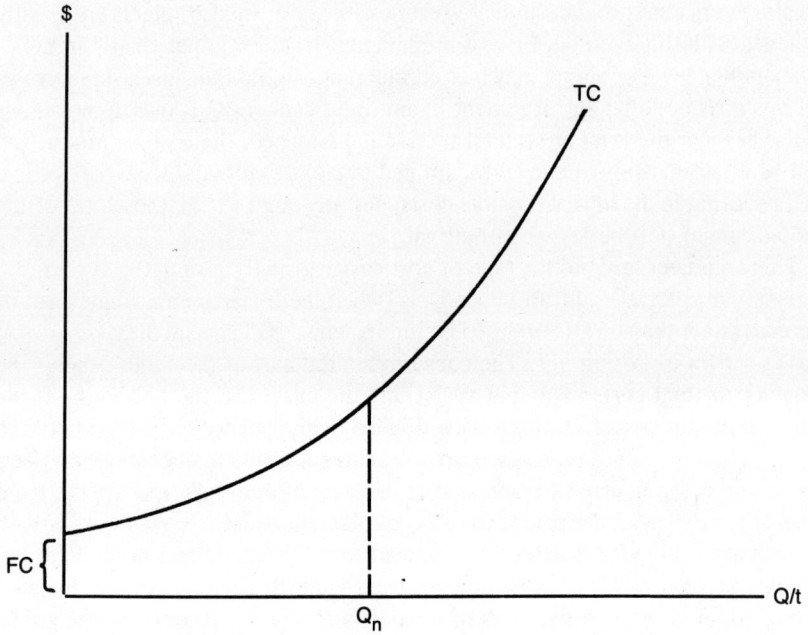

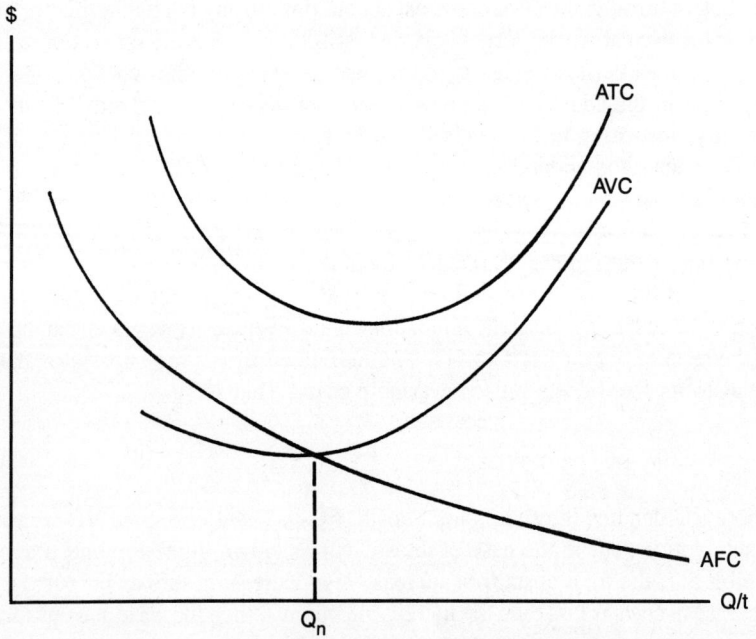

Exhibit 5.8

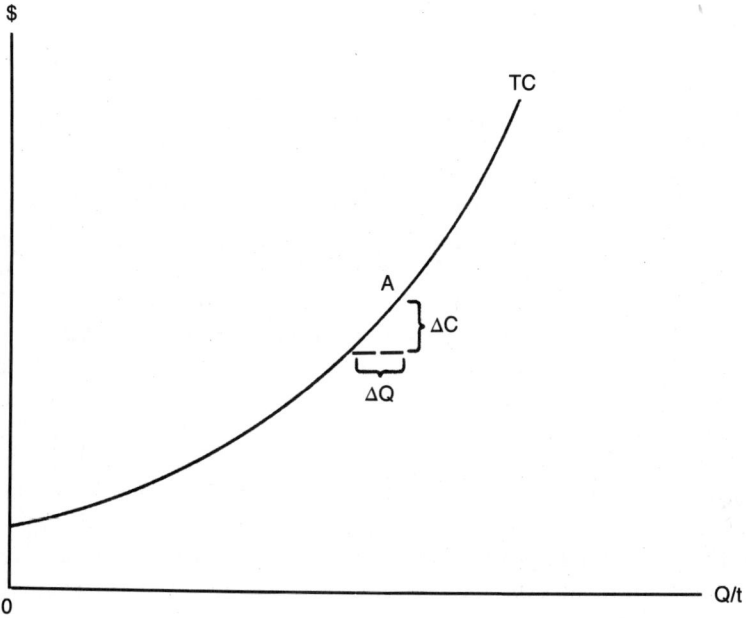

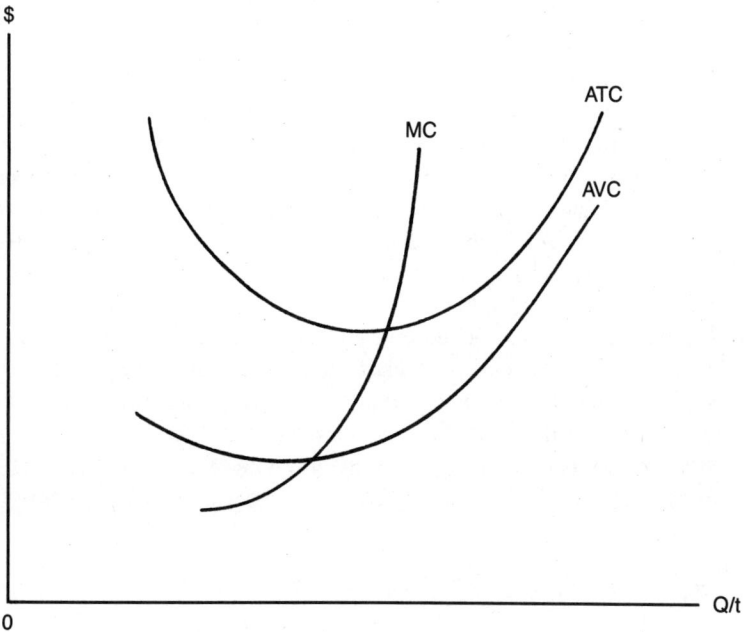

(momentarily at Q_n), and finally increase at an increasing rate. This is how the condition of variable returns to scale manifests itself in the case of the total cost curve that is usually specified in a Marshallian analysis. Precisely the same relationship between cost and output is reflected when, as in the set of curves shown in the bottom half diagram, the total costs are divided by the quantity of output to give the per unit costs of production. Only in this set of curves the relationship is manifested in the U-shaped average variable cost (AVC) curve.

The neoclassical short-run (i.e., short-period) analysis attaches great importance to the changes taking place at the margin. Consequently, it focuses on the marginal cost of production—the change in the total cost of production as output varies. This marginal cost is represented by the changing slope of the total cost curve shown in the top half diagram and by a separately drawn MC curve in the bottom half diagram. As can be seen from exhibit 5.8, the marginal cost rises, once the average variable costs begin falling at a decreasing rate, so that the MC curve intersects the AVC and ATC curves at their respective lowest points. The MC curve rises more rapidly than either the AVC or ATC curves, thereby indicating that the marginal costs are more sensitive than the variable costs to a change in the level of output. All of these relationships are simply mathematical properties of the applicable cost curves once it can be established that certain of the inputs essential to production cannot be varied in the short period and that therefore, in order to expand output, it is necessary to combine greater or lesser quantities of the variable inputs with those fixed inputs—with the consequence that there are necessarily variable returns to scale.

The cost curves shown in exhibit 5.8 apply most clearly in the case of the neoclassical proprietorship that is the representative firm within the agricultural sector and even forms the small-firm periphery of industries within the industrial sector. This is because the neoclassical proprietorship has available to it in the short period only a limited quantity of capital inputs (the single plant it operates) and only a limit quantity of managerial inputs (those the small group of owner-managers can provide). In the analysis that follows, the cost curves shown in exhibit 5.8 will be assumed to be those of a neoclassical proprietorship even though, despite the considerable time that has passed since cost curves of this type were first specified, there has yet to be published an empirical study confirming the existence of such cost curves, at least within the nonagricultural sectors of the economy. However, they will not be assumed to be the cost curves of a megacorp, the representative firm within the oligopolistic sector. This is because the mega-corp, with its more elastic managerial structure, is able to operate multiple plants, with these multiple plants, in turn, giving rise to a quite different set of cost curves.

5.3.2 Plant segments and the megacorp's costs

Each plant owned by the megacorp consists of one or more plant segments. A plant segment is a unit within the plant that is self-sufficient in terms of equipment or capital inputs. It includes enough of each piece of equipment to produce the good or service with which the plant as a whole is identified. Usually there is one piece of equipment, such as an assembly line, with which multiple units of other equipment must be combined to form the individual plant segment. In any case, the various pieces of equipment which constitute the plant segment represent the optimal combination of capital inputs, that is, the combination which enables a particular good or service to be produced at the lowest possible cost. A plant segment therefore represents the smallest unit, or "quantum," of capital that can be identified as an input into the production process. For it is not until various heterogeneous capital goods have been organized into a plant segment that production can proceed, at least within the industrial sector where the combination of those capital inputs is the critical factor in the technology, or mode of production, employed.

What distinguishes the megacorp from the neoclassical proprietorship, at least insofar as production is concerned, is that the megacorp is able to vary its level of output in the short period by utilizing a larger or smaller number of plant segments. Assuming that each plant as well as each plant segment employs the same technology (an assumption to be relaxed shortly), with that technology indicated by the same a_{ij} and l_j technical coefficients which apply to each of the different plants, a portion of the megacorp's AVC curve can be represented by the series of points shown in exhibit 5.9. The diagram indicates that a megacorp can produce the output Q_n utilizing n plant segments, the output Q_{n+1} utilizing $n+1$ plant segments, and so on, all at the same average variable cost. What this means is that as the megacorp varies its output, the average variable costs will remain constant—even though it is jumping, discontinuously, from one discrete level of output to another.

It is tempting, from the perspective of the more conventional Marshallian model, to view each of the points in exhibit 5.9 as being the lowest point on the U-shaped AVC curve that represents one of the megacorp's plant segments. This interpretation transforms the discrete set of points shown in exhibit 5.9 into the series of U-shaped cost curves shown in exhibit 5.10. Such an interpretation would be unwarranted, however, for several reasons. First, to the extent that the production system is characterized by fixed technical coefficients, as was argued in the preceding subsection, the material and labor inputs must be used in certain invariant combinations not just with one another but also with the capital inputs embodied in each plant segment. In other words, there is no reason to assume greater flexibility in combining the variable inputs with the fixed capital (and managerial) inputs than there is in combining the variable inputs with each other. To assure the lowest possible production costs, all the inputs—fixed as well as variable—may have to be employed in the same ratios as those given by the technical coefficients in the A and L matrices. A plant segment is simply the smallest quantum of capital to which those technical coefficients apply. The technology of the industry may in fact be such that it permits virtually no flexibility in those technical coefficients. For example, with the type of integrated

Exhibit 5.9

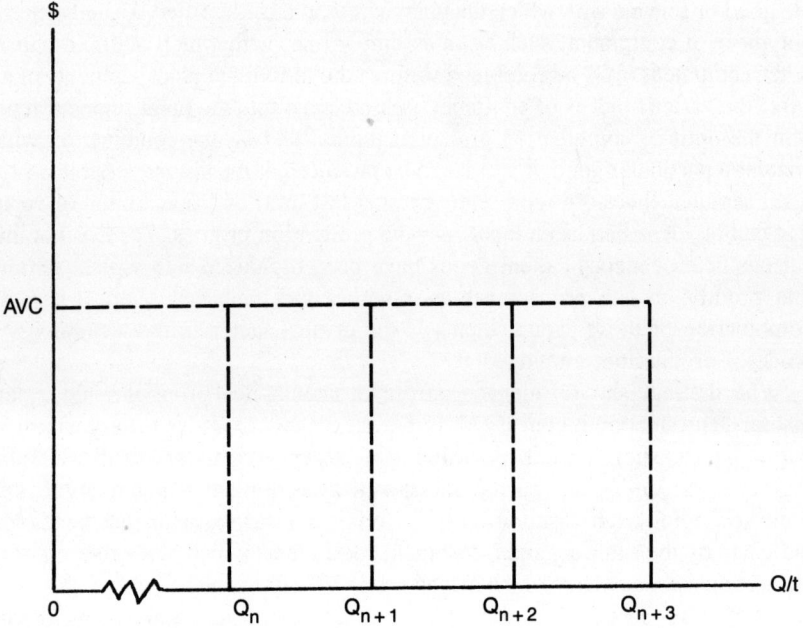

Exhibit 5.10

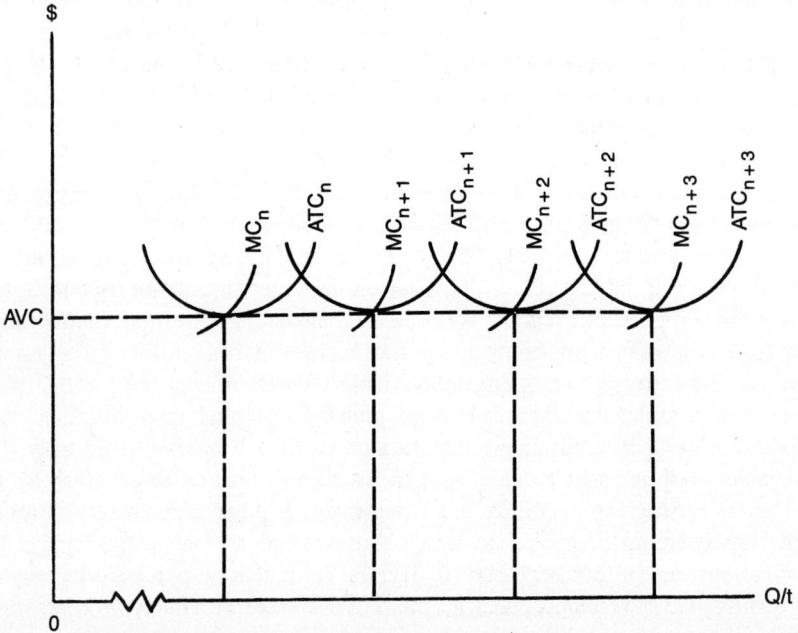

steel mill in use in 1978, it may have required no less and no more than 0.95 tons of coal to produce a single ton of carbon steel. Moreover, what little flexibility the technology permits may well be lost as a result of the work rules which the workers and the management have jointly established through collective bargaining. These work rules, for example, may well ensure that, until a new plant is constructed and/or new work rules negotiated, no less and no more than 8.15 hours of human resources will have to be used to produce a ton of carbon steel.

There is, however, an even more important reason why the curves shown in exhibit 5.10 are inapplicable to a megacorp. Those curves imply that the megacorp can produce at the lowest possible average variable cost only when sales happen to be at one or more discrete levels: Q_n, Q_{n+1}, Q_{n+2}, etc. When sales fall between these discrete points—for example, between Q_n and Q_{n+1}—the curves imply that the megacorp will be forced to utilize at least one of its plants more intensively and thus will experience the same rising marginal costs to which the neoclassical proprietorship, with its single plant, is subject. (The megacorp may, of course, choose to use several plant segments more intensively rather than just one plant segment, but this hardly changes the thrust of the argument. Whether any of the plant segments can be used more intensively, that is, whether the technical coefficients are sufficiently flexible to permit this option, is the issue.)

The trouble with this argument is that it overlooks the role played by finished goods inventories in enabling a firm like the megacorp to adjust its output discontinuously, that is, by quantum leaps from one point of least cost production to another, even through sales may vary continuously, that is, by smaller quanta. The fact is that when current sales fall between Q_n and Q_{n+1}, the megacorp has one of two options. It can operate $n+1$ plant segments and allow its finished goods inventories to rise; or, alternatively, it can operate n plant segments and allow its finished goods inventories to fall. Which option it elects will, of course, be influenced by the current direction in which sales are moving. If sales are rising, and especially if they are expected to continue rising, then the first option is likely to be the more attractive one. But if sales are falling and the expectation is that they will continue to fall, then the second option is likely to be the more attractive one. This argument, it should be noted, ties in with what has already been said about the role of inventories in the macroeconomic adjustment process (see chapter 3, section 2.3). The point is that, by using its finished goods inventories to offset any discrepancy, either positive or negative, between sales and current output, the megacorp is able to avoid operating any of its individual plant segments except at their most efficient level of output. With its finished goods inventory providing the necessary cushion or "slack," the megacorp is still able to produce at the lowest possible average variable costs. This means that its AVC curve is simply the locus of the points shown in exhibit 5.9 and takes the form shown in exhibit 5.11.

The megacorp, then, is able to expand production by utilizing additional plant segments and it is able to reduce production by closing down, or temporarily

Exhibit 5.11

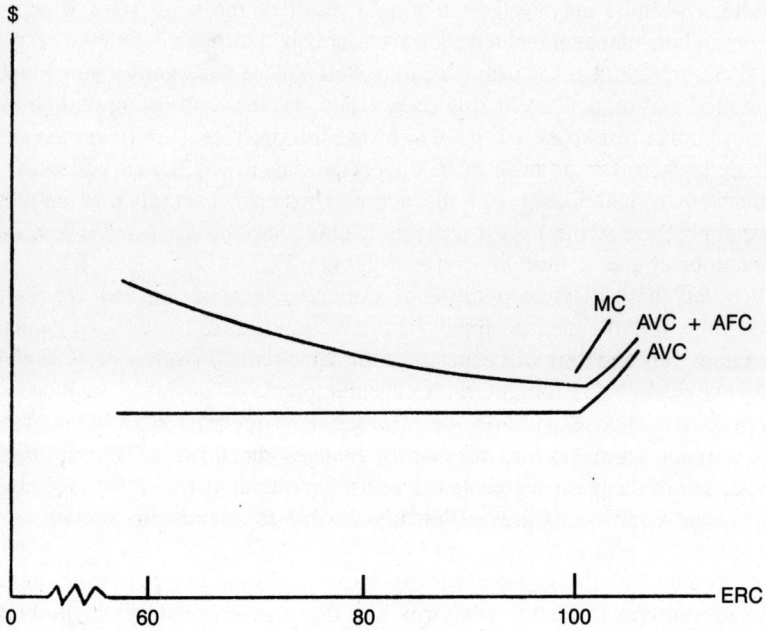

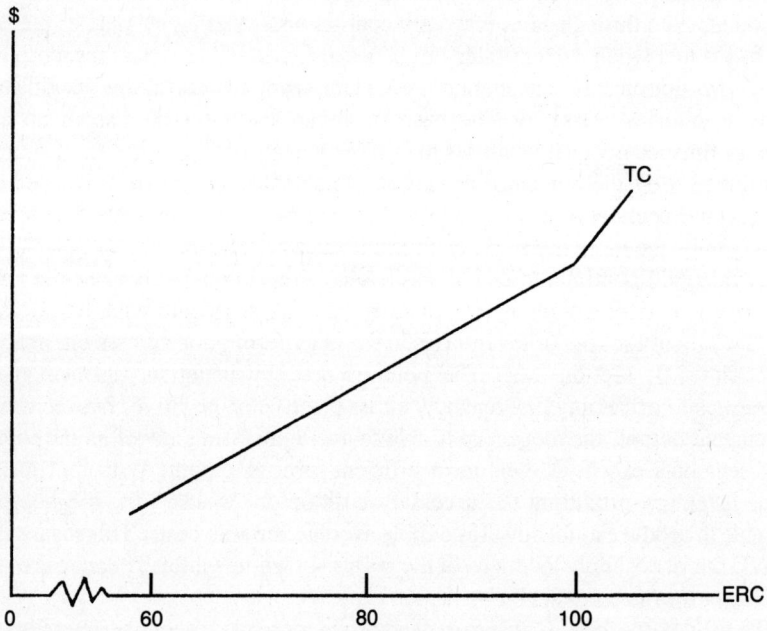

idling, one or more of those same plant segments. In either case, it is able to avoid the rise in marginal costs which occurs when any single plant or plant segment must be used more or less intensively in order to expand or reduce output. Nonetheless, insofar as the short period is concerned, the megacorp is not able to expand production in this way indefinitely, for the megacorp at any given moment in time has only a limited number of plant segments. Each of these plant segments will be able to produce only a certain amount of output at the lowest possible cost. This can be termed its "engineer-rated capacity," and when the quantity that can be produced most efficiently in all of the different plant segments is aggregated, it constitutes the megacorp's total engineer-rated capacity (ERC) within that particular industry.

The megacorp is therefore able to produce at constant average variable costs up to 100 percent of ERC. With the average variable costs constant, the marginal costs, too, will be constant, for up to that point the two curves will coincide. This means that the TC curve will, for all practical purposes, be linear as shown in exhibit 5.11, rather than taking the curvilinear form shown in exhibit 5.7. However, beyond 100 percent of ERC, when the megacorp no longer has additional plant segments it can utilize, the logic behind the notion of variable returns holds and the megacorp's average variable costs will rise. Moreover, since the 100 percent ERC point marks a discontinuity in the AVC curve, the marginal costs will jump before rising at an even more rapid rate. It is for this reason that the curves shown in exhibit 5.11 take the form they do. (It is better, when making comparisons among different firms, to change the variable measured along the horizontal axis from the quantity produced per time period, Q/t, as in earlier exhibits, to the percent of ERC being utilized, as in exhibit 5.11. In this way, the differing sizes of firms can be ignored, on the grounds that the critical factor insofar as the returns to scale are concerned is how close to "full capacity" the firm is operating.)

The constancy of costs associated with the megacorp, it should be noted, applies only to the average variable and to the marginal costs. With the fixed costs being divided by an ever greater quantity as output expands, average fixed costs will necessarily decline, though at a decreasing rate, as production rises. It is for this reason that the curve which combines average variable and average fixed costs falls continuously until it reaches its minima just to the right of 100 percent ERC. Both the fact that the average variable, and hence marginal, costs are constant and the fact that the average variable and average fixed costs combined necessarily fall as output increases are important to the arguments which follow (see chapter 6, section 3, and chapter 7, section 3.1).

It might appear that the curves shown in exhibit 5.11 are not really that different from the more conventional cost curves shown in exhibit 5.8. The U is bent somewhat out of shape but still eventually the curves turn up, with the result that both average variable and marginal costs then rise. To take this view, however, is to miss the key difference between the megacorp's short-period situation and that of the neoclassical proprietorship as posited by the conventional theory. This is that the megacorp is unlikely to operate beyond 100 percent of ERC. The full justification for making this statement must wait until the megacorp's investment behavior is analyzed (see chapter 7, section 2.1, although the point has already been touched on briefly in connection with the accelerator effect outlined above in chapter 4, section 1.3). Suffice it for now to point out that, as part of the forward planning it normally carries out, the megacorp can be expected to increase its capacity in each of the industries to which it belongs so as not only to satisfy the normal growth in demand over time but also to provide sufficient reserve capacity to handle any unanticipated surge in sales. It is the existence of this reserve capacity, together with the substantial inventory of unsold output, which provides the necessary "slack" so that an economic system with the megacorp as the representative firm is better able to cope with any fluctuations in demand. Such a system will behave quite differently, macrodynamically, from one in which, as a normal practice, neither reserve capacity nor inventories of unsold goods are available to absorb the changes in the level of demand. Thus, in modeling any system of production, it is necessary to distinguish an economy with slack, such as the corporate economy of the United States, from the type of "taut" economy which economists usually assume exists in the advanced countries of the West but which is actually found only in certain East European countries.

Because of its reserve capacity, the megacorp normally operates at between 60 and 95 percent of ERC, with 80–85 percent of ERC the expected or "standard operating rate." Only as a result of unforeseeable circumstances (such as a war mobilization) is it likely that sales will exceed 100 percent of ERC; and even then, whether the industry normally produces to order or not, the response is likely to be a delay in the delivery dates rather than a more intense utilization of the existing plant segments that would cause unit costs to rise significantly. The relevant portion of the cost curves shown in exhibit 5.11 is therefore the interval between 60 and 95 percent of ERC. The portion beyond 100 percent ERC where both average variable and marginal costs rise as the level of output increases is virtually of no practical import. The existence of reserve capacity is readily confirmed by not just the statistics regularly reported by the U.S. Federal Reserve Board on the rates of capacity utilization within the manufacturing sector but also by direct observation of the operating practices of megacorps.

What has just been said about the constancy of the megacorp's average variable and marginal costs was based on the assumption that each plant or plant segment employs the same technology and therefore can be characterized by the same technical coefficients. This is an assumption which does not hold when there has been technical progress, as reflected by a change in the A and L matrices in the interval between the construction of the first and last plant segments. Indeed, if technical progress has been constant over that period, as is quite likely to be the case, the cost of operating different plants will be represented by the points shown in exhibit 5.12 rather than the points shown in exhibit 5.10. As output is expanded, it will be necessary to utilize older and less efficient plant segments so that the cost of operating $n+1$ plant segments will be greater than that of operating the n plants, the cost of operating the $n+2$ plants will be greater than that of operating the $n+1$ plants, and so on. This, in turn, means that the AVC and MC curves, rather than being horizontal as in exhibit 5.11, will rise as output is expanded, the MC curve step-wise and the AVC curve continuously, as shown in exhibit 5.13.

While the fact that an industry has, over time, experienced technical progress clearly makes a difference in terms of the cost curves shown in exhibit 5.11, one should not exaggerate the difference this factor actually makes. For one thing, the same technical progress will enable the firm, through investment in newer equipment, to improve the efficiency of its older plant segments as well. This, in fact, is one of the types of investment to be considered below (see chapter 7, section 2.2). And while the newer equipment in an older plant may not lead to the same low costs as when the same equipment is part of a new facility which has been designed and built with the new equipment in mind, still it can narrow considerably the differential in costs among plants, as measured by the vertical distance between the points in exhibit 5.12. It is for this reason that, within the vicinity of the standard operating ratio, or SOR—this being the level at which the megacorp is most likely to find itself producing—the differential in costs when plants are either reactivated or idled will not be that great. Moreover, even though the direct costs of operating a marginal plant may be somewhat higher, there may be offsetting cost advantages—even beyond the greater volume over which the overhead expenses can be spread—from operating a larger number of plant segments.

For all these reasons, the upward drift of the average variable and marginal costs depicted in exhibit 5.13 which, on theoretical grounds, seems so likely when there has been steady technical progress may, in reality, be barely perceptible. The increase in costs may actually be so slight that it makes no difference to assume, as will be done in the chapters which follow, that in the case of a megacorp the average variable and marginal costs are constant within the relevant range of 60 to 95 percent of ERC and that therefore the cost curves depicted in exhibit 5.11 are the appropriate ones for the oligopolistic subsector. This assumption, it turns out, is consistent with the evidence from the empirical studies which have carried out on how the costs of multi-plant firms respond to changes in the level of output, once proper allowance is made for the different vintages of those plants. The nature of the megacorp's cost curves having now been described, we can return to the question of how reasonable it is to assume constant returns to scale, in the short period, as the Leontief model does for the enterprise sector as a whole.

5.3.3 Constant returns to scale

Whatever the actual shape of the megacorp's cost curves—whether it be those

Exhibit 5.12

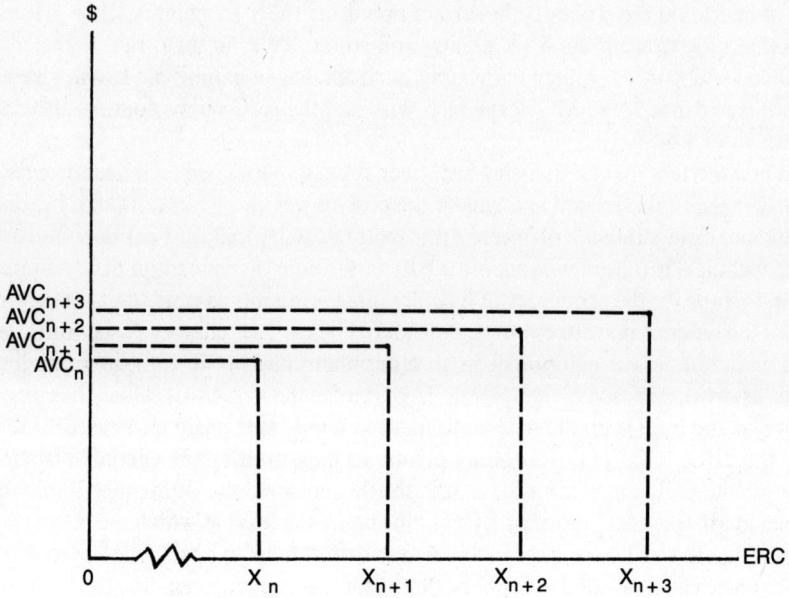

Exhibit 5.13

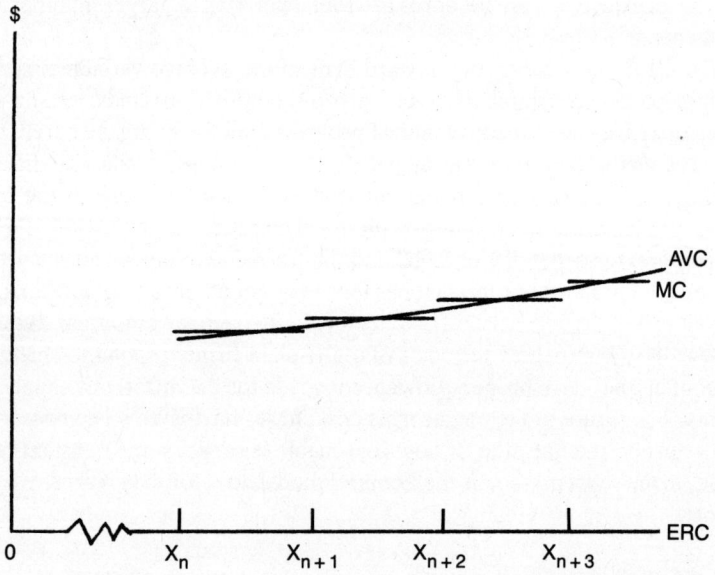

depicted in exhibit 5.11 or those in exhibit 5.13—it seems clear, at least insofar as the oligopolistic subsector is concerned, that a change in the scale of production will leave the technical coefficients unchanged. Even if costs do rise somewhat as less efficient plant segments are brought into operation, this reflects not a change in the technical coefficients themselves but rather the different technology, and thus the different technical coefficients, of the plant segments being activated. Thus a change in the level of aggregate output, as measured by G, which leads to a change in the demand for an oligopolistic industry's output will not alter the A, L and the soon-to-be-introduced K matrices. It is in this sense that the technical coefficients are "fixed," at least in the short period. They will change only as a result of the technical progress occurring in the long period. With the technical coefficients in this sense fixed, it is then possible to vary production in the short period, that is, over the cycle, at what is for all practical purposes constant average variable and marginal costs. One is therefore on fairly solid ground in assuming, at least insofar as the oligopolistic subsector is concerned, constant returns to scale such that

$$(1+\lambda)G = (1+\lambda)Q_0 \qquad (5.44)$$

where Q_0 is the vector of output produced by the oligopolistic subgroup of industries identified in exhibit 5.2.

An important implication of the constant returns which can be posited, aside from its effect on the costs of production over the cycle, is that the size of the individual firm is thereby left unexplained. The megacorp, it can be assumed, is able to operate any number of plants at the same constant costs (ignoring the different vintages of those plants) up to the number of plants required to supply all the demand for an industry's output. How many plants or plant segments the megacorp will in fact operate, and thus how large a share of the market it controls, will depend, once aggregate demand factors have determined total industry sales, on the outcome of the nonprice competition among firms which is the more important form of competition within the oligopolistic subsector (see chapter 7, section 2.3). Whether constant returns to scale can also be posited for the nonoligopolistic component of the industrial sector is a more open question.

There is a long tradition in economics which asserts that, in the case of a single-plant firm (with its single group of owner-managers), production involves combining variable quantities of certain inputs with the fixed inputs so as to enable the scale of production to be altered in the short run (or short period). Indeed, it is the changing ratio of these variable inputs (material and labor) to the fixed inputs employed (plant and equipment, management) which results in the variable returns to scale which are then postulated. These variable returns to scale, were they in fact to be observed empirically, would belie the assumption of fixed technical coefficients, and hence constant returns to scale, on which the Leontief short-period model of production is based. The technical coefficients derived from the input-output model of the U.S. economy would at most represent only a long-period set of relationships—an averaging out over time of the changing, or flexible, coefficients that hold in the short period. They would thus represent only a snap-shot picture taken at a particular moment in time, one that fails to capture the back-and-forth movement which is no less a part of the reality.

The flexibility with which at least the neoclassical proprietorship is assumed to be able to combine various inputs is, however, only a theoretical argument. Despite the unquestioning manner in which this flexibility is assumed in the standard microeconomic textbooks, it has yet to be substantiated by any empirical evidence from the industrial sector. It may well be that, just as the rise in cost experienced by the megacorp when it utilizes a somewhat less efficient plant segment is an imperceptible one, so the rise in cost experienced by the neoclassical proprietorship when it is forced to use its single plant more intensively is also imperceptible. Indeed, it was Piero Sraffa who, in an article first published in English in 1926 (a slightly different version appeared the year before in Italian), first questioned the assumption of variable returns to scale, particularly the decreasing returns that were said to occur beyond a certain point, upon which the Marshallian partial equilibrium analysis rests.

What Sraffa pointed out was that the assumption of decreasing returns was based largely on the argument Ricardo had made concerning land and other natural resources. The argument therefore applies only to the primary sector. It was a mistake, Sraffa pointed out, to extend the argument Ricardo had made about land to the industrial sector where the mode of production is quite different. Indeed, there is no reason—at least not one that had been offered by Marshall or any other economist so far—why the industrial sector, as distinct from the primary sector, should necessarily be subject to decreasing returns to scale. Nor is there any reason why the industrial sector should necessarily be subject to increasing returns either. Although the growth of output per worker is sometimes cited as evidence of the latter, this argument, like so many based on the Marshallian framework, violates the critical *ceteris paribus* assumption of that partial analysis. Sraffa's point was that, holding time and all the other parameters of the Marshallian demand and supply curves constant, there is no axiomatic basis for assuming either decreasing *or* increasing returns and thus no basis for assuming variable returns to scale.

Several points need to be made stressed in connection with this seminal article written by Sraffa ten years before the appearance of *The General Theory*, fifteen years before Leontief produced the first input-output table and thirty-four years before Sraffa would finally made clear, at least to those outside the relatively small world of Cambridge, England, what he was really driving at by publishing his work long in progress, *The Production of Commodities by Means of Commodities*. The first point is that Sraffa was not really concerned with whether the industrial sector was subject to decreasing or increasing returns. The then raging controversy on this question was largely beside the point. Nor was Sraffa simply trying to call attention to some flaw in the Marshallian demand-and-supply framework so that, by modifying that framework in the appropriate way, it could still be used to answer the same types of questions. Rather what Sraffa was trying to suggest was that the supply-and-demand framework is an inappropriate one for trying to analyze the industrial sector of the economy. This was a point that was not lost on Keynes (see chapter 3, section 2.4); and it is a point the significance of which will become clearer once it can be shown, following Sraffa, that it is possible to explain the $\mathbf{P}$ and $\mathbf{Q}$ vectors without having to posit supply and demand curves of any sort (see chapter 6, section 4.5). For the moment, however, what is most pertinent about the 1926 article is its denial of any axiomatic basis for assuming variable returns, at least within the industrial sector. If the assumption of variable returns is warranted, it can only be on the basis of the empirical evidence.

So far, in examining that empirical evidence, we can find a strong case for assuming *constant* returns to scale, holding technology constant, only within the oligopolistic subcomponent of the industrial sector. Insofar as the nonoligopolistic sector is concerned, the empirical evidence is virtually nonexistent. The nonoligopolistic subsector, however, accounts for less than a fifth of the output produced by the industrial sector (see section 5.1.1, exhibit 5.2). Given the relative size of the nonoligopolistic subsector and the lack of any evidence for either decreasing or increasing returns, it seems not unreasonable merely to extend the argument about constant returns within the oligopolistic subsector to the industrial sector as a whole. That is,

$$(I+\lambda)\mathbf{G} = (I+\lambda)\mathbf{Q_I} \tag{5.36}$$

where $\mathbf{Q_I}$ is the vector of output, in real terms, produced by all the industries outside the primary sector. Indeed, the burden of proof is on those who would argue the contrary.

It follows from what has just been said that the technical coefficients which can be derived from the input-output table for the U.S. and other advanced market economies are no more affected by the scale of production than they are by the price vector. But if the $\mathbf{A}$ and $\mathbf{L}$ matrices are not determined by the scale of production, $(I+\lambda)\mathbf{Q}$, or the price vector, $\mathbf{P}$, then what does determine the specific value those coefficients take? To answer this question, it is necessary to turn to the third explanation that can be found in the literature, the rate of technical progress.

5.4 The Rate of Technical Progress

Technical progress can take either of two forms. One is the development of new techniques for producing the existing set of products and the other is the development of entirely new products. The first type of technical progress stems from what is known as process innovation and the second, from product innovation. In talking about the latter, one needs to distinguish a minor product innovation from a major one. A minor product innovation is one that, by increasing the variety of goods and services being produced by an already existing industry, adds to the industry's product line. A major product innovation, in contrast, leads to the creation of an entirely new industry, one not previously represented along the columns and rows of the input-output table. This second type of product innovation is more difficult to analyze since it represents a change in the very categories used to describe the enterprise sector. It is for this reason that the emphasis in this and the chapters which follow will be primarily on process innovation, with only product innovation of the minor sort also taken into account. This, however, is not to scant the importance of major product innovation. As Joseph Schumpeter was among the first to emphasize, it is difficult to account for the dynamism of an advanced market economy like that of the United States without allowing for the effect of periodic product innovations of a major sort. Nor will the discussion which follows be without relevance to an understanding of major product innovation since it does deal with product innovation of the minor sort, and major product innovations such as the railroad and the computer usually begin as minor innovations on an unrelated product. It is just that the Leontief model more readily lends itself to the analysis of process innovation.

The A and L matrices which are intrinsic to the Leontief model represent the technology, or techniques of production, currently in use by each of the industries which make up the enterprise sector. Technical progress which takes the form of process innovation occurs when those techniques, and thus the coefficients denoted by the A and L matrices, change so as to enable more final output, as represented by the D vector, to be produced relative to the inputs that must be obtained from without the economic system. The inputs which must be obtained from without are, as has already been pointed out (see chapter 1, section 2.4, and chapter 4, section 4.1), both the human resource inputs obtained from the parallel anthropogenic system and the natural resource inputs obtained from the ecological environment. It is in terms of the former, that is, the human resource inputs, that technical progress based on process innovation is usually measured. This is because an economic system is judged by its ability to provide for the material needs of the individuals who constitute the larger society; and it is the growth of output relative to the necessary human resource inputs that determines how well the material needs of the society's individual members can be met. One may, of course, want to add the proviso, in recognition of the environmental constraints, that the balance between the natural and social systems not be upset so as to impair either the health of those same individuals or the eventual availability of natural resource inputs (see chapter 13, part 3). Still, subject to this ecological proviso, it is the increase in output relative to the human resource inputs that will determine the society's ability to meet the material needs of its members—and thus the measurable rate of technical progress.

The technical progress which stems from process innovation can therefore be distinguished from just any change in the technical coefficients by the fact that it leads to an increase in the growth of output per worker in the aggregate, $\overset{\circ}{Z}$. Indeed, this increase in the growth of output per worker in the aggregate can be termed the measurable rate of technical progress. It represents the quantitative as distinct from the qualitative dimension of technical progress, the latter being the introduction of new products. Once the Leontief model of production has been extended in the way suggested by Pasinetti so as to provide a vertically integrated model of production, it is possible to analyze this growth of output per worker on an industry-by-industry basis, with $\overset{\circ}{Z}$ simply the weighted average of the growth of output per worker, $\overset{\circ}{z}_j$, in each of the h industries producing items for final use. Indeed, the growth of output per worker in the aggregate, as the weighted average of the growth of output per worker in each of those h industries, can itself then be explained in terms of the induced effect of investment on the rate of technical progress. The first step, therefore, in explaining what determines the rate of technical progress—and thus the coefficients denoted by the **A** and **L** matrices at any one point in time—is to derive the Pasinetti model of vertically integrated production from the more basic Leontief model.

5.4.1 A vertically integrated model of production

The material inputs used in the production process—the intermediate output of the enterprise sector—can be reduced to an even more basic set of inputs. These are the labor and other inputs which must be obtained from outside the enterprise sector. It is possible to determine the direct and indirect requirements for each of these more basic inputs by extending the Leontief model along the lines suggested by Pasinetti. In this way, a vertically integrated model of production, showing the transformation of the more basic inputs into the net output of the enterprise sector, can be derived.

The Leontief inverse, as already explained (see section 5.2.3), indicates the direct and indirect requirements for the material inputs produced by each of the n industries shown in an input-output table. These direct and indirect material requirements can be reduced to a set of direct and indirect labor requirements by pre-multiplying the Leontief inverse by the **L** vector. That is,

$$\underline{L} = L \, (I - A)^{-1} \tag{5.46}$$

where $\underline{L}$ is a row vector the elements of which, $\ddot{l}_1, \ddot{l}_2, \ddot{l}_3, \ldots, \ddot{l}_n$, are the number of hours of labor required, directly and indirectly, to produce a single unit of output in each of the n different industries which comprise the enterprise sector. The right-hand side of equation 5.46 can then be post-multiplied by the final demand vector, **D**, to determine the direct and indirect labor required to produce that particular amount of net output.

A similar vector can be derived for the unit direct and indirect residual income earned by each of those same n industries. That is,

$$\underline{\pi} = \pi(I - A)^{-1} \qquad (5.47)$$

where π is a row vector the elements of which, $\ddot{\pi}_1$, $\ddot{\pi}_2$, $\ddot{\pi}_3$, . . . $\ddot{\pi}_n$, represent the unit residual income earned directly and indirectly by each of the same n industries. The right-hand side of equation 5.47 can also be post-multiplied by the final demand vector, D. But in this case what is then determined is not the direct and indirect labor requirements but rather the direct and indirect residual income earned by each industry in producing that particular amount of net output.

So far the intermediate output supplied by each of the n industries which constitute the enterprise sector has been reduced to only one type of more basic input, the labor services obtained from the household sector via the parallel anthropogenic system—plus any direct and indirect unit residual income thereby earned. Whether there are any more basic inputs to which the intermediate output of the enterprise can be reduced is the very question which has divided the various schools in economics for more than a century. Marxists, relying on the labor theory of value, believe there are no other more basic inputs, aside from these labor services, and for them the unit direct and indirect residual income simply represents the "surplus value" (not the same as, and therefore not to be confused with, the "surplus" generated by each industry "in value terms" defined in section 5.2.3) which the "capitalists" as the owners of the means of production (the plant and equipment used in the production process) are able to expropriate for themselves. Neoclassical economists, on the other hand, believe that there is at least one other more basic type of input, this being the "capital" which the same plant and equipment represents, and for them the direct and indirect residual income is the payment required to induce certain households to lower their consumption so that these capital inputs can be obtained.

We are not yet in a position to address the fundamental question raised by this dispute between the Marxists and the neoclassical economists. The Leontief model itself still requires further elaboration—so it can encompass the long period as well as the short. Moreover, there is still the role of the government and of natural resources (non-reproducable goods) to be taken into account. For the moment, therefore, we shall leave the question open and specify only a set of direct and indirect labor coefficients, to be represented by the L vector, plus a set of direct and indirect unit residual income coefficients—with the latter, represented by the π vector, to be subsequently explained as either the payment for some basic input similar to the labor services obtained from the household sector or, alternatively, as simply the transfer of income in whole or in part from those supplying a more basic input to some other group in society.

As already noted, both the L and π vectors can be post-multiplied by the final demand vector, D, to indicate the amount of labor that will be required, directly and indirectly, to produce that amount of net output as well as the amount of residual income that will be earned per unit of output, directly and indirectly, in the process. This gives rise to the following vertically integrated model of production:

$$
\begin{array}{ccccccccc}
0 & + & 0 & + & 0 & + \ldots + & 0 & + & p_1 q_{1.h+1} & = & p_1 Q_1 \\
0 & + & 0 & + & 0 & + \ldots + & 0 & + & p_2 q_{2.h+1} & = & p_2 Q_2 \\
0 & + & 0 & + & 0 & + \ldots + & 0 & + & p_3 q_{3.h+1} & = & p_3 Q_3 \\
\vdots & & \vdots & & \vdots & & \vdots & & \vdots & & \vdots \\
0 & + & 0 & + & 0 & + \ldots + & 0 & + & p_h q_{h.h+1} & = & p_h Q_h
\end{array} \quad (5.48)
$$

$$
\begin{array}{cccc}
+ & + & + & + \\
w\bar{l}_1 Q_1 & +w\bar{l}_2 Q_2 +w\bar{l}_3 Q_3 + & \ldots & + w\bar{l}_h Q_h \\
\ddot{\pi}_1 Q_1 & + \ddot{\pi}_2 Q_2 + \ddot{\pi}_3 Q_3 + & \ldots & + \ddot{\pi}_h Q_h \\
= & = & = & = \\
p_1 Q_1 & p_2 Q_2 \quad p_3 Q_3 + & \ldots & + p_h Q_h
\end{array}
$$

Comparing this equation set with the equation set representing the Leontief model (see section 5.1.1, equation set 5.1), one can see a number of important differences. The first is that the inner matrix consists entirely of zeroes, reflecting the fact that each industry, being vertically integrated to the fullest extent possible, no longer need obtain its material inputs from other industries. The direct material requirements are instead now reflected in the larger values for the labor and residual income coefficients, with the inner matrix in effect eliminated. The other important difference is that the n industries represented by equation set 5.1 have been reduced to the smaller number of h industries which produce items for final use. This means that the $n-h$ industries which supply only intermediate goods have in effect also been eliminated. They are instead incorporated as vertical components of the h industries producing items for final use. Indeed, it is from the fact that the resulting model applies only to these h vertically integrated industries—an artificial restructuring of the n different industries which actually exist in an advanced market economy like that of the United States—that the model takes its name. Artificial though the model may be, it nonetheless is more useful for certain purposes than the Leontief model from which it is derived.

As Pasinetti noted in first formalizing the vertically integrated model of production, the view that the economy consists only of vertically integrated industries has been implicit in the work of most economists since the time of Adam Smith. It is what economists are in effect assuming when, following the example of Walras, Marshall and Keynes, they ignore the complications arising from intermediate output, or production. The virtue of the formal model developed by Passinetti is that it makes clear how the type of Leontief model which is directly observable, with any intermediate output explicitly taken into account, can be transformed into a vertically integrated model of production so that the use of any basic inputs, labor *et al.*, can then be directly related to the net or final output produced by the economic system.

Because the inner matrix of the vertically integrated model consists entirely of zeros and is therefore equal to a zero matrix $\mathbf{0}$, the final demand column, $\hat{\mathbf{P}}\mathbf{D}$, is equal to the total output column, $\hat{\mathbf{P}}\mathbf{Q}$. Moreover, the value added row, $\hat{\mathbf{V}}\mathbf{Q}$ or $(w\hat{\mathbf{L}} + \hat{\boldsymbol{\pi}})\mathbf{Q}$, is also equal to the total output column (and row). Equation set 5.48 can therefore be rewritten as follows:

$$
\begin{array}{ccccc}
\begin{array}{|c|}
\hline
p_1 q_{1.h+1} \\
p_2 q_{2.h+1} \\
p_3 q_{3.h+1} \\
\cdot \\
\cdot \\
\cdot \\
p_h q_{h.h+1} \\
\hline
\end{array}
&
\begin{array}{c}
= \\
= \\
= \\
\\
\\
\\
=
\end{array}
&
\begin{array}{|c|}
\hline
p_1 Q_1 \\
p_2 Q_2 \\
p_3 Q_3 \\
\cdot \\
\cdot \\
\cdot \\
p_h Q_h \\
\hline
\end{array}
&
\begin{array}{c}
= \\
= \\
= \\
\\
\\
\\
=
\end{array}
&
\begin{array}{|c|}
\hline
w\ddot{l}_1 Q_1 + \ddot{\pi}_1 Q_1 \\
w\ddot{l}_2 Q_2 + \ddot{\pi}_2 Q_2 \\
w\ddot{l}_3 Q_3 + \ddot{\pi}_3 Q_3 \\
\cdot \quad \cdot \\
\cdot \quad \cdot \\
\cdot \quad \cdot \\
w\ddot{l}_h Q_h + \ddot{\pi}_h Q_h \\
\hline
\end{array}
\end{array}
\qquad (5.49)
$$

What equation set 5.49 makes clear is that, in a vertically integrated model, the net output of each industry is the same as its total output; and the value of this output, $p_i Q_i$, is equal to the industry's wage bill plus any residual income. That is,

$$
p_i Q_i = w\ddot{l}_i Q_i + \ddot{\pi}_i Q_i \qquad (5.50)
$$

Dividing equation 5.50 through by Q_i, one can see that the price, p_i, is equal to the wage rate multiplied by the direct and indirect labor coefficient plus the direct and indirect unit residual income. That is,

$$
p_i = w\ddot{l}_i + \ddot{\pi}_i \qquad (5.51)
$$

For the entire set of h vertically integrated industries, this means that

$$
\mathbf{P} = w\underline{\mathbf{L}} + \underline{\boldsymbol{\pi}} \qquad (5.52)
$$

The significance of this last equation will become clearer once we turn in the next chapter to the subject of pricing. Indeed, as we shall see when the focus shifts in later chapters from the set of relative prices represented by the $\mathbf{P}$ vector to the growth of the aggregate price level, $\overset{\circ}{P}$, the Pasinetti vertically integrated model of production is indispensable for analyzing both the distribution of income and, as a reflection of the struggle over relative income shares, the inflationary process. At the moment, however, we are concerned only with the rate of technical progress as a possible determinant of the $\mathbf{A}$ and $\mathbf{L}$ matrices, with the first task being to derive a measure of that technical progress—or at least the portion due to process innovation. In this connection, the vertically integrated model is particularly useful because it enables us to calculate the direct and indirect labor requirements for producing any given amount of final output. These direct and indirect labor requirements, as represented by the $\mathbf{L}$ vector, can then be compared at various points in time so as to provide an estimate of the secular growth of output per worker, both for each industry and for the enterprise sector as a whole.

5.4.2 Measuring the growth of output per worker

By post-multiplying the $\mathbf{L}$ vector by the Leontief inverse, it is possible to derive a set of direct and indirect labor coefficients for each of the years in which an input-output table exists. In the case of the United States, these are the business census years of 1947, 1958, 1963, 1967, 1972 and 1977. This new $\mathbf{L}$ vector represents the quantities of labor, in hours worked, that were required both directly and indirectly to produce the net output of each industry in real terms, $q_{i.n+1}$, in each of those years. For each industry the direct and indirect coefficient, l_j, can be compared over the interval for which data are available, with the value which l_j takes then expressed in the following manner as a function of time:

$$l_j(t_n) = (1 + \overset{\circ}{z}_j)^x \, l_j(t_0) \tag{5.53}$$

where $l_j(t_0)$ is the direct and indirect labor coefficient for an industry in some initial time period; $l_j(t_x)$ is the direct and indirect labor coefficient x time periods later; and $\overset{\circ}{z}_j$ is a negative fraction (i.e., $-1 < \overset{\circ}{z}_j < 0$), the absolute value of which is the rate of growth of output per worker in that industry. Equation 5.53 can be rewritten in natural logs as follows:

$$ln \, l_j(t_x) = ln \, l_j(t_0) + ln \, (1 + \overset{\circ}{z}_j) \, (t_x) \tag{5.54}$$

so that the β_j coefficient in the following equation can then be estimated econometrically:

$$ln \, l_j(t_x) = ln \, l_j(t_0) + \beta_j(t_x) \tag{5.55}$$

where β_j is defined as follows:

$$\beta_j = ln \, (1 + \overset{\circ}{z}_j) \tag{5.56}$$

Once the value of the β coefficient has been determined, it is possible to calculate the growth of output per worker in each industry, $\overset{\circ}{z}_j$, by taking the antilog of β and subtracting 1.

Edward Ochoa, in a line of work initiated by Anwar Shaikh, has used this approach to calculate the value of $\overset{\circ}{z}_j$ over the 1947–72 period for 71 of the 79

Exhibit 5.14

Secular Growth of Output Per Worker Within 71 Major Industry Groupings,*
1947–1972

SIC #	Industry Grouping	$\overset{\circ}{z}$	y
62	Communications except broadcasting	6.9%	1.44%
52	Radio, TV and communications equipment	6.3	1.11
53	Electronics components, accessories	6.2	0.47
24	Plastics and synthetic materials	5.9	0.61
25	Drugs, cleaning, toilet preparations	5.9	0.95
15	Miscellaneous fabricated textile products	5.8	0.32
59	Photographic, optical goods	5.5	0.30
27	Petroleum refining	5.2	2.12
12	Fabrics, yarn and thread mills	5.1	1.40
23	Chemicals, allied products	5.0	1.62
48	Service industry machines	5.0	0.40
47	Office and computing machines	4.8	0.43
50	Household appliances	4.7	0.46
13	Miscellaneous textiles, floor coverings	4.7	0.35
14	Apparel	4.6	1.90
1	Agriculture	4.6	5.92
64	Public utilities	4.4	3.01
28	Rubber, miscellaneous plastic products	4.4	1.03
60	Miscellaneous manufacturing	4.2	0.71
46	Machine shop products	4.1	0.24
4	Coal mining	4.1	0.35
9	Ordnance and accessories	4.1	0.62
10	Food and kindred products	4.1	7.72
63	Radio and TV broadcasting	3.9	0.22
6	Stone, clay mining and quarrying	3.9	0.18
5	Crude petroleum, natural gas	3.9	0.97
21	Paperboard containers, boxes	3.9	0.47
61	Transportation	3.8	4.27
29	Leather tanning	3.8	0.11
55	Motor vehicles	3.7	3.57
11	Tobacco manufactures	3.7	0.70
18	Household furniture	3.6	0.43
17	Wooden containers	3.6	0.05
16	Lumber, wood products except containers	3.5	1.10
19	Other furniture, fixtures	3.5	0.21
39	Engines and turbines	3.5	0.30
20	Paper and allied products	3.5	1.23
31	Glass and glass products	3.5	0.30
3	Nonferrous metal ores mining	3.5	0.14
56	Aircraft and parts	3.4	1.42

49	Electric transmission equipment	3.3	0.70
38	Other fabricated metal products	3.3	0.90
32	Stone and clay products	3.3	0.90
26	Paints and allied products	3.3	0.24
30	Footwear and other leather products	3.3	0.38
58	Professional, scientific instruments	3.2	0.46
7	Chemical, fertilizer mineral mining	3.2	0.06
67	Hotels, repair places except autos	3.2	1.58
71	Medical, educational services except nonprofessional	3.2	3.56
36	Heating, fabricated metal products	3.1	0.98
54	Miscellaneous electrical machinery	3.1	0.24
34	Primary nonferrous metals manufacturing	3.0	1.45
22	Printing and publishing	3.0	1.68
68	Business services, R&D	2.9	3.79
57	Other transportation equipment	2.8	0.59
35	Metal containers	2.8	0.27
65	Wholesale and retail trde	2.8	2.81
33	Primary iron and steel manufacturing	2.7	2.46
40	Farm machinery and equipment	2.7	0.33
42	Materials handling equipment	2.6	0.18
45	General industrial machinery, equipment	2.6	0.54
51	Electric wiring, lighting equipment	2.4	0.32
44	Special industry machinery, equipment	2.4	0.40
37	Screw machine products	2.3	0.63
69	Auto repair and services	2.2	1.16
41	Construction machinery, equipment	2.2	0.45
43	Metalworking machinery, equipment	1.8	0.54
8	New and repair construction	1.8	8.76
70	Amusements	1.5	0.74
2	Iron and ferroalloy ores mining	1.2	0.09
66	Finance and insurance	1.0	3.69

*Excludes real estate as well as seven other industries.

Source: Edward M. Ochoa, "Labor-Values and Prices of Production: An Interindustry Study of the U.S. Economy, 1947–1972," unpublished doctoral dissertation, New School for Social Research, March 1984.

industries delineated within U.S. input-output tables. (Because data on capital outlays are not available separately for seven of the other eight industries—see section 5.5.2—they are treated by Ochoa as vertical components of the remaining 71 industries. The real estate industry has, in addition, been eliminated on the grounds that the labor employed therein is not "socially necessary." Thus the value of n in the study carried out by Ochoa is 71, with the reduction in the number of separately delineated industries dictated in all but one case by the absence of corresponding data on capital outlays.) The values for $\mathring{z}_j$ estimated by Ochoa are given in exhibit 5.14. As can be seen from the table, all 71 industries experienced a secular rise in output per worker over the period, ranging from 6.9 percent in the communications industry to 1.0 percent in finance and insurance.

Together, these growth rates represent the elements of a 1-by-h **Z** vector such that

$$\mathbf{Z} = \{\mathring{z}_1 \ \mathring{z}_2 \ \mathring{z}_3 \ \ldots \ \mathring{z}_h\} \tag{5.57}$$

(Ochoa's 71 industries, like the slightly larger number of major industry group-ings from which they have been derived, are sufficiently broad that each produces at least some net output. Thus h like n is equal to 71 for the **Z** vector obtained by Ochoa.) The elements of this **Z** vector, if they are first weighted by the average value, for the period as a whole, of the final output produced by each industry (the elements of the **Y** vector defined in section 5.1.4), will sum up to the growth of output per worker in the aggregate, $\mathring{Z}$. That is,

$$\mathring{Z} = \sum_{j=1}^{h} y_j \mathring{z}_j \tag{5.58}$$

The value of $\mathring{Z}$ for the period 1947–1972, as calculated in this manner by Ochoa, is 3.7 percent. (Alternatively, the value of $\mathring{Z}$ can be calculated by weighting the elements of the **Z** vector by the value added in each industry, v_j, averaged for the period as a whole. Since the value added by all h industries together is the same as the value of the net output produced *in toto* by the same h industries, the figure obtained for $\mathring{Z}$ will be the same, even though each element of the **Z** vector is being weighted differently.)

The growth of output per worker in each industry can be compared with the growth of output per worker in the aggregate to indicate the relative growth of output per worker in each industry, $\mathring{z}_j - \mathring{Z}$. These relative growth rates, as shown in exhibit 5.14, would then constitute a 1-by-h Ω vector defined as follows:

$$\Omega = \{\mathring{z}_1 - \mathring{Z} \ \mathring{z}_2 - \mathring{Z} \ \mathring{z}_3 - \mathring{Z} \ \ldots \ \mathring{z}_h - \mathring{Z}\} \tag{5.59}$$

To the extent that the cost of labor, both direct and indirect, is the only cost that needs to be taken into account, this Ω vector indicates the relative decline in costs likely to be experienced over time by each of the h vertically integrated indus-tries. (To the extent that prices can be expected to vary in line with costs, the Ω vector will also indicate the change in relative prices over time. See section 5.5.4.)

The reason for examining the decline in cost within just the h vertically integrated industries, rather than for all n industries, is that what may appear from the data to be an increase in output per worker in one industry, when the output of the different industries must necessarily be measured in value terms, may actually be the result of technical progress in some other industry. Remember that the surplus per unit of output that is generated by each industry in value terms, s_j, is equal to the value added per unit of output, v_j. As a proportion of the price, p_j, obtained by each industry for its output, s_j is therefore equal to 1 less the cost per unit of the material inputs obtained from other industries, $[p_1 a_{1,j} + p_2 a_{2,j} + p_3 a_{3,j} + \ldots + p_n a_{n,j}]$ (see section 5.2.3). This means that if technical progress enables one industry to supply some material input at a lower cost, measured by the amount of direct and indirect labor required to produce that good, and if the industry then sells that input at a lower price to an industry which continues to sell its own output at the price that was previously being charged, then the technical progress will be reflected in the greater value added by the second industry—either in the form of a higher wage paid to its workers or in the form of increased residual income— despite the fact that the second industry is not the one in which the technical progress has actually occurred.

It need not be the case, of course, that the first industry will lower its price while the second industry will hold its price constant. Just the opposite could be true—or, as seems more likely, both industries could share in the gain. The point is that relative price movements make it impossible to determine, from just the data on direct labor productivity, which industry within an interdependent system of production is actually the source of any technical progress due to process innovation. The problem is compounded by the fact that the technical progress which leads to a reduction in the costs of one industry, with a subsequent increase in the surplus being generated in value terms by that industry and/or by the industries to which it supplies material inputs, may be due to product innovation in yet another industry—without the product innovation necessarily lowering the costs of the industry that has introduced the new product. It is for this reason that it is best to base any measure of technical progress on the vertically integrated model of production. The secular declines in the $\bar{l}_j$ and $\bar{\pi}_j$ direct and indirect labor and unit residual income coefficients—as distinct from just the l_j and π_j direct labor and unit residual income coefficients—are unaffected by the interindustry pricing of material inputs. Moreover, all the industries which, as the suppliers of inputs, might possibly be responsible for that increasing output per worker because of some product and/or process innovation they have implemented, are included as part of the same vertically integrated industry.

The Z vector can be interpreted as measuring the absolute rate and the Ω vector as measuring the relative rate at which mechanization—the replacement of labor with machines and other capital inputs—is occurring in each of the h vertically integrated industries. It is, of course, possible that the labor is being replaced, not by any capital inputs directly but rather by certain nondurable material inputs, e.g., by plastics or other materials which require less handling. Even so, the use of the new materials is likely to require a concomitant investment in new equipment so that the reduction in labor inputs is nonetheless associated with the acquisition of the requisite capital inputs. The Z and Ω vectors can therefore be viewed as indicating the absolute and relative rates of technical progress that is due to increased mechanization within each vertically integrated industry. While the replacement of labor with machines and other capital inputs is thus what underlies any technical progress, this does not mean that labor is necessarily being replaced by some other type of input—one that is obtained from without, and therefore is exogenous to, the enterprise sector. It may just be that the labor in the industries utilizing the capital inputs is being replaced by the labor in the industries producing the goods that serve as capital inputs. This point will be elaborated on shortly (see section 5.5.2). For the moment, we shall continue to ignore the question of whether there are any other basic inputs aside from the labor services provided by the household sector and instead view the Z and Ω vectors as simply measuring the rate of technical progress due to the increased mechanization that stems from process innovation—without thereby implying that one exogenously supplied input is being substituted for another (but see chapter 13, part 3). Having derived these two measures of the technical progress which is occurring—and indeed with the measures themselves indicating the rate at which the direct and indirect labor requirements for producing any given amount of aggregate output are likely to decline over time—we can now turn to the question of what determines that rate of technical progess. We shall begin with a discussion of the noneconomic factors before turning to the economic determinants of technical progress as measured by the growth of output per worker in the aggregate, $\overset{\circ}{Z}$.

5.4.3 Science, technology and institutional development

The economic system, as pointed out in chapter 1, is but one of four institutional dimensions of society; and, as such, it derives important inputs from those other institutional dimensions. One of those other institutional dimensions is the value orientation, consisting of the beliefs held by the various members of society, including any supposed knowledge. (The value orientation, it will be recalled, is different from the other three institutional dimensions in that it need not be systemic, or coherent. See chapter 1, section 2.4.) A part of the value orientation consists of beliefs as to how physical processes work. In modern times, these beliefs have been systematized under the rubric of astronomy, physics, chemistry and the other natural sciences, with this part of the value orientation further divided into basic and applied areas. Indeed, the development of science in the relatively brief span of time since the Copernican-Newtonian Revolution of the 17th century is what sets modern society apart from all earlier civilizations. The salient characteristic of this latest epoch is the increased control over the natural environment which the knowledge gained from scientific inquiry has given humankind. This knowledge has transformed not only the economic system, enabling a far higher material standard of living to be achieved, but also every other dimension of human activity as well.

The precise factors responsible for the emergence of science and for the subsequent growth of scientific knowledge is a matter of intense debate among historians of science. It lies beyond the scope of this text to enter into that debate. All that need be noted is that science, viewed as a social system that produces as its output certain types of beliefs—those validated through the experimental method—is governed by its own quite distinctive dynamic, one that should not be confused with the dynamic that operates along the economic or any of the other institutional dimensions of society. Among the key factors in determining the distinctive dynamic of science, and thus the growth of scientific knowledge, is the dialectical process itself, the rules which scientists have adopted for determining what is a validated theory and the incentive structure which has evolved within the community of scientists. (Within that incentive structure, it should be noted, money compensation plays only a secondary role.)

It is, of course, true that economic factors, along with political and anthropogenic factors, are important in determining the growth of scientific knowledge. Both the availability of scientific instruments, as the counterpart of the economic means of production, and the ability of those who carry out scientific research to free themselves from other pursuits depend, in the first instance, on how great is the economic system's net output or surplus and, in the second instance, on what disposition is made of that surplus. It is for this reason that one must take into account the interaction between the growth of scientific knowledge and the growth of an economic surplus—the growth of scientific knowledge making possible a larger economic surplus and the larger economic surplus, in turn, providing the material means of support for increased scientific activity. Still, it would be a mistake to view these economic factors as having more than a moderating effect on the basic dynamic of science, especially in the period since science first succeeded in establishing itself as a separate domain of human endeavor. The growth of scientific knowledge follows an internal logic of its own, with the next discovery depending on what have been the prior discoveries. At most, economic factors determine only the pace, and not the direction, of scientific advance. Moreover, it does not follow that more economic resources devoted to science will necessarily lead to an increased output of scientific knowledge. It is just as likely, because of the distorting effect which the judgments of those determining the allocation of resources may have on the direction of scientific inquiry, for the greater largesse to have the opposite effect.

It is the growth of scientific knowledge, as regulated by the internal logic of science, that determines the intellectual milieu in which the technology of a society evolves. One should not assume, however, that technology is the mere derivative of science. The relationship is a more subtle one. Indeed, there was a steady growth of technology over many eons before the emergence of modern science, and it was not clear even as late as the 19th century what precise role science was playing in that era's dramatic breakthroughs in technology. Certainly few of the inventors from that period were trained as scientists or consciously applied scientific principles. Only by the second half of the 20th century has it become apparent that the growth of scientific knowledge is what sets the ultimate limit on the evolution of technology. At the same time one must recognize that so much unexploited knowledge has been accumulated to date that, even if there were to be no further increment in the stock, the evolution of technology would continue far into the foreseeable future.

The technology of a society consists of the techniques used to achieve various social ends. Among these techniques are the ones used in the production of goods and services. These techniques represent the society's economic technology. They are embedded in the A and L matrices, and will change as the A and L matrices themselves change as a result of technical progress. Although the term technology, when used without a qualifying adjective, generally refers only to these economic techniques, it should be kept in mind that there are other techniques, not directly related to the production of goods and services, which are no less critical to the functioning of a society. Among the latter are the techniques for making group decisions, for rearing and educating the next generation and indeed even for organizing the set of institutions that will make it possible to distribute, whether through markets or not, the material surplus which the economic technology makes it possible to produce. It is these techniques that determine how advanced are a society's social institutions, the economic ones among them. The more advanced those institutions are, the greater the society's ability to exploit the technology that has emerged from the scientific revolution of the past 400 years.

A political system capable of responding to the changing economic needs of the population and an anthropogenic system capable of producing the necessary number of skilled workers define the minimal level of institutional development that needs to be achieved if the growth of scientific knowledge and technology is to be reflected in rising output per worker. (See chapter 10, part 1, and chapter 13, part 1, for a further elaboration of this point.) It is no less essential, however, that the economic institutions, such as the representative type of business enterprise and the monetary-financial system, reach a certain level of maturity. Indeed, the continued evolution of these economic institutions, no less than the continued evolution of the non-economic institutions, may be a necessary condition for maintaining the growth of output per worker. Thus the eclipse of the neoclassical proprietorship by the megacorp and the subsequent further evolution of the latter into the diversified, multinational corporation—together with the replacement of commodity and fiat money by a system of credit money (as described in chapter 12, section 1.1)—may have been no less critical to the growth of the U.S. and other advanced economies in the 20th century. It is for this reason that the existing level of development, insofar as the entire panoply of social and economic institutions is concerned, must be considered at least an implicit parameter of any growth model.

The rate of technical progress as measured by $\overset{\circ}{Z}$ therefore depends on two sets of noneconomic factors. One is the accumulated stock of technical knowledge to which the interplay between science and technology has given rise. It is this accumulated stock of technical knowledge that will determine the maximum rate at which output per worker can increase—especially in the case of an economy, like that of the United States, which cannot simply borrow the technology of some more advanced economy (see chapter 4, section 2.5). The other limiting factor is the present state of development insofar as the society's institutions—political, economic and anthropogenic—are concerned. It is this current level of development that will determine the society's ability to exploit the existing stock of technical knowledge. What still remain to be identified are the economic determinants of technical progress.

5.4.4 The economic determinants of technical progress

The technology of each industry has been represented, up to this point, by a set of direct material and labor coefficients. These coefficients, however, are an imperfect representation of each industry's technology. For one thing, they indicate only the quantity of each input that must be used, not the process that enables the industry to convert those inputs into its own distinctive product line. To describe that process would require a flow diagram, giving the sequence in which the various inputs are used, together with instructions for combining those inputs. That is, one needs a "recipe," not just a "list of ingredients." More significantly, however, the direct material and labor coefficients leave unspecified what are perhaps the most important inputs of all. These are the capital inputs—the plant and equipment used in the production process.

It is the capital inputs which largely determine the technology being employed. This is especially true in the most recent historical period during which a capitalist mode of production, based on the crucial role played by the capital inputs, has been the dominant one. Some would argue that, with the disproportionate growth of the service sector, there has been a shift within recent decades to a postindustrial society—with a different mode of production, based on the critical role played by human resource inputs, gradually supplanting the capitalist one. Whether or not this is the case, the capitalist mode of production will continue to prevail within at least the industrial sector.

With a capitalist mode of production, it is the capital inputs—the plant and equipment—around which the rest of the production process is organized. The other types of material inputs that are required, along with the types of workers, are largely dictated by the nature of those capital inputs. This is why it has been possible, at least up to this point, to represent the technology being used in each industry by a set of direct material and labor coefficients. The capital inputs are already implicit in those coefficients, with a different set of capital inputs giving rise to a different set of a_{ij} and l_j coefficients. These capital inputs will soon be made explicit as the first step in extending the Leontief model of production to encompass the long period as well as the short. The present discussion is in fact meant to lay the foundation for that extension of the Leontief model in the main section which next follows. For the moment, however, it will suffice simply to note that the nature of the technology being employed depends critically on the capital inputs. Indeed, it is difficult to conceive of any change in technology which does not involve a change in the capital inputs. What this means is that technical progress is, to a large extent, capital embodied, with the secular rate of growth of investment, $\mathring{I}$, determining the rate of technical progress as measured by $\mathring{Z}$.

The reason for this dependence of the rate of technical progress on the rate of growth of investment is, in part, the vintage nature of much of the existing capital stock (see chapter 4, section 1.1 for a discussion of what is meant by the "vintage" component of the capital stock). With continuous technical progress, as measured by the secular decline over time in the relevant labor coefficients, it necessarily follows that the different plants constructed at different points in time will require different amounts of labor inputs both directly and, in the form of material inputs, indirectly—with a different average variable cost of production associated with each of those different plants. (See section 5.3.2, for a discussion of the different costs associated with plants acquired at different points in time when there has been continuous technical progress.) All but the most recently constructed of these plants constitute the vintage capital stock. The more quickly this vintage capital stock is being replaced by new plants embodying the most up-to-date technology, the more rapid will be the growth of output per worker.

The process of replacing the vintage capital stock with new plants embodying the most up-to-date technology will, of course, ultimately come to an end unless there is continuous growth in technical knowledge. Without further additions to the knowledge base, it is only a matter of time until all the plants embody the most efficient techniques presently available and there are no more vintage plants to be replaced. It might seem, therefore, that it is necessary only to posit continuous growth in technical knowledge, without having to mention the vintage capital stock. The existence of the vintage capital stock is important, however, for two reasons. First, it explains why the growth of output per worker is not limited to the rate at which technical knowledge is increasing. With at least part of the existing capacity taking the form of vintage plants, output per worker can increase more or less rapidly than the growth of technical knowledge, depending on the rate at which the vintage plants are being replaced. Second, once it is recognized that the growth of output per worker can vary independently of the growth of technical knowledge, one must then allow for the further effect which the investment in new plant and equipment necessary for replacing any vintage capital stock will have. This further effect is on the growth of technical knowledge itself.

As already indicated, while the growth of technical knowledge depends ultimately on the progress of science, the relationship between the two is a complex one. This is because, while scientific knowledge can exist in the abstract, the growth of technical knowledge requires actual working models. In the case of the technology embodied in the plants used to produce goods for sale in the market, the only working models are the plants currently being operated by firms, with improvements in the technology embodied in those plants requiring either the introduction of new equipment or the construction of entirely new plants. This means that the rate at which technical knowledge advances within the industrial sector of the economy depends on the rate at which new plant and equipment is being acquired and hence on the secular growth of investment, $\mathring{I}$. The corollary of this proposition is that replacing any part of an industry's vintage capital stock will lead to further improvements in the technology so that even the plants that previously embodied the best techniques will no longer be the least-cost production units. In this way, the process will be a cumulative one, with the replacement of the vintage capital stock leading to further advances in technical knowledge which then make a new group of plants eligible for replacement because they no longer embody the most up-to-date technology.

There is no reason to assume, however, that the relationship is a linear one, with technical knowledge increasing at the same constant rate as each new plant is contructed. It may well be that, once the rate at which new plants are being constructed exceeds a certain limit, a separate industry will be formed to produce or assemble the various types of capital inputs which go into each plant. Indeed, a separate industry may be formed to produce just one of those specialized pieces of equipment. The emergence of the new investment goods industry, because of the more intensive commitment of resources it fosters, may then accelerate the growth of technical knowledge. On the other hand, it may well be that, because of the limit imposed by progress within the scientific discipline upon which the technology is based and/or because of the constraints on the society's development along some other institutional dimension, the further construction of new plants will, beyond a certain point, lead to increasingly smaller advances in technical knowledge. The point is that the relationship between the secular growth of investment, $\mathring{I}$, and the growth of technical knowledge may be a nonlinear one.

There are two separate reasons, then, for positing that technical progress, as measured by $\mathring{Z}$, will be a decreasing power function of the secular growth of investment, $\mathring{I}$. One is the effect that the expenditure on new plant and equipment will have on the rate at which the vintage capital stock is being replaced. At low levels of investment, as measured by $\mathring{I}$, the rate at which the vintage capital stck is being replaced will be less than the growth of technical knowledge. Through the disproportionate reduction in costs which can be achieved by stepping up the rate at which the vintage capital stock is being replaced, it is then possible for the growth of output per worker, $\mathring{Z}$, to exceed the secular growth of investment, $\mathring{I}$. However, because there is only a limited amount of vintage capital to be replaced, $\mathring{Z}$ can increase more rapidly than $\mathring{I}$ only at a decreasing rate. The second reason for positing that $\mathring{Z}$ is a decreasing power function of $\mathring{I}$ is the endogenous effect that any expenditures on new plant and equipment will have on the growth of technical knowledge. Again, at low levels of investment, as measured by $\mathring{I}$, a separate capital goods sector is unlikely to flourish—or even to emerge as the complement of whatever new final goods industries are being established. Through the disproportionate growth in technical knowledge that is likely to occur as the size of the investment goods sector expands, it is then possible for the growth of output per worker, $\overset{\circ}{Z}$, to increase more rapidly than the secular growth of investment, $\overset{\circ}{I}$. However, beause of the ultimate limit imposed by the rate of scientific progress and/or by the level of development along the other institutional dimensions, $\overset{\circ}{Z}$ can increase more rapidly than $\overset{\circ}{I}$ only at a decreasing rate.

This nonlinear relationship between $\overset{\circ}{I}$ and $\overset{\circ}{Z}$ is represented by the Z curve depicted in exhibit 5.15. The shape of the curve reflects the critical role played by the growth of technical knowledge relative to the rate at which investment in new plant and equipment is being carried out. While a higher rate of growth of investment, $\overset{\circ}{I}$, will always lead to some increase in the growth of output per worker as long as there is some vintage capital stock to be replaced and/or the investment itself leads to further improvements in technique, the gains will be proportionately less once $\overset{\circ}{I}$ exceeds the exogenously given growth of technical knowledge, as determined by the rate of scientific progress and/or the level of the society's institutional development. This exogenously determined growth of technical knowledge is represented by point A on the Z curve shown in exhibit 5.15 where the slope is equal to 1. Up to that point, with $\overset{\circ}{Z}$ increasing more rapidly than $\overset{\circ}{I}$, it can be assumed that technical progress is being constrained, not for lack of the necessary scientific understanding or institutional development but rather, only for lack of the necessary investment in new plant and equipment. However, beyond that point, with $\overset{\circ}{Z}$ increasing less rapidly than $\overset{\circ}{I}$, it can be assumed that the opposite situation prevails, with technical progress constrained by the lack of more rapid advancement in the scientific understanding of natural phenomena and/or by the failure of the society to develop sufficiently along its other institutional dimensions. Thus it follows that the point on the Z curve where the slope is equal to 1 indicates the rate at which whatever is the exogenous constraint on technical progress—whether it be the growth of scientific knowledge or the level of institutional development—is being relaxed.

The Z curve alone, however, is not sufficient to determine the rate of technical progress. One needs to know, in addition, what is the secular growth of investment so that one can then determine where, along the relevant Z curve, the economy falls. This, in turn, means that one needs to know what secular growth of investment, $\overset{\circ}{I}$, will satisfy one or more of the necessary conditions for continuous economic expansion.

5.4.5 Technical progress and the sustainable growth rate

The secular growth of investment, $\overset{\circ}{I}$, can be derived endogenously within the model by first equating the growth of output per worker, $\overset{\circ}{Z}$, with the secular growth of aggregate demand and then imposing the aggregate supply condition that the growth of investment must necessarily match the growth of aggregate

Exhibit 5.15

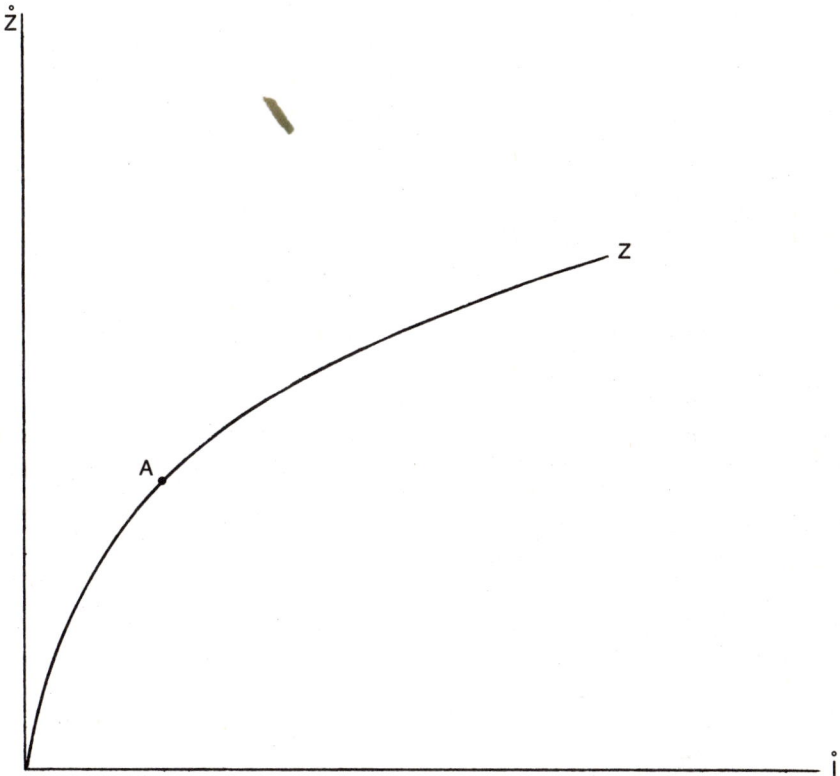

output. The reason the growth of output per worker can be equated with the secular growth of aggregate demand is that the growth of aggregate demand is limited in the long period to the rate at which real income is rising—and the rate at which real income is rising will, in turn, be equal to the rate at which output per worker is increasing (see chapter 4, section 3.2). This argument will be further elaborated on in the main section which next follows when a long period model of production will be developed. Suffice it for now to note that, with the growth of aggregate demand equal to the growth of output per worker, it then follows that, if capacity is to increase at the same rate as aggregate demand, the rate of growth of investment must be equal to the growth of output per worker.

Thus the relationship between the growth of output per worker, $\overset{\circ}{Z}$, and the secular growth of investment, $\overset{\circ}{I}$, is a dual one—indicating that the two variables are interdependent. On the one hand, reflecting the capital-embodied nature of technical progress, the growth of output per worker, $\overset{\circ}{Z}$, will be a decreasing power function of $\overset{\circ}{I}$—as indicated by the Z curve depicted in exhibit 5.15. On the other hand, reflecting the dependence of aggregate demand on the growth of output per worker and the aggregate supply condition that must hold in the long period, the secular growth of investment, $\overset{\circ}{I}$, must necessarily be equal to the growth of output per worker, $\overset{\circ}{Z}$. Where this latter condition is satisfied can be seen by juxtaposing the Z curve on a set of axes with a 45° line emanating from the origin, as in exhibit 5.16. The condition is satisfied only at the point where the Z curve intersects the 45° line. It is at that point, and that point alone, that the secular growth of investment, $\overset{\circ}{I}$, representing the rate at which aggregate supply is increasing, will be equal to the growth of output per worker, $\overset{\circ}{Z}$, representing the rate at which aggregate demand is increasing. For with the secular growth of aggregate output, $\overset{\circ}{G}$, assumed to be identical to the secular growth of output per worker, $\overset{\circ}{Z}$, it then follows that $\overset{\circ}{I}$ will at that point also be equal to $\overset{\circ}{G}$—with the aggregate supply condition for continuous economic expansion thereby satisfied (see chapter 4, section 1.3).

As can be seen from exhibit 5.16, it is the position of the Z curve that will determine where it intersects the 45° line and thus where the aggregate supply condition is being satisfied. The position of the Z curve, in turn, depends on the noneconomic determinants of technical progress. A change in one of those parameters will lead to a shift of the Z curve and hence to a new point at which the growth of output per worker, $\overset{\circ}{Z}$, is equal to the secular growth of investment, $\overset{\circ}{I}$. As already indicated, the noneconomic determinants of technical progress, and thus the parameters of the Z curve, are (1) the growth of technical knowledge due to the progress of science and (2) the level of development of the society's institutions, economic as well as noneconomic. It is these parameters which will determine the position of the Z curve and therefore where it intersects the 45° line. Where the Z curve intersects the 45° line and thus where the growth of output per worker, $\overset{\circ}{Z}$, is equal to the secular growth of investment, $\overset{\circ}{I}$, will, in turn, determine the economic system's sustainable rate of expansion—insofar as that rate of expansion depends only on satisfying the aggregate supply condition.

There are, of course, other conditions besides the aggregate supply condition that must be satisfied if whatever is the current secular growth rate, $\overset{\circ}{G}$, is going to be a sustainable one (see chapter 4, section 1.4). A major question to be explored in the chapters which follow is what, besides the secular growth of investment being equal to the secular growth of output per worker, is necessary for those other conditions—the value, sectoral balance and monetary conditions in particular—to be satisfied. For the moment, however, the only requirement is that $\overset{\circ}{I} = \overset{\circ}{Z}$. This equality not only ensures that, with the growth of aggregate output, $\overset{\circ}{G}$, the same as the growth of output per worker, $\overset{\circ}{Z}$, the aggregate supply condition will be satisfied. It also ensures that, with the growth of aggregate savings, $\overset{\circ}{S}$, adjusting to whatever is the secular growth of aggregate investment, $\overset{\circ}{I}$, and with aggregate savings and aggregate investment the only types of discretionary funds and discretionary expenditures so far allowed for within the model, the aggregate demand condition for continuous economic expansion will also be satisfied.

Exhibit 5.16

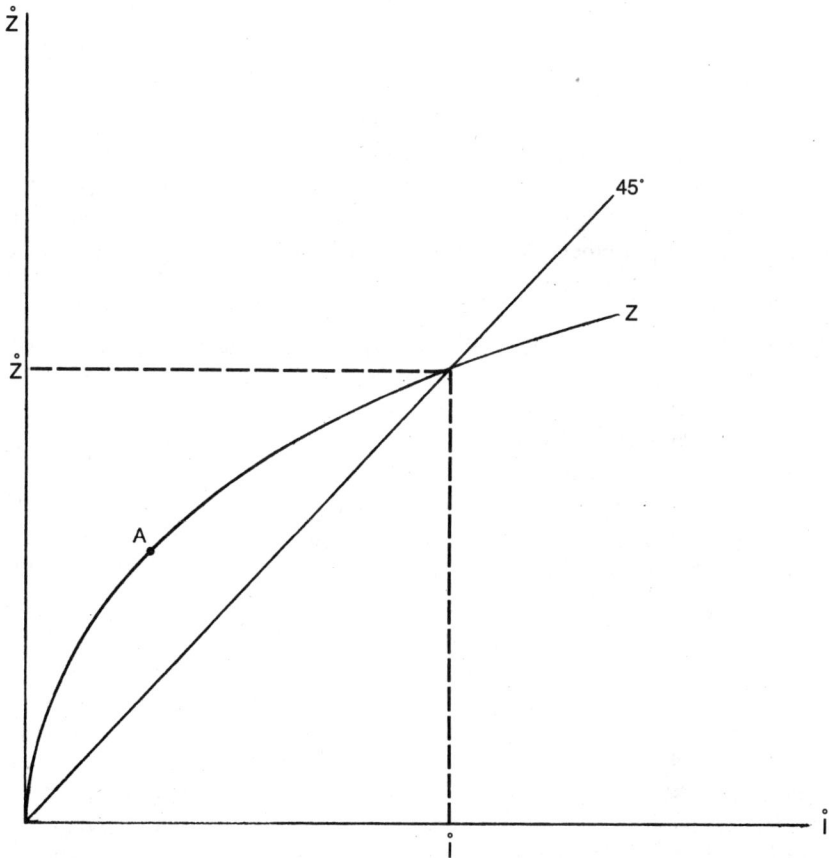

Indeed, it will not be until chapter 6 when the analysis will be extended to encompass the value relationships, chapters 9 and 10 when the analysis will be extended to encompass the sectoral balance relationships and chapter 12 when the analysis will be extended to encompass the monetary-financial relationships that additional conditions for continuous economic expansion will need to be imposed. Still, the fact that there are those other conditions should be kept in mind.

Besides not assuming that the aggregate supply and aggregate demand conditions are the only ones that need to be satisfied, one must not make the mistake of assuming that there is only one sustainable rate of economic expansion—for example, a secular growth rate equal to $\overset{\circ}{Z}$ as shown in exhibit 5.16. This is the significance of $\overset{\circ}{I}$ and $\overset{\circ}{Z}$ (or at least the variables for which they serve as proxies) being interdependent.

So far, only the effect of a higher rate of investment in inducing a more rapid rate of technical progress (as measured by $\overset{\circ}{Z}$) has been taken into account. However, one cannot exclude the possibility that the secular growth of investment, $\overset{\circ}{I}$, will simply adjust over time to whatever happens to be the secular rate of expansion (as determined by the value of $\overset{\circ}{Z}$). Indeed, in light of what will be said later about the determinants of business investment, this is a quite plausible line of argument—as long as there is no improvement over time in the capital goods being supplied to one or more industries (see section 5.5.2 and chapter 7, section 2.4). The possibility that $\overset{\circ}{I}$ will adjust to $\overset{\circ}{Z}$ rather than the reverse cannot be excluded since the Z curve has yet to be derived empirically and thus there is no way of knowing whether it passes through the origin, as in exhibit 5.16, or whether, alternatively, it cuts the 45° line at two separate points, as in exhibit 5.17. The difference in the situations represented by the two diagrams is whether there are certain types of investment being carried out that add to the productive capacity of a vertically integrated industry without increasing output per worker and thus whether the Z curve has a positive intercept, or constant term, such as $\overset{\circ}{I}_1$ in exhibit 5.17. With the Z curve having a positive intercept, the economy could just as well be at point B in exhibit 5.17 as at point C.

At point B, the growth of output per worker is constrained not by the exogenously determined growth of technical knowledge but rather by the low rate of investment, or accumulation. The secular growth of investment, $\overset{\circ}{I}$, may nonetheless have adjusted to the secular rate of economic expansion, as determined by $\overset{\circ}{Z}$, so that, with $\overset{\circ}{Z} = \overset{\circ}{I}$, both the aggregate supply and aggregate demand conditions for sustained growth are being satisfied. However, this sustainable rate of expansion would be a relatively low one. If the secular growth of investment were to increase to $\overset{\circ}{I}_2$, with that higher rate of accumulation causing the growth of output per worker to rise to $\overset{\circ}{Z}_2$, then the secular rate of economic expansion associated with that growth of output per worker would not only be a higher one, it would also be a sustainable one since, with $\overset{\circ}{Z}_2 = \overset{\circ}{I}_2$, both the aggregate supply and aggregate demand conditions for sustained growth would again be satisfied. Thus, until the Z function has actually been derived empirically for the group of advanced market economies represented by the OECD and the position of any one of those countries along the curve then determined, it is not possible to say whether there is only one sustainable rate of economic expansion (as in exhibit 5.16), two sustainable rates of economic expansion (as in exhibit 5.17)—or more (depending on the shape of the as-yet-to-be-derived Z curve). At present, the Z curve is simply a theoretical construct which, however coherent a basis it provides for analyzing the determinants of technical progress, still remains to be validated empirically.

In summary, then, the rate of technical progress, as measured by $\overset{\circ}{Z}$, depends on where along the Z curve the secular growth of investment, $\overset{\circ}{I}$, places the economy. In other words, it depends on the rate of accumulation, reflecting the capital-embodied nature of technical progress. This argument holds both in the short period, as a manifestation of how rapidly any vintage plants are being replaced (see chapter 7, section 2.2, for the further development of this point),

Exhibit 5.17

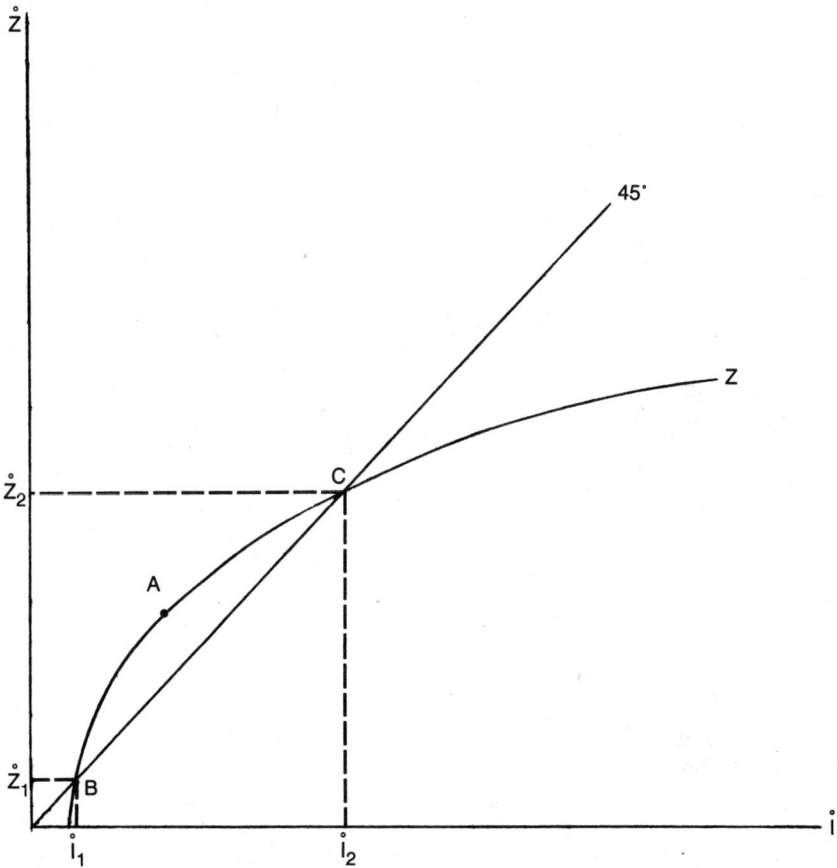

and in the long period, as a manifestation of how much the relative expansion of the capital goods sector is likely to spur the growth of technical knowledge (see chapter 7, section 2.4). The secular rate of economic expansion, $\overset{\circ}{G}$, to which the growth of output per worker gives rise will be a sustainable one, provided the growth of output per worker, $\overset{\circ}{Z}$, is matched by the growth of capacity, as determined by $\overset{\circ}{I}$. Whether $\overset{\circ}{G}$ is a sustainable rate of economic expansion or not, however, it is $\overset{\circ}{Z}$ which, as the weighted average of the growth of output per worker in each separate industry, will then determine the values taken by the Z and Ω vectors.

What still remains to be explained is what determines the rate of technical progress that takes the form of a reduction in the use of some basic input other than the labor services, or human resource inputs, supplied by the household sector. To address this question, it will be necessary to develop a long period model of production—with the capital inputs no longer assumed to be given—as an extension of the short period model of production developed so far in this chapter. This long period model will, in turn, enable us to explain what determines the set of prices represented by the **P** vector, both in the long period and in the short. With the explanation that has just been given for what determines the **Z** and Ω vectors, the first, and most critical, step in developing that pricing model has already been taken.

5.5 A Long-Period Model of Production

In the model of production developed in the preceding sections, the amount of productive capacity was taken as given. This assumption means that output can be increased only to the extent there is reserve capacity and/or firms are willing to use the existing capacity more intensively. It also means that any capital goods that might be produced, rather than being endogenously determined like the other material inputs based on a set of technical relationships, must be treated as part of the net output of the system—and that therefore the amount of investment being carried out by firms is left unexplained. The model, in other words, holds only in the short period.

To extend the Leontief model so that it can encompass the long period as well, it is necessary to drop the assumption that the amount of productive capacity is fixed. Indeed, it is only by taking into account the growth of productive capacity over time that, as already pointed out, a short-period analysis can be transformed into a long-period model (see chapter 4, part 1). The difference is that instead of taking into account just the increase in aggregate capacity, we will now carry out the analysis on an industry-by-industry basis so as to make the previous set of arguments about the effects of any increase in capacity consistent with an input-output framework. This long-period model of production differs from the short-period model previously developed in a number of important ways. For one thing, it means that the increase in output over time will be limited only by the rate of growth of investment by each industry, $\overset{\circ}{I}_j$, and not by the amount of reserve capacity. It also means—and this is the key change that needs to be made in the short-period model previously developed—that a separate **K** vector of capital inputs must first be specified and then incorporated within the inner matrix of the input-output table, with the flow of goods to other industries on capital account in this way eliminated from the final demand vector.

5.5.1 How to represent the capital inputs

While it has long been recognized that the capital inputs play a key role in the process of production within the industrial sector, it has not been clear how those inputs should be represented in a formal model of the economy. Indeed, much of the controversy in economics has revolved around this question. The prevailing view among economists, at least since the triumph of marginal analysis early in the 20th century, is that the capital inputs can best be represented by a single-valued scalar, K, denoting the amount of capital goods which, in the form of productive capacity, have been accumulated to date. It is this treatment of the capital inputs which, in the most frequently encountered type of model, leads to the specification of the individual industry production function as follows:

$$Q_j = f(K_j, L_j) \qquad (5.60)$$

where K_j is the stock of capital inputs previously accumulated by the jth industry and L_j is the amount of labor inputs used in conjunction with those capital inputs. The aggregate production function already discussed in connection with the neoclassical growth model is simply this individual industry production function with the subscripts omitted to indicate that it applies to the enterprise sector as a whole (see chapter 4, section 3.5, equation 4.14). This treatment of the capital inputs can be criticized on a number of grounds.

The first is that it improperly combines stock and flow variables. To the extent that other inputs besides the labor services of certain individuals must be used in producing an industry's output, those inputs should be represented by a flow, and not a stock, variable. In this connection one must be careful to distinguish the long-period production function from the short-period one. For it is only in the long period that the capital inputs can be represented as a flow. In the short period the capital inputs are by definition fixed and, as such, cannot be monotonically related to output as implied by equation 5.55. Rather, the relationship between the amount of output produced in the short period and the industry's capital stock reduces itself to the simple dichotomous one that either the necessary capital stock is already in place—in which case production is possible—or, alternatively, no output can be produced. However, once the requisite plant and equipment is in place, the amount of capital inputs will no longer determine how much, within the existing capacity limits, is produced. The amount of output will instead depend on the flow of direct material and labor inputs. That is why, in developing a short period model of production, there is no need to denote the capital inputs separately. Being a fixed parameter, they are already implicit—like the existing set of social institutions—in whatever $\mathbf{A}$ and $\mathbf{L}$ matrix has been specified. The situation is, of course, different in the long period. Within that time frame output can be expanded only by increasing the amount of productive capacity and this, in turn, means that the capital stock can no longer be taken as fixed. It therefore follows that, whatever the time frame adopted, the production function given by equation 5.60 has been misspecified. Either the K_j variable needs to be placed outside the parenthesis with a bar $^-$ over it to indicate that it is a fixed parameter—this would be the case if equation 5.60 were meant to denote the short-period production function—or, alternatively, the K_j variable needs to be replaced by the change in the capital stock, ΔK_j or I_j. Only in the latter case would equation 5.60 encompass, as it must if it is to apply in the long period, the flow of capital inputs needed to expand capacity in line with the growth of output.

A second reason for criticizing the conventional treatment of the capital inputs, as represented by equation 5.60, is that it confuses one of the system's outputs, the flow of investment goods, for one of the basic inputs into the production process. While the investment goods produced by an industry can serve as the inputs into some other industry's production process (or even into the industry's own production process), they cannot be considered basic inputs insofar as the system of production itself is concerned. Rather they are simply part of the total output produced by each industry, no different, except for how quickly they are used up, from the other intermediate goods and services that are being produced. Like any other intermediate output, these investment goods can be reduced to the more basic inputs of labor services (plus any nonreproducible natural resoures that may be needed). While their durability is what sets the investment goods apart from other types of intermediate output, and indeed creates an additional set of complications, this does not make them a basic input into the system of production as a whole. It only makes them a durable intermediate output.

Thus the type of production function represented in equation 5.60 not only mistakes the stock of capital available in the short period for the flow of capital inputs needed in the long period, it also confuses an intermediate output of the system for some exogenously supplied input. Still, the more important and fundamental reason for rejecting the type of production function represented by equation 5.60 is that it fails to take into account the heterogeneous nature of the capital inputs used in the production process. The goods supplied by the subset of industries which comprise the investment goods sector are each different from one another, consisting as they do of various pieces of equipment—motors, lathes, dies and the like—together with the plant needed to house them. Indeed, this is what makes these investment goods the output of different industries. With no common measure, such as tons or gallons, by which these capital inputs can be denominated in physical terms, it is misleading to represent them as a singular quantity K, either at the industry or aggregate level. This was precisely the point of Joan Robinson's 1953 *Review of Economic Studies* article, "The Production Function and the Theory of Capital," that launched the Cambridge attack on the conventional treatment of capital inputs.

To avoid this source of error, it is necessary to represent the capital inputs, not as some single-valued scalar, K, but rather as an *n*-by-*n* **K** matrix each element of which, $k_{i,j}$, represents the quantity of some capital input, $q(k)_{i,j}$, supplied by industry i which industry j needs to increase its productive capacity by a given quantum, $\hat{q}_j$. That is, one can specify an *n*-by-*n* **K** matrix such that

$$K = \begin{Bmatrix} k_{1.1} & k_{1.2} & k_{1.3} & \dots & k_{1.n} \\ k_{2.1} & k_{2.2} & k_{2.3} & \dots & k_{2.n} \\ k_{3.1} & k_{3.2} & k_{3.3} & \dots & k_{3.n} \\ . & . & . & & . \\ . & . & . & & . \\ . & . & . & & . \\ k_{n.1} & k_{n.2} & k_{n.3} & \dots & k_{n.n} \end{Bmatrix}$$ (5.61)

where $k_{i.j}$ is the quantity of the capital good produced by industry i relative to the increase in industry j's capacity which that capital good, together with the capital goods supplied by other industries, would make possible. That is,

$$k_{i.j} = \frac{q(k)_{i.j}}{\hat{Q}_j}$$ (5.62)

where $q(k)_{i.j}$ is the quantity of some capital input supplied by industry i to industry j and $\hat{Q}_j$ is the additional output that can be produced by industry j with that capital input, together with the capital inputs supplied by other industries in a certain fixed ratio.

5.5.2 The K matrix

As can be seen by comparing the elements of each, the **A** and **K** matrices are similar in concept. The most important difference is that while the coefficients of the **A** matrix represent the flow of material inputs from one industry to another, the coefficients of the **K** matrix represent the flow of capital inputs. A second, less important, difference is that the $\hat{Q}_j$ term, which serves as the denominator for the elements of the **K** matrix, reflects the discontinuous or "lumpy" nature of any expansion in capacity. The fact is that capacity can be expanded, not continuously, but only in discrete amounts equal to the minimal plant size in each industry. The $\hat{Q}_j$ term in equation 5.62 reflects this fact just as the $q(k)_{i.j}$ term indicates that the **K** matrix represents the interindustry flow of capital inputs rather than the interindustry flow of material inputs.

In theory it should be possible to distinguish the n-h industries which supply inputs to other industries from the h industries which produce items for final use and then, among the former, to distinguish the industries supplying material inputs from the industries producing investment goods, that is, supplying the items needed either to replace or add to an industry's existing capacity. Indeed, each of the n industries would then fall into one, and only one, of the following three categories:

1) investment goods (capital inputs) industries
2) material inputs industries
3) final goods industries

However, the industries for which input-output data are available in the case of the U.S. economy are so highly aggregated that it is not possible to fit them neatly into just one of these categories. Instead, each industry has to be viewed as supplying some mix of investment goods, material inputs and final goods. Thus the same 79 industries represented within the **A** matrix are also represented within the **K** matrix—though with the coefficients for the corresponding cells of the two matrices taking quite different values. Indeed, for some industries, the horizontal rows of the **A** matrix consist mostly of zeros while along the rows of the **K** matrix for the same industries many more of the cells will have positive coefficients. These are the industries which are primarily investment goods industries. In contrast, for some industries, the rows of the **K** matrix consist mostly of zeros while along the rows of the **A** matrix for the same industries many more of the cells have positive coefficients. These are the industries which primarily supply material inputs to other industries. Of course, there are also industries for which the rows of both the **K** and **A** matrix consist mostly of zeros—but with a certain amount of net output being supplied to the household and government sectors. These are the industries which primarily supply goods for final use.

The closest it is possible to come at the present time to producing an estimate of the **K** matrix for the U.S. economy is the capital flow table (CFT) that, based on the estimates of Gross Domestic Private Investment (GDPI) in each of the quinquennial census years, is derived as a supplement to the input-output tables prepared by the U.S. Department of Commerce. The CFT shows how the capital goods produced in the 42 of 79 major industry groupings which account for all of GDPI are distributed among 72 of those same 79 industries. (The 42 two-digit major industry groupings which, since they produce all of the capital goods included in GDPI, constitute the U.S. economy's investment goods sector, are further broken down into 150 six-digit commodity groups, or industries. On the other hand, two major industry groupings, representing Federal government and state and local government enterprises, receive no capital flows as measured by GDPI and thus are not shown in the table. Moreover, data on the capital flows into certain industries are not available and so they have had to be combined with other industries to form larger industry groupings. For example, all four of the agricultural industries shown in exhibit 5.1 are treated as a single industry—as are the construction and maintenance/repair industries separately delineated in exhibit 5.1. The CFT is therefore actually a 150 by 72 matrix.)

The CFT, however, shows only the flow of capital goods (measured in value terms) from one industry to another without relating that flow to the change in the latter's productive capacity. It is therefore not possible to either (a) distinguish the flow of capital goods to replace worn-out parts and equipment from the flow of capital goods to expand capacity, or (b) determine the change in capacity resulting from these flows. In other words, the figures shown in each cell of the 150 by 72 matrix indicate only the quantity of some capital input actually supplied by one industry to another, $q(k)_{i,j}$, and not the quantity required to increase capacity by a given quantum, $q(k)_{i,j}/\hat{Q}_j$. To obtain an estimate of the latter, and thus to derive the $\mathbf{K}$ matrix as specified above, one would need to collect additional information from each of the 79 industries so that the figures shown in the cells of the CFT, net of any replacement flows, could be scaled in terms of the increase in capacity thereby made possible. Still, there is no reason why, at least in theory, this additional information could not be collected and an estimate of the $\mathbf{K}$ matrix thereby obtained.

With the flow of capital inputs needed to expand capacity in the long period represented, as it should be, by an n-by-n $\mathbf{K}$ matrix, it is possible to specify the short-period production function as follows:

$$\mathbf{Q} = f_S(\mathbf{A}, \mathbf{L}), \ \bar{\mathbf{K}} \qquad (5.63)$$

and the long-period production function as follows:

$$\mathbf{Q} = f_L(\mathbf{A}, \mathbf{L}, \mathbf{K}) \qquad (5.64)$$

Comparing equation 5.64 with equation 4.14 (equation 5.60 without the subscripts), one can readily see the difference between the type of long-period production function that will be relied on henceforth and the comparable neoclassical production function. It is not just that the former replaces the single-valued K scalar with an n-by-n $\mathbf{K}$ matrix. It is also that it avoids mixing stock and flow variables to represent the relevant inputs into the production process. Yet a third point of difference can be seen when equation 5.64 is replaced by the vertically integrated version of the same production function.

The capital inputs, just like any other intermediate output of the enterprise sector, can be reduced to the quantities of direct and indirect labor needed to produce the h different types of final output. In the case of this vertically integrated model, the long-period production function then takes the following form:

$$\mathbf{Q} = f_L(\underline{\mathbf{L}}) \qquad (5.65)$$

where $\mathbf{L}$ is the amount of labor required directly and indirectly by each of the final goods industries in order to produce a given quantity of output. As indicated by the $=$ sign, the indirect labor includes not only the labor needed to produce any nondurable material inputs but also the labor needed to produce the capital inputs used to expand capacity in line with the growth of output in those h different industries. One can therefore distinguish this long-period production function from the corresponding short-period production function, which takes the following form:

$$\mathbf{Q} = f_S(\mathbf{L}) \qquad (5.66)$$

In the case of the latter, the indirect labor includes only the labor using in producing any nondurable material inputs, not the labor used in producing any additional capital inputs.

Thus the type of long-period production function that will be relied on henceforth—whether in the form of equation 5.64 or, alternatively, in the form of equation 5.65—neither ignores the need for capital inputs altogether, which all too often is the case in economic analysis, nor misrepresents them as some exogenously supplied basic input, or "factor of production." Rather the capital inputs are represented, in the case of equation 5.64, by a separate $\mathbf{K}$ matrix which is then included as one of the technical relationships determining the method of production and, in the case of equation 5.65, by the somewhat higher values which the direct and indirect labor coefficients take, reflecting the indirect labor required to produce the capital inputs needed to expand capacity in line with the growth of output. As equation 5.65 makes clear, these capital inputs are not exogenously supplied from outside the enterprise sector. Rather they are an intermediate output which, like any other type of intermediate output, can be reduced to the more basic input of the labor services supplied by the household sector. In contrast, the neoclassical production function fails to take into account the role played by any other intermediate output besides the capital inputs while it misrepresents those capital inputs as being exogenously supplied in the same way the labor inputs are supplied.

5.5.3 The industry incremental capital-output ratios

Based on the capital input coefficients represented by the $\mathbf{K}$ matrix, it is possible to derive the incremental capital-output ratio, b_j, for each of the n industries which comprise the enterprise sector. For the incremental capital-output ratio is simply the sum of all the different capital inputs needed to increase capacity by a given quantum, measured in value terms, relative to the value of the output that can be produced with that additional capacity. That is,

$$b_j = \frac{\sum_{j=1}^{n} p_i k_{i,j}}{p_j \hat{Q}_j} \qquad (5.67)$$

The entire set of these incremental capital-output ratios can then be represented as a 1-by-n $\mathbf{B}$ vector such that

$$\mathbf{B} = \{b_1 \ b_2 \ b_3 \ \ldots \ b_n\} \qquad (5.68)$$

The incremental capital-output ratio for the economy as a whole, v, is simply the weighted average of these incremental capital-output ratios for each of the n different industries. That is,

$$v = \sum_{j=1}^{n} v_j b_j \qquad (5.69)$$

where the weights, v_j, are the value added by each of the n industries. Alternatively, v can be calculated by weighting the value of the similarly derived incremental capital-output ratios for each of the h vertically integrated industries by the share of final output, in value terms, produced by each of those h industries. That is,

$$v = \sum_{j=1}^{n} y_j \ddot{b}_j \qquad (5.70)$$

where $\ddot{b}_j$ is the incremental capital-output ratio for each of the h vertically integrated industries, derived as follows:

$$\ddot{b}_j = \frac{\sum_{j=1}^{n} p_i k_{i,j}}{p_j \hat{Q}_j} \qquad (5.71)$$

with the entire set of these incremental capital-output ratios then constituting a separate $\underline{\mathbf{B}}$ vector; and the y_j terms are the elements of the $\mathbf{Y}$ vector previously specified (see section 5.1.4). Although the $\underline{\mathbf{B}}$ vector includes fewer elements than the $\mathbf{B}$ vector (h instead of n elements), this is offset by the fact that each element, because of the capital inputs needed to produce the material inputs used earlier in the production process, takes a higher value. This different set of incremental capital-output ratios, moreover, is then multiplied by a different set of weights. Nonetheless, the aggregate figure, v, is the same whichever of the two formulas, equation 5.69 or 5.70, is used—just as it was when the aggregate growth of output per worker, $\overset{\circ}{Z}$, was calculated (see section 5.4.2).

Since the product of any column and row vector is the sum of the multiplied elements of the two vectors, equation 5.69 can be rewritten, in matrix notation, as follows:

$$v = \mathbf{B}\mathbf{V} \qquad (5.72)$$

and equation 5.70, rewritten as follows:

$$v = \underline{\mathbf{B}}\mathbf{Y} \qquad (5.73)$$

As can be seen from these last two equations, the effect of omitting the $\hat{}$ or "hat" over a vector, such as $\mathbf{B}$, which is being multiplied by another vector is that the set of products of the two factors will then be summed up, or combined, to form a single-valued scalar, such as v, rather than simply remaining as a new vector.

Just as it is possible to derive the incremental capital-output ratio for the enterprise sector as a whole by taking the weighted average of the incremental capital-output ratio for each of the h vertically integrated industries, so it is possible to derive the rate of growth for the enterprise sector as a whole—and thus the rate of growth, $\mathring{G}$, for the economy itself—by taking the weighted average of the growth rates for each of those same h vertically integrated industries, g_j. That is,

$$\mathring{G} = \sum_{i=1}^{h} y_j \mathring{g}_j \qquad (5.74)$$

or, in matrix notation,

$$\mathring{G} = GY \qquad (5.75)$$

where G is an h-by-1 column vector such that

$$G = \left\{ \begin{array}{c} g_1 \\ g_2 \\ g_3 \\ . \\ . \\ . \\ g_h \end{array} \right\} \qquad (5.76)$$

with $g_1, g_2, g_3, \ldots g_h$, the secular rates of expansion in vertically integrated industries $1, 2, 3, \ldots, h$. While it is possible to derive the same aggregate growth rate by weighting the growth rate for all n industries by the value added within each industry, this alternative approach does not then permit one to explain what determines those individual industry growth rates. It is therefore only on the basis of the Pasinetti vertically integrated model of production that the G vector can be endogenously derived as the next step in developing a long-period model of production to complement the short-period model previously specified.

5.5.4 Individual industry growth rates

As was brought out in section 5.2.1, the total output produced by each of the n industries which constitute the enterprise sector will depend on the final demand vector, D, and the Leontief inverse $(I - A)^{-1}$ or $\mathring{A}$. That is,

$$Q = (I - A)^{-1} D \qquad (5.24)$$

Thus, to explain what determines the *change* in the total output of each industry over time, one need only explain what determines the change in the final demand vector. (This, of course, assumes that the Leontief inverse can be treated as a fixed parameter which, if it changes over time, does so at a rate slow enough so that this complication can simply be ignored or, alternatively, that $\dot{\mathbf{A}}$ changes in such a way that the shift in that parameter over time can readily be taken into account.)

The change in the final demand vector from one time period to the next can be represented as follows:

$$\mathbf{D_0} = \mathbf{D_{-1}} + \hat{\mathbf{G}}(\mathbf{D_{-1}}) \qquad (5.77)$$

or, alternatively,

$$\mathbf{D_0} = (\mathbf{I} + \hat{\mathbf{G}})\mathbf{D_{-1}} \qquad (5.78)$$

where $\mathbf{D_0}$ is the final demand vector which can be observed in the current time period, $\mathbf{D_{-1}}$ is the final demand vector which can be observed in the preceding time period, $\mathbf{G}$ is some growth vector such as the one specified in equation 5.76 and $\mathbf{I}$ is the identity matrix previously denoted. This change in the final demand vector may be either a short-period one, reflecting the cyclical movement of the economy during the most recent period of time to have elapsed, or it may be a long-period one, representing the continuation over that interval of some previously determined trend. In the former case, the model needed to explain the $\mathbf{G}$ vector is a more complicated one that we are as yet prepared to go into. Indeed, it will not be until the end of chapter 10 that all the necessary groundwork will have been laid—although the essential outline of that model has already been presented (see chapter 4, part 4). We shall therefore confine ourselves, for the moment, to explaining what determines the $\mathbf{G}$ vector when the change in the final demand vector, as given by equation 5.78, is simply the continuation, within a long-period context, of some past trend. The long-period model we shall use, at least initially, is one of vertically integrated production, with the enterprise sector thus viewed as consisting of h separate industries, each producing a different item for final use.

The growth of output in each of those h vertically integrated industries will depend on the growth in the demand for the types of consumption goods, both private and public, which those h different industries produce. In this chapter we shall limit the analysis to the growth in the demand for the (final) consumption goods which flow from the enterprise sector to the household sector. Later, when the difference between private and public goods has been brought out in chapter 10, the model will be extended to include the growth in demand for the final (consumption) goods which flow from the enterprise sector to the government sector as well.

Insofar as the growth of demand for just private consumption goods is concerned, the principal determinant is the growth of real income over time, based on the growth of output per worker, $\overset{\circ}{Z}$. To the extent it is possible to produce more net output using the same number of workers, there will be a greater amount of net output available for distribution among households. There is, of course, no reason to assume that this greater output will actually go to the workers employed in producing these goods and services. There are two other possibilities, each just as likely. One is that the greater amount of net output will be distributed among a larger number of workers, with employment thereby rising (but with output per worker as a consequence necessarily falling). This can be accomplished either by reducing the average number of hours worked each year, h (thereby increasing the amount of leisure time) or by adding to the number of persons employed within the public sector. The other possibility is that the greater net output will go to others besides the workers employed in producing those goods and services. These nonworkers to whom a part or all of the additional net output goes may be either rentiers with some form of property rights or the recipients of transfer income from the government.

The effect on the *composition* of final demand, and hence the growth of one industry relative to another, will be different depending on how the increase in net output is distributed. Indeed, this is why it will be be necessary, in the chapters which follow, to take into account the other two possibilities besides an increase in the real income of the existing work force through higher real wages. Still, since the effect on the *growth* (as distinct from the *composition*) of aggregate demand will be the same whatever the distribution of the increased social surplus, we shall for the moment confine ourselves to the simpler case in which all of the increase in output per worker worker is reflected in higher real wages—especially since this is in large part what has actually happened over long periods of time in advanced economies like that of the United States. As long as the growth of output per worker is matched by an increase in the real income of at least some households, the only difference which the distribution of the increased social surplus will make is in the composition of final demand and hence in the relative growth rates of the different industries which constitute the enterprise sector.

With the growth of output per worker assumed to be matched by an increase in the real wages of the existing labor force and their successors, we can posit a corresponding set of income elasticities of demand for the consumption goods produced by each of the h vertically integrated industries. (For a discussion of how these income elasticities are determined, see chapter 9, section 1.1.) This set of income elasticities can be represented as an *n-by-1* Υ vector such that

$$\Upsilon = \left\{ \begin{array}{c} \eta_1 \\ \eta_2 \\ \eta_3 \\ . \\ . \\ . \\ \eta_h \end{array} \right\} \tag{5.79}$$

where $\eta_1, \eta_2, \eta_3, \ldots, \eta_h$ is the income elasticity of demand in industries *1, 2, 3, . . . , h*. To the extent that the growth of demand depends solely on the real income effects of the rise in output per worker, the growth rates for each of the *h* vertically integrated industries will then be equal to this Υ vector premultiplied by the $\mathring{Z}$ scalar. That is,

$$\underline{G} = \mathring{Z}(\Upsilon) \qquad (5.80)$$

where $\underline{G}$ is a vector representing the growth rates for each of the *h* vertically integrated industries. Of course, with a different distribution of the growing social surplus made possible by the increase in output per worker, the values taken by the elements of this Υ vector would be different.

In addition to the real income effects of increasing output per worker, it may be necessary to take into account the relative-cost and—to the extent relative prices depend on relative costs—the relative-price effects of the same technical progress. As already pointed out (see section 5.4.2), it is possible to derive a Ω vector, indicating the difference between the growth of output per worker within each industry, $\mathring{z}_j$, and the growth of output per worker for the enterprise sector as a whole, $\mathring{Z}$. This differential movement in the growth of output per worker can, within the context of a long-period model, be equated with the differential movement in costs and—to the extent that relative prices depend on relative costs (see chapter 6, section 4.5)—with the differential movement in price. Thus, to determine the effect that a change in relative prices is likely to have on the growth rate of each vertically integrated industry, it is necessary only to multiply each element of the Ω vector by the corresponding price elasticity of demand, e_j. This means that, in order to encompass the possible effect that changing relative prices may have on each industry's growth rate, equation 6.80 needs to be expanded as follows:

$$G = \mathring{Z}(\Upsilon) + \mathring{\Omega}(\Psi) \qquad (5.81)$$

where Ψ is an *h-by-1* vector such that

$$\Psi = \left\{ \begin{array}{c} e_1 \\ e_2 \\ e_3 \\ . \\ . \\ . \\ e_h \end{array} \right\} \qquad (5.82)$$

with $e_1, e_2, e_3, \ldots, e_h$ the price elasticity of demand for the goods supplied by industries *1, 2, 3, . . . , h*.

It should be noted that the values taken by the Ψ vector may be so close to zero (see chapter 9, section 1.6) that, for all practical purposes, the possible substitution effect on each industry's growth rate can be ignored. In any case, the value of e_j compared with η_j and the value of $\mathring{z}_j - \mathring{Z}$ compared with $\mathring{Z}$ alone is likely to be so small that the possible substitution effect will only slightly modify the influence of what is the primary factor determining the growth of each vertically integrated industry—the real income effect of technical progress. For this reason, equation 5.80 may well be sufficient for actually estimating the value of the **G** vector. Nonetheless, it is only on the basis of the more comprehensive equation 5.81, with the possible substitution effect of technical progress also taken into account, that the growth rates for each of the vertically integrated industries can be said to be fully determined. With the **G** vector thus explained, all that now remains to be done, to complete the long-period model of production, is to indicate how the growth rates for each of these composite industries can be translated into a separate **G** vector representing the growth rates for all n of the industries which actually make up the enterprise sector.

For each of these n industries there will be three sources of expansion over time—the increased demand for any items of final consumption the industry may produce, the increased demand for any material inputs it supplies to other industries and the increased demand for any investment goods it produces. The relative importance of these three growth factors will depend on how the total output of each industry, Q_j, is divided among the goods entering into final consumption, the material inputs supplied to other industries and the investment goods that will become the capital input of some other industry. The overall growth rate for each of the n industries, g_j, will in fact be the weighted average of the growth in demand for each of the three types of goods supplied by the industry. That is,

$$g_j = w_1 g_{j_1} + w_2 g_{j_2} + w_3 g_{j_3} \tag{5.83}$$

where g_{j_1} is the rate of increase in the demand for the items of final consumption produced by the jth industry; g_{j_2} is the rate of increase in the demand for the material inputs supplied by the industry; g_{j_3} is the rate of increase in the demand for the investment goods supplied by the industry, and the w's are a set of weights—with w_1 the ratio of the amount of goods entering into final consumption produced by the industry, $q(C)_j$, to total industry output, Q_j; w_2 the ratio of the amount of material inputs supplied by the industry, $q(a)_j$, to total industry output, and w_3 the ratio of the amount of investment goods produced by the industry, $q(k)_j$, to total industry output. The weights, w_1, w_2, and w_3, are not likely to be the same. Indeed one, or even two, of the weights may well be zero, indicating that the industry does not supply a particular type of good. Still, it will be easier to proceed on the assumption that each industry produces all three types of goods—including a zero amount of any one type of good. In this way, the argument will be sufficiently general to cover every possibility. It should further be noted that, with w_1, w_2 and w_3 each taking a different value, these weights will change from one time period to the next and will therefore need to be recalculated after each iteration of the model.

The growth in demand for any items of final consumption supplied by an industry, g_{j_1}, has already been explained. Indeed, one can specify a $\mathbf{G}_1$ vector, representing the rate of expansion by each of the n industries that is due to the increased demand for the items of final consumption produced by the industry, with the values taken by this $\mathbf{G}_1$ vector determined on the basis of equation 5.81. This means that, to explain the overall rate of expansion by each industry, it is necessary only to develop a set of corresponding equations to explain the growth in the demand for any material inputs supplied by an industry, g_{j_2}, and the growth in the demand for any investment goods supplied by the same industry, g_{j_3}. This would then give rise to separate $\mathbf{G}_2$ and $\mathbf{G}_3$ vectors analogous to the $\mathbf{G}_1$ vector.

The growth in demand for the material inputs supplied by an industry, g_{j_2}, will depend on the rate of expansion by each of the industries to which it supplies those material inputs. To be more precise, g_{j_2} will be equal to the rate of growth by each of the n industries that is due to the increased demand for final consumption items, weighted by the relative amount of material inputs supplied to each of those industries. With the rate of growth by each of the n industries that is due to the increased demand for final consumption items given by equation 5.81 and with the relative amount of material inputs supplied by the jth industry to every other industry represented by the jth row of the $\mathbf{A}$ matrix (converted to percentages of the total material inputs produced by that industry), it is therefore necessary only to premultiply the former, an n-by-1 column vector, by the latter, a 1-by-n row vector, in order to determine the value of g_{j_2}. That is,

$$g_{j_2} = \mathbf{A!}_j [\mathring{\mathbf{Z}}_s(\Upsilon) + \hat{\Omega}(\Psi)] \tag{5.84}$$

where $\mathbf{A!}_j$ is industry j's row within the $\mathbf{A}$ matrix as a proportion of the industry's total intermediate output. For all n industries, one can therefore derive a $\mathbf{G}_2$ vector, representing the growth due to the increased demand for material inputs, by means of the following equation:

$$\mathbf{G}_2 = \mathbf{A!} [\mathring{\mathbf{Z}}(\Upsilon) + \hat{\Omega}(\Psi)] \tag{5.85}$$

where $\mathbf{A!}$ is the entire set of rows which make up the $\mathbf{A}$ matrix, taken as a proportion of the total output produced by the industry which the row represents, and not just the jth industry's row within the set.

Similarly, the growth in demand for the investment goods produced by an industry, g_{j_3}, will depend on the rate of expansion by each of the industries to which it supplies those capital inputs. Only in this case the vector representing those growth rates, as given by equation 5.81, will have to be premultiplied not by the jth industry's row within the $\mathbf{A}$ matrix (converted to percentages) in order to weight those growth rates but rather by the jth industry's row within the analogous **K** matrix (again converted to percentages). That is,

$$g_{j_3} = \mathbf{K}!_j[\overset{\circ}{\mathbf{Z}}(\Upsilon) + \hat{\Omega}(\Psi)] \tag{5.86}$$

where $\mathbf{K}!_j$ is industry j's row within the **K** matrix as a proportion of the total capital goods supplied by the industry. Moreover, one needs to keep in mind that this relationship, unlike that of equation 5.84, holds only in the long period when (a) each industry can be expected to increase capacity in line with the growth of demand (that is, when the aggregate supply condition is likely to hold both at the industry and at the aggregate level) and (b) when the discontinuous, or "lumpy," nature of capital expansion can therefore be largely ignored. In the short period, when neither of those two assumptions is appropriate, equation 5.86 does not apply. Indeed, this is why, in the short period, any investment goods that may be produced by an industry must be treated as part of that industry's exogenously determined net output, and hence as part of the final demand vector. It is only in the long period that, based on equation 5.86, any intermediate output that consists of investment goods, or capital inputs, can be incorporated within the inner matrix of the input-output system by taking into account the technical relationships that are given by the **K** matrix as the counterpart to the **A** and **L** matrices.

For all n industries one can then derive a $\mathbf{G}_3$ vector, representing the growth due to the increased demand for capital inputs, by means of the following equation:

$$\mathbf{G}_3 = \mathbf{K}![\overset{\circ}{\mathbf{Z}}(\Upsilon) + \hat{\Omega}(\Psi)] \tag{5.87}$$

where $\mathbf{K}!$ is the entire set of rows which make up the **K** matrix, taken as a proportion of the total output produced by the industry which the row represents, and not just the jth industry's row within the set. With this $\mathbf{G}_3$ vector, together with the $\mathbf{G}_1$ and $\mathbf{G}_2$ vectors and the relevant sets of weights, it is possible, based on equation 5.83, to explain the secular increase in output for all n industries. The resulting **G** vector, given some initial value for **D**, the final demand vector, then makes it possible to explain, based on equation 5.78, the level of final demand, and hence the quantity supplied, by those same n industries in each succeeding time period. This, however, is only the quantity solution to the long-period model of production which has now been derived. To determine not just the corresponding set of relative prices but also, even more important, the value terms which appear as part of the weights in the long-period model of production, it is necessary to derive the dual price solution as well. This will be done in the chapter which follows as part of specifying the value condition that must hold for an expanding economy as the counterpart of the supply conditions, at both the industry and aggregate level, which have just been delineated.

Recommended Readings

Gardiner Means's distinction between trading and administered price markets can be traced back to his 1934 memorandum to the Secretary of Agriculture, "The Reality of Administered Prices," published as Senate Document no. 13 in January 1935, and republished in Means's collection of essays, *The Corporate Revolution in America*, New York: Crowell-Collier, 1962. The distinction between flex-price and fix-price markets will be found in John Hicks, *Capital and Growth*, Oxford: Clarendon Press, 1965, ch. 7. Paul Davidson's emphasis on the distinction between spot and forward markets can be found in his *Money and the Real World*, London, Macmillan, 1972. The salient characteristics of the megacorp which distinguish it from the neoclassical proprietorship are described in somewhat greater detail in Eichner, *The Megacorp and Oligopoly*. See also Eichner, *Toward a New Economics*, Armonk, N.Y.: M. E. Sharpe, 1985, ch. 2. In connection with these and other efforts to draw a distinction between the sectors of the economy dominated by megacorps and the sectors in which smaller firms prevail, see Robert T. Averitt, *The Dual Economy*, New York: Norton, 1968.

William G. Shepherd's analysis of the extent of oligopoly in the U.S. economy will be found in *Market Power and Economic Welfare*, New York: Random House, 1970, and in "Causes of Increased Competition in the U.S. Economy, 1939–1980," *Review of Economics and Statistics*, November 1982. Despite the title of the latter work, it shows that the concentration ratios within the manufacturing sector have remained basically unchanged over the period surveyed.

The similarity between the Keynesian multiplier and the Leontief inverse has not previously been noted in the literature—nor has the rate at which a surplus is being generated, either in physical terms or in value terms, previously been identified. On the actual computation of the Leontief inverse, see Miernyk, *Input-Output Analysis*, ch. 7. See also the other works on input-output analysis under the recommended readings for chapter 2.

The argument presented in part 3 of this chapter about the nature of the megacorp's cost curves was originally put forward in Eichner, *The Megacorp and Oligopoly*, pp. 28–37. For a further discussion of this point, as well as a survey of the empirical evidence, see Fred Lee, "Post Keynesian View of Average Direct Costs: A Critical Evaluation of the Theory and the Empirical Evidence," *Journal of Post Keynesian Economics*, Spring 1986, together with the comment published in the same issue. On the econometric evidence, see also J. Johnson, *Statistical Cost Analysis*, New York: McGraw-Hill, 1960; Alan A. Walters, "Production and Cost, An Econometric Survey," *Econometrica*, 1963; Bela Gold, *Explorations in Managerial Economics, Productivity, Costs, Technology and Growth*, New York: Basic Books, 1971.

The 1926 article by Sraffa, "The Laws of Returns under Competitive Conditions," originally published in the December issue of the *Economic Journal*, has been reprinted in American Economic Association, *Readings in Price Theory*, Chicago: Irwin, 1952. A somewhat different version was published in Italian the year before.

Parts 4 and 5 of this chapter reflect the argument originally presented in *Toward a New Economics*, ch. 3. See *The Megacorp and Oligopoly*, pp. 231–33, as well. Parts 4 and 5 also draw heavily on Luigi L. Pasinetti, *Structural Change and Economic Growth*, London: Cambridge University Press, 1981. On the vertically integrated model of production, see Pasinetti, *Structural Change and Economic Growth*, chs. 2, 6; Pasinetti, "Vertical Integration in Economic Analysis," *Metroeconomica*, 1973, reprinted in *Essays on the Theory of Joint Production*, L. L. Pasinetti, ed., New York: Columbia University Press, chs. 2; Pasinetti, *Lectures on the Theory of Production*, New York: Columbia University Press, chs. 2–4. For the empirical work reported in exhibit 5.14, see Edward Ochoa, "Labor-Values and Prices of Production: An Interindustry Study of the U.S. Economy, 1947–1972," unpublished doctoral dissertation, New School for Social Research, March 1984 and "An Input-Output Study of Labor Productivity in the U.S. Economy, 1947–72," *Journal of Post Keynesian Economics*, Fall 1986.

On technical progress in general, see Robinson, *The Accumulation of Capital*, ch. 9; Clarence C. Ayres, *The Theory of Economic Progress*, New York: Schocken, 1962 [lst ed: North Carolina State Press, 1944]; Joseph Schumpeter, *The Theory of Economic Development*, New York: Oxford University Press, 1961 [lst ed., 1919], and *Business Cycles*, New York: McGraw-Hill, 1939; Nathan Rosenberg, *Perspectives on Technology*, New York: Cambridge University Press, 1976, and *Inside the Black Box, Technology and Economics*, New York: Cambridge University Press, 1982; John Jewkes *et al.*, *The Sources of Invention*, 2nd ed., New York: Norton, 1969; Lynn White, *Medieval Technology and Social Change*, Oxford: Oxford University Press, 1962; David Landes, *The Unbound Prometheus*, New York: Cambridge University Press, 1969, and *Revolution in Time*, Cambridge, Mass.: Harvard University Press, 1983. See also Walt W. Rostow, "Technology and the Price System," *Science and Ceremony, The Institutional Economics*, C. E. Ayres, William Breit, and William G. Culbertson, Jr., eds., Austin: University of Texas Press, 1976; Stoneman, *The Economic Analysis of Technological Change*. For a more comprehensive survey of the literature, see Rosenberg, *Inside the Black Box*, ch. 1.

On the capital-embodied nature of technical progress, see Paul Davenport, "Embodied Technical Change: A New Approach," *Canadian Journal of Economics*, February 1983. See also the work of John Cornwall cited under the recommended readings for chapter 4.

On the long-period model of production, see Pasinetti, *Structural Change and Economic Growth*, chs. 3–5, 9; John Blatt, *Dynamic Economic Systems*, Armonk, N.Y.: M. E. Sharpe, 1983, part II; Eichner, *Towards a New Economics*, ch. 3.

Chapter 6

The Enterprise Sector:
Prices and Pricing

Contents

Chapter 6

The Enterprise Sector:
Prices and Pricing

In a market economy it is not possible to analyze production solely in physical terms. Production must be analyzed in value terms as well, that is, with prices explicitly taken into account. How those prices are established—the process as well as the determinants—is an essential part of the analysis, one that must be consistent with the theory of production itself. What this means is that, with the Leontief model identified as the most appropriate one for analyzing the enterprise sector as a system of production, both in the short period and in the long, a separate pricing model needs to be developed as the complement of that production model. Such a model is necessary not only so that the nominal flows shown within the cells of the input-output table can simultaneously be broken down into their price and quantity components but also so that any increase in the price level over time, and hence the rate of inflation, can be explained.

There are two somewhat different pricing models which are available to meet this need—at least insofar as the long-period set of relative prices is concerned. One of these models is the Sraffian model, to be found in Piero Sraffa's book, *Production of Commodities by Means of Commodities*, published in 1960 but whose essential thrust was long known to Sraffa's colleagues at Cambridge University. The Sraffa model has the advantage of enabling distributional issues, like the ones that will be taken up in chapter 8, to be addressed directly; and it is this model which will therefore provide the starting point for the analysis of prices and pricing behavior in this chapter. The Sraffian model, however, deals only with the case of an economic system which is merely reproducing itself over time, with no change in the techniques being used and no increase in the amount of net output, or economic surplus, being created. To encompass the historically more relevant case, that of an economic system which is growing over time as a result of technical progress, it is necessary to incorporate into the Sraffian model certain elements of the von Neumann model. This is the model which the mathematician John von Neumann published 15 years before *Production of Commodities* appeared but which, like the Sraffian model, is still ignored in standard intermediate level textbooks. The von Neumann model skirts the distributional issues to focus on the set of relative prices which must be established in an economic system that is growing over time. The two models are not necessarily incompatible with one another but rather have been formulated with different questions in mind. The long-period pricing model to be developed in this chapter will attempt to synthesize these two complementary approaches.

This combined Sraffa-von Neumann model, however, serves only to explain the set of relative prices, together with residuals, that must prevail in the long period. That is, it enables one to specify only the value condition that must hold, as represented by the dual price solution to the model of production, for an economic system that is expanding along some secular growth path. It does not enable one to understand what prices will actually be established. To explain the latter, it is necessary to supplement the long-period model of relative prices, or values, with a short-period model of pricing behavior. Indeed, this distinction between the value relationships that must hold in the long period and the process by which prices are actually established is the distinction between prices and pricing on which the chapter rests.

Again, there are two different models to be considered— only in this case they are not easily reconciled. One is the Walrasian pricing model which is usually presented as the paradigmatic one in economic textbooks. As will be seen, this model cannot explain the residual income vector, π, except as a disequilibrium phenomenon within an equilibrium framework; and in any case the model seems to apply only to the commodity sector where firms tend to be price takers rather than price setters. The other model is the markup pricing model which was first introduced into economics in the 1930s by Gardiner C. Means in the United States and by the Oxford Pricing Group in England but which was incorporated into the larger theoretical framework on which this text is based only by Michal Kalecki later in the same decade. The Marshallian pricing model, it turns out, is but a special case of this markup model. Since the markup model is the model that applies throughout the statistically more significant industrial sector, it is this pricing model that will be treated as the prevailing one within the enterprise sector.

Still, the first step in explaining the actual pricing behavior of firms within the industrial sector will be to derive the dual price solution to the long-period model of production developed at the end of the last chapter so that the value condition that needs to be satisfied if there is to be continuous growth can be determined. While this set of relative prices need not actually prevail, it is the only set of prices that will enable firms to cover the full costs of production as they expand over time, and hence it serves as a useful benchmark for analyzing any short-period price movements. In this respect, the P vector plays the same role as the output solution to the same long-period model of production when, weighted and averaged for all n industries over time, it yields the benchmark growth rate, $\overset{\circ}{G}$ for analyzing short-period quantity movements.

6.1 The Necessary Value Condition in an Expanding Economy

So far, in extending the Leontief model of production to cover the long period, all that has been explained is what determines the rates of expansion by each of the n industries which constitute the enterprise sector. What still remains to be explained is what prices must be charged by each of those n industries if they are going to be able to cover their costs of production—and thereby reproduce and grow, not just in real terms but also, in value terms as well. The set of prices sufficient to enable each of the n industries to cover their costs of production in the long period is what is meant by the value condition that must be satisfied if an advanced market economy like that of the United States is going to be able to continue expanding along whatever is presently its secular growth path. This value condition is given by the **P** vector which, since it can be determined simultaneously, serves as the dual price solution to the long-period model of production outlined at the end of chapter 5.

Within the framework of a Leontief model, the value of the **P** vector depends, ultimately, on the amount of residual income earned by each industry per unit of output, as represented by the $\boldsymbol{\pi}$ vector. This can be seen by examining, once again, that model's dual price solution as previously derived (see chapter 5, section 2.2):

$$\mathbf{P} = \mathbf{V}(\mathbf{I} - \mathbf{A})^{-1} \tag{5.30}$$

As already expained, the value added by each industry per unit of output, v_j, will be equal to the unit labor costs, wl_j, plus the unit residual income, π_j. That is,

$$\mathbf{V} = w\mathbf{L} + \boldsymbol{\pi} \tag{5.18}$$

Thus, with the technology as represented by the **A**, **K** and **L** matrices assumed to remain unchanged, the set of relative prices, **P**, will depend only on the money wage rate and the unit residual income in each of the n different industries. That is,

$$\mathbf{P} = f(w, \boldsymbol{\pi}), \bar{\mathbf{A}}, \bar{\mathbf{K}}, \bar{\mathbf{L}} \tag{6.1}$$

Within a Leontief model in which prices are free to change but the technology is fixed, there are, then, only three variables that need to be determined in order to arrive at the dual price solution—with an explanation for any two of those variables being sufficient to explain the third. These three variables are the wage rate, w (or the set of wage rates, **W**), the unit residual income earned by each of industry, $\boldsymbol{\pi}$, and the set of relative prices, **P**. The point can be seen even more clearly by starting with the vertically integrated version of the same Leontief model (see chapter 5, section 4.1). Indeed, that is one of the advantages of starting from that model.

While the set of relative prices that needs to be established in the long period thus depends only on the wage rate and the unit residual income earned by each industry once the values taken by the **L**, **K** and **L** matrices are known, the wage rate can be treated as yet another parameter if it is simultaneously being determined in some other part of the same more general model. This is in fact how the wage rate will be accounted for in the model to be developed within this text (see chapter 8, part 3). With the wage rate as an additional parameter, equation 6.1 reduces to the following:

$$\mathbf{P} = f(\boldsymbol{\pi}), \ \bar{\mathbf{A}}, \ \bar{\mathbf{K}}, \ \bar{\mathbf{L}}, \ \bar{\mathbf{w}} \tag{6.2}$$

In other words, once the wage rate, and hence the unit labor cost, is known, it is necessary only to explain what determines the residual income in each of the n industries in order to derive the dual price solution to the Leontief model of production.

As already noted (see chapter 5, section 4.1), the unit residual income earned by each industry can be interpreted in either of two ways—as the cost of some essential input or, alternatively, as the income "expropriated" by one group at the expense of another. The approach that will be followed in this chapter, at least initially, will be to examine the extent to which the residual income earned by each industry can be explained as the necessary cost of supplying some essential input and thus of producing whatever output is being demanded of that industry in the long period. Only by first ascertaining this "full cost" of production will it be possible to determine, not just the value condition for continuous expansion but also the need, if any, for a residual income vector.

The most appropriate starting point, in attempting to explain the set of prices that must be established in the long period if the value condition for continuous growth is to be satisfied, is the model that is found in Piero Sraffa's 1960 classic, *Production of Commodities By Means of Commodities*. This is not because that model is a long-period one. On the contrary, since it abstracts from growth and technical progress, it would appear to apply, if at all, only in the short period. Rather the reason for starting with the Sraffian model is that it marks a return to the classical tradition in economics wherein it is the cost of production that determines the "natural" or long-period set of prices. It thus marks the first break with the alternative view that has now become the dominant one among economists, namely, that it is supply and demand factors that determine the long-period or, using the conventional terminology, the long-run set of relative prices.

6.1.1 The Sraffian model

In the model presented in the first part of *Production of Commodities*—a model that abstracts from fixed investment—the residual income vector is explained in terms of a uniform rate of profit, r, on the material inputs that must be obtained in advance of production. While the amount of these material inputs will vary by industry, depending on the values which each industry's technical coefficients take, the rate of profit is assumed by Sraffa to be uniform across industries in keeping with the classical tradition upon which he was drawing. Thus the amount of residual income earned by any one industry per unit of output is given by the following equation:

$$\pi_j = r \sum_{i=1}^{n} p_i a_{i \cdot j} \qquad (6.3)$$

where r is some rate of return on "capital," with $0 < r < 1$. The residual income vector for the enterprise sector as a whole can then be specified as follows:

$$\pi = rPA \qquad (6.4)$$

Substituting rPA for π, the value added vector can be specified as follows:

$$V = wL + rPA \qquad (6.5)$$

and the equation representing the different components of the price vector would then take the following form (with the order of the wage and profit components reversed):

$$P = PA + rPA + wL \qquad (6.6)$$

The first two elements can be combined, with the common PA terms then factored out, so that equation 6.6 takes the following form:

$$P = (1 + r)PA + wL \qquad (6.7)$$

Indeed, this is the form in which the Sraffian model is usually specified. However, it is easier to see the relationship to a Leontief model by focusing on equation 6.6 instead. The first element on the right-hand side of equation 6.6 corresponds to the inner matrix of a Leontief model (with the Q vector factored out) while the second and third elements correspond to the value added row (with the Q vector again factored out).

Despite the limitations soon to be pointed out, the Sraffian model as represented by equation 6.7 has three features which make it a useful starting point for a long-period analysis of relative prices. The first is that the Sraffian model does not slight the importance of working capital in a time-delineated system of production, and the second useful feature is that it makes clear that wages and "profits" represent competing claims against any economic surplus which the system of production is able to generate. Indeed, it is this last feature which distinguishes the entire family of Sraffian pricing models, including the model that will be developed in this chapter, from the more usual way of explaining what determines the value of the residual income vector. The contrast between the two approaches can be seen more clearly by substituting the rate of return, r, for the unit residual income earned by each of the different industries, π, so that equation 6.1 can be rewritten as follows:

$$P = f(w, r), \bar{A}, \bar{L} \qquad (6.8)$$

Both the Sraffian model and the alternative neoclassical theory can be reduced to equation 6.8. The difference is in the interpretation placed on the w and r variables.

The conventional theory in economics views the wage rate, w, as measuring the marginal productivity of labor in each industry and the rate of profit, r, as measuring the marginal productivity of "capital." The value added by each industry, v_j, is then simply the sum of the marginal contribution made by each of these two "factors" of production, weighted by the quantities of each input which are used in the production process. (See chapter 8, section 4.3, for a further discussion, and critique, of the marginal productivity theory.) The Sraffian model, in contrast, views the wage rate and the rate of profit as depending on the outcome of a struggle between two antagonistic groups over what disposition is to be made of the surplus the system of production is capable of generating. While the size of the surplus may be explainable within the parameters of an economic model, the division of that surplus between workers and "capitalists" is not. It depends instead on the noneconomic factors that have, in the historical past, determined the relative bargaining power of the two groups.

As already explained, the surplus generated by an economic system is the net, or final, output produced by each of the n industries (see chapter 5, section 2.3). The essential point which the Sraffian model brings out is that while the total surplus, both in physical and value terms, may be fixed, based as it is on technological factors—and even the surplus generated by each industry in physical terms may be fixed once the final demand vector has been determined—the surplus generated by each industry in value terms is not. This is because the surplus generated by each industry in value terms is the same as its value added, and only the sum of value added by all n industries, the national income, is fixed, not the value added by each industry individually, v_j. The latter will vary as the wage rate, w, and thus the industry's wage bill, wLQ, varies relative to the rate of profit, r.

A change in the wage rate, w, relative to the rate of profit, r, will almost certainly lead to a change in the value added by each industry, v_j—and hence, since P depends on V, to a change in relative prices as well. Indeed, as long as the factor to which the rate of profit, r, is applied in determining the residual income of an industry (this factor, in the Sraffian model, being the amount of "capital" employed) is different across industries from the factor to which the wage rate, w, is applied in determining the same industry's wage bill (this factor being the amount of labor employed), any redivision of the national income between wages and "profits" will have this relative price effect—in addition to its more obvious effect on the distribution of income between workers and "capitalists." Moreover, since the value added by each industry, v_j, is the same as the amount of surplus being generated by that industry in value terms, the new V vector (and the new P vector derived from that V vector) will also have the effect of redistributing the surplus in value terms across industries while leaving the total value added, as represented by the national income, unchanged.

Thus prices serve the function in a Sraffian model, not of allocating resources—this is precluded by the fixed technical coefficients—but rather of implementing the redistribution of income that any change in the rate of profit relative to the wage rate implies. Once it is realized that the division of each industry's value added between a certain size wage bill and a certain amount of residual income is indeterminate within any fixed technical coefficient model of production and depends instead on the set of exogenous sociopolitical factors determining the value of w relative to r, it then follows that the set of relative prices, as given by the **P** vector, is the means by which this division of the economic surplus between workers and "capitalists" or, as perhaps is more accurate, between workers and nonworkers is actually effectuated within a market economy. Indeed, what distinguishes a Sraffian from other types of models is the important insight that any correctly specified model of a production system will lack at least one behavioral equation necessary for determining the distribution of income—with the one variable which is left unexplained necesarily being some distributional variable such as the wage rate and/or the rate of profits.

Sraffa was able to develop a model along these lines, however, only by relying on certain restrictive assumptions, namely, that the "capital" to which the rate of profit is applied consists of the "means of production," or material inputs, purchased in advance of production. Still, the same argument can be shown to hold, as we shall see in the sections which follow, as long as the residual income of each industry is determined by a different set of factors from the wage bill. This condition is satisfied in the model developed in the first part of *Production of Commodities* by applying the rate of profit, r, to the material inputs of each industry so as to determine the residual income of each industry. It thus explains the residual income of each industry in terms of the industry's need for "circulating" or "working" capital. But, as will be clear from what follows, there are other, more realistic ways to take into account the need for working capital while still having the residual income vector determined by a quite different set of factors from those determining the size of each industry's wage bill. We now turn, therefore, to a discussion of the cost of working capital within the framework of a Sraffian model.

6.1.2 The cost of working capital

The Sraffian model, in the form of equation 6.7, can be viewed as an explanation for what determines the values taken by the π vector—at least insofar as that vector depends on the working capital requirements of each industry. The model is predicated on the assumption that any material inputs which must be purchased in advance of production will have to earn a return, r, that is the same for all n industries. While the Sraffian model does not explain what value r must take—it merely makes the point that any increase in the rate of profit on the material inputs purchased in advance will be at the expense of wages—this uniform value of r across industries is then sufficient, once the **A** and **L** matrices are known, to determine the π vector and hence the **P** vector itself.

It should be noted that Sraffa was not trying to provide an explanation of how the cost of working capital affects relative prices. Nor was his purpose that of identifying all the necessary costs of production. Rather he was simply trying to make it clear that, within the type of fixed technical coefficient model of production favored by the classical economists—a model which can now be empirically implemented thanks to the work of Leontief and others in deriving input-output tables for the U.S. and other advanced market economies—only the total surplus being generated is uniquely determined. The distribution of that surplus between workers and any other group, such as the "capitalists," is left unexplained. It is just that, by abstracting from fixed capital as he did (at least in the first part of *Production of Commodities*), Sraffa was perforce presenting a model in which only the need for working, or "circulating," capital can explain what determines the values taken by the π vector. Still, one must keep in mind that Sraffa interpreted the rate of profit, r, not as the cost of obtaining working capital but rather as the factor determining what portion of any surplus would *not* go to workers. Moreover, he made a simplifying assumption that is questionable insofar as the actual working capital requirements of any industry are concerned. This is the assumption that no provision need be made in advance to cover the material needs of workers during the time required to complete the production process. Thus, to incorporate the cost of working capital in a more realistic way within a Sraffian model, it is necessary to modify Sraffa's own approach in at least three respects.

The first is to extend the argument of the classical economists beyond what Sraffa was prepared to do and acknowledge that the cost of working capital is a necessary cost of production—just like the cost of the material and labor inputs purchased with the funds which the "working capital" represents. The need for working capital reflects the time required not just to produce any output but also to sell that output so that funds will then be available to purchase the necessary inputs—both any material inputs and any human resource, or labor, inputs as well (see chapter 2, section 2.3). Indeed, without some provision for obtaining those inputs in advance, production would not be possible. Production cannot begin without the necessary inputs. Yet without the proceeds from the sale of the output produced with those inputs, it is not possible, at least within a market economy, to obtain the necessary inputs. Thus, unless some means can be found to finance the purchase of the necessary inputs in advance, a system of production—like that represented by the Leontief and Sraffian models—will find itself at a standstill: While the process of production can be maintained indefinitely at a certain level once it is under way, there is no way to get the process under way.

It was, of course, the "capitalists" who, at a critical juncture in history, during the transition from merchant to industrial capitalism, provided a solution to this problem. They were able to meet the working capital needs of the new types of industrial activity out of their profits from trade. Indeed, it was this purpose which the profits from trade historically served that may explain Sraffa's treatment of working capital in *Production of Commodities*. At the present time, however, the provision of working capital is the specialized function of a particular industry (as distinct from a particular class of individuals). That industry is the commercial banking segment of the financial sector—just one of the n industries that comprise the enterprise sector but an industry which, because of the strategic role it plays within the economy, requires its own separate analysis. Indeed, the recognition that the commercial banking segment of the financial sector specializes in the provision of working capital so that the production process will not be disrupted for lack of funds will be the point of departure for the subsequent analysis of the role played by money and credit in the economy (see chapter 12, part 1).

Once it is recognized that the provision of working capital is at present the specialized function of a particular industry (rather than that of a particular social class), the argument for treating the cost of working capital as a necessary cost of production is further strengthened. The financial services purchased from the commercial banking industry by each of the other industries differ from the other intermediate inputs that must be obtained in advance only in that the "price" is specified in terms of some market rate of interest—that is, some fraction, i, of the funds advanced, rather than just a flat sum, p. All the other arguments that have been made so far about an input supplied by one industry to another still hold— including the argument that the price of the input can be reduced to the cost of the labor that is required, both directly and indirectly, to supply that input plus a certain amount of residual income. What this means is that the cost of working capital is not only a necessary cost within any system of time-delineated production but also that this cost can be represented in terms of a certain market rate of interest, i, applied to the inputs which must be purchased in advance. Equation 6.6 therefore needs to be rewritten as follows:

$$\mathbf{P} = \mathbf{PA} + \mathbf{wL} + i\mathbf{PA} \qquad (6.9)$$

where i is the market rate of interest on short-term loans to business firms and represents the "price" of the financial services supplied by the commercial banking system to the other n industries.

The second modification that is required of the Sraffian model, in order to encompass the cost of working capital, is to recognize that it is not just material inputs that need to be obtained in advance of production. It is also any human resource, or labor, inputs as well. While the classical economists assumed that it was only the subsistence needs of workers that needed to be met in advance of production—this was the basis for what came to be known as the "wages fund" doctrine—Sraffa reversed the argument by assuming that the circulating capital of each industry consists only of the material inputs that have to be obtained beforehand. Sraffa's reasons for turning the classical argument on its head are not difficult to fathom. Aside from not wanting to be criticized for holding to the discredited wages fund doctrine, he was determined to avoid the error of viewing "capital" as something other than a heterogeneous combination of certain physical goods. While it is possible to treat a portion of the wages paid workers (the portion used to meet their subsistence needs) as the material cost of the labor inputs being provided and in this way still retain the notion of circulating capital as some combination of previously produced physical goods, this would have greatly complicated the argument. Sraffa chose instead to make the simplifying assumption that only the material inputs obtained in advance, and not the goods needed by workers to meet their subsistence needs during the period of production, constitute the circulating capital of each industry.

However, with the shift from the analytical category of "circulating" capital as a possible basis for explaining the residual income of each industry to the analytical category of "working" capital as a necessary cost of production, this simplifying assumption becomes less defensible. Firms themselves make no distinction between the funds they need to borrow in order to finance the purchase of material inputs and the funds they need to borrow in order to cover their wage bill during the period of production. Indeed, it is virtually impossible, as a practical matter, to delineate the one type of loan from the other. Whatever the reason for borrowing the funds, it will add to the amount of short-term debt that will then need to be serviced through interest payments. What this means is that the market rate of interest, i, needs to be applied both to the material inputs purchased in advance *and* to the wage bill incurred during the period of production. To incorporate the full cost of working capital within a Sraffian model, equation 6.9 therefore needs to be rewritten as follows:

$$P = PA + wL + i[PA + wL] \qquad (6.10)$$

As a means of representing the cost of working capital, equation 6.10 still suffers from a serious limitation. The Sraffian model assumes that only a single time period elapses between the purchase of any material inputs and the realization of income, or funds, from the sale of the output produced with those inputs. This is an unnecessarily simplistic and limiting assumption. While it is possible to treat the time interval between the purchase of any inputs and the realization of funds from the sale of the output produced from those inputs as an additional parameter of the model, this complication can be handled more readily by focusing on the inventory-to-sales ratio in each industry, ξ.

The inventory-to-sales ratio indicates how much additional output must be produced, beyond what is needed to meet current demand, so that the production process will not be disrupted for lack of the necessary stock of inventory. An inventory-to-sales ratio of, for example, 0.25 means that output equal in value to one-fourth of the sales during any given time interval must be set aside as a permanent stock of raw materials, goods still being worked on and unsold finished output. The cost incurred in producing this additional output can be assumed to be the same as that incurred in producing the output which is actually then sold. Thus the inventory-to-sales ratio, taken as a proportion of the labor and material costs incurred in producing any goods for sale, represents the cost to each industry of the inputs needed to maintain the necessary stock of inventory. Since this cost must be covered prior to the receipt of any income from the sale of output, it needs to be financed out of working capital—whether that working capital is provided by the enterprise itself or borrowed from some bank or other financial institution. The cost of working capital, insofar as any particular industry is concerned, is therefore simply the market rate of interest on short-term loans to business, i, multiplied by the sales-to-inventory ratio, ξ_j, as a proportion of each industry's unit material and labor costs, $\sum_{i=1}^{n} p_i a_i._j$. With a 1-by-n Ξ vector representing the entire set of these inventory-to-sales ratios, the last term in equation 6.34 would then take the following form:

$$DS_S = i[\Xi(PA + wL)] \qquad (6.11)$$

where DS_S is the amount of the enterprise sector's short-term debt service attributable to the cost of working capital. Equation 6.10 itself would then take the following form:

$$P = PA + wL + i[\Xi(PA + wL)] \qquad (6.12)$$

The values taken by the Ξ vector, it should be noted, are available as part of the input-output data published each census year and updated monthly.

The $i[\Xi(PA + wL)]$ term on the right-hand side of equation 6.12 simply indicates what is the price, i, of the input supplied by a particular industry—namely, the commercial banking industry—and the quantity, $\Xi(PA + wL)$, of that input—namely, short-term financial services—that must be supplied to each of the other n industries. As the contractual payment for a necessary input, it is no different from any of the other flows represented within the inner matrix of the input-output system and thus can no longer serve to explain what determines the values taken by the residual income vector. This point can perhaps be grasped more readily by denoting the commercial banking industry as the jth industry and then replacing i, the price of the financial services provided by that industry, with p_j and $\Xi(PA + wL)$, the quantity of those financial services, with Q_j. DS_S would then disappear as a separate term within the price equation representing the Sraffian model and equation 6.12 would be reduced to the following:

$$P = PA + wL \qquad (6.13)$$

We would then be back to equation 6.1 with the residual income vector, including the residual income earned by the commercial banking industry itself, as yet unexplained. It would seem, therefore, that with the cost of working capital viewed as a necessary cost of production—one that, with the development of a separate commercial banking industry, is already covered by the **A** and **L** matrices—we are still without any explanation for what determines the values taken by the π vector. To see what that explanation might perhaps be, we need to turn to the second part of *Production of Commodities*, where Sraffa introduces fixed capital into his model. Since the "fixed" capital takes the form of machinery which, even though it remains in use for more than one period, is assumed not to increase in quantity, we are still far short of a model that can explain the macrodynamic behavior of an advanced market economy like that of the United States which is expanding over time. Still, with the introduction of this fixed capital, we can at least analyze the role played by depreciation in a Sraffian type of model.

6.1.3 Fixed capital and depreciation

"Fixed" capital, as distinct from "working" capital, is more difficult to incorporate within a Sraffian model. The complication stems from the fact that the plant and equipment representing the productive capacity of each industry is not, like the other types of material inputs, entirely used up within the interval that defines the production period. There is thus a question of how to encompass, within such a model, the flow of capital inputs needed to replace the "fixed" capital as it is being used up. For while it would be quite unrealistic to assume that this fixed capital is entirely used up within a single production period, it would be no less unrealistic to assume that, once in place, it has a perpetual life. This complication arises, it should be noted, because of the durability of the "fixed" capital—that is, of the plant and equipment that constitutes the productive capacity of each industry. While it is the implication which this durability of the capital inputs has for the timing of investment outlays that will be stressed in the chapter which next follows, here the emphasis will be on the implication the durability has for the setting of a price for the goods produced with that "fixed" capital.

Within the economics literature, two quite different approaches have been taken in an attempt to define the cost, within any one period, of the fixed capital used in the production process. The conventional approach is to view the fixed capital as physically deteriorating over time at a certain rate so that it is entirely used up within an interval of time, T, that is some multiple of the production period. The argument is usually simplified by assuming that the fixed capital deteriorates at a constant rate but one could just as readily assume that the physical deterioration occurs at an irregular rate—or even, like the proverbial "one-horse shay," that it occurs all at once. The essential premise is that the fixed capital has a finite life denoted by T. Starting from this premise, it is possible to prorate the cost of the fixed capital over its life so that the cost during any one period can be denoted as a "depreciation charge" equal to 1/T of the purchase price. As an item of fixed expense, this depreciation charge is then added to the variable costs in determining the total costs of production.

This conventional way of handling the durability of fixed capital can be criticized on two grounds. The first is that it views the fixed capital as some singular entity rather than a heterogenous combination of previously produced goods, or capital inputs. This criticism has already led to an insistence that the K scaler normally used to denote any fixed "capital" be replaced by a K matrix representing the combination of goods produced by other industries that an industry must obtain if it is going to add to its productive capacity (see section 5.5.2). With each of the goods denoted by the K matrix likely to wear out at a different rate, it is not clear how the fixed capital's finite life is to be determined. There would seem to be, not a single finite life T, but rather a different finite life for each type of capital input required—with no obvious basis for calculating the finite life of the whole.

The doubt that an actual number can be assigned to T is reinforced by the fact that, with a program of preventive maintenance such as that routinely carried out under modern management techniques, there is no reason why a plant (as distinct from the separate capital goods comprising the plant) should physically deteriorate over time. The individual capital goods needed to keep the plant going may wear out (and may therefore need to be replaced on a certain fixed schedule) but it should be possible to maintain the plant itself indefinitely. If an entire plant needs to be replaced, it will not be because it has physically deteriorated but rather, only because it has become technologically obsolescent. Indeed, it is not the existence of "fixed" capital *per se* that is the source of the difficulty in attempting to determine the costs that need to be covered by any set of prices but rather the existence of "vintage" capital—that is, plants which no longer represent the state of the art insofar as production techniques are concerned. The virtue of the alternative approach suggested by Sraffa is that it at least attempts to come to grips with the problem of "vintage" capital.

In the second part of *Production of Commodities* Sraffa suggests that any fixed capital, such as a piece of machinery, be viewed as an input which gives rise to two quite distinct outputs, each of which is separately valued. One output is the good or service produced with the fixed capital and the other is the fixed capital itself which, being one period older, is now a capital input of a different type. It is then possible to derive the "depreciation charge" for any one type of capital input, or piece of equipment, used in the production process by comparing the value of the output that can be produced with a capital good of that vintage, holding all the other inputs constant, with the value of the output that can be produced with the same capital good when it is one period more recently acquired. This approach has the effect of shifting from a Leontief technology, with each industry characterized by a single technique of production, to a von Neumann technology. The latter, based on the growth model developed by John von Neumann, assumes that each industry can produce more than one type of good using a number of different techniques. It is thus consistent with Sraffa's assumption that for each type of capital input, or piece of equipment, used in the production process there is a joint output, with there being as many different techniques as there are different capital inputs and different periods during which each input can be used. Indeed, it is the von Neumann model that provides the mathematics for encompassing the Sraffian treatment of fixed, or durable, capital inputs as a special case of the problem of "joint production" first pointed out by Marshall, to wit, the problem of determining the cost of each when the same set of inputs produce two separate goods as their output.

The Sraffian approach has several advantages over the more conventional treatment of fixed capital. For one thing, it can encompass the heterogenous nature of the goods which constitute the productive capacity of any industry. It thus correctly denotes the fixed capital in terms of a K matrix rather than just a K scaler (even though, to simplify the argument, only one piece of durable equipment is sometimes assumed, as Sraffa himself did, in specifying the model). Moreover, it recognizes that any depreciation in the value of a capital input will be due to a relative decline in the value of what can be produced with that capital input, and not necessarily to the physical deterioration of the capital good itself. It thus can better handle the complications arising from any "vintage" capital inputs. Still, the approach suggested by Sraffa for encompassing fixed capital within a model of production will not be the basis for the analysis of long-period prices which follows. This is not because of any flaw in the logic of Sraffa's argument. Indeed, based on the mathematics of the von Neumann model, the Sraffian approach can be shown to yield a fully determinate price as well as output vector. It is rather that the Sraffian approach does not lend itself to the type of empirically testable model of a growing economy which this text is meant to provide.

Thus in what follows the durability of the "fixed" capital inputs will be dealt with in a manner quite different from that suggested by Sraffa. To the extent the capital inputs actually wear out over time, it will be assumed that they are continually replaced through a program of preventive maintenance. The cost of this preventive maintenance, reflecting the replacement parts that need to be purchased from each of the n industries, will then be viewed as simply another of the necessary costs of production already encompassed by the A matrix. Indeed, one of the 79 industries represented within the actual input-output table for the U.S. economy is the maintenance and repair construction industry serving a number of the other 79 industries. The remaining industries, it can be presumed, carry out their own preventive maintenance programs. This is the reason for positing, as will the analysis which follows, that once any fixed capital in the form of productive capacity has been acquired, it will be maintained in good working condition until scrapped, with the cost of the necessary preventive maintenance then included as part of each industry's overhead, or fixed, costs.

To the extent the capital inputs become technologically obsolescent instead of simply wearing out, it can be assumed that they will be replaced as part of the investment carried out by each industry separate from any ongoing program of preventive maintenance (see chapter 7, section 2.2, for a discussion of this component of investment). In this way, the existence of "vintage" capital inputs will be treated, as it needs to be, not as a problem of valuation but rather as a problem of determining the optimal rate of investment by the individual firms in each industry. Only indirectly, through the effect it has on the rate of investment, will the existence of "vintage" capital influence the price level—and even then the more basic factor determining the growth of investment will be the rate of technical progress. Indeed, once technical progress is recognized as part of the broader process underlying the growth of the economy over time, one can see more clearly the reasons for pursuing a quite different approach from that suggested by Sraffa, at least insofar as any "fixed" capital inputs are concerned.

For one thing, the Sraffian treatment of fixed capital implies that a value must be placed on each separate piece of vintage equipment used in the production process before the prices necessary for covering the costs of production can be determined. This argument, if true, would vastly increase the informational requirements for deriving the P vector as the dual price solution to the long-period model of production specified at the end of the last chapter. Instead of knowing the value of each capital input only at the time it was supplied by one of the capital goods industries, one would need to be able to determine the value of that capital input during each subsequent time period as well until the good was finally scrapped. This means that the K matrix, as the basis for determining the B and hence the P vector, would have to be seen as an n-by-n-by-n cube, rather than just an n-by-n square, matrix—with the entire additional dimension of that vector then, in some way, filled in. An empirical estimate of the values taken by the coefficients along just two of those dimensions has as yet to be obtained (see chapter 5, section 5.2), and adding a third dimension would only make the task more difficult. If, as will be argued in the section which next follows, it is possible to determine the value of the P vector based on an n-by-n K matrix alone, without having to take into account the effect which the passage of time has on the value of any capital goods purchased in earlier periods, then the Sraffian approach imposes additional information requirements which are unlikely to be met in practice without adding to the explanatory power of the model. It can therefore be rejected on the basis of what is known as the parsimony principle—the rule that any superfluous arguments should be ignored (see chapter 15, section 0.0).

A second reason for rejecting the Sraffian approach is that while it allows for fixed capital, it ignores the need to increase the amount of that fixed capital over time in line with the growth of the economy. It thus implicitly assumes, like the conventional neoclassical models, that the economy is not growing. As we shall now see, it is only when the need to expand capacity over time is taken into account that one can take the next important step toward explaining what determines the values taken by the residual income vector within a long-period model of production.

6.1.4 The cost of expansion

As yet, there would appear to be no explanation for the existence of a π vector. With both the provision of credit (working capital) and the replacement of any worn-out durable material inputs (physical capital) the specialized function served by one or more of the n industries which constitute the enterprise sector, all the necessary costs of production, as so far delineated, would appear to be encompassed by the A and L matrices. The need for a π vector can be understood only when, in addition to all the other costs of production, one takes into account the cost of expansion itself.

The cost of expansion is the cost of obtaining the capital inputs needed to increase the capacity of each industry in line with the growth of output. It is thus the cost of satisfying the necessary supply condition for continuous economic growth. Only by taking into account this cost of expansion, based on the growth models of von Neumann and Pasinetti, can the residual income vector, and hence the price vector itself, then be explained.

The cost of expansion will depend on two factors. One is the growth rate of each industry, g_j. It is this first factor that will determine the rate at which the capacity of each industry needs to be increased. The other key variable is the industry's incremental capital-output ratio, b_j. It is this second factor that will determine, for each quantum increase in capacity, the amount of capital inputs in value terms that will need to be obtained. The product of these two factors, $g_j b_j$, represents the industry's rate of required investment, with this rate of required investment, ϕ_j, defined as follows:

$$\phi_j = \frac{\sum\limits_{i=1}^{n} p_i q(k)_{i\,j_t}}{p_j Q_{j_t}} \tag{6.14}$$

The numerator, $\sum\limits_{i=1}^{n} p_i q(k)_{i\,j_t}$, is the amount of capital inputs in value terms the industry needs to obtain during time period t; and the denominator, $p_j Q_{j_t}$, is the value of the output that was being produced by the industry at the beginning of the period. The numerator, since it indicates the amount of investment in nominal terms that will have to be undertaken, is in fact the industry's cost of expansion during time period t. What still needs to be made clear is why this cost of expansion, when divided by the value of the industry's output at the beginning the period, will equal the product of the industry growth rate and the incremental capital-output ratio—or, in other words, why $\phi_j = g_j b_j$.

The rate at which each industry needs to expand capacity will be roughly equal to its own secular growth rate, g_j. While the increase in capacity need not exactly match the increase in demand during any one time period—indeed the unlikelihood of the two matching will be the point of departure for the short-period analysis to follow—this complication can be ignored within the context of a long-period model. The quantum increase in capacity which the acquisition of a new plant by any one firm represents will, across firms and over time, tend to average itself out. Thus the growth of investment by each industry in the long period, $\mathring{I}_j$, can be equated with the secular growth of demand for its output, g_j. That is,

$$\mathring{I}_j = g_j \qquad (6.15)$$

where $\mathring{I}_j$ is the rate of growth of investment by the jth industry. Indeed, equation 6.15, generalized for all n industries, represents the necessary supply condition for continuous growth (see chapter 4, section 1.4).

With each industry necessarily having to increase its capacity at the same rate its sales are growing, the amount by which the industry will need to increase its capacity during any one time period will be the amount it was able to sell at the beginning of the period, Q_{j_t}, multiplied by the growth rate, g_j. The value of the output which can be produced with this additional capacity will be the increment in output, $g_j(Q_{j_t})$, multiplied by the price, p_j. The amount of capital inputs in value terms that will need to be obtained in order to increase capacity by that amount will be the value of the additional output that can be produced, $p_j[g_j(Q_{j_t})]$, multiplied by the incremental capital-output ratio, b_j. Thus the value of the capital inputs the industry needs to be able to obtain in time period t—the nominal value of the investment that will need to be undertaken and therefore the cost of the industry's expansion during that period—is given by the following formula:

$$\sum_{i=1}^{n} p_i q(k)_{i\,j_t} = b_j(p_j[g_j(Q_{j_t})]) \qquad (6.16)$$

or, with the terms on the right-hand side rearranged slightly,

$$\sum_{i=1}^{n} p_i q(k)_{i\,j_t} = g_j b_j(p_j Q_{j_t}) \qquad (6.17)$$

Dividing both sides of equation 6.17 by $p_j Q_{j_t}$, one can then derive the industry's required rate of investment, ϕ_j, as follows:

$$\phi_j = \frac{\displaystyle\sum_{i=1}^{n} p_i q(k)_{i\,j_t}}{p_j Q_{j_t}} = g_j b_j \qquad (6.18)$$

The rate of required investment, when applied to the value of the industry's output at the beginning of any period, will determine the amount of capital inputs in value terms that must be obtained—and hence both the nominal amount of investment that will need to be carried out and the industry's cost of expansion during that period. For example, in the case of an industry with an incremental

Exhibit 6.1

Year	Sales	Δ Sales	Growth	Investment	Δ Invest.	Growth	Required Rate of of Invest.
0	$1,000,000	—	—	$150,000	—	—	15%
1	1,050,000	$50,000	5%	157,500	$7,500	5%	15
2	1,102,500	52,500	5	165,375	7,875	5	15
3	1,157,625	55,125	5	173,644	8,269	5	15
4	1,215,506	57,881	5	182,326	8,682	5	15
5	1,276,282	60,776	5	191,442	9,116	5	15

capital-output ratio of 3 that is growing at 5 percent a year, the rate of required investment in any one year will be 15 percent. As can be seen from exhibit 6.1, in a year when its sales were initially $1,000,000, the amount of capital inputs in value terms the industry will need to obtain, based on this required rate of investment, will be $150,000. While in the succeeding year its sales and hence its output, Q_{j_t}, will be 5 percent greater, the amount by which it will need to increase capacity will also be 5 percent greater so that its rate of required investment, ϕ_j, remains the same. However, the *amount* of investment the industry will need to undertake, and thus the cost of expansion, will be 5 percent greater. This is because the cost of expansion will be the same rate of required investment, 15 percent, applied to the 5 percent greater sales volume.

Like any other essential cost, the cost of expansion will need to be covered by the industry's sales revenues. This means that the industry's sales revenues, $p_j Q_{j_t}$, will have to exceed the industry's material and labor costs, $c_j Q_{j_t}$, by an amount at least equal to $g_j b_j (p_j Q_{j_t})$. The following condition thus needs to be satisfied:

$$p_j Q_{j_t} - c_j Q_{j_t} = g_j b_j (p_j Q_{j_t}) \qquad (6.19)$$

where c_j represents the material and labor costs of each industry, $[p_1 a_{1j} + p_2 a_{2j} + p_3 a_{2j} + \ldots + p_n a_{nj} + w l_j]$. Dividing both sides of equation 6.19 by Q_{j_t}, we obtain the following:

$$p_j - c_j = g_j b_j (p_j) \qquad (6.20)$$

Since the residual income of each industry per unit of output, π_j, is the difference between the industry price, p_j, and the unit material and labor costs, c_j, equation 6.20 can be rewritten as follows:

$$\pi_j = g_j b_j (p_j) \qquad (6.21)$$

The implication of equation 6.21 is that, if an industry is going to be able to cover the cost of its expansion over time, its unit residual income, π_j, must be at least equal to the rate of required investment, $g_j b_j$, multiplied by the industry price, p_j. This is true regardless of how the increase in capacity is financed. Even if the investment is financed externally by adding to the industry's long-term debt, the cost of servicing that debt will still need to be covered out of the industry's sales revenue. Indeed, once the cost of servicing any long-term debt has been stabilized at a certain fixed proportion of total costs—and this will necessarily have to be the case in the long period—it will no longer make any difference whether the expansion is financed externally or whether, as is more likely to be the case when an industry is dominated by megacorps with some degree of pricing power, it is financed internally. In either case the price will need to exceed the material and labor costs by an amount equal to $g_j b_j(p_j)$. Resort to external financing will merely permit a temporarily lower price, one that will then have to be offset by a higher price in the long period so as to cover the increased cost of debt service. (For the further development of this point, insofar as the individual firm's cost of finance is concerned, see chapter 7, section 3.2.)

Thus, once the cost of debt service has been stabilized at a certain fixed proportion of total costs, the unit residual income of each industry, π_j, can be explained in terms of the cost of expansion per unit of output, $g_j b_j(p_j)$. This explanation can then be generalized for all n industries as follows:

$$\pi = \hat{P}G\hat{B} \qquad (6.22)$$

where the **G** and **B** vectors are as previously specified (see above, sections 5.5.3 and 5.5.4).

Once the values which the residual income vector needs to take have been determined, the price vector itself can then be derived. One need only divide through both sides of equation 6.21 by the industry price, p_j, and in this way obtain the following relationship:

$$\mu_j = g_j b_j \qquad (6.23)$$

where μ_j is the profit margin of each industry defined as follows:

$$\mu_j = \frac{\pi_j}{p_j} = \frac{p_j - c_j}{p_j} \qquad (6.24)$$

What equation 6.23 brings out is that an industry's profit margin—that is, the rate at which it is generating any net revenue, and hence any cash flow, or "savings"—must be at least equal to the rate of required investment, $g_j b_j$ or ϕ_j. This necessary condition—what can be termed the value condition for continuous economic expansion—is simply a variant of the Harrod-Domar formula previously presented (see chapter 4, section 1.1) once that formula has been disaggregated so that it applies at the individual industry level. One can see this by shifting the terms of equation 6.23 as follows:

$$g_j = \frac{\mu_j}{b_j} \tag{6.25}$$

keeping in mind that μ_j represents each individual industry's savings rate while b_j is its incremental capital-output ratio. Indeed, the Harrod-Domar formula itself is simply equation 6.25 weighted and aggregated for all n industries.

Still, in attempting to explain what determines the industry price, it is better to focus on the markup on costs rather than the profit margin. This is because the markup, unlike the profit margin, is simply added to the labor and material costs in calculating the industry price. One does not need to know the price beforehand. The markup, m_j, is defined as follows:

$$m_j = \frac{p_j - c_j}{c_j} \tag{6.26}$$

Dividing both sides of this equation by c_j and then shifting terms, one can isolate the price variable on the left-hand side as follows:

$$p_j = (1 + m_j)c_j \tag{6.27}$$

Thus, based on equation 6.27, the industry price, p_j, can readily be determined once the material and labor costs of production are known.

While it is the markup, m_j, which must be directly applied to the labor and material costs to yield the industry price, it is the profit margin, μ_j, which, as the industry's savings rate, can more readily be explained in terms of the industry growth rate and its incremental capital-output ratio. However, the one variable can be converted into the other based on the following relationship:

$$m_j = \frac{\mu_j}{1 - \mu_j} \tag{6.28}$$

That this relationship necessarily holds can by seen by substituting $(p_j - c_j)/p_j$ for the μ_j terms and p_j/p_j for the 1 in equation 6.28 as follows:

$$m_j = \frac{p_j - c_j}{p_j} / [\frac{p_j}{p_j} - \frac{p_j - c_j}{p_j}] \qquad (6.29)$$

and carrying out the operations called for as follows:

$$m_j = \frac{p_j - c_j}{p_j} / [\frac{p_j - (p_j - c_j)}{p_j}] = \frac{p_j - c_j}{p_j} * \frac{p_j}{c_j} \qquad (6.30)$$

When the identical p_j terms in the numerator and denominator are canceled, the right-hand side of equation 6.30 reduces to the mark-up, $(p_j - c_j)/c_j$, thereby demonstrating that equation 6.28 is correct. Substituting the determinants of the profit margin, as given by equation 6.23, for the μ_j terms in equation 6.28, the size of the mark-up, m_j, can then be explained as follows:

$$m_j = \frac{(g_j b_j)}{1 - (g_j b_j)} \qquad (6.31)$$

Equation 6.27, the price equation for any one industry, is easily generalized for all h vertically integrated industries since the costs of production, c_j, for any one industry will be equal to the direct and indirect unit labor costs, $w\ddot{l}_j$. The latter term can then be substituted for c_j in equation 6.27 as follows:

$$p_j = (l + m_j)w\ddot{l}_j \qquad (6.32)$$

and this result then generalized for all h vertically integrated industries. That is,

$$\mathbf{P} = (\mathbf{I} + \hat{\mathbf{M}})\, w\underline{\mathbf{L}} \qquad (6.33)$$

where $\mathbf{I}$ is the identity matrix and $\underline{\mathbf{L}}$ is the vector of direct and indirect labor coefficients previously specified (see above, chapter 5, section 2.1 and section 4.1), and $\underline{\mathbf{M}}$ is a l-by-h vector determined as follows (based on equation 6.31):

$$\underline{\mathbf{M}} = \hat{\mathbf{G}}\hat{\mathbf{B}}[\mathbf{I} - (\hat{\mathbf{G}}\hat{\mathbf{B}})]^{-1} \qquad (6.34)$$

where $\underline{\mathbf{G}}$ and $\mathbf{B}$ are the growth and ICOR vectors for the h vertically integrated industries that were previously specified (see chapter 5, sections 5.4 and 5.3).

Substituting the right-hand side of equation 6.31 for m_j in equation 6.32, we obtain the following:

$$p_j = [1 + \frac{(g_j b_j)}{1 - (g_j b_j)}]w\ddot{l}_j \qquad (6.35)$$

which can be further reduced as follows:

$$
\begin{aligned}
p_j &= \frac{1 - g_j b_j}{1 - g_j b_j} + \frac{g_j b_j}{1 - g_j b_j} \, w\ddot{l}_j \\[2ex]
&= \frac{1 - g_j b_j + g_j b_j}{1 - g_j b_j} \, w\ddot{l}_j \qquad (6.36) \\[2ex]
&= \frac{1}{1 - g_j b_j} \, w\ddot{l}_j
\end{aligned}
$$

This result can then be generalized for all h vertically integrated industries. That is,

$$\mathbf{P} = (\mathbf{I} - \hat{\mathbf{G}}\hat{\mathbf{B}})^{-1} \, w\underline{\mathbf{L}} \qquad (6.37)$$

The generalization of equation 6.27 for all n industries, rather than for just the h vertically integrated industries, is somewhat more complicated because one needs to take into account, explicitly, the prices paid by each industry for its material inputs. Thus the generalization of equation 6.27 for all n industries takes the following form:

$$\mathbf{P} = (\mathbf{I} + \hat{\mathbf{M}})[\hat{\mathbf{P}}\mathbf{A} + w\mathbf{L}] \qquad (6.38)$$

or, shifting terms so as to isolate the $\mathbf{P}$ vector on the left-hand side:

$$\mathbf{P} = (\mathbf{I} + \mathbf{M})(w\mathbf{L})[\mathbf{I} - \mathbf{A} - \hat{\mathbf{M}}\mathbf{A}]^{-1} \qquad (6.39)$$

with $\mathbf{M}$ based on $\mathbf{G}$ and $\mathbf{B}$, rather than $\underline{\mathbf{G}}$ and $\underline{\mathbf{B}}$. In its reduced form, this equation can be rewritten as follows:

$$\mathbf{P} = (\mathbf{I} - \hat{\mathbf{G}}\hat{\mathbf{B}})^{-1} \, (w\mathbf{L})[\mathbf{I} - \mathbf{A} - \hat{\mathbf{M}}\mathbf{A}]^{-1} \qquad (6.40)$$

The $(\mathbf{I} - \hat{\mathbf{G}}\hat{\mathbf{B}})^{-1} \, w\mathbf{L}$ term in the above equation represents what has previously been specified as the value added vector, $\mathbf{V}$ (see chapter 5, section 1.4). The remaining term on the right-hand side of the equation, $[\mathbf{I} - \mathbf{A} - \hat{\mathbf{M}}\mathbf{A}]^{-1}$, is a variant of the Leontief inverse, with the elements of this inverse representing the proportion of the total value placed on each industry's output that goes to cover just the unit wage costs rather than all of the value added per unit of output (see chapter 5, section 2.3). It should be noted that the $-\hat{M}A$ term—the one point of difference between this inverse and the Leontief inverse as it has previously been specified—represents the residual income earned on the material inputs purchased from each of the other n industries. It is therefore the basis for taking into account the indirect residual income within a vertically integrated model of production. Still, the more important point is that equation 6.40, since it consists of a value added vector multiplied by a Leontief inverse, is but a variant of the dual price solution given by equation 5.30.

Based on either equation 6.37 or equation 6.40, the price vector, P, can be said to be fully explained within the context of the long-period model of production developed at the end of the last chapter. This does not mean, however, that the set of prices actually observed at any historical point in time will necessarily correspond to this price vector. To determine the actual set of prices—as distinct from the set of prices that will satisfy the value condition for continuous expansion—it is necessary to extend the long-period analysis of prices that has just been completed to the short period. This will be the task taken up in the remaining parts of this chapter.

6.2 The Megacorp and Oligopoly

We shall begin the analysis of how prices are actually determined in an advanced market economy like that of the United States by examining what is the more typical case, that of an oligopolistic industry consisting of one or more megacorps (see chapter 5, section 1.2). Only after deriving a determinate model of pricing under these circumstances will we take up, in the final part of this chapter, other models of industrial as well as commodity pricing.

The pricing model to be developed in this chapter is predicated on the very features which distinguish the megacorp from the type of firm usually assumed in economic analysis. One of these distinguishing features, the multiple plants which the megacorp operates, has already been the basis for positing a set of cost curves, and hence a cost function, that implies constant rather than decreasing returns to scale holding the A, K and L matrices and thus the technology constant (see chapter 5, part 3). Another of those distinguishing features, membership in at least one oligopolistic industry, will shortly be the basis for positing a corresponding revenue function. For the moment, however, the focus will be on another of the megacorp's distinguishing features, the separation of management from ownership. It is the separation of management from ownership, with the predominant control exercised by the former group, that suggests a quite different behavioral rule from that usually assumed in economic analysis.

6.2.1 The megacorp's behavioral rule

Ever since the publication of Adolf A. Berle and Gardiner C. Means's classic study, *The Modern Corporation and Private Property*, in 1932, it has been recognized by at least some economists that the goals pursued by the megacorp are not likely to be same as those of a neoclassical proprietorship. The reason they have questioned whether the megacorp seeks to maximize short-run profits is the *de facto* control exercised by the executive group as a self-perpetuating body of professional managers who need own no shares in the company. While there has been general agreement among this minority of economists that the megacorp cannot be described as simply seeking to maximize short-run profits, opinion has been divided over what behavioral rule should be substituted in its place. Within the literature two quite different approaches can be identified.

On the one side are those economists who have questioned whether the megacorp is able to maximize anything, be it profits or some other target variable. The reasons for doubting that the megacorp engages in maximizing behavior vary. For those who, like Herbert Simon and other behavioral theorists, have focused on the internal structure of the megacorp, it has to do with the difficulty of mobilizing any bureaucratic organization behind a single goal. Each department, it is argued, will pursue its own quite different objectives, and the outcome of this inherent conflict in the goals of the different departments can only be some compromise which falls short of what could maximally be achieved in terms of any one particular goal. For those who, like certain institutionalist economists, have focused on the megacorp's external situation, the explanation has to do with the lack of competitive pressure on the firm to maximize anything. As long as the megacorp can avoid serious blunders, its established position will enable it to survive—along with the industry or industries to which it belongs. It is thus survival, together with a ''quiet life,'' that is postulated as being the primary goal of the executives who control the megacorp. Some have even suggested that if the megacorp maximizes anything, it is likely to be the salaries, fringe benefits and other perquisites of the managerial class which controls the firm. From both perspectives, it is ''satisficing'' rather than maximizing behavior which characterizes the megacorp as a business organization.

On the other side of the question are the managerial theorists like William Baumol and Robin Marris who, while retaining the notion of maximizing behavior, have insisted that it is the growth of the firm rather than the amount of short-run profits that is being maximized. Among the managerial theorists the division of opinion has been over what is the most appropriate variable for measuring the growth of the firm. Is it sales, assets or some other variable? Still, this point of contention is less significant than the consensus among them that, for the executives who exercise effective control of the megacorp, the growth of the firm over time, because of the increase in power, prestige and remuneration which it brings in its wake, is the most important desideratum.

The model of oligopolistic pricing that will be developed in this chapter follows the latter approach. There are a number of reasons why this approach has been adopted over the other. First, while it is clear that megacorps generally pursue a number of different goals, many in conflict with one another, it is also clear that, other things being equal, one of those goals is generally given priority over the others. This is the goal of achieving the largest possible net revenue, or "profits." Indeed, the primacy attached to this goal is the basis for overcoming the diseconomies of scale that would otherwise make multiple-plant operation and other facets of the megacorp's decentralized mode of operation impractical. The recognized technique among megacorps for avoiding the diseconomies of scale inherent in large bureaucratic organizations is to establish a number of separate and coequal "profit centers," each of which is judged and evaluated by its ability to contribute to the organization's overall cash flow position. In this way, each of the subunits is given the maximum degree of freedom and discretion while still being held accountable for contributing to the success of the organization as a whole. While this argument would seem to represent a retreat from the view that megacorps do not attempt to maximize short-run profits, it will be seen that, when all the semantic confusions have been cleared up, what a firm must do to maximize the growth of profits over time is not the same as what it must do to maximize short-run profits.

Second, as much as executive group may favor a "quiet life," hoping to be left in tranquility until its members are able to retire with a pension, an examination of corporate histories strongly suggests that the megacorps which favor this goal tend to fare less well over time than those which pursue a maximum growth strategy. The reason is that, however secure the firm's position in a particular industry may be, there is no guarantee that the industry itself will survive over time, especially in the face of the rapid technical progress necessary for continous expansion of the economy. It turns out that those megacorps which are most likely to survive in the long run are the megacorps which have attempted to grow at the highest possible rate by continuously diversifying and expanding into newer, more rapidly growing industries. Thus it is the need to ensure survival that dictates maximum growth as the goal of the firm. Those firms which fail to expand apace with the economy are likely to find themselves at an increasing disadvantage on a number of fronts. These include the ability to attract new personnel as well as the ability to finance capital expenditures.

It is therefore growth maximization which, in the model of oligopolistic pricing to be developed in the sections which follow, will be the assumed goal of the megacorp as the representative firm under oligopoly. Moreover, this growth is to be measured by the rate of increase in the megacorp's internal cash flow, or residual income. It is through an increase in its internal cash flow that the megacorp's discretionary funds, and thus its command over the resources needed to assure its growth over time, will be maximized. Indeed, the megacorp's cash flow is what is meant by the term "discretionary funds" (see chapter 2, section 3.3). While the growth of assets and the growth of sales over time are likely to be closely correlated with the growth of the megacorp's internal cash flow, or discretionary funds, they are nonetheless not the same, with neither the growth of sales nor the growth of assets ensuring the maximum growth of the firm in the same way that the growth of cash flow, or discretionary funds, does.

In pursuing a growth maximizing strategy, the megacorp can be assumed to follow two simple behavioral rules.

One, insofar as any particular industry to which it is already committed is concerned, the megacorp will attempt at the very least to maintain, if not actually to increase, its current market share while simultaneously acting to minimize its costs of production. In general, a megacorp can realistically aim for a larger share of the market only if the industry is still at a relative early stage in its product-life cycle and/or the megacorp has only recently entered the industry. Once an industry has reached the mature, oligopolistic stage in its development, the share of the market held by any megacorp is unlikely to change significantly in ways that can be anticipated in advance. For a megacorp which has long been a member of a mature oligopolistic industry, maintaining the present share of that market is the only reasonable expectation. Nonetheless this goal, if realized, will assure the megacorp of a certain rate of growth of cash flow—assuming it is simultaneously able to maintain the same mark-up above costs. For with the megacorp's sales increasing at the same rate as the growth in demand for the industry's output, the megacorp's cash flow will, as long as the same mark-up is maintained, increase accordingly. Indeed, there is probably no way the cash flow being generated can grow more rapidly than by the megacorp succeeding in holding on to its present market share. Of course, to the extent that the megacorp is also able to continually reduce its costs of production, whether through the purchase of new equipment or other cost-reducing methods, while holding on to that same market share, the growth of its cash flow will be all the greater.

Two, insofar as the entire set of *n* industries is concerned, the megacorp will attempt to expand into any industry which, combining high growth prospects with an opportunity to transfer its managerial know-how, will enable the megacorp to increase the growth of its cash flow. Such an industry, it should be noted, is likely to be a relatively new one—an industry which, its economic viability having been demonstrated, now requires more resources to further develop and market the product than a neoclassical proprietorship can provide. It is in this way that not only does technical progress continually give rise to new oligopolistic industries but also megacorps are able to avoid the decline which necessarily attends any one industry. For at the same time the megacorp can be expected to undertake the investment needed to expand into newer, more rapidly growing industries, it can also be expected to begin withdrawing from the industries which, besides growing at a rate which is less than that for the economy as a whole, will require a net infusion of funds from the megacorp's sales in other industries just to maintain the existing market share. The withdrawal from the industry will entail a halt to any further capital outlays—except perhaps those which can be self-financed within the industry itself— until the existing capacity is sold or scrapped. The simultaneous expansion into newer, more rapidly growing industries and the withdrawal from older, stagnant industries is what enables the megacorp to maximize its own growth, as measured by the increase in cash flow, or discretionary funds, over time.

It should be noted, however, that the question of whether megacorps follow a growth maximizing stategy or whether, alternatively, their behavior can best be described as "satisficing" is far from being a settled one empirically. At the very least, one must acknowledge the constraints on a growth maximizing strategy suggested by some of the arguments made on behalf of the satisficing model. This means that the goal of maximizing growth is likely to be tempered by the survival-threatening factors which the heads of the various staff departments are likely to emphasize—e.g., antitrust and other legal restrictions by the chief counsel, collective bargaining and other personnel considerations by the vice president for industrial relations. There are also the constraints on the growth maximizing strategy which derive from the competing claims on the megacorp's net revenue. These claims, to be sure, include the higher salaries, fringe benefits and other perquisites required to satisfy the more individualistic goals of the managers. Still, the more important of these competing claims, quantitatively, are the higher dividends required to satisfy the income and capital gains goals of the megacorp's stockholder, or nominal owners (see chapter 8, section 3.4). All of these constraints need to be acknowledged in specifying growth as the principal goal, or maximand, of the megacorp.

The megacorp, then, can be assumed to act so as to maximize its own rate of growth, subject to a number of constraints—among them the need to maintain a certain rate of growth of dividends. In pursuit of this goal, the megacorp can be expected to follow two behavioral rules. One of these is that it will attempt to maintain, if not actually to enlarge, its share of the market in the industries to which it already belongs while simultaneoulsy undertaking whatever investment is necessary to lower its costs of production. The other behavioral rule is that it will attempt to expand into newer, more rapidly growing industries while simultaneously withdrawing from any older, relatively stagnant industries. These are the two behavioral rules which will enable the megacorp to maximize the growth of its cash flow, or discretionary funds, over time.

While the issue of whether the megacorp actually pursues a growth maximizing strategy as distinct from a satisficing one has yet to be resolved on empirical grounds, there is much less question about whether the megacorp seeks to maximize its net revenue, or profits, in the short run. As will become clear once the relationship between the firm and the industry has been clarified, it makes little sense for the megacorp, given the situation in which it typically finds itself, to pursue such a goal. Indeed, the empirical evidence would suggest that maximizing net revenue in the short run is not only contrary to what the megacorp actually attempts to do. It is also not possible.

6.2.2 The relationship of the firm to the industry

The third thing that distinguishes the megacorp from the neoclassical proprietorship, aside from the *de facto* control exercised by the executive group and the firm's ability to operate multiple plants at constant average variable costs, is its membership in at least one oligopolistic industry. This means that the megacorp is but one of several such firms which, together, account for most of the industry's sales. The fewness of the sellers, in turn, gives rise to the recognized interdependence which is the hallmark of oligopoly. As a result of this recognized interdependence, none of the firms which dominate the industry can take any action to increase its share of the market without forcing its rivals to respond in kind.

The recognized interdependence which is inherent in an oligpolistic situation has, ever since August Cournot turned his attention to the problem in the 1830s, defied the efforts of economic theorists to explain how a price is arrived at under the circumstances. Because the actions taken by any one firm to gain an advantage can readily be offset by the countermoves of its rivals, the price under oligopoly has seemed to be indeterminate. Only by making assumptions which fly in the face of the very interdependence which characterizes oligopoly, as in the classic Cournot and Bertrand-Edgeworth solutions to the problem, has it been possible to develop a determinate model of oligopolistic pricing. It is for this reason that the discussion of oligopolistic pricing in the standard microeconomic textbooks is notable mostly for the absence of any formal model.

What has long seemed an enigma to economic theorists has, however, found a practical solution among the executives of megacorps. The solution takes the form of what is known as "price leadership," with one firm—usually the one with the largest share of the market and/or the lowest costs of production—taking the initiative in announcing any change in the industry price. Still, what enables the system of price leadership to resolve the problem of recognized interdependence is not the fact that one firm can be counted on to take the initiative in announcing any change in price. Rather it is the expectation, based on past experience, that the other firms in the industry will match whatever change in price has been announced by the price leader, or dominant firm. It is the adherence to the new list price by all the other firms in the industry, once a change has been initiated by the price leader, that makes the price under oligopoly determinate. And while the system of price leadership is the particular mechanism by which this result is most generally achieved within the oligopolistic sector of the U.S. economy, any other mechanism which would induce firms to behave in a similar manner, whether it be regulation by an independent government commission or a legally enforceable cartel agreement, would serve as well. It is just that the system of price leadership, since it provides firms with a means of acting collectively that does not violate the country's antitrust laws, is the mechanism that has come to be favored by the megacorps operating outside the regulated sector of the U.S. economy.

What induces firms, under a system of price leadership, to match any change in price announced by the dominant firm is the very interdependent situation in which they find themselves. Early in the historical process by which an industry is

Exhibit 6.2

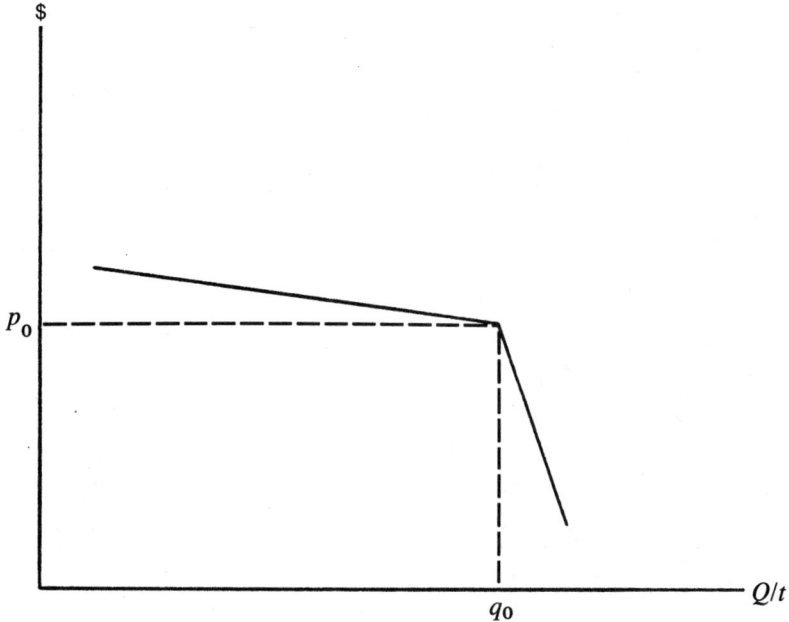

transformed into an oligopoly firms will come to recognize that they have lost the capacity to act independently of one another and that they are therefore caught on the corner point of the "kinked" demand curve shown in exhibit 6.2, which the individual firm in an oligopolistic industry faces. If the individual firm unilaterally attempts to raise its price above p_0, this as a way of increasing its profit margin, it can expect its customers to shift their business to one of the other firms which has maintained its price at p_0. It is for this reason that the individual firm's demand curve is depicted, to the left of the point representing the current price p_0, as being virtually horizontal, indicating an elasticity of demand over that range approaching, if not actually equal to, infinity. Alternatively, if the firm unilaterally attempts to lower its price below p_0, this as a way of boosting its sales, the other firms will have no choice but to lower their price by the same amount if they want to retain their customers. With all the firms now charging a lower price, the firm initiating the reduction in price will find itself frustrated in its efforts to increase its share of the market. The only gain in sales will be from whatever increase in demand the lower price has prompted. If, as is likely to be the case, the demand for the industry's product is price inelastic, then the increase in sales will be at the expense of each firm's net revenue. As a result, the profit margin on each unit sold, both by that firm and by every other firm in the industry, will be lower. It is for this reason that the individual firm's demand curve is depicted, to the right of the point representing the current price p_0, as having a slope the same as that of the industry demand curve and therefore as being inelastic.

What the kinked demand curve brings out is that, for the individual firm in an oligopolistic industry, it is best to adhere to the current list price rather than try to change it unilaterally. However, this does not mean that it is not in the interest of all the firms collectively to have a different price established. Indeed, with the circumstances in an industry changing continuously, it is unlikely that any price will remain optimal, or even tolerable, for long. This is where the system of price leadership fills an essential need. It enables the firms in an oligopolistic industry to establish a new price collectively, something they would not be able to do individually. The collective nature of the decision is evidenced by the other firms matching, rather than undercutting, the new list price announced by the dominant firm. Even if the new price is, from the point of view of any one firm, less than an optimal one, it is still likely to be a more favorable price than the one which would prevail in the absence of the price-matching behavior.

The self-interest of the individual firms in following a collective approach to pricing is only the carrot that reinforces the behavior underlying the system of price leadership. There is also the stick. When a firm refuses to abide by the rules, insisting instead on establishing its own price unilaterally, the price leader must be prepared to retaliate, either by reducing prices to the level being charged by the maverick firm or, if the price leader wishes to drive the lesson home with particular force, by cutting the price even further. Indeed, what establishes a particular firm as the price leader is its willingness to suffer the losses necessary from time to time to bring any recalcitrant member of the industry back into line. Usually it takes only a short period of vigorous price cutting to convince the firm that its demand curve is indeed kinked downward and that it only stands to lose by not matching the dominant firm's price. Thus the behavior underlying a system of price leadership is usually behavior learned from painful experience.

It is, of course, possible that the price leader will be unable to force one of the other firms to match its list price—in which case a new price leader may well emerge. The establishment of a new price leader is especially likely if the maverick firm, even if it has not yet succeeded in capturing the largest share of the market, is nonetheless the least-cost producer as a result of having invested in the newest, technologically most advanced plant and equipment. Still, once the establishment of a new price leader has been acknowledged by the other firms matching whatever change in price *it* announces, the industry will once again have settled down into the stable pattern of price leadership and, even more importantly, of "price followship" that characterizes oligopoly.

The megacorp, when it functions as the price leader, can be assumed to be acting on behalf of the entire industry. It is not just the obeissance of the other firms to whatever change in price has been announced. It is also the objective circumstances which dictate (1) that no other firm is likely to have lower costs and therefore be better able to withstand a lower price should one emerge from any interfirm rivalry, and (2) that the elasticity of demand faced by the price leader will be the same as that faced by every other firm—as well as being the same as that faced by the industry as a whole. The reason why no other firm is likely to have lower costs has already been explained. Some other firm with lower costs that wants to set a limit on the mark-up above costs and therefore on the industry price can readily do so—and in the process, if it is willing to bear the cost of any ensuing price war, become the price leader. What still remains to be explained is why the price leader is likely to be faced with the same elasticity of demand as every other firm, regardless of that other firm's market share. In clearing up this point, it will become clear why, as long as the analysis is restricted to the short period, the price within an oligopolistic industry remains indeterminate and why it is only by expanding the time frame to encompass the long period that a determinate model of oligopolistic pricing can be constructed.

6.2.3 The short-period indeterminancy of price

When, as under a system of price leadership, the other firms simply match whatever change in price is announced by the dominant firm, it is no longer the price that will determine the quantity sold by each firm. The quantity sold will instead depend on other factors—the level of aggregate demand insofar as total industry sales are concerned and each firm's individual selling effort insofar as relative market shares are concerned. What this means is that, while the quantity sold will vary inversely with the price, each firm's share of the market is likely to remain unchanged whatever the price. Indeed, a system of price leadership has come to be established in virtually every oligopolistic industry precisely because it leads to this result. Under a system of price leadership, then, the industry and individual firm demand curves will be similar to those shown in exhibit 6.3, with each firm, including the industry price leader, supplying the same relative proportion of the total quantity demanded at each possible price. While the curves shown in exhibit 6.3 have been drawn on the assumption that one firm, the price leader, accounts for half of the industry's sales and only two other firms (each supplying 25 percent of the market) account for all the rest, the relationship between the industry demand curve and the individual firm demand curves would be the same no matter how many firms constituted the industry and what were their relative shares of the market—as long as all the other firms simply matched whatever change in price was announced by the price leader. The only difference would be the number of separate demand curves that would need to be drawn to represent each firm and the relative slope of each. With this point in mind, it can now be demonstrated that the elasticity of demand faced by each firm, including the price leader, will be the same as the elasticity of demand for the industry's product as a whole at every point along the respective demand curves they face.

To see this, one need only rewrite the equation defining the elasticity of demand (see chapter 9, equation 2) so that it takes the following form:

$$e = \frac{\Delta Q}{\Delta p} * \frac{p_0}{Q_0} \qquad (6.41)$$

The price elasticity of demand at point R on the industry demand curve shown in exhibit 6.3 is thus equal to the inverse of that demand curve's slope, $\Delta Q/\Delta p$, multiplied by the price-quantity ratio, p_0/Q_0. For a megacorp price leader which, like the one represented in exhibit 6.3, accounts for half the industry's sales, the slope of its demand curve, D_a, at any given price, p_0, will be only half the slope of the industry demand curve at that point, and thus the inverse of the slope of that demand curve will be twice that of the industry demand curve. This two-fold greater value for the inverse of the slope will, however, be offset by a price/quantity ratio which is only half that of the industry—with the result that the price elasticity of demand at price p_0 is the same for both the industry and the megacorp-price leader. By a similar line of reasoning it can be shown that the price elasticity of demand at price p_0 is also the same for every other member of the industry—as, for example, the other two firms which, as assumed in exhibit 6.3, each supply 25 percent of the market.

With the demand curve faced by the megacorp-price leader virtually the same as the industry demand curve, at least insofar as the elasticity of demand at any

Exhibit 6.3

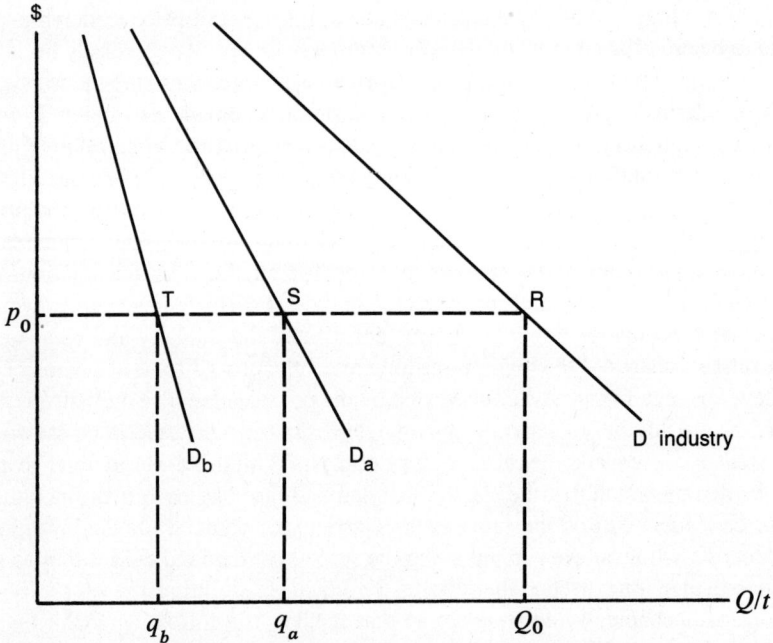

given price is concerned, it is tempting to treat oligopoly as simply a form of monopoly with the additional complication that the pricing behavior of the different firms constituting the industry must somehow be coordinated. One can then turn to the model of monopolistic pricing developed independently by Edward Chamberlin and Joan Robinson in the 1930s to explain how the price in any oligopolistic industry will be determined. With the price leader facing a negatively sloped demand curve, such as D_a in exhibit 6.3, it will then need only to equate its marginal revenue, as shown in exhibit 6.4, with its marginal cost in order to maximize its net revenue. Indeed, this is precisely what the dominant firm is assumed to do in the type of model most widely used by economists to explain oligopolistic pricing behavior. (While the megacorp's marginal costs are depicted in exhibit 6.4 as being constant over the relevant range to conform with what has previously been argued, the conclusion would be the same if, as is more commonly assumed, its marginal costs are rising. The profit-maximizing level of output will still be where the marginal cost curve intersects the marginal revenue curve.

It is a relatively easy matter, however, to show that this Chamberlin-Robinson model is of little relevance in explaining how prices are determined under oligopoly. (The usefulness of the model in explaining any differential in price *among* the firms in an industry, especially outside the oligopolistic core of the economy, is another matter—one that will be taken up shortly. See section 6.4.3). The available evidence strongly suggests that industries are likely to find themselves on the inelastic portion of their demand curves, with the absolute value of e less than 1. This means they are likely to find themselves to the right of the point of unitary elasticity which, as shown in exhibit 6.5, must necessarily bisect the demand curve when that curve is extended so that it cuts both axes. It is the cumulative effect of technical progress in lowering the cost of production, and thereby requiring an increasingly smaller portion of total income to purchase that good, which shifts the industry from the left to the right of the point of unitary elasticity on its demand curve over time (see chapter 9, section 1.4). But once the industry is to the right of that point, that is, when it is on the inelastic portion of its demand curve, the marginal revenue will, as shown in exhibit 6.5, necessarily be negative. This is because of the mathematical relationship which holds between the average and marginal revenue—in particular, because of the fact that, at any given price, the slope of the marginal revenue curve will be twice that of the average revenue curve. Since there is no way that a negative marginal revenue curve can be equated with a positive marginal cost of production (the marginal cost would be negative only if *total* costs declined as output expanded), it can be seen why the Chamberlin-Robinson model is suspect as an explanation of how the price is determined in an oligopolistic industry.

What is being questioned here is not the logic of the model but rather the validity of the underlying assumption that the representative type of firm within an oligopolistic industry, a megacorp, seeks to maximize its net revenue in the

Exhibit 6.4

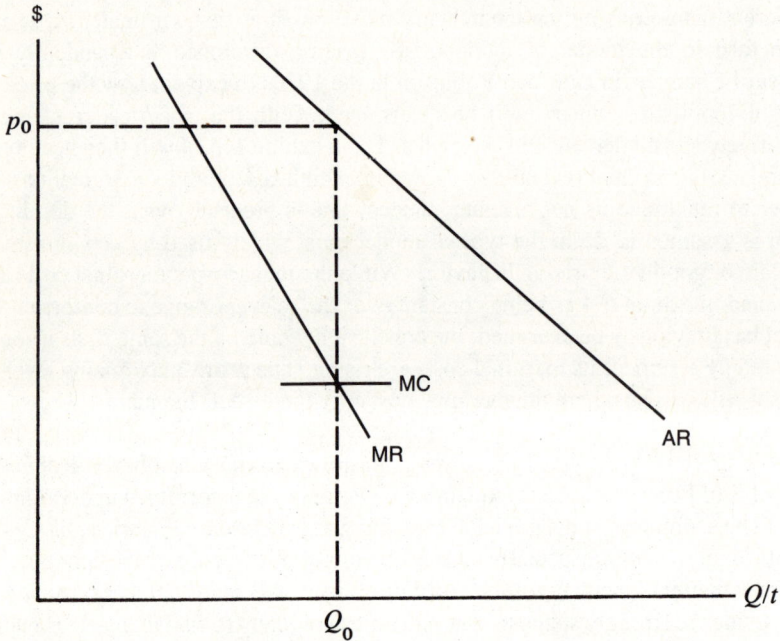

short period. It has already been pointed out, in discussing the behavioral rule of
the megacorp (see section 6.2.1) that this assumption is inappropriate, given the
nature of the megacorp's governing body—a self-perpetuating group of executives with only minimal equity holdings in the company. Now it can be seen that
the assumption is also inconsistent with what is known about the price elasticity of
demand in most oligopolistic industries. The fact is that one can understand the
pricing behavior of the megacorp and the industry for which it is the price leader
only by shifting to the same time perspective as that which governs such a firm.
This means shifting the analysis of pricing behavior from a short-period to a long-
period perspective. Any change in price will necessarily occur in the historical
moment of the short period. However, the basis for that change in price will be a
set of long-period considerations. And the most important of those long-period
considerations will be the need to finance the investment that the expansion of the
firm, along with the expansion of the industry and the overall economy, requires.

6.3 The Size of the Markup under Oligopoly

Given its own organizational goals and the role it plays as surrogate for the
industry as a whole, the megacorp-price leader, it can be assumed, will attempt to
establish a price for its output sufficient not just to cover its other costs of
production but also to provide the necessary profit margin to meet its long-term

Exhibit 6.5

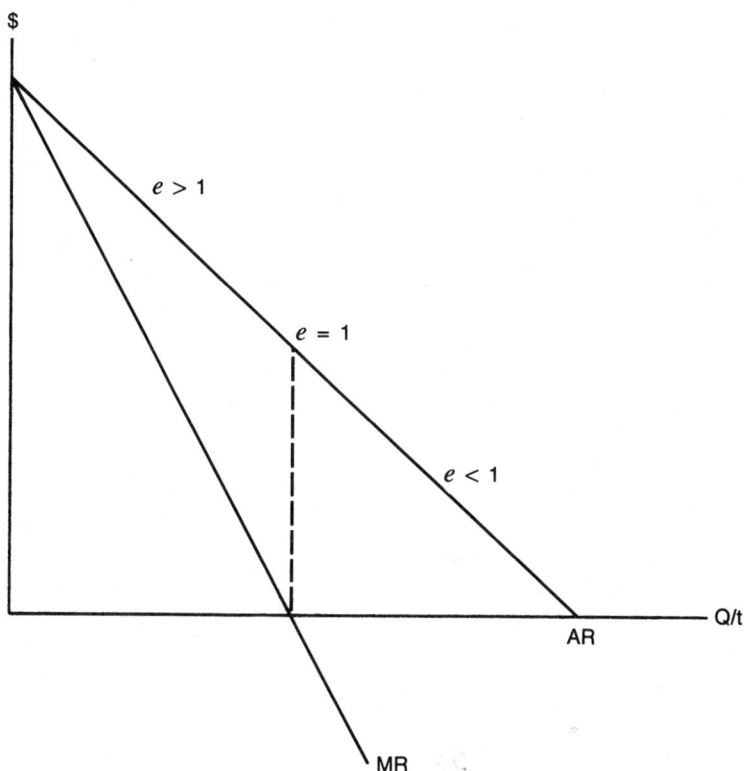

expansion needs. Indeed, it is in this way that the megacorp, as the representative firm, serves the important function of ensuring that the value condition for continuous economic growth is satisfied. There are thus two types of costs which determine the long-period price in an oligopolistic industry that is part of an expanding economy. They are (1) the costs of producing the current level of output, and (2) the costs of expansion, both within the industry itself and into other, more rapidly growing industries.

The costs of expansion, it can be assumed, will be met by applying a certain markup, m_j, to the other costs of production, c_j, so that, as previously explained (see section 6.1.4), the following relationship is satisfied in the long period:

$$p_j = (1+m_j)c_j \qquad (6.27)$$

where

$$m_j = \frac{g_j b_j}{1-(g_j b_j)} \qquad (6.29)$$

Indeed, this is simply the value condition that each industry will need to satisfy if it is going to be able to expand at the rate dictated by the growth of the overall economy. Still, one cannot simply take for granted that the megacorp-price leader will be able to establish a markup as given by equation 6.29. The markup actually established by the megacorp-price leader may be less—or it may be higher. To determine which, we need to examine the factors that actually determine the size of the markup in the short period, that is, at the point in historical time at which firms actually find themselves.

6.3.1 Short-period price movements

The megacorp-price leader, in attempting to establish any list price, will find itself buffeted in the short period by various disruptive events. The most important of these disruptive events, insofar as the price level itself is concerned, will be any change in the prices that must be paid for inputs, both material and human resource, and any change in the industry growth rate, g_j. (A third type of disruptive event would be any price "shaving" by the other firms in the industry. This third possibility will, however, be ignored—at least for the moment—by assuming that the megacorp's price leadership remains unchallenged. However, see section 6.4.3.) As a result of these short-period disruptive events to which the industry is subject, the list price will have to be adjusted periodically so as to enable the megacorp-price leader, together with the other firms in the industry, to move closer to obtaining the optimal long-period price for its output. Thus the change in list price which can be observed empirically in the short period in each oligopolistic industry will depend on two factors: (1) any change in the costs of production, c_j, since the last change in the list price, and (2) any change in the industry growth rate, g_j.

The short-period change in the costs of production has already been discussed and analyzed. These costs include both the direct, or variable, costs and the indirect, or fixed, costs of production. As already pointed out (see chapter 5, section 3.2), the megacorp's direct costs of production can be assumed either to be constant or not to vary significantly within the relevant limits, that is, between 70 and 95 percent of engineer-rated capacity (ERC). This means that, over that likely range of output, both the marginal costs (MC) and the average variable costs (AVC) will be either constant or nearly so. While the per unit indirect and/or fixed costs will necessarily fall as output is expanded, an average expected figure can be obtained by relying on the standard operating ratio (SOR). This is the percent of engineer-rated capacity at which, based on the industry's past history of cyclical movements in sales and output, the megacorp can normally expect to operate. Indeed, the expansion of productive capacity will ordinarily be planned with that cyclical volatility in mind (see chapter 7, section 2.2). The standard operating ratio, when applied to the megacorp's engineer-rated capacity, provides an estimate of the firm's expected level of output, and this estimate of expected output can then serve as the denominator for calculating the expected average fixed costs. In this way it is possible for the megacorp to determine its likely costs of production *ex ante*, that is, in advance of any actual production. Relying on the standard operating ratio to abstract from any possible cyclical movements in industry demand, the megacorp-price leader is able to estimate its costs of production, c_j, as follows:

$$c_j = \text{AVC} + \frac{\text{FC}}{\text{SOR*ERC}} \tag{6.42}$$

where AVC, FC, SOR and ERC are all as previously defined. The average variable costs, it should be noted, include both material and labor costs while the fixed costs include, aside from the material and labor costs of administration and staff services, any debt service, DS, long-term as well as short-term. With constant returns to scale, these costs will not change, at least in the short period, even if the level of output should vary, unless the prices that must be paid for those inputs—both material and labor—change. It is for this reason that one must look to a change in the prices paid for material and labor inputs in order to explain any short-period change in the megacorp-price leader's costs of production, c_j.

Any change in the megacorp-price leader's direct and indirect costs will therefore depend on the prices being charged by the other industries which supply it with material inputs (as well as with services, including financial services). It will thus depend on the same interindustry relationships which govern production, though with the input-output table viewed as a set of interdependent prices rather than a set of interdependent product flows. With each industry assumed to price its output in the same manner and the prices of the material inputs dependent on the prices being charged by other industries, the determining factor, insofar as the costs of production are concerned, becomes the cost of any inputs besides the material ones represented by the A matrix. And the only other inputs besides the material ones are the labor, or human resource, inputs. The costs of production for the enterprise sector are thus largely reducible to the cost of labor, as already brought out in the discussion of the Pasinetti model of vertically integrated production (see chapter 5, section 4.1). The same is true even for the individual megacorp since it can expect its material costs of production to change largely in line with the general trend of labor costs. The only exceptions are industries which rely heavily on material inputs which are either imported from other countries or purchased in commodity markets. (See section 6.4.1; chapter 11, section 0.0, and chapter 13, section 3.4, for a further discussion of these exceptions.) These exceptions aside, one can equate any change in the megacorp's costs of production with a change in its unit labor costs. It will be a change in those unit labor costs, wl_j, that will largely prefigure a change in the megacorp's costs of production in the short period.

To discuss what determines the change in unit labor costs in the short period would, at this point, be premature. That discussion must wait until the factors affecting the rates of compensation received by the working members of the household sector have been identified, and this will not be done until the household sector, together with the question of income distribution, can be taken up in a systematic way (see chapter 8). For now all that need be noted is that, whatever the determining factors, a change in the megacorp-price leader's unit labor costs are likely to be followed by a change in the list price so that the price leader, together with the other firms in the industry, will be able to maintain the same profit margin, μ, or, looking at it from a slightly different perspective, the same mark-up, m. If the firms in the industry must obtain a significant portion of their material inputs in foreign and/or commodity markets, then a change in world commodity prices will also be followed by a change in the list price. Otherwise, the change in list price, with the mark-up held constant, will depend solely on the change in unit labor costs. That is,

$$\Delta p = \Delta U_L, \bar{m} \qquad (6.43)$$

where U_L represents the unit labor costs, wl_j, and the industry subscript has been dropped from the other variables as well.

Should the list price not rise in line with an increase in unit labor costs, the markup, m, will necessarily fall—unless, of course, there is an offsetting decline in the other costs of production. Why the megacorp price leader will want to avoid having the markup reduced in this manner can best be understood by considering the alternative case in which the unit labor costs of production are held constant and any change in the list price will then be due to a change in the markup. In other words, it is first necessary to analyze the situation represented by the following equation:

$$\Delta p = \Delta m, \bar{U}_L \qquad (6.44)$$

This in fact is the case that will be emphasized throughout the rest of this chapter—a discussion of the alternative possibility, a rise in unit labor costs while the markup remains unchanged, being left to the later chapters.

As already pointed out, the markup is essential for enabling the megacorp-price leader and the other firms in an oligopolistic industry to obtain the net cash inflow, or discretionary funds, needed to finance their expansion over time. The failure to maintain whatever markup has been established by the megacorp-price leader acting as surrogate for the industry as a whole will therefore impair the industry's ability to expand at the rate dictated by the industry growth rate, g. It will prevent not only the necessary value condition from being realized but also the necessary supply condition as well. The size of the markup thus depends on the industry growth rate, g (as well as the incremental capital-output ratio, b). However, the precise relationship between the industry's rate of expansion and the size of the markup in the short period is a more complicated one than that which holds in the long period. On the one hand, the megacorp-price leader and the other firms in the industry must be able to discern what the industry's rate of expansion is likely to be and then translate that perceived secular growth rate into plans for adding to their productive capacity. Moreover, this use of the funds to be generated through the markup must be weighed against the alternative uses of the same funds, including diversification into other industries. This first set of factors falls under the rubric of the demand for additional investment funds, D_I. On the other hand, the megacorp-price leader and the other firms in the industry cannot increase the size of the markup without taking into account what will be the effect on their long-term position within the industry—even with all the firms fully adhering to the same set of list prices. Moreover, the internal funds generated through the markup can be supplemented by resort to external financing. This second set of factors falls under the rubric of the supply cost of additional investment funds, S_I. More precisely, then, any change in the markup in the short period, holding unit labor and the other direct costs of production constant, will depend on the demand for additional investment funds relative to the supply cost of those additional investment funds. That is,

$$\Delta m = f(D_I, S_I) \tag{6.45}$$

The megacorp-price leader's demand for additional investment funds will be discussed at greater length in the next chapter. To briefly anticipate that discussion, it need only be pointed out that the industry's expansion over time, along with that of the economy as a whole, will confront the megacorp-price leader with the need to expand its productive capacity apace, and that added to this demand for investment funds will be certain other capital spending projects for which a return above costs, or marginal efficiency of investment, r, can be calculated. The megacorp-price leader, it can therefore be posited, is governed by a demand curve for additional investment funds which, at the margin, depends on r— calculated as the increased cash flow that will be generated from the investment being carried out relative to the cash outlay required. With the megacorp-price leader's demand for additional investment funds, D_I, explained in this manner, it is possible to proceed with a discussion of the supply cost of additional investment funds, S_I.

6.3.2 The supply cost of internally generated funds

The megacorp, it must be kept in mind, has the choice of financing any additional investment outlays either internally by increasing the markup or externally by arranging for a loan. It is the first of these two options that will now be examined in depth. While the other possibility, that of resorting to external financing, will be formally incorporated into the model of oligopolistic pricing that is shortly to be presented, an extended treatment of this option must wait (see chapter 7, part 3).

If the markup could be increased without any adverse effect, there would be no limit to the size of the markup and the price itself would be unbounded. For a firm can always find some use for the additional funds a higher markup will generate—to boost the salaries of its own executives, if not to raise the dividend rate or finance a higher level of investment. Thus, the very fact that the price in an industry is not greater than it already is can be taken as evidence that there is some adverse effect from increasing the size of the markup which the firms in that industry would prefer to avoid. Properly transformed, the adverse effect becomes the implicit cost incurred by the megacorp-price leader and the other members of the industry whenever the markup is increased. It is this implicit cost which will then serve as the effective constraint on the pricing power of these firms when, acting collectively through a system of price leadership or its functional equivalent, they establish a new list price. The implicit cost of a higher markup, R, measures the adverse effect on a firm's long-run ability to generate cash flow due to (1) the substitution effect, (2) the entry factor, and (3) the possibility of government intervention.

The substitution effect reflects the fact that, as the relative price of a good increases, customers are more likely to switch to whatever is the closest substitute produced by some other industry. The resulting lost of sales is what is meant by the substitution effect, and it depends on the arc elasticity of demand, e, between the point along the industry demand curve where the current list price places the megacorp-price leader and all the other firms in the industry and the point higher up on the same industry demand curve where the new list price will place those same firms.

Consider, for example, an increase in the industry's list price from p_0 to p_1, as shown in exhibit 6.6, which follows from establishing a higher mark-up equal to that differential in price. The loss in industry sales will be the difference between Q_0 and Q_1, with this decline in industry sales dependent on the arc elasticity of demand between points G and A. This loss of sales will be shared proportionately by all the firms in the industry, including the price leader. Keep in mind that, as pointed out in the preceding subsection, the average revenue curve faced by the megacorp-price leader is but a reduced-scale version of the industry demand curve, and that therefore exhibit 6.6, with the quantities Q_0 and Q_1 shown along the horizontal axis changed to q_0 and q_1 respectively to reflect the price leader's share of total sales, would apply to that firm as well. Indeed, with Q_0 and Q_1 changed to reflect the appropriate market share, the average revenue curve shown in exhibit 6.6 would apply to any firm in the industry.

The decline in cash flow, due to the substitution effect, is represented in exhibit 6.6 by the rectangle **BGFE**. It is equal to the marginal cash flow—the difference between the price and the marginal cost—on the output which no longer be sold at the higher list price (see chapter 7, section 3.1 for an explication

Exhibit 6.6

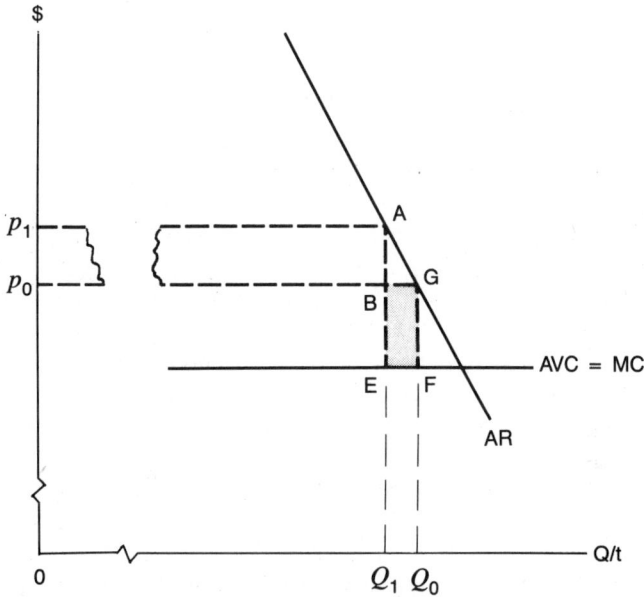

of the distinction between the marginal and average rates at which cash flow is generated). However, as shown in exhibit 6.6, this loss of cash flow is more than offset by the additional cash flow being generated, at the higher mark-up, on the output which, even after the increase in price, continues to be sold. This gain in cash flow is represented in exhibit 6.6 by the rectangle p_1ABp_0, and it is equal to the increased cash flow being generated on the reduced level of sales. Thus, in the situation depicted in exhibit 6.6, the net substitution effect is negative. This, it can be assumed, is the situation which will actually hold in an oligopolistic industry in the time period immediately following any attempt to increase the markup by raising the list price. What this means is that the megacorp-price leader will not be constrained, when deciding what markup to establish, by the immediate substitution effect. Such a result follows from the fact that, as already pointed out, the elasticity of demand in an oligopolistic industry is likely to be less than 1, with the industry thus on the inelastic portion of its demand curve. Whether, when the megacorp price leader extends its time horizon to encompass subsequent time periods, the net substitution effect becomes positive, thereby constraining the megacorp in deciding what markup to establish, is another matter—one that will be gone into shortly. First it is necessary to explain the entry factor.

The entry factor reflects the fact that, as the markup is increased due to the absolute rise in the price relative to costs, new firms will find it easier to overcome the barriers to entry that, as one of the distinguishing features of oligopoly, previously prevented them from entering the industry. This is because the higher markup, or margin above costs, will better enable them to offset the cost disadvantages they face. If, as a result of the higher markup, new firms (including those already members of other industries) should succeed in gaining entry, the established firms will find their relative shares of the market reduced. The resulting decline in the sales of these established firms, including that of the price leader, is what is meant by the entry factor, and it depends on the probability, γ, that a new firm of minimal optimum size $\hat{Q}$ will enter the industry following an increase in the markup.

Consider the same increase in the industry's list price, from p_0 to p_0, which follows from establishing a higher markup—but as now further elaborated in exhibit 6.7 to take into account the entry factor as well. The shift in the average revenue curve for all the established firms in the industry from AR to AR′ represents the expected impact of the entry by a new firm, one which must supply a certain minimal proportion, d, of the industry's total output in order to realize all the economies of production. As can be seen, the sales of the established firms will fall from Q_0 to Q_0′—a decrease equal to the output that must be sold by the new firm to minimize its costs of production, $\hat{Q}$ or $d(Q_0)$, multiplied by the probability, γ, that a firm of this size will actually enter the industry following an increase in the mark-up. Again, with the other established firms continuing to match whatever list price is announced by the dominant firm, this decline in sales will be shared proportionally by all the members of the industry including the price leader so that, with the quantity Q_0′ changed to q_0′ to reflect the latter's share of the market, exhibit 6.7 would apply to that firm as well.

Notice that the decline in cash flow in the immediate time period, due to the entry factor, is given by the rectangle G′GFF′. It is equal to the marginal cash flow on the output which, as a result of the loss of market share to the new entrant, can no longer be sold. There is also, of course, the additional decline in cash flow due to the substitution effect—equal now to the rectangle B′G′F′E′. The two together, rectangle B′GFE′, represent the combined loss, due to both the substitution effect and the entry factor, from raising the industry price in order to establish a higher markup. Even with the entry factor now taken into account, this combined loss will still be less than the gain in cash flow from increasing the markup on the output which contines to be sold, as given by rectangle p_1A′B′p_0. Thus, in the time period immediately following an attempt to establish a higher markup, as depicted in exhibit 6.7, not even the combined substitution effect and the entry factor are likely to be positive, thereby constraining the megacorp-price leader in deciding what new list price to announce.

Insofar as the entry factor is concerned, this is because the entry of a new firm into the industry cannot take place at once. At least several years will be required to give the potential new entrant time to study the situation, plan its move into the industry and then implement those plans. It is only as the megacorp-price leader

Exhibit 6.7

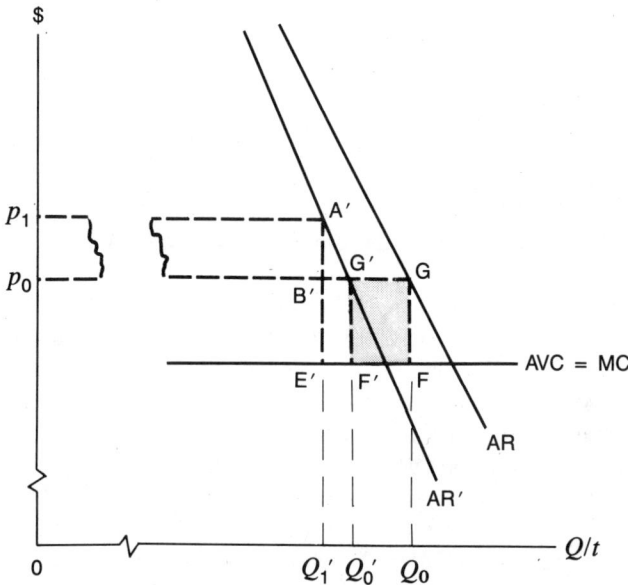

extends its time horizon beyond the immediate period and considers the longer-run impact of its decision to increase the markup that the entry factor is likely to become a significant constraint on its pricing behavior. That is,

$$\gamma = f(t) \qquad (6.46)$$

where γ is the probability of a new firm of minimal optimal size $\hat{Q}$ entering a particular oligopolistic industry, as judged by the megacorp-price leader, and t is the number of pricing periods which the megacorp-price leader takes into account in considering the long-term impact of any new price it may announce.

The perceived probability of new entry depends not only on how long is the megacorp-price leader's time horizon, as measured by t, but also on the extent to which the markup is to be increased. The greater the increase in the size of the markup being contemplated, the greater the probability of attracting new firms into the industry once the new list price is announced. This is because a potential new entrant will be better able to overcome the cost disadvantage from which it suffers, and thus the barriers to entry, the greater is the size of the markup. That is,

$$\gamma = f(\Delta m) \qquad (6.47)$$

Indeed, there is reason to believe that, because the decision to enter an industry is based on passing a certain critical point insofar as the margin above costs is concerned, the probability of new entry, γ, is an exponentially increasing function of the contemplated increase in the size of the markup, Δm. As the size of the markup becomes larger, the probability of new entry increases disproportionately. Since it will necessarily take time for any new entry to occur, the probability of entry function needs to specified as follows:

$$\gamma = f(\Delta m, t) \tag{6.48}$$

with the relationship between γ and Δm, if not between γ and t, an exponential one.

Essentially the same argument applies in the case of the substitution effect. It takes time for purchasers of a particular good to make the necessary adjustments, both in technology and, to the extent it applies, in tastes, if they are to utilize a substitute product. As a number of empirical studies have shown, the elasticity of demand increases as the time horizon is extended. Similarly, since each increase in the relative price of a good pushes the industry supplying that good further up on its demand curve, moving it closer to the elastic portion of that curve (see exhibit 6.5), the substitution effect will be greater, as reflected by the arc elasticity of demand, the larger is the increase in the list price announced by the dominant firm on behalf of the entire industry. That is,

$$e = f(\Delta m, t) \tag{6.49}$$

where the change in the markup, Δm, can be equated with a change in relative price on the assumption that the prices of all other goods remain unchanged. Indeed, with the arc elasticity of demand likely to increase disproportionately as the size of the markup is increased, there is reason to believe that the relationship between e and Δm if not between e and t is an exponential one.

Since the substitution effect and the entry factor depend on the same set of factors, they can be analyzed conjointly—even though the response will be different in each case. Holding the change in the markup, Δm, constant, one can say that both the substitution effect and the entry factor will depend on the time horizon of the megacorp-price leader. The further that firm peers into the future in considering the impact of its decision to increase the markup, the greater will be the importance of both the substitution effect and the entry factor in influencing that decision. If the time horizon extends beyond a certain point in time, the two factors together may even become positive. This means that the loss of cash flow due to both the substitution effect and the entry factor, as given in exhibit 6.7 by rectangle B$'$GFE$'$, will exceed the gain in cash flow from the higher markup on the output which continues to be sold, as given by rectangle p_1A$'$B$'p_0$. In other words, as the megacorp attempts to assess the long-term impact of a higher markup, it may come to recognize that, beyond a certain point in time, its rate of cash flow may well be reduced below what it is at present.

The fact that its cash flow, or discretionary funds, may eventually be reduced below the current level as a result of the decision to establish a higher markup does not necessarily mean, however, that the megacorp-price leader will decide against incorporating the higher markup into its list price. The eventual decline in cash flow, if it should actually be experienced, will occur some time in the future. In the interim, the megacorp-price leader, along with the other firms in the industry, will have the additional funds which the higher markup will enable them to generate. Those additional funds can be used in ways, including cost reduction and diversification into other industries, that may more than offset the eventual decline in cash flow. In effect, the markup serves as an instrumental variable for regulating the megacorp's intertemporal cash flow, with the decision of how high to set the markup depending on how great will be the eventual cost, due to the combined substitution effect and entry factor, relative to how great will be the returns from the investment which the higher markup will enable the megacorp to finance in the interim.

6.3.3 The implicit interest rate, R

It is possible, by taking into account the time pattern, both of the anticipated eventual decline in cash flow due to the combined substitution effect and entry factor and of the additional investment funds that will be obtained in the interim, to derive an implicit interest rate, R, on those internally generated funds. In determining what would be the equivalent of the interest rate that would have to be paid if the same amount of funds were to be obtained through a loan from some external source, one need only keep in mind the following:

1) The principal, which would serve as the denominator in calculating the interest rate on the loan, would be a single lump sum obtained at once rather than an amount which would build up gradually over time (though at a decreasing rate) between the time the higher markup was established and the subsequent point in time when the combined substitution effect and entry factor became positive;

2) the amount of interest specified in the loan agreement, which serves as the numerator in calculating the interest rate, would have to be paid at once rather than being delayed until the combined substitution effect and entry factor became positive, and

3) these interest payments would remain at a fixed level rather than increasing over time as both the substitution effect and the entry factor became more powerful.

With these three points in mind, it is then possible to apply the appropriate discount factors to both the eventual probable decline in cash flow and to the additional investment funds obtained in the interim so as to derive R, the implicit interest rate on any additional cash flow, or discretionary funds, generated as a result of establishing a higher markup.

The formula for calculating the value of R is as follows:

$$R = \frac{C_F}{Prin} \qquad (6.50)$$

where C_F is the implicit cost of any internally generated funds, transformed into the equivalent of a certain amount of interest paid each time period following the rise in price, with the value of C_F determined as follows:

$$C_F = \frac{\dfrac{1}{t-(s-1)} \sum\limits_{j=1}^{t} [q_0{*}MCF_0(|e_j| + \gamma_j{*}d)] - [p_0{*}q_0(1 - \dot{p}[\,|e_j| + \gamma_j{*}d])]}{(1+r)^{s-1}} \qquad (6.51)$$

and *Prin* is the principal sum obtained over the time interval t as a result of increasing the price, with the value of Prin determined as follows:

$$Prin = \sum_{j=1}^{s-1} \frac{[p_0{*}q_0(1 - \dot{p}[\,|e_j| + \gamma{*}d])] - [q_0{*}MCF_0(\,|e_j| + \gamma_j{*}d)]}{(1+r)^{j}} \qquad (6.52)$$

where t is the number of time periods taken into account by the megacorp-price leader in considering a possible change in the mark-up and hence in the industry price; s is the time period during which the combined substitution effect and entry factor is expected to become positive (with $s < t$); q_0 is the quantity of output sold by the firm prior to any change in price; MCF_0 is the marginal cash flow, or price less marginal costs, being generated on that level of output; $\dot{p}$ is the proportional change in price, $\Delta p/p$, being considered; r is some time preference factor, such as the return on investment and/or the firm's target rate of growth, which applies to the firm (see chapter 7, section 2.2), and e, γ and d are as previously specified.

It should be noted that the $[q_0{*}MCF_0(\,|e_j| + \gamma_j{*}d)]$ term in the above two equations represents the loss, in any given time period, due to the combined substitution effect and the entry factor. It therefore corresponds to the rectangle B′GFE′ in exhibit 6.7. The $[p_0{*}q_0(1 - \dot{p}[\,|e_j| + \gamma_j{*}d])]$ term, meanwhile, represents the greater cash flow being generated on the output that is still likely to be sold following the rise in price. It therefore corresponds to the rectangle p_1A′B′p_0 in exhibit 6.7. The discount factors, $(1 + r)^{s-1}$ and $(1 + r)^{j}$, in each of the two equations are used to determine the present value of both the subsequent eventual decline in the amount of cash flow being generated and the principal sum likely to be realized in the interim (see chapter 7, section 1.1, for a discussion of discounting). The

$$\frac{1}{t - (s - 1)} \sum_{j=1}^{t}$$

term in equation 6.51 converts the eventual loss, due to the combined substitution effect and entry factor, into an average loss per time period while the summation sign in equation 6.52 aggregates the net gain in cash flow between time periods 1 and s so that the principal sum that would be obtained from the rise in price can be determined.

While it is thus possible to convert the cost to the firm of establishing a higher markup, due to the combined substitution effect and entry factor, into an implicit interest rate on the additional cash flow, or investment funds, thereby obtained, it is just as likely that the megacorp-price leader will be governed by what it considers the maximum acceptable risk of new entry, γ_x. This is because the entry of a new firm into the industry, aside from whatever loss of relative market share it may portend, is likely to upset whatever price coordination and maintenance arrangements have been worked out among the existing firms within the industry. The new firm, if it is to sell enough of its product to realize the production economies upon which its decision to enter the industry was based, must capture the requisite share of the market, d. And to do this, as a firm offering an unknown and untested product, it will almost certainly be forced initially to sell its output at a price below that of the other firms in the industry. This price shaving may well lead to a breakdown of the community of interest among the established firms within the industry and to a subsequent period of sharply reduced, or even negative, margins above cost until the lesson of oligopolistic interdependence has again been fully driven home to the surviving firms. The entry of a new firm into the industry is more easily prevented than accommodated, and it is for this reason that the already established firms may not want to run more than a certain risk of encouraging the entry of some new firm. Should this be the case, it will then be this maximum acceptable risk of new entry, γ_x, which will govern the size of the markup. However, even if it is not the risk of encouraging the entry of some new firm that effectively limits the size of the markup, then it may well be the possibility of government intervention, θ, that sets the upper limit.

Even when their combined impact is taken into account, the substitution effect and the entry factor may be too weak to place any limit on the size of the markup in an oligopolistic industry. The only constraint on the pricing power of the megacorp, when acting as the surrogate for the industry as a whole, may be the fear of retaliatory action by the government. In the absence of specific legislation authorizing price controls or some equivalent form of price regulation—whether specific to the industry or applicable to the enterprise sector as a whole—the government can only react to the announcement of a higher list price by (a) initiating a suit under the antitrust laws; (b) reducing tariffs and other restrictions on imported substitutes; (c) canceling or redistributing its contracts with members of the industry; or (d) bringing pressure to bear on the members of the industry in some one of the several other extra-legal ways open to it. With specific legislation authorizing price controls or some equivalent form of price regulation already in the statute books, the power of the government to interdict any increase in the markup will, of course, be all the greater. Given the difficulty of determining in advance what form, if any, the government intervention may take and, even more importantly, how costly the intervention will ultimately prove to the industry, the megacorp price leader may be unwilling to run more than a certain risk of provoking some retaliatory action by the government. All other constraints proving inadequate, it will be this maximum acceptable risk of government intervention, θ_x, which will govern the size of the mark-up.

The megacorp-price leader, when trying to decide what change if any to make in the size of the present mark-up, will thus find itself facing a situation similar to that depicted in exhibit 6.8. This four-quadrant diagram indicates the extent to which, if the markup, m, were to be increased, the cost to the megacorp-price leader, as measured by the implicit interest rate, R, would increase relative to the additional investment funds per planning period, $\Delta F/t$, which would thereby be generated internally. (Although only three quadrants are needed to show the relationship between the three variables, Δm, R and F/t, it is easier to display the four quadrants with a single common origin and use a 45° line drawn from the origin to eliminate one of the four quadrants.)

An increase in the size of the markup, m, as measured along both axes of quadrant III, will lead to an increase in the implicit interest rate, R, on the additional funds thereby generated, as shown by the R function in quadrant IV. With only a small increase in m, the combined substitution effect and entry factor is likely to be negligible, even when the longer-term impact is fully taken into account. But as the increase in the size of the markup being contemplated becomes larger, the combined substitution effect and entry factor will become disproportionately greater. This is because, as already pointed out, both the substitution effect as measured by e and the entry factor as measured by γ are an increasing function of the change in the size of the markup, Δm. It is for this reason that the R function shown in quadrant IV is depicted as bowing up to the left. As can be seen, the value of R becomes infinite at Δm_x, which is the increase in the markup associated either with the maximum acceptable risk of entry, γ_x, or the maximum acceptable risk of government intervention, θ_x, depending on which constraint is the operative one.

Simultaneously, the increase in the size of the markup will lead to an increase in the amount of discretionary funds being generated per planning period, as shown in quadrant II. Were it not for the combined substitution effect and entry factor, the relationship between the markup and the additional funds being generated would be a linear one, corresponding to the ray OA. But since the loss

Exhibit 6.8

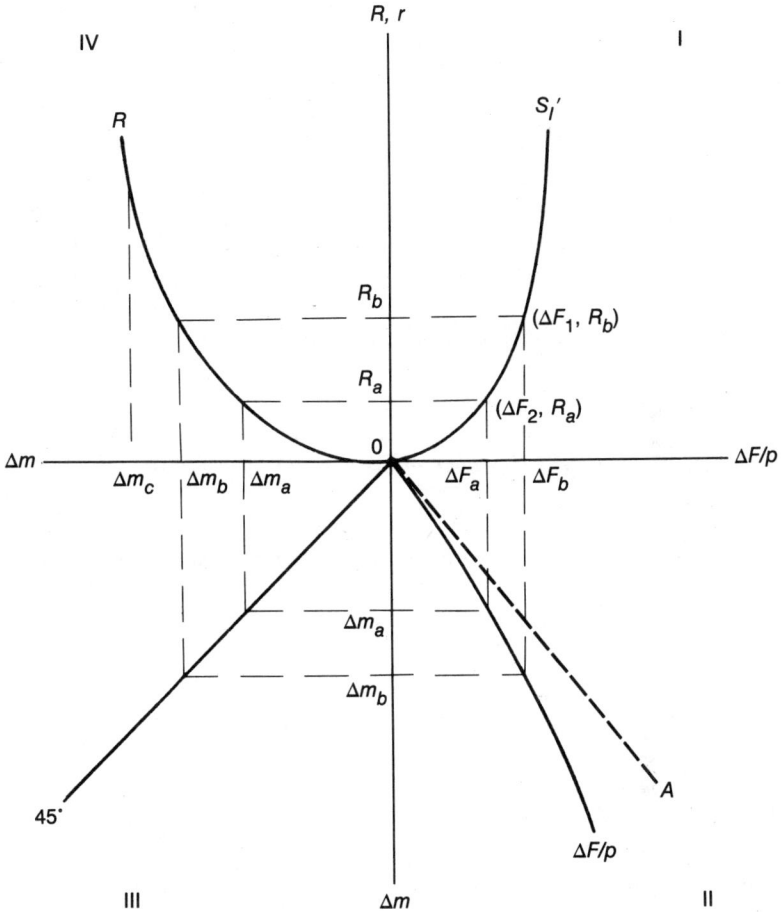

of sales due to the combined substitution effect and entry factor will be all the greater the larger is the increase in the size of the markup, the relationship is actually one in which $\Delta F/t$ increases at a decreasing rate relative to Δm. It is for this reason that the ΔF function shown in quadrant II is depicted as bowing down to the left of the ray OA. (It should be noted that the additional funds being generated, shown along the horizontal axis of quadrant II, is measured as a flow per unit of time, with that time unit the megacorp's planning horizon—that is, the number of pricing periods into the future that the combined substitution effect and entry factor are taken into account.)

Given the R function shown in quadrant IV and the ΔF function shown in quadrant II, one can then derive the supply curve for internally generated funds,

$S_I{'}$. One need only relate the implicit interest rate, R, as the size of the markup is increased to the simultaneous increase in funds per planning period, $\Delta F/p$, which the same increase in the markup will generate. This is because the supply curve for internally generated funds is meant to show how the cost of obtaining those funds, as measured by R, can be expected to increase as the amount of funds obtained, as measured by $\Delta F/t$, also increases. The two together—for example, R_a and ΔF_a if the markup were to be increased by Δm_a or R_b and ΔF_b if the markup were to be increased by Δm_b—would give the coordinates for one point on the supply curve, $S_I{'}$. It is this supply curve, defined as the locus of all possible combinations of R and ΔF as Δm varies, which is shown in quadrant I of exhibit 6.8. To derive the supply curve for all investment funds, not just those which are internally generated but also those obtained from without, it is necessary only to take into account the availability of external finance.

As already indicated, a full discussion of the role played by external finance must wait until the chapter which next follows. For now it will suffice simply to posit that the megacorp price leader has such favorable access to the credit markets that it can obtain whatever funds it wants from external sources at a constant interest rate equal to i. This means that, as shown in exhibit 6.9, the megacorp price leader will come off better if it obtains any additional investment funds it may need, up to the point F_a, by increasing the size of the markup. The implicit interest rate on the funds thereby obtained, R, will be less than the interest rate, i, on any funds obtained from external sources. But beyond ΔF_a, since R will then exceed i, the megacorp will come off better if it obtains the additional funds through external financing. Thus the total supply curve for additional investments funds which the megacorp-price leader faces is represented by S_I—which corresponds to $S_I{'}$ up to ΔF_a and then runs parallel to the horizontal axis at a height given by the interest rate on external funds, i. It is this total supply curve for additional investment funds which, when viewed together with the demand curve for additional investment funds, D_I, will determine what change in the size of the markup, if any, is optimal.

6.3.4 The optimal change in the size of the markup

When, just before the start of a new pricing period, the megacorp-price leader must decide what size mark-up to apply to its costs of production, it will find itself in one of the three situations depicted in exhibits 6.10–6.12. In all three of these possible cases, the change in the mark-up, Δm, will depend on where the demand curve for additional investment funds, D_I, and the supply curve for additional investment funds, S_I, intersect. The difference between the three situations is where the point of intersection lies relative to (a) the origin, and (b) the point where the $S_I{'}$ and S_I curves diverge.

In the first of the three possible situations, the one depicted in exhibit 6.10, the D_I and S_I curves intersect outside the positive quadrant. This means that the

Exhibit 6.9

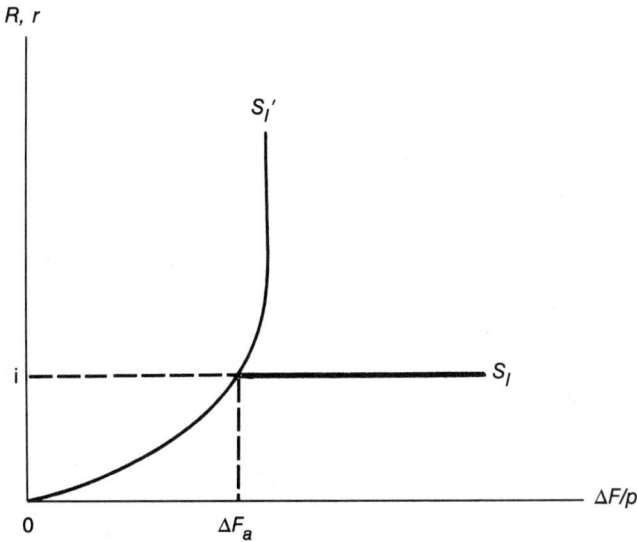

existing markup is sufficient to generate more investment funds than are required to finance the megacorp-price leader's current capital expansion program. While the megacorp-price leader might seem likely, under the circumstances, to opt for a lower markup, this need not be the case. Both the entry factor and the fear of government intervention play no role when the markup, together with the set of industry list prices, is to be reduced rather than increased. This is the reason that the discussion in the preceding subsection was predicated on a possible increase in price rather than just a more general change in price, negative as well as positive. Moreover, a reduction in the size of the markup that was accompanied by a reduction in the set of list prices might well be misinterpreted by the other firms in the industry, precipitating a period of price warfare and unstable market conditions. For both these reasons, the markup may not be reduced even if the D_I and S_I curves do intersect below the origin of the positive quadrant. Indeed, the markup is most likely to be reduced, under the circumstances depicted in exhibit 6.10, when the megacorp-price leader, faced with a rise in the costs of production, decides to increase the list price so as to offset, only in part, that increase in costs.

In the second of the three possible situations, the one depicted in exhibit 6.11, the D_I and S_I curves intersect above the origin but below the point where the S_I' and S_I curves diverge. This means that the existing markup is insufficient to generate the investment funds required by the megacorp-price leader's current capital expansion program, and that the additional funds needed can be obtained at the least cost to the firm by increasing the size of the markup. Under the

Exhibit 6.10

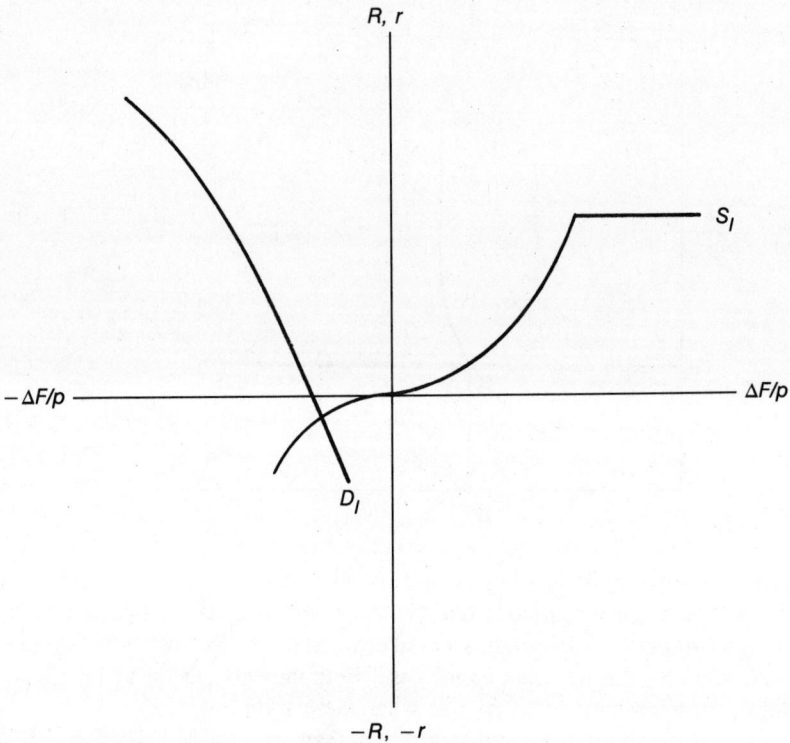

circumstances depicted in exhibit 6.11, the mark-up will be increased by Δm_a, thereby generating additional investment funds F_a at an implicit interest rate, R_a, with no resort made to external financing.

Finally, in the third of the three possible situations, the one shown in exhibit 6.12, the D_I and S_I curves intersect at a point where the S_I curve no longer coincides with the S_I' curve. This means that the existing markup is again insufficient to generate the investment funds required by the megacorp-price leader's current capital expansion program, but that now the additional funds required can be obtained at the least cost to the firm by some combination of a higher markup and resort to external financing. Under the circumstances depicted in exhibit 6.12, ΔF_b of the additional funds required will be generated by increasing the size of the markup by Δm_b, and the rest of the funds, $\Delta F_d - \Delta F_b$, will be obtained by borrowing from external sources at an interest rate equal to i. As can be seen, without access to any external funds, the megacorp-price leader would be able to obtain only ΔF_c in additional funds, and those would have to be generated by a higher markup, Δm_c, with a higher implicit interest rate, R_c.

The three situations which the megacorp-price leader may face, as shown in

Exhibit 6.11

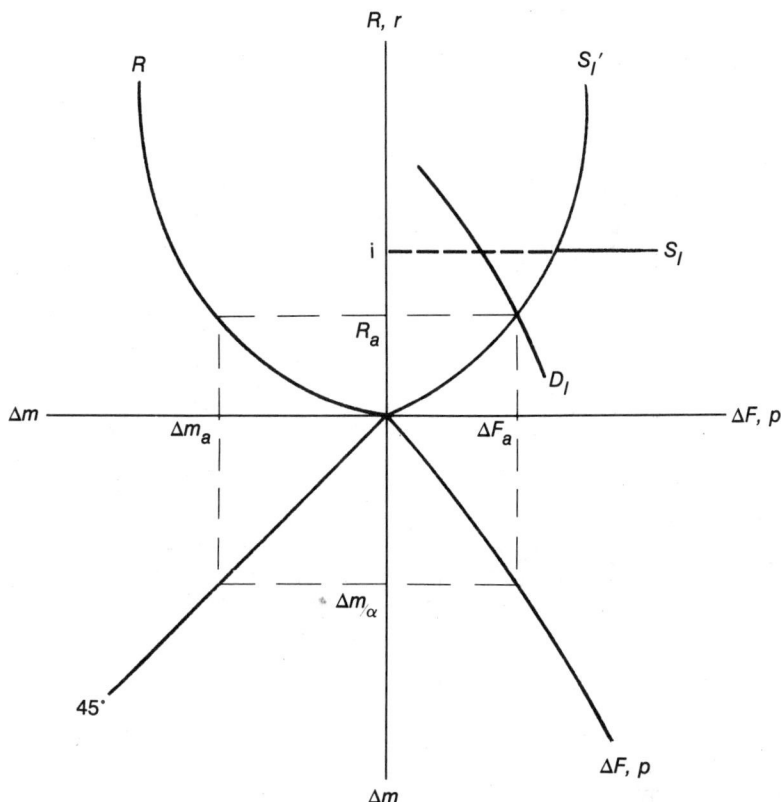

exhibits 6.10–6.12, are an exhaustive list of the discrete possibilities rather than a set of conditions that will necessarily determine, with the mathematical exactitude implied by the curves which have been drawn, the megacorp-price leader's choice of markup and the amount of additional investment funds to be generated thereby. In other words, the three diagrams merely indicate the limits which a rational decision about the size of the markup will approach. They are not meant to suggest that the megacorp-price leader or any other member of the industry will actually be able to calculate the precise point at which the D_I and S_I curves intersect. Indeed, here as in other mattters, the megacorp-price leader is likely to rely on certain "rules-of-thumb" which, though not necessarily producing an optimal decision at every moment in time, are nonetheless more easily applied and in general approximate that best possible choice. The "rule-of-thumb" in this case is that, unless there is some compelling reason to change it, the mega-corp-price leader should continue to apply whatever markup has previously been arrived at through past historical adjustments in the size of that markup. This

Exhibit 6.12

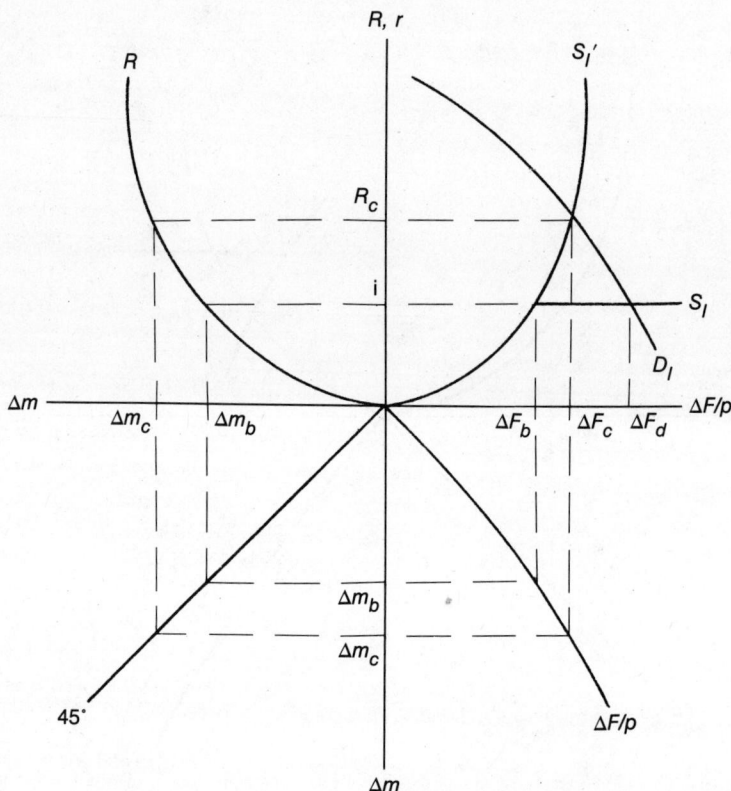

rule-of-thumb, however, does not mean that the markup will not be varied should the need arise.

In deciding whether to vary the size of the markup, the megacorp-price leader's first step will be to ascertain whether, at the existing markup, the rate at which cash flow is being generated is sufficient to finance current capital spending plans. This will be determined as part of the annual financial review which every megacorp carries out, with projected sales and the cash flow likely to be generated from those sales compared with the preliminary capital budget that has been drawn up. The likelihood, given the procedures by which various proposals are screened at the lower levels of the firm for possible inclusion in the capital budget, is that the preliminary figure will exceed the current rate at which cash flow, and hence discretionary funds, is being generated; and it is not uncommon for the executive group, in this situation, to opt for trimming the capital budget so as to keep it within the limits dictated by the amount of cash flow likely to be generated within the next twelve months—or at least within the limits of the cash flow that would be generated in the absence of any cyclical movement in sales.

The executive group, however, may be reluctant to cut back on spending for strategic or other reasons, and in that case a decision will be made as to whether the markup, or profit margin, should be increased. This decision is likely to be based on little more than an informed judgment of how long it will take for the combined substitution effect and entry factor to become positive relative to how long it will take to recover the cost of whatever investment is to be financed out of the additional funds.

If what seems like the most prudent increase in the size of the markup, taking all the relevant factors into consideration, will still leave the megacorp-price leader with an insufficient amount of cash flow, or discretionary funds, to finance all the capital spending deemed essential to the survival and growth of the firm, then the possibility of adding to the firm's long-term debt through the placement of new securities will have to be explored. Still, if the resort to external financing is likely to create difficulties of the sort that will be described in the next chapter—and if, moreover, the risk of either new entry or possible government intervention appears too great to justify an increase in the size of the markup—then the current capital spending plans will have to be reconsidered and possibly revised in light of the availability of financing, external as well as internal. It is by tracing out sequentially in this manner the interrelationship between its capital spending, pricing, and financing decisions that the megacorp-price leader will find itself in one of the three situations depicted in exhibits 6.10–6.12. In the first of these three situations, the megacorp-price leader will not need to increase the markup at all. Indeed, it can even allow the markup to decline in the face of rising costs. But in the other two situations the megacorp-price leader will need to establish, as part of any new set of list prices it may then announce, a higher markup.

The amount by which the markup will be increased in the latter two cases will depend on (a) how great has been the shift of the megacorp-price leader's demand curve for additional investment funds, D_I, and (b) how elastic is its supply curve for more internally generated funds, $S_I{}'$. The factors determining the shift in the demand curve for additional investment funds will be analyzed in the chapter which next follows. Here it is necessary only to make clear what determines how elastic will be the megacorp's supply curve for more internally generated funds, $S_I{}'$. The more elastic that supply curve—that is, the less it rises as both the markup and the amount of additional funds being generated increases—the easier it will be for the megacorp-price leader to respond to a shift in the D_I curve by simply increasing the size of the markup.

The elasticity of the $S_I{}'$ curve depends on the same factors which, for any given change in the size of the markup, determine the implicit interest rate on internally generated funds, R. It therefore depends on (1) the change in the size of the mark-up, Δm; (2) the elasticity of industry demand, $|e|$; (3) the magnitude of the barriers to entry, as measured by the probability of new entry, γ; and (4) the willingness of the government, in the prevailing political climate, to intervene directly in that particular industry, as measured by θ. That is,

$$R = f(\Delta m, \ |e|, \ \gamma, \ \theta) \tag{6.53}$$

and therefore

$$S_I' = f(\Delta m, \ |e|, \ \gamma, \ \theta) \tag{6.54}$$

In other words, e, γ and θ are the parameters of the supply curve for more internally generated funds, S_I', shown in exhibits 6.10–6.12, with the slope, and therefore the elasticity, of that supply curve reflecting the strength of all three factors. The more inelastic is industry demand (that is, the lower the absolute value of e), the higher the barriers to entry (that is, the lower the value of γ) and the less likely the government to intervene (that is, the lower the value of ϱ), the flatter will be the S_I' curve and the more likely it is that a shift in the D_I curve will be translated directly into a higher markup. This is what Kalecki meant when he said that the size of the markup depends on the "degree of monopoly." P. W. S. Andrews, characteristically, used the term "degree of competition" instead, but he was referring to essentially the same set of factors. It is perhaps better, however, to use the more neutral term "degree of pricing power" to describe the combined influence of the elasticity of industry demand, the probability of new entry, and the likelihood of government intervention in determining the ability of any one firm, or any group of firms collectively, to increase the size of the markup directly in proportion to the increased need, and hence demand, for additional investment funds.

It must be kept in mind, however, that, as already brought out by equation 6.45, the size of the markup within any given industry does not depend on the degree of pricing power alone but rather on that factor in combination with the demand for additional investment funds. This is essential for understanding what determines the size of the markup, m, across industries. Only in part will the relative size of the markup depend on the value of e, γ and θ for each industry. It will also depend on each industry's growth rate, g, and its incremental capital-output ratio, b, relative to that of other industries (see section 6.1.4). Thus, cross-sectionally, it can be posited that

$$m_j = f(e_j,, \ \gamma_j, \ \theta_j, \ g_j, \ b_j) \tag{6.55}$$

Over time, however, since the other factors can be assumed to remain largely unchanged, the size of the markup within any given industry is likely to vary only with the industry growth rate. That is, based on time series observations,

$$m_j = f(g_j) \tag{6.56}$$

with e_j, γ_j, θ_j and b_j as fixed parameters.

What can be posited in the case of any oligopolistic industry—that is, an industry dominated by a small number of megacorps, one of which acts as the price leader—is that the degree of pricing power will be at least sufficient to enable it to increase the size of the markup, m_j, as the industry growth rate, g_j, varies so that the necessary value condition (as well as the necessary supply condition) for continuous expansion by that industry in line with the growth of the economy can be satisfied. This, of course, is only a hypothesis and it therefore needs to be tested against the empirical evidence. Still, this result derived from the model of oligopolistic pricing developed in this section can be contrasted with the quite different conclusion which follows from the alternative models of pricing more commonly relied upon by economists. It is to these alternative models of pricing that we must now turn.

6.4 Alternative Pricing Models

The model of oligopolistic pricing developed in the preceding section differs significantly from the models of pricing behavior upon which economists more typically base their arguments. These alternative pricing models are of two major types: (1) models of commodity pricing based on the assumption that firms are price takers, and (2) models of nonoligopolistic industrial pricing whereby firms are assumed to be price setters rather than price takers. The first type of model, since it depends on the same excess-demand hypothesis that underlies the neo-Walrasian model of general equilibrium, can be termed the Walrasian model, while the second type of model, since it can more readily encompass the excess-supply hypothesis of Marshall, will be termed the Marshallian model (see chapter 5, section 1.2). The critical difference between these two models is whether the adjustment to any disequilibrium condition is assumed to take place through a change in price or whether, alternatively, the adjustment is assumed to occur through a change in the quantity supplied. Together, the two models constitute the microfoundation of the conventional neoclassical theory, with the incompatability between them not always recognized. Since it serves as the counterpart of the model of long-period prices presented in the first part of this chapter, we will begin with the Walrasian model before turning to the alternative Marshallian model. We shall therefore begin with an examination of the model which is perhaps the more relevant one for explaining commodity pricing.

6.4.1 The Walrasian model and commodity pricing

The Walrasian model, like the Marshallian model, assumes that the representative firm within each industry is a neoclassical proprietorship. Two of the features which distinguish this type of firm from the megacorp provide the rationale for both the behavioral rule and the type of cost curves assumed in the Walrasian and Marshallian models. These features are (1) the direct control over the firm exercised by a small number of owner-entrepreneurs and (2) the single plant or two in which all of the firm's output is produced. Since the firm is controlled by a small number of owner-entrepreneurs who derive their compensation solely from whatever residual income is earned, it can be assumed that the goal of the firm is to maximize the amount of that residual income, or "profit," earned by the firm in the short period. Moreover, since the small group of owner-managers is incapable of operating more than one or two plants, it can be assumed that the firm is subject to variable returns as it expands or contracts production, with the U-shaped cost curves depicted in exhibit 5.7 the relevant ones. The model that is most useful for analyzing how prices are determined within the commodity sector is therefore one which is predicated on

1. the short-period maximization of net revenue, and
2. a set of U-shaped average variable and average total cost curves.

To complete the model of commodity pricing, it is necessary only to add the assumption, as the Walrasian model does, that each firm is a price taker.

The assumption that each firm is a price taker means that one must shift from the level of the individual firm to that of the industry as a whole in order to understand the process of price formation. In a Walrasian model the individual firm has no pricing discretion. Prices are instead determined at the industry level by the balance between demand and supply factors—with the individual firm then having to take this market-determined industry price as a given in deciding how much to produce (the only decision left to the firm). Once each firm has determined the optimal quantity for it to produce at that price, it will then place that amount of output on the market for whatever price can be commanded (which need not be the same as the price on which the firm based its output decision). Starting from these premises, it is possible to construct a determinate model of prices and pricing behavior for which, in any disequilibrium situation, what is known as the Walrasian excess-demand hypothesis holds.

Formally, the Walrasian model entails only a separate set of demand and supply curves for each type of good represented by the national product and hence, ignoring any intermediate output, for each of the n industries which constitute the enterprise sector. As an explanation for what determines the values taken by the price vector in the long-run—the neoclassical counterpart of the long-period model of prices presented in the first part of this chapter—the Walrasian model thus takes the form of the following two equations for each of the n industries:

$$\bar{p}_i = f(D_i, S_i) \tag{6.57}$$

$$\bar{Q}_i = f(D_i, S_i) \tag{6.58}$$

where $\bar{p}_i$ is the long-period, or "equilibrium," price of the goods produced by the ith industry; Q_i is the equilibrium quantity produced and sold by the ith industry; D_i is the ith industry's demand function as given by equation 5.41, and S_i is the ith industry's supply function as given by equation 5.42 (see chapter 5, section 2.4).

--plain any short-period
-antity

currently being demanded and the quantity currently being supplied within each of those n industries, with the difference between the two viewed as the measure of the disequilibrium within the market. In that case, the price equation for any one industry takes the following form:

$$\Delta p_i = f(Q_{D_i} - Q_{S_i}) \tag{6.59}$$

where Δp_i is the change in the price of the ith industry between one period and the next, Q_{D_i} is the quantity being demanded of industry i at the beginning of the interval, and Q_{S_i} is the quantity which is meanwhile being supplied. In this way, one need only determine the balance between demand and supply at any one moment in time—and not what specific form the separate demand and supply functions take. As we shall see, this is a considerable advantage when it comes to empirically testing the Walrasian model along with the excess-demand hypothesis, as represented by equation 6.59, which underlies that model.

In the discussion which follows, the Walrasian model will be taken to mean either a set of $2n$ equations in the form of equations 6.57 and 6.58 (the long-run, or long-period, version of the model) or n equations in the form of equation 6.59 (the short-run, or short-period, version). The model cannot be said to be complete, however, until the basis for specifying the separate demand and supply functions for each industry has been explained. On the demand side, this further specification of the Walrasian model will have to wait until chapter 9, when the corresponding macrodynamic behavior of the household sector will be analyzed. For now the focus must remain on the enterprise sector and the underlying determinants of the supply functions that are a necessary part of any neoclassical model.

One approach is to posit, for each of the n industries, a set of $q+r$ isoquants, where q is the number of material inputs used in the production process and r is the number of nonmaterial inputs. However, as already pointed out (see chapter 5, section 2.4), it is not possible to derive the necessary set of isoquants from the data available for individual firms or industries and then, based on that set of isoquants, to derive the corresponding set of cost curves. Thus, in further elaborating on the Walrasian model so that it can be used as the basis for empirical work, economists are likely simply to posit a set of cost and revenue curves such as those shown in exhibit 6.13 without attempting to derive those cost curves from an underlying set of isoquants. If this expedient suggests that one of the key theoretical constructs upon which the Walrasian general equilibrium model is based may have no existence in reality, it nonetheless makes it possible to construct a model that can explain the behavior of the individual firm, along with that of the system as a whole, while still holding to the assumption that firms are price takers. Indeed, it is this modified Walrasian model, suitable only for carrying out the "partial" analysis of one industry at a time, which would appear to be the most appropriate one for explaining price movements within the primary sector of the U.S. economy, agriculture in particular.

The "equilibrium" or determinate solution to this model, both in the short run and in the long run, is well known. To maximize their net revenue, firms will necessarily have to produce at the point on their cost and revenue curves where the marginal cost is equal to the marginal revenue. This is the point q_0 in exhibit 6.13 when the price, as determined by the intersection of the industry supply and demand curve, is p_0. As industry demand varies over time, this net-revenue-maximizing level of output will necessarily change in the manner shown in exhibit 6.14, falling to q_1 when the industry price declines to p_1 and increasing to q_2 when the price rises to p_2. As each individual firm adjusts its output over time to this net-revenue-maximizing level of sales, it will be acting as though it were governed by a supply curve that coincides with its marginal cost curve above where that curve is intersected by the average variable cost curve. This supply curve for each individual firm, when aggregated for all the firms comprising the industry, then yields the industry supply curve shown on the right-hand side of exhibits 6.13 and 6.14.

It may well be that the price determined by the balance between demand and supply factors at the industry level will enable the representative firm, as shown in exhibit 6.14, to earn a profit in the short run. However, the entry of new firms into the industry, attracted by the prospective returns above cost, will eliminate those profits in the long run (just as the forced withdrawal of firms from the industry, because the price is no longer sufficient to cover all the necessary costs of production, will eliminate any losses). With allowance thus made for the entry of new firms (as well as for the exit of older, inefficient firms), the industry supply curve can be expected to shift over time so that, in the hypothetical long run as shown in exhibit 6.15, it intersects the industry demand curve at a price just sufficient to enable the representative firm to cover its average total costs of production. Indeed, it is this price (p_1 in exhibit 6.15) that is the long-period—or rather the long-run—"equilibrium" price within the modified Walrasian model.

While this determinate solution will be well known to anyone who has previously studied economics, the dynamic adjustment process that must operate if this long-run equilibrium price is to be realized in practice has received relatively little attention. This is the dynamic adjustment process previously identified in connection with the Walrasian excess-demand hypothesis (see chapter 5, section 2.4). With a shift in either the demand or supply curve so that the current market price no longer represents the long-period equilibrium price solution, the individual firm will be faced with either an excess demand for or, alternatively, an excess supply of the good it produces. If faced with an excess demand such that the quantity being demanded is greater than the amount currently being produced, the firm can be assumed to react by insisting on obtaining a higher price—and in this way causing the industry price, based on the last transaction recorded, to rise. If, alternatively, the firm is faced with an excess supply such that it cannot find a buyer for all the goods it is currently producing, the firm can be assumed to react

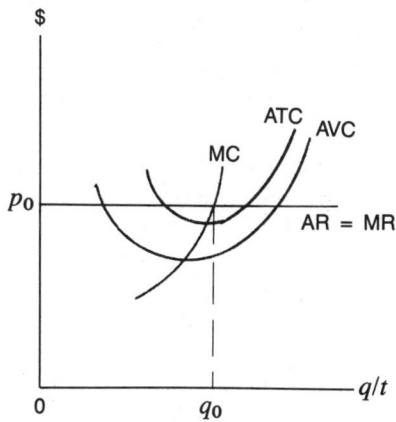

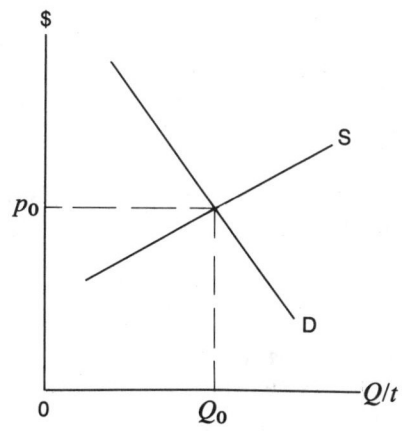

Exhibit 6.14

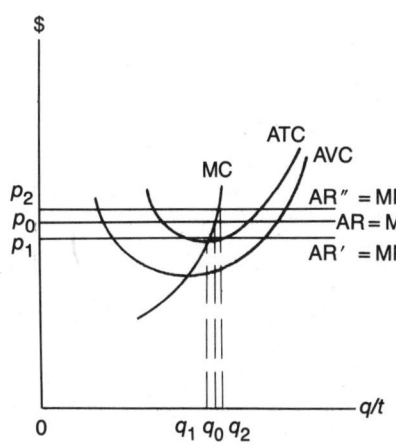

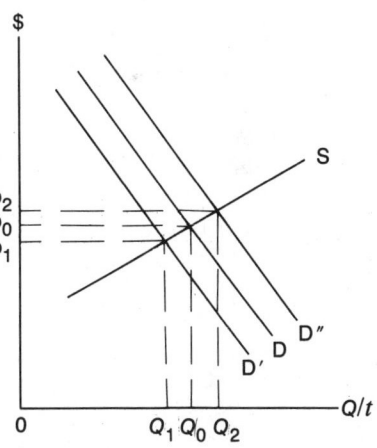

by offering to sell its output at a lower price—and in this way causing the industry price to fall. In either case, the change in price will serve to bring supply and demand back into balance with one another. Thus the following dynamic adjustment process can be specified, though now with the balance between demand and supply assumed to be restored, not necessarily within each of the n^2 cells that constitute the inner matrix of the production system but rather, only within each of the h final goods markets:

1 $Q_d \neq Q_s \longrightarrow \Delta p$ (If $Q_d > Q_s$, then $+\Delta p$; if $Q_d < Q_s$, then $-\Delta p$)

2. $+\Delta p \longrightarrow -\Delta Q_d, +\Delta Q_x$ until $Q_d = Q_s$ within each of the h final goods markets.

(The ambiguity surrounding the inner matrix is because, as already pointed out, the orthodox models, whether Walrasian or Marshallian, ignore the role played by intermediate output. See chapter 5, section 4.1.)

It is this dynamic adjustment process which, since it can be reduced to a series of discrete, observable changes over time, transforms the Walrasian model from merely a formal analysis of the necesary long-period set of relative prices into a possible explanation for any short-period price movements. Indeed, the Walrasian model in this form would appear to have considerable explanatory power—at least insofar as the agricultural sector of the U.S. economy is concerned. It is not just that the firms within this sector are neoclassical proprietorships which would appear to be price takers rather price setters. It is also that, even more important-ly, the short-period price movements within the sector closely correspond to what one would expect based on the Walrasian excess-demand hypothesis. As can be seen from exhibit 6.16, prices within the agricultural sector are indeed somewhat sensitive to fluctuations in the level of demand.

Insofar as the industrial sector is concerned, however, the observable pattern is quite different. There, as can be seen from the corresponding movement of industrial prices shown in exhibit 6.16, the excess-demand hypothesis would appear not to hold. Indeed, the lack of responsiveness by industrial prices to any short-period fluctuations in demand is the reason that has already been given for rejecting the Walrasian model insofar as determining the technical coefficients represented by the A and L matrices are concerned (see chapter 5, section 2.4). It

Exhibit 6.15

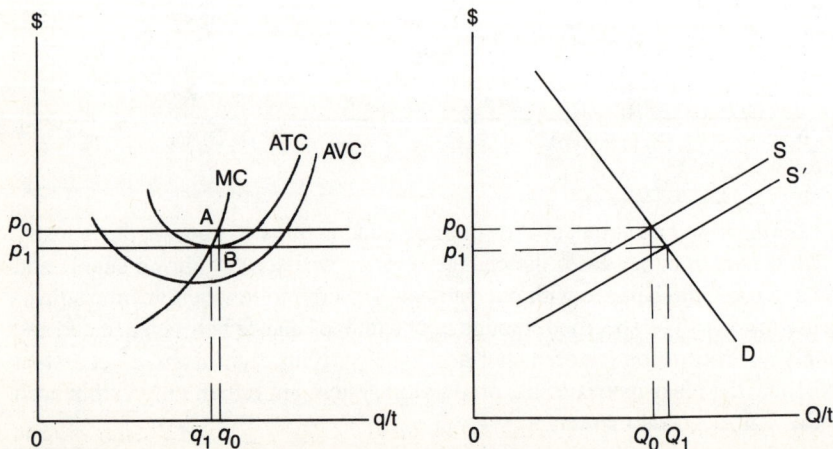

(Based on wholesale price index, 1967–69 = 100)

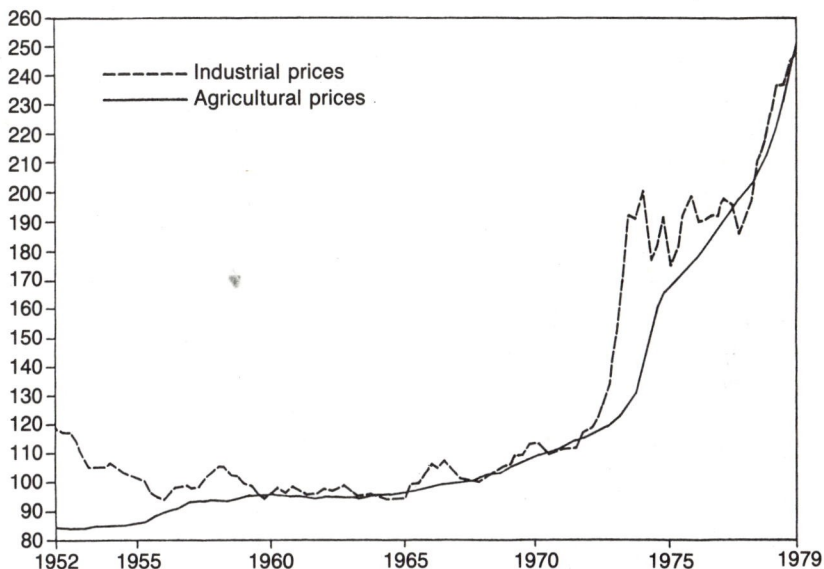

is therefore necessary, in seeking an alternative to the oligopolistic model presented earlier, to turn instead to the Marshallian model since that model does not depend in the same critical way on the excess-demand hypothesis.

6.4.2 The Marshallian model and industrial pricing

In the Marshallian model, firms are price setters rather than price takers. This means that they are forced, by the types of industrial markets in which they operate, to announce a price in advance of entering into any contract for the sale of their output, and they are then obligated by the prevailing business practice to continue honoring that "list" price for some time into the future. The Marshallian model thus applies to industries in which the price established in the "forward," as distinct from the "spot," market is the more significant one. In this type of market a temporary imbalance between supply and demand will lead, not to an immediate change in the industry price but rather, to a change in the quantity supplied by each of the different firms. The difference is brought out in exhibit 6.17, where the response under the Marshallian excess-demand hypothesis, shown in the bottom half of the exhibit, can be compared with the response under the Walrasian excess-demand hypothesis shown in the top half.

To make clear what the essential difference is, it can be assumed that the extent of the imbalance between demand and supply, $Q_{d_i} - Q_{s_i}$, is the same in both

Exhibit 6.17a

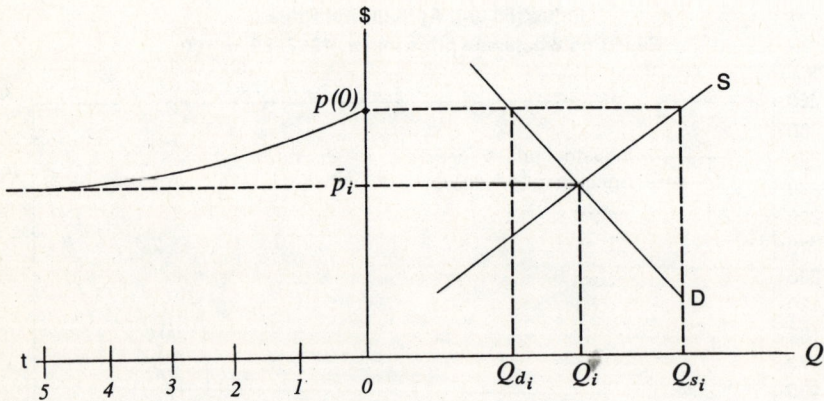

Exhibit 6.17b

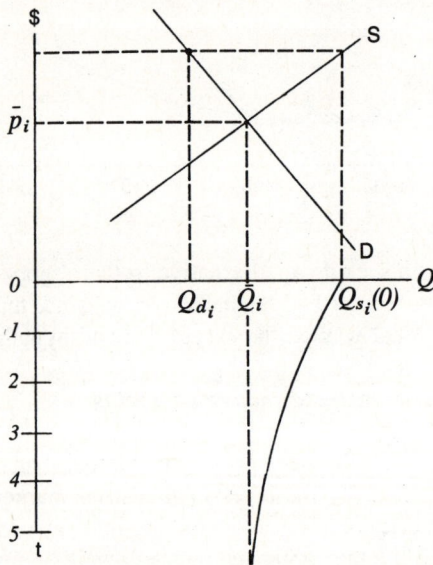

Adapted from Bent Hansen, *General Equilibrium Systems*, McGraw-Hill, 1970, ch. 2.

cases—along with the reason for the imbalance, whether a prior shift in the demand curve or, alternatively, a prior shift in the supply curve. What distinguishes the two models is that, under the Marshallian adjustment process, it is the quantity supplied by each of the firms in the industry that will fall over time until it equals the equilibrium quantity, $\bar{Q}_i$, while under the Walrasian adjustment process it is the price that will fall until it equals the equilibrium price, $\bar{p}_i$. The dynamic adjustment process under the Marshallian excess-supply hypothesis can thus be outlined as follows:

This one-step sequence, with the quantity variable playing the equilibrating role, stands in sharp contrast to the Walrasian adjustment process outlined in the previous subsection.

Since the long-run equilibrium solution will be the same in both cases, with the price and the quantity supplied equal to $\bar{p}_i$ and $\bar{Q}_i$ respectively as shown in exhibit 6.17, it can be argued that it really makes no difference whether it is the Marshallian or the Walrasian adjustment process which applies in any particular situation. However, this argument ignores the fact that the adjustment to any prior disequilibrium situation is likely to be incomplete before the system is again disturbed by a change in some exogenous factor. What one is therefore able to actually observe is not the equilibrium price and quantity, $\bar{p}_i$ and $\bar{Q}_i$, but rather only a series of incomplete, or truncated, adjustments over time to the changing homeostatic condition, $\bar{p}_i$ and $\bar{Q}_i$. Moreover, the path traced out by an industry in making this series of incomplete adjustments will be quite different depending on whether it is the Marshallian or the Walrasian adjustment process which is the operative one. Thus in the historically observable short period, when final goods markets are likely to be in disequilibrium rather than in equilibrium, it does make a difference whether it is the Marshallian or the Walrasian adjustment process which applies. In particular, with firms acting as price setters and therefore the Marshallian excess-supply hypothesis being the one that holds, quantity adjustments are likely to predominate, with the industry price changing, if at all, only slowly over time. Still, the price will change, and it is therefore necessary to explain how in a Marshallian model the price is determined.

In the absence of the commodity markets which, in a Walrasian model, determine the price at which any output can be sold, the firm has no choice but to set its own price. The only alternative is to match whatever price is being charged by other firms—in which case the firm is merely a price follower and therefore not a factor in determining the industry price. The firm may, of course, choose to set the price so as to just "break even." This is especially likely when the firm is offering a product for the first time and has no sales experience on which to base its estimate of the elasticity of demand. In that case, the firm can be expected to set its price so that, after conservatively estimating how much output it is likely to sell and thus determining as best it can what its average fixed costs are likely to be, it will be able to cover its average total costs.

The price which, as shown in exhibit 6.18, will enable the firm to cover its average total costs, ATC, at the expected level of sales, $\bar{q}$, and thus to "break even" is $\bar{p}$. It is this price which,, once it has been determined on the basis of the firm's "break-even" point, $\bar{q}$, and then established as the list price, will define the firm's supply-offer curve, S (not to be confused with a true supply curve). As can be seen from exhibit 6.19, the supply-offer curve is horizontal and thus perfectly elastic. This reflects the fact that once $\bar{p}$ has been established as the list price, the firm will supply any quantity that may be demanded at that price—at

Exhibit 6.18

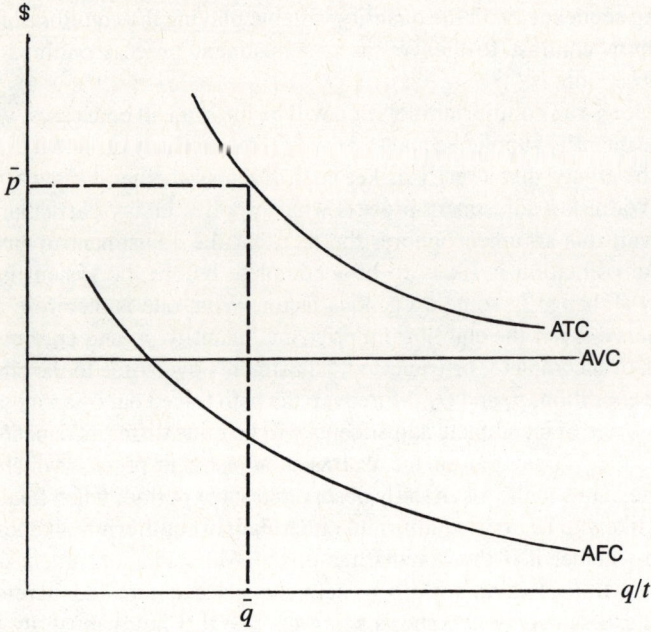

Exhibit 6.19

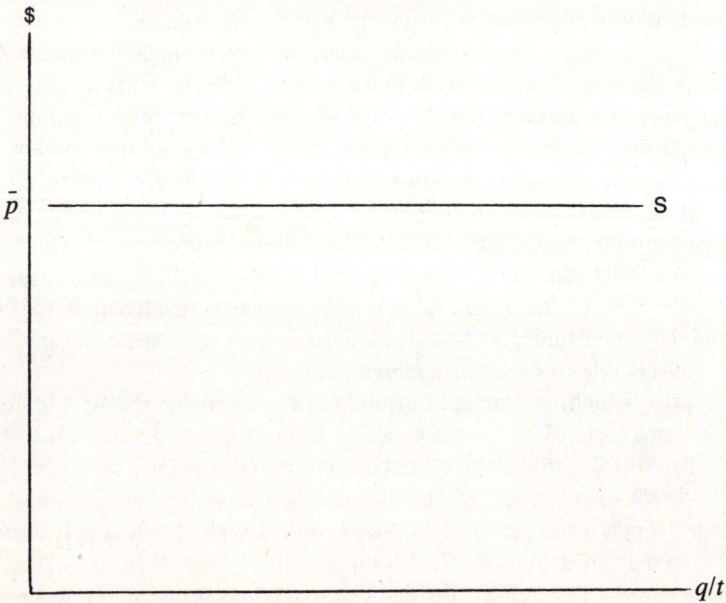

quantity supplied depends on the quantity demanded, and thus is not independent of the demand, that S is not a true "supply curve," at least as that term is generally understood by economists (see section 6.4.5).

The cost curves shown in exhibit 6.18 have been drawn on the assumption that the firm is subject to constant returns as it varies output. The curves would thus appear to be inconsistent with the nature of the representative firm within a Marshallian model (see chapter 5, section 3.1). However, as can be seen from exhibit 6.20, the price at which a firm can expect to break even will be no different even if, instead, the firm is subject to variable returns. The cost curves shown in exhibit 6.18 are, in fact, simply the limiting case when there is increasingly less likelihood that the firm's average variable costs will be affected by any change in the level of output. Since, in determining the break-even point, it makes no difference what is the slope of the average total cost curve at the point at which that curve intersects the average revenue, or price, line—all that matters is the point at which the two curves intersect—the exposition can be greatly simplified by basing the analysis on the limiting case. Indeed, it is because the analysis is thereby made simpler that the firm itself, in trying to determine the break-even point for any new product it may be offering to the market, will itself be inclined to assume constant returns to scale.

Once the firm has some experience in marketing its product, it will have a better idea of how much it can expect to sell at the price, $\bar{p}$. It may turn out that the actual quantity sold will be the anticipated amount, $\bar{q}$, so that the firm will, in fact, just "break even." However, it is more likely that the actual quantity sold will be different from what was originally expected. If the actual quantity sold turns out to be q_1, as shown in exhibit 6.21, then the firm will fail to break even and, unless it can find some way to increase its revenues by raising the price and/or expanding sales, it will be forced out of business. Alternatively, if the actual quantity sold is q_2, then the firm will succeed in more than breaking even. Indeed, it will have established a price for its product that yields a profit per unit of output equal to π, as shown by the ATC $+ \pi$ curve passing through the $\bar{p}$ and q_2 coordinates. This would be the equivalent of a list price with a built-in profit margin, μ, equal to $\pi/\bar{p}$, and hence a markup, m, equal to $\pi/$ATC, when q_2 is the expected level of output. Thus, once the firm has a better idea of what its sales are likely to be, the break-even model relied on initially can be replaced by a markup model, with the mark-up consciously set at either zero, as shown in exhibit 6.18, or at greater than zero, as shown in exhibit 6.21 (when the expected level of output is q_2).

The firm within a Marshallian model need not, of course, settle for whatever markup has previously been established. It can, since it is a price setter rather than a price taker, attempt to increase the size of the markup, m. The extent to which it is likely to be successful in this regard will be explained shortly. For the moment, all that need be pointed out is that, should the firm succeed in increasing

Exhibit 6.20

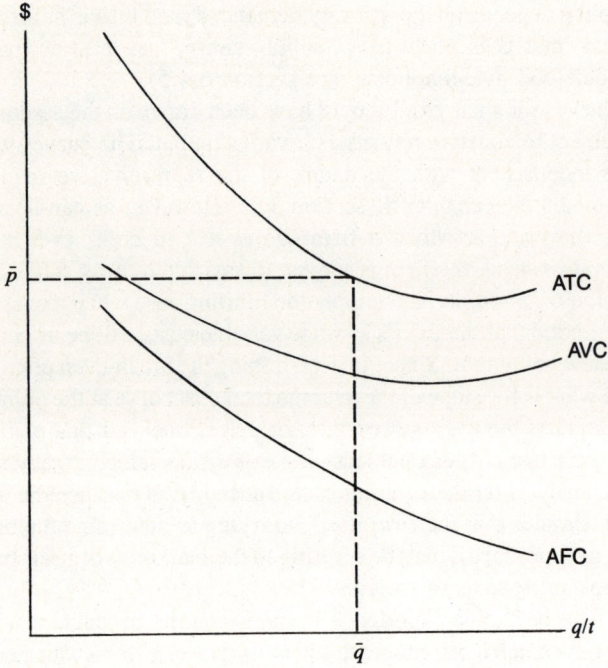

Exhibit 6.21

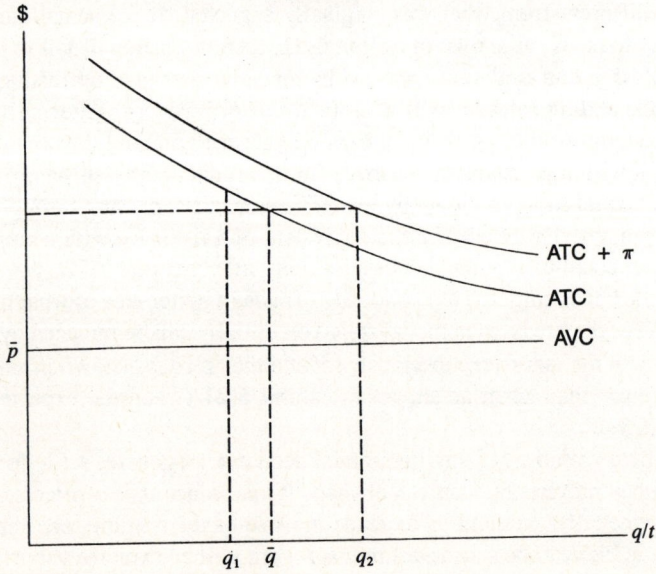

the size of that markup by what the amount of any residual income, or profit, per unit of output rises from π to π', this will lead to a change in the list price—just as would a similar change in the markup in the case of the oligopolistic industry analyzed previously (see section 6.3.1). This change in the list price from $\bar{p}$ to p' will, in turn, cause the supply-offer curve to shift from S to S' in the manner shown in exhibit 6.22, with the firm willing to supply any quantity that may be demanded at that price.

Thus, both in the way the price is determined and in the way the necessary adjustment to changing demand conditions occurs, the Marshallian model is closer to the oligopolistic pricing model presented earlier than to the Walrasian model. Like the oligopolistic model, the Marshallian model assumes that firms are price setters rather than prices takers, with the price they set being the list price that is determined by adding a certain markup, m, to the average costs of production. Moreover, this list price, once set, is likely to be maintained for some time so that, in the interim, any short-period fluctuations in demand will have to be adjusted to through changes in the level of output. It is thus not because of any lesser role played by list prices that the Marshallian model is to be distinguished from the oligopolistic model developed earlier as a possible explanation for how prices are determined within the industrial sector of an advanced market economy like that of the United States. Rather the differences between the two models lie in (1) the size of the markup, m, that is likely to be established, and thus the amount of cash flow, or discretionary funds, that is likely to be generated, and (2) the ability of firms to maintain that markup once it has been established. These differences, in turn, reflect the quite different competitive situation in which the neoclassical proprietorship as the representative firm in a Marshallian model is likely to find itself compared with that of a megacorp.

6.4.3 The size of the markup in nonoligopolistic industries

Whether the Marshallian or the oligopolistic model is the one that applies in the case of any particular industry, it can be assumed that the list price will be determined by adding a certain markup, m, to the material and labor costs of production, ATC or c_j. It is just that the markup is likely to be smaller in the case of an industry to which the Marshallian model applies. The smaller size of the markup, in turn, reflects the less protected market position of the neoclassical proprietorships which are the representative firm in the Marshallian model.

No factor is more important in this regard than the barriers to entry. The lower the cost disadvantage which a new entrant must overcome, the less protected will be the market position of the firms in that industry and the lower will be the mark-up upon which the list price is based. The extreme case is one in which the barriers to entry are negligible. This means that the technology employed is readily available to all comers, the capital costs are insignificant and/or easily

Exhibit 6.22

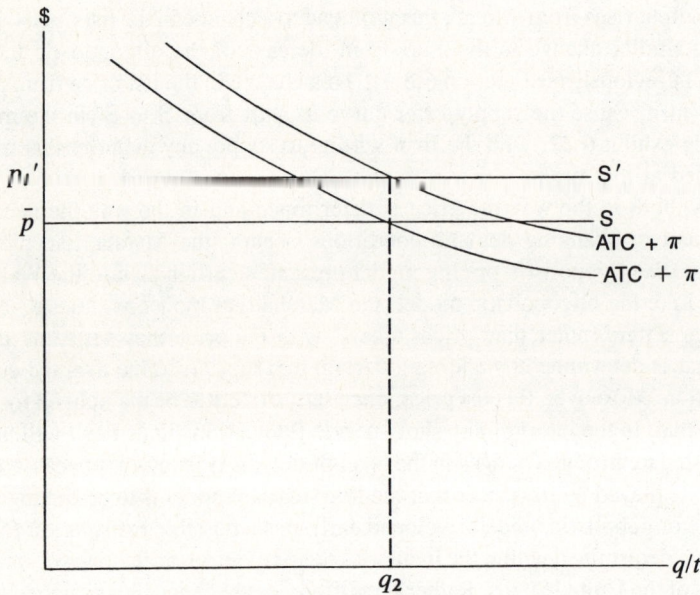

financed, all essential material and labor inputs can be obtained on equally favorable terms and there already exists an established market outlet for whatever output may be produced. In this extreme case, the markup is likely to be close to zero—once all the necessary costs of production, including compensation for the labor services of the owner-entrepreneurs as well as a minimum return on whatever funds of their own those owner-entrepreneurs have supplied, are taken into account. Indeed, except for a list price (as distinct from an exogenously given market price), it is difficult to distinguish this case from that of an industry in the long-period equilibrium of the Walrasian model.

The situation just delineated is nonetheless an extreme one, insofar as the industrial sector is concerned, since it is unlikely that entry into the industry will be unimpeded. A premium of some sort will almost certainly have to be paid, at least at the beginning, for access to the technology—even if that premium consists of little more than a higher operating cost until the technology can be mastered. Moreover, financial institutions are understandably reluctant to extend credit to new ventures, given the high rate of failure among such firms, and the availability of financing may well become problematical. It may also take time to develop dependable supplies of particular raw materials as well as to recruit, train and break in a work force—with the costs of production being higher in the interim. Finally, even if market outlets already exist, this provides no guarantee that a new firm will be able to sell its product. The potential entrant will still have to devise an effective marketing strategy, and that is likely to prove costly. In any one of these areas—technology, finance, raw materials, labor and marketing—a new firm is likely to suffer from some cost disadvantage. Thus, even in an industry to which the Marshallian rather than the oligopolistic model applies, the entry of new firms will not be unimpeded, with the result that there is likely to be a mark-up greater than zero, at least in the short run.

Still, the barriers to entry will be less than in an oligopolistic industry since this is what distinguishes the two cases. And it is these less significant barriers, as reflected in a lower concentration ratio, that in large part explains the smaller size of the mark-up in the industries to which the Marshallian model applies. However, two other factors must be taken into account as well. One is the elasticity of demand when the representative firm within the Marshallian model, the neoclassical proprietorship, produces a highly differentiated type of product—e.g., apparel. The other factor is the greater difficulty of maintaining the list price when the good produced is a fairly homogenous one supplied by more than one firm.

For the most part, it is not the industries producing a high-volume, standardized product to which the Marshallian model applies. Such an industry, because it is usually based on highly mechanized methods of production and large-scale enterprise, is more likely to be an industry to which the alternative oligopolistic model applies. The industries to which the Marshallian model applies are instead mostly those producing a highly differentiated type of product, with the goods supplied by any one firm readily distinguishable from those supplied by other firms. Indeed, it is this product differentiation which offsets the relatively low barriers to entry, thereby enabling the firm to set a price—one that, at least in the short run, includes a markup—independently of the other firms within the same broader product group. In these circumstances, the Chamberlin-Robinson model already rejected in the case of an oligopolistic industry (see section 6.2.3) can be assumed to be the applicable one.

However, what is then explained by the Chamberlin-Robinson model is not the industry price—the industry price in this case is simply the weighted average of the different prices being charged for the different types of goods—but instead the extent to which the individual firm is able to set a price that exceeds its average total costs. As can be seen from exhibit 6.23, the size of the markup will depend on the elasticity of demand for the firm's product, with this elasticity of demand merely the obverse side of the cross-elasticity of demand for the goods supplied by the other firms within the same broader product group (see chapter 9, section 1.1). The Chamberlin-Robinson model applies in this case because (1) the firm, by producing a differentiated product, need not simply match the price being charged by other firms in order to retain its customers, and (2) the demand for the firm's product, since there are close substitutes, is relatively elastic, making it possible for the firm to equate its positive marginal costs with the marginal revenue obtained as the mark-up, m, and hence the price, p, is varied.

The fact that the firm can be assumed to equate its marginal cost with its marginal revenue means that the pricing formula developed by Abba Lerner to cover this type of situation applies. That is,

Exhibit 6.23

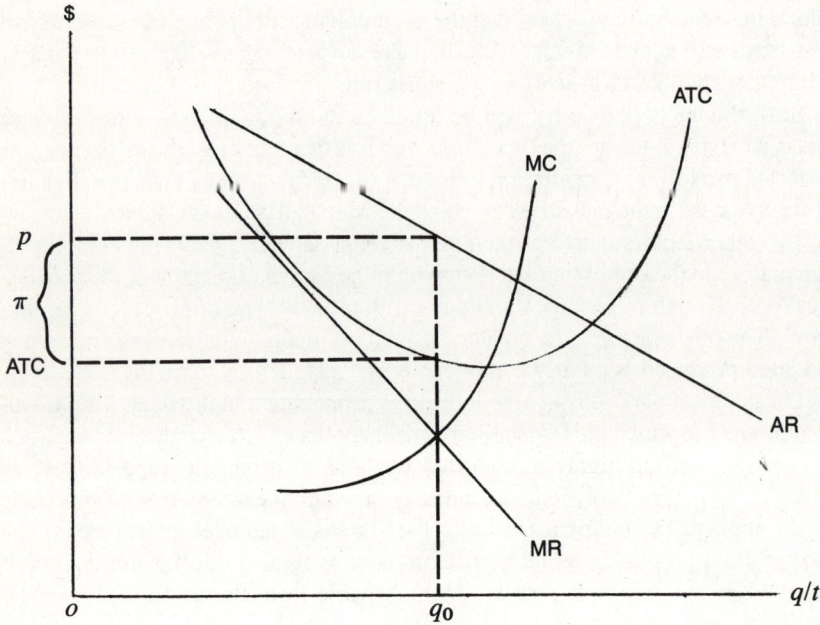

$$p = MC \frac{e_i}{e_i - 1} \quad (6.60)$$

where e_i is now the elasticity of demand for the product supplied by the individual firm—as distinct from the elasticity of demand, e_j, for the broader group of products supplied by the industry as a whole. This result is obtained by first recognizing that the firm's marginal revenue is the first derivative of total revenue with respect to quantity, derived as follows:

$$MC = \frac{dTR}{dq} = p + q * \frac{dp}{dp} = p(1 + \frac{q*dp}{p*dq}) \quad (6.61)$$

and then, based on the formula for determining the elasticity of demand (equation 6.41), substituting

$$-\frac{1}{e} \text{ for the } \frac{q*dp}{p*dq}$$

term in equation 6.61 so as to obtain the following equation:

$$MR = p\left(1 - \frac{1}{e}\right) = p - \frac{p}{e} \qquad (6.62)$$

Substituting MC for MR in equation 6.62 and then solving for p yields equation 6.60. By subtracting the firm's average total costs from the price derived in this manner and then taking the difference as a proportion of those costs, it is possible to determine the size of the markup, m—just as, by taking the difference as a proportion of the price, it is possible to determine the size of the profit margin, μ.

The same model applies, it should be noted, in the case of the smaller firms in an oligopolistic industry that supply some variant of the product produced by the megacorps which dominate the industry. Only in that case, what the model explains is the premium, if any, above the industry price which those firms are able to charge, with the size of that premium depending on where the industry price falls on the vertical axis relative to the firm's average total costs. If, as shown in exhibit 6.24, the firm's net-revenue maximizing price, $\bar{p}$, is less than the price established by the industry price leader, p_j, the firm will be able to sell its output, not at a premium but only at a discount off the prevailing industry price. As long as the smaller firm continues to supply only an insignificant share of the total market, these sales off the list price will not destabilize the industry's price-setting mechanism which, it can be assumed, is based on a system of price leadership/price followship.

Exhibits 6.23 and 6.24 give only the Chamberlin-Robinson model's short-run solution. In the longer run, with the ability of other, perhaps even new firms to duplicate whatever unique features differentiate the firm's product, the size of the markup is likely to be reduced through some combination of a more elastic demand curve and the emergence of rivals producing only a minimally different product. In the extreme case, the markup may even fall to zero. A variant of this extreme case, in which the emergence of firms able to supply nearly the same product not only reduces the markup to zero but also forces each firm to operate at below the point of optimal efficiency, gives rise to the famous "tangency solution" shown in exhibit 6.25. This is a solution that would appear to describe the situation in the areas of retail distribution not dominated by megacorps.

What has been analyzed so far is only the size of the markup in an industry supplying a highly differentiated type of product. Although this would include most of the industries to which the Marshallian model applies, there are a smaller number of industries which, even though the product is standardized, the technology employed is still relatively unsophisticated and thus the neoclassical proprietorship remains as the representative firm. The Marshallian model applies to this type of industry as well. The difference is that, without the protection a highly differentiated type of product provides, the firm has even less chance of maintain-

Exhibit 6.24

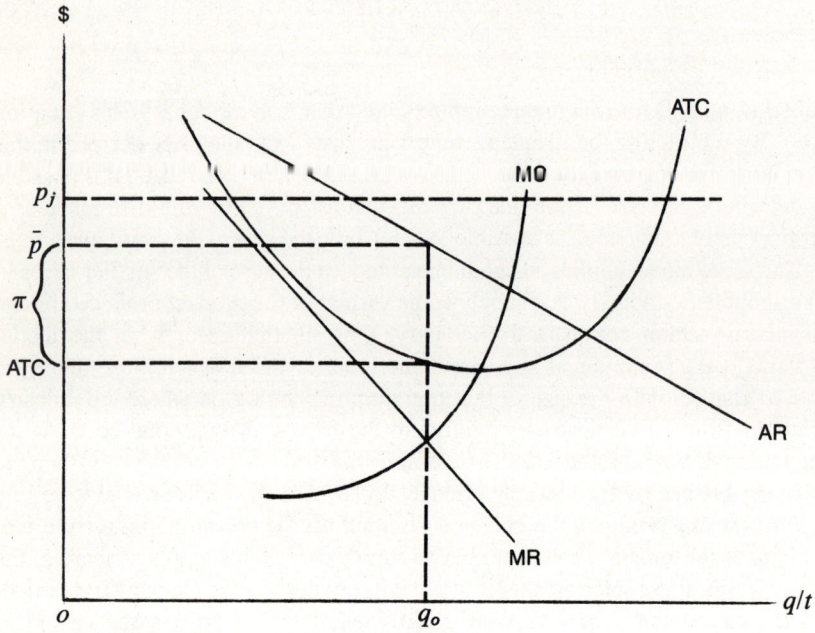

Exhibit 6.25

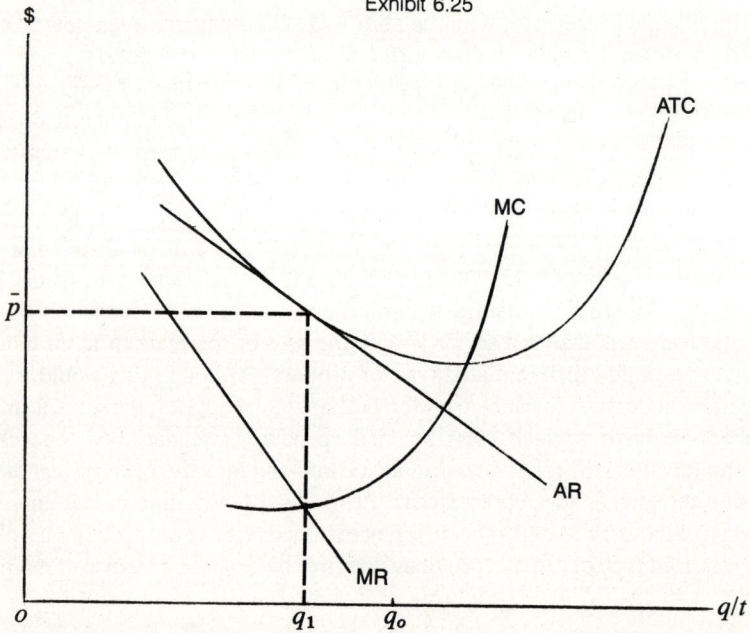

ing a price that includes a profit margin, μ, greater than zero and hence a positive markup, m. This result follows from the lack of any dominant firm which can see to it that the list price, once established, will then be adhered to by all the firms within the industry. Thus the size of the markup will depend not only on the probability of new entry and the elasticity of demand but also on whether there exists some mechanism for restraining the interfirm rivalry that takes the form of price shaving, or discounting off the list price.

Without a dominant firm both to provide leadership and to discipline any recalcitrant member of the industry, the firms supplying a fairly homogeneous product can be expected to pursue a more independent course of action in working out the price details of any transaction. This means they are more likely to discount off the list price in order to pick up a sale—especially when the demand for their product has slackened. As a result, when talking about the size of the markup within the Marshallian model, one must be careful to distinguish the transaction price from the list price. (On the distinction, see chapter 2, section 2.5.) While the list price may well be determined by firms adding a certain predetermined markup, m, to the costs of production, the margin above costs that will actually be realized on each unit of output sold may, because of the discounting off the list price, turn out to be considerably smaller. Indeed, based on the transaction price (as distinct from the list price), the profit margin, μ, may well be reduced to zero—at least at certain points in time over the cycle. However, this caveat, while it may suggest the need to modify the argument that the supply-offer curve is perfectly elastic (see section 6.4.5), does not alter any of the other conclusions which follow from the Marshallian model. Indeed, it only strengthens the argument that the markup will, over time, be reduced so that it is less than it would be if the industry were an oligopoly dominated by megacorps. The point is that, in explaining what determines the size of the markup when a group of neoclassical proprietorships all produce the same homogeneous product, one must also take into account the extent of any interfirm competition based on price. This interfirm rivalry, to the extent it leads to significant discounting off the list price, or price shaving, will cause the actual markup, and hence the profit margin, to be lower than what it would appear to be based on the list price alone.

The probability of price shaving, like the probability of entry, can be explained in terms of the industry concentration ratio. The smaller the concentration ratio, the lower the barriers to entry are likely to be. At the same time, the smaller the concentration ratio, the less likely it is that firms will adhere to the list price in working out the details of any particular transaction. Indeed, it is for this reason that it is possible to distinguish, on the basis of the concentration ratios alone, the subset of industries within the industrial sector to which the Marshallian model applies. These industries constitute the nonoligopolistic component of the industrial sector—as distinct from the industries dominated by megacorps which make up the economy's oligopolistic core (see chapter 5, section 1.2). Still, the concentration ratio merely reflects, and thus only serves as a proxy variable for, the more basic factor that will determine the size of the markup in any nonoligopolistic industry. This more basic determinant is the relative ease of entry as compounded, in the case of any one firm producing a highly differentiated type of product, by the elasticity of its own individual demand curve and, in the case of more than one firm producing the same fairly homogeneous product, by the degree of interfirm price competition.

In the nonoligopolistic sector, then, the rivalry among firms, both those waiting to enter the industry and those already members, is the principal factor determining the size of the margin above costs within each industry and hence the level of prices in the short period. It is the potential competition of new firms that largely explains the size of the markup upon which the list price is based, and it is the extent of any noncooperative, or ''competitive,'' behavior among the already established firms that largely explains what portion of that markup will actually be realized. While both sources of rivalry are important in explaining the movement of prices in the short run, it is the potential competition of new firms which will alone determine how large a markup can be maintained over time. In the extreme case, with entry into the industry unimpeded, it can be expected that the markup will, in the ''long run,'' be reduced to zero.

The long-run ''equilibrium solution is therefore the same, whether it is the modified Walrasian model or, alternatively, the Marshallian model that is thought to apply. Based on either variant of the neoclassical approach to modeling the pricing behavior of firms, it follows that any margin above costs will, over time, be eliminated so that the price is simply equal to each firm's average total costs. This conclusion, however, raises a question about the stability of any economic system (or part thereof) to which either the Walrasian or the Marshallian model applies, since it suggests that the necessary value condition for continuous growth is unlikely to be satisfied.

6.4.4 The stability of neoclassical pricing models

The argument that any margin above costs, and thus the markup, will necessarily be eliminated in the long run implies that the residual income vector previously identified in connection with the Leontief model of production (see chapter 5, section 1.4) is a null vector, the elements of which are all zeros. This conclusion is in apparent conflict with the argument (see part 1 of this chapter) that the residual income vector must take the following numerical values if the necessary value condition for continous economic expansion is to be satisfied:

$$\pi = \hat{P}G\hat{B} \tag{6.22}$$

Indeed, there are only two ways to reconcile these opposing arguments.

The first is to assume that the economy is one which is not growing over time. In that case the **G** vector would be reduced to a null vector, making the residual income vector itself, based on equation 6.22, a null vector. However, since this assumption is belied by the recent historical experience of advanced market economies like the United States, it would mean that the model is not applicable to that type of economic system. The other way to reconcile the two opposing arguments is to recognize that the necessary value condition for continuous growth need not be satisfied under actual historical circumstances. The inability to satisfy this condition may then help to explain the dynamic instability of a market economy when either the Walrasian or the Marshallian model is the one that applies.

If the residual income vector were in fact to be reduced to a null vector, this would mean that the set of prices given by the **P** vector would be insufficient to cover the costs of expansion and that the firms within each industry would therefore be unable to finance the investment in new plant and equipment needed to increase capacity in line with the growth of demand. The profit margin would be too small either to generate the necessary funds internally or to enable firms to qualify for external financing. Indeed, the insufficient profit margin is precisely what is meant by the statement that the necessary value condition for continuous growth will not be satisfied. With firms unable to finance the requisite investment in new plant and equipment, the growth of demand within each industry will not be matched by a corresponding increase in productive capacity, with the result that the necessary supply condition for continuous growth will not be satisfied either.

It is, of course, true that, with demand growing more rapidly than capacity, prices are likely to rise—with a consequent increase in the profit margin being realized within each industry. This will most clearly be the case when the modified Walrasian model is the one that applies. As shown in exhibit 6.26, the outward shift of the industry demand curve relative to the supply curve will lead to a rise in the industry price from p_1 to p_0 and thus to a shift in the representative firm's average revenue curve from AR′ to AR. The representative firm can then be expected to increase its output from q_1 to q_0, yielding a profit margin on each unit of output sold equal to the line segment $\overline{AB}$. Even when the Marshallian model is the one that applies, the realized profit margin is likely to be positive since, with the increase in demand relative to supply, fewer discounts are likely to be granted off the list price and indeed firms may even be encouraged to base their list prices on a larger markup. Nonetheless, any profit margin greater than zero is likely to be only a temporary, disequilibrium result under the conditions posited by both the Walrasian and Marshallian models.

The existence of any margin above cost will, according to either of the two neoclassical pricing models, attract new firms into the industry. As already explained in connection with the Walrasian model (see section 6.4.1), the entry of these new firms will cause the industry supply curve to shift, as shown in exhibit 6.15, from from S to S′, leading to a fall in the average revenue curve from AR to AR′ and thus to the elimination of any profit margin. Even in the case of the

Exhibit 6.26

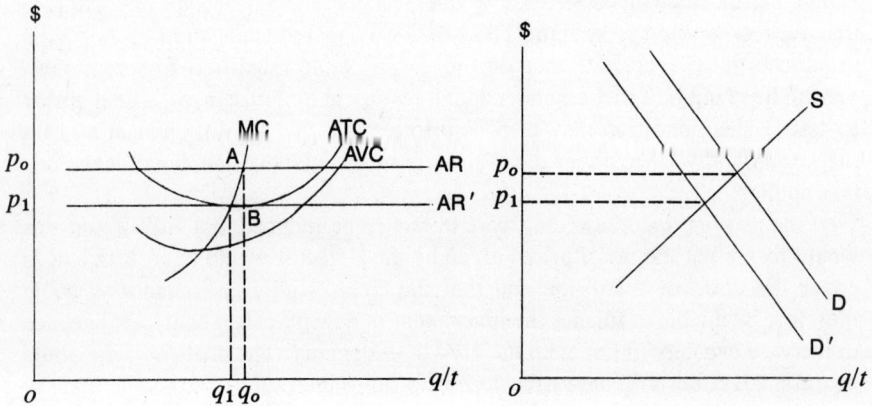

Marshallian model, the entry of the new firms can be expected to lead to increased interfirm rivalry, with the greater discounting off the list price making it difficult to maintain any margin above costs. Thus the long-run equilibrium solution posited by both the Walrasian and Marshallian models may, in time, again be realized—though only as the obverse side of the value condition for continuous growth no longer being satisfied.

The fact that it is not possible for an economic system to be in the long-run equilibrium state posited by the neoclassical price theory while simultaneously satisfying the value condition for continuous growth suggests that a growing economy—or any part thereof—to which the Walrasian or Marshallian model applies will be inherently unstable. Periods during which firms are earning a sufficient margin above cost to finance the necessary expansion of capacity because the system is, from the perspective of the neoclassical pricing models, in disequilibrium will be followed by periods during which investment will have to curtailed because the increase in capacity from the new firms entering the industry has eliminated those profit margins and therefore the system is, from the perspective of the growth model previously developed, in disequilibrium. The very process that restores the "equilibrium" insofar as the one type of model is concerned will create a disequilibrium situation insofar as the other type of model is concerned.

This inherent instability when either the Walrasian or Marshallian model is the one that applies helps to account for two observable phenomena. The first is the emergence of the megacorp as the representative type of firm and oligopoly as the prevalent type of market structure within the industrial sector. These two separate facets of the way industrial activity is organized in an advanced society like the United States can be said to have evolved so that the necessary value condition for continuous growth will be satisfied, not just temporarily as a disequilibrium outcome but rather, consistently over time as a consequence of the way in which prices are normally determined and then maintained. The second phenomenon which can be explained, once it is recognized that the equilibrium condition posited by the neoclassical price theory is inconsistent with the necessary value condition for continuous growth, is the greater instability that is likely to be observed both in agriculture, where the Walrasian model most clearly applies, and in those industries outside the oligopolistic core, where the Marshallian model instead applies.

Indeed, in analyzing the stability properties of an advanced market economy like that of the United States, a clear distinction needs to be made between its oligopolistic core and the rest of the enterprise sector. Within the former there will be little problem in satisfying the necessary value condition for continuous growth because of the pricing power of the megacorps that are the representative type of firm (see section 6.3.4). This is in sharp contrast to the rest of the enterprise sector where, since the representative firm is a neoclassical proprietorship with little or no pricing power, the value condition is likely to be satisfied only by those industries which are either not experiencing any growth (because they represent stagnant areas of the economy) or whose expansion is part of some disequilibrium growth process, such as that posited by Joseph Schumpeter in *The Theory of Economic Development* and in *Capitalism, Socialism and Democracy*. The problem posed by the existence of an oligopolistic core, then, is not that prices will be insufficient to enable firms to cover the cost of expansion. The problem will, if anything, be the opposite: that the set of prices, and hence the residual income vector, that is likely to be established by those industries will be more than is necessary to satisfy the value condition for continuous growth, with the difference representing the "excess profits" of each industry. These "excess profits," it can be argued, will not just serve to redistribute income in favor of certain groups at the expense of others. They will also, as a far more serious problem, generate additional savings beyond what is needed to match the level of investment so that the necessary aggregate demand condition for continuous growth will not be satisfied. This, however, is a point that must wait until the discussion of income distribution in chapter 8 to be developed further.

There is yet another way that the apparent conflict between the long-run equilibrium state postulated by neoclassical price theory and the necessary value condition for continuous growth can be avoided. This is by arguing that the analytical framework of the Marshallian and Walrasian models, based as it is on the posited existence of a separate supply curve for each industry that is independent of the demand curve, is invalid. We shall now examine that argument.

6.4.5 The industry supply curve

What economists normally mean by an industry supply curve is a schedule representing the different quantities of some good that firms are willing to supply as the price of that good varies. Several ambiguities surrounding this theoretical construct should immediately be noted. One is the question of what is meant by the price of a good. Is it the list price—that is, the price quoted to all buyers beforehand? Or is it instead the actual transaction price—that is, the price specified in a contract subsequently entered into by a specific buyer and seller? A second ambiguity concerns the time frame of the argument. Is it in the short run that the quantity supplied depends on the price? Or is it only in the long run that this relationship holds?

It should first be pointed out that the distinction between the list price and the actual transaction price is an important one only insofar as the industrial sector of an advanced market economy is concerned. Within the primary sector, the group of middlemen-speculators active in the sector's commodity markets will ensure that the forward price does not get too far out of line with the spot price, and indeed list prices, as such, do not exist. The situation is quite different within the industrial sector, however. There, an independent group of speculators able to "make" their own market for goods will not normally be found. Instead, as has already been pointed out, firms simply announce in advance the list price at which they are prepared to sell whatever quantity of output may be demanded, and a separate "spot" price cannot be observed except insofar as discounts are granted off the list price. Still, these discounts are such a common business practice that it is necessary to recognize the existence of a transaction price separate and distinct from the list price. This, in turn, raises the question of whether the quantity supplied by the firms within the industrial sector depends on the list price or the actual transaction price. While those who posit the existence of an industry supply curve that is independent of the demand curve are largely silent on this point, still one can begin to see what the answer must be once the private function served by any complete set of prices, such as that denoted by the **P** vector, has been distinguished from their public purpose.

The private function of prices is to determine the distribution of income between sellers and buyers. The higher the price being charged, the greater the amount of income going to sellers at the expense of buyers. Conversely, the lower the price, the greater the distribution of income in favor of buyers (see section 6.1.1). This private function which prices serve depends only on the actual transaction price. Indeed, it is for this reason that, in determining the margin about costs that is actually realized within any industry, and thus the rate at which discretionary funds are being generated, one needs to take into account any discounts off the list price. Still, this private function served by prices is not the same as the public function.

The public purpose served by prices is to indicate the relative scarcity of different material goods—that is, how readily available those goods are compared with the uses to which they can be put. To the extent that the set of prices denoted by the **P** vector reflects the relative scarcity of different material goods, it will enable the independent entities responsible for production—megacorps, neoclassical proprietorships, government agencies, nonprofit organizations and the like—to make decisions based on those prices in such a way as to economize on the society's available resources. The public function of prices, then, is to indicate which resources are relatively more abundant and therefore which resources can most economically be used in the production process. With a price vector that reflects the relative scarcity of different goods, those responsible for production will, by the very process of acting to minimize their costs, economize on the use of a society's scarce resources.

If prices are to serve this public function, they must be prices which, besides reflecting the relative scarcity of different goods, are known to all potential users of those goods. A price which is known only to the two parties directly involved in a transaction is of little value to other potential users of the good in indicating its relative scarcity. It is for this reason that, in the industrial sector, only the list prices can be said to serve a public function. The actual transaction prices, since they are likely to remain a secret, serve only the private function of determining the distribution of income between buyer and seller. Moreover, as will soon be brought out, even the list price can be said to serve the public function of assuring the best utilization of society's limited resources only to the extent it reflects the full costs of production, including the cost of expansion. Before elaborating on this point, however, and indeed before attempting to say whether the quantity supplied by an industry depends on the list price or the actual transaction price, it is necessary to clarify whether the industry supply curve itself is a short-run or a long-run relationship.

While it is possible, in the case of the Walrasian model, to derive an industry supply curve that applies in the short run (see section 6.4.1), the same is not true of the Marshallian model. Although the representative firm can be presumed to have the same upward sloping marginal cost curve as its Walrasian counterpart, the fact is that the quantity which the firm is willing to produce and then supply to the market does not depend on the marginal costs of production. It does not even depend on the average costs of production, for the latter will determine only the list price, not the quantity supplied. With firms prepared to fill any orders at whatever list price has previously been announced, the quantity supplied will in fact be independent of the price. This means that a supply curve, in the sense that economists normally use the term, does not exist.

Instead, what can be observed is only the supply-offer curve. This indicates the price that must be paid by buyers for any given quantity of output they may want to purchase, as distinct from the price that will determine how much firms are willing to supply. It turns out that, with the quantity supplied a function of price—as it is in the Walrasian model— the supply curve and the supply-offer curve are one and the same. However, with the quantity supplied independent of the price—as it will be when, as in both the Marshallian model and in the model of oligopolistic pricing developed in the previous sections of this chapter, firms are price setters—the very relationship upon which a supply curve in the true sense is based no longer holds; and only a supply-offer curve, not a true supply curve, can be said to exist.

As can be seen from exhibit 6.19, the supply-offer curve derived from the publicly known list price will be perfectly elastic. This simply means that firms are prepared to supply, at a certain fixed price, any quantity that may be demanded of them. However, if the list price is not necessarily adhered to by all firms—as may well be the case when, as in the Marshallian model, a large number of firms all produce the same fairly homogeneous product—a second supply-offer curve can be delineated based on the transaction rather than the list price. As can be seen from exhibit 6.27, this second supply-offer curve will have a positive slope to it rather than being perfectly elastic, with the distance between it and the supply-offer curve that is based on the list price narrowing as the quantity demanded increases. Beyond a certain point, with firms no longer willing to grant any further discounts off the list price, the two supply-offer curves will, in fact, coincide. Still, before that point is reached and indeed even beyond, buyers can count on being able to obtain whatever quantity they may need at a price no greater than the list price. The quantity which firms are willing to supply does not depend on the transaction price. Thus, neither of the two supply-offer curves should be confused with a true supply curve.

What has been said so far in questioning whether a true supply curve exists in the case of the Marshallian model holds only in the short run. While it might be supposed that these difficulties can be avoided by focusing instead on the long-run relationship between the price and the quantity supplied, this turns out not to be the case. Once the time frame is extended to encompass the long period, the existence of an industry supply curve, separate from the demand curve, becomes suspect even in the case of the Walrasian model. Indeed, with this shift in the time frame of the analysis, what has been only implicit in the argument so far—namely, that the quantity supplied by an industry, rather than being independent of the demand, is in fact determined by the demand—can be shown to be the general case for all industries. This means that, instead of having to specify a separate demand and supply function for each industry as the Walrasian general equilibrium model requires (see section 6.4.1), only a single equation of the following sort need be adduced:

$$Qs_i = f(Q_{D_i}) \tag{6.63}$$

Keynes had precisely this point in mind when, in turning Say's law on its head so as to create a useful body of macroeconomic theory, he argued that supply is not independent of demand as economists are wont to assume (see chapter 3, section 2.4).

A number of problems have already been pointed out in connection with the positively sloped supply curves usually specified by economists. These include (1) the lack of empirical evidence, at least within the industrial sector, for the

Exhibit 6.27

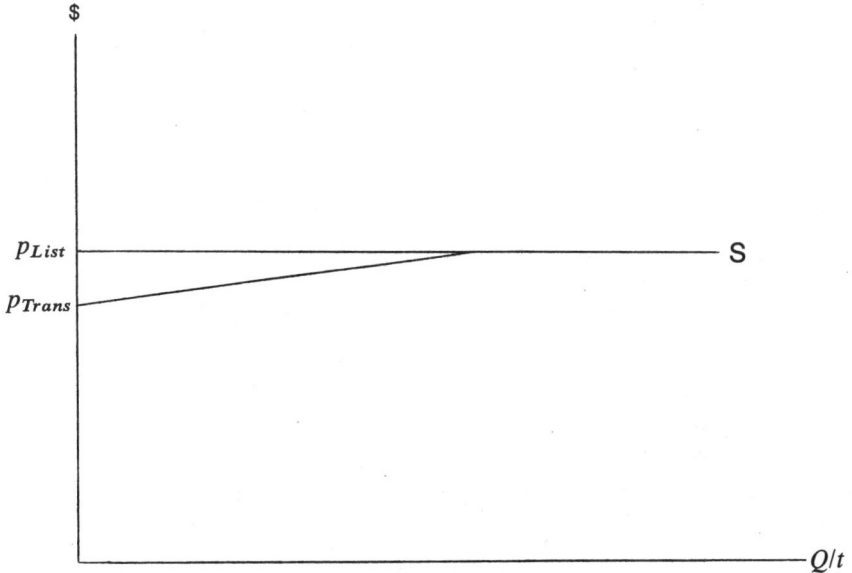

decreasing returns to scale upon which those curves are predicated (see chapter 5, section 3.3), and (2) the difficulty of incorporating such a set of separate supply curves for each industry within a general model of the enterprise sector once the necessity for intermediate output, both of capital goods and of other material inputs, is recognized (see chapter 5, section 4.1). To these problematical aspects of the industry supply curve as a theoretical construct one must add the fact that economists have so far had little success in demonstrating that the quantity supplied by an industry is a function, and a positive one at that, of the price—either in the short run or in the long run. These problems can be eliminated, however, by relying instead on the alternative post-Keynesian (and therefore post-classical) model of production that has been developed up to this point. Based on that model, it is possible to explain, without having to specify a separate supply curve for each industry, what determines both the quantity produced and the price charged by each of the n industries which constitute the enterprise sector—including even any industries, such as agriculture, in which firms are price-takers rather than price-setters. The industry supply curve as a theoretical construct can then be rejected on the grounds that it is superfluous.

The long-period model of production developed previously suggests that the quantity supplied by each vertically integrated industry can be explained in terms of the following three equations (see chapter 5, section 5.4):

$$Q = (I - A)^{-1} D_0 \qquad\qquad (5.23)$$

$$\mathbf{D_0} = \mathbf{D_{-1}} + \hat{\mathbf{G}}(\mathbf{D_{-1}}) \qquad (5.77)$$

$$\mathbf{G} = \mathring{\mathbf{Z}}(\Upsilon) + \Omega(\Psi) \qquad (5.81)$$

The dual price solution to this long-period model of production, representing the value that needs to be placed on the output of each industry if it is to cover all of its costs—including the cost of expansion—is given by the following two additional equations (see section 6.1.4):

$$\mathbf{P} = (\mathbf{I} + \hat{\underline{\mathbf{M}}}) \, w\underline{\mathbf{L}} \qquad (6.33)$$

$$\underline{\mathbf{M}} = \hat{\mathbf{G}}\hat{\mathbf{B}}[\mathbf{I} - (\hat{\mathbf{G}}\hat{\mathbf{B}})]^{-1} \qquad (6.34)$$

These last two equations can be combined so that, in its reduced form, the long-period price equation can be written as follows:

$$\mathbf{P} = (\mathbf{I} - \hat{\mathbf{G}}\hat{\mathbf{B}})^{-1} \, w\underline{\mathbf{L}} \qquad (6.37)$$

With but a slight elaboration of the argument, the same four equations—the three equations necessary for determining the output of each industry plus the one price equation—can be shown to hold in the case of all n industries, and not just for the h vertically integrated (and artificially constructed) industries.

The above equations, it can be argued, leave the output and price vectors indeterminate since there are not enough equations to account for all the unknowns. There are, in fact, seven otherwise unexplained, and thus exogenously determined, variables. These parameters of the model are $\mathbf{A}$, $\mathbf{B}$ (or, alternatively, $\mathbf{K}$), $\mathbf{L}$, Υ, Ψ, $\mathbf{Z}$ (or, alternatively, $\mathring{\mathbf{Z}}$ and Ω) and w. However, three of these variables—$\mathbf{A}$, $\mathbf{B}$ (or, alternatively, $\mathbf{K}$) and $\mathbf{L}$—depend, once their initial starting values are known, on a fourth variable, the rate of technical progress as measured by $\mathring{\mathbf{Z}}$; and this fourth variable can, in turn, be said to be uniquely determined once a technical progress curve, indicating the effect that the rate of growth of investment has on the growth of output per worker, has been derived so that the values taken by the $\mathbf{Z}$ vector will then be known. Thus four of the seven additional variables depend on the rate of technical progress, something that has already been explained, at least insofar as it depends on economic factors (see chapter 5, part 4).

Two of the model's other three parameters are the relevant sets of income and price elasticities that have yet to be taken up in any systematic way (see chapter 9, part 1). Suffice it for now to point out that, like the technical progress function, these income and price elasticities must be taken as being exogenously determined, and not as something that can be explained by an economic model. Within the orthodox framework, these elasticities are, in any case, viewed as operating on the demand, rather than the supply, side of any market. The final parameter of

the model that needs to be recognized is the money wage rate, w. This distributional variable, like the others that will subsequently be introduced as the analysis
proceeds, can be said to be exogenously determined in keeping with the model's
Sraffian framework (see section 6.4.1), with a fuller justification for this treatment to be offered when the question of what determines the money wage, as
distinct from the real wage, is examined (see chapter 8, part 3).

Even if one is willing to accept the argument that the pricing model's seven
parameters are otherwise explained, one might still object to the fact that the
model's dual price solution merely indicates what prices will need to be established if the firms in each industry are to cover their costs. These are not the
prices that will necessarily prevail at any moment in historical time. The same
criticism applies, of course, to the long-run ''equilibrium'' prices of the alternative neoclassical theory. The difference is that, while the set of prices given by
equation 6.37 (or, taking all n industries and not just the h vertically integrated
ones, equation 6.40) may not actually be observed, they are nonetheless the
prices that the firms in each industry must obtain for their output if the necessary
value condition for continuous growth is to be satisfied. Either firms must use
whatever pricing power they have to establish and then maintain the necessary
margins above cost or, alternatively, they will find their growth constrained for
lack of the necessary funds to finance the purchase of new plant and equipment.
These two separate implications of the post-Keynesian pricing model are both
subject to empirical verification. The price vector which can actually observed at
any one point in time should approximate that given by equation 6.37 (or equation
6.40), with any discrepancy between the postulated price vector and the actual
price vector tending to be eliminated over time. And any industry which, for lack
of the necessary pricing power, is as an exception to this rule should, as a
consequence, experience both greater cyclical instability and lower growth.

6.4.6 A look at the empirical evidence

The several pricing models examined in this chapter can be tested empirically by
looking at the differences in price both across industries and over time. The first
approach, relying on cross-sectional data, can be used to assess the alternative
long-period models of pricing and the second approach, relying on time series
data, can be used to assess the alternative short-period models. In this concluding
subsection, we shall look at only the cross-sectional data, thereby restricting the
comparison to the opposing long-period models. The evidence insofar as the
short-period changes in price are concerned will be taken up later, in connection
with the analysis of the inflationary process within an advanced market economy
(see chapter 14, section 3).

The long-period model of prices developed in this chapter as an alternative to
the conventional pricing models argues that, after taking into account any direct
and indirect labor costs, prices will vary across industries depending on (1) the

industry growth rate, g_j; (2) the incremental capital-output ratio, b_j; and (3) the industry's pricing power as determined by the elasticity of demand, the barriers to entry, and the likelihood of government intervention. This last factor, the industry's pricing power, is approximated, at least in part, by the concentration ratio. While the conventional neoclassical theory is not usually formulated in such a way that its long-run implications can be empirically tested, the theory would appear to argue that, after similarly taking into account any direct and indirect labor costs, prices will vary across industries depending on the amount of "capital" employed. If the amount of "capital" is measured by the incremental capital-output ratio and the industry growth rate is viewed as a separate parameter, with a zero value for that parameter as the limiting case, the differences between the two models disappear. Indeed, this is yet another way to reconcile the opposing arguments. However, if some other measure of "capital" is used and/or only a zero growth rate is thought to be consistent with the neoclassical formulation, then an empirical test of the alternative models is possible. A third long-period pricing can be identified and tested simultaneously. This is the Marxian model (see chapter 8, section 4.2) which argues that prices will vary across industries solely on the basis of the direct and indirect labor requirements.

(The rest of this subsection is not yet complete.)

Recommended Readings

On the long-period pricing model developed in part 1 of this chapter, see Pasinetti, *Structural Change and Economic Growth*, chs. 5, 7–8, 10; Eichner, *Towards a New Economics*, ch. 3.

On the Sraffian model, see, besides *The Production of Commodities by Means of Commodities*, New York: Cambridge University Press, 1960, the following: Alessandro Roncaglia, *Sraffa and the Theory of Prices*, New York: Wiley, 1978; Gilbert Abraham-Frois and Edmond Berrebi, *Theory of Value, Prices and Accumulation*, New York: Cambridge University Press, 1977; Ian Steedman, *Marx After Sraffa*, London: New Left Books, 1977; the contributions by Carlo F. Manara, Paolo Varri, Salvatore Baldone and Bertram Schefold in the collection edited by Pasinetti, *Essays on the Theory of Joint Production*, New York: Columbia University Press, 1980; Willi Semmler, *Competition, Monopoly, and Differential Profit Rates*, New York: Columbia University Press, 1984, pp. 14–47.

On the von Neumann model, see John von Neumann, "A Model of General Equilibrium," *Review of Economic Studies*, 1945–46, no. 1; Bent Hansen, *General Equilibrium Systems*, New York: McGraw-Hill, 1970, ch. 16; Blatt, *Dynamic Economic Systems*, chapter 4. On the difference between the Sraffian and von Neumann models, see Bertram Schefold, "Von Neumann and Sraffa: Mathematical Equivalence and Conceptual Difference," *Economic Journal*, March 1980.

For an elaboration of the argument presented in part 2 of this chapter, see *The Megacorp and Oligopoly*, ch. 2. See also Peter J. Wiles, *Prices, Costs and Output*, Oxford: Basil Blackwell, 1956; Romney Robinson, "The Economics of

Disequilibrium Price," *Quarterly Journal of Economics*, May 1961. On the separation of management from ownership and the question of control which is thereby raised, see, in addition to Adolf A. Berle and Gardiner C. Means, *The Modern Corporation and Private Property*, New York: Macmillan, 1933, the following: Edward S. Herman, *Corporate Control, Corporate Power*, New York: Cambridge University Press, 1981. On the behavioral rules of the megacorp, see the appendix to chapter 2 of *The Megacorp and Oligopoly* as well as the references cited therein, especially Herbert A. Simon, "A Behavioral Model of Rational Choice," *Quarterly Journal of Economics*, February 1955; Richard M. Cyart and James G. March, *A Behavioral Theory of the Firm*, Englewood Cliffs, N.J.: Prentice-Hall, 1963; Oliver E. Williamson, *The Economics of Discretionary Behavior*, Englewood Cliffs, N.J.: Prentice-Hall, 1964; William J. Baumol, *Business Behavior, Value and Growth*, revised ed., New York: Harcourt, Brace and World, 1967; Robin Marris, *The Economic Theory of 'Managerial' Capitalism*, New York: Free Press, 1964.

On the classical oligopoly models of Cournot and Bertrand-Edgeworth, see Fritz Machlup, *The Economics of Sellers' Competition*, Baltimore: Johns Hopkins Press, 1952, ch. 12; Peter Asch, *Economic Theory and the Antitrust Dilemma*, New York: Wiley, 1970, ch. 3; James W. Friedman, *Oligopoly and the Theory of Games*, New York: North-Holland, 1977. The Chamberlin-Robinson model was introduced into economics by Edward H. Chamberlin, *The Theory of Monopolistic Competition*, Cambridge, Mass.: Harvard University Press, 1933, and by Joan Robinson, *The Economics of Imperfect Competition*, London: Macmillan, 1933. Chamberlin, it should be noted, was careful not to apply the model to oligopoly while Robinson subsequently described the model as having "serious limitations." See her preface to the second edition, published in 1969. The argument against the model based on the observed elasticities of demand for oligopolistic products was first presented in Eichner, "A Theory of the Determination of the Mark-up under Oligopoly," *Economic Journal*, December 1973.

The model of oligopolistic pricing developed in part 3 of this chapter was first presented in Eichner, "A Theory of the Determination of the Mark-up under Oligopoly," *op. cit.* See also *The Megacorp and Oligopoly*, ch. 3, and Paolo Sylos-Labini, *Oligopoly and Technical Progress*, Cambridge, Mass.: Harvard University Press, 1962; Adrian Wood, *A Theory of Profits*, New York: Cambridge University Press, 1975. The model can be regarded as a further elaboration of the markup theory of pricing originally put forward by the members of the Oxford Pricing Group in Great Britain (see Robert L. Hall and Charles J. Hitch, "Price Theory and Business Behavior," *Oxford Economic Papers*, 1939, reprinted in Thomas Wilson and P. W. S. Andrews, *Oxford Studies in the Price Mechanism*, Oxford: Clarendon Press, 1951; P. W. S. Andrews, *Manufacturing Business*, London: Macmillan, 1949, and *On Competition in Economic Theory*, London: Macmillan, 1964), as well as, in two somewhat different versions, by Michal Kalecki (see his *Theory of Economic Dynamics*, New York: Rinehart,

1954, ch. 1) and by Sidney Weintraub (in *A General Theory of the Price Level, Output, Income Distribution, and Economic Growth*, Philadelphia: Chilton, 1959). In these earlier versions of the model, the size of the markup is simply taken as a given rather than being explained on the basis of the demand for, and supply cost of, investment funds. On the determination of the size of the markup, see also Donald J. Harris, "The Pricing Policy of Firms, the Level of Employment and the Distribution of Income in the Short Run," *Australian Economic Papers*, June 1974.

On the U.S. counterparts to the markup pricing models developed by the Oxford Pricing Group in Great Britain, see Abraham H. Kaplan *et al.*, *Pricing in Big Business*, Washington: Brookings Institution, 1958; Gardiner C. Means, *Pricing Power and the Public Interest*, New York: Harper & Row, 1962. For the subsequent development of the Kalecki version of the model, see Joseph Steindl, *Maturity and Stagnation in American Capitalism*, Oxford: Basil Blackwell, 1952, and Malcolm Sawyer, *Macro-Economics in Question*, Armonk, N.Y.: M. E. Sharpe, 1982, chs. 4–8. On the origins of the markup pricing model, see Fred Lee, "Full-Cost Pricing: An Historical and Theoretical Analysis," unpublished doctoral dissertation, Rutgers University, 1982. For other, earlier dynamic models of firm behavior, see Jack Downie, *The Competitive Process*, London: Duckworth, 1958; Edith T. Penrose, *The Theory of the Growth of the Firm*, New York: John Wiley, 1959 [Armonk, N.Y.: M. E. Sharpe, 1980]; John M. Clark, *Competition as a Dynamic Process*, Washington: Brookings Institution, 1961.

The argument presented in part 4 of this chapter can be traced back through *The Megacorp and Oligopoly*, pp. 126–43; Eichner, "A General Model of Investment and Pricing," in *Growth, Profits and Property*, Edward J. Nell, ed., New York: Cambridge University Press, 1980, and *Toward a New Economics*, ch. 3. The distinction made between the Walrasian excess-demand hypothesis and the Marshallian excess-supply hypothesis is based on Bent Hansen, *A Survey of General Equilibrium Systems*, New York: McGraw-Hill, 1970, especially ch. 2. See also Joan Robinson, *Economic Philosophy*, Chicago: Aldine, 1962, and *Economic Heresies*, New York: Basic Books, 1971.

On the empirical evidence with respect to the different pricing models covered in this chapter, see Semmler, *Competition, Monopoly, and Differential Profit Rates*, and Ochoa, "Labor-Values and Prices of Production," *op. cit.* See also Otto Eckstein and Gary Fromm, "The Price Equation," *American Economic Review*, December 1968; Paolo Sylos-Labini, *Trade Unions, Inflation and Productivity*, Lexington, Mass.: Lexington Books, 1974; Kenneth Coutts, Wynne Godley and William Nordhaus, *Pricing in the United Kingdom*, New York: Cambridge University Press, 1978.

Chapter 7

The Enterprise Sector: Investment and Finance

Contents

Chapter 7

The Enterprise Sector: Investment and Finance

It is the rate of investment being carried out by the enterprise sector which explains, not only the expansion path which the economic system is likely to take (see chapter 4) but also, given the input-output relationships of a Leontief production system, the residual income vector, π, and hence the set of prices, P, that can be expected to prevail—at least in the long period (see the preceding chapter). Moreover, as will become clear in the next chapter, the rate of investment is also one of the key factors determining the distribution of income. The essential question that needs to be answered, then, before the macrodynamic behavior of the American economy can be explained is what determines the rate of investment. This will be the task of the present chapter.

It is important, before proceeding any further, to explain what is meant by the term "rate of investment." The rate of investment is the value of the capital goods being produced (and purchased by other business firms) relative to the value of total output. This rate of investment, I/Y (where I is the nominal value of new plant and equipment purchases and Y, the nominal value of aggregate output) should not be confused with the rate of growth of investment, $\dot{I}$. While a change in the rate of investment necessarily implies a change in the rate of growth of investment, the two are not the same. In this chapter the focus will be on explaining what determines the increment in capital outlays from one period to the next, ΔI, with that increment in capital outlays then related to the change in nominal output, ΔY, and to the past level of investment, I_{-1}, so that, within the context of the same dynamic framework that has been developed up to this point, both the "rate" of investment and the "rate of growth" of investment can be determined.

The first step in explaining what determines the increment in capital outlays from one period to the next will be to survey the different theories of investment which can be found in the literature. These are theories which attempt to explain only the *level* of investment, I, or, at most, the *change* in the level of investment, ΔI. Still, the same theories, with only slight modification, can be used to explain the average or "the" rate of investment, I/Y, both in nominal terms and, given the rate at which the price of investment goods is increasing, in real terms; the marginal rate of investment, $\Delta I/\Delta Y$, in nominal terms, and the rate of growth of investment, $\dot{I}$. Once this review of the literature has been completed, it will then be possible, in the sections which next follow, to determine which of the theories—or combination thereof—best fit the empirical evidence. Here, as in the preceding discussion of pricing, the focus will be on the megacorp as the representative firm within the oligopolistic sector. Both the factors determining the size of its capital budget and the conditions under which it will be forced to resort to external financing will be identified. The purpose is not just to explain what determines the rate of investment by the megacorp. It is also to derive a discretionary expenditures, or E, function and a discretionary funds, or F, function for the enterprise sector and its several component parts, both corporate and noncorporate. Only in this way can the stabilizing—or destabilizing—influence of the enterprise sector be determined.

7.1 Alternative Models of Investment

There is little agreement, even among post-Keynesians, as to what is the most appropriate model of investment behavior. This is so despite the vast amount of empirical work which has been done on the question. Aside from the investment function which can be found in *The General Theory*, there are a number of other models which have been put forward by economists—largely in response to what are perceived to be the shortcomings of Keynes's own formulation. These alternative models of investment are: (1) the Kaleckian model; (2) the accelerator model; and (3) the neoclassical model. In this first part of the chapter, each of these alternative models will be taken up and examined in turn, beginning with the original Keynesian investment function.

7.1.1 The Keynesian investment function

Within *The General Theory* can be found not one but two rather different models of investment behavior. One is a static model which draws its inspiration from the earlier work of Irving Fisher on time-related problems of valuation. The other model is a dynamic one, based on the distinction which Keynes always insisted on between risk and uncertainty, even before Frank Knight made it the subject of his well-known book. Both of these models have been found to be unsatisfactory— though for quite different reasons.

In the static version of Keynes's model, the level of investment is said to depend on the marginal efficiency of capital, r, and the interest rate, i. That is,

$$I = f(r, i) \tag{7.1}$$

These two determinants, however, need to be defined with some care if Keynes's investment function is to be faithfully described.

The starting point for Keynes in defining the marginal efficiency of capital is the formula, first given by Fisher, for equating the different values of the same asset over time. Let it be assumed that a certain asset can be purchased which will then yield its owner an increment in income equal to $R_1, R_2, R_3, \ldots, R_n$ over the succeeding n time periods. (The number of time periods, n, can be viewed as being equal to infinity or, alternatively, the asset can be assumed to have a scrap, or resale value, equal to V_{n+1} in time period $n+1$.) The question that primarily interested Fisher is what will be the present value of the asset, V_0. That is, what would a rational buyer be likely to pay in order to obtain the asset? The answer Fisher gave can be represented by the following formula:

$$V_0 = \frac{R_1}{(1+i)} + \frac{R_2}{(1+i)^2} + \frac{R_3}{(1+i)^3} + \ldots + \frac{R_n}{(1+i)^n} + \frac{V_{n+1}}{(1+i)^{n+1}} \quad (7.2)$$

or, combining the R_j terms,

$$V_0 = \sum_{j=1}^{n} \frac{R_j}{(1+i)^j} + \frac{V_{n+1}}{(1+i)^{n+1}} \quad (7.3)$$

where i is the current market rate of interest.

The $(1+i)^j$ term in the above equation represents the discount factor which must be applied to the increment in income in each successive time period so that the present value of that future income stream can be determined. Equation 7.3 is therefore the most general formula for determining the present value of any asset yielding future income. Indeed, it is the formula to be used—insofar as any formula will suffice—for calculating the price at which bonds, stocks and other financial assets can be expected to trade in the various securities markets. Keynes, however, was concerned with a quite different matter. His focus was on physical assets, not financial assets; and while there are some economists who insist that the distinction is not that important, the fact is that only financial assets command a wide market. Physical assets, in the form of new plant and equipment, enable only the small number of firms constituting a given industry to generate future income, and these types of assets therefore command only a narrow market. Indeed, this is why business firms will, if they can, issue securities in the form of stocks and bonds, thereby creating a monetary, or financial, counterpart to the physical assets they own which can then command a wider market. Moreover, in the situation which Keynes was attempting to analyze, it is not the present value of some physical asset that needs to be determined. That present value, V_0, is simply the purchase price of the new plant and equipment. Rather, what is unknown is the yield, or prospective rate of return, from acquiring those assets.

Relying on equation 7.3, one can easily determine the prospective rate of return—assuming that actual numerical values can be attached to the R_j terms and V_{n+1}. One need only substitute, as Keynes did, the "marginal efficiency of capital," r, for the market rate of interest, i, as follows:

$$V_0 = \sum_{j=1}^{n} \frac{R_j}{(1+r)^j} + \frac{V_{n+1}}{(1+r)^{n+1}} \quad (7.4)$$

and then solve for r. That r represents the prospective return above cost can be seen more clearly if one ignores all but the first-period effect and then isolates the $(1 + r)$ term on the left-hand side as follows:

$$1 + r = \frac{R_1}{V_0} \tag{7.5}$$

Thus r is the "margin" by which the future return exceeds the cost of the investment.

Unfortunately, at this point in his exposition, Keynes chose to emphasize the continuity, rather than the break, with the prevailing mode of economic analysis so that, despite the clear language to the contrary, the marginal efficiency of capital as defined in *The General Theory* has come to be identified with the "marginal product of capital." One difference between the two has already been indicated (see chapter 4, section 1.1). The essential point, in this connection, is that while Keynes's concept of the marginal efficiency of capital does not require that the ratio of capital to other types of inputs vary, the marginal productivity concept does. The Keynesian concept, then, while not opposed to the neoclassical theory of distribution based on marginal productivity, is not firmly rooted in that theory either. To make sure this point is not lost sight of—and, in particular, to avoid confusing the Keynesian with the neoclassical concept—r will henceforth be termed the marginal efficiency of investment rather than the marginal efficiency of capital. The former phrase has the further advantage of making clear that what is being described is the *increment* in income, or revenue, relative to the costs of the investment project—and not all of the firm's net revenue, or profit, relative to the value of the capital stock.

To some economists, the distinction between the marginal efficiency of capital and the marginal efficiency of investment is of a different sort, with the former referring to the long-period return on investment, the latter to the short-period return. The argument of these economists is that, because of the short-period systemic effect of any rise in aggregate demand, the two may well differ. If, for example, a large number of firms rush to take advantage of the investment opportunities being created, the total demand for new plant and equipment may press against the capacity of the investment goods sector, leading either to higher prices that temporarily lower the value of r or to the sheer inability of the investment goods sector to satisfy all the current demand. While it is certainly possible that the marginal efficiency of investment will, in the short run, be depressed below its long-period value as a result of the temporarily higher cost of capital goods, the argument assumes that the industries constituting the investment goods sector are subject to decreasing returns to scale. If, as seems more likely (see chapter 4, section 1.3 and chapter 5, section 3.2), these industries normally maintain a certain amount of reserve capacity so they can increase their output without incurring higher costs, then the argument no longer holds. In any

Exhibit 7.1

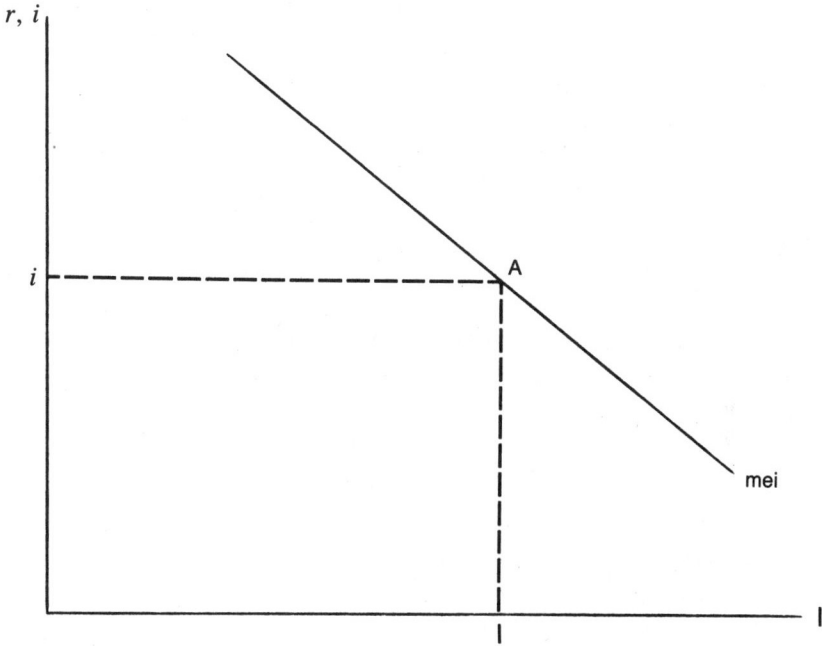

case, it seems better simply to recognize that the short-period value of the marginal efficiency of investment, r, may differ from the long-period value rather than use a separate term, and a confusing one at that, to denote the latter.

What Keynes termed the marginal productivity of capital—and what shall hereafter be referred to as the marginal efficiency of investment—is best understood therefore as simply the prospective rate of return on investment. Keynes's argument was that firms must necessarily calculate this prospective rate of return, at least implicitly, for each of the different investment projects they are considering, and that when all these different investment projects are arrayed in the descending order of their prospective rate of return, one obtains an investment demand schedule such as the one shown in exhibit 7.1. In the static version of the Keynesian investment model, this negatively sloped marginal efficiency of investment curve can then be compared with the market rate of interest, with the point at which the interest rate intersects the marginal efficiency of investment curve—point A in exhibit 7.1—determining the current level of investment, I.

What this means is that, once the marginal efficiency of investment schedule is given, the level of investment will vary only as the market rate of interest itself varies—with an increase in i leading to a decline in I and vice versa. It was this line of reasoning that led economists to expect the level of investment to be inversely correlated with the market rate of interest. Early econometric studies following the publication of *The General Theory* failed, however, to confirm the existence of any such relationship; and interviews with businessmen, both in Great Britain and the United States, cast further doubt on whether the interest rate was a significant determinant of investment behavior. Indeed, in light of what has already been said about the reliance of firms on internally generated funds (see chapter 6, sections 1.4 and 3.4) and what will be said subsequently about the marginal role played by external finance (see section 7.3.3), these empirical findings should come as no surprise. The discouraging results obtained when one relies on the static version of the Keynesian investment function explain why it has been largely abandoned as the basis for empirical research on capital expenditures.

Still, there remains the dynamic version of the same model. The estimate of r by any firm depends critically on the values assigned to the R_j terms in equation 7.3, and those values cannot be known with any degree of confidence. This is because the rate of return will depend on how well the firm's sales subsequently hold up, and the level of sales will, in turn, depend on the state of the economy at the time the new capacity comes on line and is ready to be operated—something the individual firm cannot know in advance, let alone influence. Firms are therefore forced to commit themselves to the purchase of capital goods when the prospective rate of return is uncertain. Their willingness to do so under the circumstances will depend, according to Keynes, on their state of expectations about the future.

This line of argument has been interpreted by some to mean that the actual values of the R_j and V_{n+1} terms in equation 7.3 need to be replaced by the expected values, $\epsilon(R_j)$ and $\epsilon(V_{n+1})$, where ϵ is a set of probabilities with values falling between 0 and 1. That is,

$$V_0 = \sum_{j=1}^{n} \frac{\epsilon(R_j)}{(1 + r)^j} + \frac{\epsilon(V_{n+1})}{(1 + r)^{n+1}} \tag{7.6}$$

A change in the expectations of business enterprises can then be thought of as a change in the probabilities represented by the ϵ terms in the above equation, with a more optimistic assesment of future prospects resulting in higher values for the ϵ terms and thus of r, and a more pessimistic assessment leading to lower values. The combined set of ϵ terms, as the barometer of firms' expectations, thus becomes a parameter of the marginal efficiency of investment curve, causing the curve to shift over time as the judgment of businessmen about the future direction of the economy itself fluctuates. While this interpretation is in accord with the Keynesian view that changes in the level of investment are more likely to be due to shifts of the marginal efficiency of investment curve than to movements along the curve, it nonetheless runs counter to a fundamental point stressed by Keynes.

The point is that one cannot assign probabilities, in an actuarial sense, to the future increments in income resulting from any investment which business enterprises may undertake. This is because there is no past experience relevant to the future situation that will govern the return on that investment—and thus no actuarial basis for calculating those probabilities. It is for this reason that the uncertainty surrounding investment must be distinguished from the risk of certain types of insurable accidents occurring. The probabilities which the ϵ terms represent can never be determined in advance—certainly not by the individual firms that must, by virtue of the position they occupy within the system of production, make the choice of whether to purchase any capital goods.

The marginal efficiency of investment curve, then, based on the arguments made by Keynes himself, is likely to shift back and forth over time in a way that cannot be predicted in advance. The whole thing depends, in Keynes's own words, on the "animal spirits" of the capitalist class. This, however, is a far from satisfactory state in which to leave the theory, for it means that the principal explanatory variable has been formulated in such a way that it is essentially unmeasurable. Indeed, this is one of the reasons why even economists who accept the other parts of his model have tried to improve upon Keynes's specification of the investment function. The first to do so was the independent discoverer of the basic Keynesian model, Michal Kalecki.

7.1.2 The Kaleckian model of investment

Keynes's contribution to economic theory largely ceased with the publication of *The General Theory*, in part because Keynes suffered a heart attack in 1937 and in part because he was preoccupied from 1939 until his death six years later by his wartime duties as the principal economic advisor to the British government. In contrast, Kalecki was able to continue his work in economics almost to the day he died in 1970, further refining and elaborating on the ideas he first put forward in the 1930s. As a result, even though his original treatment of investment was quite similar to that of Keynes, Kalecki's views on the subject continued to evolve until, by 1954, he could be said to have developed a model of investment which, if not necessarily opposed to the dynamic version of the model found in *The General Theory*, nonetheless had the greater virtue of identifiying the specific set of factors that might cause the marginal efficiency of investment curve to shift over time.

The Kaleckian model of investment, it should be noted, was not developed in theoretical isolation but rather was part of a broader conceptual framework for analyzing the dynamic behavior of a market economy. The centerpiece of that framework was the theory of income distribution which will be taken up at greater length in the chapter which next follows and which is perhaps Kalecki's most important contribution to post-Keynesian theory. With the simplifying assumption that there are no savings by workers and no "consumption" by "capitalists"—what has come to be termed the "classical" assumption since they were employed by the classical economists—Kalecki was able to show that the market value of any capital goods purchased, I, must necessarily be equal to the income available to business firms in the form of profits, Π (see chapter 8, section 2.1). Much the same idea was, of course, relied upon in the last chapter to explain the size of the residual vector and hence the long-period set of prices within a

Leontief model of production. From the necessary equality between I and Π under the classical assumption, it was but a small step for Kalecki to posit, as he did as early as 1933, that any addition to the capital stock, $\Delta K/K$ or I/K, will depend on the level of profit relative to the size of the capital stock, Π/K, as well as on the market rate of interest, i. That is,

$$\frac{I}{K} = f\left(\frac{\Pi}{K}, i\right) \qquad (7.7)$$

The original Kaleckian investment function, as represented by equation 7.7, is essentially the same as the Keynesian function given by equation 7.1—the principal differences being (a) that the rate of return was calculated by Kalecki at the aggregate rather than at the firm level, and (b) that both investment and the return on investment were related to the size of the capital stock. While the shift in the level of analysis had the important advantage of laying the groundwork for the macroeconomic theories of income distribution which characterize the later post-Keynesian approach, the ratios which Kalecki relied upon to highlight the distributional aspects had the unfortunate consequence of perpetuating the view that somehow the "stock of capital" was a measurable quantity. Kalecki himself grew dissatisfied with his original model for quite a different reason. The model is based on the accounting identity, under the classical assumption, that I = Π, and it therefore represents not so much a behavioral relationship as the logical outcome of defining his terms the way Kalecki did. For this reason, while still emphasizing the profits variable as the key determinant of capital outlays, Kalecki began modifying his approach so as to be able to explain why profits—besides reflecting the level of investment, based on the multiplier relationship—should induce additional capital outlays by business firms. In other words, Kalecki came to recognize that he needed a theory to explain the *ex ante* demand for investment, and not just the *ex post* equality between I and Π.

Kalecki would eventually emphasize two quite different ways in which the amount of profit being earned influences the rate of investment. Profits are important, he pointed out, first as a source of funds. Indeed, Kalecki was at the forefront of those recognizing that enterprises finance their investment outlays largely out of retained profits, together with whatever funds have been set aside for depreciation. The larger the size of those retained profits and depreciation allowances—what has earlier been defined as the enterprise sector's net cash inflow or discretionary funds, F—the greater the likelihood that firms will be able to carry through with their capital expenditure programs. It is not just that the retained profits are a direct source of funds themselves. It is also that they represent an increase in the "equity" of firms, and this increase in their "equity" will enable firms to borrow more heavily from external sources.

Corporate profits are also important, however, as an indication of whether businessmen's expectations about the future are likely to be realized. If profits are increasing, this is a sign, at least from the perspective of the enterprise, that economic conditions are improving and if, alternatively, profits are falling, this is a sign that economic conditions are deteriorating. Rising profits are therefore likely to make businessmen more optimistic about the future, persuading them to go ahead with whatever investment projects they are contemplating, while falling profits are likely to have the opposite effect. It is thus in response to the direction in which profits are moving, whether they are rising or falling, that the marginal efficiency of investment curve shifts back and forth over time.

In stressing the importance of past profits in establishing a firm's financial position, Kalecki was attempting to correct the undue emphasis which both he and Keynes had placed on the interest rate as the factor on the supply side determining the level of investment. In pointing out the effect that a *change* in profits is likely to have on business expectations, Kalecki was, moreover, attempting to identify the specific factor on the demand side which leads to the pronounced shifts of the marginal efficiency of investment curve which can be observed over time. Indeed, by relating the change in business expectations to the change in profits, Kalecki was able to take the first step toward providing an explanation for why market economies are so unstable. For if profits are rising, firms will be encouraged by that very fact to increase their capital outlays. With the stimulus to aggregate demand provided by the greater capital outlays, profits are likely to rise even higher, giving further encouragement to investment. Similarly, if profits are falling, firms can be expected to cut back on their capital outlays, precipitating a further decline in aggregate demand, profits and investment. To complete the argument, it was necessary only for Kalecki to explain what caused this process of cumulative expansion or decline to reverse itself. This Kalecki was able to do by introducing a third factor, besides the amount of profits being earned and the direction in which profits as a whole were moving, into his investment function. The third factor was the degree of utilization of the existing capital stock.

Spurred by the disproportionate rise in profits that occurs during a period of expansion, investment can be expected to increase more rapidly than aggregate demand, leading eventually to the addition of more capacity than can be effectively utilized. This means that the necessary supply condition for continuous expansion by each industry, namely, that $\dot{I}_j$ be equal to $\dot{Q}$ or g_j, will no longer be satisfied. Once firms become aware of the excess capacity within their industry, they are likely to cut back on their capital outlays. With prices weakening as a result of the excess capacity and profits turning into losses, firms will have little incentive to undertake any further investment. Paced by the decline in capital outlays, a period of cumulative decline is likely to follow. On the other hand, if investment remains depressed even though the economy has somehow managed to expand once again, the increase in demand relative to capacity will begin to put pressure on the existing plant and equipment. With prices increasing and profit margins therefore rising, firms can be expected to resume their purchase of capital goods—thereby marking the onset of another period of expansion.

The dynamic sequence outlined by Kalecki is the same as that already encountered, first, in connection with Harrod's "knife-edge" problem (see chapter 4, section 1.2) and then, subsequently, in connection with the long-run supply curve in those industries to which either the Walrasian or Marshallian model applies (see chapter 6, section 4.5). Indeed, the Kaleckian model of investment, at least insofar as capital outlays are said to depend on whether profits are rising or falling is simply a logical extension of the argument underlying the two neoclassical pricing models when they are placed in a macrodynamic context. Thus Kalecki, who otherwise is celebrated for his efforts to develop a body of theory applicable to an economy in which oligopoly predominates, specified an investment function that appears to be more appropriate to the nonoligopolistic sector of such an economy (see section 7.4.3 and 7.4.4).

The affinity between Kalecki's model of investment and neoclassical theory would, at first glance, appear to be even greater since Kalecki actually included the size of the capital stock, K, as one of the explanatory variables within his investment function. Indeed, it is this factor that determines the cyclical turning point in Kalecki's model. However, what Kalecki really had in mind was a change in the expected, or normal, rate of the capacity utilization, $\hat{C}ap$, and, without misrepresenting his argument, that variable can therefore be substituted for the K term in the investment function which Kalecki himself specified. In this way, a possible source of criticism can be avoided. This is not to suggest that determining the normal rate of capacity utilization is without statistical problems of its own. It is only to point out that a capacity utilization measure can be constructed that does not raise the same problems of valuation that a capital stock measure does, and that the average for this figure over the cycle can then be calculated.

One further refinement is necessary when specifying a Kalecki investment function. Kalecki recognized that the actual purchase of new plant and equipment occurs only with a certain lag after the decision to undertake the investment has been reached. By taking this lagged effect explicitly into account, Kalecki converted what had previously been a static, simultaneous model into a dynamic, recursive one. The amount of profits retained and the direction in which profits as a whole are moving will, together with the change in the rate of capacity utilization, determine the level of investment in the next time period, along with the amount of profits being earned—and so on for each succeeding time period. The Kalecki investment function, as modified, therefore takes the following form:

$$I_{+1} = f(F, \Delta\Pi, \hat{C}ap) \tag{7.8}$$

where I_{+1} is the amount of investment undertaken by all business firms in the subsequent time period, F is the amount of discretionary funds (net cash inflow) of the enterprise sector within the current period, $\Delta\Pi$ is the change in profits during the same period and $\hat{C}ap$ is some measure of current capacity utilization. Kalecki further specified that while F and $\Delta\Pi$ would be positively correlated with

I_{t+1}, $\hat{C}ap$ (or K) would be negatively correlated. One further point to be noted is that the amount of discretionary funds, F, actually represents the amount of business savings, and indeed Kalecki made this clear by using the symbol S instead of F. This investment equation, together with a profits equation which takes the following form:

$$\Pi = f(I, \hat{C}ap) \tag{7.9}$$

constitutes the dynamic model which Kalecki used to explain the cyclical instability of a market economy. It is a model which further elaborates on Harrod's analysis of the "knife-edge" problem.

The changes which, by 1954, Kalecki had made in his original investment function were quite consistent with the findings from the empirical research which the Keynesian revolution had stimulated. Tinbergen, Lawrence Klein and the other early econometric model builders, finding little correlation between investment and the interest rate, had instead come to rely on past profits as the principal explanatory variable in their investment equations, with some measure of the capital stock as a secondary factor. Indeed, though the equations were far from satisfactory in being able to explain cyclical fluctuations in investment, they would remain far superior to what could be explained by relying on any other model for at least another decade. By the mid 1960s, however, certain changes had been made in the alternative accelerator model which would enable it, in terms of its explanatory power, to seriously challenge the Kaleckian model.

7.1.3 The accelerator model

What has come to be known as the accelerator model of investment had its origins in a long-neglected article by John M. Clark published in 1919. Clark, examining data from the American railroad industry, noted that an increase in the amount of traffic carried by the railroads led to a disproportionate increase in capital spending by the industry, and a decrease in traffic, to a disproportionate decline in capital spending. The generalization of these findings for the economy as a whole led to two related, though quite separate conclusions: (1) that the level of investment depends on the level of aggregate demand, and (2) that the change in investment will be greater than the change in industry demand. The first of these two propositions simply says that aggregate investment is a function of real aggregate demand. That is,

$$I = f(G) \tag{7.10}$$

As already pointed out (see chapter 4, section 1.3), this reverses the direction of causation suggested by the basic Keynesian model. The second proposition means that the above functional relationship needs to specified more precisely as follows:

$$\Delta I = a(\Delta G) \tag{7.11}$$

where a is the marginal propensity to invest, $\Delta I/\Delta G$, and is assumed to be greater than 1. While it is from the second of these two relationships that the accelerator model derives its name, it is only the first which is necessarily implied when economists use the term. Any investment function in which the amount of expenditures on new plant and equipment depends on the level of demand is referred to as an accelerator model, regardless of what value a takes.

Actually, it is not necessary that the marginal propensity to invest be greater than 1 for the accelerator model, in conjunction with the multiplier, to generate endogenous cyclical movements. As was pointed out in connection with the Harrod-Domar model (see chapter 4, sections 1.1 and 1.4), the necessary condition for continuous, uninterrupted growth is that the marginal propensity to invest, a, be equal to the marginal propensity to save, s. This necessarily implies, as a corollary, that a must be equal to the product of the aggregate growth rate, $\dot{G}$, and the incremental capital-output ratio for the economy as a whole, v (the weighted average of the incremental capital-output ratio for each individual industry, b_j). As can be seen by replacing $\dot{G}$ with $\Delta G/G$ and v with $I/\Delta G$, this reduces to the following condition:

$$\dot{I} = \dot{G} \tag{7.12}$$

which is the aggregate version of the necessary supply condition which must be satisfied by each individual industry. Thus two types of accelerator models can be distinguished: those which, since they satisfy equation 7.12, are log linear and those which, since they do not satisfy equation 7.12, are nonlinear variants of that model. It is the latter type of acclerator model which, in conjunction with the multiplier, will generate endogenous cycles.

Paul Samuelson, in a classic 1939 article, has determined the entire set of possible cyclical patterns from employing a simple multiplier-accelerator model, one in which the marginal propensity to invest, a, and the marginal propensity to consume, b (and hence the marginal propensity to save, s) are the only two parameters. With the value of a allowed to vary between 0 and $4+$ and the value of b allowed to vary between 0 and $1+$, it can be shown mathematically that, with a change in the level of investment (or, in a dynamic context, with a change in the rate of growth of investment), the economic system will fall within one of the four regions delineated in exhibit 7.2. Within region A—with both a and b taking a value less than 1—the economy will move without oscillation to the new level of national income determined by the change in investment, ΔI (or by the change in the rate of growth of investment, $\dot{I}$). Within region D, on the other hand—with b either greater than 1 or associated with a relatively high value of a—the economy will expand at an explosive rate, though again without oscillation. Rather than coming to rest at some new level (or rate of growth) of national income, or even

Exhibit 7.2

b

1.0 A D

.75

.5 B C

.25

1   2   3   4   a

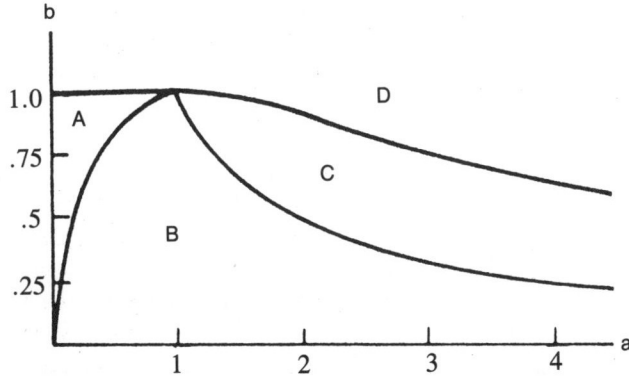

Derived from: Gardner Ackley, *Macroeconomics* (New York: Macmillan, 1978), p. 263.

oscillating around that point, the expansion can be expected to continue at an increasing rate without discernible limit. Still, the more interesting types of multiplier-accelerator models, because they come closer to simulating the cyclical behavior of a market economy, are the ones which fall within regions B and C.

Within region B—with b still less than 1 but with a taking on a higher value than in region A—the economy will oscillate around the new level (or rate of growth) of national income with cycles of diminishing amplitude until eventually the economy stabilizes at the new level (or rate of growth) of national income. Within region C—with b again less than 1 but with a taking on a higher value than in region B—the economy will also oscillate, but in this case the cycles will be of increasing amplitude so that, with each fluctuation, the economy will find itself further displaced from the mean point of the oscillations as determined by the initial change in the level (or the rate of growth) of investment and the size of the multiplier. The difference between the latter two types of models, then, is that while a region B model will eventually stabilize at some level (or rate of growth) of national income, a region C model will not. Though both models give rise to cyclical movements, the first has a long-period steady-state solution or "equilibrium" point and the second does not. The contrast between these two types of models can perhaps best be appreciated by examining exhibit 7.3. Notice that, while a region A model shifts directly to the new level (or rate of growth) of national income and a region D model simply explodes, the region B model gives rise to cycles of decreasing amplitude and the region C model to cycles of increasing amplitude. A region B model therefore implies that the economic system is endogenously stable, as previously defined, while a region C model implies that it is endogenously unstable (see chapter 4, section 4.2).

When the multiplier-accelerator model was first developed and its results generalized, it was thought to provide a relatively simple explanation for the cyclical behavior of market economies. The likely values for a and b did not appear to be different from those which would place an economy in either region

Exhibit 7.3

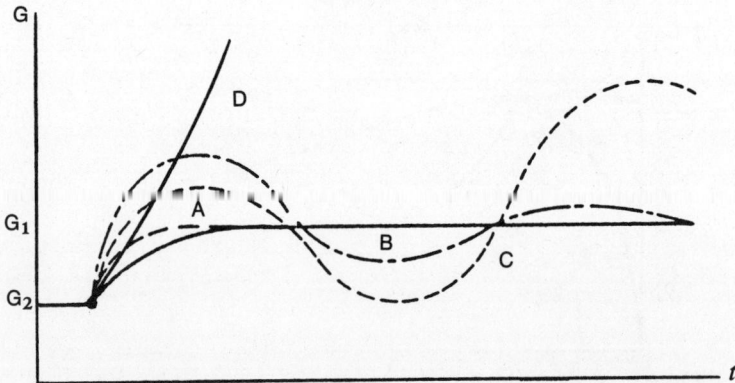

Derived from: Gardner Ackley, Macroeconomics (New York: Macmillan, 1978), p. 263.

B or region C; and the only question, it seemed, was whether the economy was likely to experience cycles of decreasing amplitude (with the system eventually stablilizing at some new level or rate of growth of income) or whether, alternatively, it was likely to experience cycles of increasing amplitude (with the system thus unstable). However, the model in this relatively simply form—with but two parameters, a and b—gives rise to a result that is somewhat unsettling.

The logic of the model requires that if, at some point in time, there should be a decline in the rate of growth of aggregate output—and, given the impossibility of maintaining the initial acceleration of investment, this inevitably happens—then investment in the next time period will necessarily be negative. It is not clear, however, how a negative amount of investment is to be interpreted. The capital stock may, of course, deteriorate physically when it is no longer being replaced and/or maintained, and this is one way to interpret the negative amount of investment to which the model eventually gives rise. But when the amount of negative investment in some period is as great, if not greater, than the amount of positive investment in earlier time periods, it is difficult to view this interpretation as a satisfactory one.

Indeed, it seems more realistic to assume that, if ΔG becomes negative, investment will simply cease rather than turn negative as well. In other words, investment may well have a floor under it, whether the floor is a zero level of investment or even some positive amount of capital expenditures needed to replace worn out plant and equipment. But if investment has a floor under it, why not also recognize that investment may have a ceiling—this being the limit imposed by the supply capacity of the investment goods industries? Indeed, this is the basis for the type of constrained multiplier-accelerator model put foward by John Hicks, Richard Goodwin and others in the early 1950s in which the economy bounces back and forth between the floor and ceiling which the limits on investment, both positive and negative, establish. This additional element of realism grafted on to the model, however, destroys its mathematical simplicity. Even more to the point, despite a conservative estimate as to what the values of a and b are likely to be, the model will still produce quite volatile movements of the economy—even within the limits imposed by the floor and ceiling.

To generate endogenous cycles that are more consistent with the actual historical experience of market economies, especially in the period since the end of World War II, it has therefore been necessary to assume that the effect of the accelerator and the multiplier will be felt, not just in the next succeeding time period but rather, over several time periods. This distributed lag effect, as it has been termed, greatly moderates the impact of the combined multiplier-accelerator effect. But again the greater realism is at the expense of the model's simplicity. What is perhaps an even more serious problem, the distributed lags are an additional set of relationships that need to be determined empirically. With these new parameters, the results of the multiplier-accelerator model can no longer be so easily generalized—although the two main possibilities, dampened oscillations and increasingly more pronounced oscillations, still hold. Indeed, what one winds up with is an *embarassement de riches* insofar as accelerator-multiplier models are concerned: Any change in the assumptions about the upper and lower limits or about the distributed lags will give rise to yet another cyclical pattern.

This is especially true if, in addition to the past level of demand as measured by G_{-t}, other variables are introduced into the investment equation. One of the more commonly stipulated of these other variables is the same measure of the capital stock, K, which Kalecki included in his investment equation. Indeed, the Kalecki and accelerator models are quite similar in the cyclical movements they can be expected to generate—the only difference being the particular factor, past profits or past levels of demand, which are assumed to cause investment to accelerate and decelerate. As will be pointed out shortly, it is not always easy to distinguish the separate influence of these two variables, despite the quite different implications for public policy depending on which is the actual determinant of investment. With other variables such as K (or, what is far preferable from a post-Keynesian perspective, some measure of capacity utilization, $\hat{C}ap$) added to the basic accelerator model, the number of permutations becomes even larger and the mathematics of the model less easily handled.

This is not to suggest that any of these more complicated models should be rejected simply because they are difficult to manipulate mathematically. One of the purposes of this text is to reorient economics away from models whose only virtue is their mathematical tractability. The point rather is that once the multiplier-accelerator model has been modified to give it greater realism, a large number of variations on the same basic model are equally plausible on *a priori* grounds, and that the choice among them then needs to be made on empirical grounds. What this means is that the basis for accepting or rejecting the accelerator model in any one of its many permutations must be its explanatory power rather than its mathematical simplicity.

Initially, the empirical results from testing the accelerator model were not encouraging. It was not just that the disproportionate change in investment relative to demand that Clark had observed in the case of the railroads earlier in the century was not mirrored in the aggregate data for the interwar and post World War II periods. It was also, even more surprisingly, that the change in aggregate investment seemed to bear little relationship to previous levels of aggregate demand. Indeed, until the mid 1960s, the Kaleckian model of investment with past profits plus some measure of the capital stock as the principal determinants seemed to have far greater explanatory power than any accelerator model. But then two significant changes were made in the way the accelerator model had up to then been specified.

The first significant change was an explicit recognition of the distributed lag associated with the accelerator effect. Rather than investment depending on the change in aggregate demand during any one time period, either current or lagged, it was seen as depending on the change in aggregate demand over a successsion of time periods—with the effect not necessarily distributed evenly over the interval. Indeed, in the original specification of a distributed lag function for investment by Leendert Koyck, the weight attached to the change in aggregate demand during any one period declined geometrically—e.g., 1/2, 1/4, 1/8, 1/16—as the effect of a particular variable, such as the change in aggregate demand, was traced further back in time. The Koyck distributed lag was but the first of many such distributed lag functions to be suggested. However, it has proven impossible to choose among any of these distributed lag specifications except on the purely pragmatic grounds of which provides the best statistical fit. It turns out that there is no theoretical basis for preferring one distributed lag specification over another. Moreover, the distributed lag function itself introduces certain statistical problems, particularly that of serial correlation, which are not easily overcome. More will be said on this point later (see chapter 9, part 2). Still, an explicit recognition of the distributed lag associated with it was the first step toward reviving the interest of economists in the accelerator model of investment.

The second, no less critical step was to disaggregate the analysis so that what was being explained was not aggregate investment but rather investment on an industry-by-industry basis. (This step was made possible by the availability of quarterly investment data, broken down by SIC two-digit industries, beginning in 1947). With the analysis of investment being carried out at the industry level, it is no longer necessary to identify the accelerator effect with a change in aggregate output. A more sensitive barometer of the change in demand, one that is more relevant to the particular circumstances of each individual industry, can be substituted. Here there are two choices. One is the change in industry sales. This was the explanatory variable emphasized by Robert Eisner when he developed his lagged-sales accelerator model in the middle 1960s. The model, in this form, can be specified as follows:

$$\Delta I_j = f(\Delta S_{j-1}, \ \Delta S_{j-2}, \ \dots, \ \Delta S_{j-n}) \qquad (7.13)$$

where ΔI_j is the change in the amount of investment by industry j over the most recent interval of time and ΔS_{j-1}, ΔS_{j-2}, . . . , ΔS_{j-n} are the change in that industry's sales, or $\Delta p_j Q_j$, over the preceding n periods. The other choice, as an explanatory variable, is the rate of capacity utilization (or, in the terminology of the preceding chapter, the percentage of engineer-rated capacity being utilized). This was the explanatory variable emphasized by Hollis Chenery in work preceding that of Eisner. The model, in this form, can be specified as follows:

$$\Delta I_j = f(\Delta Cap_{j-1}, \Delta Cap_{j-2}, . . . , \Delta Cap_{j-n}) \qquad (7.14)$$

where ΔCap_{j-1}, ΔCap_{j-2}, . . . , ΔCap_{j-n} are the observed changes in the rates of capacity utilization in the n preceding time periods.

Both variables—the change in industry sales, ΔS_j, and the change in the rate of capacity utilization, ΔCap_j—can be used to formulate a disaggregated version of the accelerater model. Although they are not entirely independent of one another, the two variables can even be used together in the same estimating equation. When this is done, it is then possible, as Michael Evans's work in the late 1960s demonstrated, to account for much of the change in business investment over time—although the relative importance of the two explanatory variables seems to vary with the industry. Formulated in this manner, the accelerator model is better able to explain business investment than the alternative Kalecki model with past profits as the principal explanatory variable. The accelerator model has the further advantage that it can be used to explain the demand for additional plant and equipment, as distinct from the availability of funds to finance that investment. It is for these reasons that, since the late 1960s, the Kalecki model has been largely abandoned in favor of the accelerator model. Moreover, the accelerator relationship has been the underlying basis for the theoretical arguments which have been made in this text about aggregate investment ever since the Harrod-Domar model was first introduced in chapter 4 to explain the process of continuous growth, and it will continue to be the underlying basis for the theoretical argument when, in the next main section, the capital expenditure decision is examined from the perspective of the individual firm, a megacorp especially.

Still, the accelerator model has not been without its subsequent challengers. One model, in particular, has been put forward in recent years, as an alternative to the accelerator model. This is the neoclassical model of investment developed by Dale Jorgenson. Although this model suffers from many of the same shortcomings as the more general theoretical approach upon which it is based, the model nonetheless deserves to be examined on its own merits. We thus need to turn to that model.

7.1.4 The neoclassical theory of investment

The static version of the investment function originally specified in *The*

General Theory can, as already pointed out (see section 7.1.1), be labeled "neo-classical" without belying Keynes's own words. By interpreting a movment along the marginal efficiency of capital schedule as a decision to vary the capital intensity of production (as well as by identifying the marginal efficiency of capital with the marginal product of capital), the investment function specified is fully in accord with the neoclassical model of production, both the aggregate version (see chapter 1, section 1.2) and the micro version (see chapter 5, section 4.5) in which the choice of inputs is between X amount of "capital" and Y amount of labor. In this specification of a neoclassical model of investment, the decision of whether to vary the capital intensity of production depends solely on the interest rate. However, it need not be the interest rate alone, especially the observed market rate, which determines the capital intensity of production (as that term is used within neoclassical theory). Indeed, the replacement of the observed market rate of interest with another variable, one that is thought to be more relevant to the choice between capital and other inputs, is the basis for the type of neoclassical investment model which has been specified by Jorgenson and others.

In the Jorgenson model, the capital intensity of production depends on what is termed the "rental price of capital" relative to the price of the output which the capital inputs make it possible to produce. It is this ratio which determines the "optimal" capital stock—that is, the quantity of capital inputs relative to other inputs which will enable an individual firm to maximize its net revenue over an extended time horizon. The same idea can expressed mathematically as follows:

$$K_j = f(\frac{p_j Q_j}{c(k)_j})\qquad(7.15)$$

where K_j is the jth industry's optimal capital stock, p_j is the price and Q_j the quantity of output sold by the firms within that industry, and $c(k)_j$ is the industry's "rental price" of capital. The implicit argument is that the firm will already, in some previous period, have achieved an optimal capital stock, with the rental price of capital equal to the marginal product of capital. That being the case, any change in the ratio $p_j Q_j / c(k)_j$ will require a change in the capital stock so as to eliminate the resulting disparity between the rental price and marginal product of capital and again make the capital stock an optimal one.

If the ratio $p_j Q_j / c(k)_j$ should increase, this means that the value of the output produced by the capital input is greater than the rental price of those inputs, indicating that the marginal product of capital has risen relative to its rental price. An addition to the capital stock will then be necessary so that, with the decline in the marginal product and/or the increase in the rental price of capital which can be expected to occur as more capital inputs are added, the marginal product and the rental price of capital will again be equal to one another. Conversely, if the ratio should fall, a reduction in the capital stock will be necessary so as to bring the marginal product and rental price back into balance with one another and make the capital stock an optimal one. It should be noted that it is not the notion of an "optimal" capital stock which is unique to the Jorgenson model of investment. That there is some quantity of capital inputs for the individual firm that is optimal is also implicit in the alternative accelerator model and, since that model of investment is integral to the long-period model of production developed in chapter 5, in the latter as well. What is unique to the Jorgenson model as well as to any other type of neoclassical investment model is the basis for determining the optimal capital stock.

In the Leontief long-period model of production, and thus in any specification of an investment function based on that model, production in the short period can be presumed to take place with technical coefficients which are fixed or invariant, not just between the material and labor inputs but also between those inputs and any capital inputs as well. The optimal capital stock—even though that term is not used—therefore depends solely on the scale of production, as given by the scalar, λ (see chapter 5, section 3.3). In the short period, if firms have some reserve capacity, the existing capital stock will be optimal within the limits already identified in connection with the relevant set of cost curves (see exhibit 5.11). Beyond the short period, however, the capital stock will remain optimal only as long as the additions to that stock, and hence the investment in new plant and equipment, keep pace with the growth of aggregate output. That is, it will remain optimal only as long as the condition given by equation 7.12 is being satisfied. Indeed, this is the underlying premise of the accelerator model, with the growth of aggregate output, $\dot{G}$, serving as the principal determinant of investment, $\dot{I}$.

In the Jorgenson and other neoclassical investment models, the optimal capital stock may or may not be a function of the growth of aggregate output. In practice, it is recognized that the expansion of the economy will create a need for additional plant and equipment, what is sometimes referred to in the context of neoclassical growth models as "capital broadening." However, since expansion of any sort is not easily handled within a neoclassical framework, the emphasis is usually on the capital intensity of production, what is referred to as "capital deepening." This emphasis is possible because, in a neoclassical model, the technical coefficients are flexible rather than fixed. Firms can, even in the absence of technical progress, adopt a variety of production techniques, each requiring a different combination of capital and labor inputs. The technique chosen, it is argued, will be the one that brings the marginal product of capital into balance with the rental price of capital. It is the additional capital inputs required by the new technique, together with the capital inputs already in place, that constitute the optimal capital stock in a neoclassical model of production and investment.

By this point enough has been said to throw into question, even without going into marginal productivity theory more deeply, much of the reasoning behind the neoclassical theory of investment. There is, first of all, the difficulty of specifying a quantity variable so that a production function with capital as a separately delineated real input can be derived empirically, either for the economy as a whole or for just the individual firm or industry (see chapter 4, section 3.7, and chapter 5, section 5.1). Moreover, it is doubtful whether the choice confronting the firm is between capital and other types of inputs. Rather the choice is more likely to be between one combination of capital inputs—together with the other types of inputs given by the technical coefficients associated with that kind of a plant or plant segment **and** another combination of capital inputs representing another kind of plant or plant segment (see chapter 5, section 3.1). Still, the neoclassical theory of investment, along with the notion of capital deepening, cannot simply be dismissed out-of-hand. Although the historical evidence suggests that economic growth is likely to be accompanied by technical progress, increasing mechanization and rising output per worker, this does not preclude the possibility of increased prior *investment* (that is, a greater stock of capital goods which have previously been acquired) per worker. Indeed, it is hard to conceive of increasing mechanization without greater prior investment per worker. Furthermore, with the size of the work force, relative to output, declining over time, there is no reason why the greater prior investment per worker need imply an increase in the incremental capital-output ratio and thus a fall in the social rate of return on investment. It is therefore possible to vary the amount of prior investment per worker while the capital intensity of production, as measured by v, remains unchanged. An increase in prior investment per worker with v constant can even be regarded as "capital deepening." If it is the prior investment per worker, rather than the substitution of capital for other inputs, that defines the optimal capital stock, then there is no reason to reject the Jorgenson model—at least as so far presented. We need instead to consider, independently of the neoclassical context in which the argument has been formulated, whether prior investment per worker, and thus the optimal capital stock, depends on the ratio, $p_j Q_j / c(k)_j$.

While the first term in the above ratio is clear enough—it is simply the value of each industry's output, or the **PQ** vector in the Leontief system—the second term, the rental price of captial, requires further explanation. In the Jorgenson model, if we ignore any capital gains from unanticipated changes in price levels, the rental price of capital is equal to the price of investment goods previously acquired multiplied by the time discount on capital investment and the rate at which capital depreciates in value over time. That is,

$$c(k)_j = p_{I_j}(r + \zeta_j) \tag{7.16}$$

where p_{I_j} is the price of the investment goods purchased by the jth industry, r is the time discount applied to capital investment and ζ_j is the rate at which capital depreciates in value over time. Since r and ζ_j can be assumed to be unaffected by cyclical factors, the jth industry's cost of capital, $c(k)_j$, in the short period depends solely on the price of investment goods, p_{I_j}. That is,

$$c(k)_j = f(p_{I_j}) \qquad (7.17)$$

Based on this relationship, equation 7.15 can then be rewritten as follows:

$$K = f(Q_j, \frac{p_j}{p_{I_j}}) \qquad (7.18)$$

In other words, the optimal capital stock depends, in addition to the level of industry output, Q_j, as in an accelerator model, on the price of the industry's output relative to the price of investment goods, p_j/p_{I_j}. It is the latter ratio which, by determining the amount of prior investment per worker, modifies the amount of capital expenditures that could be expected on the basis of the accelerator relationship alone. This is why the Jorgenson and similar neoclassical investment models are referred to as "flexible" accelerator models to distinguish them from the accelerator models which exclude any relative-cost-of-capital variable.

Whether the empirical evidence supports the specification of a flexible accelerator is a matter that will not be taken up until later. The important point to be noted here is that yet another variable, the relative cost of capital, p_j/p_{I_j}, has been identified as a possible determinant of the optimal capital stock, and thus as a factor influencing investment outlays over time. If one substitutes the Tobin version of the neoclassical investment function for the Jorgenson version, with Tobin's "Q" ratio replacing p_j/p_{I_j}, then yet another possible determinant of investment behavior can be added to the list. Since the "Q" ratio is the value of the shares in the companies which comprise the industry relative to the price of investment goods, this means that the value of those shares, V_e, replaces the price of the industry's output in the numerator and that the size of the optimal capital stock is said to depend on V_e/p_{I_j} rather than p_j/p_{I_j}. These two variables join the others already identified as possible candidates for inclusion within the investment function for the enterprise sector as a whole.

Once all the possible determinants of investment have been identified, the next step is to examine the empirical evidence to see which model, or combination of models, is most consistent with that evidence. Before attempting such an exercise, however, it may be useful to look at the question from the perspective of the individual firm. For it is the individual firm, rather than the industry, that actually decides whether to proceed with any particular investment project. Indeed, it may not be possible to make sense of the empirical evidence until we have first examined the microeconomic foundation of investment behavior.

7.2 The Firm's Investment Decision

The level of capital expenditures, or investment, is a decision made by the individual firm. A theory to explain investment must therefore be consistent with what is known about decision-making at the firm level. This is the microeconomic foundation of any model of investment behavior.

In the case of the oligopolistic sector, the representative firm is a megacorp. The goal of such a firm, and the behavioral pattern it must follow if it is going to achieve that goal, have already been identified (see chapter 6, section 2.1). The firm's goal is to grow at the highest possible rate, and this requires that the megacorp at least retain its present share of the market in the industries to which it already belongs while simultaneously reducing its costs as much as the evolving technology and the rate of capital spending will permit. In addition, if the megacorp is to avoid the decline that inevitably occurs in the case of any one industry, it must periodically expand into new, more rapidly growing industries. This requisite behavioral pattern if the megacorp is to maximize its growth over time helps to explain not only how the megacorp sets its prices but also how it determines the composition and amount of capital outlays. Indeed, as already explained, the megacorp's pricing and investment decisions are inextricably linked, with any change in the mark-up depending on the demand for additional investment funds relative to the supply cost of those funds (see chapter 6, section 3.1). It is therefore where the previous discussion of pricing left off—specifically with the as yet unexplained demand for additional investment funds—that we shall now pick up the argument.

The megacorp's demand for additional investment funds, D_I, depends on the four separate uses which can be made of those funds. They are: (1) to expand capacity; (2) to lower costs; (3) to strengthen the firm's market position; and (4) to diversify into other industries. While it is only the first two components of D_I that will necessarily lead to the purchase of new plant and equipment and therefore to investment as that term is understood by economists, all four components need to be taken into account if the megacorp's discretionary expenditures are to be balanced against its net cash inflow, or discretionary funds. In the subsections which follow, each of these four components of the demand for additional investment funds will be taken up in turn with the objective being to identify their underlying determinants. We shall begin with the megacorp's need to expand capacity.

7.2.1 The expansion of capacity

The megacorp, if it is to achieve its goal of at least maintaining its present share of the market in the industries to which it already belongs, has no choice but to expand its capacity in line with the growth of industry demand. To be caught without adequate capacity is to risk losing a share of the market to the other firms in the industry or even to new entrants. It can therefore be postulated that the same condition that must be satisfied in the long period by the industry as a whole, namely, that

$$\mathring{I}_j = g_j \qquad\qquad\qquad\qquad (6.15)$$

must be satisfied as well by each megacorp with a significant share of the market. While the *amount* of investment undertaken by the individual megacorp within any industry at any one point in time, I_{i_t}, will be only a portion of the investment undertaken by the industry as a whole, I_{j_t}—with that portion equal to the firm's share of the market—still the *rate of growth* of investment by each megacorp will necessarily have to be the same as for the industry as a whole if that firm is going to retain its present market share. This means that $\mathring{I}_i$ can be substituted for $\mathring{I}_j$ in equation 6.15 as follows:

$$\mathring{I}_i = g_j \qquad\qquad\qquad\qquad (7.19)$$

where $\mathring{I}_i$ is the rate at which the individual megacorp needs to purchase new plant and equipment for the purpose of expanding capacity within a given industry, and g_j is that industry's growth rate, one of the elements of the G vector previously explained (see chapter 5, section 5.4).

Equation 7.19 is the necessary supply condition that must be satisfied by the individual megacorp within any one of the mature oligopolistic industries to which it already belongs. It should be noted that the megacorp, as the most advanced type of business organization yet to evolve, is likely to satisfy this condition—at least in the long period. This is not just because of the megacorp's considerable pricing power which, as pointed out in the preceding chapter, will assure it of the necessary funds. It is also because of the way the megacorp itself is structured to carry out the planning of capital outlays and because of the lesser uncertainty that attends any investment in new capacity by the megacorp as compared with a firm that cannot count on retaining its present share of any growing market.

Most firms which have achieved the status of a megacorp have developed the type of managerial stucture which frees top executives from any day-to-day operational responsibilities so they can concentrate on the questions which are critical to the firm's longer run growth and survival. The answers to these questions, such as what goods should the company produce and therefore what industries should it be involved in, will then define the megacorp's growth strategy.

The megacorp can be assumed to be a member of k different industries, each of which is growing at a rate equal to g_j. The growth of demand for the megacorp's output, assuming its share of those markets remains unchanged, will be the weighted average of those growth rates. If, for example, the megacorp sells one-third of its output in an industry growing at 10 percent a year and two-thirds in an industry growing at 7 percent, then the overall demand for the megacorp's output will be increasing at 8 percent a year. That is,

$$g_i = \sum_{j=1}^{k} w_j g_j \tag{7.20}$$

where g_i is the rate at which the demand for the megacorp's output is increasing; g_j is the rate at which each of the k industries to which the megacorp belongs is expanding, and w_j is the amount of the megacorp's sales in each of those industries. Unless the megacorp's profit margin in each of those industries should change as a result of the investment it undertakes, such as the purchase of cost reducing equipment, g_i will also be the rate at which the megacorp is growing, as measured by the rate of increase in cash flow, or discretionary funds (g_i will, in addition, be the rate at which the megacorp will need to increase its capacity in all k industries as distinct from the rate, g_j, at which it will need to increase capacity in any one of those industries.)

The megacorp's goal may be to continue growing at that rate—or possibly even to grow at a higher rate. In either case, the rate at which the megacorp hopes to increase its cash flow over the next several years will be its target growth rate, with both the required rate of return on investment, $\overset{+}{r}$, and the required profit margin, $\overset{+}{\mu}$, based on it. Any return on investment less than 10 percent, if 10 percent is the target growth rate, will work against the megacorp being able to increase its cash flow at the rate it would like, while the required profit margin will simply be the target growth rate multiplied by the megacorp's average incremental capital-output ratio. The megacorp's growth strategy will, in turn, be the combination of approaches it intends to follow in order to achieve its target growth rate—e.g., broadening its product line in one or more industries so as to increase market share, relying more heavily on outside vendors so as to reduce the cost of key components.

The key to implementing any growth strategy is the annual capital budget, listing the megacorp's major investment outlays for the coming year. It is through the capital budget that the megacorp positions itself to compete in the longer run. Assisting the megacorp's top executives in drawing up the annual capital budget are likely to be various staff groups capable both of estimating the future growth of sales in any of the industries in which the megacorp is interested and of drawing up the detailed plans necessary for constructing a new production facility within any one of those industries. Thus, in the case of the megacorp, investment planning is likely to have become routinized, with the necessary staff already in place. Instead of being a unique event in the history of the firm, the purchase of new plant and equipment is carried out continuously as part of an annual planning cycle which has, as its focal point, the drawing up once a year of the firm's capital budget for the next 12-month period.

Meanwhile, the relatively fixed share of the market which the megacorp can normally expect to retain (see chapter 6, section 2.1) eliminates one of the two sources of uncertainty surrounding any investment by a firm in new plant and equipment. This is the uncertainty created by the competition of other firms. If other firms were to succeed in obtaining for themselves the entire increase in industry demand, a firm would be unable to sell any of the output that might be produced in a new plant and the return on the firm's investment would, as a consequence, be reduced to zero. The ability of the megacorp to hold on to its present share of the market eliminates this source of uncertainty. With its secure market position, the megacorp can count on its own sales within the industry increasing at the same rate as the demand for the industry's output. This leaves, as the only source of uncertainty, the rate at which the demand for the industry's output, and hence the megacorp's own sales within that industry, are likely to increase over time.

The megacorp, both because of the way it is structured and the relatively secure market position it enjoys, will therefore have little trouble in determining the rate at which it needs to increase its capacity in the long period within any one industry. Where it is likely to have difficulty is in translating this estimate of the secular growth rate for any one industry into a decision of how much new plant and equipment to purchase within that industry, as part of its capital budget, during any one 12-month period. The problem is how to time any addition to its capacity within the industry so it coincides as closely as possible with the growth of sales. On the one hand, it is embarrassing for a megacorp to be caught without sufficient capacity, for it may then be forced to concede a share of the market to rival firms or even to new entrants. It is no less embarrassing, however, to have a new plant or plant segment become operational just as part of the existing capacity is being idled for lack of demand. In the latter case the megacorp will find that it has prematurely, and perhaps even needlessly, incurred the cost of adding to its capacity.

The megacorp, it should be noted, has some room for maneuver in this regard. The existence of reserve capacity provides the megacorp with the means of supplying any unexpected increase in demand while a fall-off in sales, even if only cyclical, will end the immediate pressure to expand capacity. Indeed, it is to give itself this flexibility that the megacorp normally maintains a certain amount of reserve capacity (see chapter 5, section 3.2). Still, while the change in capacity during any one period need not match the change in sales exactly, the two do need to increase roughly in line with one another in the long period—that is, taking into account more than just the current cyclical movement. What makes the megacorp's task in this regard so difficult is that the economy follows not a steady-state growth path but rather one marked by pronounced cyclical movements and even changes in trend. One can never be certain whether the latest deviation from the secular growth of industry sales is merely a random movement, is instead part of the normal cyclical pattern, or portends a new trend. The evidence, at least initially, will be the same in all three cases. Only by taking into account the subsequent change in industry sales, thereby placing the deviation from trend in a long period context, will the megacorp be in a position to judge whether or not a new trend is emerging.

The adjustment by the megacorp to a change in the growth of industry sales,

g_j, will therefore not be immediate. A certain amount of time is likely to lapse before the change in trend can even be recognized, let alone responded to. It is for this reason that any change in the rate at which capacity is being expanded, and thus a change in $\dot{I}_i$, is likely to lag behind the change in g_j. Even so, the megacorp must make sure that the growth of capacity over time matches the growth of industry sales. Indeed, the greater the lag in the megacorp's response, the more the megacorp will need to compensate by either accelerating or decelerating its outlays on new plant and equipment. That this is possible reflects the extended period of time required to effect an increase in productive capacity and the number of discrete steps which the capital expenditure process entails.

The long lead time involved in the construction of a new facility—it can take more than a decade to find and develop a site for a major new plant such as a continuously casting steel mill—means that the planning for any one of the items to be included in the capital budget will have had to have begun many years before. At any step along the way—surveying alternative sites, acquiring land, drawing up plans, signing the necessary contracts—the project can be delayed or abandoned if the projection of industry sales should indicate that the new facility is not needed, at least not so soon. This is not to suggest that, in the face of declining sales, a magacorp will necessarily shelve its plans to build a major new facility. If the fall-off in sales is judged to be only temporary—and if the other factors to be discussed below under the heading of finance are favorable—the project may nonetheless move forward. The point rather is that, until the construction contracts are actually signed following approval of the project and its inclusion in the capital budget, the megacorp can still hold off on making the final commitment that results in the actual purchase of new plant and equipment. The obverse is that, if industry sales are increasing more rapidly than the historical trend, possibly portending a higher growth rate for the industry, the megacorp can accelerate the process by which it adds to its productive capacity.

What has just been said about the construction of a major new facility— namely, that the timing is likely to be influenced by a change in industry sales— applies no less to the purchase of any new equipment alone. A major facility is likely to be designed to house a number of plant segments, or production lines, and it is at the discretion of the firm to determine how quickly those plant segments, through the purchase of the requisite equipment (and the recruitment and training of the necessary complement of workers), will be made operational. The requisite equipment can be acquired all at once, or only gradually over time. Here, as in the case of the decision to construct a major new facility, the choice is likely to be influenced primarily by the rate at which industry sales are expanding, with the sales experience in the most recent period weighing most heavily. If there should be an unexpected change in industry sales, even after the capital budget is approved, the firm has the option of stretching out or speeding up its placement of orders for the new equipment needed to make another plant segment operational.

The purchase of new plant and equipment so that capacity can be expanded is likely, then, to be quite sensitive to any change in the rate at which industry sales are growing. One can in fact postulate that any change in the industry's secular growth rate, g_j, will be followed, after a certain lag, by a disproportionate change in the megacorp's rate of growth of investment in new capacity until the ratio of investment to the growth of sales implicit in the incremental capital-output ratio, b_j, has been reestablished and $\dot{I}_i$ and g_j are again equal to one another (see section 7.4.2). New plant and equipment may be purchased, however, not just to expand capacity but also to reduce costs. This raises the question of how any addition to capacity, or net investment, is to be distinguished from the mere replacement of existing capacity as part of the megacorp's efforts to minimize its costs.

7.2.2 *Cost reduction*

As long as technical progress does not come to a halt in the industries which supply it with capital goods, the megacorp can expect that the purchase of any new plant and equipment will have two separate, though related, effects. One will be the increase in productive capacity emphasized in the preceding subsection. The other will be a reduction in the megacorp's costs of production. For the most part, the second effect simply follows from the first. The additional capacity, to the extent it embodies the latest cost-minimizing technology, will necessarily lower the megacorp's average costs of reduction—even if all the older plants continue to be operated (see chapter 5, section 3.2). Still, there are likely to be circumstances under which the principal reason for the megacorp's purchase of new plant and equipment is that it hopes to lower its costs of production—and not that it needs to increase its capacity. It is this additional ground for the megacorp to include an item in its capital budget that now needs to be examined.

The extent to which the megacorp can lower its costs of production within an industry by purchasing new plant and equipment will depend on the rate of technical progress, as measured by the secular growth of output per worker within the industry, $\dot{z}_j$. It is the rate of technical progress since the oldest plant still in use was acquired that will determine what reduction in costs is possible, and hence the savings that can be realized, from acquiring a new plant, one embodying the most up-to-date technology. The greater the possible reduction in costs, the greater the incentive for the megacorp to increase its investment so that $\dot{I}_i$ exceeds rather than merely matches the growth of sales, g_j. This means that the megacorp's investment in new plant and equipment depends not only on the growth of industry sales but also on the differential in the cost of producing goods in a new or modernized plant compared with the cost of producing goods in the oldest plant still normally in use. The greater that differential in costs as determined by $\dot{z}_j$, the more rapid the rate at which the megacorp can expect to increase its capacity, with the difference between $\dot{I}_j$ and g_j enabling the megacorp to scrap any technologically obsolescent plants and thereby lower its costs of production.

A corollary proposition is that, the more rapidly the unit costs of production are falling as a result of technical progress, the greater will be the rate of growth of investment, not just by the individual megacorp, but also by the oligopolistic sector as a whole. Although it may appear that it is the investment which is causing the technical progress, the line of causation actually runs in the opposite direction—with the possibility of being able to lower the costs of production inducing the investment. (On the interrelationship between investment and technical progress, see chapter 5, section 4.5). Still, it is the investment in new plant and equipment which enables the technical progress to be realized, and thus it is the investment in new plant and equipment which is the key to the growth of productivity. For it is only by increasing its capacity at a more rapid rate that the growth of sales that the megacorp will be able to scrap or otherwise retire its oldest, least efficient plants.

A reduction in costs, below what can be achieved simply by increasing capacity in line with the growth of industry sales, thus requires two separate actions on the part of the megacorp. The first is that the megacorp step up its investment in new plant and equipment within the industry so that I_j exceeds g_j. The second is that the megacorp then scrap or otherwise retire the plants which, because of their higher operating costs, have become technologically obsolescent. The megacorp will need to step up its rate of investment because, with the growth of capacity merely keeping pace with the increase in industry sales, no plant is likely to be scrapped. This is because the amount of reserve capacity, like the amount of capacity represented by the plants normally in use, SOR*ERC, will need to be increased at a rate equal to g_j. Thus, with capacity increasing no more rapidly than sales, even the oldest plant still owned by the firm is likely to be retained, despite its higher operating cost, so the megacorp will be able to meet any cyclical peak in demand. At most, one or more plants will be shifted from normal to reserve use. Only by expanding capacity at a rate which exceeds the growth of industry sales will the megacorp be able to scrap or otherwise retire its obsolescent plants and thereby reduce its costs below what would be possible from just the expansion of capacity in line with the growth of industry sales.

It is, of course, possible for the megacorp to lower its costs without necessarily adding to its capacity. Indeed, the hope of being able to reduce its costs is the only reason the megacorp is likely to construct a new plant when the industry is no longer expanding—or when the megacorp, as a result of a declining market share, is no longer experiencing an increase in sales. The megacorp, however, need not construct an entire new plant. It can also lower its costs by simply substituting newer, more efficient equipment for some of its vintage equipment. In either case, the megacorp can be said to be merely replacing, rather than adding to, its capital stock—although it would not be that unusual if the new equipment enabled the firm to increase its rate of throughput (i.e., its output per unit of time), and thus its effective capacity, in addition to enabling it to lower its costs.

There are thus two types of situations in which the primary motivation for investment in new plant and equipment can be assumed to be the desire to reduce the unit costs of production. One is when, in order to be in a position to scrap one or more of its technologically obsolescent plants, the megacorp increases its capacity at a more rapid rate than the growth of industry sales. The other situation is when, with no prospect of an expanding market, the megacorp simply replaces a part of its vintage capital stock. In both cases, the investment decision is likely to depend on the expected rate of return. (The second case is but a special case of the first, with g_j equal to zero.) The rate of return, r, on this type of investment can be calculated by replacing the V_0 and R_j terms in equation 7.4 with p_I, the purchase price of the capital goods, and ΔF, the expected annual increment in cash flow, respectively—and then solving for r. The annual increment in cash flow, ΔF, from this type of investment is equal to the differential in operating costs between a new or modernized plant and the oldest plant still normally in use, Δc, multiplied by the quantity of output that can be produced in a plant of that size, $\hat{q}$. That is,

$$\Delta F = \Delta c(\hat{q}) \qquad (7.21)$$

As a practical matter, the investment decision is likely to be based on what is termed the "pay-back" period. This is the number of years required before the price that must be paid for the requisite new plant and/or equipment will be matched by the ensuing reduction in the cost of production. In mathematical terms,

$$t_r = \frac{V_0}{\Delta F} \qquad (7.22)$$

where t_r is the pay-back period; ΔF is the annual increment in cash flow from the reduction in costs which the purchase of new plant and/or equipment would make possible, and V_0 is the purchase price of the new plant and/or equipment. Thus, if purchasing a piece of new equipment which sells for $100,000 will enable the firm to reduce its costs of production by $20,000 a year ($20 a unit on 1,000 units sold), the pay-back period, is five years.

On certain assumptions, a pay-back period of five years is equivalent to a marginal efficiency of investment, r, of 20 percent. The most critical of these assumptions are (1) that the annual savings to the firm from acquiring the new plant and/or equipment will not be significantly differenct in the years following the recovery of the initial outlay from what they were on the average in the period before, and (2) that the plant and/or equipment will not depreciate in economic value (that is, its scrap price will remain equal to V_0). On these assumptions ΔF can be substituted for R in equation 7.5, with the value of r (rather than $1 + r$) determined by the resulting ratio. This means that r will be equal to $\Delta F/V_0$, which is the inverse of the pay-back period, t_r, given by equation 7.20. While the assumptions which must hold if t_r is to be equal to the inverse of r may not hold in practice, any possible distortion as to what the true value of r may be is likely to be more than offset by the advantages of relying on the pay-back criterion.

Aside from the greater ease with which t_r can be calculated, the use of the pay-back criterion to determine which cost-reducing expenditures are to be funded through the capital budget is more in keeping with the firm's desire to minimize risk while maximizing the growth of cash flow, or discretionary funds, over time. The fact is that the further into the future a firm must project the reduction in costs from the purchase of new plant and equipment, the less confident it can be about the validity of the projections. It is not just that any future benefits will need to be discounted more heavily (that is, that the discount factor becomes larger). It is also that any benefits become more uncertain the further into the future they must be projected. Indeed, the more time that must pass for the benefits to be realized, the greater the likelihood that the new plant and equipment will itself become technologically obsolescent—if not made redundant by a shift in demand to other products. A megacorp (or any other type of enterprise, for that matter) can minimize the attendant risk by giving the highest priority within the capital budget, once it is assured of sufficient capacity to meet any growth in sales, to the projects which will enable it to recoup its investment in the shortest possible time. In this way the firm will have the best chance of avoiding any loss while, if the projected reduction in the costs of production should hold up, it will have taken the steps necessary to maximize the growth of its cash flow in the long run. When the future benefits from a particular project seem likely to follow an unusual time pattern, either falling off dramatically or increasing sharply after the initial outlay of funds has been recovered, this information can readily be taken into account and the judgment that would be made on the basis of the pay-back criterion alone then modified.

Two different types of investment by the megacorp have now been identified. One is an expenditure on new plant and equipment in order to expand capacity in line with the growth of industry demand. This type of investment is best explained by a lagged-sales type of accelerator model. The other type of investment is an expenditure on new plant and/or equipment in order to reduce the costs of production. This type of investment depends on the expected return, r, as determined by the rate at which technical progress is making the capital stock obsolescent. The two types of investment are alike, not only in that both involve expenditures on new plant and equipment but also in that it is as much in the interest of the society as it is in the interest of the firm that the investment be carried out. In the case of any cost-reducing capital expenditures, the social benefits can be assumed to be the same as the private benefits. Even if the reduction in costs merely results in more income for the megacorp in the form of increased cash flow, the society as a whole will be better off because fewer real resources will be needed to produce the current level of output. Thus there is no reason to assume a discrepancy between the social and private rates of return from any investment undertaken solely for the purpose of reducing the costs of production—as long as the society maintains a ''full employment'' policy and thus the reduction in costs does not merely redistribute income within the household sector (see chapter 13, part 4). The same cannot always be said, however, for the other types of discretionary expenditures by the megacorp—expenditures which, since they lead to no increase in productive capacity, cannot be counted as part of the firm's investment outlays. Still, those other types of discretionary expenditures do play an important role in oligopolistic industries, especially in determining the degree of pricing power and hence the ability to set a markup above costs. It is to these other types of discretionary expenditures that we now need to turn.

7.2.3 Other discretionary expenditures

The key to a megacorp's ability to survive and grow over time is the use it makes of the cash flow, or discretionary funds, it is able to generate through the mark-up applied to its unit costs of production. It is for this reason that the preparation of the annual capital budget is such an important exercise for the megacorp's executive group. One possible use of the megacorp's discretionary expenditures has already been explored. This is the use of the funds to purchase new plant and equipment—whether to expand capacity, to reduce costs or, as is more typically the case, to do both simultaneously. There is another possible use of discretionary funds, however, and that is to strengthen the individual firm's market position. The most effective way a megacorp can stengthen its market position is by expending its discretionary funds so as to make the entry of new firms into the industry more difficult, and it is this use of discretionary funds which, since it is the most inclusive one, will be emphasized in this subsection. The megacorp, however, can also strengthen its market position by using its discretionary funds to differentiate its product more sharply and to create a more favorable public image.

The megacorp can erect higher barriers to entry only by placing any prospective new firms at a greater cost disadvantage. Over the years, megacorps have developed a number of techniques for accomplishing this purpose, with the techniques varying with the type of industry. (With the enactment of antirebating and similar types of laws, some of these techniques have, of course, had to be abandoned.) In the case of industries which are primarily suppliers of basic material inputs, such as steel and aluminum, the prevalent technique is one which involves tying up under long-term leases or other legal arrangements all known mineral deposits throughout the world. In the case of industries which supply high-technology intermediate goods, such as office copiers and computers, the prevalent technique is one which combines R&D, buttressed by patent protection, with some type of product servicing. And in the case of industries which produce consumer goods, such as cereals and toothpaste, the prevalent technique is one which relies on advertising, together with other forms of mass marketing. While none of these techniques would be very effective in limiting entry if they were to be employed by just a single firm, the recognized interdependence which exists in oligopolistic industries means that, if one firm undertakes the expenditures associated with a particular technique, and thus stands to gain a competitive edge, the other megacorps in the industry will be forced to carry through with similar expenditures of their own so as to neutralize any possible advantage. It is in this way that expenditures on advertising, R&D and the like, though undertaken at the initiative of the individual firm, nonetheless become an integral part of the overall collective effort to limit the entry of new firms into the industry.

A private rate of return can be estimated for this type of expenditure just as it can for the purchase of cost-reducing plant and equipment. The megacorp, by increasing its level of spending on one of the techniques available to it for erecting higher barriers, will reduce the probability of new entry, γ, and will thus be able, other factors remaining unchanged, to establish a higher mark-up. The higher mark-up, multiplied by the expected level of output, represents the additional cash flow the firm will then be able to generate. That is,

$$\Delta F = \Delta m(\text{SOR*ERC}) \tag{7.23}$$

where ΔF is now the additional cash flow which can be generated as a result of discretionary expenditures that increase the barriers to entry and where, as already noted (see chapter 6, section 5.4), SOR*ERC is the megacorp's expected level of output. Here the benefit to the individual firm derives, not from a reduction in the unit costs of production, Δc, but rather from the larger markup, Δm, which the higher barriers to entry will enable the firm to obtain.

Thus, by first estimating the value of ΔF, it is possible to determine, at least approximately, the private rate of return, r, on any expenditures by the megacorp to erect higher barriers. That rate of return will depend on the effect which the expenditures have on the probability of entry, γ. Other types of discretionary expenditures, by serving to differentiate an industry's product more sharply, may instead have an effect on the elasticity of industry demand, e. Still other types of discretionary expenditures, by serving to create a more favorable public image of the firm or industry, will have an effect on the probability of government intervention, θ. In all three cases, the calculation of the private rate of return, r, is the same. It is just that the intervening factor that enables the megacorp to obtain a higher markup and therefore a greater increment in discretionary funds will be different. Whatever the variable that is affected by the discretionary expenditures, however—whether it is γ, e or θ—the higher markup that can be obtained relative to the implicit cost of the funds thereby generated represents a shift to the right of the S_r' curve and therefore an increase in the firm's pricing power (see chapter 6, section 3.4).

The funds spent by the megacorp on advertising, R&D and the like are thus an important aspect of the non-price competition that characterizes oligopolistic industries. The traditional emphasis in economics has been on price competition—the shaving of the profit margin, or markup, in order to gain additional sales. The fact that this type of competition is likely to be considerably muted, as already pointed out (see chapter 6, section 2.2), does not mean that competition is absent from oligopolistic industries. Rather the competition takes a different form. With a certain size markup assured through the industry's collective pricing behavior, the competition consists of each megacorp trying to obtain the largest possible return from the cash flow it is able to generate. The competition, in other words, is over how best to employ any discretionary funds. The megacorps which are most successful in this regard are the ones most likely to achieve the highest growth rates and will thereby have the best chance of surviving in the long period.

The funds spent on advertising, R&D and the like, no less than the funds spent on new plant and equipment, are integral to the megacorp's struggle to achieve the highest possible growth rate. It is only by spending part of its discretionary funds to maintain sufficiently high barriers to entry, differentiate the industry's product more sharply and forestall government intervention that a megacorp can obtain the markup on its products that will enable it to finance an optimal level of other types of discretionary expenditures, including expenditures on new plant and equipment. Thus the size of the markup which the megacorp is able to obtain (see chapter 6, part 3), is itself a function, at least in part, of the discretionary expenditures which the markup makes it possible to finance—this being the portion of those funds used to strengthen the megacorp's market position. Although the expenditures on advertising, R&D and the like may appear to be intended only to enhance the individual megacorp's position vis-à-vis the other firms in the particular industries to which it belongs, the interdependence among the firms in oligopolistic industries is such that the actual impact is likely to be on the size of the markup which can be obtained in those industries rather than on the megacorp's relative market share.

A complete accounting of the discretionary expenditures by the corporate sector of the U.S. economy would therefore have to include, at the very least, any outlays on advertising and R&D. These outlays, being unrelated to current production and thus postponable, are no less discretionary than the outlays on new plant and equipment. Still, there are critical differences. One important difference is that the megacorp's outlays on advertising and R&D will have, at most, a demand-stimulating effect. They will not have a supply-enhancing effect as well. The capacity to produce will, in fact, be left unchanged by these types of expenditures, which is why they are not considered investment. If anything, they represent a diversion of funds from capital formation.

A closely related difference is that, in the case of the sums budgeted for advertising and R&D, one cannot assume that the social return, ϱ, will be at least equal to, if not actually greater than, the private return, r. Indeed, one can question whether there is any benefit at all to society from expenditures which simply serve to reinforce the market position of the established firms in oligopolistic industries. While there may be some value in fostering a certain amount of stability so that the capital accumulation process will not be impaired by the inability of firms to establish the necessary profit margins and thereby satisfy the value condition for sustained growth, it seems unlikely that the benefit to society is commensurate with the substantial sums spent each year on advertising, R&D and the other techniques used to strengthen the market position of firms. It could just as well be said—and this is what economists have usually argued—that the general interest would be better served by weakening rather than strengthening the hold which the established firms have on oligopolistic markets.

If the outlays on advertising and R&D served only to strengthen a firm's market position, the judgment about the social rate of return from these types of expenditures would be an easy one to make. Whatever may be the benefit to society from the market power of megacorps, it cannot be as great as the benefit to the megacorps themselves. The outlays on advertising and R&D, however, serve other purposes besides that of merely strengthening the market position of the established firms. Advertising, for example, can be justified as meeting the informational needs of buyers. While this claim cannot be accepted at face value—the informational content of advertising is, after all, usually negligible, with the message designed to subvert rational choice—neither can the claim be discounted altogether.

An even stronger case can be made on behalf of R&D outlays because of the role they play in technical progress. Here, too, the claim is often an exaggerated one. For the most part, R&D outlays simply lead to new variants of old products, thereby contributing, like advertising, to the product differentiation which is so important a part of the competitive dynamic in oligopolistic industries. Still, there are times when R&D expenditures lead, not just to new variants of old products but rather, to entirely new products which then become the basis for some major new industry, transforming the industrial structure (as represented by the input-output matrix) in the process. Even when an entirely new product is not created, the improvement in an old product may be such that, because of the reduction in the costs from using the product, technical progress is nonetheless promoted. This is especially true when the improvement is in the capital goods purchased by other industries. Should R&D expenditures lead to product innovation rather than just product differentiation, the social returns are likely to be quite significant. To understand what makes the difference, it is necessary to probe in somewhat greater depth the megacorp's non-price-competitive strategy, showing how, in the case of R&D expenditures, this is likely to result in product innovation and technical progress.

7.2.4 Product innovation and technical progress

With the price variable neutralized as a competitive weapon in oligopolistic industries (in much the same way nuclear weapons have been neutralized in the political arena), the rivalry among firms usually takes other forms. The key to a successful competitive strategy within a given industry lies, on the selling side, in the development of a product line. This means providing a sufficient number of variations on the same basic product that every specialized need of buyers— whether for different steel shapes or for different size copying machines—is met. The more of the buyers' specialized needs the firm can meet through its product line, the larger the share of the market it can expect to capture.

On this front, too, the firm is likely to discover that whatever initiative it takes to gain a competitive advantage will simply evoke a defensive response from its rivals. For the most part, the megacorps in oligopolistic industries offer similar product lines. (It is the fact that the industry supplies a product line, rather than just a single product, that creates the need for an index to measure price changes even in the case of the individual industry. See chapter 2, section 2.5.) Still, since there is always the hope of gaining an edge in sales, even if only temporarily, megacorps are constantly modifying their product line, adding new variations of the same basic product so as to give their salesmen an additional talking point and their advertising a fresh focus. When a new item in the product line actually leads to improved performance along some dimension, the new item represents techni- cal progress through product innovation (see the introduction to part 4 of chapter 5). While technical progress through product innovation is also important in the case of consumer goods, leading as it does to an improvement in the quality of life, there is a more direct impact on the system of production when the product innovation involves either some material input or some capital good—with the latter being especially important. Even when a new, better performance material input is developed, new types of capital equipment are likely to be required to handle the new material inputs so that technical progress through product innova- tion is closely approximated, insofar as the system of production is concerned, by product innovation in the capital goods sector. It is this type of product innova- tion—one that manifests itself in the capital goods sector—which is likely to lead to a reduction in the costs of production for some other industry and thus an increase in the available social surplus. Indeed, it is this type of product innova- tion which serves as the critical link in the process by which the growth of scientific knowledge is eventually translated into a higher material standard of living.

The other steps in this process have already been identified—the antecedent ones in chapter 5, where the interface between science and industrial technology was discussed, and the subsequent ones in the earlier subsections of this chapter, where the megacorp's reasons for purchasing new plant and equipment were analyzed. The essential link, between the growth of technical knowledge on the one hand and the embodiment of the improved technology in new plant and equipment on the other, is the action of the megacorps within the investment goods sector of adding, as part of their non-price competitive strategy, new items to their product line so as to enable their customers to reduce their costs of production. Once the state of the art has advanced to the point where a cost-reducing technique has become available, whether the new technique requires only a new type of capital good or a new type of material input along with the equipment needed to handle it, the item is almost certain to be added to the product line of the megacorps in the investment goods sector. For if one firm does not exploit the opportunity, another is likely; and the prospect of thereby being placed at a competitive disadvantage will usually be sufficient to induce the megacorps in the investment goods sector to upgrade their product line as rapidly as the technology and their own vintage capital stock will permit. With the product line in the various investment goods industries continuously being upgraded so as to make the latest technology available in the form of new plant and equipment, the rate at which the vintage capital stock is being replaced, and thus the rate at which technical progress itself is occurring, will then depend on the rate of investment in each and every industry. What this suggests is that, as long as the rivalry among firms within an investment goods industry is such that they each develop their own independent product line, the rate of technical progress is unlikely to be impeded by the existence of oligopoly. Indeed, the existence of oligopoly, to the extent it is associated with continuous efforts to upgrade the product line within the investment goods sector and with a higher level of capital outlays more generally, is likely to result in a more rapid growth of technical progress.

The process just outlined is a significant modification of the usual view as to how firms achieve cost reduction. In the conventional treatment of the subject, it is the firm experiencing the lower costs which is seen as controlling the process, exercising what discretion there may be in the matter. This is the import of setting up the model so that the decision rests entirely with the firms benefiting directly from the reduction in costs. As should now be clear, however, this is much too simplistic a view. In the first place, much of the cost reduction which takes place in the oligopolistic sector occurs as a concomitant of the megacorp's decision to expand capacity in line with the growth of industry demand. When adding to its capacity, the megacorp can be expected to purchase the most efficient plant and equipment it can obtain from the firms in the investment goods sector. The rate of product innovation in the industries supplying the megacorp with its capital inputs—and thus the differential in the cost of operating new and vintage plants—has to be especially great for a megacorp to be induced to expand capacity more rapidly than the growth of industry demand. Secondly, even when cost reduction takes place independently of capacity expansion, the megacorp is likely to be merely responding to the new products being offered by the firms in the investment goods sector—many of whom are also likely to be megacorps. For this reason, the impetus for technical progress can be said to come primarily from the investment goods sector, together with the industries supplying material inputs, rather than from the firms directly experiencing the reduction in their costs of production.

If it is the investment goods sector which, through its own product innovation, plays the key role in fostering technical progress, the question naturally arises as to what it is that determines the rate of product innovation in the investment goods sector. It is in this connection that the megacorp's discretionary expenditures on R&D need to be considered.

In many of the conventional models, the rate of product innovation is simply a function of the level of R&D expenditures. Again, however, this is too simplistic a view. The growth of industrial technology does not proceed at a constant rate but rather in spurts, dictated by the dynamics of the learning process. This is especially true of the technology underlying any particular industry. While there may be times when a breakthrough can be exploited more effectively by committing more funds to the R&D effort, this fact should not be misinterpreted to mean that more funds will lead to earlier breakthroughs and thus to a more rapid rate of product innovation. To a large extent, the breakthroughs will occur at points in time which cannot be anticipated in advance and which the megacorp is unlikely to be able to influence through its own outlays on R&D. It is for this reason that product innovation should not be regarded as a monotonic function of an industry's R&D expenditures. The best the megacorp can do is maintain an R&D staff of sufficient size and quality that the company will be able to keep abreast of technological developments—and in this way be in a position to take advantage of whatever breakthroughs may occur by upgrading its product line. In the intervals between the breakthroughs in technology which lead to real improvements in a product's performance characteristics, the R&D effort can still contribute to the further rounding out of the product line and thus to a greater differentiation of the firm's product. Indeed this point holds for megacorps in the consumer goods sector no less than for those in the investment goods and material inputs sectors, and this is why R&D expenditures tend to fluctuate so little from year to year.

The megacorp's expenditures on R&D, then, in contrast to its expenditures on advertising and the other means of strengthening its market position, can be said to give rise, at least potentially, to significant social benefits besides those inherent in the stability of market shares. These additional social benefits are the product innovation the R&D expenditures foster—which then serves, especially when it occurs in the investment goods sector, as the underlying source of technical progress. Even though the expenditures on R&D may, routinely, simply play the same product differentiating role as the expenditures on advertising, they may also, from time to time, serve the more important function of enabling the megacorps in the oligopolistic sector to offer an improved set of products to their customers. The expenditures on R&D, however, are not the only use of discretionary funds which may have social benefits unrelated to the reasons for which those expenditures are being undertaken. The use of discretionary funds to finance diversification and conglomerate expansion may also have unintended social benefits. Indeed, as the next subsection will attempt to bring out, diversification and conglomerate expansion may be the only competitive dynamic sufficiently strong to ensure that the rate of return on investment is equalized through-out the oligopolistic sector and thus that a misallocation of investment funds cannot be inferred simply from the prevalence of oligopoly.

7.2.5 Diversification and conglomerate expansion

As long as the megacorp remains tied to its present set of industries, it cannot be sure of its own survival over the long run. For industries typically experience a life cycle, beginning with the initial period of infancy when, after some techno-logical breakthrough has given birth to the industry, the subsequent combined effect of falling costs and a high income elasticity of demand enables the industry to experience rapid growth. The initial period of infancy, during which the industry may not yet be oligopolistic in structure, is likely to be followed by a period of maturity when the industry has come to be winnowed down to a few firms, some of which are megacorps, and the industry is growing at roughly the same rate as the oligopolistic sector itself. Finally, there may be a period of senescence when the industry finds itself losing markets to the products of other, more recently established industries. It is during this last period that, if a mega-corp has not learned to transcend the boundaries of the industry which originally spawned it, one is likely to witness the company's eventual demise.

The megacorps which are able to survive over time are, then, the megacorps which have learned how to carry out a program of diversification and even conglomerate expansion. Diversification involves expansion into a different in-dustry, one based on a similar technology, while conglomerate expansion involves entry into an unrelated line of business. The difference between the two types of expansion may be of little practical import, however. For one thing, the technol-ogy is never really the same, even when two industries are so close technological-ly that they fall within the same three-digit SIC. A diversifying firm must still gain access to what is, at least in part, an unfamiliar technology, and usually this will involve absorbing learning costs of one sort or another. Secondly, whether the expansion involves diversification or conglomerate expansion, the motivation is likely to be the same—to enable the firm achieve the highest possible rate of increase in its cash flow, or discretionary funds, over time. Indeed, the difference between diversification and conglomerate expansion is usually only a matter of whether the megacorp can transfer some of its managerial expertise from the one industry to another or whether it must be content with simply creating another independent "profit center" within the firm.

To ensure that it is continually in a position to expand into newer, more rapidly growing industries, the megacorp must always be weighing its possible entry into at least one more industry besides those to which it already belongs. This means that it must constantly be on the alert for more rapidly growing industries into which to expand, either by acquiring some smaller firm already established within the industry or by setting up a new division and constructing its own facilities. The basis for a megacorp's decision to go ahead with plans to enter a new industry will be the same as for any other commitment of its discretionary funds. This is the expected rate of return, r, or its close approximation, the estimated pay-back period, t_r. The main difference is that, since entry into a new industry is likely to involve a substantial commitment of the company's resources, one that cannot readily be abandoned should the calculations prove wrong, the estimate of t_r is likely to be made more conservatively and the decision itself more carefully considered.

If the megacorp is to maximize its growth over time, the expected rate of return from a diversification move or conglomerate acquisition must at least match the return from the other uses to which the megacorp can put its discretionary funds, such as lowering its costs or strengthening its market position within the industries to which it already belongs. The megacorp will therefore need to determine how great an outlay will be required over an extended period of time in order to establish a secure position in the industry it hopes to enter. This is the principal sum the megacorp will need to recover in order to break even. The megacorp will then need to estimate the number of years that are likely to elapse before it can expect to recover that sum, given the industry's profit margin, μ_j, and the amount of output it can expect to sell based on its projected share of the market. This will provide it with an estimate of the pay-back period, t_r—and therefore, by inverting that figure, with an estimate of the likely rate of return, r. While the industry's higher growth, g_j, compared with the megacorp's own growth rate, g_i, may make it attractive as an investment prospect, the megacorp must be careful that the amount it needs to expend in order to secure a certain fixed share of the market is not so great that, despite the higher growth rate (and the higher profit margin based on that growth rate), the estimated pay-back period exceeds a certain limit, one that will jeopardize the megacorp's chances of achieving its target rate of growth. The megacorp may be inclined, for strategic reasons, to settle for a longer pay-back period than on other types of investment. Still, it cannot ignore the pay-back criterion entirely, especially if a substantial portion of its discretionary funds are going to be tied up by the diversification move or conglomerate acquisition for a long time.

The expected return, r, from using the megacorp's discretionary funds to enter a new industry is only the private return. It might appear that the social return, ϱ, would be considerably less—especially if the entry is effected through the acquisition of an existing firm without any investment in new plant and equipment. In the latter case, the expected return can be considered primarily a financial one since the resulting increase in cash flow, ΔF, will not be matched by a corresponding increase in output, ΔQ. This view, while not without validity, nonetheless ignores the crucial role played by the diversification and conglomerate expansion process in allocating investment funds among different industries, thereby providing some assurance that, despite the substantial barriers to entry which exist within the oligopolistic sector and the minimal reliance that is placed on the capital funds market by megacorps, there is nonetheless a tendency for the rate of return on investment, r, to be equalized across industries.

The fact is that the megacorp as a conglomerate enterprise functions in a manner analogous to a centrally planned economy. Investment funds are generated, based on the prevailing mark-up, in the k industries which delimit the megacorp's present lines of business; and these funds, or savings, are then apportioned so as to bring the highest possible return across $k+1$ industries—the $+1$ industry being a potential new line of business for the megacorp. While, for the most part, the funds are likely to be invested in the industries from which they are being generated, still, if the highest possible return is going to be obtained, some of the funds will have to be shifted to other industries. For it is only in this way that the megacorp can finance expansion into new, more rapidly growing industries. With the megacorp committed to employing its funds where they will bring the highest possible return, the resulting pattern of capital expenditures is likely to lead over time to the equalization of the rate of return, r, across the $k+1$ industries where investment prospects are being scouted. For if the rate of return is higher in one of the $k+1$ industries than in the others, the megacorp can be expected to step up its investment in that industry, shifting funds from other industries if need be, until the rate of return is again being equalized across all $k+1$ industries. With the rate of return the same at the margin, the amount of investment funds allocated to each of the $k+1$ industries will, of course, vary.

The manner in which the conglomerate enterprise generates investment funds—by a markup on costs—and the manner in which those investment funds are then apportioned—so as to bring the highest possible return—is precisely how the accumulation process is supposed to work, at least in theory, in a centrally planned economy. The difference is that, while for the economy as a whole the social rate of return on investment needs to be equated at the margin for all n industries, the individual megacorp acting alone—even when it is a diversified, conglomerate enterprise—will be able to equate only the private rate of return, r, across $k+1$ industries. Even ignoring the discrepancy between the social and private rates of return on certain uses of the megacorp's discretionary funds, one must recognize that the $k+1$ industries among which the megacorp is prepared to shift investment funds is likely to be far fewer than the n industries which constitute the enterprise sector as a whole. This, in turn, raises the possibility that the investment funds which the megacorp is able to generate as a result of its pricing power may not go to the industries where the social rate of return is highest. Concern on this point would appear to be all the more justified given that the newest, most rapidly growing industries are likely to lie outside the oligopolistic sector while within that sector even a megacorp is likely to face significant barriers to entry if it is not already a member of that industry.

The reason for concern largely disappears, however, when one takes into account, not just the individual megacorp but rather, the entire set of diversified and/or conglomerate enterprises. The investment horizons of the different megacorps can be assumed to overlap so that all n industries will, in fact, be covered. This, in turn, ensures that the condition necessary for equalizing at least the private return on investment across all n industries will be satisfied. For if any industry should experience a higher rate of growth than the others—thus indicating that the value of r is perhaps greater in that industry—at least one megacorp not previously associated with that industry can be expected to try to gain entry as a means of increasing its own growth rate. This is likely to be true whether the industry is a relatively new one, having not yet settled down into a stable oligopolisitic pattern, or an older one which, because of some change in the composition of final demand, is experiencing a recrudescence.

In the case of a relatively new industry, one that may have only recently emerged in the wake of some technological breakthrough and still consists entirely of neoclassical proprietorships, the barriers to entry are likely to be quite low. This is a situation that is conducive to the expansion into that industry by one or more megacorps—especially if the industry has reached the stage in its development where it can continue to grow only through a major infusion of new funds. In the case of an already mature industry, one that is now experiencing a recrudescence because of some change in the composition of final demand and/or because of some technological breakthrough, the barriers to entry are likely to present a much greater obstacle. Still, if the industry's rate of growth is sufficiently high, at least one megacorp not already a member of the industry can be expected to try to gain entry. The temptation will be especially great if the megacorp has reason to believe that it can, through a somewhat different product line, serve a segment of the market that has previously being neglected.

The megacorp's need to expand into new, more rapidly growing industries if it is to maximize its own growth will therefore ensure, if one takes into account the entire set of diversified and conglomerate megacorps, that at least the private rate of return on investment will tend to be equalized across all n industries. Note that conglomerate expansion does not ensure that the markup, μ, will tend to be equalized. The markup will, in fact, differ for each industry, depending on the values taken by the $\mathbf{G}$ and $\mathbf{B}$ vectors, as well as on the degree of pricing power within each of those industries (see chapter 6, part 3). Nor does conglomerate expansion ensure that the rates of growth by each of the different industries will tend to be equalized. In the face of continuous but uneven technical progress across industries and the different income elasticities of demand for each industry's output, the elements of the $\mathbf{G}$ vector will not all have the same value (see chapter 5, section 5.4). Conglomerate expansion only ensures that the funds generated in some industries will be shifted to other industries—those experiencing a higher rate of growth—so that there will be at least some tendency, because of the underlying competitive dynamic, for the private rate of return on investment, r, to be equalized across all n of the industries which make up the enterprise sector. Conglomerate expansion thus represents an alternative to the theoretical working of the capital funds market as a mechanism for assuring the optimal allocation of investment funds across industries—as well as an alternative to the system of centralized planning found, for example, in the Soviet Union. This point will be further elaborated on in the main section which next follows.

7.3 Finance

The focus in the preceding part of this chapter was on the demand for new plant and equipment by the megacorp—among other types of discretionary expenditures. Still to be analyzed is the process by which these expenditures are financed, especially when the economy is proceeding not along some steady-state growth path but rather, as is almost certain to be the case, along a growth path marked by pronounced cyclical movements and perhaps even the shift from one secular rate of economic expansion to another. For this purpose, it is necessary to construct a flow of funds table for the individual megacorp and then, based on that table and the relationships which underlie it, to identify the types of financial problems which a megacorp is likely to face, both in the short period and in the long. Once this has been done, it will then be possible to compare the model of accumulation which is implicit in what has already been said about the megacorp's pricing power with the more conventional view of the accumulation process which is implicit in the notion of a "capital" market that determines the flow of "savings" to business firms.

7.3.1 The individual firm's flow of funds

Based on a method of financial analysis first developed by Matthew Fung, one can set up a table, such as the one shown in exhibit 7.4, listing the individual megacorp's sources and uses of funds. As already pointed out (see chapter 2, section 3.1), a table of this type is essential for analyzing the monetary counterpart of the real flows emanating from the system of production. The same flow of funds table, generalized so that it applies to the entire enterprise sector, financial as well as nonfinancial, will, together with similar tables for the other sectors of the economy, serve as the basis for the monetary analysis to be carried out in chapter 12.

The principal source of funds for a business firm like the megacorp is its sales revenue while the principal use of those funds is to cover its labor and material costs of production. When the labor and material costs, together with the megacorp's profits tax liability, are netted out from both sides of the table shown in exhibit 7.4, what remains on the right-hand side is the megacorp's current cash flow while what remains on the left-hand side, besides the cost of debt service, are the various uses to which the megacorp's discretionary funds can be put. It is not because the labor and material costs are unimportant that, together with the megacorp's profits tax liability, they need to be netted out. On the contrary, wage payments are the major source of funds for households, purchases of material

Exhibit 7.4

The Megacorp's Sources and Uses of Funds

Uses	Sources
Mandatory Uses	Sales Revenue
Employees Compensation	Less: Employees' Compensation
Cost of Material Inputs	Cost of Material Inputs
Accrued Profits Tax	Equals Gross Profits
Debt Service	Less: Accrued Profits Tax
Interest and Principal on	Equals Cash Flow
Fixed-Interest Obligations	(internally generated funds)
Dividend Payments	Depreciation Allowances
	Retained Profits
Discretionary Uses	
Capital Outlays	Sale of Assets
Purchase of Financial Assets	Physical Assets
Short-Term Financial Assets	Financial Assets
Acquisitions	
Other Long-Term Financial Assets	External Sources of Funds
	Bank and Other Short-Term Credit
	Long-Term Liabilities
	Fixed-Interest Obligations
	Sale of New Equity Shares

inputs are the major source of funds for the firms that produce intermediate goods and even the corporate income tax, although it generates less revenue than other taxes, is nonetheless an important source of funds for the U.S. government. Indeed, it is for this reason that considerable effort has already been made and will continue to be made to identify the factors determining those flows. Rather the labor and material costs, along with the profits tax liability, need to be subtracted from both sides of the table shown in exhibit 7.4 so as to reveal more clearly what is the megacorp's net position insofar as the flow of funds is concerned. That net cash position is critical for assessing not only the megacorp's financial condition but also the macrodynamic impact of the megacorp's discretionary expenditures.

As can be seen from exhibit 7.4, the megacorp's cash flow is just one of two sources of internal funds. However, the other source of internal funds, the income realized from the sale of physical and/or financial assets, is not one that the megacorp can count on over an extended period of time. The sale of its physical assets, unless they represent redundant or obsolescent plant and equipment, will reduce the megacorp's ability to produce the goods and services which are the source of its revenue while any financial assets the megacorp may hold can be sold only to the extent that its cash inflow has in the past exceeded its cash outlays. The sale of assets, physical or financial, can therefore be considered only a temporary expedient and, for this reason, will be ignored in the discussion which follows. If the sale of financial assets is to be excluded as a source of internal funds, then the use of the megacorp's funds to acquire financial assets also needs to be excluded—on the grounds that, in the long period, the two must necessarily balance each other off. The analysis can be further simplified by ignoring the possible use of funds for advertising and R&D, leaving the megacorp's expenditures on new plant and equipment as the only discretionary use of funds. Together with the netting out of the labor and material costs of production, along with the megacorp's profit tax liability, these deletions enable the flow of funds table shown in exhibit 7.4 to be reduced to the simpler one shown in exhibit 7.5.

The advantage of the flow of funds table shown in exhibit 7.5 is that it brings out more sharply the relationship between the megacorp's cash flow, or discretionary funds, on the one hand and its capital outlays, or discretionary expenditures, on the other hand. The megacorp's capital outlays, E_i, will in fact be limited to the amount of cash flow being generated, F_i, except insofar as the megacorp is willing and able to obtain additional funds from external sources by increasing its external debt, D. That is, the following relationship must necessarily hold:

$$E_i = F_i + \Delta D_i \qquad (7.24)$$

where E_i is the amount of capital outlays or, more generally, the amount of discretionary expenditures by the individual megacorp; F_i is the amount of cash flow, or discretionary funds, being generated by that same megacorp, and ΔD_i is the change in the amount of that megacorp's debt hold by outside parties, with ΔD_i itself then further specified as follows:

$$\Delta D_i = \Delta Cr + \Delta Se \qquad (7.25)$$

where ΔCr is the increase in the amount of short-term credit extended by banks and other lenders, and ΔSe is the increase in the amount of new securities issued by the megacorp, both fixed-interest obligations, Bd, and equity shares, ΔEq.

The amount of cash flow currently being generated by the individual megacorp, F_i, will depend on its current level of sales and its average profit margin. That is,

$$F_i = \mu_i(S_i) \qquad (7.26)$$

where μ_i is the weighted average of the megacorp's profit margin in each of the different industries to which it belongs, and S_i is the megacorp's total sales $(p_i q_i)$ within a given period. In the last chapter, it was argued that the markup, and

Exhibit 7.5

The Megacorp's Sources and Uses of Funds
(Simplified Set of Accounts)

Uses	Sources
Mandatory Uses	Internally Generated Funds
Debt Service (DS)	Cash Flow (F)
Discretionary Uses	External Sources of Funds (D)
Capital Outlays (E)	Bank and Other Short-Term Credit (Cr)
	Long-Term Liabilities (Se)

hence the profit margin, is likely to have been set so as to enable at least the dominant firm within each oligopolistic industry to finance all of its capital outlays from internal sources, with $\dot{F}_i$ therefore equal to $\dot{E}_i$ for that one firm. Only if the dominant firm is not able to maintain the necessary markup above costs (or if sales should fall short of expectations) will it need to obtain additional funds from external sources. (The other megacorps within the same industry, those which are price followers rather than price leaders, may need to resort to external financing if, in addition, (a) they have a greater need for investment funds than the price leader, or (b) their costs of production are higher and thus their profit margin, μ_i, is lower.) Any resort to external financing will, however, add to the amount of debt held by outside parties, increasing the cost of debt service to the individual megacorp. That is,

$$\Delta DS_i = i(\Delta D_i) \tag{7.27}$$

where ΔDS_i is the change in the cost of debt service for the individual megacorp, and i is the interest and other types of payments that must be made on the debt held by outside parties. Since the short-term interest rate, i_{ST}, is not the same as the long-term rate, i_{LT}, equation 7.26 needs to be rewritten as follows when both the megacorp's short-term debt and its long-term debt are being added to:

$$\Delta DS_i = i_{ST}(\Delta Cr_i) + i_{LT}(\Delta Se_i) \tag{7.28}$$

The individual megacorp's total cost of debt service during any one time period, it should be noted, will be equal to its cost of debt service during the previous time period plus the change over the intervening time period. That is,

$$DS_i = DS_{i-1} + \Delta DS_i \tag{7.29}$$

Any increase in the cost of debt service will, in turn, reduce the amount of funds available to finance capital outlays in subsequent time periods. This is because the cost of debt service, DS_i, must be subtracted from the total funds available to the megacorp from both internal and external sources, $F_i + \Delta D_i$, in order to determine the amount of funds available to finance any discretionary expenditures. That is,

$$E'_i = (F_i + \Delta D_i) - DS_i \qquad (7.30)$$

where E'_i is the amount of funds available to finance any discretionary expenditures (as distinct from E_i, the amount of funds actually expended on new plant and equipment and other types of discretionary outlays). Thus the resort to external funds is likely to prove self-defeating, at least as a long-term strategy. While more funds can be obtained in the immediate period because of the effect on the ΔD_i variable in equation 7.30, fewer funds will be available in subsequent periods because of the effect on the DS_i variable. Whether the resort to external funds makes sense as a short-run expedient is another matter, one that will be taken up in the subsections which follow.

Based on the flow of funds table shown in exhibit 7.5, together with the relationships represented by equations 7.24–7.30 which underlie that table, we can now proceed to identify the types of financial problems which megacorps are likely to face. Because of their pricing power—as reflected by the elasticity of the S_I' curve and thus the size of each industry's markup (see chapter 6, section 3.3)—the megacorps which dominate the oligopolistic sector can be expected to be financially self-sufficient, at least in the long period. This means that they should be able to cover the cost of any discretionary expenditures, including additions to their productive capacity, out of the discretionary funds, or cash flow, being generated by the markup which has been established in each industry. A problem of finance is likely to arise for the megacorps which dominate the oligopolistic sector only insofar as (1) the economy is temporarily displaced from its secular growth path, thereby creating a short-period gap between desired capital outlays on the one hand and the cash flow, or discretionary funds, being generated on the other hand; and (2) the marginal efficiency of investment curve, D_I, has unexpectedly shifted to the right, creating a greater demand for investment funds than can, for the moment, be met from internal sources. The first is the problem of arranging for cyclical finance, the second the problem of adjusting to some new secular trend. Each of these two types of financial problems which megacorps may face will be taken up in turn.

7.3.2 Cyclical finance

As already pointed out, the markup which enables the firms in an oligopolistic industry to cover all their costs, including the cost of expansion, will have been set on the assumption that, on the average over the cycle, they will be able to produce at the standard operating ratio (see chapter 6, section 3.1). As long as this assumption holds—and it will hold only as long as the industry continues to expand at the anticipated secular growth rate—the amount of discretionary funds, F, obtained from the markup established in each of the *m* different oligopolistic industries should be equal to the level of discretionary expenditures, E, which needs to be financed (including the purchase of any new plant and equipment). However, in an economy subject to pronounced cyclical movements, the mega-corps within the oligopolistic sector will find themselves operating at their standard ratio only episodically—and then only coincidentally. Most of the time, that is, in the short period, their level of capacity utilization will either exceed or fall short of the standard operating ratio—with important implications for the rate at which discretionary funds are being generated. This is because the *average* rate at which any discretionary funds will be generated is not the same as the *marginal* rate.

The *average* rate at which discretionary funds will be generated is the price being charged less the costs of production, including any fixed or overhead costs. It is thus equal to what has previously been defined as the profit margin, μ (see chapter 6, section 1.4). There is, to be sure, a difference between the planned, or *ex ante*, profit margin and the realized, or *ex post*, profit margin. The former—what businessmen themselves refer to as the target rate of return on sales—is implicit in whatever size markup, is used as the basis for setting the list price; while the *ex post* profit margin, the realized rate of return on sales, depends on the level of demand subsequent to the establishment of any new list price. In either case, however, it is the average total costs, both fixed and variable, which need to be subtracted from the price in order to determine the average rate at which discretionary funds are being generated. In contrast, the *marginal* rate at which discretionary funds will be generated is the transaction price (when it differs from the list price) less only the direct, or average variable, costs of production. This is because the fixed costs, being invariant, will have no effect on the amount of residual income, and hence the amount of discretionary funds, actually being realized as output varies in the short run. Thus, to determine the *marginal* rate at which discretionary funds will be generated, one need only subtract the average variable costs of production, AVC, rather than the total costs of production, AVC + AFC, from the list price. That is,

$$\mu' = p - \text{AVC} \tag{7.31}$$

where μ' is the marginal rate at which descretionary funds, or cash flow, will be generated.

Since the average variable costs are less than the total unit costs of production, it follows that the marginal rate at which discretionary funds will be generated is necessarily greater than the average rate—unless, as is unlikely, the actual transaction prices are significantly below the list price. For example, in the steel industry, as already noted (see chapter 5, section 4.1), the average variable costs are only 85 per cent of total costs—with the average fixed costs accounting for the rest. Thus, while the average rate at which discretionary funds were being generated in the steel industry in 1977 may have been 9.7 percent, based on the actual profit margin in that year, the marginal rate was 23.2 percent. This is because, while the difference between the price of $309.51 a ton and the total costs of production was only $29.92, the difference between the price and the average variable costs was $71.86, or $41.94 a ton more. This $41.94 a ton more represented the additional cash flow, or discretionary funds, being realized at the margin by the megacorps in the steel industry in 1977 due to the invariant nature of their fixed costs.

The fact that μ' is greater than μ means that, as production and sales vary over the cycle, the cash flow of megacorps, and thus their discretionary funds, will rise and fall at a more rapid rate. When sales are increasing, requiring a higher rate of capacity utilization, the cash flow of megacorps will be on the rise—and will increase more rapidly than either sales or output. Conversely, when sales are declining, leading to a lower rate of capacity utilization within the oligopolistic sector, the cash flow will fall—and will decline more rapidly than sales or output. The rate at which discretionary funds are being generated is therefore quite sensitive to demand conditions, as reflected by the level of industry sales and/or the rate of capacity utilization.

No less important than whether sales are rising and falling is whether the level of sales, and thus the rate of capacity utilization, exceeds or falls short of the standard operating ratio. When sales and output exceed the standard operating ratio, the megacorps within the oligopolistic sector will have little trouble financing their capital outlays. Indeed, they are likely to have a surplus of discretionary funds, becoming in the process net savers in the sense that their discretionary funds, F, will exceed their discretionary expenditures, E. The only financial question the megacorps will need to address is in what form to hold the increasing amount of financial assets being acquired as a result of the excess cash inflow relative to current cash outlays. However, when sales and output fall short of the standard operating ratio, the situation will be quite different. Under these circumstances, the amount of discretionary funds being generated will not be sufficient to cover current outlays, including the purchase of capital goods, and the megacorps within the oligopolistic sector will have a problem of finance.

A megacorp can thus expect to find itself in any one of four possible situations insofar as its finances are concerned. The first situation, representing the continuation of greater than anticipated growth by the oligopolistic sector, is when sales exceed the standard operating ratio and are still rising. In this situation, the megacorp will have no problem of finance, and indeed has no reason to anticipate one. The opposite situation is when sales are less than the standard operating ratio and are still falling. In this situation, representing the prolongation of a previous cyclical downturn, a megacorp will indeed have a finance problem, one that is the most serious it can face. Not only is the rate of cash inflow below the level needed to cover current outlays but, in addition, the shortfall in cash is becoming worse. In this second of the four possible situations in which it may find itself, the megacorp can respond in either of two ways. The first is by trimming its capital outlays. Indeed, this is almost certain to be the megacorp's more immediate response, with any capital expenditures not essential to maintaining its market share in some industry likely to be postponed. However, even with whatever cutback in discretionary expenditures is possible, the rate of cash inflow may still be inadequate to cover current outlays. In that event, the megacorp will be forced to seek funds from external sources.

Under ordinary circumstances, the megacorp will have little trouble in borrowing whatever funds it needs. As a Fortune 500 company, it is likely to have an excellent credit rating, with any number of financial instititions prepared to satisfy its need for short-term loans. Indeed, the megacorp is likely to have arranged for a line of credit at a number of these institutions which it can draw upon as the need arises. Short-term loans can therefore usually be obtained without difficulty. (Long-term loans are another matter, one that will be taken up shortly.) The problem of finance will take on the character of a crisis, threatening the viability of the megacorp, only if the cyclical downturn is unusually sharp and/or prolonged and if the central bank at the same time refuses to play its part in providing financial institutions with the necessary liquidity. This last possibility—an extreme one that may precipitate a breakdown of the financial system—will be discussed more fully below when the monetary constraints on economic expansion are analyzed (see chapter 12, section 2.3).

More typically a megacorp, because of its favored access to credit institutions, will have little difficulty in coping with any shortfall in cash flow, or discretionary funds, due to a cyclical downturn of the economy. The megacorp is likely to have a certain amount of short-term debt already outstanding, this as a means of financing whatever level of inventories are necessary to maintain the current level of production (see chapter 6, section 1.2). It will therefore merely need to add to that short-term debt, with the cost of its debt service consequently rising, based on the relationships given by equations 7.27 and 7.28. The increase in the cost of debt service is likely to be only a temporary one, however, for with the recovery of the economy and the return to its standard operating ratio, the megacorp will no longer experience any shortfall in cash. Indeed, once the economy enters the opposite phase of the business cycle and the megacorp finds itself operating in excess of its standard ratio, the cash flow being generated will be greater than was anticipated when the markup was established and the megacorp should then be able to reduce its short-term debt to the level it prefers. Thus, in the face of a cyclical downturn, the megacorp may be forced to add to its short-term debt beyond the level it considers optimal, with the cost of debt service increasing temporarily as a result. The megacorp may even be forced to trim its capital outlays, at least for a while. But this is likely to be the extent of the untoward consequences.

How much short-term debt the megacorp will consider optimal depends on the cost of short-term credit, i_{ST}, compared with the implicit cost of generating additional funds internally, R (see chapter 6, section 3.4). If i_{ST} is greater than R, the megacorp may choose to finance all or a portion of its working capital needs out of its own internal funds. Alternatively, if i_{ST} is less than R and if financial institutions are prepared to supply the megacorp with short-term credit irrespective of the purpose for which it will be used, then even a portion of the megacorp's fixed capital investment may be financed out of bank loans. Thus, how much short-term credit the megacorp considers optimal will depend on the same relationship that determines the need for long-term external funds. It is just that, based on the value of i_{ST} compared to R, the megacorp can be assumed to have already obtained whatever amount of short-term loans from banks it considers optimal so that, should the need arise for additional funds from external sources, the megacorp will opt for selling new securities. That is why, for the remainder of this chapter, no further effort will be made to distinguish the short-term interest rate from the long-term rate—with the cost of long-term external funds therefore denoted simply by i. Indeed, it will not be until chapter 12, when the nature of credit money is explained, that explicit allowance will need to be made for short-term, as distinct from long-term, external financing.

The other two of the four possible situations in which a megacorp may find itself as a result of the economy's cyclical movements are hybrids of the two situations already discussed, marking the transition from one state to the other. In one of these other two situations, when sales are still in excess of the standard operating ratio but are now declining, megacorps will experience no immediate cash flow problem. They can, however, anticipate a problem if sales continue to decline. In this situation, which corresponds to the immediate downturn phase of the cycle, the megacorps within the oligopolistic sector are likely to begin cutting back on their capital outlays so as to protect their cash flow position. The revised estimate of the secular growth rate which the decline in sales is likely to produce means that they can cut back on their capital outlays without being left with insufficient capacity. Similarly, in the other of the two remaining situations, when sales are below the standard operating ratio but are now increasing, megacorps can anticipate that the cash flow problem they are currently experiencing will begin to ease. In this situation, which corresponds to the recovery phase of the cycle, whatever capital spending plans have had to be delayed are likely to be revived.

So far, all that has been discussed is the effect of the economy's cyclical movements on the megacorp's need for finance in the short period. What has been argued is that the list price which is established in each of the oligopolistic industries to which the megacorp belongs can be expected to include a sufficient markup, or margin, so as to enable the long-period rate of capacity expansion to be financed out of the cash flow, or discretionary funds, being generated; and that a short-period problem of finance is likely to arise only during the below-trend phase of whatever cycles may occur when megacorps are operating at less than their standard ratio and the amount of discretionary funds, F, actually being realized falls short of the level of discretionary expenditures, E, to which they are currently committed. Even so, the problem is likely to be solved through the provision of short-term credit by financial institutions. This still leaves unanswered the question of what role, if any, the provision of long-term credit plays in the financing of investment within the oligopolistic sector. It is to this question that we shall now turn. The first step is to explain how the cost of external finance, i, is determined.

7.3.3 The cost of long-term external finance

An increase in the megacorp's long-term debt, ΔSe, needs to be distinguished from an increase in its short-term debt, ΔCr. Although the two can, at times, serve as substitutes for one another, the rules which govern the financial system in the United States (and in the other countries which follow the British rather than the Prussian model) generally preclude the use of short-term debt, such as unsecured commercial loans, to finance capital outlays. A megacorp may borrow short in anticipation either of increased cash flow in the future or of a subsequent securities issue, but the resort to short-term borrowing can be only a temporary expedient. Over the longer run, if a megacorp wants to tap external funds to finance its investment outlays, it must be prepared to add to its long-term debt. This means that it must issue new securities, either fixed-interest obligations (bonds) or equity shares (stocks). The only source of external finance which is more than a temporary expedient, then, is the capital funds market and the securities which can be sold through it.

The cost of long-term external finance, i, is a weighted average of the cost of issuing the two types of securities which can be sold in the capital funds market—fixed interest obligations and equity shares. That is,

$$i = (\beta)i_d + (1-\beta)i_e \qquad (7.32)$$

where β is the ratio of fixed-interest obligations to total long-term debt, i_d is the cost incurred by selling new fixed-interest obligations and i_e is the cost incurred by selling new equity shares. With e, the debt-equity ratio, defined as the amount of fixed-interest obligations, B_d, relative to the amount of equity shares, Eq, one can replace β in the above equation with $e/e+1$.

The cost incurred in selling new fixed-interest obligations, i_d, is the amount of annual contractual interest that must be paid on the bonds, taken as a percentage of the sums actually realized from the sale of the securities—that is, as a percentage of the funds actually obtained by the megacorp net of any commission or other brokerage fees. This cost of fixed-interest debt will vary, both in the short period and secularly, depending on conditions in the long-term credit market. In particular, it will depend on the demand for long-term credit relative to the supply, with the latter depending on the policies of the central bank (see chapter 12, section 1.4).

The cost incurred in selling new equity shares, i_e, is the inverse of the price-dividend ratio for the company's stock. The higher the quoted price of a company's shares on one of the organized stock exchanges relative to the current dividend rate, the lower the cost to the megacorp of obtaining external funds through the sale of new shares in the company. Moreover, the higher the quoted price of a company's shares, the lower the risk of a successful take-over bid and displacement of the incumbent executive group (see chapter 8, section 3.4). The executive group therefore has a strong incentive to maintain as high a price-dividend ratio for the company's outstanding shares as is consistent with the megacorp's goal of maximizing its own growth. While the price of shares in general will rise and fall with conditions in the stock market, reflecting many of the same monetary factors which govern the cost of fixed-interest debt (see chapter 12, section 2.4), the price of a company's shares relative to those of other megacorps will depend to a large extent on the actions taken by the company itself. In particular, it will depend on the megacorp's past success in increasing its dividend rate.

The fact is that the price of a megacorp's stock is simply the present discounted value, as determined by the market for such securities, of the expected future flow of dividends. An increase in the dividend rate (the R_j term in the discount formula given by equation 7.3) will lead to a higher price for the stock (the V_0 term in the same formula). While it is true that many stocks are purchased on speculation, in the hope of a "capital gain" from later selling the securities at a higher price (with that resale price equal to the V_{n+1} term in equation 7.3), this hope has little chance of being realized unless there is a reasonable prospect of the dividend rate being increased over time. Without a prospective rise in dividends, there is no reason for the stock to be valued more highly, and without any reason for the stock to be valued more highly, there is no basis for speculation. (The only exception is when, following a take-over bid, the company's stock temporarily commands a premium. See chapter 8, section 3.4) Indeed, were it to become clear that the dividend rate was going to be maintained indefinitely at the current level, the price of the stock would settle down to a value equal to some multiple of the current dividend (depending on what the prevailing long-term interest rate was) and speculation in the stock (except that due to anticipated changes in the interest rate) would most probably cease. It is therefore only an increase in the dividend rate or, even more to the point, only the *expectation* of an increase in the dividend rate that will lead to a higher price for the stock of a megacorp. Nothing is likely to have a more telling effect in this regard than an actual increase in dividends above the previous level, and indeed even above the previous trend line—whether that rate of growth of dividends is then maintained or not. It is in this way that the megacorp's executive group can act on its own to lower the cost of new equity funds, i_e, as part of the overall cost of obtaining additional long-term external funds, i.

The megacorp's executive group can act in yet another way to lower, not just the cost of equity funds but also the cost of fixed-interest obligations as well. It can do this by timing its sale of new securities so as to coincide with the point in the cycle when conditions in the long-term credit markets are most favorable to borrowers. Normally, this is when the level of economic activity has fallen below the secular trend and the central bank has been forced to respond by increasing the financial sector's liquidity. With its favored access to short-term credit, the megacorp will generally have little trouble waiting until this point in the cycle has been reached and it can arrange for long-term loans on the most favorable terms. It is therefore not the values for i_d and i_e at just any point in the cycle, or even on average over the cycle, that are relevant but rather, the lowest values these variables are likely to take at any point in the cycle. In addition to these values for i_d and i_e, one need know only the firm's preferred debt-equity ratio, e, in order to calculate the value of i.

The megacorp's debt-equity ratio, e, is the amount of fixed interest obligations relative to the amount of equity shares within the megacorp's long-term debt structure. The preferred debt-equity ratio, which need not be the same as the actual debt-equity ratio, is the one that best suits the megacorp's own particular circumstances. Typically, the executive group will determine this preferred, or "optimal," debt-equity ratio as part of its long-range financial planning, depending on what it sees as the relative advantage of the two different types of long-term securities it can issue.

The advantage of fixed-interest obligations is that they are likely to involve less of a drain on the megacorp's cash flow over the longer run than an equal amount of funds obtained through the sale of equity shares. The reason is that, in the case of fixed-interest obligations, the amount of the annual interest payment is frozen at the level stipulated in the original contract and will not, like the dividends paid by the megacorp, increase over time. For the fact is that, while the megacorp is not legally required to pay any dividend, let alone increase it, the practice, reflecting the power of the stockholders to depose the incumbent executive group, is for the megacorp to raise the dividend rate over time in line with the growth of employee compensation (see chapter 8, section 3.4). Thus, even though the cash payout on fixed-interest obligations may be greater at the outset, it actually works out to be less over the life of the securities than if the same amount of funds were to be obtained by issuing additional shares in the company. This is especially true in a period of secular inflation when the dividend rate is likely to be increased at an even more rapid rate so as to offset the rise in prices. Indeed, the continued ability of the megacorp to raise funds by issuing bonds can be explained only by the fact that certain financial institutions are required by law to invest a sizeable portion of the funds they hold as fiduciary agents in fixed-interest obligations. It is this institutional feature of the capital funds market which assures the megacorp of being able to find buyers for its fixed-interest obligations, even though the long-term financial return is likely to be less than that on equity shares. (It is the greater financial advantage to the firm in issuing fixed-interest obligations which, in turn, invalidates the thesis put forward in the 1950s by Franco Modigliani and Merton Miller—namely, that the capital funds market will necessarily function so as to equalize the return on fixed-interest obligations and equity shares, thereby eliminating any advantage of the one over the other as a source of external finance.)

Megacorps, then, have a strong incentive to rely primarily on fixed-interest obligations as a source of external finance. The disadvantage is that fixed-interest obligations carry with them a greater risk—at least for the megacorp's executive group. Should the megacorp be unable to make the required payment on its fixed-interest obligations, it is likely to face bankruptcy or, falling short of that, to face reorganization (and, along with reorganization, the replacement of its top management by another executive group). While dividends can be temporarily lowered or even suspended altogether without causing the megacorp to default on its legal obligations, the interest payments cannot. Once a megacorp comes even close to being unable to meet its interest payments, or debt service, the control of the company is likely to pass from the incumbent executive group to the financial institutions which are the principal holders of its fixed-interest obligations. Even if the megacorp does not actually reach the point of having to default, it is this group of financial institutions which, by setting the conditions for any further loans, is likely to assume control. With the economy subject to unexpected shifts in demand, raising the possibility of a precipitous fall in cash flow and therefore of the megacorp being unable to service its external debt, the risk of losing control is a factor the executive group must keep in mind in making its financial plans.

It is this risk of losing control which sets the upper limit on the desired debt-equity ratio, e. The lower limit, meanwhile, reflects the executive group's desire to minimize the cost of external funds. As long as fixed-interest obligations represent less of a drain on the megacorp's cash flow over time, the executive group will have a strong incentive to rely primarily on that type of security to meet its need for long-term external finance. Whether the desire to minimize the cost of external finance, when balanced against the desire to avoid more than a certain risk of default on its fixed-interest obligations, gives rise to a single debt-equity ratio, e, which is optimal for the megacorp or whether, instead, there is a range of values for e that will be acceptable need not concern us. (On the difference between optimizing and satisficing behavior, see chapter 6, section 2.1.) The point rather is that, after considering the relative advantages of fixed-interest obligations versus equity shares, the megacorp will decide on some value for e which will then serve as the basis for calculating the cost of external finance, i.

7.3.4 The importance of i as a parameter

Once it has been calculated on the basis of equation 7.32, the cost of external funds, i, serves as an important parameter for the megacorp in the sequence of decisions it needs to make in determining its capital outlays for the next 12-month period. The role of i in determining the size of the markup, m, has already been pointed out (see chapter 6, sections 3.4). No less important, however, is its role in determining: (a) the amount of investment that will be financed externally rather than internally, and (b) the subsequent increase in the megacorp's cost of debt service, ΔDS_i. It is these two roles which i as a parameter plays that explain why the megacorp is likely to rely only marginally on external funds to finance any capital outlays.

The value of i relative to the implicit cost of generating additional funds internally, R, will determine what portion of the megacorp's capital outlays are to be financed by selling new securities. The lower the value of i, the more attractive external financing becomes as an alternative to generating additional funds internally through an increase in the markup. As already pointed out, the megacorps within each oligopolistic industry can be assumed to have sufficient pricing power, as measured by the slope of the S'_I curve, that R will normally be less than i. Indeed, this is one of the two reasons why, as can be seen from exhibit 7.6, virtually all of the investment within the corporate sector of the U.S. economy is financed from internal sources. Nonetheless, if the demand for investment funds is sufficiently great or if for some other reason the megacorp should find itself far enough to the right on its S'_I curve that i is less than R, then the megacorp can be expected to give serious consideration to floating a new securities issue.

The value of i, moreover, will determine the increase in the megacorp's cost of debt service from whatever increase in long-term debt is viewed as being optimal. As can be seen from equation 7.27 (see section 7.3.1), the increase in the cost of debt service, ΔDS_i, will be equal to the amount of new securities issued, ΔSe, multiplied by i. Only if the megacorp can avoid adding to its long-term debt, and ΔSe is therefore zero, will the cost of debt service remain unchanged. Otherwise, with ΔSe taking a positive value and i a constant (based on the lowest values for i_d and i_e over successive cycles), the cost of debt service will increase in direct proportion to the amount of new securities being issued. However, as can be seen from equation 7.30, any increase in the cost of debt service will reduce the amount of funds available to finance capital outlays, E'_i. If this untoward effect of relying on external financing is to be avoided, one of two things will have to happen. Either the megacorp must increase the price it charges for the goods it produces and in this way offset the higher cost of debt service or, alternatively, it must increase the quantity of goods and services it is able to sell.

The first of those two alternatives can be disposed of rather quickly. If the megacorp is the price leader in one or more of the k industries to which it belongs, one can assume that it will have already determined what price is the optimal one to charge, given the demand for investment funds in that industry, D_I, relative to the supply cost, S_I (see chapter 6, section 3.4). An increase in price solely to offset a rise in the cost of debt service would in fact be no different, the timing

Exhibit 7.6
The Generation and Use of Domestic Private Savings
(1978, $billion)

Gross Savings (Discretionary Funds)			542.0
Business		203.7	
Corporate	174.1		
Noncorporate	29.6		
Household		338.3	
Durable Goods Purchases (Discretionary Expenditures)			516.9
Business		224.6	
Corporate	174.2		
Noncorporate	50.4		
Households		292.3	
Net Savings (Gross Savings Less Durable Goods Purchases)			35.1
Business		−10.9	
Corporate	−0.1		
Noncorporate	−10.8		
Households		46.0	

Sources: Exhibits 2.18, 2.19, 2.20, 2.21.

aside, from an increase in price to provide a higher markup, and therefore a higher profit margin, so the same amount of additional investment funds could be generated internally. Indeed, this is the reason why, as was argued previously (see chapter 6, section 1.4), the necessary value condition will be the same, once the cost of expansion is being taken into account, whether the required capital outlays are financed internally or externally. Of course, if the megacorp is not the price leader, then it must take the industry price as a given. Thus, whether the megacorp is a price leader or merely a price follower, it cannot expect the higher cost of debt service to be offset by a rise in price.

The only way, then, that a megacorp which relies on external financing can prevent its cost of debt service from subsequently increasing relative to its cash flow is by selling a larger quantity of output. However, with the megacorp's share of the market in the k industries to which it belongs fixed, the megacorp can expect the quantity of output it sells in each of those industries to increase only at the same rate the industries themselves are expanding. The weighted average of these growth rates will, in fact, determine the rate at which, for any given level of costs and prices—and therefore for any given set of profit margins—the megacorp's cash flow will increase over time. That is,

$$\dot{F}_i = g_i \qquad (7.33)$$

where $\dot{F}_i$ is the rate of growth of the megacorp's cash flow over time, and g_i is the average rate at which the k industries to which the megacorp belongs are expanding (see section 7.2.1, equation 7.20).

As already explained, g_i is also the average rate at which the megacorp will need to increase its capacity within that same group of industries. It will thus determine what the megacorp's rate of growth of expenditures on new plant and equipment, $\dot{E}_i$, must be. The following relationship, then, must hold if the necessary supply condition within those k industries is going to be satisfied:

$$\dot{E}_i = g_i \qquad (7.34)$$

This, in turn, means that the following relationship must hold:

$$\dot{E}_i = \dot{F}_i = g_i \qquad (7.35)$$

Indeed, it can be assumed that the markup, m_j, will have been set in each of those k industries, whether by the megacorp itself or by some other firm acting as the price leader, so as to enable equation 7.35 to be satisfied.

Not only must the growth of the megacorp's cash flow, $\dot{F}_i$, be equal to the growth of its discretionary expenditures, or capital outlays, $\dot{E}_i$, but, in addition, the amount of cash flow being generated during any one period, F_i, must be equal to the amount of capital outlays, E_i. That is, the following condition must also be satisfied:

$$E_i = F_i \qquad (7.36)$$

Otherwise, as can be seen by shifting the terms in equation 7.24, the difference, $E_i - F_i$, will have to be made up for through an increase in the amount of external debt, either ΔCr_i or ΔSe_i. However, as has already been pointed out, any increase in the amount of external debt will lead to a proportional increase in the cost of debt service, ΔDS_i, and this will, in turn, reduce the amount of funds available for capital outlays, E'_i.

If the prices being obtained by the megacorp for the goods and services it produces are already sufficient to cover a certain amount of debt service, DS_i, in addition to whatever funds are needed to finance capital outlays, then the growth of demand in the k industries to which the megacorp belongs, g_i, will provide a sufficient increase in sales revenue to cover a rise in the cost of debt service at the same rate. That is, with $\Delta DS_i > 0$, the growth of sales revenue will be sufficient to satisfy the following condition,

$$\dot{DS}_i = g_i \qquad (7.37)$$

This, in turn, means that the amount of long-term debt, Se, can increase at the same rate. Thus, while equation 7.36 will still hold, equation 7.35 must be modified as follows:

$$(\dot{E}_i + \dot{DS}_i) = (\dot{F}_i + \dot{Se}_i) = g_i \qquad (7.38)$$

Indeed, in its most general form, the relationship represented by equation 7.35 needs to be specified as follows:

$$(\dot{E}_i + \dot{DS}_i) = (\dot{F}_i + \Delta D_i) = g_i \qquad (7.39)$$

Even so, with $\dot{DS}_i$ necessarily equal to $\dot{Se}_i$ (or, more generally, necessarily equal to $\Delta \dot{D}_i$), equation 7.35 still holds. This is because, with $\dot{DS} = g$ as given by equation 7.37, it then follows that

$$\dot{E}_i = \dot{DS}_i = \dot{F}_i = \dot{Se}_i = g_i \qquad (7.40)$$

or, alternatively,

$$\dot{E}_i = \dot{DS}_i = \dot{F}_i = \Delta \dot{D}_i = g_i \qquad (7.41)$$

It is just that, once the price being obtained is sufficient to cover a certain amount of debt service, then the megacorp's long-term debt (indeed, the long-term debt of any firm) can increase, assuming the amount of short-term debt remains unchanged, at a rate equal to g_i. This, as can be seen from equation 7.41, is also the rate at which the cost of debt service will be increasing (as well as the rate at which both discretionary funds and discretionary expenditures will be growing) so that equation 7.39, along with equation 7.35, then holds.

This set of relationships which the megacorp, like any firm, will need to satisfy both in the long period and in the short helps to explain why, in contrast to what is usually assumed by economists, investment is financed primarily from internal sources. It is not that the megacorp will be precluded from issuing any new securities to finance its capital outlays. For one thing, the growth of cash flow will allow a certain rate of increase, g_i, in the amount of external debt. Second, the megacorp can even exceed that rate if it is willing to bear the greater debt burden, as measured by the ratio of debt service, DS_i, to sales revenue, X_i. Rather what equation 7.35 brings out is that, unless the megacorp—or indeed any firm—limits its use of external funds, the ability to finance capital outlays will, over the longer run, be impaired. Moreover, this consideration, together with the generally lower cost to the megacorp of generating funds internally through an increase in the markup, may explain why, as is brought out in exhibit 7.6, new securities issues play only a marginal role in the financing of corporate investment. The less any megacorp has relied on external funds in the past, as indicated by its debt burden ratio, the less it will be able to rely on them to finance current investment without reducing the amount of funds that will subsequently be available to finance capital outlays. This is because the amount by which the megacorp can increase its long-term debt while holding DS_i/F_i, and hence its debt burden ratio, DS_i/X_i, constant, is equal to $g_i(Se_{-1})$. Still, megacorps do rely on external funds, even if only marginally, and it is this fact which now needs to be explained.

7.3.5 Adjusting to a change in trend

The advantage of external financing is that it provides the megacorp with a means of adjusting to some new secular trend—one that has either temporarily increased the megacorp's need for additional investment funds or, alternatively, has temporarily reduced the megacorp's ability to generate those funds internally. External financing is able to play this role because the reduction, ΔDS_i, in the amount of funds, E'_i, that will subsequently be available to finance capital outlays will be only a fraction, i, of the additional funds immediately obtained, ΔF_i, from adding to the megacorp's long-term debt, ΔD_i, by issuing new securities. This can be seen by setting ΔD_i equal to $E_i - F_i$, based on equation 7.24, and then substituting the new level of debt service, as calculated on the basis of equations 7.27 and 7.29, for DS_i in equation 7.30. External funds, therefore, provide the megacorp—or indeed any other firm—with a certain "grace period" while it waits hopefully for the returns from whatever investment is being financed to offset the increase in debt burden. This, in fact, is why the megacorp is likely to resort to external financing when its investment demand curve, D_I, shifts unexpectedly to the right, as shown in exhibit 7.7. However, for the megacorp to give serious consideration to an increase in its long-term debt, even in this case, the investment demand curve must shift sufficiently to the right so that it intersects the investment funds supply curve, S_I, beyond where, as denoted by point A, it diverges from the S_I' curve. Otherwise, the implicit cost of internal funds, R, will be less than the cost of issuing new securities, i, and generating the additional funds internally by increasing the markup will seem preferable.

It should be noted that only some unexpected development, such as a government-induced change in the composition of final demand or a technological breakthrough, is likely to produce the type of shift in the megacorp's investment demand curve shown in exhibit 7.7. Whatever may have caused the exogenous shift in the D_I curve, however, it will create a gap between the amount of investment funds currently being generated and the amount of funds needed to take advantage of the available investment opportunities. After comparing the cost of external funds, i, with the implicit cost, R_j, of generating the additional funds internally through an increase in m_j in one or more of the industries in which, as the price leader, it has this option, the megacorp may decide to close the gap by issuing new securities. On the other hand, if it is merely the price follower in every one of those industries or for some other reason is unable to effect a

Exhibit 7.7

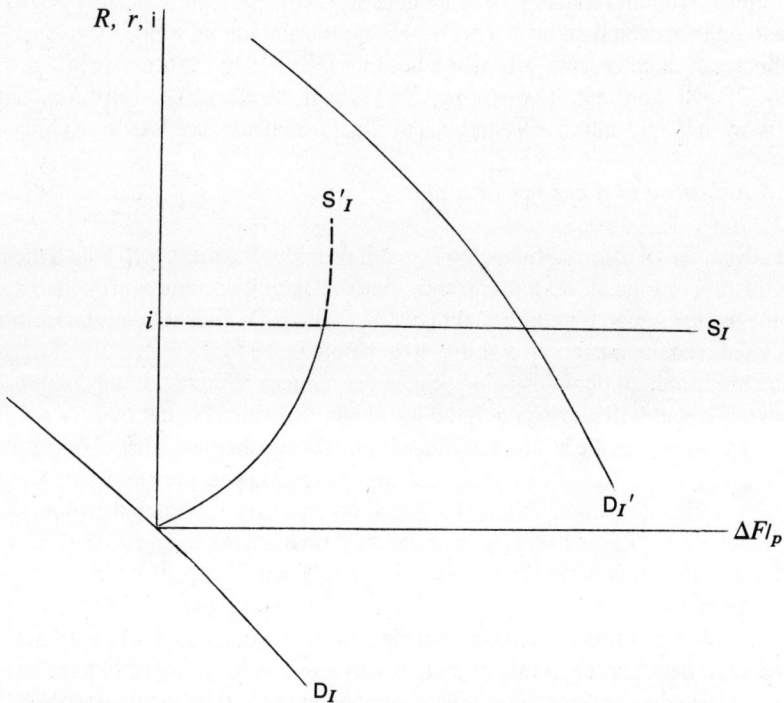

change in the average size of its markup, the firm will have no choice but to resort to outside sources of funds. The availability of external finance thus provides a supplemental source of investment funds when, in the face of some newly emergent investment opportunity, the internal funds being generated by means of the markup no longer suffice. It is in this way that the capital funds market, though relied upon only occasionally, does enable more investment to be financed than would otherwise be the case. Moreover, the type of investment likely to be financed in this way is the type of investment associated with the traverse from one growth path to another (see chapter 4, section 2.4)—or with maintaining the uneven rates of technical progress across industries which underlie whatever is presently the secular growth rate (see chapter 5, section 5.4).

It might seem that a megacorp would also be likely to resort to external financing when, instead of the investment demand curve shifting to the right as shown in exhibit 7.7, the supply curve for investment funds shifts either to the left (as a result of a decline in pricing power) or down (as a result of a decline in the cost of external finance). While the possibility of the S_I curve shifting in either of these two ways cannot be excluded, they are unlikely to be the precipitating factor in the megacorp's resort to external financing. A decline in pricing power—

represented by a more sharply rising S_I' curve and thus a shift to the left of the supply curve for all investment funds, external as well as internal, as shown in exhibit 7.8—will still leave the megacorp in a situation in which it is able to finance all the investment it needs out of the funds being generated by the existing markup. While the implicit cost of obtaining additional funds internally by increasing the markup will be greater, and thus if it were to need additional funds it would be more likely to turn to external sources, it will have no need for additional funds solely as a result of the S_I curve having shifted to the left. Only a shift to the right of the investment demand curve, as shown in exhibit 7.7, will create that need. It should be noted, moreover, that any shift of the S_I curve to the left due to a decline in its pricing power will have the effect of making the megacorp less capable of generating the funds needed to service its debt. Even if the megacorp is still able to sell long-term securities, the executive group will be reluctant to enter the capital funds market—and thereby make its financial position even more precarious—unless the investment that is to be funded is essential to the company's survival and/or offers a relatively secure and unusually high rate of return.

A fall in the cost of external finance—and thus a downward shift of the S_I curve such as the one shown in exhibit 7.9—will also still leave the megacorp in a position where it has no need for additional funds. It is only following a shift to the right of the D_I curve, as shown in exhibit 7.10, that the megacorp will have reason to consider whether, instead of obtaining an increase in the markup, it should seek funds from external sources. While a downward shift of the S_I curve due to a fall in i will not pose the same threat to the megacorp's financial viability as a leftward shift due to a decline in pricing power, still it needs to be pointed out that not much of a decline in i can be expected during any one time period. The reason is that i, representing as it does the composite cost of issuing new fixed interest obligations and equity shares at the most favorable point in the cycle, will change only slowly over time, if at all. This relative "permanence" of i, in turn, helps to explain the inability of the central bank to influence, through its open market operations, the level of investment in the oligopolistic sector—at least in the short period.

This is not to suggest that the cost of external finance, i, is of little importance. As already pointed out, the lower the value of i, the greater will be the amount of capital outlays and the more attractive external financing becomes as an alternative to generating the needed funds internally through an increase in the markup. Indeed, the decline in the cost of external funds shown in exhibit 7.10 means that not only is additional investment equal to $\Delta F_b - \Delta F_a$ likely to be carried out because it can be financed externally at a sufficiently low cost but also some of the investment that would otherwise have been financed internally, $\Delta F_c - \Delta F_d$, will now be financed externally as well. The greater reliance on external financing means, of course, that the megacorp's average markup, m, will not need to be quite as high. Thus, lowering the cost of external finance not only leads to

Exhibit 7.8

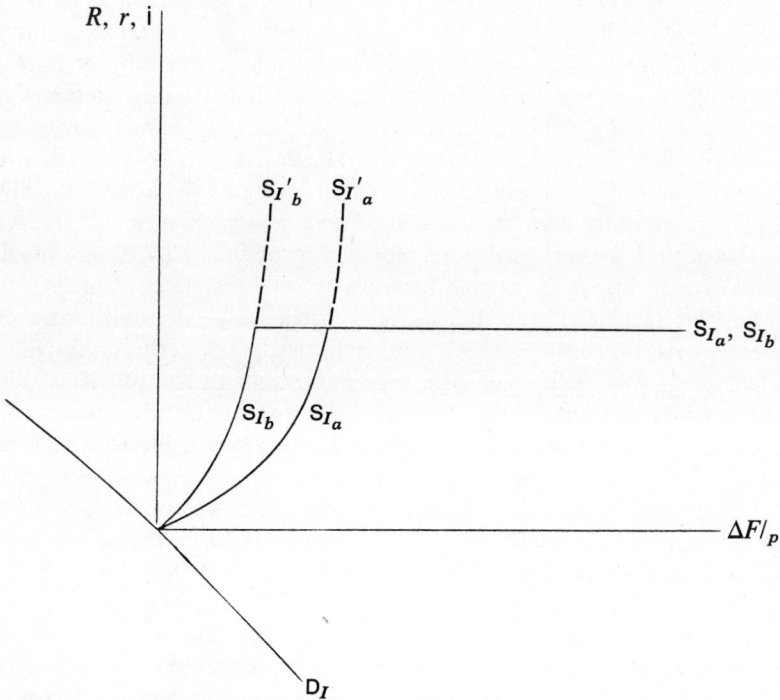

increased investment, it also serves to reduce profit margins, leading to lower prices. It was not without good reason that Keynes always argued for keeping the long-term interest rate, and thus the cost of external funds, as low as possible.

Still, as crucial as the cost of external finance may be, one should not exaggerate the importance of the capital funds market as a source of investment financing. The fact remains that, except for the regulated industries, virtually all of the investment within the oligopolistic sector is financed from the funds generated internally by the markup. The capital funds market is able to serve as a supplemental, or back-up, source of financing only because it is not relied upon to any great extent. If it were the only, or indeed even the primary, source of investment financing, the amount of capital expenditures which megacorps would be able to fund would be considerably less, and the rate of capital accumulation, along with the rate of economic expansion, would be lower. This can be seen by the situation which prevails in the regulated subcomponent of the oligopolistic sector where, as a result of the rules imposed by the regulatory authorities, firms must obtain a significant portion of their investment funds from external sources—and thus where the more conventional view of how the capital funds market functions has greater applicability.

Exhibit 7.9

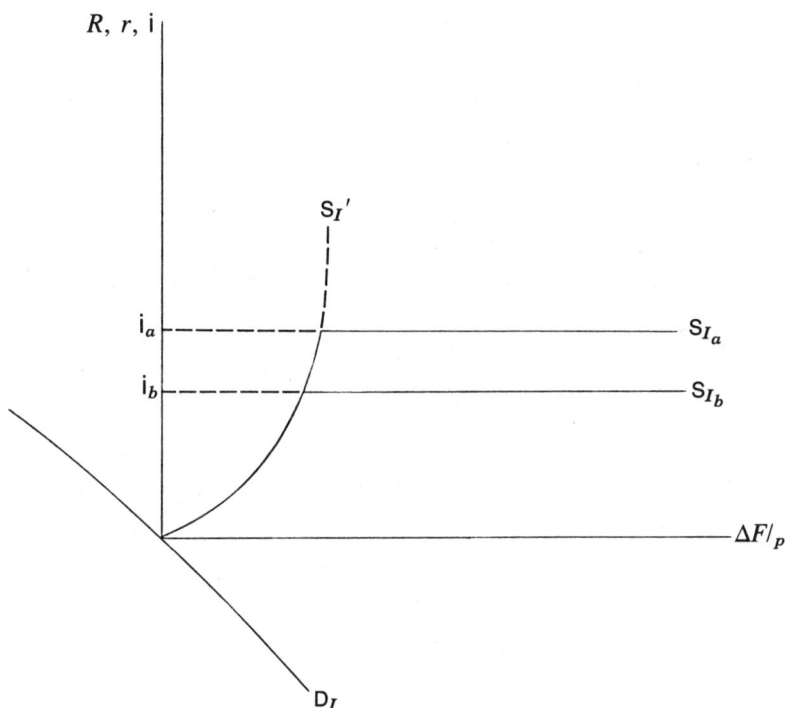

7.3.6 The regulated sector

The regulated industries, like the rest of the oligopolistic sector, are dominated by firms with many of the characteristics that define a megacorp. These firms differ from other megacorps only in that the rules of regulation generally limit the size of the markup to a depreciation allowance—that is, to the amortized value of whatever investment in new plant and equipment has previously been carried out. They cannot obtain additional investment funds, as other megacorps can, by simply increasing the size of the markup. It is this restriction on generating funds internally which creates the problem of finance for regulated megacorps. Since they must obtain whatever additional funds they need by selling securities in the capital funds market, the regulated megacorps will find themselves at a disadvantage both because of the higher cost of obtaining the funds from external sources and the limited capacity of the capital funds market to supply those funds. Both factors can be expected to hold the rate of investment below what it would be in the absence of regulation.

That the regulated megacorp is likely to be confronted by a higher cost for the funds needed to finance investment can be seen by comparing its supply curve for

Exhibit 7.10

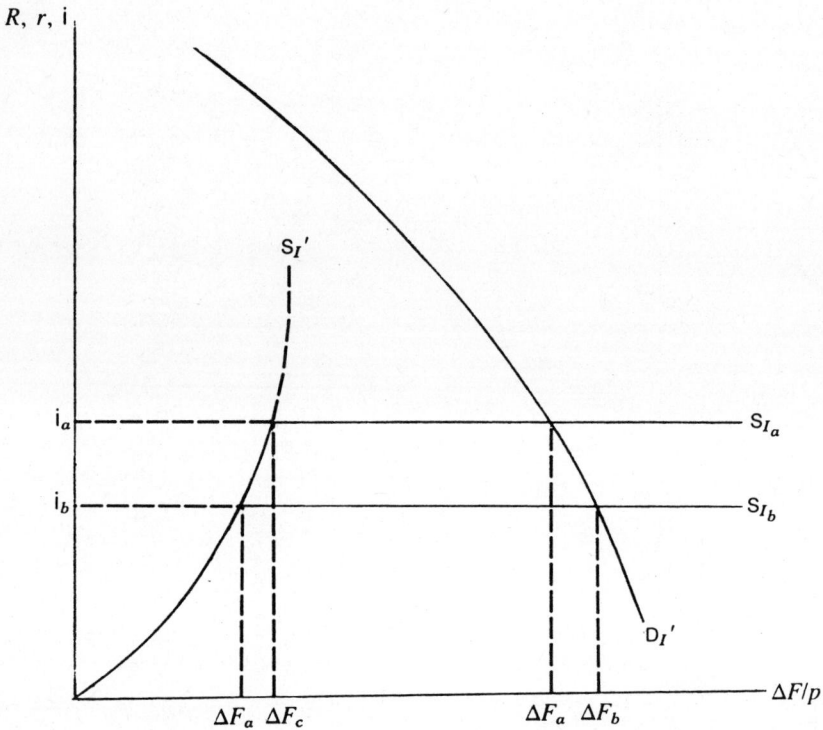

investment funds, S_{I_r}, with that of an unregulated megacorp, as shown in exhibit 7.11. On the assumption that the regulated megacorp is not a significant factor in the long-term finance (securities) markets, and thus can obtain any amount of external funds it needs at a cost equal to i_r, its supply curve will run parallel to the horizontal axis at a height equal to i_r. Since the regulated megacorp generally enjoys a more protected market position by virtue of the legislation upon which the regulation is based, its cost of external funds, i_r, as calculated from equation 7.32, may well be less than that of an unregulated megacorp. Even so, the unregulated megacorp is able to finance any amount of investment up to ΔF_a at a lower implicit cost by increasing its markup rather than by selling additional securities. This in turn means that any marginal investment projects—those whose prospective rate of return falls below i_r—are more likely to be funded by an unregulated megacorp than by a regulated one.

The relative advantage of the unregulated megacorp in funding its investment is even greater than the diagram in exhibit 7.11 would suggest. This is so for two reasons. First, the diagram depicts only the situation which holds for any incre-

Exhibit 7.11

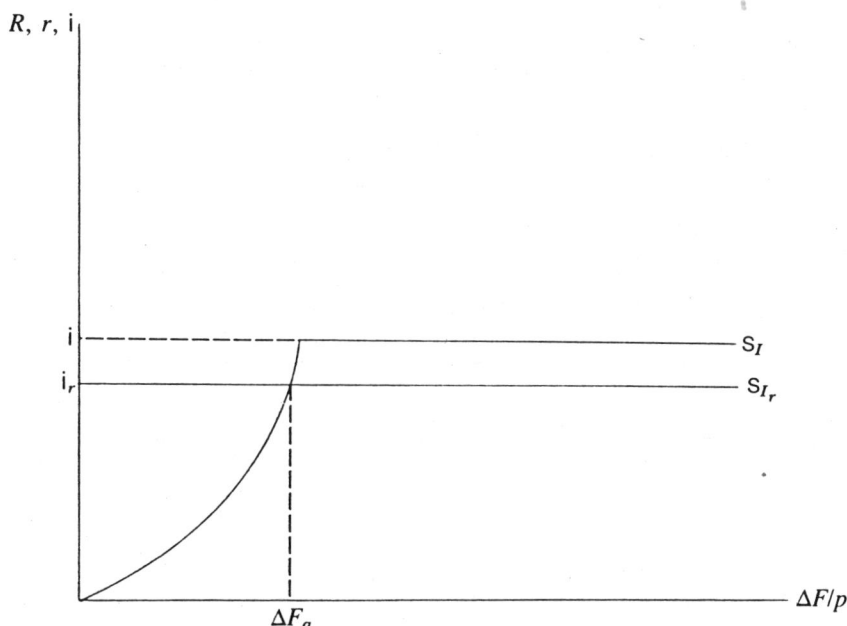

ment in investment. It ignores the fact that the unregulated megacorp, by means of a markup in excess of the depreciation allowance, is able to generate a certain amount of investment funds (even without having to increase the size of its markup) which a regulated megacorp would be able to match only by tapping external sources. Second, the assumption that the regulated megacorp is not a significant factor in the capital funds market may not hold. Indeed, before its court-ordered break-up, one regulated megacorp, AT&T, at times accounted for up to one-third of all new equity issues in the United States within a single year. As some regulated megacorp finds itself forced to issue new securities in order to obtain additional investment funds, the cost of those funds, i_r, may well be a function of how large an issue it plans to sell. In that case, the supply curve for investment funds, S_{I_r}, will be positively sloped rather than perfectly elastic.

Taking into account both these points, one can see that the regulated megacorp's supply curve for investment funds, compared to that of the unregulated megacorp, may well give rise to the situation shown in exhibit 7.12. Notice that the total amount of investment funds, F, and not the increment, ΔF, is shown along the horizontal axis of exhibit 7.12. The regulated megacorp can expect to generate F_a investment funds (equal to its depreciation allowance) at zero cost, and can expect to obtain additional investment funds only from external sources at a cost which increases with the amount of the securities which must then be sold.

Exhibit 7.12

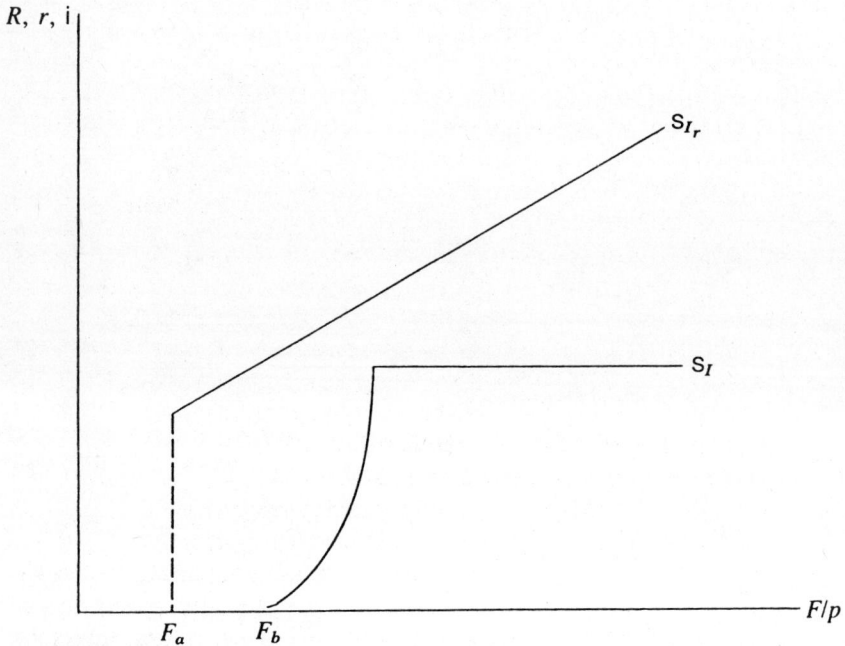

It will, beyond F_a, have to pay a higher cost for its investment funds than the unregulated megacorp unless: (a) the markup, in excess of any depreciation allowance, for the unregulated megacorp is relatively small (that is, unless F_b lies close to F_a); and/or (b) the unregulated megacorp's supply curve for investment funds, instead of being perfectly elastic beyond the point of inflection as shown in the diagram, has an even greater slope than the regulated megacorp's supply curve. While the relative positioning of the two supply curves thus cannot be determined *a priori*, the disadvantage of the regulated megacorp in terms of the cost of investment funds seems clear.

However, it is not just with respect to the cost of funds that the regulated megacorp is at a disadvantage. Because it must rely so heavily on external financing, the regulated megacorp is likely to find that, unless it limits the amount of any new issue, it will exhaust the capacity of the long-term capital funds markets to absorb its securities—at least for the time being. It may well be that, beyond a certain point, the regulated megacorp simply cannot market any more of its securities except at such a large discount as to undermine the financial viability of the company. While the unregulated megacorp may face a similar limit on the amount of any new issue, the lesser extent to which it needs to rely on external funds makes this less significant a constraint on the amount of investment that can be financed.

The regulated megacorp, then, is likely to experience greater difficulty in financing capital outlays than its unregulated counterpart. Unable to raise additional funds internally by increasing its markup, it is forced to rely instead on external funds. Not only is the cost of those funds likely to be higher, thereby closing out certain investment opportunities at the margin, but, in addition, the regulated megacorp is likely to face an absolute limit on the amount of external funds it can obtain. While there is a certain body of literature which argues that, because of the incentive provided by the rules of regulation, public utilities are likely to opt for the more capital intensive method of production, there is nothing in this argument to contradict what has just been said. Indeed, the bias toward more capital intensive methods of production is simply another factor exacerbating the regulated megacorp's problem of finance. This problem of finance is a matter of general concern because, to the extent that the megacorps in the regulated sector are unable to obtain the investment funds they need, the expansion of that sector over time is likely to be constrained, with the sector giving rise to one or more supply bottlenecks. Even though the nonoligopolistic sector has a similar problem of finance, as we shall see, that sector is less crucial insofar as the interindustry flows are concerned, and the resulting supply bottlenecks are less likely to affect the overall expansion of the production system. The salient fact about the financing problem in the regulated sector is that, unlike the similar problem facing the neoclassical proprietorships within the nonoligopolistic sector, it is due entirely to the rules of regulation. These rules, in turn, reflect the preference among economists for what can be termed the premegacorp model of accumulation.

7.3.7 Alternative models of accumulation

The model of accumulation favored by most economists is the one in which savings are generated entirely within the household sector and are then allocated to enterprises on an auction basis through what is termed the "capital market." This can be labeled the premegacorp model of accumulation. The alternative model, at least insofar as a monetarized system of production is concerned, is the one that is implicit in what has been said so far about savings and investment when the representative firm within the oligopolistic sector is a diversified, or conglomerate, megacorp. In this model, savings are generated almost entirely by means of the markup established in each industry, and the funds are then allocated among alternative investment projects by the firms themselves, bypassing the capital funds market.

The reason most economists favor the premegacorp model is not that it assures a higher level of savings. As already pointed out, the savings will be greater when megacorps and other firms are able to generate funds internally by means of a markup—especially if the internal funds thereby generated are in addition to those available externally. But this is not the point, as most economists see it. For them the primary consideration is whether any savings that might be generated will be put to the best possible use—that is, whether the savings will be optimally allocated. Only a "capital market," it is said, with the potential users of any savings forced to pay the going interest rate in order to obtain any funds, will ensure such a result. And while it may be true that only a small part of the total savings being generated—those which originate within the household sector—actually flow through the "capital market," still the amount which does is enough to ensure that savings will be optimally allocated.

Indeed, it is argued that the "capital market," such as it exists, will ensure that even any savings generated by business firms themselves will be optimally allocated. For if firms can obtain a higher return by placing their funds in the "capital market," they will do so; and this, in turn, means that whatever projects are financed out of internally generated funds must offer the prospect of at least as high a rate of return as can be obtained elsewhere. In this view of things, the interest rate—as determined by the demand for and supply of the savings which flow through the "capital market"— represents for firms the "opportunity cost" of capital. Firms which may be tempted to use all the internally generated funds themselves, even if the return is not as great, will be dissuaded from doing so by the "opportunity cost"—that is, by the higher return which can be earned by shifting the funds to others. The capital market, then, by means of the interest rate determined in that market, serves as an essential allocative mechanism, directing the flow of savings to where they can most profitably be employed.

From this argument about the allocative role played by the "capital market," it follows that the cost of internally generated funds is not the implicit interest charge, R, previously identified (see chapter 6, section 3.2) but rather the "opportunity cost" of capital, i, as determined in the "capital market." The markup, m, may well be increased in order to generate additional funds; but the extent to which it will be increased will depend on i alone, and not at all on R. For if, as shown in exhibit 7.13, i should exceed R at the point where the firm's marginal efficiency of investment curve, D_I, intersects the supply curve for investment funds, this point of intersection (point A) will be ignored. Instead, the firm will increase its markup until R and i are equalized—that is, up to the point where S_I becomes perfectly elastic (point B), with the additional funds thereby generated, $\Delta F_b - \Delta F_a$, being placed in the larger pool of societal savings rather than being used by the firm itself. The size of the markup, m, therefore depends not on the intersection of the D_I and S_I curves with i simply representing the maximum height of the S_I curve but rather on i alone. Moreover, with each firm forced to pay the going rate of interest if it wishes to obtain any of those funds, the allocation of those funds among different firms will also depend on i alone. Thus, even with a markup that generates most of the savings out of which investment is financed, it is still the "capital market" and the opportunity cost of capital, i, determined within that market which governs the allocation of those investment funds.

There are, however, several reasons to question this idealized view of how the

Exhibit 7.13

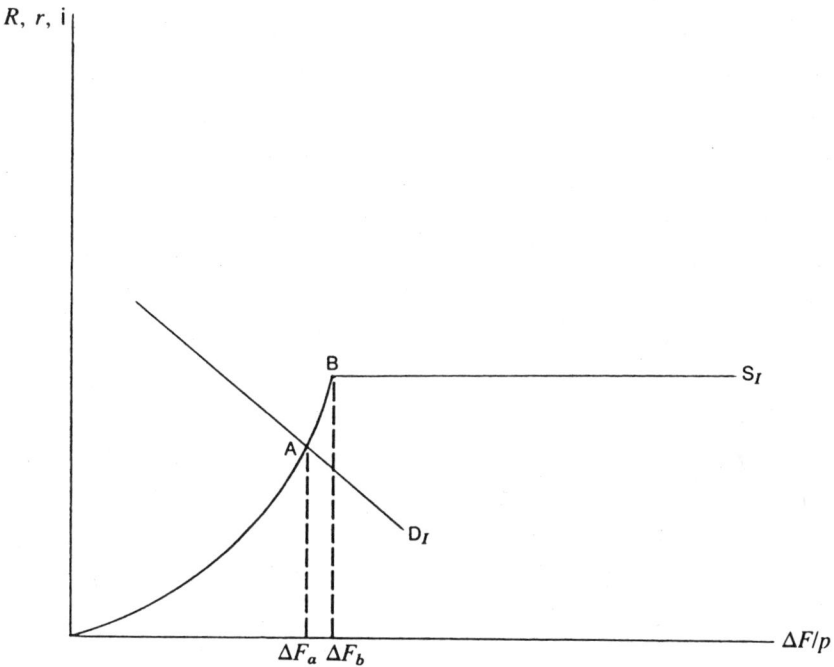

"capital market" functions. The first point that needs to be made is that what is being talked about is not a market for capital—that term connotes the set of markets in which the investment goods industries sell their output—but rather a market for capital funds, or long-term credit. While this point may seem to be only a semantic quibble, it leads to a second point which is actually the heart of the matter. Once one begins to think in terms of a capital funds market rather than a "capital market," one must recognize that what firms must pay to obtain funds through that market is not the same as the return that can be earned by supplying it with funds. The former, what has previously been denoted as i, is likely to be significantly higher than the latter—with only part of the difference being due to the cost of intermediation by the financial institutions which have organized the capital funds market.

The firm's marginal efficiency of investment curve, D_I, has a perfectly elastic addendum, such as the one shown in parts a and b of exhibit 7.14, which has not previously been taken into account. As the counterpart to the perfectly elastic portion of the firm's supply curve for investment funds, the addendum allows for the fact that, once the firm has exhausted the more profitable investment projects it can directly undertake itself, it has the option of placing any amount of funds it

Exhibit 7.14

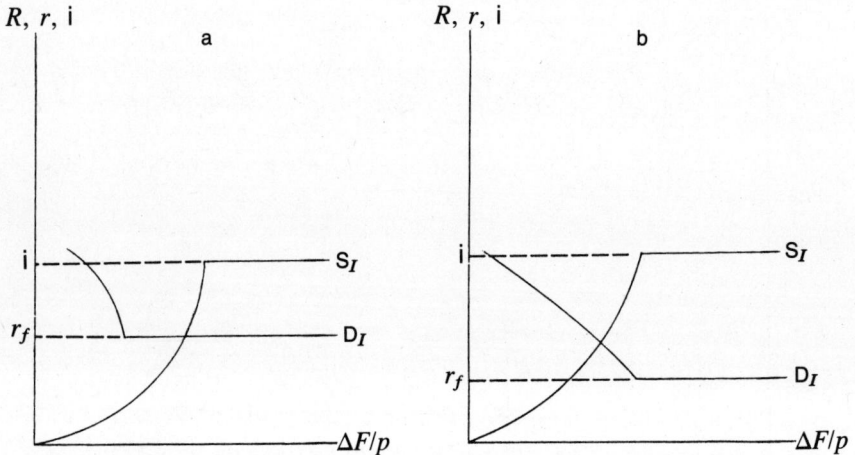

wishes in the capital funds market at a return equal to r_f, the going financial return to holders of long-term securities. On occasion, as shown in part a of exhibit 7.14, the firm's supply curve for investment funds, S_I, may intersect the D_I curve on the perfectly elastic portion of that curve. This will be the case when, due to a decline in the perceived secular growth rate or to some other factor that has lowered the return on investment, the D_I curve has shifted sharply to the left. In that event, the perfectly elastic portion of the D_I curve will be the more relevant portion. More generally, however, as shown in part b of the same exhibit, the S_I and D_I curves are likely to intersect at a point where the D_I curve has not yet become perfectly elastic. This will be the case when, as is normally true of any competently managed enterprise, the firm is able to earn a higher return on the funds it invests itself than on those it lends to others. While this means that the perfectly elastic portion of the D_I curve will no longer be the relevant one, still this portion serves, when juxtaposed with the perfectly elastic portion of the S_I curve which runs parallel to it, to indicate how great is the gap, or spread, between the cost of external funds, i, and the return that can be earned by supplying funds to the market, r_f. This difference between i and r_f is the difference between financial intermediaries' "offer" and "bid" prices for excess funds, or savings—with the firm's marginal efficiency of investment not necessarily equal to either.

The marginal efficiency of investment, r, will depend on the quasi-rents, R_j, the firm is able to earn from the purchase and integration within the production process of various types of capital goods (see section 7.1.1). These quasi-rents, in turn, depend on the intimate knowledge the firm has of the industry in which the investment is being made. The knowledge comes from being able to compete successfully in that industry and learning, in the process, what is the physical form investment must take to be profitable. It is because of this intimate knowledge, and the established market position on which it is based, that the rate of return to the firm from investing in any one industry, r_j—and thus, if the firm is a diversified megacorp which apportions its discretionary funds so as to equalize r_j across any number of different industries, the firm's overall rate of return, r—is likely to be greater that the rate of return, r_j, from supplying the same amount of funds to the "capital market." On the other hand, to the extent the firm is able to generate internally at an implicit cost equal to R all the funds it needs to finance any investment, the rate of return, r, is likely to be less than the cost of external funds, i.

From an orthodox perspective, these varying rates of return are simply "imperfections" of the "capital market," and can be dismissed as being of no great analytical significance. However, from a post-Keynesian perspective they reflect an important aspect of reality. This is that only the firms which constitute a given industry can invest—in the sense of purchasing new plant and equipment—and that therefore the entrepreneurial return from investment, r, is not the same as the financial return, r_f. The latter will always be lower because those supplying the funds, even if they are another firm (though one outside the industry), will lack the intimate knowledge—and the established market position—necessary for capitalizing on the quasi-rents upon which the entrepreneurial return is based. The lower financial return, r_f, nonetheless translates into a higher cost of external funds, i, due to two factors. They are: (a) the cost of intermediation, that is, the cost of the services provided by any financial institutions in bringing the suppliers and users of any excess funds together, and (b) the premium that must be paid to cover the greater uncertainty that arises from placing funds with others rather than employing the funds directly oneself. Together, these two factors account for the spread which normally exists between i and r_f.

These two rates, as the "offer" and "bid" prices by financial intermediates for any excess funds or savings being generated by business firms or households, merely establish the upper and lower limits on r in the short period. Where r actually falls within those limits will, under normal circumstances, be determined by the implicit cost, R, of generating additional funds internally. The exceptions are when, due to an unexpected shift to the right of the investment demand curve in the short run, the cost of external funds, i, supplants R as the determinant of r or when, due to an unexpected shift to the left of D_I, it is the return which can be earned by lending funds on a long-term basis to others, r_f, that supplants R as the determinant of r. Still, both of these exceptional circumstances, especially the latter, are more likely to arise in the case of a single industry than for all n industries together. A collapse of the marginal efficiency of investment throughout the economy will simply discourage all capital outlays while an increase in the secular growth rate, such as would be necessary to cause the marginal efficiency of investment curve for all firms to shift sharply to the right, is more likely to be accompanied by a rise in each industry's markup. What is termed the "capital market" therefore plays only an ancillary role, not just in determining the amount of savings but also in allocating those funds for actual investment purposes.

The fact is that all but a small portion of aggregate savings are generated by business firms themselves through the markup they are able to establish in each industry. Most of those funds are then used by the firms generating them to finance their own capital outlays. Even most of the savings orginating within the household sector are retained within that sector to finance the purchase of consumer durables (see exhibit 7.6). Thus, only a tiny fraction of the excess funds, or "savings," generated within either the enterprise or household sector actually flows through the capital funds market. It is the megacorp rather than the "capital market" which, at least in the case of the U.S. economy, serves as the primary mechanism not just for generating whatever savings are needed but also for allocating those investment funds within the enterprise sector.

How well these funds are allocated will depend on how efficacious is the process of diversification and conglomerate expansion already analyzed (see section 7.2.5). To the extent megacorps are able to shift the major portion of their investment outlays over time from relatively slow growing to more rapid expanding industries, any savings they generate by means of the markup will be diverted to the sectors of the economy where at least the private returns are highest. The social returns, since these are not the same as the private returns on certain types of discretionary expenditures, are a different matter. This one point aside, however, there will be at least some tendency for the marginal efficiency of investment, r, to be equalized across all n industries. Given the "imperfections" of the real world, this may be as close as it is possible to come in practice to an optimal allocation of investment funds.

7.3.8 The greater efficacy of decentralized planning

The megacorp's efficacy in generating and allocating investment funds can be compared not only with the hypothetical "capital market" of economic theory but also with the quite different mechanism which is relied upon for that purpose in a centrally planned economy like that of the Soviet Union. As already indicated (see section 7.2.1) the diversified and conglomerate megacorp can be viewed as the basic planning unit within the U.S. economy—or indeed within any other market economy in which that more advanced type of business enterprise has evolved. The principal difference between the two types of economic systems is that while in a centrally planned economy there is a single public authority to oversee all capital outlays, in a market economy like that of United States no such supreme body exists. Each of the hundreds of megacorps is sovereign unto itself, limited in its capital expenditures only by its ability to obtain the necessary funds (and avoid bankruptcy). Indeed, the closest to a supreme planning body that exists in the case of the U.S. economy (ignoring, until chapter 10, the role played by the government in purchasing more than a fifth of total output) is the relatively small number of financial intermediaries which control access to the capital funds market. However, as just pointed out, the ability of these financial intermediaries to determine the allocation of investment funds is limited. One can therefore describe the system of planning which exists in the case of the U.S. economy as a decentralized one, with each megacorp functioning as an independent planning body. This autonomy of the individual enterprise is one of the features what distinguishes the system of planning within the U.S. economy from the system of centralized planning found in the Soviet Union.

Another important difference between the two types of economic systems is, of course, the way in which the interindustry flow of inputs is controlled. In a centrally planned economy, the interindustry flow depends on the directives issued by the same authority that oversees the allocation of investment funds (though not necessarily by the same branch of that agency). In contrast, the interindustry flow of inputs depends, in a market economy like that of the United States, on the set of relative prices which have been established. The experience under both types of economic systems would suggest that the coordination of interindustry flows so that each firm obtains the inputs it needs in a timely manner is best achieved through a system of market-mediated prices under which each firm is free to purchase whatever types and amounts of inputs it wishes as long as the price it can obtain for its output is sufficient to cover the cost of those inputs. This is especially true when the firms are megacorps which, because of the high degree of vertical integration they have achieved, are able to use the market-mediated prices to measure the efficiency of their own internal allocative procedures.

The freedom of the individual firm to obtain whatever inputs it needs as long as it can cover the cost leads to one of the major advantages of a decentralized system of planning like that of the United States. This is the greater incentive it gives firms to undertake the investment necessary for minimizing, over time, their costs of production. To the extent any firm actually succeeds in lowering its costs, it will directly benefit itself, at least initially, from the higher profit margin on any output that can be sold. Indeed, it is the increment in cash flow from the higher profit margin that provides the inducement for firms to purchase the requisite capital goods (see section 7.2.2). The benefit to just the one firm alone, however, is likely to be only temporary. To the extent the investment in reducing the costs of production is part of the process by which output per worker rises over time, the initial benefit to just the one firm alone will eventually be translated into a more general benefit to the society as a whole. This is especially true if the other firms in the industry, in order to avoid being left at a cost disadvantage, are forced to match the cost-reducing outlays on new plant and equipment. As already suggested (see chapter 4, section 3.2, and chapter 5, section 4.2), it is only through this growth of output per worker within each of the industries that constitute the enterprise sector that the necessary condition for continuous growth, along with a steady improvement in the standard of living, will be satisfied.

This argument assumes, of course, that there is some process which will ensure that the growth of output per worker within any one industry leads to an increase in aggregate demand rather than to just an increase in the industry's profit margin. As already indicated, the competition among firms with respect to price cannot be counted on to produce any such result, at least within the oligopolistic sector of the U.S. economy (see chapter 6, section 2.2). A somewhat different process, one that is no less effective in limiting the size of each industry's profit margin, can nonetheless be assumed to operate—even if it makes a secular rise in the price level more likely. This alternative mechanism for ensuring that any reduction in the costs of production will lead to an increase in aggregate demand is the power of the trade unions to push up money wages in line with the growth of output per worker (see chapter 8, section 3.3).

Another important advantage of a decentralized system of planning like that of the United States, one that bears more directly on how investment funds are allocated, is the greater likelihood, due to the very multiplicity of autonomous planning units, that any worthwhile investment opportunity will be seized. With each megacorp free to make its own independent judgment as to how its discretionary funds should be spent, there is less chance that some project with a high social rate of return will be overlooked. This is because the ability to ferret out profitable investment opportunities can be assumed to be randomly distributed among the organizations which are similarly placed, strategically, to take advantage of the situation. The larger the number of autonomous decision-making units, the less likely it is that a profitable investment opportunity will go unrecognized. The better chance of investment opportunities being seized under a decentralized system of planning is a particularly important consideration when it comes to the type of investment that leads either to product innovation or to expansion into new industries. Both types of investment are especially risky, with the potential returns difficult to estimate in advance. Because of the attendant risk, they are the types of investment least likely to receive approval from a central planning authority—and yet, as pointed out in the preceding main part of this chapter, they are the types of investment that are essential to the continuing dynamism of the economy.

Indeed, it is only in determining the overall level of investment, and thus the rate of accumulation, that a decentralized system of planning like that of the United States would appear to be at a disadvantage compared with the system of planning relied upon by the Soviet Union. While fewer resources are likely to be diverted from capital formation in the case of the latter so that the market position of individual firms can be strengthened through advertising and the like, this is but a minor point of difference between the two systems. The more trenchant criticism that can be made of a decentralized planning system is that it is likely to prove less successful in coordinating the investment outlays of the different firms—even when they are megacorps—so that continuous growth by the system as a whole, at a sufficiently high rate, will be possible. We are not yet at the point, however, where we can properly evaluate this argument. We first need to shift the analysis of investment from the micro back to the macro level, with the focus on deriving an empirical estimate of the E and F functions for the enterprise as a whole based on what is known about the behavior of the megacorp as the representative firm.

7.4 The E and F Functions

Based on the discussion of investment and financing just completed, it is possible to specify a discretionary expenditures, or E, function and a discretionary funds, or F, function, for the entire enterprise sector as well as for its separate components—the corporate, the farm and the noncorporate nonfarm sectors. The E function identifies the determinants of durable goods purchases, or investment, by the sector and the F function, the determinants of the sector's net cash inflow, or gross savings. These E and F functions can be used in two ways. The first is to provide the necessary theoretical framework, consistent with the macrodynamic theory set forth above in chapter 4, for examining the empirical evidence with respect to both investment and finance. The second useful purpose served by the E and F functions is to indicate, once the parameters of these two functions have been estimated empirically, what is the contribution of the enterprise sector to the macrodynamic stability of the overall economy.

The general form which these E and F functions take has already been indicated (see chapter 4, section 4.3). It is as follows:

$$\dot{E}_i = \overset{\circ}{E}_i + f(\dot{G} - \overset{\circ}{G}, X_1, X_2, \ldots, X_m) \qquad (4.35)$$

and

$$\dot{F}_i = \overset{\circ}{F}_i + f(\dot{G} - \overset{\circ}{G}, Y_1, Y_2, \ldots, Y_n) \qquad (4.36)$$

In estimating the parameters of equation 4.35, it is the growth of discretionary expenditures in real terms, $\dot{A}_i$, rather than in nominal terms, $\dot{E}_i$, that needs to be specified as the dependent variable. This is done so that the factors determining the change over time in the price of the durable goods which constitute the sector's discretionary expenditures can be distinguished from the factors determining the demand for those goods—and indeed so the effect of any change in the price of those goods on the level of demand can be separated out. The relationship between the growth of discretionary expenditures in nominal terms, $\dot{E}_i$, and the growth of discretionary expenditures in real terms, $\dot{A}_i$, is as follows:

$$\dot{E}_i = \dot{A}_i + \dot{P}_E \qquad (7.42)$$

where $\dot{P}_E$ is the growth of the price index for the goods represented by the sector's discretionary expenditures. Based on this relationship, equation 4.35 can be rewritten as follows:

$$\dot{A}_i = \mathring{A}_i + f(\dot{G} - \mathring{G}, X_1, X_2, \ldots, X_m) \qquad (7.43)$$

The growth of discretionary expenditures in real terms which can be observed during any one period, $\dot{A}_i$, can thus be divided into two parts: (1) the continuation of whatever trend has previously prevailed, $\mathring{A}_i$, and (2) a cyclical movement, $\dot{A}_i - \mathring{A}_i$. The latter, henceforth to be denoted as $\overset{*}{A}_i$, depends on the cyclical movement of aggregate output, $\dot{G} - \mathring{G}$ (or $\overset{*}{G}$), as well as a set of additional factors, or parameters, $X_1, X_2, \ldots, X_m$, with one of those parameters necessarily being the growth of the price index, $\dot{P}_E$. That is,

$$\overset{*}{A}_i = f(\overset{*}{G}, X_1, X_2, \ldots, X_m) \qquad (7.44)$$

Meanwhile, based on equation 4.36, the growth of discretionary funds within any one period, $\dot{F}_i$, can be divided into the same two components, the continuation of the trend, $\mathring{F}_i$, and a cyclical movement, $\dot{F}_i - \mathring{F}_i$ (or $\overset{*}{F}$), with the latter dependent on $\overset{*}{G}$ and a different set of parameters, $Y_1, Y_2, \ldots, Y_n$. That is,

$$\overset{*}{F}_i = f(\overset{*}{G}, Y_2, Y_2, \ldots, Y_n) \qquad (7.45)$$

It should be noted that while the growth of discretionary expenditures in real terms, $\dot{A}_i$, needs to be determined directly and then inflated by some price index in order to explain the growth of discretionary expenditures in nominal terms, $\dot{E}_i$, the growth of discretionary funds in nominal terms, $\dot{F}_i$, can be determined directly. The additional equation needed to explain the growth of discretionary expenditures in nominal terms reflects the critical role played by the price level in bringing the real and nominal flows throughout the economy into balance with one another. The significance of this last point will become clearer once the inflationary process itself has been explained (see chapter 14, part 3).

In the discussion which follows, we shall begin by identifying the factors that determine the trend values for the growth of discretionary expenditures in nominal terms within each of the three parts of the enterprise sector, $\mathring{E}_i$, as well as the growth of discretionary funds within those same three parts, $\mathring{F}_i$—with the former set of trend values then deflated by the growth in the price of investment goods so as to yield the secular growth of discretionary expenditures in real terms, $\mathring{A}_i$. In this way, the trend values, $\mathring{A}_i$ and $\mathring{F}_i$, can be subtracted from the actually observed growth of discretionary expenditures in real terms, $\dot{A}_i$, and the actually observed growth of discretionary funds, $\dot{F}_i$, with the cyclical movements of these two variables thereby isolated. Once this has been done, it will then be possible to estimate the parameters of the following two short-period behavioral equations for the three parts of the enterprise sector:

$$\overset{*}{\dot{A}}_i = a\overset{*}{\mathring{G}} + b_1 X_1 + b_2 X_2, \ldots, b_m X_m \tag{7.46}$$

and

$$\overset{*}{\dot{F}}_i = \alpha\overset{*}{\mathring{G}} + c_1 Y_1 + c_2 Y_2, \ldots, c_n Y_n \tag{7.47}$$

where a, b_1, b_2, $\ldots$, b_m and α, c_1, c_2, $\ldots$, c_n are sets of parameters, or coefficients, whose values need to be determined empirically. The a and α coefficients, it should be noted, represent the slopes of the respective short-period E and F curves, such as those depicted in exhibits 4.23 and 4.24, and indicate the magnitude of the accelerator and income redistributive effects of a cyclical movement in aggregate demand, $\overset{*}{\mathring{G}}$. (In the short period, the effect of changing prices on the demand for durable goods can be largely ignored so that the value of the accelerator, a, will be nearly the same whether $\overset{*}{\dot{A}}_i$ or $\overset{*}{\dot{E}}_i$ serves as the dependent variable.) As previously pointed out (see chapter 4, section 4.3), the question of whether the enterprise sector exerts a stabilizing or destabilizing influence on the overall economy will depend on which of those two effects, the accelerator effect measured by a or the income redistributive effect measured by α, is greater.

7.4.1 The trend values

The task of estimating the E and F functions for the enterprise sector would be considerably easier if one could assume an unchanging trend. The cyclical movement would simply be the difference between the observed growth rate over any one time period, $\dot{A}_i$, $\dot{E}_i$ or $\dot{F}_i$, and the constant trend value, $\mathring{A}_i$, $\mathring{E}_i$ or $\mathring{F}_i$. However, one cannot exclude the possibility, at least *a priori*, that these trend values will themselves be changing over time, with at least part of the change observed during any one time period due to that very change in trend. It is therefore necessary to identify the factors that will lead to a change in the trend values, $\mathring{A}_i$ and $\mathring{F}_i$ before proceeding with the analysis of the cyclical movement, $\dot{A}_i - \mathring{A}_i$ (or $\overset{*}{\dot{A}}_i$) and $\dot{F}_i - \mathring{F}_i$ (or $\overset{*}{\dot{F}}$). (The value of $\dot{P}_E$ will, for the remainder of this chapter, be assumed to be a given so that $\mathring{E}_i$ is known once $\mathring{A}_i$ has been determined. The discussion of what determines the value of $\dot{P}_E$ as well as any of the other price indexes used to convert real into nominal flows will be left for chapter 14. Since, ignoring any advertising and R&D outlays, the discretionary expenditures of the enterprise sector consist of the expenditures by firms on new plant and equipment, the price of investment goods, P_K, can be substituted for P_E in the case of the enterprise sector.)

The theoretical basis for explaining any change in the trend values for the enterprise sector's discretionary expenditures and discretionary funds is the long-period analysis of the preceding chapters. If the economy is to expand continuously at some secular growth rate, $\overset{\circ}{G}$, then productive capacity within the enterprise sector must increase at the same rate. This is the necessary supply condition for continuous growth (see chapter 4, section 1.4), and it holds not just for the enterprise sector as a whole but also at the industry level and subsectoral level as well. That is,

$$\overset{\circ}{I}_i = g_i \qquad (7.48)$$

This equation is the same as equations 6.15 and 7.19 except that the i subscript now denotes an individual industry or subcomponent of the enterprise sector. Since the discretionary expenditures of the enterprise sector are its purchases of new plant and equipment (ignoring any outlays on advertising and R&D), $\overset{\circ}{A}_i$ can be substituted for $\overset{\circ}{I}_i$ in equation 7.48 as follows:

$$\overset{\circ}{A}_i = g_i \qquad (7.49)$$

Thus the trend value for the growth of discretionary expenditures can be assumed to be the same as the trend value for the growth of output within the individual industry or subcomponent of the enterprise sector, with a change in g_i leading to an equal change in $\overset{\circ}{A}_i$.

Moreover, if the economy is to satisfy the necessary value condition as it expands at some secular growth rate, $\overset{\circ}{G}$, then the firms within the individual industries which comprise the enterprise sector must be able to establish a mark-up sufficient to generate, on the average over time, an amount of discretionary funds so that the following relationship will hold:

$$\overset{\circ}{E}_i = \overset{\circ}{F}_i \qquad (7.50)$$

where $\overset{\circ}{E}_i$ is equal to $\overset{\circ}{A}_i$. Equation 7.50 does not preclude the possibility of a cash deficit (or surplus) within any industry or subsector as measured by the *level* of discretionary expenditures, E_i, relative to the level of discretionary funds, F_i. It only implies that, whatever the size of that cash deficit (or cash surplus), it will remain a constant share of the discretionary funds being generated as both the amount of discretionary expenditures and the amount of discretionary funds increase over time at the same rate. This, in turn, means that if $\overset{\circ}{E}_i$ should change as a result of a change in g_i (or $\dot{P}_K$), then $\overset{\circ}{F}_i$ will need to change as well.

As far as can be determined from the available evidence, the underlying factor in determining the secular growth rate in real terms—the rate of technical progress—has not varied, in the case of the U.S. economy, since the end of World War II. While the growth of output per worker would appear to have fallen in the

1970s following the rise in oil prices, the data from the most latest available input-output table fail to confirm that any such decline has occurred. The rate of technical progress, $\overset{\circ}{Z}$, as measured by the reduction in the direct and indirect labor coefficients, remains unchanged at 3.7 percent. (See chapter 5, section 4.4. Data from the 1977 census have not yet been analyzed and data from the 1982 censuses are not yet available.) Indeed, what was thought by some economists to be a decline in output per worker during the 1970s was probably only the effect of the increased labor force participation rate, especially among married women, on the other, less reliable measures of labor productivity which are frequently used.

The secular growth of aggregate output, $\overset{\circ}{G}$, has nonetheless varied over the same period. It was approximately 1.9 percent from 1952 to 1961, 4.3 percent from 1960 through 1969 and 2.7 percent from 1969 through 1979 (see exhibit 7.15). This is consistent with the argument, to be developed more fully in chapter 10, that the secular growth of aggregate output depends on the policies of the government as well as on the rate of technical progress and thus can deviate from $\overset{\circ}{Z}$. Still, it should be noted that, based on data for the period 1952–1979, the value for $\overset{\circ}{A}_i$ for the corporate component of the enterprise sector, which accounts for almost four-fifths of that sector's total output over the period, was 4.5 percent. This is not significantly different from the sector's secular growth rate. Moreover, the value of $\overset{\circ}{F}_i$ for the same corporate sector, after allowing for the rise in the price of the capital goods purchased by that sector, was nearly the same. While the values for $\overset{\circ}{E}_i$ and $\overset{\circ}{F}_i$ for the other components of the enterprise sector are somewhat lower, still the weighted average for the enterprise sector as a whole was approximately the same as the aggregate growth rate, $\overset{\circ}{G}$.

Once the trend value for the growth of the enterprise sector's discretionary expenditures in real terms, $\overset{\circ}{A}_i$, has been determined (along with the trend value for the growth of its discretionary funds, $\overset{\circ}{F}_i$, and the trend value for the growth in the price of the durable goods which represent the sector's discretionary expenditures, $\overset{\circ}{P}_K$), the next step is to explain how the purchase of new plant and equipment is likely to vary over the cycle, that is, in the short period. This requires that we resume the analysis of the accelerator relationship, picking up where the argument was left off in explaining how the megacorp decides what projects to include within its annual capital budget (see section 7.2.1). Now, however, instead of focusing on how just one of the several firms within an oligopolistic industry will respond to a change in sales, we will examine the response by the industry as a whole, with I_{j_t}, the capital expenditures by all the firms in the industry in time period t, replacing I_{i_t}, the capital expenditures by the ith firm in that same period, as the dependent variable.

7.4.2 The accelerator relationship

As already explained, the growth of investment by an industry in new capacity, $\overset{\cdot}{I}_j$, can be expected to match the growth of industry sales, g_j, as long as the industry

Exhibit 7.15

$ Billions

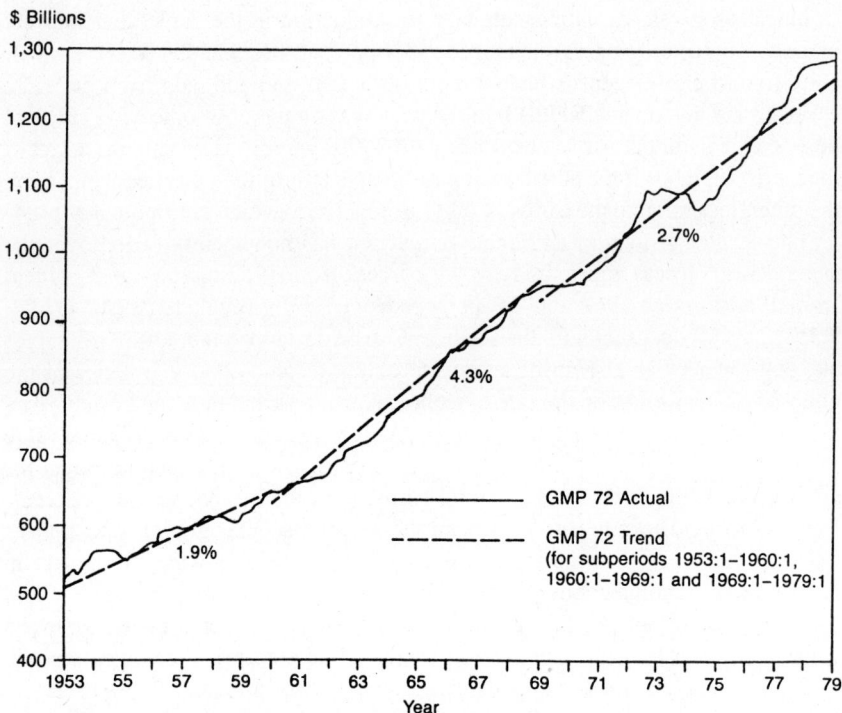

does not deviate from whatever happens to be its secular rate of expansion (see chapter 6, section 1.4, especially exhibit 6.1). It is not likely, however, that an industry's sales will increase over time at a constant rate. Due to the continuous change occurring in the exogenous factors that determine the level and composition of final demand, the growth of sales within any one industry is almost certain to vary over time, with the firms in that industry forced to adjust their capital expenditures accordingly. As previously pointed out, these firms face a difficult problem in having to decide—as they must if they are to expand capacity in line with the growth of demand—whether the latest variation in the growth rate of sales is simply a random movement, part of the industry's normal cyclical pattern or the start of a new trend. The initial piece of evidence, a rate of growth of sales that causes the industry to deviate from its secular growth path, will be the same in all three cases; and only the passage of time, with the additional sales experience it brings, will clarify the situation (see section 7.2.1). Thus it can be assumed that, should there be a change in the rate at which an industry's sales are increasing, the necessary adjustment in the rate at which the industry is adding to its capacity will occur, not at once but rather, only after a certain lag. How long it will take the firms in the industry to make the necessary adjustment in their capital outlays will depend on a number of factors and therefore cannot be determined except empirically. The one thing that can be said with assurance, based on the logic of the accelerator model, is that the longer it takes the firms in the industry to respond, the greater will have to be the change in the rate of growth of investment, I, relative to the change in the growth of industry sales, g.

As an example, let us take the case of an industry that, with an incremental capital-output ratio equal to 3, has been expanding at a rate equal to 5 percent for five periods. Whether the 5 percent is a constant growth rate or only an average of the varying growth rates over the interval makes little difference to the argument. As was previously brought out in exhibit 6.1 and now can be seen even more clearly in exhibit 7.16, the industry's required rate of investment over the period, ϕ, will be g_b or 15 percent, and this required rate of investment, to the extent it corresponds to the actual amount of investment in each of those five periods, will enable the industry to expand capacity exactly in line with the growth of sales. But now let us suppose that in time period 6 the industry's sales increase by 6 percent rather than by 5 percent and, as far as can be determined from all the information presently available, will continue to grow *ad infinitum* at that rate. With the industry maintaining the same rate of growth of investment as before, the increase in sales will exceed the rate at which the industry is adding to its capacity and, as a consequence, the amount of unutilized, or reserve, capacity will decline. Indeed, if the difference between the two rates of growth is allowed to continue long enough, the industry will eventually find itself in a position where all of its reserve capacity is being utilized and it can no longer satisfy the growing demand for its output. Well before that point is reached, however, the firms within the industry can be expected—if they are megacorps—to increase the rate at which they are adding to their capacity.

The firms in the industry could, of course, simply increase the rate of growth of investment to match the projected growth of sales. But that would leave them with less reserve capacity than they need to handle the normal fluctuations in demand. They can therefore be expected to increase the rate of growth of investment so as not just to match the more rapid growth of sales but also to reestablish the normal rate of capacity utilization within the industry. As can be seen from exhibit 7.16, this will lead to a rate of growth of investment which, temporarily, beginning in period 9, will exceed the growth of industry sales. How much I will need to exceed g will depend, among other factors, on how much time elapses before the firms in the industry respond to the change in the growth of industry sales.

For example, if the lag in the industry's response is only one period, as in exhibit 7.17, then the rate at which capacity is being increased will need to accelerate only to 14.5 percent for the normal rate of capacity utilization to be reestablished by the beginning of time period 12. If instead the lag is three

Exhibit 7.16

The Accelerator Relationship
(for an industry with b = 3)

(1)	(2)	(3)	(4)	(5)	(6)
t	Sales (S)	q	ΔS	Φ	Req. Inv.
0	$1,000,000	—	—	15%	$150,000
1	1,050,000	5%	$50,000	15	157,500
2	1,102,500	5	52,500	15	165,375
3	1,157,625	5	55,125	15	173,644
4	1,215,506	5	57,881	15	182,326
5	1,276,282	5	60,776	15	191,442
6	1,352,859	6	76,577	18	243,515
7	1,434,031	6	81,172	18	258,126
8	1,520,072	6	86,041	18	273,613
9	1,611,277	6	91,205	18	↑
10	1,707,953	6	96,676	18	1,103,187*
11	1,810,430	6	102,477	18	↓
12	1,919,056	6	108,626	18	345,430
13	2,034,200	6	115,144	18	366,156
14	2,156,251	6	122,051	18	388,125
15	2,285,627	6	129,376	18	414,413

Explanation:
(4) $\Delta S_t = S_t + - S_{t-1}$; (5) $\Phi_t = \overset{\circ}{g}_t b$; (6) Req. $Inv._t = \Phi_t(S_t)$;
(9) $\Delta Cap_t = (I_{t-1})/b$; (10) ΔReserve Cap = ΔCap − ΔS

*This figure calculated as follows:
  $642,774 ΔSales, periods 6–12
 −275,045 ΔCap, periods 6–9

  $367,729 Additional capacity needed by period 12
      x3 Incremental capital-output ratio

 $1,103,187 Required investment over the period 9–11

(7) Act. Inv.	(8) i	(9) ΔCap	(10) ΔReserve Cap
$150,000	5.0%	—	0
157,500	5.0	$ 50,000	0
165,375	5.0	52,500	0
173,644	5.0	55,152	0
182,326	5.0	57,881	0
191,442	5.0	60,776	0
201,014	5.0	63,814	−$12,763
211,065	5.0	67,005	−14,167
221,618	5.0	70,355	−15,686
282,683**	27.6	73,873	−17,332
360,575**	27.6	94,228	−2,448
459,928**	27.6	120,192	+17,715
345,430**	−24.9	153,309	+44,683
366,156**	+6.0	115,144	0
388,125**	6.0	122,051	0
414,413**	6.0	129,376	0

**Assumes a constant rate of increase in investment, periods 9–11

Exhibit 7.17

The Accelerator Relationship
(for an industry with b = 3)

(1)	(2)	(3)	(4)	(5)	(6)
t	Sales (S)	q	ΔS	Φ	Req. Inv.
0	$1,000,000	—	—	15%	$150,000
1	1,050,000	5%	$50,000	15	157,500
2	1,102,500	5	52,500	15	165,375
3	1,157,625	5	55,125	15	173,644
4	1,215,506	5	57,881	15	182,326
5	1,276,282	5	60,776	15	191,442
6	1,352,859	6	76,577	18	243,515
7	1,434,031	6	81,172	18	↑
8	1,520,072	6	86,041	18	
9	1,611,277	6	91,205	18	1,535,865*
10	1,707,953	6	96,676	18	
11	1,810,430	6	102,477	18	↓
12	1,919,056	6	108,626	18	345,430
13	2,034,200	6	115,144	18	366,156
14	2,156,251	6	122,051	18	388,125
15	2,285,627	6	129,376	18	414,413

Explanation:
(4) $\Delta S_t = S_t + - S_{t-1}$; (5) $\Phi_t = \overset{\circ}{g}_t b$; (6) Req. Inv.$_t = \Phi_t(S_t)$;
(9) $\Delta Cap_t = (I_{t-1})/b$; (10) ΔReserve Cap = ΔCap $- \Delta$S

*This figure calculated as follows:
$642,774 ΔSales, periods 6–12
$-130,819$ ΔCap, periods 6–9
——————
$511,955 Additional capacity needed by period 12
    x3 Incremental capital-output ratio
——————
$1,535,865 Required investment over the period 9–11

(7) Act. Inv.	(8) i	(9) ΔCap	(10) ΔReserve Cap
$150,000	5.0%	—	0
157,500	5.0	$ 50,000	0
165,375	5.0	52,500	0
173,644	5.0	55,152	0
182,326	5.0	57,881	0
191,442	5.0	60,776	0
201,014	5.0	63,814	−$12,763
230,130**	14.5	67,005	−14,167
263,463**	14.5	76,710	−9,331
301,625**	14.5	87,821	−3,384
345,314**	14.5	100,542	+3,866
395,332**	14.5	115,105	+12,628
345,430**	−12.6	131,777	+23,151
366,156	+6.0	115,144	0
388,125	6.0	122,051	0
414,413	6.0	129,376	0

**Assumes a constant rate of increase in investment, periods 9–11

Exhibit 7.18
The Accelerator Relationship
(for an industry with b = 3)

(1)	(2)	(3)	(4)	(5)	(6)
t	Sales (S)	q	ΔS	Φ	Req. Inv.
0	$1,000,000	—	—	15%	$150,000
1	1,050,000	5%	$50,000	15	157,500
2	1,102,500	5	52,500	15	165,375
3	1,157,625	5	55,125	15	173,644
4	1,215,506	5	57,881	15	182,326
5	1,276,282	5	60,776	15	191,442
6	1,352,859	6	76,577	18	
7	1,434,031	6	81,172	18	↑
8	1,520,072	6	86,041	18	
9	1,611,277	6	91,205	18	1,736,880*
10	1,707,953	6	96,676	18	
11	1,810,430	6	102,477	18	↓
12	1,919,056	6	108,626	18	345,430
13	2,034,200	6	115,144	18	366,156
14	2,156,251	6	122,051	18	388,125
15	2,285,627	6	129,376	18	414,413

Explanation:
(4) $\Delta S_t = S_t + - S_{t-1}$; (5) $\Phi_t = \overset{\circ}{g}_t b$; (6) Req. Inv.$_t = \Phi_t(S_t)$;
(9) $\Delta Cap_t = (I_{t-1})/b$; (10) ΔReserve Cap $= \Delta Cap - \Delta S$

*This figure calculated as follows:
  $642,774 ΔSales, periods 6–12
  − 63,818 ΔCap, periods 6–9
_____
  $578,960 Additional capacity needed by period 12
      x3 Incremental capital-output ratio
_____
$1,736,880 Required investment over the period 9–11

(7) Act. Inv.	(8) i	(9) ΔCap	(10) ΔReserve Cap
$150,000	5.0%	—	0
157,500	5.0	$ 50,000	0
165,375	5.0	52,500	0
173,644	5.0	55,152	0
182,326	5.0	57,881	0
191,442	5.0	60,776	0
214,314**	11.9	63,814	−$12,763
239,918**	11.9	71,438	−9,734
221,618**	11.9	79,973	−6,068
300,670**	11.9	89,527	−1,678
336,591**	11.9	100,233	+3,547
376,805**	11.9	112,197	−9,720
345,430**	−8.3	125,602	+16,976
366,156	+6.0	115,144	0
388,125	6.0	122,051	0
414,413	6.0	129,376	0

**Assumes a constant rate of increase in investment, periods 9–11

Exhibit 7.19
The Accelerator Relationship
(for an industry with b = 3)

(1)	(2)	(3)	(4)	(5)	(6)
t	Sales (S)	q	ΔS	Φ	Req. Inv.
0	$1,000,000	—	—	15%	$150,000
1	1,050,000	5%	$50,000	15	157,500
2	1,102,500	5	52,500	15	165,375
3	1,157,625	5	55,125	15	173,644
4	1,215,506	5	57,881	15	182,326
5	1,276,282	5	60,776	15	191,442
6	1,365,622	7	89,340	21	286,781
7	1,461,215	7	95,593	21	306,855
8	1,563,500	7	102,285	21	328,335
9	1,672,945	7	109,445	21	↑
10	1,790,051	7	117,106	21	1,494,309*
11	1,915,355	7	125,304	21	↓
12	2,049,430	7	134,075	21	430,380
13	2,192,890	7	143,460	21	460,507
14	2,346,392	7	153,502	21	492,742
15	2,510,640	7	164,248	21	527,234

Explanation:
(4) $\Delta S_t = S_t + - S_{t-1}$; (5) $\Phi_t = \overset{\circ}{g}_t b$; (6) Req. Inv.$_t = \Phi_t(S_t)$;
(9) $\Delta Cap_t = (I_{t-1})/b$; (10) ΔReserve Cap $= \Delta Cap - \Delta S$
*This figure calculated as follows:
  $773,148 ΔSales, periods 6–12
  $-275,045 ΔCap, periods 6–9

  $498,103 Additional capacity needed by period 12
        x3 Incremental capital-output ratio

  $1,494,309 Required investment over the period 9–11

(7) Act. Inv.	(8) i	(9) ΔCap	(10) ΔReserve Cap
$150,000	5.0%	—	0
157,500	5.0	$ 50,000	0
165,375	5.0	52,500	0
173,644	5.0	55,152	0
182,326	5.0	57,881	0
191,442	5.0	60,776	0
201,014	5.0	63,814	− $25,526
211,065	5.0	67,005	− 28,589
221,618	5.0	70,355	− 31,930
324,398**	46.4	73,873	− 35,572
474,845**	46.4	108,133	− 8,973
695,066**	46.4	158,282	+ 32,978
430,380**	− 38.1	231,688	+ 97,613
460,507	+ 7.0	143,460	0
492,742**	7.0	153,502	0
527,234**	7.0	164,248	0

**Assumes a constant rate of increase in investment, periods 9–11

Exhibit 7.20
**The Accelerator Relationship
(for an industry with b = 3)**

(1)	(2)	(3)	(4)	(5)	(6)
t	Sales (S)	q	ΔS	Φ	Req. Inv.
0	$1,000,000	—	—	15%	$150,000
1	1,050,000	5%	$50,000	15	157,500
2	1,102,500	5	52,500	15	165,375
3	1,157,625	5	55,125	15	173,644
4	1,215,506	5	57,881	15	182,326
5	1,276,282	5	60,776	15	191,442
6	1,352,859	6	76,577	18	243,515
7	1,434,031	6	81,172	18	258,126
8	1,520,072	6	86,041	18	273,613
9	1,611,277	6	91,205	18	↑
10	1,707,953	6	96,676	18	
11	1,810,430	6	102,477	18	1,814,772 *
12	1,919,056	6	108,626	18	
13	2,034,200	6	115,144	18	↓
14	2,156,251	6	122,051	18	
15	2,285,627	6	129,376	18	414,413

Explanation:
(4) $\Delta S_t = S_t + - S_{t-1}$; (5) $\Phi_t = \overset{\circ}{g}_t b$; (6) Req. Inv.$_t = \Phi_t(S_t)$;
(9) $\Delta Cap_t = (I_{t-1})/b$; (10) ΔReserve Cap = ΔCap $- \Delta$S

*This figure calculated as follows:
$879,969 ΔSales, periods 6–12
−275,045 ΔCap, periods 6–9
—————
$604,924 Additional capacity needed by period 12
     x3 Incremental capital-output ratio
—————
$1,814,772 Required investment over the period 9–11

(7)	(8)	(9)	(10)
			ΔReserve
Act. Inv.	i	ΔCap	Cap
$150,000	5.0%	—	0
157,500	5.0	$ 50,000	0
165,375	5.0	52,500	0
173,644	5.0	55,152	0
182,326	5.0	57,881	0
191,442	5.0	60,776	0
201,014	5.0	63,814	−$12,763
211,065	5.0	67,005	−14,167
221,618	5.0	70,355	−15,686
259,120**	16.9	73,873	−17,332
302,968**	16.9	86,373	−10,303
354,236**	16.9	100,989	−1,488
414,180**	−16.9	118,079	−9,453
484,267**	16.9	138,060	+22,916
388,125**	−20.0	161,422	+39,371
414,413	6.0	129,376	0

**Assumes a constant rate of increase in investment, periods 9–11

Exhibit 7.21
The Accelerator Relationship
(for an industry with b = 3)

(1)	(2)	(3)	(4)	(5)	(6)
t	Sales (S)	q	ΔS	Φ	Req. Inv.
0	$1,000,000	—	—	20%	$200,000
1	1,050,000	5%	$50,000	20	210,000
2	1,102,500	5	52,500	20	220,500
3	1,157,625	5	55,125	20	231,525
4	1,215,506	5	57,881	20	243,101
5	1,276,282	5	60,776	20	255,256
6	1,352,859	6	76,577	24	324,686
7	1,434,031	6	81,172	24	344,167
8	1,520,072	6	86,041	24	364,817
9	1,611,277	6	91,205	24	↑
10	1,707,953	6	96,676	24	1,470,916*
11	1,810,430	6	102,477	24	↓
12	1,919,056	6	108,626	24	460,573
13	2,034,200	6	115,144	24	488,208
14	2,156,251	6	122,051	24	517,500
15	2,285,627	6	129,376	24	548,550

Explanation:
(4) $\Delta S_t = S_t + - S_{t-1}$; (5) $\Phi_t = \overset{\circ}{g}_t b$; (6) Req. Inv.$_t = \Phi_t(S_t)$;
(9) $\Delta Cap_t = (I_{t-1})/b$; (10) ΔReserve Cap = ΔCap − ΔS

*This figure calculated as follows:
  $642,774 ΔSales, periods 6–12
 −275,045 ΔCap, periods 6–9

  $367,729 Additional capacity needed by period 12
       x4 Incremental capital-output ratio

 $1,470,916 Required investment over the period 9–11

(7)	(8)	(9)	(10)
Act. Inv.	i	ΔCap	ΔReserve Cap
$200,000	5.0%	—	0
210,000	5.0	$ 50,000	0
220,500	5.0	52,500	0
231,525	5.0	55,152	0
243,101	5.0	57,881	0
255,256	5.0	60,776	0
268,019	5.0	63,814	-$12,763
281,420	5.0	67,005	-14,167
295,491	5.0	70,355	-15,686
376,911**	27.6	73,873	-17,332
480,767**	27.6	94,228	-2,448
613,237**	27.6	120,192	+17,715
460,573**	-24.9	153,309	+44,683
408,288**	+6.0	115,144	0
517,500**	6.0	122,051	0
548,550**	6.0	129,376	0

**Assumes a constant rate of increase in investment, periods 9–11

Exhibit 7.22
The Accelerator Relationship
(for an industry with b = 3)

(1)	(2)	(3)	(4)	(5)	(6)
t	Sales (S)	q	ΔS	Φ	Req. Inv.
0	$1,000,000	—	—	15%	$150,000
1	1,050,000	5%	$50,000	15	157,500
2	1,102,500	5	52,500	15	165,375
3	1,157,625	5	55,125	15	173,644
4	1,215,506	5	57,881	15	182,326
5	1,276,282	5	60,776	15	191,442
6	1,327,333	4	51,051	12	159,280
7	1,380,427	4	53,093	12	165,651
8	1,435,644	4	55,217	12	172,277
9	1,493,069	4	57,425	12	↑
10	1,552,792	4	59,722	12	384,513*
11	1,614,903	4	62,111	12	↓
12	1,679,500	4	64,596	12	201,540
13	1,746,680	4	67,180	12	209,602
14	1,816,547	4	69,867	12	217,986
15	1,889,209	4	72,662	12	226,705

Explanation:
(4) $\Delta S_t = S_t + - S_{t-1}$; (5) $\Phi_t = \overset{\circ}{g}_t b$; (6) Req. Inv.$_t = \Phi_t(S_t)$;
(9) $\Delta Cap_t = (I_{t-1})/b$; (10) ΔReserve Cap $= \Delta Cap - \Delta S$
*This figure calculated as follows:
  $403,218 ΔSales, periods 6–12
  −275,045 ΔCap, periods 6–9

  $128,171 Additional capacity needed by period 12
    x3 Incremental capital-output ratio

  $384,513 Required investment over the period 9–11

(7) Act. Inv.	(8) i	(9) ΔCap	(10) ΔReserve Cap
$150,000	5.0%	—	0
157,500	5.0	·$ 50,000	0
165,375	5.0	52,500	0
173,644	5.0	55,152	0
182,326	5.0	57,881	0
191,442	5.0	60,776	0
201,014	5.0	63,814	+ $12,763
211,065	5.0	67,005	+ 14,167
221,618	5.0	70,355	+ 15,686
128,177**	−42.2	73,873	+ 17,332
128,177**	0.0	42,724	− 16,998
128,177**	0.0	42,724	− 19,387
201,540**	+ 57.2	42,724	− 21,872
209,602**	+ 4.0	67,180	0
217,986**	4.0	69,867	0
226,705**	4.0	129,376	0

**Assumes a constant rate of increase in investment, periods 9–11

periods, as in exhibit 7.16, then the rate at which capacity is being expanded will need to accelerate to 27.6 percent. Thus it can be seen that, the greater the amount of time that elapses before the industry responds to the change in the growth of industry sales, the greater will be the ensuing acclerator effect. Even if the lag is zero, however, there will still be an accelerator effect as long as the increase in capacity is not instantaneous but rather follows by at least one period the capital outlays themselves. This can be seen from exhibit 7.18 where it is assumed that the industry's response to the more rapid growth of sales is immediate. To compensate for the increase in sales relative to capacity during the one period required for the gestation of investment, the rate at which capacity is being expanded will still need to accelerate to 11.9 percent between periods 6 and 11. However, while the length of the gestation period cannot be ignored, it is less likely to vary than the amount of time required for the industry to respond to the change in the growth rate of sales and thus can be treated as a constant (one that then adds to the amount of time represented by the response lag).

The same method of comparative dynamics can be used to indentify the other factors, besides the response lag (and the length of the gestation period), that determine the magnitude of the accelerator effect. For example, comparing exhibit 7.19 with exhibit 7.18, it can be seen that, if sales should begin rising by 7 percent instead of just 6 percent, then the rate at which capacity is being expanded will need to accelerate to 46.4 percent during periods 9 through 11 rather than just 27.6 percent. Comparing exhibit 7.20 with exhibit 7.16, it can also be seen that, if the firms in the industry are willing to wait 8 periods instead of 6 to reestablish the normal rate of capacity utilization, then the rate at which capacity is being expanded will need to accelerate to only 16.9 percent. On the other hand, as can be seen from exhibit 7.18, the value of the incremental capital-output ratio will make no difference. While the required rate of investment, ϕ, and thus the level of investment in any period will be greater, the value of I in each period will nonetheless be the same when b is equal to 4 instead of 3. The magnitude of any accelerator effect, following a change in the growth of industry sales, will thus depend on three factors only. They are: (1) the magnitude of the change in the rate at which industry sales are increasing; (2) the amount of time which then elapses before the necessary adjustment is made in the rate at which capacity is being expanded (with this interval then added to the length of the gestation period so as to determine the overall response lag); and (3) how quickly the industry's normal rate of capacity utilization is going to be reestablished so that whatever change has occurred in the amount of reserve capacity in the interim period will be fully offset.

As can be seen from exhibit 7.22, the same three factors will determine the rate at which capacity expansion will need to *de*celerate when the growth of industry sales slows. The only difference is that it is not possible to assume, as in exhibits 7.16–7.21, that, following whatever lag there is in the industry's response, investment will then increase at some constant rate. Instead, investment will first need to fall in absolute terms before then increasing at a rate which is less than the growth of sales so that eventually the normal rate of capacity utilization can be reestablished. The initial absolute decline in investment is the counterpart of the absolute decline in investment that occurs in the opposite case, that of a more rapid growth of industry sales, once the normal rate of capacity utilization has been reestablished. In both cases, the absolute decline in investment is simply the consequence of assuming a constant rate of growth of investment, $\dot{I}$, once the necessary adjustment has been made in the rate at which capacity is being expanded. However, there is no reason to assume that the rate of growth of investment will be constant following the industry's lagged response to either a more or a less rapid growth of sales. It is, in fact, more likely that the firms in the industry will attempt, to whatever extent they can given the normal gestation period for investment, to effect as gradual a change as possible. Thus all that can be determined is the average amount of investment that will be required during the period of acceleration (or deceleration) and, as the next step in the analysis, the *average change* in the rate of growth of investment, $\dot{I}$.

What the average change in the rate of growth of investment must be during any period of acceleration can be seen by examining exhibits 7.23-7.24 where the logarithm of I has been plotted against time for the case represented by exhibit 7.16. Exhibit 7.23 shows the divergence, in periods 5 through 9, between the actual growth of investment (line segment **OB**) and the rate of growth of investment, $\dot{I}$, that would be required if the increase in capacity were going to match exactly the growth of industry sales (line segment **OA**). Thus the distance **AB** represents the gap between the growth of industry sales and the growth of capacity by the beginning of time period 9—and hence the amount of reserve capacity that will have to be activated, measured by the value of the output that can be produced with that amount of capacity. This distance, as can be seen from exhibit 7.23, is uniquely determined once the divergence between the growth of industry sales, g, and the growth of investment, $\dot{I}$, and the number of time periods represented by the response lag as an addition to the gestation period for investment are both known. (In this case, they are 1 percent and four periods respectively.)

Exhibit 7.24 shows the average rate at which the growth rate of investment, I, would have to be increased, or accelerated, so as to eliminate any gap between the growth of industry sales and the growth of capacity by the beginning of time period 12. That average rate at which the growth of investment would have to be accelerated is given by the slope of line segment **BC**. As can be seen from exhibit 7.24, the slope of that line segment is uniquely determined once the distance **AB** and the time period by which the normal rate of capacity utilization will be reestablished are both known. It should be noted that the slope of **BC** only indicates the *average rate* at which investment will have to be accelerated between periods 9 and 12. As already pointed out, the firms in the industry can be expected to try to effect as gradual a change in their capital outlays as possible, with the actual time path of investment thus indeterminate. Still, being able to

Exhibit 7.23

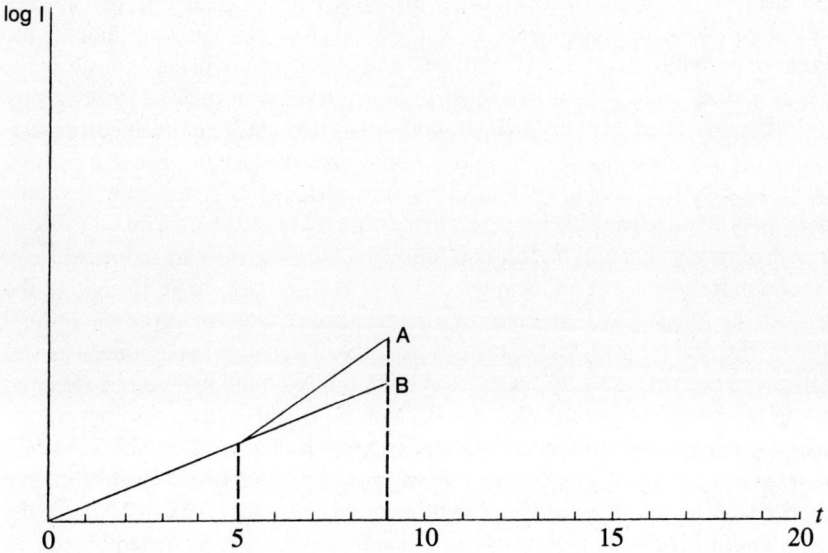

Exhibit 7.24

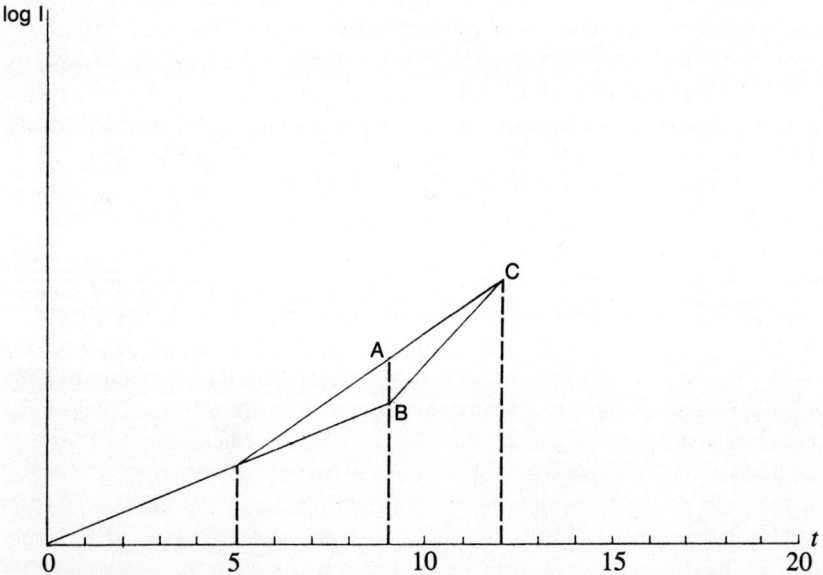

identify the average rate at which investment will have to be accelerated following a change in the growth of industry sales may be all that is necessary to explain
the observable fluctuations in capital outlays.

Exhibit 7.25 shows that what has just been said about the period of acceleration, following a more rapid growth of industry sales, applies equally to the
period of deceleration that occurs, with a lag, when the growth of industry sales
slows. The average rate at which investment will need to decelerate is again given
by the slope of line segment BC, with the slope of that line segment uniquely
determined once the change in the rate of growth of industry sales, the response
lag (added to the gestation period for investment) and the time period by which
the normal rate of capacity utilization is going to be reestablished are all known.
The only difference is that the slope of BC will be negative rather than positive.
This similarity of the way in which periods of acceleration and deceleration can
be analyzed takes on added significance once it is realized that the cyclical pattern
of investment which can be observed empirically is simply a series of alternating
periods similar to those depicted in exhibits 7.24 and 7.25.

For example, suppose that, in the case represented by exhibit 7.16, it becomes
clear to the firms in the industry by the end of time period 15 that sales have been
increasing by only 5 percent over the preceding three periods instead of the 6
percent previously projected, and that as far as can be presently determined sales
are likely to continue increasing at only 5 percent. As can be seen from exhibit
7.26, the firms in the industry can be expected to decelerate their investment in
new capacity in the manner suggested by exhibit 7.25. Moreover, by the end of
time period 22, they may once again be forced by their actual sales experience to
revise, in this case upward, their projection of the growth in demand for the
industry's output, thereby necessitating a subsequent acceleration of capital outlays in the manner suggested by exhibit 7.24. In this way, simply as a result of
firms attempting to expand capacity in line with the growth of demand, a pattern
will be traced out whereby disproportionate changes occur in the rate of growth
of investment, $\dot{I}$, relative to the growth of industry sales, g, similar to what can be
observed in many industries. While the actual time path of investment may be
difficult to pin down, the average rate at which investment is likely to accelerate
or decelerate from one phase of each succeeding cycle to the next will be uniquely
determined. It will depend on: (1) how much the perception as to the secular
growth of sales, g, itself fluctuates (with that perception some sort of weighted
average of the industry's most recent sales experience); (2) the length of time it
takes the firms in the industry to respond to the perceived change in the secular
growth rate (added to the length of the gestation period for investment in new
capacity); and (3) how quickly the firms in the industry act to restore the normal
rate of capacity utilization.

7.4.3 Estimates of a and the E function's other parameters

By comparing the capital outlays of each industry with its rate of growth of sales
over time, it should be possible to obtain estimates for each of the above three
factors in the case of that particular industry. It is simply a matter of determining

Exhibit 7.25

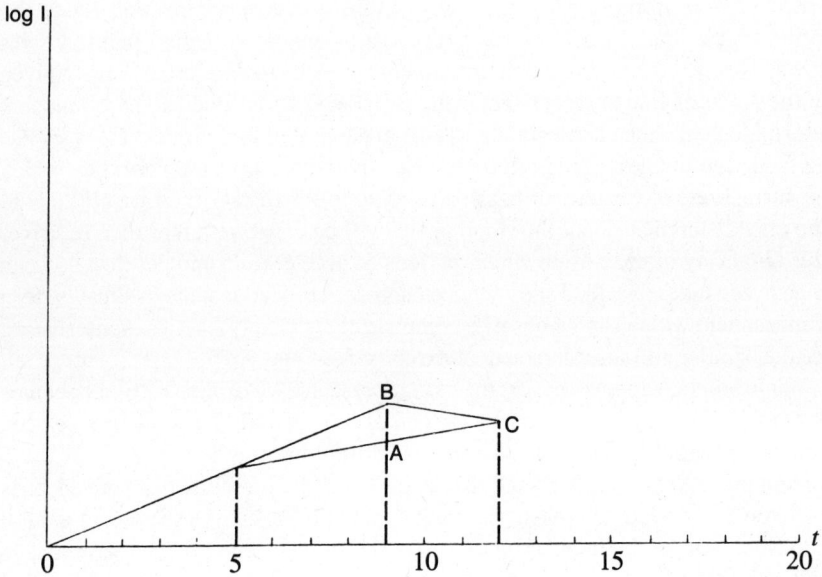

what is the average length of the two time intervals and of the line segment $\overline{AB}$ shown in exhibits 7.24 and 7.25 for the alternating periods of accelerated and decelerated investment that, when joined end to end, constitute the cyclical pattern within that industry. Once estimates of those three factors have been obtained, it should then be possible to say what is likely to be the average rate at which investment will accelerate or decelerate following any change in the growth rate of industry sales. (The average rate at which investment will accelerate during the upswing phase of the cycle, it should be noted, need not be the same as the average rate at which investment will decelerate during the downswing phase since neither the response lag nor the number of periods by which the normal rate of capacity utilization will be reestablished need be the same.)

This program of research has yet to be carried out, however. All that has been determined, in the case of the U.S. economy, is the rate at which investment will accelerate or decelerate for the corporate sector as a whole. Based on data for the period 1952–1978, it can be shown that a one percentage point increase in the growth of corporate sales above the trend value of 4.5 percent will be accompanied during the same period by a 1.9 percentage point increase in expenditures on new plant and equipment (the corporate sector's discretionary expenditures in real terms, A_1). Moreover, a one percentage point increase in the growth of corporate sales, on the average, over the preceding four quarters will lead to another 1.9 percentage point increase in expenditures on new plant and equip-

Exhibit 7.26

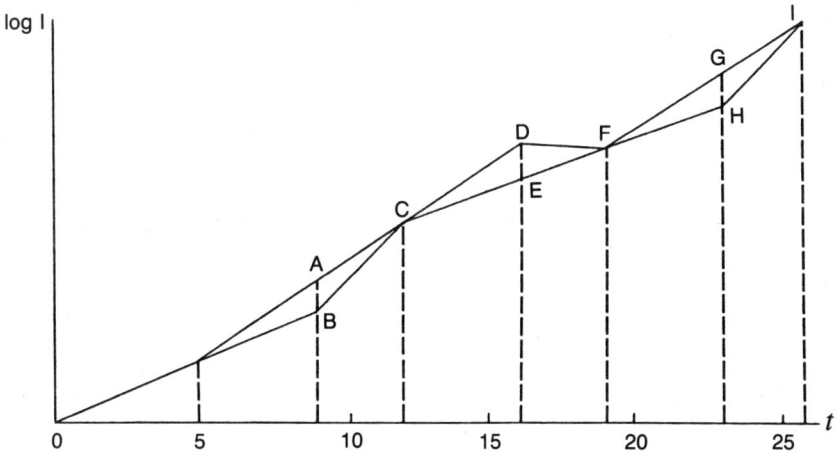

ment. The same relationship also holds for the downswing phase of the cycle, with expenditures on new plant and equipment declining by 1.9 percentage points for each one percentage point fall in sales below trend both during the current period and on the average over the preceding four quarters. This suggests that the average length of the acceleration (and deceleration) period is five quarters and that the average rate of acceleration (and deceleration) over that period is 1.9 percentage points above (or below) the secular growth of corporate sales. For the corporate sector, then, the value of a in equation 7.46 is in the neighborhood of 1.9.

It should be added that the cyclical growth of the corporate sector's discretionary expenditures, $\overset{*}{A}_{B1}$, also seems to depend on the change in the average rate of capacity utilization, $\dot{C}ap$. Based on data for the same 1952–1978 period, it can be shown that a one percentage point change in the rate of capacity utilization either above or below the average rate of 83 percent will, independently of $\overset{*}{G}$, cause the rate of growth of corporate investment to vary in the same direction by 0.13, or approximately an eighth, of a percentage point (see exhibit 7.27). This finding is not surprising in view of what has just been said about the nature of the accelerator. It does, however, identify another important parameter of the corporate sector's E function besides $\overset{*}{G}$ and $\dot{P}_I$, with X_2 in equation 7.46 thus any deviation in the normal rate of capacity utilization, $\dot{C}ap$.

The argument developed so far, and indeed the evidence offered in support of that argument, would seem to apply only to the corporate component of the enterprise sector—the portion dominated by megacorps. Nonetheless, by modifying the argument only slightly, it can be applied to the rest of the enterprise sector as well. The fact that the representative firm within those other industries

---

Exhibit 7.27

Cyclical Movement of Discretionary Expenditures in Real Terms Enterprise (Business) Sector

Corporate Sector

$$\overset{*}{\dot{A}}_{B1} = -0.0001 + 1.9(\overset{*}{\dot{G}}) + 1.86(1/4 \sum_{t=-3}^{0} \overset{*}{\dot{G}})_{-1} + 0.133(\hat{C}ap)$$
$$\quad\quad (0.04)\quad (8.0)\quad\quad (4.0)\quad\quad\quad\quad\quad (2.3)$$

$$-0.001(\dot{E}_1 - \dot{F}_i) - 0.24(1/4 \sum_{t=-3}^{0} \hat{L})_{-5}$$
$$\quad (2.1)\quad\quad\quad (2.5)$$

$R^2_a = 0.92 \quad R^2_b = 0.63 \quad R^2_c = 0.97 \quad \text{D-W} = 1.89 \quad w_1 = 0.24$

Noncorporate farm sector

$$\overset{*}{\dot{A}}_{B2} = 0.025 + 1.38(\overset{*}{\dot{G}})_{-2} + 0.45(1.2 \sum_{t=-1}^{0} \overset{*}{\dot{P}}_{food})$$
$$\quad (1.3)\quad (2.1)\quad\quad\quad (2.4)$$

$$-0.08(1/3) \sum_{t=-2}^{0} (E_{B2}/F_{B2})_{-1} + 0.0011 (X_1 - X_{1-4})$$
$$\quad (1.5)\quad\quad\quad\quad\quad\quad\quad (2.0)$$

$R^2_a = 0.72 \quad R^2_b = 0.12 \quad R^2_c = 0.75 \quad \text{D-W} = 2.1 \quad w_2 = 0.02$

Noncorporate nonfarm sector

$$\overset{*}{\dot{A}}_{B3} = 0.028 + 1.06(\overset{*}{\dot{G}}) + 0.15(1/2 \sum_{t=-1}^{0} \overset{*}{\dot{F}}_{B3}) - 0.33(1/2 \sum_{t=-1}^{0} \hat{L})_{-3}$$
$$\quad (2.2)\quad (2.3)\quad\quad (3.3)\quad\quad\quad\quad (1.9)$$

$$-0.0068((i_{1-2} + i_{1-4})/2) + 0.38(X_2)_{-1}$$
$$\quad (2.7)\quad\quad\quad\quad\quad (2.4)$$

$R^2_a = 0.76 \quad R^2_b = 0.27 \quad R^2_c = 0.82 \quad \text{D-W} = 1.8 \quad w_3 = 0.04$

---

is likely to be a neoclassical proprietorship rather than a megacorp means that the expansion of capacity will be less closely calibrated to the growth of industry sales. It is not just that a neoclassical proprietorship is almost certain to lack the staff resources needed to project the future growth of industry sales. It is also that, without a secure market position and being limited to but a single plant or two, a neoclassical proprietorship will have little reason to try to anticipate the future growth of industry sales. Indeed, any increase in capacity is likely to occur, not through the internal expansion of the existing firms but rather, through the entry of new firms (see chapter 6, section 4.3).

Even so, the same supply condition will have to be satisfied in the long period, namely, that the growth of capacity must match the growth of industry sales. Thus there are likely to be the same alternating periods of accelerated and decelerated investment. The difference is that the response lag is likely to be greater in the case of a nonoligopolistic industry, depending as it does, during the upswing phase of the cycle, on how quickly new firms are attracted into the industry by the above normal profits and depending, during the downswing phase, on how long it takes for any excess capacity to be eliminated through the withdrawal of firms from the industry, voluntarily or not. These same two factors, it should be noted, will also determine how many periods will be required to bring the amount of capacity within the industry back into line with the growth of industry sales and thus the length of the cycle itself. As a further point of difference, the rate of growth of investment, $\dot{I}$, is likely to depend more directly on whether profits within the industry are rising or falling, as Kalecki argued, rather than on the growth of industry sales *per se* or even on the rate of capacity utilization. Indeed, it is not really possible to determine the rate of capacity utilization within a nonoligopolistic industry.

Again, while a study of investment at the industry level has yet to be carried out within this theoretical framework, results are available for the farm and nonfarm noncorporate sectors. The estimated value of a for these additional two components of the enterprise sector is as follows (see exhibit 7.27): farm sector, 1.38 (lagged two quarters); and nonfarm noncorporate sector, 1.06 (current quarter only). It should be added that while the rate of capacity utilization does not appear to influence the cyclical movement of capital outlays in either sector, a proxy measure of the change in profits, $\Delta\Pi$, does—at least in the farm sector. The proxy measure is the change in food prices over the preceding two quarters (see equation 2 in exhibit 7.27). This finding would be consistent with the model of investment subsequently specified by Kalecki (see section 7.1.3). However, not too much weight can be placed on this as well as any other finding with respect to the farm and noncorporate nonfarm sectors since considerable work still remains to be done in further refining the parameter estimates of the E function for those two components of the enterprise sector.

Once the value of a, and thus the magnitude of the accelerator, has been determined, the next step is to identify the other parameters of the enterprise sector's E function besides the rate of capacity utilization, $\hat{C}ap$ (or, alternatively, the change in profits, $\Delta\Pi$), and the rate of increase in the price of capital goods, $\dot{P}_I$. One such possible additional parameter is the growth of discretionary expenditures relative to the growth of discretionary funds—or the net cash deficit, E_i–F_i—during a given time period. This variable can be interpreted as measuring the availability of internal funds to finance any capital outlays. To the extent it turns out to be a significant parameter, it would lend support to the argument that the cyclical behavior of investment depends on the availability of internally generated funds. The same argument can be tested in a slightly different form, one that is closer to the investment function later specified by Kalecki, by replacing the net cash deficit, $E_i - F_i$, with the cyclical movement of discretionary funds, $\overset{*}{F}_i$. As can be seen from exhibit 7.27, the net cash deficit, $E_i - F_i$, would appear to be a parameter of both the corporate and the farm sectors' E functions while the cyclical movement of discretionary funds, $\overset{*}{F}_i$, would appear to be a parameter of the noncorporate nonfarm sector's E function.

Yet another possible parameter is the interest rate, as measured by the long-term yield on high-grade corporate bonds. This variable would be consistent with the original Keynesian (and Kaleckian) formulation of the investment function. Yet, as can be seen from exhibit 7.27, this variable appears as a parameter only in the E function for the noncorporate nonfarm sector. Its absence in the E functions for the corporate and farm sectors can be explained, in the former case, by the nearly total reliance on internal financing and the more favorable access which megacorps have to financial institutions and, in the latter case, by the availability of publicly subsidized loans. Indeed, the amount of government-sponsored loans to farmers, the policy variable X_1, appears as one of the parameters in the farm sector's E function. The influence of monetary policy on the enterprise sector's capital outlays is instead likely to be felt through a variable quite different from the interest rate. This other variable is the liquidity position of the banking system, as measured by the ratio of bank loans to bank assets (relative to the norm), $\hat{L}$. As will be explained when the monetary-financial sector is examined in depth (see chapter 12, section 2.3), any pressure by the central bank or monetary authority on the liquidity position of the banking system, as measured by $\hat{L}$, will force banks to cut back on, or "ration," their loans to business, and if this "tight money" policy is applied when sales are falling and/or capacity utilization is below the normal rate, even megacorps may be forced to slow down, at least temporarily, their rate of capital spending. Thus the $\hat{L}$ variable appears as a parameter in the E function not just of the noncorporate nonfarm sector but of the corporate sector as well (see exhibit 7.27).

One last type of parameter can be identified in the case of the E functions for the enterprise sector. This is the set of policy variables, X, through which the government is able to influence the sector's growth of discretionary expenditures in real terms, $\dot{A}_i$. One of these policy variables has already been identified. It is the amount of government-sponsored loans to the farm sector. At least one other policy variable would appear to be a significant insofar as the enterprise sector's discretionary expenditures are concerned. This is X_2, the investment tax credit. It should be noted, however, that this variable appears as a statistically significant parameter only in the E function for the noncorporate nonfarm sector—and not in the E function for the corporate sector, which accounts for four-fifths of the capital outlays within the enterprise sector as a whole.

Thus, four types of parameters can be identified insofar as the E functions for the enterprise sector are concerned. These four types of parameters are: (1) the aggregate demand variables—$\overset{*}{G}$, $\hat{C}ap$ and $\Delta \underset{*}{\Pi}$ (or some proxy thereof); (2) the cash flow variables—E_i-F_i or, alternatively, $\overset{*}{F}_i$; (3) the monetary-financial variables—i_{LT} and $\hat{L}$; and (4) a set of policy variables, $\mathbf{X}$. The cyclical movement of discretionary expenditures within each of the three component parts of the enterprise sector, $\overset{*}{\mathbf{A}}_i$, first needs to be determined, based on the behavioral equations shown in exhibit 7.27, and the trend component, $\overset{\circ}{\mathbf{A}}_i$, then added to explain the growth of discretionary expenditures in real terms, $\dot{\mathbf{A}}_i$, which can be observed during any one period. The observed growth of discretionary expenditures in real terms for the enterprise sector as a whole, $\dot{\mathbf{A}}$, will be a weighted average of the growth of discretionary expenditures in real terms for each of those three component parts—with the growth rate of the relevant price index, $\dot{\mathbf{P}}_K$, added to this figure to explain the growth of discretionary expenditures in nominal terms, $\dot{\mathbf{E}}$. The discussion of the enterprise sector's E function having been completed, we now need to carry out a similar analysis of the sector's F function, beginning with the relationship between $\overset{*}{\mathbf{F}}_i$ and $\overset{*}{\mathbf{G}}$.

7.4.4 The cyclical behavioral equation for discretionary funds

As already explained, the marginal rate at which firms generate any cash flow, μ', will be greater than the average rate so that, as aggregate demand varies over the cycle, the change in the amount of discretionary funds being generated will be disproportionate to the change in the level of sales. This necessarily implies that the value of α in equation 7.47, which measures the magnitude of the income redistributive effect produced by a cyclical movement in aggregate output, will be greater than 1. (The nature of this redistributive effect will become clearer once the post-Keynesian theory of income distribution has been presented in the chapter which next follows. For now it will suffice simply to point out that the disproportionate change in the amount of cash flow being generated within the enterprise sector as the level of demand varies over the cycle will necessarily lead to a *relative* change in the distribution of income between that and at least one other sector of the economy.) While it can thus be assumed that the value of α will be greater than 1, the more important question is whether it is greater or less than the value of the accelerator, $\mathbf{a}$. As was pointed out at the beginning of this chapter part, the $\mathbf{a}$ and α coefficients represent the slopes of the enterprise sector's E and F curves respectively. Which coefficient is larger will therefore determine whether the enterprise sector, through its investment behavior and net cash generation, exerts a stabilizing or destabilizing influence on the economy as a whole.

To obtain a reliable estimate of the α coefficient in equation 7.47, it is first necessary to identify the other possible parameters of that F function—just as, to obtain a reliable estimate of a, it is first necessary to identify the other parameters of equation 7.46. The other parameters of the enterprise sector's F function, it can be posited, are a set of intersectoral compensation rates, $Y_1, Y_2, \ldots, Y_n$, with each of these variables governing the distribution of income over time between the enterprise sector and at least one other sector of the economy. The entire set of these intersectoral compensation rates can be regarded as the long-period determinants of the distribution of income—as distinct from the short-period determinant, $\overset{*}{G}$.

One of the intersectoral compensation rates that serves as a parameter of the enterprise sector's F function is the money wage rate, w. An increase in the money wage rate, other factors remaining the same, will reduce the rate of growth of the enterprise sector's net cash inflow, or discretionary funds, $\dot{F}_i$. This is because the increase in the money wage rate will cause the enterprise sector's unit labor costs, U_L, and thus its wage bill, wLQ, to rise. Unless prices rise to offset the higher costs of production, the average profit margin within the enterprise sector, μ, and thus the rate of growth of discretionary funds, $\dot{F}_i$, will decline. At the same time, since an increase in the wage bill will lead to a rise in the household sector's disposable income, the rate of growth of that sector's discretionary funds will be greater. Conversely, a fall in the money wage rate will, other factors remaining the same, lead to a more rapid growth of the enterprise sector's discretionary funds and a less rapid growth of the household sector's discretionary funds. However, in determining the relative distribution of income between the enterprise and household sectors, one cannot just take into account the money wage rate, w, or even the growth of the money wage rate, $\dot{w}$. The rate at which the enterprise sector's unit labor costs are rising, $\dot{U}_L$, will depend on the growth of the money wage rate, $\dot{w}$, relative to the growth of output per worker, $\overset{\circ}{Z}$. That is,

$$\dot{U}_L = \dot{w} - \overset{\circ}{Z} \qquad (7.51)$$

where U_L is a weighted average of the wL vector. Moreover, whether the average profit margin within the enterprise sector, μ, is falling or rising will depend on the rate at which the prices of any net, or final, output are increasing relative to the growth of unit labor costs. That is,

$$\mu = f(\dot{P}_C, \dot{U}_L) \qquad (7.52)$$

where P_C is a price index of the goods entering into final use, or consumption. Thus, to avoid confusing the long-period redistribution of income between the enterprise and household sectors with the short-period redistributive effect, α, all three variables—$\dot{w}$, $\overset{\circ}{Z}$ and $\dot{P}_C$—need to be included as parameters of the enterprise sector's F function, although only $\dot{w}$ and $\dot{P}_C$ are actually intersectoral compensation rates. Inclusion of $\overset{\circ}{Z}$ as a parameter of the F function simply reflects the role this variable plays in setting the limit as to the sustainable rate of economic expansion (see chapter 4, section 3.2, and chapter 5, section 4.5). That $\overset{\circ}{Z}$ is not an intersectoral compensation is indicated by the fact that it is a parameter of the enterprise sector's F function alone. Indeed, as a reflection of the unique role $\overset{\circ}{Z}$ plays, it is the only variable that will be identified in this and subsequent chapters that serves as a parameter of just one sector's F function.

The immediate flow of income between the enterprise and household sectors will depend not just on the rate of growth of wages (relative to the price of consumption goods) but also on the rate of growth of dividends. However, to the extent that the rate of growth of dividends simply corresponds, as will be argued shortly (see chapter 8, section 3.4), to the rate of growth of money wages, no separate variable need be included as an additional parameter of the enterprise sector's F function. Moreover, even if the rate of growth of dividends, $\overset{\cdot}{D}iv$, should differ from the rate of growth of money wages, $\overset{\cdot}{w}$, the discrepancy will affect only the distribution of real income within the household sector between workers and rentiers (as well as the rate of growth of prices), and not the distribution of real income between the enterprise and household sectors (see chapter 8, section 2.2).

Another intersectoral compensation rate that needs to be included as a parameter of the enterprise sector's F function is one or more of the various tax rates, t_1, $t_2, \ldots, t_x$, that apply to that sector (see chapter 10, part 3, for a further discussion of these various tax rates). An increase in any one of these tax rates, other factors remaining the same, will reduce the enterprise sector's after-tax, or net, income and thus the growth of its discretionary funds, while at the same time adding to the growth of the government sector's discretionary funds. Conversely, a decline in any one of these tax rates will, *ceteris paribus*, lead to a more rapid growth of the enterprise sector's discretionary funds and a less rapid growth of the government sector's discretionary funds. Again, however, one cannot look at just these various tax rates alone in determining the relative distribution of income between the enterprise and government sectors. In addition, the price of the goods being sold to government agencies and not-for-profit organizations, P_G (along with any subsidies to private enterprises), needs to be taken into account. Thus both the various tax rates, $t_1, t_2, \ldots, t_x$ (including any negative tax, or subsidy, rates), and the price index for the goods purchased by the government and not-for-profit sector (to the extent it differs from the price of other consumption goods, P_C, and/or the price of other investment goods, P_K) need to be included as parameters of the enterprise sector's F function.

With the possibility of income also being redistributed, in the long period, between the domestic economy and the rest-of-the world sector, the F function for the enterprise sector will need to include, as additional parameters: (1) the price of imported goods, P_M, relative to the price of exported goods, P_X; and (2) the set of various exchange rates, $ER_1, ER_2, \ldots, ER_y$, between the domestic and various foreign currencies. With the enterprise sector itself divisible into several component parts, each with a separate F function, still other variables will need to be included as parameters of the F functions for the corporate, farm and noncorporate nonfarm subsectors which have so far been delineated. These additional parameters are the variables, such as relative prices and/or relative costs, that will determine the distribution of income among these several component parts of the enterprise sector. Besides the corporate, farm and noncorporate farm components of the enterprise sector, a separate monetary-financial subsector can also be delineated. While a systematic analysis of this subsector must wait until the topic of money and credit is taken up in chapter 12, it should be noted here that the general level of interest rates, while primarily affecting the distribution of income between the monetary-financial subsector and the rest of the enterprise sector, will also determine, along with the rate of growth of dividends, the relative distribution of income between workers and rentiers (see chapter 9, section 4.4).

Once the F function for each of the several components of the enterprise sector has been fully specified, including the set of intersectoral compensation rates, Y_1, $Y_2, \ldots, Y_n$, the next step is to obtain estimates of the $c_1, c_2, \ldots, c_n$ coefficients in equation 7.47. (This step has yet to be carried out for the U.S. economy.) The separate F functions of each of the enterprise sector's component parts can then be aggregated to yield an F function for the enterprise sector as a whole, with the estimated value of α compared to the estimated value of a to see if the enterprise sector exerts a stabilizing or destabilizing influence on the overall economy. The E and F functions for the enterprise sector having thus been derived, we now need to see if it is possible to obtain a similar set of E and F functions for the household sector and, in this way, proceed further with our disaggregated analysis of the stability properties of an advanced market economy like that of the United States.

Recommended Readings

On the original Keynesian investment function, see *The General Theory*, chs. 11–12, 16. Both Kalecki's initial formulation and his subsequent investment equation can be found in Michal Kalecki, *Selected Essays on the Dynamics of the Capitalist Economy, 1933–70*, London: Cambridge University Press, 1971, chs. 9, 10. See also A. Asimakapulos, "Profits and Investment: A Kaleckian Approach," in *The Microeconomic Foundations of Macroeconomics*, Geoffrey C. Harcourt, ed., London: Macmillan, 1977. On the accelerator model, see John M. Clark, "Business Acceleration and the Law of Demand," *Journal of Political Economy*, March 1917; Hollis B. Chenery, "Overcapacity and the Acceleration Principle" *Econometrica*, January 1952; Leendart M. Koyck, *Distributed Lags and Business Investment*, Amsterdam: North-Holland, 1954; Nicholas Kaldor, "A Model of Economic Growth," *Economic Journal*, December 1959, and "Capital Accumulation and Economic Growth," in *The Accumulation of Capital*, F. A. Lutz and D. C. Hague, eds., London: Macmillan, 1961; Robert Eisner, "A Distributed Lag Investment Function, *Econometrica*, January 1960,

"Investment: Fact and Fancy," *American Economic Review*, May 1963, and "A Permanent Income Theory for Investment—Some Empirical Explorations," *American Economic Review*, June 1967; Michael K. Evans, "A Study of Industry Investment Decisions," *Review of Economics and Statistics*, May 1967. On the neoclassical investment function, see Dale W. Jorgenson, "Capital Theory and Investment Behavior," *American Economic Review*, May 1963, and "Econometric Studies of Investment Behavior," *Journal of Economic Literature*, December 1971. On Tobin's variation of this model, see John Ciccolo, Jr., "Money, Equity Values and Income," *Journal of Money, Credit and Banking*, February 1978. See also James S. Duesenberry, *Business Cycles and Economic Growth*, New York: McGraw-Hill, 1958, chs. 3–7.

On the efforts by economists to obtain an empirically satisfactory model of investment behavior, also see Michael K. Evans, *Macroeconomic Activity*, New York: Harper & Row, 1969, chs. 4–5; Dale W. Jorgenson, "Econometric Studies of Investment Behavior: A Survey," *Journal of Economic Literature*, June 1971; Robert Eisner, *Factors in Business Investment*, Boston: National Bureau of Economic Research, 1978, Gardner Ackley, *Macronomic Theory and Policy*, New York: Macmillan, 1978, chs. 8, 18–19. Eisner, it should be noted, has criticized Jorgenson for the inability of others, including Eisner himself, to reproduce Jorgenson's empirical results. See Robert Eisner and M. I. Nadiri, "Investment Behavior and the Neo-Classical Theory," *Review of Economics and Statistics*, August 1968, and "Neoclassical Theory of Investment Behavior: A Comment," *Review of Economics and Statistics*, May 1970.

Paul Samuelson's classic article on the combined multiplier-accelerator effect is "Interaction Between the Multiplier Analysis and the Principle of Acceleration," *Review of Economics and Statistics*, May 1939. See also John Hicks, *A Contribution to the Theory of the Trade Cycle*, Oxford: Oxford University Press, 1950, and Richard M. Goodwin, "The Non-linear Accelerator and the Persistence of Business Cycles," *Econometrica*, January 1951.

The literature on investment by the individual firm is quite meager (aside from the macro-oriented body of work surveyed in the preceding paragraphs). Most of the discussion is theoretical, focusing on what is termed "capital deepening." With the exception of the textbooks used in business finance and similar courses, little attention has been paid to the investment behavior of the megacorp specifically—and even in the case of those textbooks, the emphasis is on how investment decisions should be made as distinct from how they are in fact made. On the megacorp's investment strategy, see H. Igor Ansoff, *Corporate Strategy, An Analytical Approach to Business Policy for Growth and Expansion*, New York: McGraw-Hill, 1965; Michael Porter, *Competitive Strategy*, New York: Free Press, 1980; Thomas H. Naylor, John M. Vernon and Kenneth L. Wertz, *Managerial Economics*, New York: McGraw-Hill, 1983. For the type of argument found in business finance textbooks, see Ezra Solomon, *The Management of Corporate Capital*, New York: Free Press, 1959; Jan Moss, *Theory of Financial Markets*, Englewood Cliffs, N.J.: Prentice-Hall, 1973; J. Fred Weston and E. F.

Brigham, *Essentials of Managerial Finance*, 5th ed., Hinsdale, Ill.: Dryden Press, 1979.

The argument presented in part 2 of this chapter can be traced back through *The Megacorp and Oligopoly*, pp. 89–96, and "The Micro Foundations of the Corporate Economy," *Managerial and Decision Economics*, November 1983, pp. 138–39 (subsequently revised and reprinted in *Toward a New Economics*, ch. 3. On the role of the industry life-cycle on the behavior of megacorps, see Nina Shapiro, "Pricing and the Growth of the Firm," and Nai-Pew Ong, "Target Pricing, Competition and Growth," *Journal of Post Keynesian Economics*, Fall 1981. Shapiro, it should be noted, has argued for a further delineation of the life-cycle's three phases, with the first phase divided into product invention and product development sub-periods. See her "Innovation, New Industries and New Firms," *Eastern Economic Journal*, January 1986.

On the flow of funds framework relied upon in part 3 of this chapter, see Matthew Fung, "Internal Versus External Financing of the Growth of Corporate Firms," unpublished paper, Rutgers University, May 1986. See also Douglas Vickers, *The Theory of the Firm: Production, Capital, and Finance*, New York: McGraw-Hill, 1968, and *Financial Markets in the Capitalist Process*, Philadelphia: University of Pennsylvania Press, 1978; Myron J. Gordon, *The Investment, Financing, and Valuation of the Corporation*, Homewood, Ill.: Irwin, 1962; Lawrence S. Ritter, "The Flow of Funds Accounts: A Framework for Financial Analysis," in Murray E. Polakoff *et al.*, *Financial Institutions and Markets*, Boston: Houghton Mifflin, 1970; M. Chapman Findlay and Edward E. Williams, "A Post Keynesian View of Modern Financial Economics: In Search of Alternative Paradigms," *Journal of Business Finance & Accounting*, Spring 1985. For the more conventional treatment of corporate finance, see, besides the business finance textbooks already cited, the following: Eugene F. Fama and Merton H. Miller, *The Theory of Finance*, Hinsdale, Ill.: Dryden Press, 1972; Jan Mossin, *Theory of Financial Markets*, Englewood Cliffs, N.J.: Prentice-Hall, 1973.

The argument that firms should be indifferent between fixed-interest obligations and new equity shares because the financial markets will equalize the cost to the firm of relying on these alternative methods of financing investment derives from Franco Modigliani and Merton H. Miller, "The Cost of Capital, Corporation Finance and the Theory of Investment," *American Economic Review*, June 1958, and "Dividend Policy, Growth, and the Valuation of Shares," *Journal of Business*, October 1961, and has since become a prevailing assumption among economists. See also Friedrich Lutz and Vera Lutz, *The Theory of Investment of the Firm*, Princeton: Princeton University Press, 1951. For the antecedents of the alternative view on which part 3 of this chapter is based, see Kalecki, "The Principle of Increasing Risk," 1937, reprinted in *Selected Essays on the Dynamics of Capitalist Economy*, ch. 11; A. Asimakopulos, "Kalecki and Keynes on Finance, Investment and Saving," *Cambridge Journal of Economics*, September 1983. See also *The Megacorp and Oligopoly*, especially pp. 86–88, 111–16, 122–26, 164–68, and "The Micro Foundations of the Corporate Economy," *op. cit.*

On the influence of a possible take-over bid on the cost of equity shares, see Robin Marris, *The Economic Theory of 'Managerial' Capitalism*, New York: Free Press, 1964, chs. 1–2; Adrian Wood, *A Theory of Profits*, New York: Cambridge University Press, 1975.

On the presumed tendency of regulated firms to adopt more capital-intensive methods of production, see Harvey Averch and Leland Johnson, "Behavior of the Firm Under Regulatory Constraint," *American Economic Review*, December 1962, pp. 1052–69; Alfred E. Kahn, "*The Economics of Regulation*, New York: Wiley, 1970, I, pp. 49–59. On the regulated megacorp, see *The Megacorp and Oligopoly*, pp. 109–16, as well as both volumes of the Kahn book.

On the U.S. system of planning, see Neil Chamberlain, *Private and Public Planning*, New York: McGraw-Hill, 1965; John R. Munkirs, *The Transformation of American Capitalism*, Armonk, N.Y.: M. E. Sharpe, 1985. See also Alfred D. Chandler, Jr., *The Visible Hand*, Cambridge, Mass.: Harvard University Press, 1977. On the Soviet-type system of centralized planning, see Janos Kornai, *Growth, Shortage and Efficiency*, Berkeley: University of California Press, 1982.

On the estimation of the behavioral equations for the corporate, farm, and noncorporate nonfarm components of the U.S. enterprise sector, see Leonard Forman and Alfred S. Eichner, "A Post Keynesian Short-Period Model: Some Preliminary Econometric Results, *Journal of Post Keynesian Economics*, Fall 1981, pp. 117–35. For the results of the corresponding effort to estimate similar equations for the U.K. enterprise sector, see Philip Arestis, Ciaran Driver and J. Rooney, "The Real Segment of a UK Post Keynesian Model," *ibid.*, Winter, 1985–86, pp. 163–81.

Chapter 8

The Household Sector: Income Distribution

Contents

Chapter 8

The Household Sector: Income Distribution

In deriving the E and F functions for the enterprise sector, three of the topics most central to any dynamic analysis have been explored in depth. These are the production, pricing and investment decisions of the firms that constitute the enterprise sector. There remains, however, one topic which has yet to be taken up in any systematic way. In a certain sense this is the most important topic of all since, as will soon become clear, it is the way of approaching this subject which, more than anything else, serves to set post-Keynesian theory apart, not just from the neoclassical orthodoxy which reigns within the OECD community of nations but also from the Marxian alternative preferred in much of the rest of the world. The remaining question is that of income distribution, and it lies at the heart of most of the controversy in economics.

In taking up the topic of income distribution, it will no longer suffice to focus on the enterprise sector alone. The household sector as well must be brought within the purview of the analysis. This is because questions of income distribution touch on not just the relationship between the household sector and other sectors but also the relationship among the different family units which make up the household sector. A systematic exploration of the topic, therefore, requires an in-depth examination of the household sector, beginning with the class structure which delineates the subaggregates within that sector in the same way that the industrial structure delineates the enterprise sector. Only after this class structure has been laid bare, and its relationship to the productive activities which take place within the enterprise sector made clear, will it then be possible to proceed with an exposition of the post-Keynesian theory of income distribution.

This post-Keynesian theory emphasizes the same factors already pointed to in earlier chapters as determining the macrodynamic behavior of the economic system—the rate of accumulation, or investment, and the accompanying set of prices required to finance that rate of accumulation. The theory of income distribution merely traces out the impact which investment and pricing decisions have on the household sector insofar as relative shares of income, or claims on the available output, are concerned. The analysis of income distribution, then, merely extends the line of argument begun in the preceding chapters. Once the topic of income distribution has been covered, it will then be possible, in the next chapter, to develop appropriate sets of E and F functions for the household sector, thereby extending that same line of argument even further.

There are, of course, other theories of income distribution besides the post-

Keynesian one, and a number of them will be taken up in the present chapter. Some of them, it turns out, are easily incorporated within the post-Keynesian macrodynamic framework, supplementing and enriching the basic model. This is certainly true of the sociologically based theories offered by various institutionalist writers to explain both the nominal wage rate and the set of wage differentials, or premiums, across skill and/or occupational categories. Other theories, however, are clearly incompatible with a post-Keynesian approach. Both the neoclassical theory based on "marginal productivity" and the Marxian theory based on a simplistic labor theory of value fall in the latter category. Thus, before completing this discussion of the factors that determine the distribution of income, it will be necessary to take up at some length each of those two alternative theories.

8.1 Class Structure

Class structure is not a concept which economists, like many others steeped in a democratic age's egalitarian values, are likely to be comfortable with. The possibility that most adults may have reached their present station in life because of factors over which they have little control—with important implications for their relative well-being—is simply too threatening at a personal level. The natural tendency is to ignore, deny or explain away the phenomenon. It is no doubt partly for this reason that the division of income into wages for laborers, profits for capitalists and rent for landowners which characterized classical economic theory has been transformed, by neoclassical writers, into "rates of return" for "n factors of production" based on their marginal productivity without even the hint of an underlying class structure. This subterfuge, understandable though it may be, will not do, however. A class structure does exist—and not just in "capitalist" or market economies. Without making clear what is the basis for that class structure, it is not possible to give a satisfactory explanation for the distribution of income, either in the United States or in any other country. The class structure, then, needs to be understood rather than explained away—or just ignored.

In the socialist tradition from which the separate discipline of sociology emerged only in the 20th century, it is the ownership of property which sets one social class apart from another. Marx, by distinguishing "the means of production" from other types of property, merely took this line of argument one step further, albeit an important one. Nonetheless, while a simple two-fold division of classes into workers and capitalist—or even a three-fold distinction between workers, capitalists and landowners—may have been good enough for analyzing 19th century social conditions, these categories no longer serve to describe the class structure of today's advanced market economies. The term, "worker," still remains descriptive enough—though one cannot continue blinking at the important class distinctions within the "working" class itself. The term, "landowner," however, though still applicable, no longer connotes the economically dominant social class it once did. This is because of the decline in the economic position of the feudal nobility, following first the commercial and then the industrial revolution. Indeed, it causes little or no distortion to ignore the role of landowners altogether.

Even more important, however, the term "capitalist," which Marx himself popularized, no longer has the same clear meaning. This is because of the corporate revolution, beginning at the end of the 19th century but continuing into the 20th, the significance of which as yet to be fully appreciated by economists and other social scientists. The effect of this corporate revolution, aside from creating the megacorps which dominate the oligopolistic sector of the economy, has been to radically transform the nature of property ownership. Although the means of production remain nominally in private hands, thus preserving a portion of the class structure insofar as the distribution of income is concerned, the locus of decision-making power has shifted to a new class of professionally trained managers and executives. It is to this new class as the group controlling the most important means of production within an advanced industrial society that the residual income which once accrued to the capitalist class now flows. As a result, the first and most important division of income is not between "workers" and "capitalists," as was true in the 19th century, but rather between households and enterprises. Only after the share of income going to households has been determined does the division between wage and property income, and thus the distinction between a "working" and a "rentier" class, become germane.

8.1.1 The corporate revolution and private property

The corporate revolution can be defined as the historical process, spread over several decades, by which the numerous neoclassical proprietorships previously constituting the industrial sector of advanced market economies like that of the United States were transformed into a smaller number of megacorps. The transformation which occurred can be explained by the inability of an advanced market economy to satisfy the necessary value condition for continuous growth when firms lack sufficient pricing power to finance the required expansion of capacity (see chapter 6, part 2). A salient feature of the corporate revolution, as Alfred Chandler has demonstrated in his historical studies, was the emergence of multiunit business enterprises, or megacorps, controlled by a hierarchy of middle- and top-level salaried executives. Indeed, these distinguishing characteristics of the megacorp have already been pointed to in explaining the behavioral rule and cost relationships that govern the pricing of output in the oligopolistic sector. Another crucial feature of the corporate revolution, though less commonly acknowledged as such, was the radical transformation of the property relationships affecting what are the most important means of production in a modern, technologically advanced society. As Adolf Berle and Gardiner Means noted in their classic work, the replacement of owner-entrepreneurs by salaried executives has fundamentally altered the nature of the private property represented by the nation's largest industrial enterprises. The corporate revolution, then, transformed not just the nature of the representative firm and the type of market structure in which it operates but also the nature of the property relationships that determine the ultimate decision-making authority within such a system of production.

It is a transformation which has been largely overlooked or, when perceived, misinterpreted. Marx had correctly predicted that such a transformation would occur but, by suggesting that it would lead to the nationalization of private property, threw most subsequent observers off the track. The point is that the corporate revolution led not to the nationalization of the most important means of production within the industrial sector but rather only to their "socialization." Nationalization would have meant the expropriation of the property by the state. What happened instead was that control was ceded by the original owner-entrepreneurs to a new class of professionally trained managers in return for assurances of a continued flow of income in the form of dividend payments. In effect, the original owner-entrepreneurs were pensioned off, their reward being stock ownership sufficient to enable them and their heirs to enter the ranks of the rentier class.

Although the outward forms of property ownership were thus maintained, the means of production can nonetheless be said to have been socialized. This is because what now generally enables groups of individuals to gain control over the physical and other assets held in the megacorp's name are not so much legally purchased or inherited titles of ownership as successful progression up a managerial career ladder. The progression itself is part of a social process, the outcome of whatever screening devices have been adopted by the members of the executive group for choosing their successors. Although personal considerations unrelated to job performance are not entirely absent, the fact is that eventual succession to the top levels of management depends on what is judged to be the individual's personal competence as an executive rather than on any property holdings. Indeed, insofar as rising to the top levels of management are concerned, and thus to a position where significant control over the means of production can be exercised, personal holdings within the company have been all but eliminated as a prerequisite condition. What counts is the ability to assume increasingly broader ranges of responsibility within the corporate hierarchy. It is in this way that a new class drawn from the larger body of university-trained professionals has come into being, reserving for itself the positions within society through which control over the means of production within the industrial sector of the economy can be exercised. If not exactly the revolution Marx and his followers had in mind, it is nonetheless a revolution of considerable consequence.

This interpretation of the changes which have taken place within the corporate sector of the U.S. and other advanced market economies is likely to be disputed both by those disappointed that the revolution has not gone further and by those with a need to believe that nothing, in fact, has changed. For many social critics, the phrase "socialization of the means of production" implies not just that control over the megacorp no longer derives from property rights but also that, as an even more radical departure from the mores of 19th century capitalism, the control is directed toward public, or "social," ends. It is for this reason that they favor the "nationalization," and not just the "socialization," of the means of production. Although a professional class of managers may have replaced the former owner-entrepreneurs, it is still the narrow interest of the firm itself which continues to be pursued. Indeed, the managerial class can be viewed as merely providing greater competence in the pursuit of that narrow interest, all for the benefit of the stockholders who, retaining the property rights under the existing legal system, ultimately reap the reward.

On this point, the social critics find themselves largely in agreement with those economists and other social scientists who insist that nothing has really been changed by the corporate revolution. Although a new managerial class may exercise day-to-day control, it does so only at the sufferance of the older property-owning class, now tranformed into rentiers. These observers point out that, should the incumbent management fail to pursue policies which maximize the welfare of the stockholders, it will be replaced by a new executive group, one that will better serve the interests of the stockholders. The existence of outside groups, ready to take advantage of any fall in the value of a company's stock by staging a "raid," more than suffices to protect the interests of the stockholders—even if the stockholders are a large, amorphous group. The salaried managers must strive to achieve the highest possible growth of dividends, it is argued. Otherwise the value of the company's stock will fall and the managers will be deposed through a successful take-over bid. The fact that a new managerial class exercises effective control is therefore an inconsequential detail insofar as how the "capitalist" system actually works.

A full and adequate response on these points must wait until the determinants of the dividend rate can be discussed (see section 8.3.5). For now it will suffice merely to point out the irreconcilable conflict between the interests of the stockholders in the highest possible growth of dividends and the interests of the managerial group in the highest possible growth for the firm itself. The conflict arises because the funds paid out as dividends are funds no longer available to finance the growth of the firm through capital outlays of one sort or another. How this conflict is resolved can be judged by how the firm's net revenue, or "profits," are divided between dividends and retained earnings. Only the former, it should be noted, is a source of income for the household sector. The retained earnings portion remains within the enterprise sector as part of its cash flow, or discretionary funds. If nothing else, then, the corporate revolution has made the term "profits" somewhat of an anachronism—at least insofar as the corporate sector is concerned. Indeed, for the purpose of explaining the distribution of national income, it is better to drop the term altogether, speaking of the dividends paid out as part of the megacorp's quasi-contractual obligations which, along with the wages paid to workers (including managers), are the principal sources of compensation for the household sector while including the retained earnings as part of the firm's, and hence the enterprise sector's, residual income (see chapter 2, section 3.4).

Note that, while prior to the corporate revolution (and still within the noncorporate sector), the division of the firm's net revenue between distributed and retained earnings still had to be made, the decision rested with the owner-entrepreneurs. Now the amount of distributed earnings, or dividends, is primarily at the discretion of the executive group as members of the new managerial class. It is this shift in the locus of decision-making on so vital a matter that lies at the heart of the corporate revolution. That the executive group may be constrained in the decision it makes by the need to placate the nominal owners is less important than the fact that the decision now rests with a different social class with a different set of interests to defend (though, admittedly, a class not thoroughly differentiated from the older owner-entrepreneurial class in every case and not necessarily antagonistic to that older social class, except on the issue of dividend pay-out rates).

Once the residual income which accrues to the firm itself as a social organization is separated out from the larger, though now somewhat anachronistic category of "profits"—and this is done by distinguishing the retained earnings from any dividend payments—it is possible to develop a post-Keynesian theory of income distribution in which the size of that residual share is precisely what is explained. This will be the task of the next main section. First, however, it is necessary to trace out the implications for the class structure found within the household sector of the categories into which the megacorp's payments to the household sector fall. These, of course, are the categories of rentier income (i.e., dividends) and wages. What will be found is that these two categories, together with any transfer payments made by the government, give rise to what is essentially a three-class society, with one of those classes, the working class, further divided into a number of subclasses.

8.1.2 The three-class society

By recognizing the transformation of private property which has occurred as a result of the corporate revolution, it is possible to describe the household sector, for the purpose of explaining the distribution of income, in terms of three principal classes. They are: (1) a property-owning class supported primarily by rentier income, the most important source of which are corporate dividends; (2) a working class supported primarily by wage and salary income (though not necessarily without some property income); and (3) a dependent class supported primarily by transfer payments. The last of these three classes, though not previously mentioned, derives from the fact that not every household is able to obtain a subsistence level of income either from property holdings or from employment, whether within the oligopolistic sector or outside that sector. In an advanced industrial society this class, rather than being left to scrounge for whatever subsistence it can find outside the formal structure of society, is usually provided with a certain amount of income through the taxing power of the state. While a full discussion of the transfer income from which this third class draws its material support must wait until the topic is taken up as part of a more general examination of the government sector's economic impact (see chapter 10, section 3.4), the existence of the dependent class, along with the transfer income it receives, must be acknowledged here so as to include all the categories necessary for analyzing both the class structure of the United States and the distribution of income within that type of advanced industrial society.

Based on the three types of income which serve to delineate the class structure of the household sector in an advanced industrial society like that of the United States, it is possible to set up the following accounting identity:

$$Y_D = \text{P}rop + \text{NW}g + \text{T}r \tag{8.1}$$

where Y_D is the disposable income of the household sector, $\text{P}rop$ is the total amount of property income received by the household sector (net interest, net dividends and proprietor's income); $\text{NW}g$ is the take-home pay, or net wages, received by workers (the wage bill of the enterprise sector, WB, less whatever is withheld for taxes, pensions, etc.), and $\text{T}r$ is the amount of transfer income received by the household sector (see chapter 2, section 3.4). To explain the change in household disposable income over time—the cyclical fluctuations as well as the secular growth trend—it is necessary to focus on the change in each of the above three components.

It should be noted that while analyzing the changing distribution of income among households in this way helps to shed light on the relative fortunes of the three principal classes, it does not tell the whole story. This is because no one class is necessarily dependent on a single type of income. Those who depend primarily on property income may also receive wages (or salaries) and, in the case of the elderly retired, even transfer income. Similarly, those who depend primarily on wage income may also obtain some property and/or transfer income. Even those who depend primarily on income transfers may have other sources of income. The situation is further complicated by the fact that different members of the same household may obtain their principal income from different sources— some from wages, some from transfer payments and some even from property ownership. Still, though the members of a particular class may have other sources of income besides the principal type which defines their social class, it is the change in that principal source of income which will primarily affect their material well being. For this reason, the relative fortunes of the different social classes are closely tied to the change in the amount of the above three types of income being paid out—property, wage and transfer income. It is with respect to these three types of income, therefore, that the distribution of income is to be analyzed, even though the categories do not correspond precisely to the amount of income obtained by each of the three social classes—rentiers, workers and dependents.

The members of the rentier class have two primary sources of income, the dividends paid by corporations and interest payments. The dividends derive from the equity holdings which the members of the rentier class have in megacorps and other corporations; the interest income from whatever fixed-interest obligations they also hold. While it might seem that the latter would consist primarily of the bonds issued by megacorps and other corporations, they are in fact more likely to be the tax-exempt securities issued by state and local governments. The reason is the obvious one, that holding the latter type of asset reduces the tax liability of the rentier class. As for the fixed-interest obligations of megacorps and other corporations, they are principally held, as already pointed out, by various financial institutions (see chapter 7, section 3.2). To the extent the dividends paid out by megacorps are (as will be argued in section 8.3.4) quasi-contractual obligations, the two principal types of income received by the rentier class share a common characteristic of being relatively fixed—though it is the rate of growth of payment rather than the absolute amount that tends to be fixed in the case of any equity holdings.

As for the rents which were the principal source of income for the rentier class at the time the classical economists were writing, these have largely disappeared as a separate category within the framework of modern national income accounting. While firms, not just within agriculture but throughout the mining and other sectors as well, continue to earn economic "rents" from their land and other natural resource holdings, these income flows are simply included as part of whatever "profits," or net income, are reported by firms. What is listed in the National Income and Product Accounts as the "rental income of persons" is, as already pointed out (see chapter 2, section 3.4), merely the imputed rental value of owner-occupied housing and has little to do with the classical concept of rent. (For a further discussion of the rents to which natural resource and other nonreproducible inputs give rise, see chapter 13, section 3.4.)

The property income of the rentier class thus consists of only two parts: (1) a flow of dividends, Div, and (2) a flow of interest payments, Int, as some percentage, i, of the fixed-interest obligations, A_f, held by the members of that class. That is,

$$Prop = Div + i(A_f) \qquad (8.2)$$

What determines the flow of dividends will be explained in a later section of this same chapter while what determines the interest rate, i, will be explained in chapter 12.

The members of the working class *qua* workers have only a single primary source of income. This source is the wages and salaries they receive in exchange for their labor services. Nonetheless, within the working class, there are important differences. The distinction between wages and salaries hints at one of these differences, between those workers who are hired by the hour (they constitute the "blue-collar" group at one end of the spectrum) and those workers whose pay is specified in terms of a longer time interval (they constitute the "white-collar" group at the other end of the spectrum). Closely related to the distinction between blue-collar and white-collar workers is the difference between those workers who must be closely supervised and those workers who, having committed themselves to some transcendent goal, can be left to work largely on their own. The latter include not just managers and other professionals but also the self-employed— that is, the owner-entrepreneurs who play so critical a role in the orthodox theory. The transcendent goal of the self-employed, like that of the megacorp's professional managers, is to ensure the survival of the business organization, or enterprise, from which they principally derive their income. It is just that, the neoclassical proprietorship being a less advanced form of business organization, owner-entrepreneurs need a more direct personal stake in that type of enterprise if they are going to commit themselves to its survival above other goals.

It is the self-employed who, since they do not exactly fit the definition of either "capitalists" or "workers," tend to be ignored in a Marxian analysis. Control over the means of production is instead assumed to be exercised by those previously identified as members of the rentier class, with those who manage their own businesses assumed either not to exist or to contribute no labor of their own to the production process. Since this characterization of owner-entrepreneurs can be shown to be false—one may not like the type of control they exercise over other workers but this does not mean that their managerial services can be dispensed with—it tends to discredit the entire Marxian line of analysis (see section 8.4.2). Moreover, it fails to recognize the important division within the working class, and the antagonisms which it creates, between those responsible for making sure the system and all its various subcomponents are able to continue functioning, whatever may be the imperfections of the system, and all the other workers who are largely without any voice as to how things will be done.

As fundamental as is the distinction between the self-employed, corporate managers and other professionals who, on the one hand, can be left to work largely on their own and all the other workers who, on the other hand, must be closely supervised, this dichotomy is not sufficient to explain the differential in the rates of compensation earned by the members of the working class. Differences in training and prior work experience, and thus differences in skill, also need to be taken into account. The existence of different skill categories has already been pointed to in suggesting that the vector of labor coefficients, L, is actually an m-by-n matrix, with m the number of different skill categories (see chapter 5, section 1.4). Based on the U.S. government's Dictionary of Occupational Titles (DOT), the working class can be divided into a large number of skill categories—in fact, into more skill categories than can easily be handled as part of any simple exposition. Still, what are significant for our purposes here are only the major skill categories between which, because of the requisite training and other barriers, it is difficult for workers to move. Managerial and other administrative personnel is, of course, one such category but it is only one of several on which the input-output table prepared for *Scientific American* by Leontief and his associates is based. The other major skill categories are: (1) professional and technical workers; (2) other white-collar workers; and (3) blue-collar, or production, workers—making four major skill catetories in all which are delineated within the most readily accessible input-output table.

With the **L** vector expanded to an *m*-by-*n* matrix, as it must be to take into account the different skills represented by the members of the working class, it is no longer possible to base the determination of the wage bill on just the scalar, **w**. Instead, an *m*-by-*1* **W** vector, representing the different wage rates that must be paid to workers in each of the different skill categories, first needs to be specified and then the number of hours of employment offered by each industry within the several skill categories, **LQ**, must be premultiplied by that **W** vector. That is,

$$\mathbf{WB} = \mathbf{W(LQ)} \tag{8.3}$$

By dividing **LQ** matrix by **h**, the average number of hours worked by the members of the working class, the *m*-by-*n* matrix of labor coefficients can be converted into an *m*-by-*n* matrix of employment and/or job slots, with equation 8.3 then rewritten as follows:

$$\mathbf{WB} = \mathbf{W(N)} \tag{8.4}$$

where **N** is an *m*-by-*n* matrix each of whose elements, $N_{i,j}$, represents the number of job slots within the *i*th skill category in the *j*th industry. As can be seen from equation 8.4, total employment, **N**, and thus the wage bill, **W(N)**, depends on the level of aggregate demand, as given by the quantity solution to the Leontief model, $\mathbf{Q} = (\mathbf{I} - \mathbf{A})^{-1} \mathbf{D}$ (see chapter 5, section 2.1).

The **W** vector assumes that the same wage rate is paid within each skill category across industries. This, however, is not necessarily the case. The workers within a particular skill category in one industry may be paid at a rate that is higher than what is paid workers within the same skill category in another industry. This is especially likely when the first industry is one of the technologically more advanced industries dominated by megacorps while the second industry is one that consists primarily of neoclassical proprietorships with little or no pricing power. Thus another important difference among the members of the working class, one that also gives rise to certain conflicts in their interests, is the nature of the industry in which the workers are employed. That is the *n* dimension of the *m*-by-*n* matrix of labor coefficients. While this further complication can be taken into account simply by adding another dimension to the **W** vector, it is actually more revealing to suppress some of the distinctions as to the industry in which workers are employed and their relative skill level. For in this way one can see more clearly the major subdivisions that exist within the working class.

8.1.3 The major subdivisions within the working class

Five major subdivisions can be identified within the working class of an advanced market economy like that of the United States. They are:

1. The dominant white-collar group
2. Other white-collar workers
3. The intermediate class of workers
4. Premium blue-collar workers, and
5. The secondary labor force.

Each of these five major subdivisions consist, in turn, of several components. The dominant white-collar group, for example, includes: (a) the self-employed owner-entrepreneurs; (b) high-level corporate executives; and (c) the top civil servants. The other major subdivisions within the working class consist of similar components.

The self-employed owner-enterpreneurs, as a component of the dominant white-collar group, actually consist of two separate subgroups. One is represented by the professionals in practice for themselves, primarily doctors and lawyers but also the elite among accountants, architects, psychologists and a few other professional groups. The effective limitations on the number of persons entering these professions, due to educational and other barriers, gives these members of the working class an edge, even over the other owner-entrepreneurs, in terms of the income they are able to earn. The second subgroup among the self-employed owner-entrepreneurs is represented by the remnants of the capitalist class that dominated the U.S. economy in the 19th century. They are the individuals who still own their own companies, or neoclassical proprietorships (although, for tax purposes, those neoclassical proprietorships may actually take a corporate form, with the owner-entrepreneurs listed as salaried executives. Similarly, for tax purposes, the practices operated by the professionals may be organized as "professional associations," with the professionals who have organized them also drawing a salary. Still, this is only a facade designed to minimize tax liability. The fact remains that the residual income of these firms accrues to the owner-entrepreneurs, including professionals, as individuals, unlike the situation that holds in the case of megacorps.) There are significant gradations within this second subgroup of self-employed owner-entrepreneurs—the income that is earned as a residual share being greater in those sectors of the economy, especially in manufacturing, where there are barriers to entry which even a neoclassical proprietorship can take advantage of. The income earned by owner-entrepreneurs is lowest, on average, within the agricultural sector.

It is the entire group of owner-entrepreneurs, together with the top and middle-level salaried managers of megacorps, who stand at the pinnacle of the working class. It is they who, benefiting from the barriers which prevent others from joining their ranks, receive the highest rates of remuneration (even though, in the case of some of the owner-entrepreneurs, the remuneration may take the form of "proprietor's income" and show up in the national income accounts under that category rather than as wages and salaries). Among the salaried managers of the megacorps, there are also gradations, depending both on the individual's position within the corporate hierarchy and on the relative standing of the firm itself among megacorps. The rates of remuneration—not just salaries but also fringe benefits and various perquisites—are likely to be highest for those at the top levels of management in those megacorps which have become highly diversified multinational enterprises, able to compete effectively in world markets. Still, since only a relatively few reach those top levels, and thus are able to wield the influence that goes with being a high-level executive for a world-class company, proportionately more of the self-employed owners-entrepreneurs are better off—at least financially.

What makes the group of top- and middle-level salaried managers, along with the group of surviving owner-entrepreneurs, the dominant class within an advanced market economy like that of the United States is not just the relatively higher incomes they earn. Indeed, on this score they are likely to compare unfavorably with the members of the rentier class. Rather what makes the two groups dominant is the control they exercise over the means of production, the top- and middle-level salaried managers being somewhat more influential because the means of production they control are more basic to the system of production. The differentially higher incomes which the members of the dominant class receive can, in fact, be explained largely by this control they exercise. The dominant class' principal rivals in this regard are not the members of the rentier class but rather the top-level civil servants in whatever government agencies have been created to regulate the enterprise sector. In societies where the government exercises considerable control over the enterprise sector, this group of top-level civil servants can be regarded as a third component of the dominant white-collar group. Thus, the struggle over how much control the government should exercise over the enterprise sector—a recurrent political issue not just in the United States but in many other advanced societies as well—is closely tied to the struggle among the salaried corporate managers, owner-entrepreneurs and civil servants for relative dominance. To understand what is at stake in this struggle, it is necessary to understand more fully what is meant by class structure.

The class structure is not just the way the various positions in society can be stratified. It is, even more fundamentally, the outcome of the process by which those better positions are reserved for certain groups in society to the exclusion of other groups. The groups for whom the better positions in society are reserved— and this would include, *a fortiori*, the positions of control—need not be groups for which family ties and/or property holdings are essential for gaining entry.

This was predominantly the case only in the heyday of capitalism before the corporate revolution. With respect to the two groups which today challenge the survivng owner-entrpreneurs as the dominant group—the salaried managers and the top civil servants—membership depends primarily on successfully completing the prescribed educational requirements for the professions that provide entry at the bottom level of the organizational hierarchies over which the two groups preside and then successfully rising within that hierarchical structure to at least a middle-level position. What counts, in this social process by which the two groups replicate themselves over time, is not so much family ties and/or property holdings (though these continue to be important) but rather the skills required for being singled out as being exceptionally competent (or at least promising) first within the educational system and then within the organizational hierarchies with which the singled out individuals subsequently become affiliated. The only difference between the salaried managers and the top civil servants in this regard is the different type of organizational hierarchy to which they become affiliated at the crucial point of commitment in their careers—a megacorp in the case of salaried managers and a governmental agency in the case of the top civil servants.

Thus the struggle for relative power and influence among the three groups which constitute the dominant social class in an advanced industrial society like that of the United States is not just a struggle for control among those currently holding the key positions in society. It is also, even more basically, a struggle over which positions will be the key ones in the future. The latter struggle involves a broader class interest since the outcome will determine the opportunity structure for those hoping to advance from the entry level and middle ranks to the top positions within each of the two types of hierarchies that dominate economic and political life in an advanced industrial society. These are the individuals who fall within the next most desirable substratum within the working class. For just below the dominant group of corporate executives, top civil servants and self-employed owner-entrepreneurs is a subordinate class consisting of other white-collar workers. (This group excludes the clerical workers who, in recognition of their predominant sex and, even more importantly, their blocked upward mobility, are best thought of as a separate, pink-collar group.) This second class of other white-collar workers is distinguished by the fact that, while a large part of the dominant group is drawn from it, its members exercise little or no control over the means of production. They are, by virtue of their positions, excluded from the crucial decision-making within the society. As a consequence, they are likely to be ambivalent, on the one hand feeling alienated by their exclusion and on the other perhaps still hopeful of gaining entry to the dominant social class.

Two separate subgroups can be delineated within this subordinate class of other white-collar workers. One is the group of salaried professsionals, those not in practice for themselves. It is this group of salaried professionals who, among other roles, fills the ranks of the lower-level management in both the corporate and governmental hierarchies. Again there are gradations, depending on the sector in which the professionals are employed—especially whether it is private or public. The other subgroup within the subordinate white-collar class consists of all the sales personnel working on commission. Together with the owner-entrepreneurs who manage their own companies, they are all that remain of the once ascendant commercial class that, by the end of the feudal period, had carved an important place for itself in society because of the skill of its members in carrying out market transactions. It was that commercial class which then gave rise, in the 19th century, to a new class of industrial entrepreneurs from which today's dominant class of corporate executives and top civil servants has devolved. It should be added that even today employment in a small business of one's own, or even employment as a salesperson on commission, is one of the principal means by which those who would otherwise lack the necessary educational prerequisites can obtain a well-paying job.

Between the white-collar workers at the top and the blue-collar workers below, there can be found a separate class which fits neither category—though its members often aspire to the former while being drawn in large part from the latter. This intermediate class of workers consists of three subgroups: (1) low-level supervisors, such as foremen and crew chiefs; (2) technicians, those performing tasks which require some advanced training in a specialized area; and (3) secretaries and the other clerical workers who comprise the "pink-collar" group. This class is distinguished not only by the educational and other barriers that must be overcome in order to gain entry but also by the considerably more restricted degree of autonomy its members enjoy on the job. As a result of the positions they hold, the members of this intermediate class exercise some authority but usually only under the close supervision of at least a lower-level manager. The compensation and other benefits they receive from their jobs reflect both factors: the barriers they must overcome to gain their positions and the relatively limited decision-making role they serve.

Below the intermediate class of supervisors, technicians and clerical workers can be found the modern counterpart of what Marx and the other classical economists meant by the "working class." These are the production workers, receiving wages rather than salaries, and they fall into two separate groups. One category consists of the premium blue-collar workers who are sheltered from the competition of other workers for the jobs they hold. Their relatively protected position is based on one or more of the following factors: (1) that, as skilled craftsmen, they are members of a craft union; (2) that, as workers in an industry that has been organized, they belong to an industrial trade union; (3) that, as government employees, they are covered by civil service regulations; or (4) that, as employees of a megacorp whose blue-collar workers have not yet been organized, their employment, along with their rate of compensation, is governed by the company's personnel policies (see chapter 13, section 2.2, for a discussion of the megacorp's personnel policies). The second category of production workers consists of all the members of the blue-collar work force who, being employed outside the overlapping unionized, oligopolistic and governmental sectors, are not sheltered from the competition of other workers. It is this latter group of workers, together with the employable members of the dependent class, who constitute what has been termed the peripheral, or secondary, work force; and it is this peripheral work force, in turn, whose employment and earnings depend more nearly on what economists refer to as the "labor market." The employable members of the dependent class, it should be noted, are the modern counterpart of what Marx termed the "industrial reserve army," and are often in transition intergenerationally between the "disguised unemployment" which exists in the rural hinterlands of the world and full integration into the work force of an industrial society (see chapter 13, section 2.4).

In terms of the autonomy and authority which they enjoy on the job, there is little difference between the two groups of blue-collar workers. They typically work under the close supervision, not just of members of the white-collar managerial group but also, even more directly, of the members of their own class who have advanced to supervisory positions as foremen and crew chiefs. They are expected, indeed instructed, to do little more than what they are told. The difference between the two groups, then, is solely in the degree of protection which the members of each enjoy from the competition of other workers, it being this difference in the degree to which they are sheltered that explains both the greater job security and the higher rates of compensation that go with entry into the more favored of the two lowest segments of the working class. Not unexpectedly, those who find themselves a member of the less advantaged blue-collar group hope to gain entry, not just for themselves but also for their progeny, into the premium blue-collar labor force while those workers who have achieved at least that station in life try to avoid slipping backward.

With the working class divided into the above subgroups, the class structure of the household sector can then be delineated in terms of the following seven categories:

1. Rentier class
2. Dominant working class—corporate executives, top civil servant and self-employed owner-entrepreneurs
3. Other white-collar workers—salaried professionals and commission salespersons
4. Intermediate working class—supervisors, technicians and pink-collar workers
5. Premium blue-collar workers
6. Secondary labor force
7. Unemployable dependent class

It should be noted that social class is not just a matter of where an individual falls within the employment opportunity structure of a society. It involves a whole constellation of beliefs and the types of customary behavior to which those beliefs give rise. Still, the above seven categories represent the most parsimonious schema for disaggregating the household sector by social class, this as the first step toward explaining the variation in the amount of income obtained by different households. The next step is to identify the factors that determine where, within this class structure, the members of a particular household are likely to fall.

8.1.4 The determinants of a society's class structure

The underlying factor giving rise to the class structure of a society is the limited number of opportunities for becoming a member of the rentier class and the limited number of positions which provide their holders with a source of income—especially the more coveted positions, those that offer the highest rates of remuneration, the greatest personal satisfaction and the best prospects for further advancement. The opportunities for joining the rentier class aside, the total number of positions available to be filled will depend on: (1) the size of the labor force required to produce the national product, as determined by the current level of output, Q, the relevant set of labor coefficients, L, and the average number of hours worked a year, h; and (2) the number of positions, N_G, which the government decides to fund through its taxing power. The number of more coveted positions will depend on the number of managerial and professional positions that form the top row of the N (or $1/hQL$) matrix plus the similar subset from among the government-funded positions, N_G. With only a limited number of even the less coveted positions, the problem is how those positions are to be filled from among the far larger number of persons seeking them. The answer to this question depends on the type of position. This is especially true if one includes among the positions to be filled those that may enable an individual (or his or her heirs) to become a member of the rentier class. What determines the number of households with dividend and other types of property income sufficiently large that their members do not need to work is different from the factors that determine which individuals will obtain the positions that provide monetary compensation—though not as different as the prevailing ideology of the white-collar and even the premium blue-collar segments of the working class would suggest.

The rentier class, as it presently exists in the United States, had its origins in the individuals who founded the first megacorps at the turn of the century. Today it consists primarily of their successors—both their direct blood descendants and those who, in more recent decades, have similarly founded companies that were then able either to ''go public'' themselves or merge with some company whose shares were already listed on one of the stock exhanges. This characterization of the rentier class is especially true if one excludes from consideration any retired corporate executives and others who have become members of the rentier class only because of the financial assets they were able to accumulate from their disproportionately high salaries while they were still working.

To a certain extent, then, being a member of the rentier class is simply a matter of being lucky enough to inherit sufficient holdings of corporate shares or other forms of property that one does not need to work, at least to support oneself and one's family. Still, it is not entirely a matter of good fortune, at least for the generation that first accumulates the wealth. One must be at least sufficiently competent that one can found a major business enterprise that has the prospect of being acquired by, if not actually evolving into, a megacorp. If, as was suggested in the preceding subsection, the self-employed entrepreneurs who establish such companies must be considered a part of the working class, at least during their active years; and if, moreover, as was argued in the subsection before that, there is considerable skill involved in overseeing a company during its formative years, then the factors determining the first generation of rentiers are not qualitatively different from those determining how the other coveted positions in society, those available to the active members of the working class, will be filled. For both groups the determining factors are (1) the competence to manage a major organization within the larger socioeconomic structure and (2) the good fortune of having the organization survive the competitive struggle for a place within that structure. Of course, for the former group—the first generation of rentiers—it requires the added good fortune of being able to exchange any privately held shares in their company for publicly traded shares and, for their progeny, it requires the good fortune of being born into such a family. Even this distinction becomes less significant, however, once the factors determining the competence of individuals, including that of owner-enterpreneurs, are understood.

The competence needed to oversee and direct any type of social organization, like all the other types of competence upon which the everyday functioning of a society depends, is not something that is innate but rather is something that must be acquired through a long process of socialization, beginning shortly after birth and continuing for as long as the individual remains an active member of the labor force (see chapter 13, part 1). Though it depends on the individual being able to seize upon and exploit the opportunities that become available, it also depends on the factors beyond the control of any individual that will determine what opportunities are available. These opportunities include not just the entry-level position in some organization that marks the bottom rung of some job ladder but also the place in the academic program providing the prerequisite training for such an entry-level position.

The point is perhaps easier to grasp in the case of the salaried managerial class, for whom the relevant career paths are more clearly mapped. But it holds no less for the group of self-employed owner-entrepreneurs. Somehow they must obtain the prerequisite training and the on-the-job experience—whether in a family-owned firm during their formative years, while employed as a salaried manager or other type of professional by others, or during some previous unsuccessful venture. And even then any success they may enjoy will depend, at least in part, on good fortune—just as will any success by the other members of the dominant working class in rising to positions of influence and power. The reason that not just competence and a determined effort on the part of the individual are needed but also good fortune is the limited number of more coveted positions, and thus the limited number of opportunities, which any society is able to provide. While it will be argued later that these opportunities need not be as limited as they presently are, even in the case of a relatively advanced society like that of the United States (see chapter 13, part 4), the fact remains that only a portion of the society can enjoy a significant differential, in terms of real income, and that to the extent any such differential in the income and other advantages of holding certain positions in society exists, there will be intensive competition for those positions.

As a means of moderating this competition, in much the same way advertising and other nonprice forms of rivalry among firms moderate the competition for market shares, the implicit rule has evolved that one must first qualify as a member of the subordinate white-collar group before one can advance any higher within the working class. This rule reflects, of course, the very real consideration that one must be tested at a lower level of responsibility before one can be trusted to hold a key position in the society. But it also represents a practical means of restricting the number of persons who can hope to qualify for one of the positions that provides significantly greater income and other advantages. This is particularly so because of the educational requirements that must be satisfied to qualify for membership in the subordinate white-collar group. These education requirements again reflect a very real consideration, in this case the minimum levels of familiarity with certain concepts one needs to function in an entry-level white-collar position. But they also, aside from limiting the number of individuals who can qualify for those positions, favor the children of the present white collar group without blocking altogether the channels of social mobility.

Individuals are often concerned, not only about their own opportunities but also about the opportunities open to their children. At the very least, they want their children and any succeeding generations not to fall below them in social class. Toward this end, they are prepared to expend considerable effort and money in providing their children with the educational and other opportunities they need to remain within the same social class—if not to rise higher. This is true of the blue-collar group no less than the white-collar workers. It is just that the blue-collar group has fewer resources, including life experiences and other forms of knowledge, with which to aid their children. Still, when it comes to the things they know the most about, such as qualifying for a craft-based apprenticeship program or a civil service blue-collar job, the members of at least the premium blue-collar group can be just as effective in helping their children gain a secure place in the society. This is done by making sure the children have access to the prerequite training and other types of experience needed to qualify for an entry-level position in some relatively sheltered part of the labor force. Of course, the white-collar members of the work force are in an even better position to help their children, not just because they themselves are already ensconced within one of the more desirable positions but also because they are better able, by virtue of their own life experience, to guide their children across the dividing line that separates the white-collar and blue-collar labor force.

What therefore determines where, within the class structure, a household falls is the differential access to developmental opportunities the adult members have had during their formative years. This differential access begins at the time of birth into a particular family. Indeed, for rentiers whose income is based on inherited wealth, social class is determined at that very moment. However, even for those who can look forward only to the income earned through their own efforts, the family into which they are born provides the first of the differential development opportunities to which they will have access. It is the family into which they are born (or with which they are subsequently placed) that will determine how adequately their emotional and physical needs are met. It is also the family that will serve as their first tutor and decide what more formal institutions of learning they will subsequently attend. A family can in fact, by providing an emotionally stable home environment and arranging for admission to the best available schools, largely offset any disadvantage from not being born into the rentier class. Whatever relative advantage has been gained from being born into a particular family will then be compounded by the differential opportunities from becoming affiliated with whatever educational institutions are subsequently attended until finally, upon graduation and the "landing" of an entry-level position, the individual is placed on a career path within one of the five segments of the labor forced delineated above. In other words, the social class of a household depends, aside from other types of good fortune, on the differential access of its adult members to developmental opportunities during their formative years.

Now that the determinants of social class have been identified, and thus the basis for the differentials in income among households indicated, we need to turn to the factors that will determine the distribution of income between the enterprise and household sectors—that is, between the residual and non-residual income obtained from marketing the output of the enterprise sector, or production subsystem. Only after the non-residual, or household, share of income has been accounted for can the distribution of that income among the different social classes which make up the household sector then be explained.

8.2 The Non-residual Share of Income

A monetarized system of production—what some would call a "capitalist" system of production—can be defined as one in which at least one group in society, generally the group which controls the means of production, receives the residual share of income after all the contractual and quasi-contractual claims of the other groups supplying material and labor unputs have been met out of the revenue obtained from the sale of the system's output. The obvious advantage of being the group that receives the residual income is that, if the claims of the other groups can be held to a minimum—and control over the means of production, with the power this gives to contract for the other inputs, makes this a real possibility—then all, or at least a goodly share, of the surplus in value terms which is being generated will accrue to the residual income recipients. It is one of the principal functions of the price system, as already pointed out (see chapter 6, section 1.1), to ensure this outcome. Of course, being the group that receives the residual income also carries with it a significant risk. This is the possibility that the revenues earned from the sale of the output will be insufficient to cover the contractual and quasi-contractual obligations that have been incurred in the production process. In that event, unless sufficient loans can be obtained through the financial system, the group receiving the residual share may lose its control over the means of produciton and thus its right to continue in business.

While it might seem that being in a position to contract for the other inputs used in the production process would preclude the possibility that the costs will exceed the revenue earned from the sale of any output, the salient fact about a market economy is that the net revenues accruing to the group entitled to the residual income depends only in part on the prices (including wages) agreed to in purchasing any inputs. It also depends, even more critically, on the level of sales, and thus on the level of demand throughout the system. Whatever the price established for the firm's product, it will not be sufficient to cover all the contractual and quasi-contractual obligations if the level of sales falls below a certain point (what businessmen themselves refer to as the "break-even" point). The risk that the level of demand will be insufficient is one that the group receiving the residual income share cannot avoid. This is because the risk is inherent in the type of economic system that gives rise to a residual share of income—that is, a system in which the costs of production are incurred prior to the sale of any output, with those costs taking the form of contractual obligations which must be met out of any subsequent sales revenue. An economic system organized in this manner can be described as a monetarized production system—or, alternatively, as a "capitalist" system. The terms are interchangeable, and they apply not just to the market-oriented systems found in the United States and the other OECD countries but also to the centrally planned economics of the Soviet Union, Eastern Europe and mainland China. Indeed, this is why the latter are sometimes referred to as systems of "state capitalism"—although the term "managerial capitalism" would perhaps be more appropriate, just as it is for the type of economic system found in the United States and the other OECD countries.

In the case of a monetarized production system, the residual share of the income generated from production needs to be distinguished from the nonresidual share. The latter is equal to $\hat{P}AQ + wLQ$ or, based on the vertically integrated model of production, $w\underline{L}Q$, and thus clearly depends on the rates of compensation agreed to in advance for supplying whatever direct inputs, particularly the human resource ones, are needed to keep the production process going. But since the total income generated, VQ or $wLQ + \pi Q$, is simply the sum of the residual and non-residual shares, the latter also clearly depends on the factors which, independently of any contractual and quasi-contractual obligations, determine the size of the residual share. To sort out these interrelationships, and in particular to indicate what factors actually determine the non-residual share of the income being generated, it is necessary at this point to introduce the post-Keynesian theory of income distribution. This is the theory which derives from Kalecki's separate model of national income determination but which was fully worked out only in the seminal works by Joan Robinson and Nicolas Kaldor in 1956 which marked the emergence of a distinctly different post-Keynesian paradigm. We shall begin with the theory in its simplest form, first invoking the classical assumptions that Kalecki himself employed and then relaxing those assumptions as subsequent post-Keynesian theorists have done. Only after this exercise has been carried out will it be possible to explain what determines the wage, or nonresidual, share of income, both in the long period and in the short.

8.2.1 The classical assumptions

In classical economic theory, it was generally assumed that workers received only a subsistence wage which, by definition, was spent entirely on consumption (or "wage") goods. In other words, the marginal propensity to save of workers, s_w, was assumed to be zero. In contrast, the profits obtained by capitalists as the residual income of the system were assumed to be spent not at all on consumption goods but instead were thought to be used as a fund out of which to make capital outlays—as much to provide working capital, hence the prevailing "wages fund" doctrine, as to finance fixed investment. In other words, the marginal propensity of the capitalist class (nonworkers) to save out of its residual income or "profits," s_n, was one. It was these classical assumptions about savings that Kalecki invoked in making his argument that, the higher the rate of investment by the capitalist class, the larger the share of income that would accrue to that class in the form of profits. Or, as he put it more pithily, "Capitalists get what they spend and workers spend what they get." The point is easily demonstrated within a long-period framework, relying as Robinson did in *The Accumulation of Capital* on the national income and product totals.

Looking at the input-output table from which the national income and product accounts are derived (see over, exhibit 2.6 reproduced), one can see that the value-added (next-to-bottom) row gives the same total, $1,748.9 billion, as the final output (next-to-last) column. Indeed the necessary equality between the two sets of figures within an input-output framework has already been demonstrated (see chapter 2, section 1.1), and this is nothing more than the accounting identity, NI = NP, which underlies all macroeconomic analysis (see chapter 3, section 1.1). In the matrix notation in which the Leontief production model has been specified, the same accounting identity means that the value-added vector multiplied by the industry total output vector, VQ (or, in prose, the national income), will be equal to the price vector multiplied by the final demand vector, PD (that is, the national product in nominal terms—see chapter 5, section 1.4). In the

Exhibit 2.6
Expanded Input-Output Table
(1978, $billion)

Inputs obtained from industry ↓ / Outputs sold to industry →	A	B	C	D	E	Intermediate output	Change in inventories	Sales to other industries on capital account	Sales to households	Sales to government	Net sales abroad	Final output	Total	Total
A	—	23.7	85.0	22.8	35.3	166.8	2.8*	28.9*	157.0*	27.3*	1.1*	217.1	383.9	
B	43.1	—	3.5	14.6	47.8	109.0	7.0*	73.2*	397.5*	68.3*	3.2*	549.2	658.2	
C	16.9	3.8	—	43.1	10.4	79.2	3.5*	35.8*	194.5*	33.3*	1.6*	268.7	342.9	
D	24.1	22.5	19.5	—	56.6	122.7	7.8*	81.8*	444.8*	76.4*	3.7*	614.5	737.2	
E	5.6	132.1	65.4	15.3	—	264.4	1.2*	13.3*	72.0*	12.3*	0.6*	99.4	363.8	
Employees' compensation	188.9*	362.3*	129.0*	488.1*	162.5*									1,330.8
Property income	43.4*	83.3*	29.7*	122.2*	37.4*									306.0
Indirect business taxes	15.9*	30.5*	10.8*	41.1*	13.8*									112.1
Total, other outlays (value added)	248.2	476.1	169.5	641.4	213.7							1,748.9		
Total outlays	383.9	658.2	342.9	737.2	363.8	757.1	22.3	233.0	1,265.8	217.6	10.2		2,486.0	

*Estimated

vertically integrated version of the same model, **PQ** replaces **PD** as the national product so that **VQ** is equal to **PQ** with **V** therefore necessarily equal to **P**.

The classical assumptions, as revived by Kalecki, transform the single cell in which this accounting identity is represented—the cell containing the figure $1,748.9 in exhibit 2.6—into a two-fold matrix. On the one hand, the value-added row is divided into separate wage and nonwage (or "profits") components. Indeed, this has already been done in specifying the Leontief production model, and it is one less subdivision than that actually found in the input-output tables available for the United States (the indirect business taxes shown in exhibit 2.6 are best thought of for the moment as part of the nonwage or residual component.) On the other hand, the final output column is divided—following Kalecki's lead—into consumption ("wage") goods and investment goods, with each type of good produced by separate consumption and investment goods sectors. This last step, which Kalecki was inspired to take by the Marxian distinction between Department I and Department II goods, gives rise to the two-fold matrix, along with the accompanying totals, shown in exhibit 8.1.

Invoking the classical assumptions within this framework, one can readily show that for a given level of national income, the nonwage, or capitalists', share will depend on the rate of investment. For with workers doing all the consuming and the nonworkers, or capitalists, doing all the saving, the total wage bill, **WB** or $w\underline{L}Q$, must be equal to the total output of consumption goods in value terms, $P_C C$, where **C** is the portion of the net output vector, **D**, which represents the goods entering into final use by households for consumption purposes, and P_C is the portion of the **P** vector representing the prices of those consumption goods. But, as can be seen from the matrix in exhibit 8.1, the total wage bill, **WB**, is equal to the wage bill of the consumption and investment goods sectors combined ($WB_C + WB_I$). Similarly, the total output of consumption goods, $P_C C$ or **C**, is equal to the wage bill in the consumption goods sector plus the residual, or nonwage, income generated in that sector ($WB_C + \Pi_C$). Hence, with **WB** equal to **C**, it follows that $WB_C + WB_I = WB_C + \Pi_C$ or, canceling the WB_C terms on both sides of the equal sign, that

$$WB_I = \Pi_C \qquad (8.5)$$

In other words, the residual income generated in the consumption goods industry must be equal to the wage bill in the investment goods sector. If, therefore, the output of the investment goods sector is to be increased relative to that of the consumption goods sector—and this is a necessary step, as pointed out above (see chapter 4, section 2.1), if a higher rate of economic expansion is to be achieved— then the ratio of residual income to wages in the consumption goods sector, and thus the residual share of national income, will have to be higher. This can be seen by comparing exhibit 8.1, where the rate of investment, I/Y, is 20 percent, with exhibit 8.2, where the rate of investment for the same level of national income is

Exhibit 8.1

Distribution of Income Between Workers and Nonworkers
with a (I/Y) = 0.2 $S_W = 0$ $S_N = 1$

		Consumption Goods Sector Value of Output $P_C C$	Investment Goods Sector Value of Output $P_I I$	Enterprise Sector as a Whole Value of Output PQ
Nonresidual Income	Wage Bill wLQ	WB_C 1,119.3	WB_I 279.8	WB 1,399.1
Residual Income	Reinvested Profits ΠQ	Π_C 279.8	Π_I 70.0	Π 349.8
Total Income	VQ	C 1,399.1	I 349.8	Y 1,748.9

only 10 percent. The residual income share, Π/Y, will have to be higher in the first case so that the increase in the output of consumption goods for the workers who will have to be added to the labor force in the investment goods sector, and thus the larger wage bill in that sector, can be met.

It should be noted that the increase in the output of investment goods relative to that of consumption goods implies a change in the composition of final demand, as denoted by the **Y** vector, and thus a change in the **Q** and **V** (or **P**) vectors. It will also give rise, as hinted earlier (see chapter 4, section 1.2), to a disequilibrium dynamic in the short period. Still, the point to be emphasized here is that, with the classical assumptions holding, the increase in the rate of investment will lead to an increase in the share of national income going to nonworkers, or "capitalists," in the form of residual, or nonwage income—that is, "profits." This follows from the fact that, with all the savings out of which investment is financed being generated out of the residual income, or profits, retained by firms, the amount of "profits" as a share of national income will necessarily be equal to the rate of investment, Π/Y. In other words, with $\Pi = S$,

$$\frac{\Pi}{Y} = \frac{I}{Y} \qquad (8.6)$$

From this equality it follows that any increase in the rate of investment, I/Y or φ, must be accompanied by an increase in the "profit," or residual, share of national income, Π/Y. (The rate of investment, I/Y or Φ, should not be confused with the

Exhibit 8.2

Distribution of Income Between Workers and Nonworkers
with a (I/Y) = 0.1 $S_W = 0$ $S_N = 1$

		Consumption Goods Sector Value of Output $P_C C$	Investment Goods Sector Value of Output $P_I I$	Enterprise Sector as a Whole Value of Output PQ
Nonresidual Income	Wage Bill wLQ	WB_C 1,416.8	WB_I 157.3	WB 1,574.1
Residual Income	Reinvested Profits ΠQ	Π_C 157.3	Π_I 17.5	Π 174.8
Total Income	VQ	C 1,574.1	I 174.8	Y 1,748.9

rate of accumulation, $\Delta I/\Delta Y$ or a.)

The same rate of investment that determines the "profit," or residual, share of national income will also determine the share of aggregate output going to workers in the form of consumption goods. For if the residual share of national income should have to rise as a result of the higher rate of investment, the wage share in real terms (that is, the amount of consumption goods which can be purchased out of wage income) must necessarily fall. This is because of the need to shift workers to the investment goods sector and the relative decline in the output of the consumption goods sector which can be expected to follow. It is therefore the rate of investment, I/Y, that will determine the real wage. Of course, if real wages are already at the subsistence level, they cannot then be reduced in order to free up resources for capital formation. However, it is seldom the case historically that real wages are so low that they cannot be cut even more without causing a decline in the flow of labor services. At most, the amount of leisure time and/or the average life expectancy of workers will be reduced. Thus, under most historical circumstances, it is possible—at least technically—to increase the rate of investment even though this implies a reduction in the real wage below what it would otherwise be. Even if real wages are not reduced absolutely—something that can be avoided if aggregate output is expanding—they will still have to fall relative to the residual share of national income. This negative relationship between the rate of investment, and thus the rate of economic expansion, on the one hand and the share of the national product going to workers in the form of consumption goods on the other hand is one of the basic propositions of the post-Keynesian theory of income distribution. Indeed, to the extent that the workers can be equated with the population as a whole, it has already been encountered in the earlier discussion of the rate of savings, as a proxy for the rate of accumulation, as the principal factor determining the warranted growth rate (see chapter 4, section 2.4). It is just that now the implication for the distribution of income between workers and non-workers is being made explicit.

As developed so far, equation 8.6 is simply an accounting identity. It becomes a theory of income distribution only if one has reason to believe that it is the right-hand side of the equation, the ratio of investment to national income, that determines the left-hand side, and not *vice versa*. The reason for believing that investment determines savings rather than the opposite has already been outlined in brief (see chapter 3, section 2.3). The point is that, while an autonomous change in investment is possible because of the way in which a credit-based system of money works, an autonomous change in savings is not. As will be demonstrated more formally once a model of the monetary-financial sector is developed based on the Flow of Funds Accounts (see chapter 12, section 1.5), any increase in savings by households (or indeed even by some firms through a higher mark-up) will simply lead to a fall in aggregate demand below what it would otherwise be and hence to a decline in the residual income of at least some firms, leaving the amount of aggregate savings unchanged.

The analysis of investment behavior in the preceding chapter is fully consistent with this view. There it was argued that the megacorp as the representative firm first determines the amount of investment, or discretionary expenditures, it wishes to undertake, based on the growth of demand for the various products it sells and on other factors. If the cash flow, or discretionary funds, being generated from the mark-up in each of those industries is not sufficient to cover the cost of the projects which have tentatively been included in the capital budget, the megacorp then has the option of obtaining whatever additional funds it needs from external sources by issuing new securities or otherwise incurring more debt. Even if one takes as being more realistic the model which Kalecki himself came to favor—a model in which capital outlays depend at least in part on the amount of retained profits—this does not invalidate the more general point. As long as the predominant influence on investment derives from expectations about the future trend of profits and/or the type of demand factors encompassed by the accelerator model, the post-Keynesian view that it is investment which determines savings, and not the reverse, is still valid. Any check on capital outlays due to the limited availability of funds will simply act as a modifying force, or feedback governor, on the main channel of causation running from expectations and/or demand factors to investment expenditures and hence on the distribution of income. Moreover, any limit on the availability of funds for financing investment will be more important in explaining the economy's cyclical movements than in accounting for the secular growth rate.

8.2.2 When "capitalists" consume

As striking as the conclusion of the preceding section may be about the effect of investment on the distribution of income, one cannot be sure how much it depends on the admittedly extreme classical assumptions which were invoked. It is therefore necessary to relax each of those two assumptions to see how "robust" is the conclusion that, the greater the rate of investment, the greater will be the residual share of national income. The first of the classical assumptions to be dropped in further refining the post-Keynesian theory of income distribution was the assumption that "capitalists" (i.e., nonwage earners) only save; they do not consume. To encompass the possibility that nonwage earners, or "capitalists," may consume a portion of aggregate output, it is necessary to divide the profit share of national income into two subcomponents: (1) the amount of residual, or nonwage, income used to purchase consumption goods, Π_e, and (2) the amount of residual income saved (and re-invested), Π_s. This can be done, both for the total amount of residual income, Π, and for the amount of residual income earned in each of the separate consumption and investment goods sectors, Π_C and Π_I. The result is to transform the matrix shown in exhibits 8.1 and 8.2 into the matrix shown in exhibit 8.3.

With the matrix of final output (national product) and value added (national income) transformed in this way, one can readily show that, for a given level of national income and a given rate of expansion, any consumption by nonwage earners, or "capitalists," out of the residual income, or "profits," being obtained will have the effect of reducing the share of income going to workers, and thus real wages, below what it would otherwise be. For if C and I represent the same amounts as in exhibit 8.2, thereby implying the same level and growth of national income, then WB, the wage bill in real terms, will have to be reduced by Π_e, the amount of profits used to purchase consumption goods. This is because, with the output of the investment goods sector necessarily having to remain the same, the consumption goods which must now be diverted to non-workers, or "capitalist," can be provided only at the expense of the working class. It is not just the workers in the consumption goods sector whose wages will have to be reduced in real terms but also the workers in the investment goods sector as well. This result is assured in a market economy, through the process of price formation already analyzed above in chapter 6 and the subsequent sale of output at the prices thereby established.

In a monetarized production system, the value of the consumption goods produced, C, must be equal to the income, or claims, available to purchase that output. In the case now being considered, this means that C must be equal to the wage bill, WB, plus the amount of profits (non-wage income) expended on consumption goods, π_e. That is,

Exhibit 8.3

Distribution of Income Between Workers and Nonworkers
with a $(I/Y) = 0.1$ $S_W = 0$ $S_N = 1$

		Consumption Goods Sector Value of Output $P_C C$	Investment Goods Sector Value of Output $P_I I$	Enterprise Sector as a Whole Value of Output PQ
Nonresidual Income	Wage Bill wLQ	WB_C 1,259.5	WB_I 139.8	WB 1,399.3
Residual Income ΠQ	Consumption Out of Profits	Π_{C_e} 157.3	Π_{I_e} 17.5	Π_e 174.8
	Reinvested Profits	Π_{C_s} 157.3	Π_{I_s} 17.5	Π_s 174.8
Total Income VQ		C 1,574.1	I 174.8	Y 1,748.9

$$C = WB + \Pi_e \tag{8.7}$$

Since the total wage bill is equal to the wage bill in the consumption goods sector plus the wage bill in the investment goods sector (i.e., $WP = WB_C + WB_I$ while the residual income that will be used to purchase consumption goods will be equal to the residual income originating in the consumption goods sector which is used to purchase consumption goods plus the residual income originating in the investment goods sector which is used for that same purpose we can rewrite the right-hand side of equation 8.7 as follows:

$$C = WB_C + WB_I + \Pi_{C_e} + \Pi_{I_e} \tag{8.8}$$

But we also know that in setting the price of the consumption goods being produced, the firms in that sector will necessarily have to cover their costs. These costs, after subtracting out any interfirm sales, will be equal to the wages paid out, WB_C, plus any profits, both those that will be used to purchase consumption goods, Π_{C_e} and those that will be used to purchase investment goods, WB_{C_s}. In other words,

$$C = WB_C + \Pi_{C_e} + \Pi_{C_s} \tag{8.9}$$

Setting the left-hand side of equation 8.8 equal to the right-hand side of equation 8.9 and then cancelling the WB_C and Π_{C_e} terms found on both sides, we obtain the following:

$$\Pi_{C_s} = WB_I + \Pi_{I_e} \qquad (8.10)$$

In other words, the residual income being generated in the consumption goods sector that is saved (and re-invested) must be sufficient not only to meet the wage bill in the investment goods sector, WB_I, thereby enabling that sector to command the human resource inputs it requires (see equation 8.5), but also sufficient to cover the consumption purchases out of the residual income being generated in the investment goods sector, Π_{I_e}. What this means is that wages in the consumption goods sector will be reduced not just by Π_{C_e}, the amount of residual income earned in that sector which is used to purchase consumption goods but also by Π_{I_e}, the residual income earned by the investment goods sector which is similarly used to purchase consumption goods. Since the wage rate is likely to be equalized between the two sectors, this means that real wages in the investment goods sector will also be lowered by the amount of consumption out of nonwage income to match the reduction in real wages in the consumption goods sector. It is in this way that the overall wage bill, WB, will be reduced by an amount equal to Π_{C_e}, the total expenditures by nonworkers, or "capitalists," on consumption.

The significance of this result—namely, that real wages are reduced by any consumption out of nonwage income—may not be immediately apparent, especially if one continues to think in terms of the 19th century catergories of "workers" and "capitalists." After all, who would deny that owner-entrepreneurs must obtain some of the same consumption goods as "workers" if they are to meet their subsistence needs? The issue then becomes whether it is "fair" or "equitable" that they should receive a basket of consumption goods which, in many historical instances, is considerably larger on a per-capita basis than that received by the mass of "workers." The point just made about the effect of consumption out of nonwage income becomes a far more profound one when it is considered in the context of advanced 20th century market economies, those which like the United States have not only experienced a corporate revolution but a governmental one as well. For nonwage income can then be seen to include not just the higher standard of living enjoyed by owner-entrepreneurs as a class but also, of greater import, a significant portion of the dividends received by the megacorp's nominal owners, the higher margin above costs required to cover any taxes levied by the government, and even the discretionary expenditures by the megacorp for other than new plant or equipment.

The dividends paid out by megacorps have already been identified as a major source of income for the rentier class (see section 8.1.2). To the extent this dividend income is used only to purchase new equity shares in megacorps, it is no different from the income being retained by megacorps as part of the oligopolistic sector's savings, or discretionary funds. (If the dividends are used instead to purchase the fixed-interest obligations of megacorps, it will again be the same as though the income were simply being retained, the only difference being that the debt-equity ratios of those firms will rise rather than fall.) However, to the extent the dividend income is used by the members of the rentier class to purchase consumption goods, the effect will be quite different. Whatever amount of consumption goods is obtained by the members of the rentier class will add to Π_e, and thus will reduce the real wages of workers below what it would otherwise be. It is in this sense that the standard of living enjoyed by the members of the rentier class—whether they be retired workers with a small portfolio of corporate shares or the latter-day heirs of those originally founding the companies—comes entirely at the expense of the working class.

   The ability of the rentier class to command consumption goods that would otherwise go to workers is not necessarily limited by the amount of dividends being paid. With the existence of well-organized stock exchanges—and thus the possibility of windfall profits even on average through the buying and selling of shares in those markets, thanks to the liqidity supplied by the banking system with support from the central bank—the consumption expenditures of the rentier class can just as well be financed out of the "capital gains" from any equity share transactions. (For a further discussion of this point, see chapter 12, section 1.4.) Still, since the price of equity shares depends ultimately on the rate at which dividends are being increased (see section 8.3.5), it is the proportion of the revenue earned by firms that is paid out in dividends that will determine the share of the national product consumed by the members of the rentier class in the long period.

   What is significant about the income paid out by megacorps in the form of dividends is that these payments are not essential for obtaining the direct material and human resource inputs needed to maintain the current levels of output or even the investment goods required to ensure the expansion of the system over time. They are merely legal obligations—as distinct from current economic costs—which have been incurred as part of a tangled historical process by which megacorps have acquired their vintage capital stock (see chapter 4, section 1.1, and chapter 7, sections 3.2). For this reason, the payments can be reduced, if not halted altogether, without impairing the ability of the economic system to reproduce itself and expand over time—although there may ensue, it should quickly be added, serious financial, legal and even political consequences, depending on what are the other sources of external financing besides new equity shares, on what stance the courts take in interpreting the legal rights of the equity debt holders, on how powerful a bloc the equity debt holders are among the various political constituencies and on how potent are the ideas about "private property" which can be used to defend the interests of the equity debt holders. The point here is not that the dividend payments should necessarily be reduced but rather that the purely economic effect is quite different from what happens if the payments to the suppliers of direct material and human resource inputs are cut off, or even if the amount of retained earnings, or discretionary funds, available to purchase new plant and equipment is reduced. The same argument applies, of course, to the payments made by the megacorps in fulfillment of their fixed-interest obligations, except that what would be threatened by any curtailment of those payments (aside from the continued control of those companies by their executive groups) would not be the interests of the rentier class but rather the viability of the financial intermediaries, such as life insurance companies and pension funds, which are required to hold that type of asset as part of their portfolio.

Yet another form of consumption out of nonwage income is the flow of resources into the public sector for use by the government in ways other than to expand the economic infrastructure. In this case, the nonwage income will take the form of whatever tax revenue is collected by the government. However the tax is levied—as a percentage of the wage bill, as a percentage of the residual income earned or as a percentage of either the value added or price—it will increase the margin between the cost of any inputs used in producing the good or service and the price to the buyer. The government's share of that margin, equal to the average tax collected on each type of good produced, will, together with the level of aggregate demand, determine the total tax revenue obtained by the government. This tax revenue, any transfer payments or negative tax flows aside, will, in turn, determine the public sector's ability to command goods in the market (see chapter 10, section 3.1).

Like any other consumption out of nonwage income, the government's purchase of goods and services for other than expansion of the economic infrastructure will reduce the real wage of workers. The government's use of resources to expand the economic infrastructure will, of course, also reduce the real wage of workers. However, since these outlays can, like any other type of investment, be expected to add to the supply capacity of the economic system, the real wage of workers will nonetheless be increased in the long period. In contrast, the government's other types of expenditures, whether for national defense or for any of its domestic social, or anthropogenic, programs, will leave the capacity to produce goods unchanged, even in the long period. Although the number of workers receiving wages will increase, with the increment represented by the additional workers employed either directly by the government itself or by the firms supplying the government with goods and services, there will be no greater supply of consumption goods out of which the material needs of the enlarged work force can be satisfied. The real wage of each worker employed, as measured by the amount of consumption goods he or she can purchase, will have to fall.

While it might seem that all that is required to avoid a reduction in the real wage of workers is for the consumption goods sector to increase its output—and with the total wage bill and hence disposable income rising, lack of effective demand will not prevent this from happening—the fact is that, with the additional workers being added to the payroll in the economically nonproductive government and not-for-profit sector, output per worker will necessarily fall. It is the decline in output per worker, and hence in $\overset{\circ}{Z}$, that makes a reduction in the real wage below what it would otherwise be unavoidable. This point will become clearer as the analysis proceeds (see section 8.2.4 and chapter 13, section 4.0)—

although it is implicit in the earlier definition of aggregate economic output (see chapter 2, section 2.2). For now all that need be noted is that an increase in expenditures by the government for purposes other than to expand the economic infrastructure is the equivalent of an increment in Π_e and, like the other types of spending that fall in that category, will reduce the real income of workers below what it would otherwise be. It is for this reason that, as the recent experience of the United States demonstrates, the share of the national product going to the public sector cannot be increased while the same rate of economic expansion is maintained without the real wage of workers falling. The greater public consumption must necessarily be at the expense of the workers' private consumption.

What has just been said about the dividends paid out to stockholders and the taxes collected on behalf of the government applies no less to the megacorp's use of any discretionary funds to strengthen its market position. Included within this category are the sums spent on advertising, R&D and the other activities that serve to differentiate a firm's product more sharply and/or erect higher barriers to entry (see chapter 7, section 2.3). These expenditures are like the dividends paid out to stockholders in that they are essential neither for maintaining the current levels of output nor for ensuring the expansion of the system over time. They simply add to the cost that must be covered out of whatever price is being charged. At the same time, these expenditures are like the taxes collected on behalf of the government in that, while they enable persons to be added to the payroll, they do nothing to increase the amount of goods available for consumption. They simply cause output per worker to fall. The megacorp's use of discretionary funds to strengthen its market position, then, is the equivalent of consumption out of nonwage income, Π_e, and the effect, insofar as the distribution of income is concerned, is to reduce the real wages of workers below what it would otherwise be. Whether the expenditures on advertising, R&D and the like are necessary to maintain the stability of market shares within the enterprise sector and thus, since they serve to reduce the uncertainty surrounding investment, are a necessary social cost, is another matter. The point here is that, the greater the amount of any such expenditures, the larger the mark-up will need to be on the costs of production and, as a consequence, the lower will be the real wage of workers.

In summary, when the classical assumption that only workers consume is relaxed, one needs to include at least one additional variable, besides the rate of investment, among the factors determining the distribution of income. That additional variable is the amount of consumption out of nonwage income, Π_e— with that term encompassing any goods purchased by members of the rentier class out of the dividends they receive, any expenditures by the government for other than expansion of the economic infrastructure or any expenditures by the megacorp itself to strengthen its market position. But what about the second of the two classical assumptions? Once it is recognized that workers, too, may save, does not another variable need to be added to those already identified as determining the distribution of income? To answer this question, it is best to turn from the national income and product accounting framework that was used by Robinson and rely instead on the alternative algebraic line of argument developed by Kaldor.

8.2.3 When workers save

Kaldor, in relaxing the classical assumptions, started with the basic Keynesian accounting identity, $I = S$, and then proceeded to carry out a few simple algebraic manipulations. Total savings, he reasoned, are equal to the savings rate of workers, s_w, applied to the total national income, Y, plus whatever is the difference between the savings rate of capitalists and the savings rate of workers, $s_n - s_w$, applied to that portion of the national income which goes to capitalists (nonworkers) in the form of profits (residual, or nonwage, income). In other words,

$$S = s_w Y + (s_n - s_w)\Pi \tag{8.11}$$

Substituting this specification of aggregate savings for S in the basic Keynesian identity, one obtains the following equation:

$$I = s_w Y + (s_n - s_w)\Pi \tag{8.12}$$

Dividing equation 8.12 through by Y as follows

$$\frac{I}{Y} = s_w + (s_n - s_w)\frac{\Pi}{Y} \tag{8.13}$$

and then performing the algebraic manipulations necessary for isolating the Π/Y term on the left-hand side, one obtains the following equation:

$$\frac{\Pi}{Y} = \frac{1}{(s_n - s_w)} * \frac{I}{Y} - \frac{s_w}{(s_n - s_w)} \tag{8.14}$$

which is the most general formula for analyzing the effect that the differing propensities to save by workers and "capitalists" (nonworkers) will have on the distribution of income.

When the classical assumptions hold, that is, when $s_n = 1$ and $s_w = 0$, equation 8.14 is reduced to equation 8.6, thus confirming the argument already made that, the greater the rate of investment, the lower will be the share of national income going to workers. If only the assumption that capitalists (nonworkers) do not consume is relaxed, so that s_n can take any value while s_w

remains equal to zero, then equation 8.14 is reduced to the following:

$$\frac{\Pi}{Y} = \frac{1}{s_n} * \frac{I}{Y} \tag{8.15}$$

As can be seen from this equation, the residual (profit) share of national income will be higher, and thus the nonresidual, or wage, share will be lower—even beyond what the rate of investment dictates—by a factor equal to the reciprocal of the marginal propensity to save out of residual income. Thus, if those receiving the residual share (the group of nonwage earners) use half their income to purchase consumption goods, the residual share will be twice what it would otherwise be. Of course, if the group consumes at a higher rate, its share of national income will be even larger. This confirms another point made earlier, namely, that the greater the consumption out of nonwage income, as reflected by the value of s_n and hence Π_e, the lower will be the share of national income going to workers. It needs to be stressed that what is being analyzed here is the relative *distribution* of income, and not the absolute *level* of income. The two are not the same, and one of the key insights derived from the post-Keynesian theory of income distribution is that it is possible, especially in an expanding economy, for the absolute amount of income going to workers to be increasing at the same time that their relative share is declining.

Finally, if both the classical assumptions are relaxed so that s_n and s_w can take any value within certain limits—one of these limits necessarily being that the marginal propensity to save by workers cannot exceed that of nonworkers—equation 8.14 retains its most general form. A few numerical examples will bring out the essential point that emerges once the possiblility of workers' savings is recognized. This is that, for a given rate of accumulation and thus a given rate of economic expansion, any savings by workers will increase their share of national income. If 10 percent of the national income is being invested, that is, if $I/Y = 0.10$, then with $s_n = 1$ and $s_w = 0$, the nonworkers' share of national income must be 10 percent, limiting the workers' share in real terms to 90 percent (as shown in exhibit 8.2). If, in addition, half the nonwage income is used to purchase other than investment goods, that is, if $s_w = 0.5$, then the share of national income going to nonworkers will double to 20 percent, reducing the workers' share in real terms to 80 percent (as in exhibit 8.3). If now we must also allow for workers' savings, equal, say, to 5 percent of their income, then the share of the national income going to nonworkers will, according to equation 8.14, fall back to 11 percent, with the workers' share rising to 89 percent. Taking other values for s_w but still assuming that $I/Y = 0.10$ and $s_n = 0.5$, it is possible to determine the effect of varying the savings rate for workers. For example, if s_w is equal to 3 percent under these assumed conditions, then the workers' share of national income will be equal be equal to 85 percent; and if s_w is 7 percent, their share will be 93 percent. Thus, the greater the marginal propensity to save of workers, the larger will be their share of the national income.

In developing this type of algebraic analysis, one that is better able to take into account the possiblity of workers' savings, Kaldor overlooked one point. If workers are saving a portion of their income rather than spending it on consumption goods, there are only two possibilities. One is that the savings by workers will not be offset by business investment. In that case, the workers' relative share will increase only because aggregate income can be expected to decline and, out of the reduced total output of goods and services, workers will command a larger share—albeit a lesser absolute amount. The other possibility, one more consistent with the long-period framework of the present analysis, is that the savings by workers will be used to finance a portion of business investment equal to their share of total savings, with the workers receiving a certain return, in the form of dividend and/or interest payments, which adds to their wage income. What effect will the return on the financial assets acquired by workers have on the distribution of income? The answer was given by Pasinetti in the same 1962 article in which he pointed out Kaldor's failure to take that factor into account. It turns out that it is precisely the return on the assets acquired by workers with their savings which enables them to obtain a larger share of the national income. Only by becoming "capitalists" (actually rentiers) can workers increase their consumption relative to nonworkers. However, the share of the national income going to these individuals *qua* workers will remain the same.

Pasinetti first noted that, with workers acquiring financial assets which entitle them to a share of whatever "profits" are being earned, the total amount of residual income, Π, has to be divided into the amount paid to workers, Π_w, and the amount which goes to the "capitalists," or non-workers, Π_n. That is,

$$\Pi = \Pi_w + \Pi_n \tag{8.16}$$

Pasinetti then made the simplifying, but not unreasonable, assumption that any return on the financial assets acquired with their savings, either by workers or "capitalists," will be proportional to the amount of assets held by the two groups. In other words, the workers can expect the same return on their savings (converted into securities) as the "capitalists." On that premise, the total profit share of national income can be divided between workers and nonworkers as follows:

$$\frac{\Pi}{A} = \frac{\Pi_w}{A_w} + \frac{\Pi_n}{A_n} \tag{8.17}$$

where A, A_w and A_n are, respectively, the total amount of assets entitling the holders of those assets to the profits being earned by firms; the amount of those assets held by workers, and the amount held by the "capitalists," or nonworkers, with $A = A_w + A_n$.

How much of the profits earned by firms will go to workers—enabling them to add to their wage income—will depend on their marginal propensity to save. That is,

$$\frac{\Pi_w}{Y} = f(s_w) \tag{8.18}$$

The point is that the workers, by saving a portion of their wages, cannot increase the level of national income. They can only force the "capitalists," or non-workers, to share whatever profits are being earned by firms—provided they use their savings to acquire shares in companies. This can be seen by substituting $S = S_n + S_w$ for $A = A_n + A_w$ in equation 8.17—as is permissible given the long-period context of the argument. With the total profit share depending on the rate of investment and the amount of consumption by capitalists, or nonworkers, any savings by workers, as the above numerical examples demonstrate, will simply reduce the capitalists', or nonworkers', share of the profits being earned by firms. This means that it is not just the amount of profits going to workers, Π_w, that depends on s_w. The amount of profits going to the capitalists, or non-workers, Π_n—as the remaining portion of the profits being earned by firms—also depends on s_w. That is,

$$\frac{\Pi_n}{Y} = \frac{\Pi}{Y} - \frac{\Pi_w}{Y} \tag{8.19}$$

It is thus equation 8.15 rather than equation 8.14 which explains the division of the national product between wages and profits. Equation 8.14 explains something else—the division of the national income between workers and the capitalists, or nonworkers. The difference between the two is the amount of profits which goes to workers, not as compensation for their labor but rather as a return on the shares they hold in companies. It is this nonwage income which enables workers to increase their consumption relative to the capitalists, or nonworkers.

The Pasinetti elaboration of the Kaldor analysis leads to a number of important insights about the distribution of income. The first is that it is important to distinguish the distribution among social classes (capitalists, workers, etc.) from the distribution among types of income (profits, wages, etc.). The two are not the same. Workers can increase their relative share of the national income by saving. But this is not because they are able to increase the wage share of national income. Rather it is because, as "capitalists," they are entitled to a portion of the "profits." Indeed, the wage, or nonresidual, share of national income will remain the same, whatever the rate of savings by workers—unless, of course, the rate of savings is so great that the workers are able to take over control of enterprises and use that control to increase the wage share at the expense of consumption by the nonworking class. Short of this unlikely result—at least within the United States at the present time—the only effect of workers saving a portion of their income is to reduce the amount of profits earned by firms which goes to the "capitalists," or nonworkers. This leads to the second important insight which derives from Pasinetti's elaboration of the Kaldor analysis.

The rate of savings by workers, s_w, makes no difference insofar as the division of the national income between wages and profits is concerned, at least in the long period. Since the division between wages and profits will be the same whatever the value of s_w, the arguments of Kalecki and Robinson, based on the framework of the national income and product accounts, are not vitiated by the failure to allow for the possibility of workers' savings. The fact that workers account for a portion of total savings may affect the relative economic position of the different social classes—although even this possible effect should not be overstressed, given the extent to which the savings of workers are in fact used to finance the durable goods purchases of other workers rather than to acquire shares in firms. However, the rate of savings by workers, s_w, is of no importance in explaining the wage, or nonresidual, share of national income.

Several qualifications need to be made before the Pasinetti arguments can be accepted in full. One is that, in the aftermath of the corporate revolution, one cannot simply juxtapose the savings of workers against the savings of the "capitalists." One must first distinguish, at least insofar as the oligopolistic sector is concerned, between the profits retained by megacorps as part of their residual income and the profits distributed as dividends. Only after any retained earnings have been subtracted can the "profits" then be divided between rentiers and workers according to their respective share holdings. Indeed, by using a portion of their wages to acquire some of the securities issued by megacorps, the workers will become not "capitalists" but rather (at least to some degree) rentiers. Strictly speaking, the only savings by "capitalists" are the savings by the workers who are self-employed owner-entrepreneurs.

A second qualification derives from the assumption made by Pasinetti, in keeping with the post-Keynesian nature of the analysis, that the rate of investment, I/Y, is independent of the amount of savings by workers, as determined by s_w. If it were true that workers, by saving, were able to increase the total amount of funds available to finance investment by firms, with this greater availability of funds having a positive effect on the willingness of firms to undertake capital expenditures, either because the cost of long-term borrowing would fall or simply because of the greater availability of funds, then it can no longer be maintained, as the Pasinetti line of reasoning requires, that the rate of investment, I/Y, and thus the total profit share of national income, Π/Y, is unaffected by the marginal propensity to save of workers, s_w.

The possibility of workers' savings affecting the rate of investment is, of course, ruled out by the stringent assumptions of the long-period model on which not only the Pasinetti but also the Kalecki, Robinson and Kaldor arguments are based. However, even when those stringent assumptions are relaxed and the analysis shifted to the non-steady-state growth paths observable in the short period, with full allowance made for the role of finance in influencing investment behavior, there are still strong grounds for excluding the possibility that workers' savings will affect the rate of accumulation. As pointed out in the preceding chapter, megacorps require little in the way of external finance, with even that little amount readily available from the panoply of financial intermediaries. Still, in light of the important role played by pension funds and insurance companies in mobilizing workers' saving to serve as a source of external funds, and the critical difference those external funds can make in certain circumstances, it is best simply to assume that workers' savings have only a negligible effect, rather than no effect at all, on the rate of investment.

With these qualifications, the Pasinetti argument that workers' savings make no difference in the distribution of income between wages and profits can be accepted in full. This leaves, as the only factors determining that division, the two variables already identified: (1) the rate of investment, I/Y or, employing the notation used in chapter 7 in connection with the megacorp, Φ; and (2) the amount of consumption out of nonwage income, Π_e. However, these two factors may no longer be sufficient to explain the wage, or nonresidual, share of national income once we drop the assumption that workers do not save. This is not because workers' savings will affect the relative wage share—that possiblity has just been excluded—but rather because workers' savings imply a real wage that exceeds the subsistence level. With the real wage, w_r, greater than the physical minimal, it may well be that an additional factor, besides the rate of investment and the amount of consumption out of nonwage income, needs to be introduced to explain what determines the wage, or nonresidual, share of the national income. We therefore need to pick up the discussion of technical progress where it was broken off in chapter 5.

8.2.4 The growth of real wages over time

Technical progress, via process innovation, can be said to lead to a certain growth of output per worker, $\overset{\circ}{Z}$ (see chapter 5, section 4.2). Indeed, it is only by determining the growth of output per worker that an approximate measure of technical progress can be obtained. Starting, therefore, with a certain rate of technical progress for the economy as a whole, $\overset{\circ}{Z}$, it is possible to specify the rate at which the consumption goods sector will be able to increase its output per worker in the long run. For there is no reason to believe that the growth of output per worker in the consumption goods sector will be different from that in the investment goods sector. Indeed, the evidence from the most recent period suggests that the measurable rate of technical progress is the same within the two sectors (see exhibit 5.14). The growth of output per worker in the consumption goods sector can therefore be assumed to be equal to the growth of output per worker in the aggregate, $\overset{\circ}{Z}$. It is this growth of output per worker in the consumption goods sector (the same as the growth of output per worker in the investment goods sector) which will, in turn, determine the secular growth of real wages, w_r. For it is the amount of consumption goods available to workers that constitutes the real wage.

Other factors remaining the same, then, the growth of the real wage rate, w_r, will be equal to the growth of output per worker. The point, however, is that other factors need not remain the same. In particular, it may be decided on behalf of the society—or it may just happen without conscious design—that the rate of expansion, and hence the rate of investment, will be increased. In that event, the nonwage share of national income will have to rise, as already pointed out, with a consequent reduction in the growth of real wages, at least in relative terms, to accommodate the increased output of the investment goods sector. Similarly, it may be decided, or it may just happen, that the consumption out of nonwage income will be increased—whether because rentiers and other nonworkers (including members of the dependent class) are to have their relative standard of living improved, because public consumption is to be expanded relative to private consumption, or because the competition among firms over market shares has intensified. Again, the effect will be to raise the nonwage share of national income, with a consequent reduction in the growth of real wages, at least in relative terms, so that the output of the consumption goods sector can be diverted to uses other than meeting the consumption needs of the currently employed workers. Of course, a change in one of these two variables, Φ or Π_e, will displace the economy from whatever is presently its sustainable growth path, producing some sort of cyclical movement before the economy either returns to the old growth path or fully adjusts to some new growth path. Still, it is the rate of investment and the marginal propensity to consume out of non-wage income which, together with the growth of output per worker, will determine the growth of real wages in the long period.

The growth of output per worker, $\overset{\circ}{Z}$, and hence of the real wage, $\overset{\circ}{w}_r$, will, of course, not be independent of the rate of investment, Φ. As previously pointed out (see chapter 5, section 4.4), $\overset{\circ}{Z}$ is a decreasing power function of the secular rate of growth of investment, $\overset{\circ}{I}$. With the incremental capital-output ratio for the economy as a whole, v, and thus the social rate of return of investment, ϱ, remaining unchanged, it is the rate of investment, I/Y or Φ, that will, in turn, determine the secular rate of growth of investment, $\overset{\circ}{I}$. That is,

$$\overset{\circ}{I} = \frac{\varrho}{v} = \Phi\varrho \tag{8.20}$$

Indeed, it is the change in the relative size of the investment goods sector, as measured by I/Y or Φ, which accounts for the variable effect of $\overset{\circ}{I}$ on $\overset{\circ}{Z}$ in the long period. Thus, as long as the value of v and hence ϱ can be viewed as a fixed parameter, there is no need to include the growth of output per worker, $\mathring{Z}$, as an additional factor determining the wage, or nonresidual, share of the national income. The rate at which output per worker is increasing is already implicit in whatever is the value of I/Y, or Φ.

The point is, however, that v, and hence ϱ, is not necessarily a fixed parameter. Once an investment project has been carried out, the private rate of return, r—not to mention the social rate of return, ϱ—may be considerably lower than was anticipated when the commitment to carry out the investment, and thereby lower the real wage of workers, was made. If the investment was undertaken with the expectation that the firm would be able to increase its share of the market (or even just to gain a foothold), then that expectation may well be disappointed by the unforeseen reaction of the other firms within the industry. If the investment was undertaken with the expectation that the growth of industry sales would validate the decision to expand capacity, then that expectation may well be disappointed by a subsequent change in either the level or composition of final demand. Finally, if the investment was undertaken with the expectation that the firm would be able to reduce its costs, then that expectation may well be disappointed by the inability to achieve the promised reduction in the use of material and/or labor inputs. These reasons for why the private rate of return on investment, r, may be lower than was anticipated—and indeed even lower than is usually the case—are in addition to the investment carried out by firms so as to enable the output of the goods and services used within the public sector to be expanded. While the public consumption thereby being supported may be socially productive, the investment will not add to the amount of consumption goods available to workers and thus will not increase the real wage. It is for all these reasons that the growth of output per worker, $\mathring{Z}$, needs to be included as one of the factors, in addition to the rate of investment, Φ, which determines the real wage.

The growth of real wages over time can therefore be said to depend on the growth of output per worker, $\mathring{Z}$, on the rate of investment, Φ, and on the amount of consumption out of nonwage income, Π_e. That is

$$\mathring{w}_r = f(\mathring{Z}, \Phi, \Pi_e) \qquad (8.21)$$

With Φ and Π_e fixed parameters, $\mathring{w}_r$ then depends on $\mathring{Z}$ alone. This relationship holds for any economy, whether a market-based system or not. It is just that, in a market-based economy, the translation of the rising output per worker into ever higher real wages creates a set of problems which are unique to that type of system. While similar problems arise in a nonmarket economy, they manifest themselves in different ways.

In the case of a market-based economy, the difficulty of translating the rising output per worker into higher real wages can lead to two types of problems. One is a sudden reversal in the normal expansion of the system, often accompanied by some sort of financial crisis, leading to a long period of stagnation and high unemployment. This sort of breakdown in the functioning of a market economy can be explained by the failure of real wages to keep pace with the growth of output per worker, either through the falling price of consumption goods or through a secular rise in the nominal wage—allowing, of course, for any parameter shift in either the rate of accumulation or the marginal propensity to consume out of nonwage income. Nothing further will be said in elaboration of this point until the next chapter when, as a part of the broader assessment of the cyclical stability of an advanced market economy like that of the United States, the discretionary expenditures of the household sector will be analyzed (see chapter 9, section 3.2).

The other type of problem to which a market economy is prone is a rise in the various price indexes, or inflation. This sort of malady can be explained by the nominal or money wage rising more rapidly than is consistent with the growth of real wages as determined by $\overset{\circ}{Z}$, Φ and Π_e. To elaborate on this point, it is necessary to indicate what is meant by the nominal or money wage and how it can vary independently of the real wage. This will be the task taken up in the next part of this chapter. First, however, it is necessary to complete the discussion of what determines the nonresidual share of national income by shifting the focus from the hypothetical long period to the historically relevant short period and seeing if the post-Keynesian theory of income distribution applies in that case as well.

8.2.5 The short-period determinants

With the shift from a long-period to a short-period perspective, one needs to allow for the possibility of cyclical movements, as measured by $\dot{G}-\overset{\circ}{G}$ or $\overset{*}{\dot{G}}$. These cyclical movements will have a further effect on the division of the national income between nonresidual and residual shares besides those just identified in connection with the long-period model of steady-state, or at least sustainable, growth. A rate of expansion that temporarily exceeds the secular average will increase the residual share of national income at the expense of the nonresidual share while the reverse, a rate of expansion below the historical average, will increase the nonresidual share relative to the residual share (even though, in the first instance, the absolute levels of both wages and other income will be rising while in the second instance the absolute levels of both will be falling). The reason is the effect which the level of sales and the corresponding rate of capacity utilization have on the residual income of firms.

As was pointed out in the discussion of finance (see chapter 7, section 3.1), the marginal rate at which discretionary funds are generated, μ', is greater than the average rate, μ. This is because the fixed costs, though part of the formula for arriving at a list price, play no role in determining the megacorp's cash flow at the margin. Indeed, with constant marginal costs of production, the entire difference between μ' and μ will be equal to the fixed costs of production. The greater value of μ' means that when the economy is expanding more rapidly than might be expected given its secular growth rate, with megacorps operating above their standard ratio and with capacity utilization rates correspondingly high, the growth of discretionary funds within the oligopolistic core—if not throughout the entire enterprise sector—will exceed the growth rate of national income. Conversely, when the economy is expanding less rapidly than the secular growth rate, with megacorps operating below their standard ratio and capacity utilization rates therefore low, the growth of discretionary funds within the oligopolistic core—if not throughout the entire enterprise sector—will fall short of the growth of national income.

It then follows that the nonresidual share of national income, NWg/Y, depends on the level of aggregate demand. When aggregate demand is high, as manifest by sales exceeding the standard operating ratios within the oligopolistic core, corporate cash flow and thus the residual share of national income will increase relative to the nonresidual share, with the latter (including any dividend, interest and transfer payments) the portion accruing to the household sector. Even though the nonresidual share may be increasing in absolute terms, it will nonetheless be falling relative to the residual share. And when aggregate demand is low, as manifest by sales levels below the standard operating ratios, corporate cash flow and thus the residual share of national income will decline relative to the nonresidual share—though again both types of income are likely to be falling in absolute terms.

In speaking about the growth of household income over time, then, one needs to distinguish the long-period or secular influences from the short-period cyclical factor. It may, of course, be objected that this cyclical factor cannot be distinguished from the secular influences since both depend on the rate of investment, ϕ. And indeed in a simple model, in which the enterprise sector's purchase of new plant and equipment is the only type of discretionary expenditures taken into account, the rate of investment is both the most important long-period influence and the most important short-period factor. This critical role assigned to investment is, moreover, the essential link between the post-Keynesian long-period theory of income distribution outlined earlier and the short-period version just presented. This does not mean, however, that the long-period influences cannot be distinguished from the short-period cyclical factor.

First, it is only in the simplest of models, such as that reviewed in chapter 3, that business plant and equipment expenditures constitute the only type of outlays with a multiplier, and hence a short-period demand-enhancing, effect. In the more realistic type of model now being developed, it is the total amount of durable good, or discretionary, expenditures which will produce the short-period redistributional effect—and not just business expenditures on new plant and equipment. Second, and even more important, this short-period redistribution effect of total discretionary expenditures can be isolated from the long-period influences by focusing on the relationship between $\dot{G}$ and $\overset{\circ}{G}$ or whatever other variable, such as the change in the rate of capacity utilization, $\hat{C}ap$, serves as a proxy for the economic system's cyclical movements. The short-period redistributive effect can be observed by allowing $\dot{G}$ to vary relative to G while holding the several long-period determinants constant. Similarly, the long-period influences can be isolated by holding $\dot{G}\text{-}\mathring{G}$ or $\overset{*}{G}$ constant and allowing the long-period determinants to vary. Thus a change in Φ over the cycle will bring out the short-period redistributive effect of business investment while a change in the same ratio over several cycles, holding $\dot{G}\text{-}\mathring{G}$ or $\overset{*}{G}$ constant, will bring out the long-period redistributive effect of the same key determinant.

So far, in discussing what determines the nonresidual share of national income in the short period, it has not been made clear whether what is being analyzed are the various types of household income—wages, dividends, interest and transfer payments—in real terms or in nominal terms. This is because the crucial role of the price system in determining the distribution of income in real terms has yet to be brought out. Indeed, the earlier discussion of income distribution in the long period was somewhat incomplete because of this omission. It is this crucial role played by the price system insofar as the distribution of the national income is concerned, both in the long period and in the short, to which we shall now turn. This requires that we first distinguish between the nominal and real rates of compensation.

8.3 Nominal vs. Real Rates of Compensation

It is crucial, from the perspective of post-Keynesian theory, to distinguish the real rates of compensation received by members of the household sector from the merely nominal rates. Payments can be made only in current (undeflated) dollars or whatever other currency serves as the unit of account. Even contracts with escalator clauses and other provisions for indexing must, once the stipulated adjustments in compensation are made, provide payment in current dollars. The actual, or real, value of the payments will then depend on what changes, if any, subsequently occur in the prices of the goods and services which are to be purchased with the income. It is an inherent characteristic of a monetarized production system, and thus intrinsic to an advanced market economy, that the moment when agreement is reached on a rate of compensation is likely to be separated, by a certain interval of time, from the moment when the income is then expended on goods and services. It is therefore inherent in a market economy that the nominal and real rates of compensation may differ. Indeed, the distinction between nominal and real rates of compensation provides the starting point for understanding the process of inflation to which advanced market economies are prone.

The real rates of compensation are governed by the set of technological and economic factors which have already been identified. Specifically, the growth of *real* wages over time will depend on the growth of output per worker, the rate of investment and the marginal propensity of the society to consume out of nonwage income. The nominal, or money, rates of compensation, in contrast, depend on a different set of factors, most of them the outcome of social processes based on some dynamic other than an economic one. In other words, the *nominal* rates of compensation—including most importantly, though not exclusively, the compensation of workers—are determined sociopolitically rather than in any market. It is the fact that the nominal rates of compensation, because of their quite different set of determinants, may move independently of the real rates of compensation that creates the possibility of an inflationary spiral endogenous to the economic system. For when the growth of the nominal rates of compensation, as determined sociopolitically, exceeds the increase in real income which objective technological and economic factors permit, a rise in price levels will be the only means of bringing the two back into balance—as is required if firms are to cover their costs of production and thus the necessary value condition for continuous growth is to be satisfied.

In this section, the focus will be on the factors, primarily noneconomic, that determine the growth in the nominal rate of compensation received by workers. It is thus the growth in the money wage rate, $\dot{w}$, that will be explained. Since most of the disposable income received by the household sector consists of wage and salary payments, with even other types of household income dependent on $\dot{w}$, what will thus be explained is the rate at which the nominal income of the household sector will be rising. The analysis will begin by introducing another type of social institution as the counterweight of the megacorp insofar as representing the interests of workers is concerned. This other type of institution is the trade union as one form workers' organizations can take.

8.3.1 Workers' organizations

The conventional economic theory has been reluctant to accept trade unions and other types of workers' organizations as legitimate social institutions. Such organizations have been regarded as a form of ''monopoly,'' with all the pejorative connotation of that term. Yet this view fails to recognize the necessity for some type of organization to represent workers once a separate business organization, differentiated from households or families, has come into being, with interests quite different from those of its employees. The conflict of interests involves three separate aspects of the employment relationship: (1) the pattern of behavior and intensity of effort required of workers during their time on the job; (2) the extent to which differentials are to be paid to workers performing the same type of labor (based on seniority or some other criterion); and (3) the basic rate of compensation. As demonstrated by the experience of the various OECD countries, it is only to be expected that specialized social institutions will evolve in an advanced industrial society to represent the interests of workers in these matters and that, moreover, once such organizations have become institutionalized (i.e., they have acquired a formal organizational structure), they will become a separate factor in the dynamics of the economic system, pursuing goals determined primarily by the nature of the constituency they represent. To apply the technical term "monopoly" to these organizations is to misunderstand fundamentally the nature and function of these social institutions, and it is as misleading as when the same term is applied to megacorps.

The most fundamental conflict between workers and the organization which employs them is over the intensity of the effort to be made by the workers during their time on the job. The issue here is easily confused. It is not, as the orthodox theory would have it, that workers prefer not to work. Purposeful activity is a basic human need, and its lack will cause the individual to deteriorate, mentally if not physically. Indeed, workers seek employment as much for this reason as for the income it provides (under a system in which income is based primarily on employment). The conflict instead arises over how the workers are to apply themselves while on the job. The patterns of behavior that best suit the goals and/or accustomed rhythms of the workers are not necessarily the patterns that fit the work flow within the plant or office which the prevailing technology dictates—let alone the patterns of behavior that will enable the firm to maximize the rates of throughput.

At the one extreme, with the sweatshop conditions of 19th century British capitalism providing an historical example, the employees can literally be worked to death. With job assignments dictated entirely by the exigencies of the machine process, a frenzied pace which, under an earlier agricultural mode of production, was only seasonal can be made the year-long norm so that workers become burnt out before their time. If no effort is made to reduce the physical dangers present in the work environment—e.g., unvented fumes and unguarded machinery—the attrition through death and injury will be all the greater. At the other extreme, the employees can be allowed to establish their own job assignments and set their own pace, based on their own natural rhythms and whatever informal organization may arise to mediate the conflicts among individual workers. The danger in the latter case is that the productivity of the firm will fall below the level needed to survive. Because of this danger, successful firms are characterized by a managerial structure—whether merely a single owner-entrepreneur as for the simplest of neoclassical proprietorships or a hierarchy of lower, middle and high-level executives as found in all megacorps. Whatever the nature of the managerial structure, its interest in maximizing the rates of throughput and thus the productivity of the firm will be in conflict with the interests of the workers in having a pattern of behavior on the job and an intensity of effort which suits their own inclinations.

Without a trade union or some other formal structure, this conflict is likely to be resolved informally through the establishment of what are known as "work rules." These are the ways of carrying out particular job assignments which gradually gain the force of custom through the daily give-and-take between worker and supervisor. In the absence of a trade union, the advantage in determining these work rules tends to lie with the managerial group, as resistance beyond a certain point can be penalized by dismissal. Indeed, it is primarily to provide a counterweight to management in determining the work rules that workers historically have been willing to overcome their reluctance to organize formally; and even today it is the protection which a trade union provides its members in any dispute over work rules which is the key to the workers' continuing loyalty to the union. The importance of the work rules is attested to by the principal activity of the shop steward, the official at the bottom of the trade union's own managerial hierarchy with whom workers are most likely to come into contract. A shop steward is likely to spend most of his or her time enforcing the work rules.

Once a trade union or some other type of workers' organization has been established, the work rules are likely to become formalized through incorporation into the basic collective bargaining agreement, thereby gaining the status of legally binding rights and obligations on both the workers and management. It is this enhanced status of the work rules which, in addition to the nature of the technology, makes the labor coefficients of production fixed in the short period (see chapter 5, section 3.2), especially in the more capital intensive sectors of the economy where trade unions predominate. A dispute over work rules—rather than over the basic wage rate or even pay differentials—is more likely to lead to a strike and, once a walk-out has occurred, make a settlement more difficult to reach. The reason is that a dispute over work rules is more likely to directly threaten the survival of the firm, or at least its continued profitability, because of the potential danger to the firm's productivity. A dispute over the basic wage rate and/or pay diffferentials can, on the other hand, usually be resolved in a way that poses no threat to the firm.

Insofar as any differentials in pay are concerned, the workers' main interest is in seeing to it that the differentials are not used to reward individual employees who act in violation of the norms which have developed among the workers themselves. This means the workers are likely to oppose differentials based on the assessment of individual performance by management, fearing they will be used to encourage "rate-busting"—that is, an individual effort that exceeds what the majority of workers consider a reasonable pace—or even "union-busting." Instead they are likely to insist on an "objective" standard such as seniority, one that has been agreed to in advance. While management might prefer to base the differentials on individual performance, as a practical matter it is difficult to ascertain which workers are more productive, especially when the work they do is usually so highly interrelated.

Thus, once a trade union has become established, and the "objective" basis for wage differentials agreed to, the issue is likely to become largely moot. Indeed, it is not unheard of for a company, once the total cost of the wage settlement under a new contract has been determined, to leave it to the trade union to decide how that fixed sum is to be apportioned among the various grades of workers it represents. The difficult question here is whether the increases should be in absolute or in percentage terms—absolute increases reducing the relative differentials over time and percentage increases enlarging those differentials. It is not surprising that, faced with having to make a choice between these two alternatives, neither of which is likely to satisfy all the workers, the management will, in certain circumstances, "pass the buck" to the trade union. Only if the differentials paid to the small group of more experienced and/or more skilled workers who are essential to the continued viability of the firm should fall below the level needed to retain those workers are the differentials likely to become a serious issue in collective bargaining. Generally, however, trade unions will not insist on so flat a wage band—especially since the more skilled workers, who provide a disproportionate share of the union's bargaining strength, may be provoked to break off and form a separate union.

Insofar as the basic wage rate itself is concerned, one might think this would be the most contentious issue of all, leading to the sharpest conflict in collective bargaining and the most prolonged of walk-outs once the disagreement has led to a strike. After all, no issue would appear to be closer to the heart of the struggle between labor and management over relative income shares. Yet, as a practical matter, because of the implicit understanding by which a trade union gains the right to bargain on behalf of its members, the basic wage rate is seldom the critical issue. To win even minimal acceptance by the employer, the trade union must be able to guarantee that the same contractual terms, and thus the same rates of hourly compensation, will be imposed equally on all the firms within the industry. In this way, no employer will be put at a disadvantage because it has recognized the union as collective bargaining agent. Indeed, the failure of the trade union to impose the same contract terms throughout the industry— including even the firms with plants in other countries—will seriously undermine its bargaining position and, if not rectified, will lead eventually to the demise or impotence of the union. As long as the basic wage rate is the same for all the firms in the industry, the issue ceases to be fundamental to the survival of the individual firm. As for the competition between industries—a competition that will be affected by any difference in their basic wage rates—this is where the several wage contours to be discussed shortly play a decisive role. These wage contours ensure that the basic wage rate in the set of interconnected industries do not move too far out of line with one another.

The trade union, then, as the prototypical workers' organization, is able to establish a place for itself among the panoply of institutions in a modern, advanced society because the employees of a magacorp or any other large organization have quite divergent interests from that of their employer with respect to work rules, wage differentials and the basic wage rate. Once established, the trade union, like any organization, will try at the very least to survive and, if possible, to grow. To achieve that goal, it must demonstrate to both existing and prospective members that the benefits of belonging to the union exceed the costs. An important part of those benefits is the ability of the trade union to represent the interests of its members far better than they could themselves individually. (Thus the only effective strategy for resisting the inroads of a trade union is to make sure that the workers fare no worse than their counterparts in unionized firms and/or industries. The fact that less than a quarter of the work force in the United States is enrolled in a trade union is, for this reason, somewhat beside the point. Any benefits obtained by trade unions for their members will be matched by other employers, this so their workers will not be driven to seek representation by a trade union.)

While the most important way in which the trade union represents its members on a day-to-day basis is by seeing to it that the work rules are enforced, nonetheless it is by periodically renegotiating the contract with the firm or industry that the trade union is able to demonstrate most concretely to the majority of its rank-and-file members the value of collective representation. To ensure the continued loyalty of its members, the trade union must obtain an agreement that is "fair and reasonable." This requires that the terms be no different from those obtained by workers performing similar types of labor in other firms and in other industries. Thus the trade union's requirements for retaining the loyalty of its rank-and-file members are the same, insofar as the basic wage rate and the other cost-related contract provisions are concerned, as the requirements of the management for avoiding any competitive disadvantage *vis-à-vis* other firms and/or industries. Still, this does not explain what nominal, or money, wage rate will actually be agreed to. To be able to place a value on w, and thus to determine the size of a firm or industry's wage bill, it is necessary to divide that nominal figure into its two component parts, a certain basic wage rate, w_b, and a set of pay differentials, $\Delta w_1, \Delta w_2, \Delta w_3, \ldots, \Delta w_m$, for each of the skill and/or occupational categories into which the work force can be divided. The latter set of differentials, in the form of a W_Δ vector, constitutes the wage structure. Without an understanding of how this wage structure is determined, it is not possible to explain the growth of the money wage rate, $\dot{w}$. The next step, then, is to examine the wage structure of a firm or industry in an effort to understand not only how it is determined but also how stable it is likely to be over time.

8.3.2 The wage structure and its determinants

The wage structure encompasses any differentials in the wage rate paid workers in the various skill or occupational categories. At the point of actual production, within the plant or plant segment of a given firm, the explanation for these differentials begins with what John Dunlop has termed the "job cluster." This is the group of jobs which, because of the common technology and the common skills to which that technology gives rise, provide a natural basis for interpersonal comparisons among workers. Within the job cluster, one wage rate is usually taken as the standard to which any differentials are then applied. Typically this "key" rate is the rate for the entry-level position, that is, the first of the grade levels that define the promotion ladder within the job cluster. The task of setting wages within the job cluster then has two parts to it: (1) determining the key rate for the cluster; and (2) determining the appropriate differential for those who have advanced beyond the entry level or whatever other grade is the one to which the key rate applies.

The several or more job clusters to be found within any given firm in a particular industry are linked to one another by means of the differentials in their key rates. These differentials constitute the firm's "internal wage structure." Again, the general practice is to focus on one of the key rates—usually that associated with the firm's largest or most critical job cluster within that industry—and then to determine the other key rates as differentials with respect to that one rate. For competitive reasons, the internal wage structures of the different firms within the same industry are likely to be similar—if not actually identical. Indeed, the need to avoid being placed at a cost disadvantage will be a sufficiently strong motivation to ensure that firms act so as to equalize the wage rates for similar jobs within the same industry and thus to bring their internal wage structures into line with one another. The internal wage structure, then, is analogous to the price list for a firm's product line. Like the price list for a product line, it recognizes that the relevant figures constitute a set rather than just a single number. And like the price list, it is intended to neutralize one of the ways a rival firm can gain a competitive advantage.

Across industries the key rates, and thus the internal wage structures, are linked to one another by means of what Dunlop has termed "wage contours." These are groupings of wage rates determined in industries which are sufficiently similar to one another in terms of the types of labor, or human resource, inputs employed that a new rate or pattern established in any one of those industries is likely to serve as a ready basis for comparison with all the other industries within the same grouping. A number of wage contours have been identified in the case of the American economy, the most important being the auto-steel group of heavy industries. The rates of compensation within these several groupings of industries can be compared in terms of the difference between the basic wage in the auto-steel group of heavy industries and the basic wage in each of the other wage contours.

With the internal wage structures of the different industries linked to one another by means of the pay differentials among the several wage contours, it is then possible to talk about a single wage structure for the economy as a whole. This wage structure consists of the differentials in the hourly wage rate along three separate dimensions: (1) the separate grades, or ranks, within any one job cluster; (2) the different job clusters, or occupational categories, within any one firm or industry; and (3) the several groupings of industries that each form a separate wage contour. The rate of compensation received by any employed worker, w, will thus be equal to the basic wage rate received by all workers, w_b, plus or minus a wage differential, $\Delta w_{k.i.j}$, this being the wage differential for the

kth grade within the ith skill or occupational group that is employed by the jth industry or group of industries. What therefore needs to be explained is the basis on which each of these three sets of wage differentials is determined.

Two criteria are likely to be applied in determining the set of wage differentials within the skill or occupational categories that constitute a single job cluster. They are (a) where the position falls within the hierarchy of tasks that need to be carried out, and (b) how long the individual has held the same position. This means that, as part of its personnel policy, a firm must develop a pay scale specifying the increment in the hourly wage rate that will be paid when a worker either is promoted to the next higher level within the hierarchy of positions or has remained in the same position for an additional period of time. In the absence of a trade union or its functional equivalent, the pay scale is likely to reflect only the interests of the firm as an employing organization, with three sets of considerations determining the wage differentials within the job cluster. One is the need to maintain administrative control by making sure that supervisors receive a sufficiently higher differential that they will impose the necessary discipline on the workers they oversee. The second consideration is the need to preserve the skill level of the work force by making sure that experienced workers receive a sufficiently higher differential that the attrition rate can be kept within the desired range. (On this point, see chapter 13, section 2.1.) The third, and last, consideration is the need to minimize the discontent among workers over the relative rates of compensation by making sure that the only other differentials, besides those obtained through promotion and/or seniority, are those which can be justified by reference to some principle of equity. With a trade union to represent the interests of the workers collectively, it is not that these three considerations will no longer apply. It is rather that, in order to reach agreement on what pay scale should be incorporated into the contract, the firm will be forced to give greater weight to the third of the three principles.

Once the set of wage differentials within a job cluster has been determined, based on the above considerations, any change in the average rate of compensation for that portion of the firm's work force will depend on what change, if any, has occurred in the "key" rate. To simplify the argument, this "key" rate can be assumed to be the wage rate at the entry level. It thus possible to ignore the wage differentials for the k different grades within any skill or occupational category and focus instead on the set of wage differentials for the several or more entry-level positions within the firm. In this way, the set of $k.i$ wage differentials within any one firm can be reduced to a set of i wage differentials for the firm's entry-level positions. It should be noted that the wage differential for at least one of the entry-level positions must be zero, this being the entry-level position the rate of compensation for which serves as the basic wage rate, w_b, for the entire firm—and, by extension, since the occupational structure is likely to be the same for all firms, for the industry as a whole. The entry-level position paying only the basic rate of compensation is likely to be the one which encompasses the largest group of production, or blue-collar, workers, although it need not be.

The set of wage differentials for the i different entry-level positions within the firm, and hence within the work force for the industry as a whole, will depend, first and foremost, on the same factors that determine the major class subdivisions within the working class. These are the educational and related job requirements that limit the types of entry-level positions for which an individual can hope to qualify (see section 8.1.4). The most fundamental division is, of course, between those with a baccalaureate degree, who are thereby eligible for one of the white-collar positions, and the rest of the work force. Among the white-collar workers, however, there is the further division between those with and without a graduate degree and, among the blue-collar workers, between those with and without a high school diploma.

There are two interpretations of what these class differences, based on the highest degree obtained, actually represent. One interpretation is the "human capital" argument that a person's education is actually an investment, by the society if not the individual, in making the person a more "productive" member of the labor force. The return on this investment, it is argued, can be measured by the differential in the wage rate subsequently earned, relative to the cost of the education provided (including any foregone earnings during the period of schooling). The opposing interpretation is that any differences in the amount of education received are simply a way of justifying the higher rates of compensation which the members of the white-collar work force, by virtue of their strategic position within the firm, are able to obtain. These wage differentials simply reinforce the other advantages which accrue to the more educated members of the society. While clearly the resources used in education are a cost that needs to be covered, the largest portion of that cost is borne by the society as a whole—with most of the rest being borne by the individual's family. In any case, for the reasons that will be brought out when the marginal productivity theory of income distribution is examined critically (see section 8.4.3), it is fallacious to equate the differential in the wage rate subsequently earned by workers with the value of their "marginal productivity," whether that differential correlates with the amount of education received or not. Any such interpretation of the evidence confuses the relative gain obtained by just one group of workers with the overall benefit to the society from having a more highly educated labor force—one that is able to work with the sophisticated types of equipment that are the source of the economic system's increasing productivity over time.

This last point of criticism is supported by what one observes when one examines the rates of compensation for the various occupational and/or skill categories within the white-collar and blue-collar work forces separately. Controlling for the type of educational degree required to qualify for an entry-level position, one can nonetheless observe significant differentials in the wage rate, with those differentials explained by the following set of factors: (1) the extent of licensing and other non-degree restrictions on entry into the profession or craft;

(2) the percentage of those in the occupational or skill category who belong to a professional association or craft union; and (3) the percentage of those in the occupational or skill category who are female. These three sets of factors tend to be multiplicative rather than just additive, with the existence of a professional association or craft union reinforcing whatever licensing and other nondegree restrictions there are on entry into the profession or craft and with a preponderance of females, in contrast, reinforcing whatever disadvantage there is from the lack of either type of sheltering mechanism.

The percentage of those in the occupation or skill category who are female needs to be taken into account because of the special circumstances in which women as a group find themselves. A large number of women expect to be supported by their husbands once they marry. To the extent they can count on a reasonably comfortable standard of living based on their husband's income alone, they are less concerned about the relative rate of compensation for any job they may take after—or even before— they marry. In addition, many women who are married are limited in the degree of commitment they can make to their jobs. Even if they pursue a career—as distinct from just holding a job—they may be forced to interrupt that career during their child-bearing years or to subordinate it to the needs of their husbands and/or children. As a result, employers can count on a large pool of female applicants for certain types of jobs who will be less aggressive in pushing for a higher wage. The fact that this still leaves many other women, including those with families to support on their own, who are no less determined than any man to obtain the highest possible rate of compensation will not prevent employers from taking advantage of the situation. With a preponderance of applicants for whom the rate of compensation is of secondary importance, the relative wage is likely to be lower than one would expect based on the other factors which have been identified so far. This explains not only the intermediate status of the "pink-collar" work force consisting of secretaries and office assistants (see section 8.1.3) but also the lower wages received by workers in the various "female" occupations, such as nurses, elementary school teachers and retail clerks.

From what has just been said, it can be assumed that the overall demand for labor plays no role in determining the differentials in the entry-level wage for the various skill and occupational categories. This means it plays no role in determining the firm's, and hence the industry's, internal wage structure. That wage structure instead depends solely on the three factors identified above: (1) the extent of any educational and other restrictions on entry into the skill or occupational category; (2) the percentage of those in the skill or occupational category who belong to some type of workers' organization, whether a craft union or a professional association; and (3) the percentage of those in the skill or occupational category who are female. Moreover, these three factors are unlikely to change except gradually over time. With the wage structure therefore relatively stable, the rate at which the compensation of workers is being increased within any one firm or within the industry as a whole will depend on the rate at which the basic wage rate, w_b, is rising. This follows from the fact that the rate of compensation received by any worker will be equal to the basic wage rate plus or minus the wage differential for the worker's skill or occupational category. That is,

$$\mathbf{W} = w_b + \mathbf{W}_\Delta \qquad (8.22)$$

where $\mathbf{W}$ is the m-by-1 column vector of wage rates previously specified (see section 8.1.2) and $\mathbf{W}_\Delta$ is a second m-by-1 column vector defined as follows:

$$\mathbf{W}_\Delta = \{\Delta w_1 \ \Delta w_2 \ \Delta w_3 \ . \ . \ . \ \Delta w_m\} \qquad (8.23)$$

where Δw_1, Δw_2, Δw_3, . . . Δw_m are the differentials in the entry-level wage rates for each of the m skill or occupational categories into which the firm's, hence the industry's, work force can be divided. With the $\mathbf{W}_\Delta$ vector likely to remain unchanged and therefore a fixed parameter, the growth of the money wage rate, $\dot{w}$, will be equal to the growth of the basic wage rate, $\dot{w}_b$. That is,

$$\dot{w} = \dot{w}_b, \overline{\mathbf{W}_\Delta} \qquad (8.24)$$

If the differentials in the entry-level wage rate are the same across industries, then the above argument holds for the enterprise sector as a whole. The extent to which this is the case will become clearer once we have identified the factors that determine the growth of the basic wage rate, $\dot{w}_{b_j}$, within each of the n different industries that constitute the enterprise sector.

8.3.3 The basic wage rate

When a megacorp-price leader and the trade union which represents its production workers meet across the bargaining table, the basic wage rate on which they can be expected to agree is the basic wage rate being paid by the other industries within the same wage contour. It is this basic wage which will enable the megacorp to avoid being placed at a competitive disadvantage, even with respect to firms in the industries producing close substitutes (unless, of course, the labor coefficients are smaller in those other industries and/or the growth of output per worker is greater). The same wage rate will, moreover, enable the trade union to report triumphantly to its members that they are receiving a rate of compensation no less than that of other workers holding comparable jobs. The invidious basis for arriving at this rate of compensation is the reason that, as Michael Piore and other institutionalist writers have pointed out, the basic wage rate can be said to be sociologically determined. It depends on the social norm which has been established as to what is the "fair and reasonable" amount of compensation for workers to receive, given both the rate of economic expansion and the rate of inflation. Still, two questions remain. The first is whether there is only a single wage norm, or standard, for the entire enterprise sector or whether, instead, there are several wage contours. The second question is how the wage norm for the one or more wage contours is determined.

David Howell has identified two additional wage contours within the U.S. economy besides the group of heavy industries centered around the automobile and steel industries. They are (1) the group of industries using metal-working batch technologies to produce machinery, instruments and other capital goods, and (2) the remaining group of light manufacturing industries centered in what has been identified as the nonoligopolistic component of the industrial sector—textiles, apparel, lumber and wood products, furniture and fixtures, and leather products (see chapter 5, section 1.2). In 1972, the basic wage rate was $4.00 an hour in the second of these three wage contours, or 60 cents an hour less than the basic wage rate of $4.60 an hour for workers in the heavy industry group, while the basic wage rate was only $3.26 an hour in the third wage contour, a further differential of $1.34 an hour (compared to the average wage rate, in all of manufacturing, of $3.85 an hour). These differences in the basic wage rate, to the extent they have persisted over time, are primarily a reflection of how mechanized, or capital-intensive, are the techniques of production within the three groups of industries. As already explained (see chapter 5, section 4.4), it is the degree to which the production process has been mechanized that will determine the output per worker, or productivity of labor, within any one industry and hence that industry's relative contribution to whatever surplus is being generated by the economic system as a whole—with the total surplus (in physical terms) the underlying determinant of the real wage. How similar is the degree of mechanization thus serves as the basis both for the common wage standard within each of the three groups of industries and for the differential in the basic wage rate among them.

The basic wage rate within any one of the n different industries which constitute the enterprise sector is therefore equal to the basic wage rate within the automobile-steel orbit less a certain differential, Δw_{b_i}, depending on which of the above three wage contours the industry falls within. That is,

$$w_{b_j} = w_{b_0} - \Delta w_{b_i} \qquad (8.25)$$

where w_{b_j} is the basic wage rate in the jth industry; w_{b_0} is the basic wage rate in the automobile-steel group of heavy industries, and Δw_{b_i} is the difference in the basic wage rate between the auto-steel group and the ith wage contour (with Δw_{b_i} equal to 0 in the case of any industry that is part of the auto-steel orbit). Any further differential in an industry's basic wage rate, once the occupational structure of the work force as a fixed parameter, will be due to the influence of two additional factors: (1) the portion of the industry's output supplied by megacorps, as distinct from neoclassical proprietorships, and (2) the portion of the industry's work force which is represented by an industrial, as distinct from a craft, union. That is,

$$w_{b_j} = w_{b_o} + f(MEG, UNION) \qquad (8.26)$$

where MEG is the portion of the jth industry's output supplied by megacorps and $UNION$ is the portion of the industry's work force represented by one or more industrial trade unions. The first of these two additional factors reflects the higher entry-level wage paid by megacorps so as to ensure an adequate pool of applicants (see chapter 13, section 1.3) and the second additional factor, the greater bargaining power which an industrial union gives workers.

These two additional factors not only help explain the differentially higher basic wage rate within the auto-steel group of heavy industries. They also are the reason why the level of aggregate demand is unlikely to play any role in determining the basic wage rate, w_{b_o}, within that group of industries. Even if megacorps were prepared, as a matter of personnel policy, to couple lay-offs with a reduction in the entry-level wage, the industrial trade unions representing the production work force would successfully resist any such move. Over the years they have demonstrated their ability to secure for their own members whatever increase in the basic wage rate has been obtained by other workers within the same wage contour. Indeed this ability is one of the factors enabling them to retain the loyalty of their members and thereby remain a viable institution. The situation is, of course, different within the other two wage contours—especially the one that encompasses the group of light manufacturing industries previously identified as the nonoligopolistic component of the industrial sector. In the case of an industry that falls within either of those two wage contours, one cannot presume the existence either of megacorps or of an industrial trade union. As a result, one cannot exclude the possibility that the differential in the basic wage rate, Δw_{b_i}, will vary over the cycle. Still, that differential, reflecting the less capital intensive methods relied upon, is likely to be reestablished, once the economy is back on its secular growth path and the level of aggregate demand has returned to normal. This is why, as can be seen from equation 8.25, the basic wage rate within the other two wage contours depends—in the long period if not in the short—on the basic wage rate within the automobile-steel group of heavy industries. What still remains to be explained is that determines the value of w_{b_o}.

The key insight of Pierro Sraffa, as already pointed out (see chapter 6, section 1.1), is that in any fully specified model of a monetarized production system there is at least one less equation that is needed to provide a determinate solution. One of the distributional variables—either the wage rate, w, or the "rate of profit," r—must be derived from outside the system. This is what makes the distribution of income indeterminate on the basis of economic factors alone. The corollary is that, to explain the distribution of income, one must introduce at least one additional behavioral relationship, with a noneconomic variable as the key factor, to account for either w or r. The thrust of the argument up to this point is that the "rate of profit" or, more accurately, the return on investment, r, is determined endogenously, based on the rate of technical progress and/or the rate of economic expansion. This leaves the wage rate, w, as the distributional variable which is exogenously determined. Indeed, the task in this and the previous part of chapter 8 has been to explain how that variable, as the only remaining unknown within the value added vector of a Leontief-Sraffian model, $wL + \pi$, is in fact determined.

The one point to emerge so far is that, in a monetarized production system, one cannot just specify a wage rate variable. It is necessary to further distinguish between the real wage rate, w_r, and the nominal wage rate, w. While the former is uniquely determined, given the growth of output per worker, $\overset{\circ}{Z}$, the rate of investment, Φ, and the amount of consumption out of nonwage income, Π_e, the nominal wage rate can take any value—provided only that firms are able to pass on the higher cost to buyers through higher prices and the central bank is willing to pursue an accommodating monetary policy. The first condition, which is simply the necessary value condition for continuous economic expansion, is ensured, in the case of the U.S. economy, by the prevalence of megacorps (see chapter 6, section 4.4). Meanwhile the second condition, which is simply the necessary monetary condition for continuous economic expansion, will be assured, at least to some extent, by the nature of a credit-money system (see chapter 12, section 2.2). The fact that both prerequisite conditions are likely to be satisfied means that the basic wage rate, w_b—and therefore the nominal wage rate, w, for each of the different types of workers employed—cannot be determined, for any one industry alone or even for any group of industries, relying just on the economic and other variables so far identified. It must instead be determined for the enterprise sector as a whole, based on some exogenously derived norm, or standard, of what is a fair and reasonable rate of compensation for workers.

There is, among the OECD countries, a variety of sociopolitical mechanisms for deriving that norm. Indeed, each country is likely to have a mechanism *sui generis*, reflecting its own special history. In the case of the United States, a major influencing factor is the lack of a single, overriding body to determine bargaining strategy for the trade union movement as a whole. Instead, the bargaining is carried out by each union separately (delineated by major industry groupings). This has given rise to the pattern bargaining which characterizes the wage determination process in the United States. It is the pattern set in the bellwether industry, typically either automobiles or steel, which then serves as the wage norm, or standard, for other industries—especially those within the same wage contour. This norm, a certain percentage increase in the basic wage rate, can be termed the national incremental wage pattern, $\dot{w}_p$.

The basic wage rate within the automobile-steel group of heavy industries in any given year, $w_{b_0}(t_0)$, will therefore be equal, in the case of the United States, to the basic wage rate in the preceding year plus a certain percentage increase based on the national incremental wage pattern. That is,

$$w_{b_0}(t_0) = (1 + \dot{w}_p) * w_{b_0}(t_{-1}) \tag{8.27}$$

where $\dot{w}_p$ is the national incremental wage pattern and $w_{b_0}(t_{-1})$ is the basic wage rate, in the preceding year, within the automobile-steel group of heavy industries. This, in turn, means that, any change in the wage structure of U.S. industry aside, the growth of the nominal wage rate throughout the enterprise sector, $\dot{w}$, depends on the national incremental wage pattern, $\dot{w}_p$. That is,

$$\dot{w} = f(\dot{w}_p), \; \bar{\mathbf{W}}_\Delta \tag{8.28}$$

Yet to be explained is what determines the value of $\dot{w}_p$ and whether this variable alone is sufficient to explain the growth of the nominal wage rate within the enterprise sector, once the set of wage differentials represented by the $\mathbf{W}_\Delta$ matrix is known or otherwise can be taken as a given.

8.3.4 The wage pattern

The present system for determining the national incremental wage pattern, based on the agreement reached in the bellwether industry, was established in the United States only after industrial trade unions succeeded in gaining collective bargaining rights in the automobile and steel industries in the late 1930s and early 1940s. This wage regime, as it can be termed, is therefore a historically specific one. Before 1935, a different wage regime prevailed, one characterized mostly by the absence of any upward pressure on nominal wage rates—just as, in the period since 1980, a new wage regime may have emerged, reflecting the relative decline of U.S. heavy industry within the world economy (see chapter 11, section 0.0, for a further discussion of this point). In the analysis which follows, we will continue to assume a wage regime based on pattern bargaining, with the pattern itself being the one which is set in the bellwether industry. Even if it should turn out that some other industry besides a member of the auto-steel group of heavy industries now sets the pattern, this will not significantly alter the argument—as long as the basic wage rate within each of the several wage contours is keyed, in the long period if not in the short, to the norm which has thereby been established. It would still be necessary to explain what determines the value of $\dot{w}_p$. Only if the system of pattern bargaining were to be replaced by some other mechanism for deriving the wage norm would the argument need to be recast.

It is not a matter of indifference to the rest of the society what wage norm is established through the collective bargaining agreement reached in the bellwether industry. A higher rate of compensation for workers, holding prices constant, will affect the rate of savings within the enterprise sector and thus the amount of investment can readily be financed, while the same increase in the rate of compensation for workers, holding the markup constant, will force a rise in the price level. Because of these possible consequences, the inflationary one in particular, the U.S. government began at an early date to try to influence the outcome of the collective bargaining process by which the national incremental wage pattern is established. Initially, the government's role was limited to presidential intervention after the contract talks in the bellwether industry had become deadlocked and the companies involved refused to accede to higher wages without the tacit approval of the nation's chief executive. Later the intervention became more systematic as the United States experimented with presidential guideposts, guidelines and even a pay board. Whatever the manner of intervention, the effect was to make the national incremental wage pattern, $\dot{w}_p$, depend at least in part on the government's "incomes" policy—that is, the judgment, either by the president himself or by a group working under him, as to what rate of increase in the basic wage rate would best enable the government to achieve its economic goals. This means that it is necessary to introduce into the analysis, as one of the factors determining the national incremental wage pattern, a policy variable, X_i, representing the government's official "incomes" policy. That is,

$$\dot{w}_p = f(X_i) \qquad (8.29)$$

where X_i is a certain rate of increase in the nominal wage rate, $\dot{w}$.

One needs to distinguish the means relied upon to obtain compliance with the government's incomes policy from the value of X_i itself. Much of the debate over incomes policy, aside from whether one is necessary or desirable, has centered on what means should be used to ensure compliance. The U.S. government, as exhibit 8.4 brings out, has alternated between compulsory controls and voluntary guidelines, with neither approach able to gain more than temporary political acceptance. While other means of ensuring compliance have been suggested, such as various tax incentives and/or penalties, these other approaches have yet to be put to a practical test by the United States. The government, in opting for an official incomes policy, would, of course, like to be able to unilaterally determine the value of $\dot{w}_p$. And at times it has even succeeded in bringing $\dot{w}_p$ closely into line with X_i. Still, because of opposition from the trade unions, the government has at other times found itself unable to limit the size of the contract settlement in the bellwether industry, with the measure of its failure being the observable discrepancy between X_i and $\dot{w}_p$. This is why the government's incomes policy, X_i, needs to be distinguished from the national incremental wage pattern, $\dot{w}_p$. Even if the government has not been able to unilaterally determine the value of $\dot{w}_p$, it has nonetheless been able to exert considerable influence on the rate of growth of the nominal wage rate through its incomes policy. This, in turn, is what makes the national incremental wage pattern, $\dot{w}_p$, a sociopolitically rather than just a sociologically determined variable.

To say that the wage pattern is sociopolitically determined does not mean the

Exhibit 8.4

Types of Incomes Policies 1940–1982

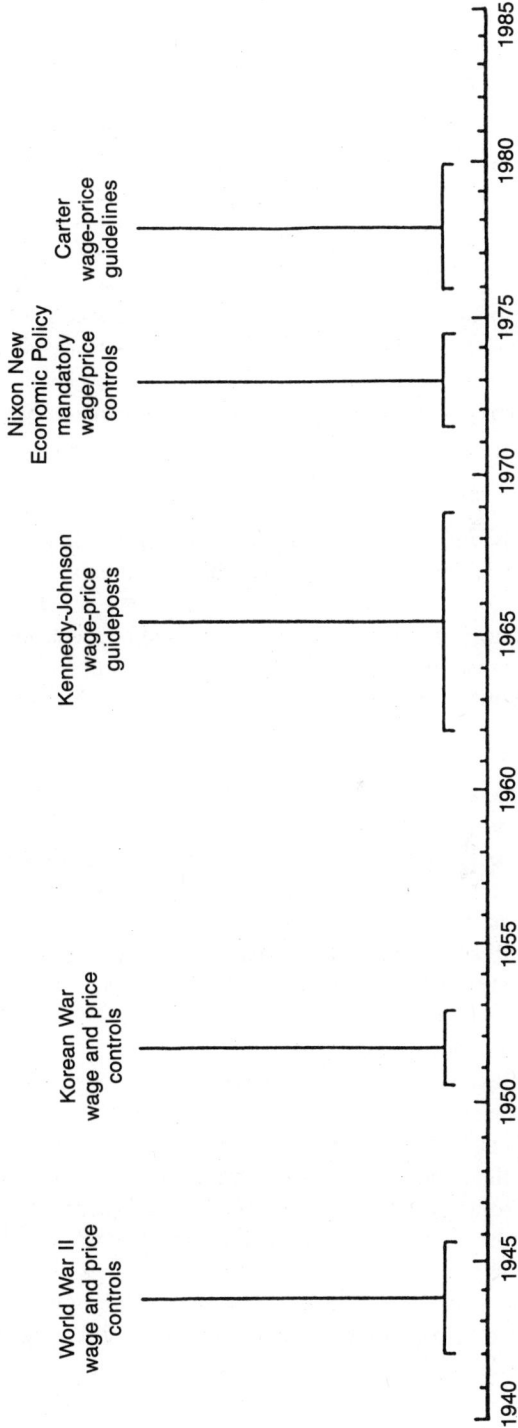

pattern is unaffected by economic factors. Given the philosophy of the trade union movement, and especially of the historically more militant leadership in the bellwether industries (this militancy being one of the factors determining which industry will be the bellwether one), the wage pattern can be correlated with certain broad economic trends. The trade union in the bellwether industry, in setting out its collective bargaining demands, can be assumed to be guided by the same two objectives as any other trade union: one, to protect its members against any loss of real income (due to rising prices for the goods the workers consume), and two, to protect its members against any loss of relative income (due to a disproportionate rise in profits). It is for this reason that the wage pattern, $\dot{w}_p$, can be correlated with the growth of the consumer price index and the growth of corporate profits—the growth of consumer prices serving as the floor under and the growth of profits as the ceiling on what trade unions are willing to accept as a "fair and equitable" wage. The inflationary implications of these goals which the trade union leadership has historically carried with it into contract negotiations, especially when the economy is expanding along anything but a steady-state growth path, will be brought out below in chapter 14. The point here is simply to make clear what are the broad goals and what are the economic variables which reflect the success of the trade union movement is achieving those goals.

One additional economic variable needs to be mentioned—if only because of the stress typically placed on that factor by economists when they attempt to explain the rate of inflation. This additional economic variable is the unemployment rate, Un. While there are a number of ways to interpret the supposed empirical finding that the rate of inflation, $\dot{P}$, is inversely correlated with the unemployment rate, one of the more plausible of these interpretations is that aggregate demand conditions, if not a factor determining the basic wage rate within the bellwether industry between contract settlements, may nonetheless influence the outcome of the negotiations by which the national incremental wage pattern is established. We shall not examine this argument any further at this point. It will be taken up later as part of a systematic discussion of the Phillips curve (see chapter 14, section 0.0). For now it is sufficient simply to indicate that the unemployment rate, Un, is another of the economic variables which may possibly influence the wage pattern, $\dot{w}_p$.

The influence of these variables does not mean that the wage pattern is uniquely determined by economic factors. At most, they will determine only the range within which $\dot{w}_p$ can be expected to fall. The actual value of $\dot{w}_p$ will instead depend on the sociological and political factors that shape the contract settlement in the bellwether industry. Indeed, from a strictly economic point of view (that is, in terms of how a monetarized production system works), there is no reason why $\dot{w}_p$ cannot take any value (ignoring, until chapter 12, the question of whether the central bank is willing to be fully accommodating). Of course, to the extent that the growth of money wages, as determined by $\dot{w}_p$, exceeds the growth of real wages, as determined by the factors identified in the preceding part of this chapter, the price level will have to rise to bring the two back into balance with one another. But that is no real constraint on $\dot{w}_p$ as the experience of the OECD countries since the end of World War II clearly demonstrates. To say that the wage pattern, and thus the basic wage rate, is sociopolitically determined, then, is to argue that it is a variable which is exogenous to the economic system, that it enters the economy, like other rules and/or social values, as an output of the political and/or other social systems. Indeed, this is what creates the possibility of supplementing the government's more conventional fiscal and monetary policies with a separate incomes policy as a more effective means of controlling the rate of inflation.

What still remains to be explained is what determines the growth, also in nominal terms, of the other components of household income. Putting aside for the moment a discussion of transfer payments (see chapter 10, section 3.4), this leaves only the growth of property income to be explained. Since any proprietors' income is but an amalgam of the labor income received by owner-entrepreneurs and the residual income of the firms they direct, it is primarily the growth of dividends which needs to be explained in order to account for all the remaining portion of the household sector's disposable income. As will become clear from the discussion which follows, the growth of dividends also depends on the national incremental wage pattern, $\dot{w}_p$—and thus the nominal income of rentiers, like the nominal income of workers, is sociopolitically determined.

8.3.5 The growth of dividends

If the company it heads is to expand at the highest possible rate, the megacorp's executive group must limit the growth of dividends to what is minimally necessary in order to avoid being deposed through a take-over bid or some other threat to its control. This, of course, assumes that megacorps pursue a "growth maximizing" strategy (see chapter 6, section 2.1). The alternative view is that firms are "equity-maximizers." This means that every increase in profits, cyclical fluctuations aside, goes to ensure the highest possible rate of growth of dividends in the long period. Through the normal functioning of the stock market, a strategy which maximizes the growth of dividends over time will also maximize the present value of the equity shares held in that firm. Hence, firms which maximize the long-period growth of profits, along with the amount of dividends paid out from those profits, will be "equity maximizers."

Whether firms are growth or equity maximizers therefore depends on how rapidly the dividend rate is being increased. If dividends are growing only at the minimum rate necessary to forestall a take-over bid or similar threat to the executive group's continued control, with $\overset{\circ}{D}iv_i$ less than the firm's growth rate as measured by the rate of increase in cash flow, or discretionary funds, then the firm must be considered a growth maximizer. Alternatively, with $\overset{\circ}{D}iv_i$ equal to g, the firm must be considered an equity maximizer. The question, then, is whether the rate at which a megacorp must increase its dividend payments in order to forestall the threat of a take-over bid will be less than the rate at which the firm is able to increase its cash flow, or discretionary funds.

A megacorp runs little risk of inviting a take-over bid as long as it succeeds in increasing its dividend payments over time at the same rate as other similarly large firms. This is because take-over bids or equivalent attacks on the incumbent management are usually organized by outsiders in the hope of financial gain, and that gain will not be realized unless the dividend rate and/or the price of the stock can subsequently be increased. When a company is already increasing dividends at the same rate as other firms, especially those within the same group of industries, there is little reason to believe that a new executive group will be able to do better, and thus there is little reason for the stockholders to support a take-over bid. This is especially true if the company's costs of production are no higher, and thus its profit margin, μ_i, no lower, than the other firms that constitute the relevant reference group. Indeed, the stockholders are likely to be convinced by the incumbent management that the bid is only a "raid," with the outside group planning to sell out once the price of the stock has been artificially jacked up, thereby leaving the stockholders with a financially gutted company. The incumbent management runs even less risk of a take-over bid the greater the value of its outstanding shares. This is because the larger the company, the greater the financial resources required by an outside group to mount a successful take-over bid. Due to this last consideration, the largest megacorps are virtually invulnerable to a take-over bid or any other type of attack by an outside group—as long as the executive group is able to keep the rate of growth of dividends, $\overset{\circ}{D}iv_i$, along with the profit margin, μ_i, up to par.

What has been pointed out so far is merely that the rate at which megacorps are increasing their dividends will tend to converge around a group norm. That this single rate of growth of dividends will not be the one that maximizes the value of equity shares still remains to be demonstrated. Indeed, the determinants of that single rate of growth of dividends have yet to be identified. Nonetheless, by pointing out that an executive group has little to fear as long as it maintains the same rate of growth of dividends as other megacorps, the first step in showing that firms within the oligopolistic sector are growth maximizers rather than equity maximizers has been taken. For if the executive group is in little danger of losing control as long as it achieves a certain minimal rate of growth of dividends, what incentive does it have to increase the dividend rate any further—especially if the higher rate of pay-out will be at the expense of the firm's own rate of expansion? In posing the question this way, one can even begin to see what are the determinants of the single rate of growth of dividends likely to prevail throughout the oligopolistic sector.

The fact is that, as already noted (see section 8.2.1), it is the executive group which determines the dividend rate, just as it is the executive group which has the final say as to what will be the rates or compensation received by the various members of the work force, including even those represented by a trade union. In making these and other interrelated decisions, the executive group is forced by its very position to view itself as the arbiter of competing claims on the revenue being generated by the company from the sale of its output. Dividends are but one claim on those revenues, originating from but one constituency—that of the stock, or equity debt, holders. Against that claim must be balanced the claims of other constituencies, particularly that of the work force (including the managers) for higher wages and that of the organization itself for the funds to finance expansion. In having to apportion the firm's revenues, especially any increment, among these several constituencies, each with their competing claims, the executive group is likely to be guided both by sentiment and by fear.

Insofar as the sentiment of the executive group is concerned, the equity debt holders have two things going for them. One is the anachronistic but nonetheless prevailing belief reflected in the law that the members of the executive group are fiduciary agents obligated to manage the firm solely in the best interests of the stockholders. Buttressing this legal myth is the close social affinity of the executive group for the stockholders. Members of the executive group are likely to be stockholders themselves—though not necessarily in the company whose fortunes they direct. It is a paradoxical consequence of the stock option plans which have been devised as part of the incentive/benefits package for top-level employees that, in order to derive the maximum financial gain, corporate executives must eventually sell the shares acquired at reduced prices under the plans. Together with the need to diversify portfolios, the way the stock option plans work may result in corporate executives owning little or no stock in their own companies. Still, the members of the executive group are likely to belong to that relatively small percentage of the population with significant equity holdings—even if the holdings are likely to be, not as yet, sufficient to enable them to maintain their present standard of living without working and thus to join the rentier class. As equity debt holders themselves, the members of the executive group can well empathize with the desire of the stockholders for higher dividends. This is a major determining factor since, once the possibility of a take-over bid can be discounted, there is little the executive group need fear in retaliation by the stockholders.

Of course, the members of the executive group can also empathize with the desire of the workers for higher wages and salaries (especially the latter). They are, after all, workers themselves with the largest part of their income still coming from wages (actually salaries). As the wages of other workers rise, so do their own salaries. Admittedly, the empathy is not likely to extend much below the ranks of managers and other white-collar employees. Offsetting this diminished empathy, however, is the power of the trade union which negotiates on behalf of the blue-collar workers (or which will gain a foothold in the company if the wages obtained by those workers do not match those received by workers in other companies). If the executive group, acting on behalf of the enterprise itself, is not able to reach agreement with the trade union, it runs the risk of having all its production brought to a halt should a significant portion of the work force walk off the job in a contract dispute. It is this threat which more than makes up for the lack of empathy which the executive group may have for the blue-collar and other production workers.

Thus, opposed to the sentiment which may argue strongly in favor of higher dividends for the stockholders is the reality of the demands being put forward on behalf of the workers by trade unions. To the extent that higher dividends are likely to become grounds for higher wage demands, the conflict between the interests of the megacorp's two most powerful constituencies will be all the sharper. In addition, of course, there is the interest of the firm itself in having more funds for its own internal expansion. It is the executive group which, having the ultimate responsibility (and also the only overall perspective), must somehow resolve these several conflicting interests (along with other claims on the megacorp's revenues). In explaining how the conflict is actually resolved, one must distinguish—as was done earlier in the discussion of the wage pattern—between what has happened historically and what is economically necessary.

Historically what has happened, at least in the United States, is that corporate managements have given first priority to generating the funds needed to finance their companies' own internal expansion. This is the argument to be found in the earlier discussion of the markup (see chapter 6, section 2.1) where it was pointed out that any other strategy would, in a highly competitive environment, jeopardize those firms' chances of survival. In other words, megacorps have been growth maximizers. Nonetheless, confronted by the power of trade unions to bargain collectively on behalf of the blue-collar workers and other employees, megacorps have been forced to accede to higher money wages—whether the increases were consistent with the growth of output per worker or not. (The inflationary inplications of this historical outcome will be brought out in chapter 14.) Because of the legal myth that the members of the executive group are simply the fiduciary agents of the stockholders and because of the close social affinity which exists between the two groups in any case, megacorps as a whole have good reason to treat their equity debt holders at least as well as their workers insofar as rates of compensation are concerned. Any other course would have left the corporate executives open to the charge that they were subordinating the welfare of the stockholders to that of the workers. Megacorps have therefore been inclined to maintain a rate of growth of dividends which is at least equal to the growth of money wages even if, reflecting the companies' first priority, the rate is less than that at which the firms themselves are expanding. Thus the extent to which firms are growth rather than equity maximizers can be determined by how closely the growth of dividends over time, $\overset{\circ}{D}iv_i$, approximates the growth of money wages, $\overset{\cdot}{w}$, rather than the growth of cash flow or discretionary funds, $\overset{\circ}{F}$.

This historical explanation for the growth of dividends, it should be noted, has little to do with economic necessity. Dividends can grow at any rate, including zero, without affecting the ability of the system to reproduce itself and expand. Insofar as dividends are an important source of household income, their reduction or even elimination would, of course, slow down the rate of consumer spending. This effect, however, can readily be offset by a higher rate of growth of wages. On the other hand, insofar as dividends are a necessary incentive if additional equity funding is to be obtained, their reduction or elimination would dry up that source of external financing. The shortfall in funds, however, could readily be met from additional internal funds or even through the sale of new fixed-interest obligations. Far more significant is the likelihood that a reduction or elimination of dividends, if mandated by law, would effectively discourage the creation of new corporations or megacorps, depending on the type of enterprise to which the legal restrictions applied. For without the prospect of increased dividend payments in the future, there would not be the capital gains to provide the requisite incentive for the original owner-entrepreneurs who have organized a firm to go "public" and thus take the first step toward becoming a megacorp. While individuals might nonetheless continue to found megacorps so that new enterprises of that sort would still emerge, the fact remains that it is not possible for an economic system like that of the United States to reproduce itself and expand with only the existing set of megacorps constituting the population of firms within the oligopolistic sector. The rate of innovation, and thus the long-period rate of expansion, might well be adversely affected. Still, this is quite different from arguing that the economic system would collapse, or even be unable to function as effectively, if dividends were reduced or eliminated altogether.

No, the main effect of holding the rate of growth of dividends to zero, or even reducing them below the rate of growth of wages, would be sociopolitical. Even if the restriction were applied to all megacorps across-the-board so that no executive group's continued control was placed in jeopardy, there would still be the almost certain political reaction of rentier groups. Since to defend the restriction on dividends would require raising questions about the nature of corporate control and accountability which many members of society, even aside from corporate stockholders, would prefer to ignore, the support rentiers could expect to receive is likely to be far greater than their relatively small numbers would suggest. One should not underestimate the convincing power of myths—such as the belief that megacorps are no different from other types of enterprises in the function they serve and that, moreover, they are managed only in the best interests of stockholders—when the myths serve a vital legitimization need for the group exercising the key decision-making power for the society as a whole. This is why it can be said that the rate of growth of dividends, like the rate of growth of money wages, is sociopolitically determined. Indeed, one can even go further and say that in the present sociopolitical context, it is the rate of growth of money wages, $\dot{w}_p$, which explains historically the secular of growth of dividends within the oligopolistic, or corporate, sector.

The short-period, or cyclical, growth of dividends will simply reflect the impact of certain transitory factors on the ability of megacorps to achieve the desired secular growth of dividends. Two of these transitory factors are especially important for the group of megacorps as a whole. One is any cyclical downturn in the economy which, as already pointed out (see chapter 7, section 3.1), can be expected to cause a disproportionate decline in corporate cash flow. This may make it necessary for the megacorp to freeze the dividend rate, if not actually to reduce it. The other important transitory factor is any need in the near future to float a new stock issue. With that prospect, assuming the new issue is intended to enable the megacorp to take advantage of an unusual expansion opportunity rather than cover unanticipated losses, the megacorp can lower its costs of borrowing funds externaly, i, by temporarily pushing the dividend rate above the growth trend, thereby hopefully boosting the price of its stock in the market and reducing its price-dividend ratio (see chapter 7, section 3.2).

With the rate of growth of dividends, both secularly and cyclically, thus explained, the only significant type of property income still to be discussed is the net interest payment received by households. Since the change over time in this component of household income depends, among other factors, on monetary policy, nothing further will be said about it until chapter 12 when the question of what determines the level of interest rates will be taken up systematically. For the moment, it will suffice to assume that the return on any fixed-interest obligations held by households, i, is exogenously determined as part of a monetary policy-making process. The discussion of the nominal income received by the household sector can therefore be limited, at least as a first approximation, to the discussion already completed of what determines the growth of the nominal wage rate, $\dot{w}$, and the closely related growth of dividends, $\mathring{D}iv$.

The arguments presented so far represent only one of the approaches favored by economists for explaining the distribution of income. (It actually represents a fusion or synthesis of two separate approaches, the arguments favored by post-Keynesian economists for explaining the growth in real income and the arguments favored by institutionalist economists for explaining the growth of nominal income.) There are, it should be noted, alternative ways of explaining the distribution of income which can be found in economics textbooks. We shall now turn to those alternatives theories of income distribution.

8.4 Alternative Theories of Income Distribution

Two major alternatives to the theories of income distribution presented so far have dominated the teaching of economics. One is the neoclassical theory of income distribution, based on the marginalist revolution which occurred in economics between 1890 and 1910. This is the theory which has gained the widest acceptance among economists outside the socialist bloc of nations and therefore serves as the orthodox theory in countries with advanced market economies. The key concept here is that of ''marginal productivity.'' The other major alternative is the Marxian theory which constitutes the orthodox approach in the Soviet Union and other Communist countries. The key concept here is that of ''the labor theory of value.'' These differing ways of explaining the distribution of income bring out most sharply what are the essential points in conflict among the three major paradigms in economics—neoclassical, Marxian and post-Keynesian. Since the division of the national income is the most fundamental of all social conflicts, the one in which all possible assistance, intellectual and otherwise, is likely to be sought, it is hardly surprising that the focus of the dispute among economists, and thus the key issue raised by the separate paradigms within which their work falls, should be the question of how income is, or ought to be, distributed.

In this section, each of the major alternatives to the post-Keynesian (and institutionalist) theory of income distribution just presented will be taken up in turn, beginning with the Marxian theory. First, however, it is necessary to acknowledge that a Marxian perspective encompasses more than just the question of income distribution, that it represents a broader philosophical system touching on all the various dimensions of society. It is this broader philosophical system which must be confronted in arguing that, to develop a suitable general framework for societal analysis, one must go beyond the ideas advanced by Marx more than a century ago.

8.4.1 Beyond Marx

There is no denying Marx's indispensable contribution to the development of the social sciences in the 19th century, just as there is no denying Keynes's important contribution to economics in the 20th century. On at least four fundamental points, Marx's scholarly work amounted to a devastating critique of the theories which dominated the nascent social sciences of his day, economics among them. The four points are: (1) the nature of social dynamics; (2) the key to social change; (3) the degree of harmony in the social order; and (4) the basis for determining social value. It is because the social sciences, at least in the non-Marxist academies of the West, have yet to effectively meet this critique of Marx that his work continues to be a source of inspiration to succeeding generations of younger scholars disaffected from the orthodox traditions within their disciplines.

At the same time, however, it would be a mistake to assume that Marx was able to completely resolve the very points he had raised. At most, he merely showed how the same issues might better be addressed. It has been the social scientists who have come after Marx, absorbing what was valid in his overall theoretical system without becoming the prisoners of any particular idea, who have finally made it possible to transcend the Marxist critique. These later scholars, many of whom would disclaim being Marxists just as they would disassociate themselves from the mainstream of the various academic disciplines, have now laid the foundation for the cumulative development of the social sciences, economics among them, as scientific endeavors. Still, since the work of these later scholars so clearly builds on Marx's ideas, it can be labeled "post-Marxian." The post-Keynesian theory being presented in this text is but one example. In outlining this body of post-Marxian social theory, it is necessary to indicate where it diverges from Marx's approach, even to the point where, on certain issues, it requires an explicit rejection of Marx's own theoretical formulation.

With regard to the nature of social dynamics, Marx was the first scholar to call into question the mechanistic view of society which dominated 19th century social thought. As an early Hegelian, trained in the dialectical method, he immediately grasped the advantage of thinking in terms of thesis, antithesis and emergent new synthesis when trying to understand social phenomena rather than in terms of simple cause-and-effect relationships. Marx's important contribution was to extend the notion of a dialectical process, originally put forward to explain the development of ideas, to the material base and other facets of social reality, thereby creating a new philosophical system based on the principle of dialectical materialism. Until relatively recently, it was the only alternative to the static, mechanistic view of society which the more orthodox academic disciplines reflected.

With the development over the past several decades of systems theory, and especially the principles of cybernetics, it is now possible to put Marx's contribution in better perspective. For the dialectical process is but a special case of the more general cybernetic processes which govern social institutions (see chapter 1, part 2). Marx was mistaken in identifying the dialectic as the characteristic cybernetic process for the other dimensions of society besides the normative one, but he was not wrong to perceive the need to posit some type of cybernetic, and thus dynamic, process for those other dimensions. Moreover, given the importance of values in determining how the other dimensions of society function, Marx was not wholly wrong to emphasize the importance of the dialectic. Still, by falling back on a more general systems approach, it is possible to go beyond Marx in developing a dynamic framework for analyzing social phenomena. Indeed, even the emergence of new social institutions can be better understood in terms of what is technically referred to, within the cybernetics literature, as "positive" feedback rather than in terms of thesis, antithesis and synthesis. Thus it is the new cybernetic viewpoint which now enables social scientists to better specify than even Marx himself could the nature of social dynamics.

As for the key to social change, it was again Marx who seemed the first to offer a reasonable explanation. Once he had the inspiration to turn the Hegelian philosophy on its head, making the material base of society the wellspring of ideas rather than the reverse, Marx had in fact isolated what he considered to be the crucial factor. This was the tension between the "forces of production" found within the material base and the "social relations" that grow up around that base.

Although Marx did not have such a model available to him, the "forces of production" can be identified with the **A** (as well as the **L** and **K**) matrix within a Leontief system of production while the "social relations" would be the institutional forms within which that set of production techniques is being exploited. Whatever the precise delineation of the two, however, they are clearly located by Marx within the material base of society, with one mode of production, such as that represented historically by feudalism, eventually giving way to another through the dialectical process. It was this analytic framework which enabled Marx to put forward his materialistic interpretation of history.

What may be objected to in Marx's argument is not the posited tension between the "forces of production" and the existing "social relations." Almost every serious student of recent history has found that technology seems to evolve at a pace with which social institutions, given their conservative character, find it difficult to remain in harmony and that this tension often produces the seeds of social change. Indeed, the point is basic to the whole notion of "positive feedback" in which an existing system must reorganize its internal structure to cope with what would otherwise be unmanageable feedback. Nor is it objectionable to rely on the concept of a material base which is represented historically by a particular mode of production. The industrial revolution, if not the preceding commercialization of economic activity, clearly marked the emergence of a different "mode of production" within Western Europe, one that would in time radically transform the other aspects of those societies. What goes against the grain is the insistence by Marx and some of his followers that the tension producing social change always originates within the material base—or what has herein been defined as the economic dimension of society. It is this primary emphasis on economic, or even technological, factors which seems arbitrary and subjective.

Max Weber, in laying the foundations for modern sociology, was one of the first to take issue with Marx on this point. Without putting all the emphasis on the normative dimension, as the Hegelians were wont to do, he nonetheless pointed out, in the part of his larger study of world religions that would be published as *The Protestant Ethic and the Spirit of Capitalism*, that ideas might be no less critical than objective economic circumstances. Sigmund Freud later criticized Marx similarly, arguing in *Civilization and Its Discontents* that history is governed as much by the basic instinctive drives of humans as by material factors. He was thus the first to place at least equal weight on what has herein been defined as the anthropogenic factor. The orthodox historians, or course, have generally focused on the decisions made by ruling elites. They have therefore argued, at least implicitly, for the importance of political factors. Those who nonetheless continue holding to a materialistic interpretation of history might respond that Weber and the mainstream historians, if not also Freud, are simply fixated on the superstructure of social institutions, ignoring the more crucial role played by the material base upon which that superstructure is erected. It has yet to be demonstrated, however, that the Marxian framework, in which the economic system is dominant, is superior to the alternative presented in part 2 of chapter 1) in which four separate dimensions are delineated—each with its own separate dynamic but with no one of those dimensions necessarily dominant over the others. At the very least, the question of which dimension of society, if any, is the key to social change remains an open one in the social sciences.

Insofar as the degree of social harmony is concerned, it was once again Marx who was the principal dissenter from the 19th century view of things. It was not just that Marx made class conflict the center of his analysis. The French socialists from whom Marx drew some of his important ideas had already emphasized the same factor, and many non-Marxist theories even today fully recognize its importance. Indeed, the preceding analysis of income distribution has highlighted the inherent conflict not just between workers and nonworkers but also between different classes of workers. What was far more novel in Marx's theories was the rejection of the view that, despite the competing interests, personal as well as class, there was a natural order which ensured a felicitous result. In contrast to Adam Smith and his followers who believed that the invisible hand of the market led to continuous growth and expansion of the economy, Marx and those who would subsequently draw their inspiration from him believed that a "capitalist," or market, economy led invariably to periodic crises. Malthus's feeble protests aside, Marx was the first major economist to dispute the notion embodied in Say's law that the economic and social system, if left alone, would remain viable. He was thus the most important anticipator of the Keynesian revolution in economics. Indeed, it was from Marx, as filtered through Rosa Luxemburg and Mikhail Tugan-Baranowsky, that Kalecki derived his own separate version of Keynes's model.

The point nonetheless is that it is not from Marx directly that we can understand the macrodynamic behavior of an economic system. That is why this is a post-Keynesian rather than just a post-Marxian text. In attempting to explain why a "capitalist" system is subject to periodic crises, Marx offered several hypotheses, not all developed to the same extent. One idea was that workers, since they received in wages less than the value they produced through their labor, would be unable to command with their income all that the economic system was capable of producing. This was what subsequent interpreters of Marx termed the "realization" problem, and it was the least systematically developed of the several ideas to be found in Marx's works about the causes of economic instability. Indeed, it was not until Luxemburg and others among the "underconsumptionist" school of Marxists further developed and refined the idea that it received significant attention. Even as further refined, however, the "underconsumptionist" view was not able to win wide support among Marxists, let alone among economists generally, until it was finally buttressed by the principle of effective demand. This text, in fact, represents the post-Marxian development of the original Marxian notion of a "realization" problem.

Among the more orthodox of Marx's followers, the emphasis has usually been put on the other explanations for the periodic crises that occur in an advanced market economy. There are two of these other explanations, and both assume that it is the "falling rate of profit" which induces the owners of the means of production to cut back on investment, thereby precipitating the crisis. In the first of these two alternative lines of argument, the falling rate of profit is attributed to the "changing organic composition of capital" and, in the other, to the nature of the recurring class struggle. While the notion that a change in the rate of investment, or accumulation, may account for the cyclical instability of the economy is hardly incompatible with the post-Keynesian theory that has been presented so far, what Marxists mean by a "falling rate of profit," especially as it relates to the "changing organic composition of capital," is. To bring out this essential point of difference between Marxian and post-Keynesian theory, it is necessary to turn to the fourth of the major points on which Marx challenged the prevailing social thought of his day. This is the basis for determining social value. While agreeing with the other classical economists that labor was the source of all value, he nonetheless succeeded in turning the classical analysis on its head, just as he had to Hegelian philosophy, thereby forcing the defenders of contemporary capitalism to seek intellectual refuge in the neoclassical theory. To see just what are the issues here, we must examine in some detail the labor theory of value which underlies an orthodox Marxian approach.

8.4.2 The labor theory of value

To the English classical economists, beginning with Adam Smith, it was only natural to assume that the labor put into a commodity was the source of that commodity's value. The earlier Lockean theory of government, with its view of the state as the defender of the labor embodied in private property, had the same intellectual roots in a society becoming increasingly dominated, in its everyday activities, by the norms of the industrious lower middle classes. That commodities would exchange in rough proportion to the labor required to produce them was an assumption which the English classical economists hardly even thought to question. First of all, there was less reason to challenge the assumption in a preindustrial society, before the adoption of modern, capital-intensive techniques made the direct labor coefficients vary significantly from one industry to another. Secondly, until Marx made it basic to his arguments, the labor theory of value was not held to that rigidly by any of the classical economists. Ricardo, for example, has been correctly described as having a "93 percent" labor theory of value. Indeed, this "loose" version of the labor theory of value underlies the vertically integrated model of production on which the earlier discussion of technical progress was based (see chapter 5, part 4). What Marx did was to develop a "tight" version of the same argument which then enabled him to use the labor theory of value in carrying out his politically powerful critique of a capitalist society.

Marx pointed out that capitalism, as the mode of production which succeeded feudalism, had made labor a commodity. Thus, to analyze a capitalist society, it was necessary to apply the labor theory of value to labor itself. This meant that the value of labor—what labor could command in the markets of a capitalist system— was only the value of the labor required to produce the commodities needed to maintain human life. In other words, it was equal only to the subsistence wage that, by and large, prevailed in the labor markets of Marx's time. But if this were true, then there might well be a discrepancy between the value of what labor can produce—what Marx referred to as the value of laboring power—and the value of the labor itself. This would be the difference between the price of a commodity and the subsistence wages of the workers employed in producing the commodity. Indeed, Marx argued, it was in the nature of a capitalist system, since the means of production are owned by a separate class besides the workers, to have such a discrepancy between the value of laboring power and the value of labor itself. This additional value that is created under a capitalist mode of production he termed "surplus value," s. Thus the value of a commodity, as represented by its price, p, can be broken down into the following components:

$$p = c + v + s \qquad (8.30)$$

where c is the value of the labor, measured by the subsistence wage, embodied in the means of production (what Marx referred to as "constant capital"); v is the value of the labor, again measured by the subsistence wage, used directly in the production of the commodity (what Marx, assuming that the wages would have to be advanced by the capitalist out of his own funds, referred to as "variable capital), and s is the surplus value created.

As it stands, the pricing formula (actually accounting identity) given by equation 8.30 is not necessarily incompatible with those developed above in chapter 6. The "constant capital," c, can be equated with the fixed costs of production arising from the purchase of plant and equipment while the "variable capital," v, can be equated with the direct or variable costs of production, the two together representing the total costs of production, c_j, in a given industry (see equation 6.1). The surplus value, s, meanwhile, can be equated with the size of the residual per unit of output, π_j, in that same industry. Indeed, Marxist writers are increasingly relying on the Sraffian or, as they often refer to it, the "neo-Ricardian" model of long-period prices given in chapter 6 to express their ideas. The point of difference between even these more sophisticated exponents of Marxian theory and other economists is the use of, and the interpretation given to, the different components of equation 8.30.

Some Marxists assert that not only is labor the source of all value but that, moreover, only the "live" labor employed directly in the production of commodities is capable of creating value. They therefore argue that the amount of surplus value, s, depends solely on the amount of variable capital, v, and not at all on the amount of constant capital, c. At the same time, they deny that the capitalist class, the group of self-employed businessmen no less than any rentiers, plays any essential role in creating value. As the owners of the means of production, and thus in a strategic position to exercise control over the system, the capitalists merely take for themselves the surplus value created by labor. Following this line of reasoning, one can define the ratio s/v as "the rate of exploitation" under a capitalist system of production. It is this rate at which the surplus value created by labor is expropriated by the "capitalists." It should be noted that this rate of exploitation, once defined, plays no further role in the Marxist analysis of a "capitalist" system. It serves only to indicate the extent to which those considered responsible for creating value are shortchanged under the system, and thus it can be used as a political rallying cry or as a basis for otherwise decrying how the system works. The use made of the other ratios derived from the same set of Marxian categories and based upon the same underlying assumptions is different. These ratios—the organic composition of capital and the (value) rate of profit— are relied upon to explain why a capitalist system is prone to periodic crises.

The organic composition of capital is the ratio of constant capital, c, to the total capital (actually total value of inputs) used in the production process, $c + v$. It is similar, though not exactly identical, to what in neoclassical theory is referred to as the "capital intensity" of production and in post-Keynesian theory as the "degree of mechanization." By itself, this ratio implies very little. But combined with the assumption that only "live" labor is capable of creating value, including any surplus value, s, it suggests a second reason, aside from the "realization" problem, why the process of capital accumulation, and thus the expansion of the economic system, may come to an abrupt halt. For it is an established historical fact that the "organic composition of capital" had been rising steadily over time. Orthodox economists and post-Keynesians alike would acknowlege that, in the words of the former, the capital intensity of production or, in the words of the latter, the degree of mechanization has been increasing. The rising organic composition of capital, however, means that v (using the Marxian categories) has been declining relative to c, and thus that production involves proportionately fewer direct labor inputs. If only "live" labor is capable of creating any value, this, in turn, implies that less surplus value, s, is being created for expropriation by the capital class through the control it exercises over the means of production. With the rate of profit defined as the ratio of s to $c + v$, it also implies a "falling rate of profit." Since it can be assumed that the capitalist class will allow the accumulation process to continue only if the rate of profit is sufficiently high, a falling rate of profit will, beyond a certain point, lead to a cessation of investment and one of the crises which periodically wracks an economic system organized on "capitalist" principles.

It should be noted that a falling rate of profit, $s/(c + v)$, and thus the intermediate cause of a major secular shift in the level of economic activity, can be explained without having to base the argument on the "changing organic composition of capital.'' As evidence, consider the third explanation which is given by Marxist economists for the instability of a capitalist system. The falling rate of profit, it is said, is simply one of the possible outcomes of the class struggle inherent in such a system of production. With the representatives of labor opposing the efforts by the capitalist class to expropriate for itself all of the surplus value being created, the rate of profit may fall, forcing the capitalist class to cut back on the rate of investment. Indeed, in the modern era, with the emergence of a powerful trade union movement and other political supports for the working class, it is the class struggle—irrespective of any changing organic composition—which is considered by some Marxist writers to be the key to the instability of a capitalist, or advanced market, economy. According to this line of reasoning, the recurrent slumps which have been deliberately induced throughout the post World War II period are simply the response one would expect when governments are controlled by the capitalist class. The recessions, or even major depressions, are essential for weakening the bargaining power of labor and thereby restoring the rate of profit needed to lay the foundation for the next period of expansion. (In support of this thesis, Marxist writers simply quote the views expressed so frequently by businessmen and their supporters in the press.)

Still, while it is possible to account in other ways for the falling rate of profit which underlies the Marxian explanation for the instability of a capitalist system, it is an increase in the ''organic composition of capital'' which, as the operative factor, follows more directly from the tight version of the labor theory of value and the uniquely Marxian concepts based on that version. (The notion of a class struggle, as should be clear from the earlier sections of this chapter, is not inconsistent with other, post-Marxian theories of income distribution. The difference, as will be made more explicit in chapter 14 is that the ''class struggle'' as part of the larger conflict over relative income shares has more to do with the problem of persistent inflation than with that of periodic crises or slumps.) Thus it is the Marxian arguments about the changing organic composition of capital which are more pertinent to the discussion at this point. Indeed, a critique of that concept encompasses the essential points in dispute between Marxist and non-Marxist economists.

Whether the changing organic composition of capital—or the increasing capital intensity of production and the greater degree of mechanizaion for that matter—leads to a falling rate of profit, $s/(c + v)$, depends entirely on the assumption made by Marxist economists as to the source of value. Certain Marxists contend that only ''live'' labor can be the source of value, from which assumption it then logically follows that, with $v/(c + v)$ falling, the rate of profit as a Marxian category must also fall. The assumption that only ''live'' labor can be the source of value seems an arbitrary one, however. It implies that capital goods such as plant and equipment produce no ''surplus value'' of their own or, using more conventional terminology, account for none of the value added. A more sophisticated view, held by Marxists who accept the neo-Ricardian framework of Sraffa, is that both "live" and "dead" labor, the latter embodied in capital goods, are the sources of value. While this concession destroys the logical link between a changing organic composition of "capital" and a falling rate of profit, it does make it possible to retain, at least in a modified form, the labor theory of value—along with the corollary concept of a rate of exploitation. Still, the critical assumption is that labor, whether as a direct input into the production process or as indirectly embodied in the capital equipment, is the only source of value—call it surplus value or value added.

The arbitrary nature of this premise can be seen most clearly by comparing it with the alternative assumptions that can be made about the source of value. One of these alternatives is the assumption that underlies the neoclassical theory of income distribution. This is the assumption that not just labor, or even just labor and "capital" together, is the source of value but rather "n factors of production" are the source of value, with the relative contribution of each being equal to its "marginal product." As can now well be shown, the assumption which underlies this marginal productivity theory is no less arbitrary that that which underlies the tight version of the labor theory of value.

8.4.3 Marginal productivity theory

Once Marx succeeded in turning the labor theory of value on its head, making it integral to his critique of "capitalism," economists of a less radical stripe became increasingly uncomfortable with having to use that theory to explain the distribution of income. The need for a quite different approach was finally met by the marginalist revolution in economics that began in the 1870s, based on the work of Stanley Jevons in England, Carl Menger in Austria and Leon Walras in the French-speaking cantons of Switzerland. Still, the one who most systematically applied the principle of the calculus to derive an entirely new theory of income distribution was the American economist, John Bates Clark. It was Clark who first appreciated the importance of being able to say, as a counter to the Marxian argument, that "capital," like labor, received only the value of its marginal product. This idea was then given its most convincing exposition in Marshall's *Principles*.

As explained by later Marshallians, the individual owner-entrepreneur faces the choice of how much labor (variable inputs) to use in conjunction with his "capital" (fixed inputs). This choice will be governed, as the quantity of labor employed in the production process is varied, by the value of the marginal product of that input (what Marshall himself referred to as its "net product"). Underlying the choice facing the owner-entrepreneur is the sort of marginal physical productivity curve shown in exhibit 8.5. As the quantity of labor employed increases (measured along the horizontal axis), the output per worker, or average physical productivity, will rise (as shown on the vertical axis), first at an increasing rate and then at a decreasing rate, until it reaches a peak value—after which it will fall.

Exhibit 8.5

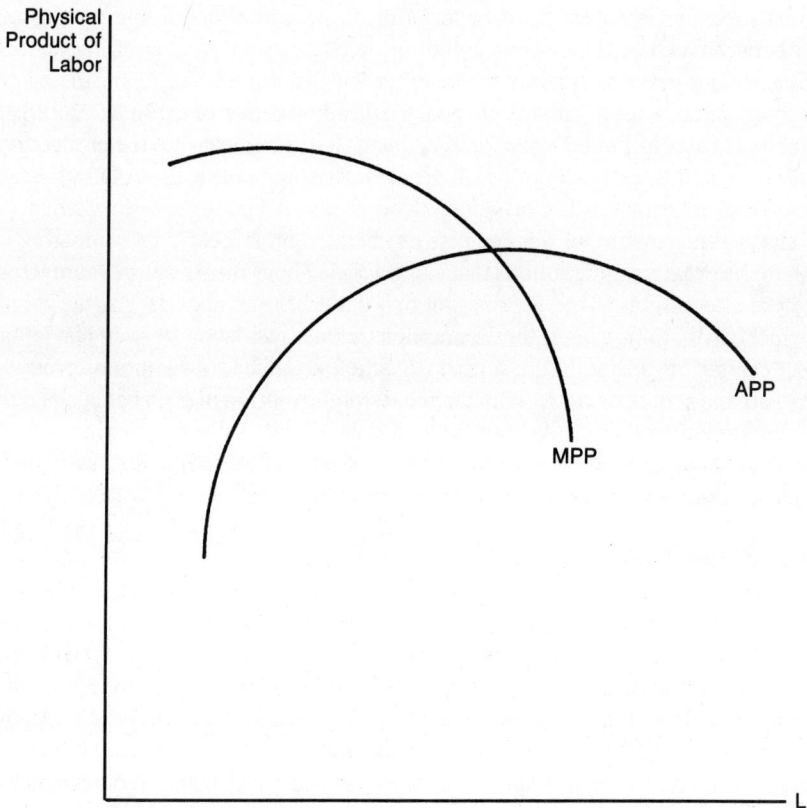

The explanation for this functional relationship is the same as that already given for the cost curves of a neoclassical proprietorship (see chapter 5, section 4.1). Indeed, the average cost curve is but an upside-down reflection of this average physical productivity curve (when labor is the only variable input). The explanation is that, with a variable input such as labor being used in conjunction with a fixed capital input, the law of variable returns holds. This means that only one quantity of the variable input labor, when used in conjunction with the fixed capital equipment, will be optimal; and that, as more or less than that amount is used, output per worker will rise or fall, depending on whether production is moving toward or away from the optimal level of output.

Given an average physical productivity (APP) curve based on the law of variable returns, such as the one shown in exhibit 8.5, a corresponding *marginal* physical product (MPP) curve can be derived using the calculus. This MPP curve indicates the change in total physical output as the quantity of labor employed varies. The output in physical terms shown in exhibit 8.5 can then be multiplied by the market price so as to determine how much is being produced in *value* terms. In this way—by in effect merely relabeling the vertical axis—the diagram shown in exhibit 8.5 can be transformed into the diagram shown in exhibit 8.6, indicating how the value of both the average physical product (VAPP) and the value of the marginal physical product (VMPP) vary as the quantity of labor employed varies. The argument which then follows is well known to anyone who has formally studied economics. A firm will employ labor only up to the point—but not beyond—where the value of the marginal physical product of labor is equal to the prevailing wage rate. The firm's demand curve for labor is therefore given by the VMPP curve shown in exhibit 8.6.

With the firm's demand curve for labor specified in this manner, a number of important conclusions then follow. One is that, given the negative slope of that curve over the relevant range (that is, where the VMPP curve is falling), the demand for labor will be inversely related to the wage rate. The other important conclusion is that labor can expect to receive in wages no more, and no less, than the value of its marginal (physical) product. For some economists, this last conclusion is merely an objective statement of how labor's share of the total value created is determined under a market system. For others, it has a normative, or ethical, connotation as well, indicating that the relative shares going to labor and "capital" are fair ones—or at least in the best interests of everyone who is a member of the society, the workers and the "suppliers of capital" alike. Whether viewed as an objective statement or a normative assessment, however, the argument is seriously flawed. For one thing, it cannot be applied to "capital," defined as a stock of durable material inputs. This, in turn, means that it cannot be used to explain the share of the firm's revenue, in the form of "profits," or residual income, which is either retained by the firm itself or distributed as a dividend.

A firm is not in a position, at least in the short period, to employ more units of capital. The firm can be assumed to already have whatever plant and equipment it needs, and all its management can decide is what quantity of the variable inputs, including labor, should be used in conjunction with those fixed, or capital, inputs. Even more fundamentally, the firm's management would be at a complete loss to say how many physical units of capital were being employed, either in the short period or the long. As has already been pointed out in several different connections (see chapter 4, sections 2.1 and 4.3; chapter 5, section 3.2), there is no physical measure that can be applied to all the heterogeneous items that constitute a firm's capital stock, and thus no physical measure of the capital inputs taken as a whole. The value of the capital stock, whether determined by taking the historical cost of whatever investment has been made or by capitalizing the expected return from that investment, cannot be broken down into its price and quantity components. Indeed, this was the very point on which Joan Robinson criticized the neoclassical theory of capital (see chapter 5, section 5.1). Without a quantity measure of the capital inputs, one cannot legitimately substitute a K or any other symbol denoting the physical units of capital for L in exhibit 8.5. This, in turn, means that it is not possible to derive a marginal physical product curve for the capital inputs, as distinct from the labor inputs.

Exhibit 8.6

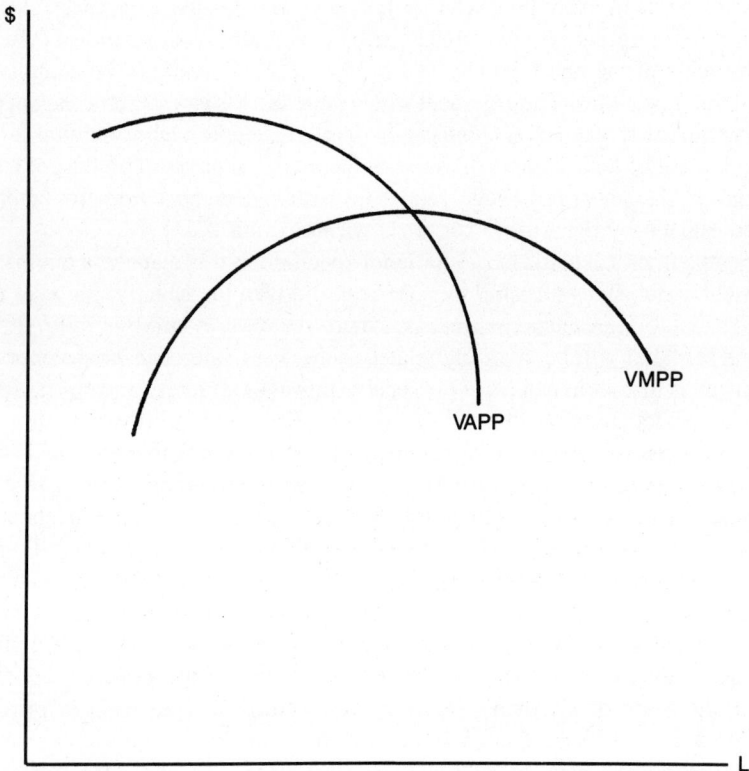

The impossibility of determining the marginal physical product of the capital inputs taken as a whole—and it makes no sense to consider any one piece of equipment or plant in isolation—undermines whatever claim might be made on behalf of the neoclassical theory as an explanation for the relative share of income going to labor. Even if it were true that the wages received by workers are equal to the value of their marginal product (more on this point shortly), it still would not then follow, as a corollary, that the return to the capital inputs is equal to the value of their marginal product. This separate argument needs to be demonstrated on its own. But how is this to be done if it is not possible to determine the marginal physical product of the firm's capital inputs taken as a whole? In truth, the "marginal physical product of capital" is not a theoretical construct which can be used in empirical work. It is instead a metaphysical concept lacking any explanatory power.

It is, of course, common for economists to assume that the residual income of the firm, Π, is equal to the amount of capital employed by the firm, K, multiplied by the value of the marginal physical product of capital, $VMPP_K$—just as the firm's wage bill is assumed to be equal to the amount of labor employed, L, multiplied by the value of the marginal physical product of labor, $VMPP_L$. From this assumption it then follows that the firm's rate of return on capital, Π/K, is equal to the value of the marginal physical product of capital, with that rate of return then providing an empirical estimate of $VMPP_K$. The objection to this line of reasoning is not just the difficulty, already pointed out, of obtaining a meaningful physical measure of K to serve as the denominator of Π. There is an additional objection no less fatal to the argument, based on what is known as the "adding up" problem.

Put simply, there is no way to prove that, were all the n factors of production—labor or otherwise—to receive a return equal to the value of their marginal product, this would exhaust the total value being created. An unexplained residual might still remain which, based on the above procedure for determining $VMPP_K$, would then be incorrectly attributed to the "productivity of capital." In light of what has already been said about how prices are determined within the oligopolistic component of the industrial sector, this possibility cannot be dismissed out of hand. As was pointed out, the mark-up used in deriving the industry's list price and hence the expected profit margin, Π/p_j or μ_j, may exceed the required rate of investment, Φ_j, depending on the elasticity of industry demand, e_j, the probability of new firms entering the industry, γ_j, and the likelihood of government intervention, θ_j (see chapter 6, section 4.6). However, even if firms were limited in the long period to a profit margin determined by an independently measurable $VMPP_K$ rather than by the firms' own pricing power, this would only account for the residual share of income going to firms. The portion of that residual income going to households in the form of dividends and other types of rentier payments would still be left unexplained.

Of course, to the extent that all of the firm's residual income, or profits, is eventually paid out in dividends and interest or—what is essentially the same thing—to the extent that the growth of dividends in the long period, $\overset{\circ}{D}iv_i$, matches the growth of the firm's discretionary funds, $\overset{\circ}{F}_i$, explaining the firm's residual share of income is the same as explaining the residual share going to rentiers. Still, one cannot take for granted that the growth of dividends will be identical to the growth of the firm's net cash inflow, or discretionary funds. As was pointed out in the preceding part of this chapter, firms may be growth maximizers rather equity maximizers, and if this is so, it is necessary to explain what determines the growth of dividends, as distinct from the growth of the firm's discretionary funds. The marginal productivity theory of income distribution, along with the closely related theory of the capital market—or rather, capital funds market (see chapter 7, section 3.7)—makes no allowance for the distinction between the two. It implicitly assumes that all the profits earned by firms will eventually be paid out in dividends and that therefore firms are equity maximizers. This means that any difference between $\overset{\circ}{D}iv_i$ and $\overset{\circ}{F}$ for the corporate sector as a whole is further evidence that the neoclassical explanation for the distribution of income among different households is, at the very least, incomplete. Still, the more significant objection to the marginal productivity theory is that one cannot obtain a meaningful measure of the capital inputs in physical terms and therefore it is not possible to determine how much of the firm's residual income actually represents a return on capital, based on its "marginal productivity," and how much is due to the pricing power which firms are able to exercise.

Even if a physical measure of the heterogeneous capital inputs could be obtained, however, it would not be enough to establish the validity of the marginal productivity theory. The essential point can best be seen by focusing on the firm's labor inputs. The number of hours workers spend on the job provides at least a quantitative, if not a physical, measure of the firm's labor inputs—ignoring, for the sake of the argument, any differences in the skill level of those employed by the firm. Despite this quantitative measure of the labor inputs, it does not then follow that the wages received by workers will be equal to the value of their marginal product. The argument, as developed by neoclassical economists, depends on the law of variable returns and, as already pointed out (see chapter 5, section 4), there is reason to question whether this law holds in the case of the oligopolistic subsector, if not for the entire industrial sphere of production. The weight of the evidence is that the labor coefficients, along with the other technical coefficients, are fixed—at least in the short period. (As for the long period, see below, chapter 13, section 3.2.) What this means is that the various types of inputs—labor, direct material and capital—cannot be varied relative to one another. Aside from the purely technical conditions of production, there are the work rules and other social constraints which ensure that the workers and the equipment they operate will be used only in certain fixed combinations. Without the one—either the crew that operates the equipment or the equipment itself—the other can produce nothing. To the extent this is the case, there is no marginal product of labor or, for that matter, of "capital" either.

Indeed, if one recognizes that the various industries are actually subsystems of production, the inadequacy of both the marginal productivity and labor theories of value is obvious. For it is in the nature of an integral system that the differential contribution of any one of its essential components cannot be determined. This is because no one of a system's elements can produce any output independently of the other elements. The fallacy of the marginal productivity theory, and thus of the neoclassical explanation for relative income shares, is that it is based on a mental experiment which assumes that the firm can do precisely what cannot be done in the case of any integral system—vary the number of components that constitute the system. Take away any one of the system's essential components or add an extra element, as the neoclassical theory would suggest is possible, and the system will no longer function properly. This is why the differential contribution of the various types of inputs used in the production process— labor, "capital" or even the "nth factor of production"—cannot be determined.

The fallacy of what has been termed the "tight" version of the labor theory of value, and thus of that explanation for relative income shares, is of a different sort. It assumes that there is but a single essential input—labor. This is what the argument that only "live" labor creates value necessarily implies. While it may be true that those who hold legal title to, and thus "own," the capital inputs contribute nothing of themselves to the current production effort—and that argument may apply as well to the members of the rentier class—it should not be misconstrued to mean that the capital inputs are not essential. Any such statement, even by implication, would be a serious error. The marginal productivity theory, by recognizing that there is more than one essential input, at least avoids this fallacy. Nonetheless, by insisting that the differential contribution of the two or more essential factors can be determined, it still manages to confuse matters.

There is an even more basic fallacy common to both the marginal productivity and the "tight" labor theories of value. This is the presumption that the sources of value are to be found in the inputs, both labor and "capital" ("variable" and "constant"), currently being employed in the production process. As essential as these inputs may be, the technology, as represented by the A (as well as the L and K) matrix, and the forms of social organization, as represented by the structure of firms and industries, are no less critical. If these factors are usually ignored in the discussion of distributive shares, it is probably because no one group in society can claim a share of the national income based on having contributed them. But, then, that is precisely the point. What may well be the most important sources of value—the technology and social organization (with the latter a special case of the former)—represent the steady accretion of the culture over the centuries. They cannot be attributed to just the presently living members of the society. Rather they are the heritage of the past that will then be transmitted to the future, thus maintaining the continuity of the culture.

Given that the sources of value are social and historical instead of particularistic and current—that they are to be found in the broader cultural endowment rather than in just the existing capital stock and the current input of human resources—the theory to explain how the value which is created is then distributed must be similarly macroscopic. It is this consideration, among others, that argues for the synthesis of post-Keynesian and institutionalist theories just presented as the most appropriate explanation for the relative distribution of income, first between the other sectors and the household sector and then within the household sector itself. The other virtues of this explanation are that it requires no arbitrary assumptions and no differentiation of what, in practice, cannot be differentiated.

Recommended Readings

On the corporate revolution, see Alfred D. Chandler, Jr., *The Visible Hand*, Cambridge, Mass.: Harvard University Press, 1977; Alfred S. Eichner, *The Emergence of Oligopoly*, Baltimore: Johns Hopkins Press, 1969, and *Toward a*

New Economics, Armonk, N.Y.: M. E. Sharpe, 1985, ch. 2; Gardiner C. Means, *The Corporate Revolution in America*, New York: Crowell-Collier, 1962. On social class in the United States and other advanced industrial societies, see C. Wright Mills, *White Collar*, New York: Oxford University Press, 1951, and *The Power Elite*, New York: Oxford University Press, 1959; Christopher Jencks *et al.*, *Who Gets Ahead?* New York: Basic Books, 1979; Lars Osberg, *Economic Inequality in the United States*, Armonk, N.Y.: M. E. Sharpe, 1984; Alfred S. Eichner, "An 'Anthropogenic' Model of the Labor Market," *Eastern Economic Journal*, October 1979, reprinted in *Toward a New Economics*, ch. 4.

The development of the post-Keynesian theory of income distribution can be traced through the following works: Michal Kalecki, "The Determinants of Distribution of the National Income," *Econometrica*, 1938; Joan Robinson, *The Accumulation of Capital*, London: Macmillan, 1956; Nicholas Kaldor, "Alternative Theories of Distribution," *Review of Economic Studies*, no. 2, 1956, reprinted in Kaldor, *Essays on Value and Distribution*, Glencoe, Ill.: Free Press, 1960; Sidney Weintraub, *A General Theory of the Price Level, Output, Income Distribution, and Economic Growth*, Philadelphia: Chilton, 1959; Luigi L. Pasinetti, "Rate of Profit and Income Distribution in Relation to the Rate of Economic Growth," *Review of Economic Studies*, October 1962, reprinted in Pasinetti, *Growth and Income Distribution*, New York: Cambridge University Press, 1974, ch. 5; Alfred S. Eichner and J. A. Kregel, "An Essay on Post-Keynesian Theory: A New Paradigm in Economics," *Journal of Economic Literature*, December 1975.

On the role of trade unions, see John T. Dunlop, *Wage Determination Under Trade Unions*, New York: A. Kelley, 1950; Arthur M. Ross, *Trade Union Wage Policy*, Berkeley: University of California Press, 1965; Richard B. Freeman and James L. Medoff, *What Do Trade Unions Do?* New York: Basic Books, 1984. On the firm's wage structure, see Peter B. Doeringer and Michael J. Piore, *Internal Labor Markets and Manpower Analysis*, Lexington, Mass.: D. C. Heath, 1971; David M. Gordon, Richard Edwards and Michael Reich, *Segmented Work, Divided Workers*, New York: Cambridge University Press, 1982. On the set of wage differentials, see Marcia Freedman, *Labor Markets: Segments and Shelters*, New York: Allenheld, Osmun, 1976; David Howell, "Production Technology, Industry Segments and Interindustry Wage Differentials," unpublished. See also Michael J. Piore, ed., *Unemployment and Inflation*, Armonk, N.Y.: M. E. Sharpe, 1979. On the determination of the basic wage rate, see Otto Eckstein, "Money Wage Determination Revisited," *Review of Economic Studies*, April 1968; Paolo Sylos-Labini, *Trade Unions, Inflation and Productivity*, Lexington, Mass.: Lexington Books, 1974; Adrian Wood, *A Theory of Pay*, New York: Cambridge University Press, 1978; James E. Annable, Jr., *The Price of Industrial Labor*, Lexington, Mass.: Lexington Books, 1984.

On Marxian theory, see Karl Marx, *Value, Price and Profit*, New York: International Publishers, 1971; Paul M. Sweezy, *The Theory of Capitalist Devel-*

opment, New York: Monthly Review Press, 1968; Ernest Mandel, *Marxist Economic Theory*, New York: Monthly Review Press, 1968; Meghnad Desai, *Marxian Economic Theory*, London: Gray-Mills, 1974. See also Joan Robinson, *An Essay on Marxian Economics*, London: Macmillan, 1960, *Collected Economic Papers*, Oxford: Basil Blackwell, 1965, Vol. III, part 3. On the neoclassical theory of income distribution, see Charles E. Ferguson, *The Neoclassical Theory of Production and Distribution*, New York: Cambridge University Press, 1969; Martin Bronfenbrenner, *Income Distribution Theory*, Chicago: Aldine, 1971; Jan Pen, *Income Distribution*, New York: Praeger, 1971; Lester C. Thurow, *Generating Inequality*, New York: Basic Books, 1975, appendix. See also George J. Stigler, *Production and Distribution Theories*, New York: Macmillan, 1941; Joseph Schumpeter, *History of Economic Analysis*, New York: Oxford University Press, 1955, pp. 909–24.

Chapter 9

The Household Sector: Expenditures and Cash Balances

Contents

Chapter 9

The Household Sector:
Expenditures and Cash Balances

If it is in explaining how relative income shares are determined that post-Keynesian theory differs most radically from the pre-Keynesian component of the "neoclassical synthesis," it is in explaining how much of the income thus obtained will be spent on various items of consumption that the theory being presented in this text goes beyond even what little of that synthesis can be attributed to Keynes himself. As fundamental as the concept of a consumption function may be to the argument made in *The General Theory* (see chapter 3, section 1.2), the way Keynes chose to model the behavior of the household sector needs to be significantly modified if the analysis is to be compatible with the rest of post-Keynesian theory. Not only is it necessary to think in terms of the secular growth of household expenditures and thus to add a long-period perspective to Keynes's short-period analysis. It is also necessary to distinguish the discretionary, or extraordinary, expenditures of households from their nondiscretionary, or routine outlays, and thereby treat the household sector in the same way as the other sectors which are being modeled.

To extend to the long period the arguments about consumption first made by Keynes, it will be necessary to develop a quite different model of household behavior from that traditionally relied upon by economists. The model will assume that decisions are made by the household as a social organization rather than by any individual person, that the material needs of households can be lexicographically ordered and that this gives rise of a set of long-period income elasticities for the major items of consumption which vary around a weighted mean of 1 and a corresponding set of price elasticities which vary around a weighted mean not significantly different from 0. Only after developing this alternative model of household behavior as the complement of the distributional theory outlined in the last chapter will it then be possible to derive a set of E and F curves, and in this way determine what effect the household sector, as distinct from other sectors, has on the macrodynamic stability of an advanced market economy like that of the United States. Before proceeding to that ultimate task, however, it will be helpful to survey the considerable body of empirical work that has been done by econometricians on the aggregate consumption function since the publication of *The General Theory*. The survey is useful for indicating both the progress economists have been able to make in understanding the determinants of aggregate consumption as better data and more sophisticated statistical techniques have become available and the inherent limit on any further progress which they face unless the prevailing micro and macroeconomic theory of household behavior is replaced by a post-Keynesian conceptual framework.

9.1 A Model of Household Behavior

Two of the key parameters in the long-period model of production presented in chapter 5 are the income and price elasticities of demand. It is these Υ and Ψ vectors which, in conjunction with the growth of output per worker, will then determine the secular rate of expansion by each vertically integrated industry. We have now reached the point where we must attempt to explain what accounts for the values taken by the Υ and Ψ vectors. Do economic factors play a role—or are the two vectors simply parameters which, insofar as any macrodynamic model of the economy is concerned, must be viewed as exogenous? The question is important, not just so the long-period model of production can now be completed but also so we can take the next step in identifying the cyclical determinants of aggregate consumption. That next step is to explain what determines the long-run demand for various types of consumption goods, including any durable items, and thus what determines the average propensity to consume in the long period. It is, of course, the same income and price elasticities which, besides determining the secular rate of expansion by each vertically integrated industry, will determine the long-run demand for the various types of consumption goods.

To explain what determines the values taken by the Υ and Ψ vectors, it is necessary to develop a model of household behavior which differs radically from the model normally relied upon by economists. The model is one in which, due to the lexicographic ordering of preferences (based on the separability and hierarchy of each household's material needs), the income effects arising from technical progress predominate over the relative price, or substitution, effects. More importantly, it is a model which does not depend on the presumed existence of utility functions or indifference curves. As it turns out, this is a model more in keeping with Keynes's original formulation of the consumption function than the more conventional theory of demand at the microeconomic level. Before presenting that alternative model, however, several preliminary matters need to be addressed—including what is meant by the income and price elasticities of demand.

9.1.1 Income and price elasticities

The income elasticity of demand for the jth item of consumption, η_j, is the proportional change in the quantity demanded relative to the proportional change in income. The price elasticity of demand for the same good, e_j, is the proportional change in the quantity demanded relative to the proportional change in price. That is,

$$\eta_j = \frac{\Delta Q_j}{Q_j} \Big/ \frac{\Delta Y}{Y} \tag{9.1}$$

and

$$e_j = \frac{\Delta Q_j}{Q_j} \Big/ \frac{\Delta p_j}{p_j} \tag{9.2}$$

where η_j and e_j are the income and price elasticities of demand previously denoted as the elements of separate Υ and Ψ vectors, (see chapter 5, section 5.4); Y is the average level of household income, and p_j and Q_j are as previously denoted (see chapter 5, section 1.1). These elasticities can be derived by estimating, in log linear form, the following demand function for each of the industries producing items for household consumption:

$$Q_{D_j} = f(p_j, \mathbf{P}_s, \mathbf{P}_c, Y, Pop, \mathbf{X}) \tag{9.3}$$

where $\mathbf{P}_s$ is a vector representing the price of all substitute goods (except at least one); $\mathbf{P}_c$ is a vector representing the price of all complementary goods; Pop is the size of the population, that is, the number of households multiplied by the average number of persons per household; and $\mathbf{X}$ is a vector of the other factors peculiar to each consumption good which influence the demand for that item.

Two separate demand curves, and thus two separate sets of income and price elasticities, can be identified, depending on whether Y denotes the level of household income in real or in nominal terms. In the latter case, part of whatever value is obtained for e will reflect the income effect of a change in relative prices. While e calculated in this manner may be adequate for determining how much pricing power a firm or industry has in the short period—the slope of the $S_I{'}$ curve, as already pointed out, depends on the potential loss of sales to some other firm or industry at or near the current level of income (see chapter 6, section 3.4)—it is not this value of e that is relevant in any long-period analysis. This is because, within that time frame, there is likely to be a significant change in the level of real income; and unless that change in real income is explicitly taken into account, the pure substitution effect of a price change—that is, the choice of one consumption good over another so as to better satisfy the same material need—cannot be isolated from the income effect. Indeed, as we shall see, it is precisely because the conventional theory of consumer behavior provides no clear basis for distinguishing the pure substitution effect of a price change from the income effect that the theory is largely useless in empirical work (see section 9.1.6). Thus, in deriving the elements of the Υ and Ψ vectors, it is necessary to specify the level of income in real terms, Y_r, rather than in nominal terms, Y_n.

In attempting to determine the values taken by those two vectors, it is best to rely on a variant of the linear expenditure model first developed by Richard Stone. The model requires that the following h-by-$h+1$ matrix be estimated, where h is the number of separate goods included within the consumption vector:

proportional change in $\longrightarrow$ relative to change in $\searrow$	p_1	p_2	p_3	$\cdots$	p_h	Y_r
Q_1	$e_{1.1}$	$e_{1.2}$	$e_{1.3}$	$\cdots$	$e_{1.h}$	η_1
Q_2	$e_{2.1}$	$e_{2.2}$	$e_{2.3}$	$\cdots$	$e_{2.h}$	η_2
Q_3	$e_{1.1}$	$e_{3.2}$	$e_{3.3}$	$\cdots$	$e_{3.h}$	η_3
.	.	.	.		.	.
.	.	.	.		.	.
.	.	.	.		.	.
Q_h	$e_{h.1}$	$e_{h.2}$	$e_{h.3}$	$\cdots$	$e_{h.h}$	η_n

Each cell within the matrix indicates the proportional change in the price and income variables shown along the top row relative to the proportional change in the quantity variables shown in the first column. Thus the main diagonal represents the (own) price elasticities of demand, $e_{j.j}$, for all h consumption goods while the elements of the matrix above and below the main diagonal represent the cross elasticities of substitution, $e_{i.j}$. Since $e_{i.ji}$ can be assumed to be equal to $e_{j.i}$, the elements of the matrix above the main diagonal are a reverse image of the elements below the main diagonal. A positive value for one of these cross elasticities indicates that the two goods are substitutes for one another and a negative value, that they are complements. In either case, the price of the one good will have an effect on the demand for the second good. On the other hand, a zero value indicates that the demand for the second good is independent of, or unrelated to, the price of the first good. The critical empirical question, as we shall see, is, first, whether these cross elasticities are significantly different from zero and then, second, whether the sign attached to them is negative or positive.

The last, or $h+1$, column, meanwhile, contains the income elasticities of demand, η_j. The above h-by-$h+1$ matrix is therefore the sum of an h-by-h matrix representing all the price elasticities of demand, cross as well as own, plus an h-by-1 Υ vector representing all the income elasticities of demand. The principal diagonal of the former constitutes what has previously been denoted as the Ψ vector. The advantage of basing the analysis of consumption on the linear expenditure model is that the conditions which the entire h-by-$h+1$ matrix must satisfy provide the same type of check on the results as the equality between final demand (aggregate output) and value added (national income) does in the case of the National Income and Product Accounts (see chapter 2, section 1.1). Indeed, based on one of those conditions, it is clear that the consumption matrix in the above form is overdetermined.

There are two conditions which the above consumption matrix must satisfy. The first is that the (own) price elasticity for each good, $e_{j,j}$, must be equal to the sum of all the cross elasticities of demand for that good, $\Sigma e_{i,j}$ (or, alternatively, $\Sigma e_{j,i}$)—though with the sign reversed. That is,

$$-e_{j,j} = \Sigma e_{i,j} = \Sigma e_{j,i}, \ i \neq j \tag{9.4}$$

In other words, the elements of the Ψ vector must be equal to the sum of the cross elasticities of demand for the same consumption good. This condition follows from the fact that, a decline in demand for one good, due to the pure substitution effect, can only be because the income that would otherwise be spent on that good is being used to purchase one or more other goods instead. The relationship given by equation 9.4 is, in turn, the reason why an h-by-$h+1$ consumption matrix is overdetermined, with one of the columns (all but the last one) redundant. Once all the cross-elasticities of demand for a good are known, the (own) price elasticity of demand is also known, given the degrees of freedom implicit in equation 9.4.

The second condition which the above consumption matrix must satisfy is that all the income elasticities, when weighted and averaged, must equal 1—unless, contrary to what has been observed for the U.S. economy (see section 9.2.2), there is some tendency for the rate of household savings to change over time, in which case the income elasticity of savings needs to be taken into account as well. (See sections 9.1.4 and 9.2.1 for a further discussion of this point.) That is,

$$\frac{\sum\limits_{j=1}^{h} w_j \eta_j}{h} = 1 \tag{9.5}$$

where w_j is the relative weight, $p_j C_j / \sum\limits_{j=1}^{x} p_j C_j$, of the jth consumption good, with x the number of items within the relevant set. In other words, the income elasticities represented by the Υ vector can be expected to vary around a weighted mean of 1.

These two constraints on the values taken by the consumption matrix derive, not from any theory of household behavior but rather, from the logic of the mathematical relationships posited in specifying the linear expenditure model. The next step is to see what additional constraints can be imposed on the consumption matrix once an empirically valid theory of household behavior has been introduced. We will now proceed to develop such a model, taking care not to base it, in any critical way, on unobservable variables. In the course of developing such a model, the argument advanced will parallel what was said earlier in connection with the enterprise sector. The locus of decision-making, it will again be assumed, is a social organization—in this case a household consisting of a number of individuals who pool their income for the purpose of meeting their routine expenses. The household may, of course, consist of only a single individual, just as a business firm may consist of only a single worker, the owner-entrepreneur. More typically, however, as can be seen from exhibit 9.1, a household consists of two or more individuals—either two adults (with or without children) or one adult with one or more children. Thus, to ensure that it applies to the more general situation that prevails throughout the household sector of the U.S. economy, the model will be based on some sort of collective rather than individualistic decision-making process.

As a second point of continuity with what was said earlier in connection with the enterprise sector, the model to be developed in the sections which follow will distinguish between the individual household's routine outlays and its extraordinary, or discretionary, expenditures. The former consist of the items which are purchased on a regular basis, with the choice governed largely by habit. In contrast, the household's nonroutine outlays consist of the items that are purchased intermittently—and then only after sufficient funds have been accumulated in the form of liquid assets and/or after the necessary financing has been arranged. While most of the latter items are durable goods of one sort or another, such as a home, a car or various household furnishings and appliances, they may also include outlays on nondurable goods and services which go beyond the amounts normally budgeted for. An example would be a child's college tuition expense or a vacation trip abroad. In what follows, the latter types of nonroutine, or discretionary, expenditures will be given short shrift and the emphasis instead placed on the household's durable goods purchases—just as, in modeling the corporate sector's discretionary expenditures, advertising and R&D outlays were all but ignored (see chapter 7, section 4.1). In this way, the parallel to the dynamic operating within the enterprise sector will be even clearer.

Besides recognizing that the effective decision-making unit is a social organization rather than just an individual person and that the household's nonroutine, or discretionary, expenditures need to be distinguished from its regularly budgeted outlays, several further modifications will be made in the usual way of modeling household behavior. The first is to recognize the discrete and variegated nature of the material needs which households have, with little or no possibility of substituting one consumption good for another. This means abandoning what Paul Davidson has termed the Gross Substitution Theorem—the assumption that each good is at least partially a substitute for every other good. A second modification will be to recognize the considerable role played by social custom and habit in determining the choice among the various types of consumption goods that are

Exhibit 9.1
Types of U.S. Households, 1984

Type	Number	Percent
Unattached individuals	19,954,000	23.3
Male	7,529,000	8.8
Female	12,425,000	14.5
Other nonfamily households	3,456,000	4.1
TOTAL, nonfamily households	23,410,000	27.4
Married couples,	50,090,000	58.6
No own children under 18	25,750,000	30.1
One own child under 18	9,546,000	11.2
Two own children under 18	9,546,000	11.2
Three or more own children under 18	5,236,000	6.1
Other family, male householder	2,030,000	2.4
No own children under 18	1,231,000	1.4
One own child under 18	506,000	0.6
Two own children under 18	224,000	0.3
Three or more own children under 18	69,000	0.1
Other family, female householder	9,878,000	11.6
No own children under 18	3,970,000	4.6
One own child under 18	2,810,000	3.3
Two own children under 18	1,985,000	2.3
Three or more own children under 18	1,113,000	1.3
TOTAL, Family households	61,997,000	72.6

Source: U.S. Bureau of the Census, "Household and Family Characteristics, March 1981," *Current Population Reports*, April 1985.

available. This means abandoning the assumption that consumer preferences are innate or in some other way exogenously determined. The third and final modification is to recognize the role played by the hierarchy of material needs in determining the changing pattern of consumption over time as household income and/or leisure increases. We shall begin this reformulation of the theory of household demand by first positing and then indicating how, based on the separability of material needs, a taxonomy of consumption can be constructed.

9.1.2 The taxonomy of consumption

The material needs of household members are discrete and variegated. This means that each household, viewed as a social organization, requires a large number of different items which are not substitutable for one another. The food that must be consumed in order to provide the minimum daily intake of calories will not provide protection against the vagaries of the climate. And among the different types of food consumed, meat does not provide the same nutrients as fruits and vegetables—just as, among the different means of sheltering the individual from the elements, clothes do not offer the same protection as a dwelling. In other words, the material needs of households are qualitatively distinct, or separable. It is for this reason that, in specifying the material needs of a household, one must speak in terms of a consumption basket—or vector of different consumption goods, C.

The different goods represented by this consumption vector can be grouped together into discrete categories, with the items that are included within any one category more nearly alike in the need they serve than the items excluded. Eight major categories of household consumption can be delineated, at least at this stage in the historical evolution of advanced market economies like that of the United States. They are:

1. Food
2. Clothing
3. Housing
4. Household durables
5. Automobiles and other means of transport
6. Personal care
7. Recreation
8. Other services

Notice that this eight-fold delineation is inclusive in the sense that there is a separate category in which to place every type of consumption good. This is the one condition that any taxonomic scheme, such as the one here being suggested for the various types of goods needed by households, must satisfy.

Within each major category, various subcategories can be further delineated on the basis of the same rule—namely, that the items included are more nearly alike in the need they serve than the items excluded. For example, in the case of food, we can identify the following subcategories:

a. meat products
b. dairy products
c. fruits and vegetables
d. grain mill products
e. bakery products
f. sugar and confectionary products
g. fats and oils
h. beverages
i. miscellaneous food products

In the case of clothing, we can identify the following subcategories:

a. male suits, coats and overcoats
b. other male clothing

c. female outerwear
d. hats, caps and millinery
e. girls', children's and infants outerwear
f. fur goods
g. miscellaneous apparel and accessories

These subcategories correspond to the three-digit breakdown of the two-digit SIC food and apparel industries. They are not arbitrary delineations but rather reflect qualitative differences, or "quantum" changes, in the degree to which a particular need is being served.

The above subcategories, even though they represent a better delineation of the representative household's material needs, are nonetheless still too broad for substitution to be a real possibility. While, in a pinch, meat can be replaced by potatoes and other vegetables as a source of calories and women's outerwear replaced by a man's suit or coat as protection against the elements, these are not normally the choices a household is forced to make in an advanced market economy. The category of meat therefore needs to be further divided into fresh and processed products, with the former subcategory further divided into beef, lamb, pork and poultry products, while the category of women's outerwear needs to be divided into blouses, shirts, dresses, suits, skirts, coats, casual wear and various other items. Even at this level of disaggregation, however, it may still not be possible, as a practical matter, to replace one good with another. For substitution to be feasible, it may in fact be necessary to disaggregate the consumption vector still further to the level of the separate items that constitute the product line of each four-digit SIC industry supplying goods to households. (For what is meant by an industry's product line, see chapter 7, section 2.4.) To what level of detail the elements of the C vector need to be specified before substitution can be considered a real possibility will depend on what is the level of disaggregation at which the $e_{i,j}$ elements within the consumption vector take on values significantly different from zero.

Once the level of disaggregation at which substitution is a real possibility has been reached—whether at the four-digit SIC industry level or below—the entire set of goods denoted by the C vector can be arranged along a continuum, with the various items lexicographically ordered. This means there are rules, based on non-numerical criteria, for grouping the goods into categories and then for determining the order in which those categories are listed—just as there are similar rules for arranging the words in a dictionary. Based on these rules, items of food need to be grouped together, separate and distinct from items of clothing—just as, in a dictionary, words beginning with the letter T are grouped separately from words that begin with P. Moreover, the various types of meat products need to be grouped separately from the different types of fruits and vegetables—just as, in a dictionary, words whose second letter is A are grouped separately from words whose second letter is E. What determines the order in which the various categories and subcategories are listed will become clearer once the concept of a hierarchy of material needs has been introduced (see section 9.1.5). For now all that need be noted is the basis for grouping the goods into major categories of consumption and a nested set of subcategories. That criterion is the extent to which the different goods serve the same type of need.

From this way in which the consumption vector needs to be specified, two propositions then follow. The first is that, in determining the degree of substitutability between any two consumption goods, it is not enough just to identify the items in broad terms, such as food or clothing. At that level of disaggregation, replacing one consumption good with another is simply not feasible. For substitution to be a real possibility, the various items of consumption need to be specified in sufficient detail that the categories at least correspond to the output of four-digit SIC industries—if not to the product line of those industries. The nested set of categories and subcategories needed to reach this level of disaggregation constitutes the taxonomy of consumption. The second proposition is that once the various elements of the C vector have been arranged along a continuum based on this taxonomy, only the items listed immediately before or after one another are likely to be close substitutes. The greater the number of other goods separating any two items, the less likely it is that one good can be used in place of the other to satisfy the same need. Thus only chicken, and not a necktie, can be considered a substitute for beef—and even then, if the recipe for making stew calls for beef, using chicken may not, as a practical matter, be an option. Indeed, the materials needs of households may be governed by technical coefficients, or the required ingredients of "recipes," no less rigid than those that determine the use of material inputs by business firms. Still, it is not just objective, technical relationships that will determine the substitutability among the different items of consumption. Habits, based on social mores, also play a role.

9.1.3 The role of social custom and habit

Viewed simply as a source of protein, pork can readily be substituted for beef or other types of fresh meat. Yet, to an orthodox Jew or Moslem, pork is unfit for human consumption—and indeed there are members of those religious communities who would rather than die than eat meat that comes from a pig. Similarly, a skirt can be used to cover the legs just as well as a pair of trousers. Yet, depending on the sex of the individual, as well as the time and place in which the person is living, wearing a skirt may well cause someone to become the object of ridicule, if not to be shunned by the other members of the community. These are but two examples of the way in which the choice among different types of consumption goods is affected by social mores. The truth is that virtually every aspect of daily living pertaining to the use of material goods is governed by what is socially acceptable—not just the types of foods eaten and the types of clothes worn but also the type of dwellings occupied, the items used to furnish those dwellings, the forms of transportation relied upon, the kind of personal care exercised and the forms of recreation pursued. Within each of these major categories of consumption, the range of choices—though not necessarily the actual choice itself—is socially conditioned and therefore limited.

In an advanced society the basic material needs of the individual are so easily satisfied, at least for the great majority of persons living in those societies, that the choice among consumption goods reflects idiosyncratic preferences rather than just objective needs. These preferences, however, are not innate or inherited. They are the result of a social conditioning, or learning, process that begins with the acquisition of language and continues throughout the individual's lifetime. First parents and relatives, then friends and acquaintances will instruct the neophyte consumer as to what items are the proper ones to use under varying circumstances. When two adults join together to form a household, they become the more immediate influence on each other's behavior, with any conflicting views necessarily having to be reconciled through some interpersonal or proto-political process. The norms developed through continuous interaction with other human beings are then modified, though only in part, by other social mechanisms such as the formal educational system and the mass media. Of course, the choice among different consumption goods never depends solely on a person's prior social conditioning or on current social mores. There is usually some room for individual discretion. A person can, for example, decide whether to have beef or lamb for the main entree at dinner—provided he or she is ordering at a restaurant or doing the cooking at home. And even if a male employee has no choice but to wear a coat and tie to work—a female employee would, of course, be governed by a different dress code—he may still be able to choose a blue shirt over a white one. Nonetheless, once both the objective and social constraints on the choice among consumption goods have been taken into account, the room for individual discretion may be quite limited. The scope for deliberate, conscious choice is even further narrowed by the need to reduce as much as possible the burden which the multiplicity of available consumption goods places on the household's decision-making capability.

An individual household must be able to make a large number of decisions on a continuous basis. Even if one ignores all the other aspects of daily living and focuses only on the question of how any income is to be spent, the number of choices is quite large. This is not to suggest that human beings, organized into households or other types of social groups, are incapable of making a rational choice. The point rather is that it is not easy for them to do so. Even if all the necessary information is at hand—something that cannot always be counted on—it requires time and mental effort to weigh the options and make a choice that everyone within the group will find tolerable. The larger the number of decisions that must be made, the greater the strain on the group's decision-making capability. The difficulty is compounded with a larger number of persons in the household. It is for this reason that, faced with the task of having to make a large number of decisions on a continuous basis, the representative, or "typical," household can be expected to adopt a two-part behavioral rule, at least insofar as the purchase of consumption goods is concerned. This two-part rule, designed to prevent the household's decision-making capability from being overtaxed, is as follows:

1. The household will continue to maintain whatever pattern of consumption has already been established, especially in the case of food, clothing and other nondurable goods. Only in response to some new information—information that indicates a change either in the household's own circumstances or in the availability of consumption goods, will the household consider altering that pattern. In this way the household is able to minimize the number of conscious, deliberate decisions it needs to make.

2. When new circumstances require that it consider a possible change in its pattern of consumption, the household will transform whatever multiple options it has into a series of discrete, preferably dichotomous, choices—such as the ones represented by the decision tree in exhibit 9.2. The household can then use whatever power of discrimination it has to rule out a succession of alternatives until only one good, the item that best meets its needs, remains to be chosen. In this way, the household is able to follow a relatively simple algorithm, one that does not place too great a strain on its ability to make decisions.

The representative household is able to tranform its multiple options into a series of discrete choices through the three-step sequential decision-making process it usually follows in selecting any particular basket of goods for purchase at the store. The first step in the process is for the household to determine the maximum amount of income it wishes to spend under each major category of consumption—usually as part of the exercise it goes through in drawing up a household budget. The minimal number of consumption goods that need to be purchased will be determined by the adult members of the household at the time they establish a separate household. At the very least, they must decide how much to spend on food, clothing and shelter while still leaving themselves enough income to cover any incidental expenses. Indeed, it is only if there is enough income to meet those minimal needs that a separate household will be established. (The exceptions form the previously delineated dependent class.) Thus an initial budget can be assumed to have been determined at the time a separate household is formed, with that budget then revised with every significant change in either the composition of the household or its real income. As long as the budget previously worked out remains in effect, the household need make no further decisions as to how its income should be apportioned among the major types of consumption goods. All it has to do is limit its purchases within any one category to the amount allowed for in the budget.

The second step in the sequential process by which the household decides which items to purchase is for the household to draw up a shopping list prior to visiting the store (or in some other way placing an order with a firm that sells to

Exhibit 9.2
Individual Household's Decision Tree

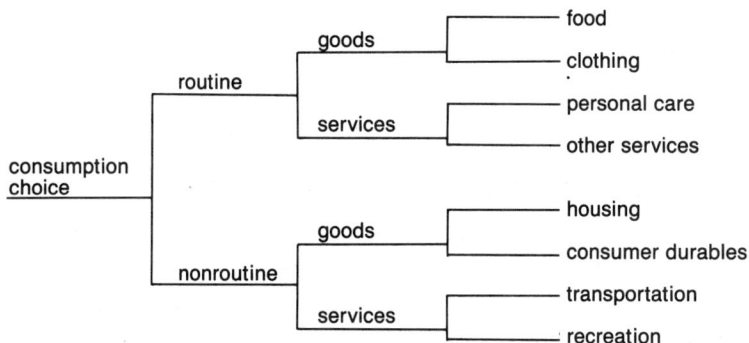

households). Once established, a household will try to keep a certain stock, or inventory, of the goods it needs, replacing those items through periodic visits to the store only as they are used up. In this way, the household can compile a separate shopping list for each of the major types of consumption goods it needs simply by noting what items have been consumed since the last visit to the store that sells those items, with the frequency of any visit to the store depending on how quickly those types of goods are normally used up. Thus the shopping list for food and other household items is likely to be compiled daily or weekly, the shopping list for clothes seasonally and the other shopping lists as items need to be replaced. The compiling of a shopping list is likely, however, be the occasion for taking into account any new information and, on the basis of that information, revising the list of items normally purchased. Adding a new item to the shopping list may, of course, mean that the household will not be able to stay within its budget. In that case the household will find itself back at the first step in the sequential decision-making process—having to decide whether to revise its budget. More typically, however, the household will simply purchase the new item instead of some other good, one that, with the inclusion of the new item, need not be purchased as frequently or indeed even at all. For example, if the new item is some type of frozen vegetable, the household will be able to cut back on its purchase of fresh vegetables. It may be, of course, that the good dropped from the regular shopping list is a more expensive one. In that case, the household will have found a way to reduce the cost of satisfying whatever are the present set of needs allowed for within the budget.

The third, and final, step in the sequential process by which the household decides which items to purchase is for some member of the household actually to visit the store (or in some other way place the order) and then, based on the shopping list previously compiled, select specific items. This third step in the process provides one last opportunity for the household's buying plans to be revised. While visiting the store (or going through a catalog), the member of the household with the responsibility for doing the shopping can take cognizance of any significant change in prices or in the items available for sale. A change in price may cause a revision in buying plans for either of two reasons. If there should be a decline in the price of some good—one that is normally kept in stock by the household but is not on the current shopping list because it does not yet need to be replaced—the person doing the shopping may decide to take advantage of the "bargain" and add the item to the basket of goods being purchased. Alternatively, if the good was already on the shopping list, there will be money left over either to spend on other items or as part of the household's unspent cash balances, thereby augmenting its discretionary funds or "savings." Conversely, if the price of some good on the list has increased, the person doing the shopping will need to reconsider the tentative choices represented by the shopping list. The individual can, of course, decide that the higher price is only a temporary deviation from the price which normally prevails and, in anticipation of the price subsequently falling, may simply avoid making a purchase at the present time. To this extent, the person will necessarily be speculating as to what is the "normal," or long-period, price of the good—in the same way that the same person would be speculating if he or she decided to snap up a "bargain." However, the individual may instead decide that the higher price is a permanent rather than a temporary one, in which case—especially if the rise in price is part of some general movement of the price level and/or involves an item of considerable expense—he or she will need to make some allowance for the loss of real income involved. This can range from going all the way back to the first step in the sequential decision-making and deciding whether to revise the household budget to merely cutting back on the purchase of some other good so as to stay within the present budgetary limits.

The three separate steps in the process—setting a budgetary limit for each major type of consumption good, compiling a shopping list within that category before visiting the store and then finally selecting the specific items to be included in the order—considerably ease the household's task of deciding what goods to purchase. Once its minimal needs have been determined and a budget drawn up, the household can then act largely on habit. Only if the composition of the household, the income of its members, the types of goods available or their prices should change will the household be forced to consider modifying or otherwise deviating from its customary buying pattern. There is still the question, of course, of how the individual household decides what goods to include as part of its normal inventory and thus what items will be found on its regular shopping list. There is also the question of how the individual household determines its nonroutine, or discretionary, outlays. We shall now turn to these questions, beginning with how the representative household is likely to respond to a change in its real income.

9.1.4 The household's response to a change in income

The flow of goods to each household is limited, in the case of a monetarized production system, by two factors. One is the amount of income received by household members (as well as the credit they can obtain) and the other is the amount of time they have both for purchasing any goods and for then making use of them. These two constraints on household consumption are, of course, not independent of one another. As has already been pointed out (see chapter 5, section 5.4), a secular rise in output per worker can be translated into either an increase in the real income and hence the purchasing power of households or, alternatively, into an increase in the amount of leisure enjoyed by household members (that is, the amount of time they need not spend in compensated employment). Moreover, an increase in leisure may be a prerequisite for the greater use of certain types of goods and services—as, for example, in the case of most recreational items. Still, it is the amount of income that, for the individual household, is likely to serve as the more immediate and binding constraint on consumption. A reduction in the average number of hours worked each year is so difficult to achieve, given the need to coordinate the activities of different workers, that it is likely to occur only intermittently—and then only through a politically mediated change in the norm that prevails throughout the society. Even with greater leisure time, however, the individual household will be unable to increase its purchase of consumption goods unless its income also rises. This is why, in the analysis that follows, the amount of leisure will be assumed to remain unchanged (or to continue increasing at the same fixed rate) while only the household's response to a change in real income is considered.

Each household can be assumed to have an order of priority in which it will select any one of the items represented by the C vector as its income increases. This order of priority will reflect both the household's objective material needs and the types of social conditioning to which the members of the household have been subject. It will therefore depend on: (1) the current stage in the life cycle of the household, as proxied by the number of persons constituting the household and their respective ages; (2) the household's social class, as proxied by the educational background and occupation of its adult members; and (3) the larger culture to which the household belongs, as proxied by nationality, language, religion and other ethnic characteristics. These three sets of factors suffice to define the household's socioeconomic profile, with the distinguishing features of that profile serving as the parameters of the household's consumption behavior.

Each household with a similar socioeconomic profile can be expected to add a particular item, C_j, to its normal inventory of consumption goods, and thus to its regular shopping list, once its income in real terms reaches a certain threshold limit—that is, once all the items with a higher priority are already being purchased on a regular basis. This means that, for any one household, the Engel curve (relating expenditures to income) will take the form shown in exhibit 9.3.

Exhibit 9.3
**Individual Household's Engel Curve
for a Particular Consumption Good**

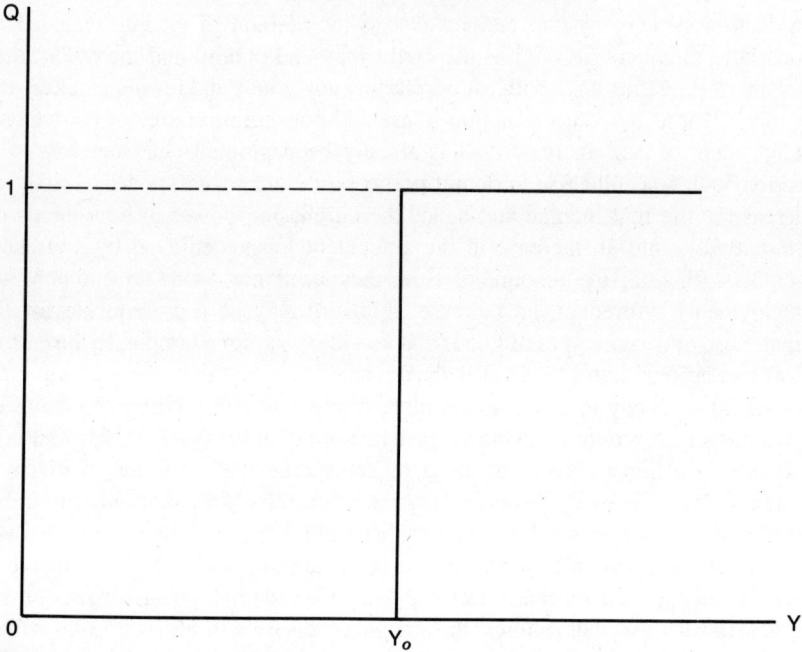

Up to the threshold limit, Y_o, the "quantity" purchased is *zero*; beyond that point, the "quantity" purchased is 1. In certain cases, only a single unit will in fact be purchased—as, for example, when the item is a television set, a vacation trip to the Caribbean or a dress suit for special occasions. For other types of consumer goods, however, the singular quantity purchased will be some multiple of the physical unit in which the item is normally priced—for example, so many pounds of meat or so many changes of clothing. In that case, what is singular about the amount purchased is the material need it enables the household to satisfy. The 1 shown on the vertical axis of the diagram in exhibit 9.3 therefore refers to the quantity of the consumption good, C_j, that must be obtained if some clearly definable purpose is to be served—whether that purpose is to be able to watch the programs broadcast over television stations, spend a certain amount of time on vacation in the Caribbean, dress in the socially approved manner on different occasions, achieve a certain level of meat consumption or something else. In this way, the household's decision of whether to purchase a particular item as its income rises can be represented as a binary, or dichotomous, choice: The item is either added to the household's regular shopping list or it is not. That is why the outcome can take only one of two values, 0 or 1.

According to this way of conceptualizing the household's decision process, the choice is never whether to purchase more of the same good. Rather the choice is whether to purchase some additional item for the first time or, what is virtually the same thing, whether to purchase some variant of an item already on the household's regular shopping list. A variant of some good already being purchased may be chosen over a new item for any one of the following reasons:

a. to obtain a better quality good—as for example when meat is purchased in the form of steaks rather than some lesser cut or when a 19-inch television set is acquired instead of a 12-inch one;

b. to provide greater variety in the way a particular need is being served—as for example when a wardrobe is expanded to include different types of skirts and blouses; or

c. to enable a more specialized set of needs to be satisfied—as for example when, instead of a single screwdriver, a set consisting of different kinds of screwdrivers is purchased.

By allowing for the additional possibility that the increment of income will not be spent on any item of consumption but will instead simply be used to increase the household's discretionary funds or ''savings,'' it is possible to encompass all the different purposes for which an increment in household income can be used.

This is not to suggest that all household savings are merely the result of a failure to make a conscious choice as to how any additional income should be spent. One of the uses to which an increment in income can be put is to provide for various types of contingencies, such as illness, loss of employment or retirement. An individual household member can even opt for the acquisition of financial assets for the deferred purchasing power they afford—to be in a position, for example, to seize some future investment opportunity or make a bequest after death. Moreover, the normal increment in income may be less than the purchase price of certain consumption goods—for example, a new home or a car—so that funds may need to be accumulated before the item with the next highest priority can be acquired. In each of these cases, the decision to add to the household's holdings of financial assets will be a conscious one and no different, in terms of the type of decision involved, from the purchase of some good or service. Nonetheless, should a household fail to make a conscious choice as to how any increment in income should be spent, the result will necessarily be an increase in the household's discretionary funds, in the form of either additional bank deposits or some other type of financial asset (see below, chapter 12, section 1.3). Thus, with the default option being an increase in its savings, the situation depicted in exhibit 9.3 is the most general one that faces a household as its income increases. (See section 9.3.1, for a further discussion of this point.)

There is no reason to assume that, for all households with the same socioeconomic profile, the threshold level of income at which a particular item of consumption will be added to the shopping list is the same. On the contrary, it seems more reasonable to assume that the threshold level will vary, with Y_o distributed

Exhibit 9.4

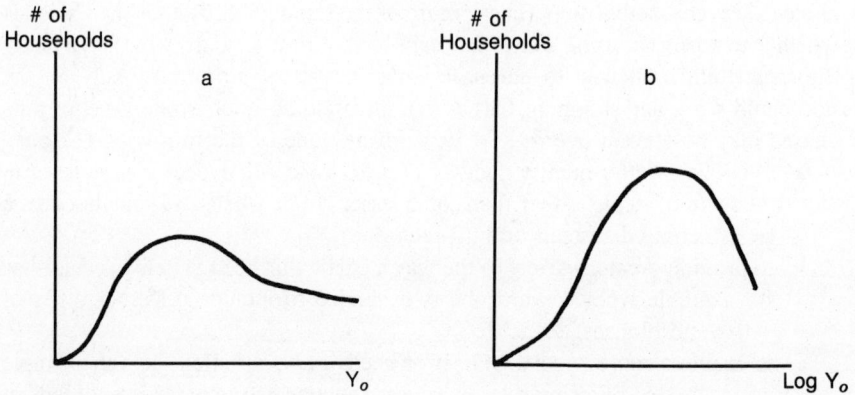

log-normally around some mean, $\bar{Y}_o$, as shown in exhibit 9.4a. This means that, once the values for Y_o are transformed into logarithms, the array takes the more familiar bell shape of a normal distribution, as shown in exhibit 9.4b. The reason for assuming a log-normal distribution is that while Y_o is bounded on the left-hand side by the fact that at zero income no purchase is possible, it is unbounded on the right-hand side, reflecting the fact that there is no upper limit to the value Y_o can take. Since the probability of any one household purchasing the item, ϵ, is also bounded by the limits of 0 and 1, the Engel curve for the entire class of such households will take the form of a sigmoid curve, such as the one shown in exhibit 9.5. This curve—in particular, the mean value, $\bar{Y}_o$, and the standard deviation, σ_Y—can be derived empirically from survey data reporting the proportion of all households within each income category that allow for that item within their budget. Indeed, by taking into account the socioeconomic profile of each household responding to the survey and weighting the responses by the relative proportion of that group within the overall population, it is possible to derive a similar Engel curve for the entire household sector. The socioeconomic characteristics which distinguish one household from another simply serve as the parameters of that Engel curve.

Once an Engel curve in this form has been derived for the entire household sector, it can be used to predict the changing income elasticity of demand for that item of consumption as the average level of household income increases over time. The income elasticity of demand, η_j, is equal to the inverse of the slope of the Engel curve depicted in exhibit 9.6, $\Delta Y/\Delta \epsilon$ multiplied by the ratio, ϵY. Moving up along that curve starting from the origin, the income elasticity of demand can be expected to reach its maximum value, with $\eta_j > 1$, somewhere to the left of the point on the curve, Y_a, where the slope is first equal to 1. From that point on, η_j will decline steadily as the average income of households rises. At the level of income Y_b, where exactly half of all households can be expected to have added the item to their inventory of goods, η_j will necessarily be

Exhibit 9.5

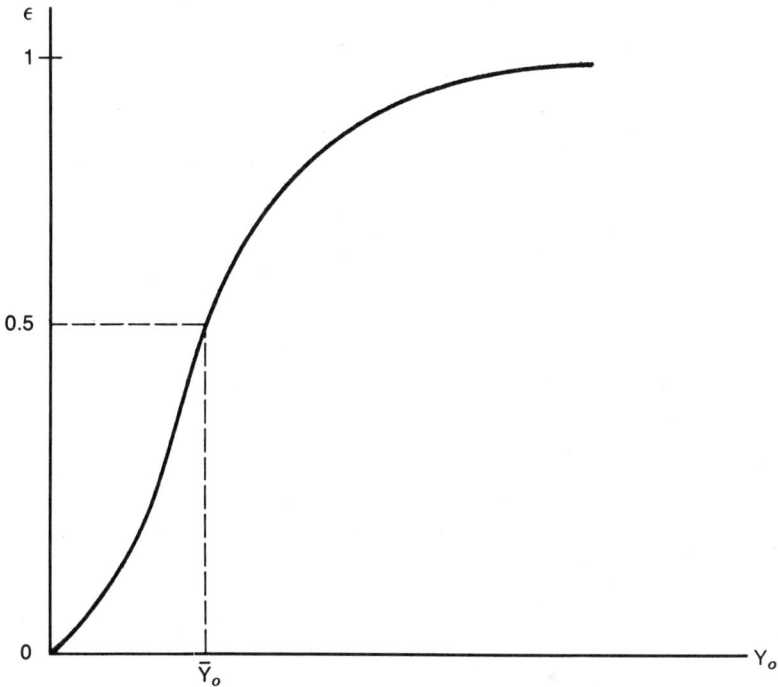

equal to 1. This is because the assumption that the threshold level of income is distributed log-normally around a mean, $\bar{Y}_o$, implies that at that point the demand for the good, instead of increasing more rapidly than income, will now increase less rapidly than income. Point B on the Engel curve shown in exhibit 9.6 therefore marks the point at which the item changes from being a "luxury" good to being a "necessity.". This is the point where, with the average income of households equal to Y_b, half of all households can be expected to have added the item to the inventory of goods they maintain.

The income elasticity of demand, η_j, will continue to decline in value beyond that point until finally, with average household income equal to Y_c, the point of saturation is reached. This is the level of household income—equal to $\bar{Y}_o$ (or Y_b) plus three times the standard deviation, σ_Y—at which virtually every household can be expected to have added the item to its inventory and the only further purchases will be to replace units of the item as they are used up. Thus, by deriving from survey data the type of Engel curve shown in exhibit 9.6 and then comparing the present level of household income with the benchmark values, Y_b (or $\bar{Y}_o$) and Y_c (or $\bar{Y}_o + 3\sigma_Y$), it is possible not only to estimate the value of η_j currently but also to project the future change in that variable as the average level

Exhibit 9.6

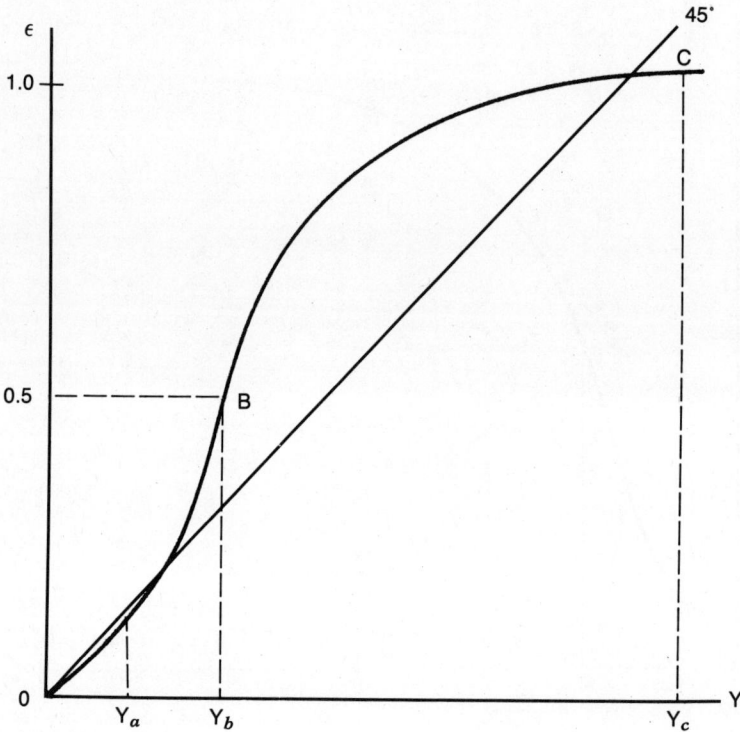

of household income continues to rise. In this way, one can determine not only the values taken by the Υ vector at the present time but also the rate at which those income elasticities can be expected to decline in the future.

Once the Υ vector has been determined in this manner, it is then possible to estimate empirically the other elements of the consumption matrix on which the linear expenditure model is based, particularly the principal diagonal which contains the Ψ vector. This is because, once the income elasticity of demand is known, the pure substitution effect of a change in price can be distinguished from the income effect. First, however, it is necessary to show how, with a complete set of Engel curves such as the one shown in exhibit 9.6, the hierarchy of material needs can be identified and the lexicographic ordering of household preferences then completed.

9.1.5 The hierarchy of material needs

Each item of consumption, C_j, will have its own Engel curve similar to the one shown in exhibit 9.6. These different Engel curves can be displayed on the same

Exhibit 9.7

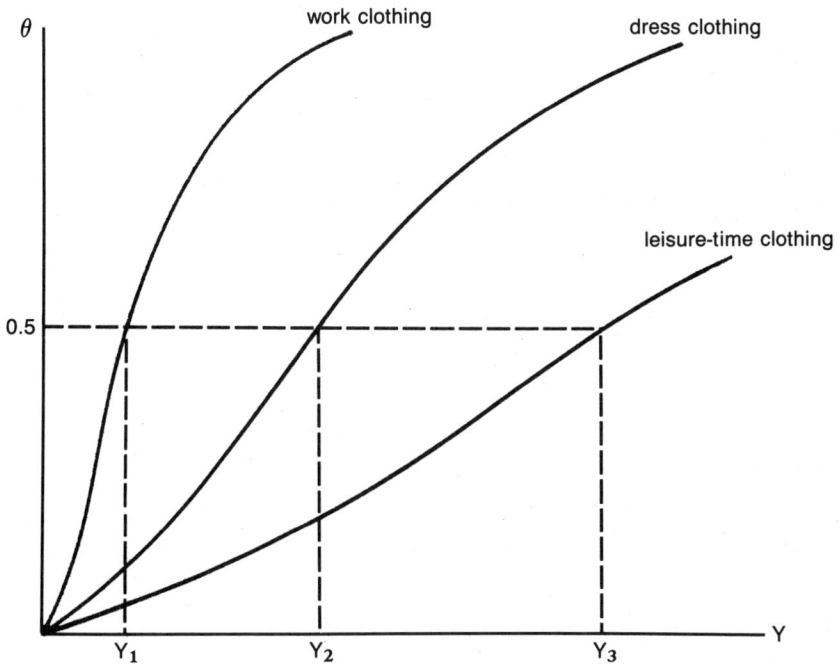

set of axes and the points of inflection at which $\eta_j = 1$ compared, as in exhibit 9.7. In this way, one can identify the order of priority in which the different items constituting that category of consumption are likely to be chosen by the group of households to which the Engel curves apply. For example, in the case of the items shown in exhibit 9.7, work clothing is likely to be added to a household's regular shopping list before dress clothing and dress clothing added before leisure-time clothing. It can therefore be said that, for that group of households, the clothing needed to hold a job ranks higher within their hierarchy of material needs than the clothing needed to dress for special occasions, and that the clothing needed to dress for special occasions ranks higher within the same hierarchy than the clothing used for leisure-time activities.

In this connection, it should be noted that the different items of consumption may be (a) complementary to one another; (b) useful for satisfying more than one need; or (c) alternative ways to spend any increment in income. For example, a variety of clothing items—including underwear, outerwear, shoes and hosiery— may be necessary to put together a complete outfit for each of the different members of the household. In that case the various items of clothing are complementary to one another. It may be, however, that the same outfit required on the job can also be used, either for dress occasions or for leisure-time activities. In that case, the same singular quantity of clothing satisfies more than one need and thus serves a multiple, or "joint," purpose. But it may also be that the type of clothing required on the job—for example, some type of uniform or heavy-duty work clothes—cannot be used for dress occasions or even during leisure hours. In that case, the different items represent alternative ways to spend any increment in income, with the order in which the choice is made reflecting the household's hierarchy of material needs.

What has just been said using the different kinds of clothing as an example applies to any group of items which, together, constitute a single category within the overall taxonomy of consumption. Once the alternative ways to spend any increment of income within that category have been identified, the order of preference for each separate item can be determined from the relative position of their Engle curves, as in exhibit 9.7. An item that half the households will include as part of their normal inventory of goods before some other item can be assumed to rank higher in the household sector's hierarchy of material needs.

Once the order of preference has been determined in this manner at one level within the taxonomy of consumption, it can then be determined for the next higher level of aggregation by making the entire category simply one item within a still broader group of goods. Indeed, by starting at the lowest level of disaggregation—the product line of each four-digit SIC industry supplying goods to the household sector—and then proceeding to each of the next higher levels of aggregation until finally the eight major categories of consumption have been covered, it is possible to determine the order of preference for the entire set of goods represented by the C vector and thus where each item falls within the hierarchy of the household sector's material needs. This order of preference, in turn, makes it possible to complete the lexicographic arrangement of the goods denoted by the consumption vector. Based on the relative position of their Engel curves, the different items within each of the nested set of consumption categories can be listed in the order that corresponds to the observed hierarchy of household needs. This rule serves as the second of the two needed to specify the elements of the C vector lexicographically, with the first rule —namely, that the items within any one category or subcategory or consumption be more alike in the need they serve than the items excluded—providing the basis for determining the nested set of consumption categories themselves (see section 9.1.2).

Once the nested set of consumption categories has been determined as part of the lexicographical ordering of household needs, it is possible to use the linear expenditure model, together with the previously obtained estimates of Υ, to derive the Ψ vector. Because of the computational difficulties which the linear expenditure model presents, the number of separate goods which can be taken into account in estimating the model's consumption matrix is not very large. Still, this is not a serious problem if one starts at the lowest level of aggregation and then proceeds, after obtaining a preliminary estimate of the values for the $e_{i,j}$ terms at that level, to the next higher level of aggregation—just as must be done in determining the household sector's hierarchy of material needs. The results obtained at each successive stage in the empirical investigation can then be checked against the conditions which must necessarily hold for the matrix as a whole.

It is not just that the (own) price elasticity of demand, $-e_{j,j}$, at any one level of aggregation must be equal to the sum of the cross elasticities of demand, $\Sigma e_{j,i}$, at that level. It is also that, once the appropriate set of nested consumption categories has been determined, the (own) price elasticity of demand at that level of aggregation, $-e_{j,j}$, must be equal to the weighted sum of the (own) price elasticities of demand of each for the separate items that constitute the jth category of consumption good. Since one effect of broadening a consumption category is that more items for which the cross elasticities of demand are negligible will be included, this means that the (own) price elasticity of demand can be expected to decrease in value as successively higher levels of aggregation are reached. Indeed, based on what has previously been said about the possibility of substituting one consumption good for another at the different levels of aggregation, the following results can be expected when the linear expenditure model's consumption matrix is estimated in the manner suggested above:

1. that the (own) price elasticities for the major categories of consumption will be negligible, that is, not significantly different from *zero*;
2. that the absolute value of the price elasticities for the goods produced at the three- and four-digit SIC level will be less than 1; that is, the demand for those goods will be price-inelastic; and
3. that it is only at the level of disaggregation represented by the separate items of each industry's product line that elasticities greater than 1 will be observed, with demand therefore price-elastic.

The income elasticity of demand, η_j, at any one level of aggregation must, of course, also be equal to the weighted sum of the income elasticities of demand for each of the separate items that constitute that larger category of consumption. But since the only other constraint is that the income elasticities for each of the major categories of consumption must, when properly weighted, sum up to 1, this condition does not lead to increasingly smaller values for the income elasticity of demand as higher levels of aggregation are reached. Indeed, η_j is free to vary around an expected mean of 1 in the case of the major categories of consumption—in contrast to an expected mean of 0 for the corresponding (own) price elasticities of demand—and around an expected mean, for the items comprising any subcategory, equal to the income elasticity of demand for the subcategory as a whole.

The elements of the Υ matrix need to be estimated prior to, and thus separately from, those of the Ψ matrix, based on the approach described in the preceding section. These income elasticities are therefore determined independently of the linear expenditure model. Still, based on the model of household behavior outlined in this chapter, the following additional result can be expected when the

Υ vector is derived from a set of Engel curves such as the ones shown in exhibit 9.7:

4. that the income elasticity of demand for the various items of consumption will vary over time, with η_j being relatively high when the item first crosses the threshold of being produced in response to some demand and then declining steadily thereafter until, when finally the point of saturation is reached, only the replacement demand remains.

This last expected result will be most clearly observable for the major items of consumption at relatively low levels of real income. However, as the consumption vector becomes more variegated over time due to technical progress (in the form of product innovation), the new goods being added to the consumption vector have proportionately the same probability of falling within any one of the eight major categories of consumption, thereby offsetting what would otherwise be a falling income elasticity of demand for that type of consumption good. This means that the expected decline in the income elasticity of demand will be observed only within an increasingly more narrow set of consumption categories—although there will still be some rough correlation between the income elasticity of demand for the major items of consumption and where they rank within the hierarchy of household needs.

We now need to see the extent to which the empirical evidence is consistent with these expected results. First, however, it is necessary to take up the alternative model of household consumption, the one based on the presumed existence of a set of utility functions and/or indifference curves, to see if that theory enables us to specify anything further about the values taken by the Υ and Ψ vectors.

9.1.6 The neoclassical model and the empirical evidence

The conventional theory either posits a utility function for each individual, such that

$$\mathsf{U} = f(C_1, C_2, C_3, \ldots, C_h) \qquad (9.6)$$

where U is the total "utility," or subjective feeling of well-being derived by the individual from the h goods represented by the consumption vector; or, alternatively, it posits a set of indifference curves, such as those shown in exhibit 9.8, with each curve within a given set representing the rate at which the individual, based on his or her "preferences," is prepared to substitute one consumption good for another. The number of these sets of indifference curves will be the number of cells above (or below) the principal diagonal of the h-by-h matrix of price elasticities. This is 28, or $\frac{1}{2}(h^2 - h)$, for just the eight major types of consumption goods and 199,990,000 for the 20,000 separate items stocked by a typical supermarket.

It is now generally acknowledged by those who hold to the conventional

Exhibit 9.8

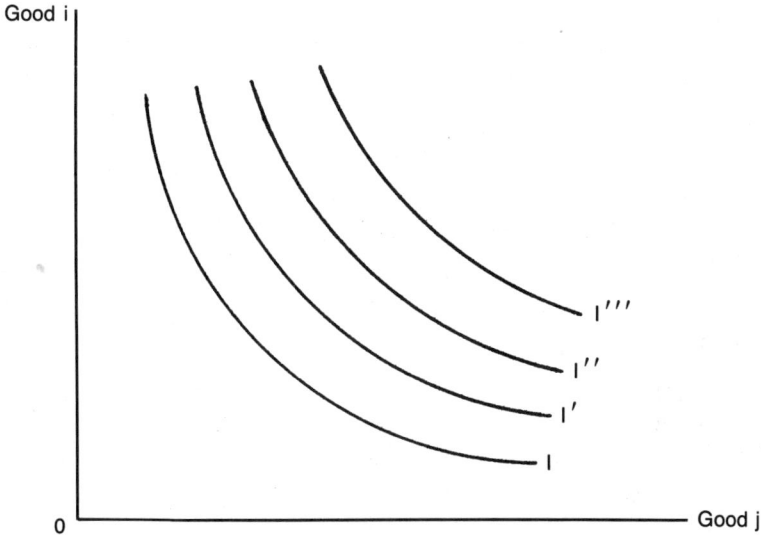

theory of consumer behavior that the dependent variable in equation 9.6 cannot be observed empirically. They nonetheless insist on the usefulness of equation 9.6 since the set of indifference curves shown in exhibit 9.8—which are thought to be observable, at least potentially—are assumed to derive from it. The question of whether a utility function of the type specified in equation 9.6 necessarily under-lies any set of indifference curves or whether, instead, a set of indifference curves can be posited independently of any utility function need not concern us. The point is that, with the dependent variable not observable, equation 9.6 does not itself add to the explanatory power of the conventional model. If that model has any explanatory power, it must derive from the sets of indifference curves which are usually specified as an integral part of that model, at least in the modern version stemming from Hicks and Samuelson's reformulation of economic the-ory along neo-Walrasian lines.

While the types of indifference curves shown in exhibit 9.8 were initially championed over the older set of arguments based on cardinal utility because it was thought that the curves were potentially observable, experience has belied that hope. Economists are no more able to derive, empirically, a set of indiffer-ence curves, such as those shown in exhibit 9.8, than they are a utility function of the type specified in equation 9.6. Thus the shift from cardinal to ordinal utility has not given the neoclassical model any more solid a foundation in the observ-able behavior of households. Even aside from this point, indifference curves, if they did exist, would require a ratiocinative process on the part of human beings which seems beyond them as individuals—let alone as members of a social group.

Before deciding on the purchase of any single item, they would need to weigh, simultaneously, the multiple options they face as represented by the $\frac{1}{2}(h^2 - h)$ sets of indifference curves. The process would, in fact, appear to be manageable only when the choice is reduced, as it usually is in presenting arguments about indifference curves, to two goods.

Although a reduction in the number of goods to two leads to a more manageable set of choices, it all but divests the model of any explanatory power. Since the various discrete needs of the individual cannot be satisfied by just two goods, one of the two "goods" has to be redefined as some composite of all the other items included within the consumption vector. It is usually then assumed, by those who hold to the conventional theory, that there are only two possible outcomes as the price of the one good specifically taken into account changes relative to the price of all other goods. One possible outcome is that less of the specific good will be purchased as its relative price rises and the other possible outcome is that more of the good will be purchased. With the latter possibility excluded for all except the rare "Giffin" good, there is only one conclusion that can be drawn. This is that less of the specific good whose relative price has risen will be purchased (or, alternatively, that more of the specific good whose relative price has fallen will be purchased). However, this line of reasoning ignores a third possibility: namely, that the change in relative price, particularly if it is due to a change in the price of all other goods, will have no effect on the quantity demanded. Without first being able to determine the real income effect of the change in relative price—and the conventional model, since it leaves the Engel curve unexplained, is of no help in this regard—one cannot rule out this third possibility. It may well be that, once the income effect of a change in the price of all other goods has been allowed for, the pure substitution effect will be zero. Indeed, this is precisely the argument, as the abnegation of the neoclassical theory, that underlies the model of household behavior developed earlier in this chapter.

According to that alternative model, the household purchases only a singular quantity of some item, whatever that quantity may be, to satisfy some quite specific need. This means that the quantity purchased is, to a large extent, independent of the price. A change in relative price will make a difference, in terms of the quantity purchased, only if it (a) implies a change in real income; (b) enables the household to satisfy the same need at a lower cost, or (c) induces the household to engage in counterspeculation, withholding its purchases in the hope that prices will subsequently rise (if the price of some good has risen above its "normal" level) or snapping up the "bargain" (if the price appears to be below the "normal" level). A fourth possibility, the one that underlies the conventional neoclassical model, is precluded. This is that the change in relative price will induce the household to purchase more or less of the same good while purchasing less or more of other goods (this is the pure substitution effect) so it can remain at the same level of subjective satisfaction or perhaps even attain a higher level of subjective satisfaction.

Which of the two models is the more appropriate one for explaining the behavior of households is primarily an empirical question—one that therefore needs to be decided on the basis of the available evidence. However, before turning to that evidence, one further point needs to be brought out. The model developed earlier in this chapter implies that the income elasticity of demand for any good will necessarily vary over time, with η_j relatively high initially and then declining steadily thereafter. It also implies that the (own) price elasticity of demand, e_j, will be (a) not significantly different from 0 in the case of the major items of consumption, and (b) not greater than -1 for the items produced by any group of firms constituting an industry. These restrictions on the values the Υ and Ψ vectors can take constitute the set of falsifiable statements by which the model can be tested empirically—just as the restrictions imposed on the values of the a and b parameters in the original Keynesian consumption function make it possible to test that theory as well, as we shall see in the main section which next follows. In contrast, the neoclassical model of consumer behavior imposes no similar set of restrictions on the values which the Υ and Ψ vectors can take. In the case of the Υ vector, this is because the income elasticities are simply left unexplained while, in the case of the Ψ vector, it is because a positive value for one of the price elasticity would simply denote a Giffin good or its counterpart on the opposite end of the spectrum, a Veblenian good. Instead there is only the strong presumption, based on the Gross Substitution Theorem, that the elements of the Ψ vector will all have values significantly greater than zero, with a negative sign attached to each of those price elasticities. Still, this is only a presumption, not a necessary implication, of the orthodox theory. Since the possibility of the price elasticity being positive cannot be wholly ruled out, the theory is irrefutable—and hence without any real explanatory power.

As already indicated, the most reliable evidence as to the values actually taken by the Ψ and Υ vectors are the estimates obtained from econometric studies based on the linear expenditure model or some variant thereof. This is because of both the comprehensive, or "general," nature of the model—the fact that it encompasses the entire set of consumption goods and not just one or two of them—and the check of any results that is provided by the conditions which the model as a whole must satisfy. The disadvantage is that, because of the data requirements for estimating its coefficients, the linear expenditure model can be applied only to a small number of consumption items. It is for this reason that estimates of the Υ and Ψ vectors, based on the model, have so far been obtained only for the major categories of consumption. While the discussion of the preceding section has suggested how the model could be extended to include the various subcategories of consumption, this suggestion has yet to be implemented in any empirical study.

The estimates of the consumption vector that were obtained by Angus Deaton for the U.K., using a variant of the linear expenditure model developed by Henry Theil and his colleagues, are among the most reliable yet obtained by empirical researchers. These results, based on data from 1900 to 1970, are presented in

Exhibit 9.9

Estimates of Own and Cross Elasticities
U.K. 1900-70

	Food	Clothing	Housing	Fuel	Drink & Tobacco	Travel & com-munication	Enter-tainment	Other goods	Other services
Food	-0.0728*								
Clothing	0.0212	-0.0165							
Housing	0.0105	-0.0270*	-0.0160						
Fuel	0.0024	-0.0035	0.0001	-0.0025*					
Drink & Tobacco	0.0107	0.0316*	-0.0045	0.0108*	-0.0622*				
Travel & com-munication	0.0421*	-0.0255*	0.0200*	-0.0051*	-0.0008	-0.0465*			
Entertainment	-0.0140*	0.0140*	0.0022*	0.0033	0.0055	0.0008*	-0.0194*		
Other goods	-0.0014	0.0102	-0.0012	0.0016	-0.0019	0.0054	0.0013	-0.0086*	
Other services	0.0011	-0.0045	0.0159	0.0030*	0.0107	0.0096	0.0063	-0.0054	-0.0467*
Value shares	0.284	0.100	0.153	0.053	0.133	0.097	0.033	0.051	0.096

* = estimates that are more than twice their standard errors
Source: Angus Deaton and John Muellbauer, *Economics and Consumer Behavior*, New York: Cambridge University Press, 1980, p. 71.

Exhibit 9.10
Income and Price Elasticities for Selected Countries
Based on Annual Aggregate Data, 1955–68

	Per Capita Disposable Income 1970 Dollars	Food		Clothing		Housing		Durables		Personal Care		Transport		Recreation		Other Services	
		η	e	η	e	η	e	η	e	η	e	η	e	η	e	η	e
U.K.	1,900	0.30	−0.27	0.62	−0.49	1.41	−0.86	1.14	−0.68	1.35	−0.78	2.53	−1.33	0.89	−0.54	2.63	−1.45
Australia	2,192	0.43	−0.27	0.45	−0.20	1.73	−0.69	1.06	−0.42	2.34	−0.85	1.70	−0.69	0.22	−0.09	1.14	−0.48
W.Germany	2,203	0.66	−0.60	0.78	−0.59	1.22*	−0.90*	1.22*	−0.90*	1.21	−0.86	1.45	−1.01	1.12	−0.80	1.74	−1.20
Sweden	2,962	0.76	−0.64	0.62	−0.44	0.92	−0.65	1.13	−0.76	1.43	−0.93	1.78	−1.11	1.09	−0.73	1.03	−0.68
U.S.	3,669	0.34	−0.26	1.14	−0.66	0.90	−0.59	1.45	−0.81	1.69	−0.92	1.14	−0.68	1.18	−0.66	2.31	−1.22
Countries	100–500	0.66	−0.48	0.97	−0.30	1.01	−0.28	1.98	−0.46	1.53	−0.34	2.46	−0.53	1.81	−0.46	1.79	−0.45
with per	500–1,000	0.82	−0.57	1.28	−0.60	0.68	−0.40	1.51	−0.67	1.10	−0.51	1.34	−0.61	1.35	−0.64	1.18	−0.49
capita	1,000–1,500	0.67	−0.40	1.09	−0.53	0.93	−0.52	1.70	−0.75	1.20	−0.61	1.60	−0.73	1.29	−0.63	1.30	−0.69
income	1,500 and up	0.50	−0.41	0.72	−0.46	1.24	−0.74	1.20	−0.71	1.60	−0.87	1.72	−0.96	0.90	−0.56	1.77	−1.01

*Housing and durables combined.

Source: Constantino Lluch, Alan A. Powell and Ross A. Williams, *Patterns in Household Demand and Savings*, published for the World Bank by Oxford University Press, 1977. Tables 3.2, 3.12, and 3.13.

exhibit 9.9. (Note that, reflecting the relative stage of Great Britain's development over the period covered, the major categories are somewhat different from those previously denoted for the U.S.) From an examination of the principal diagonal, it would appear that all the (own) price elasticities have the negative sign implied by the orthodox theory. However, it should be noted that the estimated price elasticity is significantly different, statistically, from zero for only seven of the nine categories—with only one of the price elasticities, that for drink and tobacco, greater than 5 percent. Moreover, when the same price elasticities are calculated, as a check on the results otherwise obtained, by summing up the cross elasticities which are statistically significant, the results are even less favorable to the orthodox theory. Finally, even these estimates may exaggerate the values taken by the Ψ vector. This is because Deaton was forced to assume a constant income elasticity of demand for the various items of consumption over the 70-year period covered by the study, an assumption which is inconsistent with other evidence, such as the results obtained by Constantino Lluch, Alan Powell and Ross Williams from a study of consumption patterns across countries, based on the same linear expenditure model.

As can be seen from exhibit 9.10, which presents some of the estimates from the Lluch, Powell and Williams study, the income elasticities of demand tend to decline with a rise in per-capita income. To the extent this same relationship holds not just cross-sectionally but also over time, it implies that the income elasticity of demand for the major items of consumption cannot be assumed to remain constant over time. Deaton's failure to take into account this declining elasticity means that his estimates of the price elasticities are probably exaggerated. Nonetheless, since he was able to make use of data on prices that were not available for many of the countries included in the study by Lluch, Powell and Williams, Deaton's estimates of the price elasticities are probably closer to the actual values for an advanced society like Great Britain (no comparable study has yet been carried out for the U.S.). Accepting those estimates at face value, without attempting to correct for the likely decline over time in the value of $_j$, it it would appear that the income elasticities of demand, the elements of the Υ vector, vary around a mean of 1 while the price elasticities of demand, the elements of the Ψ vector, vary around a mean of 0.04. This confirms the argument made earlier (see chapter 5, section 5.4) that the Ψ vector is only of marginal importance in determining the vector of growth rates for each industry, and that the main determinant of the G vector, aside from $\overset{\circ}{Z}$, is the Υ vector. While the evidence from this and similar studies may not yet be sufficient to reject the Gross Substitution Theorem (see, however, chapter 13, section 3.2), neither is it sufficient to reject the alternative argument that the price elasticities for the major items of consumption vary around a mean not signficantly different from 0.

9.2 The Econometrics of Aggregate Consumption

Aside from being more consistent with what is known about the price and income elasticities of demand, the model of household behavior presented in part 1 of this chapter is more in keeping with the spirit of the Keynesian consumption function (see chapter 3, section 1.2). While the former is a long-period microeconomic model and the latter, a short-period macroeconomic relationship, the principal determinant—the level of household income—is the same in both cases. This is hardly surprising since the model of household behavior has been formulated with what is known about consumption at the aggregate level clearly in mind. Indeed, it was the Keynesian consumption function that, historically, marked the first significant break with the practice in economics, at least since the marginalist revolution, of emphasizing relative price, or substitution, effects over income effects. This, however, is only one of the reasons why the Keynesian consumption function is so important in the history of economic analysis. No less important is the stimulus it gave to quantitative studies based on econometric techniques.

The consumption function which Keynes specified in *The General Theory* readily lent itself to empirical testing. There was not the same identification problem which plagued the efforts by economists to determine the shape of the Marshallian supply and demand curves. (The identification problem arose, in the latter case, from the fact that price and quantity movements could be caused by a shift of either curve, and it was not possible to "identify," from just the data on price and quantity movements, the separate contributions of the two supposedly independent curves.) Moreover, the Keynesian consumption function had just one principal determinant—unlike the Keynesian investment function. This was an important consideration in an era before economists were well versed in multiple regression techniques and could rely on high-speed computers to perform the necessary calculations. With the annual data available from the newly developed National Income and Product Accounts, it was only to be expected that Tinbergen in 1939, followed by other economists in the immediate post-war period, would attempt to test for the existence of the principal regularity underlying the Keynesian model of aggregate demand.

The results, without exception, were consistent with Keynes's specification of the consumption function. The following equation, presented in chapter 3, is typical of these results:

$$C = \$26.5B + 0.75Y_D \qquad (3.8)$$

The value of a—\$26.5 billion—is greater than 0 and the value of b (the marginal propensity to consume)—0.75—falls between 0 and 1. If there was some conflict between this result, based on time series data, and the results obtained from analyzing cross-sectional data—the former implied a linear relationship between consumption and income, the latter a curvilinear relationship—the discrepancy was easily explained by the difference in perspective implicit in the two data sets. Thus Tinbergen and those he inspired were encouraged in their efforts to make economics an empirically based science. It was only gradually, with greater sophistication in the use of econometric techniques, that they came to realize that the initial results they had obtained were not sufficient to validate empirically the Keynesian consumption function.

This greater sophistication can be seen in the three steps that mark the progress of research on the Keynesian consumption function between 1939 and 1970: (1) the use of a multiple-equation model by Daniel Suits in the early 1960s to explain aggregate household consumption; (2) the eventual recognition that the short-period determinants of consumption are different from the long-period determinants; and 3) the further refinement of Suits' approach in the large-scale econometric models constructed in the late 1960s. Indeed, it is as much to point out the lessons which have been learned about how to test a theory econometrically as to carry forward the story of the Keynesian consumption function that we shall now proceed to review that body of empirical research. While similar lessons can be learned from the efforts to test the Keynesian investment function (see chapter 7, part 1), the greater progress which has been made in identifying the determinants of aggregate consumption makes the history of that research even more instructive. Even so, as we shall see, the effort eventually floundered because economists were unable to shake from their collective minds the orthodox theory of consumer demand based on "utility" maximization.

9.2.1 The Suits set of equations

When the amount of household consumption in any given year, based on the NIPA estimate of personal consumption outlays, is regressed against the household sector's disposable income as was done in deriving equation 3.8, the amount of unexplained variance is virtually nil. Only as their statistical sophistication increased did econometricians and other economists come to realize that these results, so supportive of the Keynesian hypothesis, could not be taken at face value. As is pointed out in appendix B, the findings are vitiated by (a) the regressing of the whole with its largest part, and (b) the spurious correlation which occurs when time series data are used in a regression equation without first attempting to eliminate the common trend factor. When, in an effort to avoid these two problems, equation 3.8 is reestimated by taking the change in the variables from one year to the next, that is, their "first differences," the results obtained for the period 1929–1941 are as follows:

$$\Delta C = 0 + 0.73 \, \Delta Y_D \qquad R^2 = 0.96 \qquad (9.7)$$

Notice that the amount of unexplained variance is now 96 percent (compared to 98 percent). This indicates how much the use of the absolute amounts in the estimating equation exaggerates the correlation between aggregate consumption and household disposable income. However, it provides only a minimal estimate as to the amount of spurious correlation because, as will be explained shortly, the substitution of the first differences for the absolute values does not entirely eliminate the extraneous influence of the common trend factor.

The replacement of the absolute amounts with the first differences did more than just reduce the amount of spurious correlation. It also, together with the availability of quarterly rather than annual data, refurbished the standard by which any progress in understanding the determinants of aggregate consumption needs to be measured. The proportion of the variance which is left unexplained by the regression equation, R^2, can be viewed as a measure of how much ignorance remains as to what factors determine the value taken by the dependent variable. With the amount of this unexplained variance virtually nil when the Keynesian consumption function is estimated in level terms relying on annual data, it seems there is little more that can be learned. However, with the availability of quarterly observations for the postwar period, it became clear that there was still a great deal that was not understood about the determinants of aggregate consumption. Indeed, it turned out that the quarter-to-quarter change in consumption was barely correlated with the quarter-to-quarter change in disposable income. Thus the task which researchers in the field set for themselves in the 1960s was to reduce the considerable amount of unexplained variance which remained when the Keynesian consumption function was reestimated in first-difference form. Toward this end, they found it necessary to modify the original Keynesian formulation in two important ways.

The first was to divide aggregate consumption into its major components, and then to derive a separate equation for each of those components. Total consumption consists of expenditures on (1) durable goods, (2) nondurable goods, and (3) services (see chapter 2, exhibit 7). Moreover, the household sector's durable goods purchases, as defined in the National Income and Product Accounts, can be further broken down into (a) automobile and automobile parts purchases, and (b) other durable goods purchases. Based on the Flow-of-Funds Accounts, a third component of the household sector's durable good purchases can be identified. This is the household sector's purchases of new residences, or structures, with this category further divided into single-family and multiple-family units. By deriving a separate equation for each of these components of household spending, it has been possible for econometricians to produce a set of equations that better fits the available data.

The second way econometricians have tried to reduce the amount of unexplained variance is by introducing other factors besides disposable income as the independent, or explanatory, variable in the consumption function. Since Keynes argued only that income was the most important and not the sole determinant, the inclusion of other variables in the estimating equation does not invalidate the basic Keynesian model. That model, and the multiplier derived from it, would be inconsistent with the empirical evidence only if disposable income could be eliminated entirely from the consumption function or shown to exert only a small, marginal influence on consumption expenditues. So far, this has not been the case. Although other variables have been added to the consumption function, disposable income has continued to be the principal determinant. The inclusion of other variables has, however, required that econometricians shift from a simple regression model to a more sophisticated multiple regression model for each of the different equations that need to be estimated. (See appendix B for what this implies insofar as interpreting the statistical results are concerened.)

Quite a number of variables have been suggested for inclusion in the consumption function besides disposable income. The ones for which the empirical evidence has been strongest are (a) the household sector's liquid assets, (b) its stock of goods previously acquired, (c) credit market conditions, and (d) consumer attitudes. Moreover, for each of these four factors, there is a theoretical basis for its exerting a significant influence on consumption expenditures.

The ability of households to command goods in the market will depend not just on their current income but also on the amount of income previously obtained and then used to add to their savings—in the form of bank deposits and the other liquid assets which appear in the Flow-of-Funds Accounts as an increase in the "financial investment" of the household sector (see chapter 2, exhibit 18) and which therefore represent an increase in that sector's discretionary funds. Households, by drawing on these liquid assets, can avoid the budget constraint imposed by current income. Indeed, the evidence is that households often increase their liquid assets, especially time deposits, in anticipation of having to make major durable goods purchases. Thus an increase in the household sector's financial assets, relative to the amounts normally held, may presage a rise in that sector's discretionary expenditures.

In contrast, an increase in the stocks of physical assets held by the household sector—particularly its inventory of housing, automobiles and other durable goods—is likely to presage a fall in discretionary expenditures. The greater the size of those stocks, the less will be the need to add to those stocks and thus the lower will be the level of expenditures on the durable goods which constitute those stocks. After all, if a household has just purchased a new home, car or appliance, it is less likely to purchase another during the same period, even for replacement purposes. Conversely, as the stocks of consumer durables are reduced over time, the likelihood increases that households will act to replenish those stocks. It is for this reason that while the household sector's outlays, particularly on durable goods, can be expected to be positively correlated with the amount of financial assets held, those same outlays can be expected to vary inversely, and thus to be negatively correlated, with the stocks of physical goods already acquired.

The availability of credit, meanwhile, provides another means of transcending the budget constraint imposed by current income. If a household's income is insufficient to finance all the purchases it would like to make, the difference can be made up—at least in part—by borrowing. This is especially true with the development in recent decades of specialized credit arrangements for households, such as bank credit cards, overdraft privileges and seller-provided financing. Thus the availability of credit to the household sector, measured not just by the interest rates on consumer loans but also by such additional terms as the amount of down payment required and the length of time over which the loan is amortized, is likely to be a significant factor in determining the amount of household consumption. This is aside from just the sheer amount of funds earmarked or otherwise available for loans to households, including the funds available for home mortgages. Finally, consumer expenditures may well be influenced by psychological factors. If households have confidence that the economy will continue expanding, providing higher incomes along with job security, they are more likely to purchase "big-ticket" items such as automobiles and other durable goods than if they fear an imminent recession. The continuous monitoring of the household sector's psychological pulse by the University of Michigan's Survey Research Center has made it possible to detect any significant change in consumer attitudes.

Each of these four additional factors (as well as others) can be introduced in the aggregate consumption function, and indeed a number of empirical studies were carried out in which precisely this was done—with the result that the amount of unexplained variance was reduced. An even better result was obtained, however, by first disaggregating consumption into its major components and then introducing other explanatory variables besides disposable income into the separate equations. One of the first to demonstrate this was Daniel Suits in a body of work which was published in the early 1960s and which became the basis for the consumption block in what is now known as the "Michigan" model—one of several large-scale econometric models derived from the Tinbergen and Klein-Goldberger models, the two pioneering ventures in the large-scale econometric modeling of the U.S. economy. Suits's equations, which are presented in exhibit 9.11, invite comment on a number of points.

First, although only two additional variables besides disposable income are used to explain consumption outlays— these being the change in the household sector's liquid assets in the preceding year, ΔL_{-1}, and the similar change in the household sector's stocks of the good whose purchases are being modeled, ΔA_{-1}—the modification has been applied in a consistent way to all four categories of consumption. Moreover, there is reason *a priori* to expect both variables to be important determinants of consumption outlays. They have not been added, without any theoretical justification, simply to boost the value of the R^2 statistic.

Second, the variables are specified as first differences, and this manner of specification, as Suits argued in urging it on his fellow econometricians, serves to reduce the amount of serial correlation and the other statistical problems that arise when time series data are used.

Third, with the inclusion of the two additional independent variables, a new set of statistical issues arises. The most important question is whether the additional variables add significantly to the equation's explanatory power. As is pointed out

Exhibit 9.11

Disaggregated Consumption Equations: Postwar*

R^2

Automobiles $\Delta A = .194\Delta Y + .220\Delta L_{-1} - .551 A_{-1} + 5.042$ .74
     (2.6) (2.9)   (4.1)

Other Durables $\Delta D = .178\Delta Y + .0709\Delta L_{-1} - .0391 D_{-1} - .363$ .95
      (2.7) (4.4)   (1.2)**

Nondurables $\Delta ND = .207\Delta Y + .146\Delta L_{-1} + .299 \Delta ND_{-1} - .085$ .68
      (3.7) (2.4)** (2.0)**

Services $\Delta S = .108\Delta Y + .0447\Delta L_{-1} + .601 \Delta S_{-1} - .413$ .76
    (3.9) (1.6)** (3.9)

Total (summed) $\Delta C = .687 \Delta Y + .482 \Delta L_{-1} + \ldots + 5.007$

*Fitted in first differences to annual data, 1948–59; all variables measured in billions of 1954 dollars.
**t ratio falls outside acceptable limit.

Disaggregated Consumption Equations: Prewar*

R^2

Automobiles $\Delta A = .0893\Delta Y + .0199\Delta L_{-1} - .401 A_{-1} + 1.243$ .93
     (11.2) (1.1)**   (5.3)

Other Durables $\Delta D = .0967\Delta Y + .0403\Delta L_{-1} - .0928 D_{-1} - .484$ .93
      (12.1) (2.3)** (1.6)**

Nondurables $\Delta ND = .247\Delta Y - .0251\Delta L_{-1} + .164 \Delta ND_{-1} - .870$ .79
      (3.8) (0.2)** (0.8)**

Services $\Delta S = .130\Delta Y + .004\Delta L_{-1} + .220 \Delta S_{-1} - .166$ .87
    (4.9) (0.1)** (0.5)**

Total (summed) $\Delta C = .563 \Delta Y + .0311\Delta L_{-1} + \ldots + 25.431$

*Fitted in first differences to annual data, 1930–41; all variables measured in billions of 1954 dollars.
**t ratio falls outside acceptable limit.
Reprinted from Daniel B. Suits, "The Determinants of Consumer Expenditure: A Review of Present Knowledge," *Impacts of Monetary Policy*, Commission of Money and Credit, Prentice-Hall, 1963, p. 35.

in appendix B, this depends—aside from whether the amount of unexplained variance, as measured by $1-R^2$, is thereby reduced—on whether the t ratios fall within the acceptable range. While not all the t ratios (shown in the parentheses below the coefficient estimates) fall within the acceptable range of 2.5 or better, those for disposable income do in all four of the equations estimated for the two periods—and, in the case of the equations estimated for durable goods in the postwar period, even the t ratios for the two additional explanatory variables mostly fall within the acceptable range. More will be said shortly about the reasons for the two additional independent variables lack of explanatory power in the equations for other than durable goods purchases. For now, the important point is that the set of four separate equations developed by Suits was a considerable advance over the way consumption had previously been modeled.

And yet, even as Suits's results were becoming generally known and even incorporated into various econometric models, there was a growing uneasiness over the type of consumption function implicit in his equations. Suits himself had contributed to the uneasiness when he pointed out that if the same equations were reestimated using the quarterly data available for the postwar period rather than the annual data going back to 1929, the R^2 statistic became embarrassingly low—even close to zero for some subcategories of consumption. Indeed, based on that quarterly data and the technique of using first differences to reduce the amount of spurious correlation, there seemed to be no clear statistical association between consumption and disposable income. While this finding could be interpreted as reflecting only the poor quality of the quarterly data (see chapter 2, section 2.4), other evidence had by now become available to suggest a different explanation. The problem, this other evidence indicated, was less in the data than in their interpretation.

9.2.2 Long- vs. short-period consumption

In 1946 Simon Kuznets had published his estimates of U.S. consumption and national income for overlapping decades going back to 1869. The figures, shown in exhibit 9.12, seemed to indicate that the average propensity to consume had remained relatively constant at approximately 0.86—until the Depression decade. This constancy of the average propensity to consume, if true, would mean that the consumption function went through the origin rather than having a positive vertical intercept, or constant term, as argued by Keynes. While the data sources on which Kuznets had been forced to rely were of such a fragmentary nature that his estimates could be questioned, there was another reason to believe that the average propensity to consume was constant—despite what Keynes had argued. This was the fact that the widely predicted postwar depression had not occurred. Many economists, persuaded by Keynes that the average propensity to consume fell over time as income rose, had expected the U.S. economy to slip back to its prewar depressed state once peace returned. In their view there was simply no way that businessmen could be induced to invest enough both to make

Exhibit 9.12
**National Income and Consumption Expenditures
in 1929 Prices, 1869–1938**

Decade	National Income	Consumption Expenditures	APC
1869–78	$ 9.3 billion	$ 8.1 billion	0.86
1874–83	13.6	11.6	0.86
1879–88	17.9	15.3	.85
1884–93	21.0	17.7	.84
1889–98	24.2	20.2	.84
1894–1903	29.8	25.4	.85
1899–1908	37.3	32.3	.86
1904–13	45.0	39.1	.87
1909–18	50.6	44.0	.87
1914–23	57.3	50.7	.89
1919–28	69.0	62.0	.89
1924–33	73.3	68.9	.94
1929–38	72.0	71.0	.99

Source: Simon Kuznets, *National Product Since 1869*, New York: National Bureau of Economic Research, 1946, p. 119.

up for the sharp cutback in government spending that could be expected when the war ended and to offset the high levels of household savings which the war-time prosperity had generated. At least this was the view of the "secular stagnationists" such as Alvin Hansen. But so far, at least by the early 1960s, no depression had occurred.

At the same time, there was the mounting evidence from econometric studies, based on annual data, which seemed to confirm the existence of a Keynesian consumption function. Was the vertical intercept, the constant term a, greater than zero as postulated by Keynes? Or was the vertical intercept equal to zero as the Kuznets data strongly suggested? Since the underlying question was whether consumption expenditures as a percentage of national income declined or remained the same when the economy expanded, and thus how difficult it was for the economy to stabilize at "full employment," the issue was of more than just academic importance. Either the constant term was greater than zero, and thus consumption declined as income rose, or the constant term was not significantly differently from zero. One could not have it both ways—or so it seemed. The fact that the newly available quarterly data seemed to cast doubt on whether there was any relationship between consumption and income whatsoever only made an already contradictory body of evidence all the more difficult to assess.

It turned out, however, that there was a way to reconcile the conflicting evidence. As Arthur Smithies had first pointed out, the Keynesian consumption

Exhibit 9.13

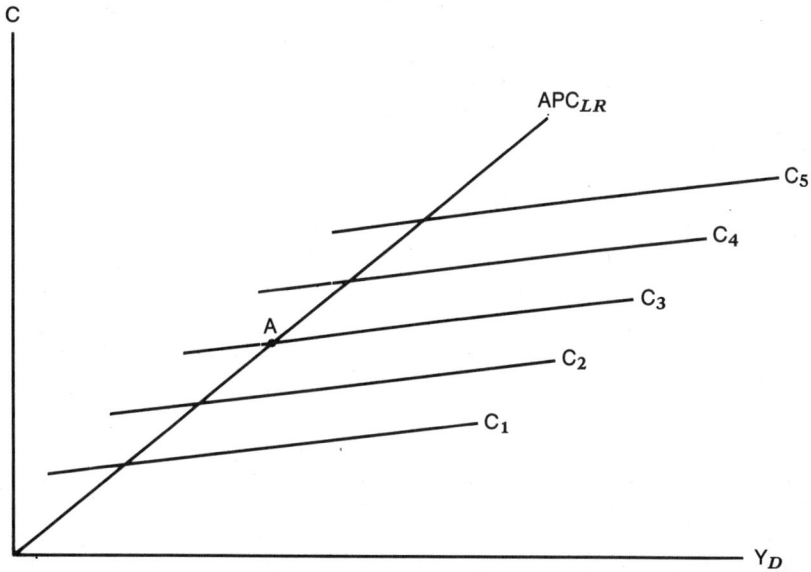

function could be viewed as a short-period relationship which, over time, shifts up to the right, tracing out, as shown in exhibit 9.13, the long-period relationship reflected in the Kuznets data. What the econometric studies—at least those based on annual data—had captured was the Keynesian short-period consumption function, represented by one of the C curves shown in exhibit 9.13. The fact that somewhat different estimates of both a and b were obtained by comparing the prewar data with the postwar data seemed to bear out this interpretation. These findings supported the view that the Keynesian short-period consumption function was shifting up to the right over time, tracing out the long-period relationship implied by Kuznets data. Indeed, the long-period average consumption line shown in exhibit 9.13 can be viewed as the locus of a particular point on the short-run consumption curve, a point such as A on curve C_3 which represents the mean value of consumption over the cycle, with that point shifting to the right over time along with the consumption curve itself. With this interpretation of the data, the question which then arose was what are the factors responsible for the shift of the short-period consumption curve. In response, three separate theories were advanced. One was the relative income hypothesis put forward by James Duesenberry, another was the permanent income hypothesis posited by Milton Friedman and the third was the life-cycle hypothesis suggested by Franco Modigliani and his collaborators.

According to Duesenberry, individual households base their day-to-day consumption on the norms established by whichever social groups, or class, they identify with. He thus denied that consumer preferences are "innate" to the individual or in any other sense can be taken as a given. Rather he argued that the preferences which can be observed from household behavior are, like other forms of social behavior, learned or acquired. The preferences of the individual household are the preferences of its social reference group, and it is the basket of goods and services considered a proper level of consumption within that social reference group that the individual household will want to purchase with its income. As the norms about consumption change within the social reference group, so will the basket of goods and services purchased by the individual household. The Duesenberry relative income hypothesis can therefore be regarded as a sociological, or Veblenesque, approach to modeling household behavior. In this respect, it is fully consistent with what has already been said about the role played in by social customs and habit (see section 9.1.3).

The relative income hypothesis carries with it a number of implications, two of which can be used to reconcile the seemingly contradictory evidence about aggregate consumption. One implication is that as the disposable income of the household sector increases over time attendant upon the growth of the economy, all the different social reference groups found within the houshold sector can be expected to revise upward their norms about consumption. In other words, there is no reason why any particular reference group should not acquire a taste for a higher standard of living as the average income within the group rises. This would explain the constant average propensity to consume over time which can be observed for the household sector as a whole. The other implication is that if the disposable income of any individual household should change relative to the average within its social reference group, the basket of goods and services purchased by that household is likely to remain the same. Instead, the changed level of income will be adjusted to by a change in savings. When the individual household's income rises, savings will increase disproportionately; and when its income falls, the individual household will attempt to maintain its present standard of living as long as it can, even going into debt if necessary. This would explain, not only the varying average propensity to consume over the cycle but also the observable "ratchet effect"—the tendency of household consumption expenditures not to fall below some previously achieved maximum. Indeed, in formulating his own version of the Keynesian consumption function, Duesenberry argued that household expenditures depended not on current disposable income but rather on the previous peak level of disposable income.

The relative income hypothesis implies that it is changing norms about consumption as per capita income rises over time which causes the short-period consumption function to shift to the right. The explanation, under the permanent income hypothesis, is somewhat different.

According to Friedman, the income received by the individual household can be divided into two components: one, a permanent component which the household expects to continue receiving indefinitely, and the other, a transitory component which cannot be counted on beyond the current time period. The household's consumption expenditures, Friedman argued, are systematically related only to its permanent income. Indeed, Friedman assumed that the individual household will spend a certain fixed proportion of its permanent income on consumption goods, this assumption being consistent with the constant average propensity to consume over time which can be observed for the household sector as a whole. However, in the case of any transitory income—e.g., overtime pay, a Christmas bonus, etc.—the individual household is as likely to save the money as it is to spend it. This means that the propensity to consume out of transitory income is, on average, equal to 0.50. The lower average propensity to consume out of transitory income can, in combination with the higher average propensity to consume out of permanent income—approximately 0.86 if Kuznets's data are to be trusted—then explain the varying average propensity to consume over the cycle found by econometricians. For it is the transitory component of household income which is likely to vary over the cycle, and with the average propensity to consume lower for that component of income, the average propensity to consume can be expected to fall as income increases cyclically and to rise as income declines—just as Keynes had postulated. The greater or lesser transitory component, with its smaller average propensity to consume, simply pulls down or raises the total consumption depending on the stage within the cycle.

In the case of the permanent income hypothesis, the emphasis is on the probabilistic nature of the income received by the individual household at any given moment in time rather than on the role of changing social norms in determining that household's consumption pattern. As an explanation for what causes the short-period consumption function to shift over time, there is no reason to prefer it to the relative income hypothesis. The two explanations, it should be noted, are not necessarily incompatible with one another, and Duesenberry's argument about the role of social norms in determining household consumption patterns can readily be incorporated into the permanent income hypothesis. The latter, however, is closer in spirit to the more conventional micro analysis of household behavior which assumes independent rather than interdependent utility functions for each household, and indeed Friedman formulated his hypothesis within that context. Still, the reason the permanent income hypothesis has come to be favored by econometricians is not because of what it has to say about the shift of the consumption function over time, or even its less radical departure from orthodox demand theory, but rather because Friedman was able to suggest a way that the concept of permanent income could be made operational in empirical studies. This was to make consumption a distributed lag function of disposable income. The permanent income hypothesis has thus been taken up by econometricians because of the difference it makes in how the short-period consumption function is specified prior to being tested.

9.2.3 The distributed lag consumption function

Any transitory component of income, Friedman argued, will tend to be viewed as permanent the longer it continues to be received. This is true for the individual household and for the household sector as a whole. Thus any increase in income which continues to be received by households can be regarded as permanent rather than transitory income. To the extent that consumption depends solely on "permanent" income, it can therefore be explained by the change in disposable income over some previous interval of time. In other words, the short-period relationship between consumption and disposable income is a distributed lag function similar to the one used by Eisner and others to explain investment outlays (see chapter 7, section 1.3). Indeed, in acknowledgment of his debt to Friedman, Eisner referred to his model as a "permanent income" theory of investment.

The distributed lag function for consumption takes the following form:

$$C_t = k(Y_t + \lambda Y_{t-1} + \lambda^2 Y_{t-2} + \lambda^3 Y_{t-3} + \ldots \lambda^n Y_{t-n}) \qquad (9.8)$$

or, more generally,

$$C_t = k \sum_{i=0}^{n} \lambda^i Y_{t-i} \qquad (9.9)$$

where C_t is the amount of consumption in year t, Y_{t-i} is the amount of disposable income in the ith prior year, k is some constant which can be interpreted as the long-period average propensity to consume, λ^i is the weight attached to disposable income in the ith year and n is the number of discrete time periods which constitute the interval over which transitory changes in disposable income are transformed into permanent income. With consumption equal to a certain fixed proportion, k, of the income in any period, the spill-over consumption from the previous time period, λC_{t-1}, can be explained as follows:

$$\lambda C_{t-1} = k \sum_{i=0}^{n} \lambda^{i+1} Y_{t-i-1} \qquad (9.10)$$

Subtracting equation 9.10 from equation 9.9 (this is referred to by econometricians as the Koyck transformation after the economist who first suggested it—see chapter 7, section 1.3) yields the following:

$$C_t - \lambda C_{t-1} = kY_t \qquad (9.11)$$

or, shifting terms,

$$C_t = kY_t + \lambda C_{t-1} \qquad (9.12)$$

It was in this form that the permanent income hypothesis was first tested empirically using time series data, with results that were encouraging. The permanent income hypothesis in this form can then be compared with the relative income hypothesis as an explanation for the short-period movements in household consumption, with the relative income hypothesis, as specified by Duesenberry, taking the following form:

$$C_t = a + b(\ddot{Y}) \qquad (9.13)$$

where $\ddot{Y}$ is the previous peak value of disposable income.

The introduction of a distributed lag function such as that used to test the permanent income hypothesis raises a number of econometric issues. The first is how the distributed lag itself is to be specified—both the interval of time to be taken into account (the value of n in the above equations) and the weight to be attached to the observation in the current or most recent period (the value of λ). The practice, following Koyck, was to use a set of geometrically decreasing weights— this is the reason the weights in equations 9.8 and 9.9 are specified as λ^i—with all the weights, or λ terms assumed to sum up to 1. When the distributed lag function takes this form, the value of n becomes unimportant. As can be seen from exhibit 9.14, even with λ as low as 0.1, the weight attached to the observation in the sixth antecedent year becomes insignificant. With λ taking a higher value, the weight attached to the observation in any year prior to t-1 becomes even less significant so that equation 9.12 is soon approximated. There is no reason, of course, why the weights need be geometrically decreasing ones. Other formulations, such as arithmetically decreasing or even equal weights, have been suggested. Still, as long as the current year's behavior is influenced by what happened previously—whatever the precise nature of the lag structure—the model can be viewed as one based on what has come to be known as "adaptive expectations." This means that those who make decisions, such as how much income should be spent on consumption, can be viewed as learning from past experience. It is this broader formulation that is intuitively appealing. (Models based on adaptive expectations have recently been criticized by some economists, who have argued for replacing them with models based on "rational expectations." See chapter 12, section 3.3).

The critical issue in any distributed lag, or "adaptive expectations," model is how the value of λ is to be determined. Efforts to estimate λ, not just in the case of the consumption function but for other types of functions as well, have been made relying on both survey and time series data. Whatever the data sources, however, it has proven difficult to obtain consistent results from one study to the next. In the case of the econometric studies based on time series data, one problem has been that of serial correlation. With consumption in the current time period assumed to depend on consumption in the preceding time period (or on

Exhibit 9.14
**Alternative Adaptive Expectations
With Declining Geometric Weights**

λ	Time period						
	0	−1	−2	−3	−4	−5	−6
0.1	0.0	.81	.66	.43	.19	.03	*
0.2	0.2	.64	.41	.17	.03	*	*
0.3	0.3	.49	.24	.06	*	*	*
0.4	0.4	.36	.13	.02	*	*	*
0.5	0.5	.25	.06	*	*	*	*
0.6	0.6	.16	.02	*	*	*	*
0.7	0.7	.09	.01	*	*	*	*
0.8	0.8	.04	*	*	*	*	*
0.9	0.9	.01	*	*	*	*	*
1.0	1.0	*	*	*	*	*	*

* less than 0.01

disposable income in the preceding time period—the two can be used inter-changeably under the permanent income hypothesis), serial correlation is almost certainly present, leading to an upwardly biased estimate of the relationship between the two variables (see appendix B). This likelihood of significant serial correlation is the second econometric issue raised by the introduction of a distributed lag into the consumption function. Indeed, unless some type of corrective measure is taken, the probable existence of substantial serial correlation will make any results obtained suspect whenever a distributed lag is employed, whether in a consumption function or in some other type of behavioral equation.

Friedman, then, was able to suggest an alternative way to reconcile the conflicting evidence about the average propensity to consume in the long period and in the short—even though it has been difficult to test the model he proposed using time series data because of certain econometric problems. While the Friedman explanation is not necessarily in conflict with the emphasis placed by Duesenberry on changing social norms and the interdependence of "utility," it certainly can be interpreted that way. Under the permanent-income hypothesis, households are assumed to maximize their individual utility, subject only to the budget constraint imposed by their income. The Friedman explanation, then, is more consistent with the neoclassical model of household behavior while Duesenberry's argument is more consistent with the model presented in the first part of this chapter. Indeed, like the original Keynesian consumption function, the latter helped lay the foundation for that alternative model of household behavior. Still, the problem is less the interdependence of "utility" than the fact that individuals cannot be certain how much income they can continue to count on. This brings us to the third way that has been suggested for reconciling the conflicting evidence about the average propensity to consume. It is the argument that was made by Modigliani, first in a joint paper with Richard Brumberg and then later in collaboration with Albert Ando. Their life-cycle hypothesis extended the logic of the orthodox model, based on the presumed maximization of utility, in such a way that the econometric problems which arose in testing the permanent income hypothesis could be avoided. This advantage was gained, however, by ignoring the very point that was central to the permanent income hypothesis—namely, the inherent uncertainty which households face as to their future income.

According to Modigliani and his several collaborators, the individual household seeks to maximize the utility from the income available to it, not just in the current time period but rather over the entire lifespan of the household. In other words, utility is maximized over an extended time horizon. (The argument, it should be noted, is usually made in terms of individuals rather than households, but in the discussion which follows we shall retain the household as the unit of analysis.) Two factors complicate the individual household's efforts to maximize the utility from its income over its lifespan. One is the uneven flow of income. Household income usually rises steadily from the time the household is first formed as a new social unit until the principal wage earner reaches his or her mid fifties. From that peak point, household income usually then falls until it reaches whatever floor is provided by pension and other retirement income. Modigliani *et al.* argue that, despite this uneven flow of income, households attempt to maintain the same standard of living over their lifespan. The other complicating factor is the similarly uneven but quite different pattern of consumption requirements over the same time interval. Typically, the household's major expenses are incurred at the time children are added and/or a home is purchased, this usually being at a relatively early point in the lifespan of the household. Indeed, at this point in the cycle, the household may be forced to go significantly into debt in order to maintain whatever standard of living seems appropriate given the lifetime income of the adult members.

Like the relative and permanent income hypotheses, the life-cycle arguments made by Modigliani *et al.* suggest why the average propensity to consume is likely to remain constant over time. In this case it is because households, anticipating the future growth of income, have already based their lifetime standard of living on it. Modigliani's life-cycle hypothesis does, however, suggest an additional set of factors, besides the growth of disposable income, likely to affect consumption over time. This is the age composition of households and other demographic factors. Moreover, as interpreted by Ando, it has a somewhat different implication for how the short-period consumption function needs to be specified.

Based on the life-cycle hypothesis, households can be expected to vary their level of consumption in the short period—on the average, assuming they share the same demographic characteristics—only to the extent their lifetime income varies. There are but two sources of a change in expected lifetime income: (a) a change in expected wage income and (b) a change in expected nonlabor, or property, income. The former is essentially what Friedman was trying to capture in using lagged income, Y_{t-1}, to measure "permanent" income. Ando merely suggested another way to approximate the change in expected wage income, one which avoids the econometric problems associated with a distributed lag function. This was to take the ratio of the labor force, L, to employment, N (the inverse of the unemployment rate).

As for a change in expected property income, this would be reflected, according to Ando, in either a change in the amount of income-earning assets held by the household sector or a change in the rate of return on those assets. In either case, it would lead to a change in the net worth of the household sector. While Friedman had included the same set of factors in formulating his permanent income hypothesis, he did not have available to him the data on household net worth which Ando was able to derive from Raymond Goldsmith's work on national wealth. It is the inclusion of this net worth variable, as well as the clear distinction between labor and nonlabor income, which distinguishes the short-period consumption function based on the Modigliani life-cycle hypothesis from other short-period consumption functions. This function is specified as follows:

$$C_t = \beta_1 Y_{L_t} + \beta_2 \ddot{Y}_{L_t} + \beta_3 W_{t-1} \tag{9.14}$$

where Y_L is aggregate labor income or the wage bill; $\ddot{Y}_L$ is expected aggregate labor income; W is the net worth of the household sector, and β_1, β_2 and β_3 are the propensities to consume out of current labor income, expected future labor income and net worth respectively. Dividing through by Y_{L_t} yields the following:

$$\frac{C_t}{Y_{L_t}} = \beta_1 + \beta_2 \frac{\ddot{Y}_{L_t}}{Y_{L_t}} + \beta_3 \frac{W_{t-1}}{Y_{L_t}} \tag{9.15}$$

It is in this form that the life cycle hypothesis is often formulated, the specification in ratio form being one way to minimize the serial correlation and other econometric problems. The ratio of the labor force to employment, L/N, is then used to approximate $\ddot{Y}_{L_t}/Y_{L_t}$ so that equation 9.15 can be simplified as follows for estimation purposes:

$$\frac{C_t}{Y_{L_t}} = \beta_1 + \beta_2 \frac{L}{N} + \beta_3 \frac{W_{t-1}}{Y_L} \tag{9.16}$$

The inclusion of the net worth variable in the consumption function and, even more critically, the availability of the data to measure it made it possible to examine the empirical significance of an old point that had been raised in the controversy surrounding *The General Theory*, the wealth effect on consumption.

Marshall's protege, A. C. Pigou, had first raised the point in denying Keynes's contention that the economy could equilibrate at less than full employment. The fall in price levels associated with an economic downturn, he argued, would increase the real value of whatever liquid assets were held by households and thus the real income of the household sector would rise. The increase in the real income of liquid wealth holders would, in turn, lead to an increase in their consumption expenditures, eventually restoring the economy to full employment. Donald Patinkin had then taken up the same argument, terming it the "Pigou effect." While the empirical significance of Pigou's point was unclear, it could not be dismissed solely on theoretical grounds. Indeed, it was one of several similar lines of argument by which the wealth of the household sector was thought to play an important role in the cyclical movements of the economy. Now, with the net worth variable included in the consumption function, the line of argument represented by that entire family of models could be assessed empirically. With just a liquid assets variable included—and thus with other types of household assets excluded—the same line of argument, but with a slightly different variable used to represent the argument, could also be tested.

This sort of test was to be carried out systematically in the course of developing the new generation of large-scale econometric models that began to appear in the late 1960s. One distinguishing characteristic of these newer models was that they were based on quarterly rather than annual data. But another characteristic was the general consensus which they tended to reflect as to the short-period determinants of consumption—the result of the close communication among those constructing the models. It was this general consensus, as presented by Evans in his textbook, *Macroeconomic Activity*, which represented the late 1960s state of the art insofar as deriving the short-period consumption function was concerned.

9.2.4 The late 1960s state of the art

There are two reasons why Evans's textbook, and the empirical results reported therein, constitute a useful benchmark for assessing what was known econometrically about aggregate consumption by the end of the 1960s. One is that the book was the first advanced macroeconomic textbook since Gardiner Ackley had initially staked out the field in 1961 with his *Macroeconomic Theory*, making Keynesian rather than business cycle models the core of the analytical framework. (By 1969, when Evans's book was published, Ackley's text was already dated. It was not revised until 1978.) Moreover, whereas the primary emphasis in Ackley had been on the theory, with the empirical evidence touched on only to inform the theory, just as it is in this text, the emphasis was almost entirely the opposite in Evans. The theory was brought out only to the extent necessary to explain the empirical findings. What this meant was that the Evans text had little theoretical bias (aside from its general Keynesian orientation). It was intended primarily to give a sense of the "empirical magnitudes."

The second reason for taking up Evans's text as the measure of what was known econometrically about the consumption function by the end of the 1960s is that it was based on, and written largely to provide a detailed explanation of, one of the most important of the large-scale econometric models of the U.S. economy then coming into prominence. This was the Wharton EFU (Economic Forecasting Unit) model developed at the University of Pennsylvania. Evans had been Klein's principal collaborator in building the model, helping to transform the earlier Klein-Goldberger model from an annual to a quarterly model. Moreover, Evans would later leave the Wharton EFU to construct, first, the Chase Econometric model and then, subsequently, his own separate model—both of which would be marketed in competition with the Wharton EFU model and the commerically even more successful Data Resources (DRI) model developed by Otto Eckstein. It was these proprietary models which, along with the Michigan, Brookings and MIT-Fed models, would represent by the end of the 1970s the fullest development of orthodox Keynesian theory—that is, the macroeconomic component of the neoclassical synthesis. However much these models might diverge from one another, and even themselves change over time, the equations to explain household consumption would easily be recognizable as those justified by Evans in his 1969 textbook.

The Evans text marks progress on a number of points—even aside from the reliance on quarterly rather than annual data. The most important advance, in comparison to Suits's earlier work, is the clear distinction made between the other components of consumption and consumer durables. It is only the former, that is, nondurable goods and services, which are explained by a Keynesian-type "consumption function." Consumer durable goods purchases—along with residential construction—are treated differently, in a manner analogous to business fixed investment. This is in fact the approach adopted in the empirical work on which this text is based (see part 3).

The second advance over Suits's earlier work is the recognition that the conflicting evidence as to the average propensity to consume in the short period and in the long somehow had to be reconciled. For Evans, the reconciliation took the form of positing a distributed lag function for consumption in the short period which, when simulated over many quarters, led to a reasonable estimate of the long-period average propensity to consume. There is, as will soon become clear, a better way to reconcile the conflicting evidence—one that avoids the econometric problems associated with a distributed lag function. Still, by making explicit allowance for the change that takes place in the propensity to consume as the time horizon is extended, the consumption equations estimated by Evans (in conjunction with Klein) represented a distinct advance over those presented earlier by Suits.

Yet a third mark of progress was Evans's effort to compare systematically the various alternative formulations of the short-period consumption function to see which of them provided the better statistical fit before deciding how household expenditures should be explained within the overall model. Indeed, this attempt to base the consumption equations on an explicit test of the major competing theories meant that the equations reflected a certain cumulative growth of knowledge—rather than simply being idiosyncratic to the author—and this is another reason to regard the Evans textbook as a benchmark in the ongoing effort to gain a better understanding of aggregate household behavior.

Evans first specified the several competing theories for estimation purposes in such a way as to facilitate comparison while at the same time attempting to minimize the problem of serial correlation. He then presented the empirical findings in two tables, here reproduced as exhibits 9.15 and 9.16, with the results shown in the first table based on annual data for the 1929–1962 period (with the war years, 1942–1946, omitted) and the results shown in the second table based on quarterly data for just the postwar period alone. It should be noted that by this time economists had come to recognize the problem posed by serial and other types of correlation among the residuals so that the Durbin-Watson statistic was routinely included among the statistics reported. (See appendix B for a discussion of this statistic.)

Equations 1–3 are alternative formulations of the permanent income hypothesis. Equation 1 is based on equation 9.12 with the first coefficient providing an estimate of k and the second coefficient an estimate of λ. Equation 2 reformulates the permanent income hypothesis in ratio form so as to reduce the amount of serial correlation, with the L/N variable taken over from Ando and Modigliani as an approximation of expected future labor income. Equation 3 is Evans's own formulation of the permanent income hypothesis, with the C/Y ratio still used to reduce the amount of serial correlation but with the growth of disposable income, $\Delta Y/Y$, replacing the L/N term. Equation 4 is Duesenberry's short-period specification of his relative income hypothesis (see equation 9.13) while equation 5 is based on the wealth variable from Ando and Modigliani's specification of the life-cycle hypothesis (see equation 9.16).

As Evans pointed out in his text, it is difficult, if one looks only at the equations in exhibit 9.15, to choose any one of the equations over the others based on the R^2 and the other statistics shown. However, when the entire set of equations is re-estimated using quarterly data, there is good reason, as can be seen from exhibit 9.16, to reject equations 2 and 5. The unexplained variance is more than 85 percent in both cases. When a lagged term is added to these two equations (see equations 2a and 5a), all the explanatory power shifts to the lagged term—as can be seen from the unacceptably low t ratio for the other independent variable. In other words, looking at the quarterly data, the L/N and W_{-1}/Y_L terms would seem to lack any explanatory power. The elimination of equations 2 and 5, based on the empirical evidence from quarterly time series, is hardly surprising. The L/N term is, after all, only the inverse of the unemployment rate and, while

Exhibit 9.15
Comparison of Various Annual Consumption Functions[a]

	$\bar{R}^2$	d	Yearly mpc	Long-run mpc
1. $C = 0.280Y + 0.676C_{-1}$ (0.041) (0.052)	0.998	1.09	0.280	0.828
2. $C/Y = 0.343 + 0.440(L/E)$ (0.042)	0.792	1.45	0.343	0.834

3. $C/Y = 0.104 - 0.402(\Delta Y/Y)$
                  (0.029)
     $+ 0.884(C/Y)_{-1}$
       (0.038)
	0.962	2.05	0.440	0.834

4. $C/Y = 0.209 + 0.267Y^0/Y$
                  (0.041)
     $+ 0.423(C/Y)_{-1}$
       (0.097)
	0.864	1.38	0.561	0.834

5. $C^*/Y_L = 0.602 + 0.085(W_{-1}/Y_L)$ (0.003)	0.959	1.53	0.447[b]	0.834[b]

[a]C, consumption of nondurables and services, billions of constant dollars; C*, consumption of nondurables and services plus use value of consumer durables, billions of current dollars; Y, personal disposable income, billions of constant dollars; Y^0, peak previous income, billions of constant dollars; Y_L, disposable labor income, billions of current dollars; L, labor force, millions; E, employment, millions.
[b]Adjusted to be comparable with the other functions.
Source: Michael K. Evans, *Macroeconomic Activity*, p. 65.

probably a good predictor of current labor income, it provides no clue as to future labor income (except to the extent that the current unemployment rate can be expected to persist). As for the W_{-1}/Y_L variable, it is only a crude measure of expected nonlabor income, the quarterly series being dominated by the immediate change in household savings. Thus there is good reason to exclude from the short-period consumption function the variables used by Modigliani *et al.* to represent the life-cycle hypothesis.

What Evans did not point out, but which nonetheless needs to be kept in mind, is that while the other equations cannot be dismissed so readily, they still fall far short of providing strong empirical support for the permanent-income or, alternatively, the relative-income hypothesis. For with each of those equations based on a distributed lag function, the possibility of substantial serial correlation cannot be excluded. The problem is most obvious in the case of equation 1. The fact that the dependent variable is specified in level terms virtually guarantees a spuriously high R^2. But even when the dependent variable is specified in ratio form, as in equations 3 and 4, the use of a distributed lag function can be expected to introduce a significant amount of serial correlation. This suspicion is

Exhibit 9.16
Comparison of Various Quarterly Consumption Functions[a]

	$\bar{R}^2$	d	Quarterly mpc	Long-run mpc
1. $C = 0.222Y + 0.738 \frac{1}{4} \sum_{i=1}^{4} C_{-1}$ (0.030) (0.038)	0.998	1.76	0.222	0.807
2. $C/Y = 0.606 + 0.189(L/E)$ (0.158)	0.007	0.49	0.606	0.803
2a. $C/Y = 0.158 + 0.038(L/E)$ (0.105)				
$+ 0.755 \frac{1}{4} \sum_{i=1}^{4} \left(\frac{C}{Y}\right)_{-1}$ (0.083)	0.570	2.31	0.765	0.803
3. $C/Y = 0.227 - 0.459 \sum_{i=1}^{4} \frac{4-i}{4}\left(\frac{\Delta Y}{Y}\right)_{-1}$ (0.049)				
$+ 0.723 \frac{1}{4} \sum_{i=1}^{4} \left(\frac{C}{Y}\right)_{-1}$ (0.051)	0.825	1.58	0.334	0.789[b]
4. $C/Y = 0.082 + 0.470(Y^0/Y)$ 0.042)				
$+ 0.313 \frac{1}{4} \sum_{i=1}^{4} \left(\frac{C}{Y}\right)_{-1}$ (0.071)	0.826	1.19	0.333	0.803[b]
5. $C^*/Y_L = 0.815 + 0.046(W_{-1}/Y_L)$ (0.014)	0.130	0.68	0.617[c]	0.803[c]
5a. $C^*/Y_L = 0.201 + 0.011(W_{-1}/Y_L)$ (0.010)				
$0.766 \frac{1}{4} \sum_{i=1}^{4} \left(\frac{C^*}{Y_L}\right)_{-1}$ (0.078)	0.658	2.09	0.152[c]	0.803[c]

[a] All the symbols are identical to those used in Exhibit 9.15.
[b] Estimated 1948–1964.
[c] Adjusted to be comparable with the other functions.
Source: Michael K. Evans, *Macroeconomic Activity*, p. 66.

supported by the Durbin-Watson statistic of less than 2. All that can be said with assurance, then, based on Evans's work, is that, while the variables representing the life-cycle hypothesis can probably be ruled out as lacking empirical support, there is no similar basis for rejecting either the permanent-income hypothesis or the relative-income hypothesis.

Moreover, based on Evans's results, it is not possible to say which is to be preferred, a short-period consumption function based on the permanent-income hypothesis or one based on the relative-income hypothesis. Both seem to account for the short-period movements of aggregate consumption equally well. The truth is that it has proven impossible to establish the superiority of either the permanent-income hypothesis or the relative-income hypothesis on the evidence from time series data. If one turns to cross-sectional data, the evidence becomes even more difficult to interpret, and in any case cannot readily be incorporated into a time series model designed to explain short-period changes in aggregate household spending.

Indeed, what remains to be said after all the evidence available up through the 1960s has been sifted is that there is probably a long-period average propensity to consume—most likely different for each major category of consumption—towards which the household sector as a whole tends to move over time as its disposable income fluctuates cyclically. This constant average propensity to consume implies, with the household sector's disposable income increasing secularly, a constant rate of growth of expenditures on consumption goods. There are thus two types of adjustments which households need to make over time: (1) one, the adjustment to the secular increase in disposable income, and (2) the adjustment to the cyclical fluctuations in the same disposable income. The dynamic factors highlighted by both the permanent-income hypothesis and the relative-income hypothesis—with no reason, really, to exclude even some of the demographic factors identified by the life-cycle hypothesis—may well be part of that two-fold adjustment process. Still, there is no empirical basis for choosing one hypothesis over the other as the single best explanation of the adjustment process.

Even before publishing his detailed empirical comparisons, Evans had ruled out two other variables from consideration. One was the amount of liquid assets held by the household sector and the other was the change in income distribution between workers and nonworkers. The reason was that these two variables added little to the explanatory power of the equations he chose to test. This does not necessarily mean, however, that these two factors are not important. It may just be that their influence on consumption, if any, needs to be brought out through a somewhat different mode of analysis, one that abandons entirely the specification of a separate consumption function, at least for nondurable goods and services.

Thus the econometric studies, whether carried out separately or as part of some larger modeling effort, had left matters pretty much up in the air by the end of the 1960s as to what factors besides disposable income are important in determining the cyclical movements of aggregate consumption. This confused state of affairs can be attributed, at least in part, to the lack of a satisfactory microeconomic foundation on which to base the analysis of the household sector's behavior. The prevailing model of household behavior, with its emphasis on the relative price effects of utility maximization, was not really compatible with Keynes's argument. And yet, those carrying out the empirical research were not prepared to shift to some other framework. We, however, need not be so inhibited. The next step, in fact, will be to show how, starting from the model of household behavior developed in the first part of this chapter and then building on what, by the end of the 1960s, had been learned about the determinants of aggregate consumption, it is possible to derive a set of E and F functions for the household sector that is more consistent with both the empirical evidence and the larger macrodynamic model developed so far in this text.

9.3 The Household Sector's E and F Curves

It is now possible, based both on the empirical work which has been done on the Keynesian consumption function and on the model of household behavior developed in the first part of this chapter, to derive the relevant set of E and F curves for the household sector. These E and F curves are based on the following more general functions, the same ones that were used previously to derive the E and F curves for the enterprise sector (see chapter 7, part 4):

$$\dot{E}_i = \dot{A}_i + \dot{P}_E \tag{7.24}$$

$$\dot{A}_i = \mathring{A}_i + f(\dot{G} - \mathring{G}, X_1, X_2, \ldots, X_m) \tag{7.25}$$

and

$$\dot{F}_i = \mathring{F}_i + f(\dot{G} - \mathring{G}, Y_1, Y_2, \ldots, Y_n) \tag{4.32}$$

where $\dot{A}_i$ is the growth of the ith sector's discretionary expenditures in real terms and $\dot{P}_E$ is the growth of the price index for the durable goods which constitute that sector's discretionary expenditures. As was brought out earlier, the growth of a sector's discretionary expenditures in real terms which can be observed during any one time period, $\dot{A}_i$, can be broken down into two parts: (1) the continuation of whatever trend has previously prevailed, $\mathring{A}_i$, and (2) a cyclical movement, $\dot{A}_i - \mathring{A}_i$ or $\overset{*}{A}_i$, which depends on the cyclical movement of aggregate output, $\mathring{G}$, as well as on a set of additional factors, or parameters, $X_1, X_2, \ldots, X_m$, one of which is the price index, P_E. That is,

$$\overset{*}{A}_i = f(\overset{*}{G}, X_1, X_2, \ldots, X_m) \tag{7.26}$$

The growth of the sector's discretionary funds during that same period, $\dot{F}_i$, can be divided into the same two components, the continuation of the trend, $\overset{\circ}{F}_i$, and a cyclical movement, $\overset{*}{F}_i$, with the latter depending on $\overset{*}{G}$ and a different set of parameters representing various intersectoral compensation rates, $Y_1, Y_2, \ldots, Y_n$. That is,

$$\overset{*}{F}_i = f(\overset{*}{G}, Y_1, Y_2, \ldots, Y_n) \tag{7.27}$$

As was done in deriving the E and F curves for the enterprise sector, we shall begin by explaining what determines the trend values, $\overset{\circ}{E}_i$ and $\overset{\circ}{F}_i$, and then proceed from there to estimate the a, $b_1, b_2, \ldots, b_m$, α, and $c_1, c_2, \ldots, c_n$ parameters of the following two behavioral equations:

$$\overset{*}{A}_i = a\overset{*}{G} + b_1X_2 + b_2X_2 + \ldots + b_mX_m \tag{7.28}$$

and

$$\overset{*}{F}_i = \alpha\overset{*}{G} + c_1Y_1 + c_2Y_2 + \ldots + c_nY_n \tag{7.29}$$

The one difference, at least in form, from the earlier analysis is that, instead of disaggregating by subsector—i.e., corporate, farm and noncorporate nonfarm—only a single E and F function will be derived for the household sector as a whole. While it should be possible, at least in theory, to derive separate E and F functions for each of the different social classes—rentier, white-collar, blue-collar and dependent—the data presently available for the United States do not permit this fine a delineation. The household sector's discretionary expenditures will instead be broken down by type of durable good purchase—housing, automobiles and other—with the E function for the household sector as a whole derived as the aggregate of those separate E functions.

9.3.1 The trend values

Just as it was possible to determine the trend values for the enterprise sector's E and F functions by falling back on the previously developed model of long-period production, so now it will be possible to derive the trend values for the household sector's E and F functions based on the model of household behavior outlined in the first part of this chapter. For each major type of durable good purchase, or discretionary expenditure—housing, automobiles and other—a separate secular growth of nominal demand can be estimated, with that trend value, $\overset{\circ}{E}_{H.j}$, the sum of two growth rates: (1) the secular growth of demand in real terms for that durable good, $\overset{\circ}{A}_{H.j}$; and (2) the secular rate at which the price of that good is increasing, $\overset{\circ}{p}_{C_j}$. That is,

$$\mathring{E}_{H.j} = \mathring{A}_{H.j} + \mathring{p}_{c_j} \qquad (9.17)$$

For the remainder of this chapter, we shall take the secular rate at which the prices of the various consumer durable goods are increasing as a given and instead focus on the growth of demand in real terms for those goods. The analysis of the changing price of these and other goods will be left for later (see chapter 14, section 0.0). However, as should be clear by now, it is the changing price of these and other goods that brings the growth of demand in nominal terms into line with the available supply in real terms, with the secular rise in the price level, that is, the inflation rate, reflecting this necessary balancing condition.

With the price of the durable goods which constitute the household sector's discretionary expenditures treated as a parameter, the secular growth of demand in real terms for any durable good purchased by the household sector, $\mathring{A}_{H.j}$, will be equal to the product of the secular growth of real income, $\mathring{G}$ (or, alternatively, $\mathring{Z}$), and the income elasticity of demand for that item of consumption, η_j. That is,

$$\mathring{A}_{H.j} = \mathring{G}(\eta_j) \qquad (9.18)$$

or, alternatively,

$$\mathring{A}_{H.j} = \mathring{Z}(\eta_j) \qquad (9.19)$$

where $\mathring{A}_{H.j}$ is the household sector's secular growth of demand in real terms for the jth item of consumption and the other variables are as previously specified.

In the case of equations 9.18 and 9.19, the jth item of consumption is a durable good. However, the same notation, and the same argument, applies to each of the other elements of the C vector as well. The entire set of these trend values are the elements of the growth vector, $\underline{G}$, previously specified for the set of vertically integrated industries producing items for final use, or consumption—especially when the relative price, or substitution effects, arising from technical progress are negligible and can therefore be ignored (see chapter 5, section 5.4). The reason for distinguishing the household sector's durable goods purchases from its other outlays, then, is not that the secular growth of demand is determined in a different manner. Rather it is because the cyclical pattern of these expenditures— along with their determinants—are different, with important consequences for how the system as a whole behaves.

Because of the role played by housing, automobiles and other consumer durables in the cyclical movement of aggregate output, these items need to be distinguished from the more general set of goods purchased by the household sector. Indeed, this is a further point, aside from the difference in the long-period and short-period propensities to consume, that had been clearly established by the empirical work done on the Keynesian consumption function up through the end of the 1960s. It had come to be recognized, by Evans among others, that because of the underlying stock-adjustment process the household sector's expenditures on durable goods over the cycle behaved in a manner that is more akin to business investment than to the other types of consumption outlays. This is why it is necessary, when modeling the short-period fluctuations in aggregate output, to separate the durable items from the other components of the C vector and treat them in a manner analogous to the durable goods purchased by the enterprise sector. It is also why the Υ vector (and the Ψ vector) used to calculate the values of the G vector needs to be respecified so that it encompasses only the income (and price) elasticities for the smaller number of durable goods that are part of the C vector. Once both these steps have been taken, with the value of the truncated Υ (and Ψ) vector explained by the model of household behavior developed in the first part of this chapter, it is then relatively easy to obtain the trend values, $\mathring{A}_{H.j}$, for the set of E functions that need to be specified for the household sector. It is simply a matter, as can be seen from equation 9.17 (or, alternatively, from equation 9.18), of multiplying the income elasticity of demand for each durable good by the secular growth of real income.

The model of household behavior developed in the preceding part of this chapter makes it possible, not just to derive an estimate of the values taken by the truncated Υ vector at any one point in time but also, to project the rate at which those those income elasticities can be expected to decline over time. One important implication of that model is that the income elasticity of demand for any consumption good, after quickly reaching its maximum value, will decline steadily thereafter as the average level of household income rises until finally the point of saturation is reached and the only subsequent demand is for replacement purposes. This argument applies, in particular, to housing, automobiles and the other durable goods purchased by households, with the declining value of the $\mathring{A}_{H.j}$ terms (based on the declining value of the income elasticity of demand, η_j) only partly offset by the introduction of new variants of older products—e.g., homes with a larger number of rooms, second cars for commuting to work—and even by the introduction of entirely new durable goods as complement of existing products, such as separate home freezers and VCRs.

The empirical work necessary for estimating the value of the $\mathring{A}_{H.j}$ terms has yet to be completed. This is because estimates of the truncated Υ vector, based on the approach outlined in the first part of this chapter, have yet to be obtained. Alternative estimates of $\mathring{A}_{H.j}$, derived by fitting a time trend to the data on consumer durable purchases in a manner similar to the way estimates were obtained for the enterprise sector, are nonetheless available. It should be noted that this approach is a less satisfactory one, making it difficult to determine what change, if any, has occurred in the income elasticity of demand for the various consumer durable goods over time. One can only determine, by dividing the estimate of $\mathring{A}_{H.j}$ by the growth of disposable income, $\mathring{Y}_D$, what was the average income elasticity of demand over the period as a whole.

Although only the income elasticities for the durable items of consumption need be taken into account, either explicitly or otherwise, in deriving the trend values for the household sector's several E functions (assuming the relative price, or substitution, effects are negligible), still the condition which the Υ vector as a whole must satisfy—namely, that the weighted average of those elements must be equal to 1—is important. For it means that the secular growth of demand for all consumption goods other than the durable items—and thus the long-period average propensity to consume insofar as nondurable goods and services are concerned—will be the complement of the weighted average of the growth in demand for durable goods. That is,

$$\mathring{C}_{ND+S} = 1 - (\sum_{j=1}^{e} w_{Cj}\mathring{A}_{H.j}) = \sum_{I=1}^{h-e} w_{Cj}\mathring{A}_{H.j} \qquad (9.20)$$

where $\mathring{C}_{ND+S}$ is the secular growth of demand for, and thus the long-period average propensity to consume, nondurable goods and services; e is the number of durable goods included among the h separate items of consumption which constitute the C vector, and w_{Cj} is the relative weight, $p_jC_j/ \sum_{j=1}^{x}p_jC_j$ of the jth consumption good when x is the number of items within the relevant set. The long-period consumption function for nondurable goods and services is therefore implicit once the trend values, $\mathring{A}_{H.j}$, have been determined. The short-period consumption function for nondurable goods and services is, however, a different matter. This is because household savings can vary in the short period in a way that is not possible in the long period.

Any one household can, of course, use a part of its income to add to its financial assets—and thereby increase its savings as conventionally defined. By exchanging the cash (or bank deposits) thereby retained for other less liquid though higher-yielding types of assets, such as bonds or common shares of stock, the individual household can even acquire an ever expanding contingency fund out of which to finance future purchases. Indeed, most households, once their more basic needs have been met, can be expected to establish such a fund, not just so they can better cope with emergencies in the more immediate run but also so they will have sufficient income, as the lifetime income hypothesis recognizes will be necessary, after the adult members of the household retire. The contingency fund itself, and the deferred purchasing power it represents, can in fact be viewed as one of the "goods" represented by the C vector. This, in turn, explains why the contingency fund, as the conscious choice made by households as to the next best use of any increment in income, will increase only at a certain secular rate—just like the other nondurable components of the C vector. That secular rate, $\mathring{S}_H$, will, relative to the growth of disposable income, $\mathring{Y}_D$, determine the long-period average propensity to save and thus the long-period average propensity to consume as well. With $\mathring{S}_H$ and $\mathring{Y}_D$ identical to one another and the income elasticity of savings therefore equal to 1, the long-period average propensity to consume will remain unchanged—as Kuznets's data suggests it has, in the case of the United States, for more than a century.

The difference between the contingency fund maintained by each household and the other nondurable components of the C vector is that the former, as the difference between current cash inflow and any cash outlays, can change as a result of factors that are beyond the control of the individual household—and even beyond the control of households as a group. While households can determine how much they wish to spend on various consumption goods, and even how much they would like to put aside as part of some contingency fund, they cannot determine the current flow of income into the household sector. That flow of income will depend on the flow of money wages and the other types of compensation paid by business firms, with the latter in turn depending on the level of aggregate demand as was brought out earlier (see chapter 8, section 1.2, especially equation 8.4, and section 3.5). Thus, if the growth of household saving during any period, $\dot{S}_H$, should differ from the expected or secular rate, $\dot{\mathring{S}}_H$, this is likely to be due, not to some conscious decision on the part of households but rather, to some change in disposable income originating from outside the household sector. Any short-period change in household savings can therefore be assumed to be involuntary.

But even if households could, through some conscious, concerted act, vary their rate of savings in the short period, the change in the size of their contingency funds would be only a temporary one. The reason is that an increase in household savings will, as long as all other factors remain the same, simply lead to a decline in aggregate demand—and thus to a subsequent fall in disposable income as business firms, faced with slumping sales, are forced to cut back on their money payments to households. Similarly, any reduction in household savings will, *ceteris paribus*, boost aggregate demand, causing disposable income and, along with disposable income, the size of the contingency fund, to rise. Indeed, this is simply the "paradox of thrift" first pointed out by Keynes. What it means is that households as a group cannot, on their own, increase their rate of savings as conventionally defined, that is, as the excess of cash inflow relative to cash outlays—except temporarily as a short-period disequilibrium outcome. (These points are elaborated on in chapter 12, section 1.3.)

Households can, however, increase their "gross savings" as defined in the Flow of Funds Accounts, both in the long period and in the short period—provided they also increase their "tangible investment." For the household sector's "gross savings" are its savings as conventionally defined plus any funds spent on durable goods—what have previously been denoted as the household sector's discretionary funds—while the household sector's "tangible investment" is the amount of durable goods purchased, or what have previously been defined as the household sector's discretionary expenditures (see chapter 2, section 3.3). Thus, the aggregate demand condition for continuous expansion will be satisfied if the household sector's "gross savings" and its "tangible investment" in nominal terms both increase at the same rate (see chapter 4, sections 1.2 and 1.4). For in that case, with $\mathring{F}_H$ and $\mathring{E}_H$ equal to one another, there will be no increase in the household sector's savings as conventionally defined. It is even possible for the aggregate demand condition to be satisfied if $\mathring{F}_H$ and $\mathring{E}_H$ diverge—provided the growing cash surplus (or deficit) in the household sector is offset by a growing cash deficit (or surplus) in some other sector. In that case, however, it is the sectoral balance condition that may not be satisfied.

9.3.2 The sectoral balance condition

As previously pointed out (see chapter 4, section 1.4), the sectoral balance condition for continuous growth requires that the relative distribution of final output among the different sectors be maintained. With only two sectors—an enterprise sector that produces all goods and services and a household sector that is the only source of demand for those goods and services in the long period—this means that the secular growth of investment, or discretionary expenditures by the enterprise sector, cannot exceed the secular growth of demand for consumption goods. That is, the following condition must be satisfied:

$$\mathring{I}_r = \mathring{C}_r \tag{9.21}$$

where I_r and C_r are aggregate investment and aggregate consumption in real terms respectively. In a simple, two-sector model, the sectoral balance condition is, in effect, the obverse of the aggregate supply condition. Just as industries cannot expand their capacity at a rate less than the growth of final demand without a supply constraint on further expansion eventually being encountered, so they cannot expand capacity at a rate greater than the growth of final demand without the returns from investment eventually being jeopardized. This means that, based on equations 9.20 and 9.21, the following condition must hold:

$$\sum_{j=1}^{n} y_j \mathring{A}_{Bj} = \sum_{j=1}^{e} w_{C_j} \mathring{A}_{Hj} + \sum_{j=1}^{h-e} w_{C_j} \mathring{A}_{Hj} \tag{9.22}$$

where $\mathring{A}_{Bj}$ is the secular rate at which the jth industry within the enterprise sector is increasing its capacity by purchasing new plant and equipment, with

$$\sum_{j=1}^{n} y_j \mathring{A}_{Bj}$$

equal to $\mathring{I}_r$; the y_j terms are the weights given by the previously defined **Y** vector (see chapter 5, section 1.4), with the w_{C_j} weights a subset of this more general set of weights, and the other terms are as previously defined. Thus it is not possible for the household sector to vary the rate at which it is puchasing durable goods,

$\overset{\circ}{A}_H$, without a fully offsetting change in the rate at which it is purchasing nondurable goods and services, $\overset{\circ}{C}_{ND+S}$, so that, taking into account the different proportion of durable to nondurable items, the secular growth of demand for all goods and services by the household sector, $\overset{\circ}{C}_r$, remains unchanged—with this last growth rate necessarily being equal both to the secular growth of real income, $\overset{\circ}{G}$, and to the secular growth of investment by the enterprise sector in real terms, $\overset{\circ}{I}_r$ (the weighted average growth of investment, $\overset{\circ}{A}_{B.j}$, by each of the n industries which constitute the enterprise sector). That is, the following condition must be satisfied:

$$\overset{\circ}{I}_r = \overset{\circ}{C}_r = \overset{\circ}{G} \qquad (9.23)$$

Indeed, the necessary equality between $\overset{\circ}{C}_r$ and $\overset{\circ}{G}$ is nothing more than the condition that the weighted sum of the income elasticity of demand for the various items of consumption must be equal to 1.

There is one last possibility that needs to be considered. This is that the household sector will increase its gross savings, or discretionary funds, relative to its tangible investment, with the growing savings as conventionally defined (the sector's increasing cash surplus) used to finance a disproportionate growth of investment, or discretionary expenditures, by some other sector. The growth of household savings, as conventionally defined, is possible, with the aggregate demand and sectoral balance conditions still being satisfied, provided the cash surplus being generated by the household sector offsets the inability of business firms to generate sufficient funds, via their markups, to finance their necesary rate of capacity expansion. However, in this case, the additional household savings will not lead to a higher rate of economic expansion and thus to a more rapid growth in the availability of consumption goods in the long period. The higher rate of household savings will only alter the distribution of real income within the household sector in the manner already analyzed for the case of consumption by rentiers out of nonwage income or even by workers out of any savings (see chapter 8, section 2.3). Indeed, this conclusion is simply a corollary of the proposition that the growth of real income depends solely on the rate of technical progress or whatever other factor determines the long-period rate of accumulation. Any increase in household savings, holding the rate of accumulation constant, will only redistribute the available output of consumption goods among the different classes of households. It will not increase the amount of real goods (and services) available for consumption.

More will be said shortly about the role of household savings in the short-period dynamics of the economy (see section 9.3.4). The point that needs to be stressed here is that, because of both the aggregate demand and sectoral balance conditions that need to be satisfied in the long period, the secular growth of the household sector's "gross" savings, or discretionary funds, $\overset{\circ}{F}_H$, can be assumed to equal the secular growth of discretionary expenditures by the household sector in nominal terms, $\overset{\circ}{\mathsf{E}}_H$, with the latter the weighted sum of the secular growth of nominal demand for each of the different types of durable goods purchased by households. That is,

$$\overset{\circ}{\mathsf{F}}_H = \overset{\circ}{\mathsf{E}}_H \tag{9.24}$$

with

$$\overset{\circ}{\mathsf{E}}_H = \sum_{j=1}^{e} w_{C_j} \, p_{C_j} \, \overset{\circ}{\mathsf{A}}_{H,j} \tag{9.25}$$

or, alternatively, with $\sum_{j=1}^{e} w_{C_j} \overset{\circ}{\mathsf{A}}_{H,j}$ denoted as $\overset{\circ}{\mathsf{A}}_H$ and $\sum_{j=1}^{e} w_{C_j} \, p_{C_j}$ denoted as $\overset{\circ}{\mathsf{P}}_{C_d}$,

$$\overset{\circ}{\mathsf{E}}_H = \overset{\circ}{\mathsf{A}}_H + \overset{\circ}{\mathsf{P}}_{C_d} \tag{9.26}$$

where $\overset{\circ}{\mathsf{P}}_{C_d}$ is the secular growth of the price index for the various durable consumption goods which constitute the household sector's discretionary expenditures.

It should be noted that, as was true of the corresponding relationship for the enterprise sector (see chapter 7, section 4.1), equation 9.24 does not preclude the possibility of a cash surplus (or deficit) for the household sector as a whole. The level of discretionary funds (or gross savings) at any one point in time, $F_H(t)$—as distinct from the growth of discretionary funds over time, $\overset{\circ}{\mathsf{F}}_H$—may well exceed the level of discretionary expenditures (what the Flow of Funds Accounts define as "tangible household investment") at that same point in time. Equation 9.24 merely implies that, whatever the discrepancy between $F_H(t)$ and $E_H(t)$, it is the rate of growth of discretionary expenditures, $\overset{\circ}{\mathsf{E}}_H$, and thus the rate of growth of discretionary funds, $\overset{\circ}{\mathsf{F}}_H$, that will determine the rate at which the household sector is either acquiring financial assets or accumulating additional debt, depending on whether $F_H(t) - E_H(t)$ is positive or negative. A full discussion on what happens when $F_H(t) - E_H(t)$ differs from zero must wait until, in connection with the analysis of money and credit, we can develop a flow of funds model for the economy as whole that encompasses the several components of the financial sector in addition to the household sector itself (see chapter 12, part 1). All that need be noted for now is that whatever the current surplus (or deficit) of the household sector, as measured by $F_H(t) - E_H(t)$, it will need to be offset by an approximately—but not exactly—equal deficit (or surplus) within the other nonfinancial sectors. The changing trend values for the growth of both discretionary expenditures and discretionary funds having thus been explained, we can now turn to the short-period behavioral equations, beginning with those for the household sector's discretionary expenditures, or durable goods purchases.

9.3.3 The cyclical behavior of consumer durables

There are not the same set of technical relationships governing the household sector's discretionary expenditures as there are in the case of the enterprise sector. While each industry will need to expand capacity in line with the growth of sales, with any belated response to a change in the rate at which sales are increasing necessarily requiring a disproportionate change in the rate of growth of investment (see chapter 7, section 4.2), households are under no similar compulsion insofar as their own durable goods purchases are concerned. Aside from replacing any old items as they wear out, households are free to purchase whatever durable goods they wish as their real income rises over time. They are not constrained by the type of technical relationships which underlie each industry's incremental capital-output ratio. In this respect, the incremental component of the household sector's durable goods purchases is truly discretionary—in the long period as well as in the short. (In this connection, see chapter 2, section 1.3, and chapter 5, section 5.2).

It is nonetheless possible to analyze the cyclical behavior of the household sector's durable goods purchases in terms of the "accelerator" effect produced by a change in the level of aggregate demand. This is because the "accelerator," as the term is used by economists (see chapter 7, section 1.3), refers simply to the influence of aggregate demand factors on a sector's investment-like expenditures. The magnitude of any such "accelerator" effect, insofar as the household sector is concerned, can be determined by substituting the cyclical movement of consumer durable goods purchases, $\overset{*}{A}_H$, for the dependent variable in equation 7.28 as follows:

$$\overset{*}{A}_H = a\overset{*}{G} + b_1X_1 + b_2X_2 + \ldots + b_mX_m \qquad (9.27)$$

and then estimating the value of a. The $\overset{*}{G}$ variable to which the a coefficient is attached measures the cyclical movement of aggregate demand. Specifying the household sector's E function in this manner is justified by the fact that, as had clearly been established by the end of the 1960s, consumer durable goods purchases behave more nearly like business investment than like other types of consumption outlays.

As was pointed out when the enterprise sector's E and F functions were derived, it is not possible to determine the value of any one coefficient, such as a, without first identifying the behavioral equation's other parameters. In the case of equation 9.26, these other parameters, $X_1, X_2, \ldots, X_m$, will be different for each major type of durable good purchased—residential structures, automobiles and other consumer durables. Indeed, this is why separate behavioral equations need to be estimated for each major type of consumer durable good—with the value of a not necessarily the same in each case. These separate behavioral equations take the following form:

$$\overset{*}{A}_{H_j} = a\overset{*}{G} + b_1X_1 + b_2X_2 + \ldots + b_mX_m \qquad (9.28)$$

where $\overset{*}{A}_{H_j}$ is the cyclical movement of the household sector's expenditures on the jth consumer durable good, with $\overset{*}{A}_H$ then the weighted average of these separate growth rates. That is,

$$\overset{*}{A}_H = \sum_{j=1}^{e} w_{C_j} \overset{*}{A}_{H.j} \qquad (9.29)$$

While not every one of the $X_1, X_2, \ldots, X_m$ parameters will affect the cyclical demand for each type of consumer durable good, the commonality of their influence on the behavior of the household sector can be seen more clearly by grouping them together within the following six categories: (1) some measure of the current stock of that type of durable good held by households; (2) the liquidity position of the household sector; (3) the availablility of credit, as measured by the appropriate interest rate and/or the liquidity position of the banking system; (4) the rate at which prices have been increasing; (5) a set of policy variables, X, and (6) and additional factors not otherwise specified.

As can be seen from exhibit 9.17, the stock variable which is important in the case of automobile purchases is the cyclical movement with respect to the number of cars registered among the driving age population, $\overset{*}{A}_{stock}$, lagged one quarter. The short-period behavior of automobile sales will also depend on the household sector's debt burden, as measured by the ratio of the interest payments on the sector's outstanding debt relative to disposable income. This variable not only reflects the household sector's liquidity position, it also indicates one of the ways in which monetary policy can affect automobile sales since any change in interest rates will alter the measure of the household sector's debt burden. The other way in which monetary policy can affect automobile sales is through the liquidity position of the banking system, $\hat{L}$, and the influence which this variable has on the amount of consumer automobile loans outstanding, Lns_A. The latter variable, and thus the cyclical movement of automobile sales, may also be affected by a selective policy of limiting consumer credit, X_5, such as was implemented by the Federal Reserve Board, the U.S. monetary authority, in 1980. Finally, the cyclical movement of expenditures on automobiles and motor vehicle parts, $\overset{*}{A}_{H.1}$, will depend on "inflationary" expectations, as measured by how rapidly automobile prices have been increasing over the preceding four quarters, and by whether there is an actual or even an anticipated strike by the workers in the automobile industry. Both the "inflationary" expectations and the anticipated work stoppage will increase automobile sales above what they would otherwise be while an actual strike, because of the supply interruption, will lead to a temporary fall in sales. Once these other parameters have been identified, the value of the "accelerator" effect, a, due to the cyclical movement of aggregate demand, $\overset{*}{G}$—along with the value of the other coefficients, $b_1, b_2, \ldots, b_m$, can be determined. The value of a in the case of automobiles, based on quarterly data for the period 1952–1978, is approximately 4.2 (see exhibit 9.17).

Exhibit 9.17

**Cyclical Movement of Discretionary Expenditures in Real Terms
Household Sector**

Autos and motor vehicle parts

$$\overset{*}{A}_{H1} = -0.06 + 4.23(\overset{*}{G}) - 5.92(\overset{*}{A}_{stock})_{-1} + 0.34(P_a - P_{a-4})/P_{a-4}$$
$$\quad\;\;(2.1)\quad\;\;(8.0)\quad\quad\;\;(3.1)\quad\quad\quad\;(2.6)$$

$$\quad\quad\quad -1.43\,(\text{Debt}) - 0.0000078\,(\text{Strkhrs}) + 0.0000067\,(\text{Strkhrs})_{-1}$$
$$\quad\quad\quad\;\;(2.5)\quad\quad\quad\;\;(4.3)\quad\quad\quad\quad\quad\quad(3.5)$$

$$R^2_a = 0.92 \quad R^2_b = 0.67 \quad R^2_c = 0.97 \quad \text{D--W} = 2.2 \quad w_4 = 0.13$$

Other durable goods

$$\overset{*}{A}_{H2} = 0.0009 + 0.84(\overset{*}{G}) + 0.34(\overset{*}{G})_{-1} - 0.17(1/4 \overset{0}{\underset{t=-3}{\sum}} L) - 0.04(D_{65.4})$$
$$\quad\quad\;\;(0.7)\quad\;\;(4.7)\quad\quad\;(2.1)\quad\quad\;\;(2.6)\quad\quad\quad\quad(3.0)$$

$$\quad\quad - 0.03(D_{74.4}) - 0.07(D_{78.1})$$
$$\quad\quad\;\;(2.2)\quad\quad\;\;(4.8)$$

$$R^2_a = 0.97 \quad R^2_b = 0.54 \quad R^2_c = 0.99 \quad \text{D--W} = 2.1 \quad w_{4b} = 0.16$$

Single-family residential construction

$$\overset{*}{A}_{H3} = 0.02 + 0.98(\Delta\overset{*}{G})_{-1} - 0.29(1/2 \overset{0}{\underset{t=-1}{\sum}}(E_H/F_H))_{-1} - 1.60(1/2 \overset{0}{\underset{t=-1}{\sum}} L)$$
$$\quad\;\;(0.01)\;\;(2.5)\quad\quad\quad(2.8)\quad\quad\quad\quad\quad\quad\quad\;(3.8)$$

$$\quad\quad -0.02(i_2) + 0.40((P_{C-1} - P_{C-9})/P_{4C-9}) + 0.53(\text{Mtg}) + 0.09(D)$$
$$\quad\quad\;\;(3.4)\quad\quad(2.8)\quad\quad\quad\quad\quad\quad\quad\quad(1.7)\quad\quad\;\;(5.0)$$

$$R^2_a = 0.59 \quad R^2_b = 0.63 \quad R^2_c = 0.85 \quad \text{D--W} = 2.0 \quad w_{4c} = 0.12$$

The cyclical demand for single-family homes, $\overset{*}{A}_{H.2}$, does not depend on any stock variable. It does, however, depend on the liquidity position of the household sector, as measured by the ratio of discretionary expenditures to discretionary funds, E_H/F_H, over the preceding two quarters (lagged one additional quarter). It also depends on "inflationary expectations," as measured by the rise in the cost of new houses over the preceding eight quarters. Most importantly, however, it depends on the liquidity position of the banking system, as measured both by $\hat{L}$ and the share of their assets which savings and loan institutions have set aside for mortgages. Indeed, due to the primary reliance on monetary policy in the efforts to control inflation between 1952 and 1978, with the impact of that policy felt more by the housing industry than perhaps any other industry, the cyclical movements of single-family residential construction have been particularly severe. This is reflected in the relatively small portion of the period-to-period movement that is explained by the trend (only 60 percent, as measured by the value of the $R^2{}_a$ statistic, with the remaining 40 percent representing the cyclical component of that period-to-period movement).

Once these other parameters of the behavioral equation for single-family residential construction have been identified, it is then possible to derive an estimate of a, along with the other coefficients, $b_1, b_2, \ldots, b_m$. As can be seen from exhibit 9.17, the estimated value of a is not significantly different from zero. Only a change in the cyclical movement of aggregate output, $\Delta \overset{*}{G}$ (lagged one quarter), and not the cyclical movement itself, $\overset{*}{G}$, has a positive coefficient— and even then the t ratio for the coefficient barely falls within the acceptable range. This zero value for the a coefficient again reflects the greater importance of the monetary variables, as distinct from the aggregate demand variables, in determining the cyclical movement of single-family residential construction.

In the case of other durable goods, the cyclical movement, $\hat{A}_{H.3}$, depends, aside from the level of aggregate demand, on the liquidity position of the banking system as measured by $\hat{L}$. (There are also outliers, or extreme values, for the 4th quarter of 1965, the fourth quarter of 1974 and the first quarter of 1978 which have not yet been satisfactorily accounted for, as indicated by dummy variables for those periods.) Insofar as can presently be determined, the cyclical movement of other durable goods purchases does not depend on: (1) any stock variable; (2) the liquidity position of the household sector; (3) the level of interest rates; (4) price expectations; or (5) any policy variables. With only the liquidity position of the banking system as an additional parameter, the value of a for other durable goods would appear to be 0.84 (for cyclical movements of aggregate output during the current period) and 0.34 (for any cyclical movement in the preceding quarter), thus indicating a lagged as well as a current accelerator effect (see exhibit 9.17).

The estimates of a for each of the three major types of consumer durable goods can be weighted and then added together to determine the slope of the overall E curve for the household sector. Based on this approach, with the weights for automobiles, single-family residential construction and other durable goods being .317, .293 and .390 respectively, it would appear that the slope of the household sector's E curve is approximately 1.5 during the current period (based on the assumption that the value of a for single-family residential construction is close to zero). Now that an estimate of the accelerator effect on consumer durable goods purchases due to the cyclical movement of aggregate demand has been obtained, it is necessary to see how this value, a, compares with the income redistributive effect of the same cyclical movement of aggregate demand, α, as estimated from the corresponding F function.

9.3.4 The household sector's F function

Again, it is not possible to estimate the value of the α coefficient without first being able to specify the other parameters of the household sector's F function. As was pointed out when the F function for the enterprise sector was derived, those other parameters, $Y_1, Y_2, \ldots, Y_n$, are various intersectoral compensation rates. Indeed, they are in several cases the identical variables. The same increase in the rate of growth of money wages, $\dot{w}$, that will reduce the rate of growth of the enterprise sector's new cash inflow, or discretionary funds, $\dot{F}_B$, will simultaneously increase the rate of growth of the household sector's net cash inflow, or discretionary funds, $\dot{F}_H$. Similarly, the same increase in the rate of growth of consumer goods prices, $\dot{P}_C$, that will produce a more rapid rise in the enterprise sector's discretionary funds will cause the household sector's discretionary funds to rise less rapidly. However, not all the parameters of the household sector's F function are those it shares with the enterprise sector.

Of particular importance, besides the growth of money wages, $\dot{w}$, relative to the growth of consumer goods prices, $\dot{P}_C$, are the several factors that will determine the distribution of income in the long period between the household and government sectors. These are the various tax rates, $t_1, t_1, \ldots, t_x$ (including any negative tax, or transfer payment, rates, $t_{n_1}, t_{n_2}, \ldots, t_{n_m}$), that apply to households. The principal one of these tax rates is the personal income tax rate, t_p. An increase in this tax rate will, *ceteris paribus*, reduce the rate of growth of the household sector's discretionary funds, $\dot{F}_H$, while at the same time increasing the rate of growth of the government sector's discretionary funds, $\dot{F}_G$. Conversely, a decline in t_p will increase the value of $\dot{F}_H$ while simultaneously lowering the value of $\dot{F}_G$. (It should be added that the personal income tax rate, since it applies to unincorporated enterprises, will affect the distribution of income between the enterprise and government sectors as well as between the household and government sectors).

The rate of growth of the household sector's discretionary funds will also be affected, at least indirectly, by any excise tax rates, $t_{e_1}, t_{e_2}, \ldots, t_{e_n}$, and even by the corporate income tax rate, t_c, as well. This is because, as will be pointed out shortly (see chapter 10, section 3.3), the burden of these two taxes falls ultimately on the household sector. Still, it is through the price of consumer goods, P_C, rather than through the $t_{e_1}, t_{e_2}, \ldots, t_{e_n}$ and t_c variables directly, that the redistributive effect of those taxes will be felt. This is why the latter set of tax variables do not need to be included as separate parameters of the household sector's F function. For the same reason, even though a shift in the terms of trade will primarily affect the real income of households, the variables by which any such shift would be measured—the ratio of the price of imported goods, P_M, to the price of exported goods, P_X, and/or the set of various exchange rates, ER_1, $ER_2, \ldots , ER_y$—do not need to be included as parameters of the household sector's F function. Their influence will already be reflected in the price of consumer goods, P_C. Only to the extent households receive wages from business firms and/or transfer payments from governments (as well as pay taxes) beyond the national borders will the distribution of income between the household sector and the rest-of-the-world be directly affected by the terms of trade.

Like the enterprise sector, the household sector is divisible into various component parts—to wit, the rentier, working and dependent classes. While it is not possible, based on the available data, to derive separate E and F functions for each of these components of the household sector, still the factors that will determine the long-period distribution of income among the several classes (and thus would serve as the parameters of any separate F functions that might be estimated) should be noted. The relative distribution of income between the rentier and working classes will depend on the rate of growth of dividends, $\overset{\circ}{D}iv$, relative to the growth of money wages, $\overset{\cdot}{w}$ (should those two growth rates differ) as well as on the level of interest rates, i. Rentiers will gain, relative to workers, if dividends are increasing more rapidly than money wages and if, moreover, interest rates are rising. The differential gain will be due, not just to the increased income flows which the higher dividend and interest payments represent but also to the capital gains produced by the higher dividend and interest payments on the financial assets held by rentiers. With an accommodating monetary policy, rentiers will be able to translate the capital gains into a further increment in their purchasing power relative to that of the two other social classes which make up the household sector (see chapter 12, section 2.4). Whether the household sector as a whole will be better off will depend on the rate of growth of dividends, $\overset{\circ}{D}iv$, and the level of interest rates, i, relative to the growth of consumer prices, $\overset{\cdot}{P}_C$. The relative distribution of income between the working and dependent classes will, meanwhile, depend on what changes, if any, are being made in the various negative tax rates, $t_{n_1}, t_{n_2}, \ldots , t_{n_m}$ (as well as what change, if any, is being made in the guaranteed annual income, Y_g, for those living in the society) relative to the positive tax rate, t_p, on the wages earned by workers (see chapter 10, section 3.4).

Thus the parameters of the household sector's F function can, for all practical purposes, be limited to the following intersectoral compensation rates: (1) the rate of growth of money wages, $\overset{\cdot}{w}$ (along with the rate of growth of dividends, Div; (2) the rate of growth of the price index for consumer goods, P_C; (3) the personal income tax rate, t_{PY} (which, along with the various negative tax rates, $t_{n_1}, t_{n_2}, \ldots , t_{n_m}$, will determine the transfer income of households and thus the distribution of income between workers and the members of the dependent class);

and (4) the level of interest rates, i (which, along with the rate of growth of dividends, $\overset{\circ}{D}iv$, will determine the income of rentiers relative to workers). Once these parameters of the household sector's F function have been identified, it is then possible, based on equation 7.29, to obtain an estimate of the α coefficient measuring the redistributive effect produced by a change in the level of aggregate demand, $\overset{*}{G}$. However, this next step has yet to be carried out. Until it has, the slope of the household sector's F curve relative to that of the E curve, and thus the contribution of the household sector to the stability of the overall economy, will remain unknown.

Recommended Readings

On the lexicographic ordering of preferences, see Peter E. Earl, *The Economic Imagination*, Armonk, N.Y.: M. E. Sharpe, 1983; Ray Canterbery, "Inflation, Necessities and Distributive Efficiency," in *Essays in Post-Keynesian Inflation*, J. H. Gapinski and C. E. Rockwood, eds., Cambridge, Mass.: Ballinger, 1979, and the sources cited in these two works. The emphasis on social custom and habit is part of an institutionalist tradition that can be traced back to Veblen. See Thorstein Veblen, *The Theory of the Leisure Class*, New York: Modern Library edition, 1961 [lst ed., 1899]; Wesley C. Mitchell, *The Backward Art of Spending Money and Other Essays*, New York: McGraw-Hill, 1937; James S. Duesenberry, *Income, Saving and the Theory of Consumer Behavior*, Cambridge, Mass.: Harvard University Press, 1949.

On the linear expenditure model, see Richard Stone, "Linear Expenditure Systems and Demand Analysis: An Application to the Pattern of British Demand," *Economic Journal*, 1954 and *The Measurement of Consumers' Expenditure and Behaviour in the United Kingdom, 1920–38*, I, London: Cambridge University Press, 1954. See also Angus Deaton and John Muellbauer, *Economics and Consumer Behavior*, New York: Cambridge University Press, 1980, ch. 3; J. L. Bridge, *Applied Econometrics*, Amsterdam: North-Holland, 1971, ch. 3; Henry Theil, *Theory and Measurement of Consumer Demand*, 2 vols., Amsterdam: North-Holland, 1975, 1976. How to derive the sigmoid Engel curve from household survey data was, aside from an earlier article by M. J. Farrell, first demonstrated by the group working with Stone at Cambridge University's Department of Applied Economics. See J. S. Cramer, "A Dynamic Approach to the Theory of Consumer Demand," *Review of Economic Studies*, February 1957, and *The Ownership of Major Consumer Durables*, London: Cambridge University Press, 1962; J. Aitchison and J. A. C. Brown, *The Lognormal Distribution*, London: Cambridge University Press, 1957; F. Graham Pyatt, *Priority Patterns and the Demand for Household Durable Goods*, London: Cambridge University Press, 1964; D. S. Ironmonger, *New Commodities and Consumer Behavior*, London: Cambridge University Press, 1972.

On the Suits set of equations, see Daniel Suits, "Forecasting and Analysis with an Econometric Model,'' *American Economic Review*, March 1962, and "The Determinants of Consumer Expenditure: A Review of Present Knowledge,'' in Commission on Money and Credit, *Impacts of Monetary Policy*, Englewood Cliffs, N.J.: Prentice-Hall, 1963. See also Gardner Ackley, *Macroeconomic Theory*, New York: Macmillan, 1961, chs. 10–12; Simon Kuznets, *National Product Since 1869*, New York: National Bureau of Economic Research, 1946, and *National Income: A Summary of Findings*, New York: National Bureau of Economic Research, 1946. On the efforts to reconcile the short- and the long-run average propensities to consume, see Arthur Smithies, "Forecasting Postwar Demand: I,'' *Econometrica*, January 1945; Duesenberry, *op. cit.*; Milton Friedman, *A Theory of the Consumption Function*, Princeton, N.J.: Princeton University Press, 1957; Franco Modigliani and Richard Brumberg, "Utility Analysis and the Consumption Function: In Interpretation of Cross Section Data,'' in *Post-Keynesian Economics*, Kenneth Kurihara, ed., New Brunswick, N.J.: Rutgers University Press, 1954, and Albert Ando and Franco Modigliani, "The 'Life Cycle' Hypothesis of Saving: Aggregate Implications and Tests,'' *American Economic Review*, March 1963. On the Pigou effect, see A. C. Pigou, "The Classical Stationary State,'' *Economic Journal*, December 1943. On the 1960s state of the art, Michael K. Evans, *Macroeconomic Activity*, New York: Harper & Row, 1969; Gardner Ackley, *Macroeconomics: Theory and Policy*, New York: Macmillan, 1978; Lawrence R. Klein and Edwin Burmeister, eds., *Econometric Model Performance*, Philadelphia: University of Pennsylvania Press, 1976. On the household sector's E and F curves, see Leonard Forman and Alfred S. Eichner, "A Post-Keynesian Short-Period Model: Some Preliminary Econometric Results,'' *Journal of Post Keynesian Economics*, Autumn 1981; Philip Arestis, Ciaran Driver and J. Rooney, "The Real Segment of a UK Post Keynesian Model,'' *Journal of Post Keynesian Economics*, Winter 1985–86.

Chapter 10

The Government and Not-for-Profit Sector

Contents

Chapter 10

The Government and Not-for-Profit Sector

With the enterprise and household sectors the only two sectors so far delineated in the model, the source of any cyclical instability would seem to be limited, at most, to errors in monetary policy. The thrust of the preceding five chapters has been that the rate of growth of discretionary expenditures within each of those two sectors depends primarily on the overall rate of economic expansion. This is true not just in the long period but in the short period as well. The only other parameters of each sector's E function, besides $\overset{*}{\mathsf{G}}$, are a set of financial variables (along with the sector's cash-flow position which, if negative, will make it more vulnerable to a restrictive monetary policy). The virtual absence of policy variables from the two E functions is especially significant. It suggests that, aside from avoiding errors in monetary policy, there is little that can be done to influence the economy's course over time. Indeed, the absence of these or any other exogenously determined variables from the two functions makes the pronounced cyclical movements which can be observed in the case of the U.S. and other advanced market economies something of a mystery. Without at least one such parameter whose volatility can account for the fluctuations in discretionary expenditures over time, it is difficult to explain the economy's cyclical behavior. The mystery as to what, besides errors in monetary policy, may be responsible for those cyclical movements can in fact be cleared up only by delineating, in addition to the enterprise and household sectors, a separate government and not-for-profit sector.

The state, as an analytical category, is conspicuous mostly by its absence from the models most commonly relied upon by economists. This is hardly surprising in light of the discipline's history. What is viewed by many as the first systematic treatment of the subject, Adam Smith's *The Wealth of Nations*, was essentially an extended argument for relying on the market rather than the state as the principal allocative mechanism; and on this question most economists, down to and including the present generation, have remained "Smithians." With economics defined as the study of how scarce resources are allocated through the market, the government necessarily falls outside the discipline's purview. In this respect, Keynes's *General Theory* is no exception. Despite being the work which, more than any other, has been responsible for the dramatically expanded role of the state in the U.S. and other advanced market economies since the 1930s, the government plays no role whatsoever in the book's formal analysis. As already pointed out (see chapter 3, part 1), the basic Keynesian model is a two-sector model, with only the enterprise and household sectors explicitly taken into account. Nonetheless, the ability of the government to influence the level of economic activity is implicit in the argument—as others were quick to grasp—and there are more than enough *obiter dicta* for those who might otherwise miss the point. Thus the importance of the government has come to be recognized, at least in macro if not in microeconomic theory.

Even so, there is no theory of the state to underlie the argument about the need for countercyclical policies. Government remains largely an afterthought, a *deus ex machina* to be invoked when there appears to be no other way to achieve some goal such as "full" employment or price "stability." Moreover, there is no recognition of the difference it makes to the argument if one posits an economy that is expanding continuously over time, albeit unevenly, rather than simply coming to rest at some new equilibrium point. The analysis of the government's role is usually confined to a static framework. Finally, there is no awareness of how the conclusions economists tend to draw about the effects of the government's tax and other fiscal policies need to be modified in light of the corporate revolution and the other institutional changes which have occurred in the U.S. and other advanced market economies. The analysis is usually based on the presumed existence of a precorporate and indeed even a preindustrial system. It is these limitations of the conventional theory that need to be overcome, beginning with the lack of an adequate theory of the state.

10.1 A Theory of the State

As postulated in chapter 1, the political system is one of four institutional dimensions, and one of three operative systems, that can be delineated in the case of any society or large grouping of individuals. Its unique function is to produce the decisions which provide whatever cohesion, or unity of purpose, there may be in the group's behavior.

The political system, or polity, has both its formal and informal components. For the society as a whole, the formal component is the government. It is the government which, in the form of various laws, judicial rulings and administrative acts, actually produces the decisions which are the output of the political system. While each of the organized groups occupying the middle ground between the individual and the state has its analogous form of "government," only the formal component of the political system for the society as a whole is able, by virtue of its monopoly of coercive power, to exercise sovereignty—that is, prevent any other political entity from overriding its authority. Over what geographical area each government's sovereignty will extend is, of course, the issue over which wars are usually fought. The informal component of the political system consists of all the other social groups, whether organized or not, which seek to influence the decisions of the government, together with whatever interaction may occur among them. The most significant aspect of this informal structure is the process by which the various factions, or parties, vie among themselves to gain control of the formal structure. It is usually this struggle for control that most people have in mind when they use the term "politics." Still, the formal and informal components are integral parts of the same overall system, and it is a mistake to ignore the interrelationship between them.

The focus in this first part of the chapter will be on the state as an idealized, or general, type of government. This is not to deny that there are significant differences between governments, even among the nations with advanced market economies. It is merely to indicate that what is common to all governments—at least those in societies which have achieved a certain minimal level of development—may be more significant than the differences. The effort by political scientists to understand the role played by the state has been limited to two models. They are the liberal and Marxian models of the state. We shall begin by critically examining each of those two models before turning to the quite different model which is implicit in what has already been said about the nature of the political system.

10.1.1 The conventional models of the state

The neoclassical and Marxian theories of income distribution each have their corresponding models of the state. This is hardly surprising in light of how closely the political issues of the day are linked to questions of income distribution. The counterpart, on the political side, to the neoclassical paradigm in economics is the liberal model of the state, which derives from Locke, John Stuart Mill and the political philosophers who have followed their lead. The best designed state, according to this model, is one with limited powers. Initially, the emphasis on limited government was in recognition of the overwhelming power which the state can bring to bear on the individual citizen and the state's historical tendency to lapse into tyranny. Later, after the industrial revolution, the emphasis on limited government derived from a desire to avoid interfering with the workings of the market.

In the liberal model of the state, the principal function of government, aside from maintaining law and order, or the "king's peace," is to establish the rules by which economic activity is to be carried out. Hence the primary concern among political philosophers has been with the representative nature of government: Those who are subject to the rules by which economic activity is regulated, it is felt, should have a voice in the formulation of those rules. It was, of course, recognized that in a modern state on the scale of England and France, not to mention the United States, not every individual can participate directly in the

making of the rules. Every individual can, however, vote for someone to represent him (or her, as the argument later came to be amended) in the rule-making
process, someone with similar economic and other interests. Thus a system of
republican government, based on universal or near universal suffrage, has come
to be viewed as the closest it is possible to come in practice to the democratic
ideal. It is this system that constitutes representative democracy, the implicit
assumption being that a vote for someone who will be able to participate in the
rule-making process is the next best thing to, and indeed the only practical means
of, enabling each individual to participate directly him or herself in the rule-
making process. The critical nature of this last assumption being evident, efforts
to reform the political system have generally been directed toward ensuring that
those who are elected to public office are indeed "representative" of their
constituencies. Still, representation has generally been restricted to regions or
similar geographical subdivisions rather than being based on social class or
industry affiliation. Once adequate representation in that limited sense has been
assured, and thus the various competing interest groups have been given a voice in
the rule-making process, there would seem to be little more that can be done to
improve government—except perhaps to work toward a better educated citizenry
or a more highly trained civil service.

The Keynesian revolution, though it marked a tactical retreat from laissez-
faire, has required no significant modification of the prevailing liberal political
philosophy. Although the state now has the additional task of maintaining the
economy in a prosperous state, any government that is by its representative
nature necessarily accountable to the electorate can be expected to achieve that
goal by applying the well-known Keynesian remedies. These remedies, it is true,
require a greater degree of government involvement in the economy. The necessary countercyclical fiscal policy, in particular, cannot easily be implemented
unless a significant share of the national income is channeled through the government sector, and this in turn leaves the door open to political log-rolling of one
sort or another to determine which groups will benefit from the government's
spending programs. Indeed, the government may, in this way, have evolved into
the "welfare" state, with various organized interest groups, such as defense
contractors, seeking assiduously to bend the machinery of government to their
own narrow purposes. Still, as long as representative government prevails, it can
be assumed that the benefits of public expenditures will roughly correspond to the
size of the various voting blocs, with those voting blocs in turn reflecting the
relative size of the different interest groups. Thus the Great Depression of the
1930s, though it left economics as a discipline permanently altered, has had no
similar impact on political science. The primary concern continues to be how
"representative" is the government—whatever may have been the expansion of
the government's powers.

Marxist and other radical critics of the orthodox position in political science
have argued that this liberal model of the state is simply a facade to conceal the *de*

facto control over the government exercised by the dominant social class. Whatever political reforms may have been adopted, the fact remains that those chosen
to serve as representatives in the rule-making body and, even more importantly,
as officials in the executive agency that implements the rules are selected in such a
way as to ensure that they reflect the same interests as those of the dominant social
class (which in their view is the "capitalist" class). Because of the manner in
which public officials are selected—through an election in which campaign contributions are likely to prove decisive or through the patronage of those able to
gain office only in this manner—the state merely serves as the "executive arm"
of the ruling class. Its purpose is to protect "capital," either by enacting laws
favorable to the owners of private property or by bearing the cost of the social
overhead needed to assure the profitability of private investment. There may well
be conflicts between the members of the dominant social class, with those conflicts then resolved through the "representative" bodies of government, but
when the conflict is between the dominant "capitalist" class and the far larger
working class, the government can be expected to line up solidly behind the
former.

The Marxists and other radical social theorists have mounted a critique of the
liberal state which is not easily dismissed. The top positions in government, both
elected and appointive, are seldom filled by ordinary wage or salary earners; and
when they are, the individuals tend rapidly to lose whatever affinity they might
have once had with the working class. Whether this means that the state has fallen
into the hands of a monolithic ruling class, necessarily opposed to the interests of
workers, is another matter. It has already been suggested (see chapter 8, section
1.3) that the dominant social class, at least in the United States, includes three
somewhat disparate groups, all of whom are workers themselves— with one of
those groups, consisting of the top civil servants, in a particularly favorable
position to influence public policy. Some might even argue, following Dwight
Waldo, that government has fallen into the hands of a self-perpetuating civil
service bureaucracy whose interests are opposed to those of the other groups in
society, "capitalists" and workers alike. Nonetheless, by looking at representation in terms of social class, Marxists and other radical social theorists have
exposed a certain blindness in the liberal view of the state.

At the same time, however, by continuing to pose the same question of how
"representative" is the government, these radical critics have left the prevailing
paradigm in political science undisturbed. The liberal theory of the state, which
complements the neoclassical theory in economics, and the radical view of the
state, which complements the Marxian analysis, share the same premise: The
extent to which the decisions reached by the government will correspond to the
preferences of the majority depends on the extent to which the majority is
represented in the government. The radicals differ from the liberals only in
assuming that the majority consists of the "working class," and that therefore it
is the "working class" which should control the government—either through a

"dictatorship of the proletariat" or, if one is committed to some form of political democracy, through a duly elected "labor" party. By focusing on the representative character of government, liberals and radicals alike may well be missing the essential point. At least this is what an alternative cybernetic model of the political system would suggest.

10.1.2 A cybernetic model of the political system

According to the general systems framework outlined at the very beginning (see chapter 1, section 2.4), the political system can be viewed as a complex cybernetic mechanism. The system is a cybernetic one to the extent it is governed by feedback (in the form of electoral returns and/or other types of responses to the policies adopted), and it is complex to the extent that the goals toward which the system is directed can themselves be varied. In attempting to model such a system, we need to start by identifying the output which distinguishes the political system from the other systems which operate in tandem with it. That distinctive output is the set of social decisions, or choices, by which the society as a whole is given whatever cohesion or direction it has.

Some of the decisions which emanate from the political system are purely "political" in nature. They are decisions about how decisions are to be made on behalf of the entire society. These types of decisions range from the mundane matter of administrative procedures within a particular agency of government to the most fundamental of constitutional issues. More generally, however, the decisions which emanate from the political system are concerned with the functioning of some other system besides the political system. This is because the political system is the only back-up system which can be called upon when something goes awry with one of the other two major societal systems, the economic and the anthropogenic. Indeed, even without something going awry, a decision by the political system may be necessary to effect a change in the behavior of one of those other two systems. This is not to suggest that, faced with a crisis that threatens the continued viability of the society, the political system will necessarily respond appropriately. The point rather is that it is only through its political institutions that a society has any chance of surmounting the crisis.

One can therefore delineate two major types of decisions, besides the purely political, which the government as the formal component of the political system may be called upon to make. One is the subset of decisions which, in the form of economic policies, serve as inputs into the economic system and the other is the subset of decisions which, in the form of anthropogenic policies, serve as inputs into the anthropogenic system. Some might argue that a third subset needs to be delineated, consisting of the decisions by government as to what values, or norms, should be held by the members of the society. However, the historical lesson generally embraced by advanced industrial societies—at least outside the Soviet bloc and the other countries committed to a Leninist political philosophy—

is that any attempt to establish a state religion is likely to prove inimical to the growth of the scientific knowledge that underlies technical progress and indeed social progress more generally (see chapter 5, section 4.3). For this reason, in delineating the output of the political system, we shall limit ourselves to the categories of political, economic, and anthropogenic decisions.

Within each of these three categories, the output of the political system can be further divided into two types of decisions: the routine and the not-so-routine. The routine decisions are the ones that give rise to little or no controversy. They are the decisions made either at the administrative level—for example, by an agency of the executive branch in implementing the provisions of some law—or at the lowest level of the judicial system. These are the types of decisions that are likely to be opposed, at most, only by the one individual or family unit to whom the specific ruling applies. The not-so-routine decisions, in contrast, are the decisions which are thought to be wrong, and therefore are opposed, by at least a significant minority of those affected. They are the decisions which, depending on what position is taken by those holding public office, can lead to a serious loss of political support. Thus the output of the political system consists of a set of routine political, economic, and anthropogenic decisions, X_{P_r}, X_{E_r}, and X_{A_r}, and an additional set of contentious, or not-so-routine decisions, X_{P_n}, X_{E_n}, and X_{A_n}. It is the latter group of decisions which, since it defines the field within which political conflict occurs and thus the items on the society's current political agenda, plays a key role insofar as the dynamics of the system are concerned. The routine decisions, unless they should once again be disputed by more than just a single individual or family, can be largely ignored—even though they must still be counted as part of the political system's total output.

What the actual outcome will be in the case of any contentious decision will depend, among other factors, on what type of political system is being modeled. Here one needs to distinguish a democratic from other types of political systems. Just as it can be assumed that any society at the same level of development as the OECD group of nations has an economic system in which the interindustry flow of goods and services depends on market transactions, so it can be assumed that such a society has a political system that satisfies Anthony Down's definition of a political democracy. This is a system in which at least one other political party besides the party presently in power can, through the electoral process, gain control of the government. There are thus three essential features of such a system:

1) that an opposition party be free to form and compete for public office on the same basis as the party presently in power without its members suffer-ing criminal or other penalties (provided they subscribe to the rules that define a system of political democracy);

2) that control of the government and its administrative machinery depend on which party has obtained the majority of votes in the elections held with a certain minimum frequency (typically not less than once every seven years);

3) that all members of the society (except those below a certain age) be
   eligible to vote in the elections that determine who holds public office.
The first two of these conditions define a system of republican, or electoral,
government while the third condition ensures that any such system of republican
government will also be democratic—that is, be responsive to the views of a
majority of those living under its rule.

Once a system of political democracy has been established, the key role in the
dynamic that characterizes the system's behavior will be played by the two or
more political parties that can be expected to form under such a system. While a
multiparty system can thus not be excluded as a possibility, still there is reason to
believe that a system of political democracy functions best when the contest for
public office is limited to two parties. This reflects the greater manageability of
the decision-making process when, in the face of numerous options, the process
can be reduced to a series of dichotomous choices (see chapter 9, section 2.4).
The political party is the specialized social institution which, as part of the
political system's informal rather than formal structure, develops the strategy by
which a coalition of interest groups, or voting blocs, seeks to gain control of the
government. The political party, as a social institution, therefore needs to be
distinguished from the various overlapping interest groups into which the electorate, consisting of all eligible voters, can be divided.

The political party, as a relatively permanent organization, will have its own
internal political structure as well as its separate economic and anthropogenic
dimensions. The various interest groups, in contrast, need not be organized. They
are simply groups of voters who can be identified as holding a particular position
on any one of the issues that define the society's political agenda. Still, what even
more clearly distinguishes the political party from the various interest groups and
indeed from other types of social organizations is the unique function it serves.
While the various interest groups are concerned only with prevailing on a particular issue, the party's goal is to capture control of the government. This it can do
only by taking a position on the various issues that constitute the society's
political agenda so as to enable the party's candidates for public office to win a
majority of the votes cast in the next election. The party's role, then, is to develop
a "platform" that will appeal to the largest number of voters. In this way, with an
opposition party ever present to challenge the incumbents holding office, the
voters will have at least some choice in each of the successive elections that are
held.

In developing its platform, a political party can pursue either a "majority" or
a "minority" strategy. The former requires that the party adopt the position
favored by the majority of voters on all or most issues. It is a strategy which the
party already in power is in the best position to pursue. Through its control of the
government, it can actually implement the policies favored by the majority of
voters and, in this way, preempt the "majority" position. The opposition party
may therefore have little choice but to pursue a "minority" strategy. This re-

quires that it adopt the position held by the minority of voters on a series of issues which, for each of those different groups of voters, is the decisive one in determining how it will vote in the next election. A "minority" strategy is feasible because only one vote can be cast by a person in each election and because how that single vote is cast may depend on just one issue out of the many on which a political party needs to take a position.

It can, of course, be argued that only the policies adopted by the party in power really matter. Only those policies represent the actual social choices being made through the political process. Indeed, this is why the "representative" nature of the government or, more accurately, the "representative" nature of the political party in power is so important. Still, it is premature to make any judgment about how responsive the government is likely to be to the majority viewpoint under the model of societal decision-making being presented here. The process of societal decision is not yet complete. The virtue of the cybernetic model is that, rather than the analysis ending with the adoption of a particular policy by the party in power, it encompasses the subsequent reaction to that policy by the electorate.

A societal decision is not just a single event terminating in a specific legislative act or even the implementation of a particular policy. This is to confuse one element in the dynamic sequence that constitutes decision-making with the process itself, and it leaves the analysis of social choice through the political process incomplete. It is the process as a whole, not just one intermediate step, that produces an **X** vector of societal decisions, or choices, as the output of the political system. Some of those choices, like the policies implemented by the party newly installed in office, are likely to be only temporary ones. They stand a good chance of being modified with the next swing in electoral fortunes. To understand how the social choices produced by the political system become more than just temporary disequilibrium outcomes, it is necessary to follow the process of societal decision-making beyond the point where a specific choice has been made and examine the subsequent steps whereby those policies are likely to be altered in response to the electoral feedback. In other words, we need to understand how the social choices made through the political system become, over time, routinized in much the same way as the choices made by households as to what goods they will purchase.

10.1.3 The political dynamic underlying social choice

Any policy that is adopted by the party in power is likely to be, at best, only partially successful, whether success is defined in terms of resolving the underlying social problem or simply in terms of obtaining a majority of votes in the next election. The chances of success are, of course, less the more newly emergent is the issue which the policies are intended to address. This is because the policies which the party in power adopts are part of a social experimental process, the results of which, like all experimental processes, cannot be known in advance.

More often than not, there is a considerable discrepancy between what it is hoped a particular policy will achieve and what the policy is actually able to accomplish. To the extent that any such discrepancy becomes apparent to those concerned about the issue, it creates an opportunity for the opposition party, by promising to pursue a somewhat different policy—or even by promising to carry out the present policy more effectively—to garner votes on that issue.

Knowing itself to be vulnerable on a particular issue, the party in power can be expected to try to modify its policy. However, for internal reasons, it may not be able to shift its position in time to neutralize the issue before the next election. This is especially true if the issue is a critical one for the "ideologues" among the party stalwarts—those who give of their time and/or money to the party because of their views on certain issues—as distinct from the "regulars" who are interested only in patronage. In that event, the issue may well become one of the crucial ones in determining the outcome of the next election, or at least it will be perceived as such if the issue is prominently raised during the election campaign. Should the opposition party win the election, the policy is, of course, more likely to be changed. But even if the opposition party should fail to gain control of the government, any policy which has clearly reduced the margin of victory is likely to be modified so as to avoid losing votes in the next election—provided the change does not run counter to the "basic principles" of the party. Thus, to the extent a particular policy proves unsuccessful, as measured by the response of voters, it is likely to be modified over time under a system of political democracy. Indeed, it is this pressure to abandon unsuccessful policies which, more than the "representative" nature of the government, is the principal virtue of such a system.

A subsequent change in policy, whether by a party newly installed in office or by an incumbent party which has just avoided defeat, may still not succeed in removing the issue from the nation's political agenda. The new policy may be no more effective than the old. This is especially true if the state of knowledge is such that the party in power, in considering what policy to adopt, is forced to take a "shot in the dark." All that can be said with any confidence is that the party in power is likely to eschew policies which have already proven ineffective. In other words, it will try to avoid repeating the failed experiments of the past—even if the change in policy at any one moment in time is only a slight one. It is in this way, through trial and error, that policies which are less successful in achieving a particular social goal will gradually be supplanted by policies which are more successful. The political system, like all cybernetic mechanisms, relies on adaptive behavior based on what, in systems theory, is referred to as deviation-reducing or "negative" feedback. This means that, to the extent the system achieves any one of its goals, it does so by reducing the discrepancy between that objective and its actual performance. In the case of the political system, the goals are social ones. At least they are the closest one can come to identifying social goals, given the multiplicity of irreconcilable interests among the individual members of the society and the inherent limitations of political institutions, even under a system of political democracy. The political system being a complex cybernetic mechanism, the goals themselves are likely to change over time as certain issues disappear from the political agenda and others emerge to take their place. This raises the question of how an issue is finally resolved and thus when a certain social goal can be said to have been achieved through the political process.

Under a system of political democracy, an issue is not finally resolved until an opposition party can no longer hope to pick up crucial votes in the next election by promising to pursue a different policy. This will occur when the issue can no longer induce a significant segment of the electorate to switch its vote from one party to another. It is only at this point that the issue will disappear from the political agenda, and the policy which has been adopted can be judged a success. This does not mean that no more decisions will have to be made. Even with the policy no longer a matter of contention among the political parties, a continuous flow of decisions may still be necessary—though now at the departmental-administrative or judicial level rather than at the legislative or cabinet level. In other words, the decision-making process will have become depoliticized and therefore, it is hoped, routinized. Of course, an issue which has in this way become dormant may at any time be revived as a result of dissatisfaction among a significant bloc of voters, especially if the disaffected group is able to organize itself politically. Nonetheless, the longer an issue remains off the political agenda, the more confidence one can have that the underlying problem has been successfully resolved through the political process. To that limited extent, one can assume that a particular goal of society has been achieved—at least for the moment.

In summary, then, one can identify a set of n issues which, as a group, constitute the society's current political agenda. These are the issues on which the two or more political parties that exist under a system of political democracy have taken different positions. Over time, as the different parties move to a common position on any one of those issues—a reflection of the fact that the members of both the majority and any strongly committed minority can no longer be induced to switch their votes as a result of the position taken on that issue by the competing parties—the problem which has given rise to that issue can be said to have been successfully resolved through the political process. At that point, the issue joins the r number of other issues for which the societal decision-making process has become routinized within the executive and judicial branches of government. The total output of the political system consists of both these routine decisions and any decisions made by the party in power which are still a matter of contention among the different parties. In other words, the output of the political system consists of an X vector of decisions, divided into an $X_{P_n} + X_{E_r} + X_{A_r}$ set of routine political, economic and anthropogenic decisions and an $X_{P_n} + X_{E_n} + X_{A_n}$ set of nonroutine or contentious decisions, with the latter constituting the items on the society's current political agenda. This output of the political system is produced by a "negative" feedback process in which, through the response of voters, any discrepancy between the implicit goals of the society on the one hand and the results of the policies presently being pursued on the other hand is gradually reduced over time. Indeed, as a result of the same cybernetic process, the elements of the 1-by-$r+n$ $\mathbf{X}$ vector, along with the relative weights attached to them, will change over time, thereby leading to a change in both the goals of the society and the items that constitute the society's political agenda.

An important question is, of course, what can be done to increase the output of the political system, qualitatively as well as quantitatively. Assuming the cybernetic model of the political system just outlined is the correct one for analyzing the behavior of a political democracy—just as the input-output model of a monetarized production system presented in the earlier chapters is the correct one for analyzing the behavior of an advanced market economy—one can proceed to examine the different features of such a system, such as the length of time between election, the relationship between the several branches of government and the means of financing political activity, to see what differential effect they have on the output of the system. However, before turning to that question and thereby identifying the sources of government failure, we first need to see why the political system must produce a subset of $\mathbf{X}_{E_r} + \mathbf{X}_{E_n}$ economic decisions as an essential input into the economic process. This will require that we identify the sources of market failure—as distinct from government failure.

10.1.4 The sources of market failure

It was long an article of faith among economists that a market-based economic system was a self-regulating mechanism, requiring little intervention by the state aside from the enforcement of contracts. Indeed, the primary purpose of the logico-deductive mode of reasoning that passed for economic analysis was to demonstrate the truth of that proposition. This explains the near universal belief in Say's Law and other propositions which argued against the government assuming any significant role in the economy. Although Marx and a number of other dissidents were to voice skepticism on this point, it was not until Keynes brought out *The General Theory* that a significant body of economists began to have doubts about the self-regulating nature of a market economy. Their doubts were, of course, prompted by the widespread unemployment that prevailed in market economies during the 1930s. Still, it was Keynes's distinctive contribution to provide the first convincing explanation, at least in terms that other economists would accept, as to why a market economy would not necessarily achieve "full employment." As soon as this one source of market failure was widely acknowledged, economists were more willing to recognize other types of market failure— encouraged to do so, in part, by the expanded role which government had come to play in the market-based economies of the OECD group of nations following the Keynesian "revolution" in political economy if not in economic theory itself. Keynes, with his prescient essay on "The Decline of Laissez-Faire," had set the tone for the subsequent debate over the relationship between politics and economics.

Economists sympathetic to the new Keynesian philosophy were able to identify several sources of market failure—even aside from the tendency of a market-based system to operate at less than full capacity. One type of market failure had, in fact, long been recognized by economists. This was the failure of the market to produce socially optimal results when certain essential elements were absent or insufficiently robust. It was this type of market failure that forced the state to assume a certain minimal regulatory role in the economy. The problem of maintaining full employment which Keynes identified merely added a macroeconomic dimension to that previously acknowledged need for certain forms of regulation.

On the demand side of the market, what was most likely to be absent, or at least unavailable in sufficient amounts, was the information needed to make a rational choice in purchasing certain types of goods. Laws regulating the provision of foods and drugs had long since been enacted for precisely that reason, and now those statutes were to be supplemented by other laws requiring the disclosure of information in the case of securities and other financial offerings, setting standards for product safety and performance, and limiting the sale of toxic and other dangerous substances. Judgments might differ as to how much information was needed to ensure a rational choice by consumers and whether this minimal amount of information must necessarily be provided by the government. Still, there was little doubt that when the requisite information was not available to buyers, or amounted to less than full disclosure of all the pertinent facts, the results of the market process could fall short of what was socially optimal.

On the supply side, what was most likely to be absent, or at least inadequate, was the amount of competition among suppliers. The weakness of competition was, in turn, likely to cause prices to deviate from the costs of production in the long run, leading not only to "monopoly" profits and hence quasi-rents but also to a set of market prices which gave misleading signals as to the relative scarcity of economic resources. Economists might differ as to how serious the problem was and what should be done about it, with some economists favoring antitrust and similar measures designed to strengthen the forces of competition while others favored various forms of regulation, including even outright nationalization. Still, what was not in dispute was the likelihood of resources being misallocated, and thus of the market failing in perhaps its most important task, when the forces of competition were insufficiently robust.

Problems could arise, it was realized, if suppliers had too little power in the market place as well as too much power. At least this was the argument of those who favored government intervention on behalf of workers, either in the form of laws regulating working conditions and setting minimum wages or in the form of legislation giving workers the right to organize and bargain collectively. Workers, as individuals, were viewed as no match for the employer; and thus to equalize the bargaining power of the two parties, it was necessary either for the government itself or, with the government playing the role of mediator, for a trade union to negotiate on behalf of the workers. Here there was considerable disagreement, with a large number of economists continuing to insist that the market provided the individual worker with more than sufficient protection. On this issue, however, economists carried less weight than the sizeable number of voters who constituted the industrial work force. Hours and wage legislation, together with strong support for collective bargaining, became an integral part of the legal environment in which business firms would operate in the United States during the post-World War II period.

It was recognized, as a result of the experience during the Great Depression, that not just workers but also firms might have too little power in the market place. This was the rationale for placing the coercive power of the state behind the efforts of producers to fix prices—whether the legislation enacted by the government involved "orderly" marketing orders in the case of agriculture, "conservation" laws in the case of crude oil, or "fair trade" in the case of retail distribution. That these measures might be inconsistent with other policies designed to strengthen the forces of competition was beside the point. Like those other policies, they reflected a growing belief that, unless the government intervened in some manner, the market would lead to results that fell short of what was socially optimal. In the case of the measures permitting prices to be fixed, the result feared was the disappearance of the producers themselves, along with the output they supplied and the jobs they provided. This was market failure of the worst sort.

In addition to the growing support for regulation at the micro level, there was, as a result of the Keynesian revolution, an increasing awareness of the need to regulate the economy at the macro level as well. The likelihood that the economy would, on its own, fail to stabilize at "full employment" was only the first of several such aggregate economic problems to be identified—though clearly it prepared the way for economists to recognize the others. One further issue raised by the Keynesian revolution was that of economic growth. It had long been held by economists (and indeed is still maintained by a significant number of them) that the rate of savings, and thus the rate of economic growth, depends on the interest rate. With the rate of interest, in turn, assumed to depend on the balance between the supply and demand for savings in the "capital" market, it could then be argued that the rate of economic growth simply reflects the social choice made by individuals, via the "capital" market, between present and future consumption. This is the argument already encountered in the earlier discussion of the "capital" market (see chapter 7, section 3.5). Thus Keynes, by denying that the level of savings depends on the rate of interest, did more than just undermine the long-held belief in Say's Law. He also destroyed an essential link in the chain of reasoning by which it was presumed that whatever was the current rate of economic expansion was the socially preferred, if not indeed the socially optimal, rate of growth. This disturbing implication of the Keynesian analysis has already been touched on (see chapter 4, section 2.1). What should be clear from that discussion is that no market mechanism exists for determining the rate at which it is in the best interests of the society to expand economically. It must necessarily be a political decision.

Yet another macro issue to emerge following the Keynesian revolution was that of aggregate price stability. Keynes had avoided the problem by assuming a constant money wage (or, what was essentially the same thing, a money wage equal to some unchanging efficiency of labor). However, the experience of the post World War II period quickly demonstrated that, with government committed to a "full employment" policy and with workers free to bargain collectively, money wages were unlikely to remain constant. In fact, the logic of the system was such that, with output per worker rising and with industrial prices "sticky" downward due to the market power of megacorps, money wages could not remain constant—not if the economic expansion was to continue, spurred by the steady growth of household income (see chapter 5, section 5.4). Money wages had to rise.

But at what rate did money wages need to rise? The market was no more help in answering this question than it was in determining the optimal rate of accumulation. Only in this case it was the "labor" market rather than the "capital" market which failed to provide a satisfactory solution. It was not just that trade unions gave workers an enhanced bargaining power which they could use to increase money wages more rapidly than the growth of output per worker. The more basic point, as Keynes had recognized, was that workers could only bargain over wages within a single industry. This still left the general level of wages indeterminant, as the preceding discussion of the money wage rate has made clear (see chapter 8, section 3.3). To limit the growth of money wages and thus to moderate any inflationary pressure, governments in the period since the end of World War II have been forced to fashion some type of incomes policy. That they have not been very successful in doing so, at least in the United States and the other English-speaking countries, is largely beside the point. The fact is that the market can no more be counted on to ensure that money wages will grow at the socially optimal rate than it can be counted to ensure that the economy itself will expand at a socially optimal rate.

What have been identified so far are the types of market failure that force the government to play a regulatory role both at the micro and at the macroeconomic level. There are at least two other types of market failure. One is the type of market failure that leaves the government with no choice but to provide certain types of "public" goods itself. The traditional view, before the Keynesian revolution in macroeconomic policy, had been that any expenditures by government were simply a form of public consumption that reduced the real income of individuals. Now it came to be recognized, following a series of suggestive articles by Paul Samuelson in the 1950s, that there might exist a certain class of goods and services which, by their very nature, could only be supplied in optimal quantities by the government. The source of the market failure which necessitates that these goods be at least subsidized, if not actually supplied, by the government will be explained more fully in part 2 of this chapter when the expenditure side of the government's fiscal policy will be examined. For now it will suffice simply to point out the role of producer, or supplier of public goods, which this second type of market failure forces the government to assume.

The third, and final, type of market failure is the one that leaves certain households without the income they need to satisfy their material needs under the rules that govern the allocation of resources within a market economy. The several sources of this type of market failure will be explained more fully in part 3 of this chapter when, as part of the analysis of the government's tax-based fiscal policy, the various income transfer, or negative tax, programs will be described. For now it will suffice simply to indicate the redistributive role which this third type of market failure forces to government to assume. All three of the roles which the government must necessarily take on if the economic system is to function properly—that of regulating the economy at both the micro and macro level, that of producing certain types of goods and services, and that of redistributing income—then define the subset of economic decisions, $X_{E_r} + X_{E_n}$, that must emanate from the political system. Still, to speak of market failure without at the same time recognizing the possibility of government failure would be misleading. We therefore need to turn to the latter.

10.1.5 Government failure

The state, like the market, is an imperfect social mechanism, prone to its own particular types of failure. There is, first and most important of all, the possibility that the state, rather than serving as the means for arriving at collective decisions, will become the instrument for tyrannizing all but the small clique presently in control of the government. History is replete with examples of the state being corrupted in this manner—up to and including the present. To avoid this type of government failure, it is essential that certain constitutional safeguards be established, whether formally or otherwise. Indeed, these constitutional safeguards are the hallmark of a political democracy. In the absence of such safeguards, providing what are viewed by many as basic political, civil and even "human" rights, the state is likely to degenerate into a despotism which not only tyrannizes the majority but also is incapable of correcting the inevitable mistakes in public policy that will occur. In terms of the cybernetic model presented this means the state loses its ability to move closer over time to an optimal set of social choices.

The mere establishment of political democracy is not sufficent, however, to ensure against government failure. Even at its best, political democracy is an imperfect system, it simply being preferable, as Winston Churchill once noted, to any of the alternatives. The potential sources of government failure are many. For one thing, the system of political democracy may be in need of further refinement. Only the minimum conditions necessary to avoid a lapse into tyranny have so far been specified. What more precise forms both the formal and informal components of the system need to take in order to ensure the best possible societal decisions still remains unclear. Indeed, this question represents the uncompleted research program of political science. One cannot assume, therefore, that the political system as presently structured will be without serious defects. The informal component of the system, especially the party structure, may have failed to mature. The linkages between the executive and legislative branches may be insufficient to assure policy coherence and electoral accountability. For these and many other reasons, the political system may behave in an unsatisfactory manner.

Even with further refinements, however, one cannot be sure that the decisions emanating from the political system will produce decisions that reflect the majority sentiment—let alone decisions that will deal effectively with the underlying problem. The election results are seldom unambiguous enough to resolve even a single issue, let alone the many likely to arise during the course of a campaign. And whatever new policies are adopted following the election are more likely to reflect the outcome of the jockeying for power within the winning coalition than the majority sentiment of the electorate. While it might seem that results more consistent with the sentiments of the majority could be obtained by holding a series of referendums on each of the contentious issues, reliance on this device, since there is nothing to ensure that the preferences expressed by the voters will be consistent with one another, is likely to lead to a set of policies that operate at cross purposes with one another. Elections for public office could, of course, be scheduled with greater frequency, thereby ensuring that unpopular policies will be reversed or abandoned more quickly. But this "reform," since those seeking reelection must run on what they have accomplished while in office, is likely to lead to policies based on a more short-sighted view.

The point is that the political system has only a certain limited capacity to produce societal decisions. This is one reason for narrowly restricting the role played by the state in the economy. The greater the number of decisions the government must make, the greater is the likelihood that the society's decision-making capability will become unduly strained so that even the most basic decisions can no longer be made in a way that meets the needs of the society. What this suggests is that the society's decision-making capability via its political institutions is too precious a social resource to be relied upon if there is any alternative, such as the market, which comes even close to being just as effective.

The government's inability to make the right decisions may be due, not just to the shortcomings of the political system, either inherent or otherwise, but also, just as likely, to some deficiency along some other dimension of society. The economic system may not produce a sufficiently large surplus to support the required level of government. The anthropogenic system may not produce the numbers of educated persons needed to operate a system of political democracy.

Finally, the civic culture, reflecting the dominant norms within the society, may not place a sufficiently high value on political activity. Indeed, it is along the normative dimension, and the set of beliefs which that value orientation represents, that the most serious obstacles to better decision-making by the government are likely to lie, especially when the political institutions themselves are fairly advanced ones. A system of political democracy, even when further refined beyond the minimal conditions necessary to avoid a relapse into tyranny, can at most ensure only that the decisions produced will be minimally responsive to the views of the majority. It cannot ensure that the decisions will be socially optimal—or even minimally adequate.

The matters left for the government to decide because the market or some other social mechanism cannot be relied upon are, for that very reason, among the most difficult ones to resolve satisfactorily. This is especially true of the issues which, because they cannot be handled in a routine manner at the administrative or judicial level, must finally be resolved through legislative action or even by the electoral process. Usually the reason the issues cannot be easily resolved is that the necessary information and, even more critically, the necessary understanding of the underlying process is lacking. This is not to argue that the government cannot be expected to intervene constructively in the economy. In view of the serious problems that can be caused by market failure, strict adherence to a laissez-faire policy may be a sure prescription for social impotence, if not disaster. The point rather is that the government should attempt to keep its intervention, and thus the number of economic decisions that must be made politically, to a minimum. Certain political decisions are unavoidable—for example, what programs should be funded through the public sector budget and how should the taxes needed to support that level of spending be raised. Other decisions, though avoidable, are far too important to be left to the market—such as the rate of accumulation and the growth of money wages. The government is better advised to devote what limited decision-making capability it has to these and other fundamental issues rather than attempt to regulate every facet of the economy. Although this may mean that some market-derived results will be less than optimal, one should not jump to the conclusion that government intervention will necessary lead to any better results. Given the limited capacity of government, the chances of an even less satisfactory political solution increase as the burden placed on the state grows.

It should be noted that this argument for restricting the role of the government, based on the limited decision-making capability of government, is different from those which follow from a laissez-faire political philosophy. The latter links the amount of political freedom to the amount of government intervention in the economy. The less the government intervenes in economic matters, it is said, the greater will be the amount of freedom enjoyed by all. This argument, however, glosses over the fundamental distinction between the government (or rather the party in control of the government) acting to suppress its political opponents and the government acting to alter the outcome of some market process. It is only the former which represents a direct threat not just to the civil liberties of those subject to the government's jurisdiction but also to the effectiveness of the political system itself, and thus it is only the former that needs to be proscribed through various constitutional safeguards. Any action by the government to alter the outcome of a market process, since it poses no direct threat to civil liberties, should be judged on purely pragmatic grounds—that is, by whether it is likely to make the majority (or perhaps even a particular minority) better or worse off. The class bias of the laissez-faire argument is revealed when those who urge that the government's role in the economy be curbed so as to protect civil liberties make no protest when the government otherwise acts to suppress its political opponents. It then becomes clear that what is meant by ''freedom'' is the absence of restraint on a particular social class in its efforts to maximize its own economic well-being at the expense of the other groups in the society.

It is, of course, true that if the government's role in the economy should become all pervasive, with too many individuals' income dependent on political decisions, the government may well degenerate into a political spoils system in which the general interest becomes secondary to the distribution of patronage and the political opposition is forced to remain quiescent by the threat of losing its contracts and/or jobs with the government. Two points need to be made in response to this argument. The first is that the possibility just outlined is not that far removed from how the governments of the OECD countries such as the United States have been observed to function in practice—with minimal constitutional safeguards nonetheless being maintained and with the political system able to respond to at least the most serious threats to the overriding public interest. The second point that needs to be made is that the possibility just outlined simply provides an additional reason for limiting the government's role in the economy to correcting the types of market failure that are likely to have the most serious consequences. It is, in other words, a further argument for keeping the economic system's political inputs to a relatively few so as not to overtax the political system. Even with the political inputs into the economic system limited, however, government failure is still to be expected—for all the reasons already indicated. It is only gradually over time, as a result of electoral feedback, that the failure of the government is likely to be less than that of the market. For while certain types of market failure are inherent in the case of a monetarized production system, government failure is, under a system of political democracy, potentially self-correcting.

In summary, the government is no less subject to failure than the market. Still, government intervention in the economy is unavoidable. The economic system requires as essential inputs a certain amount of output, in the form of societal decisions, from the political system. These are the decisions—such as the optimal rate of accumulation and the noninflationary growth of money wages—which, as the analysis of the preceding chapters has brought out, cannot be produced endogenously within the economic system and which, if left to the market or some other nongovernmental mechanism, may leave the party in power vulnerable at the polls. It is the possibility of losing control because of the economy's unsatisfactory performance overall which forces the government, under a system of political democracy, to assume at the very least a màcroeconomic regulatory role. In addition, there are the types of market failure which, because of the potential electoral fall-out, leave the government with no choice but to take on separate micro regulatory, production and redistributive roles as well. These several roles and the various forms of intervention to which they give rise—especially the provision of public goods, along with transfer payments—are then reflected in the composition and size of the public sector budget, a topic to which we shall now turn. The point to be stressed here is that these are the roles which the inherent limitations of a market-based economic system as a self-regulating mechanism have thrust on the government. It is not that the state has sought out those roles simply as a means of increasing its sway over the members of the society. And while there is little reason to believe that the government will be successful in correcting every instance of market failure, at least initially, there really is no other back-up system. The hope is that, because of the political system's cybernetic aspects—particularly, the learning, or "positive" feedback, that occurs through the successive policies adopted by the political parties hoping to gain power—any government failure will be only temporary.

10.2 The Public Sector's Budget

The government, as the formal component of the political system, requires a certain level of material support if it is to function. It must obtain a portion of the enterprise sector's output: the quantities of steel, cement, paper, typewriters, etc. needed by the various agencies to carry out their responsibilities. The agencies must, in addition, be staffed with workers, or personnel, who will contribute their labor, or human resource inputs, only if the government sees to it that their material needs are met. The government could, of course, use its monopoly of coercive power to commandeer the requisite material resources. However, such a method would be incompatible with the principle of voluntary exchange upon which a market system of production is based. Hence, in an advanced industrial society, the government tends to rely (except under emergency wartime conditions) on a different means of obtaining control over the resources it needs. It uses the income available to it from tax revenues to purchase the requisite material and human resources. How the government is able to obtain the necessary tax revenues is a question that will be taken up in part 3 of this chapter. The focus in this section will be on the amount of material and human resources the government must obtain in order to carry out its regulatory, production and redistributive roles in the economy. These are the resources provided for in the public sector's budget. We shall begin the analysis by sketching a theory of public, as distinct from private, goods and then indicating what are the special characteristics of the goods and services which fall within that category.

10.2.1 Types of public goods

Two types of public goods can be delineated. One is the "pure" public good and the other is the "quasi" public good. Though the underlying factors are somewhat different, both kinds of public goods reflect a type of market failure which only the government, either by subsidization or direct production, can overcome. This type of market failure is one that occurs whenever there are external, or "third-party," effects from a transaction and/or the use of resources. The third-party effects mean that the principle of internalized costs and benefits—the presumption that only the two parties to any transaction will bear the social costs and realize the social benefits—no longer holds. While some type of government intervention may be necessary to neutralize the external, or third-party, effects, what the government will minimally need to do will vary, depending on whether the good or service in question is a "pure" or only a "quasi" public good.

The pure public good is distinguished, first of all, by its "lumpiness," or indivisibility. This refers to the fact that a certain minimal configuration, or quantum, of resources must be obtained as an input before production of the good or service can begin. For instance, it may be necessary to connect every residence and place of business in the community to a central switchboard before an adequate level of telephone service can be provided to all. Or it may be necessary to have not just a hospital in the community itself but also a group of more specialized hospitals serving the larger region before the provision of medical care can be considered adequate. The resources needed to connect every building to a central switchboard in the case of telephone service and to provide the full complement of general and more specialized hospitals in the case of medical care are both examples of "lumpy," or indivisible, inputs. So are the various capital goods that, when combined in a certain manner, constitute the plant and equipment, or productive capacity, of each industry.

The existence of indivisible inputs has long been a source of recognized difficulty in demonstrating that resources will be optimally allocated through the market. In the extreme case, indivisible inputs create a "natural monopoly"—an industry in which the economies of scale are such that only a single firm can achieve the lowest possible costs and thus only a single firm can expect to survive. Even without being pushed to that extreme, however, indivisible inputs will preclude a good or service from being supplied in small quantities. They are, in fact, the basis for the fixed costs which make short-run marginal cost pricing incompatible with the long-run recovery of the costs of expansion and thus they are the reason why, in the industrial sector of the economy, markup pricing generally prevails (see chapter 6, section 4.4), and, in the extreme case, government regulation may be necessay (see chapter 7, section 3.6). Still, while indivisible inputs would seem to preclude the type of atomistic competition usually assumed in economic theory, this is not the same as saying that the goods or services produced with such inputs cannot be obtained through the market and that therefore the government must supply them at a zero or below-cost (that is, a subsidized) price. For the output of an industry to be classified as a pure public good, a second condition besides the "lumpiness," or indivisibility, of the inputs must hold.

The second distinguishing characteristic of a pure public good is the nondeniability of the benefits to other parties once the good or service has been provided to a single individual or group of individuals. This nondeniability of the benefits—giving rise to what economists refer to as the "free rider" problem—makes it virtually impossible to secure payment for the resources needed to produce the good or service. The inability to secure payment is, in turn, what precludes the good from being supplied through the market. Without some means of enforcing payment, anyone who might supply the good or service cannot hope to recover the cost of the inputs and therefore will be unwilling to supply the good or service. A classic example is a flood control project in an isolated valley. The series of upstream dams that would have to be constructed represent a "lumpy" outlay, requiring expenditures beyond the financial resources of any one individual or family living in the valley. And yet if any one individual were to assume that burden, constructing the series of dams at his or her own expense, then everyone else living in the valley would benefit equally as much—without having to contribute a cent to the cost of construction. Under the circumstances, the series of dams are unlikely to be built, at least by any private party.

One could, of course, appeal to the common interest of all those living in the valley and attempt to raise the necessary funds through voluntary contributions. Some would undoubtedly refuse to contribute, however, contending that they cannot afford to do so; and whatever social sanctions might be applied—for example, by their neighbors threatening to shun them as "cheapskates"—might not suffice to secure payment. Only the government, with its taxing power as an essential attribute of its sovereignty, can circumvent the problem by financing the flood control project through a levy imposed on all the individuals or households living in the valley. In this way, the inability to supply the good or service through the market can be overcome. The same is true in the case of other "pure" public goods, such as national defense, domestic law and order, some types of public health services and all forms of basic research. It should be noted that what is needed to correct the failure of the market is not necessarily for the government itself to supply the good or service—although it may, for some other reason, choose to do so—but rather for the government to use its taxing power to ensure that the costs of providing the good or service, which are beyond the capacity of any one individual or group of individuals to absorb, will be apportioned in some manner among all those expected to benefit from the provision of that good or service.

The second type of public good is the "quasi" public good. In contrast to the condition that pertains in the case of a pure public good, the use of a quasi-public good can be denied to those who benefit directly. For example, an individual who wants to travel on an interstate highway can be denied access unless he or she pays a toll. Similarly, a person who wishes to attend college or be treated in a hospital can be turned away unless he or she pays a fee. There are, nonetheless, certain indirect or "spillover" benefits to other groups in society, groups not directly involved in the sale or purchase of the good. While those who will benefit directly can be forced, via the market mechanism, to contribute to the cost of supplying the good or service, those who will benefit only indirectly cannot. As a result, the revenue obtained from the sale of the good or service may be less than the total benefits, direct and indirect. In some cases, the shortfall in revenue will lead to the good being supplied in amounts less than the socially optimal quantity. In other cases, it will lead to the good or service being supplied not at all.

A classic example of the latter is a rail or some other type of transportation link between two cities. Those who will benefit directly from the transportation link, by being able to travel themselves or ship goods over it, can be denied access unless they pay the stipulated fare. In this way, the direct beneficiaries can be forced to contribute to the cost of the project. But there is another group which will benefit from the transportation link, though only indirectly. They are the individuals who own land along the right-of-way. Because of the stimulus to economic activity which the improved means of transportation will provide, their property will increase in value. These property owners, however, cannot be forced to contribute anything to the cost of the transportation link—at least not in their role as landowners. And if the revenues generated from fares or tolls are not sufficient to cover the cost of constructing the transportation link plus any out-of-pocket expenses, private investors will not be willing to undertake the project. Hence, the transportation link will not be constructed, at least by private investors responding to market signals.

Again, one could appeal to the landowners' "public spirit," urging them to contribute to the cost of constructing the transportation link and citing as the reason for their making a voluntary contribution the eventual rise in the value of their property once the projected line had been completed. The more certain remedy, however, is for the government to levy a tax on all the property owners along the right-of-way sufficient to cover any difference between the cost of constructing the transportation link and the revenues which can be generated from the subsequent traffic along the line. In this way, the market failure would again be corrected, irrespective of how "public spirited" any of the property owners might be. In the case of this and other quasi-public goods, it is again not necessary that the government provide the good or service itself—or even that it use its taxing power to cover the full cost. The state need only provide a tax-financed subsidy to match any indirect benefits to third parties. The indirect effects on third parties, it should be noted, may be negative as well as positive. In the former case, they represent the pollution, congestion and other socially detrimental externalities that are a by-product of certain industries. This other side of the coin will be discussed later in connection with the natural resource contraints on production (see chapter 13, section 3.1). The positive indirect benefits on the other hand give rise, in the extreme case when the third parties represent everyone but a single individual or group, to the pure public good.

The positive indirect benefits, or externalities, which characterize quasi-public goods are of two types: (1) the indirect economic benefits which are reflected in the increased output of goods and services; and (2) the indirect anthropogenic benefits which are reflected in the increased skills and competence of the labor force and, even more broadly, the general population. These two types of indirect benefits are what distinguish the quasi-public economic goods and services from the quasi-public anthropogenic goods and services. Transportation, communications and energy projects, because of the indirect economic benefits to which they give rise, fall under the first category of quasi-public goods. They represent an addition to the economic system's "infrastructure" and, because of the stimulative effect they are likely to have on other types of economic activity, they often serve as the prime instrument of a government's developmental policy. The resources required to add to this infrastructure are as much a part of any investment by the society as the new plant and equipment purchased by private firms—whether the resources are brought together by private parties relying on public subsidies or are instead mobilized directly by some public agency.

Education, health and social services fall under the second category of quasi-public goods. To the extent a society is limited in its rate of progress by the lack of competent individuals, they, too, play an important developmental role. Expenditures on these types of anthropogenic services, although a form of public consumption, may nonetheless give rise to indirect social benefits no less than those arising from additions to the economic infrastructure. It is the extent of these indirect social benefits that will then determine how much of the anthropogenic quasi-public good or service the state will need to make sure is supplied, either by subsidizing the activity or by providing the service itself directly.

Whether the quasi-public good merely needs to be subsidized or is best supplied directly by the government will depend on an additional set of factors. In the case of urban highway systems, for example, the difficulty of collecting tolls is such that it is generally more convenient for the government to provide access to the system of roads simply as a free public good. In the case of elementary and secondary education, the transmission of values is so closely linked to the provision of specific skills that public control is insisted upon—at least at the present time in the case of the United States. These and other considerations have led to a situation in which the government does not merely subsidize the private provision of certain public goods but rather supplies those goods and services itself. This is no less true of certain pure public goods. For example, because of the obvious problem of exercising public control over the coercive means employed, the government tends to supply directly itself the pure public goods of national defense and domestic law and order. It is in this way that the state has come to assume a production role in the economy, with that role, together with its redistributive role, largely accounting for the public sector budget. What still remains to be explained is why the government needs to assume a redistributive role in addition to its regulatory and production roles.

10.2.2 The redistributive role of government

The actual observed pattern of income distribution has long been a source of uneasiness among the more affluent members of advanced industrial societies. It is not immediately clear why the rapid economic proress which has brought such an improved standard of living to them should leave others, a significant minority, with a level of income barely sufficient for survival. Indeed, Alfred Marshall had originally been attracted to economics, like many others both before and since, because of his concern about the widespread poverty he observed in his time. Nonetheless, the answer which Marshall and others came to after studying the question was that there was little that could be done that would not make matters worse. Before the marginalist revolution in economic theory, the reasoning was that any improvement in the wages of workers would simply lead to an increase in population and thus, when the additional ''hands'' sought employment, to a reduction in wages. The controlling principle here was a Malthusian dynamic, with wages held to the subsistence level by demographic factors. After the marginalist revolution and the shift to the neoclassical theory of income distribution, the argument changed. Now it was that workers could not expect, under a system of private enterprise, to earn more than the value of their marginal product (see chapter 8, section 4.3). If this meant that workers earned close to subsistence, this was simply because they were not more ''productive.'' The Malthusian dynamic, to the extent it still applied, operated on the supply side of the market, assuring a degree of competition among workers that precluded wages from rising any higher. The possibility that some who wished to work would be unable to find employment was excluded by the near universal belief, at least among economists, in Say's Law.

Keynes, of course, effectively destroyed at least the last part of that argument. By demonstrating that aggregate demand could equilibrate at a level which still left large numbers of workers unemployed, he not only showed why Say's Law was invalid, he also called into question the assumption that any members of society who wanted or needed income could obtain it by offering their labor services in the market. This assumption had been the basis for the belief long held by economists, beginning with the campaign by the classical writers against the poor relief laws, that it was a mistake for the government to provide income to those out of work. If individuals were unable to find employment, so the argument ran, it was because they refused to accept a lower wage, one that was more in line with the value of their labor. Government transfer payments, whether in the form of "poor relief" or some modern equivalent, simply encouraged individuals to choose leisure over work. Such a policy not only made labor artificially scarce, thereby increasing its cost, it also forced those actually performing the necessary toil of an advanced industrial society to support others in their idleness, thereby undermining belief in the fairness of how the workload was being apportioned.

These arguments became less convincing, however, once Keynes demonstrated that, even if those seeking jobs were willing to lower their wage demands, they still would not be able to obtain employment. Keynes emphasized the effect lower money wages were likely to have on the psychological factors governing the "marginal efficiency of capital" (see chapter 7, section 1.1). An even more fundamental reason, one would now have to point out based on the model developed in this text, are the fixed labor coefficients that characterize modern, technologically advanced production techniques (see chapter 5, section 1.4, and chapter 12, section 1.2). Still, whatever the underlying reason, once it is understood that workers may be unable to obtain employment, and thus the income they need, regardless of what actions they as individuals may take, the arguments against the government providing relief to those out of work become less persuasive. And indeed governments, influenced in part by the change in the intellectual climate brought about by the Keynesian revolution in political economy and in part by a more generous social ethic, began to develop a wide range of income transfer programs. The upshot was what has come to be known as the "welfare state"—a government which acts as though the socially preferable pattern of income distribution is different from the one that would emerge from market processes alone. The welfare state is, in fact, simply the government functioning in its redistributive role.

The income transfer programs which have been established under the aegis of the welfare state can be grouped under three broad headings, each reflecting a different type of market failure. One group consists of the social insurance programs. These are the programs which provide transfer income based on a condition which may occur with an estimable frequency to any member of society and which therefore represents an actuarial risk to all. Unemployment benefits were the first of these social insurance programs to be established in the United States, the risk being the involuntary loss of a job and the inability, because of labor market conditions, to obtain a substitute position. The insurance concept was then extended to cover the risk of being unable to hold a job because of physical disability and/or old age. The earlier view had been that workers should protect themselves against these risks by setting aside a part of their earnings, in the form of savings, as a contingency fund for just such a "rainy day." But by the time of the Keynesian revolution it had come to be recognized that only a relatively small number of self-employed "capitalists" were in a position, be cause of their much higher levels of income, to exercise the foresight which this required. For most workers, the wages earned were too meager, the possibility of being unable to find work too remote and the struggle to make ends meet too immediate. The result was a level of savings by most workers which left them destitute whenever they could no longer obtain employment. Since the cost of providing for those who became destitute was a social one—mores had evolved to the point where the unemployed were no longer allowed simply to starve—the cost might as well be borne through a system of social insurance, with those currently employed taxed to provide income to those who were not. To the extent that any worker might, if need be, receive benefits, the equity issue was muted. Thus it was that, with the enactment and subsequent liberalization of the social security program in the United States (the counterpart of similar programs in other countries), a comprehensive system of social insurance came into being.

A second group of income transfer programs consists of the programs intended to establish a minimum floor under income, whether the individual has ever worked or not. The social insurance programs serve only those who have success-fully entered the labor force and been able to hold on to their jobs for a certain minimal period of time. This group, as already pointed out (see chapter 8, section 3.2), constitutes the "permanent" work force and its size depends, aside from the level of aggregate demand, on the labor coefficients represented by the L vector. The size of the permanent work force thus depends on the nature of the current technology. Since that technology evolves independently of the demographic factors which determine the size of the working-age population, the permanent work force need not include all those in need of employment as a source of income. A significant number of individuals, even after excluding those with property income and those supported by other family members, may be left out. If those individuals are not to be allowed simply to starve, they must be provided with some form of transfer income. This is done through various minimum-floor income transfer programs. In the United States, these programs are administered at the state and local level of government and are often referred to, derogatorily, as "welfare" or "relief."

The reason why such programs are needed under a market system remains a matter of debate. A prevalent view is that there are always jobs available to those willing and able to work, and that therefore there must be something socially pathological about those dependent on "welfare." This view is reinforced by the fact that individuals with psychological problems sufficiently severe to preclude them from holding a job are among those covered by the minimum-floor income transfer programs—even though they represent only a small segment of the eligible population. The argument being developed in this text (see especially chapter 13, section 2.3) points to a somewhat different explanation as to why the minimum-floor income transfer programs are needed. The expansion of the economy over time, together with the changing set of labor coefficients, allows for a permanent labor force of only a certain size. Any additional persons who need or want to obtain employment will be relegated to the "peripheral," or secondary, work force (see chapter 8, section 1.3)—without any certainty of then being hired.

The number of individuals within the secondary work force who are able to find employment, unlike the number of persons holding jobs within the primary work force, is somewhat sensitive to the prevailing wage rate. It depends, in particular, on how large is the differential in wage rates between the oligopolistic and nonoligopolistic sectors of the economy. The larger that differential, the greater the ability of marginal firms to survive and the more jobs they will be able to offer (see chapter 8, section 3.2). Still, this does not mean that those who have been relegated to the secondary work force are in a position to determine their own chances of obtaining employment. Whatever the differential between wage rates in the oligopolistic and nonoligopolistic sectors of the economy, only a certain number of persons will be able to obtain jobs with the marginal firms which, because of the lower wages they pay, are able to survive. The number of persons able to obtain those jobs will depend on the labor coefficients within the nonoligopolistic sector as well as on the labor coefficients for the marginal firms within the oligopolistic sector itself. The members of the secondary labor force, moreover, have no control over how large is the wage differential between the oligopolistic and nonoligopolistic sectors. It depends on the labor market conditions previously identified. Thus the members of the peripheral work force unable to find employment, even of a transient nature, are no more in a position to do anything about their situation than those members of the permanent work force who, as a result of the economy's cyclical behavior, find themselves temporarily laid off. Both are part of the anthropogenic slack which enables the supply of human resource inputs to adjust to the demand without interrupting the flow of goods and services (see chapter 13, part 2).

The trauma of being unable to find employment, and thus failing to become economically integrated into the society, is likely to lead, the longer it continues, to the very social pathologies which make the members of the dependent class the object of scorn among other groups in society—particularly those at the greatest risk of succumbing themselves to the same pathologies. These pathologies include alcoholism, drug addiction and other forms of mental illness; criminal and other anti-social behavior, and most serious of all, the disintegration of the family unit. Indeed, even jobs which offer only transient employment, with little hope of advancement to a better paying, more secure position, are likely to increase the incidence of the same pathologies. Those who fall prey to these pathologies are, in effect, the victims of a situation in which the economic system's dynamic growth is able to create only a certain number of "good" jobs—those that enable an individual to support himself (or herself), together with other members of the family unit, at some minimum socially acceptable level. If these victims are nonetheless blamed for their plight, it is largely because other groups, those already fully integrated economically into the society, do not want to be saddled with the burden of supporting them.

The third, and final, group of income transfer programs consists of those programs intended to provide the necessary material support for those members of society who are below working age or who, for some other reason, need to be supported economically until they can enter the work force. These are the counterpart, at the other end of the age spectrum, of the income transfer programs for the elderly, both those which are part of the system of social insurance and those which simply provide a minimum income floor for the uninsured. Traditionally, it had been the family or, when the family unit was weakened or destroyed, communal religious and other private groups which were expected to provide the necessary support for the young before they entered the labor market. The prevailing social ethic held, almost as a matter of necessity given the levels of per capita income, that in the absence of this support from family and confraternal groups, it was simply the child's ill fortune if he or she grew up impoverished. There was nothing the state could, or should, do—unless both parents were lost, in which case the state might provide temporary shelter until relatives or another family unit could be found to take in the child. However, as part of the shift from a darwinistic to an existentialistic social ethic (the same transformation of values which, reflecting the rise in general living standards, led to a more humanitarian spirit overall), children came to be recognized as, if not a valuable social resource, then at least a group entitled to special protection even if they were still living with one or more of their natural parents. If the family could not be counted on, then the state had to provide a certain minimal amount of income to those responsible for the child's upbringing. The result was the establishment of the Aid to Families with Dependent Children (AFDC) program in the United States and similar child support income transfer programs in other countries. These programs, it should be noted, reflect the failure not of the market system, at least directly, but rather that of another societal system, the family (though the breakdown of the family could, in turn, be traced back to the inability of the economic system to provide a sufficient number of employment opportunities). Still, since the need in any case was for a source of income, this meant that the state, as the only remaining back-up system, had to enlarge upon its redistributive role.

The nature and extent of these child support programs have remained controversial, just like the minimum-floor transfer programs. In part the controversy has been over the cost of the program and which groups should be forced to bear the burden. But even more fundamentally the controversy has reflected a fear of undermining existing social relationships—particularly, the nexus between work and income. The fear is that, if eligibility for and benefits under the AFDC program are not narrowly restricted, then so many families might qualify at a sufficiently high level that compensated employment would no longer be essential as a source of income for individuals. They would instead be able to support themselves from the transfer income received for rearing the young, with the result that the compelling pressure which now exists for individuals to seek employment outside the home would be considerably reduced. However, it was not just the nexus between work and income which the child support programs seemed to threaten. If women in their traditional role of nurturing the young were now to be assured of adequate income, whether they accepted a male partner or not, then the power which men have traditionally held over women, especially after the women have given birth to children, would be weakened. For these reasons, eligibility for and, especially important, benefits under the child support programs have been severely limited so the programs would not become an attractive alternative to either work or marriage. This has meant that the programs have been unable to ensure an adequate level of material support for the young before they are old enough to join the work force. Meanwhile, the programs themselves, because some believe them to be too restrictive while others believe them to be too liberal, have remained controversial within the United States, an unresolved issue on the nation's political agenda.

These three types of income transfer programs are not the only way in which the government redistributes income. How the government raises the revenue to cover the cost not just of the various public goods it supplies but also of any income transfer programs themselves is a further way in which the government affects the distribution of income. Indeed, the entire set of tax rates, positive as well as negative, is the primary means by which the government carries out its redistributive role. This is a point that will be elaborated on in the main section which next follows when the government's tax-based fiscal policy will be examined. First, however, it is necessary to see how both the production role of government, along with the redistributive role, determines the programmatic structure of the public sector's budget.

10.2.3 The programmatic structure of the public sector budget

The activities of government are not just capricious but rather reflect the tasks which, for lack of any other social mechanism able to perform them, have devolved upon the state. There are, first, the tasks which have grown out of the government's having reserved for itself—as a principal attribute of its sovereignty—a monopoly of any and all deadly force directed at individuals (with severe restrictions placed on when and how that deadly force can be applied). These are the tasks which, as part of preserving the society's decision-making capability, involve maintaining an adequate defense against foreign attack, along with other forms of international security, and of preserving domestic law and order. They constitute the political functions of government. Then there are the tasks which the government has been forced to take on because of various types of market failure. These are the tasks of regulating the economy (at both the micro and macro levels), of ensuring the provision of certain pure and quasi-public goods (as additions to the economic infrastructure), and of redistributing income. They constitute the economic functions of government. Finally, there are the tasks which have fallen to the government because of the inherent limitations of the family and other human developmental institutions. These are the tasks of ensuring an adequate level of education, health and other social services. They constitute the anthropogenic functions of government.

All three of these functions, along with the more particular tasks they encompass, define the major program categories needed to make sense of the government's budget. Exhibit 10.1 gives the entire set of these program categories for the U.S. public sector, with only one of these categories, "subsidies to industry and/or the provision of credit," requiring a further explanation. The subsidies to industry can be viewed either as a necessary means of ensuring the adequate provision of certain quasi-public goods or, alternatively, as an unwarranted transfer payment from government to a few favored industries. Which is the case depends on whether the industry receiving the subsidy actually supplies goods or services which give rise to the indirect social benefits being claimed for it. Since exhibit 10.1 already includes separate categories for business services, basic industrial research, transportation and communications, energy and natural resources and municipal services, one can question whether the additional subsidies to industry—such as those received by the maritime industry and farmers both in the United States and in many other countries—are justified. The subsidies to industry are nonetheless included, despite their questionable nature, precisely because they are a significant component of the government's budget in most countries. As for the provision of credit, this represents an intrusion of the government into the financial sector of the economy and therefore needs to be examined as an additional aspect of the government's monetary policy (see chapter 12, section 2.3). Suffice it for now to point out that the argument for government-subsidized loans in certain cases is based on the indirect benefits said to arise from the activities being financed, with the provision of credit justified as being the least costly way of providing the necessary assistance.

As one further comment on exhibit 10.1, it should be noted that international security, domestic law and order, regulation of the economy and basic industrial research are all examples of pure public goods. Domestic law and order (along with the regulation of the economy, to which it is closely related) is a special type of pure public good. The "cost," or burden, which in this case the government must use its coercive powers to force all the members of society to share equitably is the advantage to the individual foregone by adhering to certain rules or laws. While any one individual might be better off by being able to violate a particular law (and would indeed be best off if he or she alone could violate that law without penalty), it is in the nature of a law that has the character of a pure public good that everyone in the society (or at least a majority) is better off when everyone eschews the proscribed behavior. A violation of such a law is thus analogous to the refusal of someone who will benefit from a more conventional type of pure public good, such as an upstream flood control project, to contribute to the cost of that good. Of course, not every law enacted by the legislature has the character of a pure public good. Some laws benefit only a portion of the society at the expense of others, and these laws reflect the redistributive role which the state also plays in

Exhibit 10.1

Major Program Categories within the Public Sector

I. Political Functions of Government
    1. General
       a. Office of the Chief Executive
       b. Legislative
    2. International Security
       a. Military
       b. Diplomatic
    3. Domestic Law and Order
       a. Judicial
       b. Police
       c. Correctional
II. Economic Functions of Government
    1. Regulation
       a. Macro
       b. Micro
    2. Provision of Pure and Quasi-Public Economic Services (additions to economic
       infrastructure)
       a. Business Services
       b. Basic Industrial Research
       c. Transportation and Communications
       d. Energy and Natural Resources
       e. Municipal Services
       f. Other
    3. Redistribution of Income
       a. Social Insurance
       b. Minimum-floor Income Transfer Programs
       c. Child Support Programs
       d. Other
    4. Subsidies to Industry and/or Provision of Credit
III. Anthropogenic Functions of Government
    1. Education
    2. Health Services
    3. Other Social Services

society. Indeed, the danger every time the legislature enacts a new law is that the broader social benefits being claimed may be illusionary, and that the law may simply benefit one group in society at the expense of others.

The program structure of the public sector's budget delineated in exhibit 10.1

needs to be further refined in three ways. The first is to include various subcategories of programs under the major headings. For example, the military component of the U.S. international security program, that is, national defense, includes the subcategories of strategic nuclear deterrence, conventional armed forces and support services. The transportation and communications program includes the subcategories of air, rail, water and highway transportation as well as postal and telecommunications. The education program can be subdivided into preschool, elementary, secondary, college and graduate programs, with these in turn further subdivided into regular, vocational and remedial programs. These and the other program categories can be broken down into even more specific subcategories. The purpose in doing so is to develop a detailed programmatic structure so that alternative means of achieving the same or similar objectives are grouped together and a comparison can then be made. For example, submarine-launched and land-based intercontinental ballistic missiles are alternative means of maintaining a strategic nuclear deterrent; strategic nuclear weapons and conventional armed forces are alternative means of putting military pressure on another country, and a military build-up and diplomacy are alternative means of influencing other nations. Similarly, foot and motor patrols are alternative means of providing police protection; increased police patrols and greater inmate capacity for penal institutions (permitting longer prison terms) are alternative means of dealing with crime and more resources for the criminal justice system and a more generous system of income transfers are alternative means of maintaining domestic law and order.

The second way in which the program structure shown in exhibit 10.1 needs to be elaborated is to take into account the different levels of government at which public goods and services, along with transfer payments, are provided. The most important distinction, in the case of the United States, is between the federal government on the one hand and state and local governments on the other—with various nonprofit organizations and even certain profit-oriented private enterprises forming a third tier of service providers. Certain types of public goods (e.g., national defense and basic research) and certain types of transfer payments (e.g., Social Security and veterans' benefits) are provided by the Federal government directly. Others, such as domestic law and order, education and local "relief," are provided by state and/or local governments. In some cases (e.g., urban renewal and AFDC), the funds are provided by the Federal government through grants-in-aid but the programs themselves are administered by state and local agencies. In still other cases (e.g., defense procurement, highway construction and employment training) public monies are used to hire private contractors, either nonprofit organizations or profit-oriented private enterprises. The point is that separate budgets need to be drawn up for each of the different levels of government, with a distinction made between the funds merely provided and the goods and services actually produced at each level.

Once appropriate budgets have been developed for each of the different levels of government, based on a comprehensive set of program categories, it is possible to elaborate on exhibit 10.1 in a third important way. That is to distinguish between resources currently being expended under the various program categories and resources which, because of their durable nature, are actually part of a growing social stock. It is necessary, in other words, not to confuse the current operating budget with the capital budget. The latter identifies the discretionary expenditures of government, and thus it represents not only the public sector's contribution to capital formation but also its contribution to the macrodynamic stability of the economic system as a whole. A part of that growing social stock, like the analogous capital formation occurring in the household sector, will be nonproductive in an economic sense and therefore will not count as investment. These are the discretionary expenditures, or durable goods purchases, required to support the government's noneconomic functions, such as national defense and education. However, this does not mean that the expenditures are socially nonproductive. It only means that they will not add to the productive capacity of the economic system and, if socially productive, they are socially productive only in a noneconomic manner (see chapter 2, section 2.2). Moreover, whether or not they are economically productive, and thus whether or not they have a supply-augmenting effect, the government's discretionary expenditures will have a multiplier, or demand-enhancing, effect. Thus the government's discretionary expenditures are comparable to those of the enterprise and household sectors, and can be analyzed in much the same way—at least insofar as their macrodynamic impact is concerned.

There is nonetheless a crucial difference between the government's discretionary expenditures and the other types of discretionary expenditures considered up to now. This is the absence of a market-determined income constraint on those expenditures, and it points to both the advantage and the disadvantage which the government has in drawing up its capital budget. The advantage is that the government's capital budget does not depend on projected market sales—either of the output to be produced with those durable goods or, as in the case of the household sector, of the essential input, labor services, which is being supplied. Indeed, it is precisely this ability to transcend the constraints normally imposed by the market that enables the government to overcome any market failure. The disadvantage is that, in determining what level of expenditures to finance, the government cannot count on the market for guidance. The nature of the public goods and services it provides requires that the government discount, or even disregard entirely, any market signals—and in the case of certain programs, the military ones for example, there are not even market signals to disregard.

What this means is that the agencies which provide public goods and services are without the type of feedback information which the market automatically provides, based on the willingness of buyers to give up income in exchange. The agencies themselves have no way of knowing what level of output or service is needed to realize the social benefits to which public goods give rise and therefore they have no way of knowing what amount of resources should be budgeted for in the various programs they oversee. The market as a cybernetic mechanism being of little or no help to them, these agencies must fall back on some other device in making their budgetary decisions. In practice, this means that the decisions are based on political considerations, with questions of resource allocation and responsiveness to consumers being important only insofar as they affect the struggle for control of the government.

The political nature of the budgetary choices made within the public sector presents no problem in analyzing the macrodynamic impact of the government's discretionary expenditures. The rate of growth of these expenditures, $\dot{E}_G$, can be considered an exogenous variable, one that is determined outside the economic system. Indeed, this will be the approach followed in the later analysis of the government's macrodynamic impact. Still, to the extent some broader public interest is involved in the public sector's budgetary choices—and the resources involved, if not the external effects being claimed, would suggest there is—this narrow concern with the macrodynamic impact of the government's discretionary expenditures will not do. If public officials and voters are to behave in a responsible manner, then it is necessary to indicate, as an integral part of the economic analysis, what set of principles the government should follow in drawing up its budget so that the broader public interest will be served. This brings us to the problem of determining the effectiveness of the different programs funded through the public sector budget.

10.2.4 Program effectiveness

The public sector of the United States consumes aproximately one-fourth of the national product. The choices made through the political system are therefore no less important in determining the overall allocation of resources than the choices that are made relying on the market mechanism. It is not just a matter of deciding which programs should be funded and at what levels. It is also a matter of deciding how large the public sector itself should be—that is, what portion of aggregate output the government should command. The question is, what set of principles needs to be followed in drawing up the public sector's budget so as to assure the socially optimal use of the resources involved.

The answer usually given to this question, at least by economists, is that the budgetary decisions should be based on some sort of "cost-benefit" analysis. The social benefits from the various types of public outlays should first be identified, it is said, and then an effort made to place a monetary value on those benefits. In this way the benefits, in monetary terms, can be compared with the costs, also in monetary terms, and a cost-benefit ratio derived. If the ratio is less than 1, this means that the social benefits outweigh the costs and the public outlays are warranted. If the ratio is greater than 1, the opposite is true. Determining the size and composition of the public sector's budget in this manner is consistent with the more general rule put forward by economists for assuring an optimal allocation of the society's resources, namely, that the benefits to society at the margin from the use of any resources should be equal to the marginal social cost.

As a practical matter, however, it has proven difficult, if not impossible, to place a monetary value on the social benefits from most types of public expenditures. The task would appear to be more manageable in the case of transportation, water reclamation and the other types of public outlays that add to the society's economic infrastructure. The benefits, since they take the form of an increase in the capacity to produce goods and services, are more easily quantified and a monetary value placed on them. It should therefore come as no surprise that cost-benefit analysis was first developed by the U.S. Army Corps of Engineers to support its requests for funds to carry out various types of "public works" projects. Still, even for these economically oriented programs, the cost-benefit ratio turns out to be largely a matter of subjective judgment. Whether the ratio is less than or more than 1 usually depends on what value is placed on the indirect social benefits, and there is considerable room for dispute as to what precisely those indirect social benefits are—let alone what value should be placed on them.

If one turns from the economic to the noneconomic goods and services provided by government, the task of placing a monetary value on the putative social benefits becomes even more difficult—and may well be impossible. How, indeed, is a value to be placed on a new military weapons system, even assuming the weapons system will have the effect claimed of reducing the probability of enemy attack? And how is a value to be placed on an expansion of the health care delivery system, again assuming the expansion will have the effect claimed of reducing mortality and/or morbidity? Cost-benefit analysis, as applied to the noneconomic functions of government, requires measuring the unmeasurable: the value of life itself, both communal and individual. It is for this reason that, together with the subjective nature of the estimates even in the case of the economic goods and services supplied by government, public officials have found cost-benefit analysis to be of little help in making budgetary decisions. The technique, as a guide to public policy, has largely failed the praxis test (see chapter 15, section 1.1, for a discussion of what is meant by the praxis test). There is, however, another technique, or set of budgetary principles, which, because it avoids the need to place a monetary value on the putative benefits from government programs, may actually be of greater practical use to public officials. This technique requires only that the relative cost effectiveness of different government programs, and not their cost-benefit ratio, be determined.

The economic goal, insofar as the public sector's budget is concerned, is to minimize the economic resources required by the government to carry out its essential functions. This goal can best be achieved by basing the funding of government programs on their relative cost effectiveness—that is, on their ability to achieve a particular social objective, whether political, economic or anthropogenic, utilizing less of the society's economic resources than any other program.

There are three steps to determining the relative cost effectiveness of government programs. The first is to identify the essential functions of government, noneconomic as well as economic, and then to develop a set of budget categories that will facilitate the comparison of different programs in terms of the social objectives they are intended to serve—in much the same way the taxonomy of consumption facilitates the choice among private goods (see chapter 9, section 2.2). The preceding discussion of market and other types of societal failure, together with the delineation of the relevant program categories in exhibit 10.1, has been structured with that first step in mind.

The second step in determining the relative cost effectiveness of government programs is to identify the social benefits, or "output," produced by any two or more programs and then to derive a measure of the output that is common to all those programs. Thus any output measure that is developed must have a quantitative dimension to it—that is, one must be able to determine if more or less of the "output" is being produced—and the measure itself must be applicable to more than just one program. This second step has been the most difficult one to carry out in any systematic way, in large part because of the intellectual confusion over what is meant by the "output" of government programs. The social systems framework outlined at the very beginning of this text (see chapter 1, part 2) and now more fully elaborated on in this chapter should, however, make it possible at least to specify correctly the output of any government program. With the political system identified as the social system which, in addition to producing societal decisions as its own unique output, serves as the back-up to every other societal system, it follows that the output of any government program is the increased output of the major societal system the program in question is meant to shore up. Once the output of any government program has been defined in this manner, the way should be cleared for deriving a quantitative measure of that program's social benefits, or "output."

The availability of the National Income and Product Accounts makes it somewhat easier, as already pointed out, to derive a quantitative measure of the "output" produced by the government's economic programs. It is necessary only to determine how much lower aggregate economic output would be in succeeding years in the absence of those outlays. Nonetheless, by pursuing a similar line of reasoning while at the same recognizing the quite different type of output produced by the political and anthropogenic systems, it should be possible to define and even measure the output of the government's other types of programs. For any political programs, the "output" is either the enhancement of the society's decision-making capability or, alternatively, the preservation of whatever decision-making capability already exists. For any anthropogenic programs, on the other hand, the "output" is the increase in the numbers and kinds of competences acquired—or even just preserved—by the persons living within the society as a result of those programs (see chapter 13, part 1). Thus, insofar as the government's international security programs are concerned, the output can be equated with the reduction in the probability of violent attack from without and, insofar as the government's domestic law and order programs are concerned, it can be equated with the reduction in the amount of crime, violent and nonviolent—the output common to both types of political programs being the preservation of the government's sovereignty within its own territory. Insofar as the government's health programs are concerned, the output can be equated with the reduction in mortality and morbidity rates and, insofar as the government's educational programs are concerned, it can be equated with the number of persons completing various levels of schooling—the output common to both types of programs being the change in the number of persons alive and well who have certain competences. Implicit in this suggested approach to measuring the output of government programs is the need to develop comparable sets of social accounts for the political and anthropogenic systems to complement the National Income and Product Accounts used to measure the output of the economic system.

The critical step, then, in determining the relative cost effectiveness of government programs is obtaining a reliable measure of the social benefits, or "output," produced by those programs. However difficult a task this may be, and however feeble have been the previous efforts to develop such output measures, the step cannot be avoided—not if the allocation of resources through the taxing and other coercive powers of the state is to be improved. Public officials are forced to make judgments all the time about the social benefits from the various government programs and the only question is whether, in deciding budgetary questions, they will have the benefit of the best available technique for determining what the level of funding should be. Even if reliable quantitative estimates of the social benefits, or output, produced by the various government programs cannot be obtained, it may still be of some value that the relevant measure of output has at least been identified. In any case, the alternative technique that has been argued for by economists, some sort of cost-benefit analysis, requires that the same judgments be made about the output of the different government programs. It simply imposes the additional requirement that, once the output has been identified and measured, a monetary value be placed on it.

With a measure of the output attributable to each program—either the additional goods and services the economic system is able to provide as a result of the expenditures or the additional noneconomic output available from one of the other major societal systems—it is then possible to compare the relative cost effectiveness of the different government programs. This is the third and final step in carrying out any cost-effectiveness analysis. The programs must first be aligned, as in the programmatic structure delineated in exhibit 10.1, so that all programs providing the same or similar types of social benefits are grouped together. For example, all rail freight programs need to be considered as a group, then all of the freight transportation programs, the rail ones included. Next, whatever is the output measure common to all of those programs needs to be identified. In the case of the various freight transportation programs, this common output measure would be the ton mileage carried. Finally, the cost of each program—that is, the resources in value terms needed as inputs if the programs are to achieve a certain level of output—needs to be divided by the common output measure so as to obtain a measure of each programs's relative cost effectiveness.

In the example so far given, that of freight transportation, the cost-effectiveness measure would be the cost per ton mile of freight carried. But in the case of a military or police program, it would be the estimated reduction in the probability of violent attack per dollar expended while in the case of some anthropogenic program it would be the increased supply of individuals with a certain minimum level of competence per dollar expended. Not just different rail freight programs but also different freight transportation programs more generally could be compared on the basis of the cost per ton mile. When it comes to examining freight transportation vis-à-vis the other economic programs of government—for example, energy or basic industrial research programs—the basis for comparison becomes the additional dollar of aggregate output likely to be generated relative to the cost. And when the government's economic programs must be compared with the noneconomic ones, the basis for comparison becomes—however difficult it may be to quantify the variables—the increase in individual options relative to the cost from the greater availability of material goods compared with the increase in individual options relative to the cost from greater personal security and/or the enhanced competence of the members of society.

Once the relative cost effectiveness of the different government programs has been determined in this manner, it would then be possible to determine the optimal combination of such programs. Any one program is likely to be most cost effective only within a narrow range of the total output which must be supplied by the government. The task, then, is to determine the optimal *combination* of government programs, this being the mix of programs which are the most cost effective in producing each of the different types of public goods and services which must be provided by the government. When that optimal combination of government programs has been determined, it can then serve as the basis for drawing up the budget for the public sector, with the costs to be covered by the budget broken down, first, by program category and then, within each of those categories, into their material and human resource components. The former will indicate the necessary purchase of goods and services by the government and not-for-profit sector from the enterprise sector; the latter the necessary purchase of labor services from the household sector. Thus the public sector budget, once it has been determined through the political process, will have a significant effect on the macrodynamic behavior of the economic system. In order to be able to analyze what that effect is likely to be, it is necessary to relate what has just been said about the public sector budget to the input-output model of the economy previously developed.

10.2.5—The public consumption component of final demand

As has already been pointed out (see chapter 5, section 1.4), the final demand vector within an input-output model of the economy includes the net output entering into public consumption as well as the net output entering into private consumption. The latter has already been analyzed in chapter 9 in connection with the household sector's purchase of goods and services. Yet to be carried out is a similar analysis of the public consumption component of final demand. Two points, in particular, need to be clarified in order to bring out the relationship between the public sector budget and the public consumption component of final demand. One is the difference it makes whether the resources provided for within the budget are material or human resource ones. The second is whether the programs to be funded are economic or noneconomic ones.

As already indicated, the resources which the public sector budget enables the government to command fall into two categories. They are (1) the material goods and services purchased from the enterprise sector and (2) the labor services obtained from the household sector. The latter are provided for within a separate personnel budget—often in the form of a complete listing, by job title, of the various positions which public officials are authorized to fill. This separate personnel budget will determine the amount of employment within the public sector, an important policy variable in its own right. Indeed, the amount of government employment, N_G, multiplied by the average wage rate of public employees, w_G, equals the government's wage bill, and the size of that wage bill is one of the factors that will determine the household sector's disposable income, Y_D, and hence the level of demand for private consumption goods. However, the government's wage bill does not constitute any additional economic output. Rather it is the equivalent, as already pointed out (see chapter 2, section 2.2), of a transfer payment since it enables those employed by the government to command the consumption goods they need without, at the same time, adding to the supply of those goods. Only the government's direct purchase of goods and services from the enterprise sector represents additional economic output—and thus it is only those purchases which, as the elements of a separate Gov component, need to be included as part of the input-output model's final demand vector. The consumption goods purchased by government employees will already be included as part of the private consumption component, C. Thus, to derive the public consumption component of final demand without any double counting, it is necessary to subtract from the total outlays to be financed out of the public sector budget, first, any transfer payments and, then, the wage bill incurred by the government in connection with each of the separate programs being funded. Still, this procedure will suffice only for the short period; and even then, because it includes whatever additions have been made by the government to the economic infrastructure, the resulting Gov vector will encompass both public consumption and public investment. To isolate the public consumption component of the final demand vector, it is necessary to net out all of the government's economic programs as well, leaving only the material goods and services purchased by the government in order to carry out its noneconomic functions. It is these resources, the means by which the government is able to implement its political and anthropogenic programs, that constitute the public consumption component of final demand. They are in fact the net output, or surplus, produced by the economic system which is then used to satisfy the material needs of the public sector.

The question of what goods and services need to be supplied to the government, and in what quantities, so that the government can in turn carry out its necessary functions can thus be answered as a subset of the general output solution to the input-output model (see chapter 5, sections 2.1 and 5.4). Each of the major programs delineated in exhibit 10.1 represents a separate type of output produced in the public sector (with the income transfer programs, as already noted, an exception), and these programs are the equivalent, within an input-output model, of separate industries. Thus the delineation of the separate programs, like the delineation of the other industries shown along the columns and rows of an input-output table, depends on the same technological characteristics that distinguish one good from another within the overall system of production. Whether the goods need to be produced by the government itself, or at least partially subsidized, rather than being left to be supplied through ordinary market processes then depends on an additional set of factors, largely technological in nature, which may or may not preclude the cost of producing those goods from being fully met out of sales revenue. Once the various programs funded by the government have, in this way, been incorporated into the model of production, the required output of those programs—the level of goods and services they must provide—can be determined in the same manner as the output of the other industries: to wit, by multiplying the final demand vector (including any final demand for public goods) by the Leontief inverse.

The pure and quasi-public economic goods produced by the government, representing as they do an addition to the economic infrastructure, can be regarded as an intermediate output of the economic system, just like any of the other forms capital accumulation can take, and thus they are a part of the final demand vector only in the short period. In the long period they are necessarily a part of the inner matrix (see chapter 5, section 5.2, for a further discussion of this distinction in the case of any capital goods). The expansion of the economic system over time will require that rail, air, water and highway transportation facilities, along with the other components of the economic infrastructure such as urban water, sewer and other utility systems, be increased proportionately. To the extent these necessary additions to the economic infrastructure cannot be supplied in the socially optimal quantities by private firms relying on the revenue generated from sales to cover their costs, the government will need either to undertake the investment itself directly or—what is probably more desirable—to provide a subsidy equal to the difference between the private returns and the total social benefits. While the amount of any such investment that will need to be carried out over any relatively brief interval is indeterminate, and thus is part of the final demand vector in the short period, the amount by which the economic infrastructure will need to be increased in the long period is governed by the same types of technical relationships that determine the overall rate of capital accumulation. In the long period, then, the government's programs to supply various quasi-public economic goods and services fall within the inner matrix of the input-output system of production.

The other public goods supplied by the government, the pure and quasi-public noneconomic goods and services, are a different matter. The types and amount of these services which must be supplied do not depend, even in the long period, on the sort of technical relationships that make any additions to the economic infrastructure a part of the inner matrix. They depend instead on the imperatives of the separate political and anthropogenic systems, with the amount of economic resources needed to support those programs at whatever is the necessary level then determining the flow of material goods and services to the government that constitutes the public consumption component of the final demand vector.

The noneconomic programs delineated in exhibit 10.1 represent the types of services that must be supplied, relying on the coercive powers of the state, if the political and anthropogenic systems are to function at a certain level. The sums budgeted for those programs represent the value of the material and human resource inputs that must be obtained for a certain level of those services to be maintained. For example, a certain amount of material and human resources are required by the government's international security and domestic law enforcement programs, these as necessary inputs from the economic and anthropogenic systems, to guard against the possibility of foreign conquest and the breakdown of internal law and order. The funds budgeted for the international security and domestic law enforcement programs represent the value of those material and human resources. Similarly, a certain amount of resources are required by the government's anthropogenic programs, again as necessary inputs from the economic and anthropogenic systems, to ensure that the anthropogenic system will be able to provide the human resource inputs needed not just within the economic system but rather more generally throughout the society.

The material inputs that need to be purchased by the government from the enterprise sector fall under two categories. There are first the direct material inputs which are immediately used up in whatever activities are being carried out. Then there are the other material inputs which, not being immediately used up, represent an addition to the public sector's capital stock. These other material inputs are the durable goods purchases, or discretionary expenditures, of government; and they fall within a separate capital budget. Each government program will have its own capital budget. This is no less true of the government's political and anthropogenic programs than of the specifically economic programs which are designed to add to the economic infrastructure. Whatever material inputs are not immediately used up—such as the ships being added to the navy's fleet, the building being constructed to house a major new research facility along with the equipment to go inside it, and the books acquired for a school library—all fall within the capital budget of some specific program. As in the case of the other types of durable goods purchases we have examined (i.e., those made by the enterprise and household sectors) there is considerable discretion as to the timing of these expenditures. It is this fact, together with the lack of any income constraint on the amount of those expenditures and the relative size of the government's purchases, which enables the government to play the predominant role in determining the macrodynamic behavior of the economy as a whole, at least in the case of the United States. Before exploring that matter any further, however, it is necessary to examine the means by which the public sector is able to finance its budget, whether the budget which has been drawn up is an optimal one or not. This involves a consideration of government taxes and other unilateral income transfers.

10.3 Taxes and Other Transfer Payments

The essence of sovereignty is the monopoly of coercive power it gives the state. As an extension of that sovereignty, the government is able to impose taxes—that is, effect the unilateral transfer of income to itself. These unilateral income transfers are the means by which the government is able to finance its outlays, including any discretionary expenditures. The flow of income may, of course, be in the opposite direction, from the government to other groups in society. In that case, the taxes are negative ones and, like the government's other budgetary outlays, will need to be financed out of the positive tax revenues the government is able to generate. The unilateral income transfers in the form of taxes, both positive and negative, create a flow of income outside market channels. They are the principal means by which the government is able to transcend, and thereby control at the macro level, the economic system.

   The government's taxing power gives it a significant leverage over the economy in two ways. First, it provides an immediate source of revenue which is not conditional on the government being able to sell something in exchange. This nonmarket source of revenue enables the government to choose a rate of growth of discretionary expenditures, $\dot{E}_G$, independently of the type of income constraint that limits discretionary expenditures in the other sectors of the economy. The growth of discretionary expenditures by the government is likely, in turn, to be the critical factor, for the reasons soon to be pointed out, in determining both the growth of total discretionary expenditures, $\dot{E}$, and the growth of aggregate output, $\dot{G}$. Second, the government's taxing power gives it preferential status as a borrower in the financial markets, even over any megacorps. This more favored access to credit, based on the certainty of repayment out of future tax revenues, enables the government to readily finance any cash deficit—that is, any discrepancy between its current tax revenues and budgetary outlays. The size of the government deficit is likely, in turn, to play a key role in determining the cyclical behavior of the economy, both because of the cash-flow feedback effect (see chapter 3, section 2.5) and because of the impact on the monetary-financial sector (see chapter 12, section 2.3).

In the subsections which follow, we shall first examine why the burden of any tax is likely to be quite different from that suggested by the conventional analysis of tax incidence, based on the neoclassical models of the firm and income distribution. We shall then turn to the dynamic model of a monetarized production system which has been developed up to this point to see what the longer run impact of any taxes, as distinct from the more immediate incidence, is likely to be. Once the positive flow of tax revenue to the government has been examined, we shall turn to the negative tax flows, or transfer payments made by the government.

10.3.1 The burden of taxation

Taxes can be viewed as the "price" of public goods and services. Like any price, they provide a means of financing the purchase of the economic resources, or inputs, needed to produce the particular goods or services being supplied. As previously pointed out, what distinguishes a public good from other types of goods and services is that it gives rise to benefits which extend beyond the payment-enforcing limits of any market. In the case of a pure public good, the benefits accrue to the entire society, with the relative distribution of those benefits impossible to determine because of their indivisible nature. In the case of a quasi public good, only the indirect or "third-party" benefits cannot be financed by means of a market price. Still, those indirect benefits will, to no less an extent, accrue to the entire society. It is for this reason that any public good will need to be financed out of the government's tax revenues. Of course, in some cases, the benefits will be limited to a particular subgroup, such as the persons living within a certain region or the those engaged in a specific activity (e.g., hunting or traveling by air). Even in those cases, however, the costs will still need to be apportioned in some manner among all the members of the subgroup, relying on the taxing power of the government to ensure that those costs are fully covered.

Precisely how, based on a system of taxation, the cost of providing any public goods and services should be apportioned among the different members of society is a question that is not easily answered. While it might seem only reasonable that the cost should be borne equally by all, this only reduces the question to what is meant by the term "equally." Does it mean the same tax rate on a per-capita basis or the same rate on a per household basis? However, it is not just a question of what is the entity to be taxed, the individual or some other social unit such as the household. Governments, recognizing the advantage of being able to tap the income flows generated by a market economy, have generally abandoned "head" taxes for various types of direct and indirect taxes. The former are based on the so-called "factors" of production, labor and "capital" (actually wage and nonwage income) while the latter, such as a sales or excise tax, are levied as a percentage of the price at which some good or service is sold in the market. The question then becomes, which of these two types of taxes will result in a more equitable sharing of the tax burden. Moreover, it is not just a matter of choosing between direct and indirect taxes. It is also a matter of choosing within each of those two categories. The government can levy a direct tax either on wages or on profits and it can levy an indirect tax either on "necessities" (items of consumption relatively high in the hierarchy of material needs) or on "luxuries" (items relatively low in the hierarchy). Finally, there is the question, at least in the case of a direct tax, whether the rate should remain the same, regardless of the level of income, or whether the tax rate should vary with the level of income and/or wealth. It is, of course, when the rate varies positively with the level of income and/or wealth that the tax is labeled "progressive" by economists. Still, the question of how progressive a "progressive" tax should be—that is, at what rate the tax rate itself should increase—remains.

Whatever the mix of taxes used to finance government outlays, the choice will have a significant effect on the distribution of income among households. While the overall burden will remain the same—it depends entirely on the share of aggregate output represented by public consumption—the relative burden will vary depending on what types of taxes are imposed. What is meant by the relative tax burden are the differing proportions by which the real income of the various subgroups within the household sector, including the several social classes, is reduced by whatever tax or set of taxes is used by the government to finance its outlays. Of course, with allowance made for transfer payments and thus for negative tax flows, some households may actually come out ahead instead of suffering a loss of real income. Still, this only means that the relative tax burden is unevenly distributed.

The relative burden of any tax will depend on the extent to which it can be shifted. Will the tax be absorbed out of the income or revenue generated by the input or good on which the tax has been levied, or will it instead by offset by increasing the rate of compensation and/or the price of that input or good? This is the immediate incidence of any tax, and until it has been determined, one cannot say what the long-run effect of the tax will be on the distribution of income within the household sector. The immediate incidence of the direct and indirect taxes imposed by government has been analyzed at considerable length by economists. However, the analysis has been based, almost without exception, on the neoclassical paradigm, making it necessary to discard virtually all that has been written on the subject. It is not just the doubts which have already been cast on the essential features of any neoclassical model—among them the assumption that firms are price takers rather than price setters and that the choice of technique is governed by a set of isoquants rather than the fixed technical coefficients represented by the **A**, **K** (or **B**) and **L** matrices. It is also that the post-Keynesian theory developed in the preceding chapters leads to a quite different conclusion about the immediate incidence, or shifting, of the corporate income, or "profits," tax—and indeed even about the longer run effect of such a tax.

10.3.2 The immediate incidence of the corporate income tax

According to the orthodox theory, a direct tax on either profits or wages is borne primarily by the recipients of that income, either "capital" or labor. This conclusion follows from the assumption that firms are profit maximizers facing a perfectly elastic demand curve, selling a good that can be produced with variable amounts of labor and "capital." Thus it is argued that when either capital or labor as an input is taxed, firms cannot simply pass the tax on to consumers in the form of higher prices. That possibility is precluded by the perfectly elastic demand curve firms face. Their only recourse is to switch to a different technique, one that requires less of the input which is being taxed and more of some other input, thereby enabling them to move along the relevant isoquant (see chapter 5, section 3.1). In this way firms can, by altering the capital-labor ratio, at least minimize their costs of production. Only to the extent that the new capital-labor ratio implies a different profit-maximizing level of output for the firm and this new profit-maximizing level of output in turn, generalized for all firms, leads to a shift of the industry supply curve will the price paid by the consumers of the good be affected. Even so, the tax is unlikely to be shifted fully on to consumers. The burden will fall primarily on the individuals supplying the input being taxed, either "capitalists" or workers, causing their real income to fall. It is with this objective in mind that a large number of economists, hoping to alter the distribution of income in favor of workers, argue for a corporate income and similar taxes on "profits." The previous analysis of how prices are established within the oligopolistic sector of the economy suggests why these hopes may be unfounded.

The megacorps within the oligopolistic sector, to the extent they have sufficient pricing power to finance any discretionary expenditures out of internally generated funds, can be expected to treat the corporate profits tax as simply another of the factors that must be taken into account in determining the optimal size markup within any industry. Indeed, they cannot fail to offset a tax on their net income through higher prices without being forced to reduce their capital outlays, and thus their own internal rate of expansion. To avoid a reduction in the rate at which they are generating cash flow, or discretionary funds, the megacorps within the oligopolistic sector will need to increase the size of the average markup by some multiple, T_c, calculated as follows:

$$T_c = \frac{1}{1 - t_c} \tag{10.1}$$

where t_c is the corporate profits tax rate. Thus, with corporate profits subject to a tax of 33.3 percent, the markup will need to be increased by a multiple of 1.5 in order to generate the same amount of cash flow or discretionary funds. This means that equation 6.31, the formula for determining what size markup must be obtained by the firms within an industry in the long period, needs to be modified as follows:

$$m_j = \mathsf{T}_c[\frac{g_j b_j}{1-(g_j b_j)}]$$ (10.2)

while the corporate profits tax rate, t_c, needs to be added to the set of factors identified in equation 6.55 that will determine what size markup will actually be established in the short period within any oligopolistic industry.

Megacorps could, of course, reduce the rate at which they are paying out dividends. In this way, they would be able to finance the same level of capital expenditures, despite the tax on profits, without having to increase the size of the markup. The tax would then not fall, even indirectly via higher prices, on the working class. Such an outcome is at least theoretically possible since the reduced flow of dividends, in response to the tax on corporate profits, will merely alter the distribution of income between the rentier class and the public sector. It will have no effect either on the level of aggregate demand or on relative prices. Indeed, as already pointed out (see chapter 8, section 2.2), both any private consumption by rentiers financed out of dividend payments and any public consumption by government agencies financed out of tax revenues are merely separate components of the overall consumption out of nonwage income, Π_e, and it is the total amount of such consumption, not the division between rentier and public consumption, that will determine the real wage of workers.

Nonetheless, while shifting at least a part of the burden of government on to rentiers through a reduction in the dividend rate is a theoretical possibility, and indeed would appear to be the result hoped for by those who advocate a tax on corporate profits, this is unlikely to be the actual outcome, given the present balance of noneconomic factors that determine the growth of dividends within the U.S. economy. As already pointed out (see chapter 8, section 3.4), the failure of any one megacorp to maintain the same rate of growth of dividends as other megacorps, especially those in the same industry or sector, would threaten the continued control of the firm by its executive group. While this threat could be neutralized if all megacorps were to act together to reduce the dividend rate, there is no reason to expect megacorps to behave in such a concerted manner. The norm which presently prevails among corporate executives is that dividends should increase over time to match the growth of money wages. They are therefore unlikely to reduce the rate of growth of dividends, simply to offset the tax on corporate profits, while the rate of growth of money wages is left unchanged.

They are more likely to increase the markup instead—especially since it can be assumed that megacorps, as a group, have sufficient pricing power to do so.

The factors that would otherwise limit the size of the markup in an oligopolistic industry—the substitution effect, the entry factor and the fear of government retaliation (see chapter 6, section 3.3)—will be largely inoperative when the markup must be increased to offset a tax, or even an increase in the tax rate, on corporate profits. With all corporations subject to the same tax, relative prices will, for the most part, be unaffected. Only to the extent that the growth rate and/or the incremental capital output ratio varies among the different industries will the profit margins themselves vary, and even then, the magnitude of any substitution effect will depend not just on the differences in the size of the profit margin across industries but also on any differences in the price elasticity of demand. With both any differences in the size of the markup across industries and any differences in the price elasticity of demand likely to be relatively small, the substitution effect as the product of those two sets of factors can be all but ignored in assessing the ability of megacorps to shift forward, through a higher price, any tax on their profits. As for the entry factor, any advantage a new firm might have as a result of its profits being subject to a lower rate of taxation will count for little, given both the higher costs it faces in attempting to capture the minimal share of the market needed just to break even and the relatively low level at which corporate profits are subject to the maximum tax rate. Finally, the possibility of government retaliation can be discounted entirely unless the government specifically prohibits companies from passing the tax on to buyers in the form of higher prices.

On the reasonable assumption, then, that any tax on corporate profits will be offset by a higher markup, as determined by the value of T_c in equation 10.1, it follows that a tax on corporate profits is not significantly different, in terms of its immediate effect or incidence, from an excise or some other type of indirect tax. The price of the goods sold by the firm will, in either case, need to be increased by the amount of tax collected on each unit of output sold. This per unit, or average, incidence will, in the case of an excise tax, be equal to the price, p_j, multiplied by the tax rate, t_e. In the case of a corporate profits tax, it will be equal to the amount of profit on each unit of output sold (including what is paid out in dividends and interest), $\hat{\pi}_j$, multiplied by the tax rate, t_c—with $\hat{\pi}_j$ in turn equal to the profit margin, $\hat{\mu}_j$, multiplied by the price. That is,

$$\mathsf{ATR}_{e_j} = t_{e_j}(p_j) \tag{10.3}$$

and

$$\mathsf{ATR}_{c_j} = t_c(\hat{\pi}_j) = t_c(\hat{\mu}_j * p_j) \tag{10.4}$$

where ATR_{e_j} and ATR_{c_j} are the tax revenue generated from the sale of each unit of good j from the excise tax on that good and from the corporate profits tax respectively; t_{e_j} is the excise tax rate on good j; $\hat{\pi}_j$ and $\hat{\mu}_j$ are the absolute amount of profits and the profit margin respectively (including what is paid out in dividends and interest) on good j, and the other variables are as previously defined. It should be noted that the relationship between the amount of profit and the profit margin that includes any dividends and interest, $\hat{\pi}_j$ and $\hat{\mu}_j$, and the amount of profit and the profit margin net of dividends and interest, $\hat{\pi}_j$ and $\hat{\mu}_j$, is as follows:

$$\hat{\pi}_j = \frac{1}{1-d}\,(\pi_j) \tag{10.5}$$

and

$$\hat{\mu}_j = \frac{1}{1-d}\,(\mu_j) \tag{10.6}$$

where d is the ratio of the firm's debt service, DS_i—that is, dividends and interest on long-term debt—as a share of cash flow, F_i (including dividends and interest). It is thus the proportion of the total discretionary funds available to the megacorp which must go to servicing its external debt (see chapter 7, section 1.1).

As can be seen by comparing equation 10.4 with equation 10.3, the average tax revenue generated from a corporate profits tax will be less than what an excise tax itself will generate by a factor equal to the profit margin. Nonetheless, by taking this factor into account, it is possible to generate the same amount of tax revenue per unit of output sold simply by increasing the corporate profits tax rate, t_c, relative to the excise tax, t_e. Thus a corporate profits tax rate of 33.3 percent which, with a profit margin equal to 10 percent, yields 3.3 cents in tax revenue for each dollar's worth of output that is sold is the equivalent of an excise tax of 3.3 percent. In the one case it is corporate profits which are being taxed, with the tax rate itself relatively high; in the other case, it is the value of the goods sold which is being taxed, with the tax rate relatively low. The effect, however, as measured by the amount of tax revenue obtained by the government and the amount by which the price level will need to be increased, will be the same. Indeed, it is possible to determine the similar equivalence between a value added tax and an excise tax—or indeed between any two taxes, direct or indirect.

What this means is that any tax which can be shifted forward, whether a value added or even a corporate profits tax, can be transformed into the equivalent of an excise tax, t_e, with $t_e(p_j)$ representing the difference between the price of some good to the buyer, p_j, and the revenue earned by firms by supplying the good, Rev_j. That is,

$$p_j - t_e(p_j) = \text{Rev}_j \tag{10.7}$$

or, alternatively,

$$p_j = \frac{1}{1-t_e} \; (Rev_j) \tag{10.8}$$

where Rev_j is the revenue earned by the firm on each unit of output sold. In the case of a corporate income tax, $t_c(\mu_j)$ can be substituted for t_e in equation 10.8 while, in the case of a value added tax, $t_v(v_j)$ can instead be substituted for the t_e term. That is,

$$p_j = \frac{1}{1-[t_c(\mu_j)]} \; (Rev_j) \tag{10.9}$$

and

$$p_j = \frac{1}{1-[t_v(v_j)]} \; (Rev_j) \tag{10.10}$$

where t_v is the value added tax rate and v_j, as previously specified, is the amount of value added, or surplus in value terms, as a proportion of the industry price (see chapter 5, section 2.3). As can be seen from the above equations, any excise tax (or its equivalent, such as the corporate income or even a value added tax) is analogous to the markup obtained by the firm. The difference, of course, is that the revenue generated from a tax, instead of accruing to the firm as part of its discretionary funds, instead flows to the government.

The hope on the part of those who favor a tax on corporate profits is, of course, that not all of the tax will be shifted forward through a rise in the price of the goods being sold, that at least part of the tax will fall on the rentier class through a forced reduction in dividends. While this possibility cannot be dismissed altogether in light of the quasi-rents, or differential returns, that enable firms to profitably undertake other forms of investment besides those needed to increase capacity in line with the growth of industry demand (see chapter 7, sections 2.2 and 2.3), one must at the same time recognize that any tax on corporate profits is likely to have other effects which, even from the perspective of workers, may be undesirable. To understand what these possible untoward effects are likely to be, it is necessary to carry the analysis beyond just the immediate incidence and consider what the longer run impact of any tax, such as the corporate income tax, is likely to be once it has been shifted forward on to buyers through a higher price.

10.3.3 The longer run impact of taxes

The thrust of the preceding section is that, whatever tax is imposed to finance government outlays, it will be the equivalent of some excise tax so that prices will be higher than they would otherwise be by a factor equal to $t_e(p_j)$—with the equivalent rate, in the case of a tax on corporate profits, equal to t_c multiplied by the profit margin, μ_j. While in terms of its impact on the price level, a corporate profits tax can thus be viewed as the equivalent of an excise tax once the necessary adjustment in the rate has been made, still an important difference between the two types of taxes should be recognized. This is the additional effect that a corporate profits tax is likely to have on the required rate of return, $\overset{+}{r}$, and hence on the level of investment within the oligopolistic sector. As already pointed out (see chapter 7, section 2.1), the megacorp first determines, as a derivative of the broader growth strategy it hopes to pursue, the target rate of return on investment, $\overset{+}{r}$, with that target rate of return then serving as the basis for screening the various investment projects emanating from within its operating divisions. With the target rate of return having to be increased by some multiple, T_c, as brought out in equation 10.1, to offset the effect of any tax on corporate profits, investment projects will necessarily have to promise a higher rate of return before they are likely to be funded through the capital budget. In this way, a corporate income tax is likely to reduce the level of investment within the oligopolistic sector, at least insofar as cost-reducing and similar types of projects unrelated to the expansion of capacity are concerned.

It is not just that the corporate income tax is likely to be shifted forward on to buyers and thus ultimately to be borne by consumers while at the same time, if it is a tax on corporate profits, inhibiting investment. It is also that the tax, contrary to the orthodox microeconomic theory, is likely to have little or no effect on the techniques of production within the oligopolistic sector—at least in the short period. In large part, this is because production within the oligopolistic sector is characterized by fixed technical coefficients, with the coefficients, as part of the **A** matrix, changing only as a result of technical progress (see chapter 5, part 4). To the extent the capital and labor inputs need to be employed in a fixed ratio to one another, a tax on either type of input will produce no change in the relative proportion of those two inputs used in the production process. The tax will instead simply add to the cost of the input which the firm's revenues will need to cover. For example, if a tax is levied on wages to finance a system of social insurance transfer payments, the prices charged for the goods produced by those workers will need to be increased by a percentage equal to the tax rate multiplied by the proportion of the price represented by the wage bill. However, the number of workers employed will be unaffected, at least in the short period. (On the longer run effect, see chapter 13, section 3.2.) Similarly, if a tax is levied on any residual income, or profits, the price is likely to be increased by a percentage equal to the tax rate multiplied by the profit margin, μ. However, the capital intensity of the production process, as determined by the value of the incremental capital-output ratio, b, will be unaffected. Indeed, any argument to the contrary, such as is frequently made by economists relying on the neoclassical model, involves a confusion over the term "capital" itself. In an industrial economy, the capital inputs take the form of new plant and equipment, and thus only an indirect tax on the output of the investment goods sector would constitute a tax on those capital inputs. A tax on profits is instead a tax on the firm's residual income, and such a tax will influence the choice of technique only to the extent it alters the required rate of return on investment, $\overset{+}{r}$ —and even then it would affect the choice of technique only in the long period, not in the short period.

To the extent the corporate income tax is simply shifted forward on to buyers in the form of higher prices without significantly affecting the technique of production, at least in the short period, the burden of the tax will fall primarily on the working class or, more generally, on the household sector— and not on "capital." It is the real income of households rather than the after-tax return on investment which will be reduced by the higher prices resulting from the corporate income tax (and, of course, from any equivalent indirect tax as well as any tax on wages themselves). Even if the industry does not supply consumer goods directly, it is likely to produce goods used as inputs by industries which do supply consumer goods so that, with the type of markup pricing which prevails within the oligopolistic sector, the tax can be expected to lead to higher prices for the consumer goods purchased by households, including the members of the working class. This point, derived from a microeconomic analysis of oligopolistic pricing within the context of an input-output model of production, is consistent with the macroeconomic model of income distribution previously presented (see chapter 8, part 2). A change in the corporate income tax rate and/or a change in the indirect tax rate (including a change from zero to some positive figure) is the same as a change in the marginal propensity to consume out of nonwage income, Π_e, and it will have exactly the same effect: It will reduce the real income of households, including those receiving wages and salaries. While it may be that the working class will benefit from the public goods and services thereby being financed, this is not a necessary consequence of the tax being imposed. Indeed, it is just as likely that the tax revenue will be used to redistribute income in favor of the nonworking classes, either rentiers or members of the dependent class, or from one group of workers to another, such as from workers in general to those employed by the government or in specific industries such as aerospace and ordinance.

The ensuing reduction in the real income of households is only the general effect of using any tax which is then shifted forward, such as the corporate income tax, to finance the public sector budget. The more specific effect of such a tax will be two-fold: (1) on the relative consumption levels of different households, and (2) on the relative fortunes of different industries.

The general effect which any fully shifted tax will have in reducing the real income of households will be independent of the factors that, in addition to the tax rate itself, determine the relative magnitude of the offsetting price changes—as long as all goods and services are subject to the same tax rate. As was brought out in the preceding subsection, the factors determining the relative magnitude of the required offsetting change in prices will, in the case of a change in the excise tax rate, be the initial set of relative prices, **P**, while, in the case of a change in either the corporate income or value added tax rates, the determining factors will be, in addition to the $\mathbf{P}$ vector, the set of profit margins, μ_1, μ_2, μ_3, . . . , μ_n, represented by a μ vector and/or the set of v_j terms represented by the value added vector, $\mathbf{V}$ (the columns of the $\mathbf{I} - \mathbf{A}$ matrix). That is,

$$\mathbf{P}_e = (1 - \Delta t_e)^{-1}\, \mathbf{P} \tag{10.11}$$

$$\mathbf{P}_c = [\mathbf{I} - \Delta t_c(\mu)]^{-1}\, \mathbf{P} \tag{10.12}$$

and

$$\mathbf{P}_v = [\mathbf{I} - \Delta t_v(\mathbf{V})]^{-1}\, \mathbf{P} \tag{10.13}$$

where $\mathbf{P}_e$ is the set of prices that will be established after the imposition of a uniform excise tax or a change in t_e; $\mathbf{P}_c$ is the set of relative prices after the imposition of a corporate profits tax or a change in t_c; $\mathbf{P}_v$ is the set of relative prices after the imposition of a uniform value added tax or a change in t_v; $\mathbf{P}$ is the price vector derived previously, based on the costs of production, including the costs of expansion (see chapter 6, section 1.4); μ is a vector the elements of which are μ_1, μ_2, μ_3, . . . , μ_n, and the other variables are as previously defined.

Besides indicating what will be the magnitude of the change in relative prices from imposing a uniform excise, corporate profits or value added tax on all goods, the above three equations make it possible to determine what will be the amount of tax revenue obtained by the government and what will be the corresponding loss of real income by households. Both the tax revenue obtained by the government and the corresponding loss of real income by households will be equal to the difference between the price vector with the tax included, $\mathbf{P}_e$, $\mathbf{P}_c$ or $\mathbf{P}_v$, and the price vector net of any taxes, $\mathbf{P}$. That is,

$$\Delta T = -\Delta Y_D = \mathbf{P}_e - \mathbf{P}(C) \tag{10.14}$$

where ΔT is the change in the amount of tax revenue obtained by the government; $-\Delta Y_D$ is the corresponding change in the real income of households due to a change in the excise tax rate, Δt_e, and $\mathbf{C}$ is the vector of consumption goods previously specified (see chapter 9, section 1.2), with $\mathbf{P}_c$ or $\mathbf{P}_v$, based on equations 10.12 and 10.13, substitutable for $\mathbf{P}_e$ if the change is in the corporate profits or value added tax rate instead of in the excise tax rate. While equation 10.14 indicates how much the real consumption of households will be reduced by an increase in the excise or some other tax rate, it leaves unexplained which are the specific items of consumption households will no longer be able to afford and thus which are the industries which will suffer a decline in demand as a result of the increase in the tax rate. The actual choice of which items not to purchase from among the consumption goods currently being produced will, in fact, be governed by the hierarchy of household needs. It will not depend, at least to any significant extent, on the change in the relative prices of the consumption goods themselves as a result of the change in the tax rate. This is the implication of the model of household behavior presented in the preceding chapter.

When, due to the imposition of some tax, the amount of consumption goods households can afford to maintain as part of their normal inventory declines (or fails to increase at the rate it should, given the growth of output per worker), the choice of which goods not to purchase will depend on which items, moving down the hierarchy of household needs, are the threshold, or marginal, ones. While different consumption goods will be at the threshold point of being dispensed with, depending on the household's real income and socioeconomic profile, the basis for making the choice will be the same for all households, regardless of their income. The choice will be dictated by which objective need among those currently being satisfied the household considers the least essential. This is the opposite of the situation previously considered (see chapter 9, section 1.4) in which, with real income rising, different consumption goods are at the threshold point of being added to the household's normal inventory. Only to the extent that a corporate profits or value added tax has a sufficiently significant differential effect on the relative price of two goods capable of satisfying the same objective need (because of the difference in the value of μ_j or v_j in the two industries which supply the good) will households have any reason to substitute the one item for the other rather than just forego a single item of consumption altogether. But this possibility, while it cannot be excluded altogether, seems a remote one.

An excise tax, or indeed even a corporate profits or value added tax, may nonetheless have a significant impact on the relative consumption levels of different households. This will be the case if (a) only some among the h different final consumption goods are affected by the tax (either directly or, through the effect on the industries which supply it with material inputs, indirectly), and/or (b) different tax rates apply to the various items of final household consumption. The first situation, it should be noted, is but a special case of the second, with the tax rate—t_e, t_c or t_v—either some fixed value or zero. It is nonetheless easier to begin by taking up that special case.

If only certain items of consumption are subject to a particular tax, then the differential impact will depend on where those goods fall within the hierarchy of household needs. If the items are among the first that would be budgeted for by any household, such as unprocessed food or undergarments, then the tax will fall on the largest possible number of households, with a disporportionately greater impact on the households with the lowest income. Conversely, if the items are those which, like an annual trip abroad or a recreational motor boat, are normally budgeted for only by households at the upper end of the income distribution curve, the tax will be borne by only a relatively small number of households. Indeed, by knowing where any particular item of consumption falls within the hierarchy of needs, both for households in general and for various demographic and other subgroups, it is possible to achieve a wide range of differential effects insofar as the burden of taxation is concerned. This can be done by (a) exempting certain categories of consumption goods from whatever tax is being imposed, or (b) subjecting the different categories of consumption to different tax rates. In this way—but in this way only—public officials can make any tax as "progressive" as they want. The corollary is that, without knowing where the various items of consumption fall along the hierarchy of household needs, it is not possible to determine how "progressive" (or, what is essentially the same thing, how "regressive") any tax is likely to be, whether it takes the form of an excise tax or one of its equivalents, a corporate profits or value added tax.

So far all that has been examined is the differential effect of any tax on households. Still to be considered is the differential effect on firms and, *pari passu*, on various industries. Of course, with the revenue generated by any tax implying a reduction in the real income of households so that a larger portion of aggregate output can be used for public consumption, the relative fortunes of different industries will necessarily be affected. The industries which supply the goods and services needed by the government will find their sales increasing more rapidly while the industries which supply consumption goods to the household sector will find their sales increasing by less than would otherwise be the case. However, this is only the effect of deciding how large the public sector should be, irrespective of what taxes are used to finance that level of public consumption. The pertinent question here is what further effect will the type of tax—and the rate at which it is being collected—have on the relative fortunes of different industries.

The relative fortunes of different industries will be affected only to the extent that whatever taxes are relied upon to finance the public sector lead to a significant change in the price vector, $\mathbf{P}$, and that change in relative prices then leads to a change in the relative growth rates of those industries. The extent to which any tax will lead to a change in relative prices is given by equation 10.11 (or, alternatively, equations 10.12 and/or 10.13) while the extent to which the change in relative prices will affect the growth rate of the different industries can be determined by adding to the two terms previously identified as determining the $\underline{\mathbf{G}}$ and hence the $\mathbf{G}$ vector (see chapter 5, section 5.4), a third term representing the difference between the initial and subsequent price vectors, $\mathbf{P} - \mathbf{P}_e$ (or, alternatively, $\mathbf{P} - \mathbf{P}_c$, and/or $\mathbf{P} - \mathbf{P}_v$), multiplied by the (own) price elasticities of demand, $\mathbf{\Psi}$. Thus, once allowance has to be made for some excise or other type of tax, equation 5.81 needs to be further elaborated as follows:

$$G = \overset{\circ}{Z}_s(\Upsilon) + \hat{\Psi}(\Omega) + \hat{\Psi}(P - P_e) \qquad (10.15)$$

Still, unless the elements of the $\mathbf{\Psi}$ vector, representing the (own) elasticities of demand, are significantly different from zero—and there is no reason to believe they are (see chapter 9, section 1.6)—the relative growth rates and hence the relative fortunes of the different industries will be unaffected by the type of tax relied upon by the government or the rate at which the tax is being collected. The relative price effects of the tax, as determined by equation 10.11 (or, alternatively, equations 10.12 and/or 10.13), will, in that case, not matter insofar as the growth rates of the different industries are concerned. The sole effect of the tax will, in fact, be on the relative consumption levels of different households. This is especially true if one takes into account the redistributive effect of any negative tax flows, or income transfers, as well as of the additional taxes that will have to be imposed to finance those transfer payments.

10.3.4 Negative tax flows

The government's transfer payments represent a unilateral disbursement of funds, without anything being obtained in return. For this reason, they can be viewed as negative tax flows. The total amount of these transfer payments at each of the different levels of government, Tr, along with the government's expenditures on nondurable goods and services, Gov_{ND+S}, needs to be subtracted, or netted out, from the total tax revenue collected by the government, T, in order to derive the government and nonprofit sector's discretionary funds, F_G. That is,

$$F_G = T - (Tr + Gov_{ND+S}) \qquad (10.16)$$

Subtracting just the amount of transfer payments alone from total tax revenue merely indicates the government's net tax revenue.

The government's transfer payments, or negative tax flows, fall into two categories: (1) subsidies to business for producing certain goods and services, the opposite of the excise and other types of taxes levied on business firms, and (2) income transfers to individuals, the opposite of the taxes collected from the household sector. The primary focus in this subsection will be on the latter. For one thing, this category represents by far the largest portion of the transfer payments made by the government of the United States and that of most other advanced industrial countries. Second, the transfer payments to individuals are most clearly intended to redistribute income within the household sector. The subsidies to business firms, to the extent they can be justified, will have to be no greater than is necessary to cover the cost of the indirect social benefits from the provision of certain "quasi-public" goods and services (see section 10.2.1). If the activities being subsidized do in fact give rise to indirect social benefits which are (a) equal to the amount of the subvention and (b) widely diffused, then there will not be any redistribution of income within the household sector. Finally, the transfer payments to individuals constitute the income of the dependent class, an important component of the household sector's disposable income (see chapter 8, section 1.2). For all three of these reasons, the subsidies to business will be ignored in the discussion which follows and the government's transfer payments,

Tr, equated with the amount of income transfers to individuals. The only thing that needs to be said further about the subsidies to business is that, just as an excise tax will add to the price that must be paid for some good or service, any subsidies, or negative tax flows, to the enterprise sector will enable some good or service to be supplied to the market at a price less than the full costs of production.

The amount of transfer income received by individuals—and hence both the amount of offsetting tax revenue that will need to be collected and the level of material well-being enjoyed by the members of the dependent class—will be the product of two factors: (a) the size of the eligible population, Pop_D, and (b) the size of the average stipend received, Y_{tr}. That is,

$$Tr = Y_{tr} * Pop_D \qquad (10.17)$$

The size of the eligible population, Pop_D, will, in turn, depend on the rules for determining an individual's eligibility for each of the different types of income transfer programs which have been established. As pointed out previously (see section 10.2.2), income transfer programs can be grouped under three main categories, with the eligibility rules varying for each. The three categories are: (1) social insurance programs for the elderly, the disabled and the temporarily unemployed; (2) programs to provide income support for children and others before they are ready to enter the labor force; and (3) programs to provide a minimum-income floor.

It is the size of the population eligible for the last of these three types of programs which will be most sensitive to economic factors, such as the level of aggregate demand. For this reason, as well as the residual nature of the programs, any change in the size of the dependent class, Pop_D, will be equated, in the analysis which follows, with a change in the number of persons eligible for the minimum-floor income transfer programs. The number of persons eligible for the other two types of income transfer programs will, of course, also be sensitive to economic factors, even if not to the same extent. It is just that, since the eligibility rules for those other types of programs are more stringent, demographic and other noneconomic factors are likely to weigh more heavily in determining the size of the eligible population. For example, the number of elderly persons receiving transfer payments under the social insurance programs will depend on both the retirement age, a policy variable, and the average life expectancy—with the latter in turn depending, among other factors, on the past levels of expenditure by the government on health care. These factors will be more important in determining the size of the eligible population than the unemployment rate or the prevailing wage rate. Similarly, the number of families receiving child support will depend on both the birth rate and the rate of family dissolution, with these noneconomic factors again the primary, though not the only, determinants.

The most important of the economic factors determining the size of the population eligible for any minimum-floor income transfer program will be the secular unemployment rate, Un. (In the case of the social insurance program for the temporarily unemployed, the cyclical unemployment rate, as distinct from the secular unemployment rate, will be the more important determinant. See chapter 4, section 3.4, for a discussion of the difference between the two.) The fewer the employment opportunities—as determined by the expansion of the economy over time and the increased demand for human resource inputs which this implies relative to the growth of output per worker—the larger will be the number of persons without any means of obtaining income except through the transfer payments provided by the goverment. No more need be said about this point for the moment. It will be picked up and elaborated on in the subsequent chapters of this text (see chapter 13, section 0.0, and chapter 14, section 0.0). For now, the secular unemployment rate, Un, can simply be taken as a parameter of the number of persons eligible for any minimum-floor income transfer program and thus of Pop_D. This will permit us to focus on the factors determining the size of the average stipend, Y_{tr}, under a miniumum-floor income transfer program— along with the more controversial question of whether the amount of income an individual or household can obtain under such a program will affect the size of the eligible population, making Pop_D and Y_{tr} interdependent.

The size of the average stipend received by anyone eligible for a particular income transfer program, Y_{tr}, will depend on three factors: (1) the minimum, or guaranteed, income, Y_g, which an individual or household can expect to receive under the program; (2) the negative tax rate, t_n, that is, the rate at which the individual or household will lose benefits as the income from other sources increases; and (3) the amount of wage and other earned income, Y_e. More specifically,

$$Y_{tr} = Y_g - t_n(Y_e) \qquad (10.18)$$

Thus, if an individual is guaranteed $1,000 in income under a particular program (that is, if $Y_g = \$1,000$) and loses $1 in benefits for every $2 in wage and other income (making $t_n = 33\frac{1}{3}$ percent), then with $1,200 in earned income (i.e., $Y_e = \$1,200$) the individual will obtain $600 in transfer payments ($1,000 less $33\frac{1}{3}$ percent of $1,200 or $400), giving him or her a total income from all sources equal to $1,800 ($1,200 plus $600).

The relationship between Y_{tr} and Y_e, holding Y_g and t_n constant, can be represented by the line segment $\overline{AB}$ in exhibit 10.2. The vertical intercept, A, is the guaranteed income, Y_g, and the slope of the line is the negative tax rate, t_n. At any point along that line, such as point C, the amount of transfer income which can be obtained, when the amount of earned income is Y_{e_0}, will be Y_{tr_0}. By moving to a different point along $\overline{AB}$, for example point D, one can see how the size of the stipend will decline, from Y_{tr_0} to Y_{tr_1}, as the amount of earned income increases from Y_{e_0} to Y_{e_1}. What equation 10.12 and exhibit 10.2 make

Exhibit 10.2

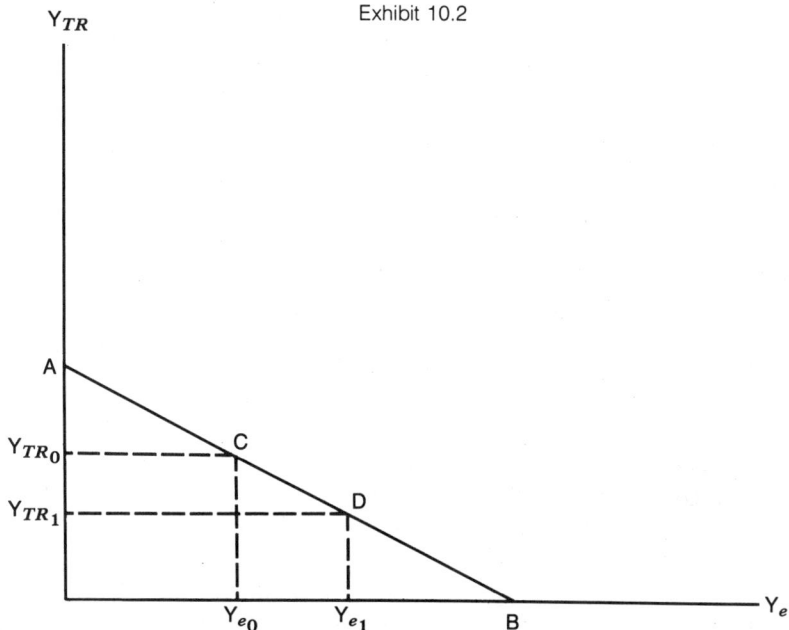

clear is that the size of the stipend received under any income transfer program, Y_{tr}, will depend not only on the amount of income earned, Y_e, in addition to that stipend but also on the negative tax rate, t_n—and, no less important, on the effect which that negative tax rate is likely to have on the incentive to earn any income.

At the one extreme, the stipend received by an individual or household can be reduced by a dollar for each dollar of other income earned. This would constitute a negative tax rate, t_n, equal to 100 percent. While a negative tax rate equal to 100 percent might seem best if one wishes to minimize the burden on the rest of the society, it may in fact, because of the disincentive it creates to earn other income, actually result in a higher average stipend. Whatever other income is earned will simply be substracted from the stipend, leaving the individual or household no better off—and thus without any incentive to earn income in addition to the minimum stipend, Y_g, for which the individual or household is eligible. Without any earned income, and thus without any reduction in the size of the stipend based on the negative tax rate, t_n, the burden on the rest of the society will be at the highest possible level, Y_g. With a lower negative tax rate—for example, the 33⅓ percent rate postulated in the above example—those eligible for the program will have a greater incentive to earn other income and the burden on the rest of society, because of the reduced size of the average stipend, will be lower.

At the other extreme, the negative tax rate can be set at zero. This would mean that, once found to be eligible for a particular program, the individual or household would continue to receive the same stipend regardless of how much wage and other income was being earned. It would thus be possible for those eligible for payments under the program to have a larger total income than those who, not being eligible, were being taxed so as to provide the necessary transfer payments. The same might be true even if the negative tax rate were greater than zero but still relatively low and/or the guaranteed income under the program were relatively high. In the case of the social insurance programs for the elderly and even the child support programs, this situation would not raise the same question of equity and/or practicality. Those not at present receiving benefits under the program would, at some point over their life cycle, also become potentially eligible—either when they reached a certain age or if and when they became parents. However, under the minimum-floor and indeed under the other income transfer programs, a question either of equity or of practicality will necessarily arise.

It should be noted that the negative tax rate, t_n, together with the guaranteed income, Y_g, will be sufficient to distinguish one income transfer program from another. Indeed, with t_n a constant, each income transfer program can be uniquely characterized, at least insofar as the level of benefits directly provided and the total income permitted under the program are concerned, by a line segment in Cartesian space, such as the one shown in exhibit 10.2. (If t_n is not a constant, then the functional relationship defining the curvilinear segment $\overline{AB}$ will need to be specified as well.) Once an income transfer program has been uniquely characterized by a line segment, such as $\overline{AB}$ in exhibit 10.2, based on the value of the Y_g and t_n parameters, one can see more clearly the constraints imposed by the conflicting objectives of assuring, on the one hand, an adequate level of income under the program and, on the other hand, of minimizing the burden on the rest of the society.

The vertical intercept, Y_g, is the minimal amount of income that any individual or household can count on receiving under the program. Among the three types of income transfer programs, it can be assumed that the value of Y_g will be lowest for the minimum-floor programs, with that value of Y_g then defining the minimal standard of living which anyone living in the society can count on. At the very least, if members of the society are not going to perish for lack of the necessary material goods, the value of Y_g for those programs must be equal to the cost of purchasing a subsistence basket of consumption goods. If the value of Y_g is greater than subsistence (a somewhat elastic standard, depending as it does on the particular circumstances of each individual and/or household as well as on social norms), then that minimum level of income will determine what standard of living those eligible for the program can expect to enjoy even if they have no other source of income (or they prefer not to seek one out). While it might seem that the burden on the rest of the society would be minimized if that amount of income and only that amount on income were to be specified as the the value of Y_g in the case of the minimum-floor income transfer programs, this is not necessarily true. As has already pointed out, the average stipend, Y_{tr}, and thus the burden on the rest of the society, will also depend on the negative tax rate, t_n. This, in turn, raises the question of what limits, if any, there are to the amount of transfer income the government can provide.

10.3.5 The limits on transfer payments

The essential nature of an income transfer program is that income, and hence purchasing power, is redistributed within the household sector. (As should be clear by now, income cannot be redistributed between the household and the other sectors without impairing either the growth rate or the level of public consumption. See chapter 8, part 2.) This means that, as a practical matter, it is not possible for more than a certain portion of all households to be eligible for the entire set of income transfer programs. What that portion is will depend on the amount of labor required to produce the current level of output, based on the value of the L vector, relative to the number of persons encompassed by the household sector. The equity question, as distinct from the practicality question, is why some individuals and/or households, and not others, should receive transfer payments. When those receiving a stipend would not otherwise be able to meet their minimal material needs, there is at least an answer to this question, one which is in accord with what most people consider fair and just. The prevailing social norm in the United States and in other advanced societies is that no one should be allowed to starve. Moreover, when the income transfer programs merely redistribute income over the life cycle, as in the case of the social insurance and even the dependent care programs, the equity question can be parried by pointing out that every individual and/or household has the same chance of qualifying at some point in the interval between birth and death. However, when those obtaining transfer payments under a minimum-floor or some other type of income transfer program (e.g., agricultural price supports) have a total income that exceeds, or even merely approximates, the income of those being taxed to finance the transfer payments, the equity question can no longer be dismissed so readily.

The total income of an individual or household eligible for some income transfer program will be the stipend received under the program, Y_{tr}, plus whatever other income the individual or members of the household can earn. That is,

$$Y_t = Y_{tr} + Y_e \qquad (10.19)$$

where Y_t is the total income of any individual or household eligible for an income transfer program. Substituting the right-hand side of equation 10.18 for Y_{tr} in the above equation, we obtain the following:

$$Y_t = Y_g + (1 - t_n)Y_e \qquad (10.20)$$

On the assumption that the other income earned will be labor and not property income, we can set Y_e equal to some wage rate multiplied by the number of hours worked. That is,

$$Y_t = Y_g + (1 - t_n)(w_d * h_d) \qquad (10.21)$$

where w_d is the average wage per hour earned by the members of the dependent class and h_d is the average number of hours worked, with the product of those two variables being substituted for Y_e in equation 10.20.

The total income of those eligible for an income transfer program, as given by equation 10.21, can then be compared with the total income of those receiving only a wage. The latter, it can be assumed, will be subject to a personal income tax equal to t_p on any income earned so that the cost of income transfer and other government programs can be covered. (If the government relies on other types of taxes as well, such as an excise or profits tax, it can instead be assumed, based on the argument of the preceding subsections, that those taxes, taken together, will be the equivalent of a personal income tax equal to t_p.) Thus the total income of those receiving only a wage can be specified as follows:

$$Y_w = (1 - t_p)(w_w * h_w) \qquad (10.22)$$

where Y_w is the total income of those whose only income is from wages and salary; w_w is the average wage per hour they earn, and h_w is the average number of hours worked. Taking the difference between this total income earned by a member of the working class and the total income obtained by those eligible for some income transfer program, we can derive the following relationship:

$$\Delta Y_w = Y_w - Y_t$$
$$= [(1 - t_p)(w_w * h_w)] - [(Y_g + (1 - t_n)(w_d * h_d)] \qquad (10.23)$$

where ΔY_w is the differential in the total income of any worker receiving only a wage compared to someone who is eligible for transfer payments under one or more programs.

One needs to impose the condition that ΔY_w cannot be negative. This is not just a matter of equity—that those being taxed to finance the transfer payments should not be left with a lower standard of living than those receiving the transfer income. It is also a matter of ensuring that there is a sufficient amount of income subject to a positive tax rate, t_p, that the total cost of transfer payments by the government can be financed out of tax revenues. If the total income of those eligible for a minimum-floor program should exceed what can be earned by those not covered, one would have to assume that, unless other restrictions are imposed, so many individuals will find a way to qualify that the income still subject to a positive tax will no longer be sufficient to cover the cost of the transfer payments. Long before that crisis point is reached, the program is likely to be abolished as being impractical if not unfair. It should be added that the greater the government's expenditures on public goods and services, the greater will be the amount of tax revenue the government will need to generate to cover, in addition, any transfer payments—making even larger the amount of income which must be earned by those not eligible for that or any other income transfer program if adequate tax revenues are to be generated.

As can be seen from equation 10.23, how large ΔY_w is—and indeed whether it is positive or negative—will depend on three sets of factors: (1) the positive tax rate, t_p, on wage and other personal income; (2) the negative tax rate, t_n, on any transfer income; and (3) the differential between the amount of earned income by someone who, receiving only a wage, is a member of the working class compared to the total income of someone eligible for the minimum-floor or some other type of income transfer program, with that differential, $Y_w - Y_t$ in turn dependent on (a) the differential between the wage earned by workers and the wage that can be earned by members of the dependent class, $w_w - w_d$, and (b) the differential in the number of hours worked by the two groups, $h_w - h_d$. That is,

$$\Delta Y_w = f(t_p, t_n, w_w - w_d, h_w - h_d) \qquad (10.24)$$

There is some reason to believe that both the hourly wage earned by members of the dependent class and the number of hours they work will be less than what at least white-collar and organized blue-collar workers can count on. Nonetheless, holding those two sets of factors constant—as seems appropriate when the unorganized blue-collar work force is the relevant basis for comparison since, as already pointed out (see chapter 8, section 1.3), there is no clear dividing line between this group and the employable members of the dependent class)—the differential in the amount of income earned by workers, ΔY_w, will depend on the value of t_p relative to the value of t_n. This, in turn, means that, to judge the fairness and practicality of any income transfer program, and indeed the entire set of such programs, the analysis needs to shift from the type of diagram shown in exhibit 10.2, where only the transfer payments, or negative tax flows, are measured along the vertical axis, to the type of diagram shown in exhibit 10.3. With the positive tax flows appearing on top and the negative tax payments relegated to the bottom quadrant, line segment $\overline{AB}$ now approaches the horizontal axis from the opposite direction. This permits $\overline{AB}$ to be extended to point C, with the slope of the additional segment, $\overline{BC}'$, indicating the rate at which any wage or other income, Y_e, will be taxed as it exceeds the amount, Y_{e_m} (at point B), at which the individual or household is no longer eligible for any transfer payments. With the diagram reflecting the positive tax rate, t_p, as well as the negative tax rate, t_n, one can better understand the constraints on any set of income transfer programs.

Where point B lies along the horizontal axis in exhibit 10.3 will determine the liberality of the minimum-floor and other income transfer programs relative to its

Exhibit 10.3

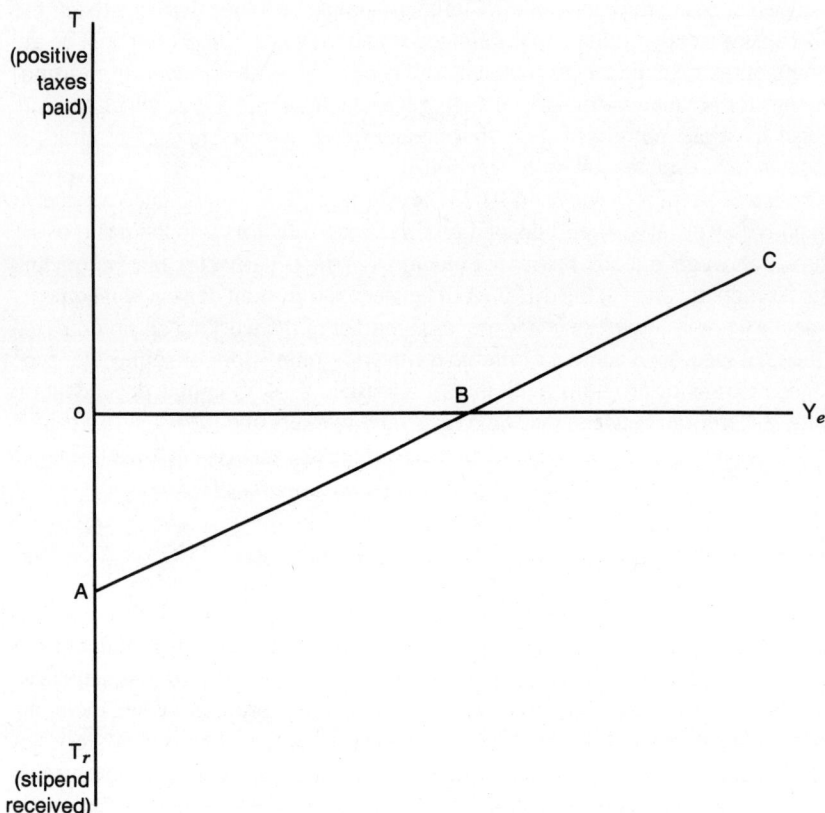

burden on the rest of the society. The further to the right of the origin point B lies, the larger will be the guaranteed, or minimum, payment under the program, Y_g, and/or the lower will be the negative tax rate, t_n. The liberality of any income transfer program can therefore be equated with how large is the area of triangle AB0 in exhibit 10.3, with the average stipend under the program, Y_{tr}, equal to that area divided by the number of persons eligible for benefits, Pop_N. The same triangle, however, also measures the tax burden imposed by the program on other households. These are the households which, since they are ineligible for transfer payments under the program, find themselves on the other side of point B. Their tax burden will be greater both because the cost of the program itself will be greater and because there will be fewer other individuals and/or households among whom to share the tax burden. For both these reasons, the burden on any one individual or household will be greater, as measured by the positive tax rate, t_p, required to fund the government's budget, whatever goods and services are purchased as well as the entire set of income transfer programs. Thus, the further to the right point B lies, the more liberal will be the program in terms of the average stipend provided but, at the same time, the greater will have to be the personal tax rate, t_p. Conversely, the further to the left point B lies, the less liberal will be the program but also the smaller the tax burden on other households.

The relationship between the average stipend, Y_{tr}, under the various income transfer programs and the positive tax rate, t_p, is not quite as rigid as exhibit 10.3 would suggest. For one thing, the positive tax rate, t_p, need not be the same as the negative tax rate, t_n. Indeed, the two rates are unlikely to be the same. Since the total amount paid out under any program will need to be matched by additional tax revenues, the positive tax rate is in effect determined once the values of Y_g and t_n have, as a matter of policy, been fixed. While there may a level of benefits which, taking into account the other factors that will determine the overall tax burden, will enable t_p to be set equal to t_n, still this will be only one of the many possible levels of benefits which can be provided under the entire set of income transfer programs. Secondly, as already indicated, the negative tax rate can increase exponentially or, as is more likely to be the case, in graduated steps so that, as shown in exhibit 10.4, point B lies further to the left, for any given level of guaranteed income, Y_g, and thus for any fixed degree of liberality. Indeed, the positive tax rate, as shown in the same diagram, can also increase in graduated steps. Finally, as shown in exhibit 10.5, $\overline{AC}$ may be discontinuous, with a gap, $\overline{BB}'$, between the amount of other income, Y_{e_m}, at which an individual and/or household is no longer eligible for payments under the minimum-floor program and the amount of income, Y_{e_n}, at which a positive tax will have to be paid. The greater that gap, the more clearly differentiated the dependent class will be from the working class—at least at that moment in time. However, with even fewer households earning a level of income that will subject them to a positive tax, the greater will be the burden on the remaining households, those that find themselves to the right of point B'. It is just that those households will not have to be taxed to provide a stipend for the "working poor"—those households which, since they earned too much income to qualify for transfer payments but too little income to be taxed, fall between points B and B'.

Still, once the size of the average stipend, Y_{tr}, and thus point B in exhibit 10.5, has been determined by the government as a matter of its income redistribution policy, the tax burden on the households whose wage and other types of income exceed the taxable level will also be determined. This means that it is not possible to increase the liberality of any income transfer program and thus of the entire set of such programs without, at the same time, increasing the tax burden on the households subject to a positive tax rate, that is, the households which find themselves to right of point B' in exhibit 10.5. It is this set of relationships, and the constraints which they impose on the amount of transfer payments, which indicate why, once Y_g exceeds the socially determined subsistence level, any

Exhibit 10.4

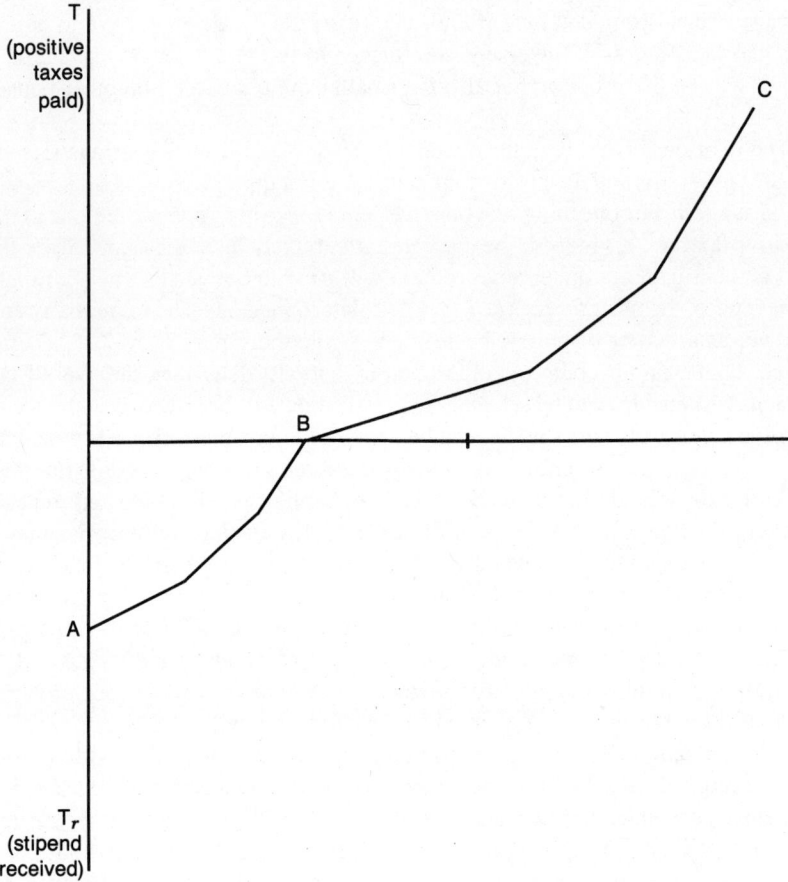

further liberalization of the minimum-floor income transfer program, aside from lowering the negative tax rate, t_n, is likely to be strongly opposed by the working class, making it a dubious strategy for improving the condition of the dependent class. The better strategy, in turns out, at least insofar as the employable members of the dependent class are concerned, is to increase the number of employment opportunities so that there are jobs for all who wish them. This is a topic to which we shall return in chapter 13. First, it is necessary to explain how the government, through its combined expenditure and tax policies, can determine what growth path the economic system will follow and thus what will be the rate at which the demand for labor is increasing.

10.4 The Government's Controlling Hand

Thanks to Keynes, it is no longer a novel idea that the government, through its

Exhibit 10.5

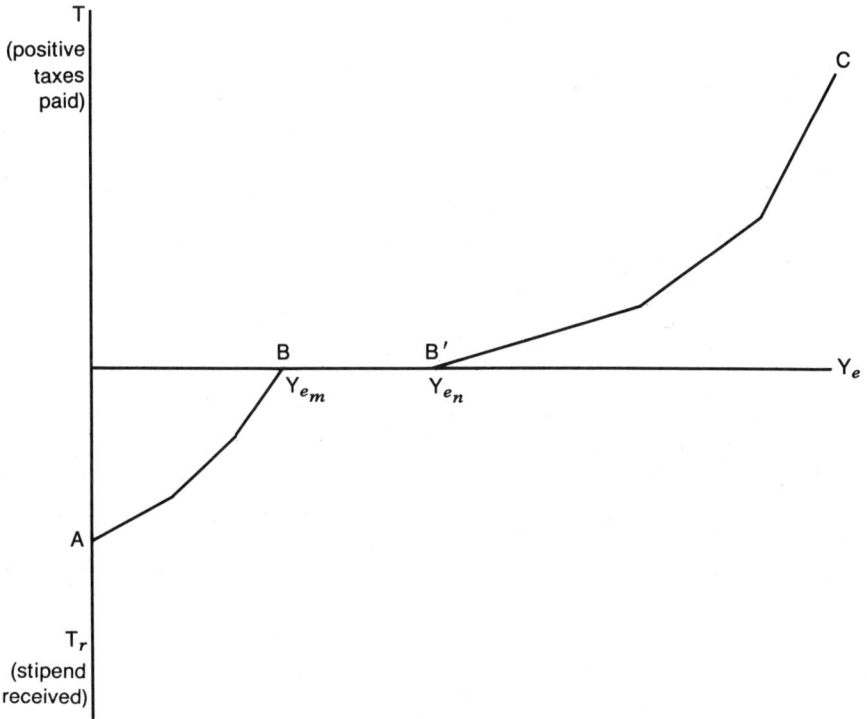

fiscal policy, can determine the economic system's expansion path and thus the number of employment opportunities being created. What is not well understood is the actual dynamic process by which the combination of spending, taxing and borrowing decisions by the government determines the economy's secular growth rate. This is because of the static Keynesian model generally relied upon by economists. Within that framework, the imperatives of continuous growth— including the need for the public sector to expand over time in balance with the rest of the economy—are likely to be overlooked. The last part of this chapter, by further elaborating on the macrodynamic model developed so far, will attempt to fill this gap in the conventional macroeconomic theory. The aim will be to indicate how the government, as the society's formal decision-making mechanism, is able to exercise a controlling hand on the economy.

The government's fiscal policy has three parts to it. There is first the set of decisions reflected in the size and composition of the public sector's budget. This is the expenditure side of fiscal policy, already examined in part 2. Especially important insofar as the macrodynamic behavior of the economy is concerned is the capital component of the public sector budget. The outlays on structures and other durable goods constitute the government's discretionary expenditures, and these discretionary expenditures, E_G, represent a significant portion of total discretionary expenditures. Then there is the set of decisions reflected in the various tax schedules, each associated with a different type of public levy. This is the taxation side of fiscal policy, previously described in part 3. The various tax schedules, depending on the level of economic activity, will determine the government's net cash inflow, or discretionary funds, and these discretionary funds, F_G, are no less significant a portion of the total discretionary funds being generated. Finally, there is the set of decisions reflected in the way any cash deficit, the difference between E_G and F_G, is to be financed—at the federal level in particular. This is the debt management side of fiscal policy.

In the subsections that follow, only the first two of these three aspects of fiscal policy will be taken up. The federal government's debt management decisions, since they are so closely linked to monetary policy, will be left to be analyzed in chapter 12. For now it will simply be assumed that the central bank adopts a passive policy, making sure that the federal government is able to fund whatever additional debt it incurs as a result of its spending and taxation decisions. The analysis will begin by deriving the E and F curves for the government and not-for-profit sector before proceeding to show how, through the relative position of those two curves which its fiscal policy establishes, the federal government is able to choose what secular growth path the economy will follow.

10.4.1 The E and F functions for the government sector

A set of E and F functions can be specified for the government and not-for-profit sector similar to those already derived for the enterprise and household sectors (see chapter 7, part 4, and chapter 9, part 3). Based on what has already been learned about the determinants of discretionary expenditures and discretionary funds within the enterprise and household sectors, one would expect these E and F functions to take the following form:

$$\overset{*}{A}_{G_i} = f(\overset{*}{G}, E_{G_i} - F_{G_i}, \overset{\circ}{L}, i_{LT}, X) \tag{10.25}$$

and

$$\overset{*}{F}_{G_i} = f(\overset{*}{G}, X_T, \overset{\circ}{P}_{G_i}, \overset{\circ}{w}_{G_i}) \tag{10.26}$$

where $\overset{*}{A}_{G_i}$ is the cyclical movement of discretionary expenditures in real terms within the ith component of the government and not-for-profit sector (the difference between the actually observed rate, $\dot{A}_{G_i}$, and the trend value, $\overset{\circ}{A}_{G_i}$); $\overset{*}{F}_{G_i}$ is the cyclical movement of discretionary funds (in nominal terms) within the same subsector; $\overset{*}{G}$ is the cyclical movement of aggregate demand; $E_{G_i} - F_{G_i}$ is the subsector's current cash deficit; $\overset{\circ}{L}$ is the degree of liquidity pressure being exerted by the central bank; i_{LT} is the set of long-term interest rates relevant to the capital outlays made by that subsector; X is a set of policy variables that affect the level of discretionary expenditures within the subsector; X_T is the set of tax schedules established by the government; $\overset{\circ}{P}_{G_i}$ is the secular growth of the price index for all the goods and services purchased by the subsector, and $\overset{\circ}{W}_{G_i}$ is the secular growth of the wage rate within that component of the government and not-for-profit sector.

The cyclical movement of discretionary expenditures in nominal terms for the government sector as a whole, $\overset{*}{E}_G$, can then be calculated as follows:

$$\overset{*}{A}_G = \sum_{i=1}^{n} \overset{*}{A}_{G_i} \tag{10.27}$$

and

$$\overset{*}{E}_G = \overset{*}{A}_G + \overset{\circ}{P}_E \tag{10.28}$$

where $\overset{*}{A}_G$ is the cyclical movement of discretionary expenditures in real terms for the government sector as a whole, and $\overset{\circ}{P}_E$ is the secular growth of the price index for just the structures and other durable goods purchased by the government (rather than all goods and services). The cyclical movement of discretionary funds (in nominal terms) for the government sector as a whole, $\overset{*}{F}_G$, can be calculated in a similar manner as follows:

$$\overset{*}{F}_G = \sum_{i=1}^{n} \overset{*}{F}_{G_i} \tag{10.29}$$

The U.S. economy's government and not-for-profit sector, it should be kept in mind, is divided into three components: (1) the federal government; (2) all state and local governments; and (3) all nonprofit organizations, so that n in equations 10.27 and 10.29 is equal to 3.

For estimation purposes, equations 10.25 and 10.26 need to be specified as follows:

$$\overset{*}{A}_{G_i} = a(\overset{*}{G}) + b_1(E_{G_i} - F_{G_i}) + b_2(\hat{L}) + b_3(i_{LT}) \\ + b_4(X_1) + \ldots + b_n(X_m) \tag{10.30}$$

and

$$\overset{*}{F}_{G_i} = \alpha(\overset{*}{G}) + c_1(\overset{\circ}{P}_G) + c_2(\overset{\circ}{W}_{G_i}) + c_3(X_{T_1}) \\ c_4(X_{T_1}) + \ldots + c_n(X_{T_n}) \tag{10.31}$$

where a is the value of the accelerator for the ith component of the government sector and thus is equal to the slope of the E curve for that subsector; α is the value of the redistributive effect of any cyclical movement of aggregate demand and thus is equal to the slope of the corresponding F curve, and $b_1, b_2, \ldots, b_h$ and

$c_1, c_2, \ldots, c_n$ are the coefficients for the parameters of those two curves, indicating the direction and magnitude of the shift in those curves which will occur as the parameters themselves vary.

So far, the argument is no different from what has already been said about the growth of discretionary expenditures and of discretionary funds within the enterprise and household sectors. This includes the condition that the secular growth of discretionary expenditures in nominal terms within any subsector, $\mathring{E}_i$, must be equal to the secular growth of discretionary funds, $\mathring{F}_i$. The analysis of the government sector breaks new ground only as one turns to the actual empirical work of estimating equations 10.32 and 10.33. The first significant difference arises in connection with the trend values, $\mathring{E}_i$ and $\mathring{F}_i$.

The trend values, in the case of the enterprise and household sectors, can be postulated *a priori*, based on the long-period model of economic growth that has been developed in the preceding chapters. Each industry can be expected to expand over time at a rate determined by the average growth of output per worker for the economy as a whole, $\mathring{Z}$, multiplied by the income elasticity of demand for the output produced by that industry (ignoring any relative price, or substitution, effect). This growth rate will then determine the rate at which each industry will need to expand its capacity and thus the rate at which it will need to add new plant and equipment. The growth of discretionary expenditures in real terms for the enterprise sector as a whole, $\mathring{A}_B$, will be the weighted average of the growth of real expenditures on new plant and equipment for all n industries (which, together with the secular growth of the price index for durable goods, $\mathring{P}_K$, will give the secular growth of discretionary expenditures in nominal terms, $\mathring{E}_B$). Meanwhile, the secular growth of discretionary expenditures in real terms for the household sector as a whole, $\mathring{A}_H$, will (again ignoring any possible relative price, or substitution, effect) be equal to the weighted average of the income elasticity of demand for the various types of durable goods purchased by households (which, together with the secular growth of the price index for those types of durable goods, will give the secular growth of discretionary expenditures in nominal terms, $\mathring{E}_H$).

The government sector is different in that there is no long-period model that will enable the secular growth of discretionary expenditures to be specified *a priori*, either for any one component of the government sector individually or for the sector as a whole. The closest parallel to what has been said in connection with the enterprise and household sectors is what can be termed the income elasticity of demand for "public" as distinct from "private" goods. This phrase refers to the observed rate at which the size of the public sector increases relative to the growth of real income. However, there is reason to question whether the "income elasticity of demand for public goods" is a valid theoretical construct. For one thing, as already pointed out, the government at each of the different levels of jurisdiction is not subject to the same type of income constraint as business firms and households. The government has the power to tax, or unilaterally tap income flows, for its own purposes independently of what is being provided in return so that the income elasticity of demand for public goods is a politically rather than a market-determined variable. No less important, while there are many state and local governments so that the erratic, or unpredictable behavior, of any one governmental unit does not preclude the possibility of being able to generalize about the trend over time, there is only one federal government—accounting for more than half of all the tax revenue collected in the United States. Its behavior can be shown to be highly unpredictable, subject as it is to the influence of political factors unrelated to any immediate, or even longer run, need for durable goods. This makes the federal government's E and F functions, along with the E and F curves derived from those functions, unique.

The secular growth of discretionary expenditures by the federal government can be said to be largely a matter of policy, unrelated to any of the economic variables that determine the secular growth of discretionary expenditures in the other sectors. This is especially true since, for the U.S. federal government, virtually all of its durable goods purchases are for military purposes. Thus

$$\mathring{A}_{FG} = f(\mathbf{X}) \tag{10.32}$$

where $\mathring{A}_{FG}$ is the secular growth of discretionary expenditures in real terms by the federal government and $\mathbf{X}$ is a set of policy variables, including X_1, the level of expenditures on defense and other international security programs (with X_2, $X_3, \ldots, X_n$ the level of expenditures for the other types of programs delineated above in exhibit 10.1). Moreover, in the absence of any long-period model to explain the trend, $\mathring{A}_{FG}$ is merely the result of averaging the growth of the federal government's discretionary expenditures in real terms during any one period, $\mathring{A}_{FG_t}$, for a given interval of time, such as the length of a particular political regime or administration. That is,

$$\mathring{A}_{FG} = \sum_{t=1}^{n} \dot{A}_{FG_t} \tag{10.33}$$

with n a certain number of time periods greater than the length of the normal business cycle but otherwise is undefined. This, in turn, means that $\mathring{A}_{FG_t}$ can be substituted for $\dot{A}_{FG_t}$ in equation 10.32, as follows:

$$\dot{A}_{FG_t} = f(\mathbf{X}) \tag{10.34}$$

While, as a practical matter, the trend value for any variable will need to be estimated on the basis of some equation similar to 10.34, there is a considerable difference between that estimate being used as a check on the *a priori* argument of a long-period model and that estimate being all that can be said about the trend. In the latter case, the estimate is simply a statistical artifice. It amounts to little more than the tautological statement that the trend is whatever it happens to be.

Nonetheless, if what has just been said about the secular growth of the federal government's discretionary expenditures accurately describes the reality, this has an important implication for how a change can occur in the economy's secular rate of expansion. It means that, based on equation 10.34, the growth of the federal government's discretionary expenditures in real terms during any one time period, $\dot{A}_{FG_t}$, can be changed as a matter of policy, and that if the higher (or lower) rate of growth is then maintained for an extended period of time, the secular growth rate, $\dot{A}_{FG}$, will be changed as well, placing the economic system on a different secular growth path. However, it is not just that the E function for the federal government includes a set of policy variables, represented by the X vector, which are the means by which the rate of growth of discretionary expenditures within that sector can vary independently of current economic conditions. It is also that those policy variables are the only determinants of the rate of growth of the federal government's discretionary expenditures, even in the short period, so that equation 10.30 is reduced to equation 10.34. This, in fact, is the second important way in which the E and F functions for the government sector, together with the E and F curves derived from those functions, differ from those of the enterprise and household sectors. The federal government's E function includes none of the economic variables that serve as parameters of the other sectors' E curves in the short period.

10.4.2 The actual E and F curves

It turns out that when econometric techniques are used to estimate the parameters of equation 10.30 for the federal component of the U.S. government and not-for-profit sector, relying on quarterly data for the period 1952–1978, the value of a is not significantly different from zero. This finding is not inconsistent with the results obtained by other investigators. What it means is that the accelerator model does not apply and that therefore the $\overset{*}{G}$ variable needs to be dropped from the federal government's E function. Furthermore, it turns out that the value of the b_2, b_2 and b_2 coefficients in the same equation is also not significantly different from zero. This means that the rate at which the federal government's durable goods purchases are increasing is unaffected by the size of the federal deficit, the degree of liquidity pressure being applied by the central bank or the level of long-term interest rates. With these variables also dropped from equation 10.30, one is left with the set of policy variables represented by the X vector as the only determinants of $\dot{A}_{FG_t}$—and hence, with $\overset{\circ}{P}_K$ a constant, as the only determinants of $\dot{E}_{FG_t}$ as well. Indeed, this is why exhibit 10.6, reporting the empirical results obtained for the government sector, contains no separate equation for the federal government. None of the economic variables for which time series estimates are available help to explain the quarter-to-quarter movement of the federal government's discretionary expenditures in real terms. As a result, all the variance has to be attributed to the unmeasurable policy variables denoted by the X vector.

Exhibit 10.6

**Cyclical Movement of Discretionary Expenditures in Real Terms
Government Sector**

Federal Component

(no equation)

State and Local Government Component

$$\overset{*}{A}_{SL} = \underset{(3.2)}{0.12} + \underset{(1.5)}{0.064(\overset{*}{X}_4)} - \underset{(2.5)}{0.06(1/3 \sum_{t=-2}^{0} (E_6/F_6))_{-1}} - \underset{(4.4)}{0.009(i_1)}$$

$R^2_a = 0.96 \qquad R^2_b = 0.16 \qquad R^2_c = 0.97 \qquad \text{D–W} = 1.8 \qquad w_{6a} = 0.10$

Not-for-profit Component

(no equation)

Exhibit 10.7

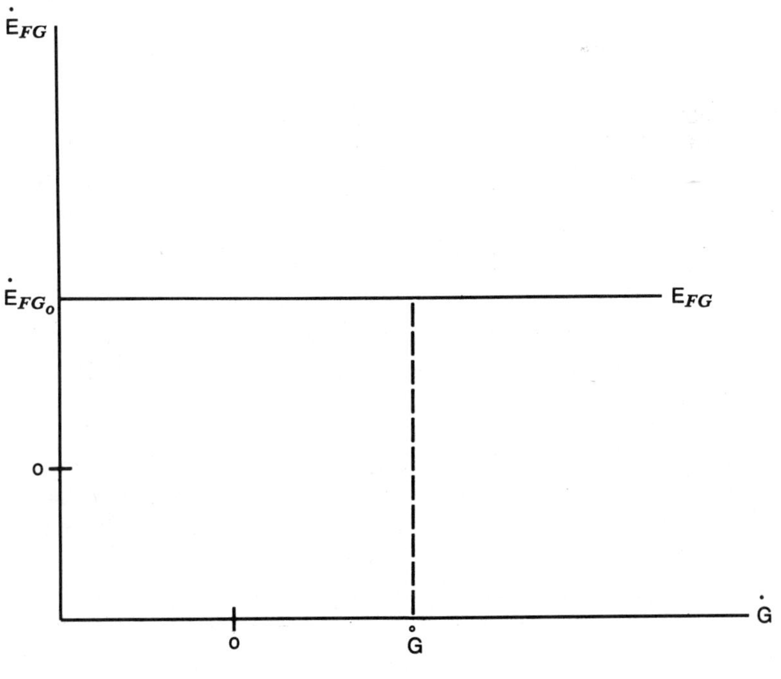

On the basis of these empirical findings, one can assume that the discretionary expenditures, or E, curve for the federal government takes the form shown in exhibit 10.7. Influenced by the political factors identified earlier in this chapter (see section 10.1.3), the party in power can be assumed to have chosen a rate of growth of discretionary expenditures for the current period, $\dot{E}_{FG_t}$, which will remain invariate whatever the level of aggregate demand, $\overset{*}{G}$. It is for this reason that the E_{FG} curve is depicted in exhibit 10.7 as running parallel to the horizontal axis at a height equal to some constant, $\dot{E}_{FG_0}$. The way the curve is drawn means that it will shift up and down (while remaining parallel to the horizontal axis) only as the policy variables represented by the X vector change.

The above argument needs to be modified only slightly to take into account the durable goods purchases, or discretionary expenditures, by state and local governments. For one thing, there is a pronounced secular trend to the growth of discretionary expenditures at the state and local level. Indeed, for the period 1952–1978, the trend component, $\overset{\circ}{A}_{SL}$, accounts for virtually all of the quarter-to-quarter movements in $\dot{A}_{SL}$. (This can be seen by examining the R^2_a statistic reported for the state and local government sector equation in exhibit 10.6. This statistic measures how much of the quarter-to-quarter movement in $\dot{A}_{SL_t}$ can be explained by a simple exponential time trend. In contrast, the same time trend accounts for very little of the quarterly movement in $\dot{A}_{FG_t}$.) This empirical finding is consistent with the fact that the economic and anthropogenic types of public goods supplied by government, the demand for which can be expected to increase over time at the same rate the economy is growing, are provided almost entirely at the state and local level.

Moreover, while the value of a also turns out to be not significantly different from zero when equation 10.30 is estimated econometrically for the state and local government sector, the E curve derived from that function would appear to have two parameters in addition to the policy variables represented by the X vector. They are: (1) the size of the sectoral deficit, $E_{SL} - F_{SL}$, reflecting the constitutional and other strictures which state and local governments are under to balance their budgets; and (2) the long-term interest rate, i_{LT}, reflecting the dependence of state and local governments on the bond market to finance major capital outlays. Finally, an additional policy variable can be identified in the case of the state and local government sector's discretionary expenditures. This is the amount of grant-in-aid by the federal government, X_4 (involving, essentially, the transfer of tax revenue, or income, from the one level of government to the other.) With but these two modifications—the one affecting the placement of $\overset{\circ}{G}$, the benchmark growth rate, along the horizontal axis and the other affecting the number of shift parameters which need to be taken into account—the E curve for state and local government will be the same as that for the federal government shown in exhibit 10.7. (The not-for-profit component of the government sector is so small that it can, for all practical purposes, be ignored.) Thus, for the government sector as a whole, the growth of discretionary expenditures, both in real terms, $\dot{A}_G$, and in nominal terms, $\dot{E}_G$, can be assumed to be independent of aggregate demand conditions as measured by $\dot{G} - \dot{G}$, or $\overset{*}{G}$.

While the $\overset{\cdot}{G}$ variable can be omitted from the E function—and indeed must be dropped, given what is known about the growth of discretionary expenditures within the government sector—the same is not true of the corresponding F function. On the contrary, since the amount of revenue generated under a fixed schedule of tax rates depends on the level of economic activity, it is the cyclical movement of aggregate output, $\overset{*}{G}$, which is the principal factor determining the cyclical movement of discretionary funds within the government sector. This is especially true for the federal component of that sector.

The federal government's two main sources of tax revenue, the personal income tax and the corporate profits tax, are both highly income elastic. Indeed, because of the corporate profits tax, the federal government is a junior partner of every corporate enterprise, with the amount of revenue generated by the tax varying directly with the growth of corporate profits. With corporate profits themselves an increasing function of aggregate demand (see chapter 7, section 4.4), the amount of revenue generated by the tax can be expected to vary over the cycle at a greater rate than whatever change is occurring in the level of demand. When the economy is expanding at a rate that exceeds the secular average, the revenue from the corporate income tax will be increasing at an even more rapid rate, and when the economy is growing at a rate less than the secular average, the revenue from the tax will be increasing at an even lower rate—and indeed may actually decline. This relationship, along with the income elasticity of the personal income tax, is the reason why the discretionary funds, or F, curve of the federal government takes the form shown in exhibit 10.8, with a slope greater than 1.

Where exactly the federal government's F curve will intersect the vertical plane at the point $\overset{\circ}{G}$ will depend on the curve's parameters, as identified in equation 10.31. Those parameters, especially the various tax rates, X_{T_1}, $X_{T_2}, \ldots, X_{T_n}$, are the means by which the F curve can be shifted, whether as a conscious policy decision or not. An increase in any one of the various tax rates will, other factors remaining the same, cause the F curve to shift upward. This is because the higher tax rates will, at any given level of aggregate demand, generate additional tax revenues and thus will produce additional discretionary funds for the federal government. Lower tax rates will, of course, have the opposite effect. (The above argument assumes that the government's expenditures on nondurable goods and services remains unchanged. The government's discretionary funds, it will be recalled, are the difference between its net tax revenue—total tax revenue less transfer payments—and its outlays on nondurable goods and services.) At the same time, a more rapid increase in the price of the goods purchased and/or the wages paid by the federal government, relative to the secular growth of those variables, will cause the F curve to shift downward. This is because the higher prices and/or wages will require a greater outflow of funds

Exhibit 10.8

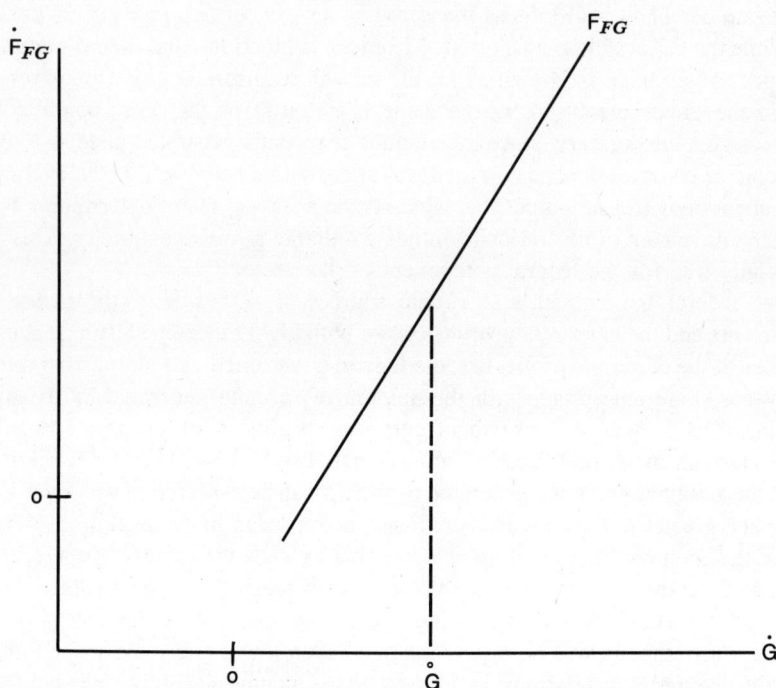

to the enterprise and/or household sectors, leaving the federal government with fewer funds in excess of its nondurable goods purchases. A slower growth of prices and wages will, of course, have the opposite effect.

What has just been said about the F function for the federal government applies, in general, to the state and local government component and thus to the government sector as a whole. The one caveat is that because of the different types of taxes relied upon, as well as the different rates that may apply even when the different levels of government rely on the same type of tax, the slope of the state and local government's F curve, together with the point at which it intercepts the vertical plane at $\overset{\circ}{G}$, will be somewhat different. Nonetheless, the overall shape of the F curve will be the same.

10.4.3 The macrodynamic nexus

Once E and F curves such as those shown in exhibits 10.7 and 10.8 have been derived for the government sector, one can see what effect the sector will have on the short period macrodynamic stability of the economic system. One need only display the two curves on the same set of axes, as in exhibit 10.9. (To simplify the exposition, the state and local government component will be ignored from this point on and the government sector identified with the federal component alone.)

Exhibit 10.9

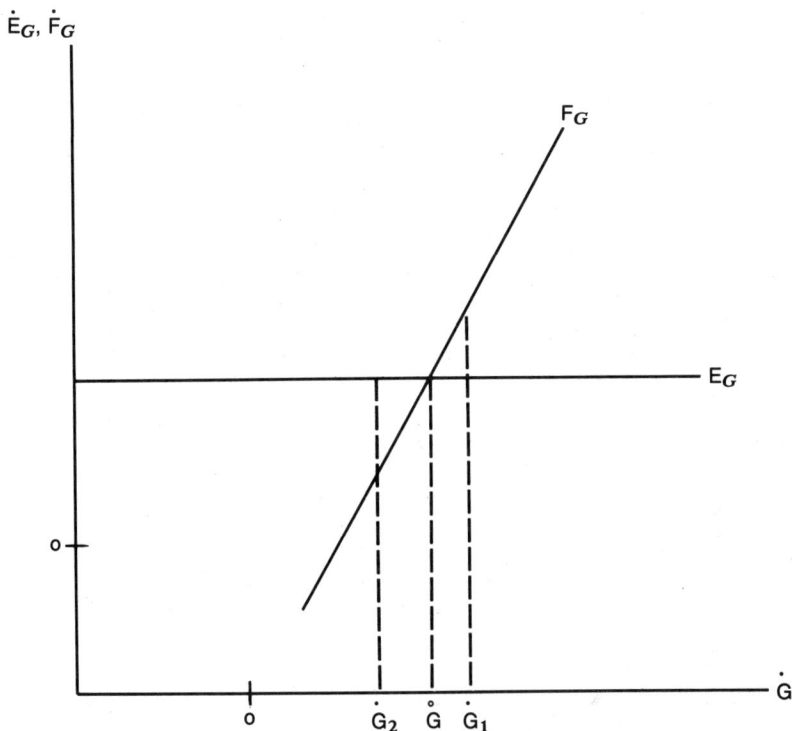

As can be seen from the diagram in exhibit 10.9, the government sector, like the enterprise and household sectors, has the effect of making the economy as a whole endogenously stable. (See chapter 4, section 4.2, for an explanation of what is meant by endogenously stable.) With the slope of the government's F curve greater than that of its E curve, any displacement of the economy from its secular growth rate, $\overset{\circ}{G}$, will create a cash flow feedback effect—measured by the difference between E_G and F_G—which will tend to push the economy back on to that secular growth path. (On the cash-flow feedback effect, see chapter 3, section 2.5.) For example, with the economy located to the right of $\overset{\circ}{G}$ in exhibit 10.9 and therefore expanding at a rate, let us say $\overset{\bullet}{G}_1$, which is greater than the secular average, the rate of growth and hence, most likely, the absolute level of discretionary funds within the government sector will be greater than the growth and level of discretionary expenditures. This excess inflow of funds into the government sector will serve to dampen the rate of economic expansion, reducing it eventually to $\overset{\circ}{G}$ if other factors do not first intercede. The dampening effect of the government's discretionary funds, or tax revenues, increasing more rapidly than its discretionary expenditures during the expansionary phase of the cycle is the "fiscal drag" that was first noted during the 1960s and served as the justification for the 1964 tax cut. Similarly, with the economy located to the left of $\overset{\circ}{G}$ in exhibit 10.9 and therefore expanding at a rate, say $\dot{G}_2$, which is less than the secular average, the growth and absolute level of discretionary expenditures will be greater than the growth and absolute level of discretionary funds. This excess of cash outlays will serve to quicken the pace of economic activity, restoring it to $\overset{\circ}{G}$ if other factors do not first intercede. The tendency of the government sector's discretionary expenditures to continue growing at the same rate even as its discretionary funds, or tax revenues, fall off sharply during an economic downturn is perhaps the most important of the "automatic stabilizers" that were first identified in the 1950s.

The above argument, it should be noted, is based on the assumption, reflected in exhibit 10.9, that at the secular growth rate $\dot{E}_G$ is equal to $\dot{F}_G$, meaning that the government's discretionary expenditures and discretionary funds are both increasing at the same rate—although, to satisfy the necessary monetary condition for continuous growth (see chapter 12, section 1.6), one must further assume that at any one moment in time the *level* of the government's discretionary expenditures, E_G, exceeds the *level* of discretionary funds, F_G, by an amount equal to $\overset{\circ}{Y}(F_G)$ where $\overset{\circ}{Y}$ is the secular growth of the national income (the secular growth of the price level, $\overset{\circ}{P}$, added to the secular growth of aggregate output, $\overset{\circ}{G}$). What this last proviso means is that, at $\overset{\circ}{G}$, the government sector can be assumed to be running a deficit equal to the annual increment in aggregate income, measured in current dollars, but that, with the government's discretionary expenditures and discretionary funds both increasing at the same rate, the size of the deficit relative to the level of aggregate income will remain unchanged. These assumptions will be relaxed shortly. For the moment, however, they provide a convenient starting point for the analysis of the government sector's macrodynamic impact on the rest of the economy.

With the last of the economic system's three major sectors having now been examined in terms of their E and F curves—only the rest-of-the-world sector remains to be taken up—one can infer more than just the short-period stability properties of the government sector alone or indeed even the short-period stability properties of the other two sectors. One can proceed to postulate a set of E and F curves for the entire economy and thereby bring out the relationship between the whole and its several parts. With all three sectors, the enterprise and household as well as the government, having an F curve whose slope is greater than that of the corresponding E curve, one can be reasonably certain that the aggregate E and F curves will be similar to those shown in exhibit 10.10—with the slope of the aggregate F curve also necessarily greater than that of the aggregate E curve. One can be confident on this point because the aggregate E and F curves are simply the sum, algebraically and geometrically, of the entire set of sectoral E and F curves (see chapter 4, section 4.3). The rest-of-the-world sector, given its relative size, is unlikely to change the picture presented in exhibit 10.10. Indeed, it turns out that this sector's F curve also has a slope greater than that of the corresponding E curve (see chapter 11, section 0.0).

Exhibit 10.10

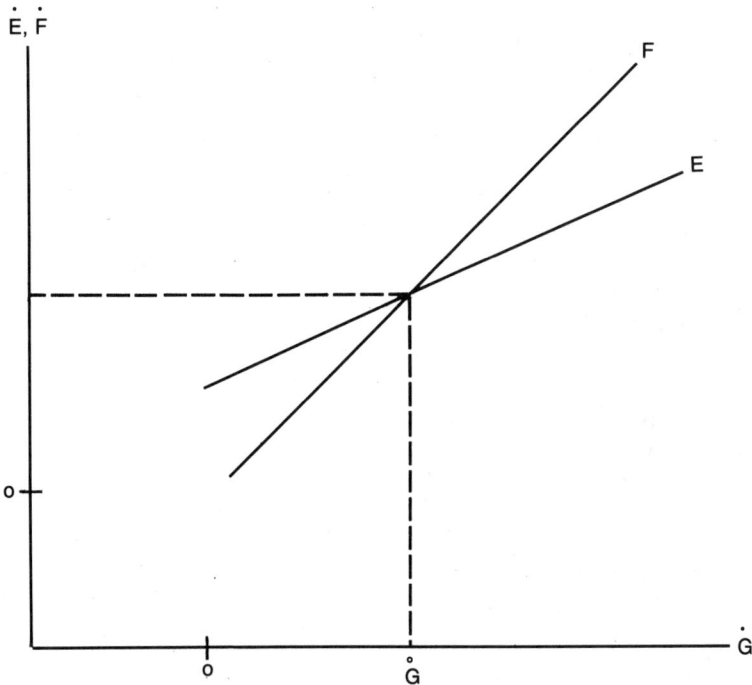

An examination of just the aggregate E and F curves alone, as represented in exhibit 10.10, is sufficient to establish a number of important points. For one thing, it is now possible to say whether the U.S. economy is endogenously stable in the short period. As previously explained (see chapter 4, section 4.2), the economy's endogenous stability will depend on how great is the slope of the aggregate E curve relative to that of the aggregate F curve. Given the curves shown in exhibit 10.10, one can be reasonably certain that an advanced market economy like that of the United States is endogenously stable. This means that any displacement of the economy from its secular growth path will give rise to a dynamic adjustment process, based on the cash-flow feedback effect, which will return the economy back to that growth path. An important corollary is that, with the endogenous forces represented by the aggregate E and F curves acting in such a way as to maintain whatever secular growth rate has previously been established, it will not be easy to place the economic system on a different growth path. The significance of this point will be clearer as the discussion proceeds (see section 10.4.5).

Examining just the aggregate E and F curves alone, one can also determine at what rate, given the current balance of macrodynamic factors, the economy as a whole will be expanding. This currently applicable growth rate—which is approximated as a practical matter by the actually observed growth rate, $\dot{G}$—is determined by where the aggregate E and F curves intersect. It is the counterpart, in a dynamic analysis, of the equilibrium level of national income, Y, in a static Keynesian model (see chapter 3, section 2.1). Still, it is more instructive to examine the aggregate E and F curves, not by themselves alone as in exhibit 10.10 but rather, in conjunction with one or more of paired sets of sectoral E and F curves, such as those that apply to the government and not-for-profit sector. Indeed, it is only in this way one can trace out the macrodynamic nexus, that is, the relationship between what is happening at the sectoral level and what is happening at the aggregate level—or indeed understand why $\mathring{G}$ in exhibit 10.10 is the currently applicable growth rate. In order to make clear what is meant by the macrodynamic nexus, let us see what will be the effect on the aggregate E and F curves, and thus on $\mathring{G}$ itself, when there is a change in the government's expenditure policy, as represented by the appropriate shift of its E curve.

10.4.4 A change in expenditure policy

At any one point in time, the government's discretionary expenditures will necessarily be increasing at some rate, $\dot{E}_G$. That rate could be zero or even negative—although, in an advanced industrial society, $\dot{E}_G$ is likely to be greater than zero for the reason that will be made clear at the beginning of the next subsection. Thus, the government cannot avoid having an expenditure-based fiscal policy, even if it is arrived at only by default. That policy will then determine the height above the origin at which the government's discretionary expenditures curve, as shown in exhibit 10.9, runs parallel to the horizontal axis. Still, one E curve alone is not enough to determine the macrodynamic impact of a change in the government's expenditure policy. A second E curve needs to be drawn, as in part a of exhibit 10.11. Only in this way can a change in the government's expenditure policy be posited and the effect of that change on the rate at which the economy as a whole is expanding then determined.

The change in expenditure policy shown in part a of exhibit 10.11 can be regarded, as it will in the discussion which follows, as a shift from E_{G_0} to E_{G_1} and thus as a move to higher rate of growth of discretonary expenditures. However, it could just as well be viewed as a shift from E_{G_1} to E_{G_0} and thus as a move to a lower rate of growth of discretionary expenditures. The change in policy shown in part a of exhibit 10.11 can, in turn, be interpreted in either of two ways: 1) as what would happen if E_{G_1} rather than E_{G_0} represented the government's current expenditure policy, or 2) as what would happen if E_{G_1} were actually to succeed E_{G_0} as the government's expenditure policy. An exercise in comparative dynamics can readily be carried out, based on the first interpretation. However, for analyzing the more complicated case of an actual traverse through historical time, only the second interpretation will suffice.

A shift of the government's E curve from E_{G_0} to E_{G_1}, as shown in part a of exhibit 10.11, will produce a corresponding shift of the E curve for the economy as a whole from E_0 to E_1, as shown in part b of the same exhibit. The shift of the

Exhibit 10.11

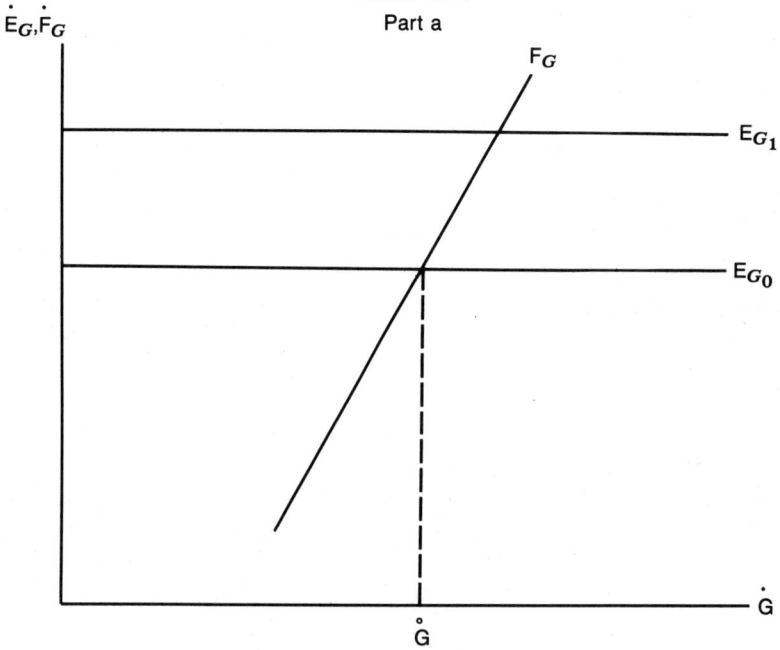

Part a

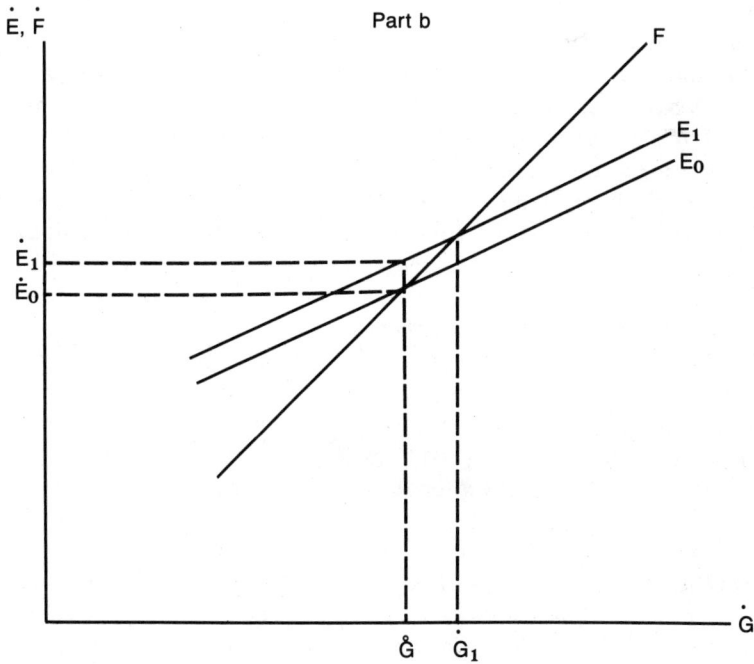

aggregate curve will, however, be less pronounced than that of the sectoral curve because the government's discretionary expenditures are only a part of total discretionary expenditures (approximately one-sixth in the case of the United States). In its new position the aggregate E curve will, together with the aggregate F curve (which, it can be assumed, has remained unchanged), make $\dot{G}_1$ the aggregate growth rate which is now the applicable one. This is the growth rate which, were it not for the incomplete adjustment process, one would expect to observe during the current period. Why the shift to the new aggregate growth path is likely to be incomplete, with the value taken by $\dot{G}_1$ therefore likely to be only approximated rather than actually attained, can be understood only by examining in greater depth the process by which, as a result of the shift in either the aggregate E or F curve, the economy will find itself on a different growth path.

The shift of the aggregate E curve, the result of the more pronounced shift of the government's E curve, means that, at least initially or *ex ante*, total discretionary expenditures will be increasing more rapidly than total discretionary funds. Whereas previously $\dot{E}$ was equal to $\dot{F}$, now as can be seen in part b of exhibit 10.11, $\dot{E}$ exceeds $\dot{F}$ by an amount equal to $\dot{E}_1 - \dot{E}_0$. This more rapid growth of total discretionary expenditures will, in turn, have a stimulative effect on the economy due to both the multiplier effect and the cash-flow feedback effect. These two effects are not the same and should not be confused with one another (see chapter 3, section 2.5).

The multiplier effect arises from the increased spending on nondurable goods and services induced by the shift of the aggregate E curve. While the usual practice is to derive the multiplier mathematically, based on an empirical estimate of the various marginal propensities (to invest and tax as well as to consume and save), this is not an approach that can be recommended for constructing a macrodynamic model. The reason is only in part that, with each sector having a different marginal propensity to "consume" and "save," this method of deriving the value of the multiplier is unreliable. It is also that, with the dynamic adjustment process associated with the multiplier likely to be truncated in the historical time of actual experience, k is unlikely to reach the full value given by the relevant mathematical formula, whether equation 3.17 or some elaboration thereof. This is why, as already explained, the value of k is best estimated directly, on the basis of equation 3.29, by taking the change in the aggregate growth rate, $\overset{*}{G}$, which follows from or, more accurately, is statistically associated with the change in total discretionary expenditures, $\overset{*}{E}$.

The cash-flow feedback effect, on the other hand, arises from whatever discrepancy, if any, exists between total discretionary expenditures and total discretionary funds. It therefore depends on the difference between E and F rather than on the cyclical movement of E alone. Moreover, while the multiplier effect builds up over time until it approaches as a limit some value greater than 1, the cash-flow feedback effect diminishes in value over time until, with $E - F$ equal to

Exhibit 10.12

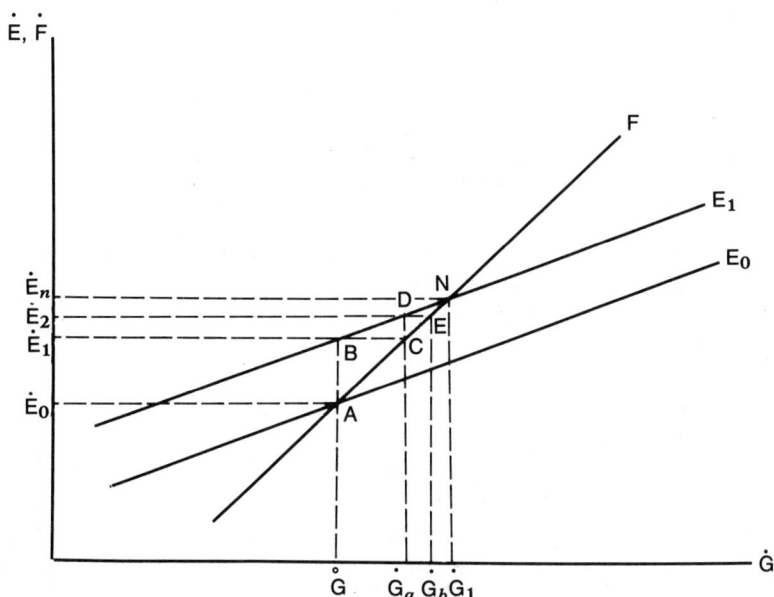

zero, it ceases to play any further role in the dynamic adjustment process. Thus the multiplier and the cash-flow feedback effects not only depend on different variables, they also work in different ways. As an example, let us take the situation shown in exhibit 10.12, an elaboration of exhibit 10.11, part b, where, as a result of an upward shift of the government's E curve, the rate of growth of total discretionary expenditures has increased from $\dot{E}_0$ to $\dot{E}_1$.

Were the growth of total discretionary expenditures to remain fixed at $\dot{E}_1$ without increasing any further, the rate of expansion for the economy as a whole would be only $\dot{G}_a$ and not $\dot{G}_1$. Part of the movement from $\dot{G}$ to $\dot{G}_a$ will be due to the multiplier effect of the increase in the growth of total discretionary expenditures from $\dot{E}_0$ to $\dot{E}$ but how much, without knowing the value of k for that time period, cannot be said. It is nonetheless the multiplier effect associated with the increased rate of growth of discretionary expenditures that will provide the initial impetus for the economy as a whole to begin expanding more rapidly.

The rest of the increase from $\dot{G}$ to $\dot{G}_a$ will be due to the fact that, with the economy moving from point A in the direction of point B as a result of the more rapid rate at which durable goods are being produced and sold, total discretionary expenditures, E, will be greater than total discretionary funds, F. With more cash funds thus being put into the circular flow than are being withdrawn, the pace of economic activity can be expected to quicken. This cash-flow feedback effect, together with the multiplier effect, will push the economy in the direction of point C. As the economy approaches that point on its F curve, the discrepany between

E and F will be eliminated, due to the more rapid increase in total discretionary funds relative to discretionary expenditures, and the cash-flow feedback effect will tend to lose its force. Meanwhile, the full multiplier effect of total discretionary expenditures increasing from $\dot{E}_0$ to $\dot{E}_1$ will already have been felt, marking the first round of the dynamic adjustment process. That first round can be traced out in exhibit 10.12 by the movement of the economy from point A to point C via point B, with the economy expanding at a rate equal to $\dot{G}_a$ as it reaches point C.

The growth of total discretionary expenditures cannot be expected to remain at $\dot{E}_1$, however. This is why the increase in the aggregate growth rate from $\dot{G}$ to $\dot{G}_a$ marks only the first round of the dynamic adjustment process. Since durable goods purchases are in part endogenously determined (reflecting the influence of the accelerator model in the enterprise and household sectors), the growth of total discretionary expenditures will, with the economy expanding at a rate equal to $\dot{G}_a$, increase still further from $\dot{E}_1$ to $\dot{E}_2$. This will lead to total discretionary expenditures again being greater than total discretionary funds, with the difference between E and F having a further stimulative effect on the economy. The cash-flow feedback effect during this second round will not be reduced to zero until, with the aggregate growth rate having increased to $\dot{G}_b$, the economy has moved to point E on its F curve where the growth of total discretionary expenditures is again being matched by the growth of discretionary funds. This second round of the dynamic adjustment process is traced out in exhibit 10.12 by the movement of the economy from point C to point E via point D. Again, it is the increase in total discretionary expenditures, because of the multiplier effect, which serves as the catalyst but it is the subsequent disproportionate increase in total discretionary funds that, by reducing the cash-flow feedback effect until it becomes negligible, will bring this second round of the adjustment process to an end.

The subsequent rounds in the dynamic adjustment process could easily be traced out as well. The only difference would be that, with the slope of the aggregate E curve being less than that of the aggregate F curve, the increment in the aggregate growth rate, $\dot{G}$, will be less with each succeeding round until it finally becomes negligible. There are, however, two reasons why it makes little sense to proceed any further with this round-by-round explanation now that the underlying dynamic has been made clear. The first reason is that the ultimate limit to the increase in the aggregate growth rate, and thus the point that will eventually be reached, can be determined without having to go through that exercise. The ultimate limit is given by the intersection of the E_1 and F curves. When that point is reached—this being point N in exhibit 10.12 with an aggregate growth rate equal to $\dot{G}_1$—the movement of the economy along its F curve will have finally caught up with the shift of and subsequent movement along the aggregate E curve, and the combined multiplier and cash-flow feedback effects will be fully exhausted. That is why, with a shift of the total discretionary expenditures curve from E_0 to E_1, it is $\dot{G}_1$ which represents the new rate at which the economy can be expected to expand.

At the same time, it is unlikely that the economic system will actually reach the point where the new aggregate E curve intersects the aggregate F curve. It may happen in the logical time of a comparative dynamics approach, but the story in the historical time that can actually be observed is almost certain to be different. This is because the dynamic adjustment process just described is not likely to continue for more than one or two rounds without being cut short, or truncated, by a subsequent shift in one or the other aggregate curve. When that shift occurs, it will be some other growth path besides G_1 to which the economy will move via a similar adjustment process. Still, since one can only indicate the eventual stopping point of whatever dynamic adjustment process is already known to have been initiated, it is $\dot{G}_1$ that is explained by the shift of the aggregate E curve relative to the aggregate F curve. This is what makes $\dot{G}_1$ the currently applicable growth rate. Moreover, were there to be no further shift in either the aggregate E or aggregate F curve, due either to a shift of the government's E curve or to the shift of some other sectoral curve, $\dot{G}_1$ would in time become the new secular growth rate.

An analysis of the government's expenditure-based fiscal policy, relying on the appropriate set of E and F curves for both the government sector and the economy as a whole, therefore leads to the following conclusion: An increase in the rate of growth of durable goods purchases by the government, implying as it does an upward shift of the government's E curve similar to that shown in part a of exhibit 10.11, will produce an upward shift of the aggregate E curve as well, though not of the same magnitude; and this upward shift of the aggregate E curve will, in turn, lead to a more rapid rate of expansion for the economy as a whole. The argument also holds in reverse. If the shift of the government's E curve, as a result of a reduction in the rate of growth of durable goods purchases, is from E_{G_1} to E_{G_0}, thereby implying the adoption of a less, rather than a more, expansionary expenditure policy, the aggregate E curve will shift from E_1 to E_0, and the rate of expansion for the economy as a whole will decline.

This conclusion, it should be noted, is not significantly different from what one would expect, based on a static Keynesian model. The only difference is that the analysis is now being carried out in terms of growth rates, with the adjustment to any change in policy divided into separate multiplier and cash-flow feedback effects which, it was pointed out, may not have fully worked themselves out by the time a shift in one of the relevant parameters leads to a new situation. The thrust of the argument, however, remains the same. The government can, by choosing the appropriate value for $\dot{E}_G$, place the economic system on whatever growth path seems socially most desirable. Even if the economy can only be nudged in the desired direction, the government can, by making further adjustments in $\dot{E}_G$, compensate either for any errors on its own part or for any of the exogenous disturbances to which the economic system is subject. The government's growth of discretionary expenditures can therefore be viewed as the instrumental variable by which the society, through its political institutions, can determine the economy's rate of expansion. The argument up to this point has

nonetheless ignored a number of complications which can arise when the placement of the economy on a different growth path is meant to be permanent, or at
least hold for the long period. These complications, which do not arise within the
static framework of the more conventional macroeconomic theory, explain why
any change in the currently applicable growth rate may be just a temporary one,
thereby defeating the government's purpose in altering its expenditure-based
fiscal policy.

10.4.5 Placing the economy on a different growth path

Any effort by the government to place the economy on a different growth path
will be beset by a number of problems. One of these arises from the sectoral
balance condition that must be satisfied. As already pointed out (see chapter
9.3.2), the growth of private consumption will need to match the growth of
aggregate output, and thus the rate at which business firms are expanding capacity, if the expansion process is not going to be interrupted for lack of effective
demand. The argument was previously formulated, however, without taking into
account the considerable amount of public consumption in an advanced market
economy like that of the United States. Now that the role of the government in
providing certain goods and services as a form of public consumption has been
acknowledged, it is necessary to modify the argument accordingly.

The main difference in the argument, once a government sector is allowed for
in addition to the enterprise and household sectors, is that it will be the growth of
total consumption, public as well as private, which will need to match the rate at
which business firms are expanding capacity. Equation 9.23 therefore still holds.
It is just that it needs to be elaborated on as follows:

$$\mathring{I} = c(\mathring{C}) + 1{-}c(Gov) = \mathring{G} \qquad (10.38)$$

where Gov is the secular rate at which the government is increasing its purchases
of real goods and services, nondurable as well as durable; c is the ratio of private
consumption by households, C, to total consumption, D (including the government's expenditures on goods and services, Gov), and the other variables are as
previously defined. Indeed, it is actually D, the amount of total consumption,
public as well as private, which replaces C in equation 9.23. (It should also be
noted that, to the extent all the relevant price indexes are changing at the same
rate, it will make no difference whether the variables in equation 10.38 are
specified in real or in nominal terms.)

This more general statement of the sectoral balance condition for continuous
growth implies that, if the demand for private consumption is increasing either
more or less rapidly than the rate at which aggregate output is growing and thus
more or less rapidly than the rate at which new capacity is being added within the
n industries that constitute the production subsystem, the government sector will
need to adjust its own secular rate of expansion, as measured by Gov, so that the

growth of total consumption, public as well as private (the middle term in equation 10.38), will be equal to $\overset{\circ}{G}$ (as well as equal to $\overset{\circ}{I}$). If the ratio of the government's discretionary expenditures to total outlays, d, can be considered a constant, then what the government must do to ensure that the sectoral balance condition is being satisfied can be stated in terms of the secular rate at which the government's own durable goods purchases are increasing. In that case, $\overset{\circ}{A}_G$, can be substituted for Gov in equation 10.38 so that the sectoral balance condition then takes the following form:

$$\overset{\circ}{I} = c(\overset{\circ}{C}) + 1-c(\overset{\circ}{A}_G) = \overset{\circ}{G} \tag{10.39}$$

The problem is that there is no set of economic forces—or political ones either, for that matter, except the possible electoral feedback—which can be counted on to ensure that $\overset{\circ}{A}_G$, and thus $\overset{\circ}{E}_G$ will take the value needed to satisfy either equation 10.39 or, should d vary, equation 10.38.

As already pointed out (see section 10.4.1), the value which $\overset{\circ}{A}_G$ actually takes is merely the cumulative effect of the government's expenditure policy over time. The government, by maintaining $\overset{\cdot}{A}_G$ at a higher value for a sufficient number of periods, will cause $\overset{\circ}{A}_G$ to rise—just as, by maintaining $\overset{\cdot}{A}_G$ at a lower value for a sufficient number of periods, it will cause $\overset{\circ}{A}_G$ to fall. Thus there is no reason why equation 10.39 or, with d free to vary, equation 10.38 will necessarily be satisfied. This is the corollary of the government being able, simply by shifting its own E curve, to place the economy on a different growth path. The aggregate growth rate which the government has implicitly opted for through its expenditure policy need not be a sustainable one in the long period—as indeed it will not be unless the sectoral balance condition is being satisfied.

Still, it is only that the government will have fewer options, insofar as its own rate of growth of discretionary expenditures, $\overset{\cdot}{E}_G$, is concerned, if the economic system's expansion is not eventually going to be brought to an end by the failure of final demand to keep pace with the growth of supply capacity. It is not that the government will be precluded from placing the economy on a particular growth path, such as $\overset{\cdot}{G}_1$ in exhibit 10.13. With c remaining unchanged, an aggregate growth rate equal to $\overset{\cdot}{G}_1$ will be sustainable provided the government makes sure its own expenditures, as denoted by $\overset{\cdot}{Gov}$ (or, with d remaining constant, as denoted by $\overset{\circ}{A}_G$), increase at the same rate. Moreover, $\overset{\cdot}{G}_1$ will still be a sustainable growth rate even if the government, by taking advantage of its ability to redistribute income through taxes, opts for a change in the value of c. Policymakers merely have to make sure that, taking into account the differential growth of private and public consumption implicit in the changing value of c, total consumption, D (the middle term in equation 10.38), increases at a rate equal to $\overset{\cdot}{G}_1$.

Satisfying the sectoral balance condition is only the first of the several problems the government will need to overcome if it is going to place the economy on a different growth path, one which will be sustainable in the long period. The

Exhibit 10.13

Part a

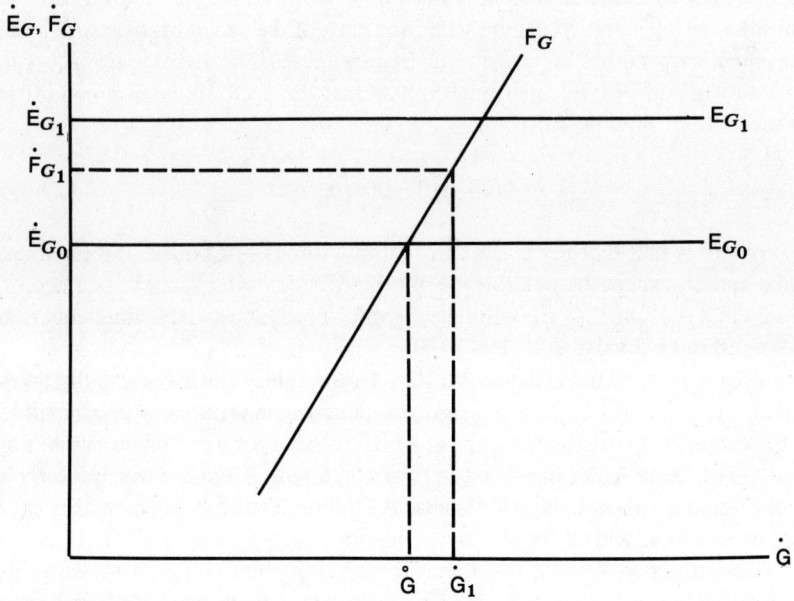

Part b

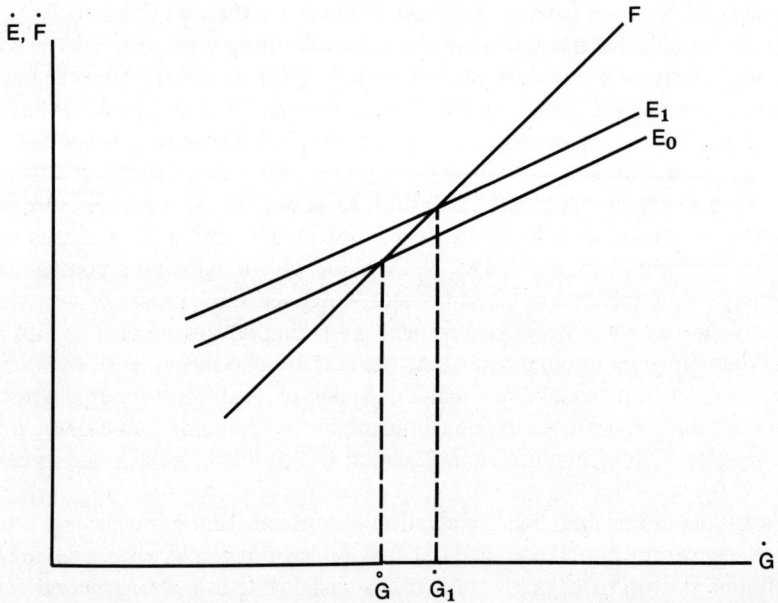

government will, in addition, need to successfully cope with the temporary increase in the relative size of its cash deficit when, through an upward shift of its own E curve, it attempts to place the economy on a more rapid growth path, such as the one represented by $\dot{G}_1$ in exhibit 10.13. With the shift of its discretionary expenditure curve from E_{G_0} to E_{G_1}, the government will no longer find itself at the point where its own E and F curves intersect. While the increase in the aggregate growth rate from $\mathring{G}$ to $\dot{G}_1$ due to the combined multiplier and cash-flow feedback effect of the more rapid growth of the government's discretionary expenditures will lead to an increase in tax revenues and thus to a higher rate of growth of discretionary funds, still, as can be seen from exhibit 10.13, the rate of growth of discretionary funds, $\dot{F}_{G_1}$, will be less than the rate of growth of discretionary expenditures, $\dot{E}_{G_1}$, at the higher aggregate growth rate, $\dot{G}_1$. This, in turn, means that whatever the size of the government's deficit previously, it will increase relative to the amount of tax revenue being obtained, T, and hence relative to the amount of discretionary funds, F_G.

The increase in the relative size of the government's deficit should not be viewed as more of a problem than it actually is. For one thing, it will not preclude the economy from remaining on the higher growth path represented by $\dot{G}_1$. Indeed, it is precisely the increase in the size of the government's cash deficit which, by requiring the government to put more funds into circulation than it is withdrawing through taxation, will enable the economy to eventually reach $\dot{G}_1$— at which point, the cash deficit within the government sector will be balanced by the corresponding cash surpluses in the other sectors, the result of business firms enjoying above-normal sales and the household sector experiencing above-normal employment. The deficit within the government sector will be a problem only because it will have to be financed in some manner. Even that will not cause any difficulty if the central bank is prepared to accommodate its monetary policy to the fiscal needs of the government. (The argument that this type of accommodation will, through its effect on the "money supply," lead to a more rapid rise in prices and thus to a higher rate of inflation, will be taken up in connection with the analysis of the role played in the economy by money and credit. See chapter 12, as well as chapter 14, part 3. There the argument will be shown to be unfounded.) The most that will happen in an untoward way as a result of $\dot{F}_G$ being less than $\dot{E}_G$ is that the amount of interest being paid by the government, as a share of its total budget, will have to be increased.

The cash deficit within the government sector will create a serious problem only if it is perceived by those responsible for economic policy as being undesirable *per se*, and they then take precipitous action to eliminate it—for example, by reducing the rate of growth of the government's discretionary expenditures. If that happens, with the government's E curve necessarily shifting down, the aggregate E curve will be lowered as well, and the currently applicable growth rate will then be less than $\dot{G}_1$. Indeed, instead of placing the economy on a more rapid secular growth path, the government's expenditure policy will have simply produced another fluctuation around the trend line, $\mathring{G}$. It will mark the next phase of what Kalecki first identified as the political trade cycle. The point here is that if those responsible for economic policy act precipitously to reduce the government's cash deficit, they will defeat their purpose in adopting a more expansionary fiscal policy. Not only will they fail to place the economy on a higher secular growth path. They will also add to the cyclical instability of the system. While the analysis so far would seem to suggest that policymakers must choose between either a mounting cash deficit within the government sector, at least temporarily, or the abandonment of their efforts to place the economy on a politically more desirable growth path, there is in fact a way out of the dilemma. Indeed, there are two ways.

If the more rapid rate of expansion by the economy as a whole caused by the upward shift of the government's E curve can be maintained over several periods, thereby giving rise to a belief that the economy's secular growth rate has in fact increased, both the enterprise and household sectors can be expected to respond in a way that leads to their own E curves shifting upward as well. This is because the secular growth rate, $\mathring{G}$, is a parameter of discretionary expenditures in both the enterprise and household sectors. Once convinced that the above-normal sales and employment are more than just temporary cyclical phenomena, business firms can be expected to embark upon a more vigorous capital expansion program and households, to add to their inventory of durable consumption goods at a more rapid rate. This upward shift of the E curves for the enterprise and household sectors, which will be reflected in an upward shift of the aggregate E curve as well, should not be confused with the movement along those two curves described earlier as the aggregate growth rate increases (see section 10.4.3). The latter is the immediate, endogenous response of discretionary expenditures to a higher aggregate growth rate in the current time period. The increase in the growth of discretionary expenditures now being described is that due to the belief of business firms and households that the secular growth rate has increased and their willingness, as a result, to step up the rate at which they are purchasing durable goods. This likely response by business firms and households will, in fact, give policymakers two options regarding the timing of expenditure policy.

10.4.6 The two expenditure policy options

The first option involves a one-time change in expenditure policy—with the desired growth path being reached only after the E curves of the enterprise and household sectors have fully shifted. This is the delayed-response option available to policy makers for guiding the economy across the traverse of historical time from one secular rate of economic expansion to another. Under this option, policymakers are forced to make a judgment as to the rate at which the public sector will need to grow if the desired rate of expansion for the economy as a whole is going to be achieved. Let us assume that the aggregate growth rate which policymakers prefer is $\mathring{G}_2$, as shown in exhibit 10.14. If the relative balance between private and public consumption is going to be left unchanged, then the

Exhibit 10.14

Part a

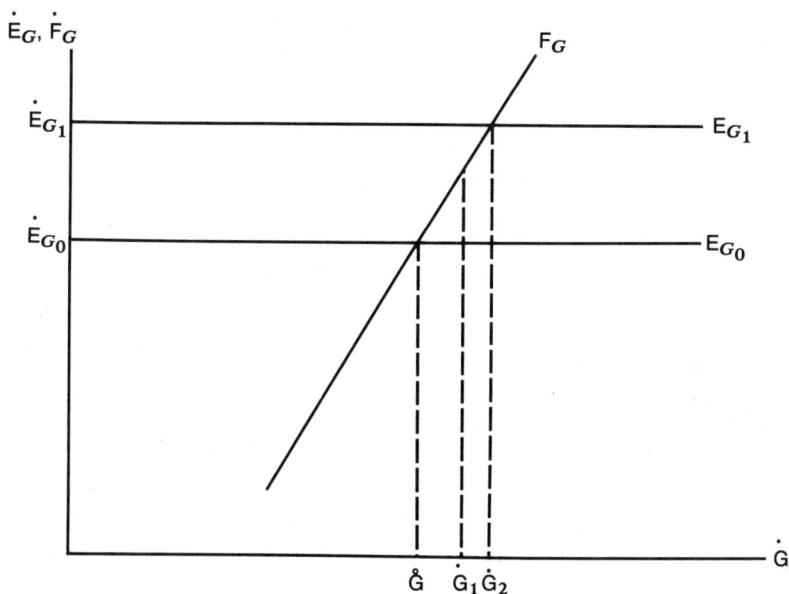

Part b

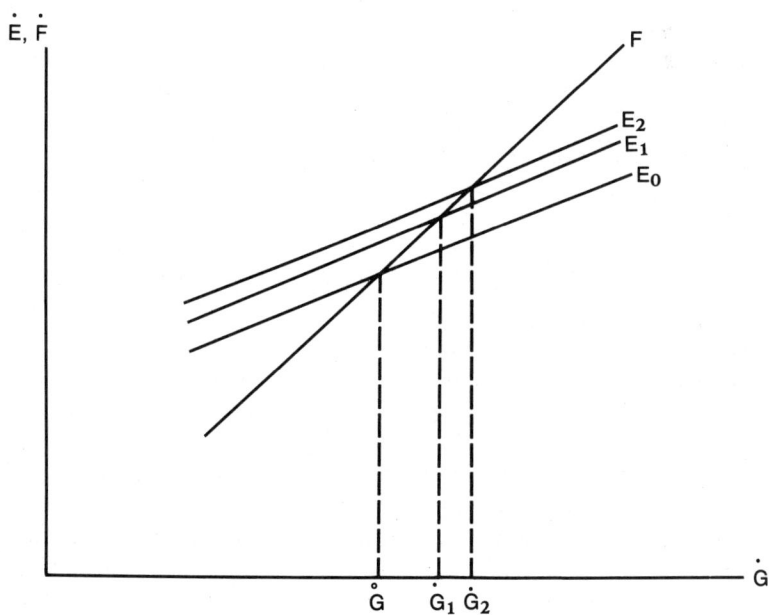

public sector will need to grow, in real terms, at the same rate. Indeed, if the relative balance between the government's discretionary and nondiscretionary expenditures is going to be left unchanged, $\mathring{A}_G$ need only match $\dot{G}_1$. Otherwise, with both c and d free to vary, the public sector will need to grow at a rate, $\dot{G}ov$, which, by offsetting the higher or lower rate at which private consumption is increasing, will enable equation 10.38 to be satisfied. Let us assume that this rate, after taking into account the growth of the price index for the durable goods purchased by the government, is $\dot{E}_{G_1}$.

Once the necessary growth of the public sector has been determined, policy-makers must then make sure that the growth of the government's discretionary expenditures not only increases at the required rate, $\dot{E}_{G_1}$, but also, no less important, remains at that rate. This policy, if pursued for a sufficient length of time, will convince business firms and households that the secular growth rate is now higher and indeed approaching $\dot{G}_1$. Once business firms and households become convinced that the secular growth rate has increased, they can be expected to step up the rate at which they are themselves acquiring durable goods, producing an upward shift of the enterprise and household sectors' E curves. The result, as can be seen from part b of exhibit 10.14, is that the aggregate E curve will itself shift to the right, placing the economy on a more rapid growth path than that represented by $\dot{G}_1$. Indeed, when the subsequent response by the enterprise and household sectors is complete, one can expect that the rate at which the economy as a whole is expanding will be $\dot{G}_2$ making this rather than $\dot{G}_1$ the currently applicable growth rate. The diagrams shown in exhibit 10.14, it should be stressed, represent a subsequent point in time rather than an alternative to the earlier situation shown in exhibit 10.13.

As can be seen from exhibit 10.14, when the economy eventually reaches the secular growth path represented by $\dot{G}_2$, the government will no longer be troubled by a cash deficit that is increasing relative to the amount of discretionary funds being generated. This is because, with the additional tax revenues which can then be collected, the growth of discretionary funds will match the growth of the government's discretionary expenditures, $\dot{E}_{G_1}$, which has enabled that higher rate of economic expansion to be achieved. It is in this way that the government's deficit will eventually be stabilized relative to the size of the public sector under the first of the two options available to policymakers. Notice that, under this first option, the desired growth rate, $\dot{G}_2$, is achieved in two stages. The government's fiscal policy is first used to move the economy from the growth path given by $\dot{G}$ to $\dot{G}_1$. The subsequent response by the enterprise and household sectors, based on the long-period income effect of the more rapid rate of growth, is then relied on to effect a further movement of the economy from $\dot{G}_1$ to $\dot{G}_2$.

Under the second option available to policymakers, the economy is immediately placed on the desired growth path—but the far more pronounced increase in the government's discretionary expenditures which this requires must subsequently be curbed if the economy is not going to overshoot the mark. If $\dot{G}_2$ is again the secular growth path on which policymakers would like to place the

Exhibit 10.15

Part a

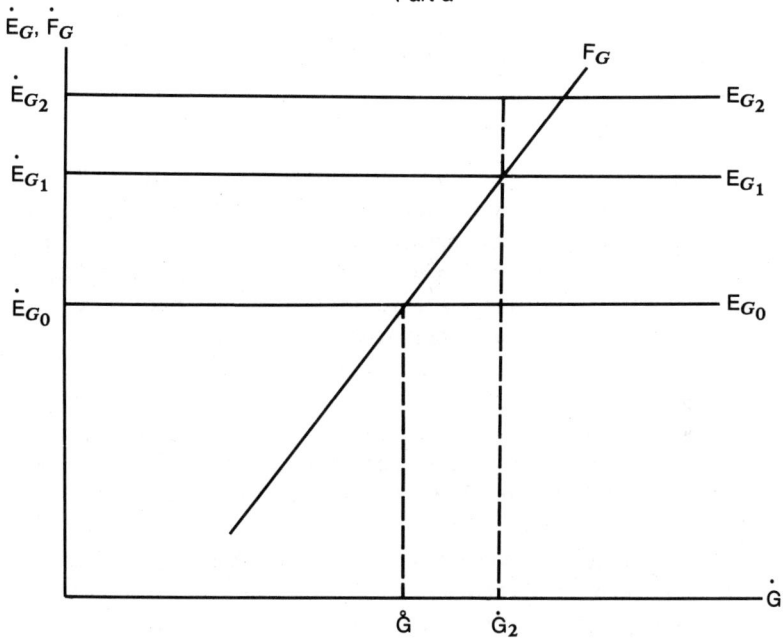

Part b

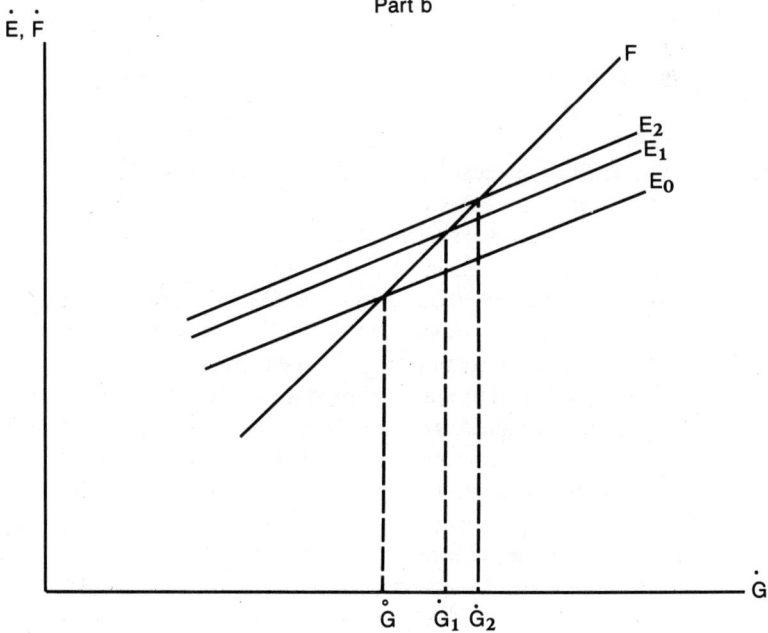

economy—though without the same delay—then the higher rate of growth of discretionary expenditures by the government which will have to be maintained is $\dot{E}_{G_2}$, as shown in part of exhibit 10.15 (rather than $\dot{E}_{G_1}$ as in exhibit 10.14). This higher rate of growth of discretionary expenditures, following the same line of reasoning as before, will mean that, with the shift of the aggregate curve from E_0 directly to E_2, the currently applicable growth rate will be $\dot{G}_2$. The difference is that, if the economy is to remain at $\dot{G}_2$ and not expand at an even more rapid rate, the growth of discretionary expenditures within the government sector will subsequently have to be reduced to offset the upward shift of the enterprise and household sectors' E curves. This means that, if the aggregate E curve is to remain unchanged, with $\dot{G}_2$ not just the currently applicable growth rate but also the new secular rate of expansion, the government's discretionary expenditure curve will eventually have to be lowered from E_{G_2} to E_{G_1}.

As the government's discretionary expenditure curve shifts down from E_{G_2} to E_{G_1}, the size of the cash deficit within the government sector will be stabilized relative to the amount of discretionary funds being generated. This is indicated in exhibit 10.15 by the government's discretionary funds curve, F_G, intersecting its discretionary expenditures curve, E_G, at an aggregate growth rate equal to $\dot{G}_2$. The way in which the size of the deficit is stabilized under this second option—through a subsequent reduction in the government's rate of growth of discretionary expenditures—needs to be distinguished from a policy which precipitously cuts back on the government's discretionary expenditures, without waiting for the higher aggregate growth rate to produce an upward shift of the E curves for the enterprise and household sectors. The latter policy will simply lead to a cyclical movement around the old secular growth path rather than to the economy being placed on a new, more rapid growth path. Indeed, with the precipitous reduction in the government's discretionary expenditures merely initiating a cyclical downturn, the problem of the government's growing cash deficit will only be exacerbated.

What the above analysis suggests is that using the government's expenditure policy to place the economy on a more rapid growth path is likely to prove more complicated a task than a static Keynesian model would suggest. It is not so much that the dynamic adjustment process, based on the combined multiplier and cash-flow feedback effects, is likely to be truncated so that $\dot{G}_2$ will only be approximated rather than actually attained. Rather the difficulty arises from the income effect on the enterprise and household sectors which, by causing the E curves within those sectors to shift, will produce a shift of the aggregate E curve as well. Still, once this complication is understood, policymakers will find that there are two paths the economy can successfully follow in making the necessary transition to the new secular rate of expansion. One path requires a one-time increase in the rate of growth of the government's discretionary expenditures, with the government then holding to that higher rate while the subsequent increase in the rate of growth of discretionary expenditures within the enterprise and household sectors leads to a further upward shift of the aggregate E curve. The alternative path requires an even greater increase in the rate of growth of the government's discretionary expenditures, at least initially, but then permits a gradual reduction in the government's rate of growth of discretionary expenditures so that, with the subsequent increase in the rate of growth of discretionary expenditures within the enterprise and household sectors, the aggregate E curve remains unchanged.

While the second option might seem preferable since it will enable the economy to achieve the desired long-period rate of expansion more quickly, policymakers will find themselves facing two problems if they should elect to follow that path across the traverse that separates one secular growth path from another. The first is that they will need to closely calibrate the subsequent reduction in the rate of growth of the government's discretionary expenditures so that the downward shift of that sector's E curve merely compensates for the upward movement of the enterprise and household sectors' E curves. Otherwise, the economy will either exceed or fall short of the target growth rate. The second problem is that, even if policymakers should succeed in fully offsetting the subsequent upward movement of the other sectors' E curves, the change in the government's rate of growth of discretionary expenditures will introduce a cyclical movement of its own within the industries which produce the structures and other durable goods purchased by the government. Whichever of the two paths is successfully followed, however, policymakers can count on the government's deficit being reduced to a fixed proportion of its tax revenues, or discretionary funds, once the income effect of the higher secular growth rate on discretionary expenditures within the enterprise and household sectors fully manifests itself. If, on the other hand, policymakers fail to take into account the subsequent income effect from the higher secular growth rate, they run the risk of either increasing the cyclical instability of the economy or placing it on a more rapid growth path than is desired—the disadvantage of the latter being an unsatisfactory rate of increase in consumption (see chapter 4, section 2.1).

So far the discussion has been solely in terms of a more expansionary expenditure policy and the complications likely to arise therefrom. The arguments, and the complications, would be the same for the opposite case of a less expansionary expenditure policy. It is just that the arguments would need to be reversed—with the rate of growth of the government's discretionary expenditures, $\dot{E}_G$, in that case being reduced and then maintained at a lower level. A reduction in the value of $\dot{E}_G$, it should be noted, means only that the rate of *increase* is less, not that the government's durable goods purchases actually decline. Were the government's discretionary expenditures to fall in absolute terms, the most likely result would be a cyclical downturn rather than just a movement to a lower secular growth rate. How pronounced the cyclical downturn would be would depend on the extent to which there was an offsetting increase in the rate of growth of private consumption and/or how quickly the government's expenditure policy was reversed. The arguments presented so far need to be significantly modified only when the discussion shifts from an expenditure-based to a tax-based fiscal policy.

10.4.7 A change in tax policy

Just as a change in expenditure policy can be equated with a shift of the government's E curve, so a change in tax policy can be represented by a shift of that sector's F curve. If tax rates decline, the government's F curve will shift downward, and this change in the position of the government's F curve can be viewed as having a stimulative effect on the economy similar to that produced by an upward shift of the government's E curve. However, a change in tax policy is only superficially the obverse of a change in expenditure policy. Indeed, another reason for abandoning the static framework of the conventional macroeconomic theory is so the quite different effect produced by a change in tax policy, compared to a change in expenditure policy, can be made clear.

There are three things about a change in tax policy that will lead to a quite different result, insofar as $\mathring{G}$ is concerned. One is that the government can specify by law only the *rate* at which it taxes the various income flows—sales revenue, wages, profits, etc. It cannot specify the *amount* of taxes it will actually collect. The latter depends, in addition to the various tax rates, on how large are the income flows being taxed. This means that once the tax rates represented by the X_T vector has been enacted into law, the amount of tax revenue actually collected by the government, and thus the rate of growth of discretionary funds, $\dot{F}_G$, will depend on a factor over which the government has no direct control—namely, the level of aggregate demand, both secular, as measured by $\mathring{G}$, and cyclical, as measured by $\overset{*}{G}$. This stands in sharp contrast to the government's ability to directly control, through the legislation by which it enacts a budget, the rate of growth of discretionary expenditures, $\dot{E}_G$. The difference is reflected in the fact that, as already pointed out, the government's F function includes $\overset{*}{G}$ as one of the key explanatory variables while its E function does not (see section 10.4.2). It should be noted that being unable to directly control the growth of discretionary funds is not a condition unique to the government sector. For megacorps, too, it is only the *rate* at which funds are being generated which they can hope to control directly—with the relevant rate, in their case, being the value of μ implicit in their choice of what markup they will attempt to establish. The actual amount of cash flow generated, and thus the rate of growth of discretionary funds, will then depend on the level of aggregate demand (see chapter 7, sections 3.2 and 4.4).

The dependence of $\dot{F}_G$ on $\overset{*}{G}$ means that a change in the various tax schedules, as represented by the X_T vector, will primarily alter the slope of the government's F curve. As can be seen from exhibit 10.16, a change in the slope of the F curve will, of course, also produce a change in the vertical position of that curve at whatever growth rate is used as the point of reference. Moreover, even the constant term, or vertical intercept, of the F curve (the point at which it intersects the vertical axis) will be altered if the minumum amount of income subject to a tax, Y_m, changes along with the rates themselves. Nonetheless, a shift of the government's F curve will be different in a fundamental way from a shift of the corresponding E curve. As can be seen from exhibit 10.16, the F curve will rotate

Exhibit 10.16

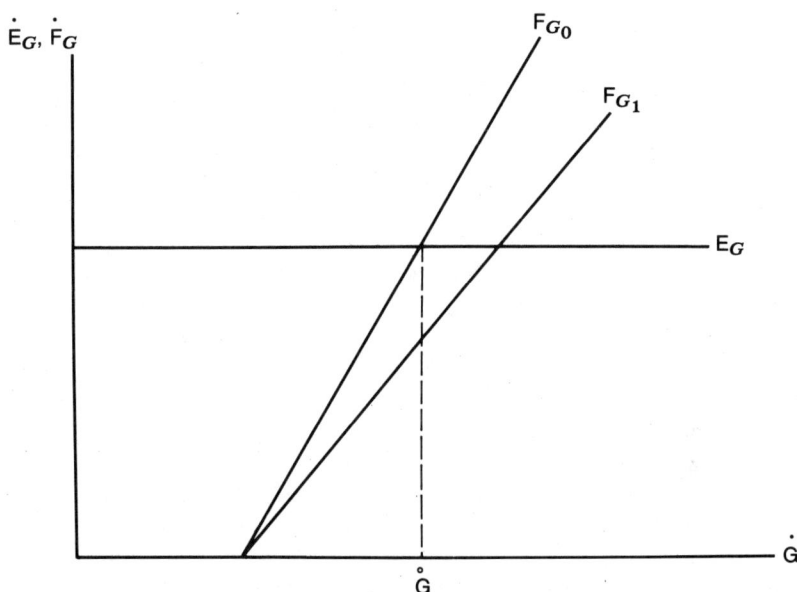

around the point at which it intersects the horizontal axis rather than simply shift up and down, as the E curve will, in a parallel movement. This quite different way in which the F curve shifts is more than just a minor mathematical point. It reflects a second important difference between a change in the government's expenditure policy and a change in its tax policy.

As already pointed out, a change in expenditure policy will give rise to a combined multiplier and cash-flow feedback effect as the shift of the E curve leads directly, via the attendant shift of the aggregate E curve, to a new rate of expansion that will then be the currently applicable growth rate for the economy as a whole. In contrast, a change in tax policy will have no multiplier effect of its own. This is because the new tax rates will not be sufficient, in themselves, to induce a subsequent change in expenditures by the other sectors on nondurable goods and services. The change in tax rates will, instead, give rise only to a cash-flow feedback effect, based on how much the new tax rates affect the size of the current cash deficit within the government sector, $E_G - F_G$. It is, of course, true that the size of the government deficit, through the role it plays in determining the discrepancy between total discretionary expenditures and total discretionary funds, $E - F$, and thus the magnitude of the overall cash-flow feedback effect, will be one of the factors determining the level of aggregate demand. However, it does not follow that a shift of the government's F curve will *per se* make a difference insofar as the level of aggregate demand is concerned. The reason is that, while a shift of the government's E curve will lead to an attendant shift of the aggregate E curve as well, a shift of the government's F curve will leave the aggregate F curve unchanged. This, in turn, reflects a third crucial difference between a change in expenditure policy and a change in tax policy.

The parameters that cause the sectoral E curves to shift up and down tend to be variables, such as the size of the cash deficit or some policy variable, which apply only to that particular sector. Even when the variable is one that affects the rate of growth of discretionary expenditures more generally, such as the degree of liquidity pressure being exerted by the central bank or the level of long-term interest rates, it will cause all the E curves to shift in the same direction. In contrast, the parameters of the government's and the other sectoral F curves consist of various intersectoral compensation rates. A change in any of those variables, while causing a sector's F curve to rotate in one direction, will cause the F curve of the other sector with which it shares that parameter to rotate in the opposite direction.

For example, an increase in the personal income tax rate will cause the government's F curve to rotate upward but it will, at the same time, cause the household sector's F curve to rotate downward. Since there is no parameter of its own F curve that a sector does not share with some other sector—the $\overset{\circ}{Z}$ parameter of the enterprise sector's F curve being the only exception—there is no sectoral F curve which can shift without producing at least a partially offsetting shift of some other sector's F curve. As a result, the position of the aggregate F curve will remain unchanged despite whatever may be the shifts occurring in the sectoral curves. Indeed, this is why the parameters of each sector's F curve are termed intersectoral compensation rates: They only determine the distribution of income, or funds, between sectors—and not the rate at which income is increasing within the system as a whole. This distinguishing characteristic of the aggregate and sectoral F curves' parameters is, in turn, one of the reasons why a change in tax policy cannot be counted on, in the same way that a change in expenditure policy can, to effect a change in the aggregate growth rate, G.

A change in any one of the various tax schedules will make a difference, insofar as the aggregate growth rate is concerned, only if the sector subject to the tax can be expected to respond differently from the government to the resulting change in the size of its cash deficit. If, for example, the corporate income tax rates were to be reduced, this would lead to a lower rate of growth of discretionary funds for the government sector but, at the same time, to a higher rate of growth of discretionary funds for the corporate component of the enterprise sector. The resulting reduction in the corporate sector's cash deficit (or, as it may be, the resulting increase in its cash surplus) would thus be offset by an increase in the government sector's cash deficit (or, alternatively, by a decrease in the government's cash surplus). This is why the aggregate F curve will remain unchanged. However, the two sectors may respond quite differently, insofar as their durable goods purchases, or discretionary expenditures, are concerned, to an equal though opposite change in the size of the sectoral cash deficit. As can be seen from equation 10.25, the size of the sectoral deficit, $E_i - F_i$, can be considered one of the factors that will determine each sector's rate of growth of discretionary expenditures. If the value of the coefficient attached to that explanatory variable differs across sectors, then a change in tax rates may indeed cause the aggregate E curve to shift, thereby making some other growth rate the currently applicable one even if the aggregate F curve itself remains unchanged.

Thus the possibility of the economy being stimulated through a reduction in tax rates cannot be ruled out. This is especially so since the rate of growth of discretionary expenditures by the federal government, unlike the rate of growth of discretionary expenditures within the other sectors of the economy, is unaffected by the size of the sectoral cash deficit (see section 10.4.2). This means that the decline in tax rates, while making no difference insofar as the federal government's outlays are concerned, can be expected to induce business firms and/or households to step up their rate of expenditures on durable goods. Indeed, it is precisely this anticipated response by business firms and households that provides the rationale for cutting taxes as a means of placing the economy on a more rapid growth path.

Still, one must not exaggerate the likely stimulative effect of a reduction in tax rates. For one thing, the increased rate of growth of discretionary funds, or net cash inflow, may simply mean more ''savings''—in the form of bank deposits and other short-term liquid assets—by the sector for which the applicable tax rates have been reduced. In other words, the reduction in taxes may lead to ''financial'' as distinct from ''tangible'' investment (to use the actual terminology of the U.S. Flow of Funds Accounts). This is especially true if it is the corporate sector which has benefited from the reduction in tax rates. Without some other stimulus to aggregate demand so that the rate of growth of sales (or the rate of capacity utilization) is increased, megacorps will have no reason to step up their rate of capital spending, leaving the aggregate E as well as the aggregate F curve unchanged by the reduction in tax rates.

A reduction in the personal income and other tax rates directly applicable to households is, of course, more like to have a stimulative effect on the economy. As previously pointed out (see chapter 9, sections 1.4 and 3.1), any increase in income will cause households to add new items, durable ones among them, to the inventory of consumption goods they normally maintain. Thus, even if the first response by households to the reduction in tax rates is to increase their ''savings,'' still as they come to realize that their cash flow has actually increased, households can be expected to step up their rate of spending on durable and other consumption goods. While an increase in the size of their contingency funds may be one of the ways in which households choose to use the additional flow of income, it is unlikely that this will be considered the next best use of the increased income by all households. One can therefore expect the household sector's E curve, and thus the aggregate E curve as well, to shift up as a result of the reduction in tax rates.

Even so, the reduction in the tax rates applicable to households cannot be just a temporary one. It must be maintained long enough to convince households that their ''permanent'' income—that is, the income they can count on in the long period—has actually increased. If this happens, and the additional cash flow leads to a more rapid growth of expenditures by households, then business firms will eventually be induced, by the more rapid growth of sales, to step up their capital outlays as well. However, this means that the stimulative effect produced by a shift of the government's F curve will not be as immediate as that produced by a shift in the opposite direction of its E curve. As a result, the government will need to incur the same increase in the relative size of its cash deficit over a longer period of time just to achieve the same stimulative effect. Moreover, the stimulative effect is likely to be negligible, even allowing for the additional time required, unless it is the household sector, rather than the enterprise sector, which directly benefits from the reduction in tax rates. This is why a change in tax policy is less immediately effective, if not altogether useless, as a means of placing the economy on a more rapid growth path.

Varying the tax rates represented by the X_t vector can, instead, be used to serve a different purpose. A change in any of those rates will, as already pointed out, alter the slope of the government's F curve. It will thus alter the slope of the aggregate F curve as well—although only proportionately as much. A change in the average profit margin, because of the effect on the slope of the enterprise sector's F curve, will, of course, produce a similar result. The change in the slope of the aggregate F curve will, in turn, alter the stability properties of the economic system. On the one hand, a reduction in tax rates, by making the government's F curve and thus the aggregate F curve less elastic, will make the economy itself endogenously less stable. This can be seen from exhibit 10.17 where it is assumed that a reduction in tax rates has caused the total discretionary funds curve to shift from the position represented by F_0 to that represented by F_1. With the aggregate F curve thus having a lesser slope, any displacement of the economy from the secular growth path will give rise to a lesser cash-flow feedback effect, as measured by the discrepancy between $\dot{F}$ and $\dot{E}$ at $\dot{G}_1$, with more time therefore required to return the economy to its secular growth path. On the other hand, the same reduction in tax rates, by giving the aggregate F curve less of a slope, will make it easier to place the economy on a more rapid growth path. This can be seen from exhibit 10.18, where a shift of the total discretionary expenditures curve from E_0 to E_1 is what is required to place the economy on the growth path represented by $\dot{G}_1$ when the total discretionary funds curve is in the position represented by F_0 while a shift of the total discretionary expenditures curve from E_0 to E_2 is what is required to achieve the same secular rate of expansion when, due to a change in tax rates or some other set of parameters, the total discretionary funds curve has rotated so that it is now in the position represented by F_1.

The argument also holds in reverse. An increase in the various tax rates will cause the aggregate F curve to have a greater slope, and while this will make the economy endogenously more stable, it also means that a more pronounced shift of the aggregate E curve will be required to place the economy on a different growth path. Thus there are trade-offs in making the economic system endogenously more or less stable. This point will not be pursued any further until chapter 14.

Exhibit 10.17

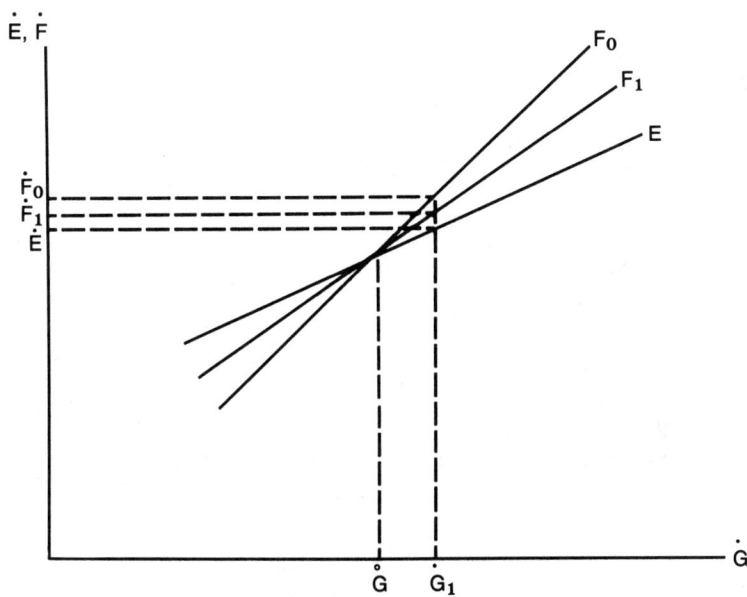

Exhibit 10.18

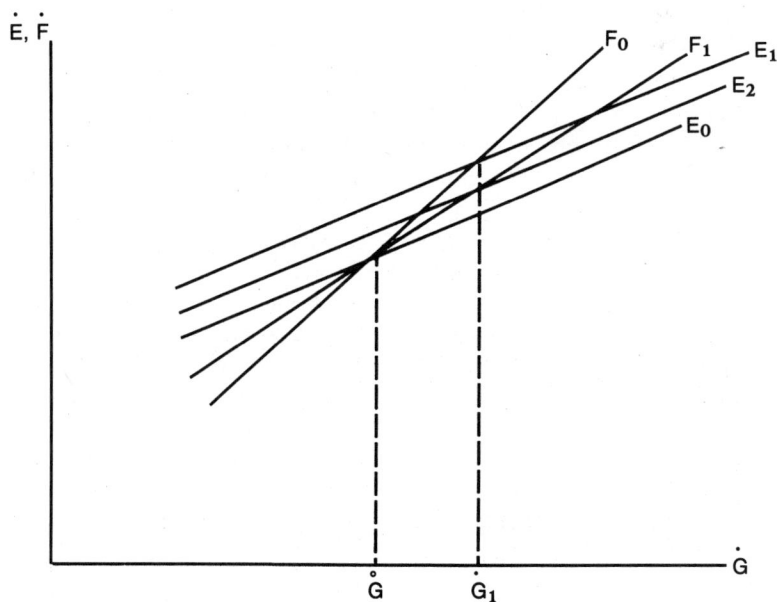

We first need to examine the rest-of-the-world sector and then, once the sectoral analysis has been completed, see what constraints there may be, monetary or otherwise, on the growth path which the society through its political institutions can choose.

Recommended Readings

The model of democratic government developed in this chapter draws heavily on Anthony Downs, *An Economic Theory of Democracy*, New York: Harper & Row, 1957, as well as on the efforts by others to apply the principles of cybernetics to the political system. For the latter, see Karl Deutsch, *The Nerves of Government*, New York: Free Press, 1966; Amitai Etzioni, *The Active Society*, New York: Free Press, 1968; Talcott Parsons, *Politics and Social Structure*, New York: Free Press, 1969. For a quite different approach to modeling the governmental process, see James Buchanan and Gordon Tullock, *The Calculus of Consent*, Ann Arbor: University of Michigan Press, 1962. On the liberal model of the state, see David B. Truman, *The Governmental Process*, New York: Knopf, 1971.

On market failure, see Francis M. Bator, "The Anatomy of Market Failure," *Quarterly Journal of Economics*, August 1958; William Baumol, *Welfare Economics and the Theory of the State*, Cambridge, Mass.: Harvard University Press, 1965; Mancur Olson, *The Logic of Collective Action*, Cambridge, Mass.: Harvard University Press, 1965. See also Robert H. Haveman, *The Economics of the Public Sector*, New York: Wiley, 1970. The essay by Keynes on "The Decline of Laissez-Faire" can be found in his collection, *Essays in Persuasion*, reprinted as vol. 9 in *The Collected Writings of John Maynard Keynes*, London: Macmillan for the Royal Economic Society, 1973. The case of a pure public good was first identified by Paul Samuelson. See his "The Pure Theory of Public Expenditures," *Review of Economic and Statistics*, November 1954; "Diagrammatic Exposition of a Theory of Public Finance," *ibid.*, November 1955, and "Aspects of Public Expenditure Theories," *ibid.*, November 1958. However, the concept has required further refining by other economists. See J. C. Head, "Public Goods and Public Policy," *Public Finance*, no. 3, 1962; Peter O. Steiner, "Public Expenditure Budgeting," in *The Economics of Public Finance*, Washington: Brookings Institution, 1974.

On the problem of determining which governmental programs should be funded, see Charles Schultze, *The Politics and Economics of Public Spending*, Washington: Brookings Institution, 1968; Alice Rivlin, *Systematic Thinking for Social Action*, Washington: Brookings Institution, 1976; Alfred S. Eichner and Charles Brecher, *Controlling Social Expenditures*, Montclair, N.J.: Allenheld & Osmun, 1979. On cost-benefit analysis, see A. R. Prest and R. Turvey, "Cost-Benefit Analysis: A Survey," *Economic Journal*, December 1965, reprinted in American Economic Association and Royal Economic Society, *Surveys of Economic Theory*, III, London: Macmillan, 1966; E. J. Mishan, *Cost-Benefit Analysis*, New York: Praeger, 1971.

On the post-Keynesian theory of tax incidence, see Michal Kalecki, "A Theory of Commodity, Income and Capital Taxation," *Economic Journal*, 1937, reprinted in his *Selected Essays on the Dynamics of the Capitalist Economy*, London: Cambridge University Press, 1971, ch. 4; John Eatwell, "On the Proposed Reform of Corporation Tax," *Bulletin of the Oxford Institute of Economics and Statistics*, November 1971; A. Asimakopulos and John B. Burbridge, "The Short-Period Incidence of Taxation," *Economic Journal*, June 1974. As for the empirical evidence on the shiftability of the corporate income tax, see Marian Kzyzaniak and Richard A. Musgrave, *The Shiftability of the Corporate Income Tax*, Baltimore: Johns Hopkins Press, 1963; J. G. Cragg, Arnold C. Harberger and Peter Mieszkowski, "Empirical Evidence of the Incidence of the Corporation Income Tax," *Journal of Political Economy*, December 1967; John B. Burbridge, "Internally Inconsistent Mixtures of Micro- and Macrotheory in Empirical Studies of Profits Tax Incidence," *Finanzarchiv*, no. 2, 1976. For the conventional analysis of tax incidence, see Richard A. Musgrave, *The Theory of Public Finance*, New York: McGraw-Hill, 1959. On the analysis of transfer payment programs, see Christopher Green, *Negative Taxes and the Poverty Problem*, Washington: Brookings Institution, 1967.

Chapter 12

Money and Credit

Contents

These last two parts are not yet completed.

Chapter 12

Money and Credit

So far, little has been said about the role which money plays in an economy, national or international. This may seem surprising in view of the claim made at the outset that post-Keynesian theory is meant to apply to a monetarized, as distinct from a barter, system. The neglect of money has been more apparent than real, however.

First, the existence of a monetarized system has been implicit in all that has been said up to this point. There would be no dual solution to the Leontief model of production if money did not play an intervening role in all transactions. Only when goods are exchanged for money, and not simply bartered for other goods or allocated physically, is it necessary to ensure that the revenue obtained from the sale of any output will be sufficient to cover all the costs of production, including the cost of expansion. The fact that the disaggregated, sectoral analysis of the preceding seven chapters has been based on a Leontief input-output model with a dual price solution is therefore one clear sign that the system being described is a monetarized one. Moreover, in the absence of money, there would not be separate E and F curves for each of the different sectors. It is only because of the same intervening role of money that investment and savings—or, more broadly, discretionary expenditures and discretionary funds—can deviate from one another. Thus the adoption of a flow-of-funds framework and the derivation of separate E and F curves for each of the different sectors based on that set of accounts are a further sign that what is being modeled is a monetarized production system.

Nonetheless, the role which money plays in an advanced economy like that of the United States has yet to be made explicit. This lack of attention to money *per se* is no accident. It reflects the belief among post-Keynesians that while monetary factors are clearly important—and indeed, under certain circumstances, may be critical—they are typically less important than the real factors which have been emphasized up to this point. It is not, as some critics of this and other Keynesian-inspired theories have charged, that "money does not matter." It is rather that other factors matter more, and until those other factors have been identified, one cannot distinguish the separate influence of money. This is why it is only now that the disaggregated, sectoral analysis of the preceding chapters has been completed that the question of what role monetary factors play can be properly addressed.

Monetary factors, to the extent they influence business investment and other durable goods purchases, are perhaps most important in explaining any short-period change in real output and thus the economy's cyclical movements. Even within that time frame, however, monetary factors normally play only a marginal role. It is not just that business investment is likely to be financed primarily from internal funds. It is also, even more significantly, that the existing set of monetary institutions is designed to be largely accommodating to whatever need for credit business firms, and indeed purchasers of durable goods in general, may have. This, in turn, makes the amount of money—or rather, the amount of funds in circulation—an endogenously determined variable.

12.1 The Endogeneity of Money

It has been the practice among economists—at least since the Hicks-Hansen interpretation of the *The General Theory* became the prevailing one—to posit the existence of an exogenously determined stock of money. It is then assumed, as an extension of the Marshallian supply-and-demand framework to the monetary sphere, that the central bank can vary the stock of money independently of the demand. It is precisely this assumption which is challenged by the argument that what serves as the means of payment under a credit-based system of money is endogenously determined. To present this alternative line of argument, we shall first need to explain what a credit-based system of money is and how it differs from both commodity and fiat money. We shall then expand upon the flow of funds model which has underlain the analysis of the preceding chapters to include a financial sector consisting, at the very least, of banks. Finally, we shall use this expanded flow of funds model to trace out the separate real, financial and monetary effects of a net increase in debt as well as a net increase in savings.

12.1.1 Credit-based money

The necessary starting point, in analyzing the role of money and credit, is to recognize that an advanced industrial economy like that of the United States is a monetarized production system (see chapter 1, section 1.1), and that such a system presumes the existence of credit-based, as distinct from commodity or even fiat, money. A credit-based system of money has two distinguishing features. One is the means by which payment is normally made in any business transaction, and the second is the means by which the amount of funds in circulation is increased.

Under a credit-based system of money, payment is normally made by check, or bank draft. A check is a piece of paper authorizing the bank holding the funds of the party making the purchase (i.e., the buyer's bank) to transfer a certain amount of those funds to the individual or organization designated as the payee (i.e., the seller). Ordinarily, the payee will then deposit the check in its own account at some bank so that the transaction, on the monetary side, actually entails a shift of funds from one bank account to another, whether with the same bank or two different banks. It is, of course, possible to hold funds in the form of some national currency rather than depositing the funds in a bank. This, however,

Exhibit 12.1
Income Statement of Representative Economic Entity

	Gross Income	$150,000
—	Current Outlays	80,000
=	Net Cash Inflow	$ 70,000
—	Durable Goods Purchases	60,000
=	ΔBank Balance	$ 10,000

Exhibit 12.2
Change in Balance Sheet of Representative Economic Entity
(Nonfinancial)

ΔAssets		ΔLiabilities	
ΔBank Balance	$10,000	ΔLoans Outstanding	0
ΔOther Assets	0	ΔNet Worth	$10,000
Total Change	$10,000	Total Change	$10,000

is typical only for those engaged in small, retail transactions, including those active in what is termed "the underground economy." For virtually all other business firms, and indeed even for most households, payment is normally made by check.

This system for effecting payment presumes that every economic entity— whether it be a business firm, household, separate level of government or non-profit organization—has an account at some bank, with a positive balance maintained at all times. Any sums received in payment by one of these entities will be deposited in its bank account, and any sums paid out will be transferred, by check, to the bank account of the different economic entity to whom the amount is due. The difference between the amount received, over a given interval of time, and the amount paid out will determine what change, if any, has occurred in the economic entity's bank balance, that is, the amount of funds deposited in some bank (see exhibit 12.1). While the change in its bank balance will be only one of the factors determining the economic entity's current financial position (see exhibit 12.2), there are two reasons for focusing on that variable, at least for the moment. First, an increase in the amount of funds deposited in some bank must precede the acquisition of any other type of financial asset. Second, it is through a change in the amount of funds held in some bank that the economy's real and monetary flows are linked. Both these points will be further elaborated on as the analysis proceeds.

A system of payment based on checks also presumes the existence of one or more banks as part of a separate financial sector. A bank is a business enterprise which, alone, is legally empowered to do two things:

1) accept deposits and then, up to the limit set by the amount of funds deposited with it, honor checks ordering funds transferred from one account to another, either within the same bank or between two different banks; and

2) make loans by crediting the borrower's account at the bank with a stipulated amount of funds in return for signing a "note" agreeing to pay back an even larger sum in the future.

The deposits which, on the one hand, it accepts and the loans which, on the other hand, it makes give rise to the type of asset and liability structure which uniquely characterizes a bank (see exhibit 12.3). The bank's liabilities necessarily include the funds which have been deposited with it while its assets necessarily include, in addition to any "currency" or other "reserves," the notes it holds as evidence of the loans it has made. In contrast, a nonfinancial economic entity, like the one represented in exhibit 12.2, need have no financial liabilities. Moreover, its assets necessarily include the balance maintained at some bank rather than the notes obtained from making loans to other economic entities. Making loans to credit-worthy customers is, in fact, the specialized function which banks serve.

The financial sector need not be limited to banks alone. Indeed, as will be pointed out shortly, the financial sector cannot be said to be fully developed unless it includes, along with a significant number of private banks, a publicly accountable central bank to serve as both the monetary authority and the fail-safe mechanism for the system as a whole. Moreover, a well developed financial sector may well encompass, as the case of the United States demonstrates, various other types of financial institutions. These include brokerage firms and other financial market makers to help arrange for the sale of long-term securities, nonbank financial intermediaries such as life insurance companies and mutual funds, and specialized lenders such as factors and household finance companies. Still, the indispensable component of the financial sector is a group of banks, or depository institutions. These banks, together with the monetary authority, or central bank, and the various nonbank financial institutions constitute the financial as distinct from the nonfinancial component of the enterprise sector.

Once a financial sector with banks as the key component has evolved, payment relying on commodity or even fiat money is likely to be superseded, in the majority of business transactions, by a system of payment based on checks. This

ΔCurrency	$ 0	ΔDeposits	$10,000
ΔOther Reserves	10,000	ΔOther Liabilities	0
ΔLoans	0	ΔNet Worth	0
ΔOther Assets			
Total Change	$10,000	Total Change	$10,000

is not just because of the greater ease and security with which large sums can be transferred. It is also because a system of payment based on checks makes it possible, through the process by which banks make loans, to vary the amount of funds in circulation. Indeed, this advantage helps to explain why a system of credit-based money is likely to evolve coincidental with the process of industrialization itself. As already pointed out, the financial problem inherent in any market-regulated system of production is that goods cannot be produced until the necessary material inputs have first been obtained and those inputs cannot be purchased except out of the proceeds from the sale of the output produced from the inputs. This creates the need, on the part of business firms, for working capital, and while this need can be satisfied, at least initially during the early stages of industrialization, out of the profits from trade, it is likely to be only a matter of time until a group of specialized firms known as banks emerge to provide other firms with working capital on a routine basis (see chapter 6, section 1.2). The advantage of relying on banks to provide business firms with working capital is that the amount of funds in circulation will then be responsive to the level of economic activity. This is in sharp contrast to what happens when the only means of payment is some form of either commodity or fiat money.

Commodity money is a physical good which is then used as the means of payment in most, if not all, transactions. While in theory the physical output of any industry can serve as money, the choice had, as a practical matter, come to be limited until relatively recent times to the two precious metals, gold and silver. The very same attribute which enabled these two metals to serve so effectively as money, namely, their relatively limited supply, became the source of increasing dysfunction once the world, or at least the countries straddling the English channel, entered the modern period of continuous economic expansion. The growth of the Dutch and British economies after 1600 was constrained by, among other factors, the inelastic supply of gold and silver. There were, in fact, only two ways in which the money supply in this form could be increased. One was to work goods. Not until the new nation states learned how to exploit the invention of the printing press would an alternative to commodity money finally become available. That alternative was fiat money.

The fiat money created when the government declares that paper engraved in a certain way shall be legal tender also takes a physical form, but the paper on which the currency is printed is itself intrinsically of little value. Unlike gold or silver, it cannot be diverted to other, nonmonetary uses. Fiat money instead takes its value from the fact that it can be used to pay whatever taxes are owed the government. Once acceptable to the government, it is then likely to become acceptable more generally as a means of making payment, at least within that one political jurisdiction. However, the very same attribute which recommends fiat money over commodity money, namely, the greater control which the government can exercise over its supply, soon became a source of dissatisfaction with that form of money. The problem was the difficulty the government had in making sure there was enough money in circulation—but not too much. Indeed the task appeared to be beyond the capability of any public body subject to political pressures that reflected a different dynamic from that governing the economy. What was needed was some other mechanism for ensuring an adequate supply of money, one that would respond automatically and independently of the political authorities to the changing need for a circulating medium as the level of economic activity fluctuated over time. This alternative mechanism turned out to be the various private banks, linked to one another in such a way as to form a credit-based system for effecting payment, initially by means of bank notes and then, subsequently, by means of checks or bank drafts.

Under a credit-based system of money, the amount of funds in circulation depends on the need for working capital by business firms (along with the need for other types of short-term credit). Whenever business firms experience an increase in orders and therefore must act to expand output, they can be expected to seek bank loans to finance the purchase of the inputs, labor and material, they need. With a contract in hand for the delivery of goods some time in the future, a business firm will, under ordinary circumstances, have no trouble obtaining a loan from any one of the banks with which it maintains an account. The bank, on its part, will simply credit the firm's account with the amount sought as a loan. In this way, the firm will gain a bank balance it did not previously have—and against which it can then write checks in payment for any labor services or material inputs. Meanwhile, both the bank's assets (under the heading of loans) and its liabilities (under the heading of deposits) will increase by the amount of the loan

---

Exhibit 12.4

Change in Balance Sheet as a Result of Bank Lending

Business Firm

ΔAssets		ΔLiabilities	
ΔBank Balance	$5,000	ΔLoans Outstanding	$5,000
ΔOther Assets	0	ΔNet Worth	0
Total Change	$5,000	Total Change	$5,000

Business Firm's Bank

ΔAssets		ΔLiabilities	
ΔCurrency	0	ΔDeposits	$5,000
ΔOther Reserves	0	ΔOther Liabilities	0
ΔLoans	$5,000	ΔNet Worth	0
ΔOther Assets	0		
Total Change	$5,000	Total Change	$5,000

(see exhibit 12.4). With the amount of funds which can circulate in payment for goods and services limited to the amount of funds held as deposits by banks, any loan by a bank, since it will also increase the bank's deposits, necessarily increases the amount of funds in circulation.

The process also works in reverse. As loans are paid off without being renewed or offset by loans to other parties, the total amount of funds held as deposits by banks will decline. Indeed, this is why the term "credit-based system of money" applies. Any change in the amount of funds circulating as drafts against bank deposits will depend on the demand for loans, or credit. Nonetheless, some form of fiat, if not commodity, money is likely to be retained as an essential component of the credit-based system. This is because, in order to induce a bank's customers to deposit their funds with it, the bank must be able to repay them in something other than a check drawn on the bank's own account. In other words, the bank needs some type currency to serve as a reserve, and this can only take the form of commodity or fiat money. While in the earlier stage of their evolution, banks would have little choice but to hold a certain amount of gold or silver so as to be able to satisfy the demand of depositors for repayment, more recently with the establishment of stable governments prepared to use their considerable taxing power to support a national currency, commodity money has generally been replaced by fiat money as the form in which banks hold at least part of their reserves. However, before going into this matter of reserves more thoroughly, we need to expand upon the flow of funds model that has been relied on up to this point.

12.2 An expanded flow of funds model

It is not difficult to make the argument in the preceding chapters consistent with what has just been said about how payment is effected and the amount of funds in circulation increased under a credit-based system of money. All that is necessary is to show the interchangeability of the different terms which are used to describe the same set of real and monetary flows. The net cash inflow of an economic entity is what, in the official U.S. Flow of Funds Accounts, is termed its "Gross Savings" and what, in this text, has been relabeled the entity's discretionary funds. Meanwhile, any durable goods purchases are what, in the same Flow of Funds Accounts, are termed "Tangible Investment" and what in this text have been relabeled discretionary expenditures. The difference between the two is what, in the Flow of Funds Accounts, is termed "Financial Investment" and what, in this text, has been designated as the entity and/or sector's cash surplus or, when that balance is negative and thus the entity and/or sector is in deficit, its net borrowing (see chapter 2, section 3.5). However, despite the differences in terminology, only one set of real and monetary flows is being described. The real flows are those reflected in the income statement shown in exhibit 12.1 and the monetary flows are those reflected by the corresponding change in the balance sheet for the same economic entity shown in exhibit 12.2. By further tracing out the effect that a change in the balance sheet of some nonfinancial entity has on the balance sheet of some bank or other type of financial institution, we can show the link between the economy's real and monetary flows. First, however, the income statements and balance sheets for the different types of economic entitites—those for banks and other types of financial institutions as well as those for nonfinancial economic entities—need to be aggregated so the analysis can be carried out at the macro as well as at the micro level.

It is the unique source of its gross income, as delineated in exhibit 12.1, that distinguishes one type of nonfinancial economic entity from another. For the type of nonfinancial entity previously denoted as a business firm, or enterprise, that unique source of gross income is sales revenue. For the type of nonfinancial entity previously denoted as a household, the unique source of its gross income is wages, supplemented by dividends and transfer payments. And for the type of nonfinancial entity previously denoted as a sovereign government, the unique source of its gross income is tax revenue. Thus all nonfinancial entities with sales revenue can be grouped together as the constituent parts of a separate business, or enterprise, sector; all the nonfinancial entities with wages, dividends and/or transfer income, can be grouped together as a separate household sector, and all the nonfinancial entities with tax revenue can be grouped together as a separate government and not-for-profit sector. (We shall, for the moment, ignore the rest-of-the-world sector.) These differences in the source of gross income aside, the income statements for each of the different nonfinancial sectors, together with the resulting change in its balance sheet, will be the same as those shown in exhibits 12.1 and 12.2. These two exhibits, together, can therefore be used to represent the flow of funds into and out of any particular nonfinancial sector of the economy. Indeed, this is how the flow of funds tables for the various nonfinancial sectors were previously derived (see chapter 2, part 3).

One can similarly aggregate the income statement and resulting change in balance sheet for each bank and, in this way, derive an additional sectoral account. This would be an account showing the flow of funds into and out of the banking component of the financial sector. The income statement for an individual bank is the same as that shown in exhibit 12.1, except that any difference between a bank's net cash inflow and its durable goods purchases will appear, at least initially, as a change in its net worth and not as a change in the amount of funds deposited with some other entity. For any one bank and for the banking system as a whole, then, the category "Change in Bank Balance" needs to be replaced in the income statement by the category "Change in Net Worth." Still, it is a change in the balance sheet for the banking system as a whole, due to a change in the balance sheets for the various nonfinancial sectors, that serves as the link between the economy's real and monetary flows. For this reason, we can largely ignore the banking sector's current income flows and focus entirely on the changes in its balance sheet.

To obtain a model which can be used to analyze the economy's real and monetary flows simultaneously, we therefore need only augment the flow of funds accounts for at least two of the nonfinancial sectors with a set of accounts representing the banking system's balance sheet, as in exhibit 12.5. The real flows are those shown in the top part of the consolidated account under the headings of gross income, current outlays and durable goods purchases for each of the two nonfinancial sectors. The monetary flows, meanwhile, are the changes in the assets and liabilities of the banking system shown at the bottom, with the changes in the two or more nonfinancial sectors' financial position that is shown in between serving as the connecting link between those monetary flows and the real flows shown at the top. Once the flow of funds model has been expanded in this way, it is then possible to trace out the quite different monetary effects of: (1) a nonfinancial transacton; (2) a net increase in savings; (3) a portfolio shift; and (4) a net increase in debt. The first two of these four possible events will be examined in this subsection, the rest in the subsections which follow. We are now in a position to carry out this type of exercise because the factors causing a change in the various nonfinancial sectors' real flows—the change in their gross income, current outlays and durable goods purchases—have already been identified in the preceding chapters. We can therefore start with a change in one of these real flows, taken as a given, and proceed from there to trace out the subsequent financial and monetary effects, together with any feedback effects on the system's real flows.

Exhibit 12.5

Flow of Funds Model with Separate Financial Sector

Nonfinancial Sector A	Nonfinancial Sector B
Gross Income	Gross Income
− Current Outlays	− Current Outlays
= Net Cash Inflow	= Net Cash Inflow
− Durable Goods Purchases	− Durable Goods Purchases
= Net Financial Change	= Net Financial Change
= ΔBank Balance	= ΔBank Balance
+ ΔOther Assets	+ ΔOther Assets
− ΔLoans Outstanding	− ΔLoans Outstanding
− ΔOther liabilities	− ΔOther liabilities
= Net Financial Change	= Net Financial Change

Banking System

ΔAssets	ΔLiabilities
ΔCurrency	ΔDeposits
+ ΔOther Reserves	+ ΔOther Liabilities
+ ΔLoans	+ ΔNet Worth
+ ΔOther Assets	
= Change in Assets	= Change in Liabilities

A nonfinancial transaction is one that involves two different nonfinancial entities. While a large number of transactions take place between the same type of nonfinancial entity—as, for example, when a business firm purchases a material input from another business firm—a transaction will make a difference in the sectoral accounts only when it occurs between two different types of nonfinancial entities. Any such transaction will necessarily lead to a change in the net cash inflow of the two sectors involved. For example, the purchase of a consumption good by some household will cause the net cash inflow of the enterprise sector to increase and the net cash inflow of the household sector to decline (see exhibit 12.6). Similarly, the payment of the wages due a production worker will cause the net inflow of the enterprise sector to decline and the net cash inflow of the household sector to rise.

The change in the net cash inflow of the two sectors from any such transaction will be mirrored by a change in the bank balances of the same two sectors—if payment is made by check. The bank balance of the sector receiving the payment will increase and the bank balance of the sector making the payment will decline. While one bank may gain and another bank lose deposits as a result of the transaction, the banking system as a whole will be unaffected. The total amount of funds deposited in banks will thus be the same after the transaction is completed as was the case before. This is why, even with a credit-based system of money, the role played by banks need not be made explicit as long as the analysis is restricted, as it has been up to now, to the change in the net cash inflow of the different sectors.

Payment need not, of course, be made by check. As already noted, some form of fiat, if not commodity, money is likely to be retained as an essential component of the credit-based system. Moreover, it is not just the banks which are likely to hold, as a reserve asset, a certain amount of fiat money. Each of the different types of nonfinancial entities—business firms, households and even sovereign governments—will need to keep a certain amount of fiat money on hand as well. This is especially true if the entity engages in frequent, small transactions for which payment in currency and even coins has an advantage over checks. If payment is made in currency, with the currency then being retained by the party receiving the payment, the total amount of funds deposited in banks will again be unaffected by the transaction. The difference is that the transaction will take place outside, rather than through, the banking system. Only if the currency is deposited with or, alternatively, is withdrawn from a bank will the financial sector be affected. We shall take up this further possibility shortly in connection with other types of portfolio shifts. For the moment, all that need be noted is that a nonfinancial sector's cash balances include, besides the funds deposited in some bank, any currency in its own possession and that these funds make it possible to effect payment independently of the banking system. Still, as long as the currency remains part of some nonfinancial sector's cash balances, the total amount of funds deposited in banks will be unaffected. The next step is to see what happens when, instead of a nonfinancial transaction there is a net increase in savings.

An act of saving is a decision by a nonfinancial entity not to use some of its cash inflow to make a purchase. It is the opposite of a transaction in that the net cash inflow of the economic entity making the decision will increase rather than show a decline. The difference can be seen by comparing, as in exhibit 12.6, a transaction between two nonfinancial sectors, such as the purchase of nondurable goods by a household, with an act of saving by the type of economic entity found within just one of those sectors. The act of saving, in the example shown in exhibit 12.6 entails a decision by some business firm to reduce its current outlays by $1,000 while its gross income remains unchanged. As can be seen from exhibit 12.6, the act of saving implies a $1,000 increase in the firm's net cash inflow, a $1,000 increase in the firm's net financial position and a $1,000 increase in the amount of funds deposited in one or more banks. While it might seem that the $1,000 increase in bank deposits would also necessarily imply a $1,000 increase in the assets and liabilities of the banking system—and thus a $1,000 increase in

Exhibit 12.6

Effect on the Flow of Funds of a Transaction Compared to an Act of Saving

Purchase of Nondurable Goods by Households
(Nonfinancial Sector B)

	Nonfinancial Sector A			Nonfinancial Sector B	
	Gross Income	+$1,000		Gross Income	0
−	Current Outlays	0	−	Current Outlays	+$1,000
=	Net Cash Inflow	+$1,000	=	Net Cash Inflow	−$1,000
−	Durable Goods Purchases	0	−	Durable Goods Purchases	0
=	Net Financial Change	+$1,000	=	Net Financial Change	−$1,000
=	ΔBank Balance	+$1,000	=	ΔBank Balance	−$1,000
+	ΔOther Assets	0	+	ΔOther Assets	0
−	Loans Outstanding	0	−	Loans outstanding	0
−	ΔOther liabilities	0	−	ΔOther liabilities	0
=	Net Financial		=	Net Financial	
=	Net Financial Change	+$1,000	=	Net Financial Change	−$1,000

Banking System

	ΔAssets			ΔLiabilities	
	ΔCurrency	0		ΔDeposits	0
+	ΔOther Reserves	0	+	ΔOther Liabilities	0
+	ΔLoans	0	+	ΔNet Worth	0
+	ΔOther Assets	0			
=	Change in Assets	0	=	Change in Liabilities	0

the total amount of funds available for effecting payment as the monetary effect of the firm's net increase in savings—it would be a mistake, as we shall see shortly, to jump to any such conclusion. We first need to be sure we fully understand what, within the expended flow of funds model, is meant by an increase in net savings.

Although it is usually assumed that any increase in the rate of savings will be the deliberate act of some household, exhibit 12.6 makes clear that it could just as well be the deliberate act of some other type of nonfinancial entity, such as a business firm or even a sovereign government. Moreover, the increase in the rate of savings could just as well be the consequence of actions by some other nonfinancial entity besides the one experiencing the greater net cash inflow so that, in this sense, the increase in the rate of savings is involuntary. Besides recognizing that any sector can save (in the sense that its net cash inflow is being increased), it is therefore necessary to distinguish a deliberate act of saving, such as the one shown in exhibit 12.6, from an involuntary one. The former involves a

Exhibit 12.6 (continued)

Reduction in Current Outlays by Business Firms
(Nonfinancial Sector A)

	Nonfinancial Sector A			Nonfinancial Sector B	
	Gross Income	0		Gross Income	0
−	Current Outlays	−$1,000	−	Current Outlays	0
=	Net Cash Inflow	+$1,000	=	Net Cash Inflow	0
−	Durable Goods Purchases	0	−	Durable Goods Purchases	0
=	Net Financial Change	+$1,000	=	Net Financial Change	0
=	ΔBank Balance	+$1,000	=	ΔBank Balance	0
+	ΔOther Assets	0	+	ΔOther Assets	0
−	ΔLoans Outstanding	0	−	ΔLoans outstanding	0
−	ΔOther liabilities	0	−	ΔOther liabilities	0
=	Net Financial Change	+$1,000	=	Net Financial Change	0

Banking System

	ΔAssets			ΔLiabilities	
	ΔCurrency	0		ΔDeposits	+$1,000
+	ΔOther Reserves	0	+	ΔOther Liabilities	0
+	ΔLoans	0	+	ΔNet Worth	0
+	ΔOther Assets	0			
=	Change in Assets	0	=	Change in Liabilities	+$1,000

reduction in some nonfinancial entity's current outlays, the latter an increase in its gross income. Still, it is not whether the greater savings are due to a reduction in current outlays or to an increase in gross income that will determine the subsequent monetary effect.

Actually, as can be seen from exhibit 12.6, what must first be ascertained, even before attempting to determine what the monetary effect, if any, will be is the *net* increase in savings. This is the amount by which a nonfinancial entity's net cash inflow, or *gross* savings, exceeds its durable goods purchases, or investment. The example given in exhibit 12.6 is merely the limiting case of when a nonfinancial entity's durable goods purchases remain unchanged while its gross savings have increased. When a nonfinancial entity purchases a durable good, the effect, insofar as its net cash inflow, or gross savings, is concerned, is no different from when it purchases a nondurable good. Both its net cash inflow and its bank balance will decrease while the net cash inflow and bank balance of the capital goods component of the enterprise sector will rise (see exhibit 12.7). For there to be a *net* increase in a nonfinancial entity's savings with a resulting improvement in its financial position, then either its net cash inflow must increase relative to its durable goods purchases or, alternatively, its durable goods purchases must be reduced while its net cash inflow remains unchanged (see exhibit 12.8).

To summarize, an increase in a nonfinancial sector's net savings, with whatever monetary effect this is likely to have, can come about in any one of the following ways:

1. through an increase in gross income;
2. through a reduction in current outlays; or
3. through a reduction in durable goods purchases.

Either of the first two changes implies an increase in the entity's net cash inflow, or gross savings—with the former, an increase in gross income, giving rise to involuntary savings and the latter, a reduction in current outlays, representing a deliberate act of saving. Still, it is the increase in the entity's gross savings (or net cash inflow) less any change in its durable goods purchases which will then determine the *net* change in its savings—with that net change in savings giving rise to a separate financial effect which takes the form of an increase in the economic entity's bank balance.

A net increase in savings, then, in contrast to a nonfinancial transaction, implies that the financial sector—initially, the banking system—will gain funds at the expense of the nonfinancial sectors. Moreover, and this is the next point that needs to be understood, the banks and other financial institutions cannot, on their own, put those funds back into circulation. As will become clearer when we shortly examine the monetary effect of a net increase in debt (the obverse of a net increase in savings), the funds can be recirculated only if some nonfinancial entity is prepared to take out a loan. The point is an important one. It explains why it is wrong to assume that any income which is saved rather than spent on goods and services will nonetheless be kept in circulation by the banks. The fact is that the funds, once deposited in a bank, can remain unspent indefinitely. Indeed, it is by holding funds as the unspent balances of depositors that banks are able to absorb any excess monetary flows relative to the real flows—and thereby play a key role in stabilizing the monetarized system of production.

The ability of banks to absorb funds, in the form of idle balances, is in turn the reason why savings—or, to use the terminology of the preceding chapters, discretionary funds—need to be distinguished from business investment and the other types of durable goods outlays that fall under the rubric of discretionary expenditures. With the banks able to absorb any net increase in savings, it is possible for a nonfinancial sector's discretionary funds to increase relative to its durable goods outlays, or discretionary expenditures; and this explains, among other things, how there can be the various types of "leakage" from the spending stream, or circular flow, that are the basis for the cash-flow feedback effect previously identified (see chapter 3, section 2.5). Still, our concern at the moment is with the monetary, rather than the real, effect of a net increase in savings. This monetary effect can be observed by tracing out, as in exhibits 12.6 and 12.8, the resulting

Exhibit 12.7

Monetary and Financial Effects of a Durable Goods Purchase

	Capital Goods Sector			Other Nonfinancial Sector	
	Gross Income	+ $1,000		Gross Income	0
−	Current Outlays	0	−	Current Outlays	0
=	Net Cash Inflow	+ $1,000	=	Net Cash Inflow	0
−	Durable Goods Purchases	0	−	Durable Goods Purchases	+ $1,000
=	Net Financial Change	+ $1,000	=	Net Financial Change	− $1,000
=	ΔBank Balance	+ $1,000	=	ΔBank Balance	− $1,000
+	ΔOther Assets	0	+	ΔOther Assets	0
−	ΔLoans Outstanding	0	−	ΔLoans outstanding	0
−	ΔOther liabilities	0	−	ΔOther liabilities	0
=	Net Financial Change	+ $1,000	=	Net Financial Change	− $1,000

Banking System

	ΔAssets			ΔLiabilities	
	ΔCurrency	0		ΔDeposits	0
+	ΔOther Reserves	0	+	ΔOther Liabilities	0
+	ΔLoans	0	+	ΔNet Worth	0
+	ΔOther Assets	0			
=	Change in Assets	0	=	Change in Liabilities	0

change, first, in the bank balance of the nonfinancial sector with the net increase in savings, and then, as the corollary of that financial effect, the corresponding change in the banking system's balance sheet. To trace out the full monetary effect, however, we still need to consider (a) the possibility of a subsequent portfolio shift, and (b) the real, or income, effect of the increase in net savings on at least one other nonfinancial entity. We shall begin with the former.

12.1.3 Portfolio shifts

Each nonfinancial entity, it can be assumed, will determine from experience how large a cash balance it needs to maintain, either as a checkable deposit in some bank or as currency in hand, so that its ability to continue making payments will not be impaired. This minimal cash balance will be the entity's first priority insofar as holding financial assets is concerned. However, once this minimal cash balance is established (or restored, following a net outflow of funds), the entity

Exhibit 12.8

Monetary and Financial Effect of a Reduction in Current Outlays Combined with a Durable Goods Purchase

Capital Goods Sector		Other Nonfinancial Sector	
Gross Income	+ $1,000	Gross Income	0
− Current Outlays	0	− Current Outlays	− $2,000
= Net Cash Inflow	+ $1,000	= Net Cash Inflow	+ $2,000
− Durable Goods Purchases	0	− Durable Goods Purchases	+ $1,000
= Net Financial Change	+ $1,000	= Net Financial Change	+ $1,000
= ΔBank Balance	+ $1,000	= ΔBank Balance	+ $1,000
+ ΔOther Assets	0	+ ΔOther Assets	0
− ΔLoans Outstanding	0	− ΔLoans Outstanding	0
− ΔOther liabilities	0	− ΔOther liabilities	0
Net Financial Change	+ $1,000	= Net Financial Change	+ $1,000

Banking System

ΔAssets		ΔLiabilities	
ΔCurrency	0	ΔDeposits	0
+ ΔOther Reserves	0	+ ΔOther Liabilities	0
+ ΔLoans	0	+ ΔNet Worth	0
+ ΔOther Assets	0		
= Change in Assets	+ $2,000	= Change in Liabilities	+ $2,000

will prefer to hold other types of assets. This is because little or no interest can be earned on whatever funds are held as a checkable deposit or as currency. Any net increase in savings, then, assuming the nonfinancial entity already has the minimal cash balance it needs, can be expected to lead, after the initial increase in its bank balance, to a portfolio shift, with the nonfinancial entity using the excess cash to acquire other types of financial assets.

The possibility of a portfolio shift implies the existence of other financial assets besides bank deposits and currency. Some of these other assets, such as a noncheckable time deposit, may be issued by the banks themselves. Others, such as a mutual fund share, imply that the financial sector consists of more than just banks. Thus, before proceeding to trace out the monetary effect of a portfolio shift, following a net increase in saving by some nonfinancial sector, it is necessary to expand on the earlier description of the financial sector to allow for (a) other types of financial assets besides bank deposits and currency, and (b) other types of financial institutions besides banks.

Exhibit 12.9
Types of Financial Assets

Securities
  Public
    Federal government securities
    State and local government securities
    Other publicly issued securities (government backed)
  Private
    Mortgages
    Other fixed interest obligations (bonds)
    Equity shares
Intermediary Obligations
  Mutual Fund Shares
  Pension Rights
  Insurance Policies
  Trust certificates
    Real estate
    Other
  Savings Institution Shares
  Credit Union Shares

In an advanced industrial economy with a sophisticated financial sector, there are two other types of financial assets which can be found in the portfolios of nonfinancial entities besides the bank deposits and currency which constitute their cash balances (see exhibit 12.9). They are (1) securities, or the long-term liabilities of other nonfinancial entities, and (2) intermediary obligations. The latter are the liabilities of another type of financial institution—the nonbank financial intermediary (see exhibit 12.10). The need for this other type of financial institution arises from the advantages of intermediation. This is the process of issuing some new type of debt instrument, e.g., a share in a mutual fund or in a savings and loan association, as the offsetting liability against the financial assets of a different sort, usually longer term and/or less liquid, which make up the financial intermediary's portfolio. The advantages of intermediation are twofold. For those holding the debt instrument issued by the financial intermediary, it provides a higher and/or more secure financial return. For the nonfinancial entities whose debt instruments are held as assets by the financial intermediary, it provides a firmer and more dependable market for the securities they issue.

As can be seen from exhibit 12.9, one can distinguish the securities, or long-term debt, of public agencies from those issued by private parties, with the latter further divided into fixed-interest obligations and equity shares. These securities are the principal means by which nonfinancial entities are able to finance any net investment, or discretionary expenditures, in excess of the discretionary funds currently being generated. Their role in enabling nonfinancial entities to finance more outlays than would otherwise be possible makes them a critical point of interface between the real and financial sectors. However, it is not easy for a nonfinancial entity, even a megacorp, to successfully market any securities it may wish to issue (see chapter 7, part 3). There has to be a party with sufficient funds to purchase the securities. While it might seem that banks, as the repository of excess funds, would be the logical party to take on such a role, this possibility is precluded by the prohibition, at least in the United States, against banks ''lending long.'' The stricture reflects a belief, based on historical experience, that with their liabilities consisting of deposits which are immediately redeemable, banks run too great a risk of becoming illiquid—thereby rendering the system of payment inoperative—if they are permitted to include, as part of their loan portfolio, the long-term securities issued by nonfinancial entities. Indeed, this is why, in the United States and in the other countries that follow the British rather than the European continental model, not only financial intermediaries but also a third type of financial entity, the market maker, has had to evolve to supplement the activities of the banks (see exhibit 12.10).

Market makers serve as the middlemen speculative interest in the markets, both initial and secondary, for the securities issued by nonfinancial entities. They thus play the key role of (a) linking the buyers and sellers of securities; (b) making it easier to convert securities back into cash; and (c) ensuring that the securities markets function like commodity markets (see chapter 6, section 4.1). In addition, they often take the initiative in organizing new types of nonbank financial intermediaries, such as mutual and money market funds. It is through the activities of these market markers that the price of the various securities is determined—with that price, reflecting the balance between supply and demand, then determining the current yield from holding that type of asset. Indeed, the current yield, or financial return, is simply the stipulated interest payment or anticipated dividend as a proportion of the security's present market value, or price. The supply of securities, meanwhile, depends on the need for additional external funding by each of the different nonfinancial sectors, beyond what can be raised through short-term loans from the banks, and the demand depends on how much those same nonfinancial sectors are able to add to their net savings, beyond the cash balances they normally maintain. This is true even if, in the case of any net savings by the household sector and a subsequent portfolio shift, the funds eventually accrue to some nonbank financial intermediary so that the demand for securities is largely the demand for that type of asset by the financial intermediaries, such as mutual funds, pension funds and insurance companies, to which at least a significant portion of the household sector's excess cash holdings are likely to flow.

However, even the excess cash which remains within the banking system is likely to soon be converted, through a portfolio shift, into some other type of

---

Exhibit 12.10
Types of Nonbank Financial Institutions

Market Makers
  Investment Bankers
  Securities Dealers
   Public
   Private
  Other Brokerage Firms
Nonbank Financial Intermediaries
  Mutual Funds
  Pension Funds
  Insurance Companies
  Savings Institutions
  Real Estate Investment Trusts
  Other Investment Trusts
Other Financial Institutions
  Factors
  Household Finance Companies

---

higher yielding financial asset. This is the process of intermediation which occurs within the banking system itself. It entails converting a checkable bank deposit into a somewhat less liquid and/or less secure asset, such as a certificate of deposit, so that a higher financial return can be obtained. One therefore needs to distinguish two types of portfolio shifts (aside from the possible conversion of a bank deposit into currency, or vice versa). They are (1) a portfolio shift in which a checkable bank deposit is converted into a noncheckable deposit and (2) a portfolio shift in which a checkable deposit is converted into the liability of some nonbank financial intermediary. In the first case, the total amount of bank deposits will remain unchanged. It is just that the amount of checkable deposits will decline (see exhibit 12.11. Note that the banking system's noncheckable deposits are now listed separately from its checkable deposits). While there will be a decline in the bank balance of the nonfinancial entity reponsible for the portfolio shift, with the banking system's noncheckable deposits increasing at the expense of its checkable deposits, the banks themselves will still hold the same amount of funds. Indeed, because banks need to retain a smaller amount of reserves against the noncheckable deposits they hold, they will actually have more funds available for making loans. This is why they are willing to pay a higher rate of interest on the funds deposited in a noncheckable account. In the second case, there will be no change either in the total amount of funds held by the banks or in the amount of checkable deposits. It is just that the assets of the nonfinancial entity making the

portfolio shift will now include the liabilities of some nonbank financial intermediary, with the latter showing a larger bank balance in return (see exhibit 12.12.
Note that the flow of funds model has now been further expanded to include a
separate nonbank financial sector). Thus, whatever the type of portfolio shift
following a net increase in savings, the amount of funds circulating as checkable
deposits will be no greater. If anything, the amount of such funds will decline.

It might seem that any net savings which flow, via the household sector, to
nonbank financial intermediaries would, through the types of securities purchased by those entities, make additional funds available to either the enterprise
or government sectors. However, the amount of securities available for purchase
is, at any given moment in time, fixed. It depends on how business firms and
public bodies have, in the past, decided to finance their cash deficits. An increase
in the demand for securites will therefore only cause the price of securities to rise,
with the higher price fully absorbing the additional funds. Indeed, the resulting
rise in asset prices is the second way, in addition to whatever excessive cash
balances are held as bank deposits or currency, that the financial system is able to
play a stabilizing role by adjusting the monetary flows so they match the real
flows.

It is, of course, true that an increase in the price of securities will cause their
yields, and hence the cost of external finance, to fall so that at least one of the
nonfinancial sectors will have a greater incentive to undertake expenditures in
excess of its current cash inflow. The stimulative effect which the lower long-
term interest rates are likely to have on aggregate demand cannot be ignored—
even if this relative price effect is likely to be more than fully offset by the
dampening income effect of the increased leakages from the spending stream.
Still, insofar as the amount of funds in circulation is concerned, the acquisition by
households and other nonfinancial entities of the debt instruments issued by
financial intermediaries, following a net increase in savings, will make no difference. The only way the amount of funds circulating as checkable deposits can be
increased is if some nonfinancial sector is prepared to increase, not its net savings
but rather, its net debt.

12.1.4 A net increase in debt

A nonfinancial entity can incur a cash deficit—the obverse of a net increase in
savings—in either of two ways. It can, quite deliberately, increase its total outlays
relative to its current cash inflow. Usually, any such increase in outlays relative to
the amount of cash inflow will be because the entity wishes to increase its durable
goods purchases, or investment. The outlays on nondurable goods and services
are likely either to remain unchanged, as in the case of a household, or to be
closely geared to the current rate of sales and thus to the rate of cash inflow, as in
the case of a business firm. This is why an increase in outlays relative to current
cash inflow can usually be assumed to represent an increase in durable goods

purchases, or discretionary expenditures. Still, it is possible for a household to incur a cash deficit in order to finance some nondurable purchase, such as a holiday trip, and it is even common for a business firm to incur a cash deficit so it can finance the purchase of the additional inventory and labor services it needs to fill a sales order. More generally, then, a deliberately incurred cash deficit will be the result of some nonfinancial sector increasing its total outlays, whether for durable goods or not, relative to its current cash inflow. Alternatively, a nonfinancial entity may incur a cash deficit because its current cash inflow has declined, for reasons beyond its control, and it is not able to reduce its outlays by a corresponding amount without jeopardizing its ability to continue in operation. In this latter case, the cash deficit will be an involuntary one.

Any cash deficit, whether deliberately incurred or not, will have the same monetary effect. The nonfinancial entity experiencing the shortfall in cash inflow will need to cover the deficit by arranging for a loan—either from a bank or from some other source. Otherwise, it will lack the funds to maintain its current level of payments. While the nonfinancial entity may initially respond to the deficit by allowing its balance at the bank to fall, this can be only a temporary solution. To restore its minimal cash balance, the nonfinancial entity, and thus the sector to which it belongs, will need to obtain a loan from a bank, thereby adding to its net debt. The nonfinancial entity experiencing the shortfall in cash inflow may, of course, seek funds from some other source. Indeed, it may even force its creditors to grant it an involuntary loan by refusing to make the required payments. Still, the more typical response of a nonfinancial entity, in the face of an impending cash deficit, is to arrange for a bank loan, thereby adding to the net debt of the sector to which it belongs.

Any time a nonfinancial sector adds to its net debt by arranging for a bank loan, the amount of funds circulating as checkable bank deposits will necessarily rise (see the first part of exhibit 12.13). This is true whether the cash deficit necessitating the loan has been deliberately incurred or not. Moreover, it is only through a bank loan that the amount of funds circulating as checkable deposits can increase. If, instead, funds are borrowed from a nonbank financial intermediary, the latter will need to draw down its cash balance at some bank in order to make the funds available and, as a result, the total amount of checkable bank deposits will remain the same (see the second part of exhibit 12.13). Thus, just as was true in the case of a portfolio shift following a net increase in savings, the existence of nonbank financial intermediaries makes little difference—the only effect being on the availability and cost of external finance. Indeed, this is why the existence of nonbank financial intermediaries can usually be ignored and the flow of funds model simplified by eliminating the nonbank financial sector.

In the type of economic system which the flow of funds model describes, any increase in the amount of funds available for making payment depends, then, on the willingness of some nonfinancial sector to add to its bank-held debt. An increase in the demand for bank loans, provided that the banking system is willing and able to satisfy that demand, will lead to an increase in the amount of funds

Exhibit 12.11
Portfolio Shift Following Net Increase in Savings

Net Increase in Savings (exhibit 12.6)

Nonfinancial Sector A			Nonfinancial Sector B		
	Gross Income	0		Gross Income	0
−	Current Outlays	−$1,000	−	Current Outlays	0
=	Net Cash Inflow	+$1,000	=	Net Cash Inflow	0
−	Durable Goods Purchases	0	−	Durable Goods Purchases	0
=	Net Financial Change	+$1,000	=	Net Financial Change	0
=	ΔBank Balance	+$1,000	=	ΔBank Balance	0
+	ΔOther Assets	0	+	ΔOther Assets	0
−	ΔLoans Outstanding	0	−	ΔLoans Outstanding	0
−	ΔOther liabilities	0	−	ΔOther liabilities	0
=	Net Financial Change	+$1,000	=	Net Financial Change	0

Banking System

ΔAssets			ΔLiabilities		
	ΔCurrency	+$1,000		ΔCheckable Deposits	0
+	ΔOther Reserves	0	+	ΔNoncheckable deposits	+$1,000
+	ΔLoans	0	+	ΔOther Liabilities	0
+	ΔOther Assets	0	+	ΔNet Worth	0
=	Change in Assets	+$1,000	=	Change in Liabilities	+$1,000

circulating as checkable deposits. The argument also holds in reverse. A reduction in the amount of bank loans outstanding, with borrowers on balance reducing their debt to the banking system as their loans come due, will cause the amount of checkable deposits to fall. This last point can be demonstrated as well, relying on the same flow of funds model developed so far. However, there are two restrictions on the model which derive from the very nature of a market economy, and both these restrictions need to be kept firmly in mind. The first restriction is that one cannot posit an *increase* in outlays by one of the nonfinancial sectors without indicating how the purchase is going to be financed. The other restriction is that one cannot instead posit a *decrease* in outlays without tracing out the effect of the reduced flow of income on at least one of the other nonfinancial sectors. Unless these restrictions are kept in mind, the argument can easily go astray.

To see why the first of the two restrictions is necessary, let us return to exhibit 12.7. While, in that example, a $1,000 purchase of durable goods was postulated, all that was actually shown was how the payment was handled through the

Exhibit 12.11 (continued)

Portfolio Shift (Substitution of Noncheckable for Checkable Deposit)

Nonfinancial Sector A			Nonfinancial Sector B	
Gross Income		0	Gross Income	0
− Current Outlays		−$1,000	− Current Outlays	0
= Net Cash Inflow		+$1,000	= Net Cash Inflow	0
− Durable Goods Purchases		0	− Durable Goods Purchases	0
= Net Financial Change		+$1,000	= Net Financial Change	0
= ΔBank Balance		0	= ΔBank Balance	0
+ ΔOther Assets		+$1,000	+ ΔOther Assets	0
− ΔLoans Outstanding		0	− ΔLoans Outstanding	0
− ΔOther liabilities		0	− ΔOther liabilities	0
= Net Financial Change		+$1,000	= Net Financial Change	0

Banking System

ΔAssets		ΔLiabilities	
ΔCurrency	+$1,000	ΔCheckable Deposits	0
+ ΔOther Reserves	0	+ ΔNoncheckable deposits	+$1,000
+ ΔLoans	0	+ ΔOther Liabilities	0
+ ΔOther Assets	0	+ ΔNet Worth	0
= Change in Assets	+$1,000	= Change in Liabilities	+$1,000

banking system. Not explained was how the sector purchasing the durable goods was able to finance the increase in its outlays—and thus an important detail was left out. This omission can now be corrected by postulating, as in exhibit 12.14, that the sector first obtained a bank loan for $1,000. It should be noted that, without the bank loan, it is not clear how the sector would be able to pay for the goods it purchased. The only other way would be if its gross income had previously increased by $1,000. But that would imply a $1,000 increase in outlays by some other sector, and one would still have to explain how a nonfinancial sector can, without adding to its debt, finance an increase in its outlays while its gross income remains unchanged. The eluctable fact about a market economy (at least one based on credit money) is that an increase in outlays by one of the nonfinancial sectors relative to its gross income, and thus an autonomous increase in outlays by all the nonfinancial sectors taken as a whole, is possible only by assuming, as in exhibit 12.14, that the purchase is financed by a loan from the banking system.

What exhibit 12.14 makes clear is that, as a result of some nonfinancial sector

Exhibit 12.12
Portfolio Shift Following Net Increase in Savings

Net Increase in Savings (exhibit 12.6)

	Nonfinancial Sector A			Nonfinancial Sector B	
	Gross Income	0		Gross Income	0
−	Current Outlays	− $1,000	−	Current Outlays	0
=	Net Cash Inflow	+ $1,000	=	Net Cash Inflow	0
−	Durable Goods Purchases	+ $1,000	−	Durable Goods Purchases	0
=	Net Financial Change	+ $1,000	=	Net Financial Change	0
=	ΔBank Balance	+ $1,000	=	ΔBank Balance	0
+	ΔOther Assets	0	+	ΔOther Assets	0
−	ΔLoans Outstanding	0	−	ΔLoans Outstanding	0
−	ΔOther liabilities	0	−	ΔOther liabilities	0
=	Net Financial Change	+ $1,000	=	Net Financial Change	0

Banking System

	ΔAssets			ΔLiabilities	
	ΔCurrency	+ $1,000		ΔCheckable Deposits	+ $1,000
+	ΔOther Reserves	0	+	ΔNoncheckable deposits	0
+	ΔLoans	0	+	ΔOther Liabilities	0
+	ΔOther Assets	0	+	ΔNet Worth	0
=	Change in Assets	+ $1,000	=	Change in Liabilities	+ $1,000

Other Financial Institutions

	ΔAssets			ΔLiabilities	
	ΔBank Balance	0		ΔShares Issued	0
+	ΔSecurities Held	0	+	Other Liabilities	0
+	ΔOther Assets	0	+	ΔNet Worth	0
=	Change in Assets	0	=	Change in Liabilities	0

being willing to add to its bank-held debt in order to finance the purchase of durable goods, the amount of checkable deposits, and thus the amount of funds which can be used to effect payment, will increase by $1,000. This is the monetary effect of the loan deliberately entered into by one of the nonfinancial sectors. It is not, however, the only effect of a credit-financed purchase. Once a check is issued in payment for the durable goods and then redeposited in the banking system, the gross income of the capital goods sector will increase by

Exhibit 12.12 (continued)

Portfolio Shift

Nonfinancial Sector A		Nonfinancial Sector B	
Gross Income	0	Gross Income	0
− Current Outlays	−$1,000	− Current Outlays	0
= Net Cash Inflow	+$1,000	= Net Cash Inflow	0
− Durable Goods Purchases	0	− Durable Goods Purchases	0
= Net Financial Change	+$1,000	= Net Financial Change	0
= ΔBank Balance	0	= ΔBank Balance	0
+ ΔOther Assets	+$1,000	+ ΔOther Assets	0
− ΔLoans Outstanding	0	− ΔLoans Outstanding	0
− ΔOther liabilities	0	− ΔOther liabilities	0
= Net Financial Change	+$1,000	= Net Financial Change	0

Banking System

ΔAssets		ΔLiabilities	
ΔCurrency	+$1,000	ΔCheckable Deposits	+$1,000
+ ΔOther Reserves	0	+ ΔNoncheckable deposits	0
+ ΔLoans	0	+ ΔOther Liabilities	0
+ ΔOther Assets	0	+ ΔNet Worth	0
= Change in Assets	+$1,000	= Change in Liabilities	+$1,000

Other Financial Institutions

ΔAssets		ΔLiabilities	
ΔBank Balance	+$1,000	ΔShares Issued	+$1,000
+ ΔSecurities Held	0	+ ΔOther Liabilities	0
+ ΔOther Assets	0	+ ΔNet Worth	0
= Change in Assets	+$1,000	= Change in Liabilities	+$1,000

$1,000, thereby enabling that sector to increase its outlays by a similar amount. This is the quite separate income effect of a credit-financed purchase, and it is traced out in the top set of the accounts shown in exhibit 12.14—with that permanent increase in the flow of income a combination of the separate multiplier and cash-flow feedback effects previously delineated (see chapter 10, section 4.4).

While the monetary effect, at least in the first instance, will be the same, whether the bank loan has been arranged to finance an increase in outlays or to cover an involuntary deficit, the income and hence the real effects on the system

Exhibit 12.13
Bank Loan vs. Nonbank Loan

Bank Loan

Nonfinancial Sector A		Nonfinancial Sector B	
Gross Income	0	Gross Income	0
− Current Outlays	0	− Current Outlays	0
= Net Cash Inflow	0	= Net Cash Inflow	0
− Durable Goods Purchases	0	− Durable Goods Purchases	0
= Net Financial Change	0	= Net Financial Change	0
= ΔBank Balance	+$1,000	= ΔBank Balance	0
+ ΔOther Assets	0	+ ΔOther Assets	0
− ΔLoans Outstanding	+$1,000	− ΔLoans Outstanding	0
− ΔOther liabilities	0	− ΔOther liabilities	0
= Net Financial Change	0	= Net Financial Change	0

Banking System

ΔAssets		ΔLiabilities	
ΔCurrency	0	ΔCheckable Deposits	+$1,000
+ ΔOther Reserves	0	+ ΔNoncheckable deposits	0
+ ΔLoans	+$1,000	+ ΔOther Liabilities	0
+ ΔOther Assets	0	+ ΔNet Worth	0
= Change in Assets	+$1,000	= Change in Liabilities	+$1,000

Other Financial Institutions

ΔAssets		ΔLiabilities	
ΔBank Balance	0	ΔShares Issued	0
+ ΔSecurities Held	0	+ Other Liabilities	0
+ ΔOther Assets	0	+ ΔNet Worth	0
= Change in Assets	0	= Change in Liabilities	0

as a whole will be quite different, depending on the reason for the loan. This is because, within the constraints imposed by the flow of funds model, an involuntary cash deficit can occur in one of the nonfinancial sectors only as a result of a reduction in outlays by some other nonfinancial sector. To see what this second restriction on the flow of funds model implies, let us return to the second part of exhibit 12.6, where a deliberate act of saving by one of the nonfinancial sectors was postulated. The only effect that was traced out in that earlier example was the

Exhibit 12.13 (continued)

Nonbank Loan

Nonfinancial Sector A			Nonfinancial Sector B	
Gross Income		0	Gross Income	0
− Current Outlays		0	− Current Outlays	0
= Net Cash Inflow	+$1,000		= Net Cash Inflow	0
− Durable Goods Purchases		0	− Durable Goods Purchases	0
= Net Financial Change		0	= Net Financial Change	0
= ΔBank Balance	+$1,000		= ΔBank Balance	0
+ ΔOther Assets		0	+ ΔOther Assets	0
− ΔLoans Outstanding	+$1,000		− ΔLoans Outstanding	0
− ΔOther liabilities		0	− ΔOther liabilities	0
= Net Financial Change	+$1,000		= Net Financial Change	0

Banking System

ΔAssets		ΔLiabilities	
ΔCurrency	0	ΔCheckable Deposits	0
+ ΔOther Reserves	0	+ ΔNoncheckable deposits	0
+ ΔLoans	0	+ ΔOther Liabilities	0
+ ΔOther Assets	0	+ ΔNet Worth	0
= Change in Assets	0	= Change in Liabilities	0

Other Financial Institutions

ΔAssets		ΔLiabilities	
ΔBank Balance	−$1,000	ΔShares Issued	0
+ ΔSecurities Held	0	+ ΔOther Liabilities	0
+ ΔOther Assets	+$1,000	+ ΔNet Worth	0
= Change in Assets	0	= Change in Liabilities	0

financial effect on the sector which, by reducing its current outlays, was able to increase its cash balance at the bank. What was not brought out was the income effect on the sector from which the funds were diverted—an important detail that, again, was left out. This omission is corrected in exhibit 12.15.

As can be seen by examining the top set of accounts in that exhibit, should a nonfinancial sector reduce its current outlays as the means it has chosen to increase its net savings, the gross income of some other nonfinancial sector will necessarily fall by the same amount. This, no less than the inability of a nonfinancial sector to increase its outlays while its gross income remains unchanged unless

Exhibit 12.14
Bank Financed Durable Goods Purchase

Bank Loan

Capital Goods Sector A		Other Nonfinancial Sector B	
Gross Income	0	Gross Income	0
− Current Outlays	0	− Current Outlays	0
= Net Cash Inflow			0
− Durable Goods Purchases	0	− Durable Goods Purchases	0
= Net Financial Change	0	= Net Financial Change	0
= ΔBank Balance	0	= ΔBank Balance	+ $1,000
+ ΔOther Assets	0	+ ΔOther Assets	0
− ΔLoans Outstanding	0	− ΔLoans Outstanding	0
− ΔOther liabilities	0	− ΔOther liabilities	0
= Net Financial Change	0	= Net Financial Change	0

Banking System

ΔAssets		ΔLiabilities	
ΔCurrency	0	ΔCheckable Deposits	+ $1,000
+ ΔOther Reserves	0	+ ΔNoncheckable deposits	0
+ ΔLoans	+ $1,000	+ ΔOther Liabilities	0
+ ΔOther Assets	0	+ ΔNet Worth	0
= Change in Assets	+ $1,000	= Change in Liabilities	+ $1,000

it is prepared to go further into debt to the banking system, is an ineluctable fact about a market economy. Furthermore, because of this income effect, the banking system, rather than gaining deposits as a result of the net increase in savings by the one nonfinancial sector (see exhibit 12.6), will be left with the same amount of deposits as before. This is because the reduction in the gross income of the other sector will reduce that sector's bank balance, and thus the total amount of funds deposited in banks, by $1,000. Indeed, as the second part of exhibit 12.15 makes clear, it is only if and when that other sector arranges for a bank loan to cover the involuntary deficit it has incurred that the total amount of checkable deposits within the banking system will increase.

While in exhibits 12.6 and 12.15 it has been assumed that one of the nonfinancial sectors has reduced its current outlays so as to be able to increase its net savings, this may in fact not be possible when one takes into account, as one must, not just the restrictions imposed by the flow of funds model but also those which

Exhibit 12.14 (continued)

Purchase of Durable Goods

Capital Goods Sector A		Other Nonfinancial Sector B	
Gross Income	+$1,000	Gross Income	0
− Current Outlays	0	− Current Outlays	0
= Net Cash Inflow	+$1,000	= Net Cash Inflow	0
− Durable Goods Purchases	0	− Durable Goods Purchases	+$1,000
= Net Financial Change	+$1,000	= Net Financial Change	−$1,000
= ΔBank Balance	+$1,000	= ΔBank Balance	0
+ ΔOther Assets	0	+ ΔOther Assets	0
− ΔLoans Outstanding	0	− ΔLoans Outstanding	0
− ΔOther liabilities	0	− ΔOther liabilities	0
= Net Financial Change	+$1,000	= Net Financial Change	−$1,000

Banking System

ΔAssets		ΔLiabilities	
ΔCurrency	0	ΔCheckable Deposits	+$1,000
+ ΔOther Reserves	0	+ ΔNoncheckable deposits	0
+ ΔLoans	+$1,000	+ ΔOther Liabilities	0
+ ΔOther Assets	0	+ ΔNet Worth	0
= Change in Assets	+$1,000	= Change in Liabilities	+$1,000

the complementary input-output model of production imposes. The enterprise sector, in particular, cannot reduce its current outlays on labor without its output of goods and services, and thus its gross income, declining. While both the household and government sectors may have greater discretion in this regard, they, too, are likely to experience some difficulty if they attempt to reduce their outlays on nondurable goods and services. The preceding argument is therefore strengthened if, instead of positing a reduction in current outlays, one posits a reduction in durable goods purchases. As already pointed out, a reduction in a sector's durable goods purchases will have the same effect on its net savings as a reduction in its current outlays.

It is, of course, possible that the sector which has reduced its outlays either on durable or nondurable goods, and thereby imposed a cash deficit on some other nonfinancial sector, will use the net increase in its savings to reduce its debt to the banking system. This can be accomplished by the sector paying off rather than renewing its bank loans as they come due. In that event, as can be seen from

Exhibit 12.15

Monetary and Income Effects of a Net Increase in Savings

Reduction in Current Outlays (by Nonfinancial Sector A)

Nonfinancial Sector A		Nonfinancial Sector B	
Gross Income	0	Gross Income	$ − 1,000
− Current Outlays	− $1,000	− Current Outlays	0
= Net Cash Inflow	+ $1,000	= Net Cash Inflow	− $1,000
− Durable Goods Purchases	0	− Durable Goods Purchases	0
= Net Financial Change	+ $1,000	= Net Financial Change	− $1,000
= ΔBank Balance	+ $1,000	= ΔBank Balance	− $1,000
+ ΔOther Assets	0	+ ΔOther Assets	0
− ΔLoans Outstanding	0	− ΔLoans Outstanding	0
− ΔOther liabilities	0	− ΔOther liabilities	0
= Net Financial Change	0	= Net Financial Change	0

Banking System

ΔAssets		ΔLiabilities	
ΔCurrency	0	ΔCheckable Deposits	0
+ ΔOther Reserves	0	+ ΔNoncheckable deposits	0
+ ΔLoans	0	+ ΔOther Liabilities	0
+ ΔOther Assets	0	+ ΔNet Worth	0
= Change in Assets	0	= Change in Liabilities	0

exhibit 12.16, the amount of checkable deposits within the banking system, and thus the amount of funds available for making payment, will be reduced by the amount the one sector's loans are repaid, thereby negating the increase in bank deposits from the loan to the other sector to cover its deficit. But the sector with a cash surplus need not reduce its bank debt. It may instead elect either to maintain a larger cash balance or, what is more likely, acquire some type of other financial asset. In that case, the demand for financial assets will increase and hence their price will rise inversely with the decline in their yield. However, the amount of funds circulating as checkable deposits will be unaffected. This is why the amount of funds in circulation depends on the demand for credit. The amount of those funds will, in fact, increase over time at a rate determined by the willingness of the nonfinancial sectors, on net balance, to add to their bank-held debt. It is only if and when the loans are, on balance, repaid that the amount of funds will actually decline.

Exhibit 12.15 (continued)

Financing of Involuntary Cash Deficit (by Nonfinancial Sector B)

	Nonfinancial Sector A		Nonfinancial Sector B	
	Gross Income	0	Gross Income	−$1,000
−	Current Outlays	−$1,000	Current Outlays	0
=	Net Cash Inflow	+$1,000	Net Cash Inflow	−$1,000
−	Durble Goods Purchases	0	Durable Goods Purchases	0
=	Net Financial Change	+$1,000	Net Financial Change	−$1,000
=	ΔBank Balance	+$1,000	ΔBank Balance	0
+	ΔOther Assets	0	ΔOther Assets	0
−	ΔLoans Outstanding	0	ΔLoans Outstanding	+$1,000
−	ΔOther liabilities	0	ΔOther liabilities	0
=	Net Financial Change	+$1,000	Net Financial Change	−$1,000

Banking System

	ΔAssets		ΔLiabilities	
	ΔCurrency	0	ΔCheckable Deposits	+$1,000
+	ΔOther Reserves	0	ΔNoncheckable deposits	0
+	ΔLoans	+$1,000	ΔOther Liabilities	0
+	ΔOther Assets	0	ΔNet Worth	0
=	Change in Assets	+$1,000	Change in Liabilities	+$1,000

In summary, then, any change in the amount of funds that uniquely, within a credit-based system of money, serve as the means of payment will depend on the demand for bank credit. That is,

$$\Delta Dep = f(\Delta Cr) \qquad (12.1)$$

where ΔDep is the change in the amount of checkable deposits and ΔCr is the change in the amount of bank loans. Indeed, since the change in deposits is simply the offsetting entry on the liability side of the banking system's balance sheet when a loan is made, the change in the amount of checkable deposits will closely approximate the change in the amount of bank loans. That is,

$$\Delta Dep \cong \Delta Cr \qquad (12.2)$$

Equation 12.1, then, merely supplements equation 12.2, indicating that the

Exhibit 12.16
Reduction in Bank Loans (by Nonfinancial Sector A)

Nonfinancial Sector A			Nonfinancial Sector B		
	Gross Income	0		Gross Income	$ − 1,000
−	Current Outlays	− $1,000	−	Current Outlays	0
=	Net Cash Inflow	+ $1,000	=	Net Cash Inflow	− $1,000
−	Durable Goods Purchases	0	−	Durable Goods Purchases	0
=	Net Financial Change	+ $1,000	=	Net Financial Change	− $1,000
=	ΔBank Balance	0	=	ΔBank Balance	0
+	ΔOther Assets	0	+	ΔOther Assets	0
	ΔLoans Outstanding	− $1,000	−	ΔLoans Outstanding	+ $1,000
−	ΔOther liabilities	0	−	ΔOther liabilities	0
=	Net Financial Change	+ $1,000	=	Net Financial Change	− $1,000

Banking System

ΔAssets			ΔLiabilities		
	ΔCurrency	0		ΔCheckable Deposits	0
+	ΔOther Reserves	0	+	ΔNoncheckable deposits	0
+	ΔLoans	0	+	ΔOther Liabilities	0
+	ΔOther Assets	0	+	ΔNet Worth	0
=	Change in Assets	0	=	Change in Liabilities	0

direction of causation is from right to left—an important addendum, the significance of which will shortly be made clear. This relationship between the amount of funds in circulation and the amount of bank loans can be seen by tracing out, as in exhibits 12.14 and 12.15, not just the financial and monetary effects of a net increase in debt but also, when the increase in debt is voluntary, the *attendant* income effect or, alternatively, when the increase in debt is involuntary, the *precipitating* income effect. Still, the relationship is apt to be lost sight of unless one keeps firmly in mind the two restrictions that apply to a monetarized production system. The first is that the nonfinancial sectors individually, and thus the nonfinancial sectors as a whole, cannot increase their current outlays without at least one of the sectors adding to its bank debt. The second restriction is that one of the nonfinancial sectors cannot reduce its total outlays without, at the same time, reducing the gross income of some other nonfinancial sector.

This last restriction explains why it is fallacious to assume that one of the nonfinancial sectors can increase its net savings and thereby add to the total amount of savings. As can be seen by tracing out, as in exhibit 12.15, the full income effect of a net increase in savings by one of the nonfinancial sectors, this

Exhibit 12.17

Increase in National Income from Rise in Credit-Financed Expenditures

Period	Cr	ΔCr	Dep	ΔDep	Exp	ΔExp	Y	ΔY
0	450	—	450	—	600	—	600	—
1	600	150	600	150	750	150	600	—
2	700	100	700	100	850	100	750	150
3	733	33	733	33	883	33	850	100
4	745	12	745	12	895	12	883	33
5	748	3	748	3	898	3	895	12
6	749	1	749	1	899	1	898	3
7	750	1	750	1	900	1	899	1
8	750	—	750	—	900	—	900	1

Source: Adapted from Wynne Godley and Francis Cripps, *Macroeconomics*, Oxford University Press, 1983, pp. 62–63.

will simply reduce by an equal amount the net savings of one or more of the other nonfinancial sectors, leaving aggregate savings unchanged. If additional investment is going to be undertaken, it can only be financed, as exhibit 12.14 makes clear, through bank loans. That increase in debt to the banking system will, however, be sufficient in itself to finance the additional investment—irrespective of what is happening to aggregate savings. Indeed, as can be seen from exhibit 12.14, the credit-financed purchase of any goods, whether for investment purposes or not, will produce a net increase in savings within the sector from which the goods are being purchased so that aggregate savings will then rise to match the net increase in outlays. This, in fact, is the basis for the assertion that has been made throughout the text, as a further extension of the arguments by Keynes and Kalecki, that it is investment (or, more generally, credit-financed purchases) that determines savings—and not the reverse.

It is nonetheless maintained by a large number of economists—even by some who call themselves "Keynesians"—that a higher rate of saving by households is a necessary precondition for increased business investment and thus more rapid economic growth. This argument, we can now see, is doubly wrong. First, it assumes that households are the only source of the savings needed to finance business investment. It thus ignores the fact that investment by the enterprise sector is financed primarily out of the cash flow, or savings, that business firms themselves generate. Indeed, for the reasons that were brought out in the earlier analysis of business finance (see chapter 7, section 3.1), it can hardly be otherwise. Second, as the flow of funds model makes clear, a higher rate of savings by households will only reduce the cash flow of business firms, leaving aggregate savings unchanged. Indeed, the only way to increase aggregate savings is through a prior increase in investment and other discretionary expenditures, with bank credit providing the necessary interim financing. The role of bank credit in enabling investment and other discretionary expenditures to vary independently of aggregate savings has a further implication, however, one which then makes it possible to derive the monetary condition for continuous economic expansion.

12.1.5 The monetary condition for continuous economic expansion

To the extent that expenditures can be financed, not out of current income but rather, through bank credit, the level of sales at any one moment in time is not limited to the amount of income flowing into each of the nonfinancial sectors. Sales to one of the nonfinancial sectors can exceed that sector's current income, or total cash inflow, by the amount the sector is willing and able to increase its debt to the banking system. Indeed, it is the possibility of the nonfinancial sectors being able to make credit-financed purchases that, by relaxing the income constraint that would otherwise preclude any such possibility, explains how the level of national income can increase from one time period to the next. This argument applies not only to the increase in autonomous, or discretionary, expenditures that initiates the multiplier process by which the level of national income increases but also to the subsequent rounds of that same multiplier process as business firms seek and obtain bank credit to finance the larger inventory they will need to hold in order to satisfy the greater demand for non-discretionary consumption goods. Of course, once the sector obtains the loan and uses the proceeds to make payment for additional goods and services, the borrowed funds will enter the income stream and remain in circulation from that point on in time. The level of income, Y, will therefore increase by the amount of additional credit obtained from the banking system. That is,

$$\Delta Y = \Delta Cr \tag{12.3}$$

where Y is the level of national income in nominal terms (the level of output in real terms, G, multiplied by the aggregate price level, P). Alternatively, since based on equation 12.2 ΔDep can be substituted for ΔCr,

$$\Delta Y = \Delta Dep \tag{12.4}$$

Equation 12.4 can be interpreted as stating the necessary monetary condition for a one-time, permanent increase in the level of national income as a result of the multiplier effect of a rise in credit-financed durable goods purchases. It indicates how much the amount of funds circulating as checkable bank deposits must increase, through the willingness of the nonfinancial sectors to go more heavily into debt to the banking system, if a higher level of aggregate expenditures is going to be achieved. It should be noted that, as will soon be made quite clear, the direction of causation is from left to right rather than the reverse, with the increase in income requiring the increase in credit and therefore inducing the increase in bank deposits.

Wynne Godley, in addition to first making clear this monetary condition for a one-time rise in the level of national income, has pointed out that the movement of the economy to the permanently higher level of expenditures cannot occur instantaneously. There will necessarily be a lag between the time the banking system credits the nonfinancial sectors with the additional funds and the time the funds are actually used to effect payment for goods and services, thereby adding to the flow of income. One can, in fact, posit the following sequence of events following an increase in debt by the nonfinancial sectors to the banking system so a higher level of expenditures can be carried out:

1. $\Delta Cr \cong \Delta Dep \longrightarrow$ Sales
2. ΔSales $\longrightarrow \Delta$Payments and hence ΔY

The first step in this dynamic adjustment process is the same as that outlined earlier in the case of a disequilibrium situation created by investment exceeding savings (see chapter 3, section 2.2)—only now the excess of investment over savings is represented by the increase in the amount of credit being extended by the banking system and the simultaneous increase in the amount of checkable bank deposits. With the amount of funds available for making payment augmented in this way, the increase in bank credit will be followed, with a certain lag, by an increase in the level of sales by the enterprise sector as a whole. The lag will depend on how much time normally elapses between when a loan agreement is entered into with the banks and contracts are then signed for the purchase of goods and services with the borrowed funds.

In the second step of the adjustment process, the increase in sales by the enterprise sector will be followed, again with a certain lag, by an increase in the flow of payments through the banking system, as traced out in exhibits 12.6 and 12.7. This second lag will depend on the amount of time allowed in the sales contract for making payment (as distinct from the amount of time allowed for delivery of the goods themselves, a lag that will affect only the real flows within the input-output model of production). Once payment has actually been effected, the level of national income will rise, as indicated by equations 12.3 and 12.4, by the amount the nonfinancial sectors have, on net balance, increased their debt to the banking system.

While the total amount of time required for this dynamic adjustment process to fully work itself out cannot be determined *a priori*—it is an empirical question, dependent on how quickly contracts are entered into and payment actually effected following the provision of bank credit—still the lag itself must be recognized. It implies that the level of expenditures on goods and services in any one time period, Exp_0, and thus the level of aggregate demand, will necessarily be equal to the level of national income in that period, Y_0, plus the increase in the amount of bank credit, Cr—with the level of national income rising in the next period to match the level of aggregate demand. That is,

$$Exp_0 = Y_0 + \Delta Cr_0 \tag{12.5}$$

with $Y_0 = Y_{-1} + \Delta Cr_{-1}$, based on equation 12.3. This sequence is traced out in exhibit 12.17 for an economic system in which the nonfinancial sectors have decided to increase their expenditures by $300 billion relying on bank credit, with the timing of the expenditures over the seven-period interval reflecting how quickly the necessary financing can be arranged.

The relationship represented by equation 12.5 and traced out in exhibit 12.17 is important for two reasons. First, it indicates why, in the interval between any one discrete time period and the next, the national product, as measured by total expenditures on goods and services, need not equal the national income. It is only by ignoring the short-run adjustment process by which any credit-financed expenditures lead to a permanent increase in the level of national income that the necessary condition for macrodynamic balance previously identified (see chapter 3, section 1.1) will appear to be satisfied. The point can be seen more clearly if NP_0 is substituted for Exp_0 and NI_0 for Y_0 in equation 12.5 as follows:

$$NP_0 = NI_0 + \Delta Cr_0 \tag{12.6}$$

Second, the relationship represented by equation 12.5 helps explain why the cash deficit incurred by any one of the nonfinancial sectors need not, and indeed can not, be offset by a cash surplus in one or more of the other nonfinancial sectors— not if the monetary condition for a one-time, permanent increase in the level of national income given by equation 12.4 is going to be satisfied. The point can be seen more clearly if the expenditures on nondurable goods and services by the nonfinancial sectors, taken as a whole, are subtracted from both sides of equation 12.5, leaving as the residual the following aggregate equation:

$$E = F + \Delta Cr \tag{12.7}$$

Equation 12.4, along with equation 12.3, specifies only the greater amount of checkable bank deposits that is necessary for a one-time increase in the level of national income. It says nothing about the monetary condition that must be satisfied to finance a constant rate of increase in the level of national income. However, by taking the requisite increase in deposits as a proportion of some prior level of deposits, it is possible to rewrite equation 12.4 in terms of growth rates as follows:

$$\dot{Y} = \dot{D}ep \tag{12.8}$$

With equation 12.4 replaced by equation 12.5 and the variables again specified in terms of their rate of increase, this necessary condition for continuous economic expansion then takes the following form:

$$\dot{E}xp = (\dot{Y} + \Delta Cr) \tag{12.9}$$

However, if equation 12.8 is simultaneously being satisfied, as both equation 12.3 and exhibit 12.17 indicate will necessarily be the case, equation 12.9 reduces to the following:

$$\dot{E}xp = \dot{Y} = \dot{C}r \tag{12.10}$$

That is why, at both the sectoral and aggregate level, the growth of expenditures need only match the growth of income once the amount of expenditures in any one time period exceeds the level of income by the amount required to previde the necessary increase in the means of payment.

Of course, in the long period, the increasing efficiency with which the banking system is able to carry out its function of effecting payment will reduce the need for bank loans as a means of increasing the amount of checkable deposits. That is, the following relationship, rather than equation 12.8, must necessarily hold in the long period:

$$\overset{\circ}{Y} = \overset{\circ}{D}ep + \overset{\circ}{V} \tag{12.11}$$

where $\overset{\circ}{V}$ is the secular rate at which the banking system is increasing the efficiency with which it carries out its payments function, measured by the ratio of bank deposits to national income, Dep/Y.

Equation 12.11 would appear to be identical to the equation of exchange, upon which the monetarist model of the inflationary process is based. The resemblance is all the more striking if $\overset{\circ}{Y}$ is broken down into its component parts and any increase in the desire of the nonbank public to hold currency is taken into account so that 12.10 can then be rewritten as follows:

$$\overset{\circ}{G} + \overset{\circ}{P} = \overset{\circ}{M} + \overset{\circ}{V} \tag{12.12}$$

where M is equal to the amount of bank deposits, Dep, and the amount of currency held by the nonbank public, Cur_P; and V is now the "income velocity" of circulation, based on the Irving Fisher equation of exchange, as distinct from the efficiency of the banking system in carrying out its payments function (see section 12.3.0 for a fuller explanation of the distinction). Equation 12.12, however, is merely a statement of the monetary condition that must be satisfied if the expansion of the economy in real terms is not going to be interrupted for lack of the funds needed to effect payment. Like the other necessary conditions for continuous growth which have been identified—such as the aggregate demand condition that $\mathring{I} = \mathring{S}$ (see chapter 4, section 1.4)—the equality does not imply anything about the direction of causality. Whether the variables on the right-hand side of the equal sign determine the variables on the left-hand side or vice versa has to be ascertained on some other basis. This, by the way, is also true of the strong statistical association that can be observed over time between the growth of money income and the growth of the means of payment. The correlation between these two growth rates indicates nothing about the direction of causation.

However, now that the process by which the amount of funds in circulation increases over time has been explained, the direction of causation is clear. The fact that what serves as the means of payment under a credit-based system of money is endogenously determined, based on the demand for credit, means that it is the left-hand side of equation 12.12 that determines the right-hand side rather than, as the monetarists would argue, the reverse. (It is also why the rate at which investment and other credit-financed expenditures are being carried out can be assumed to determine the level of aggregate savings rather than, as even many orthodox Keynesians seem to believe, the reverse.)

Only one point still remains to be clarified before the flow of funds model of a monetarized production system can be considered complete. This is the role played by bank reserves in the process by which any purchases of goods in excess of current cash inflow are financed. Indeed, it is because they believe that the amount of bank reserves is exogenously controlled by the monetary authority that monetarists would argue that the direction of causation in equation 12.12 is from right to left. The next step, then, is to introduce bank reserves formally into the flow of funds model developed so far and see to what extent the arguments which have been made about the endogeneity of money need to be modified—or perhaps even abandoned altogether. To further extend the model in this way, we shall also need to introduce, in the section which next follows, the central bank which the monetary authority regulates so that we can then trace out the effect of whatever policy that monetary authority adopts.

12.2 Monetary Policy

Business firms, households and other economic entities can be expected to retain their trust in the banking system, holding most of their cash balances as deposits in some bank, only as long as they have reason to believe they can withdraw the funds whenever they need or want to do so. It is not enough that they can order the funds transferred to the bank account of some other economic entity. To retain their confidence in the banking system, depositors need to know that they can withdraw the funds from the system itself. This means there must be some other type of asset, besides a deposit in a bank, which an economic entity can hold as part of its cash balance, with any bank deposits readily convertible into that other type of asset. To be acceptable in exchange for the funds deposited with the banking system, this other type of asset will need to take the form of a circulating "currency." This means it must be no less acceptable in exchange for goods and services than a check or bank draft. The banking system, knowing that it must be prepared to redeem in this other form of cash the funds deposited with it, will in turn need to hold, as part of its own assets, a certain amount of the circulating currency as a "reserve." To proceed any further and explain, at least within the context of the U.S. economy, what constitutes either the circulating "currency" or bank reserves more generally, it is necessary to expand upon the flow of funds model by adding, as a separate sector within the financial subsystem, a central bank with its own distinctive assets and liabilities. The first step will be to explain the role played by a central bank, like the U.S. Federal Reserve System, in an advanced industrial economy.

12.2.1 The role of the central bank

As attested to by the historical experience of the past three centuries, a system of payment based on credit money is susceptible to cataclysmic breakdown. One source of potential danger arises from the asset structure of the banking system. If, for some reason, the loans made by a bank should "go bad"—that is, if borrowers are unable to maintain the agreed upon schedule of payment for servicing their debt—then the bank will find itself financially weakened by the reduced rate of cash inflow. If enough of the loans it has made should, in this way, become "delinquent," the bank will be unable to convert its deposits into some other form of cash and the bank will become "illiquid." Under ordinary circumstances, it would then be forced into receivership. Of course, if only one bank suffers from a problem of bad loans and is forced into receivership, the system as a whole will not necessarily be threatened. Indeed, this is the argument for a system of payment based on a large number of banks, each of which assumes both the responsibility for judging the credit-worthiness of prospective borrowers and the attendant risk should its judgment prove to be wrong. Still, experience has shown that it is possible for banks as a group, through no fault of their own, to be suddenly confronted by a widespread condition in which borrowers are unable to continue making the payments required of them in settlement of their outstanding debt. This possibility is created by the volatility of the income and real output flows in a monetarized system of production.

Even without the problem created by delinquent loans, the banking system may find itself in a crisis. Whatever is the alternative to allowing funds to remain as deposits within the banking system—whether it be converting the deposits into some form of commodity money or, with fiat money having replaced commodity money, converting them into whatever happens to be the circulating currency of the country—the banking system may find itself being drained of that particular type of asset. This means the banking system will lose a portion of what normally serves as part of its reserves. If the loss of reserves continues unchecked, the banking system may no longer be able to convert deposits into cash, causing the system to become just as illiquid as when faced with delinquent loans on a large scale. Historically, this type of threat to the liquidity of the banking system has been created by events originating outside the country itself—e.g., by a significant decline in exports relative to imports which has to be covered by drawing on domestic bank balances. The U.S. banking system, because of the unique status of the dollar as an international currency, is not presently susceptible to a loss of reserves through the net outflow of funds abroad. It can, nonetheless, still suffer a significant loss of reserves, thereby threatening the liquidity of the system.

It is because the system of payment, based on checks issued against the funds deposited in banks, is vulnerable in each of these two ways that the governments of advanced industrial societies have found they must establish a central bank to serve as the overall regulator of the financial system. Each government has arrived at this solution by following a different historical path, reflecting the country's own unique experience in attempting to exploit the advantges of industrial development. Still, since the need for a central bank derives from the very nature of the credit-based system of money common to all advanced industrial societies, the central banks which have been established by each of the different governments have certain features in common. Thus, while the analysis that follows will be based on the specific example of the Federal Reserve System, the type of central bank the U.S. government has established, much of the argument also applies to other countries with a different type of central bank. This is true despite the fact that, unlike the situation in other countries, the Federal Reserve System consists of 12 separate central banks, each covering a different region of the United States, with those 12 banks forming a system that is overseen by a single monetary authority, the Federal Reserve Board or the "Fed" (officially known as the "Board of Governors of the Federal Reserve System").

The central bank's first and foremost responsibility, given its *raison d'être*, is to act as a fail-safe mechanism, preventing the system of payment from suffering a cataclysmic breakdown. The central bank is able to play this role because of its unique powers. They include the following:

1) the right to issue, as a liability of the central bank itself, notes which then serve as the circulating currency, or fiat money, within that political jurisdiction.

2) the right to require all other banks to deposit with it certain types of assets as a reserve against the amount of funds they themselves held as deposits;

3) the right to make loans, or advances, to the other banks either by providing them with additional currency or, alternatively, by simply crediting them with additional amounts of the reserves they are legally required to maintain with the central bank; and

4) the right to purchase, in the open market, certain types of assets—including those held by the banks in return for the loans they have made—thereby shoring up the asset structure of the banking system.

These powers which the central bank has, at least in the United States, are reflected not just in the balance sheet of the central bank itself but also in the balance sheet of the depository institutions (i.e., other banks) the central bank regulates.

What constitutes the ''currency'' and ''other reserves'' of banks has, up to this point, been left deliberately vague (see exhibits 12.3–12.9, 12.11–12.16). It can now be seen that the ''currency'' which banks hold as part of their reserves so that depositors can be assured of being able to withdraw their funds should they wish to do so are in fact the liabilities which the central bank is empowered to incur by issuing its own notes. (In the case of the United States, these liabilities are the Federal Reserve notes which individuals use in everyday, small transactions). The notes issued by the central bank (actually, by each of the 12 Federal Reserve Banks) are, in turn, one of the items included on the liability side of its balance sheet (that is, the balance sheet for the Federal Reserve System as a whole—see exhibit 12.18). The total Federal Reserve note issue consists of (a) the currency held by banks; (b) the currency held by the nonbank public; and (c) the U.S. Treasury's own cash holdings. However, it is only the currency held by the banks (what is termed their ''vault cash'') that constitutes a part of the banking system's reserves, with the figure shown under that category on the liability side of the central bank's balance sheet necessarily the same as the figure shown on the asset side of the banking system's balance sheet. Yet to be explained is the remaining portion of the banking system's reserves—the reserve balances shown on the liability side of the central bank's balance sheet and the equal amount of other reserves shown on the asset side of the banking system's balance sheet.

The banking system's other reserves are the balances which the members of the Federal Reserve System maintain at one of the 12 Federal Reserve Banks, depending on the region in which they are located. Initially, at the formation of the Federal Reserve System, these balances were created by the member banks exchanging the gold, or commodity money, they held as reserves for shares in one of the 12 regional Federal Reserve banks. Since then, with the complete displacement of gold from the domestic system of payment, the balances maintained by member banks at the ''Fed'' (i.e., with the Federal Reserve System as a whole) has come to depend on the central bank's open market operations—that is, on its purchase and sale of U.S. government securities. The right to engage in open market operations has, in fact, become the most important of the powers exercised by the Fed as the central bank of the United States. Aside from shoring up the asset structure of the banking system (along with the asset structure of other institutions, nonfinancial as well as financial), it is the principal means by which the monetary authority, the Federal Reserve Board, is able to implement its policies.

The Federal Reserve System, acting through its agent in the financial markets, the Federal Reserve Bank of New York, is able to effect the purchase of government securities only by issuing in payment a check drawn on its own account. If the securities have been purchased from a member bank, the check will pass

Exhibit 12.18

Balance Sheets of Central Bank (Federal Reserve System) and Banking System

Central Bank

Assets	Liabilities
Gold Stock	Federal Reserve Notes
SDRs	Currency held by banks
U.S. Government Securities	Currency held by public
Loans to Member Banks	Treasury cash holdings
Float	Reserve Balances
Other Assets	Other Liabilities

Banking System

Assets	Liabilities
Currency	Checkable Deposits
Other Reserves	Noncheckable Deposits
Loans	Other Liabilities
Other Assets	Net Worth

directly into the hands of that bank. If, alternatively, the securities have been purchased from some other private party, the check will pass into the hands of a member bank only after it has been deposited in that bank by the party which has sold the securities to the Fed. In either case, the check issued in payment will come into the possession of a member bank, and the only way the Fed can clear the check (that is, make good on it) is by crediting the member bank with a greater reserve balance. It is in this way that the purchase of government securities by the Fed, while necessarily adding to the assets of the central bank, also leads to an increase in the amount of bank reserves that are shown both on the liability side of the central bank's balance sheet and on the asset side of the banking system's own separate balance sheet. The sale of government securities by the Federal Reserve System has the opposite effect, with the check written by either a bank or other private party to pay for the securities necessarily reducing, once the check clears, the reserves of the banking system.

Another of the central bank's powers is, of course, the right to determine the amount of reserves each member bank needs to hold as a proportion of its deposits, noncheckable as well as checkable. These are the bank's required reserves, as distinct from its actual reserves. A common error among economists is to assume that, since banks can be expected to hold no more than the required amount of reserves and will, in pursuit of maximum earnings, use whatever additional funds they have to make loans, the central bank can, by determining the amount of bank reserves through its open market operations, also determine the amount of funds circulating in the form of bank deposits. Indeed, it is for this reason that economists usually assume that what they term the ''supply of money'' is exogenously determined as a matter of monetary policy. This line of argument, as we shall now see, is incorrect for a number of reasons. To begin with, it ignores the very purpose for which the governments of advanced industrial societies have established central banks like the U.S. Federal Reserve System—a purpose which is reflected in the way the central bank conducts its open market operations.

12.2.2 Open market operations

The Fed's primary objective, in conducting its open market operations, is to ensure the liquidity of the banking system. This means that its open market operations necessarily consist, for the most part, of two elements: (1) defensive behavior, and (2) accommodating behavior.

The defensive component of the Fed's open market operations requires that it offset the flows into and out of the domestic monetary-financial system so as to leave the total amount of baank reserves unchanged. The flows into and out of the domestic monetary-financial system are those represented by the other items on the Fed's balance sheet shown in exhibit 12.18 besides the reserve balances on the liability side and the loans to member banks on the asset side. The defensive component of the Fed's open market operations thus consists of buying or selling government securities so that, on net balance, it offsets these flows into or out of the monetary-financial system. An increase in the amount of cash held by the nonbank public will, for example, reduce bank reserves while an increase in the amount of bank float (the number of checks issued but not yet cleared) will add to bank reserves. In order to maintain bank reserves at the same level, the Fed will need to purchase in the open market government securites equal in value to whatever additional currency the nonbank public has decided to hold. If, instead, the nonbank public decides to reduce the amount of currency it holds, the Fed will need to sell government securities. The same is true of the other items on the liability side of the Fed's balance sheet shown in exhibit 12.18, with an increase in any of those items necessarily having to be offset by the purchase of government securities and a decline in any of those items, by the sale of government securities. For the items on the asset side of the Fed's balance sheet, the argument holds in reverse. To maintain bank reserves at the same level, the Fed will need to purchase government securities to match any reduction in those items and it will need to sell government securities to match any increase.

To demonstrate that the Fed must act in this way if total bank reserves are to be held at a fixed level, it is necessary only to set the two sides of the Fed's balance sheet equal to one another as follows:

$$\text{G}old + \text{SDR}s + \text{FGS} + \text{Res}_{BOR} + \text{F}lt + \text{Oth}\text{A} =$$
$$\text{Cur}_V + \text{Cur}_P + \text{Cur}_G + \text{Res}_{Bal} + \text{Oth}\text{L} \qquad (12.13)$$

where $\text{G}old$ is the amount of gold and $\text{SDR}s$, the amount of Special Drawing Rights (within the International Monetary Fund) held by the Fed; FGS is the amount of U.S. government securities held by the Fed; Res_{Bor} is the amount of borrowed reserves, or loans made by the Fed to members banks; $\text{F}lt$ is the amount of bank float; OthA is the amount of other assets held by the Fed; Cur_V is the amount of currency held by the banks in their vaults; Cur_P is the amount of currency held by the nonbank public; Cur_G is the U.S. Treasury's cash holdings; Res_{Bal} is the amount of reserve balances held at the Fed by member banks, including any borrowed reserves, and OthL is the amount of the Fed's other liabilities. Rewriting equation 12.13 in first-difference form and then isolating the net change in total bank reserves, ΔRes_T, on the right-hand side, we obtain the following equation:

$$\Delta\text{Res}_T = + \Delta\text{G}old + \Delta\text{SDR}s + \Delta\text{FGS} + \Delta\text{F}lt + \Delta\text{Res}_{Bor} + \Delta\text{Oth}\text{A}$$
$$- \Delta\text{Cur}_P - \Delta\text{Cur}_G - \Delta\text{Oth}\text{L} \qquad (12.14)$$

where ΔRes_T is the net change in total bank reserves and is equal to the banking system's non-borrowed reserves, ΔRes_{NB}, plus the amount of borrowed reserves, ΔRes_{Bor}, and the amount of currency held by the banks, ΔCur_V. The amount of borrowed reserves, it should be noted, continues to appear on both sides of the equation. Whereas in equation 12.13 it appeared on the right-hand side as part of the reserve balances held at the Fed by member banks, in equation 12.14 it appears on the left-hand side as part of total bank reserves.

From equation 12.14 it can be seen that, if bank reserves are to remain at the same level, the Fed needs to offset any change in the other variables on the right-hand side by an opposite change in the amount of U.S. government securities it holds. For example, with an increase in the amount of currency held by the nonbank public, total bank reserves will fall (as indicated by the negative sign attached to the ΔCur_P variable) unless the Fed's holdings of government securities, FGS, increase by the amount the nonbank public has added to the currency it holds—just as an increase in the amount of bank float will cause total bank reserves to rise (as indicated by the positive sign attached to the $\Delta\text{F}lt$ variable) unless the Fed reduces its holdings of government securities by the amount the float has increased.

The point can be seen even more clearly by holding total bank reserves constant (so that the ΔRes_T variable, being equal to zero, drops out of equation 12.14 along with the ΔRes_{Bor} variable on the right-hand side) and then isolating, on the left-hand side, the ΔFGS variable as follows:

$$\Delta\text{FGS} = - \Delta\text{G}old - \Delta\text{SDR}s - \Delta\text{F}lt - \text{Oth}\text{A}$$
$$+ \Delta\text{Cur}_P + \Delta\text{Cur}_G + \Delta\text{Oth}\text{L} \qquad (12.15)$$

While equation 12.14 indicates the net change in the total bank reserves that will occur as a result of a change in the other balance sheet items (including the Fed's portfolio of government securities), equation 12.15 indicates the change in the Fed's holdings of government securities that is required to offset a change in the other balance sheet items (besides the Fed's portfolio of government securities) so that bank reserves will remain unchanged. Thus the Fed needs to reduce its holdings of government securities in order to offset an increase in the amount of bank float or any of its other assets (as indicated by the negative sign attached to those variables in equation 12.15) while it needs to add to its holdings of government securities to offset an increase in the amount of currency held by the public or any of its other liabilities (besides those which serve as reserves for the banking system).

Equation 12.15 explains why there is no observable relationship between the Fed's open market operations, as represented by the FGS variable, and the amount of bank reserves. The Fed's purchases or sales of government securities are intended primarily to offset the flows into or out of the domestic monetary-financial system and thereby hold bank reserves constant. The central bank, however, cannot just maintain bank reserves at a fixed level. As already explained (see section 12.1.1), the reason the earlier systems of commodity and fiat money alone were replaced by a credit-based system was the need for a means of payment that would vary with the level of economic activity and thus with the need for additional funds. Under a credit-based system of money, the amount of funds in circulation will increase automatically in response to the need for additional working capital by business firms (as well as in response to the need for other forms of short-term credit). But this presumes that banks are not precluded, by the lack of reserves, from making the requisite loans. It is the banking system's need for additional reserves as the demand for credit increases that explains the other part of the Fed's open market operations, its accommodating behavior.

Whenever the banks, responding to the need for additional credit, increase their outstanding loans to one or more of the nonfinancial sectors, the amount of funds deposited with the banking system, as the offset on the liability side of the additional assets being acquired by banks, will necessarily increase. The amount of reserves which the banking system is legally required to maintain, either as cash in the vault or as a balance maintained at the Fed, depends on the amount of funds deposited in the system. Thus an increase in bank loans, by increasing the amount of bank deposits, will add to the banking system's required reserves. If the banking system is not going to be left with insufficient reserves, the Fed will need to take offsetting action. This means it must purchase additional government securities equal to the amount by which the banking system's required reserves are increasing. The amount by which the Fed must increase its holdings of government securities so as to accommodate the demand for bank loans is therefore given by the following equation:

$$\Delta FGS_A = \Delta Res_R \qquad (12.16)$$

where ΔFGS_A is the change in the Fed's holdings of government securities that is needed solely to accommodate the demand for bank loans. However, unless the Fed also, at the same time, acts to fully offset the flows into and out of the domestic monetary-financial system, the banks may still be left either with insufficient reserves or, if there has been a net inflow of funds into the system, with excess reserves. Thus, to fully accommodate the demand for bank loans without providing the banks with excess reserves, the Fed will need to conduct its open market operations according to the following rule:

$$\Delta FGS_A = - \Delta Fed_A + \Delta Cur_P + \Delta Res_R \qquad (12.17)$$

where Fed_A is the net change in the various items, besides the amount of currency held by the nonbank public, shown on the right-hand side of equation 12.15. That is,

$$\Delta Fed_A = \Delta Gold + \Delta SDRs + \Delta Flt + \Delta OthA - \Delta Cur_G - \Delta OthL \qquad (12.18)$$

The change in the Fed's holdings of government securities in response to a change in the first two items on the right-hand side of equation 12.17 represents the defensive component of the U.S. central bank's open market operations, and the change in the Fed's holdings of government securities in response to a change in the last item on the right-hand side represents the accommodating component. As can be seen from exhibit 12.19, approximately 80 percent of the change in the Fed's holdings of government securities in the period between 1953 and 1978 can be accounted for by these three explanatory variables. In other words, the change in the Fed's holdings of government securities and thus its open market operations, instead of being strictly a policy variable, is for the most part endogenously determined by the need to maintain the liquidity of the banking system. Indeed, this is why it is an error to assume, as macroeconomic theorists normally do, that the monetary base, or high-powered money—consisting of the currency held by the nonbank public, Cur_P, and total bank reserves, Res_T (that is, all but the third and last items on the right-hand side of equation 12.13)—is an exogenously determined policy variable. The fact is that the nonbank public cannot be prevented from adding to the amount of currency it holds—not if its confidence in the banking system is going to be maintained. And if the banking system is going to be left with enough reserves to meet its legal requirements, the Fed then has no choice but to offset through its open market operations not just the change in the ΔCur_P variable but also any change in the ΔRes_R variable as well.

This is not to say that the Fed, as the monetary authority for the United States, will necessarily pursue a fully accommodating policy. The same evidence presented in exhibit 12.19 that the Fed's open market operations are largely an

Exhibit 12.19

Variables Affecting the Federal Reserve Board's Open-Market Operations (as Measured by ΔFGS)

Variables	Interval	1953–1978	1953–1961	1962–1978	1962–1972	1972–1978
ΔFed$_A$	coeff	−.76	−.66	−.77	−64	−.81
	t ratio	14.84	6.70	12.10	6.35	8.39
ΔRes$_R$	coeff	.75	.35	.81	.61	.92
	t ratio	6.89	2.79	5.58	4.15	3.88
ΔCur$_P$	coeff	1.10	1.42	1.04	.90	1.17
	t ratio	14.00	3.74	8.40	3.65	3.14
Constant	coeff	25.37	−24.89	82.12	230.08	−169.91
	t ratio	.35*	.55*	.56*	1.42*	.28*
R^2		.80	.63	.74	.60	.76
D–W		2.95	2.22	3.12	2.22	3.57
Observations		104	36	68	44	28

*Not statistically significant at 5% level of probability.

endogenous response to the demand for credit also indicates that the monetary authority is not without some discretion as to how accommodating a policy it will actually follow. While approximately 80 percent of the change in the Fed's holdings of government securities between 1953 and 1978 can be accounted for by the need both to offset the flows into and out of the domestic monetary-financial system *and* to provide banks with the reserves they require, there is the remaining 20 percent of the Fed's portfolio changes still to be explained. This requires an analysis of the Fed's nonaccommodating behavior, both the impact which such a policy is likely to have on the economy's macrodynamic behavior and the reasons for such a policy—despite the threat it poses to the liquidity of the banking system.

12.2.3 A nonaccommodating policy

The U.S. Federal Reserve System, in carrying out its open market operations, need not just offset the flows into and out of the domestic monetary-financial system while simultaneously making sure that banks have adequate reserves. It can pursue a less than fully accommodating policy or, alternatively, it can pursue a more than fully accommodating policy. In either case, the effect will be a change in the amount of free reserves held by the banks, ΔRes$_F$—with a less than fully accommodating policy necessarily leading to a reduction in free reserves and a more than fully accommodating policy, to an increase in free reserves. This can be seen from the very definition of free reserves.

The banking system's free reserves are its total reserves —borrowed as well as nonborrowed—less the amount of required reserves. That is,

$$\Delta Res_F = \Delta Res_T - \Delta Res_R \tag{12.19}$$

The offsetting balance sheet items, for any change in total reserves, is given by equation 12.14. By means of equation 12.18, we can substitute the net change in the Fed's assets, ΔFed_A, for all the variables on the right-hand side of equation 12.14—with the exception of the change in Fed's holdings of government securities (ΔFGS), the amount of credit it has extended to member banks (ΔRes_{Bor}), and the amount of currency held by the nonbank public (ΔCur_P)—so that, for any change in total bank reserves, the following relationship necessarily holds:

$$\Delta Res_T = \Delta Fed_A + \Delta FGS + \Delta Res_{Bor} - \Delta Cur_P \tag{12.20}$$

The amount of borrowed reserves can be subtracted from both sides of equation 12.20, eliminating that variable from the right-hand side and leaving only the banking system's nonborrowed reserves on the left-hand side as follows:

$$\Delta Res_{NB} = \Delta Fed_A + \Delta FGS - \Delta Cur_P \tag{12.21}$$

The total change in the Fed's holdings of government securities can then be divided into (a) the change necessary to fully accommodate the demand for credit, ΔFGS_A, and (b) the difference between the total change and the accommodating change, $\Delta FGS - \Delta FGS_A$ or ΔFGS_{NA}. Equation 12.21 can therefore be rewritten as follows:

$$\Delta Res_{NB} = \Delta Fed_A + \Delta FGS_A + \Delta FGS_{NA} - \Delta Cur_P \tag{12.22}$$

Substituting the accommodating change in the Fed's holdings of government securities, as given by equation 12.17, for ΔFGS_A in the above equation, we found that the ΔFed_A and ΔCur_P variables cancel out and we obtain the following:

$$\Delta Res_{NB} = \Delta Res_R + \Delta FGS_{NA} \tag{12.23}$$

Since the banking system's total reserves are the sum of its borrowed and nonborrowed reserves, the change in borrowed reserves, ΔRes_{Bor}, can be added to both sides of equation 12.23 so as to yield the following equation:

$$\Delta Res_T = \Delta Res_R + \Delta FGS_{NA} + \Delta Res_{Bor} \tag{12.24}$$

Finally, substituting the right-hand side of this last equation for the ΔRes_T variable in equation 12.19, the ΔRes_R variable cancels out and we obtain the following:

$$\Delta Res_F = \Delta FGS_{NA} + \Delta Res_{Bor} \qquad (12.24)$$

Thus the change in the banking system's free reserves is equal to the nonaccommodating change in the Fed's holdings of government securities, ΔFGS_{NA}, plus the change in borrowed reserves, ΔRes_{Bor}.

To the extent the monetary authority puts pressure on banks to curtail their lending activity rather than avail themselves of the Fed's credit facilities, the change in borrowed reserves will be closer to zero and all of the Fed's nonaccommodating behavior will be reflected by the change in free reserves. Substituting $X_{M \cdot 1}$ for FGS_{NA} to indicate that the Fed's nonaccommodating change in the amount of government securities it holds is a policy variable, this means that equation 12.24 can be rewritten as follows:

$$X_{M \cdot 1.} = \Delta Res_F \qquad (12.25)$$

with $X_{M \cdot 2}$, the change in the required reserve ratio (that is, the amount of reserves banks must hold relative to their deposits), and $X_{M \cdot 3}$, the rediscount rate (that is, the interest charged by the Fed on loans to member banks), constituting the other monetary policy variables insofar as the U.S. economy is concerned. (It should be noted the required reserve ratio varies both with the type of deposit and with the type of depository institution, so that $X_{M \cdot 2}$ is actually a set of monetary policy variables.) Now that it has been shown that the Fed's more-or- less-than-fully-accommodating behavior can be approximated, as a policy variable, by the change in the banking system's free reserves, the next step is to explain what effect such a policy is likely to have on the economy's real flows.

Any open market operations by the Fed which are either less or more than fully accommodating will have two quite separate effects. One is the obvious effect on the banking system's reserve position. With a reduction in the amount of free reserves, and thus a decline in the ratio of free to total reserves, at least some banks can expect to find themselves short of reserves and they will be forced to respond in one of two ways. Most immediately, they will need to acquire additional reserves. While they can, if necessary, arrange to borrow the additional funds from the Fed, this will invite an official inquiry into their lending operations. They are therefore more likely to borrow the excess reserves of other banks in what is known as the federal funds market. This resort to the federal funds market, when bank reserves are being squeezed by a nonaccommodating policy, will cause the rate that must be paid on those funds to rise. As will be brought out in the subsection which follows, the increase in the federal funds rate will put upward pressure on interest rates more generally. Once past the immediate need to square their accounts at the Fed, member banks can be expected to cut back on their loans so that, with the corresponding reduction in bank deposits, they can satisfy their reserve requirements without having to borrow. The longer term effect of the Fed's nonaccommodating policy, then, will be to make the banks less willing to provide credit. It should be noted that, in this last respect, a more than fully accommodating policy is not simply the obverse of a less than fully accommodating policy—and thus the two types of policies are not entirely symmetrical. While the federal funds rate can be expected to fall with an increase in the ratio of free to total bank reserves, thereby putting downward pressure on interest rates, banks are not inclined to approve loan applications just because they have excess reserves. They will, in fact, be willing to grant loans only to those who can demonstrate that they are "credit-worthy," and once this demand for loans has been satisfied, no additional credit is likely to be extended.

There is a second effect of a nonaccommodating policy, one that is not generally appreciated. This is the effect on the amount of funds within the banking system itself—as distinct from the amount of funds held as reserve balances at the Fed. The banks can lend out to others only the funds which have been deposited with them. As funds are lent out, the amount of funds available for making further loans will be reduced and, in time, exhausted. The Fed, through its open market operations, not only increases the amount of reserve balances. It also, when it purchases government securities from the nonbank public, increases the amount of funds deposited with the banking system. This is because the checks issued in payment for those securities will, before they are returned to the Fed causing the amount of bank reserves to increase, be deposited in some bank so that bank balances themselves will rise. It is, in fact, only in this way that a cash deficit by the U.S. federal government can be translated into an increase in bank deposits. Unless the Fed purchases the securities issued to cover the cash deficit, thereby "monetizing" the debt, total bank deposits will remain unchanged. When, therefore, the Fed decides as a matter of policy not to fully accommodate the demand for credit, the banking system as a whole is likely to find itself short, not just of reserves but also, no less critically, of deposits as well. Indeed, the balance which the banks normally maintain between their loans (on the asset side of their balance sheets) and their deposits (on the liability side) will be upset, putting further pressure on the banks to curtail their lending activity. The key policymaking group within each bank is its ALCo, or Assets and Liabilities Committee, and when a bank finds itself short of the funds it needs, in the form of deposits, to make further loans, the ALCo will have to decide what class of loans to cut back on.

The ratio of bank loans to bank deposits can, in fact, be regarded as a measure of the banking system's lending capacity, with any deviation from the secular, or normal, ratio, $\hat{L}$, a disequilibrium condition created by the Fed's nonaccommodating behavior. A less than fully accommodating policy, as indicated by an increase in the value of $\hat{L}$, will put pressure on the banks to cut back on their loans to business firms and households—even beyond what will be happening as a result of the simultaneous rise in interest rates. Indeed, this is why the $\hat{L}$ variable appears as one of the parameters of the E curve for the enterprise and household sectors, with that variable exerting an even greater influence on the cyclical movement of real discretionary expenditures, $\overset{*}{A}_i$, than whatever is the relevant long-term interest rate, i_{LT}. The $\hat{L}$ variable in effect captures the extent to which the banking system is being forced to ration credit when the Fed, as the U.S. monetary authority, decides to pursue a nonaccommodating policy. This is why $\hat{L}$ can also be viewed as measuring the "degree of liquidity pressure," with an increase $\hat{L}$ indicating greater pressure on the liquidity of the banking system and a decline in $\hat{L}$, a reduction in liquidity pressure.

Any nonprice credit-rationing by the banks will, of course, be reinforced by the simultaneous rise in the level of interest rates. As already pointed out, a nonaccommodating policy on the part of the Fed will cause the federal funds rate, i_{FF}, to rise as banks with insufficient reserves are forced to compete for a diminished amount of excess reserves. With the Fed itself no longer as significant a factor on the demand side of the government securities market, the Treasury bill rate, i_{TB}, is also likely to rise, adding to the upward movement of short-term interest rates. Eventually, because of the differential which normally exists between short- and long-term interest rates (see the next subsection), the cost of servicing any newly acquired external debt will increase, discouraging prospective borrowers from seeking long-term loans, at least for the time being. Still, the more powerful influence in forcing a cutback in credit-financed durable goods purchases will be the reluctance of the banks to countenance any further deterioration in their balance sheet position, as measured by $\hat{L}$, and the subsequent cutting off of credit to certain entire classes of borrowers.

One can therefore expect to observe the following dynamic sequence whenever the Fed decides to pursue a less than fully accommodating policy:

1. $- \Delta \text{Res}_F$ and $\therefore - \Delta(\text{Res}_F/\text{Res}_T) \longrightarrow + \Delta i_{FF}, + \Delta i_{TB}, + \Delta \hat{L}$
2. $+ \Delta i_{FF}, + i_{TB}, \longrightarrow + \Delta i_{LT}$
3. $+ \hat{L}, + i_{LT} \longrightarrow - \overset{*}{A}$
4. $- \overset{*}{A} \longrightarrow - \overset{*}{G}$

The effect of a less than fully accommodating policy on the part of the Fed is clear. It will, by putting upward pressure on interest rates and, even more significantly, by forcing banks to ration credit, lead to a cyclical downturn in the rate of growth of real discretionary expenditures, $\overset{*}{A}$, and of aggregate output, $\overset{*}{G}$. (The effect of a more than fully accommodating monetary policy is not so clear cut. It may simply lead to lower interest rates and excess bank reserves, without a significant cyclical effect on the economy.) This, however, is only the minimal effect which a less than fully accommodating policy on the part of the Fed may have. If pursued long or hard enough, the less than fully accommodating policy may lead, as Hyman Minsky has pointed out, to a collapse of the entire monetary-financial system.

A cyclical downturn, whether initiated by a nonaccommodating monetary policy or not, will cause the enterprise sector, along with one or more of the other nonfinancial sectors, to run an involuntary cash deficit. This is because of the effect which the cyclical downturn will have on the rate of capacity utilization within the enterprise sector and hence on the rate of cash flow into that sector (see chapter 7, section 3.2). To the extent the cyclical downturn also reduces employment and tax revenues, the household and government sectors will incur involuntary deficits as well. With the banks willing and able to provide short-term loans, the involuntary cash deficits will not be a serious problem. At most, some marginal business enterprises—or those with a temporarily exposed financial position because they have committed themselves, at least for the moment, to large fixed-interest payments—will be forced into receivership. But if, because of the Fed's restrictive monetary policy, those cash deficits cannot be financed, business firms will eventually be forced on a large scale to default on their financial obligations, thereby undermining the asset structure of the banks and other financial institutions. At that point in the process of cumulative debt deflation and contraction, the banking system will become illiquid, with economic entities unable to continue making payment, and the financial system will find itself in crisis.

The central bank can, of course, easily avert such a crisis. All it need do is reverse its restrictive monetary policy and, instead of putting pressure on the banks to curtail their lending activity, encourage them to provide whatever credit business firms and other economic entities need to tide themselves over. The central government also needs to do its part, deliberately incurring a large cash deficit—if it has not already done so involuntarily. Only the total cash deficit, $E - F$, and not the distribution of that deficit among the different nonfinancial sectors, is uniquely determined by the level of aggregate demand, $\overset{*}{G}$, so that the central government, by running a larger cash deficit, can reduce the deficit of the other nonfinancial sectors. Meanwhile it is the total cash deficit, including whatever portion is accounted for by the central government, which, by giving rise to a stimulative cash-flow feedback effect, will enable the economy to recover and eventually resume its secular expansion (see chapter 10, section 4.3). Still, if the central government insists on balancing its own budget, even during a cyclical downturn, so that the aggregate cash deficit, $E - F$, is largely shifted on to the other nonfinancial sectors while the central bank continues to hold to its nonaccommodating policy, a collapse of the monetary-financial system is all but certain. This, in fact, is the Minsky explanation for the various financial crises—and near crises—the United States has experienced over the last century or more.

Only one further point need be made in connection with a nonaccommodating policy by the Fed. Such a policy often gives rise to one or more subsequent financial innovations as the banks and other financial institutions seek to avoid the limits the Fed might otherwise be able to impose in the future on their lending activity. This explains the emergence in recent decades of CDs (certificates of deposit), negotiable CDs, money market accounts, repurchase agreements and a number of other new financial practices. The innovations are simply the banking system's longer term response to a nonaccommodating policy on the part of the Fed—a response that is no more surprising than the banking system's more immediate response of having to ration credit while it tries to make do with its existing reserve balances. The financial innovations are but an example of a positive (i.e., learning) feedback response, as distinct from the negative (adaptive) response which credit rationing represents.

While it is clear what will happen if the Fed should opt for a less than fully accommodating policy, there is still the question of why it would choose such a policy. After all, the best it can hope to achieve is a cyclical downturn in economic activity which, hopefully, can be reversed before it becomes a full-blown financial crisis. The reason usually given for the Fed's pursuing a nonaccommodating policy is the need to curb inflation. To see what validity there may be to this argument, we need to turn to what is the one thing the Fed, as the U.S. monetary authority, clearly controls. This is the level of interest rates.

12.2.4 The level of interest rates

From what has already been said, it is clear that the Fed is able to set short-term interest rates at whatever level it wishes. The Fed itself decides on the rediscount rate, that is, the rate of interest on any funds borrowed from it by member banks. Indeed, the rediscount rate, $X_{M \cdot 3}$, is one of the three monetary policy variables within the U.S. economy. In most countries, the central bank's control over this "bank rate," as it is termed, is sufficient to determine the entire set of short-term interest rates since all other short- and even long-term interest rates are keyed to it. However, in the United States the situation is a little more complicated since the key short-term rate is not the rediscount, or "bank, rate but rather the federal funds rate, i_{FF}. This is because, with the rediscount rate a policy variable and hence a politically "administered" price, it is the federal funds rate that is more sensitive to credit market conditions. Changes in the rediscount rate are, in fact, more likely to lag behind than to anticipate changes in the federal funds rate.

Even though the federal funds rate is the more sensitive barometer of credit market conditions, the Fed is fully able to determine i_{FF}—along with the other key short-term interest rate, the Treasury bill rate, i_{TB}. As was pointed out in the preceding subsection, the Fed can cause the federal funds rate to rise simply by forcing, through its open market operations, a reduction in the banking system's free reserves—just as, by increasing the amount of free reserves, it can cause the federal funds rate to fall. The same less than fully accommodating policy, meanwhile, by lowering the price at which U.S. government securities can be bought and sold in the open market, will cause the Treasury bill rate to rise while a more than fully accommodating policy, by raising the price of government securities, will cause the Treasury bill rate to fall. In this way, the Fed can stabilize the entire set of short-term interest rates at whatever level it wishes. All it need do is first reduce or increase the banking system's free reserves until the desired level of short-term interest rates has been reached and then switch from a nonaccommodating to a fully accommodating policy. Whether short-term interest rates remain fixed at that level will, in fact, be the best indication of whether the Fed has adopted a fully accommodating policy.

The set of short-term interest rates, i_{ST}, therefore depends on the the Fed's open market operations in the following way: As long as the banking system's free reserves remain unchanged, with $X_{M \cdot 1}$ consequently equal to zero, short-term interest rates will stay at the same level. This means that those in need of bank loans can obtain all the additional credit they need at a fixed rate, i_0, and the supply of additional funds, or bank credit, can be represented by the type of curve shown in exhibit 12.20. With $X_{m \cdot 1} < 0$, short-term interest rates will rise while, with $X_{M \cdot 1} > 0$, short-term interest rates will fall. Indeed, they will continue to rise or fall until the Fed again opts for a policy that is just fully accommodating, with $X_{M \cdot 1}$ equal to zero (or the Fed reverses policy and hence the direction in which short-term interest rates are moving). Thus the perfectly elastic supply curve for additional credit shown in exhibit 12.20 may shift up or down, depending on whether the Fed is pursuing a less than or a more than fully accommodating policy. However, this shift of the supply curve for additional credit should not be confused with a movement along the curve, with the quantity supplied assumed to vary positively with the interest rate—or even to be perfectly inelastic with respect to i. That would involve the fallacy of positing a supply curve for additional credit that was separate from, and therefore independent of, the demand for additional credit.

The fact is that, under a credit-based system of money, with the central bank responsible for providing the banks with the reserves they need, the amount of additional credit supplied by the banks is determined solely by the demand. It depends not at all on the interest rate. That is,

$$S_{\Delta Cr} = f(D_{\Delta Cr}) \tag{12.26}$$

In setting the prime or any one of the other short-term rates they charge borrowers, banks will simply "mark up" by a certain amount the cost of funds to themselves, as determined by i_{FF} or whatever else represents the effective "bank" rate. The short-term interest rate, then, is determined independently of demand and supply conditions in the credit markets—with the only "supply curve" which can actually be observed being the type of supply-offer curve shown in exhibit 12.20 as the analogue of the supply-offer curve for the goods supplied by megacorps and other industrial firms at some similarly "fixed" price. This makes the entire set of short-term interest rates—the federal funds and Treasury bill rates no less than the rediscount rate—a set of politically administered rather than a set of market-determined prices. Indeed, the short-term

Exhibit 12.20

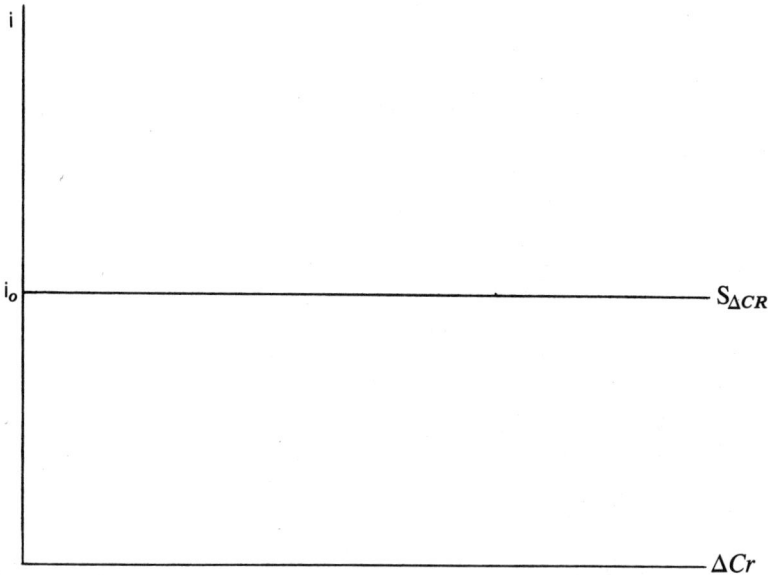

interest rate is simply another of the distributional variables that, within a Leontief-Sraffa model of the production subsystem, is indeterminate on the basis of technological and/or economic factors alone (see chapter 6, section 1.1)—just like the wage and dividend rates (see chapter 8, sections 3.4 and 3.5). The only difference is that i determines the distribution of income between fixed-interest debt holders and the rest of the household sector rather than the distribution of income between workers and nonworkers or between equity share holders and the rest of the household sector.

It should be noted that it is possible to speak of "the" interest rate, i, for the same reason that it is possible to speak of "the" wage rate, w. Although there are a large number of short- and long-term interest rates, each of these different interest rates can be viewed in terms of a certain risk premium, Δi, which is added to the basic interest rate, i—just as each of the different wage rates can be viewed in terms of a certain wage differential, Δw, which is added to the basic wage rate, w (see chapter 8, section 3.2). The risk premium, in the case of the various short- and long-term interest rates will depend on (a) the type of borrower; (b) the nature of the assets which serve as security or collateral; and (c) the duration of the loan. Thus the risk premium is less on loans to the Federal government than on loans to households or even to business firms, including megacorps; less on loans secured by real estate (mortgages) than on unsecured loans or even on loans for which other types of assets serve as collateral; and, finally, less on 30-day notes than on 20-year bonds. The combination of all three factors will determine the risk premium, Δi, on any particular type of loan, with that risk premium tending to stabilize around a certain mean value in the long period. Indeed, this risk premium is what accounts for the differentials which can be observed as a long-period, or secular, phenomenon among the various short- and long-term interest rates. That set of differentials will, however, vary in the short period due to the portfolio shifts that must take place before a change in the set of short-term interest rates, i_{ST}, can lead to a corresponding change in the set of long-term interest rates, i_{LT}, thereby reestablishing the long-period risk premiums that normally hold.

There are, then, two sources of the changes in interest rates which can be observed in the short period. One is a temporary reduction or increase in the differentials that normally prevail among the different interest rates until subsequent portfolio shifts can reestablish the risk premiums that hold in the long period. The second source of change is the effect of a less than or more than fully accommodating policy by the Fed on the basic interest rate, i. Any change in the basic interest rate will initially manifest itself as a change in the federal funds rate, i_{FF}, but it will then be confirmed only as the Treasury bill rate, i_{TB}, and the rediscount rate, $X_{M \cdot 3}$, change so as to reestablish the normal differentials among those three short-term interest rates. It is, of course, this second source of change that will then induce the first. Indeed, this is why the first source of change can be ignored and the emphasis instead placed on the Fed's ability to control, or "fix," the basic interest rate, i.

The argument that the basic interest rate, i, is a politically determined distributional variable rather than a market-determined price involves more than just a rejection of the Marshallian demand-and-supply framework for analyzing changes in the interest rate and other monetary variables. It also means that the interest rate cannot be used to measure social time preference—that is, the value to society of goods that become available at different points in time and therefore the social time discount factor. Indeed, as should be clear by now, the more appropriate social time discount factor is the secular growth rate, $\overset{\circ}{G}$, rather than any interest rate. This argument that the basic interest rate, i, is an exogenously determined policy variable should not be taken to mean, however, that the Fed's ability to "fix" interest rates is without limits. There is, in fact, a floor below which the Fed cannot push interest rates without initiating a commodity price inflation. That floor is the rate at which commodity prices, due to demand and supply conditions, are currently rising and expected to continue rising. If the interest rate on bank loans is less than the rate at which commodity prices are rising, then it will be to anyone's advantage to borrow funds for speculating in commodity futures (that is, on the future direction of commodity prices). Indeed, there will be no limit to the demand for bank credit—as long as the rate at which commodity prices are increasing exceeds the rate of interest on bank loans. Moreover, as the prices of commodities begin to rise due solely to the speculative demand, the process will begin to feed upon itself. The windfall profits will encourage further speculation, and this, in turn, will lead to an even more rapid increase in prices and still greater speculative buying.

The very nature of a credit-based system of money makes it difficult for the banks to avoid fueling this type of commodity price inflation. The banks' function, within a credit-based system of money, is to make sure that business firms have the working capital, or credit, they need so that production is not halted for lack of material (and labor) inputs. Whether the price of those inputs is rising or holding steady is beside the point. Firms have to be able to purchase the requisite inputs if production levels are going to be maintained (or perhaps even increased), and the function of the banks is to provide them with the credit they need to purchase those inputs—whatever the rate at which the prices of those inputs are increasing. This is why the banking system, in the very process of satisfying the demand for credit, will be forced to "accommodate" whatever is the rate of growth of the prices for the material (and labor) inputs used in the production process. In the case of a commodity price inflation, the firms purchasing the commodities as material inputs, since they cannot avoid taking a position in those commodities (through the inventories they hold), will in fact be among the principal speculators.

Two points need to be quickly noted, however, before jumping to the conclusion that, as the monetarists themselves put it, "inflation is always and everywhere a monetary phenomenon," one that can be avoided only by limiting the growth of the money supply. The first point is that what has been described so far is only the case of a commodity price inflation. A secular rise in the price of industrial goods is something quite different, with a quite different dynamic as the underlying explanation. This will become clear once the secular inflationary process is analyzed within the context of the larger macrodynamic model that is being constructed (see chapter 14, part 3). The second point that needs to be noted is that, even to the extent a more general rise in prices can be attributed to commodity speculation, there is a relatively simple cure, one that does not require the central bank to adopt a nonaccommodating policy and thereby induce a cyclical downturn in economic activity. The central bank need only ensure that the interest rate on bank loans, i, exceeds the anticipated growth of commodity prices.

Thus the floor, or lower limit, below which the Fed cannot push interest rates without fueling a commodity price inflation is given by the rate at which commodity prices are currently increasing and expected to continue rising. It should be noted that there is no corresponding ceiling, or upper limit, on how high the Fed can push the basic interest rate. It just that, the higher the basic interest rate, and thus the greater the cost of external funds, the less willing business firms and other economic entities will be to undertake any discretionary expenditures in excess of their current net cash inflow, or internally generated (i.e., discretionary) funds. This, in turn, will affect not just the economy's cyclical movements, as determined by $\overset{*}{A}$ and $E - F$, but also the economy's secular rate of expansion, as determined by $\overset{\circ}{I}$ and $\overset{\circ}{Z}$. More will be said in elaboration of this point once the complete macrodynamic model has been presented (see chapter 14). For now all that need be noted is how radically different from the conventional monetary theory is the model of the monetary-financial system which has just been outlined as one part of the larger complete macrodynamic model. To see this, we need only turn, as we shall in the next part of this chapter, to the conventional monetary theory.

12.3 The Conventional Monetary Theory

The monetary theory found in the standard macroeconomics textbooks, orthodox Keynesian as well as monetarist, differs radically from the preceding argument in that it assumes— implicitly if not explicitly—a system of either commodity or fiat money so that a stock, or supply, of money can be said to exist independently of the demand for credit. The failure to take into account the role played by credit-based money as the successor to systems based entirely on either commodity or fiat money is, by itself, sufficient reason to reject that body of theory. There are, however, further grounds for criticizing each of the different variants of the conventional monetary theory, as we shall see in the survey that follows. We shall begin with the Patinkin model which, since it does not posit a separate demand curve for money, is perhaps the simplest of the conventional models. We shall then take up, in turn, the Friedman, rational expectations, Hicks-Hansen LM, and Tobin models.

(The rest of this chapter, covering parts 3 and 4, has not yet been sufficiently revised to permit its publication in the provisional first edition of the textbook.)

Recommended Readings

The post-Keynesian theory of money and credit can be traced back to *The General Theory*, particularly ch. 17. See, in this connection, Jean DeLargentaye, "A Note on the General Theory of Employment, Interest and Money," *Journal of Post Keynesian Economics*, Spring 1979. The two works which first developed, in a systematic way, this alternative approach to money are Paul Davidson, *Money and the Real World*, London: Macmillan, 1972, and Hyman P. Minsky, *John Maynard Keynes*, New York: Columbia University Press, 1975. See also Joan Robinson, "The Theory of Interest," in *The Rate of Interest and Other Essays*, London: Macmillan, 1952; Nicholas Kaldor, *The Scourge of Monetarism*, New York: Oxford University Press, 1983. The most comprehensive treatment, representing a synthesis on the monetary side which matches that of Pasinetti on the real side, is Basil Moore, *The Macroeconomics of Credit Money, Horizontalists and Verticalists*, New York: Cambridge University Press, 1988. See also the articles by Moore, "The Endogenous Money Stock," *Journal of Post Keynesian Economics*, Fall 1979, and "Unpacking the Post-Keynesian Black Box: Bank Lending and the Money Supply," *ibid.*, Autumn 1983. In addition, see Marc Lavoie, "The Endogenous Flow of Credit and the Post-Keynesian Theory of Money," *Journal of Economic Issues*, September 1984;

Marc Jarsulic, *Money and Macro Policy*, Boston: Kluwer-Nijhoff, 1985; Stephen Rousseas, *Post Keynesian Monetary Theory*, Armonk, N.Y.: M. E. Sharpe, 1986; Philip Arestis, "The Post Keynesian Theory of Money, Credit and Finance," *Thames Papers in Political Economy*, Spring 1987. For the empirical evidence in support of the post-Keynesian theory of money, see, in addition to Moore, "Unpacking the Post-Keynesian Black Box," the following: Philip Arestis and Ciaran Driver, "A Comparison of the Monetary-Financial Blocks of Two Post-Keynesian Short-Period Models," *British Review of Economic Issues*, Autumn 1984; Leonard Forman, Miles Groves and Alfred S. Eichner, "The Demand Curve for Money Further Considered," in Jarsulik, *op. cit.* (as well as in Eichner, *Toward a New Economics*).

The flow of funds model developed in this chapter can be compared with that presented in Jacob Cohen, *Money and Finance: A Flow-of-Funds Approach*, Ames: Iowa State University Press, 1986. See also Andrea Terzi, "Savings Expenditure and the Financial Conditions of Production: Two Views," unpublished doctoral dissertation, Rutgers University, January 1986; and "The Independence of Finance from Saving: A Flow-of-Funds Interpretation," *Journal of Post Keynesian Economics*, Winter 1986–87. The argument by Wynne Godley will be found in Godley and Francis Cripps, *Macroeconomics*, Oxford: Oxford University Press, 1983. On the Minsky financial instability hypothesis, see Minsky, *Can "It" Happen Again?* Armonk, N.Y.: M. E. Sharpe, 1982; Martin Wolfson, *Financial Crises*, Armonk, N.Y.: M. E. Sharpe, 1986.

Chapter 13

The Exogenous Supply Constraints

Contents

Chapter 13

The Exogenous Supply Constraints

As previously pointed out, the economic system requires, as inputs, both the output of the parallel anthropogenic system and a continuous flow of raw materials from the surrounding environment (see chapter 1, section 2.4). These two types of essential inputs are, of course, in addition to the economic policies which, as the output of the parallel political system, give the economy its direction. Still, it is the human resource inputs representing the output of the anthropogenic system and the natural resource inputs from the engirding ecological system which, once a set of economic policies has been decided upon, will serve as the exogenous supply constraints on the rate of economic expansion. These two limits on the rate of expansion are important, not just because they determine the potential growth rate (see chapter 4, section 3.1) but also, because they provide the basis for the variant of the "excess-demand" theory of inflation that needs to be examined now that the monetarist explanation would seem to be untenable.

It is the "excess-demand" theory of inflation which, in one form or another, has generally been relied upon by economists and others to explain the secular rise in the price level over the last several decades. "Too much money chasing too few goods," the variant favored by monetarists, is only one form the argument can take. The alternative form, the variant favored by orthodox Keynesians, is that inflation is caused by too great an increase in demand (on the real side of the economy due to the growth of nominal income and/or credit) relative to the available supply. Whatever may be their differences as to where the inflationary pressure originates, whether on the monetary side of the economy or on the real side, monetarists and orthodox Keynesians hold to the same "excess-demand" theory of inflation —in contrast to the "cost-push" explanation on which this text is based (see chapter 14, part 3). In either of its two variants, the "excess-demand" theory necessarily implies some sort of shortage, or "bottleneck," on the supply side, whether of labor or some other type of exogenously obtained input. Otherwise, the growth of demand would not be "excessive." It is for this reason that, in positing one or more exogenous supply constraints as this chapter does, one cannot avoid addressing the question of whether, as many economists would argue, inflation is caused by an "excess demand" for goods and services relative to the available supply.

To answer this question, we will need to analyze in greater depth than was previously possible (see chapter 4, part 3) the two exogenous constraints on the rate of economic expansion—the amount of labor, or human resource inputs, supplied by the parallel anthropogenic system and the amount of raw materials, or natural resource inputs, available from the surrounding environment. We shall begin by first describing the human developmental process which constitutes the internal dynamic of the anthropogenic system. This is so the factors determining the flow of human resource inputs into the economic system can be identified. Once the nature of the anthropogenic system's internal dynamic has been explained, it will become clear why the rate of economic expansion is not likely to be constrained for lack of the necessary human resources and we can then turn our attention to the natural resource constraints. After explaining how technical progress serves to reduce not just the natural resource but also the human resource constraints on economic growth, the chapter will indicate what determines the value of nonreproducible, as distinct from reproducible, goods. Finally, the chapter will describe the set of policies that must be followed if there is to be a better utilization of the society's human resources and thus if the economic system is to come closer to achieving "full employment."

13.1 The Human Developmental Process

To determine the possible role of labor "shortages" in the inflationary process, we need to know how business firms and other types of employing organizations obtain their human resource inputs. This requires an understanding of the human developmental process by which individuals acquire the competence they need to fill whatever employment opportunities the economic system is able to offer. Since the various types of competence individuals may acquire are the output of a separate anthropogenic system operating parallel to the economic system, we need to begin by modeling that system in much the same way we began the discussion of the government's economic policies by modeling the parallel political system (see chapter 10, part 1). Modeling the anthropogenic system will enable us to trace out the career path each individual follows over his or her lifetime in the course of acquiring the competence needed to fill various social roles. In this way we will be able to juxtapose, against the conventional view of how the labor "market" functions to allocate workers and determine wage rates, the alternative human resource model on which this text is based.

13.1.1 The anthropogenic system

The anthropogenic system has already been defined as the set of institutions which, *qua* system, enable individuals to develop the competence they need to perform the society's essential tasks. Among these essential tasks are the work assignments, or jobs, represented by the N vector—that is, the labor coefficients denoted by the L vector, multiplied by Q, the level of total output, and then divided by h, the average number of hours each worker is employed. While there are other societal tasks for which individuals must be prepared, it is the work assignments represented by the N vector which are critical to the performance of the economy itself (see chapter 5, section 1.4, and chapter 8, section 3.2, for a discussion of how the N vector is determined). Without individuals able to carry out those work assignments, there could be no production and hence no economic output. It is the anthropogenic system, as distinct from the economic, which prepares individuals so they can perform these and all other essential societal tasks.

The anthropogenic system, then, is concerned with human development. This means it is concerned with a process that is sequential, cumulative, discrete, discontinuous and nonreversible—all characteristics which make the process difficult to model. The process of human development is actually several processes overlaid on one another. There is first a process of physical development, governed by the genetic endowment of each individual and the physiological principles which apply to all human beings. On top of the physical development there is a process of emotional development and a separate process of cognitive development, both of which influence the other as well as being conditioned by the individual's physical well-being. Finally there is a process of interpersonal development which, building on the other, more basic developmental processes, sets the stage for the acquisition of one or more particular competences. These multiple levels to the developmental process, and especially the dependence of any acquisition of competence on the antecedent types of development, are important to keep in mind so that the availability of workers to perform even the simplest type of economic task will not be taken for granted as economists are wont to do.

The anthropogenic system which enables individuals to acquire various types of competence consists of three types of developmental institutions—the family, the school and the employing organization. It is through affiliation with each of these three types of institutions, beginning with birth into a particular family, continuing with enrollment in a series of schools and ending with placement in one or more employing organizations, that individuals are enabled to carry out the tasks which a society needs performed. Affiliation with one or more of these developmental institutions is to the anthropogenic system what a market transaction is to the economic system—the system's quintessential activity.

Affiliation involves acceptance by the developmental institution of a certain responsibility for the individual and acceptance by the individual, in turn, of a certain obligation to the institution. These commitments on both sides, though intangible and not always explicit, are nonetheless quite binding—as long as the affiliation continues. They are based, in the case of the family, on strong personal bonds; and even though those ties are likely to become more formalized and less personal as the individual progresses through the educational system and enters the world of work, they never cease to serve as an effective constraint on the behavior of both parties. It is because the individual accepts the institution's limits on his or her behavior, this as the *quid pro quo* for being taken care of and nurtured, that the individual is allowed to have the experience and involvement with the institution which is so essential to his or her development. Part of the *quid pro quo* is, of course, a certain loyalty by the individual to the institution and a certain loyalty in return by the institution to the individual. The personal ties and loyalties which characterize the affiliation with any anthropogenic institution, be it the family, the school or the employing organization, are precisely what are absent in the case of a pure market transaction.

To the extent the developmental process proves successful, it will result in the individual acquiring one or more types of competence. Each competence has two parts to it. One is a particular configuration of motor-cognitive skills, such as those listed for the 12,100 different jobs delineated in the Dictionary of Occupational Titles (DOT) for the United States. The other part of any competence is the ability to function within a particular social setting, such as the classroom, the office or the factory. The one part of competence without the other, it should be noted, is not sufficient to enable the individual to carry out a work assignment or perform some other important societal task. For example, a typist, no matter how proficient, will not meet the employng organization's needs if he or she is unable to get along with other workers while someone unable to touch type, no matter how well he or she may get along with others, is similarly ill suited for the position.

The various types of competences which each individual acquires through affiliation with a succession of developmental institutions represent the output of the anthropogenic system—just as the goods and services supplied by business firms represent the output of the economic system. This output of the anthropogenic system is two-dimensional, based as it is on (a) the number of individuals with the competence to perform one or more of society's essential tasks, and (b) the number of different competences each of these individuals has. The output of the anthropogenic system can thus be represented by an m-by-x $\mathbf{H}$ matrix, with x the number of persons within the society and m the number of different competences which each of those individuals is in a position to acquire. This m-by-x $\mathbf{H}$ matrix represents the society's stock of human resources. While it is customary to limit x, the number of persons to be included in the inventory of the society's human resources, to those above a certain age, it should be noted that, even from the first moment of birth, individuals are engaged in the process of acquiring various competences (though of a rudimentary sort, to be sure), and that once they enter the formal educational system, these competences become increasingly measurable. Nonetheless, for the purposes of the present discussion, x will be limited to the number of persons 16 years and older—thus including only those who can be considered, even minimally, to be a part of the potential labor force.

Although other types of competence may be no less important to society, it is the types of competence needed to carry out one or more work assignments, such as those represented by the production system's matrix of labor coefficients, which are (a) most pertinent to the present discussion, and (b) more easily ascertained. The evidence that individuals have acquired the competence necessary to carry out a particular work assignment can be found in the jobs which those individuals actually hold at present or have held in the past. An individual retaining a job beyond some initial probationary period is likely to have the competence, at least to some minimal degree, which the job requires. In contrast, the competence to perform other essential societal tasks, such as discerning false ideas, selecting knowledgably among electoral candidates and successfully rearing children, is difficult to validate. Thus m will be limited in the analysis which follows to the number of employment-related types of competence which each member of society is in a position to acquire through a succession of affiliations with developmental institutions, beginning with the family, continuing with the formal educational system and culminating with one or more employing organizations.

The m categories in the above matrix can be specified as follows, as the first step in delineating the major types *and levels* of competence which it is possible for individuals to acquire: (1) managerial; (2) professional; (3) technical (which covers salespersons working on commission); (4) low-level supervisory; (5) secretarial and other clerical (including salespersons not on commission); (6) skilled production (craft); (7) semi-skilled production; and 8) all other competences, no matter how minimal. Each of these main categories would include any number of subcategories, reflecting more specific types of skills, and thus the various types of competence an individual can acquire, like the various types of goods that make up the consumption vector, can be lexicographically ordered (see chapter 9, section 1.2). Each of the skill subcategories would, in turn, include various grades, reflecting the years of experience, beginning with grade 1, the entry level, and continuing through the remaining r grades.

The cells in this m-by-x **H** matrix (with the m dimension subdivided into r ranks) can be filled in by examining the vita for each of the persons, 16 years and older, who are members of that society. Each vita, were it available, would list (1) the individual's family background (e.g., parents' occupation, education, income, ethnicity); (2) schools attended and other educational experiences; and (3) work history. It thus would indicate the succession of affiliations which the individual has had with the three principal types of developmental institutions. From the work history, beginning with the present job and going backwards in time, it would then be possible to determine which of the various types of work-related competences the individual has acquired and thus whether the entry, under each of the m categories, is yes or no. If the entry is yes, then one would want to know the years of experience and/or the grade level attained as well. While a vita of the sort described has yet to be assembled for all the persons 16 years or older in the United States, the critical data could readily be pieced together from various sources so as to provide a reasonable estimate of the relevant figure for each of the cells within the rectangular matrix.

When all the necessary entries have been made and an **H** matrix of the sort described thereby created, the results are likely to reflect a certain triangular pattern, with those who have the competence to carry out a managerial work assignment likely to have the competence to carry out a large number of other work assignments as well but those with only some lower level types of competence not necessarily able to carry out managerial work assignments. The same is true as one moves to each of the lower levels of competence. An individual having that competence may also have the competence, as indicated by his or her vita, to carry out some even lower level work assignment but not the competence to carry out a higher level assignment. This m-by-x **H** matrix, with its triangular pattern of nonzero entries, will reflect the society's stock of human resources at a given moment in time, based on the flow of output from the anthropogenic system. The entries for each of the cells will change continuously as individuals reach the relevant age of 16, graduate from various types of educational institutions, obtain new work assignments and withdraw from the work force (involuntarily through layoffs and death as well as voluntarily). Still, by carefully monitoring the relevant flows, it should be possible to keep the matrix up to date.

The question which arises, and which needs to be answered if the role of human resource factors in limiting the rate of economic expansion is to be understood, is how the anthropogenic system is able to produce as its output this vector of x individuals with m types of competence so as to match the economic system's need, at each and every moment in time, for m categories of competence, or skill, distributed over n industries, as represented by the **N** vector. How are the individuals who at birth can potentially acquire any competence (assuming no physical disability) subsequently prepared so that they acquire only the limited and specific types of competence for which the society has a need? In other words, how are the **H** and **N** vectors made compatible with one another, with the various types of competence developed as an output of the anthropogenic system fitted to the limited employment and other opportunities that a society, through its economic system, is able to provide? The answer to these questions can be found in two features of the anthropogenic system which have yet to be brought out. One is the career path by which each individual progresses through the anthropogenic system and the other is the dual role which the employing organization plays as both a utilizer and a developer of competence.

13.1.2 The individual's career path

A career path is what every individual follows as he or she progresses through the anthropogenic system—even though the terminus may fall far short of what anyone would consider a "career." This career path is traced out, for each individual, in the vita listing his or her affiliations with various developmental institutions. No less important than the affiliations actually obtained, however, are the affiliations not obtained. The latter determine which career paths will be foreclosed to the individual.

Nearly every affiliation marks a critical juncture, or fork, along an individual's career path. Any affiliation, whatever may be the developmental opportunities it affords, will close out other options. It is for this reason that, as an individual progresses through the anthropogenic system, he or she is almost certain to become more specialized in the types of tasks he or she can perform as the necessary corollary to becoming more competent. The closer an individual comes to being able to carry out the work assignment represented by a particular labor coefficient, the less likely it is that he or she will be able to carry out some other work assignment, one represented by a different labor coefficient. This is especially true at the higher levels of competence. For example, by the time one has become an experienced accountant or elementary school teacher, one has little chance of qualifying for a job as an electrical engineer—or indeed for any job outside the area of one's specialization. Such a progressive closing out of options is the counterpart to the alternative use of resources which are foregone when, through the economic system, a particular use of those resources is decided upon. The immediately limiting factor, in the case of the anthropogenic system, is not the amount of material resources but rather the amount of time each individual has during his or her lifetime for various activities, maintenance as well as developmental ones.

The affiliation which, more than any other, is likely to close out an individual's options is the one over which the individual has absolutely no control. This is the affiliation at birth with a particular family unit (assuming it is actually a family unit, and not just an isolated and/or abandoned female to whom the individual is born). Even if the individual must subsequently be placed with another family unit (or, there being no family willing to take in the child, the individual must either remain in some type of institutional care or roam the streets), much of the individual's subsequent fate will already have been determined. The critical importance of this initial affiliation is not just that so much of the earliest, and most essential, development takes place within the family. It is also that the family unit is likely to play the key role, second only to that of the larger society, in determining any subsequent affiliations with other developmental institutions, particularly various schools and such educational alternatives as social clubs and summer programs. Indeed, no other single factor is as important as the affiliated family unit in determining the career path which the individual is likely to follow. It is for this reason that the socioeconomic characteristics of the family are generally viewed as the principal determinant of an individual's social class— whether social class is defined in terms of the categories delineated in chapter 8 or on the basis of some narrower set of sociological criteria.

Still, family background is only one of several factors determining the individual's differential access to developmental institutions. And it is this differential access to developmental institutions which, in turn, will determine where, within the occupational-industry structure represented by the N matrix—and thus where, within the class structure of the society—the individual's career path will take him or her. The other factors determining the individual's differential access to developmental institutions are (2) the individual's own existential, or free-willed, performance during earlier affiliations with educational institutions and employing organizations, and (3) the effectiveness, known or otherwise, of the developmental institutions with which the individual has previously been affiliated. It is the question of how much the individual's own existential performance during earlier affiliations actually matters compared to family background (and the types of schools and other developmental opportunities that family connections make possible) that lies behind the controversy over how equal are the opportunities which a society like that of the United States provides. While the relative importance of these three factors may be in question, the fact that all three play a significant role, with the relative weight they carry varying both with the type of society and with the type of opportunity, cannot be denied.

Differential access to developmental institutions, then, rather than the ownership of property *per se* or any other economic factor is what, as already explained (see chapter 8, section 1.4), underlies the class structure of a society. This is not to say that the ownership of property, through the income and other advantages it affords, is unimportant. Nor is it to say that rentier income, even without any salary or other labor income to supplement it, will not be sufficient to support the style of life one may wish. It is only to make the point that, membership in the rentier class aside, the class structure of a society is based on differential access to developmental institutions. And even the highly advantageous position which the members of the rentier class enjoy no longer stands as an exception to what has just been said if one recognizes that the family is a developmental institution to which one can, through birth, have differential access.

The class structure of a society reflects the fact that, as previously pointed out, the employment opportunities which the society is able to provide are not all equally desirable. They differ both in terms of the amount of income they enable individuals to earn and in the other advantages they confer, especially the degree of autonomy enjoyed on the job and the amount of influence which can be exerted over other people. Indeed, this is the basis for the subdivision of the working class, with the eight principal types of competence—the m categories identified in the previous section—thereby reduced to five major groupings of occupations, or careers, in terms of their relative attractiveness. They are (1) the dominant white-collar group of top corporate executives, active owners of major companies and high-ranking public officials; (2) other managerial and white collar workers; (3) technicians; secretaries and other "pink" collar workers, and foremen and other low-level supervisors; (4) skilled and semiskilled production workers (with the latter included only if they are represented by a trade union); and (5) other blue-collar workers. Together with the specific industry or industries with which the occupation is associated, these five categories—the basis for the class subdivisions within the working class—reflect how attractive to the holder any particular job is likely to be.

The competition is, of course, greatest for the jobs which offer the highest income and/or the most other advantages—including the opportunity to qualify for even more desirable positions. This competition is moderated, however, by the protection, or shelters, which incumbent job-holders are able to erect through seniority and similar types of rules. These sheltering mechanisms serve to ensure that workers will be replaced only when positions become vacant through death, retirement or dismissal (the later usually limited, after an initial probationary period, to cases involving a clear violation of the rules)—and not just because there are others wishing to work at a lower wage. This is one of the reasons why, as will soon be explained more fully, the model of a commodity market does not apply to the human resource inputs used in the production process. Moreover, these same sheltering mechanisms ensure that when an opening does occur, even at a senior level, employees are likely to be promoted from within the organization until all intermediate positions have been filled, leaving an opening only at the entry level. The competition, then, is not so much for specific jobs as for the entry-level positions the employing organization is able to offer and then, once an entry-level position has been obtained, for promotion along the job ladder (or continuation of the career path) for which that entry-level position represents the bottom rung.

Obtaining an entry-level position, then, marks an especially critical juncture along the career path each individual follows. Once a particular entry-level position has been obtained, the individual will gain access to certain career paths from which he or she would otherwise be excluded. This is especially true for those hoping to become professionals and/or managers. However, even for blue-collar workers, obtaining an entry-level position is the essential first step in the process by which one's occupation, and hence one's social status, is determined. Until the prerequisite entry-level position has been obtained and sufficient work experience accumulated, one cannot really claim to have a particular skill and/or occupation. The individual will instead find him or herself relegated to the queue of applicants, without any skill or occupation, who are hoping to gain an entry-level poisition. Indeed, it is among the individuals waiting on this and the other queues for an entry-level position that the competition for jobs is most intense.

In the competition for an entry-level position, those with the prerequisite educational background and/or prior work experience will, of course, have an advantage. Indeed, they may be the only ones with a real chance of being hired. Thus the failure to gain admission to a particular educational program or even to obtain certain types of prior work experience will close out a number of career options for the individual. This means that the competiton to gain a certain type of entry-level position is likely to be preceded by the competition to gain entrance to the prerequisite educational programs and/or to acquire the prerequisite work experience—with the greater competition at the one juncture often moderating, because of the narrower field left, the competition at a later juncture. Those who miss out in the competition to gain a place on a particular career path because, at a critical point, they failed to make the necessary affiliation and thus had that option closed out for them, will be forced to settle for some alternative career path, one usually leading to a less desirable type of job. It is in this way that the individual's employment prospects are gradually restricted so that he or she is part of the eligible pool of applicants only for certain jobs and not for others. The employment opportunities for which the individual is no longer eligible, because of the failure either to progress beyond a certain point in the educational system or to gain a particular type of entry-level position, then set the upper limit on the social class to which the individual can aspire. It is for this reason that social class can be said to depend on differential access to the developmental institutions which constitute the anthropogenic system.

The restricted access to developmental institutions, reflected in what does not appear on an individual's vita, is one way in which those born into a society are gradually molded to fit the employment opportunities the society is able to provide. A second way the adjustment occurs is through the dual role the employing organization plays, both as the source of demand for various types of competence and as the indispensable means by which those same competences are further developed and refined. It is this dual role which the employing organization as an anthropogenic institution plays that now needs to be explicated.

13.1.3 The employing organization's dual role

The educational system, no matter how highly developed it may be in terms of both the level and variety of instruction it provides, will still turn out graduates with less competence than that required by most employing organizations. This is because didactic learning cannot match the demands placed on the individual by the actual job itself. Even the graduates of a medical school, who remain within the educational system as long as anyone else, must still complete severals years of internship and residency before becoming even minimally competent to practice medicine without being closely supervised by a more experienced doctor. In this respect, the educational component of the anthropogenic system produces, at most, only a semi-finished set of outputs. The final finishing process requires the on-the-job training which only some employing organization can provide. It is for this reason that affiliation with some employing organization is essential if an individual is to progress beyond a certain point along any career path. This creates the Catch-22 situation in which the new entrant into the labor force often finds him or herself: It is difficult to obtain employment without prior work experience, and it is difficult to become experienced without first obtaining employment. One of the ways in which the family connection frequently proves crucial is in arranging for that work experience, either in a family-owned business or at a place where some relative is already employed.

The employing organization's role is therefore a critical one in the development of any competence. Providing the on-the-job training is, however, only incidental to the employing organization's primary purpose—which, in the case of a business enterprise, is to produce the goods and services that, upon being sold, will provide the organization with the revenue it needs to cover its costs of production. In the case of a government agency, the reason the organization exists is to carry out some legally mandated public task, and in the case of the school or some other educational organization the reason is to mount a curriculum (the two purposes overlapping in the case of the public school). Employment opportunities are made available by an organization, not because this will enable an individual to obtain the on-the-job training he or she needs but rather, because the organization must be staffed by human beings if it is to function. Any on-the-job training, and hence any contribution to the output of the anthropogenic system, is merely incidental to what the organization is attempting to accomplish. Indeed, this is what makes the on-the-job training so indispensable. Because employing organizations are primarily attempting to accomplish something else, with the performance of workers judged in terms of the contribution it makes to that objective, the individual's experience on the job has a "real" quality to it that the previous educational preparation, no matter how much effort has been made to simulate the actual work environment, will almost certainly lack. The only real work experience is experience on the job.

For the employing organization, then, the overriding consideration is whether the individual seeking a position already has sufficient competence so that, with the on-the-job training he or she will then receive, that individual can be absorbed into the work force without impairing the organization's operating effectiveness. This is particularly true when the employing organization is a megacorp or some other large-scale bureaucratic entity. The need to ensure that anyone hired will fit within the existing structure of the work force can be seen most clearly in how such an employing organization is likely to fill its entry-level positions—that is, the openings at the bottom of whatever job ladders, or continuations of career paths, originate within the employing organization itself. (Although the entry-level positions may represent only a small portion of the jobs available within the organization, they are likely to be a majority of the jobs which need to be filled at any given moment. This is not only because of the tendency to fill more advanced positions from within, as already noted, but also because the quit rate is likely to be higher at the entry level.)

In the case of entry-level positions, the starting wage will normally be set sufficiently high so that, given the prevailing wage norms within the region or industry, whichever is the more relevant basis for comparison (see chapter 8, section 3.3), a large enough pool of applicants will be attracted to give the employing organization a choice of whom to hire. This enables the executives responsible for the hiring to feel they have chosen the best person among those applying (something they could not be sure of, however incorrectly, if only one person were available). It also provides some assurance that the organization will continue to be able to fill that position when there are future openings. In other words, the employing organization attempts, as a matter of policy, to ensure that for each of its entry-level positions there is a queue of qualified applicants—that is, more applicants than there are job openings.

Thus for each of the employing organization's entry-level positions, there is likely to be, especially when the employing organization is a megacorp or some other large organization, a pool, or queue, of qualified applicants awaiting an opening, with the size of that pool equal to a certain proportion, u, of the number of entry-level positions. This pool serves the same purpose, insofar as the human resource inputs are concerned, as the inventory of raw materials which firms maintain to preclude any disruption of their production schedules for lack of nonhuman inputs. In the case of the human resource inputs, the inventory consists of a set of resumés of qualified applicants which are kept on file in case an opening at the entry level should occur, with the file periodically updated to keep it current. The executives responsible for hiring who set the entry-level wage may, of course, err on the low side, leaving the employing organizations with too small a pool of qualified applicants. In that case, either the starting wage will need to be increased and/or a greater effort made to attract qualified applicants. The objective in either case is to avoid having the choice of whom to hire depend on precisely the factor which economists emphasize in their models of "the labor market"—namely, the wage rate.

Given the pool of qualified applicants, the employing organization will then fill the available positions on the basis of which individuals, in light of their past education and prior work experience, seem most likely to "work out." Those hired will undergo a period of probation during which the competence previously acquired and their ability to learn on the job can be tested under conditions the employing organization itself can control. The ability to get along with fellow workers and otherwise "fit into the organization" can also be assessed. Those not separated from the employing organization before the end of the probationary period can be considered to have the minimal competence necessary to fill that particular entry-level position. They will then become part of the employing organization's permanent work force and, in that sense, will become fully affiliated with the organization. There is thus a double screening of those who initially constitute the pool of qualified applicants (from among those queued up seeking a position): first, at the point in time when a conditional offer of employment is made and then, later, at some point before the probationary period ends. The intent is to avoid hiring anyone who cannot be absorbed into the permanent work force without impairing the operating effectiveness of the various teams of workers that constitute the organization.

The filling of positions beyond the entry level follows much the same process—though with certain important differences. Again, the policy is to ensure a sufficient pool of qualified applicants so that the choice does not actually depend on the wage rate. The main difference is that, with any positions beyond the entry level likely to be filled by promotion from within, what economists term the labor market plays even less of a role. The pool of applicants will normally consist of those who already hold the next lower level position within the organization, with the choice then made from among this group. The organization may, however, decide to enlarge the pool by recruiting from outside—in which case the selection process will more closely resemble that for an entry-level position. Even if the choice is someone from within the organization, however, that individual will have to complete a probationary period so that there is again a double screening of the qualified applicants. Only in this way can the organization be assured that, in replacing one member of its permanent work force with another, it will be able to continue functioning without serious impairment.

The employing organization thus plays a dual role within the anthropogenic system. On the one hand, it is the ultimate source of the demand for any and all competences. On the other hand, it is the sole provider of the on-the-job training without which competence cannot be fully developed—and hence it is an important developmental institution in its own right. Because of this dual role it plays, the employing organization operates at the critical interface between the anthropogenic and economic systems, regulating the output of the one in response to the need of the other for human resource inputs. It is therefore the employing organization, even more than any labor "market," which acts as an equilibrating device, making sure that the flow of human resources into the economic system is always sufficient to meet the system's need for labor inputs. Indeed, this dual role played by the employing organization, whereby the "demand" for human resource inputs creates the supply which satisfies that demand, precludes the use of separate supply and demand curves to analyze what happens at the point of interface between the anthropogenic and economic systems. In this respect, the supply of human resource inputs, or labor, is no different from the supply of goods and services and the supply of credit. In all three cases, the quantity supplied depends on the demand rather than the two being independent of one another, as the conventional theory assumes. As previously pointed out, the recognition of this fact is what underlies the Keynesian revolution in economics (see chapter 3, section 2.1). To better appreciate this point, at least insofar as it pertains to the human resource inputs into the production process, we need to turn now and examine the conventional treatment of what is termed the labor "market," based on the Marshallian demand and supply framework.

13.1.4 The conventional treatment of the labor 'market'

The model developed up to this point—with a separate anthropogenic system providing the economic system with the human resource inputs it needs through the process by which individuals become affiliated with a particular employing organization, often for the rest of their working years—differs signficantly from the conventional view of how the labor "market" operates. That alternative model, part of the same neoclassical theory which at various points in this text has been examined critically and found wanting, assumes that the decision of whether to commit a portion of one's time to a particular job can be analyzed and understood in the same way as the sale of commodities in world markets. It thus postulates the existence of a market for labor, on a national scale, that is the analogue of the commodity markets that operate globally. It further assumes that the sale and purchase of labor in this market is governed by an implicit contract specifying the wage rate and the attendant working conditions, with that contract automatically renewed each time an employee reports back to work. The argument so far presented in this chapter, by positing the existence of a separate anthropogenic system and by insisting that employment is based on affiliation rather than on any implicit contract, has already in effect rejected these two basic assumptions of the conventional theory. Still, the perhaps more significant difference between the two approaches, at least insofar as understanding the dynamics of an advanced industrial economy is concerned, is in the role attributed to the wage rate itself.

In the conventional model of the labor "market," it is the wage rate that brings the demand for and supply of labor into balance with one another, thereby ensuring—in the long run if not more immediately—"full employment." As has already been pointed out in passing, the wage rate in fact plays a quite different role. The money wage, w, is the numeraire upon which the entire set of prices represented by the P vector is based (see chapter 5, sections 1.4 and 5.2; chapter 6, section 1.1). The rate at which the money wage is increasing, $\overset{\circ}{w}$, relative to the growth of the real wage, as determined by the growth of output per worker, $\overset{\circ}{Z}$, the rate of accumulation, ϕ, and the amount of consumption out of nonwage income, Π_e, will then determine the rate at which the aggregate price level is increasing and hence the rate of inflation, $\overset{\circ}{P}$. The money wage rate, then, is one of the key distributional variables within the Leontief-Sraffa-Pasinetti model of the production subsystem that has been relied on in this text. Still, the distributional role which the money wage rate, like other prices, plays does not mean it cannot simultaneously serve the market equilibrating role attributed to it by the conventional theory. It is therefore necessary to examine and deal explicitly with that argument.

The equilibrating role which the wage rate is thought to play depends on two further assumptions of the conventional theory besides the two already identified. The first of these two additional assumptions is that there exists at the firm and/or the industry level a demand curve for labor, based on the value of labor's marginal physical product, which can then be aggregated for the economy as a whole. The second additional assumption is that there exists a supply curve for labor, based on each worker's preference for earned income over leisure, which can also be aggregated for the economy as a whole. The equilibrating role which, according to the conventional neoclassical theory, the wage rate plays therefore depends on the presumed existence of separate demand and supply curves for the labor, or human resource, inputs used in the production process. To refute the argument that the wage rate plays the equilibrating role attributed to it by the conventional theory, one need only show that no such separate demand and supply curves for labor actually exist. We shall begin by examining the putative demand curve for labor.

According to the conventional theory, the individual firm's demand curve for labor is derived from a marginal physical product curve which relates the change in the firm's output to the change in the amount of labor employed—holding other inputs constant. The descending portion of this marginal physical product curve, multiplied by the price of the output being produced, will yield a demand curve for labor which is negatively sloped, implying that the firm's demand for labor is inversely related to the wage rate (see chapter 8, section 4.3). Even at the microeconomic level, before attempting to derive an aggregate demand curve for labor, there is a serious objection to this formulation. The objection is to the assumption—a necessary one if the marginal physical product of labor is to be derived or even to make sense as a theoretical construct—that firms are free to vary the amount of labor employed relative to other inputs. This assumption runs counter to the fixed technical coefficients, including the fixed labor coefficients, which have been posited from the very outset in specifying, as part of this macrodynamic analysis, a model of production. Indeed, with fixed technical coefficients, like those which would seem to apply in the short period within the industrial sector, no such thing as a "marginal physical product of labor" exists (see chapter 5, part 3). It can neither be derived mathematically from the relevent production function (the vertical columns within the input-output table which indicate the quantities of inputs required to produce a given unit of output) nor equated with anything else which can be observed empirically.

The objection is more than a formal one, based on some obscure mathematical point. Under modern techniques of production, with workers employed in teams to operate a fixed stock of equipment, it is not possible to determine the "marginal product of labor" in any meaningful sense of that term. Once an operating rate has been set, neither the size of the work teams (the relationship of workers to one another in the production process) nor the manning scales (the relationship of each worker to the equipment he or she operates) can be varied—at least within the oligopolistic core of the industrial sector dominated by megacorps. Even when union work rules do not prohibit a change in staffing, the nature of the production process itself, together with the need for standardized rules in managing the process, will. While it might seem that this argument would apply only to those working directly with equipment, it is in fact even more difficult to determine the marginal contribution of the other employees, including any white-collar professionals and middle-level managers. Indeed, no evidence that it is possible to vary the amount of labor inputs in the short period, relative to the other inputs, while still maintaining the same level of output has ever been adduced, not just in connection with the oligopolistic core but indeed for the entire industrial sector.

Those who believe in the existence of a negatively sloped demand curve for labor, while perhaps prepared to concede that the fixed nature of the technical coefficients makes it impossible to determine the marginal product of labor in the short period, would contend that firms can nonetheless vary the amount of labor employed, relative to other inputs, in the longer run. We shall take up this argument later in connection with the natural resource constraint on the rate of economic expansion (see section 13.3.2). For now it need only be noted that the demand for labor can be assumed to be independent of the wage rate—at least in the short period. This is not to say that there is no demand for labor, or human resource inputs. On the contrary, the demand for labor is given by the set of labor coefficients, L, and the level of output in each of the n different industries, Q— with Q itself determined by the final demand vector, D, premultiplied by the Leontief inverse, $\dot{A}$. The point, rather, is that a demand curve for labor cannot be derived with the wage rate, w, as the principal determinant shown on the vertical axis.

Nonetheless, a certain level of demand for labor, or rather for human resource inputs, can be posited both at the industry level and in the aggregate, depending on the value of the L and Q vectors, and this, in turn, leads to the possibility that the demand for labor may be greater than the available supply—as implied by the excess-demand theory of inflation. To assess this possible explanation for the secular inflation that has bedeviled the advanced industrial economics of the world, including the United States, in the post-World War II period, it is necessary to turn to, and critically examine, the conventional supply curve for labor— which also includes the wage rate as the principal determinant shown on the vertical axis. In particular, we need to see to what extent the labor force participation rate actually depends on the wage rate.

13.1.5 The labor force participation rate

According to the conventional theory, the decision of how many hours to work is made by the individual worker, with that decision depending, among other factors, on the wage that can be earned. A higher wage, it is posited, will induce the individual worker to supply a greater amount of labor inputs, measured in hours spent on the job; and this direct relationship between the wage rate and the number of hours worked, when aggregated for all the potential members of the labor force, leads to an aggregate supply curve for labor which is positively sloped—at least in the area where it intersects the aggregate demand curve for labor. A higher wage is said to be necessary to induce the greater supply of labor because otherwise, having already determined the optimal balance between work and leisure at the old wage rate, the individual worker would no reason to spend any more time on the job.

This conventional way of setting up the analysis on the supply side of what is thought to be a labor "market" in fact misrepresents the options available to the individual worker in at least two critical respects. First, it assumes a choice about the number of hours to be spent on the job that most workers do not in fact have. The reality is that it is social convention, reinforced by law and collective bargaining agreements, which determines the number of hours that must be worked by those holding "full-time" jobs—the jobs which provide a sufficient amount of income so that an individual can support not only him- or herself at a minimally acceptable level but also any children or other dependents. An individual must either work those minimum number of hours (which, on a week-to-week basis, may fluctuate around some norm) or else give up any hope of obtaining a full-time position (and thus the advantages, other than just more hours of work, which a full-time position carries with it). The first thing the individual must decide, then, is not how many hours to work but rather whether or not to seek a full-time position. Once the individual has opted for the latter, the number of hours that must be spent on the job will be determined by what is considered the "normal" work week.

Second, the conventional way of setting up the analysis on the supply side assumes a choice between work and leisure, paralleling the choice over how many hours to work, which, again, most workers do not have. The reality is that only those potential members of the labor force who have other sources of income—or belong to families with other sources of income —can avoid having to take a full-time position. They include, primarily, those with significant property income (which, typically, for those not already working full-time, is inherited), those with relatives (husbands, wives, parents or children) holding a full-time position who are willing to support them, and those eligible for government transfer payments even if they should continue working (primarily the elderly receiving Social Security or other retirement income). It is only these individuals for whom a part-time job, giving them a choice of how many hours to work, is likely to seem at all preferable—and even for many of these individuals a full-time position may still be what they would choose, if one were available, because only a full-time position will provide them with a sufficient amount of income and/or enable them to feel personally self-fulfilled.

What these two constraints on the individual's choice about how many hours to work suggest is that the potential labor force needs to be divided into two segments, one consisting of those for whom a full-time position is the desired type of employment and the other consisting of those for whom part-time employment, with its accompanying choice as to the number of hours worked, is preferred. In the case of the first group, the number of hours worked represents a dichotomous decision. Either the individual works full time, in which case he or she must put in the conventional number of hours each week, or else that person will remain outside the full-time work force. For this first group of potential workers, one would not expect the wage rate, however calculated, to affect the labor force participation rate. These individuals are forced to seek full-time positions, either because this is the only means of obtaining the income they need to support themselves and any dependents, or because of the other rewards that come only from full-time employment; and any small variation in the wage rate is unlikely to lead to a different decision. Aside from some change in their personal situation (e.g., graduation from school, the anticipated birth of a child), the only factor likely to affect the willingness of these individuals to enter the labor force and actively seek employment is the availability of jobs. It is this line of argument, rather than the notion of a positively sloped supply curve for labor, which is supported by the empirical evidence. Studies, such as the one by William Bowen and T. Aldrich Finegan, have shown that the labor force participation rate depends primarily on the unemployment rate, with individuals on balance ''withdrawing'' from the labor force as the prospects of obtaining a job diminish. The wage rate, it would appear from the evidence, plays no role in determining the willingness of individuals to actively seek employment and thus to be officially counted as part of the labor force.

It is therefore only for the second group of workers, those who prefer a part-time to a full-time position, that the conventional supply curve for labor would seem to apply, if at all, with the number of hours those individuals are willing to work positvely related to the wage rate. However, the size of this group—and its response to a change in the wage rate—should not be exaggerated. This segment of the potential labor force includes only those with other sources of income and, among those with other sources of income, only those who would not still, for noneconomic reasons, prefer full-time to part-time employment. It thus excludes those who have taken a part-time job because nothing else is available. Even among those for whom part-time employment is the preferred alternative, the notion of a positively sloped supply curve applies only if they would be willing to work longer hours at a higher wage rate (or would insist on working fewer hours at a lower wage rate). Thus in identifying the segment of the potential labor force to which the conventional argument on the supply side holds, one must further exclude (a) those who are willing to work only a fixed number of hours, regardless of the wage rate, because they prefer to devote the greater part of their time to other, noncompensated activities such as attending school or caring for children, and (b) those who would be willing to work additional hours if the opportunity arose (though still less than a full work week) even without any increase in the wage rate. For the first subgroup, the supply curve is perfectly inelastic (or perhaps even backward bending) while for the second subgroup it is perfectly elastic. In either case, the supply curve is not positively sloped as the orthodox theory would suggest.

Indeed, the only reasonable conclusion is that the supply of labor, and thus the labor force participation rate, does not depend to any significant degree on the wage rate. Rather the supply of human resource inputs will depend on the demand. As more jobs become available with a rise in the level of economic activity, more indivduals will step forward to take those jobs. In the case of any more advanced positions which may open up within the same organization, the individuals who step forward will be those at lower levels awaiting promotion. In the case of any positions at the entry level that may become available, the individuals who step forward will be those queued up awaiting an opening. This point will be elaborated on shortly when, in the next part of this chapter, we examine the human resource constraint on the rate of economic expansion. Here we need only note that neither the demand for nor the supply of labor can be said to depend on the wage rate, and thus the wage rate cannot play the equilibrating role which is attributed to it by the conventional theory in economics. Indeed, as we shall see, a quite different adjustment mechanism operates. This, in turn, argues for replacing the conventional model, based on the presumed existence of separate supply and demand curves for labor, with the model that has just been presented of an anthropogenic system that operates parallel to and, beyond the key point of interface representing the transition from school to work, inter-actively with the economic system.

13.2 The Human Resource Constraint

Given the level of output in each industry, $\mathbf{Q}$, the relevant set of labor coefficients, $\mathbf{L}$, and the average number of hours that must be worked to hold a job, h, the economic system will generate a certain number of job slots, or employment opportunities (see chapter 8, section 1.2). These employment opportunities will increase secularly at a rate, $\overset{\circ}{\mathsf{N}}$, equal to the growth of aggregate output less the growth of output per worker. That is,

$$\overset{\circ}{\mathsf{N}} = \overset{\circ}{\mathsf{G}} - \overset{\circ}{\mathsf{Z}} \tag{13.1}$$

where N is the product of the $\mathbf{Q}$ and $\mathbf{N}$ matrices divided by h. It is both the number of these employment opportunities and the rate at which they are increasing that, through the on-the-job training thereby being provided, will determine the growth of the anthropogenic system's own distinctive output, the x number of persons with m types of competence which the $\mathbf{H}$ matrix denotes. But this is only one side of the interdependent relationship which exists between the economic and anthropogenic systems. The other side of the symbiosis is that the rate at which the various elements of the $\mathbf{H}$ matrix are increasing will determine whether the economic system is able to obtain the human resource inputs it needs to expand at a given rate, $\overset{\circ}{\mathsf{G}}$. Indeed, the x dimension of the $\mathbf{H}$ matrix represents the potential labor force, with $\overset{\circ}{\mathsf{H}}$ the rate at which that potential labor force is growing.

There are two possibilities. One is that the growth of the potential labor force, $\overset{\circ}{\mathsf{H}}$, will exceed the rate at which the demand for workers is increasing, as measured by $\overset{\circ}{\mathsf{N}}$. Unless there was previously a shortage of workers, with $\mathbf{N} > \mathbf{H}$, this will mean a growing number of unemployed and/or underutilized workers, with the secular unemployment rate, $\bar{\mathsf{U}}n$, thus rising. Even if there was previously a shortage of workers, however, it will be only a matter of time until the unemployment rate will again be positive and rising. The other possibility is that the rate at which the demand for workers is increasing, $\overset{\circ}{N}$, will exceed the growth of the potential labor force, $\overset{\circ}{H}$. Unless there was previously an excess of workers, with $H > N$, this will mean that firms face a shortage of workers, with the growth of output constrained for lack of the necessary human resource inputs. It is therefore the dependence of the economic system on the anthropogenic system for its human resource inputs, rather than the dependence of the anthropogenic system on the economic system for on-the-job training, that would appear to be more relevant when considering whether the secular rise in the price level in recent decades can be explained in terms of an "excess demand" for labor. But to take this position is to ignore the anthropogenic system's endogenous response to any increased demand for its output. Once the anthropogenic system's endogenous response is allowed for, one can see more clearly why the rate of economic expansion is not likely to be constrained for lack of the necessary human resource inputs and thus why the excess-demand-for-labor explanation for inflation is not a tenable one.

The anthropogenic system of an advanced industrial society like that of the United States is able to supply any additional workers who may be needed both because of the slack which normally exists within such a system—the counterpart of the slack in the form of inventories and reserve capacity which exists within the economic system—and because of its ability to draw upon the human resources of less developed societies. The latter represent the slack of the global anthropogenic system. Insofar as just the domestic system alone is concerned, one needs to distinguish between the slack found within each employing organization and the slack found at the interface between the anthropogenic and economic systems. We shall begin by focusing on the former.

13.2.1 The employing organization's anthropogenic slack

For the individual member of society, the optimal rate of development is one which enables that person to advance to the next higher level within the anthropogenic institution to which he or she is already affiliated, or to obtain an affiliation with the anthropogenic institution which next follows along the career path he or she has chosen, just as soon as the prerequisite level of competence has been acquired. What is optimal for the individual, however, will not necessarily be optimal for any particular anthropogenic institution. This is especially true of the employing organization since, as already pointed out, its primary purpose is not to enable the members of the work force to develop greater competence but rather to produce a certain type of output using the resources available to it, including any human ones (see section 13.1.3). The difference between the rate of advance along a particular developmental path which is optimal for the individual and the rate of advance which is optimal for the anthropogenic institution with which the individual is affiliated will, besides being the source of the conflict between the interests of the two, give rise to a certain amount of slack within the anthropogenic system. This slack plays a key role in enabling the anthropogenic system to adjust to the changing demand for its output.

A certain amount of slack can be found within each of the three types of developmental institutions which constitute the anthropogenic system. It arises when the family, whether intentionally or not, "infantilizes" one of its younger members instead of enabling that person to continue developing emotionally and socially. It also arises when the school, to make things easier for its staff or to meet some other need of the organization *qua* organization, forces students to "mark time" instead of moving on to the next task in their intellectual development. Still, it is the slack which exists within the employing organization as an anthropogenic institution—as well as the slack that can be found just prior to the point of entry into the employing organization, at the interface between the educational system and the world of work—that is most important in enabling the anthropogenic system as a whole to adjust to the changing demand for its output. This is because the employing organization will be the first of the three types of anthropogenic institutions to feel the effect of any change in the need for human resource inputs, and it will then transmit that signal back through the rest of the anthropogenic system by creating more or fewer employment opportunities for those exiting from the educational system.

The amount of anthropogenic slack within each employing organization will vary, depending as it does on the following factors: (1) the amount of time required to become fully competent in each of the skill categories into which the employing organization's labor force can be divided; (2) the attrition rate within each of those same skill categories due to death, disability, retirement or disaffection, (3) the employing organization's rate of growth within the product line requiring that particular group of skills; and (4) the steepness of the organizational pyramid, this being the one additional factor, besides the firm's attrition rate and its growth rate, needed to determine the promotion rate within those skill categories. Each of these four factors is only marginally under the control of the employing organization—even when the employing organization is of a more advanced type, such as a megacorp or some similar large-scale bureaucratic entity.

To see why the amount of any anthropogenic slack depends on the amount of time required to become competent within a given skill category, let us suppose that the number of job slots, or employment opportunties, within the organization's jth skill category, N_j, is 90. Let us further suppose that employees in this skill category are first hired, on the average, when they are 25 years old and that they remain in that skill category, again on the average, until they are 55 years old. The average number of years actually spent within that grade, t_g, is then 30, and the average number of workers within that skill category who are in the same cohort, in terms of work experience, will be N_j/t_g or, in this case, 3. Suppose, finally, that while the average employee within that skill category spends 30 years in grade, it takes only four years before he or she is ready to take on a more demanding work assignment. This implies that, of the 90 persons employed in that skill category at any point in time, all but about 12 (the three in each cohort with the same amount of work experience, multiplied by the four years required to become fully competent in the position) are stalled along the relevant career path, with further advancement blocked. The general formula for calculating the *amount* of this anthropogenic slack is as follows:

$$U''_j = N_j * \frac{t_g - t_c}{t_g} \tag{13.2}$$

where U''_j is the amount of slack within the jth skill category, that is, the number of workers unable to advance any further along the relevant career path; N_j is the number of job slots within that skill category; t_g is the average amount of time spent by employees within that grade, and t_c is the amount of time the position must be held before an individual is fully competent and ready for a more demanding work assignment. The *degree* of anthropogenic slack, U''_j/N_j, can then be calculated as follows:

$$u''_j = \frac{t_g - t_c}{t_g} \tag{13.3}$$

where u''_j is the degree of anthropogenic slack within the jth skill category, that is, the proportion of workers within that category awaiting further advancement. In the above example, this proportion is 0.86 and thus the degree of anthropogenic slack is 86 percent.

As can be seen from equation 13.3, the degree of slack within a given skill category increases with the size of the gap between the amount of time typically spent in grade by workers and the amount of time required before an individual is ready for a more demanding work assignment. The greater that gap, the greater the degree of slack within that skill category. Equation 13.3 also indicates that to eliminate any anthropogenic slack, that is, to reduce u''_j to zero, the average time spent in grade, t_g, would have to be no greater than the amount of time required to become fully competent in that position, t_c. The latter variable will, of course, depend on the amount of skill involved in the particular work assignment and thus must be viewed as an exogenously determined parameter, much like the labor coefficient that will determine the number of workers needed in that position. With t_c a given, the degree of anthropogenic slack within a given skill category can be reduced only through attrition.

The attrition rate, a_j, is the proportion of workers within a given skill category who will voluntarily quit or whose affiliation with the employing organization will otherwise end within the year (or within whatever else is the relevant time period) through death, disability or retirement. It is the value of a_j which, in the absence of any promotion from within, will determine the average amount of time spent in grade by those workers who remain affiliated with the employing organization. Thus, in the above example, if the attrition rate is 20 percent, then 18 of the 90 workers employed within that skill category will no longer be with the organization at the end of the year. These workers will, of course, need to be replaced, leading to an increase in the relative proportion of employees in that skill category with less than the four years experience needed to become fully competent. As the relative proportion of workers with less than four years work experience increases, the average amount of time spent in grade, t_g, and thus the degree of anthropogenic slack, u''_j, will decline. The attrition rate, a_j, and the degree of anthropogenic slack, u''_j, are therefore inversely related to one another, with an increase in the one necessarily implying a decrease in the other. However, one cannot ignore the possibility of workers being promoted and the degree of anthopogenic slack thereby being reduced still further. To encompass this additional factor, it is necessary to elaborate on the above example, allowing not only for a certain rate of attrition within each skill category but also for the hierarchical nature of the employing organization as well as for any expansion by the organization itself.

Let us suppose that the *j*th skill category previously specified is actually the first of three levels of a certain type of competence required by the employing organization, and thus the entry level position along a three-step internal job ladder—with four years experience required at each level to become fully competent and ready for a more demanding work assignment. The 90 positions would then represent the *j.1st* skill/grade category. Let us further suppose that the employing organization needs only one person at the next higher level of competence for each three workers at a lower level. The employing organization will thus need a work force of 130, consisting of 90 persons at the entry level, 30 persons at the next higher level and 10 persons at the highest level. These ratios, the three employees at the entry level for each employee at grade level 2 and the three employees at grade level 2 for every employee at grade level 3, reflect the relative "steepness" of the organizational pyramid for that unit within the overall organization. This relative steepness, s, can be measured by the number of positions at one level, $N_{j.i}$, relative to the number of positions at the next higher rank, $N_{j.i+1}$. Thus the value of s at the entry level is 3 (the same as it is at grade level 2). Finally, let us suppose that the attrition rate at grade level 2 is 33.3 percent a year and at grade level 3 it is 50 percent (compared to 20 percent at the entry level).

The 33.3 percent attrition rate for those at grade level 2 means that about 10 openings will occur at that level each year. If those openings were to be filled entirely from within the organization, it would mean 10 promotions a year for those at the entry level—with a corresponding reduction both in the average amount of time spent in grade and in the amount of anthropogenic slack at the entry level. The attrition rate at the next higher level is not the only source of promotions, however. Any growth by the employing organization will also enable individuals to advance more rapidly along the relevant career path. Let us therefore assume that the employing organization is growing at the rate of 15 percent a year. Here we need to distinguish between a growth in sales—or whatever else serves as the measure of output—and the growth of the work force itself. As a result of the more general technical progress which is occurring throughout the economy, output per worker within the employing organization will be increasing at a certain rate, $\overset{\circ}{z}$, and this growth of output per worker, when subtracted from the growth of sales, $\overset{\circ}{g}$, will give the rate at which the organization's work force is expanding, $\overset{\circ}{n}$. That is,

$$\overset{\circ}{n} = \overset{\circ}{g} - \overset{\circ}{z} \tag{13.4}$$

where $\overset{\circ}{n}$ is the growth rate of the employing organization's work force. Thus the 15 percent growth in sales, less the five percent growth in output per worker, means a 10 percent growth each year in the size of the employing organiation's work force.

The 10 percent growth in the size of the work force, indeed any growth in the size of the work force, will reduce the degree of anthropogenic slack by increasing the rate at which workers can be promoted beyond what would be possible as a result of attrition alone. Thus, in the above example, the 10 percent growth in the number of job slots at grade level 2 will make it possible for another three employees to be promoted each year from entry-level positions. If the new slots were to be filled entirely from within the organization, this would reduce the *amount* of anthropogenic slack at the entry level still further by three, and the *rate* of slack by $\overset{\circ}{n}/s$, or 3.3 percent. Generalizing this result, one can calculate the rate of promotion within the j.i skill/grade due to the growth of the employing organization as follows:

$$\overset{\circ}{p}_g = \frac{1}{s} \, \overset{\circ}{n} \tag{13.5}$$

where $\overset{\circ}{p}_g$ is the rate of promotion due to the growth of the employing organization and s is the ratio, $n_{j.j}/n_{j.i+1}$. This rate of promotion will be in addition to that due to the rate of attrition at the next higher grade level, $a_{j.i+1}$. Taking both of these factors into account, the promotion rate within the ith grade of the jth skill category, $p_{j.i}$, can be calculated as follows:

$$p_{j.i} = \frac{1}{s} \, (a_{j.i+1} + \overset{\circ}{n}) \tag{13.6}$$

It is, of course, possible that not all the new openings will be filled from within the organization. If only a certain percentage, k, are filled from within, then equation 13.6 takes the following more general form:

$$p_{j.i} = \frac{1}{s} * k(a_{j.i+1} + \mathring{n}) \tag{13.7}$$

where k is the percentage of new job openings which are normally filled from within the employing organization.

Whatever the promotion rate, this will be an additional factor, besides the attrition rate, in reducing the average amount of time spent in grade, t_g, and thus the degree of anthropogenic slack, $u''_{j.i}$. Still, from the employing organization's viewpoint, the promotion rate must be considered a fixed parameter. This is because the determinants of $p_{j.i}$, as identified in equation 13.7, are largely beyond the direct control of the employing organization. The growth of sales, assuming the firm is able to retain its share of the market, will depend on aggregate demand conditions while the growth of output per worker, assuming the firm takes advantage of any cost-reducing investment opportunities, will depend on the rate of technical progress within the industry. Even the organization's pyramidal structure will be dictated largely by the need to maintain administrative control over the production process. Indeed, it is only in deciding what proportion of its higher-level positions are to be filled from within, and thus in determining the value of k, that the employing organization can directly influence the promotion rate.

With the promotion rate a fixed parameter (except to the extent it depends on k), the degree of anthropogenic slack, $u''_{j.i}$, will vary inversely with the attrition rate, $a_{j.i}$—a higher attrition rate necessarily implying a lesser degree of anthropogenic slack and vice versa. The attrition rate will, in turn, depend on (1) the mortality and disability rates among the workers within a given skill/grade category and thus, given those first two factors, the retirement rate within the same skill/grade category, that is, the proportion of workers who live long enough to reach whatever is the retirement age; and (2) the quit rate. Since the death and disability rates, and thus the retirement rate as well, can also be viewed as fixed parameters, any change in the attrition rate can be equated with a change in the quit rate. It is therefore by means of whatever control it has over the quit rate that the employing organization can hope to affect the degree of anthropogenic slack. The ability to control the degree of anthropogenic slack through the quit rate is, in turn, what makes it necessary for each employing organizaton to have a personnel policy which goes beyond merely screening applicants for whatever openings may occur.

13.2.2 Personnel Policy

It might at first seem that an employing organization, such as the megacorp or any other large bureaucracy, would not need to be concerned about the degree of anthropogenic slack since it is the employee, and not the organization, that will find its development thwarted. Indeed, to the extent that an increase in the average amount of time spent in grade implies a more experienced work force, a greater rather than a lesser degree of anthropogenic slack within each of the various skill categories would appear to be in the employing organization's best interest. Too much anthropogenic slack, however, will create a problem for the employing organization—as will too little.

The longer employees find themselves remaining in grade without being promoted, the more likely it is that they will become disaffected, with an adverse effect on productivity. The problem arises not from the employees who, out of frustration, quit to take other jobs. It stems rather from the workers who, despite being disaffected, remain as employees because they cannot obtain a better position elsewhere. Even if not disaffected to the point of actually "dogging it" on the job, they are likely to stop giving that extra effort which is so essential to the performance of any group, or team, of workers. The extent of any such disaffection is an especially critical factor in the case of the managerial and other white collar workers, as distinct from the production work force, since it is among the former that the organization's decision-making power must be shared.

On the other hand, the employing organization will not want to be left with so little slack that it has an insufficient number of experienced workers in each of the various skill categories. In that case, too, productivity will be adversely affected. Here it is not a matter of being unable to fill all the available positions. An employing organization such as the megacorp, because of the differential in wages it can offer, will almost always be able to fill any and all positions. Rather it is a matter of having a sufficient number of experienced workers in key positions so that the skill level which the organization as a whole has built up over the years can be maintained through the exposure which the less experienced workers have to the cadre of more experienced workers.

For the employing organization, then, there is, if not an optimal degree of anthropogenic slack, then at least an acceptable range of values which $a_{j,i}$ can take without impairing the organization's operational effectiveness. The employing organization is able to keep the degree of anthropogenic slack within these limits through the control it is able to exercise over its quit rate as the key component of the attrition rate. As brought out in the preceding section, the degree of anthropogenic slack and the quit rate within each of the various skill categories are inversely related to one another so that, by altering the latter, the former can in effect be regulated. The several steps the employing organization can take to alter the quit rate, and hence the degree of anthropogenic slack, within each of the various skill categories that constitute its work force will be one component of its overall personnel policy—the other component being the several steps it must simultaneously take to assure an adequate flow of new workers to take the place of those leaving, or quitting, the organization. There are thus two components to the employing organization's personnel policy, and each needs to be taken up in turn, beginning with the steps the employing organization can take to keep the quit rate within acceptable limits.

The most important of these steps has to do with the nature and content of the job itself. Employment is sought, beyond any income it may provide, primarily for the sense of personal accomplishment that comes from successfully meeting the challenge posed by the job itself. Human beings derive their sense of self-worth in large part from their ability to function effectively in the various spheres of life, including most importantly the world of work. Indeed, it is for this reason that, until a worker has become fully competent in the position he or she presently holds, the problem of disaffection is unlikely to arise. It is not just that the worker, having yet to become fully competent at that level, will not expect to be promoted. It is also that the worker, having still more to learn on the job, will continue to feel sufficiently challenged. Thus, even without an increase in the rates of compensation, the employing organization can reduce the quit rate in each of the skill categories which comprise its work force by making the work assignments more challenging. This, in fact, is likely to be the first step taken by the employing organization in any concerted effort to hold down the quit rate.

The problem is that there are inherent limits to what can be done to make jobs more challenging and hence more satisfying. These limits reflect the constraints that must be placed on the autonomy of the individual worker if the organization as a whole is to achieve its goals. The challenge posed by each job, once the technical, or skill, component has been mastered, is directly proportional to the amount of autonomy, or independent decision-making power, the individual worker has in that position. The greater the autonomy, the greater the challenge and—to the extent it depends on either of these two factors—the greater the job satisfaction. Yet if the employing organization is to act in a unified, coordinated manner that is responsive to the executive group's goals, this autonomy needs to be circumscribed, particularly at the lower levels.

In the simplest type of firm that can be postulated, the only employee with any real autonomy is the owner-entrepreneur, or "boss." The rest of the work force, consisting of an undifferentiated mass of unskilled helpers, merely "do what they are told." For this type of firm—one that bears a close resemblance to the type of firm usually postulated in microeconomic theory—the problem of ensuring that the rest of the work force acts in a unified, coordinated manner that is responsive to the goals of the executive group is largely obviated. The executive group consists of but a single person, the owner-entrepreneur, and the rest of the work force simply follows to the letter the instructions of this one individual. A firm of this type, however, is able to use only the simplest of production techniques, involving only the simplest of machinery. This is because the rest of the work force, apart from the owner-entrepreneur, is unable to exercise the independent judgment which more complex and sophisticated types of equipment require. Thus, as the level of technology advances, the firm is likely to evolve as an employing organization in one or both of the following two ways:

First, the responsibility, and hence the autonomy, of certain of the production workers will need to be increased. It is not just that as the number of production workers expands, at least some of them will need to be made into foremen and other types of low-level supervisors. It is also that, as the machinery to be operated becomes more complex and sophisticated, the production workers will need to be able to take greater initiative. They cannot simply "do what they are told." They will, in fact, need to develop a certain amount of competence based on their work experience. In this way a cadre of experienced production workers, able to keep the complex set of machinery going, will need to be developed and retained.

Second, the managerial tasks will become greater than any one owner-entre-preneur or even group of partners can handle. An entire managerial structure, consisting of a hierarchy of executives enjoying varying degrees of autonomy, must also be created. In this way, the distinguishing organizational structure of the megacorp and the other types of large organizations that provide most of the better job opportunities will emerge, together with the more highly differentiated class structure to which it gives rise. It is an organizational, and thus a class, structure with separate production and managerial groups—each with their own job ladders linking the lowest, entry-level positions to a succession of higher level positions which offer promotion opportunities.

Within this opportunity structure, reflecting the reality of the different types of competences that are required by the employing organization and the way the higher level competences build on the lower ones, the challenge posed by each job is essentially time-delimited. The job remains challenging only until it has been mastered—at which point either the individual must be given a new job, one that renews the challenge, or else the organization will have to cope with the disaffection that comes from the employee being stuck in a job that is no longer challenging. While it is possible to rotate job assignments among workers without having to advance any of them to positions of greater responsibilty and/or autonomy, the effectiveness of these lateral shifts in holding down worker disaffection is likely to be limited. Eventually, for a new job assignment to be considered more challenging, it will need to involve greater responsibility and/or autonomy—with an accompanying promotion and increase in compensation. But it is precisely the ability to move on to a more responsible position that, within the hierarchical structure of the megacorp and similar types of employing organizations, is limited. It is limited by the slope of the organizational pyramid at each point from the base up, as measured by the value of what has previously been defined as s— the ratio of the number of positions at the next higher level, n_{i+1}, relative to the number of positions at the ith level, n_i.

With the number of true promotional opportunties thus limited, the only alternative is to try to maintain as long as possible the challenge posed by each position. This, in turn, depends on how autonomous is the decision-making associated with each position. The greater this autonomy, the greater the challenge—and the longer it will take before the individual will have gained sufficient experience in exercising that autonomy to feel that he or she "has seen it all." The degree of autonomy in decision-making will, of course, increase as the individual advances within the organization—with the members of the managerial group starting, of course, from a much higher level than the production workers. However, while it is possible for the degree of autonomy enjoyed by the individual worker to increase as he or she advances within the organization, the degree of autonomy enjoyed by the entire work force, managers and well as production workers, will remain unchanged. This is because it is not possible to increase the autonomy, or decision-making authority, of workers at a lower level without limiting the control being exercised by those above them in the organizational hierarchy. This does not mean that a greater sharing of responsibility and/or authority between workers at different levels is not possible and, in some cases, even desirable. What it means, rather, is that once an optimal number of levels of authority have been established as the vertical dimension of the organizational structure, there is likely to be little play within the structure for increasing the autonomy of the individual worker. Just as the challenge which the opportunity for promotion provides is limited by the width of the organizational pyramid as measured by the number of entry-level positions, so the challenge which the degree of autonomy provides is limited by the height of the pyramid, as measured by the separate levels of authority. For both these reasons, there are inherent limits to what the employing organization can do to make the job more satisfying by making it more challenging. A certain amount of worker disaffection, for lack of further advancement, is unavoidable. The employing organization is therefore likely to have to resort to other measures, besides trying to make the job itself more satisfying, if it wants to hold down the quit rate.

One of these other measures is to make the factory or office a more pleasant place in which to work. Individuals seek employment, not just for the income or challenge, but also for the opportunity it provides to interact with other human beings—that is, to socialize. Thus, even with no increase in either the rate of compensation or the challenge posed, the quit rate can be held down by improving the work place as a social milieu. This can be accomplished by (1) permitting the workers to socialize more on the job, even if this means less time spent on the tasks that the organization needs carried out; (2) recruiting workers on the basis of their social compatibility, even if this means giving less weight to other qualifications; or (3) developing a program of after-work leisure activities for employees, even if this means the employing organization will have to absorb a large part of the cost itself. However, any such strategy for holding down the quit rate, like the strategy of trying to increase individual job satisfaction, has inherent limitations. Beyond a certain point, efforts to further improve the work place as a social milieu are likely to become increasingly less effective in countering worker disaffection.

The final means available to the employing organization for keeping the quit rate within acceptable limits is to adjust the premium paid for the time spent in grade. This premium can take the form either of a higher rate of current compensation, that is, a differential above the starting rate for that position, or of deferred compensation (e.g., a pension). The larger this time-in-grade premium, the lower the quit rate is likely to be. Whatever the level of disaffection among workers, they can be dissuaded from quitting if the premium for staying in their present position is sufficiently high. The retention of the disaffected workers will, of course, impair the organization's operating effectiveness. It is for this reason that the organization will need, as part of its personnel policy, to make both the jobs themselves and the work place as a social milieu as satisfying as possible. Still, it is primarily by varying the time-in-grade premium paid to workers that the employing organization can bring the quit rate for each of the various skill categories within the target range. This is true whether the quit rate, and thus the degree of anthropogenic slack, is too high or too low.

If there is too much anthropogenic slack so that, due to the lack of turnover, productivity has begun to suffer, then the time-in-grade premium can be reduced. The most practical means of doing this is by freezing the premium while the base wage itself continues rising. The resulting decline in the premium, at least relative to the base wage, will lead to a higher quit rate and thus a reduction in the degree of anthropogenic slack. Indeed, if reducing the time-in-grade premium fails to increase the attrition rate sufficiently, the employing organization can complement this strategy with a policy of forcing workers to leave the organization if they are not promoted within a certain period of time. Alternatively, if there is too little slack so that, due to the lack of experienced workers, the employing organization has trouble reproducing the skills of its work force, the time-in-grade premium relative to the base wage can be increased. The quit rate will then be slowed and the degree of anthropogenic slack increased.

Thus it can be assumed that the employing organization will normally operate with a certain degree of anthropogenic slack, reflecting the positive value of $u''_{j.i}$ for each of the $j.i$ types of jobs it has to offer. This slack within the employing organization will be complemented by the slack without—the latter consisting of the pool of qualified applicants for each entry-level position, as measured by the value of u_j. Just as the time-in-grade premium can be counted on to ensure a suffucent degree of internal slack, so the differential in the entry-level wage rate paid by megacorps and other large bureaucracies can be counted on to ensure a sufficient degree of slack at the point of interface between the employing organization and the antecedent set of anthropogenic institutions. It is this considerable degree of anthropogenic slack, both within and without, at least when the employing organization takes the form of a megacorp or some other large bureaucratic entity, which will facilitate the adjustment the anthropogenic system will need to make to any change in the rate of economic expansion.

13.2.3 A change in the rate of economic expansion

A change in the rate of expansion by the economic system will mean a change in the rate at which the economic system must obtain human resource inputs from the anthropogenic system, and hence a change in the demand for the output of the anthropogenic system. This change in the rate of economic expansion to which the anthropogenic system must respond may be a secular one, involving a shift to a different long-period growth path, or it may be simply a cyclical movement around the present trend line and hence just a short-period fluctuation. Besides distinguishing a cyclical change in the rate of economic expansion from a secular change, it is necessary to distinguish an increase in the rate of economic expansion and, hence an increase in the demand for the output of the anthropogenic system, from a decrease. The necessary response by the anthropogenic system will be different, depending on which is the case.

A cyclical decline in the rate of economic expansion will require the least adjustment by the anthropogenic system. On the assumption that the labor coefficients are fixed, at least in the short period, the decline in the rate of economic expansion will reduce the need for human resource inputs directly in proportion to the decline in output. As sales fall below current levels of output, the first response of business firms, especially megacorps, will be to reduce the hours of paid employment—and in particular to eliminate any overtime. In this way, if the decline in sales is only a modest one and/or appears to be only temporary, firms will not be forced to dismiss employees. The work force will remain intact and the cost of layoffs, not just the pecuniary ones but also the less tangible ones for workers and employers alike, will thereby be avoided. However, if the decline in sales is quite pronounced and/or continues for long, firms will be forced to let workers go (i.e., end their affiliation with that organization), with a resulting increase in unemployment.

An increase in the unemployment rate will disrupt the normal flow of individuals advancing through the anthropogenic system. With firms forced to lay off workers, those exiting from the school system will find it all but impossible to obtain the entry-level positions necessary for the further development of their competence as workers. This is especially true of those seeking entry-level positions within the production, or blue collar, work force. Joined by those who have lost their jobs, they will find themselves in a queue which is no longer moving forward, only growing longer. The situation of those with the educational and other qualifications needed to obtain an entry-level position within the white-collar work force may be less hopeless. Still, with a cyclical downturn, even the queue for those positions will lengthen as firms respond to the deterioration in their financial position by placing a freeze on hiring. Together with the longer line of individuals hoping to obtain an entry-level position within the blue-collar work force, this will create a greater degree of slack at the point of interface between the anthropogenic and economic systems. Meanwhile, within the employing organizations themselves, the amount of slack will also increase. The halt in the rate of expansion will reduce the opportunities for advancement, with a corresponding increase in the number of individuals eligible for promotion but for whom there are no openings at a higher level.

If the decline in output and employment is only a cyclical movement that will shortly be reversed, then the formal education component of the anthropogenic system, the schools, will not have to make any significant adjustment. Although there will, for the moment, be a sharp fall-off in the demand for their output, educational institutions will not need to reduce the rate at which they are turning out graduates. Those temporarily unable to obtain the employment they need to complete the acquisition of a particular competence will only have to wait for the subsequent recovery of the economy. The longer run need for that type of competence will be unchanged. It is only if the cyclical downturn presages a decline in the secular rate of economic expansion that a significant adjustment by the anthropogenic system, the formal education component in particular, will be necessary. In that case, the schools will find themselves under pressure to curtail their output so as to produce fewer graduates, thereby reducing the slack building up at the point of interface between the anthropogenic and economic systems. The pressure will come from those still at an early stage in their education and their parents who, observing that graduates of the schools are unable to obtain employment in the areas for which they have been trained, will begin to question the appropriateness of the curriculum.

The necessary adjustment will not be an easy one for the anthropogenic system to make, caught as it is between the demographic factors which, on the one hand, determine the rate of enrollment in the schools and the economic factors which, on the other hand, determine the demand for the system's output. Indeed, there are only two means of adjustment available—aside from reducing the rate of net inmigration (and this third option will only relieve the pressure for the least desirable jobs). One means of adjustment is to increase the amount of time that must be spent at each of the various levels of schooling, thus retaining individuals for a longer period of time within the formal education component of the anthropogenic system. The other means of adjustment is to reduce the number of graduates by imposing more stringent criteria for graduation. The first adjustment mechanism is limited by the amount of time individuals can profitably spend within a formal educational setting, divorced from actual work or other real-life experiences, and it runs the risk, if pushed too far, of "infantilizing" the school-age population. Indeed, it can be argued that, in the case of the United States and other advanced countries, this first means of adjustment has already been pushed too far, at least without alternating in a way that has yet to be systematically attempted the periods of employment, and thus of on-the-job training, with periods of formal schooling.

The second adjustment mechanism, meanwhile, provides a solution which only seems to be a better one. Imposing more stringent criteria for graduation, as a way of rationing the limited number of employment opportunities, merely increases the number of persons failing to complete a particular course of study. While it may be thought that the schools will, as a result, turn out a "better" product—and it may even be that, with greater pressure being put on them, those attending school will become somewhat more diligent—the degree of anthropogenic slack in the form of those queued up waiting for jobs to become available will in fact be unchanged. The reduced number of graduates will simply be offset by the increased number of dropouts, with only the relative lengths of the different queues changing. The queues of applicants for the better jobs may become shorter but the queues for the less desirable jobs will become longer.

It should be noted that, in adjusting the output of the anthropogenic system to the lower rate of economic expansion, the burden falls entirely on the anthropogenic system—and on the formal education component in particular. The economic system will, in this case, have no trouble obtaining all the human resource inputs it needs. Indeed, employing organizations will be able to choose from among a larger pool of qualified applicants and, with the increase in the degree of slack at the point of interface between the anthropogenic and economic systems, the upward pressure on the entry-level wage rate will be reduced. While worker disaffection may increase as a result of the greater slack within employing organizations themselves, the adverse effect which this might have on productivity will be offset by the pressure on workers to perform at a higher level because of the less favorable labor "market" conditions. Thus a change in the rate of economic expansion will create a significant adjustment problem for the economic, as distinct from the anthropogenic, system only if the shift is to a higher rather than a lower growth rate. Let us see what happens in that opposite case.

Again, an increase in the rate of economic expansion which is merely cyclical, and thus temporary, will not create much of an adjustment problem—either for the anthropogenic system or for the economic system. In analyzing this short period situation, it is necessary to distinguish a cyclical recovery from an increase in the rate of economic growth which, though above the secular average, is only temporary. In the case of a cyclical recovery, employing organizations will need only to restore the normal work week and/or recall any workers who have been temporarily laid off—provided that new equipment has not been installed which makes those workers redundant. The differentially higher wages paid by megacorps and other large-scale bureaucratic organizations will mean that even the workers who have found other employment in the interval can be expected to return to their jobs once the recall notices go out. Indeed, anticipating the recall, the laid off workers will not normally try to obtain another job in the interim. Other employing organizations, many of the neoclassical proprietorships in particular, may have to hire new workers to bring their work force back up to the levels they once were—as even some megacorps may have to do at the entry level. However, the stepped up rate at which new hiring is taking place will merely reduce the queues of qualified applicants, restoring them to the length they would have been had the secular rate of economic expansion been maintained, and thus it will only reestablish the normal degree of anthropogenic slack.

If the recovery continues beyond the point represented by the secular growth path, with the result that both final sales and output are increasing more rapidly than the most recent trend, then the problem of obtaining the necessary human resource inputs for the economic system becomes somewhat more problematic. Simply restoring the normal work week and/or recalling previously laid off workers will not suffice. While some further increase in the work week may be possible through overtime or even double shifts, there is a limit to how much additional output can be produced with the same size work force. Beyond a certain point, megacorps and other employing organizations will be forced to add to their work force. It is in this latter case that the degree of anthropogenic slack becomes important, providing the anthropogenic system with the cushion it needs to adjust to the cyclically higher rate of economic expansion. Employing organizations can increase the size of their work force to whatever extent they need, as long as either the degree of slack within each of the various skill categories or the queue of qualified applicants seeking entry-level positions is greater than zero.

Thus it is the degree of anthropogenic slack, both within employing organizations themselves and at the point of interface between the formal education component of the anthropogenic system and the economic system, which will determine the point at which any further increase in the rate of economic expansion is likely to be constrained for lack of the necessary additional human resource inputs. There are a number of reasons for doubting, however, whether this limit is likely to be exceeded—except under extraordinary circumstances. One reason is that the amount of anthropogenic slack within the existing work force is a variable over which, as was pointed out in the preceding subsection, the employing organization has some control. In determining how much slack is optimal, the employing organization will need to keep in mind the normal fluctuations in output, especially during the expansionary phase of the typical business cycle. The degree of slack within the employing organizations which are megacorps should therefore be sufficient to encompass whatever might be the cyclical demand for human resource inputs, even when the rate of economic expansion is above the secular average.

For this reason it would appear that, if the rate of economic expansion is, to any significant extent, limited by the availability of human resource inputs, it is not the growth of the corporate or oligopolistic component—as distinct from the rest of the enterprise sector—which is likely to be slowed. The differentially higher wage at the entry level, together with the time-in-grade premiums paid to the members of the permanment work force, are likely to ensure a considerable amount of anthropogenic slack, enabling the megacorp as the representative firm within the corporate subsector to obtain all the human resource inputs it needs, whatever the rate at which the economy as a whole is expanding The same would appear to be true of the government sector where a similar type of bureaucratic organization is the representative employer. If, then, the rate of expansion is constrained by the availability of human resource inputs, this can only be a problem for the nonoligopolistic component of the enterprise sector where the representative firm, and thus the representative employing organization, is of a quite different sort. To determine the possible human resource constraint on the rate of economic expansion, it is therefore necessary to examine the degree of anthropogenic slack and thus the availability of human resource inputs for the system of production as a whole and not just for the oligopolistic and governmental components. This, in turn, requires that we focus on the exogenous, as distinct from the endogenous, determinants of the potential labor force.

13.2.4 The exogenous determinants of the potential labor force

The output of the anthropogenic system has already been specified as an m-by-x **H** matrix, with x the number of persons, 16 years and older, who constitute the potential labor force and m the different types of competence acquired by those individuals through affiliation with family, school and employing organization (see section 13.1.1). With a sufficiently developed set of anthropogenic institutions so that the process of human development internal to the system can be taken for granted, the rate at which the **H** matrix and thus the rate at which the potential labor force will increase over time depends primarily on two factors: (1) the rate of growth of the working age population, $\overset{\circ}{e}$; and (2) the rate of net inmigration, m. However, this assumes no change in either the labor force participation rate, f, or the average number of hours worked each year, h. If either of these two parameters should vary, not just cyclically as is likely to be the case but secularly as well, reflecting a shift in longer-term social norms and hence behavioral patterns, the rate of growth of the potential labor force, $\overset{\circ}{H}$, will change as well (see chapter 4, section 3.1).

Little will be said about what determines the natural rate of increase in the society's working age population. This subject is best left to the demographers. Only two points need be noted. The first is that, with the working age population, and hence the potential labor force, limited to those 16 years and older, the natural rate of increase over the next decade or so can be predicted with reasonable accuracy. Since those who will make up the labor force over that interval have already been born, one need only know the mortality rate for each age cohort. The birth rate, which is far more difficult to predict, will not matter. The second point that needs to be noted pertains to one of the "stylized" facts about the experience of the developed countries, including the United States, over the past century or more of sustained economic expansion. What can be observed in the case of these countries is a tendency for the natural rate of increase in population to decline over time as income levels rise until it is just sufficient to enable the society to reproduce itself in number. This tendency for the native-born population to stabilize at a certain fixed level can be explained by the strain on the family unit, emotional as well as economic, by the increasingly higher levels of competence that must be developed in the next generation if the family's relative position in the society is to be maintained. In other words, in the more advanced societies the further development of the family as the basic social unit takes the form of ensuring greater competence among the younger members rather than just ensuring that the family will be able to survive intergenerationally.

The more important immediate factor in determining the rate at which the potential labor force will expend over time is the rate of net inmigration—that is, the rate of inmigration less the rate of outmigration. This factor is particularly important in the case of an already industrialized urban society whose natural rate of increase has stabilized at zero growth. The rate of net migration into an already industrialized urban society will depend on the difference between the minimum wage in that society and the wage that can be earned by those with an equivalent level of competence in the societies from which any migrants might come. As long as this difference exceeds the amount needed to provide the migrant with a higher level of real income should he or she succeed in becoming integrated into the work force of the more advanced society, the rate of migration can be assumed to be great enough, not just to fill any openings at the entry level for unskilled workers but also to provide the necessary reserve labor force. It is in this way that even the nonoligopolistic sector within an advanced industrial society will be assured of sufficient anthropogenic slack to handle any unexpected increase in the demand for its output. What can be counted on to ensure this continuous flow of workers from the rural countrysides of the world to the industrialized urban centers is the pattern of uneven development which has so far characterized the growth of the world's economy.

Industrialization, which began a little over two centuries ago in Great Britain, has since spread to an ever growing number of urban centers—not just in the United States and the other OECD group of nations but even in many of the less developed countries as well. This process of industrialization has been accompanied by the emergence of a specialized work force, attracted from distant agricultural areas as well as from the more immediate rural hinterlands by the higher real wage which can be earned. Indeed, with a push from the Malthusian pressure created by the simultaneous reduction in mortality rates and the improvement in agricultural and animal husbandry techniques which has lowered the labor-output ratio (i.e., the labor technical coefficients) in the primary sector, the displaced rural workers have streamed into the urban centers of the industrialized countries where they have swamped the available job opportunities, creating a reserve labor force quartered in the less desirable parts of the world's cities. For the representative firms within the nonoligopolistic sector located in those cities, this has meant a virtually inexhaustible source of labor inputs and thus a labor supply curve which, for all practical purposes, is perfectly elastic. As long as the minimum wage remains above the level needed to provide the migrants with a higher real income, employing organizations, even 20th century neoclassical proprietorships, have been assured of all the workers they need to fill any entry-level positions.

Moreover, this process of industrialization, accompanied by a vast migration of the agriculturally underemployed into the world's urban centers, shows no signs of abating. Although new urban centers, located in countries previously considered to be economically less developed, continue to join the older urban centers in the competition for a share of the world's industrial markets, the supply of rural peasants willing to relocate to some urban ghetto appears to be unlimited, at least at the present time in the history of the world's economy. Indeed, with the large number of countries which have yet to experience even the first stages of sustained industrial development, there seems no reason to believe that the supply will, in the foreseeable future, be exhausted. On the contrary, the prospect is that, as soon as one generation of migrants has been absorbed into the industrial labor force of the advanced economies, another will take its place. For this reason it can be assumed that, insofar as the advanced industrial societies like the United States are concerned, any openings in the opportunity structure which are not filled through the natural increase in the native born working age population will be filled through net inmigration. These include any openings in the least desirable jobs which those societies have to offer as well as any openings in the reserve labor force itself.

With a sufficient flow of inmigrants from the rural countrysides the world over to supplement the natural increase of the native-born working age population, it can be assumed that the growth of the potential labor force, $\overset{\circ}{H}$, will not fall much below the growth in the demand for human resource inputs, as determined by the economy's secular growth rate, $\overset{\circ}{G}$ (or the rate at which the D and hence the Q vector is expanding over time), and the currently applicable set of labor coefficients, L (divided by h, the number of hours that must be worked each year). An increase in the rate of economic expansion, and thus an increase in the demand for human resource inputs, will generate its own supply—in the form of increased inmigration, if not through the better utilization of the indigenous labor force. What this means is that the availability of human resource inputs is not likely to be a constraint on the rate of economic expansion. The problem, as the economy expands over time, is more likely to be of the opposite sort—that the growth of aggregate output, $\overset{\circ}{G}$, will not be sufficient to generate enough compensated employment so that every member of the society who would like a paying job can obtain one. We shall return to this point shortly (see part 4). For the moment it need only be noted that the anthropogenic system will have little trouble adjusting to a change in the secular rate of economic expansion.

The adjustment of the anthropogenic system to an increased demand for its output takes the following form: With the shift to a more rapid growth path, megacorps and other employing organizations will need to increase the rate at which they expand the size of their work force, both at the entry level and beyond.

It is not just that more new positions will have to be filled. It is also that the cushion represented by the degree of anthropogenic slack will need to be restored. This means that the pace of recruiting will have to quicken, putting pressure on the schools to increase the rate at which they turn out graduates able to fill the various entry-level positions. The schools will need to respond by either reducing the amount of time that must be spent within a given curriculum and/or by lowering the standards for graduation. In addition, the rate of inmigration from the rural hinterlands will need to increase to maintain the same size reserve labor force. These adjustments will, of course, require time so that, if the shift to a higher growth path occurs too rapidly, firms may have some difficulty, at least temporarily, in obtaining all the additional human resource inputs they need, especially the more skilled workers, including managers, that will be required if entirely new operating units are to be added. Indeed, it is the difficulty of expanding the organizational structure, as distinct from the number of workers themselves, which is likely to prove the more significant anthropogenic constraint on the rate of economic growth. Still, this only implies a limit on how quickly the anthropogenic system can adjust to a more rapid rate of economic expansion. It does not mean that, with the shift to the higher secular growth path occurring at a more gradual pace, the anthropogenic system will not be able to match the pace of the economic system by increasing the rate at which it produces its own distinctive output—the x number of individuals with m different types of competence who supply the human resource inputs into the economic system.

The experience of the United States in the post-World War II period supports the above argument. The American economy was able to shift from a 1.9 percent rate of secular growth in the 1950s to a 4.3 percent rate of secular growth in the early 1960s without any apparent strain on the anthropogenic system (see chapter 7, section 4.1, especially exhibit 7.15). Although the unemployment rate fell, there is no evidence that employing organizations were unable to obtain all the human resource inputs they needed, including skilled workers. The degree of anthropogenic slack also proved to be more than sufficient to meet the need for human resource inputs during the following decade, even at the two cyclical peaks, in 1973 and again in 1979, when the rate of expansion more closely matched the secular rate for the preceding decade. It is therefore surprising to find that the reason most frequently offered for the inflation experienced by the United States and the other advanced industrial countries since the end of World War II is the "excess demand" for labor produced by too rapid a rate of economic expansion. With this explanation clearly not a tenable one, the next step is to examine the natural resource constraints on the rate of economic expansion to see whether this factor can account for the secular rise in the price level in recent decades.

13.3 The Natural Resource Constraint

The n different industries which constitute the production subsystem require various raw materials, or natural resource inputs, from the surrounding environment. To the extent the supply of these raw materials cannot be increased to match the higher rate at which goods and services are being produced—and there is reason to view the supply of these inputs as being fixed—the economic system will be subject to a natural resource constraint as it expands over time. Now that the "labor shortage" argument has been shown to be without foundation, we need to see whether the inflation experienced by the United States and the other advanced industrial countries in recent decades can instead be explained by the natural resource constraint on the rate of economic expansion.

A strong case can be made for the existence of a natural resource constraint— indeed a much stronger case than for any human resource constraint on the rate of economic expansion. We shall examine that argument, based on the laws of thermodynamics, in the next subsection. The real question is not whether there is a natural resource constraint but rather how much it limits the prospects for any further improvement in the material standard of living enjoyed by the world's population. The answer to this question, it turns out, depends on whether future technical progress will ensure a sufficient supply of inanimate energy so that the process of replacing labor with machinery, the basis for the industrial revolution of the past 300 years, will not have to be abandoned. What will become clear as the argument unfolds is that the only two inputs which can be substituted for one another are not "capital" and labor, as the conventional theory would suggest but rather, inanimate and animate forms of energy—with the reduction in the need to rely on the latter the source of all human progress. However, before the argument can be considered complete, we shall have to go beyond the question of how limiting is the natural resource constraint and explain how the prices of natural resources, including fossil fuels, are determined. This is because the model of pricing previously put forward applies only to reproducible goods, and the natural resource inputs do not fall in that category.

13.3.1 The laws of thermodynamics

Following the lead of Nicholas Georgescu-Roegen, we can identify the following two types of natural resource inputs: (1) the combination of arable soil, available water and suitable climate which is found only in certain areas along the earth's surface and without which the production of food, fiber and other organic output by the agricultural sector would not be possible, and (2) the concentration of mineral deposits which is also found only at certain points along or just below the earth's surface and without which, in this case, the extraction of inorganic raw materials by the mining sector would not be possible. Within the latter category we can further distinguish between (a) the mineral deposits of coal, oil and uranium which serve, under present technology, as the inanimate sources of the energy used in the production process, and (b) all other mineral deposits. What these several types of natural resource inputs share in common is the fact that they must be obtained by human beings from the larger natural environment, or geosphere, consisting of the earth's biosphere (the thin layer of water and air surrounding the earth) and the lithosphere (the rock and soil that constitute the earth's crust). This means that, in considering the availability of natural resource inputs, one must take into account three sets of overlapping laws. They are the laws governing natural, biological and social systems respectively. The emphasis up to this point has been only on the last of these three sets of laws. It is now necessary to indicate the relevance of the other two sets of laws—at least with respect to the availability of the natural resources needed as inputs by the social system of production.

The earth's biosphere, so far the only macro ecological system known to exist anywhere in the universe, is viable only because it is able to draw on the sun for energy. There are two reasons why the sun's energy is such a critical factor. First, it helps to create, along with the earth's rotation, the wind and water currents that determine not just the amount of rainfall in the various regions of the world but also, more generally, the earth's climate. Second, perhaps even more important, the rate at which plants can grow depends, aside from climatic conditions and the amount of chemical nutrients in the soil, on how much energy in the form of sunlight can be captured through the process of photosynthesis. How rapidly plants can grow will, in turn, determine the amount of animal life which can be supported. It is not just that plants are the source of all the food consumed by animals, both directly (by herbivores) and indirectly (by carnivores). It is also that the oxygen which enables animals to "burn" food for energy is a joint product of the same photosynthetic process by which plants initially capture the sun's energy. Indeed, if one takes into account the process by which fossil fuels were created in the geological past, it becomes clear that the sun is the ultimate source of the energy without which all life, including human life, could not be sustained. The earth's biosphere thus needs to be viewed as a solar-powered "engine" which, like all engines, is subject to the laws of thermodynamics.

Still, this is only part of the story. The earth's biosphere is also a system which, based on the physical and chemical laws governing the universe as a whole, has evolved in its own distinctive way. As the solar system was formed through a process that is still unclear, the earth's geosphere came to embody a particularly fortuitous mixture of chemical elements. These include not just the elements such as carbon, hydrogen, oxygen, nitrogen, phosphorus and potassium which are necessary for life but also the elements such as iron, copper, aluminum, nickel, zinc and lead which serve as the essential mineral inputs for any social system of production. It is both groups of elements which, since they are virtually fixed in quantity for the likely duration of human life on earth, represent nature's true "original endowment." (It should be noted that this "original endowment" is augmented each year by the nearly 10,000 tons of meteorites and other solar debris that are trapped within the earth's gravitational field and survive their subsequent descent through the earth's atmosphere.)

Moreover, at a critical point in the formation of the earth, enough gases had escaped from the interior to initiate the process by which the earth's atmosphere and hydrosphere have subsequently evolved. Without this thin band of air and water, life as we know it would not be possible. This ecological system continues to evolve—increasingly due to the influence of human beings and not necessarily in a way compatible with the preservation of life. Thus the present level of air and water quality must be considered a separate part of the natural resource endowment human beings have inherited. Indeed, it may well be the part which, as some fear, is most in danger of being squandered. Nonetheless, it is the total natural resource endowment—the previously accumulated solar energy and the fixed quantity of essential chemical elements as well as the thin band of air and water surrounding the earth—which one needs to take into account when considering whether the rate of economic expansion is subject to a natural resource constraint. The possibility of such a constraint follows from the laws of thermodynamics.

The first law of thermodynamics is the principle of the conservation of matter and energy. This law states that matter and energy can be neither created nor destroyed. An important implication of this law is that the social system of production represented by the n different industries does not actually "produce" any of the physical goods considered to be its output. It merely reorganizes, or reconstitutes, the minerals and other chemical elements which are the natural resource inputs into the system, converting them from the original state in which they are found in nature into the quite different forms and combinations which enable them to serve the needs of human beings. This is why the economic system was defined at the very outset of this text as the set of specialized social institutions for "transforming" whatever resources are found in nature (see chapter 1, section 1.1). The first law of thermodynamics is not sufficient by itself, however, to preclude further economic expansion. While new matter and/or energy cannot be created, neither can they be destroyed. Thus human beings at most face only the need to continually recycle the matter and/or energy already a part of or being added to the earth's biosphere. It is the second law of thermodynamics, the entropy law, which strongly implies a natural resource constraint on the rate of economic expansion.

The second law of thermodynamics states that the operation of any heat-powered engine, such as the earth's biosphere, necessarily entails a net energy loss. In other words, there is no such thing as a perpetual motion machine. The universe as a whole is steadily "running down" in the sense that all the energy that now gives it coherence and order is gradually being dissipated. The solar system itself will cease to exist in its present form once all the sun's hydrogen fuel has been consumed and the earth as a viable biosphere comes to an end. While this event is likely to occur so far in the future that it can for all practical purposes be ignored, still in the interim the number of human beings whom the earth can support at some level comfortably above the physiological minimum is limited by the amount of vegetation that can be grown. This amount, in turn, is limited by three factors: (1) the amount of arable land on the earth's surface that receives sufficient rainfall or, alternatively, can be irrigated; (2) the amount of sunlight reaching those areas; and (3) the rate at which cells can divide in the course of producing vegetable matter. It is these limits on the rate at which food, fiber, and the other organic products can be grown that argue for the existence of a natural resource constraint on the rate of expansion—at least within the agricultural sector of any social system of production.

This constraint on the rate of economic expansion has been recognized by economists ever since Thomas Malthus. Indeed, it is the basis for positing "decreasing returns," and hence a rising supply cost—at least within the agricultural sector. Still, whatever the tendency toward decreasing returns in the short period, continuous improvements in agricultural technique have, over the longer run, caused economists to discount almost entirely the possibility of any significant constraint on the rate at which food, fiber, and other organic products can be grown. Such optimism, it can be argued, ignores the second law of thermodynamics—as well as the "free ride" human beings have had so far in exploiting the thin band of air and water necessary for all life, animal as well as vegetable. Europeans were at first able to avoid the natural resource constraint on agricultural production by extending their area of cultivation to the other temperate regions in North America, South America, South Africa, and Oceania which were not already preempted by advanced civilizations. In more recent times, as the effective limit to new settlement was reached, these European colonizers, joined by farmers from the other advanced civilizations, have come to rely on large quantities of industrial fertilizers (and pesticides) to achieve ever higher yields per acre. However, in surmounting in this way what would otherwise be the natural resource constraint on increased agricultural production, they have only made more acute the problem posed by the earth's fixed quantity of mineral resources.

Industrial fertilizers are simply a more concentrated form of the nutrients essential for plant growth. The chemical components are the same—principally nitrogen, phosphorus, and potassium. It is just that, in the case of industrial fertilizers, those elements have been reduced through one or more processes to a "purer," or more highly organized state, with any extraneous material eliminated. In this respect, industrial fertilizers are no different from any of the other physical goods produced by the n industries which constitute the social system of production. Each industry's physical output represents a higher degree of organization, insofar as the mineral components of those goods are concerned—and thus the very opposite of the disorder, or entropy, which increasingly characterizes the universe as a whole. However, this local reduction in the amount of entropy does not contravene the second law of thermodynamics. An unavoidable by-product of whatever industrial process is relied upon will be some loss of "free energy"—that is, the energy which, in one form or another, can be used to do the work of biological and/or mechanical systems. This loss is represented by the heat that must be vented into the surrounding air or nearby flowing water. An additional by-product will be a certain amount of waste material. Even if the effluvia does not flow untreated into the surrounding environment, thereby creating "bads" in the form of air and water pollution, it will add to the overall disorganization, or entropy, of the biosphere. This is because the waste material consists of the same mineral resources used in the production process, but with those minerals transformed by the production process into a more chaotic, or less organized, state. Only an unusable residue of the minerals embodied in the physical "goods" being produced will remain, and this residue will be combined in a more random manner with other chemical elements having little or no economic value. In the form of slag, the residue may even be costly to remove, giving it a negative value.

It is the fact that raw materials are, in this way, necessarily "used up" in the production process which is the source of the growing pressure on the earth's fixed quantity of mineral resources. Even without any increase in the level of economic activity, these minerals will need to be replaced as they become embodied in not just the physical goods but also, perhaps even more significantly, the "bads" which are the joint output of the economic system. This means having to resort over time to deposits which are less accessible and which therefore require a greater expenditure of the society's scarce resources, including its fossil and other fuels, if those deposits are to be converted through mining and similar extractive operations into the types of materials inputs which can be used in the industrial production process. With the economy expanding over time, the pressure on the earth's mineral resources will be all the greater. Since additional mineral resources can always be tapped by expending greater energy, both human and inanimate, it is the amount of solar energy stored in the form of fossil fuels (as well as leafy plants) which serves as the ultimate limit on the rate of economic expansion. It should be noted that recycling the minerals embodied in the goods previously produced will ease the problem only somewhat. For one thing, recycling itself uses up resources, including energy. Second, and ultimately even more limiting, recycling does not solve the problem of waste materials and the increase in the amount of entropy within the earth's biosphere which they represent.

Thus the net effect of any industrial activity is to increase the amount of entropy within the earth's biosphere. The reduction in entropy from whatever output in the form of goods is produced is more than offset by the loss of "free" energy and the more disorganized state in which the earth's fixed quantity of mineral resources is then left. Indeed, even the reduction in entropy from the goods produced represents only a temporary, and local, reversal of the longer run tendency toward increasing disorder postulated by the second law of thermodynamics. Since whatever goods are produced will become "scrap" and thus waste material once they can no longer efficiently serve the needs of human beings, all of the natural resource inputs will in time be reduced to a more entropic state.

If economists have paid too little attention to the limits on economic expansion which the laws of thermodynamics impose, it is largely because of the belief that an insufficient supply of some natural resource input will simply lead to an increase in the relative price of that resource, causing other, less expensive inputs to be substituted for it. Indeed, the same argument ought to apply to the human resource, or labor, inputs—even if this point is conveniently forgotten by economists when they attribute the secular rise in the price level to an "excess demand" for labor. Still, whether applied with consistency or not, the argument that any resource, natural or otherwise, which has become relatively scarce will simply be replaced by some other type of input, one which, as indicated by its price, is more plentiful, needs to be examined on its merits. This will be our next task.

13.3.2 Substitution among inputs in the long period

A major thrust of this text has been to call into question the gross substitution theorem which underlies the conventional economic theory. In its more extreme form, the theorem states that a change in the relative price of any two goods, or resources, will cause the one which has become cheaper to be substituted, at least in part, for the one which has become more expensive. This implies, as a corollary, that any two goods or resources are potential substitutes for one another. The less extreme version of the same theorem states that a change in the relative price of any good or resource will, as a result of the ensuing substitution effect, lead to a change in the demand for that good or resource. This implies only that there is at least one other good or resource which can be used instead, not that each good or resource is a potential substitute for every other good or resource.

The alternative model of household behavior presented in chapter 9 was meant to explain why the gross substitution theorem does not hold for the consumer goods represented by the **C** vector—not unless the analysis is first disaggregated to the level of a four-digit SIC industry's product line and the large number of elements which the **C** vector would then contain is lexicographically ordered based on the types of material needs being satisfied. Even then, the theorem holds only in its less extreme form. The Leontief model of production presented in chapter 5 was, meanwhile, meant to explain why the gross substitution theorem, even in its less extreme form, does not hold for the material inputs represented by the **A** matrix—at least not in the short period. This last restriction, however, still leaves open the possibility of substitution among the different material inputs in the long run as a result either of a change in their relative price or some other manifestation of increased scarcity. Indeed, with firms assumed to be cost-minimizers (see chapter 6, section 2.1), they can be expected to substitute over time other inputs for those which are becoming more expensive and/or less readily available.

It might seem a minor quibble to insist that substitution among different inputs can occur only in the long period. However, the distinction is a critical one. It means that substitution can occur only through the conscious decision by a firm to replace a part of its existing capacity. Regardless of how much the cost of any input may increase, using some other, less expensive input in its place will be precluded by the fixed technical coefficients that hold as long as the firm is restricted to the use of its existing plant and equipment. It is only by acquiring new equipment—if not a new plant altogether—that a firm will be able to adopt some new technique, one that requires less of some input which has become more expensive and/or is less readily available. It is thus only through investment, either by existing firms or new ones, that the technical coefficients represented by the $\mathbf{A}$, $\mathbf{K}$ and $\mathbf{L}$ matrices can change. Even so, reliance on a particular input cannot be reduced unless there has previously been technical progress, in the form of product innovation, in the industries which produce material inputs and/or capital goods. Thus substituting other inputs for those which have become scarce depends on the outcome of the complex process by which technical progress occurs over time in the n different industries which constitute the social system of production. A change in relative price is not a sufficient, or indeed even a necessary, condition. Nonetheless, once the intervening role of the capital accumulation process and technical progress is taken into account, one cannot rule out the possibility that, in the long period, other inputs will be substituted for those which have become relatively scarce.

While the possibility of substitution in the long period cannot be ruled out, one must be careful not to fall into the error of assuming that it is "capital" that will be used in place of the inputs which have become relatively scarce and/or whose relative price has increased. Since any substitution among inputs requires that the firm make an investment in new equipment, if not in a new plant altogether, it is easy to fall into this error. However, as was pointed out in the earlier discussion of the capital inputs (see chapter 5, section 5.1), the heterogeneous items that constitute the plant and equipment of an industry are an output of the production subsystem—albeit an intermediate one. They are in fact the output produced by the subset of investment goods industries, with that output then used as an input, like other intermediate goods, by the entire set of n industries. But this does not make the investment goods an input into the production subsystem itself.

The only exogenous inputs, insofar as the production subsystem and hence the economic system itself are concerned, are the human resource, or labor, inputs obtained from the parallel anthropogenic system and the natural resource inputs obtained from the surrounding ecological system. The capital inputs supplied by the investment goods industries are simply an intermediate output of the economic system, one that is produced using those more basic inputs. This can be seen from the fact that, relying on the Leontief inverse, the capital inputs can be reduced to a certain amount of direct and indirect labor, $\underline{\mathbf{L}}$, and, as will be brought out shortly, a certain amount of direct and indirect natural resources, $\underline{\mathbf{R}}$.

The labor and natural resource inputs, in contrast, cannot be reduced to any more basic inputs, "capital" or otherwise. This is why it is a mistake to assume that "capital" can be substituted for either the labor or the natural resource inputs. The "capital" in fact consists of varying amounts of labor and natural resources, and all that can be altered, even in the long period, is the relative proportion of labor and natural resources used (indirectly as well as directly) in producing the economic system's output—including any capital goods for investment purposes.

While the labor and natural resource inputs cannot be replaced by "capital" as they become relatively scarce and/or more costly, this still leaves open the possibility that, as suggested by the conventional economic theory, the one type of input can be substituted for the other. Here one needs to recognize that, although it is the labor inputs which have become more costly over time as a result of the higher real wage that has to be paid, it is only the natural resource inputs that can be said to have become—or, to be more accurate, to have remained—relatively scarce. As the preceding part of this chapter brought out, there would appear to be no shortage of human resources, or labor inputs. The most that can be pointed to is a shortage of certain types of skilled workers—particularly those able to set up and manage a business enterprise on their own. Still, the relative costliness of labor, given the fact that it is the natural resource inputs rather than the human resource ones that are relatively scarce, would seem to belie the principle of substitution that is basic to the orthodox theory in economics. The steady rise in the real wage of labor, despite the fact that it is the natural resource inputs that are relatively scarce, is not surprising, however, in light of the alternative model that has now been developed to explain the secular rate of expansion by advanced industrial economies like that of the United States. Indeed, that model indicates why the natural resource constraint on the rate of economic expansion cannot be overcome through substitution—not without bringing to a halt the human progress of the last several centuries.

The natural resource constraint can be avoided only if there are other inputs which can be used in place of the minerals, including fossil fuels, which are essential to the industrial system of production. It is on this point that the faith of economists in the possibilities of substitution would appear to be misplaced. The laws of thermodynamics imply that, with continuous growth, it is only a matter of time until all the essential natural resource inputs—the arable soil in which food and fiber can be grown, the minerals essential to life and industrial production, and the thin band of air and water surrounding the earth—will become scarce in *absolute* terms. Even if the first two of these obstacles can be overcome by relying on more energy-intensive techniques of cultivation, extraction, and resource recovery while imposing stringent environment controls to protect the world's air- and watersheds, this only reduces the problem to that of ensuring an adequate supply of fossil fuels and other inanimate sources of energy. That it is the amount of energy resources which serves as the ultimate limit on the rate of economic expansion becomes even clearer once one understands the profound transformation in the relationship of human societies to nature which underlies the industrial revolution of the past 300 years.

The steadily improving material standard of living which an increasing portion of the human race has enjoyed since 1800 has been based on the replacement of animate energy (mostly human) with inanimate, or mechanical, energy. Earlier in human history, a standard of living significantly above subsistence was possible only for those able to command the labor of other human beings, either through slavery or some functional equivalent. This effectively limited the number of persons who could enjoy a civilized life. Since the industrial revolution, however, the ever greater reliance on mechanical "slaves" has freed the majority of human beings in a growing number of societies from the type of unremitting toil which previously made them little better than intelligent beasts of burden. It has been the substitution of mechanical for human energy, together with a better understanding of the physical and chemical properties of nature, which has made possible the continuous growth of output per worker, and thus the steady improvement in the material conditions of human life, over the past three centuries. How long the process can continue depends critically on the availability of fossil fuels and other inanimate sources of energy.

Indeed, this is what makes the fossil fuels, along with the uranimum ores that serve as a nuclear fuel, qualitatively different from the other mineral resources which are part of the same "original endowment" of nature. Only the minerals resources that, like fossil fuels and uranium, are convertible into energy can directly replace human labor as an input into the production process. While labor can also be "saved" through the substitution of other material inputs for the mineral resources which are no longer easily extracted from the geosphere, still, as the second law of thermodynamics makes clear, this expedient will only temporarily ease the natural resource constraint on economic expansion.

As already pointed out, an overall increase in entropy is the unavoidable by-product of all industrial processes, with a greater expenditure of energy, human or otherwise, the only means of counteracting that effect. And the only alternative to a greater expenditure of human energy is an even greater dependence on the limited supplies of fossil fuels and the other inanimate sources of energy. The advantage of fossil fuels over nuclear ones is, of course, that the waste by-product is not radioactive. Still, in light of the "greenhouse" effect produced by the burning of fossil fuels, this advantage may well be an illusionary one. The fact is that there is only a limited supply of both fossil fuels *and* uranium ores—these being the only inanimate sources of energy that, aside from whatever portion of the sun's energy is tapped directly, can be used under present technology as an alternative to greater reliance on human effort. While there is not the same problem of a deleterious waste by-product in the case of solar energy, an efficient means of harnessing that power for most industrial and transportation purposes has yet to be discovered. This is what makes the mineral sources of energy, the supply of fossil fuels in particular, the ultimate natural resource constraint on the rate of economic expansion.

One could, of course, give up the hope of being able to continually economize on the use of human labor. But that would bring to an end the secular trend of the past 300 years whereby an ever increasing portion of the world's population has been able to count on a steadily improving material standard of living. In other words, a solution that requires substituting human resource, or labor, inputs for the various inanimate sources of energy would be self-defeating in terms of the purpose an economic system is intended to serve. The natural resource constraint must therefore be accepted as a real limit on the rate of economic expansion, one that cannot be overcome through substitution. The question is, just how severe a constraint is the availability of fossil fuels and other natural resources.

13.3.3 How limiting is the natural resource constraint

Based on the preceding discussion and the input-output model of the world economy constructed for the United Nations by Wassily Leontief and his associates, certain minerals can be identified as essential natural resource inputs into the social system of production. They are: (1) copper; (2) bauxite; (3) nickel; (4) zinc; (5) lead; (6) iron; (7) petroleum; (8) natural gas; and (9) coal. The last three of these minerals, as the principal sources of inanimate energy, are especially important. Still, all nine minerals need to be included, at the very least, as the elements of a natural resource vector, $\mathbf{R}$.

The specification of this vector is important for a number of reasons. First, it indicates what are the only other exogenous inputs, insofar as the economic system is concerned, besides the human resources represented by the $\mathbf{L}$ matrix. It thus provides the answer to the question posed earlier as to what, if not "capital," is the nonlabor input into the production process (see chapter 5, section 4.1). The identification of the elements of the $\mathbf{R}$ vector as the other exogenous inputs into the production process means that we can now replace the π vector within the equation that defines the value relationships for a vertically integrated system of production so that equation 5.52 (see chapter 5, section 4.1) then takes the following form:

$$\mathbf{P} = w\mathbf{L} + \mathbf{P}_R\mathbf{R} \tag{13.8}$$

where $\mathbf{P}_R$ is the set of prices, $p_{R_1}, p_{R_2}, \ldots, p_{R_k}$, for the essential mineral inputs into the production process and $\underline{\mathbf{R}}$ is a vector indicating the amounts of essential mineral inputs required, both direct and indirectly, to produce any one unit of the national product. How $\mathbf{P}_R$ is determined will be explained in the next subsection. The vector of direct and indirect mineral inputs, meanwhile, can be derived, in a manner analogous to the $\underline{\mathbf{L}}$ vector (see chapter 5, section 4.1), as follows:

$$\underline{\mathbf{R}} = \mathbf{R} \, (\mathbf{I} - \mathbf{A})^{-1} \, \mathbf{D} \tag{13.9}$$

Exhibit 13.1

The Economic System in Context

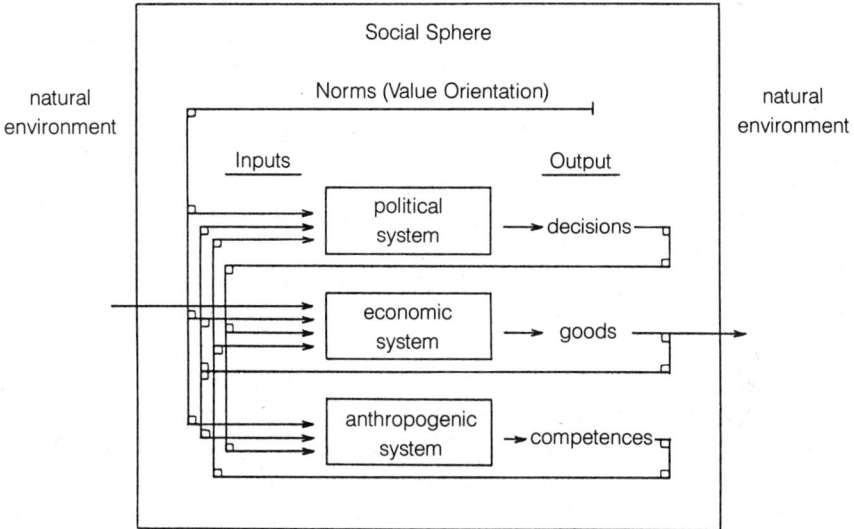

With the specification of the **R** vector, one can then fill in the last detail of the systems diagram that describes an advanced industrial society (see exhibit 13.1). This, of course, assumes that one of the outputs of the political system is the set of laws necessary for maintaining the natural environment as a viable biosphere. Otherwise, the **R** vector needs to be expanded to include the quantity of oxygenated air, potable water and arable soil. Finally, the specification of the actual components of the **R** vector indicates what are the minerals for which substitutes will in time have to be found if the rate of economic expansion is not eventually going to be slowed for lack of the necessary natural resource inputs.

Over the years, beginning with William Stanley Jevons's 1863 examination of the coal question, economists have attempted to estimate when the available supply of fossil fuels and other essential natural resources will be exhausted. While these exercises—including the studies prompted by the energy ''crisis'' of the 1970s—have been useful in calling attention to the natural resource constraint on the rate of economic expansion, they cannot be expected to answer the question to which they are addressed. This is because the answer depends on two factors about there is considerable uncertainty—in the sense that Keynes himself used the term to indicate what is inherently unknowable. The two factors are (1) the rate of growth of population and (2) future technical progress.

How quickly the available supply of essential mineral resources will be exhausted depends, to a large extent, on the rate at which human population is growing. With the growth of population unchecked, it will be only a matter of time—well within the next several centuries—until the capacity of the earth's biosphere to sustain human life, even at a reduced standard of material well-being, will be exceeded. On the other hand, if the world's population were to stabilize at a level not significantly greater than at present, it may be possible not only to avoid a deterioration in the material standard of living due to the pressure on the natural resource endowment but also, perhaps, to achieve even further improvement in that standard of living. To the extent any subsequent economic growth takes the form of providing increased services and/or leisure rather than additional physical goods, the chances of further improvement in the material standard of living are all the better—provided the world's population can be stabilized at the present level. How limiting is the natural resource constraint thus depends critically on the rate of population growth, $\mathring{P}op$. Human societies are no different in this respect from other biological organisms—as Charles Darwin, drawing upon Thomas Malthus's *Essay on the Principle of Population*, recognized in developing his theory of evolution. The critical role played by population growth is, in fact, the starting point in any ecological analysis such as the one which, in this section, is being attempted.

As critical as the growth of human population may be in determining the pressure on available natural resources, there is no way of knowing what that growth rate is likely to be in the decades ahead. All that can be said with any confidence is that population growth tends to fall toward zero as per capita income rises, but even that statement is based on what has happened in the past to the relatively small number of advanced industrial societies (see exhibit 4.12). One cannot be sure it applies to the other societies, with quite different cultural traditions, which have yet to achieve a comparable level of development. The less developed countries include such a large portion of all human beings presently alive that the growth of the world's population will, in the future, depend primarily on what happens in those societies. This makes it difficult, if not impossible, to say what will be the future growth of the world's population since both the success of those countries' industrialization efforts and the likely effect on their rate of population growth are unknown (and, most probably, unknowable).

While it might seem that the world's advanced industrial societies should be able to continue insulating themselves from the pressure of population growth beyond their borders, just as they have in the past, by severely limiting inmigration while relying on the foreign exchange needs of the less developed countries to ensure the availability of sufficient natural resources (see chapter 11, section 0.0), one has to recognize that the advanced industrial societies can, by this means, only temporarily avoid the natural resource constraint on the rate of economic expansion. As the less developed countries succeed in establishing their own industrial base, they can be expected to become increasingly unwilling to supply essential mineral inputs, including fossil fuels, to other countries. In this way, the pressure on the world's natural resource endowment from not just the growth of world population but also the efforts of the less developed countries to overcome their relative backwardness will eventually be felt even by the advanced industrial societies. If not forced to do without certain essential mineral inputs altogether, they will find themselves forced to pay a higher price for any of those inputs they need to import. While one effect will be an unfavorable shift in the terms of trade, the more significant consequence will be a decline in the growth of output per worker as industrial enterprises within those countries find that, in order to lower their costs, they must conserve the increasingly more expensive natural resource inputs instead of the human resource, or labor, inputs. It is thus through a decline in the growth of output per worker, $\overset{\circ}{Z}$, that any depletion of the essential mineral inputs represented by the **R** vector, due to the pressure of world population growth on the earth's natural resource endowment, will most clearly manifest itself. (As will be brought out in the subsection which follows, a rise in the price of some essential mineral input, such as petroleum, may be due to factors other than a growing shortage of that natural resource so that one cannot infer, from just the rise in price, that the natural resource is becoming depleted. However, whether due to a growing shortage or not, the rise in the price of the natural resource, especially if it is one of the fossil fuels, may well lead to a decline in the value of $\overset{\circ}{Z}$, at least temporarily, as firms nonetheless come under pressure to reduce their reliance on that input.)

How quickly the available supply of essential mineral resources will be exhausted will also depend on future technical progress. It is clear that, in the absence of further technological advance, the growth of the world's population, together with the efforts by the less developed countries to overcome their relative backwardness, will lead before long to an increasing shortage of the natural resource inputs represented by the **R** vector, forcing even the advanced industrial societies like the United States to concentrate of conserving the natural resource inputs rather than the human resource inputs. But this would happen, eventually, even if the world's population were to stabilize at the present level (and even if the material standard of living by that fixed number of persons increased no further). In the absence of further technological advance, it is only a matter of time until the natural resource inputs represented by the **R** vector will be depleted—with their real cost and hence their price necessarily rising even before that point is reached. It is just that an increase in the world's population, whatever that rate of growth may be, will further exacerbate the problem, creating even greater pressure on the limited natural resource endowment. This is why, in analyzing the natural resource contraint on the rate of economic growth, it is best to treat the growth of population, $\overset{\circ}{P}op$, as a fixed parameter and focus instead on what is the even more critical factor, namely, future technical progress.

The problem, once the issue comes down to whether there will be any further technological advance, is that one cannot know until the question has been been answered in the affirmative—at which point the question simply arises anew. In other words, it is not possible to answer the question in the negative and even a positive answer is not a permanent answer. For example, it is known that, if some practical means of exploiting the energy derived from the fusion of hydrogen atoms can be developed, human societies would be assured of adequate energy for considerable time to come and they will have taken another quantum leap in freeing themselves from the natural resource constraint on economic growth. But how can one know for certain that the development of fusion energy is possible until it has in fact been demonstrated? Moreover, the development of fusion energy is not the only hope for reducing the present reliance on fossil fuels. It is possible that better ways of harnessing solar energy will be discovered or some more efficient means of utilizing the existing supply of fossil fuels will be found. Again, how can one possibly know if or when this will happen until it actually occurs? Indeed, only a few weeks before this chapter was completed one would have had no reason to believe that the discovery of materials with superconductivity properties would promise to ease significantly the pressure on existing energy sources. But even this unexpected news does not ensure the further technological advance needed to exploit the scientific breakthrough.

The point is that future technical progress is inherently uncertain (in the sense of being unknowable) and this in turn, even aside from the problem of population growth, makes unanswerable the question of how severe is the natural resource contraint on economic growth. If one could count on future technical progress as an infinite extrapolation of what has happened in the past, then there would be nothing to worry about. On the other hand, in the absence of further technological advance, particularly in the critical area of developing new energy sources (or making better use of the existing energy sources), then human societies will eventually find themselves severely constrained, in attempting to improve their material standard of living, by the lack of the natural resource inputs represented by the R vector and the only question would be how soon.

Indeed, this is how it has always been—beginning with the agricultural revolution that first enabled human beings to capture more efficiently, for their own ends, the solar energy stored in leafy plants and continuing with the industrial revolution that, in more recent times, has placed other energy sources at the disposal of human societies. In every epoch, human beings have been stymied for lack of more abundant natural resources (or for lack of the implements produced with those resources), and it is only by finding a way around each new natural resource constraint that human beings have been able to make further progress in meeting their material needs— as evidenced by the growth of output per worker, $\overset{\circ}{Z}$. It is as true today, when the advanced industrial societies find themselves constrained by the lack of fossil fuels and other essential minerals, as it was in the past when arable land was more likely to be the limiting factor.

How limiting is the natural resource constraint is thus virtually the same question as how rapid is the rate of economic growth. The underlying determinant—the rate of technical progress, as measured by $\overset{\circ}{Z}$—is the same in both cases. This is why it can be said that the model of economic growth developed in this text has, from the very beginning, taken into account the natural resource constraint (see chapter 4, section 3.2, and chapter 5, part 4). It is just that the role played by the availability of natural resources has been implicit rather than explicit—at least up to now. Still, it is one thing to identify the natural resource constraint on the rate of economic expansion and quite another to show that too rapid a rate of economic expansion, by creating an "excess demand" for the natural resource inputs, will give rise to the type of secular inflation that has been experienced by the United States and the other advanced industrial societies since the end of World War II. Before reaching any such conclusion, we need to be sure that the prices of natural resources do, in fact, depend on demand factors. In other words, we have to be able to explain how the $\mathbf{P}_R$ vector specified at the beginning of this subsection is determined.

13.3.4 The pricing of nonreproducible goods

The explanation for how prices are determined that was previously offered (see chapter 6) can be said to apply, without qualification, only to the types of goods and services that are reproducible. These are the goods and services which can be replenished as they are used up and indeed even increased in quantity over time. For any other goods and services—those which are not reproducible—a different model of pricing is required.

Two types of nonreproducible goods and services can be identified. They are (1) masterpieces of various sorts, and (2) natural endowments, such as a beachfront property or a deposit of some essential mineral. The first type of nonreproducible good reflects the impossibility of duplicating the creative output of certain individuals, such as a Rembrandt, a Mozart or a Newton; and the second type of nonreproducible good reflects the impossibility of adding to the endowment of nature beyond what the earth's evolution permits. These two types of nonreproducible goods, it should be noted, are but extreme examples of the more general case in which some product of human effort or some "original gift of nature" can be replicated only imperfectly or at a higher real cost. After all, imitations of Rembrandt—if not of Mozart and Newton—are possible, both by disciples and by mechanical means, while another beachfront property or some other deposit of the same mineral can usually be found (though it may not be as accessible or as easily worked). This means that both "masterpieces" and natural endowments can be analyzed, like any nonhomogenous and/or differentially higher-cost good or resource, in terms of the Ricardian "rents" and Marshallian "quasi-rents" to which they give rise.

For each nonreproducible good, and indeed even for each not easily replicated good or service, one can assume an available substitute that is reproducible. This assumption is a reasonable one in light of the fact that (a) there are reproducible goods readily available to meet the needs of human beings for food, clothing and shelter—the most basic among the six to eight major categories of consumption (see chapter 9, section 1.2), and (b) the inanimate sources of energy can, if necessary, be replaced by human labor. One can then proceed to explain the price of any nonreproducible good, such as a masterpiece or a deposit of some essential mineral, in terms of how much the demand for it exceeds the supply of its closest reproducible substitute, with that "excess demand" then determining the "rent" (in the case of some natural resource input) or the "quasi-rent" (in the case of some unique human resource input) the nonreproducible good or service is able to command. In this way, the supply-and-demand framework of the orthodox theory can be brought to bear on the problem, as shown in exhibit 13.2.

An unlimited supply of the reproducible substitute can be assumed to be available at a constant cost, and hence a constant price, equal to $p_{i,j}$. The nonreproducible good, it can further be assumed, is preferred over that substitute because it offers certain advantages. (In the case of an exhaustible fossil fuel such as petroleum, for example, it may provide a faster means of transport.) At the same time, however, an increased supply of the nonreproducible good can be obtained only at an ever greater real cost to the society (as measured, for example, by the amount of labor, or human resource, inputs required to work some less accessible deposit). This is reflected by the divergence, beyond a certain point, of the supply curve for the nonreproducible good, S_R, from the supply curve for the reproducible good, S_M. (Where the point of divergence occurs is less important than the fact that the two curves will, because of the greater real cost incurred in obtaining the preferred good, necessarily diverge.) The price of the nonreproducible good, p_{R_j}, will then be determined by where its demand curve, D_R, intersects its supply curve, S_R. (The demand curve, D_R, is depicted as being perfectly inelastic on the assumption that the demand for the nonreproducible good depends solely on the level of income, Y. To the extent the demand for the nonreproducible good is price sensitive, the D_R curve will have a negative slope to it. However, since the price of the nonreproducible good depends only on the point of intersection with S_R, the slope of the D_R curve makes no difference in the argument which follows.)

The "rent" earned by the nonreproducible good will depend on how large is the differential between the price that can be obtained for that good, given the demand for it, and the price of its closest reproducible substitute. It is thus equal, in exhibit 13.2, to the vertical distance between point A, where the demand and supply curve for the nonreproducible good intersect, and point B on the supply curve of the reproducible substitute. This means that the price of the nonreproducible good, p_{R_j}, can be analyzed and explained in terms of the cost, and therefore the price, of the closest reproducible substitute, $p_{i,j}$, plus the "rent" which the nonreproducible good is able to obtain. That is,

$$p_{R_j} = p_{i,j} + R_j \qquad (13.10)$$

where p_{R_j} is the price of the jth nonreproducible good, $p_{i,j}$ is the price of its

Exhibit 13.2

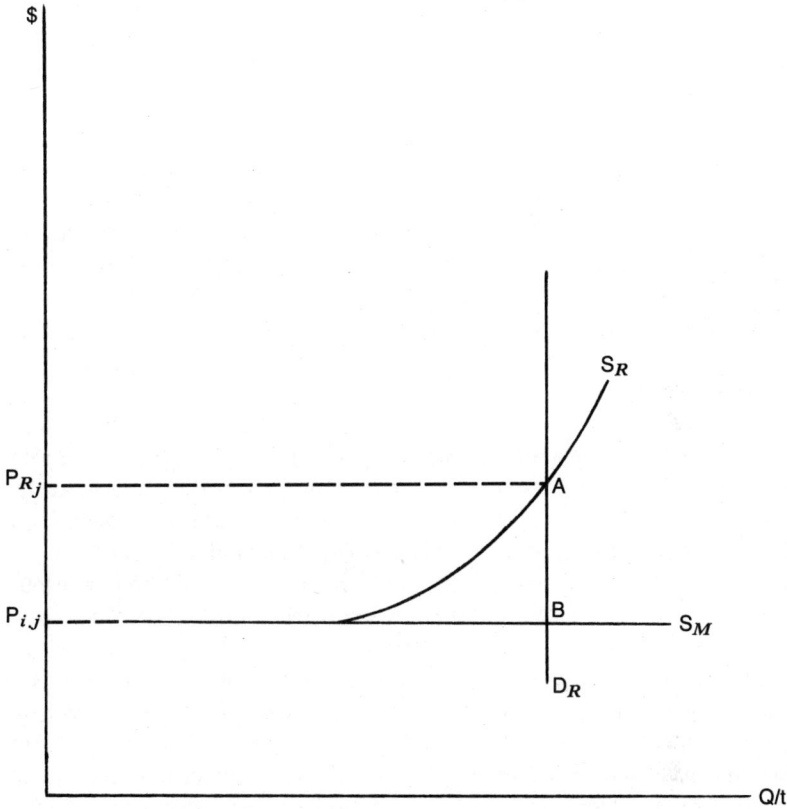

closest reproducible substitute and R_j is the per-unit rent obtained by that nonreproducible good. The price of the closest reproducible substitute, $p_{i,j}$, will depend on the factors previously analyzed (see chapter 6) while the per-unit rent obtained, R_j, depends on how much the nonreproducible good is valued, based on the market-mediated level of demand, over that substitute good. Once the size of the per-unit rent, R_j, has been explained for the somewhat more easily handled case of an exhaustible natural resource whose supply flow can be increased only at an ever greater real cost, the same line of reasoning can be extended to cover two additional cases. They are (1) the nonreproducible good whose supply is absolutely fixed, such as a Rembrandt or Van Gogh masterpiece, and (2) the good, whether reproducible or not, whose supply is fixed by the suppliers acting collectively. In this way, by returning to the case of oligopoly and even monopoly, we shall close the circle in the analysis of pricing behavior.

The case of the exhaustible natural resource whose supply flow can be increased only at an ever greater real cost is easier to analyze since, with a supply curve that is independent of the demand curve, the conventional Marshallian theory can still be applied. Indeed, it was Sraffa's great insight, pointing to the need for an alternative mode of microeconomic analysis, that the Marshallian theory holds only in this one case. The situation is more difficult to analyze when, instead of being able to assume a greater supply flow of some nonreproducible good at a higher price, one must concede that the supply is absolutely fixed so that the quantity available remains the same regardless of how much the price may rise. This is the situation, not only with art masterpieces but also, perhaps more significantly, with any parcel of land offering a locational advantage, such as access to a central business district or the seashore. In these cases, it is the supply curve, S_R, that will be perfectly inelastic, as shown in exhibit 13.3, and, unless the demand is price-responsive (and thus not perfectly elastic as well), the price will be indeterminate based on the Marshallian model.

Reverting back to Ricardo, one can nonetheless posit a differential rent, R_j, which the nonreproducible, and fixed, good and/or asset is able to command over its closest substitute, whether that substitute is reproducible (as, for example, in the case of a print of a Rembrandt or Van Gogh masterpiece) or, alternatively, is itself nonreproducible and fixed in quantity (as in the case of the next closest and/or the next most fertile parcel of land). The amount of differential rent, R_j, will depend either on the cost advantage the nonreproducible good or resource affords—as, for example, in the case of the next most fertile parcel of land—or, alternatively, on the growth of nominal income and where such items as an original art masterpiece or a beachfront property fall within the hierarchy of some economic entity's material needs (see chapter 9, section 1.5). While it is still where point A lies on the supply curve, S_R, relative to point B that will determine the amount of differential rent, point A is just that—a point whose position is determined by other than the intersection of two separate curves. This implies a pricing dynamic virtually the opposite of that which holds for reproducible goods.

Instead of the quantity demanded determining the quantity supplied, with the price depending on the cost of production (see chapter 6, section 4.5), the supply is absolutely fixed—with the price then determined by how much income has been set aside for purchasing that particular type of good and/or asset and where any one item which may be purchased is ranked by the successful bidder relative to the other available items within the same category. Indeed, the demand for the nonreproducible good and/or asset will be determined as part of the more general process by which economic entities decide on their portfolio of assets, physical as well as financial. (This means that the monetary policy adopted by the central bank will be an additional factor determining the price, p_R, and hence the per-unit rent, R_j. See chapter 12, sections 1.4 and 2.3).

It should be noted that it is only the nonreproducible good or asset which offers a cost (or net return) advantage that can be ranked, relative to any other items

Exhibit 13.3

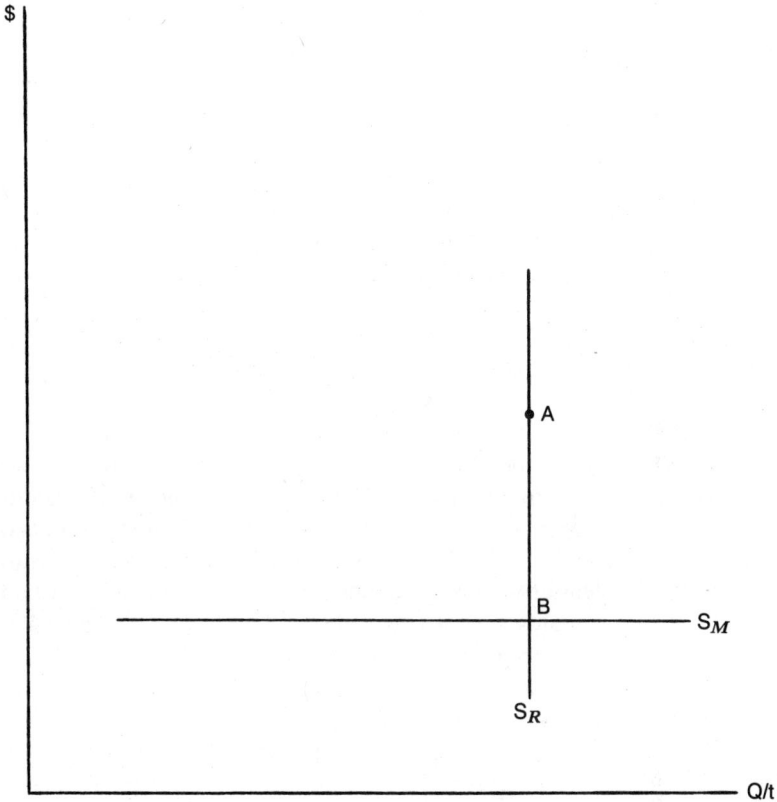

within the same more general category of goods or assets, on the basis of some objective standard. For any other type of good or asset whose supply is absolutely fixed, the ranking will necessary have to be subjective. While it would shed additional light on the matter if a utility function or some other indication of subjective preferences could be derived for the latter type of good or asset, the fact is that, as already pointed out (see chapter 9, section 1.6), this is not possible. All we can observe is the differential rent obtained, as measured by the distance between points A and B in exhibit 13.3. We have no empirical basis for inferring what determines the size of that differential.

The supply of some good or resource may be fixed, not by the inherent nature of the item—as in the case of some parcel of land or an art masterpiece—but rather through the collective action of the economic entities that control all the available supply. This, for example, was the situation in the 1920s when a small number of international oil companies controlled most of the known deposits of petroleum and again in the 1970s when control passed into the hands of OPEC (the Organization of Petroleum Exporting Countries). In this type of situation, it is again the supply curve shown in exhibit 13.3 that applies—not the one shown in exhibit 13.2. Indeed, it is a serious error to confuse the two. In the case represented by exhibit 13.2, the per-unit rent, R_j, reflects the higher real cost incurred as the supply is increased. In the case depicted in exhibit 13.3, where the supply is instead being controlled so it either remains fixed or else increases in line with the growth of demand so that a fixed per-unit rent, R_j can be maintained, the cost no longer plays any role in determining p_R. The price depends solely on the level of demand, as determined by nominal income. It thus depends on where point A lies on the supply curve relative to point B.

It should be added that, to the extent the price in some oligopolistic or other type of industry exceeds the costs of production (including the cost of expansion), exhibit 13.3 applies even to the case of reproducible goods. In this way, the analysis of how prices are determined can be brought back full circle to where the argument left off at the end of chapter 6. One can then see that the critical consideration in determining whether any differential rent, or "excess profit," can be obtained is whether the industry is able to arrive at and enforce a collective pricing and/or output decision. The pricing power to which the cooperative solution to the problem of oligopolistic interdependence gives rise will be the same, provided new entrants can be barred, whether the good being supplied is an industrial product which is reproducible or a primary product that is exhaustible. Indeed, this insight will set the stage for the discussion, in chapter 14, of the wage-price inflationary spiral as the dynamic underlying the secular rise in the price level in the United States and the other advanced industrial societies throughout the post-World War II period. Before following through on that point, however, we need to complete our discussion of the human resource inputs by addressing the question of how, in light of the likely response of the anthropogenic system to an increase in the demand for labor, the government can hope to implement a "full employment" policy.

13.4 A 'Full Employment' Policy

The thrust of the argument presented in the first two parts of this chapter is that the response of the anthropogenic system to any change in the rate of economic expansion will be such that the endemic condition in an advanced industrial economy like the United States is not an "excess demand" for (or supply shortage of) labor. The endemic condition, rather, is one in which significant numbers of individuals, representing the amount of anthropogenic slack, are either unemployed or underemployed (that is, underutilized). This means that the available stock of human resource inputs, H, will exceed the opportunity structure, N— with the difference between H and N equal to the number of persons unemployed, U, and the number of persons underemployed, U''. That is,

$$H - N = U + U'' \qquad (13.11)$$

Taking into account the different types of competence involved, the aggregate variables can be replaced by their corresponding matrices so that equation 13.11 then takes the following form:

$$\mathbf{H} - \mathbf{N} = \mathbf{U} + \mathbf{U}'' \qquad (13.12)$$

where $\mathbf{U}$ and $\mathbf{U}''$ are column vectors respresenting respectively the number of individuals within each skill or occupational category who are either unemployed or underemployed.

Two questions still remain to be answered. The first is how, in the absence of a market mechanism able to perform such a task, the excess human resource inputs are allocated among the limited employment opportunities which the economic system, even one expanding at a certain rate, can provide. The answer to this question, given in a subsequent subsection, will complete the analysis of how an individual's social class is determined—beyond whatever differential access to educational institutions and other developmental organizations the individual may have enjoyed before having had to make the transition from school to work.

The second question is by far the more important of the two. This is the question of what can be done, as a matter of public policy, to reduce the number of persons who find themselves either unemployed or even underemployed. It is the question of how close an advanced industrial society like the United States, with an equally advanced anthropogenic system, can come to achieving "full employment"—that is, maximize the utilization of its human resources. As we shall see, the answer to this second question is not unrelated to the first. However, before either of these two questions can be addressed, we need to clear away some of the misconceptions that surround the labor, or human resource, inputs into the production process. This, in turn, requires that we make explicit the human resource, or anthropogenic, perspective that underlies this text so it can be juxtaposed against the more conventional view of the matter.

13.4.1. The human resource perspective

Based on the analysis up to this point and the human resource, or anthropogenic, perspective it reflects, we can identify three errors that are commonly made with respect to the labor inputs. They are:

1. The presumption of full employment. This error consists of ruling out the possibility that a market economy will, in the long run, leave a significant portion of the labor force unemployed. It is difficult to understand how anyone familiar with conditions in the world's advanced market economies over the past century or more could fall into such an error. There would seem to be only two possible explanations. One is that some economists confuse a model's equilibrium condi-

tions—conditions which, as underlying assumptions, may or may not be satisfied—with the reality the model is meant to explain. The other is a desire by some economists not to let what is considered a minor imperfection obscure the considerable accomplishment of the advanced market economies in providing both increased and better employment opportunities, along with an ever rising material standard of living, for the majority of individuals living in those countries even during the periodic contractions to which such systems seem to be prone.

2. The labor parity fallacy. This error consists of viewing labor as but one of n inputs into the production process—and no more important than any of the other n inputs. The error here is in confusing the means to an end, namely, the economic system as the set of specialized social instititutions for satisfying the material needs of individuals, with the end itself. The fact is that the other inputs, both the natural resources derived from the surrounding environment and any other types of material inputs produced as an output of the economic system—including the capital inputs—are not on a par with labor. The labor inputs, because they cannot be disembodied from the individuals who constitute the society, are from a humanistic perspective quite different from the other inputs into the production process. Any presumption to the contrary is likely merely to serve as the justification for treating one group, or social class, within the society as simply the instrument of some other group, and thus to lay the foundation for rationalizing the exploitation of the one group by the other.

3. The consumption bias. This error consists of judging the economic well-being of an individual solely in terms of the goods available for consumption—and ignoring the types of employment opportunities thereby being provided. The fact is that the way in which an individual must spend his or her time in order to earn the necessary income may be no less important to that person's well-being than any goods or services purchased with the income earned. This is especially true as the level of income itself rises. It is thus a distortion of the reality to focus exclusively, as the conventional theory does, on the individual's role as consumer to the virtual neglect of his or her role as producer.

The human resource perspective which informs the argument of this chapter is based on three quite different premises. They are as follows:

1. The living members of any society are its most valuable resource. The greatest challenge any society faces, once it has made itself secure against foreign domination and established the necessary ecological balance, is to ensure that its human resources are being utilized to the fullest extent possible. This statement, it can be argued, is simply an objective description of the situation in which an advanced industrial society like the United States finds itself, once it is no longer willing to permit any of its members to perish for lack of the necessary material sustenance. With the right to life guaranteed, the output needed to maintain the existing stock of human resources becomes a fixed cost to the society, and the only matter then left to be determined is how effectively those human resources will be utilized.

2. Each individual member of the society is as valuable a resource, at least at

birth, as every other member of the society. If, within the same age cohort, differences in competence are likely to manifest themselves at a later point in time, this will be due primarily to whatever differential access to developmental institutions those individuals have had. This statement needs to be qualified in two ways before it can be considered defensible. First, some individuals may suffer from birth defects or other objectively measurable physiological handicaps which will place them at a disadvantage, in terms of developing certain skills, relative to the other individuals within their age cohort. Their chances of achieving the same level of competence are therefore less. Second, experience has demonstrated that an individual can, by dint of his or her own efforts, attain a level of competence within some area of endeavor beyond what would seem likely, given the opportunities the individual has had. For the same reason, some individuals may achieve less than can be expected of them. The above statement is therefore not meant to deny that each individual is, to some extent, the master of his or her own fate. The point rather is that the social structure in which the individual must find a place is by far the more decisive influence in determining what types of competence will be acquired and even, along any particular career path, what level of competence will be achieved.

3. An advanced industrial society requires, if its essential work is to be done, various types of competence—as represented by the L matrix previously specified. However, there is no objective basis for judging any one of those types of competence as being more valuable to society than any other. Each type of competence, being necessary for the functioning of the system as a whole, is equally essential. There is thus no objective basis for whatever differential there may be in the amount of compensation earned and the other rewards that go with holding any particular position. This statement, again, needs to be qualified in two ways before it can be considered defensible. First, some types of competence require more years of prior education than others before an individual can be expected to hold an entry-level position within the field, and this differential in the amount of prior education will need to be offset by a differential in subsequent earnings to cover the greater cost entailed. Second, the argument applies only to the m and n dimensions of the L matrix. Along a given career path, subsequent to any entry-level position which may be held, a differential in earnings may be justified in terms of the greater competence required and/or the greater responsibility demanded. These two qualifications aside, the burden of proof is on those who would argue that those holding a particular position within the opportunity structure represented by the L, and hence the N, matrix should receive a differential in wages or other benefits.

It is not just that the human resource perspective of this text is based on a quite different set of premises. There is also the conscious effort to avoid the three errors frequently made with respect to the labor inputs. Thus, instead of assuming that the way in which a market economy functions will necessarily lead to full employment, this text has indicated that, as an extension of the argument initially made by Keynes, the endemic condition is one in which a significant portion of the potential labor force is left unemployed (if not, in other ways, remaining underutilized). The next subsection will, in fact, attempt to explain how the limited number of employment opportunities which a market economy is able to provide is apportioned among the larger number of persons who wish to work, thereby determining the actual pattern of human resource utilization. Moreover, instead of assuming that the labor of human beings is no different from the other inputs used in the production process, this text views the individual members of any society—each and every one of them, without invidious distinction—as the society's most valuable economic resource, with the economic system judged, in terms of its efficiency, by how fully that resource is being utilized. The second subsection that follows will, in fact, attempt to indicate the means available to any society for more effectively utilizing its human resources as the possible compo-nents of a full employment policy by the government. Finally, instead of viewing the economic well-being of individuals solely in terms of the amount of goods and services available to them as part of the net output of the economic system, this text considers the types of employment provided, and in particular the opportuni-ty afforded to each and every member of society to realize his or her full potential, as no less important a consideration. The final subsection of this chapter will, in fact, examine the types of labor supply management policies required if the goal of enabling each individual to realize his or her full potential is to be attained.

13.4.2 The pattern of human resource utilization

A society's opportunity structure, that is, the amount and types of compensated employment it is able to offer, will be equal to the number of jobs available with private firms, N_E, plus whatever additional employment is provided by the government and not-for-profit sector, N_G. While the total opportunities for exer-cising competence will be considerably greater, including as they do various types of socially necessary activity such as keeping abreast of current events and rearing children, it is only the opportunity structure represented by $1/h$, the product of the Q and L matrices plus whatever jobs are financed by the govern-ment's taxing power, which provides individuals with the income needed to purchase the output of a market economy. Thus it is only this opportunity struc-ture, consisting of a certain number of compensated positions, or paying jobs, that is constrained by economic factors. The discussion that follows will be limited to that opportunity structure. The society's potential labor force, as represented by its H matrix, will be distributed across this opportunity structure according to certain rules. These rules, by determining which individuals will obtain the more desirable jobs and which individuals will be left without any jobs at all, will lead to the observed pattern of human resource utilization—and thus to the culmination of the process by which an individual's social class is determined. The rules that govern the distribution of the potential labor force among the available employment opportunities can be specified as follows, at least for the United States:

1. Anyone holding a particular job beyond an initial probationary period (usually not more than six months) can expect to retain that position until or unless (a) he or she reaches a predetermined retirement age (and thus becomes eligible for a pension or some other type of transfer payment in lieu of wage income); (b) he or she becomes physically incapacitated (and thus eligible for disability payments); (c) he or she refuses to comply with the rules governing behavior during working hours (in which case, the employee must be told the rules he or she has violated and, in many cases, given a fair hearing); or (d) the employing organization no longer needs to fill that position, either because of a temporary decline in the demand for its output or because of a more permanent restructuring of its labor force. In the former case, the laid-off worker will have the first claim on the job when and if it is restored.

This first rule precludes the possibility that an individual already affiliated with an employing organization will be replaced by someone else solely because the second person is willing to accept a lower wage. It means that a job, once filled, can be expected to stay filled until the person holding it voluntarily quits, retires, becomes physically incapacitated or violates an important work rule, or until the structure of the employing organization's required work force changes as a result of technical progress, eliminating the need for that position. (In the case of a temporary lay-off, the position continues to exist, though with the person holding it forced, for the moment, to vacate it.) This first rule thus denies, as the orthodox theory would have it, that employing organizations are continually contracting and recontracting with their workers for labor services. Rather, employing organizations need only contract with any new workers hired to fill the openings that occur through attrition and/or expansion. In this way, despite the continuous turnover, the integrity of the work force as a reproducible social group can be maintained.

2. Whenever an opening occurs, or is anticipated, a pool of qualified applicants will be formed through the joint actions of the employing organization and the individuals who would like to fill the position. The employing organization will first announce the opening, listing the starting salary and the minimal qualifications; and those who want to be considered for the position will respond by submitting an application and/or a resume to show that they meet those qualifications. The employing organization, after screening out those who lack the necessary education and prior work experience, is then free to hire, at the announced starting wage or higher, whomever it wishes from among the pool of qualified applicants.

This second rule precludes the possibility that, even in filling the openings continually occurring in the opportunity structure, the choice will be dictated by the wage (or price of labor services) that the employing organization is willing to pay and the new worker is willing to accept. Rather, a starting wage is announced that is sufficient to attract a large enough number of qualified applicants so that the employing organization can be assured of filling the opening without impairing the effectiveness of its work force. In effect the employing organization, especially when it is a megacorp, fixes in advance the starting wage for any workers it may hire in the same way it fixes the price of the goods it produces, with the wage, like the price, thus becoming an "administered," or fixed, as distinct from a "market," or flexible, price. And even if the employing organization lacks the power to fix the price of the goods it produces, as is often the case with a neoclassical proprietorship, it is still likely to be able to fix the starting wage. Indeed, the employing organization is likely to have positioned itself with respect to one of the pools of under- and unemployed workers so as to have at least that minimum amount of wage-setting power.

3. An individual can apply for any position, even if there are at present no openings and even if he or she is presently holding another job. Indeed, as part of the incessant competition that goes on among workers for the better jobs, those presently employed can be expected continually to seek advancement to a higher-level position, either within the organization with which they are already affiliated or, if that route is blocked, within another organization. The only limit on the type of job that the individual worker can hope to obtain is that imposed by the educational background and prior work experience one must have to qualify for one of the better positions within the overall opportunity structure.

A corollary of this third rule is that anyone holding a job may, upon giving advance notice, relinquish that position either to take a better job or simply to withdraw from the labor force. Wage payments to that individual will, of course, cease, along with the affiliation. The individual worker, in recognition of his or her weaker bargaining position vis-à-vis the employing organization, is thus subject to fewer constraints when it comes to terminating the relationship. This third rule provides the essential dynamic by which the available openings within the opportunity structure, especially the better ones, are filled. It is a dynamic that leads to the individual worker continually seeking to move up through the opportunity structure and, to the extent he or she is successful, creating openings below—until the only openings are those at the entry level for the least desirable jobs, those for which individuals can most easily qualify.

These rules lead to the x individuals with j types of competence who comprise the society's stock of human resources being distributed across the N employment opportunities the economic system is able to provide so that each individual is either (1) employed in a position requiring the highest level of competence the individual has so far demonstrated, or (2) unemployed. The latter group consists of three subcategories: (a) those who, though they wish to continue working, have nonetheless voluntarily quit their jobs without first obtaining another position; (b) those who, either because their labor services are no longer needed or because they are unable to perform satisfactorily on the job, have as the most recent addendum to their work history been involuntarily separated from an employing organization, and (c) those who have so far been unsuccessful in making the transition from school to work.

Only a portion of the first two groups of unemployed workers are likely to be interested in obtaining an entry-level position. The rest—those who have already progressed beyond the entry level—can instead be expected to form part of the pool of applicants seeking a position at a more advanced level (until such time as, having become discouraged, they lower their aspirations, perhaps even shifting to a different occupation or career ladder). In the queue for one of the positions beyond the entry level, they will be competing with those currently employed at a lower level but hoping to be promoted, either within the same organization or by another organization. The two groups together—those who have either relinquished or lost a position beyond the entry level and those who, having the necessary qualifications, would like to be promoted—constitute the anthropogenic slack which exists in the form of a pool of qualified applicants for each of the $j.1 \rightarrow r$ positions available beyond the entry level. Meanwhile, those who have voluntarily relinquished or lost a position at the entry level, together with those who have so far failed to make the transition from school to work, will constitute the anthropogenic slack in the form of a pool of qualified applicants for each of the $j.0$ entry level positions which are available within the same opportunity structure. The first component of the overall anthropogenic slack can be represented by a $\mathbf{U}''$ vector, with $u''_{j.1 \rightarrow r}$ as the individual elements of this first vector, and the second component can be represented by a $\mathbf{U}$ vector, with $u_{j.0}$ as the individual elements of this second vector. The two components together, $\mathbf{U}'' + \mathbf{U}$, when considered in relation to the $\mathbf{H}$ vector, represent the degree to which the potential labor force is being underutilized, with $\mathbf{U}$ alone the unemployed component and thus, relative to $\mathbf{H}$, the unemployment rate, $\mathsf{U}n$.

This formulation, it should be noted, is somewhat different from how the unemployment rate is officially defined in the United States. It includes not only those unable to obtain a job but also those who, having decided there are no openings for anyone with their qualifications, have become discouraged and thus have given up looking for a job. The assumption being made here is that individuals prefer activity to inactivity, and compensated employment to uncompensated activity. While a person might like to obtain income without having to work for it, the rules do not, for the most part, permit this. There are, of course, exceptions— most notably the rentiers with sufficient dividend, interest, and other income from the property they own that they can limit the number of hours they work. Everyone else, however, has only their compensated employment as a source of income to purchase the goods and services they need and desire, and hence must work whatever number of hours is required by the nature of the job they hold.

The rules specified above will also determine which individuals obtain the better jobs, and which individuals will be left with no choice but to accept the least desirable positions within the society's opportunity structure (unless they wish to remain unemployed). With the total number of positions fixed, for the moment, at N, workers can only determine, through the nonprice competition that goes on among them, where within that opportunity structure they will end up. They cannot through their own efforts, either individually or as a group, increase the number of employment opportunities. (The only exception is if, after going into business for themselves and thus becoming self-employed, they can increase the real income of the society through the additional output produced by the new firm they have established.) Individual workers may obtain a better job, even shifting from an unemployed to an employed status, but their gain will be at the expense of those not selected for the same position. The overall degree of anthropogenic slack, as measured by $U'' + U$, will remain unchanged. This is why the responsibility for the number of persons unable to find employment, or even unable to utilize their talent to the fullest, rests not with the individuals who are thereby put at a disadvantage but rather with the political mechanisms through which the society as a whole determines its economic (and anthropogenic) policies. For it is only at the macro level that not just the amount of residual income, Π, is determined (see chapter 6, section 1.4, and chapter 8, sections 2.4 and 2.5), but also the amount of employment, N. Both depend on the level of aggregate demand. This point is an essential one to keep in mind as we now turn to consider what a society can do through its political institutions to utilize more effectively its human resources.

13.4.3 Maximizing the utilization of human resources

The government, if it wishes to reduce the number of persons who are unemployed (or, more generally, are being underutilized), can proceed in any one of three ways to create a need for additional workers. They are (1) by increasing the amount of government and/or government-subsidized employment; (2) by stepping up the rate of economic expansion, and (3) by increasing the amount of leisure time. We shall take up each of these options in turn.

The most direct and surest way to reduce the number of persons who are unemployed is for the government to provide them with a job, either directly by placing them on its own payroll or indirectly by using its tax revenues to cover the cost of the wages being paid them. The problem with implementing a full employment policy in this manner, as will soon be made clear, is that it is likely to lower the growth of output per worker, $\overset{\circ}{Z}$, and thus reduce the growth of real income for those already employed. Before elaborating on this point, however, it is necessary to explain more fully what is meant by government-subsidized employment.

As already explained, both the number of persons employed by the government, N_G, and the government's wage bill, $w_G(N_G)$, must be considered policy variables. This is because, rather than being the result of a market-mediated process, the number of persons employed by the government, N_G, and the average rate of compensation received by those individuals, w_G, are entirely at the discretion of the government (or, more accurately, depend solely on the outcome of whatever is the political process for making decisions on behalf of the entire society). It is for this reason that, by increasing N_G and thus the total number of persons employed, N, the government is able to reduce the number of unemployed persons, U, by whatever amount it wishes. The government, however, need not add persons directly to its own payroll in order to reduce the amount of unemployment. It can instead increase the amount of subsidized employment. This it can do in either of two ways: (a) through grants to nonprofit (or even profit-seeking) organizations, or (b) through stipends to individuals.

A number of reasons have already been adduced for restricting the activities of the government as much as possible (see chapter 10, section 5.1). As was subsequently pointed out, the types of market failure that necessitate the provision of public goods by the government can be overcome by contracting with private parties for the delivery of the desired goods and services, provided the government uses its taxing power to cover the cost (see chapter 10, section 2.1). Thus, the government need not produce military equipment itself in one of its arsenals. It can contract with a private party for the delivery of the weapons. Similarly, it need not carry out research itself in one of its own laboratories. It can contract with a nonprofit organization, such as a university, for the work to be done. Although the individuals employed in the activities being funded will not appear on the government's own payroll, it is nonetheless the government's taxing power that enables their wages to be paid and, in this respect, their employment is government-subsidized. Indeed, based on this definition, virtually all of the employment generated by the government's purchase of goods and services can be considered to be government-subsidized. Still, it is necessary to distinguish between the government's purchase of goods and services for the purpose of public consumption, as in the case of any national defense (political) or educational (anthropogenic) programs, and the purchase of goods and services for public investment, such as any economic infrastructure outlays. While in both cases the employment generated must be considered to be government-subsidized, only in the latter situation will there be an increase in the amount of economic output (at least in the short period) as a result of the increase in employment.

The employment subsidized by the government through grants to nonprofit organizations (or even for-profit enterprises) can be supplemented by stipends to individuals. Instead of contracting with an organization, the government can provide a certain amount of income, or compensation, to a person directly so as to ensure that a certain type of activity will be carried out. The distinction between a stipend and some other form of transfer payment (to an individual) is that, while in the latter case there is no *quid pro quo*, an individual receiving a stipend is obligated to perform what is the equivalent of a labor service involving some goal-directed use of the individual's time. Thus if, under the AFDC program (see chapter 10, section 2.2), an adult is eligible to continue receiving income only if he or she provides proper care for one or more minor dependents, the payment would be a stipend paid for performing a valuable social task rather than being a more general type of income transfer. In the same way, if an individual were to receive income from the government in return for engaging in some other type of socially useful activity, such as serving as an official in a political party or carrying out a prescribed program of study, that payment, too, would be a stipend. The point is that, whether it takes the form of a grant to some nonprofit organization or a stipend to a particular individual, the wage compensation provided through the government's taxing power will enable a larger number of persons to be employed usefully than would otherwise be the case. It will thus increase the value of N.

Effective as either government or government-subsidized employment may be in reducing the number of unemployed persons, it will nonetheless leave the level of aggregate economic output, G, unchanged. This is because, as a form of public consumption, the government's purchase of goods and services represents a subtraction from the net output produced by the enterprise sector, not an addition. The only exception is the additional employment generated as a result of the government's expenditures on the economic infrastructure—and even in the case of any such public investment, the net output available for final use, or consumption, will remain the same (see chapter 2, section 2.2). What this means is that output per worker, Z, and thus the growth of output per worker, $\mathring{Z}$, will necessarily be lower than it would otherwise be as a result of the increase in N_G. While aggregate output, G, and hence the numerator of Z will be the same, total employment, N, and hence the denominator of Z will be larger.

The decline in Z as a result of the increase in government and government-subsidized employment creates a problem because, as already pointed out (see chapter 5, section 4.5), the sustainable rate of economic expansion and therefore the growth of real income depends primarily on the growth of output per worker, $\mathring{Z}$. Thus, an increase in the amount of government and government-subsidized employment will, through the effect it has on the growth of output per worker, create a potential conflict over the distribution of income. The conflict, if it does not force the government to rescind its decision because of the adverse political reaction (see chapter 10, section 3.5), may well add to the rate of inflation (see chapter 8, section 2.4).

It should be noted that the reduction in the growth of output per worker from an increase in government and government-subsidized employment is but the extreme case of the more general situation in which the growth of output per worker, $\mathring{z}_j$, in the industries expanding most rapidly is less than the growth of output per worker for the enterprise sector as a whole, $\mathring{Z}$. Whenever the industries supplying the bulk of any additional output have below-average rates of labor productivity growth, the overall growth of output per worker, $\mathring{Z}$, will necessarily decline. It is just that, with the increase in subsidized employment (or public outlays) representing only a transfer of purchasing power from the private to the public realm and not any additional economic output (with the possible exception of any infrastructure outlays), an increase in the proportion of total employment accounted for by the government directly or indirectly, N_G/N, will lower $\mathring{Z}$.

This is not to rule out an increase in the amount of government and government-subsidized employment as one component of a full employment policy. Although the growth of output per worker, $\mathring{Z}$, may slow, making it more difficult to control inflation, this disadvantage of the increase in subsidized employment may be outweighed by the noneconomic benefits from the activities being funded.

After all, as was previously pointed out (see chapter 2, section 2.2, and chapter 10, part 2), the fact that government expenditures may not add to aggregate economic output does not preclude the possibility of the society benefiting from the outlays in other, no less important ways—for example, through an increase in the stock of human knowledge or an improvement in the functioning of either the political or anthropogenic systems. An increase in public consumption, at the expense of private consumption, may well be warranted. Indeed, the subsidization of employment by the government, if the noneconomic benefits are sufficiently great, may well represent a better utilization of the society's human resources—especially if the only alternative is for those resources to remain unemployed. In addition to whatever the society as a whole may gain from the better utilization of its human resources, there is the benefit to the individuals themselves of having a job, both in terms of self-esteem and the opportunity, through the on-the-job training provided, to realize further their potential as human beings. Finally, if the individuals were previously receiving a certain amount of transfer income, Y_{tr}, under one of the programs for the unemployed, the net change in income flows will not be as great as just the wage received from the subsidized employment, $w_G(h)$, would suggest. Still, any government or government-subsidized employment may well, for the reason indicated, exacerbate the problem of inflation, and it is for this reason that it is necessary to examine the other two options for reducing the number of persons who are unemployed.

A second way to reduce the number of persons who are unemployed is for the government to place the economy on a more rapid growth path in one of the ways that has already been identified (see chapter 10, sections 4.5–4.7). The problem with this alternative approach to implementing a full employment policy is that any increase in the secular rate of economic expansion, $\mathring{G}$, necessarily presumes an increase in the rate of accumulation, I/Y or ϕ, and thus will be accompanied by a certain redistributional effect with the same potential for exacerbating the problem of inflation as the decline in the growth of output per worker from an increase in government and government-subsidized employment (see chapter 8, section 2.4).

It should be pointed out that, in order to place the economy on a more rapid growth path, the government will need to increase, at least temporarily, the growth of its expenditures, discretionary or otherwise. However, this disproportionate increase in government and government-subsidized employment during the period of the traverse—that is, until the increase in $\mathring{G}ov$ induces the enterprise and household sectors to step up their own rate of growth of discretionary expenditures—will not necessarily lead to a decline in $\mathring{Z}$. This is because the increase in N_G relative to N will be only cyclical, and not secular. Once the disproportionate increase in N_G has succeeded in placing the economy on a more rapid growth path, the subsequent increase in both business investment and household consumption should have the effect of restoring the ratio of government and government subsidized employment to total employment, N_G/N, to whatever was previously its long-period value so that the growth of output per worker, $\overset{\circ}{Z}$, need not decline.

Whether in fact $\overset{\circ}{Z}$ will decline depends on what change, if any, occurs in the composition of final demand, Y, as a result of the economy being placed on a more rapid growth path and what effect this change in the relevant set of weights has on YZ or $\overset{\circ}{Z}$. It is precisely this compositional effect that distinguishes the first from the second means of reducing the number of persons who are unemployed. The option previously discussed—that of increasing the amount of government and government-subsidized employment, N_G—implies a change in the composition of final demand (if the increase in employment is to be more than just a temporary one) with the relative proportion of total employment that is subsidized through tax revenues, N_G/N, rising. It therefore represents an increase in public consumption at the expense of private consumption, with the potential inflationary effect arising from the unwillingness of workers (and others) to accept the reduction in private consumption, at least in relative terms, that a disproportionate increase in public consumption entails. The second option now being discussed differs from the first in that, once the traverse to the more rapid growth path has been completed, the ratio of subsidized employment to total employment, N_G/N, is likely to be unchanged from what it was previously. During the interim period itself, that is, during the traverse, any possible adverse effect on the growth of output per worker due to the increase in government and government-subsidized employment is likely to be offset by the short-period cyclical effect on labor productivity of the higher rate of capacity utilization within the enterprise sector.

The distributional problem created by placing the economy on a more rapid growth path is not that the growth of output per worker, $\overset{\circ}{Z}$, will necessarily decline but rather, that the rate of accumulation, ϕ, will have to increase, thereby reducing, at least temporarily, the rate at which money wages and hence household income can grow without putting upward pressure on the price level (see chapter 8, section 2.4). This distributional effect will, again, be only a temporary, or cyclical, one. Once the traverse to the higher secular growth path has been successfully completed, money wages and hence household income will be able to grow at an even more rapid pace without adding to the rate of inflation. Moreover, if the rate of technical progress can be speeded up sufficiently as a result of the increase in the rate of accumulation, the higher secular growth rate will be a sustainable one. Nonetheless, that same increase in the rate of accumulation, because of the higher profit margins it will require, is likely to exacerbate the conflict over the distribution of income which underlies the inflationary process. In particular, it is likely, in the absence of the institutional mechanisms needed for the successful implementation of an incomes policy, to touch off a wage-price inflationary spiral (see chapter 14, section 3.0). This possible adverse effect of placing the economy on a more rapid growth path is the reason we need to examine the third option available to a society for reducing the number of unemployed persons. That third option is to increase the amount of leisure time.

The amount of employment, N, can be increased by reducing the average number of hours worked each year by an individual member of the labor force, h. This is because N is equal to **LQ** divided by h. The lower the value of h, the higher will be the value of N. A reduction in the value of h can be accomplished in any one of a number of ways: (a) by reducing the number of days, or hours, that constitute the normal work week; (b) by increasing the norm as to the number of vacation days allowed each year; (c) by increasing the number of mandated holidays throughout the year, or (d) by allowing for sabbaticals or other extended absences from the job with the worker continuing to receive at least partial compensation. In addition to reducing h, a society can increase the amount of employment by adopting policies that enable an individual to remain out of the labor force until a later age or to retire earlier.

Reducing the number of unemployed persons in any of the above ways requires, however, that the members of the society be willing to sacrifice some further improvement in their material standard of living for an increase in leisure. They must, in effect, be prepared to devote a portion of whatever technical progress is being achieved to reducing the amount of time they must spend in compensated employment—instead of using it to increase the amount of goods and services available for consumption. The members of a society, acting through their political institutions, may be unwilling to accept this trade-off. They (or at least the employed members of the society) may, on the one hand, insist on maintaining whatever is the present rate of growth of real income (as determined by the growth of output per worker) by refusing to countenance any further reduction in the average number of hours worked each year, h. They may, on the other hand, seek both to maintain the present rate of increase in real consumption *and* to obtain greater leisure—in which case the result will be the same as if they acted, through their political institutions, to increase the amount of government and government-subsidized employment, N_G. With nominal income rising more rapidly than the growth of output per worker, the rate of inflation, $\dot{P}$, will necessarily increase. Only if the members of a society are prepared to forego greater consumption for increased leisure can they reduce the number of unemployed persons, U—and in the process distribute more equitably within the society the total amount of leisure, involuntary as well as voluntary. If they try to "have their cake and eat it, too"—by reducing h while leaving the rate of growth of money wages, $\dot{w}$, unchanged—they will either touch off a wage-price inflationary spiral or exarcerbate whatever problem of inflation already exists.

Thus, whatever the means chosen to implement a full employment policy, the effort will be beset by difficulties. There is, first, the likely political resistance—though the reason for the resistance will be different, depending on which of the three approaches is adopted. In the case of the subsidized-employment option, the resistance is likely to be to the use of tax revenues to underwrite the wages of others. In the case of the higher-growth option, the resistance is likely to be to the increased government deficits that are necessary during the interim period of the traverse. And in the case of the greater-leisure option, the resistance is likely to be to any slowing of the rate at which the material standard of living is improving.

More generally, there is likely to be political resistance because of the fear that a full employment policy will exarcerbate the problem of inflation. And indeed this fear is not without some basis in reality—though again the source of the problem is different, depending on which of the three approaches is adopted. In the case of the subsidized-employment option, the problem arises because of the adverse effect which an increase in N_G relative to N is likely to have on the growth of output per worker. In the case of the higher-growth option, the problem arises because the necessary increase in the rate of accumulation, ϕ, will lower, at least temporarily, the rate at which money wages can grow without forcing a rise in price levels. And in the case of the greater-leisure option, the problem arises because the members of the society may insist on maintaining the same rate of growth of money wages, $\dot{w}$, despite the reduction in the average number of hours worked each year.

Still, the possible inflationary impact of a full employment policy can be avoided. One purpose in writing this text is, in fact, to explain how that is possible. While a full explanation must wait until we can deal more systematically with the inflationary dynamic of an advanced market economy like the United States (see chapter 14, section 3.0), it should be noted here in passing that adding to the rate of inflation is only a *possible effect* of a full employment policy. It is not a necessary consequence. Indeed, depending on what are the specific components of such a policy and thus what offsetting action the government needs to take insofar as its incomes policy is concerned, the number of persons who are unemployed (or otherwise underutilized) can be reduced without exacerbating the problem of inflation.

Just as there are different sources of political resistance and different distributional effects that complicate the task of controlling inflation—depending on what are the actual components of the government's full employment policy—so too there are different benefits besides the reduction in U itself. The subsidized-employment option makes it possible, as we shall see in the next subsection, to adjust the composition of final demand to fit the career objectives of the individual members of society rather than insisting, as is now the case, on the reverse. The higher-growth option makes it possible to expand the opportunity structure with only a temporary slowing of the secular rise in the material standard of living. And the greater-leisure option will lessen the second constraint, besides the amount of household income, on the ability of the individual to satisfy his or her needs, nonmaterial as well as material (see chapter 9, section 1.4). It is because of these different secondary benefits, as well as the different set of problems they create, that all three approaches need to be considered as possible components of a comprehensive full employment policy. However, even these several elements may not be enough to enable each member of the society to realize his or her full potential as a human being. The steps taken on the demand side will probably need to be complemented by a set of labor supply management policies.

13.4.4 Labor supply management

Two types of labor supply management policies need to be distinguished. One is the set of policies by which the x dimension of the $\mathbf{H}$ matrix, and hence the growth of the potential labor force, $\overset{\circ}{\mathsf{H}}$, can be affected. The other is the set of policies by which the m dimension of the same matrix, and hence the potential labor force's level of competence, is determined. We shall take up each of these two types of labor supply management policies in turn.

The natural tendency of any biological population is to expand until it has fully occupied its biological niche, at which point the homeostatic, or "equilibrium," growth rate will be zero. This biological principle goes a long way toward explaining why, as has previously been pointed out, the endemic condition in an advanced industrial society is a surplus rather than a shortage of labor, with the relevant supply management problem being how to limit the growth of the potential labor force, $\overset{\circ}{\mathsf{H}}$, so as to minimize the unemployment rate, $\mathsf{U}n$. While technical progress may ease somewhat, at least temporarily, the environmental constraint on population growth, the goal of maintaining a steady improvement in the material standard of living actually leaves little room for an increase in $\overset{\circ}{\mathsf{H}}$ without a consequent increase in $\mathsf{U}n$.

It is of course possible, as was brought out in the preceding subsection, to increase the number of employed workers, $\overset{\circ}{\mathsf{N}}$, and thus to reduce the unemployment rate without the growth of output per worker, $\overset{\circ}{\mathsf{Z}}$, falling and thereby slowing the growth of real income. Indeed, $\overset{\circ}{\mathsf{N}}$ and $\overset{\circ}{\mathsf{Z}}$ may both rise. Such an outcome is possible, however, only to the extent that the economy can be placed on a more rapid growth path—and even then the reduction in the unemployment rate will be only a temporary one unless something is done to offset the subsequent response of the anthropogenic system to the increased rate of economic expansion. This is why it is essential, as a matter of policy, to limit the growth of the potential labor force, $\overset{\circ}{\mathsf{H}}$.

As has already been explained (see chapter 4, section, 3.1), the growth of the potential labor force, $\overset{\circ}{\mathsf{H}}$, depends on the growth of the working-age population, $\overset{\circ}{\mathsf{e}}$, and the rate of net inmigration, m—with the labor force participation rate, f, and the average number of hours worked each year, h, as additional parameters. Little more need be said about the importance of limiting both the growth of population and the rate of net inmigration (see chapter 4, section 3.2, and this chapter, sections 2.4 and 3.3). The one point worth stressing here is that, with the rate of increase in the indigenous population tending to fall to zero—as it has in the advanced industrial societies—the critical control variable becomes a country's immigration policy. It is primarily by restricting the number of foreign-born individuals allowed to take up legal residence that an advanced industrial society like the United States is able to control the rate of net inmigration, m, and hence the growth of its potential labor force, $\overset{\circ}{\mathsf{H}}$. What this means is that it is not possible for the United States or any other OECD country to reduce its unemployment rate without, at the same time, taking steps to limit inmigration.

Whatever the rate of increase in the indigenous population, a sufficiently liberal immigration policy will, given the higher real wage migrant workers can earn by relocating, cause an advanced industrial society's potential labor force to grow rapidly enough to offset whatever reduction in the unemployment rate might otherwise be achieved. This is because of the narrow limits within which it is possible to increase the growth of employment, $\overset{\circ}{N}$, above its current trend value. These limits are determined, on the one hand, by the extent to which a society is willing, through its political institutions, to devote a portion of whatever technical progess is being achieved to increased leisure and/or public consumption (with a consequent decline in the growth of output per worker, $\overset{\circ}{Z}$) and, on the other hand, by the extent to which the economy can be placed on a more rapid growth path—one that, by inducing a corresponding rise in $\overset{\circ}{Z}$, will then be a sustainable one.

It should be pointed out that the political resistance to limiting immigration is not just from naturalized citizens who want relatives and others of the same ethnic background to be able to continue entering the country. It also comes, perhaps with even more telling political effect, from those who wish to retain a source of relatively cheap domestic labor. They include both the owners of small businesses with a high labor-output, or l, coefficient and consumers who would like to be able to obtain certain personal services, such as household help, at a low cost. The continued inflow of unskilled migrant workers, with its attendant social problems, is in effect an accommodation to the economic interests of those two groups. The more humane policy, insofar as the migrant workers themselves are concerned, would be to provide the financial, trade and other types of assistance needed to ensure the more rapid economic development of the countries, and the regions within those countries, from which the migrants come (see chapter 11, section 0.0). The principal effect, then, of a liberal immigration policy—with the inflow of workers limited only by the employment and housing conditions they are willing to tolerate—is to maintain the lower wages normally received by the members of the secondary, or peripheral, labor force (see chapter 8, section, 1.3). Such a policy makes it virtually impossible to reduce significantly the secular unemployment rate, $\overline{U}n$. Indeed, the more rapid the growth of employment within that country, N, the higher will be the rate of net inmigration, m, leaving the secular unemployment rate, $\overline{U}n$, unchanged if not actually higher.

One must, at the same time, recognize that the need to maintain a certain amount of anthropogenic slack—as part of the more general slack, consisting of inventories and reserve capacity, that is essential if the production subsystem is going to adjust to changes in the rate of economic expansion without an interruption of supply. This need to maintain a certain amount of anthropogenic slack precludes the possibility of reducing the unemployment rate to zero. All that can be done as a matter of policy, without increasing the likelihood of disruption from supply bottlenecks, is to minimize the fluctuations in the level of economic activity and thereby minimize not just the amount of inventory that must be held and the amount of reserve capacity that must be maintained but also the amount of anthropogenic slack, in the form of unemployed and underutilized workers, that must be tolerated. Although the secular unemployment rate thus cannot, as a practical matter, be reduced to zero, still the government can adopt a set of policies that will minimize the adverse effect on any one individual. These are the labor supply management policies designed to affect the quality, as distinct from the quantity, of human resources.

A prerequisite step, for the successful implementation of labor supply management policies, is that a set of accounts be developed to track the change over time in the society's stock of human resources denoted by the **H** matrix (as the complement of the economic accounts described in chapter 2). This set of anthropogenic accounts, by in effect aggregating the vitas for every member of the society, would indicate the number of persons available with each type of competence (see above, section 13.1.1). In this way it would be possible either to better adjust the output of the anthropogenic system to the needs of the economic system—for example, by shifting resources among the different curriculums within the educational system—or, what may eventually come to be seen as no less valid an alternative, to adjust the composition of final demand and thus the output of the economic system to whatever are the types of competence being produced by the anthropogenic system.

The set of accounts for determining the value taken by the **H** matrix, aside from helping the government in formulating its economic policies, would serve as a check on the efficacy of the society's anthropogenic institutions. As previously pointed out, the only evidence that a particular competence has been acquired, either through the formal educational system or through any on-the-job training, is the ability of the individual to retain beyond the normal probationary period a position requiring that level of competence. It is thus each individual's subsequent work history that makes it possible to determine what types of competences, if any, have been acquired through the anthropogenic institutions with which that individual has been affiliated. Some means of checking how well specific anthropogenic institutions are performing is important because the principal means of increasing the quality, as distinct from the quantity, of human resources is to increase both the number and types of anthropogenic institutions.

The United States already has perhaps the most highly developed anthropogenic system of any country in the world—as measured both by the proportion of its population with access to higher education and by the variety of its anthropogenic institutions, noneducational as well as educational. Indeed, the system of higher education, together with the large number of megacorps, is probably the principal source of the United States' comparative advantage over other countries. Even so, a large number of Americans, even among those who have attended college, fail to develop the ability to think critically and act autonomously which should be the hallmark of a college-educated person. While a larger proportion of the population has access to higher education than in any other country, many persons are nonetheless unable to take advantage of the opportunity. This is especially true of those who, for one reason or another, fail to complete even high school or, if they do receive a diploma, remain barely literate.

Some would argue that not everyone can benefit from a college education and that, even if they could, this would leave no one to perform the society's menial tasks. While there may be some truth to the latter argument, it only adds to the suspicion that the first point is simply a rationalization for limiting access to higher education. In truth, no one yet knows the extent to which every individual can benefit from attending college. The present experiment in the United States, one of the more important initiatives in human history, has yet to run its full course. The question is a critical one in light of the fear expressed by others that the computer will eventually eliminate most of the jobs which those without a college education can expect to hold. While this fear may be exaggerated, the fact remains that the technical progress of the past several centuries is likely to continue, with the less skilled members of the labor force finding it increasingly difficult to obtain employment. The failure to take whatever steps are necessary to ensure that as large a proportion of the population as possible has the prerequisite training to qualify for the available employment opportunities will only exacerbate the types of social pathology reflected in high crime rates, mental illness, substance abuse, and family breakdown. It is in this connection that the option of expanding the anthropogenic system, even in the case of the United States with its already well-developed system, needs to be considered. This form of labor supply management policy entails an increase in the number of government-financed anthropogenic programs.

What is particularly important, in determining the proportion of individuals with the requisite competence to carry out the society's essential tasks, is the number of back-up, or "second-chance," developmental institutions. Any system is subject to a certain rate of failure. This is especially true of the institutions, such as the family and the schools, responsible for human development. Rather than attempt to improve the performance of those institutions, it may be more cost-effective to create a set of back-up, or "second-chance," institutions—such as child-protection programs in the case of the family and independently administered remedial reading and mathematics programs in the case of the secondary education system. However, the second-chance anthropogenic institutions are unlikely to perform any better than the primary ones—and indeed may even perform less satisfactorily, given the more difficult population they serve—unless there is some means of monitoring their performance. Developing the type of anthropogenic accounts previously outlined will not, in itself, be enough. To monitor the performance of the entire set of human developmental institutions, it may be necessary to create, in addition, an autonomous network of career counselors that would serve as the counterpart, on the anthropogenic side, of the stockbrokers and other types of financial advisors who help household members manage their savings (financial investment) portfolios.

Under this proposed system, each individual would select an organization to provide career counseling at the point in time when he or she decides to make the transition from school to work. The organization could be the college or other type of school from which the individual is graduating, but it need not be. The choice would be the individual's. Whatever organization was selected—the type of agency that manages the careers of professional athletes and entertainers would be the prototype—it would then be responsible for helping the individual develop and implement a career plan, with the amount of compensation received by the organization for its services (from the government) based on the subsequent earnings of the individuals who were its clients. This network of career guidance organizations would supplement the existing set of anthropogenic institutions, making up for the lack of adequate market mechanisms insofar as the allocation and use of the society's human resources are concerned (see section 13.1.4).

In helping the individual make the transition from school to work, the organization providing the career counseling would first have to determine what had been the previous set of educational and other anthropogenic affiliations. In this way, the organization would begin compiling the vita that, with the addition of the individual's subsequent work history, would serve as the basis both for constructing the set of anthropogenic accounts and for monitoring the performance of the developmental institutions involved—including the organization providing the career counseling. The organization's counselors would then have to work out, with the individual, a plan for enabling that individual to realize his or her career goals. As part of the plan, the counselors would have to indicate the appropriate entry-level position and what subsequent steps would need to be taken before the individual could hope to advance beyond that point. If the individual was not already qualified for such a position, the counselors would have to indicate what must be done to make up for the deficiency. This might include taking some other, less desirable entry-level position, at least temporarily, until the necessary education and/or prior work experience had been acquired.

Once the appropriate entry-level position had been mutually agreed to, it would be the responsibility of the counseling organization to find an opening for the individual. If one were not obtained within a certain period of time, the individual would be eligible for transfer income, with the government bearing the cost unless it could show that there were, in fact, entry-level positions available within that occupation. In this way, the individual would not be left without a source of income due to the lack of employment opportunities while the government would have a more accurate count, broken down by occupation, of the actual number of persons unable to find employment. Indeed, this information would make it possible for the government, if it wished, to alter the composition of final demand (through the pattern of its own expenditures) so as to ensure whatever employment opportunities were needed to enable the individual members of the society to realize more closely their choice of careers. In this way, the demand for labor would be adjusted to the supply rather, as at present, the reverse—with a consequent increase in the satisfaction derived from work.

Besides helping the individual make the difficult transition from school to work, the counseling organization would have to stand ready to provide assistance at any subsequent time of crisis—either because the individual had been

944   MACRODYNAMICS OF ADVANCED MARKET ECONOMIES

involuntarily separated from an employing organization and thus was left unemployed or, alternatively, because the individual was unable to advance any further along the career path which he or she had chosen and thus was being underutilized. The assistance, in the event of either type of crisis, would include finding the individual a position with another employing organization, revising the previous career plan and/or arranging for retraining. Those left without any job at all would, again, be eligible for transfer income if another position were not found within a certain period of time, with the government bearing the cost unless it could show that there were, in fact, openings within the individual's chosen occupation at the level previously held by the individual.

These supply management policies—the quantitative as well as the qualitative ones—cannot be counted on to reduce the unemployment rate to zero. This is because of the need for a certain amount of anthropogenic slack if supply bottlenecks are to be avoided. They will, however, make it possible not only to minimize the unemployment rate but also to ensure that the burden is borne equitably by all the members of the society—in part, through a system of unemployment compensation financed out of tax revenues and, insofar as the burden must fall directly on those left without a job, by merely increasing the length of time required to make the transition from school to a permanent position with a megacorp or some other type of employing organization that provides career opportunities. Now that the problem of unemployment has been examined and the means of alleviating it described, the next step will be to examine more closely the problem of inflation. As has already been indicated, it is the problem of inflation, because of the inappropriate means chosen to deal with it, that is largely responsible for the high rates of unemployment experienced by the United States and the other advanced industrial countries in the second half of the 20th century (though lower than the rates experienced in the first half, thanks to the Keynesian revolution in economic policy). We shall take up the problem of inflation in the next chapter in the context of presenting, in its entirety, the post-Keynesian model of an advanced industrial economy which has so far been presented only piecemeal.

Recommended Readings

The model of the anthropogenic system is based on the work of Eli Ginzberg. See his book, *The Human Economy*, New York: McGraw-Hill, 1976. See also Eichner, "An Anthropogenic Approach to Labor Economics," *Eastern Economic Journal*, October 1979, reprinted in *Toward a New Economics*, ch. 4, and the various works cited therein. On the corresponding model of human development see, in addition, Theodore Lidz, *The Person*, New York: Basic Books, 1968. On the vita theory, see Ray Canterbery, "A Vita Theory of the Personal Income Distribution," *Southern Economic Journal*, July 1979. On job shelters, see Marcia Freedman, *Labor Markets: Segments and Shelters*, Montclair, N.J.: Allanheld, Osmun & Co., 1976. See also her book, *The Process of Work Estab-*

lishment, New York: Columbia University Press, 1969. On the queue theory of the labor market, see Lester Thurow, *Generating Inequality*, New York: Basic Books, 1975. On the different approaches to modeling the labor market, see Lars Osberg, *Economic Inequality in the United States*, Armonk, N.Y.: M. E. Sharpe, 1984, chs. 8–10; Eileen Appelbaum, "The Labor Market" in *A Guide to Post-Keynesian Theory*, Alfred S. Eichner, ed., Armonk, N.Y.: M. E. Sharpe, 1979. On the labor force participation rate, see William G. Bowen and T. Aldrich Finegan, *The Economics of Labor Force Participation*, Princeton, N.J.: Princeton University Press, 1969, and the other references in Ingrid Rima, *Labor Markets, Wages, and Employment*, New York: Norton, 1981, ch. 3. For a more conventional treatment of the subject, see Mark Killingsworth, *Labor Supply*, New York: Cambridge University Press, 1983.

The argument by Georgescu-Roegen will be found in his book, *The Entropy Law and the Economic Process*, Cambridge, Mass.: Harvard University Press, 1971. See also Ilya Prigogine and Isabelle Stengers, *Order Out of Chaos*, New York: Bantam, 1984; Charles R. Pellegrino and Jessie A. Stoff, *Darwin's Universe*, New York: Van Nostrand Reinhold, 1983; Ervin Laszlo, *Evolution: The Grand Synthesis*, Boston: New Science Library, 1987. The world input-output model, with its specification of the critical natural resource inputs, will be found in Wassily Leontief *et al.*, *The Future of the World Economy*, New York: Oxford University Press, 1978.